THE SCOUTING NOTEBOOK 2004

Editors/The Scouting Notebook
THOM HENNINGER
TONY NISTLER
DON ZMINDA

The photographs which appear in *The Scouting Notebook 2004* are courtesy of the following Major League Baseball teams, whose cooperation is gratefully acknowledged: Anaheim Angels, Baltimore Orioles, Boston Red Sox, Chicago White Sox/Ron Vesely, Cleveland Indians, Detroit Tigers, Kansas City Royals, Minnesota Twins, New York Yankees, Oakland Athletics, Seattle Mariners, Tampa Bay Devil Rays, Texas Rangers, Toronto Blue Jays, Arizona Diamondbacks, Atlanta Braves (Courtesy of Atlanta National Baseball Club, Inc. ©2003. All rights reserved) , Chicago Cubs, Cincinnati Reds, Colorado Rockies, Florida Marlins/Dennis Bancroft, Houston Astros, Los Angeles Dodgers, Milwaukee Brewers, Montreal Expos, Mark S. Levine/New York Mets, Philadelphia Phillies, Pittsburgh Pirates, St. Louis Cardinals, San Diego Padres and San Francisco Giants.

ON THE COVER: Top: Derek Jeter photo by Bob Leverone for The Sporting News; bottom left to right: Jim Thome by Robert Seale/The Sporting News, Kerry Wood by Robert Seale/The Sporting News, Mark Mulder by Dilip Vishwanat/The Sporting News; spine: Derek Jeter by Bob Leverone for The Sporting News.

Major league statistics compiled by STATS, Inc., a News Corporation Company, 8130 Lehigh Avenue, Morton Grove, IL 60053. STATS is a trademark of Sports Team Analysis and Tracking Systems, Inc.

ISBN: 0-89204-729-1

10 9 8 7 6 5 4 3 2 1

Table of Contents

The Scouting Staff

The scouting reports on each team's ballpark, manager and significant players were written by the following people, in conjunction with our editors:

Anaheim Angels	Bill Shaikin *Los Angeles Times/ Baseball America*
Baltimore Orioles	Rick Wilton *Sports Weekly Hot Sheet*
Boston Red Sox	Mat Olkin *Sports Weekly*
Chicago White Sox*	Phil Rogers *Chicago Tribune/ Baseball America*
Cleveland Indians	Paul Hoynes *Cleveland Plain Dealer*
Detroit Tigers	Pat Caputo *Oakland (Mich.) Press/ Baseball America*
Kansas City Royals*	Marc Bowman *STATS, Inc.*
Minnesota Twins	Dennis Brackin *Minneapolis Star Tribune*
New York Yankees	Mat Olkin *Sports Weekly*
Oakland Athletics	Lawr Michaels *www.creativesports.com*
Seattle Mariners	Mat Olkin *Sports Weekly*
Tampa Bay Devil Rays	Marc Topkin *St. Petersburg Times/ Baseball America*
Texas Rangers*	Evan Grant *Dallas Morning News*
Toronto Blue Jays	Tom Maloney *STATS, Inc.*
Arizona Diamondbacks*	Ed Price *East Valley Tribune (Mesa, Ariz.)*
Atlanta Braves*	Bill Ballew *Baseball America*
Chicago Cubs	Mat Olkin *Sports Weekly*
Cincinnati Reds	Peter Pascarelli *ESPN*
Colorado Rockies*	Tracy Ringolsby *Rocky Mountain News (Denver)/Baseball America*
Florida Marlins*	Mike Berardino *South Florida Sun-Sentinel*
Houston Astros	Jim Carley *Sporting News*
Los Angeles Dodgers*	Don Hartack *STATS, Inc.*
Milwaukee Brewers	Mat Olkin *Sports Weekly*
Montreal Expos*	Trace Wood *www.longgandhi.com*
New York Mets*	Bill Ballew *Baseball America*
Philadelphia Phillies*	Paul Hagen *Philadelphia Daily News*
Pittsburgh Pirates*	John Perrotto *Beaver County (Pa.) Times/ Baseball America*
St. Louis Cardinals	Peter Pascarelli *ESPN*
San Diego Padres*	Trace Wood *www.longgandhi.com*
San Francisco Giants	Joe Roderick *Contra Costa Times*

The minor league prospect reports were written by Thom Henninger (AL), Jim Henzler (Reds, Astros, Cardinals, Giants), Ron Thompson (Tigers, Brewers), Dan Ford (Cubs) and the individual team writers as noted with an asterisk (*). We'd like to thank the player-development personnel who were willing to discuss their teams' farm systems. *Baseball America's* Jim Callis also was a big help when it came to filling in blanks. The "Other Anaheim Angels," etc., were written by the STATS, Inc. publications staff. I'd also like to thank Taylor Bechtold, Norm DeNosaquo, Don Hartack, Brian Hogan, Jacob Nuesser, Corey Roberts, John Strougal and Don Zminda for their integral roles in helping to get this edition to print.

—Tony Nistler

Introduction

Welcome to the 10th edition of *The Scouting Notebook*. This is the 15th annual book of scouting reports that STATS, Inc. has created. We get several prominent baseball analysts and have them give us detailed reports on every major league player who saw significant action last season. We think you'll agree that our scouting staff features some of the top baseball minds around. Special thanks to Marc Bowman, Paul Hoynes and John Perrotto, who have contributed to all 15 books.

This is an encyclopedia of contemporary major league baseball. We tell you about the strengths and weaknesses of hundreds of players. Our analysis extends beyond major league players, too, covering each club's top minor league prospects. We study the statistics and we talk to the scouts. We look for the true ability that may have been exaggerated or obscured by the hype.

The Ballparks

We report on each club's ballpark. We detail how each stadium affects hitters, pitchers and fielders in general, as well as which players it helps and hurts the most. We also project what the park will do to rookies and other newcomers in 2004. We provide vital statistics for each park, such as its dimensions, capacity, elevation, playing surface and the amount of foul territory.

We also present our trademark park indexes. In a variety of statistical categories, we show how the home team and its opponents performed at the park and on the road. Interleague games aren't included. By comparing the overall totals at the park and on the road, we get a measure of the stadium's impact. We divide the home totals by the road totals and multiply by 100 to get the park index. An index of greater than 100 shows that the park favors a particular statistic, while an index of less than 100 means the opposite.

Most of the indexes are calculated on a per at-bat basis. Runs, hits, errors and infield errors are figured on a per-game basis. For most parks, we present data for both 2003 and the last three years overall. If the park's configuration has changed since the end of the 2001 season, we present the data for the different setups separately.

Most of the abbreviations are common, with these exceptions:

E-Infield: Infield errors.

LHB-Avg: Batting average by lefthanded hitters.

LHB-HR: Home runs by lefthanded hitters.

RHB-Avg: Batting average by righthanded hitters.

RHB-HR: Home runs by righthanded hitters.

We also list any indexes in which the park ranked in the top or bottom three in its league in 2003.

The Managers

On these pages, we analyze each manager's strengths and weaknesses, style and strategy, and outlook for 2004. We present his 2003 and career managerial record, and we also show how often he used starting pitchers on various days of rest. We compare his use and the performance of his starters to the league average.

We also provide statistical breakdowns detailing his handling of his pitching staff and his use of strategies like the sacrifice, the hit-and-run and defensive substitutions. To qualify for the rankings, a manager had to have his team for at least 100 games in 2003. Some of the terms listed in the statistics and rankings sections may be unfamiliar.

They include:

Hit & Run Success %: The percentage of hit-and-runs resulting in baserunner advancement with no double play.

Platoon Pct.: Frequency that the manager gets his hitters the platoon advantage (lefty vs. righty and vice versa). Switch-hitters always are considered to have the advantage.

Defensive Subs: The number of straight defensive substitutions with the team leading by four runs or fewer.

High-Pitch Outings: The number of times a manager's starting pitchers threw more than 120 pitches in a ballgame.

Quick/Slow Hooks: A Quick Hook occurs when a pitcher is removed after having pitched less than six innings and given up three runs or fewer. A Slow Hook occurs when a pitcher works more than nine innings, allows seven or more runs, or his total innings and runs equal 13 or more.

First-Batter Platoon Percentage: The percentage of times a manager's relievers had a platoon advantage over the first hitter they faced (lefty vs. lefty, righty vs. righty).

Mid-Inning Changes: The number of times the manager changed pitchers in the middle of an inning.

Pitchouts with a Runner Moving: The number of times the opposition was running when the manager called a pitchout.

Sacrifice Bunt Percentage: The percentage of bunts resulting in sacrifices or hits with runners on.

Starting Lineups Used: Based on batting order, 1-8 for National Leaguers, 1-9 for American Leaguers.

2+ Pitching Changes in Low-Scoring Games: The number of times a manager used at least three pitchers in a game in which his team allowed two runs or fewer.

The Players

For each major league team, we give extensive reports on 22 players. Twelve of them get a full page of scouting information, while 10 receive half-page reports. Because we like to get this book into your hands as soon as possible, players are listed with their 2003 clubs. We keep abreast of postseason transactions, and all player moves that took place through December 12, 2003 are noted. If you can't find a particular player, check the detailed index in the back.

Pages for primary players have two columns. The left column provides an in-depth report by an analyst. The right column contains statistical information:

Position: The first position shown is the player's most common position in 2003. Positions at which he played 10 or more games also are shown. For pitchers, SP stands for starting pitcher and RP for relief pitcher.

Bats and Throws: L represents for lefthanded, R stands for righthanded, and B represents both (switch-hitter).

Ht: Height.

Wt: Weight.

Opening Day Age: This is the player's age on April 1, 2004.

Born: Birthdate and birthplace.

ML Seasons: This number indicates the number of different major league seasons in which the player has appeared. For example, if a player was called up to play in September in each of the last three seasons, the number shown would be 3. This is different from major league service, which is used to determine arbitration and free-agency eligibility.

Overall Statistics: These are traditional major league statistics for the player's 2003 season and his career.

Where He Hits The Ball

For every major league game in 2003, STATS reporters entered into our computers every single ball hit into play. They kept track of the type of batted balls—grounders, flyballs, popups, line drives and bunts—as well as the distance each ball traveled. Direction was tracked by dividing the field into 26 "wedges" projecting out from home plate. Distance was measured in 10-foot increments outward from home plate.

Below are the 2003 hitting diagrams for lefthanded-hitting Juan Pierre of the Florida Marlins. The chart on the left shows where Pierre hit the ball against lefthanders, while the chart on the right shows what he did against righties.

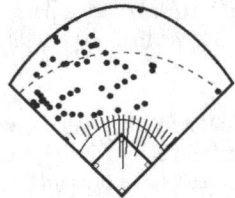 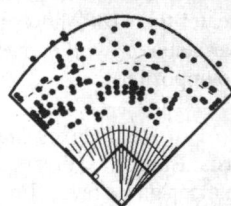

Vs. LHP   **Vs. RHP**

In the diagrams, groundballs and short line drives are shown by the lines of various lengths in the infield. The longer the line, the more groundballs and line drives were hit in that direction. As you can see from the charts on page 2, Pierre sprayed the ball

all over the field as the leadoff hitter for the World Series champion Marlins. Pierre, who rarely strikes out, took over the leadoff role a week into the 2003 season and never relinquished it.

While the lefthanded-hitting Pierre actually batted eight points higher against lefties in 2003, he took a different approach against them. The speedy center fielder tended to go up the middle with groundballs while hitting the ball beyond the infielders by going the other way. Against righthanders, Pierre sprayed the ball everywhere, though he was a bit more likely to pull grounders. Overall, he was more authoritative in his approach against righthanded pitching, driving the ball all over the outfield. Most of his extra-base hits came against righthanders.

A lot of experimentation went into producing the hitting diagrams. When we first started, we tried to show every single batted ball that was put into play by each player. We found that the charts became very cluttered for everyday players, so we began experimenting with trying to show only the most meaningful information. When all was said and done, here's what we ended up with:

a. Popups and bunts are excluded. We excluded popups because 95 percent of these are caught regardless of how fielders are positioned. We excluded bunts because defensing a bunt is an entirely different strategy primarily used against a select number of players or in specific situations.

b. For groundballs and short line drives, we include all batted balls.

c. For balls hit to the outfield, we excluded isolated points only if the chart contains more than 125 batted balls to the outfield. In such cases, if a player hits only one ball to a given area and had no other batted balls in the vicinity all season, we exclude it because it doesn't give a true indication of a tendency.

Other notes of interest:

The field is drawn to scale, with the outfield fence reaching 400 feet in center and 330 feet down the lines. Ballparks are configured differently, so a dot inside of the fence might have been a home run. Similarly, a dot outside the fence might actually have been in play.

Line drives under 170 feet are part of the infield. We give responsibility for short liners to the infielders.

No distinction is made between hits and outs.

2003 Pitching Profiles
Past readers of the *Scouting Notebook* may notice a change to our full-page reports for major league pitchers. We have replaced the charts that displayed how often a pitcher threw strikes with a more extensive breakdown of a given pitcher's performance in eight common categories, and compared them to the 2003 league averages.

The first two categories, **Overall Strike %** and **1st Pitch Strike %**, include swinging strikes, taken strikes, foul balls and balls put in play. STATS reporters tracked every pitch thrown in a major league game in 2003. Though not all batted balls come on pitches thrown within the strike zone, our theory is that most are and the ones that aren't would be difficult to judge. Our numbers reflect these assumptions.

Another statistic that may require further explanation is **Ratio**, which is the number of baserunners allowed by a pitcher per inning: ((hits + walks)/IP). This category also is commonly referred to as WHIP.

One additional note: For the category of **Groundball/Flyball Ratio**, groundballs include hits, outs and errors, while flyballs *exclude* line drives.

2003 Situational Stats
There are eight situational breakdowns for every primary player. *Home* and *Road* show performance in his home ballpark and on the road. *First Half* and *Send Half* show performance before and after the 2003 All-Star break. For hitters, *LHP* and *RHP* show how the player hit against lefthanders and righthanders. For pitchers, *LHB* and *RHB* show how the opposition lefthanders and righthanders hit against the pitcher. *Sc Pos* shows batting or pitching performance with runners in scoring position. *Clutch* shows batting or pitching performance in clutch situations, defined as the seventh inning or later with the batting team ahead by one run, tied or with the tying run on base, at bat or on deck. Our definition is consistent with save situations.

2003 Rankings
This section shows how the player ranked in his league and among his teammates. Because of space considerations, we omitted some of the less interesting rankings when a player placed high in numerous categories.

We include many less traditional categories. The Definitions and Qualifications section below provides details for these statistics.

Definitions and Qualifications

The following are definitions and qualifications for the Major League Leaders and Rankings.

Definitions:

Times on Base — Hits plus walks plus hit-by-pitch.

Groundball-Flyball Ratio — Groundballs hit divided by the total of flyballs and popups hit. Bunts and line drives are excluded.

Runs/Times on Base — Runs scored divided by times on base.

Clutch — A player's batting average in the late innings of close games, defined as the seventh inning or later with the batting team ahead by one run, tied or with the tying run on base, at bat or on deck.

Bases Loaded — A player's batting average in bases-loaded situations.

GDP per GDP situation — Groundball double plays divided by groundball double-play situations, defined as a man on first base with less than two out.

Percentage of Pitches Taken — The percentage of pitches a player lets go by without swinging.

Percentage Swings Put In Play — The percentage of swings resulting in a batted ball into fair territory or a foul-ball out.

Run Support per Nine Innings — The number of runs scored for a pitcher while he was pitching, scaled to a nine-inning figure.

Baserunners per Nine Innings — The total of hits, walks and hit batsmen allowed per nine innings.

Strikeout-Walk Ratio — Strikeouts divided by walks.

Stolen-Base Percentage Allowed — Stolen bases divided by stolen-base attempts.

Save Percentage — Saves divided by save opportunities. Save opportunities include saves plus blown saves.

Blown Saves — A blown save is charged any time a pitcher enters a game in a save situation and loses the lead. A save situation is defined as any time a reliever enters the game with a lead, isn't the pitcher of record and either a) pitches at least one inning with a lead of no more than three runs; b) enters the game with the potential tying run on base, at bat or on deck; or c) pitches effectively for at least three innings.

Holds — A hold is given to a pitcher when he enters a game in a save situation and is removed before the end of the game while maintaining his team's lead. The pitcher must retire at least one batter to get a hold.

Percentage of Inherited Runners Scored — Percentage of runners already on base when a pitcher enters a game that he allows to score.

First Batter Efficiency — The batting average allowed by a reliever to the first batter he faces in a game.

Qualifications:

In order to be ranked, a player had to qualify with a minimum number of opportunities, as follows:

Batters

Batting average, slugging percentage, on-base percentage, home run frequency, groundball-flyball ratio, runs scored per time reached base and pitches seen per plate appearance — 3.1 plate appearances per team game

Percentage of pitches taken, lowest percentage of swings that missed and percentage of swings put into play — 9.26 pitches seen per team game

Percentage of extra bases taken as a runner — .09 opportunities to advance per team game

Stolen-base percentage — .12 stolen-base attempts per team game

Runners in scoring position — .62 plate appearances with runners in scoring position per team game

Clutch — .31 plate appearances in the clutch per team game

Bases loaded — .06 plate appearances with the bases loaded per team game

GDP per GDP situation — .31 plate appearances in GDP situations per team game

BA vs. LHP — .77 plate appearances against left-handers per team game

BA vs. RHP — 2.33 plate appearances against righthanders per team game

BA at home — 1.55 plate appearances at home per team game

BA on the road — 1.55 plate appearances on the road per team game

Leadoff on-base percentage — .93 plate appearances in the No. 1 lineup spot per team game

Cleanup slugging percentage — .93 plate appearances in the No. 4 lineup spot per team game

BA on 3-1 count — .06 plate appearances with a 3-1 count per team game

BA with 2 strikes — .62 plate appearances with two strikes per team game

BA on 0-2 count — .12 plate appearances with an 0-2 count per team game

BA on 3-2 count — .12 plate appearances with a 3-2 count per team game

Pitchers

Earned run average, run support per nine innings, baserunners per nine innings, batting average allowed, slugging percentage allowed, on-base percentage allowed, home runs per nine innings, strikeouts per nine innings, strikeout-walk ratio, stolen-base percentage allowed, GDPs per nine innings, pitches thrown per batter and groundball-flyball ratio against—one inning per team game

Winning percentage — .09 decisions per team game

GDPs induced per GDP situation — .19 batters faced in GDP situations per team game

BA allowed, runners in scoring position — .77 batters faced with runners in scoring position per team game

ERA at home — .5 innings at home per team game

ERA on the road — .5 innings on the road per team game

BA vs. LHB — .77 lefthanders faced per team game

BA vs. RHB — 1.39 righthanders faced per team game

Relievers

ERA, batting average allowed, baserunners per nine innings, strikeouts per nine innings — .31 relief innings per team game

Save percentage — .12 save opportunities per team game

Percentage of inherited runners scoring — .19 inherited runners per team game

First batter efficiency — .25 games in relief per team game

Fielders

Percentage caught stealing by catchers — .43 stolen-base attempts per team game

Fielding percentage — .62 games at a position per team game (.19 chances per team game for pitchers)

Other Players

Some players didn't play enough to merit a full- or half-page essay, and aren't young enough or good enough to deserve a prospect report. But they did play in the majors last year, so we give them a brief evaluation. Following the half-page reports for each team, you'll find a page devoted to these part-timers under the heading "Other Anaheim Angels," etc. Each player gets a short summary and his 2004 Outlook is graded as follows:

A — Should be an important contributor.
B — Should play most of the season in the majors and contribute.
C — Unlikely to play much in the majors or contribute much if he does.
D — Unlikely to play in the majors.

Minor League Prospects

We present two pages of minor league prospects for each team. Prospect writers spoke directly to major league player-development personnel and also looked beyond athletic tools by analyzing statistics. Each club has seven or eight featured prospects. We try to include most of the top phenoms, but our primary emphasis is on advanced players with the best chance of contributing in the majors in 2004.

We also include an organizational overview for each team, which gives you a glimpse into the current state of each club's minor league system. In addition, we summarize a few more notable prospects per team in a section called "Others to Watch."

Where we mention that managers voted a player as the best in a specific category in his league, our source is *Baseball America*.

Major League Leaders

After the team sections, we provide a complete listing of MLB leaders for the 2003 season. The top three players in each category are shown for the American and National Leagues. You'll notice a STATS flavor to these leaders. Not only do we show the leaders for the common categories such as batting average, home runs and ERA, but you'll also find less traditional categories like steals of third and total pitches thrown.

American League Players

Edison International Field

Offense

Perhaps this is a reasonable definition of a fair park: half the lineup disappears, but the team's production at home remains fairly constant. The Angels lost Troy Glaus, Brad Fullmer, Bengie Molina, Darin Erstad and David Eckstein for much of 2003, but they hit just three fewer home runs at Edison Field than they did in their championship season of 2002.

Defense

Tim Salmon's defense has deteriorated and the Angels prefer him as their designated hitter, but they'll be losing a home-field advantage because a new right fielder must learn the peculiarities of the park. The Angels are looking at moving Garret Anderson to center or right field, but in left he successfully plays balls down the line often holding runners at first base on apparent doubles.

Who It Helps the Most

Adam Kennedy has one of the most unorthodox swings in the majors, a lefthanded uppercut that causes coaches to cringe, but his approach works well at home. The alley in right-center is 17 feet closer to home plate than the one in left-center, and many of Kennedy's flies clank off that high wall in right-center—or clear it. Kennedy hit .284 with 18 extra-base hits at home, .256 with 13 extra-base hits on the road.

Who It Hurts the Most

Flyball pitchers without dependable center fielders struggle at Edison Field. The ball flies on hot summer days, and the Angels shifted Sunday starts from 5 p.m. to 1 p.m. last year, in a season in which Gold Glover Erstad was largely unavailable to patrol the spacious outfield. Jarrod Washburn, the Angels' most pronounced flyball pitcher, has a career ERA of 4.54 at home and 3.42 on the road.

Rookies & Newcomers

New staff ace Bartolo Colon was more of a flyball pitcher in 2003, a trend he will want to reverse. The Angels moved their fastest player, Chone Figgins, from second base to center field last season. He's no Erstad, but his arm is no worse and his speed can make up for mistakes as he learns the position.

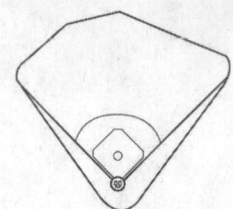

Dimensions: LF-330, LCF-387, CF-400, RCF-370, RF-330

Capacity: 45,030

Elevation: 160 feet

Surface: Grass

Foul Territory: Average

Park Factors

2003 Season

	Home Games Angels	Opp	Total	Away Games Angels	Opp	Total	Index
G	73	73	146	71	71	142	
Avg	.268	.264	.266	.266	.269	.268	99
AB	2398	2565	4963	2451	2355	4806	100
R	320	312	632	323	367	690	89
H	643	677	1320	652	634	1286	100
2B	122	132	254	131	111	242	102
3B	12	8	20	14	17	31	62
HR	59	76	135	62	94	156	84
BB	203	224	427	224	222	446	93
SO	348	472	820	392	398	790	101
E	44	32	76	44	36	80	92
E-Infield	37	26	63	36	27	63	97
LHB-Avg	.281	.245	.262	.286	.272	.279	94
LHB-HR	28	36	64	34	46	80	75
RHB-Avg	.257	.282	.270	.250	.267	.258	105
RHB-HR	31	40	71	28	48	76	93

2001-2003

	Home Games Angels	Opp	Total	Away Games Angels	Opp	Total	Index
G	217	217	434	215	215	430	
Avg	.270	.258	.264	.268	.257	.263	100
AB	7296	7618	14914	7545	7069	14614	101
R	997	949	1946	1012	950	1962	98
H	1971	1965	3936	2023	1816	3839	102
2B	372	397	769	426	317	743	101
3B	40	18	58	37	40	77	74
HR	199	218	417	192	248	440	93
BB	630	688	1318	645	685	1330	97
SO	1113	1368	2481	1224	1240	2464	99
E	137	127	264	128	153	281	93
E-Infield	119	101	220	114	121	235	93
LHB-Avg	.278	.249	.264	.274	.255	.265	99
LHB-HR	85	96	181	95	108	203	86
RHB-Avg	.262	.265	.264	.262	.259	.260	101
RHB-HR	114	122	236	97	140	237	99

2003 Rankings (American League)

- Second-lowest triple factor
- Second-lowest LHB home-run factor
- Third-lowest run factor
- Third-lowest home-run factor
- Third-lowest walk factor
- Third-lowest LHB batting-average factor

Mike Scioscia

2003 Season

Within two months of buying the Angels, new owner Arte Moreno extended the contracts of Mike Scioscia and general manager Bill Stoneman through the 2007 season. No manager could have won with the inconsistency of the Angels' starting pitchers and the injuries that depleted the starting lineup; Scioscia actually fielded more lineups than Detroit's Alan Trammell. But, for the third consecutive season under Scioscia, the Angels spiraled into a hideous skid: 5-20 in 2003, 6-14 in 2002 and 2-19 in 2001.

Offense

Garret Anderson and Tim Salmon won't be dropping a bunt any time soon, but the Angels' offensive miseries last year did not sway Scioscia from his belief that the "Moneyball" way is not the only way. The Angels led the league in stolen-base attempts and double steals, and ranked amoung the top three in the league in hit-and-run attempts, sacrifice attempts and squeeze attempts.

Pitching & Defense

For the second consecutive season, the Angels' bullpen boasted the best earned-run average in the league. Scioscia wasn't shy about using his relievers, to the point where several starters complained to him they were getting all the blame without getting a chance to work out of jams. The starters posted a 4.90 ERA last summer, up from 4.00 in 2002. Scioscia rarely extended a starter past 110 pitches, and only once used one past 120, and closer Troy Percival never pitched more than one inning.

2004 Outlook

The contract extension gives Scioscia a hammer in the clubhouse: The manager will be there for another four years, whether a player likes it or not. The Angels like that dynamic, as they don't have much patience for disgruntled players. No matter what moves the front office might make, Scioscia says no factor will be more critical to 2004 success than a return to health for Darin Erstad, Troy Glaus, Bengie Molina, Jarrod Washburn, Aaron Sele, Adam Kennedy, David Eckstein, Brendan Donnelly. . .

Born: 11/27/58 in Upper Darby, PA

Playing Experience: 1980-1992, LA

Managerial Experience: 4 seasons

Manager Statistics

Year	Team, Lg	W	L	Pct	GB	Finish
2003	Anaheim, AL	77	85	.475	19.0	3rd West
4 Seasons		333	315	.514	–	–

2003 Starting Pitchers by Days Rest

	<=3	4	5	6+
Angels Starts	0	73	65	15
Angels ERA	–	4.50	4.95	6.22
AL Avg Starts	2	79	50	22
AL ERA	3.19	4.64	4.57	4.98

2003 Situational Stats

	Mike Scioscia	AL Average
Hit & Run Success %	35.8	36.7
Stolen Base Success %	67.9	70.0
Platoon Pct.	63.9	61.7
Defensive Subs	36	23
High-Pitch Outings	1	5
Quick/Slow Hooks	26/16	19/16
Sacrifice Attempts	70	55

2003 Rankings (American League)

- 1st in stolen base attempts (190), steals of home plate (2), double steals (7) and pitchouts with a runner moving (12)
- 2nd in steals of second base (113), squeeze plays (6), hit-and-run attempts (109), defensive substitutions and quick hooks
- 3rd in sacrifice bunt attempts, starting lineups used (130) and 2+ pitching changes in low-scoring games (32)

Garret Anderson

2003 Season

On a Monday in July, Garret Anderson won the home-run derby. The next night, in his first All-Star Game start, he won the MVP award. By then, the world outside Southern California had caught on to just how good a player he is. Above all, Anderson is a marvel of consistency. He is the only player in the American League to average 190 hits over the past four seasons.

Hitting

Anderson's productivity and durability are perhaps best reflected in this statistic: In each of the past four seasons, he has topped 185 hits, 35 doubles, 25 home runs and 115 RBI. Lou Gehrig is the only player in major league history to post all those numbers in more than four seasons. The pickier fans harp on his unwillingness to draw walks, but he led the AL batting race in early September and was tied for the league lead in doubles. He combines average, power, the ability to hit lefties and righties equally well and the knack for driving in runs as well as anyone in the league.

Baserunning & Defense

The Angels consider Anderson the best defensive left fielder in the league. He positions himself smartly and reads caroms well, forcing runners to halt at first base and abandon thoughts of an easy double. His arm is adequate, and he'll seldom challenge a runner trying to score from third base if the safe play is to hold another runner at first or second. He has decent speed, but uses it less for stolen bases and more for taking an extra base.

2004 Outlook

The Angels pledged last summer to negotiate an extension with Anderson, whose contract expires after the 2004 season. He could move to right field or center, depending on the Angels' offseason moves. He played in the first 154 games before missing two because of back stiffness, and he has missed an average of just 4.3 games per year over the past seven seasons. There is no surer bet in baseball than Anderson staying healthy and hitting well.

Position: LF/DH
Bats: L **Throws:** L
Ht: 6' 3" **Wt:** 225

Opening Day Age: 31
Born: 6/30/72 in Los Angeles, CA
ML Seasons: 10

Overall Statistics

	G	AB	R	H	D	T	HR	RBI	SB	BB	SO	Avg	OBP	Slg
'03	159	638	80	201	49	4	29	116	6	31	83	.315	.345	.541
Car.	1365	5455	703	1633	349	27	193	872	66	251	732	.299	.328	.479

Where He Hits the Ball

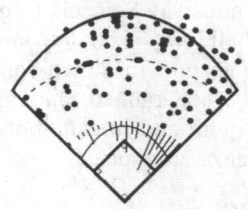
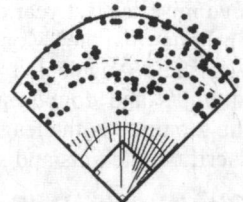

Vs. LHP **Vs. RHP**

2003 Situational Stats

	AB	H	HR	RBI	Avg		AB	H	HR	RBI	Avg
Home	316	92	12	48	.291	LHP	232	72	8	39	.310
Road	322	109	17	68	.339	RHP	406	129	21	77	.318
First Half	370	117	22	78	.316	Sc Pos	162	55	6	79	.340
Scnd Half	268	84	7	38	.313	Clutch	92	34	3	22	.370

2003 Rankings (American League)

- 1st in doubles and fielding percentage in left field (.997)
- 2nd in batting average on the road
- 3rd in cleanup slugging percentage (.583)
- 4th in hits, batting average in the clutch and fewest pitches seen per plate appearance (3.27)
- Led the Angels in batting average, home runs, at-bats, runs scored, hits, singles, total bases (345), RBI, intentional walks (10), times on base (232), plate appearances (673), games played, slugging percentage, batting average in the clutch, batting average vs. lefthanded pitchers, batting average vs. righthanded pitchers, cleanup slugging percentage (.583)

David Eckstein 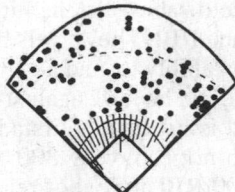 Great Bunter

Anaheim

Position: SS
Bats: R **Throws:** R
Ht: 5' 7" **Wt:** 165

Opening Day Age: 29
Born: 1/20/75 in
Sanford, FL
ML Seasons: 3
Pronunciation:
eck-STINE

2003 Season

David Eckstein started the season as one of America's darlings, the spunky little can-do shortstop for the defending World Series champions. He ended the season injured, as did many of his teammates, with his hold on his job increasingly tenuous. His batting average dropped as low as .228 in June, the Angels dropped him from first to ninth in the lineup for a spell, and his season was so crummy he actually suffered whiplash in a collision with left fielder Garret Anderson.

Hitting

Nagging spring injuries limited Eckstein's Cactus League work, and hitting coach Mickey Hatcher said Eckstein never got the repetitions he needed. He slogged through the opening weeks, and his average did not climb above .200 until April 16. He was better after the All-Star break and finished among the league leaders in sacrifice bunts, times hit by pitch and toughest to strike out. The Angels consider him one of the most effective major leaguers in executing the hit-and-run.

Baserunning & Defense

Eckstein ranked second in the league in fielding percentage among shortstops, and the Angels compare his on-field smarts to those of Alex Rodriguez. But his arm is weak and his range is limited. He may be better suited for his natural position of second base. He will be hurt if Scott Spiezio departs via free agency and the Angels replace Spiezio with a first baseman who is unable to corral Eckstein's awkward throws. Eckstein runs the bases with smarts and speed, successful on 16 of 21 stolen-base attempts.

2004 Outlook

Prospect Alfredo Amezaga is far superior to Eckstein in range, arm and speed, but he hit .210 in 37 major league games last season, so the Angels don't plan to displace Eckstein for Amezaga. They would displace him for a top free agent, though, particularly if they can acquire a leadoff hitter as well. The Angels then could cut or trade Eckstein, try him at second base where incumbent Adam Kennedy is flourishing, or use him in the utility role in which they originally envisioned him.

Overall Statistics

	G	AB	R	H	D	T	HR	RBI	SB	BB	SO	Avg	OBP	Slg
'03	120	452	59	114	22	1	3	31	16	36	45	.252	.325	.325
Car.	425	1642	248	458	70	9	15	135	66	124	149	.279	.350	.360

Where He Hits the Ball

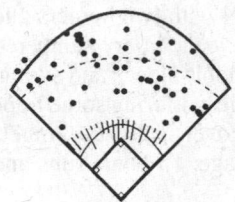

Vs. LHP   **Vs. RHP**

2003 Situational Stats

	AB	H	HR	RBI	Avg		AB	H	HR	RBI	Avg
Home	215	63	1	20	.293	LHP	133	34	2	12	.256
Road	237	51	2	11	.215	RHP	319	80	1	19	.251
First Half	304	72	3	21	.237	Sc Pos	88	24	0	27	.273
Scnd Half	148	42	0	10	.284	Clutch	72	20	1	8	.278

2003 Rankings (American League)

- 2nd in lowest percentage of swings that missed (7.7), fielding percentage at shortstop (.984), lowest slugging percentage and lowest batting average on the road
- 3rd in lowest HR frequency (150.7 ABs per HR)
- 4th in sacrifice bunts (10)
- Led the Angels in sacrifice bunts (10), hit by pitch (15), highest groundball-flyball ratio (1.6), highest percentage of pitches taken (59.6), lowest percentage of swings that missed (7.7), steals of third (4), batting average at home and lowest percentage of swings on the first pitch (12.3)

Darin Erstad

2003 Season

Nobody knew it at the time, but Darin Erstad's season was a washout from the first week. He felt a bit of pain behind his right knee, kept playing for another two weeks, then disappeared into a haze of visits to the trainer's room, to the disabled list and to medical specialists. He played 67 games, none after August 6, and began the winter with fingers crossed, hoping the hamstring injury that troubled him all summer would heal over the winter.

Hitting

When he did play, Erstad contributed little on offense and virtually nothing in the way of power. In the 49 games he played between two stints on the disabled list, he hit .224 with two homers and nine RBI. The Angels believe the injury hampered his ability to find a comfortable stance and swing. He did hit .302 against lefties, offering some hope all is not lost. If Erstad recovers fully, the Angels do not believe a .300 average, 15 home runs and 100 RBI are out of reach.

Baserunning & Defense

Erstad is a Gold Glove center fielder, and his presence in the outfield makes Anaheim pitchers better, particularly flyball pitcher · Jarrod Washburn. But the Angels might move Erstad— probably to first base, possibly to left field— thinking a less demanding defensive position might minimize the injury risk and keep his bat in the lineup. He won a Gold Glove in left field in 2000 and has impressed in several stints at first base. He is a terrific baserunner, stealing 75 bases from 2000-02 and nine of 10 even while injured last year.

2004 Outlook

Erstad decided against surgery to remove the partially torn tendon within his right hamstring, largely because the procedure offered no guarantees. So the Angels must wait to learn whether a winter of rest and therapy will allow him to play effectively. If so, they'll welcome back an offensive sparkplug and their clubhouse leader. If not, the three years and $24 million remaining on his contract will be quite an albatross.

Position: CF
Bats: L **Throws:** L
Ht: 6' 2" **Wt:** 210

Opening Day Age: 29
Born: 6/4/74 in Jamestown, ND
ML Seasons: 8
Pronunciation: ER-stad

Overall Statistics

	G	AB	R	H	D	T	HR	RBI	SB	BB	SO	Avg	OBP	Slg
'03	67	258	35	65	7	1	4	17	9	18	40	.252	.309	.333
Car.	1002	4059	645	1172	209	25	100	485	143	329	595	.289	.344	.426

Where He Hits the Ball

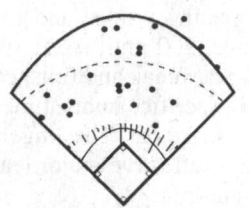 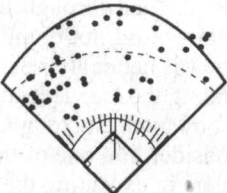

Vs. LHP　　　　**Vs. RHP**

2003 Situational Stats

	AB	H	HR	RBI	Avg		AB	H	HR	RBI	Avg
Home	143	37	1	11	.259	LHP	86	26	2	7	.302
Road	115	28	3	6	.243	RHP	172	39	2	10	.227
First Half	184	50	3	15	.272	Sc Pos	50	9	0	13	.180
Scnd Half	74	15	1	2	.203	Clutch	31	8	1	5	.258

2003 Rankings (American League)

- Did not rank near the top or bottom in any category

Troy Glaus

2003 Season

In a July game against the Devil Rays, Julio Lugo dropped down a bunt and Troy Glaus charged the ball. Pitcher Aaron Sele tipped it and Glaus slipped as he shifted direction. His right shoulder crashed into the Tropicana Field turf, and after an aborted rehabilitation assignment, he was diagnosed with a partially torn rotator cuff. Glaus never played at 100 percent all year, with wrist, hamstring, back and shoulder injuries preceding the season-ending rotator cuff tear.

Hitting

The batting average could be better, but that's an old story. Glaus prefers to focus on run production. He strikes out too much, same thing. So the most alarming aspect of Glaus' season was the drop in power. He hit 118 home runs from 2000-02—with a league-leading 47 in 2000—but just 16 in 2003, and only two in his final 35 games. He also batted .149 in that stretch, so the Angels hope they can attribute the slump to flaws in his swing, some related to injury. He does a nice job taking walks and working counts.

Baserunning & Defense

Glaus posted a poor .923 fielding percentage and committed 16 errors, many on poor throws that the Angels attribute to his sore shoulder. His ability to field the ball regressed last season, a slump coaches believe had physical and mental components. At his best, Glaus has one of the best throwing arms of any major league infielder. He runs surprisingly well for a 240-pound man and can steal one when he catches an opponent off guard.

2004 Outlook

Glaus opted against surgery to repair his rotator cuff, so spring training will tell how effective his therapy was. He will make $9.55 million for the 2004 season, the last on his contract, and owner Arte Moreno projects the payroll will drop for 2005. If Glaus recovers the form that made him a top third baseman and one of the purest power threats in the majors, the Angels should pay up happily. If he doesn't, the Angels could replace him with budding prospect Dallas McPherson.

Position: 3B
Bats: R **Throws:** R
Ht: 6' 5" **Wt:** 240

Opening Day Age: 27
Born: 8/3/76 in Tarzana, CA
ML Seasons: 6
Pronunciation: gloss

Overall Statistics

	G	AB	R	H	D	T	HR	RBI	SB	BB	SO	Avg	OBP	Slg
'03	91	319	53	79	17	2	16	50	7	46	73	.248	.343	.464
Car.	769	2755	476	696	154	6	164	473	47	439	732	.253	.357	.491

Where He Hits the Ball

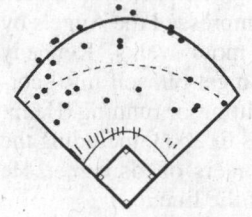 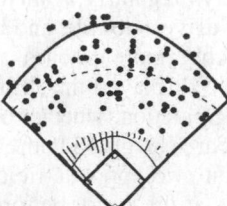

Vs. LHP   **Vs. RHP**

2003 Situational Stats

	AB	H	HR	RBI	Avg		AB	H	HR	RBI	Avg
Home	160	41	9	24	.256	LHP	89	27	2	10	.303
Road	159	38	7	26	.239	RHP	230	52	14	40	.226
First Half	303	78	15	49	.257	Sc Pos	90	25	1	31	.278
Scnd Half	16	1	1	1	.063	Clutch	40	12	2	12	.300

2003 Rankings (American League)

- 5th in errors at third base (16)
- 9th in lowest batting average with two strikes (.147)
- Led the Angels in HR frequency (19.9 ABs per HR), most pitches seen per plate appearance (4.03) and batting average with the bases loaded (.444)

Adam Kennedy

2003 Season

The second-base platoon that served the Angels so well in 2002, with Adam Kennedy playing against righthanders and Benji Gil against lefthanders, collapsed in 2003. Gil failed to keep his average above .200, and the Angels benched him in July and released him in August. At that juncture, for the first time since his rookie season of 2000, Kennedy got the chance to play every day. He batted .293 as a regular, and he hit nine of his 13 homers in his final 63 games.

Hitting

The Angels stuck Kennedy with the "can't hit left-handers" label, but he can hit lefties when he plays regularly against them. He can drop a bunt or drive a double, and he impressed the Angels by taking more pitches and more walks. Kennedy also displayed the ability to get himself into scoring position, whether by hitting or running. He hit a career-high 13 home runs in 2003, including the first two opposite-field homers of his career. He fits at the top or bottom of the lineup.

Baserunning & Defense

When the Angels acquired Kennedy four years ago, they considered him an asset at bat and a project in the field. They now consider him better afield than every second baseman in the league save Gold Glover Bret Boone, with his ability to range far and make a play on a groundball rather than simply stopping it. Kennedy isn't particularly fast, but he led the team and tied a career high with 22 stolen bases, thanks to his good jumps and astute reads of opposing pitchers.

2004 Outlook

Kennedy is on the rise, approaching his considerable potential as a middle infielder who can hit .300 with 20 home runs and 20 stolen bases. His salary could rise above $3 million in arbitration, and the Angels could cut costs by shifting the more affordable David Eckstein from shortstop or installing a minimum-wage rookie at second. But the Angels would be silly to allow Kennedy to flourish elsewhere after they invested four years in his development.

Position: 2B
Bats: L **Throws:** R
Ht: 6' 1" **Wt:** 185

Opening Day Age: 28
Born: 1/10/76 in Riverside, CA
ML Seasons: 5

Overall Statistics

	G	AB	R	H	D	T	HR	RBI	SB	BB	SO	Avg	OBP	Slg
'03	143	449	71	121	17	1	13	49	22	45	73	.269	.344	.399
Car.	613	2101	278	583	117	22	36	229	73	122	305	.277	.323	.406

Where He Hits the Ball

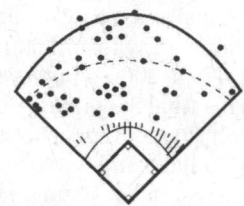
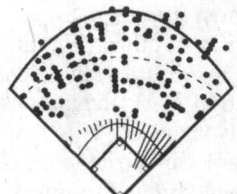

Vs. LHP   **Vs. RHP**

2003 Situational Stats

	AB	H	HR	RBI	Avg		AB	H	HR	RBI	Avg
Home	211	60	8	28	.284	LHP	115	27	2	13	.235
Road	238	61	5	21	.256	RHP	334	94	11	36	.281
First Half	227	56	4	24	.247	Sc Pos	96	23	3	37	.240
Scnd Half	222	65	9	25	.293	Clutch	67	17	1	10	.254

2003 Rankings (American League)

- 1st in fielding percentage at second base (.990)
- 3rd in lowest groundball-flyball ratio (0.7)
- 5th in caught stealing (9)
- 10th in stolen bases and lowest stolen-base percentage (71.0)
- Led the Angels in stolen bases and caught stealing (9)

John Lackey

2003 Season

John Lackey won Game 7 of the 2002 World Series, but he lost Game 1 of the 2003 season and many more thereafter. His 16 losses were the most by any American League pitcher who did not work for the Tigers, and the most by an Angels righthander since 1991. But he also had the worst run support of any AL pitcher who did not work for the Tigers. He started slowly but finished strong, with a 7.76 ERA through April and a 2.65 ERA in September, pitching 204 innings and closing with a season-low 4.63 ERA in his first full major league season.

Pitching

Lackey's opponents scored in the first inning way too often. In seven of his first eight starts, he failed to pitch a scoreless first. But he righted himself from there, and he streamlined his repertoire midway through the year by junking his curve. When he is pitching well, he throws his fastball to the corners of the plate. That fastball and a solid slider helped him strike out 6.7 per nine innings, which ranked among the league's top 10. But his fastball command was erratic and he gave up 31 home runs, also among the AL top 10. His changeup is a work in progress.

Defense

Lackey, a converted first baseman, is an above-average fielder. His pickoff move is decent at best, but he got several huge assists from Gold Glove catcher Bengie Molina. In 136.1 innings with Molina catching Lackey, opposing runners stole seven of 14 bases. In 67.2 innings without Molina behind the plate, opponents were 7-for-8.

2004 Outlook

Lackey's final start of the 2003 season was a shutout, making him the first Angel to pitch two shutouts in a season since Chuck Finley in 1994. The Angels put Lackey in the Finley mold, a tall, hard-throwing guy with competitive instincts who might not dazzle with pure stuff, yet pitches 200 innings and never backs down. Lackey won 10 games with no run support last year. He should win 15 with a revitalized offense.

Position: SP
Bats: R **Throws:** R
Ht: 6' 6" **Wt:** 235

Opening Day Age: 25
Born: 10/23/78 in Abilene, TX
ML Seasons: 2

Overall Statistics

	W	L	Pct.	ERA	G	GS	Sv	IP	H	BB	SO	HR	Avg
'03	10	16	.385	4.63	33	33	0	204.0	223	66	151	31	.278
Car.	19	20	.487	4.29	51	51	0	312.1	336	99	220	41	.274

2003 Pitching Profile

	John Lackey	AL Average
Overall Strike %	63.2	62.8
1st Pitch Strike %	62.9	58.7
Ratio	1.42	1.39
Strikeouts per 9 IP	6.66	6.11
Walks per 9 IP	2.91	3.16
Home Runs per 9 IP	1.37	1.11
Strikeout/Walk Ratio	2.29	1.93
Groundball/Flyball Ratio	1.07	1.18

2003 Situational Stats

	W	L	ERA	Sv	IP		AB	H	HR	RBI	Avg
Home	8	6	3.57	0	113.1	LHB	448	128	15	61	.286
Road	2	10	5.96	0	90.2	RHB	353	95	16	45	.269
First Half	7	8	4.99	0	119.0	Sc Pos	180	49	8	75	.272
Scnd Half	3	8	4.13	0	85.0	Clutch	28	10	0	0	.357

2003 Rankings (American League)

- 1st in shutouts (2)
- 3rd in wild pitches (11) and least run support per nine innings (3.7)
- 4th in losses and highest ERA on the road
- 5th in home runs allowed
- 6th in errors at pitcher (3) and lowest fielding percentage at pitcher (.921)
- 7th in runners caught stealing (8) and most home runs allowed per nine innings (1.37)
- 8th in games started
- Led the Angels in losses, games started, complete games (2), shutouts (2), hits allowed, batters faced (885), walks allowed, strikeouts, wild pitches (11), pitches thrown (3,291), stolen bases allowed (14), runners caught stealing (8), and GDPs induced (20)

Bengie Molina

2003 Season

The third time wasn't the charm for Bengie Molina last year. In July, he emerged unscathed from a hellacious home-plate collision with Oakland's Jermaine Dye, one in which Dye suffered a separated shoulder. Three days later, Kansas City's Ken Harvey ran him over, and again Molina was unhurt. But in September, he suffered a broken wrist in a collision with Minnesota's Dustan Mohr. His season ended three weeks too soon, but by that time Molina had established himself as one of the elite catchers in the league.

Hitting

After a winter of intensive workouts, Molina enjoyed a summer of offensive resurgence. He hit .281 with 14 home runs and 71 RBI, tying career highs in all three categories. He displays decent opposite-field power. The Angels treasure his ability to make contact, particularly in the clutch. He hit .346 with men in scoring position and struck out only six times in 107 such at-bats. The hit-and-run is always an option, not only because he seldom swings and misses, but because he is so slow that any groundball could end up a double play.

Baserunning & Defense

Molina won his second consecutive Gold Glove award, again throwing out more than 40 percent of opposing runners in 2003. He works exceptionally hard in preparing with each pitcher, and he calls a good game. However, he tends to backhand—and sometimes miss—the low and outside pitches, instead of sliding his body over to block them. He stole his first base in three years last season, on the back end of a double steal.

2004 Outlook

Molina, a finalist for the All-Star team in 2003, nonetheless will hear footsteps this year. Catcher Jeff Mathis, one of the Angels' finest prospects, finished last season at Double-A Arkansas. Molina played in 119 of the Angels' 139 games before his injury, and the Angels happily will rely on him in 2004. A productive and injury-free season should persuade them to pick up a $3 million option for 2005.

Position: C
Bats: R **Throws:** R
Ht: 5'11" **Wt:** 220

Opening Day Age: 29
Born: 7/20/74 in Rio Piedras, PR
ML Seasons: 6

Overall Statistics

	G	AB	R	H	D	T	HR	RBI	SB	BB	SO	Avg	OBP	Slg
'03	119	409	37	115	24	0	14	71	1	13	31	.281	.304	.443
Car.	500	1737	169	464	78	2	40	239	2	73	155	.267	.302	.383

Where He Hits the Ball

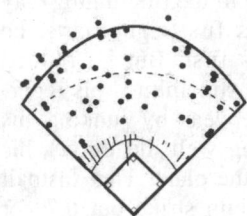
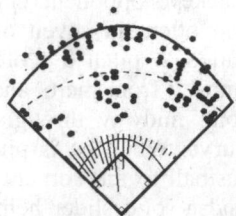

Vs. LHP   **Vs. RHP**

2003 Situational Stats

	AB	H	HR	RBI	Avg		AB	H	HR	RBI	Avg
Home	209	56	7	40	.268	LHP	114	33	7	19	.289
Road	200	59	7	31	.295	RHP	295	82	7	52	.278
First Half	270	77	9	49	.285	Sc Pos	107	37	6	58	.346
Scnd Half	139	38	5	22	.273	Clutch	58	16	1	13	.276

2003 Rankings (American League)

- 2nd in highest percentage of runners caught stealing as a catcher (40.8) and most GDPs per GDP situation (22.4%)
- 7th in batting average with runners in scoring position
- Led the Angels in GDPs (17) and highest percentage of swings put into play (53.3)

Ramon Ortiz

2003 Season

Hey, 16 wins. Pretty good, right? Ramon Ortiz became the first Angels righthander to win 16 games since 1989, the highlight of a deceptively poor year. In an otherwise sorry offensive season, the Angels provided Ortiz with the fourth-best run support of any American League pitcher. In return, he failed to complete six innings 14 times in 32 starts. His ERA leaped from 3.77 in 2002 to 5.20 last year.

Pitching

Ortiz struck out none in his one complete game, the single-most compelling statistic in noting the alarming drop in his strikeouts from 162 in 2002 to 94 last summer. He once complained, in April, of feeling "no power" in his arm, but beyond that, he and the Angels insisted no injury was evident. Nonetheless, the zip came and went on his fastball, his slider was effective but inconsistent and he had to be reminded to stop throwing his changeup so hard.

Defense

Ortiz made great strides in not letting one poor pitch or one questionable call rattle him, but he still isn't as calm as he should be when fielding, leading to needless errors. His pickoff move is better, but far from good, and even Gold Glove catcher Bengie Molina could throw out only one of the nine runners who tried to steal with Ortiz pitching.

2004 Outlook

Ortiz' father died in September after fighting emphysema for years, and Ortiz pitched with a heavy heart as the illness worsened. He vowed to dedicate the rest of his career to his late father. Ortiz, once dubbed "Pocket Pedro," is no Martinez, but can be a solid No. 2 or 3 starter when right. The Angels have a $5.5 million option on Ortiz for the 2005 season, so he must rebound this year to remain in Anaheim beyond 2004.

Position: SP
Bats: R **Throws:** R
Ht: 6' 0" **Wt:** 175

Opening Day Age: 30
Born: 5/23/73 in Cotui, DR
ML Seasons: 5
Pronunciation: or-TEEZ

Overall Statistics

	W	L	Pct.	ERA	G	GS	Sv	IP	H	BB	SO	HR	Avg
'03	16	13	.552	5.20	32	32	0	180.0	209	63	94	28	.287
Car.	54	42	.563	4.63	123	123	0	765.2	766	287	508	118	.259

2003 Pitching Profile

	Ramon Ortiz	AL Average
Overall Strike %	61.6	62.8
1st Pitch Strike %	55.9	58.7
Ratio	1.51	1.39
Strikeouts per 9 IP	4.70	6.11
Walks per 9 IP	3.15	3.16
Home Runs per 9 IP	1.40	1.11
Strikeout/Walk Ratio	1.49	1.93
Groundball/Flyball Ratio	0.91	1.18

2003 Situational Stats

	W	L	ERA	Sv	IP		AB	H	HR	RBI	Avg
Home	8	8	5.24	0	92.2	LHB	378	110	16	54	.291
Road	8	5	5.15	0	87.1	RHB	351	99	12	57	.282
First Half	11	6	4.41	0	112.1	Sc Pos	177	55	7	83	.311
Scnd Half	5	7	6.52	0	67.2	Clutch	20	5	0	2	.250

2003 Rankings (American League)

- 2nd in hit batsmen (12)
- 3rd in errors at pitcher (4) and lowest fielding percentage at pitcher (.882)
- 4th in most run support per nine innings (6.3), highest ERA and highest on-base percentage allowed (.350)
- 5th in lowest strikeout-walk ratio (1.5), highest slugging percentage allowed (.461), highest stolen-base percentage allowed (87.5) and most home runs allowed per nine innings (1.40)
- 6th in highest batting average allowed (.287) and highest ERA at home
- 7th in highest ERA on the road
- Led the Angels in wins, hit batsmen (12), pickoff throws (106), stolen bases allowed (14) and most run support per nine innings (6.3)

Troy Percival

2003 Season

The diagnosis is serious for any man, and frightening for one who must twist and turn his body to make a living. In May, doctors told Troy Percival he had a degenerative condition in his right hip. To minimize stress on the hip, and as an alternative to season-ending surgery, Percival revamped his delivery and scrapped his trademark high leg kick. Still, he earned at least 30 saves for the sixth consecutive year. He also converted a club-record 20 consecutive save opportunities between June 8 and August 22.

Pitching

At 34, Percival maintains the velocity that persuaded the Angels to convert him from catcher 13 years ago. The fastball still registers 96-98 MPH regularly and 100 MPH occasionally, and Percival insists his modified delivery improves command without a significant decline in velocity. He displayed more confidence in his curve and change-up, still thrown rarely but enough to convince Anaheim coaches he still could be an effective closer whenever his fastball decelerates to mortal speed.

Defense

Percival is so tough to hit—and so easy to run on—that many opponents will attempt to steal second. The elimination of the high leg kick gives his catchers a chance, but his delivery remains deliberate enough to tilt the balance in favor of the runner. He is not graceful in the field, but he is rarely tested in his one-inning stints.

2004 Outlook

Percival is 17 saves from 300, and 22 from passing Kansas City's Jeff Montgomery as the leader among closers who recorded all their saves for one team. Percival's contract expires this year, and he isn't sure he would want to pitch anywhere else. Owner Arte Moreno says he expects to cut player payroll after this season. So the Angels could replace Percival, who stands to earn $7.5 million in 2004, with Francisco Rodriguez, who is not eligible for arbitration until 2006.

Position: RP
Bats: R **Throws:** R
Ht: 6' 3" **Wt:** 235

Opening Day Age: 34
Born: 8/9/69 in Fontana, CA
ML Seasons: 9
Pronunciation: PURR-si-vul
Nickname: Percy

Overall Statistics

	W	L	Pct.	ERA	G	GS	Sv	IP	H	BB	SO	HR	Avg
'03	0	5	.000	3.47	52	0	33	49.1	33	23	48	7	.184
Car.	27	35	.435	3.00	527	0	283	537.0	350	234	647	56	.182

2003 Pitching Profile

	Troy Percival	AL Average
Overall Strike %	62.6	62.8
1st Pitch Strike %	57.3	58.7
Ratio	1.14	1.39
Strikeouts per 9 IP	8.76	6.11
Walks per 9 IP	4.20	3.16
Home Runs per 9 IP	1.28	1.11
Strikeout/Walk Ratio	2.09	1.93
Groundball/Flyball Ratio	0.47	1.18

2003 Situational Stats

	W	L	ERA	Sv	IP		AB	H	HR	RBI	Avg
Home	0	3	4.74	17	24.2	LHB	91	15	3	11	.165
Road	0	2	2.19	16	24.2	RHB	88	18	4	9	.205
First Half	0	2	2.48	20	29.0	Sc Pos	39	6	1	11	.154
Scnd Half	0	3	4.87	13	20.1	Clutch	117	20	4	16	.171

2003 Rankings (American League)

- 3rd in save percentage (89.2)
- 5th in saves
- 6th in fewest GDPs induced per GDP situation (2.2%)
- 7th in games finished (49)
- Led the Angels in saves, games finished (49), lowest batting average allowed vs. lefthanded batters, save percentage (89.2), blown saves (4) and relief losses (5)

Francisco Rodriguez

2003 Season

The world met "K-Rod" during the 2002 playoffs, when his fearless and fearsome performance at age 20 captivated fans. But those postseason heroics counted for nothing last year, and Francisco Rodriguez delivered an excellent rookie season that disappointed only against the backdrop of his unhittable October of 2002. He stumbled early in 2003, but by the end of the year he had held opponents to a .172 batting average, best of any American League pitcher who worked at least 60 innings.

Pitching

The Angels did not call up Rodriguez until September 2002, so hitters had no idea about him that October. By last spring, however, every team was freshly armed with scouting reports and playoff video. The message: lay off the wicked slider, because you probably won't be able to hit it and it probably will be a ball. After a few weeks of adjustment, in which he learned to throw his slider for strikes now and then so hitters could no longer sit on his fastball and rip it, he resembled a closer-in-waiting yet again.

Defense

Rodriguez, an excellent athlete, fields his position well and holds runners well. He displays remarkable composure for such a young player, enabling him to catch his breath and make a key fielding play without rushing. His slider is tough to hit but tough to catch too, and his fastball also has plenty of movement. He threw seven wild pitches in 86 innings—Jarrod Washburn threw four in 207—and in one inning walked two and threw two wild pitches, one on strike three.

2004 Outlook

Rodriguez lost his setup role to Brendan Donnelly in mid-May, in part because Donnelly had yet to give up an earned run. Rodriguez gave up an earned run in nine of his first 15 appearances, and in just nine of his other 44 games, pulling even with Donnelly by the end of the season. Rodriguez is 22 and Donnelly 32, making Rodriguez the probable successor to closer Troy Percival.

Position: RP
Bats: R **Throws:** R
Ht: 6' 0" **Wt:** 185

Opening Day Age: 22
Born: 1/7/82 in Caracas, VZ
ML Seasons: 2

Overall Statistics

	W	L	Pct.	ERA	G	GS	Sv	IP	H	BB	SO	HR	Avg
'03	8	3	.727	3.03	59	0	2	86.0	50	35	95	12	.172
Car.	8	3	.727	2.85	64	0	2	91.2	53	37	108	12	.172

2003 Pitching Profile

	Francisco Rodriguez	AL Average
Overall Strike %	62.2	62.8
1st Pitch Strike %	55.8	58.7
Ratio	0.99	1.39
Strikeouts per 9 IP	9.94	6.11
Walks per 9 IP	3.66	3.16
Home Runs per 9 IP	1.26	1.11
Strikeout/Walk Ratio	2.71	1.93
Groundball/Flyball Ratio	1.09	1.18

2003 Situational Stats

	W	L	ERA	Sv	IP		AB	H	HR	RBI	Avg
Home	4	0	2.36	2	45.2	LHB	156	29	8	29	.186
Road	4	3	3.79	0	40.1	RHB	135	21	4	12	.156
First Half	5	1	3.00	1	48.0	Sc Pos	58	12	3	28	.207
Scnd Half	3	2	3.08	1	38.0	Clutch	102	22	5	20	.216

2003 Rankings (American League)

- 3rd in relief wins (8)
- 4th in lowest batting average allowed vs. left handed batters, relief innings (86.0) and wins among rookies
- 5th in most strikeouts per nine innings in relief (9.9) and fewest baserunners allowed per nine innings in relief (9.1)
- 6th in first batter efficiency (.149) and highest percentage of inherited runners scored (43.3)
- Led the Angels in winning percentage, lowest batting average allowed vs. righthanded batters, first batter efficiency (.149), blown saves (4), relief wins (8), relief innings (86.0), lowest batting average allowed in relief (.172), fewest baserunners allowed per nine innings in relief (9.1) and most strikeouts per nine innings in relief (9.9)

Tim Salmon

2003 Season

In a typical season, Tim Salmon starts slow and heats up with the weather. In 2003, he hit .316 in April and cooled considerably thereafter. He hit six homers in April, but only five after the All-Star break. He batted .305 through June 4, which included a career-best 20-game hitting streak, and .257 afterwards. His season could be painfully encapsulated in two days. On July 5, he hit two homers. On July 6, he awoke with back pain and was taken to a hospital and diagnosed with kidney stones.

Hitting

Salmon's run production dropped dramatically as the season went on, a decline he and the Angels hope can be attributed to an injury-depleted line-up that offered him little protection. Pitching around him is relatively easy, since he accepts more than his share of walks. His bat speed is still there, and he can crush a mistake just as easily as he can flail at a breaking ball.

Baserunning & Defense

One month after Salmon said he did not "ever see myself pigeonholed solely as a DH," the Angels took away his glove after DH Brad Fullmer blew out his knee. Salmon did not contest the decision. He still can play right field without embarrassing himself, and his arm remains strong, but the Angels regularly removed him for defensive purposes before moving him to DH. They also remove him for a pinch-runner in the late innings of close games.

2004 Outlook

The Angels offered Salmon the occasional shift in right field during the second half last season, but he did not play the field in September. He found that if he played the outfield once a week his back tended to stiffen the next day. Salmon figures to play out the final two seasons of his $40 million contract at DH. He cannot be traded without his consent, so the Angels pray his .250 average as a DH last season was an aberration. Barring injury, he'll become the first player in club history to be in the Opening Day lineup for 12 consecutive years.

Position: RF/DH
Bats: R **Throws:** R
Ht: 6' 3" **Wt:** 235

Opening Day Age: 35
Born: 8/24/68 in Long Beach, CA
ML Seasons: 12
Pronunciation: SAM-en

Overall Statistics

G	AB	R	H	D	T	HR	RBI	SB	BB	SO	Avg	OBP	Slg
148	528	78	145	35	4	19	72	3	77	93	.275	.374	.464
1536	5537	941	1571	324	22	288	966	47	927	1275	.284	.389	.506

Where He Hits the Ball

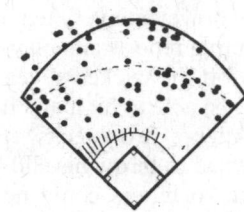 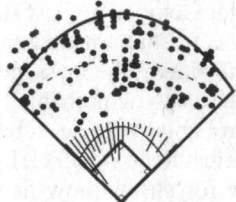

Vs. LHP   **Vs. RHP**

2003 Situational Stats

	AB	H	HR	RBI	Avg		AB	H	HR	RBI	Avg
Home	265	74	10	46	.279	LHP	157	43	7	26	.274
Road	263	71	9	26	.270	RHP	371	102	12	46	.275
First Half	315	87	14	47	.276	Sc Pos	145	41	6	55	.283
Scnd Half	213	58	5	25	.272	Clutch	77	24	2	14	.312

2003 Rankings (American League)

- 1st in errors in right field (6)
- 7th in lowest cleanup slugging percentage (.459)
- 10th in lowest groundball-flyball ratio (0.7)
- Led the Angels in walks, times on base (232), strikeouts, pitches seen (2,406) and on-base percentage

Jarrod Washburn

2003 Season

No sooner had the Angels granted Jarrod Washburn their Opening Day start than he slipped and tumbled to the ground in a spring fielding drill. He sprained his pitching shoulder and never would be 100 percent. The injury prevented him from starting the opener and left him with lingering soreness, and he also pitched through hip and back problems before leaving his final start with an ankle injury. Through it all, he pitched a career-high 207.1 innings and posted the lowest ERA among Anaheim starters.

Pitching

By the end of the season, Washburn threw an inordinately high number of sliders and changeups, and the new season will tell whether he expanded his repertoire for good or only for 2003, when the injuries robbed him of some fastball velocity. In 2002, when he won 18 games, he threw almost all fastballs, to varying spots and at speeds ranging from 83-93 MPH. He seldom topped 90 MPH last year, and Anaheim coaches hope he can become a better pitcher by integrating the slider and change with a revitalized fastball.

Defense

Washburn's biggest defensive ally is center fielder Darin Erstad, who won a Gold Glove in 2002 but spent most of 2003 nursing a hamstring injury. Washburn is a pronounced flyball pitcher, and he's not as effective without Erstad behind him. Washburn is a very good fielder, quick off the mound and alert to situations as they develop. His pickoff move is one of the best in the league.

2004 Outlook

As Washburn recovers the strength in his shoulder and the life to his fastball, he should regain his status as one of the top starters in the league. While the Angels love Washburn's competitive fire on the field, they renewed his contract in 2002 and did not offer him a long-term contract in 2003. He responded by saying he would not grant the team a hometown discount in a multiyear deal. He is eligible for free agency after the 2005 season and could be traded before then.

Position: SP
Bats: L **Throws:** L
Ht: 6' 1" **Wt:** 195

Opening Day Age: 29
Born: 8/13/74 in La Crosse, WI
ML Seasons: 6

Overall Statistics

	W	L	Pct.	ERA	G	GS	Sv	IP	H	BB	SO	HR	Avg
'03	10	15	.400	4.43	32	32	0	207.1	205	54	118	34	.256
Car.	56	41	.577	3.96	139	129	0	826.2	779	257	519	111	.248

2003 Pitching Profile

	Jarrod Washburn	AL Average
Overall Strike %	63.9	62.8
1st Pitch Strike %	60.8	58.7
Ratio	1.25	1.39
Strikeouts per 9 IP	5.12	6.11
Walks per 9 IP	2.34	3.16
Home Runs per 9 IP	1.48	1.11
Strikeout/Walk Ratio	2.19	1.93
Groundball/Flyball Ratio	0.68	1.18

2003 Situational Stats

	W	L	ERA	Sv	IP		AB	H	HR	RBI	Avg
Home	3	9	4.47	0	102.2	LHB	191	44	6	23	.230
Road	7	6	4.39	0	104.2	RHB	609	161	28	78	.264
First Half	8	9	4.22	0	128.0	Sc Pos	164	41	7	64	.250
Scnd Half	2	6	4.76	0	79.1	Clutch	58	21	3	8	.362

2003 Rankings (American League)

- 1st in home runs allowed and lowest ground ball-flyball ratio allowed (0.7)
- 2nd in most home runs allowed per nine innings (1.48)
- 4th in least run support per nine innings (3.7)
- 5th in losses
- 8th in hit batsmen (11)
- Led the Angels in complete games (2), innings pitched, home runs allowed and fewest pitches thrown per batter (3.70)

Jeff DaVanon

Position: RF/CF
Bats: B **Throws:** R
Ht: 6' 0" **Wt:** 185

Opening Day Age: 30
Born: 12/8/73 in San Diego, CA
ML Seasons: 4
Pronunciation: duh-VAN-un

Overall Statistics

	G	AB	R	H	D	T	HR	RBI	SB	BB	SO	Avg	OBP	Slg
'03	123	330	56	93	16	1	12	43	17	42	59	.282	.360	.445
Car.	186	468	70	119	21	3	19	60	19	57	101	.254	.333	.434

2003 Situational Stats

	AB	H	HR	RBI	Avg		AB	H	HR	RBI	Avg
Home	151	43	3	13	.285	LHP	38	13	2	7	.342
Road	179	50	9	30	.279	RHP	292	80	10	36	.274
First Half	157	54	10	28	.344	Sc Pos	81	27	0	29	.333
Scnd Half	173	39	2	15	.225	Clutch	53	15	0	8	.283

2003 Season

Jeff DaVanon made his major league debut in 1999 and still has yet to play a full season without a detour to the minors. Of course, he always will have the memory of a three-game run in which he homered twice in each and drove in 10 runs in all. He became the fourth player in major league history with three consecutive multi-homer games, and the third to hit a home run from each side of the plate in consecutive contests.

Hitting, Baserunning & Defense

Darin Erstad's lingering hamstring injury gave DaVanon his first extensive big league look, and he batted .344 with 10 homers in the first half. He slumped in the second half and acknowledged pitchers had adjusted to him, but not vice versa. The Angels believe DaVanon cannot hit lefthanders for an extended period. He can handle all three outfield positions, though none exceptionally.

2004 Outlook

DaVanon hit .375 (6-for-16) as a pinch-hitter, and the Angels believe his ability to get on base, hit with pop from both sides, run and play anywhere in the outfield make him an ideal bench player. If the Angels fail to acquire an outfielder over the winter, he could play right field as part of a platoon.

Brendan Donnelly

Position: RP
Bats: R **Throws:** R
Ht: 6' 3" **Wt:** 240

Opening Day Age: 32
Born: 7/4/71 in Washington, DC
ML Seasons: 2

Overall Statistics

	W	L	Pct.	ERA	G	GS	Sv	IP	H	BB	SO	HR	Avg
'03	2	2	.500	1.58	63	0	3	74.0	55	24	79	2	.200
Car.	3	3	.500	1.82	109	0	4	123.2	87	43	133	4	.194

2003 Situational Stats

	W	L	ERA	Sv	IP		AB	H	HR	RBI	Avg
Home	1	1	1.45	2	37.1	LHB	146	29	2	11	.199
Road	1	1	1.72	1	36.2	RHB	129	26	0	5	.202
First Half	0	0	0.38	2	48.0	Sc Pos	97	13	0	14	.134
Scnd Half	2	2	3.81	1	26.0	Clutch	178	39	0	14	.219

2003 Season

After Brendan Donnelly played for 14 minor league teams over 10 seasons, he emerged as a reliable reliever in 2002. He was utterly dominant in the first half of 2003, not giving up a run until May 13 and not allowing an inherited runner to score until June 11. His 0.38 ERA at the All-Star break was the lowest by an American League pitcher in 30 years (minimum 30 innings), and players voted him onto the All-Star team.

Pitching & Defense

While closer Troy Percival simply blows people away with a fastball that approaches 100 MPH, Donnelly builds his strikeouts-innings ratio behind three pitches with terrific movement—a 90-93 MPH fastball, a hard slider near 90 MPH and a split-finger pitch. His control is better than that of Percival or Francisco Rodriguez, and he is effective against lefthanded hitters.

2004 Outlook

The Angels believe Donnelly could be a closer elsewhere and would consider trade proposals, but they're perfectly happy with him and Rodriguez setting up Percival. Donnelly pitched the final four months of 2003 with bone chips floating in his right elbow, but the chips were removed after the season in routine arthroscopic surgery.

Chone Figgins

Position: CF/2B
Bats: B **Throws:** R
Ht: 5' 7" **Wt:** 160

Opening Day Age: 26
Born: 1/22/78 in Leary, GA
ML Seasons: 2
Pronunciation:
shawn

Overall Statistics

	G	AB	R	H	D	T	HR	RBI	SB	BB	SO	Avg	OBP	Slg
'03	71	240	34	71	9	4	0	27	13	20	38	.296	.345	.367
Car.	86	252	40	73	10	4	0	28	15	20	43	.290	.337	.361

2003 Situational Stats

	AB	H	HR	RBI	Avg		AB	H	HR	RBI	Avg
Home	117	35	0	11	.299	LHP	88	25	0	13	.284
Road	123	36	0	16	.293	RHP	152	46	0	14	.303
First Half	54	14	0	3	.259	Sc Pos	51	21	0	27	.412
Scnd Half	186	57	0	24	.306	Clutch	34	10	0	5	.294

2003 Season

At the start of the 2003 season, Chone Figgins was a Triple-A second baseman. By the end of it, he was the Angels' starting center fielder. The Angels recalled him four times, and after they brought him back to stay and played him every day, he hit .306. He drove in more runs than Darin Erstad, in fewer at-bats.

Hitting, Baserunning & Defense

Few major leaguers can match Figgins' pure speed, an asset he has yet to maximize. He is potential havoc every time he gets on base, so he needs to draw more walks, hit fewer flyballs and learn the pickoff moves of opposing pitchers. Still, he makes solid contact, and any line drive past an outfielder is a potential triple. The Angels threw him into center field as an experiment, figuring he could run down most balls, and discovered his arm was better suited to center than the infield.

2004 Outlook

The Angels consider Figgins in the mold of veteran Mark McLemore, a utilityman who could start four consecutive days at four different positions. Figgins prefers to play every day at one position, but the Angels are wary of his inexperience in center. He could get a shot there if the Angels move Erstad to first base.

Brad Fullmer

Position: DH/1B
Bats: L **Throws:** R
Ht: 6' 0" **Wt:** 220

Opening Day Age: 29
Born: 1/17/75 in Chatsworth, CA
ML Seasons: 7

Overall Statistics

	G	AB	R	H	D	T	HR	RBI	SB	BB	SO	Avg	OBP	Slg
'03	63	206	32	63	9	2	9	35	5	26	31	.306	.387	.500
Car.	731	2531	354	718	184	15	103	409	31	189	343	.284	.339	.490

2003 Situational Stats

	AB	H	HR	RBI	Avg		AB	H	HR	RBI	Avg
Home	98	26	3	13	.265	LHP	30	8	1	6	.267
Road	108	37	6	22	.343	RHP	176	55	8	29	.313
First Half	206	63	9	35	.306	Sc Pos	58	18	2	24	.310
Scnd Half	0	0	0	0	–	Clutch	28	10	0	3	.357

2003 Season

Brad Fullmer had a nice season for the 2002 World Series champions, but drew little interest as a free agent and took a big pay cut to return to the Angels. He hoped to earn a better deal in 2004 by playing well. Fullmer led the majors with a .392 batting average at the end of April, but he tore up his knee in June and required season-ending surgery.

Hitting, Baserunning & Defense

Fullmer worked hard to diversify his offensive game, adapting his pull-happy swing to situational hitting, driving more pitches to the opposite field and taking more pitches and walks. He runs well and aggressively; the Angels consider him among the best at scooting up one base on a ball in the dirt. He arrived in Anaheim with a good-hit, no-field reputation, but showed enough ability at first base to send Scott Spiezio to the bench when Anaheim played in National League parks.

2004 Outlook

The Angels released him in October, and Fullmer, one of the few players who actually *enjoys* the DH role, would have to prove to another club that his knee is sound. While the Angels believe he cannot hit lefties or play first base regularly, the Rangers signed Fullmer to a one-year deal, most likely to replace Rafael Palmeiro at first base.

Eric Owens

Position: CF/RF/LF
Bats: R **Throws:** R
Ht: 6' 0" **Wt:** 210

Opening Day Age: 33
Born: 2/3/71 in Danville, VA
ML Seasons: 9

Overall Statistics

	G	AB	R	H	D	T	HR	RBI	SB	BB	SO	Avg	OBP	Slg
'03	111	241	29	65	6	0	1	20	11	10	24	.270	.300	.307
Car.	806	2353	305	621	86	16	26	214	126	182	284	.264	.318	.347

2003 Situational Stats

	AB	H	HR	RBI	Avg		AB	H	HR	RBI	Avg
Home	103	25	0	8	.243	LHP	143	44	1	18	.308
Road	138	40	1	12	.290	RHP	98	21	0	2	.214
First Half	136	30	1	12	.221	Sc Pos	56	17	0	19	.304
Scnd Half	105	35	0	8	.333	Clutch	29	8	0	2	.276

2003 Season

Eric Owens happily signed with the defending World Series champions, eager to participate in the playoffs for the first time in his career. Alas, the Angels had a miserable season, and so did Owens. He couldn't keep his batting average above .220 until August. By then, still in need of a center fielder to replace the injured Darin Erstad, the Angels sat Owens and decided to try young players instead.

Hitting, Baserunning & Defense

The final batting average of .270 is deceiving, for Owens hit .216 through July and .355 over the last two months. Even at 33, he still has impressive speed and runs the bases aggressively, and he'll drop a bunt single on occasion. His walk totals are unreasonably low, given his speed and lack of power. He can play all three outfield positions, none terribly well, and his arm is average at best.

2004 Outlook

The Angels asked Owens to hit lefthanders, and he did that well. He is a free agent and a useful fifth outfielder. Owens played second base and shortstop in the minors and third base in winter ball, and he said he planned to take plenty of groundballs over the winter, hoping to increase his marketability as a utilityman.

Aaron Sele

Position: SP
Bats: R **Throws:** R
Ht: 6' 5" **Wt:** 230

Opening Day Age: 33
Born: 6/25/70 in Golden Valley, MN
ML Seasons: 11
Pronunciation: SEE-lee

Overall Statistics

	W	L	Pct.	ERA	G	GS	Sv	IP	H	BB	SO	HR	Avg
'03	7	11	.389	5.77	25	25	0	121.2	135	58	53	17	.284
Car.	122	88	.581	4.48	293	292	0	1748.0	1905	655	1217	175	.278

2003 Situational Stats

	W	L	ERA	Sv	IP		AB	H	HR	RBI	Avg
Home	3	4	4.82	0	61.2	LHB	262	66	7	41	.252
Road	4	7	6.75	0	60.0	RHB	214	69	10	34	.322
First Half	6	6	5.37	0	58.2	Sc Pos	125	38	4	56	.304
Scnd Half	1	5	6.14	0	63.0	Clutch	0	0	0	0	–

2003 Season

In the offseason, the Angels did not acquire a starting pitcher and insisted Aaron Sele would be ready for Opening Day, five months after rotator cuff and labrum surgery on his pitching shoulder. As soon as training camp opened, they revised his return date to May 1. As soon as he returned, the Angels explained his ineffectiveness as a typical part of rehabilitation from surgery. In the end, Sele spent a year doing rehab at the major league level, winning once in his final 13 starts and posting a career-worst 5.77 ERA.

Pitching & Defense

The process of rebuilding arm strength was painfully gradual, and even by season's end, Sele still lacked consistency in velocity and command. His trademark curve remains effective, but he could not maintain 90 MPH on his fastball or keep it down in the strike zone. Anaheim catchers threw out six of the seven runners that tried to steal against him.

2004 Outlook

The Angels invested $8 million in Sele's rehabilitation year and they're hoping for a payoff. They owe him $8.5 million anyway for the final year of his three-year deal, so he'll get the chance for a comeback season. The Angels will cut him if this season starts to look like 2003 all over again.

Scot Shields

Position: RP/SP
Bats: R **Throws:** R
Ht: 6' 1" **Wt:** 170

Opening Day Age: 28
Born: 7/22/75 in Fort Lauderdale, FL
ML Seasons: 3

Overall Statistics

	W	L	Pct.	ERA	G	GS	Sv	IP	H	BB	SO	HR	Avg
'03	5	6	.455	2.85	44	13	1	148.1	138	38	111	12	.247
Car.	10	9	.526	2.55	81	14	1	208.1	177	66	148	16	.232

2003 Situational Stats

	W	L	ERA	Sv	IP		AB	H	HR	RBI	Avg
Home	4	2	1.83	1	88.1	LHB	271	62	9	27	.229
Road	1	4	4.35	0	60.0	RHB	288	76	3	25	.264
First Half	2	1	1.74	1	67.1	Sc Pos	129	30	1	37	.233
Scnd Half	3	5	3.78	0	81.0	Clutch	22	4	1	3	.182

2003 Season

In his first full season in the majors, Scot Shields was the Angels' most valuable pitcher. He provided outstanding short, middle and long relief. In July, at a time when he led AL relievers in innings pitched, the Angels released starter Kevin Appier and replaced him with Shields. Shields pitched well as a starter, better as a reliever and established himself as a reliable member of the staff.

Pitching & Defense

Shields relies on four pitches, none dominant. As a starter, he needs all four—fastball, curve, slider, changeup—to succeed. His fastball sneaks above 90 MPH with good movement, but his fastball alone will not suffice the second and third times through the order. He neutralized platoon lineups by holding lefthanders to a .229 average. He is the Angels' best fielding pitcher, and Gold Glove catcher Bengie Molina threw out seven of 12 runners trying to steal off Shields.

2004 Outlook

Shields would love to start, but he is blessed with a resilient arm that could keep him in the bullpen. He posted a 1.68 ERA as a reliever and a 3.89 ERA as a starter. If a starter fails and Shields is needed in the rotation, the Angels would have no reservations about making the move.

Scott Spiezio

Position: 1B/3B
Bats: B **Throws:** R
Ht: 6' 2" **Wt:** 225

Opening Day Age: 31
Born: 9/21/72 in Joliet, IL
ML Seasons: 8
Pronunciation: SPEE zio

Overall Statistics

	G	AB	R	H	D	T	HR	RBI	SB	BB	SO	Avg	OBP	Slg
'03	158	521	69	138	36	7	16	83	6	46	66	.265	.326	.453
Car.	932	2986	402	779	183	20	91	424	28	308	410	.261	.331	.427

2003 Situational Stats

	AB	H	HR	RBI	Avg		AB	H	HR	RBI	Avg
Home	262	67	7	32	.256	LHP	148	33	3	22	.223
Road	259	71	9	51	.274	RHP	373	105	13	61	.282
First Half	271	70	9	31	.258	Sc Pos	140	35	5	68	.250
Scnd Half	250	68	7	52	.272	Clutch	74	19	3	12	.257

2003 Season

As the Angels crumbled around him, with teammates injured with disturbing regularity, Scott Spiezio played in all but four games. He started the season at first base, started at third after Troy Glaus got hurt, also played left and right field and batted in every lineup spot except leadoff. He set career highs with 36 doubles and 83 RBI.

Hitting, Baserunning & Defense

Spiezio did his best to shed his platoon tag by hitting .368 against lefthanders in 2002. He reverted toward his career norm in 2003, however, by hitting .223 against them, in part because he was a little pull-happy from the right side. At bat, he has a disciplined eye. On defense, he is terrific at first base, surprisingly good in the outfield and below average at third base. Speed is not part of his game.

2004 Outlook

The Angels pushed Spiezio into free agency, unsure whether they would move Darin Erstad to first base and very sure they had no desire to pay Spiezio anything close to his 2003 salary of $4.25 million. Spiezio wanted to return, but not as a utility player. He would be a nice $2 million first baseman for a team that could afford to bat him sixth or seventh.

Ben Weber

Position: RP
Bats: R **Throws:** R
Ht: 6' 4" **Wt:** 205

Opening Day Age: 34
Born: 11/17/69 in Port Arthur, TX
ML Seasons: 4
Pronunciation: webb-er

Overall Statistics

	W	L	Pct.	ERA	G	GS	Sv	IP	H	BB	SO	HR	Avg
'03	5	1	.833	2.69	62	0	0	80.1	84	22	46	7	.275
Car.	19	6	.760	3.18	200	0	7	249.1	248	81	143	15	.262

2003 Situational Stats

	W	L	ERA	Sv	IP		AB	H	HR	RBI	Avg
Home	5	0	2.28	0	43.1	LHB	149	40	1	9	.268
Road	0	1	3.16	0	37.0	RHB	156	44	6	22	.282
First Half	2	0	2.66	0	47.1	Sc Pos	87	20	2	22	.230
Scnd Half	3	1	2.73	0	33.0	Clutch	82	32	2	10	.390

2003 Season

While closer Troy Percival and setup men Brendan Donnelly and Francisco Rodriguez attracted the attention, Ben Weber quietly did another splendid job in the Angels' bullpen. He pitched a career-high 80.1 innings, keeping his ERA below 3.00 for the second consecutive year and posting a 1.54 ERA over the final two months of the season.

Pitching & Defense

If the Angels need a strikeout, they'll summon Donnelly, Percival or Rodriguez. If they need a double play, Weber's their guy. His fastball added a little giddy-up with improved health, rising from 87-89 MPH in 2002 to 90-92 MPH last year. His out pitch is a nasty sinker, delivered by a guy who hides the ball amid flying elbows and a violently shaking head. He can field his position, and seven of nine runners trying to steal off him were thrown out.

2004 Outlook

In three-plus years with the Angels, Weber is 19-5 with a 2.80 ERA, so on merit alone he stays. But he is eligible for arbitration for the first time, and his salary could jump to more than $1 million. The Angels might decide he can be replaced, but such a decision could be risky with Donnelly coming off elbow surgery and Percival pitching with a degenerative hip.

Shawn Wooten

Position: 1B/DH/C/3B
Bats: R **Throws:** R
Ht: 5'10" **Wt:** 230

Opening Day Age: 31
Born: 7/24/72 in Glendora, CA
ML Seasons: 4

Overall Statistics

	G	AB	R	H	D	T	HR	RBI	SB	BB	SO	Avg	OBP	Slg
'03	98	272	25	66	8	0	7	32	0	24	45	.243	.303	.349
Car.	233	615	64	173	25	1	18	84	4	35	111	.281	.322	.413

2003 Situational Stats

	AB	H	HR	RBI	Avg		AB	H	HR	RBI	Avg
Home	145	33	5	18	.228	LHP	151	36	5	21	.238
Road	127	33	2	14	.260	RHP	121	30	2	11	.248
First Half	122	34	5	19	.279	Sc Pos	83	15	1	22	.181
Scnd Half	150	32	2	13	.213	Clutch	42	13	1	8	.310

2003 Season

With Brad Fullmer injured and Scott Spiezio playing for the injured Troy Glaus at third base, career reserve Shawn Wooten finally got his chance to play every day at first base. That lasted six games, after which the Angels tried rookie Robb Quinlan and journeyman Adam Riggs before moving Spiezio back to first. Wooten made at least 15 appearances at first base, third base, catcher and DH.

Hitting, Baserunning & Defense

With his first extensive playing time in July, Wooten faded. He hit better than .300 over the first three months, then batted .203 in July, .196 in August and .190 in September. He did hit .350 as a pinch-hitter, a role in which his career average is .359. He improved dramatically at catcher and displayed surprising agility at third base, his original position, but he'll make his living with his bat. He is not a factor on the bases.

2004 Outlook

Manager Mike Scioscia bluntly told Wooten he lacked the stamina to play every day. Wooten lost nothing in translation, committing to a nutrition program and losing weight over the winter. Wooten is a solid hitter and useful bench player, but his eligibility for salary arbitration makes it uncertain whether he'll be back.

Other Anaheim Angels

Wilson Delgado (Pos: 3B/2B/SS, **Age**: 31, **Bats**: B)

	G	AB	R	H	D	T	HR	RBI	SB	BB	SO	Avg	OBP	Slg
'03	62	127	12	29	3	0	0	7	0	11	18	.228	.293	.252
Car.	211	412	48	98	11	1	3	30	4	32	79	.238	.297	.291

Injuries to Anaheim infielders and the failure of prospects sparked Delgado's acquisition from St. Louis in August. He batted .320 with a .414 OBP with the Angels, but he's shopping for work again. 2004 Outlook: C

Trent Durrington (Pos: 2B, **Age**: 28, **Bats**: R)

	G	AB	R	H	D	T	HR	RBI	SB	BB	SO	Avg	OBP	Slg
'03	12	14	5	2	0	0	0	1	1	3	0	.143	.294	.143
Car.	59	139	19	24	2	0	0	3	5	12	54	.173	.238	.187

This former second-base prospect first surfaced in 1999. He was recalled after a solid Triple-A season, then signed a minor league deal with the Brewers in November after 10 years in the Angels' and Dodgers' systems. 2004 Outlook: C

Benji Gil (Pos: 2B/SS, **Age**: 31, **Bats**: R)

	G	AB	R	H	D	T	HR	RBI	SB	BB	SO	Avg	OBP	Slg
'03	62	125	12	24	5	1	1	9	5	4	33	.192	.214	.272
Car.	604	1610	158	381	75	12	32	171	24	102	448	.237	.283	.358

The former top prospect settled nicely into a reserve role with Anaheim after losing his prospect status, but his numbers have been on the slide the last few years and he was released in mid-August. 2004 Outlook: C

Gary Glover (Pos: RHP, **Age**: 27)

	W	L	Pct.	ERA	G	GS	Sv	IP	H	BB	SO	HR	Avg
'03	2	0	1.000	4.74	42	0	0	62.2	77	22	37	6	.309
Car.	14	13	.519	5.00	130	33	1	302.1	311	107	170	43	.264

Glover was a promising righthander, but he's drifted through three systems struggling to throw strikes consistently and develop a third pitch. He moved to Anaheim for Scott Schoeneweis in July. 2004 Outlook: C

Kevin Gregg (Pos: RHP, **Age**: 25)

	W	L	Pct.	ERA	G	GS	Sv	IP	H	BB	SO	HR	Avg
'03	2	0	1.000	3.28	5	3	0	24.2	18	8	14	3	.205
Car.	2	0	1.000	3.28	5	3	0	24.2	18	8	14	3	.205

Gregg has been bouncing around the high minors since 1999, but a nice surge in his strikeout-walk ratio at two stops last summer suggests he's a better pitcher. He made three quality starts in Anaheim. 2004 Outlook: B

Tom Gregorio (Pos: C, **Age**: 26, **Bats**: R)

	G	AB	R	H	D	T	HR	RBI	SB	BB	SO	Avg	OBP	Slg
'03	12	19	1	3	0	0	0	2	0	1	8	.158	.238	.158
Car.	12	19	1	3	0	0	0	2	0	1	8	.158	.238	.158

Gregorio batted just .221 with a .290 OBP at Triple-A Salt Lake, but he got the September call when Bengie Molina was sidelined by injury. With Jeff Mathis on the rise, we may not see Gregorio again. 2004 Outlook: C

Gary Johnson (Pos: LF, **Age**: 28, **Bats**: L)

	G	AB	R	H	D	T	HR	RBI	SB	BB	SO	Avg	OBP	Slg
'03	5	8	1	3	1	0	0	0	0	1	1	.375	.444	.500
Car.	5	8	1	3	1	0	0	0	0	1	1	.375	.444	.500

Johnson has a sweet lefthanded swing and decent eye at the plate, but injuries ruined his 2002 season. He bounced back last summer, and needs to hit and show pop this spring to claim a reserve role. 2004 Outlook: C

Greg Jones (Pos: RHP, **Age**: 27)

	W	L	Pct.	ERA	G	GS	Sv	IP	H	BB	SO	HR	Avg
'03	0	0	–	4.88	18	0	0	27.2	29	14	28	3	.261
Car.	0	0	–	4.88	18	0	0	27.2	29	14	28	3	.261

Except for some trouble with the longball, Jones was solid at Triple-A Salt Lake in 2003, allowing just 36 hits in 47 innings, while walking nine and fanning 56. He couldn't post those numbers in Anaheim. 2004 Outlook: C

Bart Miadich (Pos: RHP, **Age**: 28)

	W	L	Pct.	ERA	G	GS	Sv	IP	H	BB	SO	HR	Avg
'03	0	0	–	18.00	1	0	0	2.0	5	1	3	0	.500
Car.	0	0	–	6.75	12	0	0	12.0	11	9	14	2	.256

Miadich is a fastball-slider guy who can be difficult to hit, but he issues too many walks. His best Triple-A season was in 2001, and he'll try his game in San Diego after signing a minor league pact. 2004 Outlook: C

Jose Molina (Pos: C, **Age**: 28, **Bats**: R)

	G	AB	R	H	D	T	HR	RBI	SB	BB	SO	Avg	OBP	Slg
'03	53	114	12	21	4	0	0	6	0	1	26	.184	.210	.219
Car.	107	240	28	55	11	0	2	16	0	11	53	.229	.268	.300

Molina has backed up his older brother Bengie for the past three years in Anaheim. Before accruing the highest at-bat total of his career in 2003, Jose was a .270 hitter in 54 games. 2004 Outlook: C

Julio Ramirez (Pos: CF, **Age**: 26, **Bats**: R)

	G	AB	R	H	D	T	HR	RBI	SB	BB	SO	Avg	OBP	Slg
'03	6	2	1	0	0	0	0	0	0	0	0	.000	.000	.000
Car.	72	92	12	15	1	1	1	10	2	5	35	.163	.214	.228

Ramirez was a tools-rich prospect a few years ago, but he annually struggles to post an OBP above .300. A lack of plate patience has grounded his chances, despite great speed and fielding skills. 2004 Outlook: C

Adam Riggs (Pos: 1B, **Age**: 31, **Bats**: R)

	G	AB	R	H	D	T	HR	RBI	SB	BB	SO	Avg	OBP	Slg
'03	24	61	11	15	4	1	3	5	3	9	9	.246	.343	.492
Car.	45	117	16	26	6	1	3	7	5	15	20	.222	.311	.368

A decade ago, Riggs was a Dodgers second-base prospect with some pop. Twice before he surfaced in the majors, but got his longest look with the Angels in 2003. He started well but faded in September. 2004 Outlook: C

Rich Rodriguez (**Pos**: LHP, **Age**: 41)

	W	L	Pct.	ERA	G	GS	Sv	IP	H	BB	SO	HR	Avg
'03	0	0	–	2.45	3	0	0	3.2	4	1	3	0	.308
Car.	31	22	.585	3.81	609	2	8	640.2	642	261	396	62	.264

Rodriguez is another alum of the Bob McClure School of Lefties With Nine Lives. Not counting his brief Anaheim stint in 2003, the southpaw has had only one ERA below 5.00 since a decent 1998 season. 2004 Outlook: C

Derrick Turnbow (**Pos**: RHP, **Age**: 26)

	W	L	Pct.	ERA	G	GS	Sv	IP	H	BB	SO	HR	Avg
'03	2	0	1.000	0.59	11	0	0	15.1	7	3	15	0	.140
Car.	2	0	1.000	3.54	35	1	0	53.1	43	39	40	7	.224

Turnbow surfaced in Anaheim as a promising hard-throwing reliever in 2000, but then he battled injuries the next two years. The comeback trail led to a September payoff, and he'll battle for a 2004 job. 2004 Outlook: C

Barry Wesson (**Pos**: LF, **Age**: 26, **Bats**: R)

	G	AB	R	H	D	T	HR	RBI	SB	BB	SO	Avg	OBP	Slg
'03	10	11	2	2	0	0	1	3	1	0	4	.182	.182	.455
Car.	25	31	3	6	0	1	1	4	1	1	9	.194	.219	.355

Wesson has batted .286 over the last two Triple-A seasons, but has little power and doesn't walk. He closed the gap between his strikeouts and walks in 2003, but his three-year ratio of 321:95 is ugly. 2004 Outlook: C

Anaheim Angels Minor League Prospects

Organization Overview:

The farm system has been rejuvenated, and according to *Baseball America*, the top four prospects in the high Class-A California League last summer were Angels. Rancho Cucamonga catcher Jeff Mathis, first baseman Casey Kotchman, third baseman Dallas McPherson and righthander Ervin Santana are key components of Anaheim's future. With the selection of the three position players, the standing of the organization changed markedly in just two rounds of the 2001 draft. Before that foursome alters the fate of the franchise, the Angels may get some 2004 help from infielders Alfredo Amezaga and Robb Quinlan, as well as from righthanders Chris Bootcheck and Bobby Jenks.

Alfredo Amezaga

Position: SS   **Opening Day Age:** 26
Bats: B **Throws:** R   **Born:** 1/16/78 in
Ht: 5' 10" **Wt:** 165   Obregon, Mexico

Recent Statistics

	G	AB	R	H	D	T	HR	RBI	SB	BB	SO	Avg
2003 AAA Salt Lake	75	317	55	110	20	5	3	45	14	20	39	.347
2003 AL Anaheim	37	105	15	22	3	2	2	7	2	9	23	.210

A 1999 pick, Amezaga is dependable defensively, with good hands, speed, range and instincts. His speed and ability to make contact have been assets at the plate, even as Amezaga took up switch-hitting in 2000, but he hit a wall at Triple-A Salt Lake the next two seasons. After an offseason workout program a year ago, a stronger Amezaga hit nearly 100 points higher than he did the previous two summers, showing more doubles power and reducing his strikeouts. He played with a labrum injury in his throwing shoulder late in 2003, yet he went 12-for-42 (.286) with Anaheim in September after performing poorly in place of injured Angels David Eckstein and Troy Glaus. Being more selective at the plate is critical if he wants to start in Anaheim.

Chris Bootcheck

Position: P   **Opening Day Age:** 25
Bats: R **Throws:** R   **Born:** 10/24/78 in
Ht: 6' 5" **Wt:** 200   LaPorte, IN

Recent Statistics

	W	L	ERA	G	GS	Sv	IP	H	R	BB	SO	HR
2003 AAA Salt Lake	8	9	4.25	28	26	0	171.1	194	103	43	82	19
2003 AL Anaheim	0	1	0.60	1	1	0	10.1	16	12	6	7	5

A first-rounder in 2000, Bootcheck signed too late to play until 2001. A slow start and shoulder tendinitis compromised his debut season, but he heated up and advanced to Double-A Arkansas. Again in 2002, Bootcheck was better in the second half, this time at Triple-A Salt Lake. Last spring he impressed during spring training, but a forearm injury that hurt his control was a factor in a so-so first half. As in 2002, Bootcheck had trouble with one bad inning, often the first frame, but he finished strong and posted a 2.66 ERA in his final 11 starts at Salt Lake. He works around the plate successfully when he's on, with a low-90s sinker, cutter, changeup and a less-advanced breaking pitch.

Bobby Jenks

Position: P   **Opening Day Age:** 23
Bats: R **Throws:** R   **Born:** 3/14/81 in Mission
Ht: 6' 3" **Wt:** 225   Hills, CA

Recent Statistics

	W	L	ERA	G	GS	Sv	IP	H	R	BB	SO	HR
2002 AA Arkansas	3	6	4.66	10	10	0	58.0	49	34	44	58	2
2002 A Rancho Cuca	3	5	4.82	11	10	0	65.1	50	42	46	64	4
2003 R Angels	0	0	0.00	1	1	0	4.0	2	0	0	5	0
2003 AA Arkansas	7	2	2.17	16	16	0	83.0	56	23	51	103	2

Jenks tantalized with an explosive mid-90s fastball and a hard curve as a 2000 fifth-round pick. Not throwing strikes and makeup issues have slowed his development. After an inconsistent 2002, Jenks turned a corner in the Arizona Fall League that fall. He threw his nasty curveball for strikes and worked more confidently with his changeup. He lost two months early in 2003 to a stress reaction in his throwing elbow, which might have led to a major injury if it wasn't caught. Then he enjoyed his most consistent and dominating season at Double-A Arkansas. His heater now arrives in the high 90s, but some scouts think his delivery puts his arm at risk. His 123.1 innings in 2002 are a career high, so his arm hasn't been thoroughly tested.

Casey Kotchman

Position: 1B   **Opening Day Age:** 21
Bats: L **Throws:** L   **Born:** 2/22/83 in
Ht: 6' 3" **Wt:** 210   Seminole, FL

Recent Statistics

	G	AB	R	H	D	T	HR	RBI	SB	BB	SO	Avg
2002 A Cedar Rapids	81	288	42	81	30	1	5	50	2	48	37	.281
2003 R Angels	7	27	5	9	1	0	2	6	0	2	3	.333
2003 A Rancho Cuca	57	206	42	72	12	0	8	28	2	30	16	.350

Injuries continue to plague the Angels' first-round pick from 2001. A hyperextended right forearm ended his debut season, and he missed several weeks in 2002 after jamming his left wrist during an awkward slide. Last summer he missed the first half with a torn hamstring, then took a pitch on the hand during the high Class-A California League playoffs. Still, Kotchman was productive in the Cal League, demonstrating his advanced selectivity, good bat speed and line-drive stroke. His glove is as promising as the bat. Eventually look for more power from a guy who has 47 doubles and 16 homers in 156 minor league games.

Jeff Mathis

Position: C
Bats: R **Throws:** R
Ht: 6' 0" **Wt:** 180

Opening Day Age: 21
Born: 3/31/83 in Marianna, FL

Recent Statistics

	G	AB	R	H	D	T	HR	RBI	SB	BB	SO	Avg
2002 A Cedar Rapds	128	491	75	141	41	3	10	73	7	40	75	.287
2003 A Rancho Cuca	97	378	73	122	28	3	11	54	5	35	74	.323
2003 AA Arkansas	24	95	19	27	11	0	2	14	1	12	16	.284

A first-round pick in 2001, Mathis isn't as big as many of today's catchers, but he's athletic and committed to his craft. He didn't catch much until turning pro, so he's not as refined behind the plate, but he has a strong arm, calls a good game and projects as an above-average defender. At the plate, his approach is to drive the ball up the middle, and with his line-drive stroke he's generated 80 doubles over the last two seasons between two Class-A stops and Double-A ball. While his hitting percentages weren't quite as good after his promotion to Double-A Arkansas late in 2003, his walk rate rose and his strikeout rate declined.

Dallas McPherson

Position: 3B
Bats: L **Throws:** R
Ht: 6' 3" **Wt:** 215

Opening Day Age: 23
Born: 7/23/80 in Charleston, SC

Recent Statistics

	G	AB	R	H	D	T	HR	RBI	SB	BB	SO	Avg
2002 A Cedar Rapds	132	499	71	138	24	3	15	88	30	78	128	.277
2003 A Rancho Cuca	77	292	65	90	21	6	18	59	12	41	79	.308
2003 AA Arkansas	28	102	22	32	9	1	5	27	4	19	25	.314

A second-round pick in 2001, McPherson doesn't get as much attention as Kotchman and Mathis, but he's as highly regarded. After a solid 2002 at Class-A Cedar Rapids, McPherson hit for a better average and turned up the power at high Class-A Rancho Cucamonga and Double-A Arkansas last year. He went on a home-run tear in July before reaching Arkansas, capped by a double and homer off Randy Johnson during a rehab start, and McPherson never stopped hitting to all fields with his compact swing. His defensive mobility bears watching, but with his power potential and arm strength, right field is an option if he can't cut it at third base.

Robb Quinlan

Position: 1B
Bats: R **Throws:** R
Ht: 6' 1" **Wt:** 195

Opening Day Age: 27
Born: 3/17/77 in Maplewood, MN

Recent Statistics

	G	AB	R	H	D	T	HR	RBI	SB	BB	SO	Avg
2003 AAA Salt Lake	95	393	55	122	18	4	9	68	10	25	59	.310
2003 AL Anaheim	38	94	13	27	4	2	0	4	1	6	16	.287

Never considered much of a prospect as a 10th-rounder in 1999, Quinlan has hit every step of the way and showed a steady increase in power over his first four seasons. At least until 2003, when he made as much contact but saw his slugging down more than 100 points over his 2002 mark at Triple-A Salt Lake. He was the Pacific Coast League MVP that year, when he more consistently drove the ball into the gaps for extra-base hits. He hit southpaws and righties equally well in Anaheim last summer, though his production dropped off after a fast start. Defensively, Quinlan is most comfortable at first base, but he also can play left field.

Ervin Santana

Position: P
Bats: R **Throws:** R
Ht: 6' 2" **Wt:** 150

Opening Day Age: 21
Born: 1/10/83 in Bani, DR

Recent Statistics

	W	L	ERA	G	GS	Sv	IP	H	R	BB	SO	HR
2002 A Cedar Rapds	14	8	4.16	27	27	0	147.0	133	75	48	146	10
2003 A Rancho Cuca	10	2	2.53	20	20	0	124.2	98	44	36	130	9
2003 AA Arkansas	1	1	3.94	6	6	0	29.2	23	15	12	23	4

Signed in 2000, Santana has been a strikeout machine in the minors. In 2003, the strikeouts continued to accumulate at better than one per inning at high Class-A Rancho Cucamonga, where he overpowered hitters with his mid-90s heat and tight slider. His fine season produced an invite to the Futures Game and an ERA title in the California League. The Angels were just as pleased with his improved concentration on the diamond, though Santana wasn't as dominant upon reaching Double-A Arkansas. His changeup isn't as far along and he didn't use it enough, but Santana delivers all of his offerings with a smooth, effortless motion.

Others to Watch

Second baseman **Albert Callaspo** (20) is an excellent defender who turns the double play well and can play shortstop. He uses a quick stroke to slap the ball around the field, and he won the Class-A Midwest League batting title in 2003. He has a .331 average over his first two minor league seasons and has walked more than he has struck out. . . Righthander **Rich Fischer** (23) rose rapidly through the system until reaching Double-A Arkansas late in 2002. He returned there last spring, but experienced elbow tendinitis and struggled with release point and arm slot. In 2004, look for better numbers than 5-11 with a 4.61 ERA. . . A 19th-round pick in 2001, outfielder **Nick Gorneault** (24) made himself known last summer by batting .326 with 42 doubles and 16 homers between high Class-A Rancho Cucamonga and Double-A Arkansas. He understands hitting, and executes with quick hands and bat. He's a big kid who can play all three outfield positions. . . Australian righthander **Rich Thompson** (19) excelled as a dominant reliever at Class-A Cedar Rapids, limiting hitters to 18 hits in 37.2 innings while fanning 54 and posting a 0.24 ERA. He earned a promotion to the high Class-A California League. Thompson throws two different curveballs and a high-80s fastball that can reach 90 MPH. Look for more velocity from Thompson as he matures.

Oriole Park at Camden Yards

Offense

Oriole Park at Camden Yards continues to yield fewer runs than the league average. Though it has a few odd angles, it does not yield a large number of doubles or triples. Righthanded batters hit significantly more home runs, and lefthanded batters enjoy a slight edge. Hitters from both sides do not benefit in terms of batting average. Not only is the right-center field gap expansive, the right-field wall is 25 feet high and turns its share of homers into doubles. The ball carries to left field, especially when the weather is warmer. The hitting background is one of the American League's best.

Defense

The Orioles have a reputation of keeping the infield grass higher at Camden Yards than the typical American League ballpark. This slows the ball down enough to aid Baltimore infielders who are not known for having great range. The ballpark is asymmetrical but doesn't cause a lot of odd bounces for outfielders. The foul territory is close to average among major league parks.

Who It Helps the Most

Larry Bigbie batted 110 points higher at home in 2003, and Luis Matos hit almost 100 points higher at Camden Yards than on the road. Catcher Brook Fordyce also had a noticeable advantage hitting at home. B.J. Ryan was one of the few Orioles pitches who fared well at Camden Yards. Omar Daal struggled all season, but was more effective at home.

Who It Hurts the Most

Tony Batista struggled at home in terms of home-run power. Reliever Rich Bauer allowed an ERA that was more than two runs better on the road in 2003. Rodrigo Lopez allowed 16 home runs at home and just eight away from Camden Yards.

Rookies & Newcomers

The Orioles are waiting for pitching prospects Matt Riley and Erik Bedard, both southpaws, to arrive sometime this season. Camden Yards won't provide an advantage when they are promoted. The system isn't likely to yield much help offensively this season.

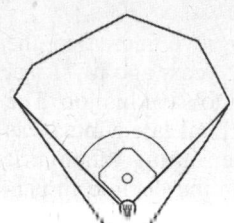

Dimensions: LF-333, LCF-364, CF-400, RCF-373, RF-318

Capacity: 48,190

Elevation: 20 feet

Surface: Grass

Foul Territory: Average

Baltimore

Park Factors

2003 Season

| | Home Games | | | Away Games | | | |
	Orioles	Opp	Total	Orioles	Opp	Total	Index
G	72	72	144	73	73	146	
Avg	.276	.262	.269	.258	.287	.272	99
AB	2431	2523	4954	2566	2507	5073	99
R	325	330	655	332	380	712	93
H	671	662	1333	663	719	1382	98
2B	130	124	254	115	146	261	100
3B	6	8	14	13	17	30	48
HR	68	90	158	63	85	148	109
BB	199	236	435	189	223	412	108
SO	368	440	808	415	432	847	98
E	36	56	92	54	50	104	90
E-Infield	31	42	73	47	45	92	80
LHB-Avg	.267	.282	.276	.266	.272	.269	102
LHB-HR	23	45	68	22	44	66	103
RHB-Avg	.281	.244	.264	.254	.300	.275	96
RHB-HR	45	45	90	41	41	82	114

2002-2003

| | Home Games | | | Away Games | | | |
	Orioles	Opp	Total	Orioles	Opp	Total	Index
G	144	144	288	145	145	290	
Avg	.261	.261	.261	.253	.283	.268	97
AB	4837	5066	9903	5049	4968	10017	100
R	617	661	1278	632	754	1386	93
H	1263	1323	2586	1277	1407	2684	97
2B	241	233	474	275	275	550	87
3B	16	13	29	25	30	01	40
HR	149	191	340	129	176	305	113
BB	406	477	883	384	465	849	105
SO	793	866	1659	847	880	1727	97
E	78	110	188	90	88	178	106
E-Infield	64	88	152	76	77	153	100
LHB-Avg	.260	.265	.263	.263	.276	.271	97
LHB-HR	53	92	145	42	93	135	106
RHB-Avg	.261	.258	.260	.248	.289	.266	98
RHB-HR	96	99	195	87	83	170	118

2003 Rankings (American League)

- Second-highest walk factor
- Lowest triple factor
- Lowest infield-error factor
- Third-lowest strikeout factor

Lee Mazzilli

2003 Season

Former manager Mike Hargrove increased the team's win total from 63 two years ago to 71 last season, but it wasn't enough to save his job. The addition of southpaw Omar Daal last winter was expected to add depth to the starting rotation. It didn't, and that coupled with the decline in performance from Rodrigo Lopez and Jason Johnson sealed Hargrove's fate. The new management team of Jim Beattie and Mike Flanagan hired its own man, Yankees first-base coach Lee Mazzilli.

Offense

Mazzilli inherits an offense with some improving young players: Jay Gibbons, Melvin Mora, Luis Matos and Brian Roberts. A healthy Jerry Hairston Jr., plus Roberts and Matos, give him plenty of options at the top of the lineup. They have the speed to be solid tablesetters. What is lacking is a marquee run producer. Gibbons is better suited further down in the order than the cleanup or fifth spot. Baltimore doesn't have any young hitting prospects waiting in the wings, so free agency and trades will be the only ways to fill holes in the lineup.

Pitching & Defense

Mazzilli's rotation lacks a staff ace. Lopez was a major surprise two years ago, but he failed to come close to duplicating his 2002 season. Johnson has not made a major developmental jump recently and probably won't fill the shoes of the departed Sidney Ponson. The Orioles need a front-of-the-rotation starter to take the burden off the returning pitchers. The bullpen, fronted by young closer Jorge Julio, is shaky. Mazzilli inherits an average defense, one that makes the expected plays but doesn't have above-average range.

2004 Outlook

The Orioles have a core of players who will continue to improve, yet they lack a couple of cornerstone hitters and a legitimate staff ace. The starting rotation remains a problem, and Julio's inconsistency hurts the bullpen. Without a major splash in the free-agent market, Baltimore again will be relegated to a fourth- or fifth-place finish in the American League East.

Born: 3/25/55 in Brooklyn, NY

Playing Experience: 1976-1989, NYM, NYY, Tex, Pit, Tor

Managerial Experience: No major league managing experience

Manager Statistics (Mike Hargrove)

Year	Team, Lg	W	L	Pct	GB	Finish
2003	Baltimore, AL	71	91	.438	30.0	4th East
13 Seasons		996	963	.508	–	–

2003 Starting Pitchers by Days Rest

	<=3	4	5	6+
Orioles Starts	0	70	61	24
Orioles ERA	–	4.95	4.64	5.22
AL Avg Starts	2	79	50	22
AL ERA	3.19	4.64	4.57	4.98

2003 Situational Stats

	Mike Hargrove	AL Average
Hit & Run Success %	42.1	36.7
Stolen Base Success %	71.2	70.0
Platoon Pct.	52.3	61.7
Defensive Subs	6	23
High-Pitch Outings	12	5
Quick/Slow Hooks	15/18	19/16
Sacrifice Attempts	68	55

2003 Rankings—Mike Hargrove (American League)

- 1st in intentional walks (35) and one-batter pitcher appearances (55)
- 2nd in starts with over 120 pitches (12)
- 3rd in pitchouts with a runner moving (7)

Tony Batista

Position: 3B
Bats: R **Throws:** R
Ht: 6' 0" **Wt:** 208

Opening Day Age: 30
Born: 12/9/73 in Puerto Plata, DR
ML Seasons: 8
Pronunciation: bah-TEESE-tah

2003 Season

While Tony Batista recorded the third-highest RBI total of his career, his doubles, walks and home runs were below his 2002 level. Overall, last season was Batista's least productive since arriving in the major leagues. After the All-Star break, Batista barely hit better than .200, the second season in a row he's been disappointing in the second half. He posted career highs with 20 errors at third base and by hitting into 20 double plays.

Hitting

The wide-open stance that Batista uses to get a better look at pitches still makes him vulnerable to outside breaking balls. This stance also produces a long swing, making him susceptible to offspeed pitches. Batista's long swing prevents him from inside-outing a pitch when he's fooled by its speed. Lefthanded pitchers give him the most trouble, mainly because they can paint the outside corner and he can't hit the pitch consistently. Batista continues to be one of the more extreme flyball hitters, yet produces few sacrifice flies.

Baserunning & Defense

Even though he began his career as a shortstop, Batista's range at third continues to decline. His ability to go behind the third-base bag and make the play is a problem, due both to his limited range and inaccurate arm. The first-step quickness that he developed as a shortstop remains, but it can't compensate for his overall lack of range. His throws to first almost always are of the long and looping variety. Bunts and slow hoppers hit in front of him no longer are routine plays for Batista.

2004 Outlook

Batista is a free agent who is unlikely to return to Baltimore. The decline in his batting average and power, coupled with a noticeable decline in his defense at third, decrease his value. Surprisingly, the 30-year-old third baseman should be in the prime of his career, but you couldn't tell that by his 2003 performance. He will have a tough time finding a full-time job unless he makes significant changes to his approach at the plate.

Overall Statistics

	G	AB	R	H	D	T	HR	RBI	SB	BB	SO	Avg	OBP	Slg
'03	161	631	76	148	20	1	26	99	4	28	102	.235	.270	.393
Car.	1022	3683	515	932	181	15	182	571	33	234	671	.253	.302	.459

Where He Hits the Ball

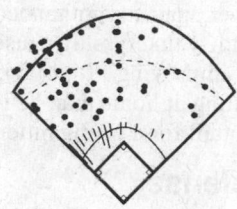
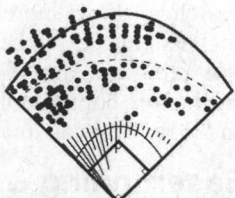

Vs. LHP	Vs. RHP

2003 Situational Stats

	AB	H	HR	RBI	Avg		AB	H	HR	RBI	Avg
Home	308	69	10	43	.224	LHP	161	31	9	22	.193
Road	323	79	16	56	.245	RHP	470	117	17	77	.249
First Half	352	87	16	61	.247	Sc Pos	172	41	7	72	.238
Scnd Half	279	61	10	38	.219	Clutch	103	28	4	21	.272

2003 Rankings (American League)

- 2nd in errors at third base (20), lowest on-base percentage and lowest fielding percentage at third base (.950)
- 3rd in lowest batting average and lowest batting average vs. lefthanded pitchers
- 4th in games played and lowest batting average at home
- 6th in GDPs (20) and lowest groundball-fly ball ratio (0.7)
- Led the Orioles in home runs, at-bats, strikeouts, GDPs (20), pitches seen (2,566) and games played

Larry Bigbie

2003 Season

Larry Bigbie earned a recall when injuries landed first baseman David Segui on the disabled list. A strained right rotator cuff compromised Bigbie's ability to make consistent contact before he landed on the disabled list in late May. His shoulder healed enough for him to return in late July. He displayed solid gap power and an improved eye at the plate over the final two months of the season.

Hitting

When Bigbie displays a level swing and sprays the ball to all fields, he's a very effective hitter. That level swing was more evident late last season, during his third stint with the Orioles. Bigbie hits pitchers from both sides of the rubber well, though he shows more power against righthanded pitchers. Inside pitches with velocity still cause him problems, but he is improving. Bigbie is much more comfortable hitting at home than he is on the road, not an unusual trait for a young hitter.

Baserunning & Defense

Bigbie has above-average speed and rarely is doubled up on the bases. His speed allows him to go from first to third on balls hit to right field. He'll steal a base when the opportunity is available, but he isn't an above-average basestealer. Bigbie is an adequate left fielder who doesn't always use his speed to his advantage to cut balls off in the gap. His arm, though average, is accurate enough to throw out some runners who test him.

2004 Outlook

The Orioles were pleased with the way Bigbie settled into the No. 3 spot in the batting order the last two months of 2003. He teased the Orioles with a little bit of power and speed when he was healthy late in the season. Yet, he'll need to generate more power and remain healthy to remain in the left-field picture. If he can't, or the Orioles sign a free agent to play in left, Bigbie will serve as a back-up outfielder. That's the more likely scenario for 2004.

Position: LF
Bats: L **Throws:** L
Ht: 6' 4" **Wt:** 215

Opening Day Age: 26
Born: 11/4/77 in Hobart, IN
ML Seasons: 3

Overall Statistics

	G	AB	R	H	D	T	HR	RBI	SB	BB	SO	Avg	OBP	Slg
'03	83	287	43	87	15	1	9	31	7	29	60	.303	.365	.456
Car.	146	452	59	123	22	1	11	45	12	47	113	.272	.339	.398

Where He Hits the Ball

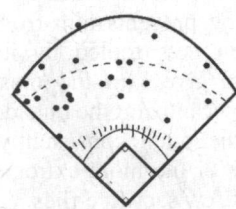 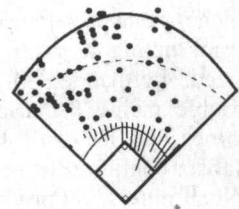

Vs. LHP   **Vs. RHP**

2003 Situational Stats

	AB	H	HR	RBI	Avg		AB	H	HR	RBI	Avg
Home	126	46	4	19	.365	LHP	71	23	1	7	.324
Road	161	41	5	12	.255	RHP	216	64	8	24	.296
First Half	67	16	1	5	.239	Sc Pos	53	11	1	18	.208
Scnd Half	220	71	8	26	.323	Clutch	47	20	1	4	.426

2003 Rankings (American League)

- 1st in batting average in the clutch
- 4th in fewest GDPs per GDP situation (3.7%)
- Led the Orioles in highest groundball-flyball ratio (2.5), fewest GDPs per GDP situation (3.7%) and batting average in the clutch

Deivi Cruz

2003 Season

Deivi Cruz provided surprising power for the Orioles last season, posting a career-high 14 home runs. Eleven of those homers were hit before the All-Star break. In the second half, he started swinging for the fences even more, and his home-run rate took a dive. His on-base percentage is always a major concern, and last year was no different because he records so few walks.

Hitting

The free-swinging Cruz routinely offers at pitches out of the strike zone, causing him to generate a large number of groundballs. He hits power pitchers much better than finesse types. Offspeed pitches and breaking balls continue to cause him problems, due to his approach at the plate. Cruz is more successful against southpaws and generates most of his power against them. Because he gets on base at a poorer rate than the average player, he's best suited to bat eighth or ninth in the line-up. Pitchers need fewer pitches to get Cruz out than most hitters at the major league level.

Baserunning & Defense

Cruz' somewhat lanky frame causes him to lumber at times in the field. He's below average at going into the hole at shortstop. He's also slow to balls hit up the middle. Cruz is adequate around the second-base bag and average at turning the double play. His arm is above average, allowing him to compensate for his below-average range. His slow first step hinders him on the bases, and he's not a threat to steal. Cruz' speed is nothing special, and he can't always go from first to third base on balls hit into the gaps.

2004 Outlook

With other alternatives at shortstop, the Orioles didn't pick up Cruz' option for 2004. Baltimore would like to upgrade at the position because his poor on-base percentage and average defense aren't likely to improve. If Cruz is to continue in the majors, he'll need to become a utility player because of his declining value at shortstop. Look for him in another uniform this season.

Position: SS
Bats: R **Throws:** R
Ht: 6' 0" **Wt:** 207

Opening Day Age: 31
Born: 11/6/72 in Nizao de Bani, DR
ML Seasons: 7
Pronunciation: DAY-vee

Overall Statistics

	G	AB	R	H	D	T	HR	RBI	SB	BB	SO	Avg	OBP	Slg
'03	152	548	61	137	24	2	14	65	1	13	49	.250	.269	.378
Car.	1006	3467	368	924	209	13	58	389	15	104	363	.267	.290	.384

Where He Hits the Ball

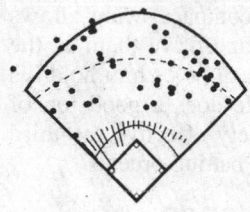 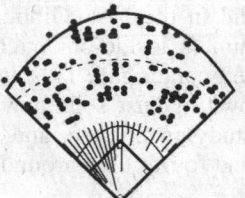

Vs. LHP   **Vs. RHP**

2003 Situational Stats

	AB	H	HR	RBI	Avg		AB	H	HR	RBI	Avg
Home	270	70	7	27	.259	LHP	140	40	7	23	.286
Road	278	67	7	38	.241	RHP	408	97	7	42	.238
First Half	300	77	11	41	.257	Sc Pos	131	36	1	45	.275
Scnd Half	248	60	3	24	.242	Clutch	88	25	1	10	.284

2003 Rankings (American League)

- 1st in lowest on-base percentage and lowest batting average vs. righthanded pitchers
- 2nd in fewest pitches seen per plate appearance (3.15)
- 4th in fielding percentage at shortstop (.975)
- 5th in highest percentage of swings put into play (52.6)
- 6th in lowest percentage of pitches taken (46.5)
- 7th in errors at shortstop (16)

Jay Gibbons

2003 Season

This former Rule 5 draftee continued to pay dividends for the Orioles. Jay Gibbons posted career highs in at-bats, doubles, RBI and batting average. It's likely his .245 batting average in September was due to a lack of stamina after two years of injuries. He made terrific strides in driving in runs as the Orioles' No. 5 hitter. Gibbons finally avoided the wrist ailments that plagued him the prior two seasons.

Hitting

Gibbons generates a lot of his power from mistake fastballs, especially ones thrown on the inside part of the plate. His plate discipline has improved, and he doesn't chase high fastballs as often as he did in the past. Gibbons' compact swing allows him to inside-out pitches and drive them to the left-center gap. This approach helps him hold his own against southpaws. He does a good job of studying pitchers and is very effective the third and fourth time around the batting order.

Baserunning & Defense

Gibbons began his career as an above-average first baseman. Over the last two seasons, he's spent most of his time in right field. He works hard on his defense and has made good progress. He aggressively charges balls hit in front of him, making spectacular catches at times. He's improved his range to nearly average, so he's no longer a liability in right. His throws are accurate, and he'll throw out runners who test his arm. He struggles at times getting to balls hit into the right-center gap because he lacks foot speed. He remains a station-to-station runner who can clog up the bases. Gibbons can go from first to third only when the ball is driven into the gap and to the wall. He rarely attempts to steal a base.

2004 Outlook

Gibbons is in the prime of his career and continues to make solid progress. This should be the year he reaches the 35-homer plateau and records a batting average better than .300. If the Orioles improve at the top of the order, his run production will improve as well.

Position: RF/1B
Bats: L **Throws:** L
Ht: 6' 0" **Wt:** 193

Opening Day Age: 27
Born: 3/2/77 in Rochester, MI
ML Seasons: 3

Overall Statistics

	G	AB	R	H	D	T	HR	RBI	SB	BB	SO	Avg	OBP	Slg
'03	160	625	80	173	39	2	23	100	0	49	89	.277	.330	.456
Car.	369	1340	178	347	78	3	66	205	1	111	194	.259	.318	.469

Where He Hits the Ball

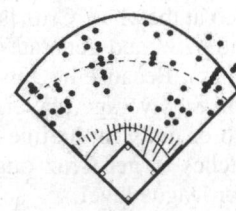
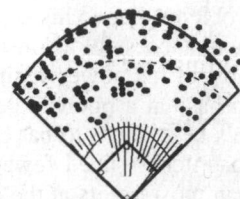

Vs. LHP   **Vs. RHP**

2003 Situational Stats

	AB	H	HR	RBI	Avg		AB	H	HR	RBI	Avg
Home	303	86	12	49	.284	LHP	187	51	5	19	.273
Road	322	87	11	51	.270	RHP	438	122	18	81	.279
First Half	347	98	14	63	.282	Sc Pos	184	53	6	77	.288
Scnd Half	278	75	9	37	.270	Clutch	99	24	0	7	.242

2003 Rankings (American League)

- 2nd in lowest cleanup slugging percentage (.377) and lowest fielding percentage in right field (.983)
- 3rd in errors in right field (5)
- Led the Orioles in runs scored, hits, singles, doubles, total bases (285), RBI, walks, intentional walks (11), times on base (225) and plate appearances (682)

Jerry Hairston Jr.

2003 Season

Jerry Hairston Jr. suffered a broken bone in his right foot on May 20. Initially, it was projected that he would miss four-to-eight weeks. He struggled at times in his rehab, especially with lateral movement, and Hairston needed 15 weeks to recover and be activated from the disabled list. Before getting hurt, he showed the improved plate patience that earned him high marks during the second half of the 2002 season.

Hitting

When healthy, Hairston has shown increased patience at the plate and an ability to get on base. He doesn't use his speed to his full advantage, hitting too many flyballs for a top-of-the-order hitter. He doesn't bunt nearly as much as he should, considering his speed and his lineup spot. The outside pitch, specifically the breaking ball, continues to give him trouble. Yet, he's reduced his swings at high fastballs. Because he has a tendency to pull the ball, he still hits too many weak groundballs to the left side of the infield. Hairston's short and compact swing allows him to make consistent contact at the plate.

Baserunning & Defense

Hairston continues to rely on a quick first step to give him an advantage in stealing bases. That and his ability to get a good lead make up for a lack of pure speed. He's one of the better Orioles in scoring from second base on hits to right field and into the gaps. In the field, his lateral quickness gets him to the ball quickly. His range is above average, especially to his left. Hairston's work around second base is above average, and he is very good at turning the double play.

2004 Outlook

Hairston is expected to be fully recovered from the fractured foot that cost him most of last season. He's made good progress in improving his ability to get on base and no longer is a liability at the top of the order. Like teammate Jay Gibbons, Hairston is entering the prime of his career and could further improve his game in 2004.

Position: 2B
Bats: R **Throws:** R
Ht: 5'10" **Wt:** 185

Opening Day Age: 27
Born: 5/29/76 in Naperville, IL
ML Seasons: 6

Overall Statistics

	G	AB	R	H	D	T	HR	RBI	SB	BB	SO	Avg	OBP	Slg
'03	58	218	25	59	12	2	2	21	14	23	25	.271	.353	.372
Car.	444	1538	198	390	79	11	24	136	81	133	200	.254	.325	.366

Where He Hits the Ball

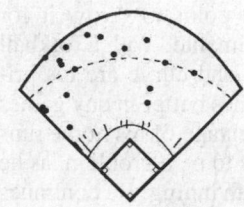 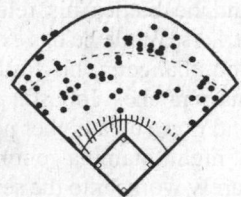

Vs. LHP **Vs. RHP**

2003 Situational Stats

	AB	H	HR	RBI	Avg		AB	H	HR	RBI	Avg
Home	107	31	1	7	.290	LHP	55	14	0	7	.255
Road	111	28	1	14	.252	RHP	163	45	2	14	.276
First Half	157	45	2	16	.287	Sc Pos	41	12	1	19	.293
Scnd Half	61	14	0	5	.230	Clutch	32	9	0	4	.281

2003 Rankings (American League)

- 1st in on-base percentage for a leadoff hitter (.389)
- 4th in sacrifice bunts (10)
- Led the Orioles in sacrifice bunts (10), highest percentage of swings put into play (54.5) and on-base percentage for a leadoff hitter (.389)

Jason Johnson

2003 Season

Jason Johnson's season began with a serious diabetic episode early in spring training. While he quickly bounced back physically, his focus on pitching took longer to come around. He posted a career high in strikeouts (118), tied his personal high in wins (10) and issued a career-high 80 walks. Johnson's 32 starts tied his career best, and his 4.18 ERA was the second best in his major league career.

Pitching

Johnson's curveball is one of the better ones in the American League. It's a sharp-breaking pitch that he sometimes struggles to keep in the strike zone. His four-seam fastball is slightly above average, and he battles his release point to throw it for strikes. While he has experimented with a forkball and changeup, his fastball and curve are his primary pitches. Johnson pitches better in day games and gives up a higher percentage of his home runs at night. Stamina continues to be a problem, as he rarely works into the seventh inning. He continues to improve his ability to generate groundballs and keep the ball in the park.

Defense

His motion to the plate is deliberate and somewhat slow, allowing runners to get a good jump on him. Runners were successful 84 percent of the time against Johnson in 2003. His pickoff move to first is slow, and he rarely catches a runner napping. Bunts and slow rollers give him trouble at times because of his size. Johnson is about average when covering first base. His throws to first are strong and accurate.

2004 Outlook

Johnson struggled down the stretch and may not be tendered a 2004 contract. Because the Orioles don't have a lot of starting pitching prospects ready for the majors, they might be forced to bring him back for another season. Johnson's leveled off in his performance with very little sign he's ready to make marked improvement in his pitching. Unless he can reduce his walk rate and build up his stamina, he'll remain an end-of-the-rotation starter.

Position: SP
Bats: R **Throws:** R
Ht: 6' 6" **Wt:** 217

Opening Day Age: 30
Born: 10/27/73 in Santa Barbara, CA
ML Seasons: 7

Overall Statistics

	W	L	Pct.	ERA	G	GS	Sv	IP	H	BB	SO	HR	Avg
'03	10	10	.500	4.18	32	32	0	189.2	216	80	118	22	.283
Car.	36	58	.383	4.91	149	133	0	806.0	874	342	518	117	.275

2003 Pitching Profile

	Jason Johnson	AL Average
Overall Strike %	61.0	62.8
1st Pitch Strike %	59.1	58.7
Ratio	1.56	1.39
Strikeouts per 9 IP	5.60	6.11
Walks per 9 IP	3.80	3.16
Home Runs per 9 IP	1.04	1.11
Strikeout/Walk Ratio	1.48	1.93
Groundball/Flyball Ratio	1.31	1.18

2003 Situational Stats

	W	L	ERA	Sv	IP		AB	H	HR	RBI	Avg
Home	6	5	3.75	0	100.2	LHB	407	115	12	48	.283
Road	4	5	4.65	0	89.0	RHB	357	101	10	39	.283
First Half	7	4	3.82	0	103.2	Sc Pos	199	47	4	60	.236
Scnd Half	3	6	4.60	0	86.0	Clutch	24	6	1	2	.250

2003 Rankings (American League)

- 1st in stolen bases allowed (32) and highest on-base percentage allowed (.358)
- 3rd in walks allowed and highest walks per nine innings (3.8)
- 4th in lowest strikeout-walk ratio (1.5)
- 5th in lowest fielding percentage at pitcher (.914)
- 6th in errors at pitcher (3)
- 7th in least run support per nine innings (4.6)
- 8th in highest batting average allowed (.283) and highest stolen-base percentage allowed (84.2)
- Led the Orioles in games started, innings pitched, hits allowed, batters faced (858), walks allowed, strikeouts, wild pitches (7), pitches thrown (3,239), pickoff throws (94), stolen bases allowed (32), runners caught stealing (6), and lowest ERA at home

Jorge Julio

2003 Season

Jorge Julio began the season as the Orioles' closer, but he never dominated except for a stretch in July. In fact, he lost the job temporarily in the second half of the season. He struggled with his control off and on last season, causing him to work deep into the count too often. On the positive side, he posted a career high 36 saves, finishing fourth in the American League.

Pitching

Julio relies on a four-seam fastball that can be clocked up to 98 MPH, but he is more effective in the 95-96 MPH range. Because of an inconsistent release point, the pitch sometimes sails out of the strike zone. His slider has a tight spin on it, but he struggles to repeat his delivery when throwing the pitch from the windup. Lefthanded hitters hit him better due to an inability to effectively pitch inside to them. Julio pitches better when he's given work on a regular basis and doesn't get a few days off. He struggles with command of his offspeed offering. He's all but abandoned the pitch, except when he wants to waste a pitch.

Defense

Typically, power pitchers are more difficult to run on because of their velocity. Julio is the exception because he does not have a good move to first base. This allows baserunners a larger than normal lead. Baserunners were 13-for-14 in stolen-base attempts with Julio on the mound last year. He fields his position adequately and covers first base without any problems. His throws to first are accurate.

2004 Outlook

Plain and simple, Julio needs to be more consistent with his release point and throw more strikes, or risk losing closer duties. Another season of eight or more blown saves would cost him his job. Julio also needs to focus better in tough situations and avoid giving up key hits. He'll need a good spring training and start of the season to quiet the grumblings about his ineffectiveness in 2003 as the closer.

Position: RP
Bats: R **Throws:** R
Ht: 6' 1" **Wt:** 223

Opening Day Age: 25
Born: 3/3/79 in Caracas, VZ
ML Seasons: 3

Overall Statistics

	W	L	Pct.	ERA	G	GS	Sv	IP	H	BB	SO	HR	Avg
'03	0	7	.000	4.38	64	0	36	61.2	60	34	52	10	.256
Car.	6	14	.300	3.22	149	0	61	151.0	140	70	129	17	.242

2003 Pitching Profile

	Jorge Julio	AL Average
Overall Strike %	58.1	62.8
1st Pitch Strike %	46.9	58.7
Ratio	1.52	1.39
Strikeouts per 9 IP	7.59	6.11
Walks per 9 IP	4.96	3.16
Home Runs per 9 IP	1.46	1.11
Strikeout/Walk Ratio	1.53	1.93
Groundball/Flyball Ratio	1.21	1.18

2003 Situational Stats

	W	L	ERA	Sv	IP		AB	H	HR	RBI	Avg
Home	0	3	4.58	20	35.1	LHB	121	33	5	17	.273
Road	0	4	4.10	16	26.1	RHB	113	27	5	19	.239
First Half	0	4	4.19	18	34.1	Sc Pos	68	17	3	27	.250
Scnd Half	0	3	4.61	18	27.1	Clutch	160	42	4	24	.263

2003 Rankings (American League)

- 3rd in blown saves (8)
- 4th in saves and relief losses (7)
- 5th in lowest save percentage (81.8)
- 6th in games finished (51)
- Led the Orioles in saves, games finished (51), save percentage (81.8), blown saves (8), relief losses (7) and relief innings (61.2)

Rodrigo Lopez

Position: SP
Bats: R **Throws:** R
Ht: 6' 1" **Wt:** 187

Opening Day Age: 28
Born: 12/14/75 in Tlalnepantla, Mexico
ML Seasons: 3
Pronunciation: rod-REE-go

2003 Season

Rodrigo Lopez suffered a strained left oblique muscle on May 1, and the injury landed him on the disabled list for six weeks. When he returned, he never was 100-percent healthy, and never displayed the 2002 form that allowed him to win 15 games. Looking beyond his health, another reason for his struggles was his inability to keep runners off the bases.

Pitching

When Lopez is pitching well, he uses his 86-88 MPH fastball to keep hitters from leaning over the plate. He doesn't have a single dominating pitch, rather he mixes his pitches to keep hitters off stride, His curve is sharp, but not of the 12-to-6 variety. It's more like a slurve. When he is on, he hits the outside corners with the pitch. Lopez does a good job of changing speeds, and that makes his fastball look a little faster than it actually is. When he's healthy, Lopez is effective against lefthanded hitters by mixing his pitches, rather than relying on any one pitch to get them out. He gets into trouble when he leaves his pitches out over the plate, something that happened often last season.

Defense

Lopez' move to first base is quick, helping to keep runners closer to the bag. He finishes his follow-through in a good fielding position, and he gets the job done. He handles bunts and slow rollers around the mound with confidence. His throws to first usually are on target. Lopez does a solid job of covering first base when needed.

2004 Outlook

The Orioles look forward to a healthy Lopez this year. He doesn't have the potential to be their staff ace, but he does add depth to a thin starting rotation. A return to his 2002 form would be the ideal, but duplicating his early success may be difficult because his stuff is average at best. He's more likely to become an innings eater who keeps his team in the game.

Overall Statistics

	W	L	Pct.	ERA	G	GS	Sv	IP	H	BB	SO	HR	Avg
'03	7	10	.412	5.82	26	26	0	147.0	188	43	103	24	.313
Car.	22	22	.500	4.81	65	60	0	368.1	400	118	256	52	.278

2003 Pitching Profile

	Rodrigo Lopez	AL Average
Overall Strike %	63.9	62.8
1st Pitch Strike %	63.8	58.7
Ratio	1.57	1.39
Strikeouts per 9 IP	6.31	6.11
Walks per 9 IP	2.63	3.16
Home Runs per 9 IP	1.47	1.11
Strikeout/Walk Ratio	2.40	1.93
Groundball/Flyball Ratio	1.21	1.18

2003 Situational Stats

	W	L	ERA	Sv	IP		AB	H	HR	RBI	Avg
Home	6	4	5.49	0	95.0	LHB	318	98	16	45	.308
Road	1	6	6.40	0	52.0	RHB	282	90	8	48	.319
First Half	2	5	5.65	0	65.1	Sc Pos	151	46	5	66	.305
Scnd Half	5	5	5.95	0	81.2	Clutch	25	8	0	1	.320

2003 Rankings (American League)

- 4th in highest ERA at home
- 7th in complete games (3) and stolen bases allowed (21)
- 8th in highest batting average allowed vs. righthanded batters
- Led the Orioles in runners caught stealing (6), highest strikeout-walk ratio (2.4) and most strikeouts per nine innings (6.3)

Luis Matos

Position: CF
Bats: R **Throws:** R
Ht: 6' 0" **Wt:** 208

Opening Day Age: 25
Born: 10/30/78 in Bayamon, PR
ML Seasons: 4
Pronunciation: MAH-tose

2003 Season

After three failed auditions with the Orioles since 2000, Luis Matos burst onto the major league scene last year. He was recalled on April 23 and hit safely in his first 15 games. Matos was batting .400 as late as June 14 and was among the batting leaders for the entire season. After missing considerable time in 2001 and 2002, he remained healthy for the entire 2003 campaign.

Hitting

Matos is a tools-rich player who has just scratched the surface of his talent. Though he remains somewhat undisciplined at the plate, he can work the count to his favor. His power is of the line-drive variety and should increase as he matures physically. Almost all of his power comes against righthanded pitchers. Southpaws get the best of him when they paint the outside of the plate with offspeed pitches and breaking balls. Righthanded power pitchers have success when they get him to chase pitches up in the strike zone. Matos sees the ball much better at night and thrives in night games. He is much more productive at home than on the road.

Baserunning & Defense

Matos can score from any base when the ball is hit into the gap. While his instincts on the bases are sound, his lack of experience can get him in trouble at times. His stolen bases are more the result of his natural speed than getting a good jump on the pitcher. Once he learns the pitchers, his stolen-base totals will improve. Matos' range in center is above average. He covers the gaps well and makes accurate throws from center field. When tested, he can throw out baserunners. On occasion, he will get a slow break on balls hit over his head, but experience should correct that problem.

2004 Outlook

Once Matos becomes more consistent at the plate, he has the ability to be a 25-25 man in home runs and stolen bases. While there will be growing pains this season, he's close to being the anchor of the Orioles' outfield for a decade.

Overall Statistics

	G	AB	R	H	D	T	HR	RBI	SB	BB	SO	Avg	OBP	Slg
'03	109	439	70	133	23	3	13	45	15	28	90	.303	.353	.458
Car.	229	750	107	199	37	6	18	75	36	52	156	.265	.321	.403

Where He Hits the Ball

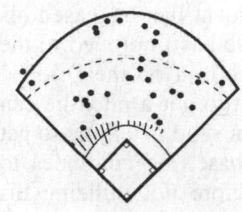

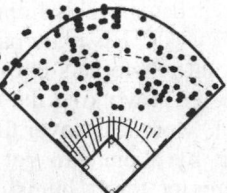

Vs. LHP   **Vs. RHP**

2003 Situational Stats

	AB	H	HR	RBI	Avg		AB	H	HR	RBI	Avg
Home	226	79	6	23	.350	LHP	108	29	1	9	.269
Road	213	54	7	22	.254	RHP	331	104	12	36	.314
First Half	183	63	6	18	.344	Sc Pos	95	26	1	30	.274
Scnd Half	256	70	7	27	.273	Clutch	67	17	2	5	.254

2003 Rankings (American League)

- 3rd in batting average at home
- 4th in sacrifice bunts (10)
- 5th in errors in center field (4) and lowest stolen-base percentage (68.2)
- 9th in bunts in play (20)
- Led the Orioles in sacrifice bunts (10), caught stealing (7), bunts in play (20) and batting average at home

Melvin Mora

2003 Season

Last season, Melvin Mora suffered two injuries that greatly impacted his play. On June 20, he was hit in the right hand by a pitch from Greg Maddux and was disabled with a painful contusion that lingered for much of the season. His season ended in mid-September when he suffered a partial tear of the medial collateral ligament in his left knee. Amazingly, Mora showed great improvement in all aspects of his game despite the injuries. He posted career highs in the three hitting percentages.

Hitting

Mora's swing has levelled off, producing more line drives and grounders and fewer popups and flyball outs. This improvement has increased his hit totals. His plate patience has improved to the point where he's one of the best on the Orioles' roster at working the count to get a pitch he can hit. Mora leans over the plate and is willing to get hit by a pitch to get on base. He continues to attempt fewer bunts, therefore not utilizing his speed as much as he should.

Baserunning & Defense

While Mora has above-average natural speed, he doesn't study pitchers to improve his jump against them. He's the team's best runner at going from first to third, scoring from second base on any hit to the outfield and even scoring from first on a gapper. His speed is an asset in the outfield, though he's better suited for left field than center. He gets a good jump on the ball from a corner spot, but is more cautious in center. His defensive versatility allows his manager to play him at any position but catcher.

2004 Outlook

The Orioles expect both of Mora's injuries to heal in time for spring training. The improving Mora makes a solid option as the No. 3 hitter in the Baltimore lineup. He's expected to be the regular left fielder and be used a lot less as a utility player. A healthy Mora should record the best power and speed numbers of his career with a full season of at-bats.

Position: LF/RF/CF/SS
Bats: R **Throws:** R
Ht: 5'11" **Wt:** 198

Opening Day Age: 32
Born: 2/2/72 in Agua Negra, VZ
ML Seasons: 5
Pronunciation: MORE-a

Overall Statistics

	G	AB	R	H	D	T	HR	RBI	SB	BB	SO	Avg	OBP	Slg
'03	96	344	68	109	17	1	15	48	6	49	71	.317	.418	.503
Car.	571	1782	269	467	97	10	49	208	47	199	357	.262	.350	.410

Where He Hits the Ball

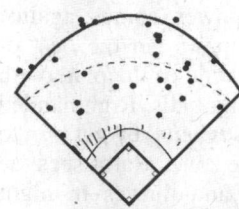
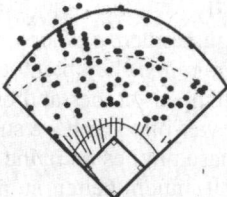

Vs. LHP   **Vs. RHP**

2003 Situational Stats

	AB	H	HR	RBI	Avg		AB	H	HR	RBI	Avg
Home	182	57	8	23	.313	LHP	74	24	5	12	.324
Road	162	52	7	25	.321	RHP	270	85	10	36	.315
First Half	275	96	13	45	.349	Sc Pos	86	22	2	33	.256
Scnd Half	69	13	2	3	.188	Clutch	57	13	3	9	.228

2003 Rankings (American League)

- 5th in fewest GDPs per GDP situation (3.8%)
- Led the Orioles in batting average, walks, hit by pitch (12), slugging percentage, on-base percentage, HR frequency (22.9 ABs per HR), most pitches seen per plate appearance (4.11), batting average vs. righthanded pitchers, batting average on the road and lowest percentage of swings on the first pitch (15.1)

Damian Moss

2003 Season

Damian Moss began the season with the San Francisco Giants and was traded to the Orioles with Kurt Ainsworth on July 31 for Sidney Ponson. The Giants grew weary of Moss' inability to throw strikes and dealt him at the trade deadline. He ended the season with more walks than strikeouts. That's why Moss is with his third team in a year's time. He also allowed 24 home runs, his highest total as a pro.

Pitching

Moss struggles to find a consistent release point. He also throws across his body, which causes control problems with all his pitches. Because he rarely repeats his delivery, his fastball has a tendency to sail out of the strike zone. Both his curveball and changeup are above-average pitches, but he fails to throw them for strikes often enough. Compounding his control problems is his approach. Moss prefers to nibble around the plate rather than go after hitters. That only adds to his walk totals. Because he throws so many pitches and always seems to be working out of jams, he almost never works deep into a game.

Defense

Moss has three different pickoff moves to first. His ability to keep runners close helps his catcher keep the running game in check when he's on the mound. Moss gets a good jump off the mound and makes all of the routine plays required of pitchers. He does a good job of covering first base when the first baseman goes into the hole between first and second base. His throws to first are quick and accurate.

2004 Outlook

If you can't throw strikes consistently, you won't hang around the major leagues, even if you are lefthanded. That's the dilemma that faces Moss. He better throw strikes and soon, or the Orioles too will lose patience waiting for him to develop as a pitcher. Unless he can fix his pitching mechanics, his future with Baltimore or any other team, is bleak.

Position: SP
Bats: R **Throws:** L
Ht: 6' 0" **Wt:** 187

Opening Day Age: 27
Born: 11/24/76 in Darlinghurst, Australia
ML Seasons: 3

Overall Statistics

	W	L	Pct.	ERA	G	GS	Sv	IP	H	BB	SO	HR	Avg
'03	10	12	.455	5.16	31	29	0	165.2	184	92	79	24	.284
Car.	22	18	.550	4.22	69	59	0	353.2	327	190	198	45	.249

2003 Pitching Profile

	Damian Moss (AL)	AL Average
Overall Strike %	55.9	62.8
1st Pitch Strike %	48.2	58.7
Ratio	1.82	1.39
Strikeouts per 9 IP	3.91	6.11
Walks per 9 IP	5.15	3.16
Home Runs per 9 IP	2.13	1.11
Strikeout/Walk Ratio	0.76	1.93
Groundball/Flyball Ratio	1.03	1.18

2003 Situational Stats

	W	L	ERA	Sv	IP		AB	H	HR	RBI	Avg
Home	5	6	4.87	0	88.2	LHB	184	63	7	27	.342
Road	5	6	5.49	0	77.0	RHB	464	121	17	63	.261
First Half	7	6	5.06	0	96.0	Sc Pos	174	45	6	62	.259
Scnd Half	3	6	5.30	0	69.2	Clutch	24	8	1	2	.333

2003 Rankings (American League)

- Did not rank near the top or bottom in any category

Brian Roberts

2003 Season

Brian Roberts was scheduled to spend most of 2003 at Triple-A Ottawa, with some time in Baltimore as a utility player. That changed when Jerry Hairston Jr. went down with a broken bone in his right foot. Roberts was a lot more productive at the plate than he was in 2002, when he lost the second-base job to Hairston. Roberts finally displayed the baserunning ability that he showed in the minors.

Hitting

Roberts has a compact swing that allows him to hit the ball to all fields. His level swing generates plenty of groundballs and infield hits. He continues to improve his ability to work the count, and he's now one of the most patient hitters on the Baltimore roster. His plate discipline doesn't produce a lot of walks, but does allow him to get a better pitch to hit. Roberts struggles with low-and-outside breaking balls from righthanders, but he's showing improvement. While he is an above-average bunter, he'll be better at it as he gains more experience.

Baserunning & Defense

Roberts uses both his slightly above-average speed and ability to get a good jump to generate his stolen bases. He's one of the Orioles' best at going from first to third on any hit to the outfield. Roberts can score from second on all but shallow hits to the outfield. With his skills and instincts, he can play both second base and shortstop, though he is more effective at second. His range is slightly above average at both middle positions. His throws to first are accurate.

2004 Outlook

The Orioles were pleased with his development, and Roberts may be the starting shortstop with a healthy Hairston back at second. As other Orioles hitters mature, Roberts is likely to move out of the leadoff spot into the No. 2 hole or further down in the lineup. A mediocre on-base percentage is keeping him from remaining at the top of the lineup. Roberts is expected to be a solid contributor—both at the plate and in the field—but his ceiling is limited.

Position: 2B
Bats: B **Throws:** R
Ht: 5' 9" **Wt:** 172

Opening Day Age: 26
Born: 10/9/77 in Durham, NC
ML Seasons: 3

Overall Statistics

	G	AB	R	H	D	T	HR	RBI	SB	BB	SO	Avg	OBP	Slg
'03	112	460	65	124	22	4	5	41	23	46	58	.270	.337	.367
Car.	225	861	125	222	40	7	8	69	44	74	115	.258	.316	.348

Where He Hits the Ball

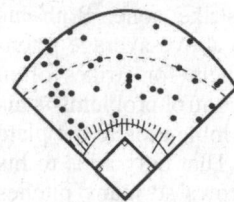 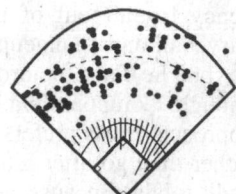

Vs. LHP   **Vs. RHP**

2003 Situational Stats

	AB	H	HR	RBI	Avg		AB	H	HR	RBI	Avg
Home	236	66	3	18	.280	LHP	129	34	2	8	.264
Road	224	58	2	23	.259	RHP	331	90	3	33	.272
First Half	193	55	3	19	.285	Sc Pos	95	25	2	37	.263
Scnd Half	267	69	2	22	.258	Clutch	66	16	1	6	.242

2003 Rankings (American League)

- 1st in lowest percentage of swings that missed (6.8)
- 5th in lowest slugging percentage and lowest HR frequency (92.0 ABs per HR)
- 8th in stolen bases and steals of third (4)
- Led the Orioles in triples, stolen bases, stolen-base percentage (79.3), highest percentage of pitches taken (60.7), lowest percentage of swings that missed (6.8), steals of third (4) and batting average with the bases loaded (.500)

Kurt Ainsworth

Position: SP
Bats: R **Throws:** R
Ht: 6' 3" **Wt:** 192

Opening Day Age: 25
Born: 9/9/78 in Baton Rouge, LA
ML Seasons: 3
Pronunciation: AYNS-werth

Overall Statistics

	W	L	Pct.	ERA	G	GS	Sv	IP	H	BB	SO	HR	Avg
'03	5	5	.500	4.08	14	11	0	68.1	72	27	52	8	.271
Car.	6	7	.462	3.75	22	15	0	96.0	97	41	70	10	.264

2003 Situational Stats

	W	L	ERA	Sv	IP		AB	H	HR	RBI	Avg
Home	3	3	3.68	0	36.2	LHB	105	30	2	9	.286
Road	2	2	4.55	0	31.2	RHB	161	42	6	19	.261
First Half	5	4	3.82	0	66.0	Sc Pos	49	16	1	16	.327
Scnd Half	0	1	11.57	0	2.1	Clutch	18	5	2	3	.278

2003 Season

The Orioles acquired Kurt Ainsworth along with Damian Moss in a July deadline deal with San Francisco for Sidney Ponson. With the Giants, Ainsworth started slowly before posting a 2.95 ERA in May and suffering a fractured scapula in his pitching shoulder. He was done for the year, save for a 2.1-inning stint with the Orioles late in the season.

Pitching & Defense

Ainsworth's four-seam fastball can be clocked up to 94 MPH. He's at his best when he spots the fastball and uses it to move hitters off the plate. When he challenges hitters up in the zone, he gets into trouble. He also throws a changeup, slider and sinker. Ainsworth continues to mature and now keeps the ball down in the zone and in the ballpark. He does a good job at holding runners with a solid move to first. Ainsworth is an average fielder who covers first base when needed.

2004 Outlook

The Orioles see Ainsworth as the key to the Ponson deal. While his shoulder injury might force him to start the season slowly, this former first rounder has ace-of-the-staff potential. Baltimore should start to see some of that potential translate into success this season.

Marty Cordova

Position: DH
Bats: R **Throws:** R
Ht: 6' 0" **Wt:** 213

Opening Day Age: 34
Born: 7/10/69 in Las Vegas, NV
ML Seasons: 9
Pronunciation: core-DOE-vuh

Overall Statistics

	G	AB	R	H	D	T	HR	RBI	SB	BB	SO	Avg	OBP	Slg
'03	9	30	5	7	1	0	1	4	1	8	5	.233	.410	.367
Car.	952	3419	480	938	192	18	122	540	57	329	730	.274	.344	.448

2003 Situational Stats

	AB	H	HR	RBI	Avg		AB	H	HR	RBI	Avg
Home	19	4	1	4	.211	LHP	8	3	0	0	.375
Road	11	3	0	0	.273	RHP	22	4	1	4	.182
First Half	30	7	1	4	.233	Sc Pos	5	2	1	4	.400
Scnd Half	0	0	0	0	–	Clutch	9	2	1	2	.222

2003 Season

Nine games into his season, Marty Cordova went on the disabled list with bone spurs in his right elbow. They were successfully removed, and he was expected back before the All-Star break. During his rehab, however, he suffered damage to the ulnar collateral ligament in his right elbow and was lost for the season. He underwent successful ligament reconstruction surgery in late August.

Hitting, Baserunning & Defense

When healthy, Cordova makes consistent contact against all types of pitchers. He's become more of a gap hitter when hitting for power, and has a knack of hitting to right field to drive in a runner from third base. Slow breaking balls on the outside of the plate and in the dirt continue to be a problem. He hits into a lot of double plays due to a lack of foot speed. On the bases, he runs with intelligence, but he doesn't always score from second on a hit to center or right field. Cordova is a competent left fielder with only an average arm.

2004 Outlook

The main question is: Will Cordova's right elbow be healed enough after two surgeries in four months? It's unlikely he'll be ready at the start of the season. The oft-injured Cordova is nearing the end of his career.

Omar Daal

Position: SP
Bats: L **Throws:** L
Ht: 6' 3" **Wt:** 193

Opening Day Age: 32
Born: 2/23/72 in
Maracaibo, VZ
ML Seasons: 11
Pronunciation:
DOLL

Overall Statistics

	W	L	Pct.	ERA	G	GS	Sv	IP	H	BB	SO	HR	Avg
'03	4	11	.267	6.34	19	17	0	93.2	134	30	53	11	.343
Car.	68	78	.466	4.55	392	164	1	1198.2	1250	441	806	140	.271

2003 Situational Stats

	W	L	ERA	Sv	IP		AB	H	HR	RBI	Avg
Home	2	5	4.83	0	50.1	LHB	77	24	1	12	.312
Road	2	6	8.10	0	43.1	RHB	314	110	10	48	.350
First Half	4	10	5.86	0	86.0	Sc Pos	109	44	3	49	.404
Scnd Half	0	1	11.74	0	7.2	Clutch	24	10	2	4	.417

2003 Season

Omar Daal was signed to a two-year contract with the hope that he would combine with Rodrigo Lopez to form an effective lefty-righty duo. It didn't happen. Lopez was a disappointment from the start, as was Daal. Daal ended the season with just four wins and one of the worst ERAs of his big league tenure.

Pitching & Defense

Daal's deceptive delivery was an asset in the past, but the decreasing quality of his pitches now makes that a moot point. The only way Daal can be effective is by keeping his pitches down in the strike zone and pitching on the black of the plate. When he has both control and command of his pitches, he can be tough. Last year that didn't happen. His fastball rarely exceeded 85 MPH and inched close to the velocity of his changeup. When the velocity difference between his pitches is diminished, he's very hittable.

2004 Outlook

The only thing saving him a roster spot with Baltimore is the second year of his two-year contract. If the Orioles are able to find enough quality starters to fill out the rotation, Daal's likely to end up as a long man out of the bullpen. He's definitely on the downside of his career.

Eric DuBose

Position: SP
Bats: L **Throws:** L
Ht: 6' 3" **Wt:** 233

Opening Day Age: 27
Born: 5/15/76 in
Bradenton, FL
ML Seasons: 2
Pronunciation:
dew-BOWES

Overall Statistics

	W	L	Pct.	ERA	G	GS	Sv	IP	H	BB	SO	HR	Avg
'03	3	6	.333	3.79	17	10	0	73.2	60	25	44	6	.222
Car.	3	6	.333	3.73	21	10	0	79.2	67	26	48	7	.229

2003 Situational Stats

	W	L	ERA	Sv	IP		AB	H	HR	RBI	Avg
Home	2	3	3.34	0	32.1	LHB	82	25	1	7	.305
Road	1	3	4.14	0	41.1	RHB	188	35	5	18	.186
First Half	0	1	2.84	0	6.1	Sc Pos	56	8	1	16	.143
Scnd Half	3	5	3.88	0	67.1	Clutch	40	10	1	4	.250

2003 Season

Eric DuBose began the season at Triple-A Ottawa, dominating hitters and earning a permanent callup in late July. He started out in the bullpen and became acclimated to the majors. When the Orioles needed a starter, he assumed that role for 10 starts. DuBose finished the season on a positive note, recording a 3.24 ERA in September.

Pitching & Defense

The southpaw throws an 88-90 MPH fastball that he uses to set up his other pitches. His out pitch at the moment is a sharp-breaking curveball. When he's on, he's spotting his breaking ball on the outside part of the plate. His offspeed offering is inconsistent. Surprisingly, he is much more effective against righthanded batters because his curveball breaks in on their hands when he throws it inside. Though he got a look as a starter, his future role might be as a lefty reliever because of durability questions. DuBose is effective against the running game and fields his position well.

2004 Outlook

DuBose has a history of injuries that may preclude a significant improvement in his game. Last year was his first as a pro during which he didn't have some sort of arm injury or surgery. Look for the Orioles to watch his workload closely again.

Brook Fordyce

Position: C
Bats: R **Throws:** R
Ht: 6' 0" **Wt:** 194

Opening Day Age: 33
Born: 5/7/70 in New London, CT
ML Seasons: 9
Pronunciation: four-DICE

Overall Statistics

	G	AB	R	H	D	T	HR	RBI	SB	BB	SO	Avg	OBP	Slg
'03	108	348	28	95	12	2	6	31	2	19	44	.273	.311	.371
Car.	569	1656	158	436	97	4	39	179	8	110	261	.263	.313	.397

2003 Situational Stats

	AB	H	HR	RBI	Avg		AB	H	HR	RBI	Avg
Home	171	50	3	14	.292	LHP	84	29	3	8	.345
Road	177	45	3	17	.254	RHP	264	66	3	23	.250
First Half	158	42	2	9	.266	Sc Pos	78	15	0	22	.192
Scnd Half	190	53	4	22	.279	Clutch	61	15	0	8	.246

2003 Season

Brook Fordyce posted career highs by appearing in 108 games and recording 348 at-bats. Unfortunately, the additional playing time did not translate into higher raw numbers and greater run production. While he was able to maintain a solid batting average, his power numbers were a disappointment, even for a catcher.

Hitting, Baserunning & Defense

One of the reasons Fordyce doesn't generate much power is because he slaps at the ball, preferring to make contact rather than drive the ball into the gaps. His hitting style allows him to make consistent contact and keep his strikeouts low. Fordyce has improved his ability to block pitches in the dirt, and he's now considered average in that skill. His throws to second base are accurate but not particularly strong. His release is slower than the average catcher's. His slow foot speed makes him a station-to-station runner and a liability on the bases.

2004 Outlook

While Fordyce has improved his play behind the plate, he barely rates as an average catcher. Offensively, he offers very little and is better suited as a backup. His next role is up in the air after the Orioles declined his 2004 option.

Pat Hentgen

Position: SP
Bats: R **Throws:** R
Ht: 6' 2" **Wt:** 195

Opening Day Age: 35
Born: 11/13/68 in Detroit, MI
ML Seasons: 13
Pronunciation: HENT-gen

Overall Statistics

	W	L	Pct.	ERA	G	GS	Sv	IP	H	BB	SO	HR	Avg
'03	7	8	.467	4.09	28	22	1	160.2	150	58	100	25	.247
Car.	129	103	.556	4.21	326	290	1	1995.0	2021	733	1257	253	.264

2003 Situational Stats

	W	L	ERA	Sv	IP		AB	H	HR	RBI	Avg
Home	4	4	3.95	0	84.1	LHB	333	79	15	41	.237
Road	3	4	4.24	1	76.1	RHB	275	71	10	29	.258
First Half	1	5	5.25	1	73.2	Sc Pos	132	29	6	43	.220
Scnd Half	6	3	3.10	0	87.0	Clutch	42	9	1	3	.214

2003 Season

After two injury-plagued seasons with the Orioles, Pat Hentgen finally remained healthy enough to start 22 games. His experience and ability to battle even when he didn't have his best stuff was evident all season long. While he gave up a high amount of home runs (25) for the innings he pitched, he was a valued member of the pitching staff.

Pitching & Defense

The velocity on his trademark four-seam fastball rarely reaches 90 MPH anymore. Hentgen now throws a cutter and two-seamer to give hitters a different look. He uses his changeup and curveball to keep hitters from sitting on his fastballs. He's more effective pitching in day games than at night because hitters have trouble picking up his pitches in daylight. His stamina isn't what it once was, and he rarely works his way into the seventh inning. Hentgen does a decent job at holding runners on first and is a solid fielder for his position.

2004 Outlook

Baltimore brought back Hentgen as a one-year stop-gap measure, and he provided more than expected. He jumped at a one-year, $2.2 million deal from Toronto early in the offseason. If Hentgen stays healthy, there isn't any reason he can't build on his 2003 season.

Kerry Ligtenberg

Position: RP
Bats: R **Throws:** R
Ht: 6' 2" **Wt:** 222

Opening Day Age: 32
Born: 5/11/71 in Rapid City, SD
ML Seasons: 6
Pronunciation: lite-en-berg

Overall Statistics

	W	L	Pct.	ERA	G	GS	Sv	IP	H	BB	SO	HR	Avg
'03	4	2	.667	3.34	68	0	1	59.1	60	14	47	9	.263
Car.	16	14	.533	3.09	322	0	45	326.0	268	129	303	36	.223

2003 Situational Stats

	W	L	ERA	Sv	IP		AB	H	HR	RBI	Avg
Home	3	2	3.60	0	35.0	LHB	87	31	4	13	.356
Road	1	0	2.96	1	24.1	RHB	141	29	5	21	.206
First Half	0	1	3.21	1	33.2	Sc Pos	65	16	2	24	.246
Scnd Half	4	1	3.51	0	25.2	Clutch	94	26	4	20	.277

2003 Season

The Orioles wanted to add a solid setup man to their bullpen last winter, and Kerry Ligtenberg provided everything they wanted. He dominated righthanded hitters, allowing them to bat only .206 against him. May was his best month, when he recorded a microscopic 0.79 ERA.

Pitching & Defense

Ligtenberg still relies on an above-average split-finger fastball, but the pitch isn't as sharp-breaking as it used to be. He now also mixes in a four-seam fastball that he can get up to 93 MPH. His slider is about average and keeps hitters from sitting on the fastball. Lefthanded hitters give him problems because he lacks a pitch that moves in on their hands. His arm is durable and he still can work in back-to-back games. But Ligtenberg also can come into a game with three or four days off and be effective. He struggles in the field, with six errors in just 34 career chances.

2004 Outlook

Ligtenberg has settled in as a good setup reliever, and it doesn't look like he'll return to the closer role, even if the opportunity presented itself. Toronto will benefit from his solid setup work after signing the righthander to a two-year, $4.5 million deal.

Willis Roberts

Position: RP
Bats: R **Throws:** R
Ht: 6' 3" **Wt:** 240

Opening Day Age: 28
Born: 6/19/75 in San Cristobal, DR
ML Seasons: 4

Overall Statistics

	W	L	Pct.	ERA	G	GS	Sv	IP	H	BB	SO	HR	Avg
'03	3	1	.750	5.72	26	0	0	39.1	41	16	26	7	.273
Car.	17	15	.531	4.62	139	18	7	247.2	265	103	172	27	.274

2003 Situational Stats

	W	L	ERA	Sv	IP		AB	H	HR	RBI	Avg
Home	1	0	3.00	0	21.0	LHB	57	17	5	13	.298
Road	2	1	8.84	0	18.1	RHB	93	24	2	18	.258
First Half	3	1	5.72	0	39.1	Sc Pos	34	14	3	25	.412
Scnd Half	0	0	—	0	0.0	Clutch	43	12	0	9	.279

2003 Season

Willis Roberts was placed on the disabled list late in June with a sprained ulnar collateral ligament in his pitching elbow. He missed the rest of the season due to the injury. He began the year with a solid April, posting a 3.95. The next two months were a struggle before he was felled by the elbow injury.

Pitching & Defense

Roberts' two best pitches are his two-seam and four-seam fastballs. The four-seamer tends to sail out of the strike zone. That's most likely due to his erratic release point. He is able to keep the two-seam fastball down in the zone, but it isn't as sharp as his other fastball. He uses his slider to keep hitters off stride. Roberts doesn't throw it at a slow-enough speed to make it a truly effective pitch. He lacks an offspeed pitch, and that prevents him from returning to the starting rotation. His pickoff move to first is just adequate. He's average at fielding his position and covering first base.

2004 Outlook

Roberts' availability for this season is in question because of the damaged ligament in his pitching elbow. He elected to avoid surgery, so the Orioles are crossing their fingers that he can avoid more elbow problems this season.

B.J. Ryan

Position: RP
Bats: L **Throws:** L
Ht: 6' 6" **Wt:** 247

Opening Day Age: 28
Born: 12/28/75 in
Bossier City, LA
ML Seasons: 5

Overall Statistics

	W	L	Pct.	ERA	G	GS	Sv	IP	H	BB	SO	HR	Avg
'03	4	1	.800	3.40	76	0	0	50.1	42	27	63	1	.227
Car.	11	9	.550	4.38	260	0	3	224.0	189	134	243	21	.229

2003 Situational Stats

	W	L	ERA	Sv	IP		AB	H	HR	RBI	Avg
Home	3	0	2.63	0	27.1	LHB	97	18	0	14	.186
Road	1	1	4.30	0	23.0	RHB	88	24	1	14	.273
First Half	3	0	5.68	0	25.1	Sc Pos	66	17	1	25	.258
Scnd Half	1	1	1.08	0	25.0	Clutch	100	27	1	22	.270

2003 Season

B.J. Ryan posted career highs in holds (19), wins and strikeouts, as well as his best ERA in the last four seasons. After the All-Star break, he recorded a 1.08 ERA—only Minnesota's LaTroy Hawkins was better among American League relievers with 20 second-half innings—and hitters batted just .191 against him after the break. Ryan is now considered one of the league's best lefthanded specialists.

Pitching & Defense

Ryan's best pitch is a plus slider that he uses to dominate lefthanded hitters. He's nearly unhittable facing lefthanders, which has been the case for five straight seasons. A deceptive pitching motion that Ryan uses hides the ball from hitters, especially those from the left side of the plate. His fastball can reach 92-93 MPH, but it lacks enough movement to be an out pitch. Righthanded batters continue to cause him problems, eliminating him from closer considerations. His move to first base is above average, and he fields bunts and slow rollers around the mound adequately.

2004 Outlook

Ryan continues to improve as a lefthanded reliever, but he may have reached his ceiling last summer. Look for him to duplicate his 2003 season, rather than improve, in 2004.

David Segui

Position: DH
Bats: B **Throws:** L
Ht: 6' 1" **Wt:** 216

Opening Day Age: 37
Born: 7/19/66 in Kansas City, KS
ML Seasons: 14
Pronunciation:
seh-GHEE

Overall Statistics

	G	AB	R	H	D	T	HR	RBI	SB	BB	SO	Avg	OBP	Slg
'03	67	224	26	59	11	1	5	25	1	26	47	.263	.341	.384
Car.	1438	4788	675	1392	281	16	138	677	17	519	674	.291	.359	.443

2003 Situational Stats

	AB	H	HR	RBI	Avg		AB	H	HR	RBI	Avg
Home	95	20	2	11	.211	LHP	50	10	0	4	.200
Road	129	39	3	14	.302	RHP	174	49	5	21	.282
First Half	204	54	4	21	.265	Sc Pos	60	15	1	19	.250
Scnd Half	20	5	1	4	.250	Clutch	43	11	0	3	.256

2003 Season

A strained right hamstring and a torn tendon in his left wrist curtailed David Segui's 2003 season. He eventually needed surgery on the wrist and was placed on the disabled list in the middle of July. When he was in the lineup, he wasn't nearly as productive as in past years.

Hitting, Baserunning & Defense

The switch-hitting Segui hits the ball to all fields. Wrist and knee injuries have greatly reduced his power and his ability to handle fastballs on the inside portion of the plate. He rarely pulls the ball for a home run from either side. The injuries also have taken a toll on his defense. He's now a below-average first baseman with limited range around the bag. Bunts to the first-base side of the infield can cause problems for him. When on base, he takes it one base at a time. Because of his slow foot speed, he needs a double to score from second base. He no longer is a threat to steal.

2004 Outlook

The only reason that Segui is returning to the Orioles is because a year remains on his contract. His role will be limited to part-time designated-hitter duties, and occasionally filling in at first base.

Rick Bauer (Pos: RHP, Age: 27)

	W	L	Pct.	ERA	G	GS	Sv	IP	H	BB	SO	HR	Avg
'03	0	0	—	4.55	35	0	0	61.1	58	24	43	5	.256
Car.	6	12	.333	4.30	97	7	1	178.0	177	69	104	24	.263

Despite his success as a Triple-A starter last season, Bauer was inconsistent in the Orioles' pen. Better in the second half, he was going to make some September starts, but shoulder tendinitis set in. 2004 Outlook: B

Hector Carrasco (Pos: RHP, Age: 34)

	W	L	Pct.	ERA	G	GS	Sv	IP	H	BB	SO	HR	Avg
'03	2	6	.250	4.93	40	0	1	38.1	40	20	27	5	.270
Car.	30	42	.417	4.22	498	1	16	605.1	596	299	482	45	.259

His walk rate always has been a concern, but Carrasco has thrown hard enough to keep getting chances. He needs to give up a lot fewer hits per inning to hold on to a significant relief role. 2004 Outlook: C

Jack Cust (Pos: DH, Age: 25, Bats: L)

	G	AB	R	H	D	T	HR	RBI	SB	BB	SO	Avg	OBP	Slg
'03	27	73	7	19	7	0	4	11	0	10	25	.260	.357	.521
Car.	65	140	15	31	9	0	5	19	0	23	57	.221	.333	.393

Cust finally turned on some power in the majors, after averaging 31 doubles and 26 homers a year in his four previous minor league seasons. He's a poor-fielding DH who walks but strikes out a ton. 2004 Outlook: B

Sean Douglass (Pos: RHP, Age: 24)

	W	L	Pct.	ERA	G	GS	Sv	IP	H	BB	SO	HR	Avg
'03	0	0	—	13.50	3	0	0	8.0	14	6	3	2	.378
Car.	2	6	.250	6.61	22	12	0	81.2	93	52	64	15	.288

Douglass lacks a dominating pitch and has struggled in the majors, despite some success at the Triple-A level. The Twins will try to get him over the hump after claiming him off waivers in October. 2004 Outlook: C

Travis Driskill (Pos: RHP, Age: 32)

	W	L	Pct.	ERA	G	GS	Sv	IP	H	BB	SO	HR	Avg
'03	3	5	.375	6.00	20	0	1	48.0	62	9	33	8	.310
Car.	11	13	.458	5.23	49	19	1	180.2	212	57	111	29	.291

Driskill has been solid as a Triple-A starter in recent years, and reached the majors at age 30 in 2002. He lives off a slider and lacks an offspeed pitch. He's struggling to turn that into a relief role. 2004 Outlook: C

Geronimo Gil (Pos: C, Age: 28, Bats: R)

	G	AB	R	H	D	T	HR	RBI	SB	BB	SO	Avg	OBP	Slg
'03	54	169	22	40	4	0	3	16	0	12	34	.237	.299	.314
Car.	196	649	58	155	25	0	15	67	2	38	129	.239	.287	.347

Known as a defensive specialist, Gil batted a lofty .339 with two of his three homers in May, but otherwise his bat wasn't very useful. Amazingly, the O's other options at catcher are hardly much better. 2004 Outlook: C

Buddy Groom (Pos: LHP, Age: 38)

	W	L	Pct.	ERA	G	GS	Sv	IP	H	BB	SO	HR	Avg
'03	1	3	.250	5.36	60	0	1	45.1	58	14	34	7	.309
Car.	26	30	.464	4.62	679	15	26	641.0	707	232	442	62	.282

After a stellar 2002 in which Groom posted a career-best 1.60 ERA at age 37, the southpaw was far more hittable last summer despite not allowing a run in his first 11 appearances. Is he too old to rebound? 2004 Outlook: C

Jose Leon (Pos: 3B, Age: 27, Bats: R)

	G	AB	R	H	D	T	HR	RBI	SB	BB	SO	Avg	OBP	Slg
'03	21	54	6	13	1	0	0	0	0	3	18	.241	.305	.259
Car.	57	143	14	35	3	0	3	10	1	6	38	.245	.289	.329

Leon hasn't done much in three Triple-A seasons, and his power has been sliding, but he got three callups from the O's in 2003. Signed to a minor league deal for '04, he'll compete for a reserve role. 2004 Outlook: C

Robert Machado (Pos: C, Age: 30, Bats: R)

	G	AB	R	H	D	T	HR	RBI	SB	BB	SO	Avg	OBP	Slg
'03	18	49	8	13	1	0	1	3	0	6	12	.265	.345	.347
Car.	216	563	61	135	33	2	10	58	0	41	117	.240	.293	.359

Never known for his bat, Machado enjoyed his best minor league season ever in 2003, batting .335 and slugging .520 at Triple-A Ottawa. He was good with the O's, too, but his throwing arm is his only weapon. 2004 Outlook: C

Carlos Mendez (Pos: 1B, Age: 29, Bats: R)

	G	AB	R	H	D	T	HR	RBI	SB	BB	SO	Avg	OBP	Slg
'03	26	45	3	10	2	0	0	5	0	0	12	.222	.217	.267
Car.	26	45	3	10	2	0	0	5	0	0	12	.222	.217	.267

Mendez made his major league debut in the course of his sixth Triple-A season last summer. His last two have been decent, but Mendez isn't likely to stick, despite signing a new minor league deal. 2004 Outlook: C

Jose Morban (Pos: SS/2B/DH, Age: 24, Bats: B)

	G	AB	R	H	D	T	HR	RBI	SB	BB	SO	Avg	OBP	Slg
'03	61	71	14	10	0	0	2	5	8	3	21	.141	.187	.225
Car.	61	71	14	10	0	0	2	5	8	3	21	.141	.187	.225

A shortstop who was a Rule 5 pick last December, Morban had to spend the entire season in the majors. He never had played as high as high Class-A, and looks destined for Double-A or Triple-A ball this year. 2004 Outlook: D

John Parrish (Pos: LHP, Age: 26)

	W	L	Pct.	ERA	G	GS	Sv	IP	H	BB	SO	HR	Avg
'03	0	1	.000	1.90	14	0	0	23.2	17	8	15	2	.205
Car.	3	7	.300	5.38	38	9	0	82.0	79	60	63	13	.256

Parrish missed all of 2002 with a torn ACL in his knee, but pitched well in Double-A ball and impressed the O's in 14 games. He's an offspeed guy who needs good command. He must show it in the spring. 2004 Outlook: C

Tim Raines Jr. (**Pos**: CF, **Age**: 24, **Bats**: B)

	G	AB	R	H	D	T	HR	RBI	SB	BB	SO	Avg	OBP	Slg
'03	20	43	4	6	1	1	0	2	0	2	12	.140	.196	.209
Car.	27	66	10	10	3	1	0	2	3	5	20	.152	.222	.227

The son of the former Montreal star has been slow to develop, but he batted .304 with a .365 OBP in the high minors in 2003. He won't get as much time to adjust to big league pitching. 2004 Outlook: C

B.J. Surhoff (**Pos**: DH/1B/LF, **Age**: 39, **Bats**: L)

	G	AB	R	H	D	T	HR	RBI	SB	BB	SO	Avg	OBP	Slg
	93	319	32	94	20	0	5	41	2	29	29	.295	.353	.404
	2133	7612	987	2142	417	39	175	1069	139	599	761	.281	.332	.415

Surhoff generated solid hitting percentages, but the oft-injured veteran endured bouts on the disabled list for a hamstring and quadriceps. Surhoff wants to play in 2004, but probably in a reserve role. 2004 Outlook: B

Pedro Swann (**Pos**: LF, **Age**: 33, **Bats**: L)

	G	AB	R	H	D	T	HR	RBI	SB	BB	SO	Avg	OBP	Slg
'03	8	14	3	3	1	0	1	2	0	1	4	.214	.267	.500
Car.	25	28	6	4	1	0	1	3	0	2	12	.143	.200	.286

Swann has played six straight seasons of Triple-A ball, hitting for a decent average but with little pop and declining plate patience. The O's inked him to another minor league deal. 2004 Outlook: C

Baltimore Orioles Minor League Prospects

Organization Overview:

Two of the Orioles' best pitching prospects, Matt Riley and Erik Bedard, got back on track last season. Both had Tommy John surgery, Riley in 2001 and Bedard in 2002. Pitcher John Maine and second baseman Mike Fontenot could offer help to the parent club by the end of the season. Outfielders Nick Markakis and Val Majewski, plus Tripper Johnson, give Baltimore several up-and-coming young hitters. Outfielder Darnell McDonald needs to show marked improvement this year or risk being passed by others in the system. The focus on pitching is now more on the power-types rather than the finesse pitchers of the past few seasons. The system is slowly being restocked with solid young arms, and young hitters like Lorenzo Scott, a 17th-round selection in 2003.

Erik Bedard

Position: P
Bats: L **Throws:** L
Ht: 6' 1" **Wt:** 191

Opening Day Age: 25
Born: 3/6/79 in Navan, Canada

Recent Statistics

	W	L	ERA	G	GS	Sv	IP	H	R	BB	SO	HR
2002 AA Bowie	6	3	1.97	13	12	0	68.2	43	18	30	66	0
2002 AL Baltimore	0	0	13.50	2	0	0	0.2	2	1	0	1	0
2003 R Orioles	0	0	1.13	3	3	0	8.0	4	1	2	11	0
2003 A Aberdeen	0	0	2.35	2	2	0	7.2	7	2	1	13	0
2003 A Frederick	0	1	7.36	1	1	0	3.2	5	3	1	2	1

Bedard needed Tommy John surgery to repair a partially torn ulnar collateral ligament in his pitching elbow in September 2002. The former sixth-round pick relies on a sharp-breaking curveball and a 92-MPH fastball with good late movement. His changeup also is above average. Before the surgery, Bedard was able to spot all his pitches for strikes and showed poise on the mound. He's not afraid to pitch inside, making him a very effective southpaw. When he returned from the surgery later in the season, his velocity was still there but his control was off due to the long layoff. Baltimore expects Bedard to start the season at Triple-A, with a late-season callup possible once he regains his control.

Mike Fontenot

Position: 2B
Bats: L **Throws:** R
Ht: 5' 8" **Wt:** 178

Opening Day Age: 23
Born: 6/9/80 in Slidell, LA

Recent Statistics

	G	AB	R	H	D	T	HR	RBI	SB	BB	SO	Avg
2002 A Frederick	122	481	61	127	16	4	8	53	13	42	117	.264
2003 AA Bowie	126	449	63	146	24	5	12	66	16	50	89	.325

Fontenot was named the Orioles' Organizational Player of the Year for 2003. He showed the ability to drive the ball into the gaps for power, but hit just 12 home runs.

His ability to reach base using either the walk, hit by pitch or base hit allowed him to record a .399 on-base percentage at Double-A Bowie last season. While some peg him as a better No. 2 hitter, his on-base skills might change minds in the organization. At the keystone, he's improving in making the double play, but his throws continue to cause problems. Still, Fontenot will move quickly and could reach the majors by September.

Tripper Johnson

Position: 3B
Bats: R **Throws:** R
Ht: 6' 1" **Wt:** 195

Opening Day Age: 21
Born: 4/28/82 in Bellevue, WA

Recent Statistics

	G	AB	R	H	D	T	HR	RBI	SB	BB	SO	Avg
2002 A Delmarva	136	493	73	128	32	6	11	71	19	62	88	.260
2003 A Frederick	123	417	43	114	25	3	5	50	7	46	92	.273

Johnson got off to a fast start at high Class-A Frederick before struggling his second time around the league. His trials against southpaws were the main reason for his problems at the plate. Johnson's power regressed last season from the prior year, and his strikeout rate increased as he pressed too hard. The Orioles still believe his solid swing will provide the kind of home-run production required from a corner infielder, once his pitch recognition improves. His foot quickness and accurate throwing arm make him a solid third-base prospect defensively. Still, inconsistent play in the field continues to plague him at times. The combination of a solid work ethic and experience at Double-A this season is expected to improve his overall game.

Rommie Lewis

Position: P
Bats: L **Throws:** L
Ht: 6' 6" **Wt:** 200

Opening Day Age: 21
Born: 9/2/82 in Bellevue, WA

Recent Statistics

	W	L	ERA	G	GS	Sv	IP	H	R	BB	SO	HR
2002 A Delmarva	1	2	2.15	53	0	25	71.0	50	19	20	77	1
2003 A Frederick	4	9	3.34	26	20	0	113.1	108	54	60	69	9

Lewis was moved to the starting rotation last season after serving as the closer for Class-A Delmarva the year before. In the closer role, he averaged more than a strikeout per inning and saved 25 games. However, the excellent command he displayed as a reliever wasn't nearly as evident as a starter in 2003. Last year, he struggled to control his breaking ball and changeup, and also ran into difficulties repeating his delivery. A 93-MPH fastball continues to improve, and remains his out pitch. Lewis will need to better command both his curveball and changeup if he's to remain a starter. The Orioles are expected to develop him as such, and he'll begin the year at high Class-A Frederick.

John Maine

Position: P   **Opening Day Age:** 22
Bats: R **Throws:** R   **Born:** 5/8/81 in
Ht: 6' 4" **Wt:** 185   Fredericksburg, VA

Recent Statistics

	W	L	ERA	G	GS	Sv	IP	H	R	BB	SO	HR
2002 A Aberdeen	1	1	1.74	4	2	0	10.1	6	2	3	21	0
2002 A Delmarva	1	1	1.36	6	5	0	33.0	21	8	4	39	0
2003 A Delmarva	7	3	1.53	14	14	0	76.1	43	16	18	108	1
2003 A Frederick	6	1	3.07	12	12	0	70.1	48	27	20	77	5

Maine proved that his late-season stop at Class-A
Delmarva in 2002 was no fluke. He recorded a 1.53
ERA with Delmarva in 2003 before being promoted to
high Class-A Frederick. After struggling his first month
in the Carolina League, Maine settled down and displayed the same effectiveness he demonstrated at lower
levels. His fastball has nice sinking movement, and he's
most effective throwing it in the 91-93 MPH range. His
slider is an improving pitch and complements his fastball. Maine is making great strides in repeating his
delivery—the consistency of his release point continues
to improve. The Orioles are thin in pitching, and he
could rise quickly through the system.

Nick Markakis

Position: OF   **Opening Day Age:** 20
Bats: L **Throws:** L   **Born:** 11/17/83 in
Ht: 6' 1" **Wt:** 170   Woodstock, GA

Recent Statistics

	G	AB	R	H	D	T	HR	RBI	SB	BB	SO	Avg
2003 A Aberdeen	59	205	22	58	14	3	1	28	13	30	33	.283

Baltimore's first-round selection and seventh overall
pick in 2003, Markakis won back-to-back Junior
College Player of the Year awards at Young Harris JC
in Georgia. A very good athlete, he led the junior-col-
lege ranks in RBI, and also wins and strikeouts. His pro
career got off to a great start in the short-season New
York-Penn League. He displayed solid ability to get the
bat on the ball and made the most of his speed by stealing 13 bases. Markakis has a strong and accurate arm
that allows him to keep runners at bay. Though he is a
talented southpaw pitcher, the organization sees a higher ceiling as a hitter in the long run.

Darnell McDonald

Position: OF   **Opening Day Age:** 25
Bats: R **Throws:** R   **Born:** 11/17/78 in Fort
Ht: 5' 11" **Wt:** 208   Collins, CO

Recent Statistics

	G	AB	R	H	D	T	HR	RBI	SB	BB	SO	Avg
2002 AA Bowie	37	144	21	42	9	1	4	15	9	22	27	.292
2002 AAA Rochester	91	332	43	96	21	6	6	35	11	32	78	.289
2003 AAA Ottawa	40	152	19	45	7	1	0	20	5	18	27	.296

The Orioles' first-round pick in 1997, McDonald went
down with a shoulder injury and subsequently underwent surgery in June. The highly athletic outfielder

continues to make progress in small steps, especially in
the power departments. His gap power hasn't yet
developed into home-run production. McDonald's plate
discipline continues to improve, but it hasn't translated
into a higher percentage of walks. He has well above-
average speed, though he doesn't utilize it to his maximum ability when on the bases. In the outfield, that
speed allows him to track down balls into the gaps, but
his defense won't be a plus. He's approaching the crossroads of his career and needs to step up to avoid being
labeled a career minor leaguer.

Matt Riley

Position: P   **Opening Day Age:** 24
Bats: L **Throws:** L   **Born:** 8/2/79 in Antioch,
Ht: 6' 1" **Wt:** 201   CA

Recent Statistics

	W	L	ERA	G	GS	Sv	IP	H	R	BB	SO	HR
2003 AA Bowie	5	2	3.11	14	14	0	72.1	56	27	23	73	4
2003 AAA Ottawa	4	2	3.58	13	13	0	70.1	70	30	28	77	4
2003 AL Baltimore	1	0	1.80	2	2	0	10.0	7	2	5	8	1

In 1999 and 2000, Riley, a former third-round pick, was
the O's top prospect. Tommy John surgery cost him all
of the 2001 campaign, however. After struggling to
regain his pre-surgery form, Riley bounced back nicely
last season. He began the year at Double-A Bowie,
striking out more than a batter an inning while walking
just 23. He relies on a 93-95 MPH fastball that complements the best curveball in the Baltimore organization.
When he was promoted to Triple-A, he maintained
nearly the same performance level. His progress earned
him a late-season recall to the majors. If Riley continues to improve his control, he'll have a good chance to
stick at the major league level this year.

Others to Watch

Righthander **Daniel Cabrera** (22) finished strong in his
first foray into a full Class-A season. He relies on a still-
improving 93-95 MPH fastball and a solid breaking ball.
Walks and control remain a problem. . . Draft-and-follow lefthander **Adam Loewen** (19) wasn't inked to a
deal until May. In just 23.1 innings in the short-season
New York-Penn League, he showed why he's so highly
though of. He'll move quickly in a system almost void
of top-flight hurlers. . . Outfielder **Val Majewski** (22)
has a solid line-drive swing that produced 12 homers at
four different levels in 2003. He can play both first base
and outfield, and has an average throwing arm. . .
Southpaw **Carlos Perez** (21) dominated the Rookie-
level Appalachian League, getting even stronger as the
season wound down. He throws a low-90s fastball, a
plus slider and decent change for strikes. He'll move to
a full- season league this year and could be on the fast
track to the majors. . . Righthander **Chris Ray** (22) has
an above-average splitter that complements a mid-90s
fastball and sharp-breaking slider. In his first season of
pro baseball, he showed lots of promise but struggled at
times with inconsistent mechanics.

Fenway Park

Offense

Fenway is a hitters' park, but not like some think. It's been 20 years since the park was a home-run haven, but its reputation is only now catching up with reality. These days, it's a singles-and-doubles park, especially for righthanded pull hitters and lefties who can go the other way. The lack of foul territory keeps at-bats going and thus boosts batting averages as well.

Defense

Fenway may be the only park in baseball where the demands on the right fielder exceed those on the center fielder. To play right, one must have enough range to cover one of the largest right fields in the majors, a strong enough arm to make throws from the 380-foot canyon and the instincts to cut off balls down the line before they kick into the canyon for three bases. Left field presents the challenge of playing caroms off the Monster, but requires little range.

Who It Helps the Most

Nomar Garciaparra always has hit for a better average here, and the effect was more pronounced than ever last year, when he had an AL-best .359 average at home. Sinkerballer Derek Lowe is 20-6 with a 2.68 ERA here over the last two years. Mike Timlin allowed only two walks and six extra-base hits at home all season.

Who It Hurts the Most

Trot Nixon consistently loses home runs at Fenway, which is to be expected for a lefthanded power hitter. Tim Wakefield is more hittable at home, perhaps because so few of the foul popups he induces stay in play.

Rookies & Newcomers

Schilling is a high-strikeout pitcher, which is vastly more important than his tendency to get slightly more flyballs than average. He will be affected by Fenway to a lesser extent than almost any other pitcher would.

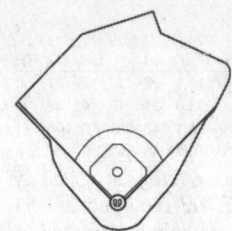

Dimensions: LF-310, LCF-379, CF-420, RCF-380, RF-302

Capacity: 33,991

Elevation: 21 feet

Surface: Grass

Foul Territory: Small

Park Factors

2003 Season

| | Home Games | | | Away Games | | | |
	Red Sox	Opp	Total	Red Sox	Opp	Total	Index
G	72	72	144	72	72	144	
Avg	.308	.259	.284	.259	.263	.261	109
AB	2480	2530	5010	2587	2507	5094	98
R	445	343	788	365	362	727	108
H	765	656	1421	671	660	1331	107
2B	178	146	324	138	150	288	114
3B	17	17	34	9	20	29	119
HR	95	61	156	108	64	172	92
BB	288	191	479	230	241	471	103
SO	359	479	838	481	536	1017	84
E	49	44	93	48	35	83	112
E-Infield	42	36	78	40	29	69	113
LHB-Avg	.301	.258	.279	.251	.267	.259	108
LHB-HR	41	28	69	53	38	91	73
RHB-Avg	.317	.261	.288	.267	.260	.264	109
RHB-HR	54	33	87	55	26	81	115

2001-2003

| | Home Games | | | Away Games | | | |
	Red Sox	Opp	Total	Red Sox	Opp	Total	Index
G	216	216	432	215	215	430	
Avg	.288	.255	.271	.269	.252	.261	104
AB	7379	7550	14929	7745	7287	15032	99
R	1171	997	2168	1138	968	2106	102
H	2128	1922	4050	2083	1834	3917	103
2B	487	429	916	436	361	797	116
3B	49	32	81	31	52	83	98
HR	253	185	438	292	201	493	89
BB	782	597	1379	702	686	1388	100
SO	1254	1624	2878	1404	1559	2963	98
E	150	137	287	137	128	265	108
E-Infield	125	117	242	114	112	226	107
LHB-Avg	.287	.249	.267	.260	.251	.256	105
LHB-HR	112	77	189	143	112	255	75
RHB-Avg	.290	.260	.275	.277	.252	.265	104
RHB-HR	141	108	249	149	89	238	105

2003 Rankings (American League)

- Second-highest batting-average factor
- Second-highest double factor
- Second-highest infield-error factor
- Second-highest RHB batting-average factor
- Third-highest hit factor
- Third-highest error factor
- Lowest LHB home-run factor
- Second-lowest strikeout factor

Terry Francona

2003 Season

Terry Francona steps into a situation where the previous manager, Grady Little, was widely blamed for Boston's failure to make it to the 2003 World Series. Little's decision not to lift Pedro Martinez with a late-inning lead in Game 7 of the ALCS caused widespread second-guessing and probably had a lot to do with his dismissal. Francona likely will enjoy something of a honeymoon, simply for not being Little. Francona was a bench coach for Oakland in 2003 and for Texas in 2002, and managed the Phillies from 1997-2000.

Offense

Francona's biggest successes in Philadelphia involved the introduction of young hitters into the regular lineup. Bobby Abreu, Scott Rolen, Mike Lieberthal and Pat Burrell all became regulars for the first time under him, and all four hit from day one. Francona preferred a set lineup, and seemed rather conventional in his use of the bunt and stolen base. As a player, he was a tremendously impatient hitter, but as a manager, he was content to use the walk-averse Doug Glanville at leadoff, which may or may not be related. On the other hand, his season on Oakland's bench might have spurred him to place more value in the base on balls.

Pitching & Defense

The intentional walk and the pitchout were two tactical options Francona showed little regard for in Philly. He seemed willing to accept poor or untested fielders at the outfield corners. He preferred a set closer, even when he had to go with a less-than-dominant veteran like Jeff Brantley or Mark Leiter. The health record of his young pitchers was less than sterling.

2004 Outlook

The only thing that's certain for Francona this year is that he'll have his hands full. He'll have an expensive, talented club, and his mandate will be to do the one thing his predecessor failed to do: take Boston to the World Series. He also may have to deal with the major distractions of Nomar Garciaparra's and Pedro Martinez' pending free agency following the 2004 season.

Born: 4/22/59 in Aberdeen, SD

Playing Experience: 1981-1990, Mon, ChC, Cin, Cle, Mil

Managerial Experience: 4 seasons

Manager Statistics

Year	Team, Lg	W	L	Pct	GB	Finish
2000	Philadelphia, NL	65	97	.401	30.0	5th East
4 Seasons		285	363	.440	–	–

2003 Starting Pitchers by Days Rest

	<=3	4	5	6+
Red Sox Starts	2	77	53	22
Red Sox ERA	3.00	4.13	4.65	4.39
AL Avg Starts	.2	79	50	22
AL ERA	3.19	4.64	4.57	4.98

2003 Situational Stats

	Grady Little	AL Average
Hit & Run Success %	42.5	36.7
Stolen Base Success %	71.5	70.0
Platoon Pct.	64.1	61.7
Defensive Subs	27	23
High-Pitch Outings	4	5
Quick/Slow Hooks	21/14	19/16
Sacrifice Attempts	34	55

2003 Rankings—Grady Little (American League)

- 3rd in pitchouts (30)

Johnny Damon

2003 Season

Johnny Damon quietly had another fine season as Boston's leadoff man and center fielder in 2003. Playing every day and setting the table for the Red Sox' big guns, he was an inconspicuous but crucial component of Boston's high-powered offense. He showed true grit in the postseason, suffering a concussion in a frightful collision with teammate Damian Jackson in the final game of the Division Series, but returning only five days later with a three-hit game.

Hitting

Damon uses the whole field well, but he knows which pitches to attack. Given something up or on the outer half of the plate, he'll line it the other way. On a pitch down and in, he can golf the ball down the right-field line with power. A patient hitter who works the count, he almost always takes the first pitch. The only thing that keeps him from drawing more walks is the fact that he is an excellent contact hitter who rarely fails to put the ball in play when he swings. Needless to say, he's a very tough two-strike hitter. He also hangs in well against lefties and is an adept bunter for either a base hit or a sacrifice.

Baserunning & Defense

Even on a team that doesn't emphasize the running game, Damon remains one of the league's best basestealers. He rarely gets thrown out, and the only thing that slows him down is a lefthander on the mound. His speed serves also him well in center, where he has great range. He's especially surehanded, and committed only one error last year. A weak throwing arm is his only defensive weakness.

2004 Outlook

There has been talk from time to time about the Red Sox considering trying to move Damon's salary, but the roles he fills on offense and defense would make him tough to replace. It's a good bet he'll remain in Boston and continue to produce the same high-quality results that he has the past two years.

Position: CF
Bats: L **Throws:** L
Ht: 6' 2" **Wt:** 190

Opening Day Age: 30
Born: 11/5/73 in Fort Riley, KS
ML Seasons: 9
Pronunciation: DAY-mun

Overall Statistics

	G	AB	R	H	D	T	HR	RBI	SB	BB	SO	Avg	OBP	Slg
'03	145	608	103	166	32	6	12	67	30	68	74	.273	.345	.405
Car.	1257	4932	833	1403	256	68	100	531	244	469	564	.284	.347	.425

Where He Hits the Ball

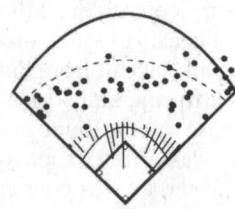 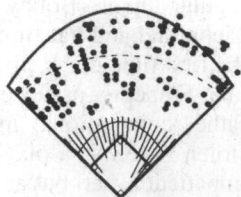

Vs. LHP   **Vs. RHP**

2003 Situational Stats

	AB	H	HR	RBI	Avg		AB	H	HR	RBI	Avg
Home	313	91	5	35	.291	LHP	193	53	3	23	.275
Road	295	75	7	32	.254	RHP	415	113	9	44	.272
First Half	366	95	7	41	.260	Sc Pos	131	35	1	52	.267
Scnd Half	242	71	5	26	.293	Clutch	92	27	3	12	.293

2003 Rankings (American League)

- 1st in fielding percentage in center field (.997)
- 2nd in pitches seen (2,850) and lowest percentage of swings on the first pitch (9.1)
- 4th in most pitches seen per plate appearance (4.13)
- 5th in stolen-base percentage (83.3)
- 6th in stolen bases
- Led the Red Sox in sacrifice bunts (6), stolen bases, pitches seen (2,850), highest ground ball-flyball ratio (1.4), stolen-base percentage (83.3), most pitches seen per plate appearance (4.13), bunts in play (20), on-base percentage for a leadoff hitter (.334) and lowest percentage of swings on the first pitch (9.1)

Nomar Garciaparra

2003 Season

Nomar Garciaparra had another great season for Boston in 2003, although he picked a most unfortunate time to slump, driving in only one run in 12 postseason games. In the regular season, he finished second in the American League in runs scored and was a contestant for the batting title before a late-season slump took him out of the running.

Hitting

What's the use in "waiting for your pitch" when you can hit anything? One couldn't blame Garciaparra for thinking that way—he swings at the first pitch more than any major league hitter, but he's also one of the most dangerous first-pitch hitters in baseball. With strong wrists and great hand-eye coordination, it's tough to get any pitch past him, even with two strikes. In the past two years, he's pulled the ball and hit it in the air more often, which has cost him some points on his average but hasn't paid dividends in the power department. Regardless, he still hits the ball hard as consistently as anyone in the game.

Baserunning & Defense

Garciaparra's throwing arm is so strong that it effectively increases his already above-average range at short. He throws on the run as well as any infielder in baseball, and since he doesn't need to set himself before making a throw from the hole, he is able to go harder to his right than most shortstops. Of course, making the play that way takes not only a strong arm but also quick feet and tremendous agility. Garciaparra also was a legitimate stolen-base threat last year, swiping 19 bases in 24 tries.

2004 Outlook

A lifelong member of the Red Sox, Garciaparra is going into his walk year. Trade rumors already have surfaced, and they could become an ongoing distraction for the entire team if an extension isn't reached. The possibility of the Red Sox and one of their defining players parting ways is sure to spark emotion all around. It may be the type of situation that would weigh heavily on any player.

Position: SS
Bats: R **Throws:** R
Ht: 6' 0" **Wt:** 190

Opening Day Age: 30
Born: 7/23/73 in Whittier, CA
ML Seasons: 8
Pronunciation:
nō-mar GARCIA par uh

Overall Statistics

	G	AB	R	H	D	T	HR	RBI	SB	BB	SO	Avg	OBP	Slg
'03	156	658	120	198	37	13	28	105	19	39	61	.301	.345	.524
Car.	928	3812	685	1231	272	47	173	669	82	271	390	.323	.370	.555

Where He Hits the Ball

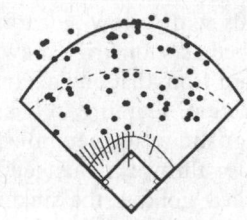 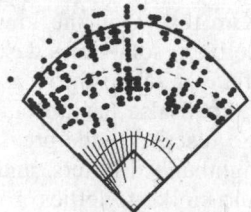

Vs. LHP   **Vs. RHP**

2003 Situational Stats

	AB	H	HR	RBI	Avg
Home	329	118	18	68	.359
Road	329	80	10	37	.243
First Half	392	125	13	60	.319
Scnd Half	266	73	15	45	.274

	AB	H	HR	RBI	Avg
LHP	171	61	7	29	.357
RHP	487	137	21	76	.281
Sc Pos	179	50	5	70	.279
Clutch	95	26	3	15	.274

2003 Rankings (American League)

- 1st in batting average at home, fewest pitches seen per plate appearance (3.12), lowest percentage of pitches taken (40.8) and highest percentage of swings on the first pitch (52.8)
- 2nd in runs scored and triples
- 3rd in sacrifice flies (10) and errors at shortstop (20)
- 4th in plate appearances (719) and batting average vs. lefthanded pitchers
- Led the Red Sox in at-bats, runs scored, hits, singles, triples, total bases (345), RBI, sacrifice flies (10), hit by pitch (11), plate appearances (719), games played and batting average at home

Byung-Hyun Kim

2003 Season

Byung-Hyun Kim's 2003 season wasn't entirely successful, but it sure wasn't boring. Coming off a 36-save season in 2002, he was moved into the rotation at the start of the year. He pitched decently but missed time in May with an ankle injury. Soon after returning, he was dealt to Boston. He remained a starter through June, but Boston needed him in the bullpen, and so he became their closer in July. He performed capably but never seemed to inspire much confidence. He looked shaky and got pulled in his only Division Series appearance, and was left off the ALCS roster with shoulder stiffness.

Pitching

Kim throws in the low 90s with a low-sidearm delivery sometimes described as submarine. Few, if any, pitchers throw as hard from that angle. His fastball also has unusual action, seeming to rise. He uses a wide-breaking slider to neutralize righthanded hitters, and also throws a changeup and sinker to lefties. Kim has gone to the sinker more often over the last two years, getting more groundballs and not quite as many strikeouts. He was only 3-6 as a starter in 2003, but had a fine 3.38 ERA in 12 starts and seemed capable of pitching well in that role.

Defense

Kim does not hold runners well and is easy to steal on. Sixteen runners attempted to steal against him last year, and only one was caught. His delivery leaves him in good position to field, and he does a good job of handling balls hit back through the box. Kim sometimes will give a fielder a hard throw to handle, however.

2004 Outlook

One of the issues new manager Terry Francona must resolve is whether Kim ought to remain the Red Sox' closer. While Kim always has been effective, questions remain about his maturity and ability to handle pressure. If the Red Sox are successful in their pursuit of a free-agent closer, one option is to return Kim to the starting rotation.

Position: RP/SP
Bats: R **Throws:** R
Ht: 5' 9" **Wt:** 180

Opening Day Age: 25
Born: 1/19/79 in Gwangju, South Korea
ML Seasons: 5
Pronunciation:
bee-yung hee-yun

Overall Statistics

	W	L	Pct.	ERA	G	GS	Sv	IP	H	BB	SO	HR	Avg
'03	9	10	.474	3.31	56	12	16	122.1	104	33	102	12	.224
Car.	29	27	.518	3.24	292	13	86	402.1	298	169	449	38	.204

2003 Pitching Profile

	Byung-Hyun Kim (AL)	AL Average
Overall Strike %	68.4	62.8
1st Pitch Strike %	64.6	58.7
Ratio	1.11	1.39
Strikeouts per 9 IP	7.83	6.11
Walks per 9 IP	2.04	3.16
Home Runs per 9 IP	0.68	1.11
Strikeout/Walk Ratio	3.83	1.93
Groundball/Flyball Ratio	1.56	1.18

2003 Situational Stats

	W	L	ERA	Sv	IP		AB	H	HR	RBI	Avg
Home	4	4	4.34	8	47.2	LHB	222	49	6	28	.221
Road	5	6	2.65	8	74.2	RHB	242	55	6	25	.227
First Half	3	7	3.52	5	84.1	Sc Pos	110	27	4	41	.245
Scnd Half	6	3	2.84	11	38.0	Clutch	133	30	2	16	.226

2003 Rankings (American League)

- 8th in relief wins (6)
- 9th in first batter efficiency (.175) and most strikeouts per nine innings in relief (9.7)
- 10th in saves (16)
- Led the Red Sox in saves (16), games finished (35), save percentage (84.2), relief ERA (3.22), relief wins (6), lowest batting average allowed in relief (.215) and most strikeouts per nine innings in relief (9.7)

Derek Lowe

2003 Season

Derek Lowe's effort to follow up his 21-win season of 2002 got off to a rough start, as he went 3-3 with a 6.53 ERA through his first eight starts. He recovered to pitch fairly well the rest of the way, winning 14 of 18 decisions with a lot of help from the offense. He provided one of Boston's biggest thrills of the year when he came on in relief in the final game of the Division Series and struck out the final two hitters—looking—with the tying run on third to preserve a one-run lead.

Pitching

Lowe comes as close as any non-knuckleballer can come to being a one-pitch pitcher. When his dandy sinker is working, he doesn't need much else. He'll change speeds with it, and mix in an occasional slider and cutter to lefthanded hitters. Year after year, he is the most extreme groundball pitcher in baseball. He therefore relies unusually heavily on his infield defense. For some reason, he was more hittable with men on base last year. It usually had been the opposite, since he always has been able to escape trouble via the double play.

Defense

Lowe had a terrific year in the field and would have been a deserving Gold Glove nominee. He handled 65 chances, the sixth-most among pitchers, and didn't commit a single error. He's fairly easy to run on, mostly because so many of his pitches end up in the dirt. Teams have an incentive to run against him, too, if they want to try to stay out of the double play.

2004 Outlook

The Red Sox exercised Lowe's $4.5 million option for 2004, and he will return to join Pedro Martinez and Curt Schilling as part of one of baseball's most formidable 1-2-3 punches. Just as Lowe was hurt the most by the downgrade in Boston's infield defense last year, he likely will be helped the most if the Red Sox obtain a new second baseman with more range. He can't expect to get the majors' best run support again, however.

Position: SP
Bats: R **Throws:** R
Ht: 6' 6" **Wt:** 214

Opening Day Age: 30
Born: 6/1/73 in Dearborn, MI
ML Seasons: 7

Overall Statistics

	W	L	Pct.	ERA	G	GS	Sv	IP	H	BB	SO	HR	Avg
'03	17	7	.708	4.47	33	33	0	203.1	216	72	110	17	.272
Car.	58	47	.552	3.57	363	87	85	907.1	859	261	607	65	.250

2003 Pitching Profile

	Derek Lowe	AL Average
Overall Strike %	61.9	62.8
1st Pitch Strike %	62.1	58.7
Ratio	1.42	1.39
Strikeouts per 9 IP	4.87	6.11
Walks per 9 IP	3.19	3.16
Home Runs per 9 IP	0.75	1.11
Strikeout/Walk Ratio	1.53	1.93
Groundball/Flyball Ratio	3.92	1.18

2003 Situational Stats

	W	L	ERA	Sv	IP		AB	H	HR	RBI	Avg
Home	11	2	3.21	0	115.0	LHB	431	119	13	52	.276
Road	6	5	6.11	0	88.1	RHB	364	97	4	43	.266
First Half	10	3	4.81	0	116.0	Sc Pos	196	54	5	74	.276
Scnd Half	7	4	4.02	0	87.1	Clutch	28	13	0	4	.464

2003 Rankings (American League)

- 1st in highest groundball-flyball ratio allowed (3.9), most run support per nine innings (7.3) and fielding percentage at pitcher (1.000)
- 3rd in highest ERA on the road
- 5th in wins
- 6th in winning percentage and lowest strike out-walk ratio (1.5)
- 7th in walks allowed and fewest home runs allowed per nine innings (.75)
- Led the Red Sox in wins, games started, innings pitched, hits allowed, batters faced (886), walks allowed, GDPs induced (21), highest groundball-flyball ratio allowed (3.9), fewest pitches thrown per batter (3.55), and most run support per nine innings (7.3)

Pedro Martinez

2003 Season

Pedro Martinez had another brilliant season, but sadly, it was overshadowed by what happened in his final inning. With a three-run lead against the Yankees in Game 7 of the ALCS, Martinez was allowed to come out to pitch the eighth, and allowed the lead to slip away. As bitter a pill as it was to swallow, the fact remains that the Red Sox couldn't have gotten there without Martinez, who led the majors in ERA.

Pitching

Ever since suffering a shoulder injury in 2001, Martinez has saved his mid-90s heat for when he has really needed it. Otherwise, he pitches in the low 90s, which works nearly as well, since his command and his other weapons are so good. He has an excellent hard curve (he calls it a slider, but its break is more downward than lateral), a cutter that he runs in on the hands of lefthanded hitters and a fading, veering changeup with screwball action. He never is afraid to back a hitter off the plate. The Red Sox try to protect him at all costs, allowing him to throw a lot of pitches only in big games and giving him an extra day of rest when possible.

Defense

Martinez has good instincts and fields his position well. He finished the year without an error for the third time in the past four seasons. He prefers not to throw over to first—he did so only 22 times all year—but he keeps runners close by looking them back or stepping off. Last year, runners stole five bases in eight attempts against him.

2004 Outlook

Martinez' contract is up at the end of the year. He'll be out to prove that he's over last year's ALCS letdown and that his shoulder is strong enough to merit a long-term investment. The situation may become a distraction, but it's hard to imagine that anything short of an injury could really slow him down. Martinez remains the team's ace, but it will be easier to limit his innings with Curt Schilling around to help save the bullpen.

Position: SP
Bats: R **Throws:** R
Ht: 5'11" **Wt:** 180

Opening Day Age: 32
Born: 10/25/71 in Manoguayabo, DR
ML Seasons: 12

Overall Statistics

W	L	Pct.	ERA	G	GS	Sv	IP	H	BB	SO	HR	Avg
14	4	.778	2.22	29	29	0	186.2	147	47	206	7	.215
166	67	.712	2.58	355	288	3	2079.0	1553	554	2426	149	.206

2003 Pitching Profile

	Pedro Martinez	AL Average
Overall Strike %	65.9	62.8
1st Pitch Strike %	60.2	58.7
Ratio	1.04	1.39
Strikeouts per 9 IP	9.93	6.11
Walks per 9 IP	2.27	3.16
Home Runs per 9 IP	0.34	1.11
Strikeout/Walk Ratio	4.38	1.93
Groundball/Flyball Ratio	1.14	1.18

2003 Situational Stats

	W	L	ERA	Sv	IP		AB	H	HR	RBI	Avg
Home	8	2	3.13	0	77.2	LHB	412	98	7	38	.238
Road	6	2	1.57	0	109.0	RHB	273	49	0	10	.179
First Half	6	2	2.36	0	103.0	Sc Pos	155	31	2	42	.200
Scnd Half	8	2	2.04	0	83.2	Clutch	65	18	0	5	.277

2003 Rankings (American League)

- 1st in ERA, lowest batting average allowed (.215), lowest on-base percentage allowed (.272), lowest ERA on the road, lowest batting average allowed vs. righthanded batters, fewest home runs allowed per nine innings (.34), most strikeouts per nine innings (9.9) and fielding percentage at pitcher (1.000)
- 2nd in strikeouts, winning percentage and lowest slugging percentage allowed (.314)
- 4th in highest strikeout-walk ratio (4.4) and lowest batting average allowed with runners in scoring position
- Led the Red Sox in complete games (3), strikeouts, winning percentage, highest strike out-walk ratio (4.4), lowest slugging percentage allowed (.314), lowest ERA at home, lowest batting average allowed with runners in scoring position, and fewest walks per nine innings (2.3)

Kevin Millar

2003 Season

It took some extra effort to get Kevin Millar into a Red Sox uniform, but it was worth it. Last winter, the Marlins sold his contract to Japan's Chunichi Dragons, but the Red Sox blocked the deal with a waiver claim. After much haggling, a deal was struck that brought Millar to Boston and satisfied all parties involved. He rewarded the Red Sox with a fine season, playing the majority of the time at first base while also filling in in the outfield. He also became a clubhouse favorite and something of a cult hero to the Fenway faithful for his "Cowboy up" rally cry and a scoreboard slip of his fearless karaoke.

Hitting

A flyball hitter, Millar's left-field power played well in Fenway, even though the Wall turned a few potential homers into doubles. He likes fastballs but will chase them up and out of the strike zone at times. He did a lot of damage against changeups last year, especially ones on the outer half of the plate that he could dive into and pull. Reasonably patient, he makes fairly good contact for a power hitter. He hits righthanders just as well as southpaws, and seems to respond to big situations.

Baserunning & Defense

First base easily is Millar's best position, although his range is rather limited. He has good hands. He didn't embarrass himself in left and right field last year, but his lack of mobility was more apparent out there, and his arm is a bit short for right field. Third base is a position he's played a little bit in past seasons, but he didn't see any time there last year. He doesn't run nearly well enough to be a factor on the bases.

2004 Outlook

Millar is another easily overlooked but crucial element of Boston's deep, relentless offense. Expect him to keep hitting, and possibly even to raise his average to back above the .300 mark, a level he exceeded both in 2001 and 2002 with Florida.

Position: 1B/LF/DH/RF
Bats: R **Throws:** R
Ht: 6' 0" **Wt:** 210

Opening Day Age: 32
Born: 9/24/71 in Los Angeles, CA
ML Seasons: 6
Pronunciation: mi-LAR

Overall Statistics

	G	AB	R	H	D	T	HR	RBI	SB	BB	SO	Avg	OBP	Slg
'03	148	544	83	150	30	1	25	96	3	60	108	.276	.348	.472
Car.	648	2043	288	593	141	13	84	347	4	216	363	.290	.362	.495

Where He Hits the Ball

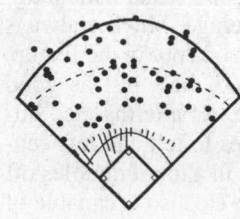
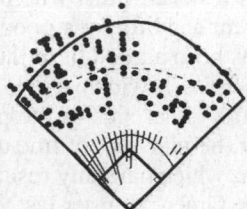

Vs. LHP   **Vs. RHP**

2003 Situational Stats

	AB	H	HR	RBI	Avg		AB	H	HR	RBI	Avg
Home	274	79	10	51	.288	LHP	149	43	5	25	.289
Road	270	71	15	45	.263	RHP	395	107	20	71	.271
First Half	309	91	14	61	.294	Sc Pos	158	48	7	75	.304
Scnd Half	235	59	11	35	.251	Clutch	83	22	5	18	.265

2003 Rankings (American League)

- 6th in sacrifice flies (9)
- Led the Red Sox in strikeouts

Bill Mueller

2003 Season

Coming off two years worth of knee problems, Bill Mueller signed a free-agent deal with the Red Sox and proved to be a terrific addition. Early in the year he split time between second and third base, and he hit so well that the Red Sox were able to trade Shea Hillenbrand and turn over the job at third to Mueller. Mueller kept on hitting and wound up winning the American League batting title, while also nearly doubling his previous career high in homers and providing a lot of big hits against the Yankees. The only blemish was that he slumped in the playoffs.

Hitting

As a switch-hitter who has good strike-zone judgment and hits for a good average, Mueller always has been a good fit in the No. 2 spot in the lineup. Despite a wider gap in 2003, he's just as good from either side of the plate. As a lefthanded hitter, he hits a lot of line drives to left and left-center, which naturally resulted in a lot of doubles off the Green Monster last year. He also is capable of jerking an inside pitch, and did so more often last year than ever before. He stays back well on breaking balls and makes excellent contact, which makes him a tough strikeout as well as a good hit-and-run man. His .358 average with men on base was second-highest figure in the AL last year.

Baserunning & Defense

As a third baseman, Mueller is in the Wade Boggs mold—he doesn't have tremendous range or a cannon arm, but his hands are soft and he throws very accurately. His ability to play second adequately is a plus. His speed is a tick above average, but he's no basestealer. He was successful just once in five stolen-base attempts in 2003.

2004 Outlook

Mueller has found a good fit in Boston, as both the ballpark and the team's offensive philosophy suit him well. He probably won't approach 20 homers or contend for the batting title again, but he likely will remain productive and well-appreciated.

Position: 3B/2B
Bats: B **Throws:** R
Ht: 5'10" **Wt:** 180

Opening Day Age: 33
Born: 3/17/71 in Maryland Heights, MO
ML Seasons: 8
Pronunciation: MILL-er
Nickname: Ferris, Muley

Overall Statistics

	G	AB	R	H	D	T	HR	RBI	SB	BB	SO	Avg	OBP	Slg
'03	146	524	85	171	45	5	19	85	1	59	77	.326	.398	.540
Car.	924	3198	507	936	197	18	60	359	17	416	432	.293	.375	.422

Where He Hits the Ball

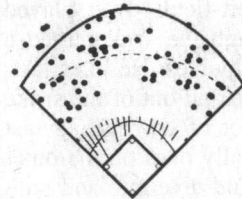 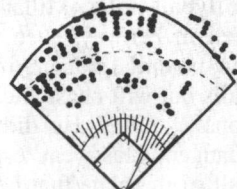

Vs. LHP   **Vs. RHP**

2003 Situational Stats

	AB	H	HR	RBI	Avg		AB	H	HR	RBI	Avg
Home	275	94	6	50	.342	LHP	173	51	8	27	.295
Road	249	77	13	35	.309	RHP	351	120	11	58	.342
First Half	283	94	8	39	.332	Sc Pos	139	46	3	61	.331
Scnd Half	241	77	11	46	.320	Clutch	76	18	1	9	.237

2003 Rankings (American League)

- 1st in batting average and batting average vs. righthanded pitchers
- 3rd in batting average with two strikes (.262) and lowest fielding percentage at third base (.951)
- 4th in lowest percentage of swings that missed (9.9) and batting average at home
- 5th in doubles and errors at third base (16)
- 6th in on-base percentage
- Led the Red Sox in batting average, doubles, lowest percentage of swings that missed (9.9), batting average vs. righthanded pitchers and batting average with two strikes (.262)
- Led AL third basemen in batting average

Trot Nixon

Position: RF
Bats: L **Throws:** L
Ht: 6' 2" **Wt:** 211

Opening Day Age: 29
Born: 4/11/74 in Durham, NC
ML Seasons: 7

2003 Season

The 2003 season was Trot Nixon's best yet, as he batted .300 for the first time while setting a new career high with 28 homers despite missing most of September with a strained calf. He was one of the most dangerous hitters in baseball against righthanded pitchers, with the second-highest average in the American League against righties (.330), as well as the third-best on-base percentage (.423) and slugging percentage (.635). He came back from his calf injury to hit three homers against the Yankees in the ALCS.

Hitting

Nixon is a good fastball hitter who gets good loft on the ball. Though mainly a pull hitter, he has the power to reach the fences in left or center field. He used to habitually take the first pitch, but he was more aggressive last season, and got results—he hit .477 and slugged .908 on the first pitch—even though he failed to work himself into hitter's counts as often as he had in the past. The one thing Nixon never has learned to do is hit left-handed pitchers, and throughout his career he's been followed by the question of whether he ought to be platooned.

Baserunning & Defense

Nixon isn't all that fast, but he covers a lot of ground in right field by getting good jumps, taking good routes and always going as hard as he can. In the same way, he gets the best out of his throwing arm, which is pretty strong, by anticipating and putting himself in good position to throw. On the basepaths, he knows when to go for the extra base and rarely misses an opportunity. Though he doesn't try to steal very often, he has been successful nearly 75 percent of the time over his career.

2004 Outlook

Even if Nixon doesn't quite match his 2003 numbers again, he'll likely remain a player with a nice package of skills. He's past the point where he could be expected to learn how to hit lefties, however, so he still could wind up platooning at some point.

Overall Statistics

	G	AB	R	H	D	T	HR	RBI	SB	BB	SO	Avg	OBP	Slg
'03	134	441	81	135	24	6	28	87	4	65	96	.306	.396	.578
Car.	696	2347	400	651	142	26	106	381	27	326	482	.277	.366	.496

Where He Hits the Ball

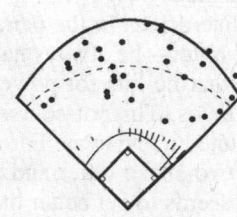

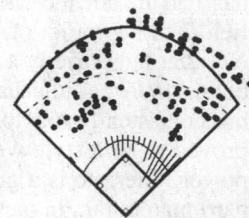

Vs. LHP   **Vs. RHP**

2003 Situational Stats

	AB	H	HR	RBI	Avg		AB	H	HR	RBI	Avg
Home	220	70	10	47	.318	LHP	96	21	3	10	.219
Road	221	65	18	40	.294	RHP	345	114	25	77	.330
First Half	273	86	14	52	.315	Sc Pos	139	42	3	56	.302
Scnd Half	168	49	14	35	.292	Clutch	66	20	6	17	.303

2003 Rankings (American League)

- 2nd in batting average vs. righthanded pitchers
- 3rd in fewest GDPs per GDP situation (3.2%) and fielding percentage in right field (.983)
- Led the Red Sox in fewest GDPs per GDP situation (3.2%)
- Led AL right fielders in home runs

David Ortiz

2003 Season

Another free agent signee who came up big for the Red Sox last year was lefthanded-hitting DH David Ortiz. As the team's No. 5 hitter, he had a huge second half on the way to his biggest season by far, receiving four first-place votes in the American League MVP balloting and finishing fifth overall. It was as much a recognition of his production and countless clutch hits (many of them having come against the Yankees) as it was of his role as a uniting force in a clubhouse full of diverse personalities.

Hitting

Where did all the power come from? Ortiz always has had it, but the Metrodome's baggie in right field had kept a lot of his line drives in the park. Not that he's strictly a pull hitter—he always has been somewhat unusual in that he hits for power but consistently hits to all fields. This, of course, proved to be a style well-suited to Fenway. For a power hitter, he is a good two-strike hitter and a hard man to fan. In fact, he seems to get better the deeper he goes into an at-bat, and all but four of his 31 homers came on the third pitch or later. He seemed quicker on fastballs last year, and few got past him. His career numbers against southpaws are respectable, but he hasn't hit them well at all the last two years.

Baserunning & Defense

Some players are quicker than they look like they ought to be, but Ortiz isn't one of them. "Plodder" is not an unduly harsh description. At first base, he catches what he gets to, but his lack of mobility is a serious handicap. He's played only 96 games in the field over the last five years.

2004 Outlook

Ortiz is eligible for salary arbitration and undoubtedly will be in line for a big raise. The Red Sox are well aware that he's a key component of the team, however, and his spot seems quite secure.

Position: DH/1B
Bats: L **Throws:** L
Ht: 6' 4" **Wt:** 230

Opening Day Age: 28
Born: 11/18/75 in Santo Domingo, DR
ML Seasons: 7
Pronunciation: or-TEEZ

Overall Statistics

	G	AB	R	H	D	T	HR	RBI	SB	BB	SO	Avg	OBP	Slg
'03	128	448	79	129	39	2	31	101	0	58	83	.288	.369	.592
Car.	583	1925	294	522	147	5	89	339	4	244	422	.271	.353	.491

Where He Hits the Ball

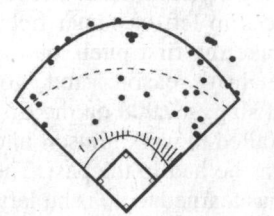 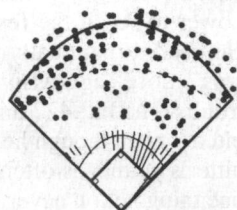

Vs. LHP   **Vs. RHP**

2003 Situational Stats

	AB	H	HR	RBI	Avg		AB	H	HR	RBI	Avg
Home	241	76	17	62	.315	LHP	116	25	4	22	.216
Road	207	53	14	39	.256	RHP	332	104	27	79	.313
First Half	221	66	10	46	.299	Sc Pos	139	38	3	65	.273
Scnd Half	227	63	21	55	.278	Clutch	72	22	6	22	.306

2003 Rankings (American League)

- 3rd in slugging percentage
- 5th in HR frequency (14.5 ABs per HR)
- 9th in most pitches seen per plate appearance (4.06)
- 10th in doubles
- Led the Red Sox in slugging percentage, HR frequency (14.5 ABs per HR) and batting average in the clutch

Manny Ramirez

2003 Season

Manny Ramirez had another fine offensive season, but the Red Sox' cleanup hitter sure stirred up a hornet's nest along the way. He missed a crucial series against the Yankees in late August due to a throat infection, amid published reports that he was seen in a hotel bar one night and that he failed to show up at the park the next day. The following day, he begged off a pinch-hitting assignment, and then was benched for a game. Amid all the controversy, it was easy to overlook that he led the league in on-base percentage and came within a point of winning his second straight batting title. After the season, the Red Sox put him on waivers, but no other team was willing to take on his contract.

Hitting

Ramirez combines power, contact and patience in a way not seen since Frank Thomas was in his prime. Ramirez has tremendous plate coverage and can drive an outside pitch to the opposite field with frightful power. His quick hands make him just as dangerous on pitches inside. He has a good eye, and will take a walk if he doesn't get his pitch. Although he never holds anything back, he has good enough bat control to be an excellent two-strike hitter.

Baserunning & Defense

The best that can be said for Manny's baserunning and defense is that it isn't as bad as it looks. He has long, loping strides, but he doesn't loaf as often as he appears to. His range is limited, however. He has a fairly strong arm. Ramirez usually runs the bases one at a time, and hamstring problems slowed him further last year.

2004 Outlook

Ramirez' role in the Red Sox' lineup is clear, but it's far from clear what kind of relationship he'll have with Boston fans, his teammates and his new manager. Sometimes he gives the appearance that he just doesn't care, a sin that's especially unforgivable in Boston.

Position: LF/DH
Bats: R **Throws:** R
Ht: 6' 0" **Wt:** 213

Opening Day Age: 31
Born: 5/30/72 in Santo Domingo, DR
ML Seasons: 11
Pronunciation:
ruh MEER oz

Overall Statistics

G	AB	R	H	D	T	HR	RBI	SB	BB	SO	Avg	OBP	Slg
154	569	117	185	36	1	37	104	3	97	94	.325	.427	.587
1383	5004	959	1585	337	14	347	1140	31	792	1106	.317	.413	.598

Where He Hits the Ball

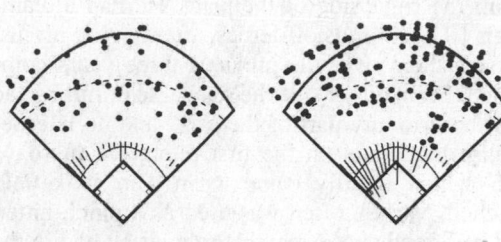

Vs. LHP   **Vs. RHP**

2003 Situational Stats

	AB	H	HR	RBI	Avg		AB	H	HR	RBI	Avg
Home	275	91	18	48	.331	LHP	143	55	8	23	.385
Road	294	94	19	56	.320	RHP	426	130	29	81	.305
First Half	345	110	21	69	.319	Sc Pos	151	51	9	66	.338
Scnd Half	224	75	16	35	.335	Clutch	73	20	2	7	.274

2003 Rankings (American League)

- 1st in intentional walks (28) and on-base percentage
- 2nd in batting average, times on base (290), batting average vs. lefthanded pitchers and cleanup slugging percentage (.587)
- 3rd in GDPs (22) and lowest fielding percentage in left field (.982)
- 4th in runs scored, slugging percentage and errors in left field (4)
- Led the Red Sox in home runs, walks, highest percentage of pitches taken (58.6), steals of third (2), batting average with runners in scoring position, cleanup slugging percentage (.587) and batting average on the road
- Led AL left fielders in batting average and home runs

Jason Varitek

2003 Season

Jason Varitek had his best season in 2003, setting career highs in homers and RBI despite slumping in August and September as well as batting ninth most of the year. The only American League catcher to have a better all-around season was Jorge Posada, who finished third in the AL MVP vote. Varitek had many big hits for the Red Sox, including eight homers in the late innings of close games, third-most in the majors. He also came up big in the postseason, batting .294 with four homers in 11 contests.

Hitting

Most of Varitek's improvement last year was seen from the right side of the plate. He had a team-high 10 home runs off lefties, after having hit just six off them over the previous three years combined. From either side, he's capable of hitting the ball hard to any part of the park, and he is especially dangerous on the first pitch. On his days off, which usually came when Tim Wakefield pitched, Varitek often was used as a pinch-hitter. He had good success in that role, as he had in the past. Perhaps due to the physical demands of catching and his willingness to play if he's at all able to, he tends to wear down late in the season, as he again did last year.

Baserunning & Defense

Defensively, Varitek is strong in every area of the game. He takes responsibility for getting the most out of his pitchers, and works hard at ensuring their success. His pitch-blocking skills are top-notch, and he throws powerfully and accurately. The makeup of the Red Sox' pitching staff likely has kept him from compiling better caught-stealing percentages. He runs well enough to not be a liability on the bases.

2004 Outlook

Varitek is going into the final year of his contract. Two of Boston's biggest stars, Pedro Martinez and Nomar Garciaparra, are in the same situation, so Varitek's fate may depend on how those other two contracts are, or are not, resolved.

Position: C
Bats: B **Throws:** R
Ht: 6' 2" **Wt:** 237

Opening Day Age: 31
Born: 4/11/72 in Rochester, MI
ML Seasons: 7
Pronunciation: VAIR-eh-teck

Overall Statistics

	G	AB	R	H	D	T	HR	RBI	SB	BB	SO	Avg	OBP	Slg
'03	142	451	63	123	31	1	25	85	3	51	106	.273	.351	.512
Car.	695	2245	296	596	152	6	79	345	11	236	450	.265	.338	.444

Where He Hits the Ball

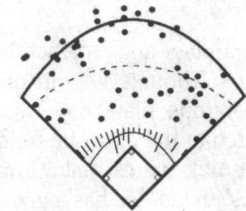 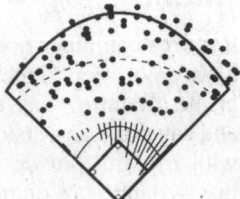

Vs. LHP   **Vs. RHP**

2003 Situational Stats

	AB	H	HR	RBI	Avg		AB	H	HR	RBI	Avg
Home	220	67	13	49	.305	LHP	136	42	10	33	.309
Road	231	56	12	36	.242	RHP	315	81	15	52	.257
First Half	255	78	16	56	.306	Sc Pos	129	39	8	65	.302
Scnd Half	196	45	9	29	.230	Clutch	84	25	8	22	.298

2003 Rankings (American League)

- 1st in errors at catcher (9)
- 2nd in lowest percentage of runners caught stealing as a catcher (23.8)

Todd Walker

2003 Season

Second baseman Todd Walker had a highly respectable season in 2003, but he mostly blended into the background until the postseason, when he batted .349 and slugged five homers in 12 games. Hitting in the second spot in the lineup, he had a solid offensive season all-around, driving in a career-high 85 runs. Walker slumped badly in July and August, but he rebounded to get some big hits in September.

Hitting

With a short, quick stroke, Walker is an excellent contact hitter with line-drive power. He uses the whole field and was able to take good advantage of Fenway's left-field wall. On the other hand, he is capable of pulling the ball, and also takes good advantage of the hole on the right side when a runner is on first. He remains tough with two strikes. Walker had made progress against lefties in recent years but went backwards last year, and sometimes was rested when a southpaw was on the mound. His career on-base percentage against lefties is just .289, a serious liability for someone who hits near the top of the order.

Baserunning & Defense

Some were pleasantly surprised with Walker's defense last year, but that probably had more to do with his reputation than anything. A bad-glove rep has followed him ever since he lost his job in Minnesota in 2000. He is below average at the keystone, but he's hardly a disaster. He lacks range and fluidity, and he sometimes hurries his throws, but he turns the double play well enough. Walker has pretty good speed but took fewer chances on the bases last year with Boston's big bats coming up behind him.

2004 Outlook

A free agent, Walker is capable of playing a supporting role on a winning team, as he did last year. He has played most of his career in parks that have boosted his average, however, and he may have trouble maintaining his numbers if he lands in the wrong park. He won't be returning to Fenway after the Red Sox declined to offer him salary arbitration.

Position: 2B
Bats: L **Throws:** R
Ht: 6' 0" **Wt:** 190

Opening Day Age: 30
Born: 5/25/73 in Bakersfield, CA
ML Seasons: 8

Overall Statistics

	G	AB	R	H	D	T	HR	RBI	SB	BB	SO	Avg	OBP	Slg
'03	144	587	92	166	38	4	13	85	1	48	54	.283	.333	.428
Car.	893	3295	476	957	217	21	71	398	63	290	437	.290	.346	.434

Where He Hits the Ball

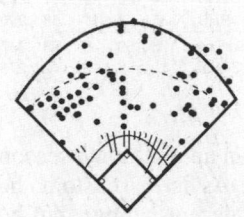 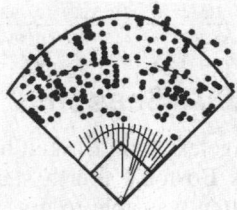

Vs. LHP   **Vs. RHP**

2003 Situational Stats

	AB	H	HR	RBI	Avg		AB	H	HR	RBI	Avg
Home	291	94	6	43	.323	LHP	158	37	4	25	.234
Road	296	72	7	42	.243	RHP	429	129	9	60	.301
First Half	366	106	8	51	.290	Sc Pos	151	45	4	68	.298
Scnd Half	221	60	5	34	.271	Clutch	82	22	2	12	.268

2003 Rankings (American League)

- 2nd in errors at second base (16)
- 3rd in sacrifice flies (10) and lowest fielding percentage at second base (.975)
- 5th in lowest percentage of swings that missed (10.0)
- Led the Red Sox in sacrifice flies (10) and highest percentage of swings put into play (49.9)

John Burkett

Position: SP
Bats: R **Throws:** R
Ht: 6' 3" **Wt:** 215

Opening Day Age: 39
Born: 11/28/64 in New Brighton, PA
ML Seasons: 15
Pronunciation: BURK-it

Overall Statistics

W	L	Pct.	ERA	G	GS	Sv	IP	H	BB	SO	HR	Avg
12	9	.571	5.15	32	30	0	181.2	202	47	107	20	.281
166	136	.550	4.31	445	423	1	2648.1	2866	700	1766	257	.277

2003 Situational Stats

	W	L	ERA	Sv	IP		AB	H	HR	RBI	Avg
Home	6	3	5.33	0	82.2	LHB	384	105	9	51	.273
Road	6	6	5.00	0	99.0	RHB	335	97	11	53	.290
First Half	7	4	5.25	0	104.2	Sc Pos	175	59	6	78	.337
Scnd Half	5	5	5.03	0	77.0	Clutch	18	5	0	2	.278

2003 Season

Ageless John Burkett had an up-and-down season as Boston's fourth starter. As is his custom, he often was able to give six decent innings, but he had more outings where he was batted around than ones in which shut the opposition down. He did manage to reach the 30-start plateau for the 10th time in his career. As he'd done in 2002, however, he fell well short of matching his 2001 level of effectiveness.

Pitching & Defense

Few major league pitchers are able to survive with as little velocity as Burkett, who usually tops out in the low to mid-80s. He works the corners with a sinker, cutter and slow curve. He's had persistent first-inning problems over the last two years, and even when he survives them, he seldom goes past the sixth.. He's tough to run on, if only because he throws over to first so often. Opposing basestealers were under .500 against him last year. He remains a capable fielder, even if he doesn't move quite as well as he once did.

2004 Outlook

Burkett became a free agent over the winter. At age 39—and three years removed from his last strong season—he's filler for the back end of a rotation, at best.

Alan Embree

Position: RP
Bats: L **Throws:** L
Ht: 6' 2" **Wt:** 190

Opening Day Age: 34
Born: 1/23/70 in The Dalles, OR
ML Seasons: 10
Pronunciation: EMM-bree

Overall Statistics

	W	L	Pct.	ERA	G	GS	Sv	IP	H	BB	SO	HR	Avg
'03	4	1	.800	4.25	65	0	1	55.0	49	16	45	5	.241
Car.	26	26	.500	4.43	497	4	7	463.0	429	192	443	58	.248

2003 Situational Stats

	W	L	ERA	Sv	IP		AB	H	HR	RBI	Avg
Home	4	1	3.95	0	27.1	LHB	99	26	4	20	.263
Road	0	0	4.55	1	27.2	RHB	104	23	1	7	.221
First Half	3	1	3.79	0	35.2	Sc Pos	45	14	1	21	.311
Scnd Half	1	0	5.12	1	19.1	Clutch	101	31	2	16	.307

2003 Season

After missing some time in April with shoulder tendinitis, Alan Embree moved back into the role he'd filled so well in the second half of 2002 as Boston's top lefthanded setup man. He pitched better than his ERA suggested, and stranded all but nine of the 44 runners he inherited. In the postseason, he appeared in eight of the Red Sox' 12 games and didn't give up a single run.

Pitching & Defense

Embree makes his living with a four-seamer in the low to mid-90s. It's straight as a string, however, and his slider is little more than a setup pitch, so he's vulnerable whenever he doesn't have the good heat. As a result, any physical problem that affects his velocity can render him suddenly hittable. He's tough on lefties, although they had slightly better success against him in 2003. Last year, showed a better move to first and held runners more effectively. He's always been a reliable fielder.

2004 Outlook

With all the uncertainty in Boston's bullpen, it's a safe bet that Embree will remain its top lefthander. He's capable of having a very good season if healthy, and a much less impressive one if not.

Casey Fossum

Position: SP
Bats: B **Throws:** L
Ht: 6' 1" **Wt:** 165

Opening Day Age: 26
Born: 1/6/78 in Cherry Hill, NJ
ML Seasons: 3

Overall Statistics

	W	L	Pct.	ERA	G	GS	Sv	IP	H	BB	SO	HR	Avg
'03	6	5	.545	5.47	19	14	1	79.0	82	34	63	9	.270
Car.	14	11	.560	4.42	75	33	2	230.0	239	84	190	25	.267

2003 Situational Stats

	W	L	ERA	Sv	IP		AB	H	HR	RBI	Avg
Home	3	3	4.94	1	47.1	LHB	87	20	1	11	.230
Road	3	2	6.25	0	31.2	RHB	217	62	8	35	.286
First Half	4	4	5.76	0	59.1	Sc Pos	70	17	1	30	.243
Scnd Half	2	1	4.58	1	19.2	Clutch	0	0	0	0	–

2003 Season

Casey Fossum opened the year in the Red Sox' starting rotation and pitched decently through mid-May, but he spent most of the remainder of the season either disabled with shoulder stiffness or pitching poorly. He logged just one inning in September and finally had minor shoulder surgery in October. In November, Fossum was traded to Arizona as part of the package for Curt Schilling.

Pitching & Defense

It's easy to see why the Red Sox valued Fossum so highly. When healthy, he throws 90 MPH from a low-three-quarters angle that makes it difficult for hitters to get on top of the ball. He also has a nice curve that he can change speeds with, as well as a cutter and changeup. His stamina had been questionable even before his shoulder problems cropped up. He has a good pickoff move and is tough to run on. He also has yet to commit an error in the majors.

2004 Outlook

Fossum is expected to be fully recovered from his shoulder surgery in time for the start of 2004, and he likely will open the season in the Diamondbacks' rotation. He probably won't pile up victories or innings just yet, but he could be an effective 180-inning pitcher.

Jeremy Giambi

Position: DH
Bats: L **Throws:** L
Ht: 5'11" **Wt:** 216

Opening Day Age: 29
Born: 9/30/74 in San Jose, CA
ML Seasons: 6
Pronunciation: yoo OM bee

Overall Statistics

	G	AB	R	H	D	T	HR	RBI	SB	BB	SO	Avg	OBP	Slg
'03	50	127	15	25	5	0	5	15	1	26	42	.197	.342	.354
Car.	510	1417	219	372	75	3	52	209	1	251	356	.263	.377	.430

2003 Situational Stats

	AB	H	HR	RBI	Avg		AB	H	HR	RBI	Avg
Home	61	12	2	9	.197	LHP	24	3	0	2	.125
Road	66	13	3	6	.197	RHP	103	22	5	13	.214
First Half	110	19	5	13	.173	Sc Pos	36	6	0	8	.167
Scnd Half	17	6	0	2	.353	Clutch	21	5	0	2	.238

2003 Season

Jeremy Giambi came to Boston last winter via a trade with the Phillies. He saw time in the Red Sox' crowded DH mix in April and May but never really got going. He had season-ending shoulder surgery to repair a torn ligament in August, and it was revealed that he'd been trying to play through the injury all season.

Hitting, Baserunning & Defense

The reason Boston obtained Giambi in the first place is that he is an on-base machine. Even last year, when he wasn't hitting at all, he continued to draw walks. He's patient, but he also preserves long counts by swinging through a lot of pitches. Against righthanders, he has respectable power; against lefties, he has less power but still gets on base. He can play left field, right field and first base, but he lacks mobility at any position and is best suited to DH. Last year, he stole the first base of his major league career—on a busted hit-and-run.

2004 Outlook

It looks like Giambi, who was released, will have to catch on somewhere as a reserve and try to play his way into a bigger role. It's hard to imagine this will be the year that he finally stays healthy from start to finish.

Damian Jackson

Position:
2B/SS/LF/CF/RF
Bats: R **Throws:** R
Ht: 5'11" **Wt:** 185

Opening Day Age: 30
Born: 8/16/73 in Los Angeles, CA
ML Seasons: 8

Overall Statistics

	G	AB	R	H	D	T	HR	RBI	SB	BB	SO	Avg	OBP	Slg
'03	109	161	34	42	7	0	1	13	16	8	28	.261	.294	.323
Car.	621	1788	270	440	104	16	22	162	117	199	421	.246	.325	.359

2003 Situational Stats

	AB	H	HR	RBI	Avg		AB	H	HR	RBI	Avg
Home	60	23	0	8	.383	LHP	87	21	0	7	.241
Road	101	19	1	5	.188	RHP	74	21	1	6	.284
First Half	76	17	0	4	.224	Sc Pos	34	7	0	12	.206
Scnd Half	85	25	1	9	.294	Clutch	23	6	0	0	.261

2003 Season

Signed as a free agent over the winter prior to 2003 season, Damian Jackson proved to be a useful bench player for the Red Sox. He played seven positions and got into 109 games, making 41 starts. His most frequent use came as a defensive replacement at second base or as a pinch-runner. He also backed up shortstop and all three outfield positions.

Hitting, Baserunning & Defense

Jackson takes a full cut and hits the ball in the air, even though he doesn't have the power to succeed with that approach. He swings through a lot of pitches and fails to shorten up with two strikes. He has very good speed, and is a good basestealer, though it became hard for him to steal successfully late last year because he so often was sent in to pinch-run for the express purpose of stealing a base. Second base is Jackson's best position, and he proved useful in center field.

2004 Outlook

After washing out as a regular earlier in his career, Jackson seems to have found his niche. If Todd Walker isn't re-signed, Jackson may become part of the solution at second base, but he shouldn't be expected to get a shot at the full-time job.

Brandon Lyon (Traded To D'BACKS)

Position: RP
Bats: R **Throws:** R
Ht: 6' 1" **Wt:** 185

Opening Day Age: 24
Born: 8/10/79 in Salt Lake City, UT
ML Seasons: 3
Pronunciation: lion

Overall Statistics

	W	L	Pct.	ERA	G	GS	Sv	IP	H	BB	SO	HR	Avg
'03	4	6	.400	4.12	49	0	9	59.0	73	19	50	6	.296
Car.	10	14	.417	4.99	75	21	9	184.0	214	53	115	26	.290

2003 Situational Stats

	W	L	ERA	Sv	IP		AB	H	HR	RBI	Avg
Home	0	2	4.61	6	27.1	LHB	120	38	5	21	.317
Road	4	4	3.69	3	31.2	RHB	127	35	1	15	.276
First Half	4	5	4.09	9	50.2	Sc Pos	73	24	1	28	.329
Scnd Half	0	1	4.32	0	8.1	Clutch	127	40	3	19	.315

2003 Season

One of Boston's biggest surprises in the first half of 2003 was Brandon Lyon, who'd been claimed off waivers from Toronto. He started strongly, moved into the closer's role in May and did a decent job until the end of June, when he began to struggle and was moved into a less demanding role. He was traded to Pittsburgh in July, but later was returned due to concern over his elbow; he admitted it had bothered him throughout the season. He was activated in September and pitched poorly, and then was traded to Arizona over the winter.

Pitching & Defense

A healthy Lyon has a fastball in the low to mid-90s, a sharp curve, a slider and changeup. He also has good command and shows plenty of poise for a youngster. He may get hit but he won't beat himself with walks. Since reaching the majors in 2001, he's been very effective at times and completely ineffective at others, which reinforces concerns about his elbow. He's an adequate fielder who doesn't hold runners well.

2004 Outlook

Lyons has some upside but obviously carries some risk as well for Arizona. He may be effective at times, though the chances of him contributing for the entire season aren't all that good.

Jeff Suppan

Position: SP
Bats: R **Throws:** R
Ht: 6' 2" **Wt:** 220

Opening Day Age: 29
Born: 1/2/75 in
Oklahoma City, OK
ML Seasons: 9
Pronunciation:
SOO-pahn

Overall Statistics

	W	L	Pct.	ERA	G	GS	Sv	IP	H	BB	SO	HR	Avg
'03	13	11	.542	4.19	32	31	0	204.0	217	51	110	23	.272
Car.	62	75	.453	4.90	222	206	0	1292.1	1424	415	720	177	.280

2003 Situational Stats

	W	L	ERA	Sv	IP		AB	H	HR	RBI	Avg
Home	9	4	3.71	0	114.0	LHB	374	116	12	54	.310
Road	4	7	4.80	0	90.0	RHB	423	101	11	38	.239
First Half	8	7	3.73	0	118.1	Sc Pos	196	48	3	64	.245
Scnd Half	5	4	4.83	0	85.2	Clutch	50	18	2	6	.360

2003 Season

Righthander Jeff Suppan signed a one-year deal with Pittsburgh in January 2003 and was putting together his best season when he was traded to Boston at the deadline to plug a hole in the back of the Red Sox' rotation. He struggled in his first few starts and quickly lost the confidence of his manager. In the postseason, he was a forgotten man.

Pitching & Defense

Suppan always is around the strike zone, but he is too hittable to get away with that consistently. He mixes a low-90s fastball, a slider and change, and tries to get hitters to chase his curve once he gets ahead. He has no real out pitch, and has trouble putting hitters away. He also is vulnerable to the longball. Durability is perhaps his biggest asset, although stamina is not—he tends to tire after five or six innings. He is a decent fielder, has a pretty good pickoff move for a righthander and is fairly tough to run on.

2004 Outlook

Suppan, once again a free agent, will shop around for a team looking for an innings-eater. Whichever club signs him will know exactly what it is getting, and will be able to rely on him to take the ball every fifth day.

Mike Timlin   (Rubber Arm)

Position: RP
Bats: R **Throws:** R
Ht: 6' 4" **Wt:** 210

Opening Day Age: 38
Born: 3/10/66 in
Midland, TX
ML Seasons: 13
Pronunciation:
TIM lin

Overall Statistics

	W	L	Pct.	ERA	G	GS	Sv	IP	H	BB	SO	HR	Avg
'03	6	4	.600	3.55	72	0	2	83.2	77	9	65	11	.239
Car.	51	55	.481	3.56	736	4	116	879.0	823	288	664	85	.248

2003 Situational Stats

	W	L	ERA	Sv	IP		AB	H	HR	RBI	Avg
Home	5	2	1.43	1	44.0	LHB	150	43	7	25	.287
Road	1	2	5.90	1	39.2	RHB	172	34	4	18	.198
First Half	3	3	3.29	2	52.0	Sc Pos	95	25	4	32	.263
Scnd Half	3	1	3.98	0	31.2	Clutch	162	35	7	21	.216

2003 Season

The Red Sox added reliever upon reliever last season, but only one was effective from beginning to end: Mike Timlin. Working as their primary righthanded setup man, Timlin proved to be one of the few constants in an often-chaotic bullpen. He posted a 3.55 ERA during the regular season, but was at his best in the postseason, working 9.2 scoreless innings over eight appearances.

Pitching & Defense

With excellent command of a sinking low-90s fastball and a slider, Timlin is able to pitch to contact and get groundballs. He issued only six unintentional walks all year, and his 65 strikeouts represented his highest output since his 1991 rookie campaign. Righthanded hitters have very little success against him. His effectiveness drops off when he works more than an inning at a time, but he needs little rest between appearances. He cuts off the running game well but is not a sure fielder, posting a pair of errors last year.

2004 Outlook

One of the first things Boston did over the winter was re-sign Timlin. While the rest of the bullpen remains unsettled, his presence stabilizes one important slot. Although he'll turn 38 this March, he's shown few signs of slowing down.

Boston

Tim Wakefield (Knuckleballer)

Position: SP
Bats: R **Throws:** R
Ht: 6' 2" **Wt:** 214

Opening Day Age: 37
Born: 8/2/66 in Melbourne, FL
ML Seasons: 11

Overall Statistics

	W	L	Pct.	ERA	G	GS	Sv	IP	H	BB	SO	HR	Avg
'03	11	7	.611	4.09	35	33	1	202.1	193	71	169	23	.246
Car.	116	101	.535	4.24	392	253	22	1878.1	1812	766	1323	232	.253

2003 Situational Stats

	W	L	ERA	Sv	IP		AB	H	HR	RBI	Avg
Home	5	4	4.25	1	112.1	LHB	379	101	7	39	.266
Road	6	3	3.90	0	90.0	RHB	404	92	16	53	.228
First Half	6	4	4.10	1	116.1	Sc Pos	188	50	2	60	.266
Scnd Half	5	3	4.08	0	86.0	Clutch	57	14	2	5	.246

2003 Season

For the first time in five years, knuckleballer Tim Wakefield was given a role and allowed to remain in it all year. The results were fine, as he served quite capably as Boston's No. 3 starter. He was especially tough late in the year, beating the Yankees in each of his ALCS starts, only to lose Game 7 in relief on a home run to Aaron Boone.

Pitching & Defense

It's no secret—a knuckleballer like Wakefield is only as good as his control of his signature pitch on a given night. When he is fully in command of it, he'll change speeds with it. When Wakefield really needs a strike, or wants to get ahead against a tough hitter, he'll often sneak in a little curveball. He's equally tough on hitters of all types. Naturally, he's much easier to run on than a conventional pitcher. He isn't as mobile a fielder as he once was, but he's become more reliable.

2004 Outlook

While the Red Sox will have a new manager this year in Terry Francona and a new workhorse in Curt Schilling, it's safe to assume Wakefield's role won't change much, except he'll likely move to the No. 4 slot. Expect more of the same from him.

Scott Williamson

Position: RP
Bats: R **Throws:** R
Ht: 6' 0" **Wt:** 185

Opening Day Age: 28
Born: 2/17/76 in Fort Polk, LA
ML Seasons: 5

Overall Statistics

	W	L	Pct.	ERA	G	GS	Sv	IP	H	BB	SO	HR	Avg
'03	5	4	.556	4.16	66	0	21	62.2	54	34	74	7	.227
Car.	25	23	.521	3.13	241	10	54	342.2	247	190	401	27	.202

2003 Situational Stats

	W	L	ERA	Sv	IP		AB	H	HR	RBI	Avg
Home	5	1	3.77	8	31.0	LHB	95	19	4	8	.200
Road	0	3	4.55	13	31.2	RHB	143	35	3	25	.245
First Half	4	3	3.38	20	37.1	Sc Pos	79	18	3	29	.228
Scnd Half	1	1	5.33	1	25.1	Clutch	146	31	6	24	.212

2003 Season

Scott Williamson began the year as the Reds' closer and did a fine job for them, converting 21 of 26 save chances before being dealt to Boston near the trade deadline. He worked in a setup role for the Red Sox and pitched fairly well despite a high ERA. His acquisition really paid off in the postseason, however. He worked all five games of the Division Series against Oakland, winning two of them, and saved all three of the Red Sox' wins in the ALCS.

Pitching & Defense

With a mid-90s fastball and a terrific hard slider, Williamson is very tough to hit when he has his command—which isn't always the case. He has a changeup for lefthanded hitters, but he tends to overthrow it. His slider is tough to lay off with two strikes. After coming back from Tommy John surgery in 2002, he's proven able to work on consecutive days. He has a pretty good pickoff move, but Williamson is slow to the plate and rather easy to run on.

2004 Outlook

Williamson is arbitration-eligible and may be non-tendered. He has proven himself as a closer and may post his first 40-save season if he lands in the right situation.

Other Boston Red Sox

Andy Abad (**Pos**: 1B, **Age**: 31, **Bats**: L)

	G	AB	R	H	D	T	HR	RBI	SB	BB	SO	Avg	OBP	Slg
'03	9	17	1	2	0	0	0	0	0	2	5	.118	.211	.118
Car.	10	18	1	2	0	0	0	0	0	2	5	.111	.200	.111

Dating back to 1998, Abad has batted better than .300 in Triple-A ball with an OBP near .400 and a slugging mark approaching .500. He got a cup of coffee in September, a week after his 31st birthday, but the Sox released him in November. 2004 Outlook: C

Bronson Arroyo (**Pos**: RHP, **Age**: 27)

	W	L	Pct.	ERA	G	GS	Sv	IP	H	BB	SO	HR	Avg
'03	0	0	−	2.08	6	0	1	17.1	10	4	14	0	.164
Car.	9	14	.391	5.15	59	29	1	204.1	227	89	125	23	.284

Arroyo enjoyed a solid Triple-A season at Pawtucket, going 12-6 with a 3.43 ERA and 155 strikeouts in 149.2 frames. He was effective in the BoSox pen late in 2003, earning his first save and an '04 chance. 2004 Outlook: B

Adrian Brown (**Pos**: CF, **Age**: 30, **Bats**: B)

	G	AB	R	H	D	T	HR	RBI	SB	BB	SO	Avg	OBP	Slg
'03	9	15	2	3	0	0	0	1	2	1	4	.200	.250	.200
Car.	417	1087	160	283	43	8	11	84	44	107	150	.260	.329	.345

The Devil Rays selected Brown from Boston in the Rule 5 draft, yet Brown didn't surface in the majors until September after Tampa Bay returned the speedster. Still, he made the ALDS squad that beat Oakland. 2004 Outlook: C

Bruce Chen (**Pos**: LHP, **Age**: 26)

	W	L	Pct.	ERA	G	GS	Sv	IP	H	BB	SO	HR	Avg
'03	0	1	.000	5.55	16	2	0	24.1	26	10	20	6	.283
Car.	20	19	.513	4.59	155	61	0	453.1	434	194	400	83	.251

Despite a promising 2000 season as a 23-year-old, Chen was dealt four times between the All-Star breaks of 2000 and 2002. He was cut by three big league teams in '03 and looks for a chance with Toronto in '04. 2004 Outlook: C

Lou Collier (**Pos**: 3B, **Age**: 30, **Bats**: R)

	G	AB	R	H	D	T	HR	RBI	SB	BB	SO	Avg	OBP	Slg
'03	4	1	0	0	0	0	0	0	0	0	0	.000	.000	.000
Car.	283	677	82	162	32	7	7	74	11	70	150	.239	.314	.338

Collier has established himself as a fairly solid Triple-A contributor over the last three seasons, but big league chances don't come around much anymore. Boston isn't a good place to be for that. 2004 Outlook: C

Bill Haselman (**Pos**: C, **Age**: 37, **Bats**: R)

	G	AB	R	H	D	T	HR	RBI	SB	BB	SO	Avg	OBP	Slg
'03	4	3	0	0	0	0	0	0	0	0	1	.000	.000	.000
Car.	589	1606	185	416	94	3	47	210	9	114	300	.259	.311	.408

The veteran catcher spent his summer at Triple-A Pawtucket, where he posted hitting percentages far below his career marks in the majors. No reason to think he won't be trying to catch on somewhere. 2004 Outlook: C

Bob Howry (**Pos**: RHP, **Age**: 30)

	W	L	Pct.	ERA	G	GS	Sv	IP	H	BB	SO	HR	Avg
'03	0	0	−	12.46	4	0	0	4.1	11	3	4	1	.478
Car.	14	20	.412	3.92	318	0	49	344.2	312	140	304	42	.244

Shoulder surgery in late 2000 cost Howry some velocity that began to return after his July 2002 trade to Boston, but a tender elbow late in 2002 led to surgery in June. He will be ready this spring. 2004 Outlook: B

Todd Jones (**Pos**: RHP, **Age**: 35)

	W	L	Pct.	ERA	G	GS	Sv	IP	H	BB	SO	HR	Avg
'03	3	5	.375	7.08	59	1	0	68.2	93	31	59	10	.323
Car.	39	42	.481	4.06	666	1	184	749.2	743	344	672	72	.261

A dreadful season with Colorado ended with his late-June release, and Jones quickly hooked on with the Red Sox. He wasn't much better with Boston (5.52 ERA), but made the ALCS roster and one appearance. 2004 Outlook: C

Gabe Kapler (**Pos**: RF/LF, **Age**: 28, **Bats**: R)

	G	AB	R	H	D	T	HR	RBI	SB	BB	SO	Avg	OBP	Slg
'03	107	225	39	61	13	1	4	27	6	22	41	.271	.336	.391
Car.	606	1908	275	519	112	12	55	248	61	184	299	.272	.335	.430

Power prospect Kapler never cashed in on his chance in Colorado after a July 2002 trade there, and the Red Sox signed him after his June release. He started 13-for-27 with Boston, followed by an 0-for-18. 2004 Outlook: B

Dave McCarty (**Pos**: LF, **Age**: 34, **Bats**: R)

	G	AB	R	H	D	T	HR	RBI	SB	BB	SO	Avg	OBP	Slg
'03	24	53	6	18	5	0	1	8	0	3	14	.340	.368	.491
Car.	528	1338	156	321	60	7	32	156	8	110	327	.240	.301	.367

McCarty contributed briefly for two contenders during the second half, the A's and Sox. Claimed off waivers in August, he batted .407 in 27 at-bats. Boston may look at him as both a pitcher and position player this spring. 2004 Outlook: C

Ramiro Mendoza (**Pos**: RHP, **Age**: 31)

	W	L	Pct.	ERA	G	GS	Sv	IP	H	BB	SO	HR	Avg
'03	3	5	.375	6.75	37	5	0	66.2	98	20	36	10	.349
Car.	57	39	.594	4.32	314	62	16	765.1	864	174	449	78	.284

What did taking off the Yankee pinstripes do to Mendoza? His 2003 ERA nearly doubled his 2002 mark. He might have settled into a starter or closer role, but ineffectiveness and injuries reigned. 2004 Outlook: B

Lou Merloni (**Pos**: 3B/2B/SS, **Age**: 32, **Bats**: R)

	G	AB	R	H	D	T	HR	RBI	SB	BB	SO	Avg	OBP	Slg
'03	80	181	24	48	8	2	1	18	2	26	41	.265	.355	.348
Car.	338	871	111	235	54	6	10	95	7	71	165	.270	.332	.380

Merloni spent five seasons as a utility infielder for Boston before he was claimed off waivers by San Diego just before Opening Day. The Sox picked him up again with a late August trade. 2004 Outlook: C

Doug Mirabelli (Pos: C, **Age**: 33, **Bats**: R)

	G	AB	R	H	D	T	HR	RBI	SB	BB	SO	Avg	OBP	Slg
'03	62	163	23	42	13	0	6	18	0	11	36	.258	.307	.448
Car.	336	863	97	203	49	2	32	115	1	106	221	.235	.324	.408

Mirabelli is a decent backup catcher who enjoyed regular duty behind the plate as knuckleballer Tim Wakefield's batterymate. He showed good pop in limited duty, especially during the second half. 2004 Outlook: C

Robert Person (Pos: RHP, **Age**: 34)

	W	L	Pct.	ERA	G	GS	Sv	IP	H	BB	SO	HR	Avg
'03	0	0	–	7.71	7	0	1	11.2	11	8	10	0	.250
Car.	51	42	.548	4.64	206	135	9	897.1	813	438	773	129	.242

Person was 15-7 (4.19) for the Phillies in 2001, but a poor 2002 was followed by elbow and shoulder procedures, and he rehabbed until May. Then a nagging hip injury sidetracked a possible closer role. 2004 Outlook: C

Ryan Rupe (Pos: RHP, **Age**: 29)

	W	L	Pct.	ERA	G	GS	Sv	IP	H	BB	SO	HR	Avg
'03	1	1	.500	6.30	4	1	0	10.0	13	1	7	4	.302
Car.	24	38	.387	5.85	89	84	0	476.2	514	162	355	81	.275

Rupe, in the closer-by-committee mix, got off to a slow spring start because of an infected boil under his right arm. He was good as a Triple-A starter (8-4, 3.26), but homers hurt him in Boston. 2004 Outlook: C

Scott Sauerbeck (Pos: LHP, **Age**: 32)

	W	L	Pct.	ERA	G	GS	Sv	IP	H	BB	SO	HR	Avg
'03	3	5	.375	4.76	79	0	0	56.2	47	43	50	6	.225
Car.	19	16	.543	3.71	367	0	5	325.1	287	209	337	24	.240

Sauerbeck was stellar in 2002, posting a 2.30 ERA with just 50 hits allowed and 70 strikeouts in 62.2 innings. He wasn't as dominant versus lefties in 2003, and Pittsburgh dealt him to Boston in July. 2004 Outlook: B

Rudy Seanez (Pos: RHP, **Age**: 35)

	W	L	Pct.	ERA	G	GS	Sv	IP	H	BB	SO	HR	Avg
'03	0	1	.000	6.23	9	0	0	8.2	11	6	9	2	.297
Car.	17	17	.500	4.54	284	0	11	287.1	253	160	287	31	.235

Seanez has been hanging around the majors since 1989, but the oft-injured pitcher struggled in Boston and Triple-A Pawtucket before a July release. A stint with the Cubs' Triple-A Iowa club wasn't much better. 2004 Outlook: C

Jason Shiell (Pos: RHP, **Age**: 27)

	W	L	Pct.	ERA	G	GS	Sv	IP	H	BB	SO	HR	Avg
'03	2	0	1.000	4.63	17	0	1	23.1	23	17	23	4	.253
Car.	2	0	1.000	5.84	20	0	1	24.2	30	20	24	4	.297

Acquired off waivers from San Diego in October 2002, Shiell bounced between Triple-A Pawtucket and Boston. He was effective at Pawtucket, which sparks hope for a better 2004 with the Sox. 2004 Outlook: C

Kevin Tolar (Pos: LHP, **Age**: 33)

	W	L	Pct.	ERA	G	GS	Sv	IP	H	BB	SO	HR	Avg
'03	0	0	–	9.00	6	0	0	4.0	5	2	3	1	.313
Car.	0	0	–	6.62	20	0	0	17.2	13	16	17	1	.203

Despite a high walk rate, Tolar was a stingy Triple-A reliever for a third year in a row, going 5-1 with a 2.27 ERA and four saves. He got a look in Boston in April, which didn't go as well, and he was released in November. 2004 Outlook: C

Steve Woodard (Pos: RHP, **Age**: 28)

	W	L	Pct.	ERA	G	GS	Sv	IP	H	BB	SO	HR	Avg
'03	1	0	1.000	5.09	7	0	0	17.2	23	5	12	3	.311
Car.	32	36	.471	4.94	162	94	0	667.1	782	149	464	90	.292

In his major league debut in 1997, Woodard worked eight innings of one-hit ball and beat Roger Clemens, 1-0. It's been mostly downhill from there, as Woodard hasn't had a sub-5.00 ERA in the bigs since 1999. 2004 Outlook: C

Boston Red Sox Minor League Prospects

Organization Overview:

The Red Sox continue to deal prospects in their pursuit of the Yankees. Among the top talent shipped elsewhere in 2003 were lefthander Phil Dumatrait (for Scott Williamson), middle infielder Freddy Sanchez (for Jeff Suppan), righthander Rene Miniel (for Lou Merloni), lefthander Jorge de la Rosa and outfielder Michael Goss (for Curt Schilling). Replenishing the system can take time, but the new Boston front office is following the Oakland model of drafting mostly college talent. In fact, the Red Sox signed just two high schoolers from their 2003 draft. While only a few players in the high minors are close to producing, recent draft choices such as David Murphy and Matt Murton offer hope that the farm system will generate major league talent soon.

Manny Delcarmen

Position: P **Opening Day Age:** 22
Bats: R **Throws:** R **Born:** 2/16/82 in Boston,
Ht: 6' 3" **Wt:** 195 MA

Recent Statistics

	W	L	ERA	G	GS	Sv	IP	H	R	BB	SO	HR
2002 A Augusta	7	8	4.10	26	24	0	136.0	124	77	56	136	15
2003 A Sarasota	1	1	3.13	4	3	0	23.0	16	9	7	16	1

A second-rounder in 2000, Delcarmen fired 92-94 MPH fastballs and hard, three-quarters curveballs past overmatched Rookie-level Gulf Coast League hitters in his 2001 debut. His curve was much more consistent late in 2002 at Class-A Augusta, and Delcarmen started calling on a changeup more as he learned that hard stuff alone didn't always work. He was off to a solid start at high Class-A Sarasota last spring when his season unraveled with a single pitch. The pain he felt led to season-ending Tommy John surgery in May. Through his rehab effort, the righthander is in terrific shape, and he may return sometime near midseason if his rehab continues to progress at its current pace.

Jon Lester

Position: P **Opening Day Age:** 20
Bats: L **Throws:** L **Born:** 1/7/84 in Tacoma,
Ht: 6' 4" **Wt:** 200 WA

Recent Statistics

	W	L	ERA	G	GS	Sv	IP	H	R	BB	SO	HR
2002 R Red Sox	0	1	13.50	1	1	0	0.2	5	6	1	1	0
2003 A Augusta	6	9	3.65	24	21	0	106.0	102	54	44	71	7

A second-round pick in 2002, Lester came to camp with less than an inning of rookie ball under his belt, yet quickly showed that an extended stay in spring training wasn't necessary. His command of three pitches, his poise on the mound and an advanced feel for pitching earned him a spot on a full-season club. Then Lester got off to a good start at Class-A Augusta, fanning 12 in his first 13 innings of work. He demonstrated the maturity and pitch command to survive full-season ball, calling on an 88-93 MPH fastball, a decent changeup and an improving curveball. With three offerings that are advanced for his age, Lester is likely to begin 2004 at high Class-A Sarasota.

Anastacio Martinez

Position: P **Opening Day Age:** 25
Bats: R **Throws:** R **Born:** 11/3/78 in Villa
Ht: 6' 2" **Wt:** 180 Mella, DR

Recent Statistics

	W	L	ERA	G	GS	Sv	IP	H	R	BB	SO	HR
2002 AA Trenton	5	12	5.31	27	27	0	139.0	152	98	75	127	12
2003 AA Portland	3	1	2.25	34	0	14	40.0	31	13	24	37	3
2003 AAA Pawtucket	2	1	1.93	8	0	0	14.0	12	3	3	15	2
2003 AA Altoona	0	0	2.25	3	0	0	4.0	6	1	1	1	1

Signed in 1998, Martinez began showing a promising combination of velocity and command at high Class-A Sarasota in 2001. Although the hard-thrower could hit the mid-90s effortlessly, his control regressed in 2002 at Double-A Trenton, and his lack of consistent secondary pitches contributed to a 5-12 record and 5.31 ERA. Last summer he made a rapid transition to relief work and did well working in more games. In a strong finish at Triple-A Pawtucket, Martinez called on his curveball more than his changeup as a reliever, but his command of the curve and his first-pitch fastball must be better to succeed in Boston. Even his trade to Pittsburgh and back didn't slow his 2003 progress.

David Murphy

Position: OF **Opening Day Age:** 22
Bats: L **Throws:** L **Born:** 10/18/81 in
Ht: 6' 3" **Wt:** 195 Houston, TX

Recent Statistics

	G	AB	R	H	D	T	HR	RBI	SB	BB	SO	Avg
2003 A Lowell	21	78	13	27	4	0	0	13	4	16	9	.346
2003 A Sarasota	45	153	18	37	5	1	1	18	6	20	33	.242

The 17th overall pick in 2003, Murphy was one of eight Baylor University players selected last June after leading the Big 12 in batting (.420) and total bases (176). He worked hard at his plate discipline at Baylor, and the results fit Boston's new organizational emphasis on on-base percentage. He set a Big 12 record with 118 hits as a junior in 2003, then kept on hitting at short-season Lowell after he signed. High Class-A Sarasota came a bit more difficult, but Murphy has a fluid lefthanded swing in addition to his plate patience. He also has good body control, plenty of raw power and a mature approach to hitting. Murphy is a big kid who runs well, though he's not a blazer. For now he's a center fielder.

Hanley Ramirez

Position: SS
Bats: B **Throws:** R
Ht: 6' 1" **Wt:** 174

Opening Day Age: 20
Born: 12/23/83 in Samana, Dominican Republic

Recent Statistics

	G	AB	R	H	D	T	HR	RBI	SB	BB	SO	Avg
2002 R Red Sox	45	164	29	56	11	3	6	26	8	16	15	.341
2002 A Lowell	22	97	17	36	9	2	1	19	4	4	14	.371
2003 A Augusta	111	422	69	116	24	3	8	50	36	32	73	.275

At the same time Ramirez' star was rising a year ago, he was sent home from instructional league because of rules violations, and he was demoted to extended spring training last May for similar infractions. Those bouts of immaturity gave way to a more mature approach by season's end. Ramirez flashed his impressive tools at Class-A Augusta, though he wasn't as successful making contact and getting on base as he was in 2002. Still, the Red Sox believe Ramirez saw his share of pitches and showed an ability to lay off breaking balls. He also showed some pop, though keeping his stroke short and quick is his ticket. He has all the tools, including a top-flight arm, to be a premier shortstop.

Kelly Shoppach

Position: C
Bats: R **Throws:** R
Ht: 5' 11" **Wt:** 210

Opening Day Age: 23
Born: 4/29/80 in Fort Worth, TX

Recent Statistics

	G	AB	R	H	D	T	HR	RBI	SB	BB	SO	Avg
2002 A Sarasota	116	414	54	112	35	1	10	66	2	59	112	.271
2003 AA Portland	92	340	45	96	30	2	12	60	0	35	83	.282

Shoppach was a second-rounder in 2001, though he didn't debut until 2002, when he impressed at high Class-A Sarasota. A downturn might have been expected in 2003, as Shoppach jumped to Double-A ball after off-season rotator cuff surgery in September. He missed most of April, but recovered remarkably, throwing out 30 percent of basestealers with his plus arm, quick release and throwing accuracy. The Red Sox also like his take-charge manner on the field. Shoppach utilized more of his raw power and improved his two-strike approach at the plate. What he needs to learn about hitting at this point is more mental than physical.

Chad Spann

Position: 3B
Bats: R **Throws:** R
Ht: 6' 1" **Wt:** 195

Opening Day Age: 20
Born: 10/25/83 in Americus, GA

Recent Statistics

	G	AB	R	H	D	T	HR	RBI	SB	BB	SO	Avg
2002 R Red Sox	57	203	20	45	8	3	6	28	1	12	37	.222
2003 A Augusta	116	414	55	129	21	3	5	63	9	40	64	.312

A fifth-round pick in 2002, Spann was a bit raw in his pro debut in the Rookie-level Gulf Coast League. An extended stay in spring training seemed likely in 2003, but the athletic Georgia native impressed in the spring and took a gigantic leap forward by playing in his home state as a teenager in the full-season Class-A Sally League. Despite being one of the younger players in the league, he demonstrated excellent bat speed, power potential and an ability to make adjustments to pitchers. He's a strong kid with good raw power and first-step quickness, and he has worked hard on groundball fundamentals. His improvement moves him closer to being an average third baseman.

Kevin Youkilis

Position: 3B
Bats: R **Throws:** R
Ht: 6' 1" **Wt:** 220

Opening Day Age: 25
Born: 3/15/79 in Cincinnati, OH

Recent Statistics

	G	AB	R	H	D	T	HR	RBI	SB	BB	SO	Avg
2002 A Augusta	15	53	5	15	5	0	0	6	0	13	8	.283
2002 A Sarasota	76	268	45	79	16	0	3	48	0	49	37	.295
2002 AA Trenton	44	160	34	55	10	0	5	26	5	31	18	.344
2003 AA Portland	94	312	74	102	23	1	6	37	7	86	40	.327
2003 AAA Pawtucket	32	109	9	18	3	0	2	15	0	18	21	.165

Youkilis never caught the attention of scouts with his tools, but he has made consistent contact and drawn walks as a pro. A young player with plate discipline often strikes out a lot, but Youkilis' eye-hand coordination and advanced two-strike approach have generated low strikeout totals. He ripped it up at Double-A Portland, earning a promotion to Triple-A Pawtucket in late July. He had reached base in 62 straight games when he arrived there, and he tied Kevin Millar's modern-day mark by reaching in 71 straight. Youkilis seemed spent by the attention given to the streak and struggled, but he rebounded during the Triple-A playoffs. There are doubts about his power potential, though Youkilis lifted the ball more at Portland. While his defensive game is better, more fine-tuning is needed.

Others to Watch

Hard-throwing **Juan Cedeno** (20) is an athletic left-hander with an above-average, 92-93 MPH fastball and a breaking ball that improved in the final months of the 2003 season. He went 7-9 with a 3.02 ERA at Class-A Augusta. Cedeno also has a good feel for a changeup. . . Righthander **Jerome Gamble** (23) ditched a history of arm trouble with Tommy John surgery in 2001. He rebounded well in 2002 and reached Double-A Portland at the end of 2003. Throwing 93-94 MPH, Gamble went 8-4 with a 3.81 ERA at two stops last summer. . . Venezuelan righthander **Harvey Garcia** (20) throws in the mid-90s already, and the 6-foot-2, 170-pounder will fill out and get stronger. His command of his fastball was impressive en route to a 3-0 (1.89) season in the Rookie-level Gulf Coast League. . . Outfielder **Matt Murton** (22) is strong with plenty of raw power. He showed good bat speed, a short stroke and plate discipline, posting a .286 average and .374 OBP in the short-season New York-Penn League.

U.S. Cellular Field

Offense

It was no surprise that the 2003 All-Star Game was won with a home run. While not many people seem to realize it, the renamed U.S. Cellular Field has replaced Wrigley Field as Chicago's true launching pad since Jerry Reinsdorf decided to move the fences in after the 2000 season. The Ballpark in Arlington, Coors Field and Miller Park were the only stadiums where more home runs were hit last season.

Defense

It's going to be interesting to see if wind conditions change this season. The latest reworking of the stadium saw some height taken off the much-criticized upper deck. Don't be surprised if some crazy things happen in the outfield in April. Groundskeeper Roger Bossard always has the infield in good shape. It's a neutral surface.

Who It Helps the Most

No surprise that Frank Thomas exercised his player option to return to the White Sox. He spent the 1990s complaining about the homers he had lost at Comiskey Park, but over the last four years, he has 85 home runs at home and 32 on the road. While conditions favor hitters, Mark Buehrle has done his best pitching at home.

Who It Hurts the Most

Carlos Lee gets caught up swinging for the fences at the Cell, and his batting average always is lower at home than on the road. Despite Buehrle's success, it's a tough place to develop young pitchers. Esteban Loaiza had more success on the road (9-4, 2.46) than at home (12-5, 3.32) during his remarkable 2003 season.

Rookies & Newcomers

There's not a ton of ground to cover in center field, which means the White Sox can use it as a way to get offensive-minded outfielders into the lineup. Carl Everett was fine there in 2003 and Jeremy Reed and Joe Borchard probably will be in future seasons. Reed could add 15-20 homer power to his high-average potential.

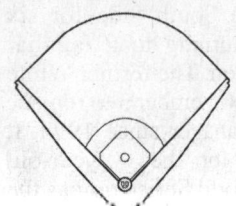

Dimensions: LF-330, LCF-377, CF-400, RCF-372, RF-335

Capacity: 47,098

Elevation: 595 feet

Surface: Grass

Foul Territory: Average

Park Factors

2003 Season

	Home Games CWS	Opp	Total	Away Games CWS	Opp	Total	Index
G	72	72	144	72	72	144	
Avg	.266	.249	.257	.264	.258	.261	98
AB	2358	2448	4806	2535	2341	4876	99
R	363	297	660	346	344	690	96
H	628	609	1237	670	605	1275	97
2B	132	122	254	143	126	269	96
3B	9	12	21	10	11	21	101
HR	115	79	194	82	65	147	134
BB	219	217	436	228	247	475	93
SO	373	511	884	425	429	854	105
E	30	46	76	52	38	90	84
E-Infield	25	40	65	44	31	75	87
LHB-Avg	.256	.256	.256	.259	.275	.269	95
LHB-HR	25	40	65	22	30	52	126
RHB-Avg	.270	.241	.258	.266	.242	.257	101
RHB-HR	90	39	129	60	35	95	138

2001-2003

	Home Games CWS	Opp	Total	Away Games CWS	Opp	Total	Index
G	216	216	432	216	216	432	100
Avg	.273	.258	.265	.266	.264	.265	100
AB	7153	7429	14582	7526	7106	14632	100
R	1156	1005	2161	1035	1057	2092	103
H	1952	1913	3865	2002	1874	3876	100
2B	381	383	764	428	377	805	95
3B	31	29	60	38	37	75	80
HR	333	259	592	244	212	456	130
BB	717	690	1407	666	694	1360	104
SO	1193	1349	2542	1306	1223	2529	101
E	114	147	261	153	131	284	92
E-Infield	103	126	229	128	105	233	98
LHB-Avg	.275	.262	.267	.252	.279	.268	99
LHB-HR	86	134	220	76	100	176	128
RHB-Avg	.272	.253	.264	.272	.249	.263	100
RHB-HR	247	125	372	168	112	280	132

2003 Rankings (American League)

- Highest home-run factor
- Highest RHB home-run factor
- Lowest error factor
- Third-lowest infield-error factor

Ozzie Guillen

2003 Season

After being away from the South Side for six years, Ozzie Guillen is returning to a familiar dugout in a brand new position. The former White Sox shortstop was hired on November 3 to replace Jerry Manuel, the club's manager since 1998. It capped a gratifying year for the 40-year-old Guillen, who picked up a World Series ring as the Florida Marlins' third-base coach. His enthusiasm for the job prompted Jerry Reinsdorf and GM Ken Williams to overlook his lack of managerial experience.

Offense

Like Manuel before him, Guillen comes to the Sox from Florida as a big believer in the importance of manufacturing runs. He'll emphasize the importance of working counts and advancing runners but, as Manuel learned, it's one thing to preach unselfishness and another to truly instill it in veteran hitters who have gotten rich by swinging for the fences.

Pitching & Defense

Guillen is a totally unknown commodity handling a pitching staff, as he has never managed or even served as a bench coach. He is likely to rely on pitching coach Don Cooper and Joe Nossek, his bench coach, and faces an immediate challenge establishing order in a bullpen that must be rebuilt. Guillen won a Gold Glove during his 16-year playing career, and good defense is obviously important to him. He might not be as quick to sacrifice fielding for hitting as was Manuel, but for the most part Manuel was only adapting to the personnel he was given.

2004 Outlook

Guillen will not have as strong of a roster as the one that finished second under Manuel in 2003, but Williams hopes players will buy into the energy the new manager brings. Unlike Manuel, who took over after the financial purge marked by the White Flag trade, Guillen will be expected to compete immediately. It's going to be an interesting year.

Born: 1/20/64 in Ocumare del Tuy, Venezuela

Playing Experience: 1985-2000, CWS, Bal, Atl, TB
Managerial Experience: No major league managing experience

Manager Statistics (Jerry Manuel)

Year	Team, Lg	W	L	Pct	GB	Finish
2003	Chicago, AL	86	76	.531	4.0	2nd Central
6 Seasons		500	471	.515	–	–

2003 Starting Pitchers by Days Rest

	<=3	4	5	6+
White Sox Starts	6	94	35	19
White Sox ERA	4.89	4.06	3.54	5.85
AL Avg Starts	2	79	50	22
AL ERA	3.19	4.64	4.57	4.98

2003 Situational Stats

	Jerry Manuel	AL Average
Hit & Run Success %	19.0	36.7
Stolen Base Success %	72.6	70.0
Platoon Pct.	56.6	61.7
Defensive Subs	64	23
High-Pitch Outings	5	5
Quick/Slow Hooks	8/14	19/16
Sacrifice Attempts	66	55

2003 Rankings—Jerry Manuel (American League)

- 1st in defensive substitutions, starts on three days rest and first-batter platoon percentage
- 3rd in steals of home plate (1), pitchouts with a runner moving (7) and pinch-hitters used (126)

Roberto Alomar

2003 Season

"Escape from New York" was the storyline of a second consecutive disappointing season for Robbie Alomar, who no longer looks like the guy who was on the short list of the best second basemen ever. His spirit, pulled down by the Mets' hopelessness, lifted when he was traded to the White Sox in early July. While he played a role in the Sox' second-half run at a Central title, his numbers in Chicago were worse than they had been in New York. It was the worst year ever for Alomar, with a drop in power continuing the deterioration of a once-great game.

Hitting

To re-establish himself, the switch-hitting Alomar must address his problems hitting righthanded. His batting average as a righty has slipped on an annual basis since 2000, when he batted .322, to his career low .189 in '03. He's still a solid hitter from the left side but does not often drive the ball. This is a guy who suddenly finds himself with bat-speed issues. He can be overpowered by good heat.

Baserunning & Defense

Alomar might have lost a tick in the field but he's still quick, especially going to his left, pulling off plenty of acrobatic catches and circus stops. He does a good job turning double plays and has a presence that steadies others on the field. He helped Jose Valentin after joining the White Sox. Alomar still has plus speed but no longer is a major threat on the bases.

2004 Outlook

This is a guy with something to prove, as he was certain to get a lukewarm response when he hit the free-agent market. Alomar appears to be at the stage of his career where he can be a useful player on an otherwise strong team, but he's not going to have a major impact on an average team.

Position: 2B
Bats: B **Throws:** R
Ht: 6' 0" **Wt:** 185

Opening Day Age: 36
Born: 2/5/68 in Ponce, PR
ML Seasons: 16
Pronunciation: AL loh mar
Nickname: Robbie

Overall Statistics

G	AB	R	H	D	T	HR	RBI	SB	BB	SO	Avg	OBP	Slg
140	516	76	133	28	2	5	39	12	59	77	.258	.333	.349
2323	8902	1490	2679	498	78	206	1110	474	1018	1109	.301	.372	.444

Where He Hits the Ball

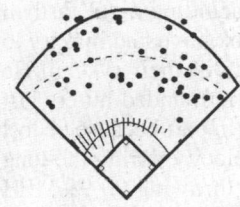 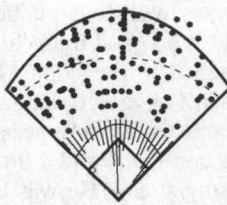

Vs. LHP   **Vs. RHP**

2003 Situational Stats

	AB	H	HR	RBI	Avg		AB	H	HR	RBI	Avg
Home	244	64	3	17	.262	LHP	140	20	2	10	.189
Road	272	69	2	22	.254	RHP	368	105	3	29	.285
First Half	298	77	2	24	.258	Sc Pos	97	27	1	34	.278
Scnd Half	218	56	3	15	.257	Clutch	66	17	0	6	.258

2003 Rankings (American League)

- 6th in bunts in play (22)
- 9th in sacrifice bunts (8) and lowest on-base percentage for a leadoff hitter (.324)
- Led the White Sox in sacrifice bunts (8), bunts in play (22) and lowest percentage of swings that missed (12.2)

Chicago (AL)

Mark Buehrle

2003 Season

While Mark Buehrle downplayed the impact, there's no denying that a spring-training contract dispute set the tone for something new—a disappointing season. Buehrle won 14 games and worked 230.1 innings, fifth-most in the league, but he also endured a nine-game losing streak over 11 starts from April 20 through June 11. That contributed to his career winning percentage dropping from .650 to .602 and his career ERA climbing from 3.52 to 3.71. If only everyone had bad years like this one. . .

Pitching

Few players Buehrle's age have better figured out the art of pitching. He works fast and throws strikes with four pitches, including a cut fastball that is so good the White Sox have had him try to teach it to the young lefties in their system. He wasn't as effective against lefthanded hitters last year as in previous seasons, in part because he lost his command and a little velocity during the long losing streak. He was back throwing 90-91 MPH after the All-Star break, when he was back to normal. One bad trend—Buehrle's ratio of strikeouts per nine innings has dropped for three years in a row, to 4.7 last year.

Defense

You run on Buehrle at your own risk. He holds runners close with one of the game's best pickoff moves. Opponents tried only five steals against him last season, succeeding just once. He is a steady fielder who has learned not to try to force the action.

2004 Outlook

For a guy who won't turn 25 until spring training, Buehrle has a ton of mileage on his arm. He appears to be extremely durable, however, showing no signs of overuse. After signing a three-year, $18 million contract in December, Buehrle is as good of a bet for 16-18 wins and 225-plus innings as anyone in the American League.

Position: SP
Bats: L **Throws:** L
Ht: 6' 2" **Wt:** 200

Opening Day Age: 25
Born: 3/23/79 in St. Charles, MO
ML Seasons: 4
Pronunciation: BURR-lee

Overall Statistics

	W	L	Pct.	ERA	G	GS	Sv	IP	H	BB	SO	HR	Avg
'03	14	14	.500	4.14	35	35	0	230.1	250	61	119	22	.278
Car.	53	35	.602	3.71	129	104	0	742.0	729	189	416	76	.258

2003 Pitching Profile

	Mark Buehrle	AL Average
Overall Strike %	64.2	62.8
1st Pitch Strike %	58.2	58.7
Ratio	1.35	1.39
Strikeouts per 9 IP	4.65	6.11
Walks per 9 IP	2.38	3.16
Home Runs per 9 IP	0.86	1.11
Strikeout/Walk Ratio	1.95	1.93
Groundball/Flyball Ratio	1.40	1.18

2003 Situational Stats

	W	L	ERA	Sv	IP		AB	H	HR	RBI	Avg
Home	8	5	3.67	0	115.1	LHB	274	72	7	38	.263
Road	6	9	4.62	0	115.0	RHB	624	178	15	75	.285
First Half	7	10	4.24	0	136.0	Sc Pos	183	57	6	87	.311
Scnd Half	7	4	4.01	0	94.1	Clutch	54	18	2	10	.333

2003 Rankings (American League)

- 1st in fielding percentage at pitcher (1.000)
- 2nd in games started and hits allowed
- 3rd in batters faced (978) and lowest stolen-base percentage allowed (20.0)
- 5th in innings pitched, pitches thrown (3,508) and GDPs induced (24)
- 7th in losses and fewest strikeouts per nine innings (4.6)
- 8th in pickoff throws (115)
- 10th in highest batting average allowed with runners in scoring position
- Led the White Sox in losses, games started and hits allowed

Bartolo Colon

Position: SP
Bats: R **Throws:** R
Ht: 5'11" **Wt:** 240

Opening Day Age: 30
Born: 5/24/73 in Altamira, DR
ML Seasons: 7
Pronunciation:
bar-TOE luh luu LONE

2003 Season

Acquired to help push the White Sox into the playoffs, Bartolo Colon did not complete the mission. It was hardly his fault, however, as he turned in a vintage season. Colon was 6-8 during the first half but bounced back to go 9-5 with a 3.52 ERA in 15 second-half starts. He worked a career-high 242 innings, throwing nine complete games.

Pitching

Colon is rightly known for his high-octane fastball, as he can seemingly run the radar gun up to 97-98 MPH at will, but he has become a pitcher in recent years. He sometimes seems willing to throw breaking balls and 93-MPH fastballs, but has the heat when he needs it. It's as if he understands how to preserve his arm throughout the long season. Colon was known as something of a wild man while with Cleveland, but last year had only three 120-pitch starts. He also walked 2.5 per nine innings. Those are Andy Pettitte numbers. He's unusually tough in day games as hitters have problems picking up the ball out of his hand.

Defense

On the mound, Colon—with legs like the trunks of Sequoia trees—is like an NBA wide-body taking up space in the lane. It should be hard to get comebackers past him, but lots of balls do shoot past him into center field. Colon has a quick release with runners on base. Opponents succeeded only once in seven stolen base attempts against him last year, and are 6-for-19 over the last two years.

2004 Outlook

The White Sox tried unsuccessfully to sign Colon to a contract extension after the season. He was one of the biggest names on the free-agent market, and the Angels gave Colon a four-year, $51 million deal that puts him at the top of the Anaheim rotation with Jarrod Washburn. As long as those massive legs hold up, Colon should be able to pitch effectively for his new club for many years to come.

Overall Statistics

	W	L	Pct.	ERA	G	GS	Sv	IP	H	BB	SO	HR	Avg
'03	15	13	.536	3.87	34	34	0	242.0	223	67	173	30	.248
Car.	100	62	.617	3.86	213	211	0	1388.2	1322	525	1120	148	.252

2003 Pitching Profile

	Bartolo Colon	AL Average
Overall Strike %	65.7	62.8
1st Pitch Strike %	63.2	58.7
Ratio	1.20	1.39
Strikeouts per 9 IP	6.43	6.11
Walks per 9 IP	2.49	3.16
Home Runs per 9 IP	1.12	1.11
Strikeout/Walk Ratio	2.58	1.93
Groundball/Flyball Ratio	0.92	1.18

2003 Situational Stats

	W	L	ERA	Sv	IP		AB	H	HR	RBI	Avg
Home	8	6	3.84	0	117.1	LHB	509	127	16	54	.250
Road	7	7	3.90	0	124.2	RHB	390	96	14	45	.246
First Half	6	8	4.14	0	134.2	Sc Pos	176	43	8	70	.244
Scnd Half	9	5	3.52	0	107.1	Clutch	95	22	2	8	.232

2003 Rankings (American League)

- 1st in complete games (9), pickoff throws (184) and GDPs induced (31)
- 2nd in innings pitched, batters faced (984) and lowest stolen-base percentage allowed (14.3)
- 3rd in balks (3) and pitches thrown (3,529)
- 4th in lowest fielding percentage at pitcher (.906)
- 5th in games started
- 6th in errors at pitcher (3)
- 7th in strikeouts
- 8th in home runs allowed
- Led the White Sox in complete games (9), innings pitched, batters faced (984), home runs allowed, wild pitches (8), balks (3), pitches thrown (3,529), pickoff throws (184), GDPs induced (31), lowest stolen-base percentage allowed (14.3), and fewest pitches thrown per batter (3.59)

Joe Crede

2003 Season

The first full big league season is a test for most players, and so it was for Joe Crede. He had whetted appetites by playing well in the second half of 2002, but didn't quite match that offensive production in '03. Crede nevertheless recovered from a disappointing first half to contribute to the White Sox' second-half run, hitting .308 with 11 homers after the All-Star break, and was steady defensively all season. He impressed many in the organization by not panicking when things went badly for him in April and May.

Hitting

Crede may have expected too much of himself after hitting 36 homers between Triple-A and the big leagues in 2002. His swing seemed a little longer earlier in the season as he tried to muscle the ball. He likes to pull the ball toward the foul pole in left field but gets more hits when he thinks about using the whole field. He struggled against righthanders last season. In his four seasons, Crede has had success jumping on first-pitch fastballs. He hit .431 on the first pitch last season. The downside is a low walks total, but he should learn to take more walks in upcoming seasons.

Baserunning & Defense

Crede looks the part at third base. He's tall, strong and flexible, with quick reactions. He does a great job coming in on grounders but has shown only average range. He has a strong, reliable arm and does not commit many errors. He's a below-average baserunner.

2004 Outlook

The White Sox hope they get more production from Crede, with 20 homers and 90-plus RBI a realistic target. He will play every day and could move up in the batting order, giving him more opportunities to drive in teammates. He could become a valuable commodity given the lack of quality third basemen in the major leagues.

Position: 3B
Bats: R **Throws:** R
Ht: 6' 2"   **Wt:** 195

Opening Day Age: 25
Born: 4/26/78 in Jefferson City, MO
ML Seasons: 4
Pronunciation: CREE-dee

Overall Statistics

	G	AB	R	H	D	T	HR	RBI	SB	BB	SO	Avg	OBP	Slg
'03	151	536	68	140	31	2	19	75	1	32	75	.261	.308	.433
Car.	228	800	99	213	43	3	31	120	2	43	129	.266	.307	.444

Where He Hits the Ball

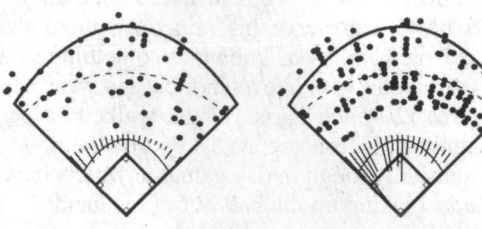

Vs. LHP   **Vs. RHP**

2003 Situational Stats

	AB	H	HR	RBI	Avg		AB	H	HR	RBI	Avg
Home	255	61	11	37	.239	LHP	150	45	6	23	.300
Road	281	79	8	38	.281	RHP	386	95	13	52	.246
First Half	302	68	8	38	.225	Sc Pos	130	37	4	52	.285
Scnd Half	234	72	11	37	.308	Clutch	69	21	2	7	.304

2003 Rankings (American League)

- 4th in fielding percentage at third base (.964)
- 5th in lowest on-base percentage and lowest batting average vs. righthanded pitchers

Carl Everett

2003 Season

In the last year of his four-year contract, Carl Everett provided proof of the talent that landed him such a big deal while he was with the Boston Red Sox. He came out of the blocks crushing the ball for Texas, hitting .306 with 14 homers and 42 RBI in 49 games through the end of May, then proved a valuable presence for the White Sox after being traded to Chicago at the beginning of July. He not only hit the ball, but did a decent job in center field as well.

Hitting

The switch-hitting Everett is a good hitter from the left side and a fairly average one batting righthanded. He is relatively tough to strike out for a guy with good power, laying off pitches outside the strike zone and cutting down his swing to put the ball in play with two strikes. There have been times in recent years when power pitchers could jam Everett on a consistent basis, but he handled the fastball better in 2003. He's never been a guy you wanted to face with men in scoring position or with a one-run lead in the ninth.

Baserunning & Defense

Everett doesn't have the speed he did five years ago but is running better than in 2002, when he was coming off surgery on his right knee. He plays all three outfield positions. Used primarily in center field last year, he sometimes had trouble in the vast open spaces of The Ballpark in Arlington but was adequate at U.S. Cellular Field, where there is less ground to cover.

2004 Outlook

Everett hit free agency at a good time in his career, but also in a buyer's market. The White Sox wanted to re-sign him, but resources dictated they would only do that if Everett found a lack of interest elsewhere.

Position: CF/LF/RF
Bats: B **Throws:** R
Ht: 6' 0" **Wt:** 215

Opening Day Age: 32
Born: 6/3/71 in Tampa, FL
ML Seasons: 11

Overall Statistics

	G	AB	R	H	D	T	HR	RBI	SB	BB	SO	Avg	OBP	Slg
'03	147	526	93	151	27	3	28	92	8	53	84	.287	.366	.510
Car.	1096	3730	583	1038	216	23	161	637	101	355	820	.278	.350	.478

Where He Hits the Ball

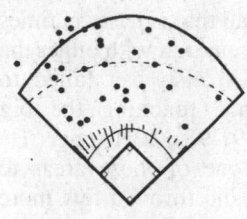 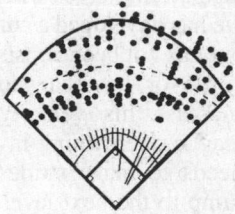

Vs. LHP   **Vs. RHP**

2003 Situational Stats

	AB	H	HR	RBI	Avg		AB	H	HR	RBI	Avg
Home	245	70	15	44	.286	LHP	138	35	4	19	.254
Road	281	81	13	48	.288	RHP	388	116	24	73	.299
First Half	307	83	18	52	.270	Sc Pos	121	41	7	61	.339
Scnd Half	219	68	10	40	.311	Clutch	67	14	4	5	.209

2003 Rankings (American League)

- 6th in hit by pitch (15)
- 9th in highest percentage of swings on the first pitch (34.8)
- 10th in errors in center field (2)
- Led the White Sox in batting average on the road (.317)

Jon Garland

2003 Season

For the second year in a row, Jon Garland had a solid but unspectacular season as a member of the White Sox' rotation. He held onto his spot all season and turned in 190-plus innings, but only matched his career-high of 12 wins. His numbers across the board were remarkably similar to 2002, with the biggest difference being that he allowed five more home runs, a disturbing trend for a sinkerballer. He had six starts in which he failed to make it through the fifth inning, the same total as a year before.

Pitching

Garland always has been a live-arm guy, with a fastball that dives when he does not overthrow it. He has developed a curveball that is nasty at times but has not been consistent enough with either the curve or his changeup. He also has failed to increase his velocity since reaching the big leagues, remaining in the 91-93 MPH range. He needs to make strides in one of those areas to jump to the next level. He did throw a few more strikes in 2003, walking only 3.5 opponents per nine innings.

Defense

Garland is an excellent fielder who handles bunts and come-backers well. He has not committed an error since 2001 and participated in four double plays over the past two years. Running on Garland is relatively easy. Runners succeeded on nine of 15 stolen-base attempts last year.

2004 Outlook

While Garland has already logged almost 600 career innings, he'll pitch almost all season at age 24. That experience should begin serving him well, and he could well blossom under new head man Ozzie Guillen. Jerry Manuel often seemed to have a quick hook with Garland, allowing him to complete only one of 94 starts. He's reached arbitration-eligible status, so it's time for him to start winning more games.

Position: SP
Bats: R **Throws:** R
Ht: 6' 6" **Wt:** 205

Opening Day Age: 24
Born: 9/27/79 in Valencia, CA
ML Seasons: 4

Overall Statistics

	W	L	Pct.	ERA	G	GS	Sv	IP	H	BB	SO	HR	Avg
'03	12	13	.480	4.51	32	32	0	191.2	188	74	108	28	.260
Car.	34	40	.459	4.60	115	94	1	571.0	581	252	323	77	.267

2003 Pitching Profile

	Jon Garland	AL Average
Overall Strike %	61.9	62.8
1st Pitch Strike %	61.5	58.7
Ratio	1.37	1.39
Strikeouts per 9 IP	5.07	6.11
Walks per 9 IP	3.47	3.16
Home Runs per 9 IP	1.31	1.11
Strikeout/Walk Ratio	1.46	1.93
Groundball/Flyball Ratio	1.38	1.18

2003 Situational Stats

	W	L	ERA	Sv	IP		AB	H	HR	RBI	Avg
Home	7	6	4.16	0	97.1	LHB	432	120	16	51	.278
Road	5	7	4.87	0	94.1	RHB	290	68	12	41	.234
First Half	6	7	4.64	0	104.2	Sc Pos	161	42	3	57	.261
Scnd Half	6	6	4.34	0	87.0	Clutch	34	6	1	2	.176

2003 Rankings (American League)
- 1st in fielding percentage at pitcher (1.000)
- 3rd in lowest strikeout-walk ratio (1.5)
- 4th in highest walks per nine innings (3.5)
- 6th in walks allowed and most run support per nine innings (6.1)
- 10th in losses, wild pitches (8) and highest ERA on the road
- Led the White Sox in walks allowed, wild pitches (8), stolen bases allowed (9) and most run support per nine innings (6.1)

Paul Konerko

2003 Season

After landing a three-year, $23 million contract, Paul Konerko could not overcome the pressure he seemed to put on himself. He got off to a terrible start at the plate, forcing him to try even harder than normal. The problem with that is he was already a max-effort guy. He seemed to be his own worst enemy until finally hitting his way out of the funk after the All-Star break. He wound up with the fewest at-bats in his five years with the White Sox, getting benched while hitting .098 in June. His average was at .184 on July 11. He hit .285 the rest of the way, but that included an all-too-familiar slump (2-for-42) to end the season.

Hitting

The weird part about Konerko's season was that he actually had his best year ever against lefties, hitting .327 with a .966 OPS. But he hit righthanders like he was swinging a wet newspaper (.187). He played on an injured left foot at the end of 2002, and there were rumors of a mysterious hip injury through 2003. It's possible physical problems restricted his ability to cover the inside part of the plate, which is why power pitchers ate him for lunch.

Baserunning & Defense

Konerko has improved his fielding. He makes the routine plays, having the highest fielding percentage among American League regulars at first base, and makes some good ones, too. He doesn't cover a lot of ground at first but does a good job scooping throws. He's a base-clogger who contributes to the White Sox' station-to-station approach.

2004 Outlook

The Sox were open to dealing Konerko but there wasn't much of a market for high-salaried guys who drive in 65 runs. The solid second half is encouraging for Konerko, but April will be the key to his season. He needs to build confidence early.

Position: 1B/DH
Bats: R **Throws:** R
Ht: 6' 2" **Wt:** 215

Opening Day Age: 28
Born: 3/5/76 in Providence, RI
ML Seasons: 7
Pronunciation: kunu- un-cue

Overall Statistics

	G	AB	R	H	D	T	HR	RBI	SB	BB	SO	Avg	OBP	Slg
'03	137	444	49	104	19	0	18	65	0	43	50	.234	.305	.399
Car.	810	2857	398	796	150	5	129	475	3	250	393	.279	.342	.470

Where He Hits the Ball

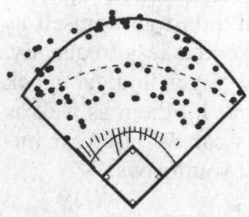 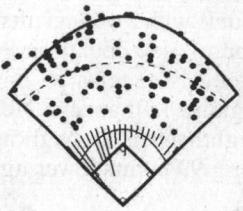

Vs. LHP   **Vs. RHP**

2003 Situational Stats

	AB	H	HR	RBI	Avg		AB	H	HR	RBI	Avg
Home	220	54	9	29	.245	LHP	150	49	10	28	.327
Road	224	50	9	36	.223	RHP	294	55	8	37	.187
First Half	233	46	5	22	.197	Sc Pos	124	27	3	42	.218
Scnd Half	211	58	13	43	.275	Clutch	64	12	3	11	.188

2003 Rankings (American League)

- 1st in GDPs (28), fielding percentage at first base (.998) and most GDPs per GDP situation (27.7%)
- 8th in lowest batting average with runners in scoring position
- 9th in batting average vs. lefthanded pitchers
- 10th in highest percentage of swings put into play (52.1)
- Led the White Sox in intentional walks (7), GDPs (28) and batting average vs. lefthanded pitchers

Carlos Lee

2003 Season

On the surface, Carlos Lee appears to have finally had a breakout season, reaching the 30-homer and 100-RBI plateaus for the first time. But it was no surprise to those who had paid attention in 2002, when he actually was a better hitter. The higher totals in 2003 were the result of an extra 131 at-bats, partly because Jerry Manuel gave him 21 more starts and partly because he was less selective at the plate.

Hitting

Lee always has had a quick bat, but he seemed to be a tick quicker this time around, perhaps because he was in better shape. His patience comes and goes, though. He attacked the first pitch with good results, but didn't get himself as many deep counts and walked far less frequently. Lee also seems to have a psychological block against lefthanders. He hasn't hit them as well as righthanders throughout his career, last year hitting 99 points lower against southpaws.

Baserunning & Defense

A good athlete with decent speed, Lee used it well in 2003, stealing a career-high 18 bases while also setting a career-high in doubles. He does not always use good judgment on the bases, however, getting himself thrown out at some bad moments. He has worked to become an average left fielder but probably never will be better than average. He occasionally gets lost on flyballs and can look bad when teams run on him.

2004 Outlook

With Magglio Ordonez, Paul Konerko and Frank Thomas locked into salaries paying them a combined $28 million, Lee was in line to become a financial casualty for the White Sox. He was a four-plus arbitration player due a significant increase from his $4.2 million salary. If he wants to stay in the upper tier of salaries, he's going to have to become an All-Star caliber player, which he has not been.

Position: LF
Bats: R **Throws:** R
Ht: 6' 2" **Wt:** 235

Opening Day Age: 27
Born: 6/20/76 in Aguadulce, Panama
ML Seasons: 5

Overall Statistics

	G	AB	R	H	D	T	HR	RBI	SB	BB	SO	Avg	OBP	Slg
'03	158	623	100	181	35	1	31	113	18	37	91	.291	.331	.499
Car.	727	2737	430	777	155	10	121	453	53	201	415	.284	.334	.480

Where He Hits the Ball

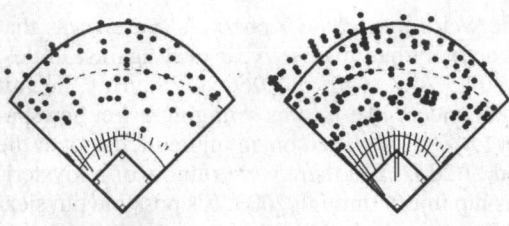

Vs. LHP   **Vs. RHP**

2003 Situational Stats

	AB	H	HR	RBI	Avg		AB	H	HR	RBI	Avg
Home	304	85	18	66	.280	LHP	165	36	5	20	.218
Road	319	96	13	47	.301	RHP	458	145	26	93	.317
First Half	340	89	14	54	.262	Sc Pos	153	53	13	85	.346
Scnd Half	283	92	17	59	.325	Clutch	89	20	2	9	.225

2003 Rankings (American League)

- 1st in errors in left field (7)
- 2nd in lowest fielding percentage in left field (.978)
- 6th in RBI, GDPs (20) and batting average with runners in scoring position
- Led the White Sox in at-bats, runs scored, singles, RBI, sacrifice flies (7), stolen bases, steals of third (2) and batting average with runners in scoring position
- Led AL left fielders in RBI

Esteban Loaiza

2003 Season

Talk about a sudden impact. After frustrating managers and pitching coaches with three different organizations, Esteban Loaiza bloomed into a Cy Young candidate (he finished second in the final AL vote) for the White Sox, who had signed him to a minor league contract. Forced to earn a job in spring training, he responded with 21 victories, tying Fernando Valenzuela's record for the most by a Mexican-born pitcher, while leading the league in strikeouts and ranking third in earned run average. An All-Star for the first time in his career, Loaiza worked five-plus innings in 32 of 34 starts and had enough left at the end to win back-to-back starts on three days' rest.

Pitching

Loaiza credits a new cut fastball for much of his new-found success. Combined with a slight increase in velocity, from 91-92 MPH to 93-94, it made him much tougher on righthanded hitters, who batted 120 points lower against him than in 2002. He has become a four-pitch pitcher, throwing both a slider and a changeup for strikes at will. He's always done a good job throwing strikes but located his pitches extremely well for most of last season.

Defense

Loaiza is a good athlete with solid fundamentals. His delivery puts him in good shape to field his position. He controls the running game well, allowing opponents to succeed on only six of their 15 stolen-base tries against him last year.

2004 Outlook

Without question, Loaiza benefited from having to prove himself as a non-roster invitee to spring training. He worked hard in the offseason and came to camp in good shape, then made an increased commitment to getting his work done between starts. It remains to be seen how he will handle success. The White Sox were wise to include a 2004 option in their minor league deal, which they exercised. They'd be happy with 15-18 wins and 200-plus innings.

Position: SP
Bats: R **Throws:** R
Ht: 6' 3" **Wt:** 215

Opening Day Age: 32
Born: 12/31/71 in Tijuana, Mexico
ML Seasons: 9
Pronunciation:
o TAY-bahn low-EYE-zah

Overall Statistics

	W	L	Pct.	ERA	G	GS	Sv	IP	H	BB	SO	HR	Avg
'03	21	9	.700	2.90	34	34	0	226.1	196	56	207	17	.233
Car.	90	82	.523	4.58	269	236	1	1480.0	1666	413	965	178	.286

2003 Pitching Profile

	Esteban Loaiza	AL Average
Overall Strike %	66.5	62.8
1st Pitch Strike %	61.9	58.7
Ratio	1.11	1.39
Strikeouts per 9 IP	8.23	6.11
Walks per 9 IP	2.23	3.16
Home Runs per 9 IP	0.68	1.11
Strikeout/Walk Ratio	3.70	1.93
Groundball/Flyball Ratio	1.44	1.18

2003 Situational Stats

	W	L	ERA	Sv	IP			AB	H	HR	RBI	Avg
Home	12	5	3.32	0	116.2	LHB		514	133	11	46	.259
Road	9	4	2.46	0	109.2	RHB		329	63	6	22	.191
First Half	11	5	2.21	0	130.1	Sc Pos		177	34	2	48	.192
Scnd Half	10	4	3.84	0	96.0	Clutch		67	12	0	2	.179

2003 Rankings (American League)

- 1st in strikeouts
- 2nd in wins, lowest ERA on the road, lowest batting average allowed vs. righthanded batters and most strikeouts per nine innings (8.2)
- 3rd in ERA, lowest batting average allowed with runners in scoring position and fewest home runs allowed per nine innings (.68)
- 4th in pitches thrown (3,511), runners caught stealing (9), lowest batting average allowed (.233) and lowest slugging percentage allowed (.350)
- Led the White Sox in ERA, wins, hit batsmen (10), runners caught stealing (9), winning percentage, highest strikeout-walk ratio (3.7), lowest batting average allowed (.233), lowest slugging percentage allowed (.350), lowest on-base percentage allowed (.286), highest groundball-flyball ratio allowed (1.4)

Magglio Ordonez

2003 Season

Here's why it's dangerous to judge a player by his standing as an All-Star. Magglio Ordonez made the American League team for the fourth time in 2003, but didn't have nearly the season he did in 2002, when he was left off the team. While Ordonez had a solid season, it was his least productive year since his rookie season of 1998. Ordonez had a very ordinary first half by his own lofty standards, but he turned up the afterburners in July and August, catapulting himself into the batting race.

Hitting

Ordonez has everything a hitter needs—good strike-zone judgment and a short, quick stroke. He pulls the ball against lefties but has opposite-field power against righthanders. Lots of his line drives hit gaps, helping him reach 70-plus extra-base hits for three years in a row. He murders pitches in the bottom half of the zone. The pitchers that have the best luck against him are breaking-ball pitchers who get him to swing at chest-high fastballs.

Baserunning & Defense

Ordonez does not have one of those eye-popping arms, but he has a quick release and accuracy. He does not have a lot of lateral range but does a good job coming in for balls—his sitting style of sliding is unique—as well as going back to the wall. He has enough speed that pitchers can't take him for granted, but he has not run a lot in the last two seasons.

2004 Outlook

Financially this is a huge season for Ordonez, whose salary jumps from $9 million to $14 million in the final year of his contract. There was not much talk about a contract extension over the off-season, in large part because of the White Sox' financial limitations. While he's a popular, home-grown star, GM Ken Williams has been forced to listen to offers for Ordonez, and a trade is not out of the question.

Position: RF
Bats: R   **Throws:** R
Ht: 6' 0"   **Wt:** 210

Opening Day Age: 30
Born: 1/28/74 in Caracas, VZ
ML Seasons: 7
Pronunciation: or-DOAN-yez
Nickname: Mags

Overall Statistics

	G	AB	R	H	D	T	HR	RBI	SB	BB	SO	Avg	OBP	Slg
'03	160	606	95	192	46	3	29	99	9	57	73	.317	.380	.546
Car.	949	3605	592	1108	232	13	178	666	82	317	409	.307	.365	.527

Where He Hits the Ball

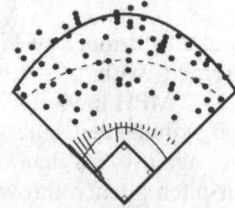   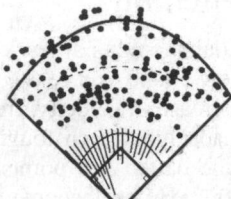

Vs. LHP   **Vs. RHP**

2003 Situational Stats

	AB	H	HR	RBI	Avg		AB	H	HR	RBI	Avg
Home	293	95	17	51	.324	LHP	164	52	12	35	.317
Road	313	97	12	48	.310	RHP	442	140	17	64	.317
First Half	346	102	17	53	.295	Sc Pos	170	53	7	69	.312
Scnd Half	260	90	12	46	.346	Clutch	80	34	2	17	.425

2003 Rankings (American League)

- 2nd in batting average in the clutch and fielding percentage in right field (.994)
- 4th in doubles
- Led the White Sox in batting average, hits, singles, doubles, total bases (331), caught stealing (5), plate appearances (674), games played, batting average in the clutch, batting average vs. righthanded pitchers, cleanup slugging percentage (.544) and batting average at home
- Led AL right fielders in batting average, home runs and RBI

Frank Thomas

2003 Season

After having his pride hurt when Jerry Reinsdorf exercised the "diminished skills" clause in his contract, Frank Thomas reasserted himself as a run-producer with his fifth career 40-homer season. Thomas' hitting was a major part of the White Sox' rise after the All-Star break, and he wasn't bad early in the year, either.

Hitting

A .321 career hitter through the 2000 season, Thomas hasn't hit above .267 since then, in part because of problems with the strike zone and frequent changes in his approach. He seemed to recognize his limitations in the second half of 2003, when he admitted that he was adopting a swing-for-the-fences mentality. The result was increased power—and some monstrous home runs—but a pedestrian average. Thomas punishes lefties but can be neutralized by righthanders who locate their fastballs. He remains patient, rarely chasing the first pitch.

Baserunning & Defense

While Thomas is content serving as the DH, for some reason he hits better when he plays first. He got 27 starts in the field in 2003 and did not embarrass himself there, committing only one error. Thomas is a station-to-station runner, which somewhat blunts the value of his taking so many walks.

2004 Outlook

Thomas had a chance to test the market as a free agent but decided to exercise his $6 million player option to return to the White Sox, who are on the hook for $8 million in 2005 and a $3.5 million buyout in '06. He is driven as much by securing his legacy as by proving anything to Reinsdorf or his peers. He's 82 homers short of 500, a level that would make him a much better bet to get into Cooperstown. It remains to be seen how Thomas will enjoy playing for former teammate Ozzie Guillen, who singled him out for criticism after being named manager.

Position: DH/1B
Bats: R **Throws:** R
Ht: 6' 5" **Wt:** 275

Opening Day Age: 35
Born: 5/27/68 in Columbus, GA
ML Seasons: 14
Nickname: Big Hurt

Overall Statistics

G	AB	R	H	D	T	HR	RBI	SB	BB	SO	Avg	OBP	Slg
153	546	87	146	35	0	42	105	0	100	115	.267	.390	.562
1851	6611	1255	2048	428	11	418	1390	32	1386	1077	.310	.428	.568

Where He Hits the Ball

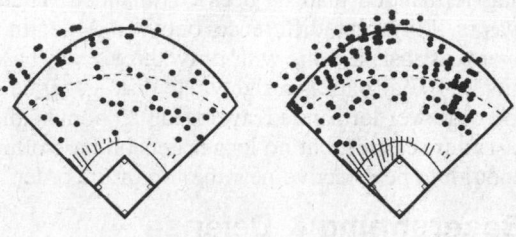

Vs. LHP   **Vs. RHP**

2003 Situational Stats

	AB	H	HR	RBI	Avg		AB	H	HR	RBI	Avg
Home	281	80	29	64	.285	LHP	149	47	17	35	.315
Road	265	66	13	41	.249	RHP	397	99	25	70	.249
First Half	301	81	20	48	.269	Sc Pos	125	35	8	52	.280
Scnd Half	245	65	22	57	.265	Clutch	76	23	7	22	.303

2003 Rankings (American League)

- 1st in lowest groundball-flyball ratio (0.5)
- 2nd in home runs, HR frequency (13.0 ABs per HR) and most pitches seen per plate appearance (4.27)
- 3rd in walks and pitches seen (2,824)
- 5th in highest percentage of pitches taken (63.4)
- Led the White Sox in home runs, walks, hit by pitch (12), times on base (258), strikeouts, pitches seen (2,824), slugging percentage, on-base percentage, HR frequency (13.0 ABs per HR) and most pitches seen per plate appearance (4.27)

Jose Valentin

2003 Season

After spending a lot of time at third base and center field the previous two years, Jose Valentin played exclusively at shortstop for the first time since his 36-error season in 2000. He continued to show signs of age at the plate, contributing with power but not as a complete hitter, but had a good year in the field. His leadership was important for a Sox team that started poorly but rallied past Kansas City and Minnesota before sliding to a second straight second-place finish.

Hitting

Why does Valentin continue switch-hitting? It's hard to imagine he'd fare worse against lefties hitting lefthanded than he does righthanded. There was a 134-point difference between Valentin's averages last season, with only three extra-base hits in 107 at-bats as a righty. He does generate a ton of power lefthanded, averaging 25 homers the last four seasons, but no longer gets on base often enough to be effective near the top of the order.

Baserunning & Defense

Valentin loved playing alongside Robbie Alomar in the second half of 2003. He had 20 errors but botched fewer routine plays than in recent seasons. He has only average range but throws well, allowing him to get outs on plays that could have gone for infield singles. Valentin has played the game hard for a long time, taking a toll on his legs. He's an aggressive baserunner who still takes chances as if he was as fast as ever.

2004 Outlook

While the White Sox would have preferred he take less this season in a renegotiated, extended contract, they nevertheless exercised a $5 million option to hang onto Valentin. He will be the primary shortstop, but could see his playing time reduced if the Sox sign a lefthanded-hitting back-up. He could extend his stay in Chicago by having a good season, as there is no heir apparent in the system.

Position: SS
Bats: B **Throws:** R
Ht: 5'10" **Wt:** 185

Opening Day Age: 34
Born: 10/12/69 in Manati, PR
ML Seasons: 12
Pronunciation: val-en-TEEN

Overall Statistics

G	AB	R	H	D	T	HR	RBI	SB	BB	SO	Avg	OBP	Slg
144	503	79	119	26	2	28	74	8	54	114	.237	.313	.463
1309	4392	708	1082	243	32	196	652	117	504	1018	.246	.324	.450

Where He Hits the Ball

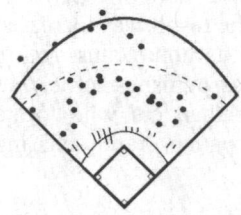   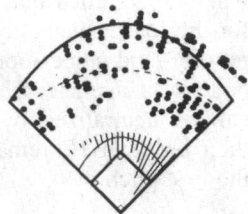

Vs. LHP   **Vs. RHP**

2003 Situational Stats

	AB	H	HR	RBI	Avg		AB	H	HR	RBI	Avg
Home	242	52	14	33	.215	LHP	107	14	2	6	.131
Road	261	67	14	41	.257	RHP	396	105	26	68	.265
First Half	298	72	13	40	.242	Sc Pos	118	27	8	44	.229
Scnd Half	205	47	15	34	.229	Clutch	63	17	4	11	.270

2003 Rankings (American League)

- 1st in lowest batting average at home
- 3rd in errors at shortstop (20) and lowest fielding percentage at shortstop (.969)
- 4th in lowest batting average
- 5th in lowest groundball-flyball ratio (0.7)
- 7th in lowest percentage of swings put into play (37.8)

Sandy Alomar Jr.

Position: C
Bats: R **Throws:** R
Ht: 6' 5" **Wt:** 235

Opening Day Age: 37
Born: 6/18/66 in Salinas, PR
ML Seasons: 16
Pronunciation: AL-loh-mar

Overall Statistics

	G	AB	R	H	D	T	HR	RBI	SB	BB	SO	Avg	OBP	Slg
'03	75	194	22	52	12	0	5	26	0	4	17	.268	.281	.407
Car.	1227	4126	485	1133	229	10	109	543	25	193	457	.275	.311	.414

2003 Situational Stats

	AB	H	HR	RBI	Avg		AB	H	HR	RBI	Avg
Home	99	23	3	10	.232	LHP	60	14	0	6	.233
Road	95	29	2	16	.305	RHP	134	38	5	20	.284
First Half	101	26	2	11	.257	Sc Pos	42	12	1	20	.286
Scnd Half	93	26	3	15	.280	Clutch	33	10	0	4	.303

2003 Season

After trading Sandy Alomar Jr. to Colorado at the deadline in 2002, the White Sox re-signed Alomar as a free agent for 2003. He turned in a solid if unremarkable season, serving as a mentor for Miguel Olivo over the first four months before taking on additional catching duties in August and September.

Hitting, Baserunning & Defense

Always an aggressive hitter, Alomar hasn't had 20 walks in a season since 1994 and these days rarely even gets to three-ball counts. He still has some power and was a dangerous hitter late in games. He has a slider-speed bat, doing most of his damage off finesse pitchers. Alomar is a skilled receiver who communicates very well with pitchers but struggles to get throws down to second base. He threw out just four of 24 basestealers (16.7 percent) last season. He's a station-to-station runner who takes few chances.

2004 Outlook

Signed in December, Alomar will return for another year as an unofficial player-coach. He is widely respected in the clubhouse and did a great job working with Olivo and the young pitchers. He is likely to stay with the White Sox' organization in some capacity when his career is over.

Tom Gordon

Position: RP
Bats: R **Throws:** R
Ht: 5'10" **Wt:** 190

Opening Day Age: 36
Born: 11/18/67 in Sebring, FL
ML Seasons: 15
Nickname: Flash

Overall Statistics

	W	L	Pct.	ERA	G	GS	Sv	IP	H	BB	SO	HR	Avg
	7	6	.538	3.16	66	0	12	74.0	57	31	91	4	.213
	113	107	.514	4.07	591	203	110	1807.0	1647	870	1637	144	.242

2003 Situational Stats

	W	L	ERA	Sv	IP		AB	H	HR	RBI	Avg
Home	6	2	1.96	9	41.1	LHB	130	30	3	17	.231
Road	1	4	4.68	3	32.2	RHB	138	27	1	6	.196
First Half	4	5	3.35	3	45.2	Sc Pos	69	16	2	20	.232
Scnd Half	3	1	2.86	9	28.1	Clutch	168	38	3	17	.226

2003 Season

Signed to a one-year contract, Tom Gordon gave the White Sox his best performance since he led the American League in saves in 1998. The key was that he was free of the elbow and shoulder injuries that allowed him to make more than 40 appearances only once in the previous five seasons. He opened the year as a setup man for Billy Koch and finished it sharing the closer's role with lefty Damaso Marte.

Pitching & Defense

There are stretches when Gordon's stuff is as electric as any reliever in baseball. But his 95-MPH fastball and knee-buckling curveball sometimes wander to the plate, missing the strike zone. The key is throwing his curveball for strikes. Once he establishes it, everything else usually falls into place. Gordon is a superior athlete who fields his position very well and can control the running game.

2004 Outlook

The White Sox wanted to re-sign Gordon, but their hands were tied by the $6.375 million commitment to Koch. Gordon filed for free agency and signed a two-year, $7.25 million deal with the Yankees. He'll set up for ace closer Mariano Rivera.

Chicago (AL)

91

Tony Graffanino

Position: SS/2B/3B
Bats: R **Throws:** R
Ht: 6' 1" **Wt:** 190

Opening Day Age: 31
Born: 6/6/72 in
Amityville, NY
ML Seasons: 8
Pronunciation:
graf-a-NEEN-oh

Overall Statistics

	G	AB	R	H	D	T	HR	RBI	SB	BB	SO	Avg	OBP	Slg
'03	90	250	51	65	15	3	7	23	8	24	37	.260	.331	.428
Car.	574	1443	234	373	75	15	32	149	31	147	280	.258	.330	.398

2003 Situational Stats

	AB	H	HR	RBI	Avg		AB	H	HR	RBI	Avg
Home	129	35	4	11	.271	LHP	165	50	6	21	.303
Road	121	30	3	12	.248	RHP	85	15	1	2	.176
First Half	141	35	5	13	.248	Sc Pos	47	12	2	17	.255
Scnd Half	109	30	2	10	.275	Clutch	30	7	2	6	.233

2003 Season

If only every major leaguer got as much out of his ability as Tony Graffanino. The veteran backup again contributed in a variety of ways in 2003, especially against lefthanded pitchers. He did a good job platooning with Jose Valentin at shortstop and getting on base when called on as a lead-off man.

Hitting, Baserunning & Defense

Graffanino historically has not had a big platoon difference, but he struggled against righthanders last season. He can drive a get-it-over fastball over the fence. He knows the strike zone and does not often get himself out. Graffanino doesn't have terrific speed but studies pitchers and gets good jumps. He plays all over the infield. While primarily a second baseman earlier in his career, he's done a good job at short and third base the last two seasons.

2004 Outlook

Graffanino, a favorite of White Sox owner Jerry Reinsdorf, filed for free agency but was expected to return to Chicago. If he does stay put, he could get significant playing time in the shortstop platoon or at second base, where the Sox had a vacancy with Roberto Alomar filing for free agency.

Billy Koch

Position: RP
Bats: R **Throws:** R
Ht: 6' 3" **Wt:** 215

Opening Day Age: 29
Born: 12/14/74 in
Rockville Center, NY
ML Seasons: 5
Pronunciation:
COTCH

Overall Statistics

	W	L	Pct.	ERA	G	GS	Sv	IP	H	BB	SO	HR	Avg
'03	5	5	.500	5.77	55	0	11	53.0	59	28	42	10	.281
Car.	27	22	.551	3.82	332	0	155	358.1	334	155	307	35	.248

2003 Situational Stats

	W	L	ERA	Sv	IP		AB	H	HR	RBI	Avg
Home	3	2	5.34	6	32.0	LHB	109	32	5	17	.294
Road	2	3	6.43	5	21.0	RHB	101	27	5	22	.267
First Half	5	5	5.63	11	38.1	Sc Pos	61	19	4	30	.311
Scnd Half	0	0	6.14	0	14.2	Clutch	100	27	4	21	.270

2003 Season

Call it Nightmare on 35th Street for Billy Koch. He came to the White Sox with huge expectations after averaging 40 saves the previous two seasons, but wound up with only 11 saves. He lost his velocity in June and his closer's job in July. He never got either back. Koch's downfall was not as simple as the injury, which was diagnosed as tendinitis.

Pitching & Defense

Koch is all about intimidation, which means he must have his fastball in the upper 90s to succeed. He seemed stripped bare when his heater dropped to 91-93 MPH on the radar gun. He throws a slider and a sinker but it does not appear either is good enough without his fastball putting hitters on the defensive. Koch is fairly quick off the mound for a big guy but is slow to the plate, making him an easy target for base thieves.

2004 Outlook

Koch represents a huge project for new manager Ozzie Guillen and Don Cooper, his pitching coach. Cooper failed to get Koch to snap out of it last year but must find a way for him to improve his mechanics, and repeat his delivery.

Damaso Marte

Tough On Lefties

Position: RP
Bats: L **Throws:** L
Ht: 6' 2" **Wt:** 200

Opening Day Age: 29
Born: 2/14/75 in Santo Domingo, DR
ML Seasons: 4
Pronunciation: da-muh-so mar-TAY

Overall Statistics

	W	L	Pct.	ERA	G	GS	Sv	IP	H	BB	SO	HR	Avg
'03	4	2	.667	1.58	71	0	11	79.2	50	34	87	3	.185
Car.	5	5	.500	2.97	167	0	21	185.0	144	70	201	16	.217

2003 Situational Stats

	W	L	ERA	Sv	IP			AB	H	HR	RBI	Avg
Home	2	0	1.69	7	37.1	LHB		125	21	1	12	.168
Road	2	2	1.49	4	42.1	RHB		146	29	2	16	.199
First Half	4	1	1.66	4	43.1	Sc Pos		75	14	1	23	.187
Scnd Half	0	1	1.49	7	36.1	Clutch		169	36	2	22	.213

2003 Season

There are few bigger bullpen weapons in the American League than Damaso Marte. Acquired in a minor league trade with Pittsburgh two springs ago, Marte has compiled a 2.12 ERA in his two seasons in Chicago, and leads the Sox with 21 saves over the last two seasons. He has proven himself durable, setting career highs for games and innings last year.

Pitching & Defense

Marte often makes hitters look silly with his two best pitches—a fastball in the 92-93 MPH range and a slider that acts like a slurve. He also has a cut fastball in his repertoire, making him even tougher for hitters to figure out. Marte struck out 9.8 per nine innings last season, holding both left- and righthanded hitters to averages below .200. He allowed only one homer in 125 at-bats by left-handed batters a year ago. Marte fields his position decently but is an easy target for basestealers.

2004 Outlook

With Billy Koch a question mark, look for Marte to play an even more important role in manager Ozzie Guillen's bullpen. This could be the year he becomes the primary closer. If not, he'll be extremely valuable in the bullpen mix.

Miguel Olivo

Position: C
Bats: R **Throws:** R
Ht: 6' 0" **Wt:** 220

Opening Day Age: 25
Born: 7/15/78 in Villa Vasquez, DR
ML Seasons: 2

Overall Statistics

	G	AB	R	H	D	T	HR	RBI	SB	BB	SO	Avg	OBP	Slg
'03	114	317	37	75	19	1	6	27	6	19	80	.237	.287	.360
Car.	120	336	39	79	20	1	7	32	6	21	85	.235	.287	.363

2003 Situational Stats

	AB	H	HR	RBI	Avg		AB	H	HR	RBI	Avg
Home	144	37	4	15	.257	LHP	86	26	4	12	.302
Road	173	38	2	12	.220	RHP	231	49	2	15	.212
First Half	191	42	5	16	.220	Sc Pos	65	15	3	23	.231
Scnd Half	126	33	1	11	.262	Clutch	38	12	1	4	.316

2003 Season

Making the jump from Double-A Birmingham last year, Miguel Olivo established himself as the White Sox' No. 1 catcher. He was a steadying presence behind the plate, especially contributing to the success of Esteban Loaiza. However, he did not hit as well as was expected.

Hitting, Baserunning & Defense

Olivo sometimes seemed overmatched against hard throwers, struggling to make contact. He did not have the plate discipline he had shown in the minors. Scouts are split on whether he has the bat speed to become a high-average hitter, but his minor league portfolio suggests he will make improvements and could become a 20-homer man. Olivo has a strong arm, which helped him rank third among qualifying AL catchers in throwing out basestealers. He has good movements blocking pitches but had too many passed balls and errors. He's a good athlete with good speed, stealing 29 bases two years ago in Double-A.

2004 Outlook

Look for improvement as Olivo's comfort level increases. He started 98 games in 2003 but could jump to 120 if he is healthy all season. He's got the potential to develop into an All-Star if he improves as a hitter.

Aaron Rowand

Position: CF/LF/RF
Bats: R **Throws:** R
Ht: 6' 1" **Wt:** 210

Opening Day Age: 26
Born: 8/29/77 in
Portland, OR
ML Seasons: 3

Overall Statistics

	G	AB	R	H	D	T	HR	RBI	SB	BB	SO	Avg	OBP	Slg
'03	93	157	22	45	8	0	6	24	0	7	21	.287	.327	.452
Car.	282	582	84	159	29	2	17	73	5	34	103	.273	.325	.418

2003 Situational Stats

	AB	H	HR	RBI	Avg		AB	H	HR	RBI	Avg
Home	81	23	5	15	.284	LHP	65	22	1	7	.338
Road	76	22	1	9	.289	RHP	92	23	5	17	.250
First Half	111	28	3	14	.252	Sc Pos	32	13	2	17	.406
Scnd Half	46	17	3	10	.370	Clutch	20	4	1	2	.200

2003 Season

After forcing his way into the lineup as the regular center fielder in the second half of 2002, Aaron Rowand tore up in his left shoulder in a dirt bike accident. It cost him the momentum he had gained. Rowand was sent to Triple-A Charlotte when his batting average dipped to .133 on May 1. He returned and hit very well in June and July (.403), but took a seat on the bench after the acquisition of Carl Everett.

Hitting, Baserunning & Defense

Rowand is an aggressive hitter who appears to be becoming less patient at the plate. He is a line-drive hitter but can generate power from his strong upper body. Rowand stole bases in the minor leagues but didn't attempt a steal last year. He doesn't look like a prototype center fielder but gets the most out of his ability.

2004 Outlook

This is a major season for Rowand, whose salary could climb if he establishes himself as a regular. He will need to prove himself for new manager Ozzie Guillen, who has rarely seen him. Even with Everett out of the picture, there's competition from Willie Harris and prospects Joe Borchard and Jeremy Reed.

Scott Schoeneweis

Position: RP
Bats: L **Throws:** L
Ht: 6' 0" **Wt:** 190

Opening Day Age: 30
Born: 10/2/73 in Long
Branch, NJ
ML Seasons: 5
Pronunciation:
show-en-weiss

Overall Statistics

	W	L	Pct.	ERA	G	GS	Sv	IP	H	BB	SO	HR	Avg
'03	3	2	.600	4.18	59	0	0	64.2	63	19	56	3	.252
Car.	30	32	.484	5.08	203	74	1	597.1	639	226	325	66	.274

2003 Situational Stats

	W	L	ERA	Sv	IP		AB	H	HR	RBI	Avg
Home	2	1	3.60	0	35.0	LHB	119	27	0	20	.227
Road	2	1	4.85	0	29.2	RHB	131	36	3	16	.275
First Half	1	1	4.13	0	32.2	Sc Pos	69	20	0	32	.290
Scnd Half	2	1	4.22	0	32.0	Clutch	24	6	0	1	.250

2003 Season

Anaheim's World Series success in 2002 came after Mike Scioscia moved Scott Schoeneweis out of the rotation to open a spot for rookie John Lackey. Schoeneweis was never entirely on board with the switch, however, and his desire to move out of the bullpen surfaced after the Angels' slow start. The result was a trade to the White Sox. Jerry Manuel used Schoeneweis exclusively in relief, saying he had not been conditioned to start. He did not have a major impact.

Pitching & Defense

Schoeneweis has a fastball that hits the low 90s and a power sinker. Those pitches allow him to be successful against lefthanders, but he never has developed the third pitch he needs to neutralize righthanded hitters. That explains his career ERA of 5.28 as a starter. The Sox will watch his change-up closely in spring training. He is a solid fielder but has an average move to first base.

2004 Outlook

Schoeneweis presented a difficult financial decision to the White Sox. He's expendable as a reliever but could add some needed depth at the end of the starting rotation, where he figures to compete for a spot.

Scott Sullivan

Signed By
ROYALS

Position: RP
Bats: R **Throws:** R
Ht: 6' 3" **Wt:** 210

Opening Day Age: 33
Born: 3/13/71 in
Carrollton, AL
ML Seasons: 9

Overall Statistics

	W	L	Pct.	ERA	G	GS	Sv	IP	H	BB	SO	HR	Avg
'03	6	0	1.000	3.66	65	0	0	64.0	48	32	56	6	.205
Car.	37	24	.607	3.91	509	0	9	677.0	598	257	577	81	.238

2003 Situational Stats

	W	L	ERA	Sv	IP		AB	H	HR	RBI	Avg
Home	2	0	6.19	0	36.1	LHB	84	20	2	11	.238
Road	4	0	0.33	0	27.2	RHB	150	28	4	18	.187
First Half	6	0	3.86	0	44.1	Sc Pos	78	14	3	25	.179
Scnd Half	0	0	3.20	0	19.2	Clutch	86	12	3	9	.140

2003 Season

It was an eventful season for the unassuming Scott Sullivan. The consummate middle reliever gave up Sammy Sosa's 500th career homer in April, then was traded for the first time in August. He pitched well for both Cincinnati and the White Sox, with the only real disappointment being that he spent a stint on the disabled list for the second consecutive year. Sullivan nevertheless made 60-plus appearances for the sixth consecutive season.

Pitching & Defense

Sullivan has regained the bite on his sinker, which had left him when he battled through shoulder troubles in 2002. He was once again tough on righthanded hitters, holding them below .200. His three-quarters motion gives him some deceptiveness. He needs to get ahead in the count to be at his best and did not have his usual control last season, walking 4.5 per nine innings. He does little these days to control the running game.

2004 Outlook

Sullivan might be on the downhill side after years of heavy usage in Cincinnati, yet could play a role in a good bullpen. The White Sox wanted to re-sign him but were in a financial bind, and Sullivan inked a two-year, $5 million deal with the Royals.

Dan Wright

Position: SP
Bats: R **Throws:** R
Ht: 6' 5" **Wt:** 225

Opening Day Age: 26
Born: 12/14/77 in
Longview, TX
ML Seasons: 3

Overall Statistics

	W	L	Pct.	ERA	G	GS	Sv	IP	H	BB	SO	HR	Avg
'03	1	7	.125	6.15	20	15	1	86.1	91	46	47	16	.277
Car.	20	22	.476	5.52	66	60	1	349.0	369	156	219	60	.273

2003 Situational Stats

	W	L	ERA	Sv	IP		AB	H	HR	RBI	Avg
Home	0	1	4.40	1	47.0	LHB	189	53	10	37	.280
Road	1	6	8.24	0	39.1	RHB	140	38	6	15	.271
First Half	0	4	5.93	0	54.2	Sc Pos	90	17	3	35	.189
Scnd Half	1	3	6.54	1	31.2	Clutch	8	3	0	1	.375

2003 Season

Elbow problems during spring training led to a wasted season for Dan Wright, who had won 14 games in 2002. Wright opened the season on the disabled list and never really got untracked. His problems had a lot to do with the team's second-place finish and Jerry Manuel's firing. That's a lot to put on Wright but, next to Billy Koch, he was the team's biggest disappointment.

Pitching & Defense

Wright's best pitch, a knuckle-curve, puts strain on the elbow. It didn't appear that he was comfortable throwing it last year. His velocity suffered at times, rarely getting above 90-91 MPH. He threw in the mid-90s in the minors but rarely has shown the same velocity during his two seasons in the big leagues. Control was also a problem for Wright last season. He fields his position decently but is slow to home plate.

2004 Outlook

This is a huge year for Wright, who won't be counted on as he was a year ago. He needs a strong spring training to reassert himself. A role change is not out of the question. Some of the Sox brass have always felt Wright's stuff would be well-suited for a bullpen role.

Other Chicago White Sox

Jon Adkins (**Pos**: RHP, **Age**: 26)

	W	L	Pct.	ERA	G	GS	Sv	IP	H	BB	SO	HR	Avg
'03	0	0	–	4.82	4	0	0	9.1	8	7	3	1	.250
Car.	0	0	–	4.82	4	0	0	9.1	8	7	3	1	.250

Acquired from Oakland for Ray Durham near the trade deadline in 2002, Adkins was a better pitcher at Triple-A Charlotte after the deal. He's in the mix for a job after going 7-8 with a 3.96 ERA there. 2004 Outlook: C

Jamie Burke (**Pos**: C, **Age**: 32, **Bats**: R)

	G	AB	R	H	D	T	HR	RBI	SB	BB	SO	Avg	OBP	Slg
'03	6	8	0	3	0	0	0	2	0	0	0	.375	.375	.375
Car.	15	13	1	4	0	0	0	2	0	0	2	.308	.308	.308

Burke got his second cup of coffee late in his second straight season of batting better than .300 at the Triple-A level. He picked up three hits and two RBI, but he likely won't do enough to ever stick. 2004 Outlook: C

Brian Daubach (**Pos**: 1B/DH, **Age**: 32, **Bats**: L)

	G	AB	R	H	D	T	HR	RBI	SB	BB	SO	Avg	OBP	Slg
'03	95	183	26	42	11	0	6	21	1	34	54	.230	.352	.388
Car.	616	1925	258	505	129	10	90	322	5	219	515	.262	.342	.480

Daubach can be a valuable role player, but the Sox were unable to get him enough at-bats with both Frank Thomas and Paul Konerko on the roster and released him in December. He had averaged 21 homers and 75 RBI a year with Boston. 2004 Outlook: B

Matt Ginter (**Pos**: RHP, **Age**: 26)

	W	L	Pct.	ERA	G	GS	Sv	IP	H	BB	SO	HR	Avg
'03	0	0	–	13.50	3	0	0	3.1	2	1	0	1	.182
Car.	3	0	1.000	5.82	63	0	1	106.2	113	43	67	14	.276

Once a highly regarded prospect, Ginter has been successful at Triple-A Charlotte in two of the last three seasons, but he's been homer-prone and hasn't shut down righthanded hitters as a major leaguer. 2004 Outlook: C

Willie Harris (**Pos**: CF/2B, **Age**: 25, **Bats**: L)

	G	AB	R	H	D	T	HR	RBI	SB	BB	SO	Avg	OBP	Slg
'03	79	137	19	28	3	1	0	5	12	10	28	.204	.259	.241
Car.	137	324	36	69	8	1	2	17	20	19	56	.213	.255	.262

Harris can play a few positions, and he batted .380 with a .470 OBP in 100 at-bats at Triple-A Charlotte in 2003. But he separated a shoulder three weeks after a May recall and hasn't hit much in the majors when healthy. 2004 Outlook: C

Jose Paniagua (**Pos**: RHP, **Age**: 30)

	W	L	Pct.	ERA	G	GS	Sv	IP	H	BB	SO	HR	Avg
'03	0	0	–	108.00	1	0	0	0.1	3	1	0	0	.750
Car.	18	21	.462	4.49	270	14	13	357.0	354	188	276	40	.262

After a poor 2002, Paniagua was cut by the lowly Devil Rays in spring training, signed with the Sox in August, arrived in September, but was cut a week later after flipping off fans after a bad outing. 2004 Outlook: C

Mike Porzio (**Pos**: LHP, **Age**: 31)

	W	L	Pct.	ERA	G	GS	Sv	IP	H	BB	SO	HR	Avg
'03	1	1	.500	6.43	3	3	0	14.0	18	1	9	2	.321
Car.	3	3	.500	5.90	51	3	0	71.2	79	34	52	17	.281

Porzio has been marginally effective as a Triple-A swingman the last three seasons, which hasn't translated well to Chicago. Lefthanders have batted .310 and slugged .531 against him, limiting his chances. 2004 Outlook: C

Armando Rios (**Pos**: CF, **Age**: 32, **Bats**: L)

	G	AB	R	H	D	T	HR	RBI	SB	BB	SO	Avg	OBP	Slg
'03	49	104	4	22	3	0	2	11	0	5	13	.212	.245	.298
Car.	419	1021	135	275	55	8	36	167	14	115	206	.269	.341	.445

Rios was a prospect with surprising pop for a guy his size, but serious injuries have plagued him nearly every time he's had a chance to get a larger role. He's past his prime and looking for a job. 2004 Outlook: C

David Sanders (**Pos**: LHP, **Age**: 24)

	W	L	Pct.	ERA	G	GS	Sv	IP	H	BB	SO	HR	Avg
'03	0	0	–	6.14	20	0	0	22.0	25	11	14	5	.281
Car.	0	0	–	6.14	20	0	0	22.0	25	11	14	5	.281

The lefty was a productive reliever in the high minors, posting four saves and a 2.41 ERA in Double- and Triple-A ball. After a decent start with the Sox in April, he bombed in July and didn't return. 2004 Outlook: B

Josh Stewart (**Pos**: LHP, **Age**: 25)

	W	L	Pct.	ERA	G	GS	Sv	IP	H	BB	SO	HR	Avg
'03	1	2	.333	5.96	5	5	0	25.2	28	16	13	4	.272
Car.	1	2	.333	5.96	5	5	0	25.2	28	16	13	4	.272

Stewart had a mildly promising 2002 campaign at Double-A Birmingham, but a blood clot in his right shoulder led to a circulatory problem in his hand last summer. He'll be back in the spring. 2004 Outlook: C

Kelly Wunsch (**Pos**: LHP, **Age**: 31)

	W	L	Pct.	ERA	G	GS	Sv	IP	H	BB	SO	HR	Avg
'03	0	0	–	2.75	43	0	0	36.0	17	25	33	1	.139
Car.	10	5	.667	3.69	209	0	1	151.1	114	82	122	12	.209

The sidearming southpaw has managed to get righthanders out, too, but he's been dominating against lefties over his career, limiting them to a .180 average and .261 slugging mark. He's a key asset. 2004 Outlook: B

Chicago White Sox Minor League Prospects

Organization Overview:

While the Sox' commitment to the minor leagues remains strong, the willingness to trade away prospects has depleted the level of talent. GM Ken Williams traded six prospects in midseason in 2003, including top-10 players Anthony Webster, a center fielder who went to Texas in the Carl Everett trade, and Royce Ring, a left-hander who went to the Mets in the Roberto Alomar deal. The Sox also lost righthander Brian West to the football program at LSU. Chicago did see catcher Miguel Olivo establish himself last season, and outfielders Jeremy Reed and Joe Borchard will try to make the jump this year. No rookie pitchers provided a major impact. The ones most likely to this season are Jon Rauch, Neal Cotts and Arnie Munoz.

Joe Borchard

Position: OF   **Opening Day Age:** 25
Bats: B **Throws:** R   **Born:** 11/25/78 in
Ht: 6' 5" **Wt:** 220   Panorama City, CA

Recent Statistics

	G	AB	R	H	D	T	HR	RBI	SB	BB	SO	Avg
2003 AAA Charlotte	114	435	62	110	20	2	13	53	2	27	103	.253
2003 AL Chicago	16	49	5	9	1	0	1	5	0	5	18	.184

Once viewed as a future star, Borchard's stock has fallen badly. His free-swinging ways have worsened the last two years at Triple-A. He no longer draws many walks, either, making his strikeouts even more of an issue. He has hit .200 with only three homers and 32 strikeouts in 85 big league at-bats. The former Stanford quarterback hits massive home runs but not enough of them. Borchard's downhill slide started after he broke a bone in his right foot in the spring of 2002, and he ended up taking last winter off for a much needed mental and physical break. The White Sox will watch him closely this spring, but he's almost certainly set for a third consecutive season at Charlotte.

Neal Cotts

Position: P   **Opening Day Age:** 24
Bats: L **Throws:** L   **Born:** 3/25/80 in
Ht: 6' 2" **Wt:** 200   Belleville, IL

Recent Statistics

	W	L	ERA	G	GS	Sv	IP	H	R	BB	SO	HR
2000 AA Birmingham	9	7	2.16	21	21	0	108.1	67	32	56	133	2
2003 AL Chicago	1	1	8.10	4	4	0	13.1	15	12	17	10	1

Not many people knew Cotts when the White Sox got him from Oakland in the Billy Koch-Keith Foulke trade. But he used his deceptive fastball to get to the big leagues one year after working for Oakland in the high-A California League. Cotts only throws about 91 MPH, but hitters don't seem to pick up his pitches well. He's

struck out 11.2 per nine innings in the minor leagues and did not seem overmatched against big league hitters. He walked way too many, however, and wound up back with Double-A Birmingham to finish out the season. Cotts goes to spring training with a chance to win a job in Ozzie Guillen's rotation, but more than likely will spend most of the season in Triple-A.

Kris Honel

Position: P   **Opening Day Age:** 21
Bats: R **Throws:** R   **Born:** 11/7/82 in
Ht: 6' 5" **Wt:** 190   Bourbonnais, IL

Recent Statistics

	W	L	ERA	G	GS	Sv	IP	H	R	BB	SO	HR
2002 A Kannapolis	9	8	2.82	26	26	0	153.1	128	57	52	152	12
2002 A Winston-Sal	0	0	1.69	1	1	0	5.1	3	2	3	8	0
2003 AA Birmingham	1	0	3.75	2	2	0	12.0	9	6	6	13	2
2003 A Winston-Sal	9	7	3.11	24	24	0	133.0	122	51	42	122	7

Honel is the crown jewel of the White Sox' pitching stable. He's a former first-round pick who led high Class-A Winston-Salem to the Carolina League title in 2003. He was one of the league's top pitchers during the regular season and won twice during the Warthogs' 5-0 playoff run. Honel was lightly pitched as a high-schooler in the Chicago's southwest suburbs and has shown a live arm as a pro. His throws 91-93 MPH with an excellent knuckle-curve. He is a polished product who expects a lot of himself. If he passes his next test at Double-A, it might not be long before he is pitching in front of hometown fans in Chicago.

Arnaldo Munoz

Position: P   **Opening Day Age:** 21
Bats: L **Throws:** L   **Born:** 6/21/82 in Mao,
Ht: 5' 9" **Wt:** 170   DR

Recent Statistics

	W	L	ERA	G	GS	Sv	IP	H	R	BB	SO	HR
2002 AA Birmingham	6	0	2.61	51	0	6	72.1	62	29	29	78	6
2003 AAA Charlotte	4	3	4.75	49	0	6	55.0	52	35	27	63	7

Few minor leaguers have bigger curveballs than Munoz' "Snapdragon," which neutralizes righthanded hitters and is downright unfair against lefthanders. He complements his curve with a sneaky quick fastball. He's already well established in his native Dominican Republic, where he was named Pitcher of the Year and Rookie of the Year in the winter of 2002-03. Munoz went directly from the Dominican to his first big league spring training and appeared to be fatigued. He spent the season with Triple-A Charlotte, starting badly but pitching well in the second half of the season. He's a little guy who has great presence on the mound, almost daring hitters to hit him. He's almost certain to be in the White Sox' bullpen before 2004 is over.

Enemencio Pacheco

Position: P   **Opening Day Age:** 25
Bats: R **Throws:** R   **Born:** 8/31/78 in Santo
Ht: 6' 0" **Wt:** 160   Domingo, DR

Recent Statistics

	W	L	ERA	G	GS	Sv	IP	H	R	BB	SO	HR
2002 A Salem	2	2	3.16	41	0	6	51.1	52	22	26	31	1
2002 A Winston-Sal	1	1	4.74	8	4	0	24.2	31	17	8	24	1
2003 AA Birmingham	12	2	2.56	30	24	0	151.1	131	51	51	116	5

Next to Jeremy Reed's rapid ascension, Pacheco was the best surprise in the Sox' system in 2003. It's hard to see why Colorado would have included a pitcher with such potential in a 2002 deal for veteran catcher Sandy Alomar Jr. Pacheco barely earned a spot in the bullpen at Double-A Birmingham out of spring training but evolved into one of the best pitchers in the Southern League. The hard-thrower greatly improved his command after being moved into the starting rotation. He throws in the mid-90s and has improved his breaking pitch. The Sox view him as a versatile pitcher who either could earn a spot in their starting rotation or help in the bullpen, possibly even as a setup man.

Jon Rauch

Position: P   **Opening Day Age:** 25
Bats: R **Throws:** R   **Born:** 9/27/78 in
Ht: 6' 11" **Wt:** 260   Louisville, KY

Recent Statistics

	W	L	ERA	G	GS	Sv	IP	H	R	BB	SO	HR
2002 AAA Charlotte	7	8	4.28	19	19	0	109.1	91	60	42	97	14
2002 AL Chicago	2	1	6.59	8	6	0	28.2	28	26	14	19	7
2003 AAA Charlotte	7	1	4.11	24	23	0	124.2	121	60	35	94	16

The 6-foot-11 Rauch should be a tough prospect to miss. But he might as well have been in the Witness Relocation program for most of 2003. He was beaten out by Esteban Loaiza and Josh Stewart for the last two spots in the Sox' rotation during spring training and never got much consideration for a job. He quietly put together a solid season at Triple-A Charlotte, putting himself back into the 2004 picture. He is not overpowering, throwing his fastball in the low 90s, but he gets some rarely seen arm angles with his height. The 2000 *Baseball America* Minor League Player of the Year has won everywhere he's been, but has not pitched consistently when he's had big league opportunities.

Jeremy Reed

Position: OF   **Opening Day Age:** 22
Bats: L **Throws:** L   **Born:** 6/15/81 in San
Ht: 6' 0" **Wt:** 185   Dimas, CA

Recent Statistics

	G	AB	R	H	D	T	HR	RBI	SB	BB	SO	Avg
2002 A Kannapolis	57	210	37	67	15	0	4	32	17	11	24	.319
2003 A Winston-Sal	65	222	37	74	18	1	4	52	27	41	17	.333
2003 AA Birmingham	66	242	51	99	17	3	7	43	18	29	19	.409

After initially flying under the radar, Reed put together a wire-to-wire performance in his first full pro season, which has him on the express train toward U.S. Cellular Field. He showed tremendous instincts to go along with one of the best bats in the minor leagues. He hit .373 overall last season, including .409 in 66 games with Double-A Birmingham. He followed that up by earning a starting spot on the Team USA squad that was upset by Mexico in the Olympic qualifier. Reed has the speed to steal bases and enough power to hit 15-20 homers. He has a strong arm and holds his own in all three outfield spots. The White Sox have juggled center fielders since the Lance Johnson era, but Reed could settle in for a long stay before the 2004 season is over.

Ryan Wing

Position: P   **Opening Day Age:** 22
Bats: L **Throws:** L   **Born:** 2/1/82 in Murrieta,
Ht: 6' 2" **Wt:** 170   CA

Recent Statistics

	W	L	ERA	G	GS	Sv	IP	H	R	BB	SO	HR
2002 A Kannapolis	12	7	3.78	25	21	0	123.2	111	64	60	109	6
2003 A Winston-Sal	9	7	2.98	26	26	0	145.0	116	62	67	107	9

Drafted one round after Kris Honel in 2001, Wing has moved up the ladder alongside him. They've given their managers a lefty-righty combination at the front of the rotation, and one day figure to be pitching in the same starting rotation for the White Sox. Wing is tough on lefthanded hitters with low-90s velocity and a nasty slider, which dives late. He has been durable as a pro but needs to improve his command. He was an All-Star in the high Class-A Carolina League last season, and will move with Honel to Double-A to start 2004. The Sox have not been hesitant to pluck pitchers from the Southern League, so Wing could put himself into consideration with a strong spring training and fast start at Birmingham.

Others to Watch

The White Sox added outfield depth by selecting the University of Arizona's **Brian Anderson** (22) and Iowa high-schooler **Ryan Sweeney** (19) 1-2 in the 2003 draft. Anderson's a center fielder with power; Sweeney is a pure hitter who is built for right field. . . Righthander **Felix Diaz** (23) might not have the stamina to get to the big leagues as a starter, but his velocity could make him a force as a setup reliever. He'll try to earn a job in spring training. . . At 27, **Ross Gload** is no kid. He's been to the big leagues with two other teams. But the White Sox saw enough of him at Triple-A Charlotte to believe he can help. He could get significant playing time if Paul Konerko is traded. . . Lefthander **Ryan Meaux** (25), who was acquired from San Francisco in 2002, had 12 saves between high Class-A Winston-Salem and Double-A Birmingham. He doesn't throw real hard but has pinpoint command, striking out 72 while allowing only four unintentional walks last season.

Jacobs Field

Offense

Historically, Jacobs Field has been a hitter's paradise. Power hitters who can drive the ball from right-center field to the right-field line can flourish at this park. A long snap of cold weather from April to mid-June hurt power production last year —141 homers were hit here in 2003 compared to 171 in 2002— but when temperatures rise, there's a natural jet stream to right-center field that smart hitters can use. The 19-foot wall that extends from the left-field line to left-center field will turn homers into doubles. Righthanded hitters with an upper cut can conquer that wall.

Defense

The Indians made the second-most errors in the American League last season, though only 44 percent came at home. Every outfield wall is padded, generating consistent bounces off the wall for outfielders. Defenders welcomed the new warning track around the field and the padded fences in front of the dugouts. There's little foul territory, so at-bats get extended. The infield and outfield grass is kept at a fair length.

Who It Helps the Most

Lefthanded-hitting Jody Gerut used the jet stream and short right-field wall to hit 13 of his 22 homers. Righthanded relievers David Riske (.200 opponent batting average), Jason Boyd (.141), Danys Baez (.205) and Rafael Betancourt (.176) pitched well because they threw hard and usually were limited to one-inning appearances.

Who It Hurts the Most

Lefties who can't keep the ball out of the air will pay a price. C.C. Sabathia (10 homers), Terry Mulholland (10) and Billy Traber (eight) were stung by the longball. Rookie righthander Jason Davis fell into the same trap, going 3-6 and allowing 12 homers at home.

Rookies & Newcomers

The Indians used 54 players in 2003, so just about every prospect got a good look at Jacobs Field. Projected starter Cliff Lee, who missed much of last year with injury, made four starts there and has to work on keeping the ball in the park.

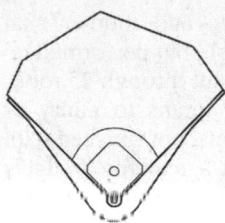

Dimensions: LF-325, LCF-370, CF-405, RCF-375, RF-325

Capacity: 43,368

Elevation: 660 feet

Surface: Grass

Foul Territory: Small

Park Factors

2003 Season

	Home Games			Away Games			
	Indians	Opp	Total	Indians	Opp	Total	Index
G	72	72	144	72	72	144	
Avg	.251	.253	.252	.260	.274	.267	95
AB	2420	2526	4946	2519	2410	4929	100
R	297	315	612	331	374	705	87
H	607	640	1247	654	660	1314	95
2B	132	125	257	133	135	268	96
3B	7	11	18	16	12	28	64
HR	63	66	129	86	94	180	71
BB	204	223	427	193	224	417	102
SO	457	461	918	474	370	844	108
E	50	60	110	61	38	99	111
E-Infield	44	53	97	53	33	86	113
LHB-Avg	.251	.248	.249	.263	.284	.271	92
LHB-HR	41	24	65	42	34	76	87
RHB-Avg	.251	.257	.254	.257	.268	.263	97
RHB-HR	22	42	64	44	60	104	60

2001-2003

	Home Games			Away Games			
	Indians	Opp	Total	Indians	Opp	Total	Index
G	215	215	430	217	217	434	
Avg	.260	.266	.263	.265	.273	.269	98
AB	7197	7577	14774	7572	7264	14836	101
R	1024	1074	2098	1082	1115	2197	96
H	1870	2018	3888	2005	1983	3988	98
2B	382	424	806	379	412	791	102
3B	25	32	57	53	54	107	53
HR	249	212	461	265	213	478	97
BB	668	764	1432	709	739	1448	99
SO	1366	1551	2917	1408	1290	2698	109
E	139	163	302	167	127	294	104
E-Infield	123	143	266	137	108	245	110
LHB-Avg	.260	.271	.265	.263	.285	.273	97
LHB-HR	149	88	237	145	83	228	102
RHB-Avg	.260	.263	.261	.266	.265	.265	99
RHB-HR	100	124	224	120	130	250	92

2003 Rankings (American League)

- Second-highest strikeout factor
- Third-highest infield-error factor
- Lowest home-run factor
- Lowest LHB batting-average factor
- Lowest RHB home-run factor
- Second-lowest run factor
- Third-lowest batting-average factor
- Third-lowest triple factor

Cleveland

Eric Wedge

2003 Season

Eric Wedge showed patience and motivational skills in his first year on the job, but performed no miracles. The Indians, who went through 25 rookies and lost most of their veterans to injury or trades, had some good moments, but finished with 94 losses. It was hard to get a feel for Wedge's managerial style because he often disdained strategy in favor of player development. He and his coaching staff played the season like a 162-game version of spring training.

Offense

Wedge envisions an offense with several players hitting 20-30 homers instead of one or two hitting 35-45. He's not crazy about the stolen base, but wants players to be able to steal, take good leads and run the bases with intelligent aggressiveness. The problem is he didn't see much of either in 2003. He showed patience with young hitters, stressing improvement from one at-bat to the next. He doesn't platoon much and wants a leadoff hitter who can steal a base in obvious situations.

Pitching & Defense

The Indians are rebuilding around pitching and Wedge, a former catcher, considers that one of his strengths. He watched his pitchers carefully last summer, monitoring pitch counts to protect his young starters. He gave the bullpen a month to flesh itself out and then established roles. He prefers to have one closer, but is not afraid to make a change. Lefties Billy Traber and Brian Tallet suffered serious elbow injuries, but Traber had a pre-existing injury and Tallet spent most of the year in Buffalo. Defensively, Wedge likes versatile players, especially in the outfield. He gives his catchers a lot of responsibility.

2004 Outlook

Wedge and general manager Mark Shapiro think the Indians might contend by midseason. That's a long shot unless the offense improves dramatically. Wedge has the security of a new contract, which runs through 2006 with options for 2007 and 2008. Wedge used 145 different lineups last season, tied for the most in the big leagues. He'd like to stabilize the order in 2004.

Born: 1/27/68 in Fort Wayne, IN

Playing Experience: 1991-1994, Bos, Col

Managerial Experience: 1 season

Manager Statistics

Year	Team, Lg	W	L	Pct	GB	Finish
2003	Cleveland, AL	68	94	.420	22.0	4th Central
1 Season		68	94	.420	–	–

2003 Starting Pitchers by Days Rest

	<=3	4	5	6+
Indians Starts	0	54	60	36
Indians ERA	–	4.36	4.33	4.74
AL Avg Starts	2	79	50	22
AL ERA	3.19	4.64	4.57	4.98

2003 Situational Stats

	Eric Wedge	AL Average
Hit & Run Success %	36.0	36.7
Stolen Base Success %	58.5	70.0
Platoon Pct.	67.1	61.7
Defensive Subs	23	23
High-Pitch Outings	1	5
Quick/Slow Hooks	24/13	19/16
Sacrifice Attempts	68	55

2003 Rankings (American League)

- 1st in starting lineups used (145)
- 2nd in double steals (6)
- 3rd in steals of home plate (1) and 2+ pitching changes in low-scoring games (32)

Danys Baez

2003 Season

Danys Baez' first full year as a closer was so erratic that he ended it as a setup man. He saved 25 games, but blew 10 and lost nine. He set a club record for righthanded relievers by making 73 appearances, but didn't pitch the last week of the season because of a twisted right ankle. Baez converted 12 of 13 save opportunities from May 2 through June 17, but blew three of his next eight chances and lost the closer's job August 18.

Pitching

Baez is strong, durable and throws 93-97 MPH. He throws a two- and four-seam fastball and a splitter. He started working on a curveball when he lost the closer's job, but it's not refined. Baez had trouble controlling his emotions as a closer. He overthrew his fastball, trying to get three outs with one pitch, instead of attacking hitters one pitch at a time. Baez has pitched in a variety of roles, but the Indians feel he's best suited for short relief because he wasn't successful developing secondary pitches as a starter. He's competitive, well conditioned and will take the ball. Last season he showed he could pitch three or four days in a row with good results.

Defense

Baez gets off the mound fast on balls hit in front of him. He has good range to his right and left and is quick to cover first base. Baez tends to rush his throws at close range. He has left the imprint of a baseball on more than one first baseman's stomach. Baez was effective controlling the running game as a starter, but ignored it as a reliever.

2004 Outlook

The Indians tried to trade Baez after outbidding the Yankees in 1999 with a four year, $14.5 million deal. They also debated non-tendering him and trying to re-sign him for less money. Instead they ran Baez through outright waivers, assigned him to the minors and then added him back to the 40-man roster, concluding they now weren't bound by the rule that he had to be offered at least 80 percent of his $5.1 million salary from 2003. Baez' future in Cleveland may hinge upon a union battle over whether the Indians can offer him less than $4.1 million for 2004.

Position: RP
Bats: R **Throws:** R
Ht: 6' 3" **Wt:** 225

Opening Day Age: 26
Born: 9/10/77 in Pinar del Rio, Cuba
ML Seasons: 3
Pronunciation: DAN-ees BUY-ez

Overall Statistics

	W	L	Pct.	ERA	G	GS	Sv	IP	H	BB	SO	HR	Avg
'03	2	9	.182	3.81	73	0	25	75.2	65	23	66	9	.229
Car.	17	23	.425	3.92	155	26	31	291.1	259	125	248	28	.238

2003 Pitching Profile

	Danys Baez	AL Average
Overall Strike %	64.0	62.8
1st Pitch Strike %	58.8	58.7
Ratio	1.16	1.39
Strikeouts per 9 IP	7.85	6.11
Walks per 9 IP	2.74	3.16
Home Runs per 9 IP	1.07	1.11
Strikeout/Walk Ratio	2.87	1.93
Groundball/Flyball Ratio	1.07	1.18

2003 Situational Stats

	W	L	ERA	Sv	IP		AB	H	HR	RBI	Avg
Home	1	5	2.89	14	46.2	LHB	151	43	4	16	.285
Road	1	4	5.28	11	29.0	RHB	133	22	5	18	.165
First Half	0	6	3.40	21	45.0	Sc Pos	95	18	3	27	.189
Scnd Half	2	3	4.40	4	30.2	Clutch	191	44	6	29	.230

2003 Rankings (American League)

- 1st in blown saves (10) and relief losses (9)
- 2nd in lowest save percentage (71.4)
- 6th in games pitched
- 8th in games finished (46)
- 9th in saves
- Led the Indians in games pitched, saves, games finished (46), lowest batting average allowed vs. righthanded batters, save percentage (71.4), lowest batting average allowed with runners in scoring position, blown saves (10) and relief losses (9)

Casey Blake

2003 Season

Casey Blake and the Indians were a good match last spring. Cleveland didn't have a third baseman ready for the big leagues and Blake spent seven pro seasons looking for a chance. Blake led the Indians in games played, hits and doubles. He started and ended the season in slumps, but hit .307 in June and .262 in July. Blake tired in September.

Hitting

Blake showed power throughout his minor league career and it translated to the big leagues in 2003. He's a gap hitter and most of his power is to the big part of ballparks. Blake can work the count, but took a lot of called third strikes on breaking balls that he thought were off the plate. Manager Eric Wedge used him in every spot in the lineup except leadoff because he recognizes hitting situations. Blake led the Indians with eight sacrifice flies and eight sacrifice bunts. He did not hit well with runners in scoring position.

Baserunning & Defense

On a team that ran the bases like its pants were on fire, Blake actually knew what he was doing. He can steal a base if needed, but excelled going from first to third or second to home. Blake had the sixth-best fielding percentage among AL third basemen despite making 19 errors. He has an accurate arm, but his range is limited. Blake starts the 5-4-3 double play quickly and charges bunts well. He made 12 starts at first and Wedge often moved him there for defensive purposes in the late innings.

2004 Outlook

Late last season, general manager Mark Shapiro named Blake his third baseman for 2004. Not bad for a guy who signed as a minor league free agent last December. Blake is perfect for a rebuilding team. He offers leadership and comes cheap after playing his first full season in the big leagues. The Indians will eventually find someone to replace Blake, but if he makes it a two- or three-year gig, he'll pay for his retirement.

Position: 3B/1B
Bats: R **Throws:** R
Ht: 6' 2" **Wt:** 210

Opening Day Age: 30
Born: 8/23/73 in Des Moines, IA
ML Seasons: 5

Overall Statistics

	G	AB	R	H	D	T	HR	RBI	SB	BB	SO	Avg	OBP	Slg
'03	152	557	80	143	35	0	17	67	7	38	109	.257	.312	.411
Car.	201	669	92	169	41	0	19	74	10	49	142	.253	.310	.399

Where He Hits the Ball

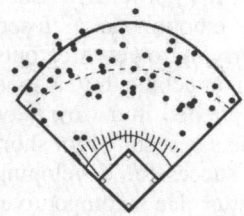
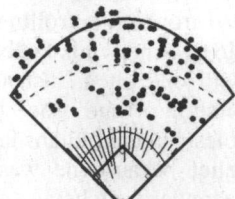

Vs. LHP   **Vs. RHP**

2003 Situational Stats

	AB	H	HR	RBI	Avg		AB	H	HR	RBI	Avg
Home	264	62	2	22	.235	LHP	159	39	7	21	.245
Road	293	81	15	45	.276	RHP	398	104	10	46	.261
First Half	295	80	10	37	.271	Sc Pos	129	30	6	50	.233
Scnd Half	262	63	7	30	.240	Clutch	84	19	2	10	.226

2003 Rankings (American League)

- 3rd in errors at third base (19)
- 4th in lowest fielding percentage at third base (.952)
- 5th in caught stealing (9)
- Led the Indians in at-bats, runs scored, hits, singles, doubles, sacrifice bunts (8), sacrifice flies (8), caught stealing (9), hit by pitch (10), times on base (191), strikeouts, pitches seen (2,414), plate appearances (621), games played, batting average with two strikes (.207) and lowest percentage of swings on the first pitch (18.1)

Milton Bradley

2003 Season

Milton Bradley's goal last year was to play 150-160 games. A strained right hamstring and a season-ending bone bruise in his lower back limited him to 101 games. Bradley opened with a 14-game hitting streak and reached base in his first 31 games. The hamstring injury put him on the DL on April 26, when he was hitting .471. The back injury ended his season on August 9.

Hitting

The switch-hitting Bradley crushed lefthanded pitching last year, but also held his own against righties. Bradley opened 2003 batting leadoff and displayed great patience. He maintained that patience when he returned from his hamstring injury and was moved to the middle of the order. Bradley is a line-drive, contact hitter who tries to pull lefties and hit the ball to the opposite field against righties. Pitchers try to get him out on inside fastballs at the waist and breaking balls down and away.

Baserunning & Defense

Bradley acted like he didn't want to steal bases in 2002, but when he opened 2003 in the leadoff spot, he suddenly started running. He led the team with 17 steals despite missing 61 games. There always seems to be something bubbling inside Bradley and it usually surfaces in his baserunning. He was benched for a game last year because he didn't run out a popup, which led to a shouting match with manager Eric Wedge. Bradley has good range and jumping ability in center field. He has 15 assists in the last two seasons, which bear testament to the strength and accuracy of his right arm.

2004 Outlook

Bradley is a handful. The Indians tried more than once last season to trade him. But general manager Mark Shapiro, while saying there's no player he wouldn't deal, seems committed to opening this year with him. He believes Bradley's talent will reduce the time it takes to rebuild. To make that happen Bradley has to play a full season, something he hasn't been able to do the last two years.

Position: CF
Bats: B **Throws:** R
Ht: 6' 0" **Wt:** 190

Opening Day Age: 25
Born: 4/15/78 in Harbor City, CA
ML Seasons: 4

Overall Statistics

	G	AB	R	H	D	T	HR	RBI	SB	BB	SO	Avg	OBP	Slg
'03	101	377	61	121	34	2	10	56	17	64	73	.321	.421	.501
Car.	318	1094	151	289	77	9	22	128	33	131	228	.264	.345	.411

Where He Hits the Ball

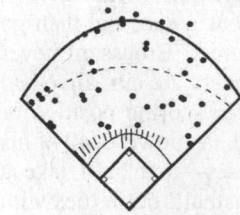
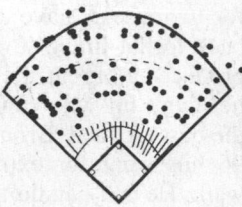

Vs. LHP   **Vs. RHP**

2003 Situational Stats

	AB	H	HR	RBI	Avg		AB	H	HR	RBI	Avg
Home	189	56	4	21	.296	LHP	112	45	4	19	.402
Road	188	65	6	35	.346	RHP	265	76	6	37	.287
First Half	293	96	7	44	.328	Sc Pos	85	27	0	41	.318
Scnd Half	84	25	3	12	.298	Clutch	55	17	0	4	.309

2003 Rankings (American League)

- 1st in batting average vs. lefthanded pitchers
- 4th in cleanup slugging percentage (.564)
- 6th in lowest stolen-base percentage (70.8)
- 10th in errors in center field (2)
- Led the Indians in batting average, stolen bases, walks, intentional walks (8), slugging percentage, on-base percentage, batting average with runners in scoring position, batting average vs. lefthanded pitchers, batting average at home and batting average on the road

Cleveland

Ben Broussard

2003 Season

Ben Broussard started 2003 on the disabled list with a strained right oblique muscle. He opened his season at Triple-A Buffalo and was promoted to Cleveland on May 13. He became the Indians' primary first baseman, hitting .292 in May and .270 through the All-Star break. Broussard's best day came on July 11, when he hit two homers and drove in five runs against the White Sox. Despite a 10-game hitting streak in September, he faded badly in the second half.

Hitting

Broussard hit 16 homers in 386 at-bats last year, but it's hard to remember any of them. His season seemed to be filled with white noise. He'd hit .250 for two weeks, have a decent game, and then go back to flat-lining it. It seemed Broussard never produced a big hit. Lefthanders ate him alive and he didn't hit with runners in scoring position or the bases loaded. Broussard has power—40 of his 96 hits went for extra bases—and he'll take a walk. He can handle the fastball, but lefties with good location give him trouble.

Baserunning & Defense

Last spring Broussard and Travis Hafner competed at first base. Broussard was much more agile and confident around the bag. He also seemed at ease because the Indians weren't going to bounce him between first and left field, as they did in 2002. But Broussard had his problems during the regular season, making nine errors and ranking 10th among AL first basemen in fielding percentage. He has decent range, but had trouble picking balls in the dirt. Broussard, who stole five bases, runs well for his size.

2004 Outlook

The Indians' front office and coaching staff are split on who'll play first in 2004. Manager Eric Wedge prefers Broussard because he's steady and consistent. In the front office, some prefer Hafner because of his power potential. They both hit left-handed so a platoon is out of the question. If the Indians don't trade one of them, the odd man out will pick up at-bats at designated hitter.

Position: 1B
Bats: L **Throws:** L
Ht: 6' 2" **Wt:** 220

Opening Day Age: 27
Born: 9/24/76 in Beaumont, TX
ML Seasons: 2
Pronunciation: brew-SARD

Overall Statistics

	G	AB	R	H	D	T	HR	RBI	SB	BB	SO	Avg	OBP	Slg
'03	116	386	53	96	21	3	16	55	5	32	75	.249	.312	.443
Car.	155	498	63	123	25	3	20	64	5	39	100	.247	.308	.430

Where He Hits the Ball

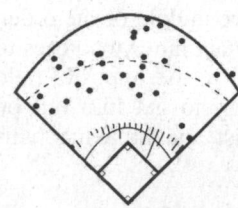 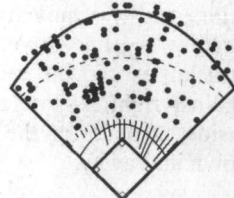

Vs. LHP   **Vs. RHP**

2003 Situational Stats

	AB	H	HR	RBI	Avg		AB	H	HR	RBI	Avg
Home	174	40	7	25	.230	LHP	103	18	2	12	.175
Road	212	56	9	30	.264	RHP	283	78	14	43	.276
First Half	174	47	8	27	.270	Sc Pos	101	23	3	35	.228
Scnd Half	212	49	8	28	.231	Clutch	66	16	1	9	.242

2003 Rankings (American League)

- 2nd in lowest fielding percentage at first base (.991)
- 5th in errors at first base (9)
- 8th in lowest batting average with the bases loaded (.111) and lowest batting average with two strikes (.146)

Coco Crisp

2003 Season

Coco Crisp made a good impression in his first extended stay in the majors. After hitting .360 at Triple-A Buffalo, he was promoted to Cleveland on June 10 when Ellis Burks went on the disabled list. He rotated between center field, left and designated hitter until he took over center following Milton Bradley's back injury in August. Crisp had a 13-game hitting streak and batted .351 (40-for-114) in July. He ended the year in a 3-for-39 slump.

Hitting

The switch-hitting Crisp understands a leadoff hitter's job. He works hard to stay on top of the ball, hitting line drives as opposed to flyballs. He put 37 bunts in play and has the speed to turn them into hits. Crisp needs to improve his on-base percentage by drawing more walks and taking advantage of favorable hitting counts. He's a spray hitter who hit lefties well. Crisp has a quick bat and has some quiet power that has yet to show itself. Right now he's vulnerable to breaking balls late in the count.

Baserunning & Defense

Crisp's game screams leadoff hitter. He's strong and wiry with an extra gear. But with all that speed, he's still learning how to steal bases. Crisp needs work on his leads because he was vulnerable to pickoffs in 2003. He has enough speed to score from first on a double, but ran into several outs because he didn't recognize situations. Crisp started 51 games in center and 38 in left and made only one error. He compensates for a below-average arm with accuracy and a quick release.

2004 Outlook

Crisp may start 2004 at Buffalo because of a crowded outfield. Milton Bradley could knock him out of center field, which means he'll be competing with Jody Gerut, Alex Escobar, Ryan Ludwick and Matt Lawton in left and right field. Crisp probably doesn't have enough power to win a corner-outfield job, but if he can improve his ability to reach base, he will be back in Cleveland sometime during the year.

Position: CF/LF
Bats: B **Throws:** R
Ht: 6' 0" **Wt:** 185

Opening Day Age: 24
Born: 11/1/79 in Los Angeles, CA
ML Seasons: 2

Overall Statistics

	G	AB	R	H	D	T	HR	RBI	SB	BB	SO	Avg	OBP	Slg
'03	99	414	55	110	15	6	3	27	15	23	51	.266	.302	.353
Car.	131	541	71	143	24	8	4	36	19	34	70	.264	.305	.360

Where He Hits the Ball

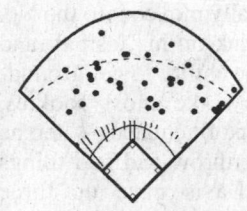 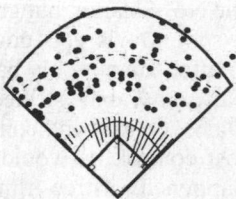

Vs. LHP   **Vs. RHP**

2003 Situational Stats

	AB	H	HR	RBI	Avg		AB	H	HR	RBI	Avg
Home	215	57	3	20	.265	LHP	112	36	0	8	.321
Road	199	53	0	7	.266	RHP	302	74	3	19	.245
First Half	126	32	0	7	.254	Sc Pos	64	19	0	23	.297
Scnd Half	288	78	3	20	.271	Clutch	61	8	0	1	.131

2003 Rankings (American League)

- 1st in lowest stolen-base percentage (62.5) and lowest on-base percentage for a leadoff hitter (.305)
- 3rd in bunts in play (37) and lowest batting average in the clutch
- 4th in highest percentage of swings put into play (53.5)
- 5th in caught stealing (9)
- Led the Indians in triples, caught stealing (9), bunts in play (37), steals of third (3) and fewest GDPs per GDP situation (7.1%)

Jason Davis

2003 Season

Jason Davis was good, bad and mediocre last year. He led American League rookies with 165.1 innings pitched, but made just two starts after August 19 because of tendinitis in his right shoulder. He pitched well against quality opponents, beating Seattle and Boston and holding the Yankees to four earned runs in 13.1 innings in consecutive no-decision starts. Yet Davis didn't win a game in a nine-start stretch from July 4 to August 19.

Pitching

Davis is a power pitcher who throws a sinking fastball, splitter and slider. The sinker, thrown at 93-97 MPH, is his best pitch. He began 2003 as the No. 4 starter, but gradually moved into the No. 2 spot. Davis gets good sink on his fastball and splitter. He not only has the ability to get ground-ball outs, but strikeouts. Like most rookies, Davis' control and command fluctuated. When he lost control, he would overthrow and bad things happened. Three times Davis gave up three homers in a game. The Indians said there was nothing seriously wrong with Davis when they limited him to two starts after August 20. He seemed very durable until then.

Defense

A former high school basketball player, Davis showed range and agility in fielding his position. But he often was moving too fast or not thinking ahead, because his six errors tied for the most in the league among pitchers. Davis, who didn't always pitch well after a mistake was made behind him, threw nine wild pitches and committed two balks. He kept runners close at first, picking off four and allowing just three steals in 11 attempts.

2004 Outlook

The Indians believe C.C. Sabathia and Davis will give them a strong one-two punch in the 2004 rotation. Manager Eric Wedge limited Davis' innings and pitches last summer. This year he's expected to loosen the reins. He'd like to see Davis reach 200 innings. The Indians haven't had a 20-game winner since Gaylord Perry in 1974. Some in the organization believe Davis one day will end that drought.

Position: SP
Bats: R **Throws:** R
Ht: 6' 6" **Wt:** 210

Opening Day Age: 23
Born: 5/8/80 in Chattanooga, TN
ML Seasons: 2

Overall Statistics

	W	L	Pct.	ERA	G	GS	Sv	IP	H	BB	SO	HR	Avg
'03	8	11	.421	4.68	27	27	0	165.1	172	47	85	25	.273
Car.	9	11	.450	4.45	30	29	0	180.0	184	51	96	26	.268

2003 Pitching Profile

	Jason Davis	AL Average
Overall Strike %	64.1	62.8
1st Pitch Strike %	60.5	58.7
Ratio	1.32	1.39
Strikeouts per 9 IP	4.63	6.11
Walks per 9 IP	2.56	3.16
Home Runs per 9 IP	1.36	1.11
Strikeout/Walk Ratio	1.81	1.93
Groundball/Flyball Ratio	1.40	1.18

2003 Situational Stats

	W	L	ERA	Sv	IP			AB	H	HR	RBI	Avg
Home	3	6	4.32	0	89.2	LHB		344	89	14	49	.259
Road	5	5	5.11	0	75.2	RHB		287	83	11	38	.289
First Half	7	7	4.60	0	105.2	Sc Pos		136	43	8	65	.316
Scnd Half	1	4	4.83	0	59.2	Clutch		40	12	1	4	.300

2003 Rankings (American League)

- 1st in ERA among rookies, errors at pitcher (6) and lowest fielding percentage at pitcher (.857)
- 2nd in losses among rookies
- 4th in lowest stolen-base percentage allowed (27.3) and wins among rookies
- 6th in wild pitches (9), least run support per nine innings (4.5) and fewest strikeouts per nine innings (4.6)
- 7th in balks (2), runners caught stealing (8), fewest pitches thrown per batter (3.54) and highest ERA
- 8th in highest slugging percentage allowed (.452), highest batting average allowed with runners in scoring position and most home runs allowed per nine innings (1.36)
- 10th in lowest strikeout-walk ratio (1.8)
- Led the Indians in losses, home runs allowed, wild pitches (9), balks (2) and pickoff throws (102)

Jody Gerut

2003 Season

Tired of being considered an extra outfielder, Jody Gerut took part in a unique conditioning program before spring training last year. Gerut had a great spring, but still spent most of April at Triple-A Buffalo. When he did get to Cleveland, he became the first rookie to lead the Indians in homers and RBI since Joe Charboneau in 1980. He led AL rookies in slugging percentage and was third in homers and extra-base hits.

Hitting

Gerut proved to be such a versatile hitter that he batted in every spot in the lineup. He spent most of his time in the third hole, which is usually reserved for the team's most complete hitter. Gerut hurt righthanders, but lefthanders neutralized him with inside fastballs and sliders and breaking balls off the plate. Gerut can use the whole field, but mostly he's a pull hitter to right field. When Gerut first joined the Indians, he struggled with information overload in preparing to face pitchers, but he gradually found a program that gave him an uncluttered focus.

Baserunning & Defense

Gerut played all three outfield positions in 2003, but spent most of his time in right. He displayed quality defense, showing range, diving catches and no fear of the outfield wall. Gerut has an above-average arm, especially from right field, and recorded nine assists. He has average speed going down the line and can steal a base now and then. He'll go into second base hard to break up a double play and knows how to go from first to third and second to home.

2004 Outlook

Unless Gerut gets hit by a falling piano, he'll be starting in left or right field in 2004. The Indians see him developing into a complete hitter along the lines of Brian Giles. They don't think he'll hit 40 homers in a season, but they do think he's capable of hitting 25-35. Gerut must improve against lefties and start showing power to left-center and center to make that happen.

Position: RF/LF/CF/DH
Bats: L **Throws:** L
Ht: 6' 0" **Wt:** 190

Opening Day Age: 26
Born: 9/18/77 in Elmhurst, IL
ML Seasons: 1
Pronunciation: GARE ot

Overall Statistics

	G	AB	R	H	D	T	HR	RBI	SB	BB	SO	Avg	OBP	Slg
'03	127	480	66	134	33	2	22	75	4	35	70	.279	.336	.494
Car.	127	480	66	134	33	2	22	75	4	35	70	.279	.336	.494

Where He Hits the Ball

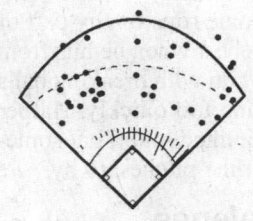 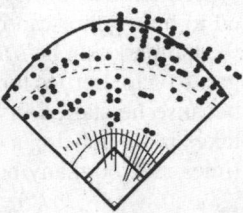

Vs. LHP   **Vs. RHP**

2003 Situational Stats

	AB	H	HR	RBI	Avg		AB	H	HR	RBI	Avg
Home	244	64	13	39	.262	LHP	134	28	0	14	.209
Road	236	70	9	36	.297	RHP	346	106	19	61	.306
First Half	219	62	10	37	.283	Sc Pos	116	29	7	52	.250
Scnd Half	261	72	12	38	.276	Clutch	77	17	0	5	.221

2003 Rankings (American League)

- 3rd in home runs among rookies
- 4th in RBI among rookies
- 5th in batting average among rookies
- 6th in batting average with the bases loaded (.500)
- 7th in errors in left field (3)
- 8th in highest percentage of swings put into play (52.1) and lowest batting average vs. lefthanded pitchers
- Led the Indians in home runs, total bases (237), RBI, GDPs (13), batting average with the bases loaded (.500) and batting average vs. righthanded pitchers

Travis Hafner

2003 Season

Travis Hafner started the season in a 4-for-32 slump because of a sore right wrist. A broken big toe on Hafner's right foot put him on the disabled list on May 13, which led to a stint at Triple-A Buffalo. Hafner returned July 12 and was the first Indian to hit for the cycle in 25 years when he executed the feat against the Twins on August 14. He hit .321-5-14 in August.

Hitting

At the start of the season, Hafner stood on top of the plate. Pitchers, especially righthanders, jammed him with fastballs and he couldn't make solid contact. Hitting coach Eddie Murray convinced Hafner to move off the plate and he started to hit. Hafner can hit home runs to any part of the ballpark, but he's at his best when he hits from gap-to-gap. Lefties fooled him with breaking balls because he started his swing too quickly. Hafner takes pride in being a disciplined hitter, but sometimes lets too many borderline pitches go by.

Baserunning & Defense

Hafner's nickname is Pronk, which stands for "half project, half donkey." Hafner definitely remains a project as a first baseman. He works hard in practice, but when the game starts and the action speeds up, he seems to get tight. He's agile for a 240-pounder and can handle routine grounders and popups, but he has trouble scooping low throws. Hafner runs the bases hard, if not fast. He completed his cycle with a triple that featured an all-out sprint around the bases and a head-first slide into third that almost knocked down the Metrodome.

2004 Outlook

If the Indians don't trade Hafner, and he doesn't beat out Ben Broussard at first, he may share time with a cast of thousands at designated hitter. The Indians see Hafner as someone who eventually could hit 25-35 homers a year and have a .365-.380 on-base percentage because of his plate discipline. They believe he's going to hit lefties because he did in the minors and doesn't bail out against them.

Position: DH/1B
Bats: L **Throws:** R
Ht: 6' 3" **Wt:** 240

Opening Day Age: 26
Born: 6/3/77 in Jamestown, ND
ML Seasons: 2
Pronunciation: HAF-ner

Overall Statistics

	G	AB	R	H	D	T	HR	RBI	SB	BB	SO	Avg	OBP	Slg
'03	91	291	35	74	19	3	14	40	2	22	81	.254	.327	.485
Car.	114	353	41	89	23	4	15	46	2	30	96	.252	.327	.467

Where He Hits the Ball

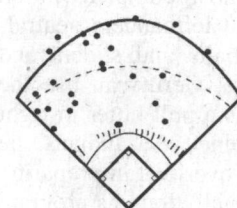
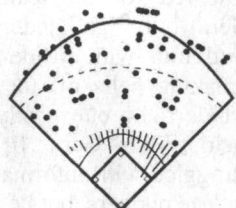

Vs. LHP   **Vs. RHP**

2003 Situational Stats

	AB	H	HR	RBI	Avg		AB	H	HR	RBI	Avg
Home	141	36	7	21	.255	LHP	84	16	2	12	.190
Road	150	38	7	19	.253	RHP	207	58	12	28	.280
First Half	104	23	4	14	.221	Sc Pos	61	14	2	21	.230
Scnd Half	187	51	10	26	.273	Clutch	53	5	1	2	.094

2003 Rankings (American League)

- 1st in lowest batting average in the clutch
- 7th in errors at first base (6)
- Led the Indians in hit by pitch (10) and HR frequency (20.8 ABs per HR)

Matt Lawton

Position: LF/DH/RF
Bats: L **Throws:** R
Ht: 5'10" **Wt:** 195

Opening Day Age: 32
Born: 11/3/71 in
Gulfport, MS
ML Seasons: 9
Pronunciation:
LAW-ton

2003 Season

Matt Lawton's career has turned into a disaster with Cleveland. He played in only 99 games last year because of a dislocated middle finger on his right hand and a sore right knee that needed surgery. Shoulder surgery and a calf injury limited him to 114 games in 2002. Lawton was hitting .315 with eight homers and 17 RBI in a 24-game stretch when he dislocated his finger July 11 swinging at a pitch. It effectively ended his season.

Hitting

Lawton still is competitive against righthanders, but his decline against lefties has been startling. In the last two seasons, he has hit .180 against them despite a .271 lifetime mark before coming to Cleveland in 2002. When he's healthy and in shape, Lawton is a patient, professional hitter. He knows how to work the count, has a solid on-base percentage and hits the ball to all fields. Lawton takes a lot of pitches, so he's vulnerable to fastballs early and breaking balls late. Lately he's tried to hit too many homers and it's hurt his swing.

Baserunning & Defense

Lawton is a good baserunner, but he'd be even better if he lost the spare tire he's been packing the last two years. He knows when to steal and gets good jumps. Lawton went 10-for-13 in 2003. Team doctors told Lawton last spring that he needed surgery on his right knee. He elected to have it after the season, but the injury cost him speed and range in left field. Lawton never had a great arm, but runners routinely challenged him last year following his 2002 shoulder surgery.

2004 Outlook

The Indians played Lawton last summer in an effort to trade him and the $14.5 million they owe him through 2005. The front office says Lawton will play this year only if he earns it. If he comes to spring training fat and limping, he'll ride the bench. If Lawton is healthy and well conditioned, his best bet for playing time will be at designated hitter.

Overall Statistics

	G	AB	R	H	D	T	HR	RBI	SB	BB	SO	Avg	OBP	Slg
'03	99	374	57	93	19	0	15	53	10	47	47	.249	.343	.420
Car.	1032	3645	575	975	212	16	105	507	124	536	450	.267	.370	.421

Where He Hits the Ball

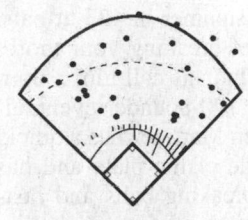 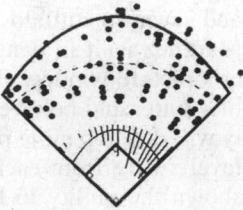

Vs. LHP   **Vs. RHP**

2003 Situational Stats

	AB	H	HR	RBI	Avg		AB	H	HR	RBI	Avg
Home	179	46	6	29	.257	LHP	90	17	3	15	.183
Road	195	47	9	24	.241	RHP	281	76	12	38	.270
First Half	323	80	15	47	.248	Sc Pos	78	18	3	36	.231
Scnd Half	51	13	0	6	.255	Clutch	57	11	2	6	.193

2003 Rankings (American League)

- 10th in on-base percentage for a leadoff hitter (.337)
- Led the Indians in stolen-base percentage (76.9), most pitches seen per plate appearance (4.01) and on-base percentage for a leadoff hitter (.337)

Victor Martinez

2003 Season

The Indians were expecting big things from Victor Martinez last year and he delivered. Not only did Martinez justify their belief that he will be their starting catcher for years to come, but he showed them he could hit in the big leagues. Martinez arrived on June 27 from Triple-A Buffalo and immediately impressed the Indians with the improvements he'd made as a catcher. Offensively, he hit safely in 24 of his last 25 games.

Hitting

Martinez is a line-drive switch-hitter who recognizes pitches early and can make adjustments during at-bats. After hitting one homer in Cleveland and seven in Buffalo last summer in 433 at-bats, Martinez isn't in danger of breaking your mother's picture window. The Indians call him a doubles hitter and believe the 190-pounder eventually will develop more power. Martinez has a quick, level swing from each side of the plate and has shown the ability to hit breaking balls and fastballs. He didn't hit well with runners in scoring position, but batted .393 (22-for-56) from the seventh inning on.

Baserunning & Defense

Manager Eric Wedge told Martinez before he started last season at Buffalo that if he wanted to make the big leagues as a catcher, he had to improve defensively. Martinez, a converted shortstop who always paid more attention to his offense, worked hard on his throwing, game-calling and ball-blocking with roving catching instructor Chris Bando. Martinez is never going to have a Pudge Rodriguez-type arm, as he threw out 28.6 percent (8-for-28) of the baserunners he faced. The Indians think Martinez and their young starting pitchers can grow together.

2004 Outlook

Martinez will go to spring training as the starting catcher, but he will be pushed by Josh Bard and Tim Laker. The Indians see Martinez becoming a complete hitter. They think someday he may develop into a catcher like Jorge Posada and hit for average and power with a high on-base percentage.

Position: C
Bats: B **Throws:** R
Ht: 6' 2" **Wt:** 190

Opening Day Age: 25
Born: 12/23/78 in Ciudad Bolivar, VZ
ML Seasons: 2

Overall Statistics

	G	AB	R	H	D	T	HR	RBI	SB	BB	SO	Avg	OBP	Slg
'03	49	159	15	46	4	0	1	16	1	13	21	.289	.345	.333
Car.	61	191	17	55	5	0	2	21	1	16	23	.288	.343	.346

Where He Hits the Ball

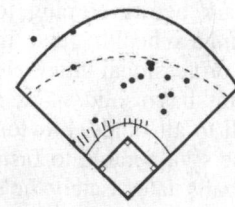 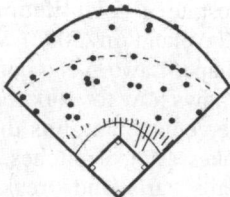

Vs. LHP   **Vs. RHP**

2003 Situational Stats

	AB	H	HR	RBI	Avg		AB	H	HR	RBI	Avg
Home	81	21	0	7	.259	LHP	59	16	1	8	.271
Road	78	25	1	9	.321	RHP	100	30	0	8	.300
First Half	44	9	0	3	.205	Sc Pos	42	10	1	15	.238
Scnd Half	115	37	1	13	.322	Clutch	34	14	0	3	.412

2003 Rankings (American League)

- Led the Indians in batting average in the clutch

C.C. Sabathia

2003 Season

C.C. Sabathia became the Indians' No. 1 starter last year in name and substance. He pitched through a winless April and a serious illness to his father, as well as getting married and becoming a father himself. Sabathia, supported by just 4.5 runs per game, made his first All-Star team on the way to his third straight season of 13 or more victories. After going 0-2 in six starts in March/April, Sabathia went 7-1 in May and June.

Pitching

Sabathia is a power pitcher, but in 2003 he refined his delivery and sharpened the command of his changeup and curveball. The improvements made him more effective in the late innings. The range on Sabathia's fastball is 92-97 MPH, but he usually sits at 93-95 MPH. He didn't reach 200 innings as he did in 2002, but he threw two complete games and reduced his walks from 88 in 2002 to 66 last year. Conditioning remains an issue with Sabathia. He was more diligent last year, but the Indians still want him to be in better shape. Sabathia reached the sixth inning in 25 of his 30 starts.

Defense

The opposition loves to bunt on Sabathia. Batters figure making a 6-foot-7, 290-plus-pound pitcher field his position will get him out of the game faster. The strategy has worked at times, but when the Twins tried it last year on July 3, Sabathia drilled Bobby Kielty and fielded everything in sight on the way to a four-hitter. Sabathia still has trouble covering first, but nine of the 14 runners who tried to steal against him were thrown out.

2004 Outlook

The Indians want Sabathia to throw 200 or more innings and set the tone for the rotation in 2004. If he could repeat his rookie year when he went 17-5, no one would complain, but the 2004 club may lack enough offense. General manager Mark Shapiro is rebuilding the Indians around starting pitching and Sabathia is his cornerstone. Sabathia, with 43 victories in three years, must get stronger in the late innings.

Position: SP
Bats: L **Throws:** L
Ht: 6' 7" **Wt:** 290

Opening Day Age: 23
Born: 7/21/80 in Vallejo, CA
ML Seasons: 3
Pronunciation:
sa-BATH oo-a

Overall Statistics

	W	L	Pct.	ERA	G	GS	Sv	IP	H	BB	SO	HR	Avg
'03	13	9	.591	3.60	30	30	0	197.2	190	66	141	19	.255
Car.	43	25	.632	4.12	96	96	0	588.0	537	249	461	55	.246

2003 Pitching Profile

	C.C. Sabathia	AL Average
Overall Strike %	64.5	62.8
1st Pitch Strike %	61.2	58.7
Ratio	1.30	1.39
Strikeouts per 9 IP	6.42	6.11
Walks per 9 IP	3.01	3.16
Home Runs per 9 IP	0.87	1.11
Strikeout/Walk Ratio	2.14	1.93
Groundball/Flyball Ratio	1.08	1.18

2003 Situational Stats

	W	L	ERA	Sv	IP		AB	H	HR	RBI	Avg
Home	7	6	3.09	0	107.2	LHB	178	49	1	17	.275
Road	6	3	4.20	0	90.0	RHB	568	141	18	59	.248
First Half	8	4	3.23	0	117.0	Sc Pos	169	36	3	48	.213
Sond Half	5	5	4.13	0	80.2	Clutch	66	18	1	5	.273

2003 Rankings (American League)

- 4th in runners caught stealing (9)
- 5th in lowest stolen-base percentage allowed (35.7) and least run support per nine innings (4.5)
- 6th in lowest ERA at home and lowest batting average allowed with runners in scoring position
- 7th in balks (2) and lowest fielding percentage at pitcher (.929)
- 10th in ERA
- Led the Indians in ERA, wins, games started, complete games (2), innings pitched, hits allowed, batters faced (832), walks allowed, strikeouts, balks (2), pitches thrown (3,148), runners caught stealing (9), winning percentage, lowest batting average allowed (.255), lowest on-base percentage allowed (.319) and lowest ERA at home

Omar Vizquel

2003 Season

He started the season as the last man standing and ended it on crutches. Omar Vizquel, the only Indian left who played in the 1995 and 1997 World Series, underwent two surgeries on his right knee to repair cartilage and played in only 64 games. The second one on September 5 ended Vizquel's season. The durable Vizquel averaged 141 games a year in his previous nine years with the Indians.

Hitting

Vizquel is still a scrappy, action-oriented offensive player. He made 56 starts in the No. 2 hole and seven in the leadoff spot to take advantage of his ability to reach base, bunt and run. Vizquel is a better hitter lefthanded than righthanded. After a sharp decline in 2000 and 2001 from the right side of the plate, Vizquel hit .293 in 2002, but he struggled again last year against lefties. Vizquel frequently walks more than he strikes out, yet he'll sometimes pop up high fastballs and jump at offspeed pitches in the dirt.

Baserunning & Defense

The universe must be off its axis—it's been two years since Vizquel won a Gold Glove. He made an uncharacteristic seven errors in 64 games last year. In 2002, he made seven in 150 games, but the award went to Alex Rodriguez to end Vizquel's nine-year run as the reigning shortstop in the American League. Vizquel remains a defensive marvel. He has range, a quick release and turns the double play fearlessly, and no one handles popups in short left field or down the line with such ease. Vizquel is one steal short of 300.

2004 Outlook

The Indians expect Vizquel to be fully recovered form his knee surgeries this year. If that's the case, he'll be back at shortstop and hitting at the top of the order. The Indians need Vizquel's run-scoring ability to improve a bad offense. Vizquel is in the final year of his contract and the Indians already are grooming potential replacements in Jhonny Peralta and Brandon Phillips. Peralta started 69 games last year when Vizquel was injured.

Position: SS
Bats: B **Throws:** R
Ht: 5' 9" **Wt:** 175

Opening Day Age: 36
Born: 4/24/67 in Caracas, VZ
ML Seasons: 15
Pronunciation: viz-KELL

Overall Statistics

	G	AB	R	H	D	T	HR	RBI	SB	BB	SO	Avg	OBP	Slg
	64	250	43	61	13	2	2	19	8	29	20	.244	.321	.336
1990	7252	1047	1982	320	51	59	656	299	728	732	.273	.340	.356

Where He Hits the Ball

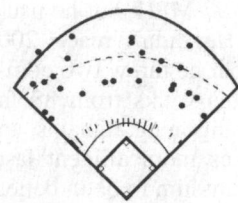 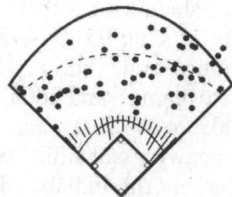

Vs. LHP   **Vs. RHP**

2003 Situational Stats

	AB	H	HR	RBI	Avg		AB	H	HR	RBI	Avg
Home	127	27	2	11	.213	LHP	67	15	0	3	.224
Road	123	34	0	8	.276	RHP	183	46	2	16	.251
First Half	231	59	2	18	.255	Sc Pos	49	11	0	13	.224
Scnd Half	19	2	0	1	.105	Clutch	39	10	0	3	.256

2003 Rankings (American League)

- 6th in most GDPs per GDP situation (19.3%)
- Led the Indians in highest percentage of pitches taken (60.7), lowest percentage of swings that missed (7.4), highest percentage of swings put into play (54.9) and steals of third (3)

Josh Bard

Position: C
Bats: B **Throws:** R
Ht: 6' 3" **Wt:** 215

Opening Day Age: 26
Born: 3/30/78 in Ithaca, NY
ML Seasons: 2
Pronunciation: baahrd

Overall Statistics

	G	AB	R	H	D	T	HR	RBI	SB	BB	SO	Avg	OBP	Slg
'03	91	303	25	74	13	1	8	36	0	22	53	.244	.293	.373
Car.	115	393	34	94	18	1	11	48	0	26	66	.239	.284	.374

2003 Situational Stats

	AB	H	HR	RBI	Avg		AB	H	HR	RBI	Avg
Home	148	34	5	19	.230	LHP	83	24	2	13	.289
Road	155	40	3	17	.258	RHP	220	50	6	23	.227
First Half	206	47	3	16	.228	Sc Pos	75	21	2	29	.280
Scnd Half	97	27	5	20	.278	Clutch	56	17	0	5	.304

2003 Season

Rookie Josh Bard opened last season as the starting catcher, but lost the job on June 27 when he was demoted to Triple-A Buffalo after hitting .228. When Bard returned on August 9, he hit .278 with five homers and 20 RBI in 31 games in a backup role, but his catching skills declined.

Hitting, Baserunning & Defense

Bard is a switch-hitter with a line-drive swing. He hit better late in the season after hitting coach Eddie Murray convinced him to open his stance and be more aggressive when he was ahead in the count. Defensively, Bard calls a good game and threw out 31.7 percent (19-for-60) of the basestealers he faced. But at times he struggled to catch the ball cleanly and block balls in the dirt. Bard worked with catching coach Joel Skinner to cut down his movement behind the plate. Bard runs like you'd think a sore-kneed, 215-pound catcher would.

2004 Outlook

Although Bard started 2003 as the No. 1 catcher, he'll probably back up Victor Martinez this year. Bard spent the offseason losing weight and improving his flexibility through yoga. If he continues to hit like he did last September—.400, three homers, 13 RBI—he will challenge Martinez for playing time.

Ellis Burks

Position: DH
Bats: R **Throws:** R
Ht: 6' 2" **Wt:** 205

Opening Day Age: 39
Born: 9/11/64 in Vicksburg, MS
ML Seasons: 17

Overall Statistics

	G	AB	R	H	D	T	HR	RBI	SB	BB	SO	Avg	OBP	Slg
	55	198	27	52	11	1	6	28	1	27	46	.263	.360	.419
	1989	7199	1247	2101	402	63	351	1205	179	790	1332	.292	.364	.511

2003 Situational Stats

	AB	H	HR	RBI	Avg		AB	H	HR	RBI	Avg
Home	100	28	2	18	.280	LHP	59	19	3	11	.322
Road	98	24	4	10	.245	RHP	139	33	3	17	.237
First Half	198	52	6	28	.263	Sc Pos	51	15	0	18	.294
Scnd Half	0	0	0	0	–	Clutch	28	11	0	6	.393

2003 Season

Ellis Burks knew something was wrong when he sprained his wrist in spring training. The veteran designated hitter kept playing until June 7, when the muscles in his right hand affected his ability to swing the bat. He underwent season-ending surgery to repair nerve damage in his right elbow on June 23.

Hitting, Baserunning & Defense

Burks is an aggressive power hitter who lives by the credo "good things happen when you swing the bat." He's a pull hitter who lives off fastballs and bad breaking balls. Pitchers give him trouble when they pitch backward—throwing breaking balls in fastball counts. Burks is a proven middle-of-the-lineup hitter and the Indians missed him when he went on the disabled list. The former 30-30 man still gets down the line well and will steal the odd base. Burks' appearances in left field have been limited to interleague games because of bad knees.

2004 Outlook

Burks wants to play this season because he didn't feel good about ending his career on the disabled list. The Indians, however, didn't pick up their $5 million option or offer salary arbitration. The team can't re-sign Burks until May 1, so he may be gone after three years in Cleveland.

Jack Cressend

Position: RP
Bats: R **Throws:** R
Ht: 6' 1" **Wt:** 195

Opening Day Age: 28
Born: 5/13/75 in New Orleans, LA
ML Seasons: 4

Overall Statistics

	W	L	Pct.	ERA	G	GS	Sv	IP	H	BB	SO	HR	Avg
'03	2	1	.667	2.51	33	0	0	43.0	40	9	28	1	.252
Car.	5	4	.556	3.97	111	0	0	145.0	150	50	96	13	.270

2003 Situational Stats

	W	L	ERA	Sv	IP		AB	H	HR	RBI	Avg
Home	2	0	1.69	0	26.2	LHB	75	19	1	3	.253
Road	0	1	3.86	0	16.1	RHB	84	21	0	9	.250
First Half	0	0	1.23	0	7.1	Sc Pos	36	9	0	8	.250
Scnd Half	2	1	2.78	0	35.2	Clutch	63	18	0	5	.286

2003 Season

The Indians took a gamble on Jack Cressend by claiming him on waivers in September 2002, even though he'd just had surgery on his right shoulder to repair a torn labrum. Cressend arrived in Cleveland on July 1 and posted a 1.26 ERA in July and a 1.33 ERA in August.

Pitching & Defense

Cressend throws a fastball, curveball, slider and changeup. He throws between 89 and 92 MPH, but his velocity still hadn't returned all the way because of the surgery. Cressend said the lack of velocity forced him to throw his breaking ball and made him a better pitcher. Cressend appeared in 24 of the Indians' 56 games in July and August, but his effectiveness suffered in September. Cressend made the first two errors of his career last year, but kept the running game under control. Four of the six runners who tried to steal against him were thrown out.

2004 Outlook

Cressend has gone from question mark to almost a sure thing when it comes to winning a job in the Indians' bullpen in 2004. He spent last summer working in middle relief, but if he has a good spring training, Cressend could move into a setup role.

Cliff Lee

Position: SP
Bats: L **Throws:** L
Ht: 6' 3" **Wt:** 190

Opening Day Age: 25
Born: 8/30/78 in Benton, AR
ML Seasons: 2

Overall Statistics

	W	L	Pct.	ERA	G	GS	Sv	IP	H	BB	SO	HR	Avg
'03	3	3	.500	3.61	9	9	0	52.1	41	20	44	7	.220
Car.	3	4	.429	3.30	11	11	0	62.2	47	28	50	7	.213

2003 Situational Stats

	W	L	ERA	Sv	IP		AB	H	HR	RBI	Avg
Home	1	2	3.67	0	27.0	LHB	54	15	4	11	.278
Road	2	1	3.55	0	25.1	RHB	132	26	3	13	.197
First Half	1	0	0.00	0	6.0	Sc Pos	32	9	2	16	.281
Scnd Half	2	3	4.08	0	46.1	Clutch	3	0	0	0	.000

2003 Season

An abdominal strain and a hernia kept Cliff Lee from pitching full-time for the Indians until mid-August. He made several rehab starts in the minors before beating Kansas City in a spot start on July 29. He returned to Triple-A Buffalo and went 4-1 in eight starts before rejoining the Indians for good.

Pitching & Defense

Lee uses a smooth delivery to throw a fastball, curveball, slider and change. He's not Randy Johnson, but he's not a soft-throwing lefty either. Lee throws 90-93 MPH with good movement. The Indians want Lee to establish his fastball more, but Lee isn't afraid to work from behind in the count with his offspeed pitches. He struck out seven batters four times in nine starts with the Tribe. Showing typical rookie jitters, Lee made some poor decisions on balls hit back to the mound, but he should improve with experience. His move to first needs work.

2004 Outlook

The Indians expect Lee to be their No. 3 starter in 2004. He had hernia surgery in October, but should be healthy by spring training. Lee was acquired from Montreal for Bartolo Colon in 2002, and the Indians expect him to join C.C. Sabathia and Jason Davis in the rotation.

Ryan Ludwick

Position: RF/LF
Bats: R **Throws:** L
Ht: 6' 3" **Wt:** 203

Opening Day Age: 25
Born: 7/13/78 in
Satellite Beach, FL
ML Seasons: 2

Overall Statistics

	G	AB	R	H	D	T	HR	RBI	SB	BB	SO	Avg	OBP	Slg
'03	47	162	17	40	8	1	7	26	2	12	48	.247	.299	.438
Car.	70	243	27	59	14	1	8	35	4	19	72	.243	.298	.407

2003 Situational Stats

	AB	H	HR	RBI	Avg		AB	H	HR	RBI	Avg
Home	85	24	2	12	.282	LHP	59	13	4	8	.220
Road	77	16	5	14	.208	RHP	103	27	3	18	.262
First Half	22	4	0	0	.182	Sc Pos	47	18	3	21	.383
Scnd Half	140	36	7	26	.257	Clutch	35	9	0	5	.257

2003 Season

The Indians acquired Ryan Ludwick from Texas for Ricardo Rodriguez and Shane Spencer on July 18. Ludwick hit .288 (23-for-80) with four homers and 17 RBI from August 12 through September 3. On September 3 he injured his right knee sliding back into first base against Detroit. The injury ended Ludwick's season and required surgery.

Hitting, Baserunning & Defense

Ludwick has power and a long, strikeout-prone swing to match. He hit 17 homers at Triple-A Oklahoma last season and is strong enough to drive a ball out of the park even when he doesn't get all of it. Ludwick can look foolish against breaking balls, but he showed the Indians an ability to make adjustments with two strikes and with men on base. He hit .383 (18-for-47) with runners in scoring position. Ludwick is a corner outfielder with a strong arm. He suffered a serious injury to his left hip in 2002 and still hasn't recovered all his speed.

2004 Outlook

The Indians acquired Ludwick because they need righthanded power. He so impressed manager Eric Wedge with his bat and hustle that he's a frontrunner to join Milton Bradley and Jody Gerut in the starting outfield. He should be fully recovered from knee surgery by spring training.

John McDonald

Position: 2B/SS/3B
Bats: R **Throws:** R
Ht: 5'11" **Wt:** 175

Opening Day Age: 29
Born: 9/24/74 in New
London, CT
ML Seasons: 5

Overall Statistics

	G	AB	R	H	D	T	HR	RBI	SB	BB	SO	Avg	OBP	Slg
'03	82	214	21	46	9	1	1	14	3	11	31	.215	.258	.280
Car.	219	530	59	125	21	4	2	26	6	22	92	.236	.275	.302

2003 Situational Stats

	AB	H	HR	RBI	Avg		AB	H	HR	RBI	Avg
Home	101	19	0	5	.188	LHP	65	14	0	4	.215
Road	113	27	1	9	.239	RHP	149	32	1	10	.215
First Half	123	31	1	9	.252	Sc Pos	46	13	0	12	.283
Scnd Half	91	15	0	5	.165	Clutch	37	10	0	2	.270

2003 Season

Infielder John McDonald deserves True Grit points. He knew in spring training that he needed micro-fracture surgery on his left knee, but tried to make it through the season. The injury sidelined him once with back pain and finally ended his season in late August. McDonald underwent surgery September 5.

Hitting, Baserunning & Defense

If McDonald could hit as well as he fields, he'd be headed for Cooperstown. He makes dazzling plays at shortstop and second base. He has quick feet, quicker hands and a strong arm. McDonald's not as flashy at third base, but still gets the job done. What he has a problem doing is hitting. He swings at too many high fastballs and doesn't hit enough line drives. Power pitchers knock the bat out his hands, yet he hit .283 (13-for-46) with runners in scoring position. McDonald has average speed, but needs to make consistent contact.

2004 Outlook

McDonald was on crutches until November because of his surgery, but he should be ready by spring training. In the past, it was said that McDonald could go to another team and start at short or second base. But at 29, he appears to be a career utility infielder.

Brandon Phillips

Position: 2B
Bats: R **Throws:** R
Ht: 5'11" **Wt:** 185

Opening Day Age: 22
Born: 6/28/81 in Raleigh, NC
ML Seasons: 2

Overall Statistics

	G	AB	R	H	D	T	HR	RBI	SB	BB	SO	Avg	OBP	Slg
'03	112	370	36	77	18	1	6	33	4	14	77	.208	.242	.311
Car.	123	401	41	85	21	2	6	37	4	17	83	.212	.251	.319

2003 Situational Stats

	AB	H	HR	RBI	Avg		AB	H	HR	RBI	Avg
Home	177	37	3	16	.209	LHP	95	17	2	8	.179
Road	193	40	3	17	.207	RHP	275	60	4	25	.218
First Half	300	63	4	24	.210	Sc Pos	105	22	2	28	.210
Scnd Half	70	14	2	9	.200	Clutch	63	9	2	7	.143

2003 Season

When the Indians gave Brandon Phillips the second-base job in spring training, they knew he'd struggle offensively. But they never expected such a failure. When Phillips was sent to Triple-A Buffalo on July 14, he was hitting .210. He responded by hitting .175 at Buffalo and .200 upon his recall on August 27.

Hitting, Baserunning & Defense

Phillips was overmatched as a big league hitter. He swung long and hard and tried to pull every pitch over the left-field fence. Pitchers worked him down and away with breaking balls and fastballs because he kept pulling his head and front shoulder off the ball. Phillips couldn't make adjustments and sulked instead of worked when he was finally demoted. He's a fine defensive player and has the arm and range to play second or short. Phillips has decent speed, but was rarely on base.

2004 Outlook

Phillips will start 2004 in Buffalo. The Indians, rushed him last year, now want him to mature and accept responsibility for his career. They went into the offseason looking for a big league second baseman. Phillips will play second and short at Buffalo and could be Omar Vizquel's eventual replacement.

David Riske

Position: RP
Bats: R **Throws:** R
Ht: 6' 2" **Wt:** 190

Opening Day Age: 27
Born: 10/23/76 in Renton, WA
ML Seasons: 4
Pronunciation: RISK-ee

Overall Statistics

	W	L	Pct.	ERA	G	GS	Sv	IP	H	BB	SO	HR	Avg
'03	2	2	.500	2.29	68	0	8	74.2	52	20	82	9	.196
Car.	7	5	.583	3.66	157	0	10	167.1	141	79	192	22	.230

2003 Situational Stats

	W	L	ERA	Sv	IP		AB	H	HR	RBI	Avg
Home	1	1	1.96	3	41.1	LHB	124	18	5	12	.145
Road	1	1	2.70	5	33.1	RHB	141	34	4	14	.241
First Half	2	1	2.60	1	45.0	Sc Pos	71	14	2	17	.197
Scnd Half	0	1	1.82	7	29.2	Clutch	179	38	7	22	.212

2003 Season

After a shaky April, David Riske put together the best season of his career. He started the year as a setup man, but replaced Danys Baez as closer on August 16 and subsequently went 7-for-7 in save situations. Riske allowed just three runs in 25.1 innings in his last 24 games.

Pitching & Defense

Riske features a deceptive motion and a sneaky 90-91 MPH fastball, but in 2003, two things may have changed the course of his career. Riske started throwing a splitter for a change of pace and stayed on a year-round exercise program to avoid the back problems that have bothered him in recent years. Before Riske started throwing the splitter, hitters waited for a mistake with the fastball. He's a strikeout pitcher with more strikeouts than innings pitched in his career. Riske, with only one career error, has a quick move to the plate, but needs to keep runners closer at first.

2004 Outlook

Riske, a 56th-round draft pick in 1996, could be the Tribe's closer this season if Bob Wickman isn't fully recovered from Tommy John surgery and Baez is jettisoned. Otherwise, Riske will ride shotgun as the top setup man. The arbitration-eligible Riske went into the winter looking for a big raise.

Jake Westbrook

Position: SP/RP
Bats: R **Throws:** R
Ht: 6' 3" **Wt:** 185

Opening Day Age: 26
Born: 9/29/77 in Athens, GA
ML Seasons: 4

Overall Statistics

	W	L	Pct.	ERA	G	GS	Sv	IP	H	BB	SO	HR	Avg
'03	7	10	.412	4.33	34	22	0	133.0	142	56	58	9	.281
Car.	12	19	.387	5.23	71	34	0	246.0	286	94	127	22	.297

2003 Situational Stats

	W	L	ERA	Sv	IP		AB	H	HR	RBI	Avg
Home	4	4	4.74	0	68.1	LHB	275	76	5	28	.276
Road	3	6	3.90	0	64.2	RHB	230	66	4	33	.287
First Half	4	4	4.34	0	66.1	Sc Pos	144	42	5	53	.292
Scnd Half	3	6	4.32	0	66.2	Clutch	40	11	0	3	.275

2003 Season

Jake Westbrook, under manager Eric Wedge, finally made it through a season healthy. He set career highs in victories, starts and innings pitched. Westbrook bounced between the bullpen and rotation before being sent to Triple-A Buffalo on June 29. He returned as a starter in July.

Pitching & Defense

Westbrook can start or relieve, but his durability has been questioned because of a sore right elbow that was surgically repaired in 2002. He throws a sinker, changeup and slider. The sinker, thrown at 89-91 MPH, has good movement and resulted in 26 double-play grounders. All his pitches have good action, but he's a nibbler who sometimes struggles to throw strikes. When Westbrook is right, he can pitch deep into a game because he gets quick outs on grounders. Westbrook is a decent fielder, but basestealers went 11-for-15 against him in 2003.

2004 Outlook

Westbrook has a chance to be the fifth starter or pitch out of the bullpen. Wedge has pushed Westbrook to trust his pitches and be more aggressive in the strike zone. Westbrook is expected to compete with Jason Stanford, Chad Durbin and Jason Bere for a spot in the rotation.

Bob Wickman

Position: RP
Bats: R **Throws:** R
Ht: 6' 1" **Wt:** 240

Opening Day Age: 35
Born: 2/6/69 in Green Bay, WI
ML Seasons: 11

Overall Statistics

	W	L	Pct.	ERA	G	GS	Sv	IP	H	BB	SO	HR	Avg
'03							Did Not Play						
Car.	59	45	.567	3.68	627	28	156	863.0	854	367	639	61	.260

2003 Situational Stats

	W	L	ERA	Sv	IP		AB	H	HR	RBI	Avg
Home	–	–	–	–	–	LHB	–	–	–	–	–
Road	–	–	–	–	–	RHB	–	–	–	–	–
First Half	–	–	–	–	–	Sc Pos	–	–	–	–	–
Scnd Half	–	–	–	–	–	Clutch	–	–	–	–	–

2003 Season

Bob Wickman missed all of last season while recovering from Tommy John surgery on his right elbow. Wickman had the surgery in December 2002 and has been rehabbing ever since. He made four minor league appearances at the end of last season, pitching 3.2 innings.

Pitching & Defense

While Wickman is a big man, he gets by on finesse and location rather than power. He's a sinker-slider pitcher who throws between 89 and 92 MPH. Wickman, who pitched nine plus years before going on the disabled list in 2002, has started, set up and closed. He's spent his last five years as a closer, a stretch during which his walks have decreased and his command has improved. Wickman is always well prepared, keeping his own records on hitters. Wickman isn't going to win any Gold Gloves, but he hustles to cover first.

2004 Outlook

The Indians are counting on Wickman to be their closer. They think he's fully recovered from surgery and liked the way he threw at the end of last year. If Wickman's comeback stalls, he could retire. He's in the final year of a three-year, $16 million deal and has said he'd never go through surgery again.

Jason Bere (Pos: RHP, Age: 32)

	W	L	Pct.	ERA	G	GS	Sv	IP	H	BB	SO	HR	Avg
'03	0	0	–	4.05	2	2	0	6.2	5	2	1	0	.208
Car.	71	65	.522	5.14	211	203	0	1111.0	1095	626	920	145	.258

Bere could throw the high fastball by nearly everyone when he arrived in 1993, but he hasn't been the same pitcher since elbow surgery in '96. Last season ended with June shoulder surgery, but he'll be back with Cleveland after signing a minor league deal in early November. 2004 Outlook: C

Rafael Betancourt (Pos: RHP, Age: 28)

	W	L	Pct.	ERA	G	GS	Sv	IP	H	BB	SO	HR	Avg
'03	2	2	.500	2.13	33	0	1	38.0	27	13	36	5	.196
Car.	2	2	.500	2.13	33	0	1	38.0	27	13	36	5	.196

A 1993 undrafted free agent who converted to the mound in '97 and pitched in Japan in 2000, Betancourt made a triumphant rise to the majors after sitting out 2002 with arm troubles. A pleasant surprise for the Tribe. 2004 Outlook: B

Nick Bierbrodt (Pos: LHP, Age: 25)

	W	L	Pct.	ERA	G	GS	Sv	IP	H	BB	SO	HR	Avg
'03	0	2	.000	9.14	18	5	0	43.1	64	27	29	9	.348
Car.	5	8	.385	6.77	34	21	0	127.2	164	66	102	26	.311

Once a highly regarded southpaw, Bierbrodt has survived a bout of Steve Blass-style wildness (spring 2002) and a drive-by shooting (June 2002). He struggled to get his career on track in 2003. 2004 Outlook: C

Jason Boyd (Pos: RHP, Age: 31)

	W	L	Pct.	ERA	G	GS	Sv	IP	H	BB	SO	HR	Avg
'03	3	1	.750	4.30	44	0	0	52.1	38	26	31	4	.200
Car.	4	2	.667	5.76	101	0	0	120.1	115	67	85	12	.254

After a strong start at Triple-A Buffalo, Boyd was recalled by Cleveland, his fourth team in four years. He was less hittable, but walks were a problem. Pittsburgh claimed him off waivers in October. 2004 Outlook: C

David Cortes (Pos: RHP, Age: 30)

	W	L	Pct.	ERA	G	GS	Sv	IP	H	BB	SO	HR	Avg
'03	0	0	–	12.00	2	0	0	3.0	8	0	1	1	.471
Car.	0	0	–	8.10	6	0	0	6.2	11	4	3	1	.355

Cortes was pitching in the Mexican League when he signed a deal with Triple-A Buffalo in August. He pitched well there before struggling in his first major league recall since 1999 with Atlanta. He now moves to Detroit after signing a minor league deal. 2004 Outlook: C

Chad Durbin (Pos: RHP, Age: 26)

	W	L	Pct.	ERA	G	GS	Sv	IP	H	BB	SO	HR	Avg
'03	0	1	.000	7.27	3	1	0	8.2	18	3	8	2	.429
Car.	11	23	.324	6.05	51	48	0	270.2	324	109	148	45	.298

Durbin's impressive strikeout rate and fewer hits per inning at Triple-A Buffalo were compromised by home runs. He made two September appearances against his former Royals teammates, who torched him both times. 2004 Outlook: C

Dave Elder (Pos: RHP, Age: 28)

	W	L	Pct.	ERA	G	GS	Sv	IP	H	BB	SO	HR	Avg
'03	1	1	.500	19.29	4	0	0	2.1	5	4	3	2	.417
Car.	1	3	.250	4.62	19	0	0	25.1	23	18	26	3	.245

Elder's 2003 started well with 12.2 scoreless innings in April at Triple-A Buffalo. He was recalled on May 1, but rotator cuff tendinitis quickly led to exploratory surgery in June and his October release. 2004 Outlook: C

Ricky Gutierrez (Pos: SS, Age: 33, Bats: R)

	G	AB	R	H	D	T	HR	RBI	SB	BB	SO	Avg	OBP	Slg
'03	16	50	2	13	3	0	0	3	0	3	5	.260	.309	.320
Car.	1074	3529	463	945	138	25	38	349	49	356	572	.268	.340	.353

A series of herniated disks led to spinal fusion surgery in 2002, but Gutierrez returned in June. Pain persisted and his season ended in July with a career-threatening compression of the spinal cord. 2004 Outlook: C

Alex Herrera (Pos: LHP, Age: 27)

	W	L	Pct.	ERA	G	GS	Sv	IP	H	BB	SO	HR	Avg
'03	0	0	–	9.00	10	0	0	7.0	7	8	6	3	.250
Car.	0	0	–	5.11	15	0	0	12.1	10	9	11	3	.213

Five scoreless outings in 2002 were followed by seven more in July. Then Herrera was roughed up in three games and returned to Triple-A Buffalo. Colorado claimed the hard thrower off waivers in October. 2004 Outlook: B

Tim Laker (Pos: C, Age: 34, Bats: R)

	G	AB	R	H	D	T	HR	RBI	SB	BB	SO	Avg	OBP	Slg
'03	52	162	17	39	11	0	3	21	2	9	38	.241	.281	.364
Car.	233	520	53	118	25	2	8	60	5	37	129	.227	.279	.329

Laker posted career highs in at-bats, hits, doubles and RBI, but it doesn't bode well to be in an organization with two young catching prospects, Josh Bard and Victor Martinez. The two parties avoided arbitration and agreed to a one-year deal in October. 2004 Outlook: C

Greg LaRocca (Pos: 3B, Age: 31, Bats: R)

	G	AB	R	H	D	T	HR	RBI	SB	BB	SO	Avg	OBP	Slg
'03	5	9	3	3	1	0	0	0	0	1	1	.333	.400	.444
Car.	39	88	16	23	6	1	0	6	1	8	11	.261	.337	.352

For three seasons, LaRocca has hit for average and drawn walks for Triple-A Buffalo, but has shown little power as a third baseman. Knowing the door is closing on him, LaRocca is considering Japan for '04. 2004 Outlook: C

David Lee (Pos: RHP, Age: 31)

	W	L	Pct.	ERA	G	GS	Sv	IP	H	BB	SO	HR	Avg
'03	1	0	1.000	4.70	8	0	0	7.2	4	6	7	1	.143
Car.	5	2	.714	4.14	92	0	1	111.0	109	68	93	14	.261

Despite a high walk total, Lee enjoyed a decent season of relief work at Triple-A Las Vegas before the Dodgers dealt him to Cleveland in September. The Indians have re-signed him to a minor league deal. 2004 Outlook: C

Chris Magruder (Pos: LF, Age: 26, Bats: B)

	G	AB	R	H	D	T	HR	RBI	SB	BB	SO	Avg	OBP	Slg
'03	9	26	3	9	2	1	1	3	0	3	6	.346	.433	.615
Car.	113	313	40	70	17	2	7	33	2	19	66	.224	.273	.358

After missing the first half with a torn thumb ligament, Magruder batted .328 for Triple-A Buffalo. After a solid September with Cleveland, he signed a minor league deal with Milwaukee. 2004 Outlook: C

Terry Mulholland (Pos: LHP, Age: 41)

	W	L	Pct.	ERA	G	GS	Sv	IP	H	BB	SO	HR	Avg
'03	3	4	.429	4.91	45	3	0	99.0	117	37	42	17	.295
Car.	119	131	.476	4.37	592	317	5	2390.1	2600	810	1740	200	.278

He isn't as old as Jesse Orosco, but in the grand tradition of Orosco and Bob McClure, Mulholland will ride his lefthandedness as long as someone will write him a paycheck. In 2004 he wants to start. 2004 Outlook: C

Aaron Myette (Pos: RHP, Age: 26)

	W	L	Pct.	ERA	G	GS	Sv	IP	H	BB	SO	HR	Avg
'03	0	0	—	23.63	2	0	0	2.2	7	2	1	1	.467
Car.	6	12	.333	8.16	42	30	0	150.0	182	98	128	26	.301

Myette has enjoyed solid stints in the high minors with the White Sox and Texas, but hasn't shown the necessary command in the majors. A July trade to the Phils is a new chance. 2004 Outlook: C

Chad Paronto (Pos: RHP, Age: 28)

	W	L	Pct.	ERA	G	GS	Sv	IP	H	BB	SO	HR	Avg
'03	0	2	.000	9.45	6	0	0	6.2	7	3	6	1	.292
Car.	1	7	.125	4.93	59	0	0	69.1	74	25	45	9	.269

Paronto hasn't exactly dominated Double-A and Triple-A hitters in recent seasons, so it isn't surprising that he didn't impress during a brief April callup. He signed with St. Louis in November. 2004 Outlook: C

Jason C. Phillips (Pos: RHP, Age: 30)

	W	L	Pct.	ERA	G	GS	Sv	IP	H	BB	SO	HR	Avg
'03	0	1	.000	9.00	3	0	0	5.0	9	2	2	1	.409
Car.	1	4	.200	6.20	17	6	0	53.2	61	28	32	10	.293

Phillips had been a solid starter at Triple-A Buffalo dating back to 2001, but he hasn't carried his success to Cleveland. He was sold to Japan's Orix Blue Wave in June. 2004 Outlook: C

Jerrod Riggan (Pos: RHP, Age: 29)

	W	L	Pct.	ERA	G	GS	Sv	IP	H	BB	SO	HR	Avg
'03	0	0	—	9.00	2	0	0	4.0	7	1	2	0	.412
Car.	5	4	.556	5.19	67	0	0	86.2	105	43	66	8	.307

A part of the Robbie Alomar deal in late 2001, Riggan has been terrific at Triple-A Buffalo but ineffective with Cleveland. A free agent in May, he signed with the Mets and later with Japan's Hashin Tigers. 2004 Outlook: C

Carl Sadler (Pos: LHP, Age: 27)

	W	L	Pct.	ERA	G	GS	Sv	IP	H	BB	SO	HR	Avg
'03	0	0	—	1.86	18	0	0	9.2	11	5	10	0	.306
Car.	1	2	.333	3.60	42	0	0	30.0	26	16	33	2	.243

Sadler made the club out of spring training and pitched better with the Indians than at Triple-A Buffalo, but he was sent down in May to make room for Jason Bere and never returned. 2004 Outlook: C

Jose Santiago (Pos: RHP, Age: 29)

	W	L	Pct.	ERA	G	GS	Sv	IP	H	BB	SO	HR	Avg
'03	1	3	.250	2.84	25	0	0	31.2	37	14	15	2	.298
Car.	17	22	.436	4.39	225	0	4	293.1	326	93	150	28	.281

Santiago has enjoyed brief flashes of success as a reliever with the Royals and Phillies, but he's been too hittable of late to hold on to a significant role in a major league bullpen. 2004 Outlook: C

Angel Santos (Pos: 2B, Age: 24, Bats: B)

	G	AB	R	H	D	T	HR	RBI	SB	BB	SO	Avg	OBP	Slg
'03	32	76	9	17	3	1	3	6	1	3	18	.224	.253	.408
Car.	41	92	11	19	4	1	3	7	1	5	25	.207	.245	.370

The infielder doesn't hit for average or for power, though he draws a few walks. Dealt from Boston to Cleveland near the All-Star break, Santos batted .239 at two Triple-A affiliates last year. 2004 Outlook: C

Bill Selby (Pos: 3B, Age: 33, Bats: L)

	G	AB	R	H	D	T	HR	RBI	SB	BB	SO	Avg	OBP	Slg
'03	27	39	3	4	1	0	0	5	0	3	11	.103	.163	.128
Car.	198	431	45	96	20	3	11	48	1	33	71	.223	.279	.360

Selby wasn't able to establish himself as even a utility-man or part-timer during Cleveland's recent retooling. His opportunity ended when Cleveland dealt him to St. Louis in June. 2004 Outlook: C

Zach Sorensen (Pos: 2B, Age: 27, Bats: B)

	G	AB	R	H	D	T	HR	RBI	SB	BB	SO	Avg	OBP	Slg
'03	36	37	2	5	1	0	1	2	0	7	13	.135	.273	.243
Car.	36	37	2	5	1	0	1	2	0	7	13	.135	.273	.243

Sorensen was up and down a few times between Triple-A Buffalo and Cleveland, and he didn't produce at either level. He batted .239 with a .299 OBP at Buffalo and produced even less with the Tribe. 2004 Outlook: C

Brian Tallet (Pos: LHP, Age: 26)

	W	L	Pct.	ERA	G	GS	Sv	IP	H	BB	SO	HR	Avg
'03	0	2	.000	4.74	5	3	0	19.0	23	8	9	2	.303
Car.	1	2	.333	3.48	7	5	0	31.0	32	12	14	2	.271

The hard-throwing Tallet was 12-4 (3.08 ERA) at Double-A Akron and Triple-A Buffalo in 2002, but was 4-4 with a 5.14 ERA at Buffalo before elbow troubles led to Tommy John surgery in August. 2004 Outlook: D

Billy Traber (Pos: LHP, Age: 24)

	W	L	Pct.	ERA	G	GS	Sv	IP	H	BB	SO	HR	Avg
'03	6	9	.400	5.24	33	18	0	111.2	132	40	88	15	.293
Car.	6	9	.400	5.24	33	18	0	111.2	132	40	88	15	.293

Reportedly, Traber has pitched with elbow pain for years, but it came to a head late in the year as his performance and numbers went into the tank. He underwent Tommy John surgery in late September. 2004 Outlook: D

Cleveland Indians Minor League Prospects

Organization Overview:

The Cleveland system is one of the game's best, with dominant pitching staffs at a few levels and promising hurlers on every minor league club. The best rotation may have been at Double-A Akron, where Jeremy Guthrie, Fernando Cabrera, Francisco Cruceta, Kyle Denney and Derrick Van Dusen worked for much of 2003. The number of young players who are close to helping in Cleveland is staggering, thanks in part to the trading acumen of general manager Mark Shapiro in 2002, when a labor stoppage loomed and few teams were parting with top prospects. Shapiro acquired a host of young talent, while scouting director John Mirabelli has done well stocking the lower levels of the system.

Francisco Cruceta

Position: P   **Opening Day Age:** 22
Bats: R **Throws:** R   **Born:** 7/4/81 in Rancho
Ht: 6' 2" **Wt:** 173   Viejo, DR

Recent Statistics

	W	L	ERA	G	GS	Sv	IP	H	R	BB	SO	HR
2002 A S Georgia	8	5	2.80	20	20	0	112.2	98	42	34	111	7
2002 A Kinston	2	0	2.50	7	7	0	39.2	31	13	25	37	2
2003 AA Akron	13	9	3.09	27	25	0	163.1	141	70	66	134	7

Acquired along with Ricardo Rodriguez for Paul Shuey in July 2002, the little-known Cruceta jumped from a low-A Dodgers affiliate to Cleveland's high Class-A Kinston and finished strongly. The skinny righthander, who was signed in 1999 and played three seasons in the Dominican Summer League, continued his rapid climb at Double-A Akron last summer. Cruceta throws a low-90s fastball that is hard to pick up because of his herky-jerky motion. He also mixes in a changeup and a slurvy breaking ball. His changeup is further along than the breaking pitch and could become a true weapon for him. Cruceta needs work on his command and overall consistency to reach Cleveland.

Alex Escobar

Position: OF   **Opening Day Age:** 25
Bats: R **Throws:** R   **Born:** 9/6/78 in Valencia,
Ht: 6' 1" **Wt:** 190   VZ

Recent Statistics

	G	AB	R	H	D	T	HR	RBI	SB	BB	SO	Avg
2003 AAA Buffalo	118	439	63	110	21	2	24	78	8	24	133	.251
2003 AL Cleveland	28	99	16	27	2	0	5	14	1	7	33	.273

A terrific athlete signed by the Mets in 1995, Escobar first excelled in 1998 with a .310-27-91 campaign in the Class-A Sally League. A fractured vertebra in his back and a shoulder injury sidetracked him in 1999 before he bounced back with a solid season at Double-A Binghamton in 2000. After an off year at Triple-A

Norfolk in 2001, Escobar was dealt to Cleveland as the key player in the Robbie Alomar trade with New York, blew out his left knee three months later in spring training and missed the 2002 season. His power was evident at Triple-A Buffalo last summer, and he made advances in pitch recognition and working counts, but his propensity to strike out continued. Still, he is young and mostly needs to improve his pitch selection.

Jeremy Guthrie

Position: P   **Opening Day Age:** 24
Bats: R **Throws:** R   **Born:** 4/8/79 in
Ht: 6' 1" **Wt:** 200   Roseburg, OR

Recent Statistics

	W	L	ERA	G	GS	Sv	IP	H	R	BB	SO	HR
2003 AA Akron	6	2	1.44	10	9	0	62.2	44	11	14	35	0
2003 AAA Buffalo	4	9	6.52	18	18	0	96.2	129	75	30	62	15

The 22nd overall pick in the 2002 draft, Guthrie signed late, pitched only in the Arizona Fall League a year ago and struggled in the big league camp last spring. Still, he was dominant at Double-A Akron, going 4-0 with a 1.30 ERA and a .189 opponent batting average in his first six starts. Guthrie worked with a 90-94 MPH fastball and good command of his pitches, including a slider and changeup. After just 10 games at Akron, he moved to Triple-A Buffalo, where things didn't go as well. Yet, it was an impressive debut for Guthrie, who's bright and has the intangibles that could elevate him to Cleveland by September, possibly for good in 2005.

Jhonny Peralta

Position: SS   **Opening Day Age:** 21
Bats: R **Throws:** R   **Born:** 5/28/82 in
Ht: 6' 1" **Wt:** 180   Santiago, DR

Recent Statistics

	G	AB	R	H	D	T	HR	RBI	SB	BB	SO	Avg
2003 AAA Buffalo	63	237	25	61	12	1	1	21	1	15	45	.257
2003 AL Cleveland	77	242	24	55	10	1	4	21	1	20	65	.227

Signed in 1999, Peralta had fared better with the glove than the bat until he showed a surge in power (28 doubles, 15 homers), made better contact and hit for a much better average (.281) at Double-A Akron in 2002. Defensively, his soft hands and strong arm make him a dependable shortstop, and the only question is whether Peralta will outgrow the position. He would have spent 2003 at Triple-A Buffalo, but Omar Vizquel's arthroscopic knee surgery in June opened the door to the 21-year-old, who adequately handled defensive chores. He's a capable fastball hitter who learned some adjustments to breaking balls and offspeed stuff in Cleveland. His time there showed he must get stronger. After an offseason workout program to bolster his strength, he is likely to start 2004 at Buffalo if Vizquel is healthy.

Grady Sizemore

Position: OF
Bats: L **Throws:** L
Ht: 6' 2" **Wt:** 195

Opening Day Age: 21
Born: 8/2/82 in Seattle, WA

Recent Statistics

	G	AB	R	H	D	T	HR	RBI	SB	BB	SO	Avg
2002 A Brevard Cty	75	256	37	66	15	4	0	26	9	36	41	.258
2002 A Kinston	47	172	31	59	9	3	3	20	14	33	30	.343
2003 AA Akron	128	496	96	151	26	11	13	78	10	46	73	.304

One of three top prospects acquired from Montreal for Bartolo Colon in June 2002, Sizemore has hit better than .300 and developed a power stroke since the deal. He already had advanced plate discipline, which he uses to work counts and draw walks. He was one of the best prospects in a talent-laden Double-A Eastern League in 2003, and was named the MVP of the Futures Game in Chicago, delivering an RBI single and a homer in a 3-2 U.S. team victory. Defensively, his speed, skills and instincts in the outfield are as solid as his bat. Sizemore could surface in the majors as a center fielder if he can strengthen his throwing arm. With his all-around game and leadership skills, he arguably is the system's best prospect.

Corey Smith

Position: 3B
Bats: R **Throws:** R
Ht: 6' 1" **Wt:** 205

Opening Day Age: 21
Born: 4/15/82 in Plainfield, NJ

Recent Statistics

	G	AB	R	H	D	T	HR	RBI	SB	BB	SO	Avg
2002 A Kinston	134	505	71	129	29	2	13	67	7	59	141	.255
2003 AA Akron	127	473	51	128	27	3	9	64	7	50	99	.271

Smith has been challenged by his minor league assignments as one of the youngest players on each team. A hard-nosed approach and extraordinary work ethic neutralize the age factor. Smith also has excellent bat speed, which he put to good use in 2003 at Double-A Akron. He cut his strikeouts dramatically, and Smith should generate more pop as he matures. He also collected 45 errors at Akron after leading all Carolina League third basemen with 34 errors in 2002. Yet he displays decent range and an adequate arm, but at times has been prone to making poor throws. There's no plan to rush Smith to Cleveland.

Jason Stanford

Position: P
Bats: L **Throws:** L
Ht: 6' 2" **Wt:** 200

Opening Day Age: 27
Born: 1/23/77 in Tucson, AZ

Recent Statistics

	W	L	ERA	G	GS	Sv	IP	H	R	BB	SO	HR
2003 AAA Buffalo	10	4	3.43	20	20	0	126.0	124	57	25	108	13
2003 AL Cleveland	1	3	3.60	13	8	0	50.0	48	20	16	30	5

The undrafted Stanford was signed in 1999 after playing ball at North Carolina-Charlotte. Despite a lack of prospect status, Stanford impressed in his 2000 debut by going 12-7 (2.62 ERA) at three different stops. He pitched at Double-A Akron and Triple-A Buffalo over the next two seasons, finishing strongly at Buffalo in 2002, with a 3-1 mark and 2.78 ERA in six games. A fast start there in 2003 led to a July 4 promotion to Cleveland. Stanford has a very good changeup. Yet, with just an average fastball and breaking pitch, he has succeeded every step of the way, displaying durability and an excellent feel for pitching. With a good spring, Stanford could be Cleveland's fifth starter, but the Indians think he'll be useful in nearly any role.

Kazuhito Tadano

Position: P
Bats: R **Throws:** R
Ht: 6' 0" **Wt:** 180

Opening Day Age: 23
Born: 4/25/80 in Tokyo, Japan

Recent Statistics

	W	L	ERA	G	GS	Sv	IP	H	R	BB	SO	HR
2003 A Kinston	2	1	1.89	7	1	0	19.0	13	5	3	28	0
2003 AAA Buffalo	0	0	3.86	2	0	0	7.0	6	3	4	6	0
2003 AA Akron	4	1	1.24	31	0	3	72.2	62	15	15	78	4

Two years ago, Tadano was a top-flight college pitcher and a likely high first-round pick in Japan. He never was drafted, however, presumably because Tadano and a few college teammates had participated in a pornographic video. Major league clubs that were aware of the video shunned him, despite a 93-94 MPH fastball and three strong secondary pitches—slider, splitter and changeup. Cleveland signed him at little cost during spring training, and Tadano responded with a rapid climb to Triple-A Buffalo last summer. The Indians consider him a complete pitcher, with multiple offerings, command, a deceptive motion that is quick to the plate, good fielding ability and mental toughness. He only needs innings to fine-tune his game for Cleveland. The Indians see Tadano as a bullpen guy.

Others to Watch

In 2003, righthander **Fernando Cabrera** (22) threw harder than anyone in Cleveland's Double-A rotation of prospects. He improved at Akron, as he generated more quality strikes and learned to put people away, using a mid-90s fastball that he kept low in the zone. . . After an uneventful North American debut in 2002, **Fausto Carmona** (20) made the front office take notice by leading the minors in wins and the Class-A Sally League in ERA last summer, going 17-4 with a 2.06 ERA. His impeccable command was impressive for someone so young. . . Righty **Jake Dittler** (21) reached high Class-A Kinston in 2003, throwing strikes and featuring a plus changeup at two levels, en route to an 11-5 season and a 2.53 ERA. . . Pitching in the Rookie-level Appy League after his selection in the 2003 draft, 6-foot-4 righty **Adam Miller** (19) showed a big league slider, an advanced changeup and low-90s sinker, which made him one of the best prospects in his league. His delivery is loose and easy, but his demeanor and hard stuff are pit-bull material.

Comerica Park

Offense

The Tigers moved the left-field wall at Comerica Park in 20 feet prior to last season, and 41 home runs were hit into the area between the previous fence and the current one. Despite Comerica Park's reputation for vastness, it is a good park for a lefthanded pull-hitter with power. The bullpen in right field extends the wall out on a straight angle, so it is short for a longer-than-usual distance before angling out to the grandstand. It remains anything but a home-run hitters' park, however.

Defense

It is imperative the Tigers have a speedy center fielder who covers a lot of ground. Range in the outfield remains important. Because the fences are deep, there are a lot of holes for base hits to fall in. In a tradition brought over from Tiger Stadium, the infield grass is slow.

Who It Helps the Most

Third baseman Eric Munson is the ideal Comerica Park hitter. He's a lefthanded hitter with pull power. Alex Sanchez has the speed necessary to cover the ground in center field. He's also an excellent bunter who benefits from the slow infield. Righthanded pitcher Nate Cornejo has a sinking fastball and doesn't strike out a lot of hitters, so he should do well in Detroit.

Who It Hurts the Most

Comerica Park is not a good ballpark for gap-to-gap power hitters such as Dmitri Young. Outfielders who can't run or throw are a real burden in the stadium. Middle infielders Omar Infante and Ramon Santiago just don't appear strong enough to do much damage as hitters in a ballpark this size.

Rookies & Newcomers

The Tigers' top prospects at the upper levels of the minor leagues don't have styles that fit Comerica Park. Outfielder Cody Ross is an example. He is good defensively, but he is a righthanded hitter whose power could be neutralized at home.

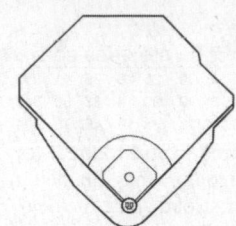

Dimensions: LF-345, LCF-370, CF-420, RCF-365, RF-330

Capacity: 40,120

Elevation: 585 feet

Surface: Grass

Foul Territory: Average

Park Factors

2003 Season

	Home Games			Away Games			
	Tigers	Opp	Total	Tigers	Opp	Total	Index
G	72	72	144	72	72	144	
Avg	.237	.271	.255	.239	.302	.270	94
AB	2409	2612	5021	2448	2422	4870	103
R	252	391	643	275	441	716	90
H	571	709	1280	584	731	1315	97
2B	84	123	207	96	155	251	80
3B	18	26	44	14	20	34	126
HR	62	87	149	74	90	164	88
BB	178	256	434	219	243	462	91
SO	464	370	834	510	313	823	98
E	55	57	112	65	36	101	111
E-Infield	46	46	92	52	31	83	111
LHB-Avg	.257	.292	.273	.246	.314	.275	99
LHB-HR	33	45	78	45	44	89	89
RHB-Avg	.209	.256	.237	.229	.292	.265	90
RHB-HR	29	42	71	29	46	75	88

2001-2002

	Home Games			Away Games			
	Tigers	Opp	Total	Tigers	Opp	Total	Index
G	143	143	286	144	144	288	
Avg	.255	.278	.267	.252	.295	.273	98
AB	4741	5053	9794	4985	4943	9928	99
R	558	713	1271	603	850	1453	88
H	1208	1405	2613	1258	1456	2714	97
2B	210	277	487	294	326	620	80
3B	66	58	124	21	39	60	209
HR	107	115	222	125	291	316	71
BB	372	447	819	368	457	825	101
SO	771	772	1493	980	740	1720	88
E	129	90	219	128	94	222	99
E-Infield	104	76	180	94	82	176	103
LHB-Avg	.272	.289	.280	.264	.290	.277	101
LHB-HR	70	77	147	60	87	147	100
RHB-Avg	.238	.270	.255	.242	.298	.270	94
RHB-HR	37	38	75	65	104	169	45

2003 Rankings (American League)
- Lowest RHB batting-average factor
- Second-lowest batting-average factor
- Second-lowest double factor
- Second-lowest walk factor

Alan Trammell

2003 Season

Alan Trammell knew that when he returned to Detroit, where he was an icon as a player, he was being presented with a difficult task as manager. But no one could have possibly predicted just how difficult. The Tigers, with 119 losses, came within a single defeat of tying the 1962 New York Mets for the most losses in major league history in a single season. The Tigers unloaded veteran players such as Randall Simon, Damion Easley, Robert Fick and Mark Redman, getting either prospects or nothing in return. They went totally into a rebuilding mode, and most of the young players did not come through.

Offense

Trammell would prefer play it conservatively. He'd like a set batting order. He'd like to hit-and-run and bunt at the obvious times and steal when necessary, but not necessarily have his team running all the time. The problem is, none of those things were options last season. Trammell juggled his lineup a lot because he had to. The Tigers not only lost a lot of games, but they were blown out of a lot of games.

Pitching & Defense

Trammell relies heavily on pitching coach Bob Cluck, who emphasizes less velocity in order to gain better command. Trammell went both ways with starters, letting them pitch deep into games and getting out the quick hook, as he searched for a way to get his team on the winning track. However, he simply was unable to establish any real pattern.

2004 Outlook

Trammell mostly kept his cool under extremely trying circumstances. While the Tigers continued to play poorly on the field, he did greatly improve what had been a glaring lack of maturity among the players in the clubhouse. It was disappointing that the Tigers continued to make an extraordinary number of mental mistakes under Trammell's watch. It was an area he vowed to improve with his teaching skills. Whether he is better able to get his message across will have much to say about his team's success this season.

Born: 2/21/58 in Garden Grove, CA

Playing Experience: 1977-1996, Det

Managerial Experience: 1 season

Manager Statistics

Year	Team, Lg	W	L	Pct	GB	Finish
2003	Detroit, AL	43	119	.265	47.0	5th Central
1 Season		43	119	.265	–	–

2003 Starting Pitchers by Days Rest

	<=3	4	5	6+
Tigers Starts	1	75	55	21
Tigers ERA	1.23	5.78	6.11	5.16
AL Avg Starts	2	79	50	22
AL ERA	3.19	4.64	4.57	4.98

2003 Situational Stats

	Alan Trammell	AL Average
Hit & Run Success %	31.1	36.7
Stolen Base Success %	60.9	70.0
Platoon Pct.	72.2	61.7
Defensive Subs	13	23
High-Pitch Outings	2	5
Quick/Slow Hooks	13/16	19/16
Sacrifice Attempts	96	55

2003 Rankings (American League)

- 1st in sacrifice bunt attempts, hit-and-run attempts (119) and saves with over 1 inning pitched (14)
- 2nd in squeeze plays (6) and relief appearances (451)
- 3rd in fewest caught stealings of third base (2), sacrifice-bunt percentage (85.4%) and mid-inning pitching changes (221)

Jeremy Bonderman

2003 Season

Jeremy Bonderman pitched his way into the Tigers' rotation during spring training and stayed there most of the season. Despite numbers that would be considered subpar on most pitching staffs, he nonetheless was the Detroit's most consistent starting pitcher. Late in the season, as he tired and his fastball lost some its life, Bonderman was pulled from the rotation. Five of his seven appearances in September came in relief, as manager Alan Trammell kept him near a predetermined limit of 160 innings.

Pitching

Bonderman has a compact delivery and consistently hits the mid-90s with his fastball. He was clocked as high as 98 MPH during spring training, but pitched with less velocity during the season. He tends to throw harder early in games and loses some gas in the middle to late innings. His fastball sinks and tails away from righthanded hitters. Bonderman's best pitch might be his slider. He throws it in the mid-80s with a sharp break and a lot of depth, and he commands it well. He needs to develop a better changeup—the pitch definitely is his weak link. He held his poise remarkably well last season for a 20-year-old making his major league debut in just his second professional season.

Defense

Bonderman is a good athlete who fields his position well. He made just one error while logging 40 total chances. He moves well side to side. He isn't particularly quick to home plate and does not pay proper attention to baserunners. He yielded 25 stolen bases last year, which was the second-highest total in the American League.

2004 Outlook

Bonderman has the arm and mental makeup to someday be a No. 1 starter. How fast he comes along depends on how quickly he develops a serviceable changeup, and how rapidly the team behind him improves. Still, the Tigers will lean on him more heavily in 2004, and he's a good bet to reach the 200-inning mark if he can stay healthy.

Position: SP
Bats: R **Throws:** R
Ht: 6' 2" **Wt:** 210

Opening Day Age: 21
Born: 10/28/82 in Kennewick, WA
ML Seasons: 1

Overall Statistics

	W	L	Pct.	ERA	G	GS	Sv	IP	H	BB	SO	HR	Avg
'03	6	19	.240	5.56	33	28	0	162.0	193	58	108	23	.294
Car.	6	19	.240	5.56	33	28	0	162.0	193	58	108	23	.294

2003 Pitching Profile

	Jeremy Bonderman	AL Average
Overall Strike %	61.5	62.8
1st Pitch Strike %	54.8	58.7
Ratio	1.55	1.39
Strikeouts per 9 IP	6.00	6.11
Walks per 9 IP	3.22	3.16
Home Runs per 9 IP	1.28	1.11
Strikeout/Walk Ratio	1.86	1.93
Groundball/Flyball Ratio	1.42	1.18

2003 Situational Stats

	W	L	ERA	Sv	IP		AB	H	HR	RBI	Avg
Home	4	8	5.22	0	88.0	LHB	382	117	14	60	.306
Road	2	11	5.96	0	74.0	RHB	274	76	9	39	.277
First Half	3	13	4.88	0	103.1	Sc Pos	181	50	3	68	.276
Scnd Half	3	6	6.75	0	58.2	Clutch	21	7	0	4	.333

2003 Rankings (American League)

- 1st in losses among rookies
- 2nd in losses, wild pitches (12), stolen bases allowed (25), ERA among rookies, lowest winning percentage, highest slugging percentage allowed (.482) and least run support per nine innings (3.7)
- 3rd in highest ERA, highest batting average allowed (.294) and highest on-base percentage allowed (.352)
- 4th in runners caught stealing (9)
- 6th in fewest pitches thrown per batter (3.54)
- 7th in balks (2) and highest walks per nine innings (3.2)
- 8th in highest ERA at home
- Led the Tigers in walks allowed, strikeouts, wild pitches (12), balks (2), stolen bases allowed (25), highest strikeout-walk ratio (1.9), fewest pitches thrown per batter (3.54) and most strikeouts per nine innings (6.0)

Nate Cornejo

2003 Season

In his first full season in the major leagues, Nate Cornejo made 32 starts and was the rare Detroit pitcher to keep his ERA under 5.00. He started out well, but experienced a rough patch in June and July when he made several poor starts in a row. He rebounded and pitched better in August and September, although he had little to show for his efforts due to a lack of run support.

Pitching

In 2001, Cornejo combined to win 20 games while pitching at the minor and major league levels. At that time, he reminded scouts of Kevin Brown because his fastball consistently reached 92-94 MPH, with uncommon sink. While the sink still is there, the velocity is gone. Cornejo sometimes hits 88 MPH, but he mostly works in the 85-MPH range. He has a late-breaking slider and a good-enough changeup, but everything he does revolves around his fastball. Detroit pitching coach Bob Cluck tried to emphasize that Cornejo worry less about velocity and more about movement, but in the process, Cornejo lost his ability to miss bats. He struck out just 46 hitters last season.

Defense

Although he had surgery on both knees before the Tigers drafted him, Cornejo is an exceptional athlete, especially considering his size. He is extraordinarily quick off the mound and surehanded. His pickoff move to first also is exceptional, and opposing big league thieves have just a 50-percent career success rate on his watch.

2004 Outlook

Cornjeo made strides last season in his mental approach by developing a bulldog attitude. But his lack of velocity raises a red flag. Where it looked like he was a potential No. 1 or 2 starter a couple years ago, it appears he now might be a No. 4 or 5 starter at best. Not throwing as hard may have helped him stay in the major leagues, but it's a double-edged sword because Cornejo simply might not throw hard enough to reach what at one time seemed like his considerable potential.

Position: SP
Bats: R **Throws:** R
Ht: 6' 5" **Wt:** 245

Opening Day Age: 24
Born: 9/24/79 in Wellington, KS
ML Seasons: 3
Pronunciation: cor-NAY-ho

Overall Statistics

	W	L	Pct.	ERA	G	GS	Sv	IP	H	BB	SO	HR	Avg
'03	6	17	.261	4.67	32	32	0	194.2	236	58	46	18	.307
Car.	11	26	.297	5.14	51	51	0	287.1	362	104	91	34	.312

2003 Pitching Profile

	Nate Cornejo	AL Average
Overall Strike %	60.5	62.8
1st Pitch Strike %	59.9	58.7
Ratio	1.51	1.39
Strikeouts per 9 IP	2.13	6.11
Walks per 9 IP	2.68	3.16
Home Runs per 9 IP	0.83	1.11
Strikeout/Walk Ratio	0.79	1.93
Groundball/Flyball Ratio	1.70	1.18

2003 Situational Stats

	W	L	ERA	Sv	IP		AB	H	HR	RBI	Avg
Home	2	8	4.63	0	89.1	LHB	375	116	12	53	.309
Road	4	9	4.70	0	105.1	RHB	393	120	6	42	.305
First Half	4	7	4.44	0	103.1	Sc Pos	201	65	4	76	.323
Scnd Half	2	10	4.93	0	91.1	Clutch	75	22	1	5	.293

2003 Rankings (American League)

- 1st in lowest strikeout-walk ratio (0.8), highest batting average allowed (.307), least run support per nine innings (3.2) and fewest strikeouts per nine innings (2.1)
- 2nd in GDPs induced (30) and highest on-base percentage allowed (.356)
- 3rd in losses and lowest winning percentage
- 5th in hits allowed and highest batting average allowed with runners in scoring position
- 6th in highest groundball-flyball ratio allowed (1.7)
- Led the Tigers in ERA, complete games (2), innings pitched, hits allowed, walks allowed, GDPs induced (30), highest groundball fly ball ratio allowed (1.7), lowest ERA on the road and fewest home runs allowed per nine innings (.83)

Bobby Higginson

2003 Season

Players being paid more than $11 million, such as Bobby Higginson last season, simply are expected produce more than a .235 batting average, 14 home runs and 52 RBI. Higginson missed three weeks in July because of a pulled left hamstring muscle, an injury that bothered him most of the season. He also was suspended for two games after "directing inappropriate comments" at umpire Doug Eddings during and after an August 10 game against Minnesota. Higginson had been angry after being ejected from the game for arguing balls and strikes after popping out.

Hitting

For three seasons, Higginson has struggled to regain the form he had in 2000, when he batted .300 with 30 home runs and 102 RBI. He consistently turned on inside fastballs then, driving them hard, and sometimes deep, but now misses a lot of those pitches. He still draws his share of walks and does not strike out a lot for a power hitter. But is Higginson still a power hitter? The last three seasons, he's averaged 14 home runs and his RBI production has gone from 102 to 52.

Baserunning & Defense

Higginson is better in left field than right, but he played almost exclusively in right last season because the Tigers' corner outfielders lack range. When he plays mostly in left field, he ranks among the American League leaders in outfield assists. When he plays mostly in right, those assist numbers drop dramatically. His arm is more accurate than strong. Higginson has below-average speed for a major league outfielder, but he gets a good jump on the ball and is surehanded. He will steal a base when it is least expected and has good instincts as a baserunner.

2004 Outlook

Because Higginson has two years and $17 million remaining on his contract, the Tigers have little choice other than to hope he will regain his form from 2000. Whether he is productive or not, Higginson will be in the lineup every day, probably in right field.

Position: RF
Bats: L **Throws:** R
Ht: 5'11" **Wt:** 195

Opening Day Age: 33
Born: 8/18/70 in Philadelphia, PA
ML Seasons: 9

Overall Statistics

	G	AB	R	H	D	T	HR	RBI	SB	BB	SO	Avg	OBP	Slg
'03	130	469	61	110	13	4	14	52	8	59	73	.235	.320	.369
Car.	1221	4436	672	1224	246	31	175	644	86	578	707	.276	.360	.464

Where He Hits the Ball

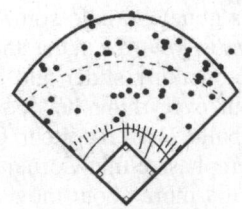 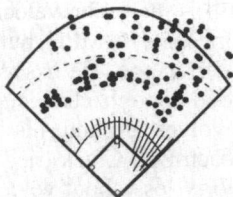

Vs. LHP   **Vs. RHP**

2003 Situational Stats

	AB	H	HR	RBI	Avg		AB	H	HR	RBI	Avg
Home	240	54	6	25	.225	LHP	154	35	3	19	.227
Road	229	56	8	27	.245	RHP	315	75	11	33	.238
First Half	268	63	5	23	.235	Sc Pos	102	22	3	36	.216
Scnd Half	201	47	9	29	.234	Clutch	81	15	0	5	.185

2003 Rankings (American League)

- 1st in lowest fielding percentage in right field (.981)
- 2nd in lowest batting average
- 3rd in errors in right field (5)
- Led the Tigers in walks, highest percentage of pitches taken (62.4), lowest percentage of swings that missed (11.5) and lowest percentage of swings on the first pitch (20.1)

Brandon Inge

2003 Season

Last season could not have gotten off to a worse beginning for Brandon Inge. Starting the year as Detroit's primary catcher, he was hitting just .150 when he was sent to Triple-A Toledo in mid-June. He returned to re-claim the starting catching job in August and hit .325 in his first 22 games back. However, he slumped in September (.188).

Hitting

Inge is a puzzle. He is strong, athletic and hard working. However, he is perpetually confused about what he is as a hitter. When he first arrived in the major leagues in 2001, he had an inside-out stroke and drove most pitches to right field. Now, he has a conventional approach with a stance that is neither open nor closed, but it hasn't improved his consistency as a hitter. Although he is not big, he does have power. At times, he will turn on a fastball and drive it a surprising distance. Inge's problem is that everything he does well as a hitter rarely shows up. In 840 major league at-bats, he is hitting .198, essentially making him an easy out.

Baserunning & Defense

Inge was a shortstop and bullpen closer at Virginia Commonwealth University when he was drafted by the Tigers and converted into a catcher. Although he is not a threat to steal, he runs well for his position, but he makes too many mental mistakes on the bases. He has a strong throwing arm and a quick release. He is agile behind the plate and has improved his pitch calling. Still, Inge tends to drop too many pitches, and like everything about his game, he lacks the consistency necessary to be an elite receiver. The tools, however, are there.

2004 Outlook

Inge did enough last season to still be considered a potential everyday catcher. The time is coming soon when the "potential" tag will be dropped and he will be viewed as a bust. In fact, that day may come in 2004 if he does not start producing on a consistent basis this year.

Position: C
Bats: R **Throws:** R
Ht: 5'11" **Wt:** 195

Opening Day Age: 26
Born: 5/19/77 in Lynchburg, VA
ML Seasons: 3
Pronunciation: inj

Overall Statistics

	G	AB	R	H	D	T	HR	RBI	SB	BB	SO	Avg	OBP	Slg
'03	104	330	32	67	15	3	8	30	4	24	79	.203	.265	.339
Car.	278	840	72	166	41	6	15	69	6	57	221	.198	.254	.314

Where He Hits the Ball

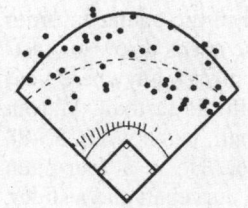 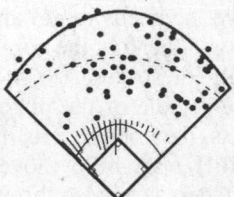

Vs. LHP　　　　　**Vs. RHP**

2003 Situational Stats

	AB	H	HR	RBI	Avg		AB	H	HR	RBI	Avg
Home	173	35	4	14	.202	LHP	110	27	5	12	.245
Road	157	32	4	16	.204	RHP	220	40	3	18	.182
First Half	167	25	4	11	.150	Sc Pos	66	9	0	16	.136
Scnd Half	163	42	4	19	.258	Clutch	65	11	2	4	.169

2003 Rankings (American League)

- 2nd in fielding percentage at catcher (.996)
- Led the Tigers in most pitches seen per plate appearance (4.06)

Mike Maroth

2003 Season

Mike Maroth made major league history last season. Problem is, it was for the dubious distinction of being the first pitcher since Oakland's Brian Kingman in 1980 to lose 20 or more games. The irony of Maroth's season is that the better he pitched, the more he lost. He was 4-13 before the All-Star break, but his ERA was 4.89. After the break, he was 5-8, but his ERA was 6.89. His primary function for the struggling Tigers essentially was to eat up innings, averaging roughly six innings in 33 starts.

Pitching

Maroth has little margin for error. He has an excellent changeup, but in order for it to be effective, he needs to get ahead in the count. In order to get ahead in the count, he needs throw his fastball for strikes. Yet, if he misses anywhere near the middle of the plate with his fastball, Maroth gets hammered. His fastball is between 85-88 MPH with little movement. He is a four-pitch pitcher, as he also throws a curveball and a slider, but the only pitch that frustrates hitters is his changeup. Despite all his problems last season, Maroth never complained. It did not phase him that he was closing in on the 20-loss mark.

Defense

Maroth fields his position well. He has some range and good presence once he gets the ball in his hands as a fielder. Maroth is quick to the plate and does a very good job of holding runners. His eight pickoffs in 2003 represented the best figure in the major leagues.

2004 Outlook

Maroth is a tough kid with a good approach to pitching, and there is a place for him in the major leagues. However, it's definitely not as a No. 1 starter. On a contending team, he would be an ideal spot starter and long reliever, or might even do well as a situational lefthander. But as long as he stays in Detroit, he will remain in the regular rotation.

Position: SP
Bats: L **Throws:** L
Ht: 6' 0" **Wt:** 190

Opening Day Age: 26
Born: 8/17/77 in Orlando, FL
ML Seasons: 2
Pronunciation: mah-ROTH

Overall Statistics

	W	L	Pct.	ERA	G	GS	Sv	IP	H	BB	SO	HR	Avg
'03	9	21	.300	5.73	33	33	0	193.1	231	50	87	34	.299
Car.	15	31	.326	5.23	54	54	0	322.0	367	86	145	41	.290

2003 Pitching Profile

	Mike Maroth	AL Average
Overall Strike %	60.9	62.8
1st Pitch Strike %	57.7	58.7
Ratio	1.45	1.39
Strikeouts per 9 IP	4.05	6.11
Walks per 9 IP	2.33	3.16
Home Runs per 9 IP	1.58	1.11
Strikeout/Walk Ratio	1.74	1.93
Groundball/Flyball Ratio	1.45	1.18

2003 Situational Stats

	W	L	ERA	Sv	IP		AB	H	HR	RBI	Avg
Home	3	12	5.08	0	102.2	LHB	171	44	5	22	.257
Road	6	9	6.45	0	90.2	RHB	602	187	29	93	.311
First Half	4	13	4.89	0	112.1	Sc Pos	174	58	8	77	.333
Scnd Half	5	8	6.89	0	81.0	Clutch	31	8	0	2	.258

2003 Rankings (American League)

- 1st in losses, home runs allowed, runners caught stealing (11), highest slugging percentage allowed (.502) and most homeruns allowed per nine innings (1.58)
- 2nd in pickoff throws (182), highest ERA, highest batting average allowed (.299) and highest ERA on the road
- 3rd in highest batting average allowed with runners in scoring position and fewest strikeouts per nine innings (4.1)
- 6th in lowest winning percentage
- Led the Tigers in wins, losses, games started, batters faced (847), home runs allowed, hit batsmen (8), pitches thrown (3,130), pickoff throws (182), runners caught stealing (11), winning percentage, lowest stolen-base percentage allowed (42.1), most run support per nine innings (5.4) and fewest walks per nine innings (2.3)

Craig Monroe

2003 Season

Given the opportunity to play every day, an opportunity he probably would not have received were he on a better team, Craig Monroe proved he is a major league-caliber player. He had 23 home runs and 70 RBI in 425 at-bats. Monroe also improved as the season moved on. Through June, he was batting just .206 with six home runs and 25 RBI. He finished the season with an eight-game hitting streak that raised his average to .240.

Hitting

Monroe is a classic power hitter with a lot of holes in his swing. He tries to pull everything and does not use the entire field. Pitchers have success pounding him with fastballs inside and working him away. Monroe is much more of a threat against lefthanded pitching. He had 14 home runs in 157 at-bats vs. lefthanders, compared to just nine homers in 268 at-bats against righties. He swings at too many bad pitches early in the count and does not draw enough walks.

Baserunning & Defense

Monroe has average speed for a major league left fielder. He does not steal many bases, but he isn't a baseclogger, either. His range is average, though he catches what he reaches. He had eight assists last season, but his arm ranks a notch above average. He definitely is an adequate left fielder, but he would be vulnerable in right or center field.

2004 Outlook

The Tigers had been looking at Monroe as a fifth or sixth outfielder, but he likely played his way into the starting lineup to begin this season. His ticket is his bat. In order to be an everyday major league player, Monroe needs to maintain the relatively consistent power production he displayed during the second half of 2003. He also will have to continue to push his batting average upward.

Position: LF/RF/DH
Bats: R **Throws:** R
Ht: 6' 1" **Wt:** 215

Opening Day Age: 27
Born: 2/27/77 in Texarkana, TX
ML Seasons: 3

Overall Statistics

	G	AB	R	H	D	T	HR	RBI	SB	BB	SO	Avg	OBP	Slg
'03	128	425	51	102	18	1	23	70	4	27	89	.240	.287	.449
Car.	168	502	62	116	20	1	26	76	6	33	112	.231	.281	.430

Where He Hits the Ball

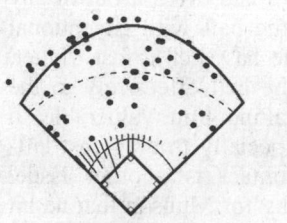
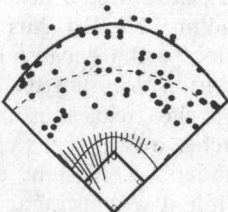

Vs. LHP	Vs. RHP

2003 Situational Stats

	AB	H	HR	RBI	Avg		AB	H	HR	RBI	Avg
Home	193	44	10	33	.228	LHP	157	46	14	34	.230
Road	232	58	13	37	.250	RHP	268	56	9	36	.209
First Half	216	49	9	33	.227	Sc Pos	103	30	10	52	.291
Scnd Half	209	53	14	37	.254	Clutch	69	11	3	10	.159

2003 Rankings (American League)

- 2nd in home runs among rookies
- 4th in errors in left field (4)
- 5th in lowest batting average with two strikes (.135)
- 6th in lowest batting average in the clutch
- 9th in highest percentage of swings that missed (23.5)
- 10th in errors in right field (3)

Eric Munson

2003 Season

Following the 2002 season, Eric Munson, a catcher at Southern Cal and a first baseman in the minors, went to the instructional league to learn how to play third base. He played well enough there during spring training to open the season as the Tigers' everyday third sacker. Munson held the position until suffering a season-ending fractured left thumb on August 11. Despite the injury, he had by far his most productive major league campaign.

Hitting

Munson has an exceptionally quick bat, which is proving to be both a blessing and a curse for him. He can turn on a fastball and drive it out of any stadium. He also hits the ball with exceptional velocity. But because he has such a fast trigger, Munson does not hit the ball effectively to the opposite field, thus making him vulnerable to pitches away. That's especially true against left-handers. Consistent contact is another issue. While it was encouraging for Munson that he hit 18 home runs last season, it was disappointing he had only nine other extra-base hits. He doesn't strike out much for a free-swinger, but Munson does not walk much, either. He's not a particularly cerebral hitter.

Baserunning & Defense

Munson does not run well and is awkward defensively. That's why it was shocking he took to third base. Still, he grades out as a below-average major league player at the hot corner. His range is limited and his footwork is not good. He also is slow transferring the ball from his glove to his throwing hand. His arm is average in terms of strength, but he shifts his feet awkwardly sometimes and it leads to throwing errors.

2004 Outlook

Munson has one positive tool: his bat. His career will be based on how well he hits. Last season was a step in the right direction, but he still has yet to have a breakout campaign. At 26, he's getting a little old for the prospect label. It's time for Munson to produce.

Position: 3B
Bats: L **Throws:** R
Ht: 6' 3" **Wt:** 230

Opening Day Age: 26
Born: 10/3/77 in San Diego, CA
ML Seasons: 4

Overall Statistics

	G	AB	R	H	D	T	HR	RBI	SB	BB	SO	Avg	OBP	Slg
'03	99	313	28	75	9	0	18	50	3	35	61	.240	.312	.441
Car.	137	443	35	96	12	1	21	62	3	44	94	.217	.286	.391

Where He Hits the Ball

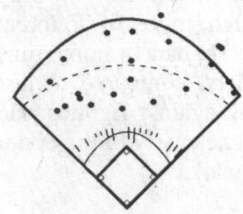
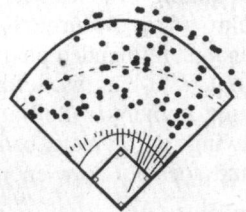

Vs. LHP   **Vs. RHP**

2003 Situational Stats

	AB	H	HR	RBI	Avg		AB	H	HR	RBI	Avg
Home	165	44	7	22	.267	LHP	77	16	3	8	.208
Road	148	31	11	28	.209	RHP	236	59	15	42	.250
First Half	254	60	12	36	.236	Sc Pos	66	16	4	33	.242
Scnd Half	59	15	6	14	.254	Clutch	58	12	2	10	.207

2003 Rankings (American League)

- 3rd in errors at third base (19)
- 4th in home runs among rookies
- Led the Tigers in sacrifice flies (7) and HR frequency (17.4 ABs per HR)

Carlos Pena

2003 Season

In his first full season in the major leagues, Carlos Pena posted below-average numbers across the board for a first baseman. He got off to a slow start, hitting just .174 with little power in March/April. He had raised his batting average to .233 when he went on the disabled list with a pulled hamstring muscle in June. When he returned, Pena played well through August but was not able to sustain his momentum in September.

Hitting

Pena likes the ball on the inner half of the plate, although he has a tendency to get jammed. Pitchers like to work him away because he does not take pitches to the opposite field very often. There is a relatively small area where Pena consistently centers the ball, so he can be pitched to easily with runners in scoring position. Because he tries to pull the ball too much, Pena often pulls off it. He has power and will hit a home run or crush a double up the gap when you least expect it. That, of course, speaks volumes about his lack of consistency as a hitter.

Baserunning & Defense

Pena is woefully slow and is not a smart baserunner. He came to the Tigers from Oakland in a trade with a reputation as an exceptional fielder. Although he showed flashes of brilliance with the glove in 2002, last season he regressed defensively. He dropped throws, booted easy fielding chances and did not throw the ball well. Compounding the issue was the timing of his mistakes. Too many were at crucial times of ball games. His lack of consistency was both alarming and puzzling.

2004 Outlook

There was a time, not long ago, when Pena was considered one of the best prospects in baseball. He's since been traded from Texas to Oakland, and from Oakland to Detroit. In major league stints at all three places, his performance has been unexpectedly underwhelming. Pena will turn 26 in May, and his career clearly is at a crossroads.

Position: 1B
Bats: L **Throws:** L
Ht: 6' 2" **Wt:** 215

Opening Day Age: 25
Born: 5/17/78 in Santo Domingo, DR
ML Seasons: 3
Pronunciation: PAIN-yuh

Overall Statistics

	G	AB	R	H	D	T	HR	RBI	SB	BB	SO	Avg	OBP	Slg
'03	131	452	51	112	21	6	18	50	4	53	123	.248	.332	.440
Car.	268	911	100	224	42	11	40	114	6	104	251	.246	.327	.448

Where He Hits the Ball

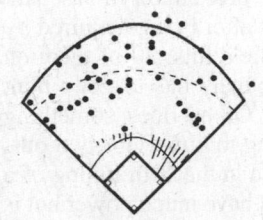 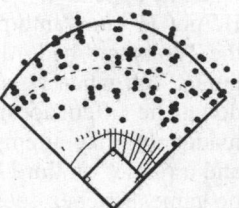

Vs. LHP   **Vs. RHP**

2003 Situational Stats

	AB	H	HR	RBI	Avg			AB	H	HR	RBI	Avg
Home	227	57	8	25	.251		LHP	149	31	5	18	.200
Road	225	55	10	25	.244		RHP	303	81	13	32	.267
First Half	212	52	8	25	.245		Sc Pos	107	23	5	36	.215
Scnd Half	240	60	10	25	.250		Clutch	76	22	4	11	.289

2003 Rankings (American League)

- 1st in errors at first base (13) and lowest fielding percentage at first base (.990)
- 3rd in lowest percentage of swings put into play (37.2)
- 5th in lowest batting average vs. lefthanded pitchers
- 6th in highest percentage of swings that missed (24.6) and lowest batting average with runners in scoring position
- 7th in lowest batting average with two strikes (.140)
- 9th in strikeouts and lowest batting average
- Led the Tigers in fewest GDPs per GDP situation (6.1%)

Alex Sanchez

2003 Season

Detroit acquired center fielder Alex Sanchez in a trade from Milwaukee on May 27 for minor league pitcher Chad Petty and outfielder Noochie Varner, two of the Tigers' better prospects. He was moved because Brewers manager Ned Yost reportedly was frustrated with his lack of fundamental play and didn't like Sanchez' work ethic. Sanchez held the regular center-field position for the Tigers the remainder of the season. Hitting in the leadoff spot, Sanchez batted .289 for Detroit and stole 44 bases.

Hitting

Sanchez is wildly inconsistent. There are times when he appears to be the best bunter in baseball. He put 71 bunts into play after being acquired by the Tigers and had 40 infield hits, 30 of them on bunts. Yet, when he absolutely has to get a bunt down, he often doesn't. Or he does something maddening like attempting to bunt with two outs and a runner on third base in the 11th inning of a tie game. Sanchez doesn't have much power but is capable of shooting the ball through the infield consistently. He hangs in well against lefthanded pitching, but doesn't work deep enough in the count or draw enough walks.

Baserunning & Defense

Sanchez is capable of stealing a base at any time. On an 80 scouting scale, he is widely considered a 70 runner, meaning he is one of the fastest players in baseball. Given that speed, he still gets thrown out attempting to steal at a relatively high rate. Defensively, Sanchez has the wheels to roam spacious Comerica Park, but he doesn't always get a good jump on the ball and sometimes takes wayward angles. His arm is below average.

2004 Outlook

Sanchez seems to respond well to the teaching style of Detroit manager Alan Trammell. Although he has a long way to go before he is viewed as a consistent performer, Sanchez did make strides last season. He has all the physical tools to be a top center fielder and leadoff hitter, and will be a regular this season.

Position: CF
Bats: L **Throws:** L
Ht: 5'10" **Wt:** 159

Opening Day Age: 27
Born: 8/26/76 in Havana, Cuba
ML Seasons: 3

Overall Statistics

	G	AB	R	H	D	T	HR	RBI	SB	BB	SO	Avg	OBP	Slg
'03	144	557	58	160	23	8	1	32	52	25	74	.287	.319	.363
Car.	286	1019	120	288	36	17	2	69	95	61	149	.283	.324	.357

Where He Hits the Ball

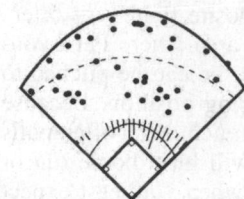
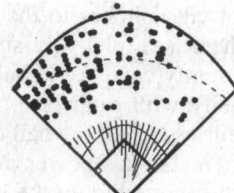

Vs. LHP   **Vs. RHP**

2003 Situational Stats

	AB	H	HR	RBI	Avg		AB	H	HR	RBI	Avg
Home	269	74	0	10	.275	LHP	152	47	0	9	.309
Road	288	86	1	22	.299	RHP	405	113	1	23	.279
First Half	330	90	1	21	.273	Sc Pos	96	21	1	31	.219
Scnd Half	227	70	0	11	.308	Clutch	92	19	0	7	.207

2003 Rankings (American League)

- 1st in caught stealing (18), bunts in play (71) and errors in center field (6)
- 2nd in stolen bases (44)
- 3rd in steals of third (7)
- 4th in lowest on-base percentage for a leadoff hitter (.317)
- 10th in lowest stolen-base percentage (71.0)
- Led the Tigers in stolen bases (44), caught stealing (18), highest groundball-flyball ratio (1.8), bunts in play (71), steals of third (7), batting average vs. lefthanded pitchers (.330), on-base percentage for a leadoff hitter (.317), and batting average on the road (.321)

Ramon Santiago

Position: SS/2B
Bats: B **Throws:** R
Ht: 5'11" **Wt:** 167

Opening Day Age: 24
Born: 8/31/79 in Las Matas de Farfan, DR
ML Seasons: 2

2003 Season

Ramon Santiago began the season as the Tigers' regular second baseman. Detroit manager Alan Trammell had decided to move him from his natural position—shortstop—to second as the Tigers broke in a new double-play combination with Santiago and shortstop Omar Infante. Santiago struggled at the keystone, however, and at one point made eight errors in 13 games and was removed from the starting lineup when Detroit called up Warren Morris from Triple-A Toledo. Because Infante struggled at shortstop and also was sent to Toledo, Santiago was moved back to short, where he played well defensively the remainder of the season. At the plate, Santiago did his best work late in the season. He had 11 RBI and hit .271 in September.

Hitting

Santiago's problem is obvious: He doesn't have enough strength to hit major league pitching. A switch-hitter who is an outstanding bunter, he seldom drives the ball, especially righthanded. He's more of a threat hitting from the left side of the plate. One statistical fact defines Santiago as a hitter—despite walking just 33 times in 444 at-bats last season, Santiago still had a higher on-base percentage than slugging percentage.

Baserunning & Defense

His struggles at second base aside, Santiago is a solid middle infielder. Before he tore a rotator cuff near the end of his first full professional season, Santiago had exceptional arm strength. After resting his arm for a full season while he was a designated hitter, he literally had to re-learn how throw. While his arm doesn't have the overwhelming zip it used to, it is at least average in strength and is accurate. Although more quick than fast, Santiago has the potential to steal 20 or more bases in a season. His problem is reaching base.

2004 Outlook

Santiago didn't do enough last season to make anyone believe he has a future as an everyday player. He is average to slightly above average as a major league shortstop defensively, but he has to hit more or teams always will be looking to replace him.

Overall Statistics

	G	AB	R	H	D	T	HR	RBI	SB	BB	SO	Avg	OBP	Slg
'03	141	444	41	100	18	1	2	29	10	33	66	.225	.292	.284
Car.	206	666	74	154	23	6	6	49	18	46	114	.231	.297	.311

Where He Hits the Ball

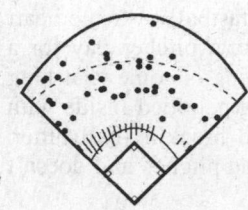 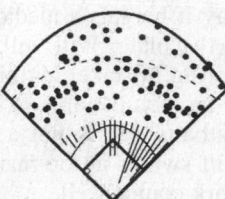

Vs. LHP **Vs. RHP**

2003 Situational Stats

	AB	H	HR	RBI	Avg		AB	H	HR	RBI	Avg
Home	224	56	1	18	.250	LHP	134	25	1	1	.197
Road	220	44	1	11	.200	RHP	310	75	1	25	.242
First Half	239	54	1	7	.226	Sc Pos	94	22	0	27	.234
Scnd Half	205	46	1	22	.224	Clutch	76	17	0	4	.224

2003 Rankings (American League)

- 1st in sacrifice bunts (18), lowest batting average, lowest slugging percentage, lowest HR frequency (222.0 ABs per HR), lowest batting average vs. lefthanded pitchers and lowest batting average on the road
- 2nd in bunts in play (49)
- 3rd in lowest on-base percentage
- 5th in fewest pitches seen per plate appearance (3.29)
- 7th in highest groundball-flyball ratio (1.8) and errors at second base (10)
- 10th in highest percentage of swings on the first pitch (33.8)
- Led the Tigers in sacrifice bunts (18), stolen-base percentage (71.4) and batting average with the bases loaded (.429)

Kevin Witt

2003 Season

Kevin Witt was signed as a minor league free agent prior to last season and was called up to Detroit May 16 after hitting .316 with nine home runs and 28 RBI for Triple-A Toledo. He hit well upon his arrival in Detroit, and was in the lineup as a regular against righthanded pitching throughout most of June and July. He played 27 games at first base, 13 in left field and five at third, though he primarily served as the team's designated hitter. As the season wore on and he slumped, Witt started less frequently.

Hitting

The knock on Witt is that he has slider bat speed. He has excellent power and will hit the ball a long way if he gets a mediocre fastball over the heart of the plate. Witt will make a pitcher pay for a glaring mistake, but his swing is somewhat long so he is vulnerable to being pounded inside with fastballs. He is not a good breaking-ball hitter. Witt swings at too many bad pitches and doesn't work counts well.

Baserunning & Defense

Witt doesn't really have a position, nor is he particularly versatile. The reason the Tigers moved him around so much last season was to get his bat in the lineup while he was hot. He is not fluid in the field and doesn't throw well. His range also is below average. An oddity, however, is that while he is considered a below-average fielder, Witt has yet to make an error in 337 chances in the major leagues. He is of little threat on the basepaths.

2004 Outlook

In the end, the Tigers were not impressed enough with Witt, and they removed him from the 40-man roster after the season. St. Louis signed him to a minor league contract with an invite to the big league camp for spring training. With Albert Pujols possibly moving to first base in 2004, Witt may not stick around the majors as long or play as much.

Position: DH/1B/LF
Bats: L **Throws:** R
Ht: 6' 4" **Wt:** 220

Opening Day Age: 28
Born: 1/5/76 in High Point, NC
ML Seasons: 4

Overall Statistics

	G	AB	R	H	D	T	HR	RBI	SB	BB	SO	Avg	OBP	Slg
'03	93	270	25	71	9	0	10	26	1	15	68	.263	.301	.407
Car.	127	338	33	84	10	0	13	36	1	19	87	.249	.287	.393

Where He Hits the Ball

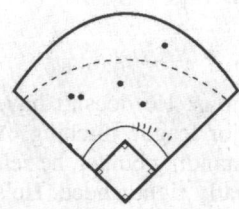
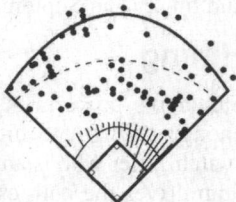

Vs. LHP   **Vs. RHP**

2003 Situational Stats

	AB	H	HR	RBI	Avg		AB	H	HR	RBI	Avg
Home	133	31	4	13	.233	LHP	29	7	0	2	.241
Road	137	40	6	13	.292	RHP	241	64	10	24	.266
First Half	147	39	6	17	.265	Sc Pos	67	13	1	17	.194
Scnd Half	123	32	4	9	.260	Clutch	39	5	0	2	.128

2003 Rankings (American League)

- Did not rank near the top or bottom in any category

Dmitri Young

2003 Season

Dmitri Young may have been the one and only bright spot for the Tigers in an otherwise dismal season. Despite not having anyone capable of protecting him in the batting order, Young arguably had his best all-around season. After hitting just .173 in March/April, he hit .355 in May and .330 in June. He also produced a 16-game hitting streak in August, during which he batted .426.

Hitting

Young is a switch-hitter who is equally proficient from the right or left side. He has exceptionally quick hands and loves fastballs. He especially likes first-pitch fastballs, and damages a pitcher who is careless with one. He hits mostly line drives, and because much of his home-run power is gap-to-gap, Young performs better on the road than at roomy Comerica Park. Just 10 of his 29 home runs were hit at Comerica Park last season. There was a time when he presented the best of both worlds, because for a big player with power, he didn't strike out that much. That trend changed last season, however, when he fanned a career-high 130 times. His previous high had been 94 whiffs in 1988.

Baserunning & Defense

Considering his size, Young is fairly athletic. He can play the outfield, and even third base for a day or two in a pinch. But in an ideal world, he would stay put at first base or DH. The Tigers, however, have been living in a far from ideal world, so Young logged 61 games in a the outfield and 16 at third last season. He hustles and has OK hands, but he is not fluid and his arm strength is below average. Young does not steal often, but he has enough speed to take an extra base when it's presented.

2004 Outlook

Young will be entering the third year of a four-year, $28.5 million contract. He is a relatively expensive player, but one who produces. At 30, he's in his prime and will be leaned on heavily to produce in the middle of the batting order.

Position: DH/LF/3B
Bats: B **Throws:** R
Ht: 6' 2" **Wt:** 245

Opening Day Age: 30
Born: 10/11/73 in Vicksburg, MS
ML Seasons: 8

Overall Statistics

	G	AB	R	H	D	T	HR	RBI	SB	BB	SO	Avg	OBP	Slg
'03	155	562	78	167	34	7	29	85	2	58	130	.297	.372	.537
Car.	900	3122	424	924	205	22	108	444	23	262	559	.296	.353	.480

Where He Hits the Ball

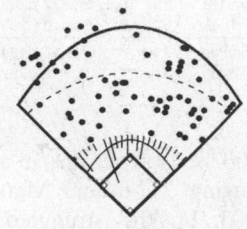 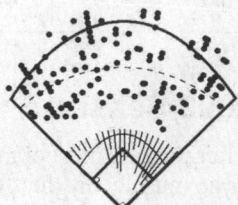

Vs. LHP   **Vs. RHP**

2003 Situational Stats

	AB	H	HR	RBI	Avg			AB	H	HR	RBI	Avg
Home	287	84	10	34	.293		LHP	191	56	9	27	.293
Road	275	83	19	51	.302		RHP	371	111	20	58	.299
First Half	325	92	18	49	.283		Sc Pos	124	37	6	55	.298
Scnd Half	237	75	11	36	.316		Clutch	91	26	3	11	.286

2003 Rankings (American League)

- 2nd in lowest percentage of swings put into play (35.4)
- 3rd in highest percentage of swings that missed (26.5)
- 4th in intentional walks (16), strikeouts and highest percentage of swings on the first pitch (39.9)
- Led the Tigers in batting average, home runs, at-bats, runs scored, hits, singles, doubles, triples, total bases (302), RBI, hit by pitch (11), times on base (236), GDPs (16), pitches seen (2,344), plate appearances (635), games played, slugging percentage, on-base percentage, batting average with runners in scoring position, cleanup slugging percentage (.536)

Matt Anderson

Position: RP
Bats: R **Throws:** R
Ht: 6' 4" **Wt:** 200

Opening Day Age: 27
Born: 8/17/76 in Louisville, KY
ML Seasons: 6

Overall Statistics

	W	L	Pct.	ERA	G	GS	Sv	IP	H	BB	SO	HR	Avg
'03	0	1	.000	5.40	23	0	3	23.1	25	9	13	5	.272
Car.	15	7	.682	4.89	245	0	26	246.2	230	146	220	27	.251

2003 Situational Stats

	W	L	ERA	Sv	IP		AB	H	HR	RBI	Avg
Home	0	0	8.44	1	10.2	LHB	35	10	2	7	.286
Road	0	1	2.84	2	12.2	RHB	57	15	3	10	.263
First Half	0	1	6.17	3	11.2	Sc Pos	31	6	2	13	.194
Scnd Half	0	0	4.63	0	11.2	Clutch	39	11	1	6	.282

2003 Season

After missing most of the 2002 season because of a torn muscle in his throwing shoulder, Matt Anderson returned in 2003, but he struggled. Ineffective early in the season, he was sent to Triple-A Toledo May 7. He did not return to the major leagues until rosters expanded in September.

Pitching & Defense

When he was drafted first overall in 1997, and in 2001 when he recorded 22 saves, Anderson often threw 100 MPH or harder. Now he sometimes will touch 95 MPH, but his fastball usually is clocked at 92-93 MPH. Since returning from a shoulder ailment, his arm angle has been down. The result is his fastball has flattened out. Anderson also throws a hard breaking ball but doesn't command it particularly well. When he was throwing harder, he induced a lot of swinging strikeouts with his breaking ball, but that's more difficult now that his velocity and control have decreased. Anderson is exceptionally athletic and an excellent fielder.

2004 Outlook

It's little secret Tigers officials have been frustrated by Anderson's lack of maturity. It's their hope he has matured from the adversity of the last two seasons because he still has a good enough arm to make him an effective closer or setup man.

Eric Eckenstahler

Position: RP
Bats: L **Throws:** L
Ht: 6' 7" **Wt:** 220

Opening Day Age: 27
Born: 12/17/76 in Waukegan, IL
ML Seasons: 2

Overall Statistics

	W	L	Pct.	ERA	G	GS	Sv	IP	H	BB	SO	HR	Avg
'03	0	0	—	2.87	20	0	0	15.2	9	15	12	0	.167
Car.	1	0	1.000	3.80	27	0	0	23.2	23	17	25	1	.253

2003 Situational Stats

	W	L	ERA	Sv	IP		AB	H	HR	RBI	Avg
Home	0	0	1.04	0	8.2	LHB	27	5	0	3	.185
Road	0	0	5.14	0	7.0	RHB	27	4	0	2	.148
First Half	0	0	—	0	0.0	Sc Pos	15	1	0	4	.067
Scnd Half	0	0	2.87	0	15.2	Clutch	9	2	0	0	.222

2003 Season

Eric Eckenstahler was called up from Triple-A Toledo during the last week of July for his second stint in the major leagues. He had pitched in seven games for the Tigers during the 2002 season. After a couple rough outings in late August last year, Eckenstahler closed the season by allowing just one run in his final eight appearances, covering 6.1 innings. Before being called up, he was 3-6 with a 3.16 ERA in 39 games for Toledo.

Pitching & Defense

At 6-foot-7, Eckenstahler throws from a three-quarters arm angle. There is a lot of movement in his delivery, which makes the ball difficult for hitters to pick up. His fastball consistently clocks in at 90 MPH, topping out at 92 MPH. That should make him tough on lefthanded hitters, although he had more success against righthanders last season. His fastball is his best pitch, but he does have a late-breaking slider. Eckenstahler is a big man who doesn't move well on the mound. He's had only two fielding chances in 27 games as a major leaguer.

2004 Outlook

If Eckenstahler has a role in the major leagues, it will be as a situational lefty. The tougher he is on lefthanded hitters, the longer his career will be.

Franklyn German

Position: RP
Bats: R **Throws:** R
Ht: 6' 7" **Wt:** 270

Opening Day Age: 24
Born: 1/20/80 in San Cristobal, DR
ML Seasons: 2
Pronunciation: her-MAHN

Overall Statistics

	W	L	Pct.	ERA	G	GS	Sv	IP	H	BB	SO	HR	Avg
'03	2	4	.333	6.04	45	0	5	44.2	47	45	41	5	.273
Car.	3	4	.429	5.26	52	0	6	51.1	50	47	47	5	.260

2003 Situational Stats

	W	L	ERA	Sv	IP		AB	H	HR	RBI	Avg
Home	0	2	6.75	2	21.1	LHB	80	19	2	13	.238
Road	2	2	5.40	3	23.1	RHB	92	28	3	12	.304
First Half	2	3	3.90	5	32.1	Sc Pos	59	16	0	17	.271
Scnd Half	0	1	11.68	0	12.1	Clutch	83	19	1	9	.229

2003 Season

Franklyn German began the season with the Tigers, but he was sent to Triple-A Toledo in late June because of control problems. German was 2-3 with a 3.90 ERA at the time of his demotion, though his numbers were misleading. He walked 32 hitters and hit two more in 32.1 innings. After going 1-4 with a 2.45 ERA at Toledo, German returned to Detroit in late August and continued to struggle with his control.

Pitching & Defense

German is the classic big, hard-throwing righthander. The ball looks small in his hand, and he constantly hits the mid-90s with his fastball. His fastball, however, is straight, and he tends to get it up in the strike zone. German commands his fastball poorly and constantly falls behind in the count. It's a shame, too, because he has an outstanding split-finger pitch. It would be a devastating offering if he were able to set it up with his fastball. He does not hold runners well and is an average fielder.

2004 Outlook

If German learns to command his fastball to set up his split-finger pitch, he quickly will become one of the best closers in baseball. But that's a huge "if" based on what he presented last season.

Shane Halter

Position: 3B/SS/2B/1B
Bats: R **Throws:** R
Ht: 6' 0" **Wt:** 195

Opening Day Age: 34
Born: 11/8/69 in LaPlata, MD
ML Seasons: 7

Overall Statistics

	G	AB	R	H	D	T	HR	RBI	SB	BB	SO	Avg	OBP	Slg
'03	114	360	33	78	5	2	12	30	2	27	77	.217	.269	.342
Car.	644	1785	191	445	88	18	41	184	16	139	384	.249	.306	.388

2003 Situational Stats

	AB	H	HR	RBI	Avg		AB	H	HR	RBI	Avg
Home	161	37	6	15	.230	LHP	152	37	6	15	.243
Road	199	41	6	15	.206	RHP	208	41	6	15	.197
First Half	193	44	6	18	.228	Sc Pos	84	17	1	19	.202
Scnd Half	167	34	6	12	.204	Clutch	65	19	3	9	.292

2003 Season

A veteran on a team going through a youth movement, Shane Halter often got lost in the shuffle. He played little early in the season, but got more playing time as the Tigers' younger players struggled.

Hitting, Baserunning & Defense

Halter does have some power. What he lacked last season was the consistent power he displayed the previous two years. While he had 12 home runs, he had just five doubles and two triples. His lack of patience at the plate also is puzzling. He hits lefthanders much better than righthanders. Halter is the classic jack of all trades, but the master of none defensively. He started at every infield position last season and played a little bit in the outfield. He's a below-average major league player defensively at each of those spots. It's not just a range issue. Halter makes too many errors on routine plays. He has below-average speed.

2004 Outlook

Put in the right position as a utilityman, Halter can be a useful major league player. He stings the ball well for a backup, and is adequate defensively if he isn't exposed at one position on a daily basis over an extended period time.

Detroit

137

Warren Morris

Position: 2B
Bats: L **Throws:** R
Ht: 5'11" **Wt:** 188

Opening Day Age: 30
Born: 1/11/74 in Alexandria, LA
ML Seasons: 5

Overall Statistics

	G	AB	R	H	D	T	HR	RBI	SB	BB	SO	Avg	OBP	Slg
'03	97	346	37	94	13	2	6	37	4	23	42	.272	.316	.373
Car.	440	1495	176	399	70	7	26	164	16	150	218	.267	.334	.375

2003 Situational Stats

	AB	H	HR	RBI	Avg		AB	H	HR	RBI	Avg
Home	166	50	4	18	.301	LHP	77	22	0	7	.286
Road	180	44	2	19	.244	RHP	269	72	6	30	.268
First Half	119	35	3	11	.294	Sc Pos	89	25	2	33	.281
Scnd Half	227	59	3	26	.260	Clutch	47	12	0	4	.255

2003 Season

Warren Morris was signed by the Tigers prior to last season as a minor league free agent and began the season at Triple-A Toledo. When youngsters Omar Infante and Ramon Santiago struggled as a double-play combination, he was called to the major leagues in early June. He subsequently had a streak from June 14-22 during which he hit three home runs in eight games and raised his batting average to .348. He cooled down after that.

Hitting, Baserunning & Defense

Morris has a consistent, level swing, but when he's able to get the bat to the ball, he is capable of doing only minimal damage. He will run into a pitch and drive it over the right-field wall every now and then, but for the most part he has struggled to match the 15-homer output he had with Pittsburgh as a rookie in 1999. Morris has little speed and shows considerably below-average range in the field, though he usually will handle the routine play.

2004 Outlook

Looking for younger players with more upside, the Tigers removed Morris from the 40-man roster after the season before re-signing him to a minor league deal for 2004. Morris is limited in too many ways to help most teams.

Danny Patterson

Position: RP
Bats: R **Throws:** R
Ht: 6' 0" **Wt:** 190

Opening Day Age: 33
Born: 2/17/71 in San Gabriel, CA
ML Seasons: 8

Overall Statistics

	W	L	Pct.	ERA	G	GS	Sv	IP	H	BB	SO	HR	Avg
'03	0	0	–	4.08	19	0	3	17.2	15	4	19	1	.227
Car.	24	18	.571	4.07	313	0	7	342.2	374	96	226	28	.282

2003 Situational Stats

	W	L	ERA	Sv	IP		AB	H	HR	RBI	Avg
Home	0	0	6.00	2	9.0	LHB	34	6	1	4	.176
Road	0	0	2.08	1	8.2	RHB	32	9	0	4	.281
First Half	0	0	–	0	0.0	Sc Pos	22	6	1	7	.273
Scnd Half	0	0	4.08	3	17.2	Clutch	22	5	0	2	.227

2003 Season

Danny Patterson underwent Tommy John surgery on his throwing elbow in June of 2002 and did not return to a major league mound until July of the last season. After just 19 appearances, many pitching through discomfort, Patterson again was shut down for the remainder of the season in early September.

Pitching & Defense

Patterson never has been a hard thrower. He usually works in the mid-80s or slightly higher with his fastball. He cuts across the ball with his fingers and throws a swing-back fastball. Patterson neither walks many hitters nor strikes out many hitters. He is a poor athlete and subsequently does little to stand out in the field. He handles what he can get to, however, and has committed just one big league error in his eight seasons. He is vulnerable to being bunted upon. He is, however, quick to home plate out of the set position. He also has an excellent third-to-first pickoff move.

2004 Outlook

Patterson is entering the final year of a three-year, $7 million contract. Ideally, he's a long reliever, perhaps even a setup man. Patterson showed enough last season to indicate he still can be an effective major league pitcher, but his health is an obvious concern.

Ben Petrick

Position: LF/CF
Bats: R **Throws:** R
Ht: 6' 0" **Wt:** 200

Opening Day Age: 26
Born: 4/7/77 in Salem, OR
ML Seasons: 5
Pronunciation:
PEET-rick

Overall Statistics

	G	AB	R	H	D	T	HR	RBI	SB	BB	SO	Avg	OBP	Slg
'03	46	122	18	27	6	0	4	12	0	8	31	.221	.269	.369
Car.	240	669	114	172	37	5	27	94	5	78	177	.257	.336	.448

2003 Situational Stats

	AB	H	HR	RBI	Avg		AB	H	HR	RBI	Avg
Home	67	15	2	4	.224	LHP	58	15	1	7	.259
Road	55	12	2	8	.218	RHP	64	12	3	5	.188
First Half	2	0	0	0	.000	Sc Pos	17	4	0	7	.235
Scnd Half	120	27	4	12	.225	Clutch	19	1	0	0	.053

2003 Season

Ben Petrick was acquired by Detroit from Colorado on July 13 for pitcher Adam Bernero. Once considered a top catching prospect, he played mostly outfield last season. He had a streak in August during which he had a couple key hits for the struggling Tigers. Yet, he slumped with just one home run and two RBI in 45 at-bats during September.

Hitting, Baserunning & Defense

In 669 major league at-bats, Petrick has 27 home runs, 37 doubles and five triples, so he has some power. He has a short swing, though he struggles with inside heat. He doesn't have a lot of speed, but he is somewhat athletic and will make a spectacular catch in the outfield now and then. Despite his sometimes alarming throwing problems, Petrick's best position is catcher. It was in the back of the Tigers' minds when they acquired him that he will return full-time behind the plate.

2004 Outlook

If Petrick has a long-term future in the major leagues, it will be as a catcher. As an outfielder, he is viewed more as a "4-A" player, meaning he ranks either as one of the best players on a Triple-A roster or the 24th or 25th man on a major league roster.

Nate Robertson

Position: SP
Bats: R **Throws:** L
Ht: 6' 2" **Wt:** 215

Opening Day Age: 26
Born: 9/3/77 in Wichita, KS
ML Seasons: 2

Overall Statistics

	W	L	Pct.	ERA	G	GS	Sv	IP	H	BB	SO	HR	Avg
'03	1	2	.333	5.44	8	8	0	44.2	55	23	33	6	.306
Car.	1	3	.250	6.45	14	9	0	53.0	70	27	36	9	.318

2003 Situational Stats

	W	L	ERA	Sv	IP		AB	H	HR	RBI	Avg
Home	1	1	5.08	0	33.2	LHB	30	9	0	2	.300
Road	0	1	6.55	0	11.0	RHB	150	46	6	19	.307
First Half	0	0	—	0	0.0	Sc Pos	36	10	0	11	.278
Scnd Half	1	2	5.44	0	44.2	Clutch	12	2	0	0	.167

2003 Season

After compiling a 9-7 record with a 3.14 ERA in 24 appearances and 23 starts for Triple-A Toledo, Nate Robertson was called to Detroit in mid-August. Thrust immediately into the starting rotation, he lasted five or more innings in seven of his eight starts. His best start was his Detroit debut against Texas August 18 when he allowed two runs on eight hits in 8.1 innings

Pitching & Defense

Robertson goes out to the mound with two pretty good pitches. His fastball is between 88-92 MPH and has decent movement. He also throws a respectable changeup, although it would probably be a stretch it to call it his out pitch. He's a tough kid with a bulldog mentality who doesn't give in easily to hitters. He fields his position adequately and pays attention to opposing basestealers, who were just 1-for-4 against him last year.

2004 Outlook

Robertson showed enough last season that he will get a shot to win a spot in the starting rotation this season. He is one of those pitchers who doesn't have a lot of room for mistakes because he doesn't have one overwhelming pitch. But he does understand how to pitch, and more importantly how to compete.

Matt Roney

Position: RP/SP
Bats: R **Throws:** R
Ht: 6' 3" **Wt:** 230

Opening Day Age: 24
Born: 1/10/80 in Tulsa, OK
ML Seasons: 1

Overall Statistics

	W	L	Pct.	ERA	G	GS	Sv	IP	H	BB	SO	HR	Avg
'03	1	9	.100	5.45	45	11	0	100.2	102	48	47	17	.262
Car.	1	9	.100	5.45	45	11	0	100.2	102	48	47	17	.262

2003 Situational Stats

	W	L	ERA	Sv	IP		AB	H	HR	RBI	Avg
Home	1	1	3.46	0	52.0	LHB	182	54	10	32	.297
Road	0	8	7.58	0	48.2	RHB	207	48	7	21	.232
First Half	1	3	3.34	0	62.0	Sc Pos	90	21	4	34	.233
Scnd Half	0	6	8.84	0	38.2	Clutch	54	17	1	5	.315

2003 Season

Matt Roney was selected by the Tigers in the Rule 5 draft prior to last season from Pittsburgh. He spent the entire year in the majors, working in virtually every role from starter to closer. He made 11 starts, going 1-7 with a 6.80 ERA. As a reliever, he was 0-2 with 4.18 ERA. Roney was given two save opportunities and wasn't able to convert either of them.

Pitching & Defense

Roney consistently throws his fastball at 95 MPH. His problems are based on command more than velocity. He tends to fall behind in the count and come in with a fastball that catches too much of the middle of the plate. Roney has a sharp breaking ball that is a nice complement to his fastball. He needs a third pitch, however, as his changeup is not major league-caliber. Roney will not win a Gold Glove anytime soon—in 20 fielding chances last season, he made two errors.

2004 Outlook

Everybody likes Roney's arm strength, but how ready is he for the major leagues? In most systems, he would have been at the Double-A level last season. If he wants to be a starter, he needs an offspeed pitch to go along with his fastball and breaking ball.

Jamie Walker

Position: RP
Bats: L **Throws:** L
Ht: 6' 2" **Wt:** 190

Opening Day Age: 32
Born: 7/1/71 in McMinnville, TN
ML Seasons: 4

Overall Statistics

	W	L	Pct.	ERA	G	GS	Sv	IP	H	BB	SO	HR	Avg
'03	4	3	.571	3.32	78	0	3	65.0	61	17	45	9	.247
Car.	8	8	.500	4.63	191	2	4	169.0	169	49	124	29	.257

2003 Situational Stats

	W	L	ERA	Sv	IP		AB	H	HR	RBI	Avg
Home	2	2	3.38	1	34.2	LHB	113	24	6	14	.212
Road	2	1	3.26	2	30.1	RHB	134	37	3	27	.276
First Half	2	2	3.28	2	35.2	Sc Pos	79	20	3	34	.253
Scnd Half	2	1	3.38	1	29.1	Clutch	121	32	7	22	.264

2003 Season

Jamie Walker had a good season statistically and was the Tigers' most consistent performer in the bullpen. He walked only 17 hitters while striking out 45 in 65 innings. He also was very durable and appeared in 78 games—the second-highest total in the American League last year. He allowed fewer hits (61) than innings pitched.

Pitching & Defense

Walker does not throw hard, with a fastball that clocks in at 86-88 MPH. He throws across his body, however, which makes his fastball deceptive. He hides the ball well. Walker's breaking ball is not a sharp one, and it rolls more than what is ideal for a situational lefthander. Although he is still much more effective against lefthanded hitters, Walker does get hurt by lefty batters at inopportune times when he hangs his breaking ball on the inside part of the plate. He allowed six home runs in 32 innings against lefthanded hitters last season. His mental make up is a strength. Walker is a consummate professional who fields his position cleanly and pays attention to the running game.

2004 Outlook

The Tigers re-signed Walker following the season. He will be their situational lefthander in 2004, and again will be called upon early and often.

Other Detroit Tigers

Steve Avery (Pos: LHP, Age: 33)

	W	L	Pct.	ERA	G	GS	Sv	IP	H	BB	SO	HR	Avg
'03	2	0	1.000	5.63	19	0	0	16.0	19	7	6	5	.302
Car.	96	83	.536	4.19	297	261	0	1554.2	1529	569	980	148	.259

It's been a dozen years since Avery burst onto the scene with an 18-8 season with Atlanta at age 21 in 1991. Lost magic and a shoulder ailment in 1999 ended his career until his brief return in 2003. 2004 Outlook: C

Hiram Bocachica (Pos: CF, Age: 28, Bats: R)

	G	AB	R	H	D	T	HR	RBI	SB	BB	SO	Avg	OBP	Slg
'03	6	22	1	1	1	0	0	0	0	0	7	.045	.045	.091
Car.	172	333	44	72	19	1	10	26	7	19	83	.216	.261	.369

His trade to Detroit in 2002 looked like a promising opportunity, but Bocachica hasn't been able to capitalize. A 1-for-22 start in April earned him a one-way ticket to Triple-A Toledo. 2004 Outlook: C

A.J. Hinch (Pos: C, Age: 29, Bats: R)

	G	AB	R	H	D	T	HR	RBI	SB	BB	SO	Avg	OBP	Slg
'03	27	74	7	15	3	1	3	11	0	3	18	.203	.247	.392
Car.	346	942	103	207	27	3	32	112	13	71	210	.220	.281	.357

Once a promising catching prospect, Hinch has fashioned a career as a backup backstop. A groin injury during the second half kept him from taking playing time from struggling incumbent Brandon Inge. 2004 Outlook: C

Gene Kingsale (Pos: CF, Age: 27, Bats: B)

	G	AB	R	H	D	T	HR	RBI	SB	BB	SO	Avg	OBP	Slg
'03	39	120	11	25	3	1	1	8	1	10	17	.208	.265	.275
Car.	211	533	65	134	17	5	3	53	15	39	96	.251	.307	.319

Kingsale enjoyed a promising stint with the Padres in 2002, when Tigers manager Alan Trammell was a San Diego coach. Detroit traded for Kingsale, who failed to win the center-field job and went to Triple-A Toledo. Kingsdale will return to San Diego after agreeing to a minor league deal in November. 2004 Outlook: C

Danny Klassen (Pos: 3B, Age: 28, Bats: R)

	G	AB	R	H	D	T	HR	RBI	SB	BB	SO	Avg	OBP	Slg
'03	22	73	9	18	3	1	1	7	0	4	26	.247	.286	.356
Car.	85	261	34	59	8	2	6	23	2	21	84	.226	.289	.341

Klassen is an infielder with some pop in his bat, but it hasn't emerged during major league trials. The slide in his batting average and strikeout-walk ratio in Triple-A ball is not a good sign. He re-signed with the Tigers in November. 2004 Outlook: C

Gary Knotts (Pos: RHP, Age: 27)

	W	L	Pct.	ERA	G	GS	Sv	IP	H	BB	SO	HR	Avg
'03	3	8	.273	6.04	20	18	0	95.1	111	47	51	14	.288
Car.	6	10	.375	5.66	50	19	0	132.0	139	64	81	21	.267

Knotts has enjoyed little success in the high minors, dating back to 1999, so it's not surprising that he has failed to establish himself in the majors. At least playing in Detroit offers more chances. 2004 Outlook: C

Chris Mears (Pos: RHP, Age: 26)

	W	L	Pct.	ERA	G	GS	Sv	IP	H	BB	SO	HR	Avg
'03	1	3	.250	5.44	29	3	5	41.1	50	11	21	5	.307
Car.	1	3	.250	5.44	29	3	5	41.1	50	11	21	5	.307

In his first stint of Triple-A ball, Mears started 5-1 (2.78) working as a swing man. He reached Detroit in June, saving five games and posting a 3.38 ERA for the month before getting roughed up a bit. 2004 Outlook: B

Dean Palmer (Pos: DH, Age: 35, Bats: R)

	G	AB	R	H	D	T	HR	RBI	SB	BB	SO	Avg	OBP	Slg
	26	86	3	12	2	0	0	6	0	9	28	.140	.235	.163
	1357	4902	734	1229	231	15	275	849	48	502	1332	.251	.324	.472

Palmer hasn't been fully healthy since the 2000 season, enduring shoulder problems in 2001 that led to cervical disc surgery in May 2002. The neck and back problems persisted in 2003 and the knife awaits. 2004 Outlook: C

Craig Paquette (Pos: 1B, Age: 35, Bats: R)

	G	AB	R	H	D	T	HR	RBI	SB	BB	SO	Avg	OBP	Slg
'03	11	33	2	5	0	0	0	0	0	0	5	.152	.152	.152
Car.	814	2591	304	620	128	10	99	377	27	120	620	.239	.274	.411

Paquette hadn't managed to get over the Mendoza line in parts of two seasons with Detroit before he was released in late April. He signed on with the Cards' Triple-A club but went home in late May. 2004 Outlook: D

Fernando Rodney (Pos: RHP, Age: 27)

	W	L	Pct.	ERA	G	GS	Sv	IP	H	BB	SO	HR	Avg
'03	1	3	.250	6.07	27	0	3	29.2	35	17	33	2	.294
Car.	2	6	.250	6.04	47	0	3	47.2	60	27	43	4	.308

Rodney is a hard thrower who lacks movement on his heater and needs solid secondary pitches. His stuff has been good enough to dominate in the high minors, and it started working for him this past September. 2004 Outlook: B

Brian Schmack (Pos: RHP, Age: 30)

	W	L	Pct.	ERA	G	GS	Sv	IP	H	BB	SO	HR	Avg
'03	1	0	1.000	3.46	11	0	0	13.0	14	4	4	1	.292
Car.	1	0	1.000	3.46	11	0	0	13.0	14	4	4	1	.292

After posting a 2.05 ERA and 29 saves at Double-A Erie, Schmack got his first cup of coffee in the big leagues. His long and winding road stopped in Detroit after stints in two other systems. 2004 Outlook: C

Chris Spurling (Pos: RHP, Age: 26)

	W	L	Pct.	ERA	G	GS	Sv	IP	H	BB	SO	HR	Avg
'03	1	3	.250	4.68	66	0	3	77.0	78	22	38	9	.266
Car.	1	3	.250	4.68	66	0	3	77.0	78	22	38	9	.266

A Rule 5 pickup from Pittsburgh, Spurling got plenty of work in the Tigers' bullpen. With the rebuilding club in flux, he even managed to pick up three saves. Some Triple-A time still seems likely. 2004 Outlook: C

Andres Torres (Pos: CF/RF, Age: 26, Bats: B)

	G	AB	R	H	D	T	HR	RBI	SB	BB	SO	Avg	OBP	Slg
'03	59	168	23	37	4	3	1	9	5	10	35	.220	.263	.298
Car.	78	238	30	51	5	4	1	12	7	16	51	.214	.264	.282

Torres is a hard-working prospect with some speed, but getting on base frequently enough to use it has been difficult since he posted a .391 OBP at Double-A Erie in 2001. He endured an off year in 2003. 2004 Outlook: C

Matt Walbeck (Pos: C, Age: 34, Bats: B)

	G	AB	R	H	D	T	HR	RBI	SB	BB	SO	Avg	OBP	Slg
'03	59	138	11	24	4	1	1	6	0	3	26	.174	.197	.239
Car.	682	2109	215	492	79	5	28	208	13	133	343	.233	.280	.315

A catcher who hit .174 (Walbeck) backing up a starter who hit .203 (Brandon Inge) tells the tale of the 2003 Tigers. Walbeck annouced his retirement at the end of October and was named as the new manager of the Tigers' Class-A West Michigan affiliate. 2004 Outlook: D

Ernie Young (Pos: DH, Age: 34, Bats: R)

	G	AB	R	H	D	T	HR	RBI	SB	BB	SO	Avg	OBP	Slg
'03	5	11	0	2	0	0	0	0	0	4	5	.182	.400	.182
Car.	285	792	108	177	33	4	27	90	10	89	211	.223	.308	.378

A multi-tool prospect a decade ago, Young is a remarkable defensive player whose bat hasn't kept pace with his glove. He got his first taste of the major leagues since his successful stint on the 2000 Olympic team. 2004 Outlook: C

Detroit Tigers Minor League Prospects

Organization Overview:

Ninety-eight wins is a good total for one season. But over two seasons? Not so much. The Tigers, having lost 225 games in 2002 and 2003 combined while running their string of losing seasons to 10, are far worse than any major league team should ever be. So it figures that anyone who shows anything in the Detroit system will soon find himself with a big league job. GM Dave Dombrowski deserves a large share of the credit for building the world champion Marlins team of 2003, but his task in Detroit is even more daunting. All that losing has provided the Tigers with some high draft picks, but it seems unlikely that any 2004 rookie will have a big impact at the major league level.

Jon Connolly

Position: P	**Opening Day Age:** 20	
Bats: R **Throws:** L	**Born:** 8/24/83 in	
Ht: 6' 0" **Wt:** 205	Oneonta, NY	

Recent Statistics

	W	L	ERA	G	GS	Sv	IP	H	R	BB	SO	HR
2002 A Oneonta	5	3	4.01	14	14	0	85.1	102	46	10	50	7
2003 A W Michigan	16	3	1.41	25	25	0	166.0	128	37	38	104	4

Connolly came out of nowhere to become perhaps the Tigers' best prospect at the end of 2003. Drafted in the 28th round in 2001 out of high school in Oneonta, New York, he had the rare pleasure of starting his minor league career pitching for his home town team in 2002. Modestly successful there, the lefthander advanced to the Class-A Midwest League in 2003 and dominated that level for the entire season, posting an ERA of 1.51 on the road and 1.35 at home. Connolly is not a classic power pitcher, averaging fewer than six strikeouts per inning, but he showed excellent control while yielding only four home runs. He likely will start the 2004 season in the rotation at high Class-A Lakeland.

Rob Henkel

Position: P	**Opening Day Age:** 25	
Bats: R **Throws:** L	**Born:** 8/3/78 in La Mesa,	
Ht: 6' 2" **Wt:** 210	CA	

Recent Statistics

	W	L	ERA	G	GS	Sv	IP	H	R	BB	SO	HR
2002 A Jupiter	8	3	2.51	14	12	0	75.1	55	22	22	82	4
2002 AA Portland	6	1	2.86	13	13	0	70.0	54	31	27	68	6
2003 AA Erie	9	3	3.38	16	16	0	82.2	67	33	27	70	7

Henkel was acquired in early 2003 in the trade that sent Mark Redman to Florida. The Marlins, under then-GM Dave Dombrowski, drafted him out of UCLA in the third round of the 2000 draft, but he did not sign in time to make his minor league debut that year. The lefthander pitched 42 innings in 13 games in 2001 before injury ended his season. He recovered nicely in 2002, but a back injury and a tender shoulder limited him to 82.2 innings in 16 starts for Double-A Erie in 2003. Henkel's best pitch is a knuckle-curve. An intelligent player with experience pitching for a top college team, he figures to become a mainstay in the Tigers' rotation, if he can stay healthy.

Omar Infante

Position: SS	**Opening Day Age:** 22	
Bats: R **Throws:** R	**Born:** 12/26/81 in Puerto	
Ht: 6' 0" **Wt:** 176	la Cruz, VZ	

Recent Statistics

	G	AB	R	H	D	T	HR	RBI	SB	BB	SO	Avg
2003 AAA Toledo	64	224	28	50	10	0	2	18	22	22	32	.223
2003 AL Detroit	69	221	24	49	6	1	0	8	6	18	37	.222

Promoted to Detroit in 2002 before his 21st birthday, Infante struggled in 2003. The Venezuelan middle infielder is an example of how bad teams can stay on a downward spiral by rushing their prospects. A talented defensive player who can play second or shortstop, Infante seems unlikely to hit for much power, though at his age there is room for considerable development. As a result of Eric Munson's thumb injury, Infante played third base in a late-September return, but he clearly does not have the power to play a corner position. His major goals must be to learn how to hit lefthanders and to hit in Comerica Park; in 2003 he batted only .155 against southpaws, and a mind-boggling .152 at home.

Preston Larrison

Position: P	**Opening Day Age:** 23	
Bats: R **Throws:** R	**Born:** 11/19/80 in	
Ht: 6' 4" **Wt:** 215	Aurora, IL	

Recent Statistics

	W	L	ERA	G	GS	Sv	IP	H	R	BB	SO	HR
2002 A Lakeland	10	5	2.39	21	19	0	120.1	86	39	45	92	6
2003 AAA Toledo	0	1	3.38	1	1	0	5.1	3	3	2	3	1
2003 AA Erie	4	12	5.61	24	24	0	126.2	161	89	59	53	10

Larrison had his own rooting section behind first base at the Futures Game last July in Chicago, as friends and family made the trip from his hometown of Aurora, Illinois, about 30 miles away. Drafted by the Tigers out of the University of Evansville (Indiana) in the second round in 2001, Larrison had an excellent first full season at high Class-A Lakeland in 2002 and almost made the major league club out of spring training in 2003. Sent instead to Double-A Erie, he got off to an excellent start, allowing no earned runs over 11 innings in his first two starts. Then the wheels came off, as Larrison allowed 79 earned runs over his remaining 115.2 innings for Erie. He'll look to rebound in 2004, probably starting at Erie.

Shane Loux

Position: P   **Opening Day Age:** 24
Bats: R **Throws:** R   **Born:** 8/13/79 in Rapid
Ht: 6' 2" **Wt:** 235   City, SD

Recent Statistics

	W	L	ERA	G	GS	Sv	IP	H	R	BB	SO	HR
2003 AAA Toledo	11	6	3.02	21	20	0	128.0	129	53	30	58	5
2003 AL Detroit	1	1	7.12	11	4	0	30.1	37	24	12	8	4

The Tigers made Loux their second-round pick in 1997. Despite undergoing elbow surgery in early 2001, he notched 33 wins at the Double-A and Triple-A levels in the three-year period from 2000-02. He continued on that pace for Toledo in 2003, earning an August recall and a shot at the 2004 Tigers rotation. American League hitters had little problem with Loux in his three-game stint in 2002, and even less problem in '03, when he allowed 24 earned runs in 30.1 innings. Loux has nothing left to prove at Triple-A, and as he enters his eighth pro season, the Tigers are going to have to run him out there every fifth day and hope for the best.

Cody Ross

Position: OF   **Opening Day Age:** 23
Bats: R **Throws:** L   **Born:** 12/23/80 in
Ht: 5' 11" **Wt:** 180   Portales, NM

Recent Statistics

	G	AB	R	H	D	T	HR	RBI	SB	BB	SO	Avg
2003 AAA Toledo	124	470	74	135	35	6	20	61	15	32	86	.287
2003 AL Detroit	6	19	1	4	1	0	1	5	0	1	3	.211

Ross is not a big man, but he has consistently hit for power, while also stealing bases, throughout his minor league career, progressing one level every year. He is that rare combination: a righthanded hitter who throws lefthanded. His size, competitiveness and surprising pop have drawn frequent published comparisons to Craig Biggio. Pressed into service for a month as a leadoff man in the absence of a suitable alternative at Triple-A Toledo, Ross cut down on his strikeouts while still hitting for power and average. After a brief major league stint in 2003, Ross tore the ACL in his left knee. He should be ready to resume baseball activities by the end of February, however, and may be ready to contribute as an outfielder for Detroit in 2004.

Andy Van Hekken

Position: P   **Opening Day Age:** 24
Bats: R **Throws:** L   **Born:** 7/31/79 in Holland,
Ht: 6' 3" **Wt:** 185   MI

Recent Statistics

	W	L	ERA	G	GS	Sv	IP	H	R	BB	SO	HR
2002 AA Erie	4	7	3.83	21	21	0	134.0	138	69	34	97	10
2002 AAA Toledo	5	0	1.82	7	7	0	49.1	41	14	11	19	4
2002 AL Detroit	1	3	3.00	5	5	0	30.0	38	13	6	5	2
2003 AAA Toledo	4	6	5.88	13	12	0	72.0	93	47	18	25	11
2003 AA Erie	5	6	4.02	13	13	0	80.2	89	41	18	32	13

In 2003, the only pitcher with an ERA under 5.40 to start a game for the Tigers was Nate Cornejo. So there's plenty of room available in the 2004 rotation. If he's healthy, this could be the year Van Hekken claims a slot. Of Dutch ancestry, Van Hekken was born in Holland, Michigan. He was drafted by the Mariners and signed in 1998, but was traded to Detroit a year later in the deal that sent Brian Hunter to Seattle. Van Hekken relies on his curveball and craftiness to compensate for a below-average fastball. After a disappointing start to 2003 at Triple-A Toledo, the lefthander was sent to Double-A Erie, where he pitched better, and then recalled to Toledo near the end of the season.

Joel Zumaya

Position: P   **Opening Day Age:** 19
Bats: R **Throws:** R   **Born:** 11/9/84 in Chula
Ht: 6' 3" **Wt:** 215   Vista, CA

Recent Statistics

	W	L	ERA	G	GS	Sv	IP	H	R	BB	SO	HR
2002 R Tigers	2	1	1.93	9	8	0	37.1	21	9	11	46	2
2003 A W Michigan	7	5	2.79	19	19	0	90.1	69	35	38	126	3

Although he reportedly threw his fastball around 90 MPH in high school in Chula Vista, California, Zumaya lasted until the 11th round of the 2002 draft before being selected by the Tigers. Zumaya is a power pitcher. He features a fastball that now reaches into the high 90s and an excellent hard curveball. In 2003, he averaged 12.5 strikeouts per nine innings, but missed six weeks with back problems and a strained oblique muscle. He figures to start 2004 at high Class-A Lakeland, pitching in the rotation, but he has the tools to move up quickly if he can smooth out his delivery and stay healthy. With Zumaya's skills and size, the Tigers may consider grooming him as a future closer.

Others to Watch

Drafted out of Tulane University in 2003, shortstop **Tony Giarratano** (21) hit .328 in the short-season New York-Penn League. The Tigers paid him a $500,000 signing bonus. He'll likely start 2004 at high Class-A Lakeland, and could move up quickly. . . Third baseman **Kody Kirkland** (20) was acquired from the Pirates in the Randall Simon trade. A draft-and-follow in 2002, he hit .303 and slugged .496 for Oneonta in the short-season New York-Penn League in 2003. . . Lefthander **Wil Ledezma** (23) was selected in the Rule 5 draft in 2002 from Boston, and therefore had to spend all of 2003 on the major league roster. He posted a 5.79 ERA in 84 innings, perhaps good enough to stay with the parent club in 2004. . . The Tigers paid a $3.35 million bonus to sign the third overall pick in the 2003 draft, Wake Forest righthander **Kyle Sleeth** (22). Sleeth did not sign until August and will make his pro debut in 2004. Armed with a mid-90s fastball, the 6-foot-5 Sleeth went 31-6 in three seasons at Wake Forest and tied a Division I record with 26 straight wins between the 2001 and 2003 seasons.

Ewing M. Kauffman Stadium

Offense

All offensive elements are enhanced by Kauffman Stadium. The park has excellent sight lines that reduce strikeouts and increase batting averages. Home-run totals at Kauffman, among the best in baseball, are likely to decline in 2004, as the fences are expected to be moved back 10 feet to their pre-1995 depths. Extra-base hits should remain plentiful due to the large outfield expanse that means more ground to cover and longer outfield throws. Recently added luxury boxes have reduced foul ground between the dugouts, occasionally giving batters an extra swing.

Defense

Fleet-footed outfielders are a must at Kauffman Stadium. The ball carries well for most of the baseball season and there's a large area to cover in each field. Very slight wall angles at the foul poles help turn singles into triples, as balls hug the wall and scoot past unwary outfielders. Glove men will enjoy the immaculately groomed infield that produces few bad hops.

Who It Helps the Most

Kauffman Stadium benefits all hitters, but speedy, slashing types with gap power gain most from the large outfield and the way the ball carries in the hot part of the summer. Groundball pitchers can avoid much of the park's hitting-friendly effects. Mike MacDougal, Runelvys Hernandez and Jeremy Affeldt should perform better at home.

Who It Hurts the Most

Pitchers who work high in the strike zone can expect to give up lots of extra-base hits. Jose Lima had trouble keeping the ball in the park at home. Outfielders who lack range will find it difficult to cover sufficient ground in Kauffman Stadium.

Rookies & Newcomers

David DeJesus and Alexis Gomez should benefit from their home park. Both have gap power and the speed to cover the outfield. Chris George and Mike MacDougal must keep the ball down to succeed. It's vital to use the infield defense and avoid giving up hits deep into the outfield.

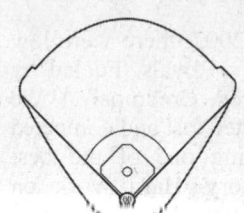

Dimensions: LF-330, LCF-375, CF-400, RCF-375, RF-330

Capacity: 40,785

Elevation: 750 feet

Surface: Grass

Foul Territory: Average

Park Factors

2003 Season

	Home Games			Away Games			
	Royals	Opp	Total	Royals	Opp	Total	Index
G	71	71	142	73	73	146	
Avg	.281	.292	.286	.264	.264	.264	108
AB	2388	2583	4971	2542	2414	4956	103
R	382	458	840	351	307	658	131
H	671	753	1424	671	638	1309	112
2B	135	142	277	111	135	246	112
3B	15	16	31	18	14	32	97
HR	60	102	162	80	70	150	108
BB	215	248	463	203	242	445	104
SO	350	373	723	464	401	865	83
E	36	59	95	54	55	109	90
E-Infield	28	53	81	46	46	92	91
LHB-Avg	.276	.297	.286	.256	.279	.266	107
LHB-HR	28	41	69	43	29	72	94
RHB-Avg	.286	.288	.287	.272	.253	.262	109
RHB-HR	32	61	93	37	41	78	120

2001-2003

	Home Games			Away Games			
	Royals	Opp	Total	Royals	Opp	Total	Index
G	215	215	430	217	217	434	
Avg	.275	.291	.283	.255	.264	.259	109
AB	7334	7808	15142	7533	7173	14706	104
R	1094	1312	2406	948	1001	1949	125
H	2017	2272	4289	1918	1895	3813	114
2B	384	435	819	356	368	724	110
3B	58	52	110	50	45	95	112
HR	200	309	509	197	244	441	112
BB	631	734	1365	611	761	1372	97
SO	1059	1197	2256	1367	1207	2574	85
E	145	171	316	162	157	319	100
E-Infield	118	146	264	134	138	272	98
LHB-Avg	.274	.295	.285	.249	.269	.259	110
LHB-HR	77	139	216	99	111	210	100
RHB-Avg	.276	.287	.282	.259	.260	.259	109
RHB-HR	123	170	293	98	133	231	123

2003 Rankings (American League)

- Highest run factor
- Highest hit factor
- Second-highest RHB home-run factor
- Third-highest batting-average factor
- Third-highest RHB batting-average factor
- Lowest strikeout factor
- Third-lowest error factor

2003 Season

After losing 100 games in 2002, there were low expectations of Tony Pena's Royals. Fueled by Pena's credo of "Nosotros Creemos" ("We Believe"), the 2003 club started fast and competed for a division title, enjoying one of the best rebounds in baseball history. Hard work on fundamentals in spring training paid off later as Pena put many facets of the game to heavy use. Genial and approachable, the infectiously optimistic Pena was named AL manager of the year

Offense

The Royals aren't blessed with a heavy power-hitting lineup, so Pena tries to make the most of scoring opportunities through high-pressure speed tactics. Everyone in the lineup is expected to contribute as Pena forces the issue with steals and aggressive baserunning. He expects all hitters to know how to bunt and utilizes sacrifices and the hit-and-run. Pena makes little use of pinch-hitters or pinch-runners.

Pitching & Defense

Pena keeps his youthful rotation on a short leash, maintaining innings limits. While he'll remove a youngster at the first sign of trouble, veterans are allowed to escape jams and pitch deep into games, even if they have no history of doing it. Pena's quick hook with youngsters means heavy use of relievers with well-defined roles. Pitching changes are based upon game situations rather than hitter matchups. To work with his young pitchers, Pena requires defensive-minded catchers who control the running game. Otherwise, he prefers good hitters throughout the lineup. He'll use intentional walks to set up double plays, but rarely uses pitchouts or makes defensive changes.

2004 Outlook

Despite some free-agent signings, expectations shouldn't be too high. Pena's challenges include sorting through young pitchers for a rotation, stretching out those young starters to save the bullpen and incorporating new outfield prospects into the lineup. Pena made headway in 2003 at rebuilding the Royals, and more progress will be expected soon.

Born: 6/4/57 in Monte Cristi, Dominican Republic

Playing Experience: 1980-1997, Pit, StL, Bos, Cle, CWS, Hou
Managerial Experience: 2 seasons
Pronunciation: PAIN-ya

Manager Statistics

Year	Team, Lg	W	L	Pct	GB	Finish
2003	Kansas City, AL	83	79	.512	7.0	3rd Central
2 Seasons		132	156	.458	–	–

2003 Starting Pitchers by Days Rest

	<=3	4	5	6+
Royals Starts	1	78	42	28
Royals ERA	7.11	4.99	4.60	4.78
AL Avg Starts	2	79	50	22
AL ERA	3.19	4.64	4.57	4.98

2003 Situational Stats

	Tony Pena	AL Average
Hit & Run Success %	35.8	36.7
Stolen Base Success %	74.1	70.0
Platoon Pct.	60.4	61.7
Defensive Subs	13	23
High-Pitch Outings	1	5
Quick/Slow Hooks	36/13	19/16
Sacrifice Attempts	81	55

2003 Rankings (American League)

- 1st in steals of home plate (2) and quick hooks
- 2nd in double steals (6) and sacrifice bunt attempts
- 3rd in stolen base attempts (162), steals of second base (101) and steals of third base (17)

Jeremy Affeldt

2003 Season

A coin toss kept Jeremy Affeldt from an Opening Day start, but it was a recurring blister that sent him to the disabled list in late April. When Affeldt returned a couple of weeks later, the Royals changed his grip, moving his fingers off the seams to avoid blistering. When that didn't help, they moved him to the bullpen to reduce his innings. He pitched well enough to eventually get closing opportunities. Although he couldn't keep his rotation job, Affeldt was a prime contributor to the Royals' success.

Pitching

Affeldt has the repertoire and stamina to be a successful starter. He calls on a low-90s fastball that reaches 96 MPH. But it's his 12-to-6 curveball—thrown 20 MPH slower than his heater—that makes Affeldt so difficult to hit. He can throw his curveball to the outside corner at will. When both the fastball and curve are working, he rarely needs his barely average slider or his mediocre, but improving, changeup. The speed differential between the heater and curve makes it difficult for batters to keep the ball fair when they make contact. While he doesn't back down from hitters and pitches inside, Affeldt lacks the bounce-back arm required of closers.

Defense

Despite a good pickoff move, Affeldt allows baserunners an advantage if they steal in non-fastball counts. Since 2002, 18 runners have stolen successfully against him in 27 tries. Although he's athletic and moves well to the ball, he's not an especially good fielder; he'll occasionally get overanxious trying to get the lead runner instead of taking the sure out.

2004 Outlook

The Royals are determined that Affeldt will be in their rotation. He's a hard worker who's committed to solving his blistering problem. He pitched through a lot of pain last year and made grip changes to avoid the problem. Affeldt has the stuff to be a No. 2 starter, and he'll have an important setup role if he cannot overcome the recurring blister that has sidelined him for parts of the last two seasons.

Position: SP/RP
Bats: L **Throws:** L
Ht: 6' 4" **Wt:** 215

Opening Day Age: 24
Born: 6/6/79 in Phoenix, AZ
ML Seasons: 2
Pronunciation: AFF-felt

Overall Statistics

	W	L	Pct.	ERA	G	GS	Sv	IP	H	BB	SO	HR	Avg
'03	7	6	.538	3.93	36	18	4	126.0	126	38	98	12	.261
Car.	10	10	.500	4.20	70	25	4	203.2	211	75	165	20	.266

2003 Pitching Profile

	Jeremy Affeldt	AL Average
Overall Strike %	62.6	62.8
1st Pitch Strike %	57.1	58.7
Ratio	1.30	1.39
Strikeouts per 9 IP	7.00	6.11
Walks per 9 IP	2.71	3.16
Home Runs per 9 IP	0.86	1.11
Strikeout/Walk Ratio	2.58	1.93
Groundball/Flyball Ratio	1.18	1.18

2003 Situational Stats

	W	L	ERA	Sv	IP		AB	H	HR	RBI	Avg
Home	2	3	4.07	2	59.2	LHB	112	25	2	16	.223
Road	5	3	3.80	2	66.1	RHB	371	101	10	37	.272
First Half	5	5	4.76	0	85.0	Sc Pos	110	25	2	38	.227
Scnd Half	2	1	2.20	4	41.0	Clutch	35	1	1	1	.029

2003 Rankings (American League)

- 7th in balks (2)
- Led the Royals in stolen bases allowed (14), highest strikeout-walk ratio (2.6), lowest slugging percentage allowed (.402), highest groundball-flyball ratio allowed (1.2), lowest ERA at home, lowest batting average allowed with runners in scoring position, fewest home runs allowed per nine innings (.86) and most strikeouts per nine innings (7.0)

Brian Anderson

2003 Season

The 2003 season began poorly for Brian Anderson. He was bothered by a sore hamstring and won just two of his first 10 outings for Cleveland. However, he rebounded to become one of baseball's winningest pitchers down the stretch, winning 12 of 22 starts over the last four months. The Royals acquired Anderson in a deadline deal and he finished strong; the club won all five of his September outings. Anderson enjoyed career bests in wins and ERA.

Pitching

Working primarily with a low-90s fastball, Anderson will aim his above-average changeup at the outside corner to induce grounders. He'll throw an upper-80s cut fastball in on righthanded hitters' hands to back them off the plate, although he rarely throws the cutter for strikes. Anderson has outstanding control. He works quickly and usually pitches ahead in the count, rarely walking more than one or two in a game. Although he hasn't been given the chance to finish many games, Anderson proved capable of regularly pitching into the eighth inning in 2003. He has been hampered in past seasons by non-arm injuries, such as the broken foot that ended his 2002 season.

Defense

Anderson is one of the premier pitchers at controlling the running game. He has a couple of different pickoff moves, one to keep runners close and another that catches unwary baserunners napping. Anderson has been among the league leaders in picking off runners, and he limited basestealers to just one successful attempt in nine tries last year. He no longer is agile off the mound, but he handles the glove well enough.

2004 Outlook

The strong finish helped showcase Anderson's talent as he headed into the free-agent market over the winter. He enjoyed the pennant race and wants another chance to pitch in meaningful September contests in 2004. The Royals allowed him to pitch deep into games, and Anderson decided to return, agreeing to a two-year deal to stay.

Position: SP
Bats: R **Throws:** L
Ht: 6' 1" **Wt:** 185

Opening Day Age: 31
Born: 4/26/72 in Portsmouth, VA
ML Seasons: 11

Overall Statistics

	W	L	Pct.	ERA	G	GS	Sv	IP	H	BB	SO	HR	Avg
'03	14	11	.560	3.78	32	31	0	197.2	212	43	87	27	.279
Car.	75	69	.521	4.58	250	213	1	1350.1	1487	280	636	224	.283

2003 Pitching Profile

	Brian Anderson	AL Average
Overall Strike %	63.3	62.8
1st Pitch Strike %	60.7	58.7
Ratio	1.29	1.39
Strikeouts per 9 IP	3.96	6.11
Walks per 9 IP	1.96	3.16
Home Runs per 9 IP	1.23	1.11
Strikeout/Walk Ratio	2.02	1.93
Groundball/Flyball Ratio	1.13	1.18

2003 Situational Stats

	W	L	ERA	Sv	IP		AB	H	HR	RBI	Avg
Home	6	5	4.22	0	100.1	LHB	182	47	9	20	.258
Road	8	6	3.33	0	97.1	RHB	577	165	18	80	.286
First Half	7	6	4.13	0	104.2	Sc Pos	154	46	5	71	.299
Scnd Half	7	5	3.39	0	93.0	Clutch	28	12	0	3	.429

2003 Rankings (American League)

- 1st in lowest stolen-base percentage allowed (11.1)
- 2nd in fewest strikeouts per nine innings (4.0)
- 3rd in most run support per nine innings (6.4)
- 4th in GDPs induced (25)
- 6th in fewest walks per nine innings (2.0) and highest slugging percentage allowed (.458)
- 7th in runners caught stealing (8)
- 10th in lowest ERA on the road (3.33)
- Led the Royals in complete games (2) and most GDPs induced per GDP situation (22.2%)

Carlos Beltran

2003 Season

Amidst speculation that he'd be traded, Carlos Beltran had another fine season for the Royals. He missed the first two weeks with a strained oblique muscle, and a hyperextended right elbow limited his throwing late in the season. In between, though, he led the club in most hitting categories and finished among league leaders in several areas, while setting career bests in steals and batting average. Beltran even put his name in the record books with some Hall of Famers, becoming just the sixth modern-era player to reach 100 RBI, 100 runs scored and 30 steals in a season for the third time.

Hitting

Beltran's compact swing helps him make contact, but his quick bat still generates good power. Although generally he's a patient hitter, he'll look fastball early in the count. When putting either of the first two pitches in play since 2001, Beltran is a .388 hitter who slugs .695. He had sacrificed a little batting average in previous years to hit for more power. Opposing managers often turn him around to hit righthanded, but Beltran fares equally well against either platoon. Beltran hasn't hit especially well in clutch situations; he's done more damage in early innings and seems to become impatient later in the game.

Baserunning & Defense

A smooth stride hides Beltran's fine speed. He has excellent baserunning instincts and seems to steal at will; he has succeeded in 91 percent of his 132 attempts since 2000. Beltran reads flyballs well and glides easily across the outfield to haul them in. Beltran has an average arm, although he throws accurately and excels at throwing home to prevent runs.

2004 Outlook

The Royals hoped to sign their arbitration-eligible center fielder to a long-term contract over the offseason, but Beltran is expected to test the free-agent market after the 2004 season. Trading Beltran at midseason is likely if the Royals fail to sign him. Wherever Beltran plays in 2004, he'll be one of the game's best players as he enters the prime of his career.

Position: CF
Bats: B **Throws:** R
Ht: 6' 1" **Wt:** 190

Opening Day Age: 26
Born: 4/24/77 in Manati, PR
ML Seasons: 6
Pronunciation: BELL-tron

Overall Statistics

	G	AB	R	H	D	T	HR	RBI	SB	BB	SO	Avg	OBP	Slg
'03	141	521	102	160	14	10	26	100	41	72	81	.307	.389	.522
Car.	726	2868	495	825	137	43	108	465	150	279	540	.288	.350	.478

Where He Hits the Ball

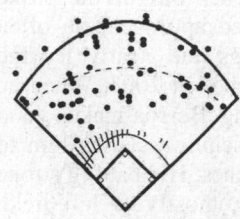

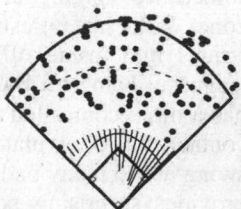

Vs. LHP   **Vs. RHP**

2003 Situational Stats

	AB	H	HR	RBI	Avg		AB	H	HR	RBI	Avg
Home	249	83	10	45	.333	LHP	151	49	7	25	.325
Road	272	77	16	55	.283	RHP	370	111	19	75	.300
First Half	277	82	12	54	.296	Sc Pos	150	52	8	70	.347
Scnd Half	244	78	14	46	.320	Clutch	52	14	4	11	.269

2003 Rankings (American League)

- 1st in stolen-base percentage (91.1) and lowest fielding percentage in center field (.987)
- 2nd in errors in center field (5)
- 3rd in triples and stolen bases
- 4th in steals of third (6)
- 5th in batting average with runners in scoring position
- 7th in batting average at home
- Led the Royals in batting average, home runs, runs scored, triples, RBI, stolen bases, walks, times on base (234), slugging percentage, HR frequency (20.0 ABs per HR), stolen-base percentage (91.1), steals of third (6), and cleanup slugging percentage (.482)

Angel Berroa

2003 Season

Despite a disappointing 2002 season, Angel Berroa was handed the Royals' starting-shortstop job. After some inconsistent defensive play early in the season, he met all challenges with a strong season that led to AL Rookie of the Year honors. Berroa made outstanding progress during the season, becoming an important part of an improving Royals lineup. Berroa finished strong and proved durable. He placed among rookie leaders in several offensive areas.

Hitting

Berroa is one of the most aggressive hitters in the league. He will attack the first hittable pitch, sometimes lunging at pitches out of the strike zone. With his unrestrained approach, he often strides into inside offerings and nearly led the league in being hit by pitches in 2003. When he has a more controlled swing, Berroa makes good contact, but poor plate discipline causes him to swing at too many bad pitches. His batting stroke provides surprising power, mostly to left field. Berroa is a good bunter who succeeded near the top of the order when asked to move runners over.

Baserunning & Defense

Despite his good speed, Berroa isn't an accomplished baserunner or basestealer. He has an aggressive approach on the bases and sometimes runs into outs. Berroa's strong arm gets him in trouble if he relies on it too much instead of using consistent footwork to make reliable throws. After beginning the year with a bunch of errors, Berroa's focus changed and he became one of the league's best defensive shortstops. He still needs to improve his double-play skills.

2004 Outlook

After a solid 2003, Berroa is considered one of the cornerstones of the Royals' organization. He still has lots of work to do, especially in developing a consistent approach to fielding and improving his plate discipline, and in 2004 he'll have to avoid a sophomore dropoff. While Berroa is not yet ready to join the pantheon of American League All-Star shortstops, he's among the best of the rest in baseball, and one of the most improved players in the game.

Position: SS
Bats: R **Throws:** R
Ht: 6' 0" **Wt:** 175

Opening Day Age: 26
Born: 1/27/78 in Santo Domingo, DR
ML Seasons: 3

Overall Statistics

	G	AB	R	H	D	T	HR	RBI	SB	BB	SO	Avg	OBP	Slg
'03	158	567	92	163	28	7	17	73	21	29	100	.287	.338	.451
Car.	193	695	108	196	37	8	17	82	26	39	120	.282	.334	.432

Where He Hits the Ball

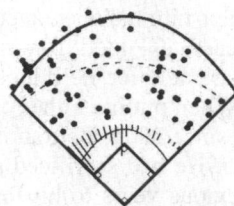 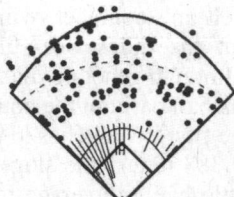

Vs. LHP   **Vs. RHP**

2003 Situational Stats

	AB	H	HR	RBI	Avg		AB	H	HR	RBI	Avg
Home	268	77	6	29	.287	LHP	179	56	9	26	.313
Road	299	86	11	44	.288	RHP	388	107	8	47	.276
First Half	311	88	9	37	.283	Sc Pos	137	36	3	53	.263
Scnd Half	256	75	8	36	.293	Clutch	78	18	2	11	.231

2003 Rankings (American League)

- 1st in errors at shortstop (24) and lowest fielding percentage at shortstop (.968)
- 2nd in sacrifice bunts (13)
- 3rd in batting average among rookies
- 4th in hit by pitch (18) and steals of third (6)
- 5th in home runs among rookies and RBI among rookies
- 9th in sacrifice flies (8)
- 10th in triples
- Led the Royals in sacrifice bunts (13), hit by pitch (18), strikeouts, games played, bunts in play (19) and steals of third (6)

Ken Harvey

Position: 1B/DH
Bats: R **Throws:** R
Ht: 6' 2" **Wt:** 240

Opening Day Age: 26
Born: 3/1/78 in Los Angeles, CA
ML Seasons: 2

2003 Season

Coming off a record-setting Arizona Fall League campaign over the offseason, Ken Harvey started the 2003 season strong, contributing several important hits to the Royals' fast start. He fell into disuse during interleague play, but later responded well in substituting for the injured Mike Sweeney. Harvey suffered two minor shoulder injuries and his power-hitting suffered while his strikeouts increased, leading to diminished playing time down the stretch. Still, Harvey put together a good first season.

Hitting

In 2003, Harvey sacrificed making contact for an exaggerated uppercut swing intended to produce more pop. It paid off early in the season, but pitchers quickly learned to work him down and away with breaking balls and throw fastballs up and out of the strike zone, leading to strikeouts or balls beaten into the turf. He's an aggressive hitter, looking to swing early at anything hittable; he took a first-pitch ball barely a third of the time in 2003. Hard-throwing pitchers who work inside, especially righthanders, enjoy an advantage against Harvey.

Baserunning & Defense

An already slow baserunner, Harvey was hobbled by foot injuries early in his career and is now just a station-to-station runner who's rarely successful when taking chances on the bases. Harvey's defensive inexperience was apparent when he frequently was caught out of position on grounders to the right side and when he wandered into the basepath and was injured in a collision with a baserunner. Harvey clearly was one of the worst first basemen in the league, but he should improve with more experience.

2004 Outlook

Few players exhibit both the raw talent and the obvious shortcomings shown by Harvey in his rookie campaign. His power may come naturally once he reverts to his line-drive stroke and once again makes good contact. Harvey may become manager Tony Pena's biggest challenge in 2004; with the type of adjustments he made in the 2002 AFL, Harvey again could become a high-average hitter with moderate power.

Overall Statistics

	G	AB	R	H	D	T	HR	RBI	SB	BB	SO	Avg	OBP	Slg
'03	135	485	50	129	30	0	13	64	2	29	94	.266	.313	.408
Car.	139	497	51	132	31	0	13	66	2	29	98	.266	.311	.406

Where He Hits the Ball

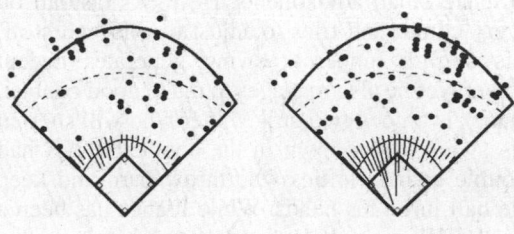

Vs. LHP   **Vs. RHP**

2003 Situational Stats

	AB	H	HR	RBI	Avg		AB	H	HR	RBI	Avg
Home	232	52	5	29	.224	LHP	156	52	7	27	.333
Road	253	77	8	35	.304	RHP	329	77	6	37	.234
First Half	282	75	9	43	.266	Sc Pos	116	34	2	45	.293
Scnd Half	203	54	4	21	.266	Clutch	57	20	3	19	.351

2003 Rankings (American League)

- 2nd in highest groundball-flyball ratio (2.5) and errors at first base (11)
- 6th in batting average vs. lefthanded pitchers
- 7th in fewest pitches seen per plate appearance (3.30)
- 8th in batting average in the clutch
- Led the Royals in GDPs (15), highest groundball-flyball ratio (2.5), batting average in the clutch, batting average vs. lefthanded pitchers and batting average on the road

Raul Ibanez

2003 Season

After his breakout 2002 season, Raul Ibanez suffered a slight dropoff in 2003. While he still hit for a useful average, his power was down, especially in the second half as the Royals battled for a pennant. He was the everyday left fielder, except when he filled in at first for the injured Mike Sweeney. It was in trying to replace Sweeney's bat as a cleanup hitter that Ibanez was found lacking. Still, Ibanez was one of the Royals' steadiest sources of run production.

Hitting

Ibanez is always tinkering with his stance and swing; even when he's hitting well, he still likes to make small adjustments. He looks fastball on every count, and tries to adjust to offspeed stuff. His slightly uppercut swing generates decent power, yet he also manages to make good contact. Ibanez is a good two-strike hitter who will shorten his swing when down in the count. He has had trouble against lefties who throw hard and keep the ball in on his hands. While Ibanez has been a good RBI man, he's fared better lower in the slugging portion of the lineup.

Baserunning & Defense

Ibanez has adequate speed for the outfield and can steal bases in a running offense like Kansas City's. He runs the bases intelligently, but rarely takes the extra base. Because Ibanez doesn't read flyballs especially well and lacks good speed, he's a mediocre outfielder. His below-average arm should limit him to left-field duty. He can fill in at first base, but is overmatched there as a regular. Ibanez also can play third base or catch in an emergency.

2004 Outlook

Ibanez became a free agent after the 2003 season. The Royals made it an offseason priority to re-sign Ibanez, who had become an important part of the lineup and a strong clubhouse presence who had assisted young Royals hitters. The Mariners, however, made Ibanez one of the early free-agent signings in mid-November, reaching a three-year, $13 million agreement that makes him Seattle's starting left fielder.

Position: LF/1B/DH
Bats: L **Throws:** R
Ht: 6' 2" **Wt:** 200

Opening Day Age: 31
Born: 6/2/72 in Manhattan, NY
ML Seasons: 8
Pronunciation: ee-BON-yez

Overall Statistics

	G	AB	R	H	D	T	HR	RBI	SB	BB	SO	Avg	OBP	Slg
'03	157	608	95	179	33	5	18	90	8	49	81	.294	.345	.454
Car.	629	1862	268	518	103	18	69	305	20	157	294	.278	.334	.464

Where He Hits the Ball

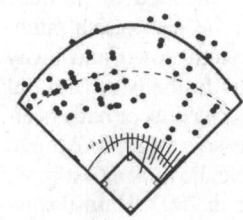
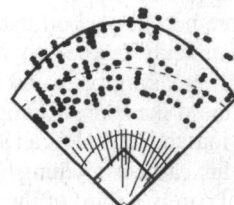

Vs. LHP   **Vs. RHP**

2003 Situational Stats

	AB	H	HR	RBI	Avg		AB	H	HR	RBI	Avg
Home	301	95	8	49	.316	LHP	204	50	7	29	.245
Road	307	84	10	41	.274	RHP	404	129	11	61	.319
First Half	357	102	12	53	.286	Sc Pos	178	51	3	68	.287
Scnd Half	251	77	6	37	.307	Clutch	69	19	2	6	.275

2003 Rankings (American League)

- 3rd in sacrifice flies (10)
- 4th in fielding percentage in left field (.988)
- 5th in batting average vs. righthanded pitchers
- Led the Royals in at-bats, hits, singles, doubles, total bases (276), sacrifice flies (10), intentional walks (5), pitches seen (2,647), plate appearances (671) and batting average vs. righthanded pitchers

Mike MacDougal

2003 Season

The Royals took a chance when they anointed rookie Mike MacDougal their Opening Day closer, but he handled the pressure very well, contributing heavily to the Royals' fast start. Despite a few stumbles, MacDougal was among league leaders in saves, earning an All-Star berth. He began to struggle at midseason, suffering from extremely poor control. In order to throw strikes he sometimes aimed his pitches, grooving straight fastballs with predictably bad results. MacDougal recovered later in the second half, although he finished the year sharing save chances with Curtis Leskanic and Jeremy Affeldt.

Pitching

MacDougal's fastball hits the mid-90s and occasionally flirts with 100 MPH. Control has been a serious problem; his moving fastball often sails up and out of the strike zone. He also throws a quality slider that can be devastating against righthanded hitters in search of high heat. Unfortunately, his command is lacking and MacDougal will often bury sliders in the dirt. Even his changeup is thrown hard, in the mid-80s, and he has occasional trouble corralling it. His lanky frame often causes his delivery to get out of whack, usually resulting in bouts of wildness that come and go from one batter to the next. Pitching on short rest has not been a problem.

Defense

MacDougal lacks a reliable pickoff move, but few runners have dared steal against his fastball. MacDougal's fielding is as erratic as his fastball. His gangly delivery leaves him out of position to field grounders and his throws to the bases sometimes sail like his pitches.

2004 Outlook

The Royals still believe MacDougal can become an ace stopper and they intend to give him the first shot in 2004. Still, they'll hedge their bets as they develop Ryan Bukvich and possibly Affeldt as alternatives. For MacDougal to succeed, he'll need to have a more consistent delivery. If the Royals are patient enough to let his natural ability come to the fore, he can become a dominant strikeout pitcher in short relief.

Position: RP
Bats: B **Throws:** R
Ht: 6' 4" **Wt:** 195

Opening Day Age: 27
Born: 3/5/77 in Las Vegas, NV
ML Seasons: 3

Overall Statistics

	W	L	Pct.	ERA	G	GS	Sv	IP	H	BB	SO	HR	Avg
'03	3	5	.375	4.08	68	0	27	64.0	64	32	57	4	.267
Car.	4	7	.364	4.28	77	3	27	88.1	87	43	74	6	.261

2003 Pitching Profile

	Mike MacDougal	AL Average
Overall Strike %	59.9	62.8
1st Pitch Strike %	53.8	58.7
Ratio	1.50	1.39
Strikeouts per 9 IP	8.02	6.11
Walks per 9 IP	4.50	3.16
Home Runs per 9 IP	0.56	1.11
Strikeout/Walk Ratio	1.78	1.93
Groundball/Flyball Ratio	2.84	1.18

2003 Situational Stats

	W	L	ERA	Sv	IP		AB	H	HR	RBI	Avg
Home	3	2	4.33	12	35.1	LHB	135	31	2	16	.230
Road	0	3	3.77	15	28.2	RHB	105	33	2	17	.314
First Half	3	3	2.59	24	41.2	Sc Pos	69	23	2	31	.333
Scnd Half	0	2	6.85	3	22.1	Clutch	128	34	4	23	.266

2003 Rankings (American League)

- 2nd in games finished (61)
- 3rd in blown saves (8) and lowest save percentage (77.1)
- 6th in saves and errors at pitcher (3)
- 7th in most baserunners allowed per nine innings in relief (14.6)
- Led the Royals in saves, games finished (61), hit batsmen (8), wild pitches (6), save percentage (77.1), blown saves (8), relief ERA (4.08), lowest batting average allowed in relief (.267) and most strikeouts per nine innings in relief (8.0)

Darrell May

Position: SP
Bats: L **Throws:** L
Ht: 6' 2" **Wt:** 185

Opening Day Age: 31
Born: 6/13/72 in San Bernardino, CA
ML Seasons: 5

2003 Season

Overlooked in spring training, Darrell May won the fifth-starter job almost by default. He strung together a series of useful starts, but couldn't win due to lack of run support. After a short bullpen stint, May returned to the rotation with a revised outlook. He worked deeper into games and became the Royals' most consistent second-half starter, winning 10 of his last 19 starts. He led the club in most pitching categories.

Pitching

May is a classic lefty finesse pitcher, with a fastball that tops out in the upper-80s. To succeed, May must hit the corners with his fastball and slider, setting up his above-average changeup. He added a cut fastball that appeared to have good movement and more utility than his straight fastball, especially against lefthanded hitters. May needs pinpoint control to succeed; he'll give up a lot of long flyballs when he gets too much of the plate. He's a true "four-corner" pitcher who can throw up, down, in or out with good command. Throwing more first-pitch strikes helped him lower pitch counts and go deeper into games in 2003, but he tends to lose his stuff after six innings.

Defense

Because he lacks an exceptional pickoff move and often works with offspeed pitches, May has learned to vary his delivery to reduce baserunners' leads, with excellent results in 2003. He allowed just four successful steal attempts all year after permitting 13 in 2002. May is barely adequate with the glove, but avoids damaging mistakes. He lacks range afield, but throws accurately to the bases and knows when to try for the lead runner.

2004 Outlook

May can look to 2003 as a career year. He can't expect to get much better, although he should be able to replicate his success if he doesn't have to assume the No. 1 starter role. May's stuff is not suitable for it. He can win as a fourth or fifth starter, but he'll have to continue making adjustments, as he did with his cutter in 2003, without losing his superior command.

Overall Statistics

	W	L	Pct.	ERA	G	GS	Sv	IP	H	BB	SO	HR	Avg
'03	10	8	.556	3.77	35	32	0	210.0	197	53	115	31	.246
Car.	16	20	.444	4.69	106	57	0	408.1	425	134	259	71	.266

2003 Pitching Profile

	Darrell May	AL Average
Overall Strike %	64.0	62.8
1st Pitch Strike %	57.8	58.7
Ratio	1.19	1.39
Strikeouts per 9 IP	4.93	6.11
Walks per 9 IP	2.27	3.16
Home Runs per 9 IP	1.33	1.11
Strikeout/Walk Ratio	2.17	1.93
Groundball/Flyball Ratio	0.71	1.18

2003 Situational Stats

	W	L	ERA	Sv	IP		AB	H	HR	RBI	Avg
Home	5	4	4.10	0	107.2	LHB	203	44	6	18	.217
Road	5	4	3.43	0	102.1	RHB	599	153	25	68	.255
First Half	4	4	3.54	0	112.0	Sc Pos	140	41	3	52	.293
Scnd Half	6	4	4.04	0	98.0	Clutch	60	17	1	7	.283

2003 Rankings (American League)

- 2nd in lowest groundball-flyball ratio allowed (0.7)
- 5th in home runs allowed
- 6th in lowest on-base percentage allowed (.292)
- Led the Royals in ERA, wins, losses, games started, complete games (2), innings pitched, hits allowed, batters faced (868), home runs allowed, walks allowed, strikeouts, pitches thrown (3,259), pickoff throws (53), lowest batting average allowed (.246), lowest on-base percentage allowed (.292), lowest stolen-base percentage allowed (44.4), fewest pitches thrown per batter (3.75), lowest ERA on the road, lowest batting average allowed vs. lefthanded batters,most run support per nine innings (5.7) and fewest walks per nine innings (2.3)

Joe Randa

2003 Season

The 2003 season was full of the usual streaks and slumps for Joe Randa. He had a strong start, struggled in May and finished very strong. He missed three weeks at midseason with a strained oblique muscle, but otherwise steadied a young Royals club. Randa moved to No. 2 in the order and responded well, hitting .349 and slugging .517 from the end of June through September, with 32 RBI in his final 39 games. Arguably it was his best all-around season.

Hitting

An aggressive hitter who looks to pull the ball, Randa sometimes will get himself out chasing high fastballs. But he makes good contact, which, along with his bunting ability, helped him succeed in the No. 2 hole. He has reduced his strikeout rate while increasing his slugging mark each of the last two years. Randa is a very streaky hitter whose good and bad spells can last a month or more. Randa has earned a reputation for good clutch hitting; he's a good two-out run producer and adjusts well to hitting behind in the count.

Baserunning & Defense

Randa really shines with the glove. He has quick feet and hands, and a strong, accurate arm. He'll usually make a few errors in a short span, then none for long stretches. Randa is accomplished at charging bunts and is surehanded enough for spot second-base duty. His 2003 campaign was deserving of Gold Glove consideration. Randa is no longer a basestealing threat. He's now a slow runner who rarely takes chances on the bases.

2004 Outlook

Randa's best season came prior to his free agency and left the Royals with one of their most difficult offseason dilemmas. The Royals have prized Randa for years because he's been a low-dollar player of moderate and adaptable talent. His tenure in Kansas City was at risk, but he agreed to a one-year deal to return in late November. Randa will continue to provide his steady defense and useful, but limited, hitting to the Royals.

Position: 3B
Bats: R **Throws:** R
Ht: 5'11" **Wt:** 190

Opening Day Age: 34
Born: 12/18/69 in Milwaukee, WI
ML Seasons: 9
Nickname: The Joker

Overall Statistics

	G	AB	R	H	D	T	HR	RBI	SB	BB	SO	Avg	OBP	Slg
'03	131	502	80	146	31	1	16	72	1	41	61	.291	.348	.452
Car.	1155	4182	538	1196	240	32	94	587	42	329	554	.286	.341	.426

Where He Hits the Ball

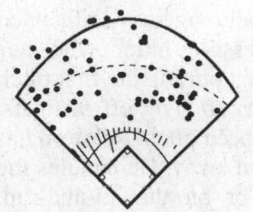
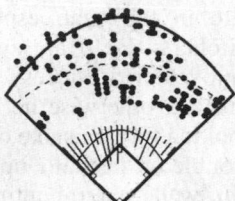

Vs. LHP   **Vs. RHP**

2003 Situational Stats

	AB	H	HR	RBI	Avg		AB	H	HR	RBI	Avg
Home	224	64	9	41	.286	LHP	151	47	6	21	.311
Road	278	82	7	31	.295	RHP	351	99	10	51	.282
First Half	278	69	10	34	.248	Sc Pos	118	34	5	52	.288
Scnd Half	224	77	6	38	.344	Clutch	56	19	3	12	.339

2003 Rankings (American League)

- 1st in fielding percentage at third base (.980) and lowest batting average with the bases loaded (.000)
- 6th in lowest percentage of swings that missed (10.3)
- 7th in sacrifice bunts (9)
- Led the Royals in lowest percentage of swings that missed (10.3) and highest percentage of swings put into play (48.8)

Desi Relaford

2003 Season

Desi Relaford began the season in his accustomed super-sub role before the Royals gave their primary offseason acquisition the full-time second-base job, replacing ineffective Carlos Febles. Relaford showed an ability to adjust to different roles and made starts at five different positions. He wore down in the second half, and a torn ligament in his left wrist limited the switch-hitter to lefthanded hitting, yet it was Relaford's most productive season as he set many new career bests.

Hitting

Relaford has hit especially well from the left side, although his wrist injury in 2003 hindered him late in the year, especially against lefthanded pitchers. He's an aggressive hitter who has enjoyed great success when putting the first pitch in play; otherwise he'll try to fight off fastballs, looking for a mistake offspeed pitch. Relaford has trouble on fastballs up and away. He handles the bat well when bunting or on the hit-and-run. Despite mediocre results leading off, Relaford gets on base well enough and runs well enough for a table-setting spot near the top or bottom of the order.

Baserunning & Defense

Relaford is both fast and a good baserunner. He's aggressive on the bases and exhibits good judgment, plus he's an adept base thief. He can play any infield or corner-outfield position temporarily without damaging the club's overall defense, but he's exposed if overused in one spot. Although he has good range afield, Relaford lacks the arm to play shortstop, third base or right field every day, and his double play pivot is weak at second base.

2004 Outlook

Having Relaford at second base full time had several negative effects for Kansas City, and for Relaford himself; he's much better as a heavily used reserve. The club's better off having him give a regular a day off or pinch-hit, and he won't wear down as easily. Relaford is a fine all-around ballplayer whose versatility is even more valuable with many clubs expanding their bullpens at the expense of bench players.

Position: 2B/3B/RF
Bats: B **Throws:** R
Ht: 5' 9" **Wt:** 180

Opening Day Age: 30
Born: 9/16/73 in Valdosta, GA
ML Seasons: 8
Pronunciation: RELL-a-ford

Overall Statistics

	G	AB	R	H	D	T	HR	RBI	SB	BB	SO	Avg	OBP	Slg
'03	141	500	70	127	27	5	8	59	20	40	70	.254	.315	.376
Car.	738	2323	304	580	120	17	33	258	73	235	393	.250	.326	.359

Where He Hits the Ball

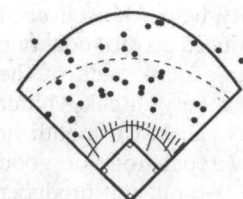 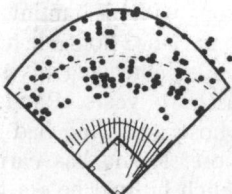

Vs. LHP   **Vs. RHP**

2003 Situational Stats

	AB	H	HR	RBI	Avg		AB	H	HR	RBI	Avg
Home	235	60	5	34	.255	LHP	130	39	3	19	.300
Road	265	67	3	25	.253	RHP	370	88	5	40	.238
First Half	292	84	6	40	.288	Sc Pos	116	38	1	48	.328
Scnd Half	208	43	2	19	.207	Clutch	65	19	0	7	.292

2003 Rankings (American League)

- 2nd in lowest batting average vs. righthanded pitchers
- 5th in stolen-base percentage (83.3)
- 6th in lowest on-base percentage for a leadoff hitter (.321)
- 7th in lowest HR frequency (62.5 ABs per HR)
- 9th in sacrifice bunts (8) and lowest slugging percentage
- 10th in errors at second base (8)

Mike Sweeney

2003 Season

The biggest surprise of the Royals' unexpected pennant drive in 2003 may be that they did much of it without the help of their biggest bat, Mike Sweeney. After getting off to a slow start, Sweeney rebounded and was among league leaders in power and average before being sidelined with back stiffness from mid-June into August. After his return, Sweeney wasn't the same hitter; he managed just 12 extra-base hits in the last two months and finished with his poorest season since 1998.

Hitting

Sweeney features a dangerous combination of power, contact hitting and strike-zone judgment. He adjusts well to pitching patterns and game situations, which allows him to be productive even when behind in the count. Although he's a good RBI producer, Sweeney is more likely to contend for a batting title than a home-run crown because his slightly uppercut stroke produces line drives and he uses all fields. A patient hitter who often succeeds against finesse pitchers, Sweeney has more trouble against power pitchers who can throw hard stuff high and tight for strikes.

Baserunning & Defense

Because he always hustles in the field and on base, Sweeney succeeds at both despite an awkward appearance. He's an average defender who has improved his range at first and has learned to scoop errant throws. His large build belies decent foot speed and he reads pitchers well enough to surprise them with a steal attempt. Sweeney has been used on the front end of double steals and also has successfully stolen home.

2004 Outlook

Sweeney's frequent injuries are becoming ever more costly. In 2004, he must prove that the back injury hasn't wrecked his powerful swing. In order to be ready for Opening Day, Sweeney avoided back surgery, gambling instead that rest can fully restore his health. Because the Royals produced a winning record in 2003, his contract was automatically extended through 2007. He knows where he'll be playing and can concentrate solely on staying in the lineup all year.

Position: DH/1B
Bats: R **Throws:** R
Ht: 6' 3" **Wt:** 225

Opening Day Age: 30
Born: 7/22/73 in Orange, CA
ML Seasons: 9

Overall Statistics

	G	AB	R	H	D	T	HR	RBI	SB	BB	SO	Avg	OBP	Slg
'03	108	392	62	115	18	1	16	83	3	64	56	.293	.391	.467
Car.	920	3306	532	1014	205	4	139	604	42	373	373	.307	.381	.497

Where He Hits the Ball

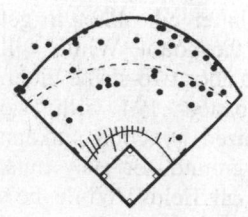 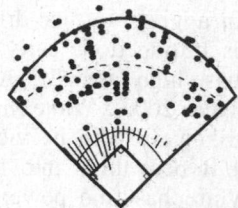

Vs. LHP   Vs. RHP

2003 Situational Stats

	AB	H	HR	RBI	Avg		AB	H	HR	RBI	Avg
Home	173	58	7	41	.335	LHP	112	31	5	20	.277
Road	219	57	9	42	.260	RHP	280	84	11	63	.300
First Half	215	69	12	50	.321	Sc Pos	108	43	6	67	.398
Scnd Half	177	46	4	33	.260	Clutch	56	19	1	12	.339

2003 Rankings (American League)

- 1st in batting average with runners in scoring position and batting average with the bases loaded (.667)
- 10th in batting average in the clutch
- Led the Royals in intentional walks (5), on-base percentage, batting average with runners in scoring position, batting average with the bases loaded (.667) and batting average at home

Rondell White

Position: LF
Bats: R **Throws:** R
Ht: 6' 1" **Wt:** 220

Opening Day Age: 32
Born: 2/23/72 in
Milledgeville, GA
ML Seasons: 11

2003 Season

Following a spring-training trade from the Yankees, Rondell White spent the next five months playing left field and hitting in an RBI spot for the Padres. A nagging hip injury slowed White, but he continued to produce with the bat and drive in runs. White became expendable when Phil Nevin returned from the disabled list in July. The Royals needed a righthanded RBI bat and White fit the bill, driving in almost a run per game during their September pennant race. Overall, White met his career norms; it was a rebound season after a disappointing 2002 campaign.

Hitting

An aggressive, line-drive hitter who likes to get his hitting done early in the count, White will chase high fastballs. He's a poor two-strike hitter. Since 2000, White has batted .194 with two strikes. He can be victimized by good sinkers; he'll beat them into the ground for easy outs. White has fine power to all fields. While he's productive against both lefthanded and righthanded pitchers, he has much better power against righthanders. White is a free swinger who still makes good contact and has hit for a good average in all but one of his nine full seasons.

Baserunning & Defense

Due to repeated knee problems, White no longer tries to steal bases. Still, he has above-average speed. While he doesn't use it much on the bases—he rarely tries for the extra base—it does help him in the outfield. White reads flyballs well and shows fine defensive range. Overall, he's an average left fielder who is hampered by a very weak arm, even for left field.

2004 Outlook

White's becoming a journeyman outfielder. He has played for five teams in the last four years and, after becoming a free agent during the off-season, likely will continue his journey to another team. His injury history and defensive limitations make White a difficult fit for most teams. His best 2004 option will be with a team that has enough depth to replace him should White again suffer an injury that costs him extensive playing time.

Overall Statistics

	G	AB	R	H	D	T	HR	RBI	SB	BB	SO	Avg	OBP	Slg
'03	137	488	62	141	23	4	22	87	1	31	79	.289	.341	.488
Car.	1119	4089	591	1179	230	28	156	590	91	287	727	.288	.343	.473

Where He Hits the Ball

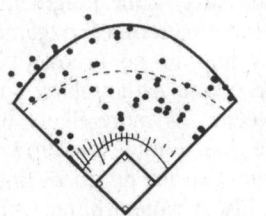
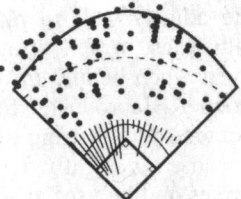

Vs. LHP   **Vs. RHP**

2003 Situational Stats

	AB	H	HR	RBI	Avg		AB	H	HR	RBI	Avg
Home	247	79	5	36	.320	LHP	137	41	4	20	.299
Road	241	62	17	51	.257	RHP	351	100	18	67	.285
First Half	309	85	16	52	.275	Sc Pos	133	38	7	65	.286
Scnd Half	179	56	6	35	.313	Clutch	73	11	4	14	.151

2003 Rankings (American League)

- Did not rank near the top or bottom in any category

Kevin Appier

Position: SP
Bats: R **Throws:** R
Ht: 6' 2" **Wt:** 215

Opening Day Age: 36
Born: 12/6/67 in Lancaster, CA
ML Seasons: 15
Pronunciation: APE-ee-er

Overall Statistics

W	L	Pct.	ERA	G	GS	Sv	IP	H	BB	SO	HR	Avg
8	9	.471	5.40	23	23	0	111.2	120	43	55	21	.269
169	136	.554	3.72	412	400	0	2591.1	2418	930	1992	232	.247

2003 Situational Stats

	W	L	ERA	Sv	IP		AB	H	HR	RBI	Avg
Home	4	2	4.89	0	42.1	LHB	249	63	14	34	.253
Road	4	7	5.71	0	69.1	RHB	197	57	7	31	.289
First Half	6	5	4.78	0	84.2	Sc Pos	97	32	6	46	.330
Scnd Half	2	4	7.33	0	27.0	Clutch	0	0	0	0	–

2003 Season

Inconsistent results and a sore elbow led to Kevin Appier's July release from Anaheim. Although he was known to be damaged goods when he arrived, the Royals were happy to acquire him for four August starts. However, his partially torn elbow ligament worsened, resulting in season-ending September surgery.

Pitching & Defense

Appier's fastball now barely reaches 90 MPH, and while he still has an above-average splitter and a good slider, he relies more heavily on sharp-breaking curveballs and low-80s sinkerballs. He must constantly change speeds and be able to throw offspeed stuff for strikes at any time. His exaggerated delivery still leaves him out of good fielding position. He has improved his move to first and will vary his delivery to hold runners.

2004 Outlook

Because Anaheim still is responsible for the last year of Appier's expensive contract, he comes cheaply in 2004. The Royals signed him for the league minimum. His elbow surgery was successful. He's been a winner for a long time and will be favored to win a lower rotation job in spring training.

Miguel Asencio

Position: SP
Bats: R **Throws:** R
Ht: 6' 2" **Wt:** 190

Opening Day Age: 23
Born: 9/29/80 in Villa Mella, DR
ML Seasons: 2
Pronunciation: ah-SEN-see-oh

Overall Statistics

	W	L	Pct.	ERA	G	GS	Sv	IP	H	BB	SO	HR	Avg
'03	2	1	.667	5.21	8	8	0	48.1	54	21	27	4	.295
Car.	6	8	.429	5.14	39	29	0	171.2	190	85	85	21	.286

2003 Situational Stats

	W	L	ERA	Sv	IP		AB	H	HR	RBI	Avg
Home	0	1	7.94	0	17.0	LHB	96	33	2	18	.344
Road	2	0	3.73	0	31.1	RHB	87	21	2	9	.241
First Half	2	1	5.21	0	48.1	Sc Pos	52	14	1	23	.269
Scnd Half	0	0	–	0	0.0	Clutch	6	0	0	0	.000

2003 Season

After surviving his Rule 5 season in 2002, Miguel Asencio was hoping to hold down a rotation role in 2003. However, he went on the disabled list with a sore elbow, and surgery to remove bone chips ended his season after just eight starts.

Pitching & Defense

Asencio's easy delivery belies a mid-90s, moving fastball. At its best, the pitch will run down and away from righthanders, inducing grounders. Unfortunately, his heater is an unruly beast that escapes Asencio's control all too frequently, causing him painful fits of poor control. He works against a hitter's timing with an above-average changeup, but his curveball remains a weak offering. Thus far, Asencio hasn't proven durable enough to handle a season-long rotation spot. He moves quickly to field grounders, but is tentative throwing to the bases and has a below-average pickoff move.

2004 Outlook

Despite the procedure for bone chips, Asencio is expected to be ready for spring training and the Royals want him to hold a mid-rotation spot. Having consistent command is the key; Asencio has the stuff to succeed if he can harness it regularly for six innings in a row.

Chris George

Position: SP
Bats: L **Throws:** L
Ht: 6' 2" **Wt:** 200

Opening Day Age: 24
Born: 9/16/79 in Houston, TX
ML Seasons: 3

Overall Statistics

	W	L	Pct.	ERA	G	GS	Sv	IP	H	BB	SO	HR	Avg
'03	9	6	.600	7.11	18	18	0	93.2	120	44	39	22	.309
Car.	13	18	.419	6.32	37	37	0	195.0	240	70	84	38	.304

2003 Situational Stats

	W	L	ERA	Sv	IP		AB	H	HR	RBI	Avg
Home	4	3	7.57	0	52.1	LHB	100	28	7	22	.280
Road	5	3	6.53	0	41.1	RHB	288	92	15	44	.319
First Half	9	6	7.11	0	93.2	Sc Pos	91	25	3	40	.275
Scnd Half	0	0	–	0	0.0	Clutch	1	0	0	0	.000

2003 Season

Chris George could do no wrong early in the season. Due to timely hitting and super run support, he kept winning, even when pitching poorly. Until Darrell May won his 10th in mid-September, George's nine wins led the club. When George continued to struggle entering the All-Star break, he was sent to Triple-A Omaha and wasn't recalled in September.

Pitching & Defense

George tends to throw low-90s fastballs at the corners, then uses the offspeed stuff to get outs. Although his curve and slider are fairly ordinary, his changeup can be deceptive. Unfortunately for George, his command suddenly leaves him and he has to throw his fastball where it can be hit. He hasn't been successful pitching down in the zone, as he was during his rise through the Royals' farm system. George fields his position well enough, but has trouble holding baserunners.

2004 Outlook

With the Royals' sudden influx of quality young starters, George will have his work cut out for him in the spring. Barring a host of spring injuries, George should start the season at Triple-A Omaha and work his way back to the majors. He needs to regain his command, however.

Jimmy Gobble

Position: SP
Bats: L **Throws:** L
Ht: 6' 3" **Wt:** 190

Opening Day Age: 22
Born: 7/19/81 in Bristol, TN
ML Seasons: 1

Overall Statistics

	W	L	Pct.	ERA	G	GS	Sv	IP	H	BB	SO	HR	Avg
'03	4	5	.444	4.61	9	9	0	52.2	56	15	31	8	.271
Car.	4	5	.444	4.61	9	9	0	52.2	56	15	31	8	.271

2003 Situational Stats

	W	L	ERA	Sv	IP		AB	H	HR	RBI	Avg
Home	1	4	4.82	0	28.0	LHB	57	15	1	6	.263
Road	3	1	4.38	0	24.2	RHB	150	41	7	26	.273
First Half	0	0	–	0	0.0	Sc Pos	58	17	3	24	.293
Scnd Half	4	5	4.61	0	52.2	Clutch	4	1	0	0	.250

2003 Season

When the Royals' decimated pitching staff needed fresh arms, Jimmy Gobble was recalled from Double-A Wichita and thrust into a big league pennant race. After a strong showing at Wichita, he was asked to make several important August starts. He pitched very well in winning his first two outings and generally enjoyed a solid major league debut.

Pitching & Defense

Gobble spots a low-90s fastballs inside or out and throws a deceptive changeup. But it's his outstanding curveball that gives hitters the most trouble. Gobble struggled to get out of big league jams, rushing his delivery, which diminished his fastball's velocity and the break of his curve. He mostly needs to build strength; he currently lacks the stamina to pitch more than six effective innings. Gobble hasn't shown much with the glove and still is working on a useful pickoff move.

2004 Outlook

The Royals see Gobble as a No. 2 or 3 starter. They like what they've seen so far but want him to build up his stamina. Gobble will battle for a rotation job in the spring. If he starts at Triple-A Omaha, he'll be among the first recalled and should become a major leaguer for good in 2004.

Aaron Guiel

Position: RF
Bats: L **Throws:** R
Ht: 5'10" **Wt:** 200

Opening Day Age: 31
Born: 10/5/72 in Vancouver, BC, Canada
ML Seasons: 2
Pronunciation: GUY-el

Overall Statistics

	G	AB	R	H	D	T	HR	RBI	SB	BB	SO	Avg	OBP	Slg
'03	99	354	63	98	30	0	15	52	3	27	63	.277	.346	.489
Car.	169	594	93	154	43	0	19	90	4	46	124	.259	.326	.428

2003 Situational Stats

	AB	H	HR	RBI	Avg		AB	H	HR	RBI	Avg
Home	179	47	4	21	.263	LHP	102	28	2	15	.275
Road	175	51	11	31	.291	RHP	252	70	13	37	.278
First Half	100	27	5	14	.270	Sc Pos	76	23	4	40	.303
Scnd Half	254	71	10	38	.280	Clutch	30	2	0	1	.067

2003 Season

Recalled from Triple-A Omaha in May as bench filler, Aaron Guiel used experience gleaned from nearly a decade in the minors to make the most of an opportunity. He hit well from the outset, first earning a platoon job, then taking over in right field and becoming a successful leadoff hitter in the second half.

Hitting, Baserunning & Defense

Guiel understands his role well. He has fine on-base ability when leading off, but will try to pull the ball for extra bases when hitting in an RBI spot. Guiel crowds the plate and doesn't give in to inside pitches. He's neither a smooth fielder, nor extremely fast. Instead, he runs good routes and gets a quick jump on the ball while exhibiting an adequate right-field arm. Guiel is a fearless baserunner who lacks basestealing ability and runs into too many outs.

2004 Outlook

The Royals view Guiel as their everyday right fielder to start the season, although they eventually may arrange a platoon for the position. Even if he fails to hold a starting job, he'll be valuable as a fourth outfielder. He won't surprise anyone in 2004. To maintain his success, Guiel will have to make adjustments as he sees fewer fastballs.

Curtis Leskanic

Position: RP
Bats: R **Throws:** R
Ht: 6' 0" **Wt:** 196

Opening Day Age: 35
Born: 4/2/68 in Homestead, PA
ML Seasons: 10
Pronunciation: les-CAN-ik

Overall Statistics

	W	L	Pct.	ERA	G	GS	Sv	IP	H	BB	SO	HR	Avg
'03	5	0	1.000	2.22	53	0	2	52.2	38	29	50	2	.204
Car.	47	29	.618	4.30	552	11	51	669.1	631	332	604	72	.251

2003 Situational Stats

	W	L	ERA	Sv	IP		AB	H	HR	RBI	Avg
Home	4	0	3.30	1	30.0	LHB	85	15	0	5	.176
Road	1	0	0.79	1	22.2	RHB	101	23	2	13	.228
First Half	4	0	2.48	0	29.0	Sc Pos	62	12	0	16	.194
Scnd Half	1	0	1.90	2	23.2	Clutch	89	19	0	10	.213

2003 Season

When the Royals needed short relief help at midseason, they acquired Curtis Leskanic from Milwaukee. After joining Kansas City, Leskanic continued in a setup role before gradually working into a part-time closer job as one of the club's most reliable relievers.

Pitching & Defense

Leskanic works mainly with two pitches, a mid-90s fastball thrown with good movement and a hard slider; he'll mix in an occasional curveball, but not as an out pitch. Although he isn't bothered by frequent use, when he pitches on consecutive days his pitches tend to lose their natural movement. He doesn't have especially good control. Still, he can get strikeouts when needed and he's had success against both lefthanded and righthanded hitters. He's a below-average fielder who has an average pickoff move.

2004 Outlook

An 11-year veteran who missed all of 2002, Leskanic talked of retirement before re-signing for 2004. Following one of his most successful seasons to date, he was interested in pitching short relief this season if the circumstances were right. Although he would be miscast as a closer, Leskanic can be useful in a setup role.

Jose Lima

Position: SP
Bats: R **Throws:** R
Ht: 6' 2" **Wt:** 205

Opening Day Age: 31
Born: 9/30/72 in
Santiago, DR
ML Seasons: 10
Pronunciation:
LEE-mah

Overall Statistics

	W	L	Pct.	ERA	G	GS	Sv	IP	H	BB	SO	HR	Avg
'03	8	3	.727	4.91	14	14	0	73.1	80	26	32	7	.280
Car.	71	77	.480	5.13	276	175	5	1211.1	1361	288	795	200	.284

2003 Situational Stats

	W	L	ERA	Sv	IP		AB	H	HR	RBI	Avg
Home	3	2	6.50	0	36.0	LHB	167	55	6	27	.329
Road	5	1	3.38	0	37.1	RHB	119	25	1	10	.210
First Half	5	0	2.52	0	39.1	Sc Pos	82	20	2	30	.244
Scnd Half	3	3	7.68	0	34.0	Clutch	8	1	0	1	.125

2003 Season

After his release from the Tigers in 2002, Jose Lima was reborn pitching for the independent Newark Bears. His fastball had new life and his changeup was sinking again, so the pitching-desperate Royals took a chance and were rewarded when they won Lima's first eight starts. The clock struck midnight when Lima suffered a groin strain in mid-July, reducing his fastball's velocity and rendering his out pitch, the changeup, ineffective.

Pitching & Defense

Although Lima's 90-MPH fastball is fairly straight and too weak to be a primary pitch, he needs it to keep hitters from sitting on his changeup. He tried to reduce the advantage lefty hitters have enjoyed against him with a decent curveball for the Royals, but it's still a secondary pitch. He lives and dies with that sinking mid-70s changeup that induces grounders. His reliance on offspeed stuff gives baserunners a big advantage despite an average pickoff move and frequent throws to first.

2004 Outlook

It's been a long fall for the animated, former 20-game winner. Still, he's proven he deserves another chance in the majors. You've got to wonder, though, how much longer Lima can get by on changeups and nerve alone.

Brent Mayne

Position: C
Bats: L **Throws:** R
Ht: 6' 1" **Wt:** 190

Opening Day Age: 35
Born: 4/19/68 in Loma
Linda, CA
ML Seasons: 14
Nickname: Mayner

Overall Statistics

	G	AB	R	H	D	T	HR	RBI	SB	BB	SO	Avg	OBP	Slg
'03	113	372	39	91	17	1	6	36	0	32	59	.245	.307	.344
Car.	1196	3424	345	909	172	7	38	388	17	343	539	.265	.333	.353

2003 Situational Stats

	AB	H	HR	RBI	Avg		AB	H	HR	RBI	Avg
Home	183	49	1	21	.268	LHP	106	25	3	13	.236
Road	189	42	5	15	.222	RHP	266	66	3	23	.248
First Half	212	54	4	21	.255	Sc Pos	93	26	2	31	.280
Scnd Half	160	37	2	15	.231	Clutch	59	14	2	6	.237

2003 Season

Brent Mayne made the most of his limited offensive contributions, hitting three of his six homers in the first two weeks as the Royals started quickly. Although his bat cooled and he managed just 15 second-half RBI, it was a good season because he helped young pitchers improve and his club won.

Hitting, Baserunning & Defense

Mayne's a weak hitter; he tries to slap pitches through the infield, but he's regularly overmatched by merely average pitching. Although he's become more aggressive at the plate, he still makes good contact. Mayne has marginal power. His bat has slowed in recent years and he rarely pulls the ball anymore. Although he runs better than most catchers his age, he's still very slow. Mayne shows surprising mobility behind the plate; his good mechanics and quick release help him control baserunners despite a merely average arm.

2004 Outlook

Despite a decent 2003 campaign, the end's near for Mayne, who's been terrific working with inexperienced Kansas City hurlers. With useful defensive abilities, Mayne can succeed as a backup catcher, but won't hit enough to contribute as a regular. The Royals didn't pick up his option for 2004 and signed Benito Santiago to be the starting catcher.

Kyle Snyder

Position: SP
Bats: B **Throws:** R
Ht: 6' 8" **Wt:** 220

Opening Day Age: 26
Born: 9/9/77 in Houston, TX
ML Seasons: 1

Overall Statistics

	W	L	Pct.	ERA	G	GS	Sv	IP	H	BB	SO	HR	Avg
'03	1	6	.143	5.17	15	15	0	85.1	94	21	39	11	.283
Car.	1	6	.143	5.17	15	15	0	85.1	94	21	39	11	.283

2003 Situational Stats

	W	L	ERA	Sv	IP		AB	H	HR	RBI	Avg
Home	0	3	6.50	0	45.2	LHB	194	53	5	23	.273
Road	1	3	3.63	0	39.2	RHB	138	41	6	25	.297
First Half	1	4	4.62	0	64.1	Sc Pos	65	21	2	32	.323
Scnd Half	0	2	6.86	0	21.0	Clutch	12	4	0	0	.333

2003 Season

A former first-round draft pick, Kyle Snyder realized some of his potential in an encouraging rookie campaign that was cut short by shoulder stiffness after one August start. Because Snyder missed almost two years due to Tommy John surgery and had only 100 professional innings entering 2003, the Royals set a strict innings limit

Pitching & Defense

Snyder's repertoire includes the standard fastball, slider, curve and changeup. His low-90s heater can reach 95 MPH, and the sinking action of his two-seamer induces grounders. He throws strikes and can work confidently with his tailing slider or an above-average curveball thrown with a late, tight break. His changeup was less effective last year, but is still a well-developed pitch for the relatively inexperienced pitcher. Snyder is an adept fielder who is quick off the mound. A poor pickoff move and slow delivery give baserunners an advantage.

2004 Outlook

Despite undergoing shoulder surgery in early September, Snyder's 2004 aim is to pitch wire-to-wire without injury worries. If he proves to be fully healthy, the Royals hope to stretch him deeper into games and develop him into a solid starter.

Michael Tucker

Position: RF/CF/LF/DH
Bats: L **Throws:** R
Ht: 6' 2" **Wt:** 195

Opening Day Age: 32
Born: 6/25/71 in South Boston, VA
ML Seasons: 9

Overall Statistics

	G	AB	R	H	D	T	HR	RBI	SB	BB	SO	Avg	OBP	Slg
'03	104	389	61	102	20	5	13	55	8	39	88	.262	.331	.440
Car.	1116	3295	510	853	167	42	106	424	103	373	788	.259	.338	.432

2003 Situational Stats

	AB	H	HR	RBI	Avg		AB	H	HR	RBI	Avg
Home	195	58	8	37	.297	LHP	123	29	2	11	.236
Road	194	44	5	18	.227	RHP	266	73	11	44	.274
First Half	322	88	13	52	.273	Sc Pos	98	30	2	38	.306
Scnd Half	67	14	0	3	.209	Clutch	55	12	1	4	.218

2003 Season

Expected to reprise his 2002 platoon-reserve role, Michael Tucker instead became the Royals' starting center fielder to start the season. When Carlos Beltran returned from the disabled list, Tucker went back to platooning until early August, when a fouled pitch caused a hairline fracture in his lower right leg, essentially ending his season.

Hitting, Baserunning & Defense

Tucker is a free-swinging, streaky hitter, prone to being overly conscious of pulling the ball for extra bases. He will chase fastballs up and out of the strike zone. He's a much better hitter when he keeps a controlled swing and hits the ball where it's pitched. To stay sharp, he requires frequent use; he hasn't succeeded in pinch-hitting roles. Tucker has good outfield range and an average arm that is barely adequate for right field. He is a good baserunner with the speed and instincts to take extra bases.

2004 Outlook

With the Royals' abundance of emerging outfield talent, Tucker, a free agent, wasn't heavily pursued. The Giants signed him to a two-year, $3.5 million deal, but whether he will start, platoon or come off the bench will depend on the Giants' spending habits over the winter.

Paul Abbott (Pos: RHP, Age: 36)

	W	L	Pct.	ERA	G	GS	Sv	IP	H	BB	SO	HR	Avg
'03	1	2	.333	5.29	10	8	0	47.2	47	26	32	8	.257
Car.	40	26	.606	4.68	142	93	0	624.2	576	335	450	79	.246

It was as recently as 2001 that Abbott was 17-4 as a starter with Seattle, but a torn labrum in 2002 has limited his effectiveness since his best season. Now age becomes a factor, though the D-Rays signed him in November. 2004 Outlook: C

Brent Abernathy (Pos: 2B, Age: 26, Bats: R)

	G	AB	R	H	D	T	HR	RBI	SB	BB	SO	Avg	OBP	Slg
'03	12	34	3	2	0	0	0	0	1	1	3	.059	.086	.059
Car.	208	801	92	196	35	5	7	73	19	53	84	.245	.295	.327

Abernathy has regressed since making a decent big league debut in 2001. The Royals claimed him off waivers from Tampa Bay in April, and he spent the second half rebounding nicely at Triple-A Omaha. He signed a minor league deal with Detroit in December. 2004 Outlook: C

Brandon Berger (Pos: RF, Age: 29, Bats: R)

	G	AB	R	H	D	T	HR	RBI	SB	BB	SO	Avg	OBP	Slg
'03	13	32	3	7	0	0	0	3	0	5	4	.219	.324	.219
Car.	70	182	23	39	6	2	8	22	1	15	38	.214	.280	.401

Berger didn't produce much in April after a solid spring, and found himself at Triple-A Omaha for the season in May. He slugged .527 at Omaha, keeping his major league dream alive. 2004 Outlook: C

Dee Brown (Pos: LF/RF, Age: 26, Bats: L)

	G	AB	R	H	D	T	HR	RBI	SB	BB	SO	Avg	OBP	Slg
'03	50	132	16	30	7	0	2	14	1	8	37	.227	.280	.326
Car.	204	616	67	141	30	1	10	65	6	39	155	.229	.277	.330

Despite three solid seasons in the high minors, Brown hasn't seized his opportunities with the Royals. Guys named Mark Quinn, Raul Ibanez and Aaron Guiel have done better and played ahead of him. 2004 Outlook: C

Morgan Burkhart (Pos: 1B, Age: 32, Bats: B)

	G	AB	R	H	D	T	HR	RBI	SB	BB	SO	Avg	OBP	Slg
'03	6	15	1	3	0	0	0	1	0	1	2	.200	.250	.200
Car.	42	121	20	30	4	0	5	23	0	19	38	.248	.366	.405

Burkhart slugged better than .500 at Triple-A Pawtucket in 2000-01 before heading to Japan in 2002. He signed with Triple-A Omaha and surfaced with the Royals in June, but didn't show enough pop to stay. 2004 Outlook: C

D.J. Carrasco (Pos: RHP, Age: 26)

	W	L	Pct.	ERA	G	GS	Sv	IP	H	BB	SO	HR	Avg
'03	6	5	.545	4.82	50	2	2	80.1	82	40	57	8	.271
Car.	6	5	.545	4.82	50	2	2	80.1	82	40	57	8	.271

Despite his status as a Rule 5 pickup from Pittsburgh, Carrasco pitched a great deal for the Royals. He made two emergency starts and earned two saves, as he was useful down the stretch until imploding in his final two outings. 2004 Outlook: B

Gookie Dawkins (Pos: 2B, Age: 24, Bats: R)

	G	AB	R	H	D	T	HR	RBI	SB	BB	SO	Avg	OBP	Slg
'03	3	2	0	0	0	0	0	0	0	1	2	.000	.333	.000
Car.	55	98	8	16	4	0	0	3	2	9	34	.163	.241	.204

Getting out of the Cincinnati system might seem like the ticket to rekindling Dawkins' career, but we're talking about a guy who hasn't enjoyed success at the Triple-A level and may never. 2004 Outlook: C

Rick DeHart (Pos: LHP, Age: 34)

	W	L	Pct.	ERA	G	GS	Sv	IP	H	BB	SO	HR	Avg
'03	0	2	.000	13.50	4	0	0	4.0	8	2	1	1	.421
Car.	2	3	.400	6.14	56	0	1	63.0	81	32	45	13	.312

The Royals tinkered with their pitching staff all season long, and that included DeHart's first big league stint since three appearances with Montreal in 1999. His stay lasted two weeks. 2004 Outlook: C

Mike DiFelice (Pos: C, Age: 34, Bats: R)

	G	AB	R	H	D	T	HR	RBI	SB	BB	SO	Avg	OBP	Slg
'03	62	189	29	48	16	1	3	25	1	9	30	.254	.299	.397
Car.	484	1431	137	345	79	7	28	155	3	88	302	.241	.290	.365

DiFelice collected his highest at-bat total since 2000 and posted a career-high 16 doubles. Yet he's searching for his next minor league contract. That's the life of a big league backup catcher. 2004 Outlook: C

Carlos Febles (Pos: 2B, Age: 27, Bats: R)

	G	AB	R	H	D	T	HR	RBI	SB	BB	SO	Avg	OBP	Slg
'03	74	196	31	46	5	0	0	11	8	13	30	.235	.299	.260
Car.	506	1656	255	414	65	18	24	146	68	163	297	.250	.328	.354

The hitting percentages continued their decline in 2003, and the Royals finally gave up on Febles, probably for good, with none of his marks above .300 in August. He'll get a chance somewhere else. 2004 Outlook: C

Nate Field (Pos: RHP, Age: 28)

	W	L	Pct.	ERA	G	GS	Sv	IP	H	BB	SO	HR	Avg
'03	1	1	.500	4.15	19	0	0	21.2	19	14	19	3	.235
Car.	1	1	.500	5.06	24	0	0	26.2	27	17	22	5	.262

Field was effective at Double-A Wichita and Triple-A Omaha, collecting seven saves and posting a 3.38 ERA. His success spurred a string of second-half callups, and he's in the 2004 mix. 2004 Outlook: B

Jason Gilfillan (Pos: RHP, Age: 27)

	W	L	Pct.	ERA	G	GS	Sv	IP	H	BB	SO	HR	Avg
'03	2	0	1.000	7.71	13	0	0	16.1	22	10	12	3	.310
Car.	2	0	1.000	7.71	13	0	0	16.1	22	10	12	3	.310

Gilfillan was solid in relief at Triple-A Omaha, going 6-0 with a 2.05 ERA. But he struggled in KC in May and June and returned to Omaha. He signed a minor league deal with Colorado in November. 2004 Outlook: C

Jason Grimsley (Pos: RHP, Age: 36)

	W	L	Pct.	ERA	G	GS	Sv	IP	H	BB	SO	HR	Avg
'03	2	6	.250	5.16	76	0	0	75.0	88	36	58	6	.299
Car.	35	47	.427	4.81	438	11	0	824.0	839	446	563	70	.265

Grimsley's three-year career with the Royals appears to document his decline. He was solid in 2001 with a 3.02 ERA, but he's posted marks of 3.91 and 5.16 with more walks the last two seasons. 2004 Outlook: C

Runelvys Hernandez (Pos: RHP, Age: 25)

	W	L	Pct.	ERA	G	GS	Sv	IP	H	BB	SO	HR	Avg
'03	7	5	.583	4.61	16	16	0	91.2	87	37	48	9	.249
Car.	11	8	.579	4.60	30	29	0	188.0	166	59	83	17	.260

Elbow inflammation in May seemed to be minor and his June return was anticipated, but Hernandez underwent Tommy John surgery in September. The Royals' ace may miss all of the 2004 season. 2004 Outlook: D

Jeremy Hill (Pos: RHP, Age: 26)

	W	L	Pct.	ERA	G	GS	Sv	IP	H	BB	SO	HR	Avg
'03	0	0	-	0.00	1	0	0	1.0	1	0	0	0	.250
Car.	1	0	1.000	3.48	11	0	0	10.1	9	8	7	1	.237

The catcher-turned-pitcher still leans too heavily on a mid-90s fastball, yet he was mentioned as a possible KC closer last spring. A horrible start at Triple-A Omaha led to a midseason trade to the Mets. 2004 Outlook: C

Rontrez Johnson (Pos: CF, Age: 27, Bats: R)

	G	AB	R	H	D	T	HR	RBI	SB	BB	SO	Avg	OBP	Slg
'03	8	3	3	1	0	0	0	0	0	0	2	.333	.333	.333
Car.	8	3	3	1	0	0	0	0	0	0	2	.333	.333	.333

Johnson was a Rule 5 pickup from Texas, and the outfielder was returned to the Rangers in mid-April. In July he was released after a poor Triple-A showing and closed 2003 with Atlanta's Triple-A Richmond. 2004 Outlook: C

Al Levine (Pos: RHP, Age: 35)

	W	L	Pct.	ERA	G	GS	Sv	IP	H	BB	SO	HR	Avg
'03	3	6	.333	2.79	54	0	1	71.0	67	29	30	9	.251
Car.	21	29	.420	3.75	342	7	10	494.1	498	208	242	58	.265

Levine put together a scoreless streak of 18 innings with the Rays from April-June, and was dealt to the Royals at the July 31 deadline. His walks were high, but he managed to post a stingy ERA. 2004 Outlook: B

Graeme Lloyd (Pos: LHP, Age: 36)

	W	L	Pct.	ERA	G	GS	Sv	IP	H	BB	SO	HR	Avg
'03	1	4	.200	5.29	52	0	0	47.2	68	14	25	2	.335
Car.	30	36	.455	4.04	568	0	17	533.0	560	161	304	51	.271

Since posting a 1.67 ERA with the Yankees in 1998, Lloyd has seen his ERA steadily climb. It's been in the fives the last two seasons, and he was of little help during the Royals' 2003 drive for a pennant. 2004 Outlook: C

Albie Lopez (Pos: RHP, Age: 32)

	W	L	Pct.	ERA	G	GS	Sv	IP	H	BB	SO	HR	Avg
'03	4	2	.667	12.71	15	0	0	22.2	41	17	15	7	.383
Car.	47	58	.448	4.94	297	92	4	841.1	938	343	558	112	.284

The Royals pulled out all the stops in trying to win the American League Central in 2003, and bringing Lopez aboard as a reliever was one of them. He was released in June after developing a sore elbow. 2004 Outlook: C

Mendy Lopez (Pos: 1B/2B/3B, Age: 30, Bats: R)

	G	AB	R	H	D	T	HR	RBI	SB	BB	SO	Avg	OBP	Slg
'03	52	94	13	26	5	1	3	11	2	4	28	.277	.306	.447
Car.	172	384	41	98	18	5	5	36	7	23	97	.255	.301	.367

Despite approaching his 30th birthday, Lopez was a candidate for his first big league starting job if rookie Angel Berroa had failed at shortstop. Berroa didn't, and Lopez lost 53 games to a strained calf muscle. 2004 Outlook: C

Sean Lowe (Pos: RHP, Age: 33)

	W	L	Pct.	ERA	G	GS	Sv	IP	H	BB	SO	HR	Avg
'03	1	1	.500	6.25	28	0	0	44.2	55	21	28	7	.301
Car.	23	15	.605	4.95	248	22	3	440.0	485	194	288	51	.285

In 2001, Lowe won nine games, saved three others and posted a solid 3.61 ERA as an effective swing man with the White Sox. Little has gone well since then, as Lowe has a 5.95 ERA in 2002-03. 2004 Outlook: C

Julius Matos (Pos: 3B/2B, Age: 29, Bats: R)

	G	AB	R	H	D	T	HR	RBI	SB	BB	SO	Avg	OBP	Slg
'03	28	57	7	15	1	0	2	7	1	1	12	.263	.276	.386
Car.	104	242	26	59	4	0	4	26	2	10	45	.244	.278	.310

The Royals called on anyone and everyone to stay in the American League Central race, and utilityman Matos got off to a hot start when he arrived in July. It didn't last, but he has some fine memories. 2004 Outlook: C

Jarrod Patterson (Pos: 3B, Age: 30, Bats: L)

	G	AB	R	H	D	T	HR	RBI	SB	BB	SO	Avg	OBP	Slg
'03	13	22	3	4	0	0	0	0	0	3	6	.182	.280	.182
Car.	26	63	9	15	1	1	2	4	0	3	10	.238	.294	.381

Patterson's hitting percentages at Triple-A Omaha weren't as good as his two previous Triple-A seasons, but he got callups in July and September. He struggled, but celebrated his 30th birthday in Kansas City. 2004 Outlook: C

Tom Prince (Pos: C, Age: 39, Bats: R)

	G	AB	R	H	D	T	HR	RBI	SB	BB	SO	Avg	OBP	Slg
'03	32	48	5	10	2	0	2	6	1	5	7	.208	.309	.375
Car.	519	1190	113	248	66	4	24	140	9	105	252	.208	.286	.331

Despite a .208 career average, Prince has managed to play 17 seasons in the majors. The Twins waived him near midseason, but the Royals quickly picked him up. He'll turn 40 with his new team. 2004 Outlook: C

Brad Voyles (Pos: RHP, Age: 27)

	W	L	Pct.	ERA	G	GS	Sv	IP	H	BB	SO	HR	Avg
'03	0	2	.000	7.18	11	3	0	31.1	47	18	24	6	.348
Car.	0	4	.000	6.45	40	3	1	68.1	83	44	56	12	.302

Voyles spent chunks of his summer on I-29 between Kansas City and Triple-A Omaha. He was far more successful at the northern outpost, Omaha, posting a 2.99 ERA in 81.1 innings. He's in the 2004 mix. 2004 Outlook: C

Les Walrond (Pos: LHP, Age: 27)

	W	L	Pct.	ERA	G	GS	Sv	IP	H	BB	SO	HR	Avg
'03	0	2	.000	10.13	7	0	0	8.0	11	7	6	2	.324
Car.	0	2	.000	10.13	7	0	0	8.0	11	7	6	2	.324

The former Cardinals prospect was solid in the high minors in 2003, both before and after the Royals picked him up with a May waiver claim. His big league debut wasn't as successful, but he'll be back. 2004 Outlook: C

Kris Wilson (Pos: RHP, Age: 27)

	W	L	Pct.	ERA	G	GS	Sv	IP	H	BB	SO	HR	Avg
'03	6	3	.667	5.33	29	4	0	72.2	92	16	42	13	.305
Car.	14	9	.609	5.32	90	19	1	235.0	291	64	136	49	.303

Elbow troubles that began in 2001 and carried into 2002 slowed his progress, but Wilson enjoyed a healthy summer and filled in for injured Royals starters. He's another year removed from injury. 2004 Outlook: B

Jamey Wright (Pos: RHP, Age: 29)

	W	L	Pct.	ERA	G	GS	Sv	IP	H	BB	SO	HR	Avg
'03	1	2	.333	4.26	4	4	0	25.1	23	11	19	1	.245
Car.	51	69	.425	5.15	178	175	0	1055.2	1159	533	560	117	.288

Escaping Colorado in 2000 looked promising for the young righthander, but he hasn't developed the necessary command. The Royals called in September, and he tossed a shutout and three quality starts. 2004 Outlook: C

Kansas City Royals Minor League Prospects

Organization Overview:

The Royals heavily tapped into their system while making a surprising run at the American League Central title in 2003. Despite falling short in the standings, Angel Berroa, Ken Harvey, Mike MacDougal, Kyle Snyder and Jimmy Gobble all arrived from the minors to make significant contributions. The draft day focus on pitching has left the Royals' farm system poorly stocked in terms of position players, although the club has some outfield prospects ready to make their mark. David DeJesus, Byron Gettis, Alexis Gomez and Chris Lubanski will compete for the center-field job should Carlos Beltran leave. Zack Greinke, Colt Griffin and Kyle Middleton lead a strong group of young hurlers.

Ryan Bukvich

Position: P **Opening Day Age:** 25
Bats: R **Throws:** R **Born:** 5/13/78 in
Ht: 6' 3" **Wt:** 250 Naperville, IL

Recent Statistics

	W	L	ERA	G	GS	Sv	IP	H	R	BB	SO	HR
2003 AAA Omaha	1	2	4.91	34	0	5	36.2	39	21	25	44	2
2003 AL Kansas City	1	0	9.58	9	0	0	10.1	12	11	9	8	2

Because Bukvich throws hard, the Royals thus far have overlooked his control difficulties. He began the 2003 season as a setup man in Kansas City, while also serving as an alternative should Mike MacDougal fail as closer. However, MacDougal succeeded and Bukvich was relegated to Triple A Omaha, where he shared closer duties and, despite good strikeout rates, continued to battle his control. Bukvich's mid-90s fastball is strong enough for the majors, especially when offset by his hard slider and splitter. He tends to overthrow, however, causing his fastball to sail and his offspeed stuff to bounce in the dirt. The Royals will give Bukvich another chance, but he must resolve his control problems soon or miss a chance to take a major league bullpen role.

David DeJesus

Position: OF **Opening Day Age:** 24
Bats: L **Throws:** L **Born:** 12/20/79 in
Ht: 5' 11" **Wt:** 175 Brooklyn, NY

Recent Statistics

	G	AB	R	H	D	T	HR	RBI	SB	BB	SO	Avg
2003 AA Wichita	17	71	14	24	4	0	2	10	1	9	8	.338
2003 AAA Omaha	59	215	49	64	16	3	5	23	8	34	30	.298
2003 AL Kansas City	12	7	0	2	0	1	0	0	0	1	2	.286

The multi-talented DeJesus has made rapid progress since being drafted in the fourth round in 2000, especially considering he lost the entire 2001 season to an elbow injury. He now is considered the frontrunner for the center-field job should Carlos Beltran leave Kansas City. DeJesus is a fine line-drive, contact hitter whose power is expected to improve once his lanky frame fills out. He began to show some power as one of the 2003 Arizona Fall League's better sluggers. DeJesus has superior strike-zone judgment, ideal for the top of a batting order and he has above-average speed. His arm is strong enough for right field and he has enough speed for any outfield spot, but DeJesus needs more experience reading flyballs. He should contend for a starting major league job late in 2004.

Byron Gettis

Position: OF **Opening Day Age:** 24
Bats: R **Throws:** R **Born:** 3/13/80 in
Ht: 6' 2" **Wt:** 220 Centreville, IL

Recent Statistics

	G	AB	R	H	D	T	HR	RBI	SB	BB	SO	Avg
2002 A Wilmington	120	449	76	127	33	2	8	70	10	48	103	.283
2003 AA Wichita	140	510	80	154	31	4	16	103	15	55	110	.302

Recognized as the Royals' Minor League Player of the Year in 2003, Gettis had an outstanding season at Double-A Wichita, showing unusual power and good on-base ability. It was his first season above Class-A, as his hitting has been very slow to develop. He has above-average speed and is an excellent defensive outfielder who displays good range and a strong arm. While his glove is ready for the majors, his bat remains a question mark. He's on the right track, following a good 2002 season in a pitchers' league at high Class-A Wilmington with his breakout year at Wichita. If Gettis shows the trend is for real, he'll reach the parent club before the end of 2004.

Alexis Gomez

Position: OF **Opening Day Age:** 25
Bats: L **Throws:** L **Born:** 8/6/78 in Loma de
Ht: 6' 2" **Wt:** 180 Cabrera, DR

Recent Statistics

	G	AB	R	H	D	T	HR	RBI	SB	BB	SO	Avg
2002 AA Wichita	114	461	72	136	21	8	14	75	36	45	84	.295
2002 AL Kansas City	5	10	0	2	0	0	0	0	0	0	2	.200
2003 AAA Omaha	121	456	49	123	23	8	8	58	4	26	91	.270

Boon turned to bust for Gomez in 2003 as he suffered from repeated hamstring pulls that diminished not only his speed, but also negatively affected his swing. After such a fine year in 2002, he was at the head of the Royals' outfield prospect class, but he has been passed by David DeJesus and has been shifted to right field. Gomez combines fine raw talent, including above-average speed and a good arm, with moderate power potential, but he has yet to turn those tools into useful skills. He's still far too undisciplined at the plate and has been plagued by inconsistent play. Gomez needs another full year in the high minors.

Ruben Gotay

Position: 2B
Bats: B **Throws:** R
Ht: 5' 11" **Wt:** 160

Opening Day Age: 21
Born: 12/25/82 in
Fajardo, PR

Recent Statistics

		G	AB	R	H	D	T	HR	RBI	SB	BB	SO	Avg
2002 A Burlington		133	509	87	145	42	9	9	83	5	73	110	.285
2003 A Wilmington		134	502	68	131	31	2	9	72	8	60	97	.261

Although he lacks any one outstanding tool, Gotay has moderate ability in many areas and no significant holes in his game. He's a versatile defender who was rated as the Class-A Midwest League's best second baseman in 2002, and he's also played some at third base. He's a very patient hitter with gap power, and while he doesn't project as a big power threat, the switch-hitting Gotay will get on base with regularity while producing more than a handful of doubles. As a fairly unheralded prospect, Gotay may surprise some folks in a hitters' environment at Double-A Wichita in 2004.

Zack Greinke

Position: P
Bats: R **Throws:** R
Ht: 6' 2" **Wt:** 190

Opening Day Age: 20
Born: 10/21/83 in
Orlando, FL

Recent Statistics

	W	L	ERA	G	GS	Sv	IP	H	R	BB	SO	HR
2002 R Royals	0	0	1.93	3	3	0	4.2	3	1	3	4	0
2002 A Spokane	0	0	7.71	2	2	0	4.2	9	4	0	5	0
2002 A Wilmington	0	0	0.00	1	0	0	2.0	1	0	0	0	0
2003 A Wilmington	11	1	1.14	14	14	0	87.0	56	16	13	78	5
2003 AA Wichita	4	3	3.23	9	9	0	53.0	58	20	5	34	5

The Royals' persistence with drafting high school pitchers in early rounds appears to have paid big dividends with Greinke. After just 11.1 professional innings in 2002, he pitched successfully against established pro players in Puerto Rico over the winter before tearing through the high Class-A Carolina League. The outstanding season earned Greinke recognition by *Sporting News* as its Minor League Player of the Year. With superior command of three plus pitches (low-90s fastball, curve, changeup) and uncanny poise, he has the talent to become a No. 1 starter in the big leagues. The wait will be excruciating, but the Royals are committed to biding their time with Greinke.

Colt Griffin

Position: P
Bats: R **Throws:** R
Ht: 6' 4" **Wt:** 198

Opening Day Age: 21
Born: 9/29/82 in
Marshall, TX

Recent Statistics

	W	L	ERA	G	GS	Sv	IP	H	R	BB	SO	HR
2002 A Burlington	6	6	5.36	19	19	0	90.2	75	60	82	66	1
2002 A Wilmington	0	1	3.86	3	0	0	4.2	3	2	5	3	0
2003 A Burlington	9	11	3.91	27	27	0	149.2	127	80	97	107	7
2003 A Wilmington	1	0	0.00	1	1	0	6.0	3	1	0	5	0

It's easy to see why Griffin is considered a prospect, and just as easy to see why he hasn't progressed as a pro. He has some of the hottest heat in baseball—his moving four-seamer is regularly thrown in the mid- to upper 90s. The pitch was clocked at 100 MPH when he was still a Texas high schooler, earning him first-round draft status in 2001. Since then, Griffin has shown poor control, walking 191 and throwing 54 wild pitches in 252.2 professional innings. His slider is erratic and he has poor command of his changeup. Although he made some progress in 2003, his career has stagnated due to inconsistent mechanics. If he finds the strike zone more often, Griffin will advance quickly, although his lack of useful offspeed stuff eventually may relegate him to the bullpen.

Mike Tonis

Position: C
Bats: R **Throws:** R
Ht: 6' 3" **Wt:** 215

Opening Day Age: 25
Born: 2/9/79 in
Sacramento, CA

Recent Statistics

		G	AB	R	H	D	T	HR	RBI	SB	BB	SO	Avg
2002 R Royals		6	17	2	3	0	0	1	3	0	2	3	.176
2003 AA Wichita		87	307	34	73	18	0	2	24	3	23	52	.238

Tonis might be a prospect, but thus far he hasn't stayed healthy long enough to tell. Since his second-round selection in 2000, he has spent more time on the disabled list than in uniform. He missed games in 2001 with knee problems, then lost almost all of 2002 to a torn labrum and, later, to a serious beaning. When in the line-up, Tonis has displayed quality defensive skills, moving well behind the plate and throwing accurately. His bat has been disappointing thus far, especially in a repeat season at a hitters' park in Double-A Wichita in 2003. Overall, he's just mediocre with a bat in his hands. If he gets to the majors, it'll be on the strength of his glove, and it may be years before he learns to hit big league pitching.

Others to Watch

The Royals looked to bolster their depleted farm system by taking **Chris Lubanski** (19) in the first round in 2003. His outstanding speed was evident in the Rookie-level Arizona League as he connected for six triples in just 221 at-bats. Focused and hard-working, Lubanski is a good defensive center fielder whose power is expected to develop. . . Not far behind the Royals' other pitching prospects is righthander **Kyle Middleton** (23), who led the high Class-A Carolina League with a 2.41 ERA in 2003 after a fine year at Class-A Burlington in 2002. Middleton has a low-90s fastball which he offsets with a good curve and changeup. He has proven durable and needs only to show more consistency. . . Although **Danny Tamayo** (24) lacks the typical prospect pedigree, he has done nothing but succeed at each level because he knows how to pitch. His fastball only reaches 90 MPH, but he works well with a curve and an above-average changeup. He may not blow hitters away, but if Tamayo keeps getting them out he'll merit a shot at the majors.

Hubert H. Humphrey Metrodome

Offense

For all its deficiencies as a ballpark—and there are many—the Metrodome plays fairly honest, provided you can pick up flyballs against the Teflon-coated roof. It's no better than an average home-run park whose deep alleys favor speedy gap hitters. The right field fence is 327 feet down the line and should be a target for lefthanded power hitters. Lefthanded pitchers generally do well in the Dome, but sinkerball pitchers can be hurt by the Dome's slick artificial surface.

Defense

Speed is a prerequisite because of the slick playing surface and deep alleys. One of the keys to the Twins' recent success is that the team has built a lineup geared to playing well in the Dome. Outfielders Torii Hunter and Jacque Jones cover as much ground as anyone, and shortstop Cristian Guzman and second baseman Luis Rivas have good range and strong arms. The most unique aspect of the park is the large blue baggie that serves as an oversized wall in right field.

Who It Helps the Most

Guzman and Rivas have the speed and gap power to take advantage of their home stadium, and both did that in 2003. Rivas batted .295 at home. Guzman hit .278 with 11 triples at home, .257 with three triples on the road. Jones is another speedy gap hitter who hit better at the Dome (.318) than the road (.289).

Who It Hurts the Most

Righthanded hitters who try too hard to pull the ball are setting themselves up for problems. Consider the 2003 season of Torii Hunter, who tried early to hit homers to provide the power the club lacked. The result: Hunter batted .217 at home, .280 on the road.

Rookies & Newcomers

Michael Cuddyer figures to get another shot in 2004. He has power potential, but needs to hit the ball to all fields before the homers will come. In time, lefthanded hitters Joe Mauer and Justin Morneau could take advantage of the short right-field fence.

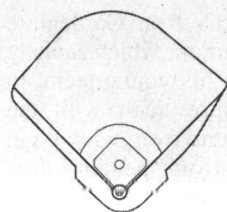

Dimensions: LF-343, LCF-385, CF-408, RCF-367, RF-327

Capacity: 48,678

Elevation: 815 feet

Surface: Turf

Foul Territory: Average

Minnesota

Park Factors

2003 Season

	Home Games			Away Games			
	Twins	Opp	Total	Twins	Opp	Total	Index
G	72	72	144	72	72	144	
Avg	.274	.266	.270	.277	.264	.270	100
AB	2436	2624	5060	2577	2425	5002	101
R	353	341	694	360	324	684	101
H	668	699	1367	713	640	1353	101
2B	139	142	281	143	122	265	105
3B	24	13	37	16	8	24	152
HR	71	85	156	69	81	150	103
BB	245	178	423	210	178	388	108
SO	452	485	937	444	389	833	111
E	32	55	87	46	56	102	85
E-Infield	24	44	68	36	44	80	85
LHB-Avg	.286	.267	.276	.294	.258	.278	100
LHB-HR	34	44	78	25	31	56	134
RHB-Avg	.262	.266	.264	.260	.268	.264	100
RHB-HR	37	41	78	44	50	94	84

2001-2003

	Home Games			Away Games			
	Twins	Opp	Total	Twins	Opp	Total	Index
G	216	216	432	215	215	430	
Avg	.274	.263	.268	.273	.267	.270	99
AB	7274	7693	14967	7649	7297	14946	100
R	1052	972	2024	1036	1007	2043	99
H	1994	2024	4018	2090	1946	4036	99
2B	459	427	886	427	367	794	111
3B	60	50	110	45	32	77	143
HR	200	228	428	231	262	493	87
BB	692	556	1248	637	592	1229	101
SO	1382	1449	2831	1445	1166	2611	108
E	109	165	274	141	151	292	93
E-Infield	83	134	217	119	128	247	87
LHB-Avg	.282	.271	.277	.282	.272	.277	100
LHB-HR	103	113	216	126	114	240	90
RHB-Avg	.264	.257	.260	.262	.263	.263	99
RHB-HR	97	115	212	105	148	253	83

2003 Rankings (American League)

- Highest triple factor
- Highest strikeout factor
- Second-highest LHB home-run factor
- Third-highest walk factor
- Second-lowest error factor
- Second-lowest infield-error factor
- Third-lowest RHB home-run factor

Ron Gardenhire

2003 Season

As a rookie manager in 2002, Ron Gardenhire dealt with the threat of contraction, which actually served as a rallying point for his young team. In his second season, Gardenhire dealt with the increased expectations that came from winning in 2002, contract distractions from pending free agents and injuries that knocked out starting pitchers Eric Milton and Joe Mays. Gardenhire, jocular and outgoing by nature, had closed-door meetings with players he felt lacked focus. In the end, he did a better job managing in 2003 and was runner up for AL Manager of the year.

Offense

Gardenhire, a feisty middle infielder as a player, favors an aggressive running game to put pressure on opposing defenses. He likes to hit-and-run, and sometimes uses the sacrifice bunt. That's not to say he wouldn't like to add power, but prospects Matthew LeCroy, Michael Cuddyer and Michael Restovich have yet to provide it. Gardenhire generally is patient, if players are focused and don't make mental mistakes. He's certainly more patient and approachable than his predecessor and mentor, Tom Kelly.

Pitching & Defense

Gardenhire likes set bullpen roles, which is why he started the season with lefties Johan Santana, J.C. Romero and Eddie Guardado in the pen, even though Santana was one of the top starters. He had consistently gone with Guardado as his closer. Gardenhire believes defense wins games. That's why he made Jacque Jones his everyday left fielder two years ago despite Jones' problems against left-handed pitchers. In key games, Gardenhire will go with defense over batting punch.

2004 Outlook

The set bullpen that has been key to the Twins' success during Gardenhire's first two seasons as manager may be a thing of the past. Both Eddie Guardado and LaTroy Hawkins have signed elsewhere, leaving Gardenhire to rebuild his pen. Also gone are starter Eric Milton and catcher A.J. Pierzynski. The budgetary restrictions could become a distraction for the team's young veterans, and Gardenhire will be tested to hold the fort in '04.

Born: 10/24/57 in Butzbach, West Germany

Playing Experience: 1981-1985, NYM

Managerial Experience: 2 seasons

Manager Statistics

Year	Team, Lg	W	L	Pct	GB	Finish
2003	Minnesota, AL	90	72	.556	–	1st Central
2 Seasons		184	139	.570	–	–

2003 Starting Pitchers by Days Rest

	<=3	4	5	6+
Twins Starts	1	68	69	15
Twins ERA	3.00	4.89	4.71	4.30
AL Avg Starts	2	79	50	22
AL ERA	3.19	4.64	4.57	4.98

2003 Situational Stats

	Ron Gardenhire	AL Average
Hit & Run Success %	29.9	36.7
Stolen Base Success %	68.1	70.0
Platoon Pct.	62.8	61.7
Defensive Subs	19	23
High-Pitch Outings	2	5
Quick/Slow Hooks	15/20	19/16
Sacrifice Attempts	61	55

2003 Rankings (American League)

- 1st in squeeze plays (8)
- 2nd in slow hooks

Eddie Guardado

2003 Season

At some point people are going to stop noting that Eddie Guardado's lack of a dominant pitch makes him an unlikely closer, and simply take note of his numbers. The lefthander has been one of baseball's top closers the last two seasons, earning saves in 86 of 96 opportunities (89.6 percent). He's earned his teammates' confidence and the Everyday Eddie moniker fits. Guardado converted a club-record 24 consecutive save opportunities from September 4, 2002 through June 5 of last season. He then converted 17 consecutive saves from August 4 through September 24.

Pitching

Although his fastball seldom breaks 93 MPH, Guardado's excellent control and his willingness to challenge hitters make the pitch effective. He is not going to beat himself, allowing only 2.17 walks per nine innings the past two seasons. He also has a better-than-average curveball and slider, plus a split-finger fastball that he added two years ago. That pitch has improved his effectiveness against righthanded hitters, who struggle to stay above the Mendoza line against him. While he might lack the 97-MPH fastball of teammate LaTroy Hawkins, Guardado will stack his bottom line up against anyone's.

Defense

Guardado isn't a natural athlete, but he fields his position with a veteran's aplomb. He has quick reflexes, allowing him to stab balls that appear headed up the middle. He holds runners well, and his quick, compact delivery makes it difficult to steal against him.

2004 Outlook

A 21st-round pick with Minnesota in 1990, the closer may have been open to staying for less money, but he opted to sign a three-year, $13 million deal that could pay $17 million if he is Seattle's closer the final two seasons of the contract. The Mariners also have righthanders Kazuhiro Sasaki and Shigetoshi Hasegawa on board, so the lefthanded Guardado may do more setup work than closing in 2004. Don't underestimate Guardado, who might lack the dominant pitch, but has a closer's temperament.

Position: RP
Bats: R **Throws:** L
Ht: 6' 0" **Wt:** 200

Opening Day Age: 33
Born: 10/2/70 in Stockton, CA
ML Seasons: 11
Pronunciation: gWar-DAH-doe
Nickname: Everyday Eddie

Overall Statistics

	W	L	Pct.	ERA	G	GS	Sv	IP	H	BB	SO	HR	Avg
'03	3	5	.375	2.89	66	0	41	65.1	50	14	60	7	.207
Car.	36	47	.434	4.50	639	25	116	697.2	662	268	605	99	.252

2003 Pitching Profile

	Eddie Guardado	AL Average
Overall Strike %	67.6	62.8
1st Pitch Strike %	65.0	58.7
Ratio	0.98	1.39
Strikeouts per 9 IP	8.27	6.11
Walks per 9 IP	1.93	3.16
Home Runs per 9 IP	0.96	1.11
Strikeout/Walk Ratio	4.29	1.93
Groundball/Flyball Ratio	0.59	1.18

2003 Situational Stats

	W	L	ERA	Sv	IP		AB	H	HR	RBI	Avg
Home	2	2	1.75	22	36.0	LHB	63	11	0	5	.175
Road	1	3	4.30	19	29.1	RHB	178	39	7	19	.219
First Half	1	4	3.75	20	36.0	Bases Emp	50	12	1	15	.240
Scnd Half	2	1	1.84	21	29.1	Clutch	171	34	6	21	.199

2003 Rankings (American League)

- 1st in save percentage (91.1)
- 2nd in saves
- 3rd in games finished (60), first batter efficiency (.136) and fewest baserunners allowed per nine innings in relief (8.8)
- Led the Twins in saves, games finished (60), lowest batting average allowed vs. righthanded batters, save percentage (91.1), lowest batting average allowed in relief (.207) and fewest baserunners allowed per nine innings in relief (8.8)

Cristian Guzman

Position: SS
Bats: B **Throws:** R
Ht: 6' 0" **Wt:** 195

Opening Day Age: 26
Born: 3/21/78 in Santo Domingo, DR
ML Seasons: 5
Pronunciation: GOOZ-mahn

2003 Season

Cristian Guzman was the team's catalyst during a surprising first-half run in 2001. The description has seldom been used since. The shortstop has been unable to recapture the promise he showed in earning an All-Star berth that season, and was criticized last year for his lack of focus and seemingly lethargic play. The organization's lack of infield depth left no option but to continue playing Guzman, and he did manage a .287 average and .355 on-base percentage after the break.

Hitting

In 2001, Guzman was a splendid combination of power and speed, with 28 doubles, 14 triples and 10 homers. That computed to an extra-base hit every 9.5 at bats. Last season, Guzman had an extra-base hit every 16.7 at bats. Twins coaches have worked with him to swing down on more pitches, believing grounders on the Dome's fast turf better utilizes his speed. Too often, however, he has appeared punchless, slapping his bat at pitches rather than taking hard swings. Guzman's other weakness is his lack of discipline, although he did show improvement in his walk rate in 2003. Still, his .311 on-base percentage last season hardly stamps him as a leadoff-type hitter.

Baserunning & Defense

Guzman has exceptional speed, but he never has refined his basestealing technique to take full advantage. He's also been bothered by a variety of knee problems, which have limited his running. Defensively, he frequently displays tremendous range, and he's a more consistent player in the field than he was a few years ago. But he still has a tendency to make his miscues on routine plays.

2004 Outlook

Team officials have tired of Guzman's inconsistent approach and lack of focus, but there isn't another quality shortstop in the organization ready. So Guzman is almost certain to be back at short in 2004, but it's the final season of his multiyear contract and prospect Jason Bartlett may be an option by 2005. Guzman needs to show more desire and focus—not to mention an improved on-base percentage—to win over the coaching staff.

Overall Statistics

	G	AB	R	H	D	T	HR	RBI	SB	BB	SO	Avg	OBP	Slg
'03	143	534	78	143	15	14	3	53	18	30	79	.268	.311	.365
Car.	696	2701	374	713	111	57	31	243	92	136	427	.264	.302	.382

Where He Hits the Ball

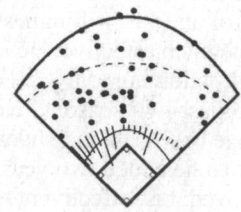
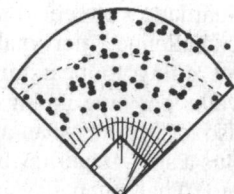

Vs. LHP   **Vs. RHP**

2003 Situational Stats

	AB	H	HR	RBI	Avg		AB	H	HR	RBI	Avg
Home	273	76	1	35	.278	LHP	164	41	1	14	.250
Road	261	67	2	18	.257	RHP	370	102	2	39	.276
First Half	339	87	0	21	.257	Sc Pos	142	36	0	46	.254
Scnd Half	195	56	3	32	.287	Clutch	71	23	0	6	.324

2003 Rankings (American League)

- 1st in triples
- 2nd in lowest HR frequency (178.0 ABs per HR)
- 3rd in sacrifice bunts (12), fielding percentage at shortstop (.980) and lowest stolen-base percentage (66.7)
- 4th in bunts in play (30) and lowest slugging percentage
- 5th in caught stealing (9)
- Led the Twins in singles, triples, sacrifice bunts (12), stolen bases, caught stealing (9), bunts in play (30), highest percentage of swings put into play (52.2), fewest GDPs per GDP situation (3.8%) and batting average with the bases loaded (.714)

Torii Hunter

Gold Glover

2003 Season

The Twins signed Torii Hunter to a long-term deal before the 2003 season, hoping he would blossom into a bona fide superstar. That didn't happen, although Hunter remains one of the game's best defensive center fielders. He drove in a career-high 102 runs, but most of his other offensive numbers declined from 2002. His batting average dipped 39 points and his on-base percentage was down 22 points. Hunter suffered a midseason swoon, batting only .231 during July and August.

Hitting

Hunter has the potential to be much more of a home-run threat. His failure to crack the 30-home-run barrier can be traced to his undisciplined approach. Although he's shown some improvement, his swing still is too long at times, which makes him especially vulnerable to inside fastballs. When Hunter falls behind in the count, he too often swings at anything near the strike zone, leaving him flailing at outside breaking balls or high fastballs. It's encouraging that his walks have increased from 29 to 35 to 50 the past three seasons.

Baserunning & Defense

There's not a better defensive center fielder in the American League than Hunter, won his second Gold Glove in 2003. He gets a great jump on the ball, and he's fearless, slamming into fences and diving for liners. Hunter also has one of the strongest and most accurate throwing arms among center fielders, and aggressive baserunners have learned to stay put. Hunter's speed has not translated to stolen-base success because of his lack of technique.

2004 Outlook

Hunter's defense makes him one of the team's most valuable players. If he could improve offensively, he might be one of the league's most valuable players. But that's a big "if." At this stage, Hunter is what he is—an aggressive, undisciplined hitter with the power to hit 25-30 homers. Unless he improves his approach, he's not going to bat .300 or hit 40 homers. Still, it's difficult to be disappointed with a player whose defensive talents produce nightly highlight material.

Position: CF
Bats: R **Throws:** R
Ht: 6' 2" **Wt:** 210

Opening Day Age: 28
Born: 7/18/75 in Pine Bluff, AR
ML Seasons: 7

(Minnesota)

Overall Statistics

	G	AB	R	H	D	T	HR	RBI	SB	BB	SO	Avg	OBP	Slg
'03	154	581	83	145	31	4	26	102	6	50	106	.250	.312	.451
Car.	691	2443	350	650	132	22	96	369	52	160	495	.266	.316	.456

Where He Hits the Ball

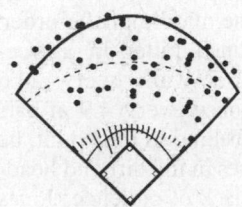
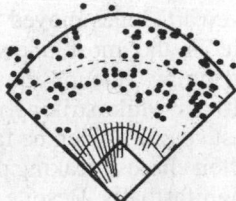

Vs. LHP   **Vs. RHP**

2003 Situational Stats

	AB	H	HR	RBI	Avg		AB	H	HR	RBI	Avg
Home	277	60	12	37	.217	LHP	167	42	9	35	.251
Road	304	85	14	65	.280	RHP	414	103	17	67	.249
First Half	337	85	14	57	.252	Sc Pos	191	47	8	76	.246
Scnd Half	244	60	12	45	.246	Clutch	81	24	2	12	.296

2003 Rankings (American League)

- 2nd in lowest batting average at home
- 4th in fielding percentage in center field (.991)
- Led the Twins in home runs, at-bats, runs scored, total bases (262), RBI, plate appearances (642) and games played

Jacque Jones

2003 Season

Jacque Jones once looked like a platoon player because of his problems against lefthanded pitching. But no one has benefited more from the managerial change from hard-nosed Tom Kelly to Ron Gardenhire before the 2002 season. Jones has been a .300 hitter the past two seasons, and batted a career-high .269 against lefties in 2003. He got off to a fast start, but a nagging groin problem limited his playing time and production over the final three months.

Hitting

Jones began the season as the Twins' leadoff hitter, but the free swinger was miscast in that role. With the midseason acquisition of Shannon Stewart, Jones moved to the middle of the order. He is the most undisciplined hitter in a free-swinging lineup, drawing a walk every 24.6 at-bats while striking out once every 4.9 at-bats last season. When he falls behind in the count, he often chases breaking pitches in the dirt and head-high fastballs. Despite his lack of patience, Jones is one of the Twins' better clutch-hitters with runners in scoring position. With his quick bat, he is a good bet to hit 35-plus homers at some point in his career.

Baserunning & Defense

Jones is one of the league's best defensive left fielders, but with the acquisition of the weak-armed Stewart, he was forced to move to right field. Jones lacks a right fielder's arm. His strength as an outfielder is his speed and his ability to get a quick jump on the ball. With 13 stolen bases in 14 attempts in 2003, Jones finally acted on his potential to steal 20-plus bases regularly.

2004 Outlook

While Jones and Stewart may be too much alike in their ability to both return in 2004, Stewart was re-signed to be the leadoff hitter. That means Jones, signed through 2004, will stay in right field. Unless, of course, the Twins decide to trade Jones, who hasn't distinguished himself in the last two postseasons (9-for-56, .161). That's a concern for an organization trying to take a step beyond winning the weak Central Division, which after all is hardly something to hang a hat on.

Position: LF/DH/RF
Bats: L **Throws:** L
Ht: 5'10" **Wt:** 200

Opening Day Age: 28
Born: 4/25/75 in San Diego, CA
ML Seasons: 5

Overall Statistics

	G	AB	R	H	D	T	HR	RBI	SB	BB	SO	Avg	OBP	Slg
'03	136	517	76	157	33	1	16	69	13	21	105	.304	.333	.464
Car.	683	2414	349	703	145	10	85	323	41	140	500	.291	.332	.465

Where He Hits the Ball

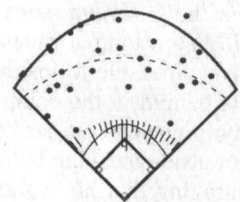
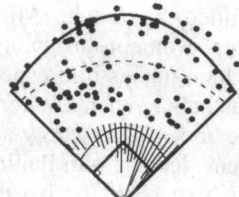

Vs. LHP **Vs. RHP**

2003 Situational Stats

	AB	H	HR	RBI	Avg		AB	H	HR	RBI	Avg
Home	264	84	7	33	.318	LHP	145	39	2	14	.269
Road	253	73	9	36	.289	RHP	372	118	14	55	.317
First Half	300	90	10	35	.300	Sc Pos	129	36	4	54	.279
Scnd Half	217	67	6	34	.309	Clutch	66	21	1	8	.318

2003 Rankings (American League)

- 1st in highest groundball-flyball ratio (2.6)
- 2nd in lowest percentage of pitches taken (42.5), highest percentage of swings that missed (27.6) and highest percentage of swings on the first pitch (46.9)
- 3rd in errors in left field (5) and lowest on-base percentage for a leadoff hitter (.314)
- 8th in steals of third (4), batting average vs. righthanded pitchers and fewest pitches seen per plate appearance (3.31)
- Led the Twins in hits, highest groundball-fly ball ratio (2.6), stolen-base percentage (92.9) and steals of third (4)

Corey Koskie

2003 Season

The 2003 season for Corey Koskie can be summed up in a single fact: He hit his last home run on July 5. That's alarming for a player who, after a .276-26-103 season in 2001, looked like the team's main source of lefthanded power. Since then his home runs have decreased each season, and his last two RBI totals would be acceptable for a slick-fielding middle infielder. He revealed after the season that he had played with a broken hamate bone in his right wrist, which provides some hope that his numbers will rebound.

Hitting

On a team of free swingers, Koskie is patient to a fault. The coaching staff compared Koskie's approach to Ted Williams', meaning the Twins third baseman looks for the absolute perfect pitch before swinging. Problem is, Koskie is not Ted Williams, which means Koskie too often is batting behind in the count and is forced to swing defensively. He is at his best when he's aggressive at the plate.

Baserunning & Defense

The Twins' recent success has been founded on pitching and defense, and Koskie is one of the league's top defensive third basemen. He has quick reflexes, a reliable glove and a strong throwing arm. The decision to pick up his 2004 option was an indication that GM Terry Ryan didn't want to weaken the team's defense to take a chance on increased power production at third base from Michael Cuddyer. Koskie's speed on the basepaths is barely adequate, but he is a smart player who has been in double figures in stolen bases each of the last three seasons.

2004 Outlook

Despite Koskie's offensive slide, the club picked up his $4.5 million option for 2004. He will be the starting third baseman, but if his power and run production don't improve, it will be his final season with the Twins. Several team officials already are weary of watching Koskie's ultra-patient approach, which has generated 462 strikeouts the past four seasons. That's a tolerable total for a legitimate power hitter, but not for a corner infielder who goes three months without a homer.

Position: 3B
Bats: L **Throws:** R
Ht: 6' 3" **Wt:** 220

Opening Day Age: 30
Born: 6/28/73 in Anola, MB, Canada
ML Seasons: 6
Pronunciation: KOSS-key

Overall Statistics

	G	AB	R	H	D	T	HR	RBI	SB	BB	SO	Avg	OBP	Slg
'03	131	469	76	137	29	2	14	69	11	77	113	.292	.393	.452
Car.	698	2366	370	675	156	11	76	366	57	336	544	.285	.379	.457

Where He Hits the Ball

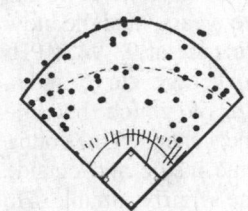
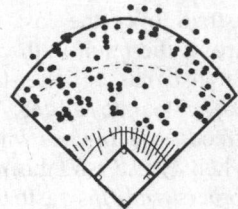

Vs. LHP   **Vs. RHP**

2003 Situational Stats

	AB	H	HR	RBI	Avg		AB	H	HR	RBI	Avg
Home	221	64	8	32	.290	LHP	170	38	3	20	.224
Road	248	73	6	37	.294	RHP	299	99	11	49	.331
First Half	319	95	14	55	.298	Sc Pos	118	32	2	50	.271
Scnd Half	150	42	0	14	.280	Clutch	63	13	0	7	.206

2003 Rankings (American League)

- 2nd in fielding percentage at third base (.973)
- 6th in sacrifice flies (9) and most pitches seen per plate appearance (4.08)
- 7th in fewest GDPs per GDP situation (3.9%)
- 8th in lowest batting average with the bases loaded (.111)
- Led the Twins in sacrifice flies (9), walks, strikeouts, pitches seen (2,292) and most pitches seen per plate appearance (4.08)

Kyle Lohse

2003 Season

Kyle Lohse took another significant step forward in 2003, picking up the slack when injuries knocked Eric Milton, Joe Mays and Rick Reed out of the rotation. There were stretches when Lohse looked like the Twins' No. 1 pitcher. He posted a 1.97 ERA in six May starts, and was 8-2 in 12 starts after August 1. He was the Twins' No. 3 starter for the postseason after failing to crack the postseason rotation in 2002. To understand just how far he has come, remember that Lohse was 3-18 with a 6.04 ERA at Double-A New Britain in 2000.

Pitching

The righthander has added several MPH to his fastball over the last three years, and he now throws the pitch with confidence at 93-94 MPH. He also has a better-than-average curve and a major league slider, both of which become effective out pitches when he's ahead in the count. When Lohse isn't hitting the inside and outside corners with his fastball, he's fairly hittable. He also lacks a changeup, which is one reason lefthanders continue to give him trouble. Whatever weaknesses he has are offset by his demeanor. Lohse doesn't rattle and won't give in to hitters.

Defense

Lohse was a three-sport athlete in high school (football, basketball and baseball), and fields his position like the top athlete he is. He has quick reflexes on balls hit up the middle, plus better-than-average speed when he's called on to cover first. He has a decent move to first, making him difficult to run against.

2004 Outlook

Lohse is certain to be in the 2004 rotation, and if his improvement continues he has a chance to develop into a top-notch starter. He's 27-19 in his first two full seasons, which is much better at that benchmark than 2003 teammates Brad Radke and Eric Milton were. Milton has been traded to Philadelphia, so Lohse joins Radke and Johan Santana at the top of the rotation. He has been durable, and his mental toughness has endeared him to the coaching staff. At age 25, he should be on the verge of a breakout season.

Position: SP
Bats: R **Throws:** R
Ht: 6' 2" **Wt:** 200

Opening Day Age: 25
Born: 10/4/78 in Chico, CA
ML Seasons: 3
Pronunciation: lowshe

Overall Statistics

	W	L	Pct.	ERA	G	GS	Sv	IP	H	BB	SO	HR	Avg
'03	14	11	.560	4.61	33	33	0	201.0	211	45	130	28	.268
Car.	31	26	.544	4.67	84	80	0	472.0	494	144	318	70	.268

2003 Pitching Profile

	Kyle Lohse	AL Average
Overall Strike %	65.4	62.8
1st Pitch Strike %	61.3	58.7
Ratio	1.27	1.39
Strikeouts per 9 IP	5.82	6.11
Walks per 9 IP	2.01	3.16
Home Runs per 9 IP	1.25	1.11
Strikeout/Walk Ratio	2.89	1.93
Groundball/Flyball Ratio	0.90	1.18

2003 Situational Stats

	W	L	ERA	Sv	IP		AB	H	HR	RBI	Avg
Home	6	4	4.12	0	89.2	LHB	446	126	16	64	.283
Road	8	7	5.01	0	111.1	RHB	341	85	12	33	.249
First Half	6	8	4.78	0	116.2	Sc Pos	165	52	9	72	.315
Scnd Half	8	3	4.38	0	84.1	Clutch	26	9	0	5	.346

2003 Rankings (American League)

- 5th in wild pitches (10)
- 7th in fewest walks per nine innings (2.0) and lowest groundball-flyball ratio allowed (0.9)
- 8th in games started and highest ERA on the road
- 9th in highest batting average allowed with runners in scoring position
- 10th in highest strikeout-walk ratio (2.9), fewest pitches thrown per batter (3.58), highest ERA and highest stolen-base percentage allowed (80.0)
- Led the Twins in wins, games started and wild pitches (10)

Doug Mientkiewicz

2003 Season

When the season started, Doug Mientkiewicz looked like he was on the way out to make room for younger, lower-priced talent. By year's end, Mientkiewicz was as much a part of the team's heart and soul as anyone in the clubhouse. Playing most of the season with an injured left wrist that required postseason surgery for frayed cartilage, he batted .300 and fielded first base like the Gold Glover he was in 2001. He flourished in the No. 3 spot in the batting order, where he moved after the Twins acquired Shannon Stewart.

Hitting

A line-drive hitter with gap power, Mientkiewicz lacks the home-run pop desired of a corner infielder. Yet he's one of the toughest outs in a free-swinging lineup, exhibiting excellent patience and knowledge of the strike zone. Mientkiewicz was the only Twins regular who had more walks than strikeouts last season. He has a quick bat and hits well against both lefthanders and righthanders. In 2003, southpaws often tried to bust him with inside fastballs. Righthanded pitchers more often worked him away.

Baserunning & Defense

Mientkiewicz's greatest asset is his defensive work at first. He has a superb glove, quick reflexes and gets down the line on foul balls with quickness that belies his actual running ability. He makes it extremely difficult for a Twins infielder to be charged with a throwing error. On a team founded on pitching and defense, Mientkiewicz and center fielder Torii Hunter are the core position players. Mientkiewicz' running speed is average, at best, but he's a heady player who knows when to take the extra base.

2004 Outlook

There was a time when some Twins officials envisioned power-hitting Justin Morneau as the starter at first base in 2004. That's not going to happen. If Morneau is in the lineup, he'll split time at DH with Matthew LeCroy. Mientkiewicz has been too valuable defensively to contemplate a lineup without him. And while he lacks home-run power, his .300 average, high on-base percentage and clutch-hitting ability make him an offensive plus.

Position: 1B
Bats: L **Throws:** R
Ht: 6' 2" **Wt:** 200

Opening Day Age: 29
Born: 6/19/74 in Toledo, OH
ML Seasons: 6
Pronunciation: mint-KAY-vich

Overall Statistics

	G	AB	R	H	D	T	HR	RBI	SB	BB	SO	Avg	OBP	Slg
'03	142	487	67	146	38	1	11	65	4	74	55	.300	.393	.450
Car.	565	1863	239	520	128	6	38	241	9	262	270	.279	.371	.415

Where He Hits the Ball

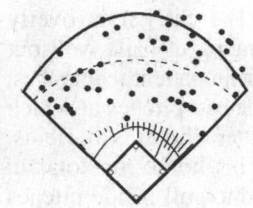
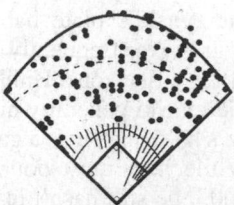

Vs. LHP   **Vs. RHP**

2003 Situational Stats

	AB	H	HR	RBI	Avg		AB	H	HR	RBI	Avg
Home	244	67	6	37	.275	LHP	168	47	8	26	.280
Road	243	79	5	28	.325	RHP	319	99	3	39	.310
First Half	284	84	7	35	.296	Sc Pos	132	38	3	48	.288
Scnd Half	203	62	4	30	.305	Clutch	63	25	2	14	.397

2003 Rankings (American League)

- 3rd in batting average in the clutch
- 4th in fielding percentage at first base (.997)
- 6th in batting average on the road
- Led the Twins in doubles, times on base (225), on-base percentage, lowest percentage of swings that missed (11.6) and batting average in the clutch

A.J. Pierzynski

Position: C
Bats: L **Throws:** R
Ht: 6' 3" **Wt:** 220

Opening Day Age: 27
Born: 12/30/76 in Bridgehampton, NY
ML Seasons: 6
Pronunciation: PEER-zin-skee

2003 Season

Name the category, and A.J. Pierzynski posted a career best in 2003. On top of that, the lefthanded-hitting catcher was a .300 hitter for the second straight season. He drew more walks than in either of his previous two full seasons, while striking out fewer times. After struggling against lefthanded pitchers early in his career, he batted .281 against them in 2003. And he didn't turn 27 until the offseason. All that, yet Pierzynski's future with the Twins was in doubt at season's end thanks to the looming presence of 2001's first overall draft pick, Joe Mauer.

Hitting

No way do you want your Little Leaguer watching Pierzynski's plate habits. The catcher is overly aggressive, frequently swinging at balls well out of the strike zone. Unlike his impatient teammates, Pierzynski generally hits the bad pitches at which he's hacking. He is a gap hitter who uses all fields. While he almost doubled his home-run total in 2003, he still hasn't learned to pull inside pitches on a consistent basis. Team officials believed he could develop into a 25-plus home-run hitter.

Baserunning & Defense

The veteran catcher also has made significant strides defensively, to the point where he's one of the league's best behind the plate. He's exceptionally good at blocking low pitches, has a better-than-average arm and calls a solid game. The one rap is that Pierzynski spends too much time debating pitch calls with umpires. Some Twins officials feared that Pierzynski's talkative nature might work against the team's pitching staff. With good speed for a catcher, Pierzynski is a smart baserunner who knows when to take the extra base.

2004 Outlook

Mauer wasn't expected to make his major league debut until at least the second half of the 2004 season, but with budget issues, the Twins decided to deal Pierzynski and a player to be named to San Francisco for pitchers Joe Nathan, Boof Bonser and Francisco Liriano. Pierzynski takes over behind the plate in San Francisco as he approaches his prime.

Overall Statistics

	G	AB	R	H	D	T	HR	RBI	SB	BB	SO	Avg	OBP	Slg
'03	137	487	63	152	35	3	11	74	3	24	55	.312	.360	.464
Car.	430	1428	184	430	106	12	26	193	6	60	193	.301	.341	.447

Where He Hits the Ball

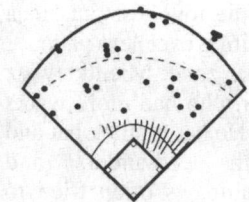
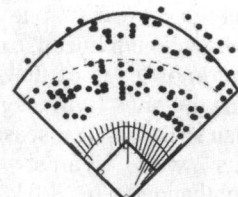

Vs. LHP   **Vs. RHP**

2003 Situational Stats

	AB	H	HR	RBI	Avg		AB	H	HR	RBI	Avg
Home	234	69	6	37	.295	LHP	135	38	4	22	.281
Road	253	83	5	37	.328	RHP	352	114	7	52	.324
First Half	276	82	9	48	.297	Sc Pos	136	44	7	66	.324
Scnd Half	211	70	2	26	.332	Clutch	82	16	1	7	.195

2003 Rankings (American League)

- 3rd in fewest pitches seen per plate appearance (3.25), lowest percentage of pitches taken (43.3) and highest percentage of swings on the first pitch (43.0)
- 4th in batting average vs. righthanded pitchers
- 5th in intentional walks (12) and batting average on the road
- 6th in hit by pitch (15) and fielding percentage at catcher (.993)
- 7th in errors at catcher (6) and batting average with two strikes (.257)
- 8th in batting average
- Led the Twins in intentional walks (12), hit by pitch (15) and batting average on the road
- Led AL catchers in batting average

Brad Radke

2003 Season

A tale of two halves was the story of Brad Radke's 2003 season. He went 0-6 in his final 10 starts before the All-Star break. Then, presto, his fortunes turned. Radke pitched like the staff ace who made three strong starts in the 2002 postseason. The righthander went 9-1 after the break, allowing a just 1.1 homers per nine innings.

Pitching

The key for Radke always is control, because he lacks a dominating fastball. His first-half problems in 2003 largely were the result of not having pinpoint control of his changeup, which is his most effective pitch. At midseason, Twins pitching coach Rick Anderson worked with Radke to release his changeup from a more vertical arm position. That helped Radke disguise the pitch and increased its sinking action. At his best, he is hitting corners with his 90-92 MPH fastball and throwing his changeup for strikes. He also mixes in a slider and curve. In his second-half surge last season, Radke walked only 0.76 batters per nine innings.

Defense

Radke isn't athletic in the mold of a LaTroy Hawkins, but he's developed into a very good defensive pitcher. He has a quick glove and can be counted on to make the correct decisions. Radke has committed only four errors his entire career. He also holds runners close for a righthanded pitcher, making him difficult to steal against despite his reliance on offspeed pitches.

2004 Outlook

While his contract expires after the 2004 season, Radke again will be a mainstay of the rotation. He might not have the dominant stuff of a prototype ace, but typically he gives his team a chance to win in the latter innings. He's extremely durable, pitching at least 212.1 innings in seven of the last eight seasons. With Johan Santana and Radke at the top of the rotation, the Twins think they have the foundation of a staff that can be a threat in short postseason series.

Position: SP
Bats: R **Throws:** R
Ht: 6' 2" **Wt:** 188

Opening Day Age: 31
Born: 10/27/72 in Eau Claire, WI
ML Seasons: 9
Pronunciation: RAD-key

Overall Statistics

	W	L	Pct.	ERA	G	GS	Sv	IP	H	BB	SO	HR	Avg
'03	14	10	.583	4.49	33	33	0	212.1	242	28	120	32	.288
Car.	116	110	.513	4.32	285	284	0	1868.1	2003	364	1124	246	.274

2003 Pitching Profile

	Brad Radke	AL Average
Overall Strike %	69.1	62.8
1st Pitch Strike %	68.5	58.7
Ratio	1.27	1.39
Strikeouts per 9 IP	5.09	6.11
Walks per 9 IP	1.19	3.16
Home Runs per 9 IP	1.36	1.11
Strikeout/Walk Ratio	4.29	1.93
Groundball/Flyball Ratio	1.01	1.18

2003 Situational Stats

	W	L	ERA	Sv	IP		AB	H	HR	RBI	Avg
Home	8	6	5.52	0	107.2	LHB	465	138	18	53	.297
Road	6	4	3.44	0	104.2	RHB	374	104	14	46	.278
First Half	5	9	5.49	0	118.0	Sc Pos	162	45	6	63	.278
Scnd Half	9	1	3.24	0	94.1	Clutch	56	21	1	6	.375

2003 Rankings (American League)

- 3rd in hits allowed, fewest walks per nine innings (1.2) and highest ERA at home
- 4th in home runs allowed and highest slugging percentage allowed (.464)
- Led the Twins in wins, games started, complete games (3), innings pitched, hits allowed, batters faced (888), home runs allowed, pitches thrown (3,130), stolen bases allowed (15), runners caught stealing (6), highest strikeout-walk ratio (4.3), and fewest walks per nine innings (1.2)

Luis Rivas

2003 Season

Early last season, the Twins considered demoting Luis Rivas to the minors and had power-hitting outfielder Michael Cuddyer, a former infielder, taking grounders at second. Rivas' future was so uncertain he nixed his plans to buy a new car at the All-Star break. By season's end, the second baseman was back in the team's future plans. Stuck with a .188 batting average on May 8, Rivas batted .300 in both May and June, .284 in July and .275 in August. He also showed a little more pop in his bat after a midseason move from the No. 9 spot in the order to the No. 2 spot.

Hitting

Rivas put a little pepper into his game—literally—last season. The longstanding baseball tradition became a staple of Rivas' pre-game routine, as the infielder tapped soft-tosses back to Twins coaches in an attempt to improve his bat control and concentration. Something must have clicked. The staff had been working on Rivas to level off his swing in an effort to hit more grounders and one-hop liners off the Dome's slick surface. His weaknesses continue to be his lack of patience and limited knowledge of the strike zone. It's unlikely he'll ever be a leadoff hitter.

Baserunning & Defense

Rivas has good speed and is steadily improving his basestealing technique. The Twins still see him as a 30-plus basestealer. He is excellent at turning the double play and displays decent range, a solid glove and a strong arm. But there were times last season where his concentration and focus appeared to lag in the field. Infield coach Al Newman preached focus and positioning, and Rivas' defense improved as the season progressed.

2004 Outlook

The Twins once thought Rivas would develop into a .300-hitting infielder with better-than-average power. Now they're just hoping he can avoid last season's troubles. He should be the club's starting second baseman, but staying there is up to him. The physical talent is there if Rivas wants to put the time and energy into improving his deficiencies.

Position: 2B
Bats: R **Throws:** R
Ht: 5'11" **Wt:** 175

Opening Day Age: 24
Born: 8/30/79 in La Guaira, VZ
ML Seasons: 4
Pronunciation: REE-vas

Overall Statistics

	G	AB	R	H	D	T	HR	RBI	SB	BB	SO	Avg	OBP	Slg
'03	135	475	69	123	16	8	8	43	17	30	65	.259	.308	.381
Car.	397	1412	193	372	64	20	19	131	59	91	219	.263	.312	.377

Where He Hits the Ball

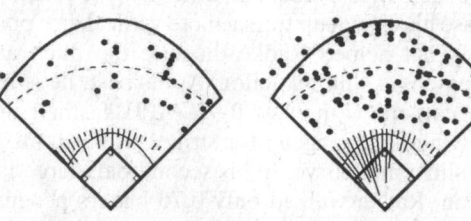

Vs. LHP   **Vs. RHP**

2003 Situational Stats

	AB	H	HR	RBI	Avg		AB	H	HR	RBI	Avg
Home	237	70	4	26	.295	LHP	130	26	1	9	.200
Road	238	53	4	17	.223	RHP	345	97	7	34	.281
First Half	249	67	1	18	.269	Sc Pos	125	28	1	32	.224
Scnd Half	226	56	7	25	.248	Clutch	54	16	0	5	.296

2003 Rankings (American League)

- 3rd in most GDPs per GDP situation (20.4%)
- 4th in triples and lowest batting average vs. lefthanded pitchers
- 5th in highest groundball-flyball ratio (2.2), lowest batting average on the road and lowest fielding percentage at second base (.982)
- 6th in GDPs (20)
- Led the Twins in GDPs (20)

Johan Santana

2003 Season

Graduating from Rule 5 draftee to staff ace over three years, Johan Santana drew the starting assignment for the team's opening postseason game against the Yankees. A long reliever on Opening Day, he moved into the rotation to stay in mid-July and went 5-0 with a 1.07 ERA in six August starts. The reason it took so long to get Santana into the rotation is that club officials felt one of the team's strengths was having lefties Santana, J.C. Romero and Eddie Guardado lined up in the bullpen.

Pitching

Santana's career turned when he perfected his changeup prior to the 2002 season. He now has ace stuff—a fastball that hits the mid-90s, a hard slider and a changeup that he throws with two different grips, giving him two different breaks. The lefty struggled with his control his first two seasons in the majors, but now he's tough on both righthanded and lefthanded hitters. The question mark is his durability. He missed the second half of the 2001 season with an elbow injury, suffered muscle-cramping problems several times last season and had a bone chip removed from his left elbow after the season.

Defense

Santana might well be the team's ace next season, but he has a long way to go to be a Gold Glover. The lefty is a decent athlete, but he lacks poise in fielding his position. He already has eight errors in 59 chances during his four major league seasons. He should improve with age and experience. Santana does have a decent move to first, making him difficult to steal against.

2004 Outlook

Team officials say they are not concerned about the bone-chip surgery, and they expect Santana to be ready for the start of spring training. A potential All-Star, Santana will open 2004 in the starting rotation. The big question is whether he's durable enough to log the innings required of a staff ace. He never has pitched more than 160 innings in a season, but he'll get that chance in 2004.

Position: RP/SP
Bats: L **Throws:** L
Ht: 6' 0" **Wt:** 195

Opening Day Age: 25
Born: 3/13/79 in Tovar Merida, VZ
ML Seasons: 4

Minnesota

Overall Statistics

	W	L	Pct.	ERA	G	GS	Sv	IP	H	BB	SO	HR	Avg
'03	12	3	.800	3.07	45	18	0	158.1	127	47	169	17	.216
Car.	23	12	.657	3.97	117	41	1	396.1	363	166	398	41	.243

2003 Pitching Profile

	Johan Santana	AL Average
Overall Strike %	64.4	62.8
1st Pitch Strike %	64.1	58.7
Ratio	1.10	1.39
Strikeouts per 9 IP	9.61	6.11
Walks per 9 IP	2.67	3.16
Home Runs per 9 IP	0.97	1.11
Strikeout/Walk Ratio	3.60	1.93
Groundball/Flyball Ratio	0.58	1.18

2003 Situational Stats

	W	L	ERA	Sv	IP		AB	H	HR	RBI	Avg
Home	5	2	4.07	0	84.0	LHB	178	34	5	14	.191
Road	7	1	1.94	0	74.1	RHB	410	93	12	37	.227
First Half	4	2	3.00	0	72.0	Sc Pos	127	21	5	31	.165
Scnd Half	8	1	3.13	0	86.1	Clutch	62	16	0	5	.258

2003 Rankings (American League)

- 1st in winning percentage and lowest batting average allowed with runners in scoring position
- 5th in lowest batting average allowed vs. lefthanded batters
- 6th in errors at pitcher (3)
- 7th in balks (2)
- 8th in strikeouts
- Led the Twins in ERA, strikeouts, winning percentage, lowest batting average allowed (.216), lowest slugging percentage allowed (.367), lowest on-base percentage allowed (.276), lowest ERA at home, lowest ERA on the road, lowest batting average allowed vs. lefthanded batters, first batter efficiency (.125), lowest batting average allowed with runners in scoring position, fewest home runs allowed per nine innings (.97), most strikeouts per nine innings (9.6), and most strikeouts per nine innings in relief (11.3)

Shannon Stewart

2003 Season

The Twins' season turned on the All-Star break trade that brought Shannon Stewart aboard in exchange for young outfielder Bobby Kielty. Stewart fit perfectly into the leadoff role on a free-swinging team that lacked a true No. 1 hitter. He batted .322 after the trade, led the Twins in second-half runs scored and made a number of excellent defensive plays. The only negative was that his weak arm limited him to left field, where Jacque Jones is one of the league's best defensive performers. Jones moved to right field.

Hitting

Stewart is a solid contact hitter with just enough patience to be an adequate leadoff man. He had one of the best half-seasons of his career after the trade to Minnesota, with his second-half hitting percentages all well above his career numbers. Having said that, he didn't play that much over his head. Stewart is more steady than flash, a career .303 hitter who has scored more than 100 runs in four of the last five seasons. For a corner outfielder, he lacks power. Still, he hits both lefties and righthanders very well and doesn't have problems with a particular pitch or location.

Baserunning & Defense

While Stewart has decent speed, his stolen-base total has dropped from a career-high 51 in 1998 to only four last season, when he was thrown out six times. Stewart still has the speed to steal 20-plus bases if he's allowed to run more often. His biggest weakness as a player is his defense. He's a natural left fielder with only average range and a below-average arm.

2004 Outlook

Timing was on Stewart's side, because he became a free agent after his excellent second half with Minnesota. The budget-conscious Twins were intent on re-signing him and cut salary elsewhere on the roster to make room for him. Stewart fit in well with teammates and coaches, and the club needed a leadoff hitter. The two sides agreed on a three-year contract reportedly worth $18 million. He'll be back in left field.

Position: LF/RF
Bats: R **Throws:** R
Ht: 6' 1" **Wt:** 210

Opening Day Age: 30
Born: 2/25/74 in Cincinnati, OH
ML Seasons: 9

Overall Statistics

	G	AB	R	H	D	T	HR	RBI	SB	BB	SO	Avg	OBP	Slg
'03	136	573	90	176	44	2	13	73	4	52	66	.307	.364	.459
Car.	920	3720	624	1127	240	32	79	394	166	340	470	.303	.368	.448

Where He Hits the Ball

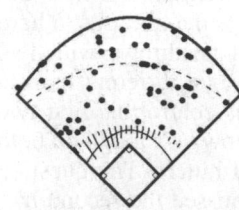

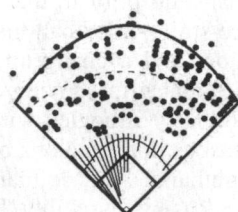

Vs. LHP　　　　**Vs. RHP**

2003 Situational Stats

	AB	H	HR	RBI	Avg		AB	H	HR	RBI	Avg
Home	287	89	7	34	.310	LHP	139	46	4	16	.331
Road	286	87	6	39	.304	RHP	434	130	9	57	.300
First Half	303	89	7	35	.294	Sc Pos	127	40	2	55	.315
Scnd Half	270	87	6	38	.322	Clutch	70	20	1	8	.286

2003 Rankings (American League)

- 2nd in sacrifice flies (11)
- 3rd in on-base percentage for a leadoff hitter (.363)
- 4th in errors in left field (4) and lowest fielding percentage in left field (.984)
- Led the Twins in batting average (.322), batting average vs. righthanded pitchers (.347), on-base percentage for a leadoff hitter (.382), batting average at home (.370) and lowest percentage of swings on the first pitch (20.3)

Grant Balfour

Position: RP
Bats: R **Throws:** R
Ht: 6' 2" **Wt:** 185

Opening Day Age: 26
Born: 12/30/77 in Sydney, Australia
ML Seasons: 2

Overall Statistics

	W	L	Pct.	ERA	G	GS	Sv	IP	H	BB	SO	HR	Avg
'03	1	0	1.000	4.15	17	1	0	26.0	23	14	30	4	.235
Car.	1	0	1.000	5.02	19	1	0	28.2	26	17	32	6	.243

2003 Situational Stats

	W	L	ERA	Sv	IP		AB	H	HR	RBI	Avg
Home	0	0	3.77	0	14.1	LHB	48	11	1	6	.229
Road	1	0	4.63	0	11.2	RHB	50	12	3	8	.240
First Half	0	0	3.24	0	8.1	Sc Pos	25	5	0	7	.200
Scnd Half	1	0	4.58	0	17.2	Clutch	20	3	0	3	.150

2003 Season

When he made his major league debut in 2001, Grant Balfour was considered a possible closer of the future. Short relief didn't pan out, and in 2003 he returned to the Twins in midseason as a long reliever. He exhibited better control, both of his pitches and nerves. The stat worth noting is that opponents batted only .235 after his recall.

Pitching & Defense

Balfour has major league pitches—a fastball that reaches 94 MPH, a heavy sinker and solid slider. The Twins' staff believes his curveball is adequate as an offspeed pitch, although that remains the biggest question mark. If Balfour could improve his offspeed assortment, he'd have a much better shot to stick. His success against both righthanded and lefthanded hitters has opened the door to making him a starter. Balfour is a good athlete who fields his position adequately and holds runners well for a righthander.

2004 Outlook

Balfour had problems controlling his emotions during his first major league stint in 2001, but in 2003 he showed team officials he had the composure to pitch at this level. If he shows he can consistently work ahead in the count, he could be the team's No. 5 starter out of spring training.

LaTroy Hawkins

Position: RP
Bats: R **Throws:** R
Ht: 6' 5" **Wt:** 214

Opening Day Age: 31
Born: 12/21/72 in Gary, IN
ML Seasons: 9

Overall Statistics

	W	L	Pct.	ERA	G	GS	Sv	IP	H	BB	SO	HR	Avg
'03	9	3	.750	1.86	74	0	2	77.1	69	15	75	4	.239
Car.	44	57	.436	5.05	366	98	44	818.0	956	290	532	105	.293

2003 Situational Stats

	W	L	ERA	Sv	IP		AB	H	HR	RBI	Avg
Home	6	2	1.21	1	44.2	LHB	122	25	4	12	.205
Road	3	1	2.76	1	32.2	RHB	167	44	0	11	.263
First Half	5	2	2.56	0	45.2	Sc Pos	87	21	0	18	.241
Scnd Half	4	1	0.85	2	31.2	Clutch	208	50	2	17	.240

2003 Season

A failed closer in 2001, LaTroy Hawkins was the American League's most dominant setup man in 2003. Last summer, he allowed only three earned runs after the All-Star break. Hawkins had a streak of 20 straight scoreless outings from July 31 through September 14, and the Twins won 18 of those games.

Pitching & Defense

Despite a live arm, Hawkins failed as a starter and a closer before finding his niche as a setup man. He struggled with his control until pitching coach Rick Anderson revamped his delivery before the 2002 campaign. Hawkins' best pitch is a fastball that hits 97-98 MPH. When he gets ahead in the count, he mixes in a hard slider, slow curve or an occasional split-finger pitch. A good fielder, Hawkins also has perfected a slide step that helps him hold runners close.

2004 Outlook

A free agent, Hawkins was one of the most attractive relievers on the market. Twins officials were pessimistic about their chances of re-signing Hawkins, a power pitcher who has the stuff to be a top closer. The Cubs won the Hawkins sweepstakes, signing him to a three-year, $11 million deal.

Matthew LeCroy

Position: DH/C/1B
Bats: R **Throws:** R
Ht: 6' 2" **Wt:** 225

Opening Day Age: 28
Born: 12/13/75 in
Belton, SC
ML Seasons: 4
Pronunciation:
LEE-croy

Overall Statistics

	G	AB	R	H	D	T	HR	RBI	SB	BB	SO	Avg	OBP	Slg
'03	107	345	39	99	19	0	17	64	0	25	82	.287	.342	.490
Car.	241	733	82	192	45	1	32	120	0	55	166	.262	.317	.457

2003 Situational Stats

	AB	H	HR	RBI	Avg		AB	H	HR	RBI	Avg
Home	161	50	9	30	.311	LHP	131	39	7	20	.298
Road	184	49	8	34	.266	RHP	214	60	10	44	.280
First Half	174	52	9	31	.299	Sc Pos	90	33	3	44	.367
Scnd Half	171	47	8	33	.275	Clutch	41	14	2	10	.341

2003 Season

The club jettisoned David Ortiz after the 2002 season, believing Matt LeCroy's righthanded power—and cheaper pay stub—would pay off. Wrong. LeCroy got off to a slow start, homering just once in his first 58 at-bats. He had a decent second half, hitting .304-6-20 in August. But he struggled mightily against the Yankees in the ALDS (1-for-11, four strikeouts).

Hitting, Baserunning & Defense

LeCroy is a born designated hitter, a slow-footed power hitter without a position at which he excels. He is a backup first baseman and catcher who must provide power to maintain a big league roster spot. His hitting improved last season when he started going to all fields, rather than pulling the ball. He has trouble catching up with inside fastballs and still needs to improve his knowledge of the strike zone. Still, he batted .367 with runners in scoring position and fared well against lefties.

2004 Outlook

LeCroy is the frontrunner at DH, but he needs to be productive out of the gate because the club is looking for playing time for its minor league power prospects. His power numbers will determine whether he's the full-time DH or platoons at the position.

Eric Milton

Traded To
PHILLIES

Position: SP
Bats: L **Throws:** L
Ht: 6' 3" **Wt:** 225

Opening Day Age: 28
Born: 8/4/75 in State
College, PA
ML Seasons: 6

Overall Statistics

	W	L	Pct.	ERA	G	GS	Sv	IP	H	BB	SO	HR	Avg
'03	1	0	1.000	2.65	3	3	0	17.0	15	1	7	2	.234
Car.	57	51	.528	4.76	166	165	0	987.1	1000	269	715	149	.259

2003 Situational Stats

	W	L	ERA	Sv	IP		AB	H	HR	RBI	Avg
Home	1	0	0.00	0	7.0	LHB	18	7	1	3	.389
Road	0	0	4.50	0	10.0	RHB	46	8	1	2	.174
First Half	0	0	—	0	0.0	Sc Pos	7	2	0	2	.286
Scnd Half	1	0	2.65	0	17.0	Clutch	0	0	0	0	—

2003 Season

It's remarkable that Eric Milton had a 2003 season at all. The lefthander underwent major knee surgery in spring training and was a long shot to return to the staff. The amount of cartilage that was removed threatened his career, but Milton returned to the rotation for three September starts. He landed a bullpen role in the postseason.

Pitching & Defense

Milton has a 94-MPH fastball, a hard slider and solid curve. When he moves his fastball in and out for strikes, and mixes in his curve and slider, he can be devastating. But the problem is consistency. Too often Milton struggles with his control and leaves too many pitches up in the strike zone. He's been prone to home runs, and many lefthanders have been successful against him. He has a good move to first and fields his position well.

2004 Outlook

While there is some concern that Milton's left knee could become arthritic, the Phillies acquired him in exchange for reliever Carlos Silva, infielder Nick Punto and a player to be named. To take pressure off his knee, Milton is attempting to lose weight. That raises a concern, too, because in September, he was 20 pounds lighter and had lost a few MPH. That may have been from inactivity or the weight loss.

Dustan Mohr

Position: RF/LF/CF
Bats: R **Throws:** R
Ht: 6' 1" **Wt:** 210

Opening Day Age: 27
Born: 6/19/76 in
Hattiesburg, MS
ML Seasons: 3

Overall Statistics

	G	AB	R	H	D	T	HR	RBI	SB	BB	SO	Avg	OBP	Slg
'03	121	348	50	87	22	0	10	36	5	33	106	.250	.314	.399
Car.	261	782	111	202	47	2	22	85	12	69	209	.258	.319	.408

2003 Situational Stats

	AB	H	HR	RBI	Avg		AB	H	HR	RBI	Avg
Home	167	42	4	17	.251	LHP	117	31	4	12	.265
Road	181	45	6	19	.249	RHP	231	56	6	24	.242
First Half	243	66	8	23	.272	Sc Pos	97	19	2	25	.196
Scnd Half	105	21	2	13	.200	Clutch	56	14	0	4	.250

2003 Season

No Twin had a greater second-half fall than Dustan Mohr, who likely played himself out of the team's future. Mohr appeared to be a key part of the present—and the future—when he batted .396-5-15 in May. But his numbers decreased thereafter. He was the only position player not to appear in a postseason game.

Hitting, Baserunning & Defense

Mohr's shortcomings as a hitter are his lack of power and his propensity to strike out. He's a good fastball hitter when he puts himself in a position where he's likely to get a fastball. But when Mohr falls behind in the count and has to contend with breaking pitches, he struggles to make contact. He's an excellent outfielder who is fearless of fences or diving turf catches. He also has adequate speed and a decent arm.

2004 Outlook

Mohr is a hard-nosed player and a solid defensive outfielder. But he needs to improve his knowledge of the strike zone, as well as his hitting ability against breaking pitches, to stay in the majors. It's unlikely that he will be back with the Twins, who have a wealth of promising, young outfielders. Prospects Michael Cuddyer and Michael Restovich have more power potential than Mohr.

Rick Reed

Position: SP
Bats: R **Throws:** R
Ht: 6' 1" **Wt:** 195

Opening Day Age: 38
Born: 8/16/65 in
Huntington, WV
ML Seasons: 15

Overall Statistics

	W	L	Pct.	ERA	G	GS	Sv	IP	H	BB	SO	HR	Avg
'03	6	12	.333	5.07	27	21	0	135.0	155	29	71	21	.285
Car.	93	76	.550	4.03	273	245	1	1545.2	1601	285	970	213	.267

2003 Situational Stats

	W	L	ERA	Sv	IP		AB	H	HR	RBI	Avg
Home	5	5	4.76	0	75.2	LHB	295	78	8	34	.264
Road	1	7	5.46	0	59.1	RHB	248	77	13	39	.310
First Half	4	9	5.03	0	87.2	Sc Pos	112	34	6	53	.304
Scnd Half	2	3	5.13	0	47.1	Clutch	25	5	1	1	.200

2003 Season

In 12 months, Rick Reed went from the Twins' most effective pitcher in the second half of 2002 to an afterthought in the closing weeks of 2003. The veteran was beset by a series of injuries, including an abdominal strain in June and a back strain in August. When he returned from the back injury, he had lost his rotation spot and pitched only in relief in September.

Pitching & Defense

At his best, Reed is a control freak who hits corners with his 90-MPH fastball and an impressive sinker. He also mixes in a changeup and slider to keep hitters off balance. He wasn't at his best very often in 2003, especially after the All-Star break. His control numbers still were solid, but he yielded too many hits in critical spots. Reed fields his position successfully. He has a quick move to first, making him difficult to steal against.

2004 Outlook

Reed's tenure with the Twins may be over. At age 38, he'll have to take a drastic pay cut, and perhaps accept a minor league contract, if he wants to continue his career. He's not a candidate to be a situational reliever, as righthanded hitters batted .310 against him last season. Only a 2004 turnaround will keep him in the majors.

Juan Rincon

Position: RP
Bats: R **Throws:** R
Ht: 5'11" **Wt:** 192

Opening Day Age: 25
Born: 1/23/79 in Maracaibo, VZ
ML Seasons: 3
Pronunciation: rin-CONE

Overall Statistics

	W	L	Pct.	ERA	G	GS	Sv	IP	H	BB	SO	HR	Avg
'03	5	6	.455	3.68	58	0	0	85.2	74	38	63	5	.231
Car.	5	8	.385	4.43	72	3	0	120.0	125	52	88	11	.267

2003 Situational Stats

	W	L	ERA	Sv	IP		AB	H	HR	RBI	Avg
Home	2	2	4.97	0	41.2	LHB	158	35	2	15	.222
Road	3	4	2.45	0	44.0	RHB	163	39	3	20	.239
First Half	1	3	3.12	0	49.0	Sc Pos	84	19	1	30	.226
Scnd Half	4	3	4.42	0	36.2	Clutch	85	25	2	7	.294

2003 Season

Juan Rincon had his first extended major league stay and became the team's most effective long reliever after lefty Johan Santana was moved into the rotation. Rincon was especially effective before the All-Star break, but posted a 4.97 ERA in 23 appearances after August 1. He also fared much better on natural grass (2.72 ERA) than on the artificial surface of the Dome (4.97 ERA).

Pitching & Defense

Rincon's best pitch is a hard slider that breaks in on lefthanded hitters, making him equally difficult to hit from either side of the plate. Those numbers make him an ideal long reliever, but a better offspeed assortment could lead to a starting role. Rincon has a fastball that hits the low 90s, plus a better-than-average curve. He's been working on a changeup and might try a split-finger fastball. Rincon fields his position well, but he needs to improve his move to first and his slide step. He's a little too inviting for potential basestealers.

2004 Outlook

Rincon likely will be the Twins' long reliever again, although he could be in the mix for the No. 5 starter job. If Rincon comes up with a split-finger fastball over the offseason, he could exceed all expectations for 2004.

Kenny Rogers

Position: SP
Bats: L **Throws:** L
Ht: 6' 1" **Wt:** 217

Opening Day Age: 39
Born: 11/10/64 in Savannah, GA
ML Seasons: 15
Nickname: The Gambler

Overall Statistics

W	L	Pct.	ERA	G	GS	Sv	IP	H	BB	SO	HR	Avg
13	8	.619	4.57	33	31	0	195.0	227	50	116	22	.292
158	114	.581	4.23	622	335	28	2455.0	2532	898	1538	247	.267

2003 Situational Stats

	W	L	ERA	Sv	IP		AB	H	HR	RBI	Avg
Home	8	3	4.50	0	106.0	LHB	215	54	6	22	.251
Road	5	5	4.65	0	89.0	RHB	563	173	16	74	.307
First Half	7	5	4.89	0	108.2	Sc Pos	210	60	6	70	.286
Scnd Half	6	3	4.17	0	86.1	Clutch	38	15	1	6	.395

2003 Season

The Twins fared well when they signed Kenny Rogers as a free agent late in spring training after Eric Milton went down with a knee injury. Rogers became a mainstay of the rotation, finishing third in victories (13), with one fewer than co-leaders Brad Radke and Kyle Lohse, and going 5-3 with a 3.36 ERA in 12 games (10 starts) after August 1.

Pitching & Defense

The veteran still has an excellent sinker and a fastball that reaches the low 90s. He also has a curve and changeup, and will throw any of his pitches at any time from a variety of arm angles. He doesn't have dominating stuff, but doesn't beat himself or give in to hitters. Rogers remains one of the best fielding pitchers in the game, with quick reflexes and a sure glove. His superb move to first makes him difficult to steal against.

2004 Outlook

Rogers is unlikely to be back with the Twins, as the club prefers to open up a spot in the rotation to one of its prospects. But Rogers' strong finish shows that there's still fuel left in the tank, and the lefty again could be a bargain pickup for a contending team. The southpaw still has enough arm, and plenty enough savvy, to be a major league starter.

J.C. Romero

Position: RP
Bats: B **Throws:** L
Ht: 5'11" **Wt:** 195

Opening Day Age: 27
Born: 6/4/76 in Rio Piedras, PR
ML Seasons: 5

Overall Statistics

	W	L	Pct.	ERA	G	GS	Sv	IP	H	BB	SO	HR	Avg
'03	2	0	1.000	5.00	73	0	0	63.0	66	42	50	7	.272
Car.	14	13	.519	4.76	185	22	1	276.1	284	132	219	28	.268

2003 Situational Stats

	W	L	ERA	Sv	IP		AB	H	HR	RBI	Avg
Home	1	0	4.04	0	35.2	LHB	103	22	1	13	.214
Road	1	0	6.26	0	27.1	RHB	140	44	6	25	.314
First Half	2	0	5.20	0	36.1	Sc Pos	84	24	4	33	.286
Scnd Half	0	0	4.73	0	26.2	Clutch	120	30	2	15	.250

2003 Season

J.C. Romero inexplicably lost control of his fastball and hard slider, and spent most of the summer pitching behind in the count as his ERA rose from 1.89 in 2002 to 5.00. His walks per nine innings rose dramatically, and opponents batted 59 points higher while hitting more than twice as many homers in fewer innings.

Pitching & Defense

Romero still has outstanding stuff: a mid-90s fastball, hard slider and solid changeup. It may be that a nagging groin injury bothered him more than he let on and compromised his control. He also needs to regain confidence in his two-seam fastball, which breaks in on righthanded hitters and was key to them batting just .211 against Romero in 2002. Even his fielding suffered a bit in 2003, though he has a good move to first and a quick slide step to counter basestealers.

2004 Outlook

Romero once was the team's closer of the future. His poor control and struggles against righthanders make that unlikely in 2004. But with Eddie Guardado and LaTroy Hawkins gone, Romero may be in the closer mix if the Twins don't sign one. That could be a disaster. Based on his 2003 season, he appears best suited as a situational lefthander.

Michael Ryan

Position: RF
Bats: L **Throws:** R
Ht: 6' 0" **Wt:** 185

Opening Day Age: 26
Born: 7/6/77 in Indiana, PA
ML Seasons: 2

Overall Statistics

	G	AB	R	H	D	T	HR	RBI	SB	BB	SO	Avg	OBP	Slg
'03	27	61	13	24	7	0	5	13	2	6	12	.393	.441	.754
Car.	34	72	16	25	7	0	5	13	2	6	14	.347	.392	.653

2003 Situational Stats

	AB	H	HR	RBI	Avg		AB	H	HR	RBI	Avg
Home	34	13	4	7	.382	LHP	16	7	0	2	.438
Road	27	11	1	6	.407	RHP	45	17	5	11	.378
First Half	0	0	0	0	–	Sc Pos	13	5	1	8	.385
Scnd Half	61	24	5	13	.393	Clutch	17	5	0	0	.294

2003 Season

No one was a bigger surprise down the stretch than Michael Ryan. Ryan got off to a horrendous start at Triple-A Rochester, but his hitting improved when he underwent an eye exam and changed the prescription on his contact lenses. He led the Twins in batting (.404) and homers (5) for the month of September.

Hitting, Baserunning & Defense

Ryan features one of the smoothest hitting strokes in the system. His bat quickness makes him an excellent fastball hitter, but he has struggled with breaking pitches. While he lacks the power desired in a corner outfielder, he can hit the gaps to all fields. Ryan started his career as an infielder, but struggled defensively. He'll never be a Gold Glove winner, possessing only average speed and an adequate arm. But he's a smart player who will take the extra base, which fits the Twins' mold. His ticket to the majors will be his quick bat.

2004 Outlook

Ryan has earned a spring training look. But there are no guarantees. The club is seeking more power, and the high-profile prospects in that regard are righthanded hitters Michael Cuddyer and Michael Restovich. But Ryan's hitting stroke could help win a spot as a spare outfielder.

Other Minnesota Twins

James Baldwin (Pos: RHP, Age: 32)

	W	L	Pct.	ERA	G	GS	Sv	IP	H	BB	SO	HR	Avg
'03	0	1	.000	5.40	10	0	1	15.0	21	4	7	6	.333
Car.	79	70	.530	5.02	236	200	1	1260.0	1376	465	814	192	.278

Baldwin pitched well enough in Triple-A before joining the Twins' pen. He earned his first save, but a rough spell in August led to his release. 2004 Outlook: C

Rob Bowen (Pos: C, Age: 23, Bats: B)

	G	AB	R	H	D	T	HR	RBI	SB	BB	SO	Avg	OBP	Slg
'03	7	10	0	1	0	0	0	1	0	0	4	.100	.091	.100
Car.	7	10	0	1	0	0	0	1	0	0	4	.100	.091	.100

The catcher reached Triple-A Rochester last summer at age 22, showing some pop and decent catching skills. But the Twins moved A.J. Pierzynski to make room for Joe Mauer, not Bowen. 2004 Outlook: C

Mike Fetters (Pos: RHP, Age: 39)

	W	L	Pct.	ERA	G	GS	Sv	IP	H	BB	SO	HR	Avg
'03	0	0	–	0.00	5	0	0	6.0	2	1	1	0	.100
Car.	31	40	.437	3.73	597	6	99	698.0	676	337	504	60	.258

Fetters was solid in five April outings before a strained hamstring put him on the disabled list. He developed a sore elbow while rehabbing the hammy and had Tommy John surgery in August. 2004 Outlook: D

Tony Fiore (Pos: RHP, Age: 32)

	W	L	Pct.	ERA	G	GS	Sv	IP	H	BB	SO	HR	Avg
'03	1	1	.500	5.50	21	0	0	36.0	32	21	23	5	.242
Car.	12	6	.667	4.39	87	2	0	151.2	136	76	94	18	.242

A 30-year-old Fiore won 10 games in 2002. He struggled in April and wasn't able to contribute as he did the year before. 2004 Outlook: C

Chris Gomez (Pos: 2B/3B/SS, Age: 32, Bats: R)

	G	AB	R	H	D	T	HR	RBI	SB	BB	SO	Avg	OBP	Slg
'03	58	175	14	44	9	3	1	15	2	7	13	.251	.279	.354
Car.	1080	3507	388	888	185	16	52	374	28	323	625	.253	.320	.360

Gomez settled into a utility role and played adequately at second base, third and short. He hit OK and took a bite out of Denny Hocking's at-bats. 2004 Outlook: C

Denny Hocking (Pos: 2B/3B/SS, Age: 33, Bats: B)

	G	AB	R	H	D	T	HR	RBI	SB	BB	SO	Avg	OBP	Slg
'03	83	188	22	45	10	2	3	22	0	15	37	.239	.291	.362
Car.	876	2204	273	556	109	17	25	215	36	188	412	.252	.310	.351

His at-bats and batting average have been on a steady dip since 2000. Hocking's ability to get on base also has been fading, but the Twins hold on to him. 2004 Outlook: C

Adam Johnson (Pos: RHP, Age: 24)

	W	L	Pct.	ERA	G	GS	Sv	IP	H	BB	SO	HR	Avg
'03	0	1	.000	47.25	2	0	0	1.1	8	1	0	1	.667
Car.	1	3	.250	10.25	9	4	0	26.1	40	14	17	7	.360

Johnson was the second overall pick in 2000, but has failed as a starter in the minors. He was better after a midsummer move to the pen. 2004 Outlook: C

Joe Mays (Pos: RHP, Age: 28)

	W	L	Pct.	ERA	G	GS	Sv	IP	H	BB	SO	HR	Avg
'03	8	8	.500	6.30	31	21	0	130.0	159	39	50	21	.302
Car.	42	55	.433	4.69	162	120	0	790.1	849	262	428	104	.274

A 17-13 season in 2001 earned him a big contract, but elbow problems surfaced in 2002 and led to Tommy John surgery in September. He returns in 2005 for the last year of his $20 million deal. 2004 Outlook: D

Mike Nakamura (Pos: RHP, Age: 27)

	W	L	Pct.	ERA	G	GS	Sv	IP	H	BB	SO	HR	Avg
'03	0	0	–	7.82	12	0	1	12.2	20	2	14	4	.339
Car.	0	0	–	7.82	12	0	1	12.2	20	2	14	4	.339

Born in Japan and raised in Australia, Nakamura played college ball and signed with the Twins. A solid second season of Triple-A ball, with a 2.99 ERA and 95 strikeouts, puts him in the mix. 2004 Outlook: C

Jesse Orosco (Pos: LHP, Age: 46)

	W	L	Pct.	ERA	G	GS	Sv	IP	H	BB	SO	HR	Avg
	2	2	.500	7.68	65	0	2	34.0	41	21	29	4	.299
	87	80	.521	3.16	1252	4	144	1295.1	1055	581	1179	113	.223

Age may be catching up with the 24-year vet, who pitched for three big league teams in 2003 and wasn't very effective for any of them. Righties clocked him for a .390 average. Lefties hit just .231. He signed a minor league deal with Arizona in November. 2004 Outlook: C

Alex Prieto (Pos: 2B, Age: 27, Bats: R)

	G	AB	R	H	D	T	HR	RBI	SB	BB	SO	Avg	OBP	Slg
'03	8	11	1	1	0	0	0	0	0	0	4	.091	.091	.091
Car.	8	11	1	1	0	0	0	0	0	0	4	.091	.091	.091

As a free-agent signee out of Venezuela, Prieto has spent 11 years in the minors. His numbers haven't varied much in four Triple-A seasons, but Prieto finally got the call in 2003 to cover for injuries. 2004 Outlook: C

Carlos Pulido (Pos: LHP, Age: 32)

	W	L	Pct.	ERA	G	GS	Sv	IP	H	BB	SO	HR	Avg
'03	0	1	.000	4.02	7	1	0	15.2	15	3	6	0	.254
Car.	3	8	.273	5.67	26	15	0	100.0	102	43	38	17	.270

Pulido debuted with Minnesota in 1994, but hadn't been seen since in the majors. He's played in Mexico and Taiwan in recent years, and pitched well enough at Triple-A to help out in August and September. 2004 Outlook: C

Brad Thomas (Pos: LHP, Age: 26)

	W	L	Pct.	ERA	G	GS	Sv	IP	H	BB	SO	HR	Avg
'03	0	1	.000	7.71	3	0	0	4.2	6	3	2	1	.316
Car.	0	3	.000	9.00	8	5	0	21.0	26	17	8	7	.306

Slowed by a sore elbow in the spring, Thomas joined Triple-A Rochester in July and went 0-3 with a 3.53 ERA. The Twins have been light in lefty relievers and he may work his way into the bullpen mix. 2004 Outlook: C

Minnesota Twins Minor League Prospects

Organization Overview:

Each spring the Twins' minor league system is asked to fill holes on the major league roster, and in recent years it has gotten the job done. Nearly every Twins regular and starting pitcher is either homegrown or rounded out his game in the system after being acquired in a trade for a veteran. In 2003, Johan Santana secured a place in the Minnesota rotation, Matt LeCroy proved productive, and Michael Ryan and Lew Ford were exceptional role players down the stretch. The new season is likely to offer greater big league opportunities to Ryan, Ford, Grant Balfour, Mike Cuddyer, Justin Morneau and Michael Restovich. And look for little known Jason Bartlett and the highly regarded Joe Mauer to debut.

Jason Bartlett

Position: SS
Bats: R **Throws:** R
Ht: 6' 0" **Wt:** 175

Opening Day Age: 24
Born: 10/30/79 in Lodi, CA

Recent Statistics

	G	AB	R	H	D	T	HR	RBI	SB	BB	SO	Avg
2002 A Lk Elsinore	75	308	57	77	14	4	1	33	24	32	53	.250
2002 A Ft. Myers	39	145	24	38	7	0	2	9	11	17	24	.262
2003 AA New Britain	139	548	96	162	31	8	8	48	41	58	67	.296

It was a minor 2002 trade that shipped outfielder Brian Buchanan to the Padres for Bartlett, a 13th-round pick in 2001. Then he impressed at Double-A New Britain in 2003. Bartlett showed quickness, range and a good arm at short, and plate discipline that suggests he could be a major league regular and a possible leadoff man. Though he lacks blazing speed, he led the system with 41 steals. While his ability to reach base is more critical, Bartlett's extra-base hits at New Britain are signs of decent gap power. He played the last 10 games with a stress fracture in his foot, discovered by a medical exam that ended plans to play in the Arizona Fall League.

Jesse Crain

Position: P
Bats: R **Throws:** R
Ht: 6' 1" **Wt:** 200

Opening Day Age: 22
Born: 7/5/81 in Toronto, ON

Recent Statistics

	W	L	ERA	G	GS	Sv	IP	H	R	BB	SO	HR
2002 R Elizabethtn	2	1	0.57	9	0	2	15.2	4	2	7	18	0
2002 A Quad City	1	1	1.50	9	0	1	12.0	6	3	4	11	0
2003 A Ft. Myers	2	1	2.04	10	0	0	19.0	10	6	5	25	0
2003 AA New Britain	1	1	0.69	22	0	9	39.0	13	4	10	56	0
2003 AAA Rochester	3	1	3.12	23	0	10	26.0	24	10	10	33	0

A Toronto native out of the University of Houston, Crain was a second-round pick in 2002. Despite this former college shortstop's lack of pitching experience, he is a fast-track guy who has dashed through the Twins' system in less than two years. Crain works with a mid-90s fastball, a sharp slider, a roundhouse curve he throws to lefties and a changeup. His command of his pitches has made him less dependent on his heater than other hard throwers. Last summer, with just 27.2 innings as a pro, Crain dominated at two levels before reaching Triple-A Rochester in July. For the season, he held batters to a .159 average. With his solid makeup, he looks like closer or setup material in the majors.

Michael Cuddyer

Position: OF
Bats: R **Throws:** R
Ht: 6' 2" **Wt:** 225

Opening Day Age: 25
Born: 3/27/79 in Norfolk, VA

Recent Statistics

	G	AB	R	H	D	T	HR	RBI	SB	BB	SO	Avg
2003 R Twins	2	5	1	4	0	0	1	3	0	1	0	.800
2003 AAA Rochester	53	186	25	57	17	0	3	34	5	25	49	.306
2003 AL Minnesota	35	102	14	25	1	3	4	8	1	12	19	.245

A 1997 first-round pick drafted as a shortstop, Cuddyer moved to third base and later the outfield in the minors. He was the Twins' primary right fielder to open 2003, but after an 11-for-58 (.190) April, he went to Triple-A Rochester. Cuddyer, who should hit for average and power, is being groomed as a utilityman who can play second base, third and the outfield corners. A bad left hamstring bothered him for much of 2003, limiting him to 32 games in the outfield, eight at second base, four at third base and three at first for Rochester, where he committed just one error in 47 games. He hit safely in the Twins' final five games, going 7-for-18 (.389) with two homers. He should play in Minnesota in 2004.

J.D. Durbin

Position: P
Bats: R **Throws:** R
Ht: 6' 1" **Wt:** 185

Opening Day Age: 22
Born: 2/24/82 in Portland, OR

Recent Statistics

	W	L	ERA	G	GS	Sv	IP	H	R	BB	SO	HR
2002 A Quad City	13	4	3.19	27	27	0	161.0	144	66	51	163	14
2003 A Ft. Myers	9	2	3.09	14	14	0	87.1	73	35	22	69	3
2003 AA New Britain	6	3	3.14	14	14	0	94.2	102	39	29	70	10

There's hardly a more outgoing and confident player than Durbin, a second-round pick in 2000. Durbin overcame early injury problems to go 13-4 at Class-A Quad City in 2002. Last summer he was 15-5 (3.12) in a career-high 182 innings between high Class-A Fort Myers and Double-A New Britain. Durbin added some zip to his fastball in 2003 and now works in the mid-90s. His fastball has good sinking action and he's added life to his slider. He's a maximum-effort pitcher who has learned that more MPH isn't enough at higher levels, and he's working to mix his stuff more effectively. Improving his changeup is critical to his career as a starter.

Minnesota

Lew Ford

Position: OF   **Opening Day Age:** 27
Bats: R **Throws:** R   **Born:** 8/12/76 in
Ht: 6' 0" **Wt:** 190   Beaumont, TX

Recent Statistics

	G	AB	R	H	D	T	HR	RBI	SB	BB	SO	Avg
2003 AAA Rochester	53	211	33	64	18	2	3	31	4	10	28	.303
2003 AL Minnesota	34	73	16	24	7	1	3	15	2	8	9	.329

A 1999 pick by Boston, Ford was acquired in a 2000 trade. He had been overshadowed in the Twins' system until he led the minors in runs, batted .318 and posted a .398 OBP in the high minors in 2002. After hitting .317 with a .372 OBP over two summers at the Triple-A level, Ford is difficult to ignore, especially after two solid stints with Minnesota in 2003. After a broken forearm sidelined him for nearly two months, Ford batted .364 with five extra-base hits in 22 at-bats with Minnesota in September, and he drove in 11 runs and batted .368 in 19 at-bats with runners in scoring position. Capable at all three outfield positions, Ford is a well-rounded player with good instincts and speed.

Joe Mauer

Position: C   **Opening Day Age:** 20
Bats: L **Throws:** R   **Born:** 4/19/83 in
Ht: 6' 4" **Wt:** 205   St. Paul, MN

Recent Statistics

	G	AB	R	H	D	T	HR	RBI	SB	BB	SO	Avg
2002 A Quad City	110	411	58	124	23	1	4	62	0	61	42	.302
2003 A Ft. Myers	62	233	25	78	13	1	1	44	3	24	24	.335
2003 AA New Britain	73	276	48	94	17	1	4	41	0	25	25	.341

Mauer is widely viewed as the game's best prospect. The Twins believe he's ready for the majors, and they dealt incumbent A.J. Pierzynski to the Giants to make room for him. Mauer showed his Gold Glove-caliber game behind the plate is ready during spring training last March, and he threw out better than 50 percent of base-stealers in 2003. It's a credit to Mauer that he batted .338 between high Class-A Fort Myers and Double-A New Britain, even though teams were gunning for the former first overall pick. His power is less developed, but the Twins aren't tampering with him. They appreciate that he is so disciplined that he drives the ball the other way when he's worked outside. More power will come.

Justin Morneau

Position: 1B   **Opening Day Age:** 22
Bats: L **Throws:** R   **Born:** 5/15/81 in New
Ht: 6' 4" **Wt:** 205   Westminster, Canada

Recent Statistics

	G	AB	R	H	D	T	HR	RBI	SB	BB	SO	Avg
2003 AA New Britain	20	79	14	26	3	1	6	13	0	7	14	.329
2003 AAA Rochester	71	265	39	71	11	1	16	42	0	28	56	.268
2003 AL Minnesota	40	106	14	24	4	0	4	16	0	9	30	.226

Like Mauer, Morneau has a sweet lefthanded swing that should generate a high average and power in the majors. His power stroke made a splash when he plowed through Double-A and Triple-A ball in 2003, batting .309 with 19 homers in just 217 at-bats before his first callup by Minnesota on June 10. Playing sporadically there ended his red-hot run. Morneau became more aggressive and swung at more borderline pitches, and he batted .236 with just three homers in 127 at-bats after he returned to Triple-A Rochester in late July. Still, his advanced plate discipline and power to all fields assure a bright future. Morneau continues to improve as a first baseman, but for now, defensive stalwart Doug Mientkiewicz stands in his way.

Michael Restovich

Position: OF   **Opening Day Age:** 25
Bats: R **Throws:** R   **Born:** 1/3/79 in
Ht: 6' 4" **Wt:** 245   Rochester, MN

Recent Statistics

	G	AB	R	H	D	T	HR	RBI	SB	BB	SO	Avg
2003 AAA Rochester	119	454	75	125	34	2	16	72	10	47	117	.275
2003 AL Minnesota	24	53	10	15	3	2	0	4	0	10	12	.283

Restovich is an impressive athlete with "Killebrew power," as farm director Jim Rantz describes it. While Restovich at Triple-A Rochester wasn't the run producer and home-run hitter that he was in 2002 in the hitting-friendly Triple-A Pacific Coast League, he is capable of reaching the seats in any park. He still strikes out frequently, but the Twins won't overreact to his strikeouts and compromise his one special tool with an emphasis on making contact. Improved plate discipline could reduce his whiffs and quicken his rise to Minnesota. Restovich is solid defensively and has good speed. His outfield play is ready for the majors.

Others to Watch

The Twins acquired **Boof Bonser** (22) in the A.J. Pierzynski trade with the Giants. The 6-foot-4 righthander throws a mid-90s fastball that sinks and moves, but his secondary pitches need work. In 2003, Bonser was better after a late jump to Triple-A Fresno, where he was 1-2 with a 3.13 ERA, and he'll compete for a starting role with the Twins. . . Outfield prospects are knocking at the door in Minnesota, and **Jason Kubel** (21) will lead the next generation after batting .298 with a .361 OBP at high Class-A Fort Myers in 2003. His short stroke and plate discipline are key assets, and so is his terrific arm. . . The 21st overall pick in 2003, third baseman **Matt Moses** (19) underwent a 20-minute procedure after a physical revealed a tiny hole in his heart. Despite the delay, Moses still batted .385 with 11 RBI in 18 games for the Twins' Rookie-level Gulf Coast League club. The lefthanded hitter showed quick hands and power to all fields. . . Ahead of Moses on the third-base depth chart is **Terry Tiffee** (24), who enjoyed his best pro season at Double-A New Britain in 2003. A switch-hitter who is better from the left side of the plate, Tiffee enjoyed a .315-14-93 season at New Britain and was named the MVP of the Eastern League All-Star Game.

Yankee Stadium

Offense

Yankee Stadium no longer measures 457 feet to left-center, but it's still a pitchers' park. This is especially true for righthanded hitters. While lefties can pull balls into the (relatively) short porch in right field, righthanders find few advantages to offset the pitchers' various advantages, including the long infield grass and the shadows that creep across the field during day games.

Defense

A left fielder with limited range can have a hard time here. He must play deep enough to be able to get back on balls hit deep to left-center, but also must be quick enough to get to flares behind shortstop. The center fielder, who must play a little deeper than normal, isn't able to give as much help on such plays. With the infield's long grass, a weak arm can be more glaring than a lack of range for an infielder. Historically, lefthanded pitchers have flourished here, for obvious reasons.

Who It Helps the Most

Andy Pettitte had a terrific record here, but he won't be back. Jorge Posada has hit better in the Bronx over the course of his career. Chris Hammond pitched exceptionally well here in his first season with the club.

Who It Hurts the Most

Alfonso Soriano's power is to left-center, the deepest part of the park. He likely would hit more homers and have a better average in almost any another venue. Jason Giambi hit most of his home runs on the road last year, but that hasn't been a consistent pattern and probably won't continue.

Rookies & Newcomers

Expectations for Aaron Boone should be dialed down a bit as he begins his first full year in Yankee Stadium, which is much less friendly to righthanded hitters than the parks he played in at Cincinnati. Jon Lieber, who had problems with lefthanded hitters even when at the top of his game, may find those problems magnified here.

Dimensions: LF-318, LCF-399, CF-408, RCF-385, RF-314

Capacity: 57,478

Elevation: 55 feet

Surface: Grass

Foul Territory: Small

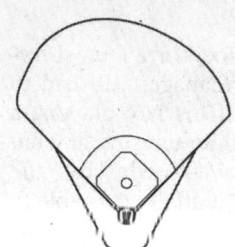

New York (AL)

Park Factors

2003 Season

	Home Games			Away Games			
	Yankees	Opp	Total	Yankees	Opp	Total	Index
G	73	73	146	72	72	144	
Avg	.263	.265	.264	.277	.267	.272	97
AB	2410	2585	4995	2583	2500	5083	97
R	349	336	685	426	309	735	92
H	633	686	1319	715	667	1382	94
2B	120	132	252	143	163	306	84
3B	5	10	15	9	13	22	69
HR	94	66	160	107	56	163	100
BB	277	177	454	321	172	493	94
SO	443	509	952	473	475	948	102
E	54	50	104	49	41	90	114
E-Infield	47	37	84	41	35	76	109
LHB Avg	.254	.273	.263	.274	.265	.270	97
LHB-HR	49	29	78	58	23	81	105
RHB-Avg	.272	.260	.265	.280	.269	.274	97
RHB-HR	45	37	82	49	33	82	96

2001-2003

	Home Games			Away Games			
	Yankees	Opp	Total	Yankees	Opp	Total	Index
G	215	215	430	216	216	432	
Avg	.271	.253	.262	.273	.265	.269	97
AB	7200	7559	14759	7727	7439	15166	98
R	1113	929	2042	1182	946	2128	96
H	1950	1912	3862	2106	1969	4075	95
2B	383	373	756	420	432	852	91
3B	17	25	42	23	42	65	66
HR	292	205	497	292	178	470	109
BB	775	539	1314	835	566	1401	96
SO	1343	1623	2966	1513	1514	3027	101
E	153	166	319	157	126	283	113
E-Infield	133	121	254	135	110	245	104
LHB-Avg	.272	.250	.261	.269	.253	.261	100
LHB-HR	164	92	256	157	77	234	115
RHB-Avg	.270	.255	.262	.276	.273	.275	95
RHB-HR	128	113	241	135	101	236	103

2003 Rankings (American League)

- Second-highest error factor
- Third-lowest hit factor
- Third-lowest double factor

Joe Torre

2003 Season

Without a doubt, 2003 was Joe Torre's most trying season as the Yankees' manager. He had to deal with injuries to many of his key players, a work-in-progress bullpen and an unusual amount of interference from above—even by the Yankees' standards. Through it all, he was able to keep his players focused on the games on the field. It might well have been his best managerial performance in pinstripes.

Offense

Torre is loyal to his veterans and won't overreact to a short-term slump. When he has an open position, as he did with right field last year, he will give a candidate several weeks to impress him before making a decision. He'll platoon if it's his best option, but he never blindly follows the percentages. He calls for the hit-and-run a bit more than average, and the sacrifice less often. He prefers hitters who take their walks and make the pitcher work, and he seems to have less patience with hitters who take a more aggressive approach, all things being equal. He also seems to have a general preference for players who have a persona similar to his own, which is professional and unflappable, rather than emotional and impulsive.

Pitching & Defense

Torre will go a long way with a veteran pitcher before giving him the hook. In the bullpen, he defines roles and sticks to them, rather than riding the hot hand. There were plenty of role redefinitions last year, but once a decision had been made, a few good outings wasn't going to reverse it. With a weak setup crew, Torre rode closer Mariano Rivera harder than ever.

2004 Outlook

Torre always plays his cards close to the vest, but 2004 could be his last season at the Yankees' helm. Long-time bench coach Don Zimmer already has left in a huff, and Torre's comments last year betrayed a certain weariness of interference from upstairs. The shape and direction of the roster, particularly the pitching staff, is unclear, though the man at the top seemed inclined to spend money as the offseason got underway. Torre may be in for another highly challenging season.

Born: 7/18/40 in Brooklyn, NY

Playing Experience: 1960-1977, Atl, StL, NYM

Managerial Experience: 22 seasons

Manager Statistics

Year	Team, Lg	W	L	Pct	GB	Finish
2003	New York, AL	101	61	.623	–	1st East
22 Seasons		1680	1509	.527	–	–

2003 Starting Pitchers by Days Rest

	<=3	4	5	6+
Yankees Starts	1	73	60	20
Yankees ERA	–	4.17	3.93	4.99
AL Avg Starts	2	79	50	22
AL ERA	3.19	4.64	4.57	4.98

2003 Situational Stats

	Joe Torre	AL Average
Hit & Run Success %	38.0	36.7
Stolen Base Success %	74.8	70.0
Platoon Pct.	65.0	61.7
Defensive Subs	10	23
High-Pitch Outings	15	5
Quick/Slow Hooks	6/17	19/16
Sacrifice Attempts	40	55

2003 Rankings (American League)

- 1st in sacrifice-bunt percentage (87.5%) and starts with over 120 pitches (15)
- 2nd in pitchouts (31)
- 3rd in stolen-base percentage

Aaron Boone

2003 Season

It was a year of big moves for Aaron Boone. First, he moved from third base to second, but was returned to his old position a few weeks into the season. In late July, his father was fired as manager of the Reds, and three days later, he was traded for the first time in his career—to the Yankees. He didn't quite play up to expectations for them, but Boone was solid overall, especially on defense. In the postseason, he struggled both at the plate and in the field, but had the Yankees' biggest hit of the playoffs, a game-winning homer in the final game of the ALCS.

Hitting

Over the last two years, Boone has become stronger and more pull-conscious, which has helped his power numbers but cut into his batting average. He's one of the few righthanded hitters in baseball who consistently is less effective against southpaws. He isn't one to try to take a lot of pitches. Finesse pitchers can get him to chase offspeed pitches out of the strike zone. Strong fundamentally, Boone can bunt over a runner if asked.

Baserunning & Defense

Boone's fielding slump in the playoffs was not indicative of his usual performance. He actually is one of the better-fielding third basemen in baseball, with good range and a strong, accurate arm. He even can play shortstop or second base if needed. His speed is not much better than average, but he's become a pretty good basestealer, rarely getting caught.

2004 Outlook

Boone re-signed with the Yankees, who won't need to lean on him to be a central offensive performer for them. He'll hit in a low-pressure slot in the bottom third of the order, and will be expected to contribute more with his glove than his bat. Yankee Stadium probably will keep him from matching his Cincinnati numbers, but he likely will be a little more productive than he was with New York in 2003.

Position: 3B/2B
Bats: R. **Throws:** R
Ht: 6' 2" **Wt:** 200

Opening Day Age: 31
Born: 3/9/73 in La Mesa, CA
ML Seasons: 7

Overall Statistics

	G	AB	R	H	D	T	HR	RBI	SB	BB	SO	Avg	OBP	Slg
'03	160	592	92	158	32	3	24	96	23	46	104	.267	.327	.453
Car.	722	2572	358	694	154	14	92	393	91	202	458	.270	.332	.448

Where He Hits the Ball

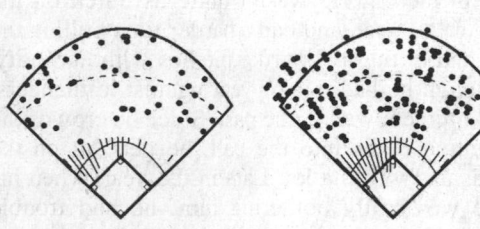

Vs. LHP   **Vs. RHP**

2003 Situational Stats

	AB	H	HR	RBI	Avg		AB	H	HR	RBI	Avg
Home	295	85	13	46	.288	LHP	153	33	5	16	.216
Road	297	73	11	50	.246	RHP	439	125	19	80	.285
First Half	349	91	16	56	.261	Sc Pos	155	45	6	67	.290
Scnd Half	243	67	8	40	.276	Clutch	95	19	5	19	.200

2003 Rankings (American League)

- Did not rank near the top or bottom in any category

Jason Giambi

2003 Season

It was a painful and often-times frustrating season for someone who ultimately finished with 41 homers and even drew one first-place vote in the American League MVP balloting. Still, for a perennial MVP candidate like Jason Giambi, the expectations always are immense. He was prevented from attaining his accustomed heights by a staph infection that caused eye irritation from late April to mid-May, and patellar tendinitis in his left knee that bothered him all year.

Hitting

Giambi takes the classic power hitter's approach, waiting patiently until he gets something he can pull in the air. He wasn't quite as quick on the trigger last year, and had a harder time pulling the ball and hitting two-strike pitches with authority. Although he had a poor year against lefthanders, he'd hit them well in the past. Since he crowds the plate and dives into the ball, he gets hit on the hands and wrists a lot. Late in the year, when his knee was really bothering him, he had trouble catching up to high fastballs. His hitting seems to suffer when he's DHing instead of playing the field.

Baserunning & Defense

Giambi isn't built for speed, and his knee problem and overall susceptibility to muscle pulls forces him to run the bases conservatively. The only thing that keeps him from hitting into more double plays is the fact that he hits the ball on the ground relatively infrequently. In the field, he has little lateral range, but does a good job handling tough hops and digging out low throws.

2004 Outlook

Despite undergoing knee surgery in November, Giambi's problem may be chronic. It could cause him to miss significant time at some point down the road. It may be something he'll be able to play through in the short term, but it likely will prevent him from being the hitter he was at his peak. Even if he's no better than he was last year, however, he obviously will remain quite valuable.

Position: 1B/DH
Bats: L **Throws:** R
Ht: 6' 3" **Wt:** 230

Opening Day Age: 33
Born: 1/8/71 in West Covina, CA
ML Seasons: 9
Pronunciation: gee-OM-bee

Overall Statistics

	G	AB	R	H	D	T	HR	RBI	SB	BB	SO	Avg	OBP	Slg
'03	156	535	97	134	25	0	41	107	2	129	140	.250	.412	.527
Car.	1264	4493	818	1358	287	8	269	904	13	824	854	.302	.415	.549

Where He Hits the Ball

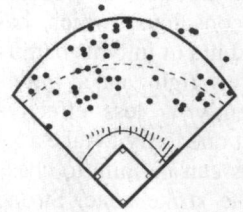 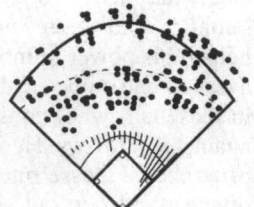

Vs. LHP   **Vs. RHP**

2003 Situational Stats

	AB	H	HR	RBI	Avg		AB	H	HR	RBI	Avg
Home	253	60	12	37	.237	LHP	146	28	6	30	.192
Road	282	74	29	70	.262	RHP	389	106	35	77	.272
First Half	318	85	26	73	.267	Sc Pos	152	39	13	71	.257
Scnd Half	217	49	15	34	.226	Clutch	53	11	2	3	.208

2003 Rankings (American League)

- 1st in walks, hit by pitch (21), strikeouts and pitches seen (2,916)
- 2nd in lowest groundball-flyball ratio (0.5) and lowest batting average vs. lefthanded pitchers
- 3rd in times on base (284), on-base percentage, HR frequency (13.0 ABs per HR) and most pitches seen per plate appearance (4.23)
- 4th in home runs and lowest percentage of swings put into play (37.3)
- Led the Yankees in home runs, RBI, intentional walks (9), times on base (284), strikeouts, pitches seen (2,916), slugging percentage, HR frequency (13.0 ABs per HR), fewest GDPs per GDP situation (5.7%), and cleanup slugging percentage (.526)

Derek Jeter

2003 Season

Three innings into the Yankees' 2003 opener, Derek Jeter suffered the first serious injury of his career, dislocating his left shoulder on a freak basepath collision. He was able to return in mid-May, but he had to contend with an unusual number of bumps and bruises over the rest of the season. Despite that, and a shoulder that might not have gotten back to full strength, he continued to perform at a high level and finished third in the American League batting race.

Hitting

No matter how he's pitched, Jeter can stay inside the ball and shoot it to right field. His power is to right as well, though he hits mostly groundballs and line drives. He's especially dangerous on the first pitch and likes to go after it. His ability to wait on the ball helps make him an excellent two-strike hitter. Although he isn't especially patient, Jeter has a good eye and will take a walk rather than chase borderline pitches. With a good batting average and a natural tendency to hit behind the runner, he's an excellent fit in the No. 2 hole in the lineup.

Baserunning & Defense

There is little agreement on the quality of Jeter's defense. It's obvious that he has a strong arm, great athleticism and terrific baseball instincts, but his work in the field somehow seems to be less than the sum of its parts. While his strengths are obvious, his weaknesses are subtle. It may be the angles he takes, his habit of throwing on the run when going to his right, his positioning, his first step, or some combination thereof, but one thing is hard to deny: other shortstops handle balls that he doesn't. He normally is an excellent percentage basestealer, but last year, understandably, he ran far less often.

2004 Outlook

With the exception of the freak shoulder injury, Jeter always has been durable and consistent. It's safe to assume he'll play a full season in 2004, and that his steal total will come back up.

Position: SS
Bats: R **Throws:** R
Ht: 6' 3" **Wt:** 195

Opening Day Age: 29
Born: 6/26/74 in Pequannock, NJ
ML Seasons: 9
Pronunciation: JEL-ter

Overall Statistics

	G	AB	R	H	D	T	HR	RBI	SB	BB	SO	Avg	OBP	Slg
'03	119	482	87	156	25	3	10	52	11	43	88	.324	.393	.450
Car.	1212	4870	926	1546	239	41	127	615	178	513	873	.317	.389	.462

Where He Hits the Ball

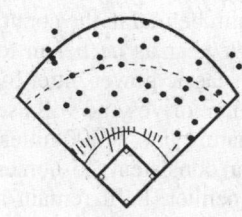 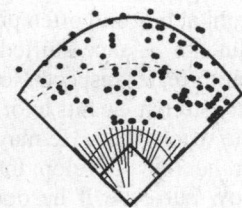

Vs. LHP   **Vs. RHP**

2003 Situational Stats

	AB	H	HR	RBI	Avg		AB	H	HR	RBI	Avg
Home	252	80	7	29	.317	LHP	100	37	3	13	.370
Road	230	76	3	23	.330	RHP	382	119	7	39	.312
First Half	231	73	5	24	.316	Sc Pos	109	36	1	39	.330
Scnd Half	251	83	5	28	.331	Clutch	46	7	1	3	.152

2003 Rankings (American League)

- 2nd in batting average with two strikes (.264) and lowest fielding percentage at shortstop (.969)
- 3rd in batting average, highest groundball-fly ball ratio (2.4) and batting average on the road
- Led the Yankees in batting average, highest groundball-flyball ratio (2.4), bunts in play (12), batting average with the bases loaded (.533), batting average vs. lefthanded pitchers, batting average vs. righthanded pitchers, on-base percentage for a leadoff hitter (.375), batting average at home, batting average on the road and batting average with two strikes (.264)
- Led AL shortstops in batting average

Nick Johnson

2003 Season

Last year, young first baseman Nick Johnson began to make good on the promise he'd shown in the minors, even as injuries continued to hold him back. He got off to a good start before suffering a stress fracture in his right hand in mid-May while swinging at a pitch, and was out until late July. He wasted little time getting going upon his return, however, and he finally had begun to establish himself as the club's No. 2 hitter by the end of the year.

Hitting

Johnson is one of the most patient hitters in the league. This had gotten him into trouble at times during his rookie campaign, when pitchers came right at him and often put him behind in the count. But the balance shifted last year as he began to earn greater respect. Not a classic power hitter by any stretch, he hits a lot of line drives and will use the whole field. He may mature into a .300 hitter, or he may develop into a consistent 25-homer guy, but even if he does neither, he'll remain a fine—if somewhat unconventional—No. 2 hitter because of his ability to get on base.

Baserunning & Defense

Johnson has been used as a DH at times, but that isn't due to any defensive deficiencies. He's a good first baseman with decent range around the bag, and three of his five errors came in a disastrous September game against Detroit. He runs deceptively well, and it can't be taken for granted he'll always stay put.

2004 Outlook

In early December, Johnson, right fielder Juan Rivera and lefthander Randy Choate were dealt to Montreal for Expos ace Javier Vazquez. Johnson should take over as the primary first baseman, but the bigger question is whether he'll be able to avoid the wrist and hand injuries that repeatedly have interrupted his progress. At 25, Johnson could take a big step forward if he's able to stay healthy. He might not put up an eye-popping batting average or big power numbers, but the overall package should be quite valuable.

Position: 1B/DH
Bats: L **Throws:** L
Ht: 6' 3" **Wt:** 195

Opening Day Age: 25
Born: 9/19/78 in Sacramento, CA
ML Seasons: 3

Overall Statistics

	G	AB	R	H	D	T	HR	RBI	SB	BB	SO	Avg	OBP	Slg
'03	96	324	60	92	19	0	14	47	5	70	57	.284	.422	.472
Car.	248	769	122	197	36	0	31	113	6	125	170	.256	.376	.424

Where He Hits the Ball

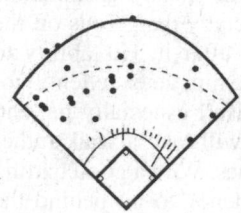
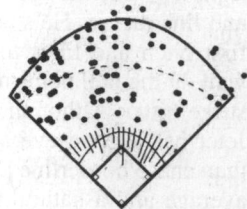

Vs. LHP　　　　**Vs. RHP**

2003 Situational Stats

	AB	H	HR	RBI	Avg		AB	H	HR	RBI	Avg
Home	150	43	8	22	.287	LHP	71	20	2	9	.282
Road	174	49	6	25	.282	RHP	253	72	12	38	.285
First Half	120	37	5	18	.308	Sc Pos	84	23	2	31	.274
Scnd Half	204	55	9	29	.270	Clutch	36	9	1	6	.250

2003 Rankings (American League)

- 3rd in highest percentage of pitches taken (64.3)
- 9th in errors at first base (5)
- Led the Yankees in on-base percentage, most pitches seen per plate appearance (4.28) and lowest percentage of swings on the first pitch (14.0)

Hideki Matsui

2003 Season

Hideki Matsui, a.k.a. "Godzilla," came to the Yankees with considerable fanfare, even by New York standards. The fascination was understandable; he had been one of Japan's premier power hitters, and he was to be the first Japanese League power hitter to try to test his mettle in the American major leagues. While he didn't attain the gaudy power numbers some had predicted, he contributed in a variety of ways. He might have won the American League Rookie of the Year award if two voters had not left him off the ballot entirely.

Hitting

Matsui was, in most respects, quite different than what people had expected. While most assumed he'd be an all-or-nothing slugger, he was very much the opposite. He was not preoccupied with pulling or lifting the ball, and seemed more focused on merely making good contact. He is capable of yanking the ball—most of his home runs went down the right-field line—but he also uses the whole field and hits a lot of groundballs and line drives. He's very patient, especially early in the count.

Baserunning & Defense

Matsui's defensive ability also came as a surprise. While some had envisioned a typical slow-moving slugger, he turned out to be a very capable outfielder, covering a lot of ground in New York's expansive left field. When Bernie Williams got hurt, Matsui moved to center and held his own there too. His only real weakness is an exceptionally weak throwing arm, which he tries to compensate for by getting rid of the ball as quickly as possible. Baserunners occasionally took advantage of his inability to read and react before throwing. He runs decently but is risk-averse on the bases.

2004 Outlook

Matsui may need to alter his plate approach in order to produce truly impressive power numbers. Even if he doesn't, though, he's shown he can be valuable. He may not be the type to be the centerpiece of an offense, but he can be an integral part of the supporting cast on a winning team.

Position: LF/CF
Bats: L **Throws:** R
Ht: 6' 2" **Wt:** 210

Opening Day Age: 29
Born: 6/12/74 in Kanazawa, Japan
ML Seasons: 1
Pronunciation: mat-soo-ee

Overall Statistics

	G	AB	R	H	D	T	HR	RBI	SB	BB	SO	Avg	OBP	Slg
'03	163	623	82	179	42	1	16	106	2	63	86	.287	.353	.435
Car.	163	623	82	179	42	1	16	106	2	63	86	.287	.353	.435

Where He Hits the Ball

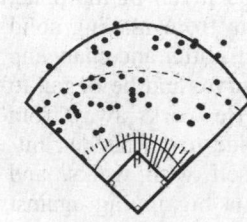

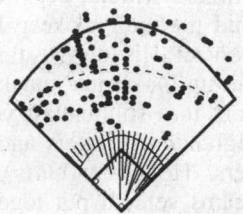

Vs. LHP   **Vs. RHP**

2003 Situational Stats

	AB	H	HR	RBI	Avg		AB	H	HR	RBI	Avg
Home	302	91	9	55	.301	LHP	195	56	3	24	.287
Road	321	88	7	51	.274	RHP	428	123	13	82	.287
First Half	381	114	9	66	.299	Sc Pos	173	58	5	90	.335
Scnd Half	242	65	7	40	.269	Clutch	77	25	2	11	.325

2003 Rankings (American League)

- 1st in games played, RBI among rookies, errors in left field (7) and lowest fielding percentage in left field (.969)
- 2nd in GDPs (25) and highest percentage of swings put into play (55.5)
- 4th in highest groundball-flyball ratio (2.2) and batting average among rookies
- 7th in highest percentage of pitches taken (62.6)
- 8th in singles and doubles
- Led the Yankees in singles, doubles, sacrifice flies (6), GDPs (25), games played, lowest percentage of swings that missed (13.7), highest percentage of swings put into play (55.5) and batting average with runners in scoring position

Mike Mussina

2003 Season

Mike Mussina was the Yankees' most consistent-ly effective starting pitcher last year, but it was an uphill battle. He always seemed to draw tough teams or tough opposing pitchers. He faced the Blue Jays six times and the Red Sox three times, and in 19 of his 31 starts he faced a team that fin-ished the season with a winning record. He twice squared off against eventual AL Cy Young-winner Roy Halladay, and also faced Pedro Martinez, Esteban Loaiza and Tim Hudson.

Pitching

Few pitchers paint the black as consistently as Mussina does. He has the command to work the corners without catching too much of the plate, and the stuff to keep hitters from making solid contact. His low-90s fastball, cutter and changeup set up his dandy knuckle-curve, and he began to mix in a splitter last year. He works away from righthanded hitters and inside to lefthanded hit-ters. He rarely hurts himself with walks, and teams seldom put together a big inning against him. If he falls behind, he will give a hitter some-thing to hit, but he works ahead in the count much more often. Mussina has good stamina and main-tains his effectiveness deep into the game. His most overlooked attribute may be his durability—last year was his ninth consecutive 200-inning season, the longest active streak in the majors.

Defense

A terrific fielder, Mussina handled all 49 chances cleanly last year and was rewarded with his sixth Gold Glove. He gets the ball to the plate quickly and is tough to run on. Basestealers went 9-for-19 against him last year and have a 53.2-percent suc-cess rate over Mussina's career.

2004 Outlook

Mussina turned 35 this winter, so it's fair to won-der when he might start slipping a bit. He showed no signs of it thus far, and until he does, he remains one of the best bets around to approach 20 wins. If free agency thins out the Yankees' rotation, he may take on the mantle as its unques-tioned ace.

Position: SP
Bats: L **Throws:** R
Ht: 6' 2" **Wt:** 185

Opening Day Age: 35
Born: 12/8/68 in Williamsport, PA
ML Seasons: 13
Pronunciation: myoo-SEE-nuh
Nickname: Moose

Overall Statistics

W	L	Pct.	ERA	G	GS	Sv	IP	H	BB	SO	HR	Avg
17	8	.680	3.40	31	31	0	214.2	192	40	195	21	.238
199	110	.644	3.53	386	386	0	2668.2	2497	597	2126	278	.247

2003 Pitching Profile

	Mike Mussina	AL Average
Overall Strike %	67.2	62.8
1st Pitch Strike %	63.8	58.7
Ratio	1.08	1.39
Strikeouts per 9 IP	8.18	6.11
Walks per 9 IP	1.68	3.16
Home Runs per 9 IP	0.88	1.11
Strikeout/Walk Ratio	4.88	1.93
Groundball/Flyball Ratio	1.13	1.18

2003 Situational Stats

	W	L	ERA	Sv	IP		AB	H	HR	RBI	Avg
Home	10	4	3.04	0	115.1	LHB	419	96	10	37	.229
Road	7	4	3.81	0	99.1	RHB	388	96	11	43	.247
First Half	10	6	3.26	0	124.1	Sc Pos	157	47	5	56	.299
Scnd Half	7	2	3.59	0	90.1	Clutch	59	13	0	4	.220

2003 Rankings (American League)

- 1st in fielding percentage at pitcher (1.000)
- 2nd in runners caught stealing (10) and lowest on-base percentage allowed (.275)
- 3rd in highest strikeout-walk ratio (4.9) and most strikeouts per nine innings (8.2)
- 4th in strikeouts and fewest walks per nine innings (1.7)
- 5th in wins and lowest ERA at home
- 6th in lowest batting average allowed (.238)
- Led the Yankees in ERA, innings pitched, strikeouts, runners caught stealing (10), lowest batting average allowed (.238), lowest slugging percentage allowed (.372), lowest on-base percentage allowed (.275), lowest ERA at home, lowest batting average allowed vs. righthanded batters, fewest home runs allowed per nine innings (.88) and most strikeouts per nine innings (8.2)

Andy Pettitte

2003 Season

Lefthander Andy Pettitte started the 2003 season slowly, compiling a 5-6 record and 5.33 ERA through June 8. Then he got rolling, going 16-2 with 3.29 ERA the rest of the way and winning three of four decisions with a 2.10 ERA in five postseason starts. It marked his first 20-win season since 1996, a year that also saw him finish with a 21-8 record.

Pitching

Pettitte throws in the low 90s, harder than he did earlier in his career, and now is able to go right at hitters with his four-seamer more often than he used to. His cutter, which used to be his big pitch, is something hitters still look for, and Pettitte uses that to his advantage. His slider has become a more important pitch for him also. A sinker and a changeup round out his arsenal. Hitters tend to have the most success against him on the first pitch of an at-bat. Earlier in his career, he would lose his edge after six innings, but over the last two years he's shown better stamina.

Defense

Pettitte had been a strong fielder in the past, but last year he made six errors, which tied for the most in the majors among pitchers. Four of them came on hurried throws to the bases. Pettitte is well known for having one of the best pickoff moves in the game, but certain baserunners may have begun to key into it last season. For the first time in years, he failed to pick off a single runner, and basestealers were successful on 13 of 14 steal attempts.

2004 Outlook

It was thought that Pettitte, a free agent, preferred to stay with the Yankees, since he pitches so well at Yankee Stadium. His career winning percentage there is .730, compared to .586 on the road, and his career ERA at home is nearly a full run lower. Yet, Pettitte decided to play for a team closer to home and gave it the hometown discount. Taking less money from Houston than he was offered by the Yankees, Pettitte agreed to a three-year, $31.5 million deal. He leaves an aging Yankees rotation to join young righthanded studs Ray Oswalt and Wade Miller in Houston.

Position: SP
Bats: L **Throws:** L
Ht: 6' 5" **Wt:** 225

Opening Day Age: 31
Born: 6/15/72 in Baton Rouge, LA
ML Seasons: 9
Pronunciation: pet-it

Overall Statistics

	W	L	Pct.	ERA	G	GS	Sv	IP	H	BB	SO	HR	Avg
'03	21	8	.724	4.02	33	33	0	208.1	227	50	180	21	.272
Car.	149	78	.656	3.94	283	276	0	1792.2	1901	579	1275	143	.273

2003 Pitching Profile

	Andy Pettitte	AL Average
Overall Strike %	64.5	62.8
1st Pitch Strike %	58.7	58.7
Ratio	1.33	1.39
Strikeouts per 9 IP	7.78	6.11
Walks per 9 IP	2.16	3.16
Home Runs per 9 IP	0.91	1.11
Strikeout/Walk Ratio	3.60	1.93
Groundball/Flyball Ratio	1.76	1.18

2003 Situational Stats

	W	L	ERA	Sv	IP		AB	H	HR	RBI	Avg
Home	10	4	3.78	0	100.0	LHB	224	72	5	25	.321
Road	11	4	4.24	0	108.1	RHB	611	155	16	66	.254
First Half	11	6	4.63	0	116.2	Sc Pos	180	45	6	68	.250
Scnd Half	10	2	3.24	0	91.2	Clutch	65	14	1	4	.215

2003 Rankings (American League)

- 1st in errors at pitcher (6) and lowest fielding percentage at pitcher (.857)
- 2nd in wins, most run support per nine innings (7.0) and highest stolen-base percentage allowed (92.9)
- 3rd in pickoff throws (165)
- 5th in winning percentage and highest groundball-flyball ratio allowed (1.8)
- 6th in strikeouts and most strikeouts per nine innings (7.8)
- 7th in highest strikeout-walk ratio (3.6)
- 8th in games started and hits allowed
- Led the Yankees in wins, games started, batters faced (896), wild pitches (5), pickoff throws (165), GDPs induced (18), winning percentage, highest groundball-flyball ratio allowed (1.8) and most run support per nine innings (7.0)

Jorge Posada

2003 Season

Last year, Jorge Posada was the most productive catcher in the American League. He was one of the Yankees' most important offensive players, and was unstoppable over the last two months of the season. He also caught more innings than all but three major league catchers. For his efforts, he was rewarded with a third-place finish in the American League MVP balloting. Perhaps his only blemish was a 3-for-19, seven-strikeout showing in the World Series.

Hitting

Earlier in his career, the switch-hitting Posada was stronger from the right side. Over the years, the disparity has shrunk, and last year he was equally effective from either side. He's a very patient hitter who works his way into hitters' counts, and he hits especially well once he gets ahead. From the left side, he has good power from left-center to the right-field line. As a righthanded hitter, he is a little more aggressive and has more of a tendency to pull. Although his home-run total increased by 10 last year, he wasn't doing much of anything differently. He simply was healthier, and perhaps as a result, some of his doubles became homers.

Baserunning & Defense

Posada has a decent arm, and last year he threw more accurately and cut down on his throwing errors substantially. He nabbed 26.5 percent of opposing basestealers in 2003. One thing he could do better is get his lower body in front of balls in the dirt, which he tends to stab at. Posada was caught stealing four times last year, but three of them came when he was put in motion on a full count. He is less of a liability on the bases than many catchers.

2004 Outlook

Although last year was the first time Posada attracted any MVP consideration, he has been performing at more or less the same level since 2000. There's no reason to think he can't keep it up, though it would be a surprise if he were to sneak into the MVP race once again.

Position: C
Bats: B **Throws:** R
Ht: 6' 2" **Wt:** 205

Opening Day Age: 32
Born: 8/17/71 in Santurce, PR
ML Seasons: 9
Pronunciation: hor-hay po-sa-da

Overall Statistics

	G	AB	R	H	D	T	HR	RBI	SB	BB	SO	Avg	OBP	Slg
'03	142	481	83	135	24	0	30	101	2	93	110	.281	.405	.518
Car.	866	2920	449	788	181	5	135	526	9	474	758	.270	.375	.474

Where He Hits the Ball

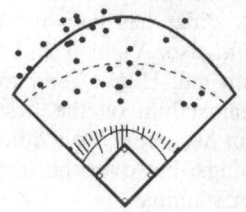 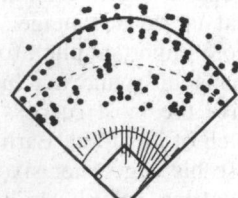

Vs. LHP   **Vs. RHP**

2003 Situational Stats

	AB	H	HR	RBI	Avg		AB	H	HR	RBI	Avg
Home	208	54	15	45	.260	LHP	122	36	8	27	.295
Road	273	81	15	56	.297	RHP	359	99	22	74	.276
First Half	278	70	17	52	.252	Sc Pos	143	41	10	75	.287
Scnd Half	203	65	13	49	.320	Clutch	61	18	3	14	.295

2003 Rankings (American League)

- 4th in fielding percentage at catcher (.994)
- Led AL catchers in home runs and RBI

Mariano Rivera

2003 Season

In 2002, Mariano Rivera suffered the first serious arm injury of his career, so it was important to see how well he'd hold up in 2003. His season got off to a late start, but once he got going, he was used more heavily than ever and held up just fine. After missing almost all of April with a strained groin and building up his arm in May, he worked at an 81-appearance, 90-inning pace over the final two-thirds of the season. He seemed no worse for the wear, saving 40 games and posting the lowest ERA of his career. He then made eight appearances and totaled 16 innings in the Yankees' 17 postseason games, with all five of his saves being of the two-inning variety.

Pitching

If anyone is capable of being a dominant one-pitch pitcher, it's Rivera. His mid-90s cutter is one of the most feared weapons in any pitcher's arsenal. Righthanded hitters find it nearly impossible to pull, and lefthanded hitters fare even worse, rarely getting the fat part of the bat on the ball. He'll work in a few two-seamers and four-seamers, always going right after the hitter. He can work up in the zone for strikeouts or down for groundballs. Rivera is a little less unhittable—but still effective—when he works on consecutive days. And as he's shown time and again in the postseason, he's quite capable of working as his own setup man when necessary.

Defense

Rivera is an agile fielder whose only weakness is an occasional hurried throw. He has a decent pick-off move but doesn't often use it; he knows that when he's on the mound, baserunners are loath to risk getting thrown out, so he pays them little attention.

2004 Outlook

Rivera remains the best closer in baseball. Having proven himself sound, there's little reason to think he will be anything less than his usual stellar self in 2004. He won't stay at his peak forever, but he's shown no signs of slowing down.

Position: RP
Bats: R **Throws:** R
Ht: 6' 2" **Wt:** 170

Opening Day Age: 34
Born: 11/29/69 in Panama City, Panama
ML Seasons: 9

Overall Statistics

	W	L	Pct.	ERA	G	GS	Sv	IP	H	BB	SO	HR	Avg
'03	5	2	.714	1.66	64	0	40	70.2	61	10	63	3	.235
Car.	43	29	.597	2.49	512	10	283	649.2	515	177	582	37	.215

2003 Pitching Profile

	Mariano Rivera	AL Average
Overall Strike %	68.8	62.8
1st Pitch Strike %	60.2	58.7
Ratio	1.00	1.39
Strikeouts per 9 IP	8.02	6.11
Walks per 9 IP	1.27	3.16
Home Runs per 9 IP	0.38	1.11
Strikeout/Walk Ratio	6.30	1.93
Groundball/Flyball Ratio	2.00	1.18

2003 Situational Stats

	W	L	ERA	Sv	IP		AB	H	HR	RBI	Avg
Home	3	1	1.78	22	35.1	LHB	147	29	1	12	.197
Road	2	1	1.53	18	35.1	RHB	113	32	2	18	.283
First Half	3	0	1.75	16	36.0	Sc Pos	81	20	0	27	.247
Scnd Half	2	2	1.56	24	34.2	Clutch	186	43	1	26	.231

2003 Rankings (American League)

- 3rd in saves and highest percentage of inherited runners scored (48.6)
- 4th in games finished (57) and save percentage (87.0)
- 7th in lowest batting average allowed vs. left handed batters and fewest baserunners allowed per nine innings in relief (9.6)
- Led the Yankees in games pitched, saves, games finished (57), lowest batting average allowed vs. lefthanded batters, save percentage (87.0), blown saves (6), relief ERA (1.66), relief wins (5), relief innings (70.2), lowest batting average allowed in relief (.235) and fewest baserunners allowed per nine innings in relief (9.6)

Alfonso Soriano

2003 Season

In 2003, Alfonso Soriano nearly matched his spectacular totals from the season before, but the reaction to it couldn't have been more different. This time, there was frustration over his inability—or, perhaps, unwillingness—to address the holes in his game. In the postseason, when he slumped so badly that he nearly got himself benched, the frustration came to the forefront.

Hitting

With incredibly powerful wrists, and swinging one of the longest, heaviest bats in the game, Soriano thinks he can hit anything. He's almost right. Few players are better at golfing a pitch at, or even below, the knees. He can get around on anyone's fastball, even on the inside half of the plate. And he always swings from the heels. Patient he is not, however. He'll take a strike, but not two, and he ends many at-bats without having seen a single one. With the success he's had as a hyper-aggressive, bad-ball hitter, it's somewhat understandable that Soriano would be reluctant to change. Still, it can be maddening to watch pitchers see how far off the plate they can get him to chase, as Pedro Martinez repeatedly did in the playoffs.

Baserunning & Defense

Soriano's defense is a lot like his hitting—alternately spectacular and maddening. A strong-armed former shortstop with good range, he can knock down a grounder up the middle and rifle it over to first base, and he can just as easily fail to anticipate a hop or throw away a routine three-hopper. He led major league second basemen in errors for the third consecutive season. A blazer on the bases, he's capable of stealing second or third at any time.

2004 Outlook

This may be the season in which it's determined whether Soriano will remain in pinstripes. Now arbitration-eligible, he certainly will be able to command top dollar, and the Yankees may be reluctant to commit to him unless he shows he'll be more responsive to their suggestions. Whether he'll actually be able to change his plate approach is another question entirely.

Position: 2B
Bats: R **Throws:** R
Ht: 6' 1" **Wt:** 160

Opening Day Age: 26
Born: 1/7/78 in San Pedro de Macoris, DR
ML Seasons: 5
Pronunciation: soar-ee-ah-no

Overall Statistics

	G	AB	R	H	D	T	HR	RBI	SB	BB	SO	Avg	OBP	Slg
'03	156	682	114	198	36	5	38	91	35	38	130	.290	.338	.525
Car.	501	2010	326	571	124	10	98	270	121	91	430	.284	.322	.502

Where He Hits the Ball

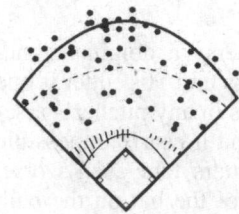
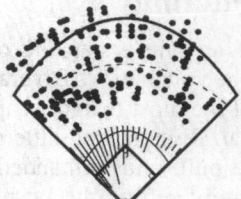

Vs. LHP   **Vs. RHP**

2003 Situational Stats

	AB	H	HR	RBI	Avg		AB	H	HR	RBI	Avg
Home	329	90	15	42	.274	LHP	138	43	7	16	.312
Road	353	108	23	49	.306	RHP	544	155	31	75	.285
First Half	407	119	22	52	.292	Sc Pos	143	37	6	54	.259
Scnd Half	275	79	16	39	.287	Clutch	76	22	2	9	.289

2003 Rankings (American League)

- 1st in at-bats and errors at second base (19)
- 2nd in plate appearances (734) and lowest fielding percentage at second base (.975)
- 3rd in total bases (358)
- 4th in stolen bases and strikeouts
- 5th in home runs, hits and lowest percentage of pitches taken (45.1)
- 6th in runs scored and steals of third (5)
- 7th in highest percentage of swings that missed (24.4)
- Led the Yankees in at-bats, runs scored, hits, triples, total bases (358), stolen bases, caught stealing (8), plate appearances (734), stolen-base percentage (81.4) and steals of third (5)
- Led AL second basemen in home runs

David Wells

2003 Season

Ageless David Wells got off to a good start in 2003, winning 10 of his first 12 decisions. His chronically balky back began to bother him in the second half, but he rebounded in September. He also pitched well in the postseason until a stiff back forced him out of Game 5 of the World Series after only one inning. There were more than a few games where he was hit hard, and it took considerable run support for him to post a 15-7 record, but he lived up to his reputation as an innings-eater, even at age 40.

Pitching

Exceptional command and a willingness to go right at hitters are Wells' defining characteristics on the mound. His stuff—a high-80s fastball, a cutter, a changeup and a big bender—is hittable, and the fact that Wells is always around the strike zone leaves him open to being hit hard when he doesn't have his good command. Most nights, however, he throws enough quality strikes to get the job done, calling upon his curve at any point in the count. He's one of the most efficient pitchers in the majors, which helps him pitch into the seventh inning fairly consistently.

Defense

Never a paragon of physical fitness, Wells has been further slowed by back problems the last few years. He handles what he gets to but can be slow to field bunts or cover first base. He throws over to first a lot, and sometimes catches someone leaning the wrong way, but he generally is slow to the plate and is one of the easier lefthanders to steal against. He did pick off four opponents last year, his highest total since 1997.

2004 Outlook

The Yankees declined Wells' $6 million option for 2004, making him a free agent. Though pitchers of his age and condition aren't supposed to be successful, he's made a pretty good case to the contrary over the past few years. While he had surgery to repair a herniated disc in December, Wells still may have another decent season or two in him.

Position: SP
Bats: L **Throws:** L
Ht: 6' 4" **Wt:** 230

Opening Day Age: 40
Born: 5/20/63 in Torrance, CA
ML Seasons: 17
Nickname: Boomer

Overall Statistics

W	L	Pct.	ERA	G	GS	Sv	IP	H	BB	SO	HR	Avg
15	7	.682	4.14	31	30	0	213.0	242	20	101	24	.286
200	128	.610	4.06	557	386	13	2826.2	2914	624	1873	330	.266

2003 Pitching Profile

	David Wells	AL Average
Overall Strike %	70.7	62.8
1st Pitch Strike %	65.7	58.7
Ratio	1.23	1.39
Strikeouts per 9 IP	4.27	6.11
Walks per 9 IP	0.85	3.16
Home Runs per 9 IP	1.01	1.11
Strikeout/Walk Ratio	5.05	1.93
Groundball/Flyball Ratio	1.22	1.18

2003 Situational Stats

	W	L	ERA	Sv	IP		AB	H	HR	RBI	Avg
Home	8	5	4.89	0	108.2	LHB	201	55	8	25	.274
Road	7	2	3.36	0	104.1	RHB	645	187	16	72	.290
First Half	11	3	3.76	0	127.0	Sc Pos	201	50	6	71	.249
Scnd Half	4	4	4.71	0	86.0	Clutch	82	19	1	6	.232

2003 Rankings (American League)

- 1st in fewest pitches thrown per batter (3.39), fewest walks per nine innings (0.8) and fielding percentage at pitcher (1.000)
- 2nd in highest strikeout-walk ratio (5.1)
- 3rd in hits allowed
- 4th in complete games (4)
- 5th in most run support per nine innings (6.3) and fewest strikeouts per nine innings (4.3)
- 7th in highest batting average allowed (.286)
- 10th in innings pitched, stolen bases allowed (16) and winning percentage
- Led the Yankees in complete games (4), hits allowed, home runs allowed, GDPs induced (18), highest strikeout-walk ratio (5.1), fewest pitches thrown per batter (3.39) and fewest walks per nine innings (0.8)

Bernie Williams

2003 Season

Bernie Williams, who was dogged by shoulder problems in 2002, hoped he'd be healthy in 2003. Instead, he had his worst year in a decade. He was hitting close to .400 in late April, but he fell into a terrible rut in May and then had surgery to repair torn cartilage in his left knee. He was out until just before the All-Star break, and it took him a month to get his stroke back. Even when he did, he didn't swing the bat with much authority.

Hitting

Last year, after Williams' knee problem flared up, he didn't drive the ball nearly as consistently as he had in the past. He also had problems getting around on good fastballs. When healthy, he's a patient, line-drive hitter who makes good contact and generates respectable power. He usually is equally effective from either side of the plate, but his knee seemed to hamper him more from the left side last year. With his tendency to hit the ball on the ground, combined with his declining speed, he grounded into 21 double plays, fourth-most in the American League.

Baserunning & Defense

Williams' long, graceful strides somewhat mask his deficiencies in center field. Though he still runs fairly well once he gets up to speed, he doesn't read balls off the bat well. As a result, his lateral range is limited, and he compounds it by playing conservatively and allowing a lot of balls to fall in front of him. It seems only a matter of time before he's moved to a position to which he's better suited. Chronic shoulder problems have rendered his throwing arm a major liability. He never has gotten the most out of his speed on the bases.

2004 Outlook

Williams has been the Yankees' center fielder and cleanup hitter for years, but he may not last much longer in either spot. The whispers that he'll be moved to left field or DH are growing louder. Still, a healthy Williams is capable of being an important offensive contributor.

Position: CF
Bats: B **Throws:** R
Ht: 6' 2" **Wt:** 205

Opening Day Age: 35
Born: 9/13/68 in San Juan, PR
ML Seasons: 13

Overall Statistics

G	AB	R	H	D	T	HR	RBI	SB	BB	SO	Avg	OBP	Slg
119	445	77	117	19	1	15	64	5	71	61	.263	.367	.411
1656	6403	1143	1950	372	53	241	1062	143	898	988	.305	.390	.492

Where He Hits the Ball

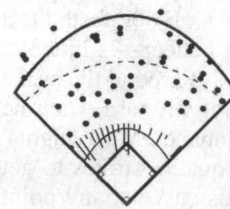 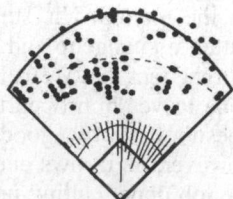

Vs. LHP	**Vs. RHP**

2003 Situational Stats

	AB	H	HR	RBI	Avg		AB	H	HR	RBI	Avg
Home	198	47	5	22	.237	LHP	132	37	4	18	.280
Road	247	70	10	42	.283	RHP	313	80	11	46	.256
First Half	195	55	7	33	.282	Sc Pos	120	32	3	43	.267
Scnd Half	250	62	8	31	.248	Clutch	49	14	1	7	.286

2003 Rankings (American League)

- 2nd in fielding percentage in center field (.997)
- 4th in GDPs (21) and lowest cleanup slugging percentage (.394)

Jose Contreras

Position: SP/RP
Bats: R **Throws:** R
Ht: 6' 4" **Wt:** 224

Opening Day Age: 32
Born: 12/12/71 in Havana, Cuba
ML Seasons: 1

Overall Statistics

	W	L	Pct.	ERA	G	GS	Sv	IP	H	BB	SO	HR	Avg
'03	7	2	.778	3.30	18	9	0	71.0	52	30	72	4	.202
Car.	7	2	.778	3.30	18	9	0	71.0	52	30	72	4	.202

2003 Situational Stats

	W	L	ERA	Sv	IP		AB	H	HR	RBI	Avg
Home	2	0	1.65	0	27.1	LHB	143	29	2	15	.203
Road	5	2	4.33	0	43.2	RHB	114	23	2	7	.202
First Half	3	1	4.62	0	25.1	Sc Pos	56	11	0	15	.196
Scnd Half	4	1	2.56	0	45.2	Clutch	22	5	0	5	.227

2003 Season

Cuba's Jose Contreras was one of the most successful pitchers in international tournaments, so he naturally became the subject of an intense bidding war when he defected last winter. The Yankees won out with a four-year, $32 million deal. He began 2003 in the bullpen, got sent down and recalled, made two excellent starts and then strained his shoulder. He came back in late August, and was the team's most effective starting pitcher in September.

Pitching & Defense

Contreras' forkball is something to behold. His unnaturally wide grip imparts so little spin that the pitch comes in almost like a low-80s knuckleball, sinking late and hard. With a mid-90s fastball to set it up, he's tough to hit and deadly once he gets ahead. He has the stamina to work deep into games, but apparently was somewhat unfamiliar with the demands of relief work. He's a good fielder who's quick off the mound, but he does little to slow the running game.

2004 Outlook

The Yankees' rotation could be a lot less crowded in 2004, and Contreras ought to be in the mix from the start. It's no exaggeration to say that a healthy Contreras could take the league by storm this year—the man has got the goods.

David Dellucci

Position: RF/CF
Bats: L **Throws:** L
Ht: 5'11" **Wt:** 189

Opening Day Age: 30
Born: 10/31/73 in Baton Rouge, LA
ML Seasons: 7
Pronunciation:
duh-LOO-chee

Overall Statistics

	G	AB	R	H	D	T	HR	RBI	SB	BB	SO	Avg	OBP	Slg
'03	91	216	26	49	12	3	3	23	12	23	58	.227	.313	.352
Car.	541	1264	163	337	63	20	27	163	21	125	308	.267	.338	.412

2003 Situational Stats

	AB	H	HR	RBI	Avg		AB	H	HR	RBI	Avg
Home	114	32	3	20	.281	LHP	38	5	1	6	.132
Road	102	17	0	3	.167	RHP	178	44	2	17	.247
First Half	145	37	2	19	.255	Sc Pos	63	13	2	19	.206
Scnd Half	71	12	1	4	.169	Clutch	56	5	0	4	.089

2003 Season

David Dellucci had a chance to win at least part of the Yankees' right-field job late in the year, but he failed to take advantage of the opportunity. He began the season in his customary fourth outfielder/pinch-hitter role for Arizona, performed below his usual standards and was traded the Yankees in late July. In New York, he didn't produce when given the chance and then missed most of September with a sprained left ankle.

Hitting, Baserunning & Defense

Dellucci is well-suited to a reserve role. He hits righthanded pitchers consistently enough to be a useful extra outfielder and bat off the bench. He has a good track record pinch-hitting, although he had only two pinch-hits in 18 tries last year. Being able to play all three outfield positions is another plus, although Dellucci is a little stretched to cover center, and his weak throwing arm is exposed in right field. He was a surprising 12-for-12 as a basestealer after coming into the season with nine career steals in 21 attempts.

2004 Outlook

As an arbitration-eligible player, Dellucci may be non-tendered. He'll remain a useful fourth outfielder wherever he ends up, but he probably won't ever earn a bigger role.

Karim Garcia

Position: RF/LF/CF
Bats: L **Throws:** L
Ht: 6' 0" **Wt:** 195

Opening Day Age: 28
Born: 10/29/75 in
Ciudad Obregon, Mexico
ML Seasons: 9
Pronunciation:
ka-REEM

Overall Statistics

	G	AB	R	H	D	T	HR	RBI	SB	BB	SO	Avg	OBP	Slg
'03	76	244	25	64	6	0	11	35	0	14	52	.262	.302	.422
Car.	403	1205	147	293	37	11	56	179	7	67	280	.243	.282	.432

2003 Situational Stats

	AB	H	HR	RBI	Avg		AB	H	HR	RBI	Avg
Home	105	25	4	12	.238	LHP	55	9	1	3	.164
Road	139	39	7	23	.281	RHP	189	55	10	32	.291
First Half	136	33	8	20	.243	Sc Pos	63	18	3	25	.286
Scnd Half	108	31	3	15	.287	Clutch	28	7	0	2	.250

2003 Season

Karim Garcia seemed to establish himself as something more than a role player in 2002 when he drove in 52 runs over the last two months of the season, but it all went down the drain in 2003. He strained his left wrist late in spring training, tried to play through it, and finally went on the DL in May. He missed the next six weeks and then was traded to the Yankees. He hit well for them, but never saw anything more than semi-regular playing time, even after right fielder Raul Mondesi was traded in late July.

Hitting, Baserunning & Defense

Garcia is an aggressive pull hitter with good power. He hits best early in the count and tends to get himself out after he falls behind. He had trouble with lefties last year but had fared decently against them in the past. Garcia moves well enough to cover a corner outfield spot but has little savvy on the basepaths. His throwing arm is strong, but he was unable to throw accurately last year—perhaps a lingering effect of his wrist problem.

2004 Outlook

Garcia is arbitration-eligible and might be non-tendered. He never seemed to win the favor of Joe Torre, but he'll land somewhere as an extra outfielder.

Chris Hammond

Position: RP
Bats: L **Throws:** L
Ht: 6' 1" **Wt:** 190

Opening Day Age: 38
Born: 1/21/66 in Atlanta, GA
ML Seasons: 11

Overall Statistics

	W	L	Pct.	ERA	G	GS	Sv	IP	H	BB	SO	HR	Avg
'03	3	2	.600	2.86	62	0	1	63.0	65	11	45	5	.270
Car.	56	59	.487	4.16	316	136	2	982.2	1020	355	621	87	.270

2003 Situational Stats

	W	L	ERA	Sv	IP		AB	H	HR	RBI	Avg
Home	1	1	1.32	1	34.0	LHB	89	26	3	13	.292
Road	2	1	4.66	0	29.0	RHB	152	39	2	16	.257
First Half	2	0	3.20	1	39.1	Sc Pos	81	18	2	25	.222
Scnd Half	1	2	2.28	0	23.2	Clutch	124	33	3	17	.266

2003 Season

Coming off a superb 2002 season, lefthander Chris Hammond signed a lucrative two-year deal with the Yankees. He pitched fairly well (and fairly often) over the first half of the year, but he never established a definite niche for himself in the bullpen. When the Yankees added lefthanded relievers late in the season, Hammond was rendered an afterthought. He was used only once in the postseason, and was left off the ALCS roster entirely.

Pitching & Defense

In some ways, Hammond is like Seattle's Jamie Moyer—a none-too-young lefthander with a beautiful changeup and good command. Hammond has little else, though. His fastball is average at best, and his breaking ball isn't much. He actually is less effective against lefthanded hitters, which prevents him from being useful as a one-out specialist. He has a very good pickoff move and didn't allow a single stolen base last year. His glovework isn't problematic.

2004 Outlook

It's hard to say how Hammond will fit in this year. Manager Joe Torre clearly was at a loss over how to put him to good use. He's capable of being effective, but he might wind up being used more in long relief than in a setup role.

Jon Lieber

Position: SP
Bats: L **Throws:** R
Ht: 6' 2" **Wt:** 230

Opening Day Age: 33
Born: 4/2/70 in Council Bluffs, IA
ML Seasons: 9
Pronunciation:
LEE-ber

Overall Statistics

	W	L	Pct.	ERA	G	GS	Sv	IP	H	BB	SO	HR	Avg
'03				Did Not Play									
Car.	86	83	.509	4.18	272	225	2	1510.1	1603	311	1121	188	.271

2003 Situational Stats

	W	L	ERA	Sv	IP		AB	H	HR	RBI	Avg
Home	–	–	–	–	–	LHB	–	–	–	–	–
Road	–	–	–	–	–	RHB	–	–	–	–	–
First Half	–	–	–	–	–	Sc Pos	–	–	–	–	–
Scnd Half	–	–	–	–	–	Clutch	–	–	–	–	–

2003 Season

Jon Lieber didn't throw a single pitch for the Yankees last year, but it was no reason for disappointment. He underwent Tommy John surgery in August 2002, and when they signed him in January 2003, they expected him to be rehabbing for most, or all, of the season. His only game action in 2003 came during a handful of minor league rehab starts in August.

Pitching & Defense

When healthy, Lieber gives righthanded hitters fits with a tight slider and terrific command. He has had trouble with lefthanded hitters, who take advantage of his unremarkable fastball and changeup. Despite his inability to corral lefties, he is so tough on righthanders that he's generally effective. He also is so efficient with his pitches that he's consistently able to work deep into the game. Lieber seems to pay a price for the heavy work, however, wearing down late in the season year after year. He's a good fielder and his slide step makes him tough to run on.

2004 Outlook

This will be Lieber's first season back from major surgery, and it will take time to rebuild his arm strength. He probably won't be able to make a contribution before the second half.

Jeff Nelson

Position: RP
Bats: R **Throws:** R
Ht: 6' 8" **Wt:** 225

Opening Day Age: 37
Born: 11/17/66 in Baltimore, MD
ML Seasons: 12

Overall Statistics

	W	L	Pct.	ERA	G	GS	Sv	IP	H	BB	SO	HR	Avg
'03	4	2	.667	3.74	70	0	8	55.1	51	24	68	4	.248
Car.	46	39	.541	3.32	714	0	31	721.2	581	382	771	48	.223

2003 Situational Stats

	W	L	ERA	Sv	IP		AB	H	HR	RBI	Avg
Home	2	0	2.78	5	32.1	LHB	77	21	2	16	.273
Road	2	2	5.09	3	23.0	RHB	129	30	2	21	.233
First Half	3	2	4.11	7	30.2	Sc Pos	56	22	1	32	.393
Scnd Half	1	0	3.28	1	24.2	Clutch	122	35	3	31	.287

2003 Season

Jeff Nelson began the year as the Mariners' primary righthanded setup man. After Seattle closer Kazuhiro Sasaki went down with bruised ribs in June, Nelson got a few save chances, but he blew some leads and soon went back to a setup role. He lashed out against the Mariners' front office in August, and soon was traded to the Yankees, where he continued in the same role and performed decently.

Pitching & Defense

Nelson comes with a funky low-three-quarters delivery, and his wide-breaking slider is his bread and butter. He sets up the slider with a 90-MPH fastball. Understandably, he's at his best against righthanded hitters. When his command wavers or he can't get hitters to chase his slider, walks can be a problem. In the field, Nelson doesn't move well but handles what he gets to, which isn't very much these days—he has logged just 10 total chances in the past two seasons combined. He no longer is all that easy to run on, however.

2004 Outlook

A free agent, Nelson is sure to find setup work somewhere. He'll be 37 this year, but his slider still has enough bite to make him an asset to any club's bullpen.

Antonio Osuna

Position: RP
Bats: R **Throws:** R
Ht: 5'11" **Wt:** 200

Opening Day Age: 30
Born: 4/12/73 in Sinaloa, Mexico
ML Seasons: 9
Pronunciation: oh-SOON-a

Overall Statistics

	W	L	Pct.	ERA	G	GS	Sv	IP	H	BB	SO	HR	Avg
'03	2	5	.286	3.73	48	0	0	50.2	58	20	47	3	.282
Car.	34	28	.548	3.58	376	0	21	449.2	391	191	465	39	.236

2003 Situational Stats

	W	L	ERA	Sv	IP		AB	H	HR	RBI	Avg
Home	2	1	3.38	0	32.0	LHB	82	25	0	15	.305
Road	0	4	4.34	0	18.2	RHB	124	33	3	14	.266
First Half	2	2	2.96	0	27.1	Sc Pos	70	18	1	26	.257
Scnd Half	0	3	4.63	0	23.1	Clutch	68	20	2	10	.294

2003 Season

Antonio Osuna came to the Yankees in a three-team trade in January 2003. He was an effective setup man with New York in the first half, although he missed time with a strained groin in April and May. He re-injured the groin in June and missed a month, and after coming back in mid-July, he was inconsistent and soon fell down the depth chart. By September, he no longer was being called upon in important situations.

Pitching & Defense

Osuna is able to get his fastball into the low to mid-90s. He also has a slider and changeup that he turns over. He did a better job of getting ahead in the count last year but paid the price for it by getting hit harder, especially early in counts. A flyball pitcher, he didn't induce a single groundball double play all year. His compact stretch delivery and tendency to throw high fastballs virtually negated the running game. A fair fielder, he hasn't erred in three years.

2004 Outlook

The Yankees declined their option on Osuna, allowing him to become a free agent. He didn't seem comfortable pitching in New York, and he may be able to establish himself as a reliable setup man elsewhere.

Ruben Sierra

Position: DH/LF/RF
Bats: B **Throws:** R
Ht: 6' 1" **Wt:** 215

Opening Day Age: 38
Born: 10/6/65 in Rio Piedras, PR
ML Seasons: 17

Overall Statistics

	G	AB	R	H	D	T	HR	RBI	SB	BB	SO	Avg	OBP	Slg
	106	307	33	83	17	1	9	43	2	27	47	.270	.327	.420
2004	7539	1027	2033	403	58	285	1224	141	572	1136	.270	.317	.452

2003 Situational Stats

	AB	H	HR	RBI	Avg		AB	H	HR	RBI	Avg
Home	173	44	7	28	.254	LHP	89	21	3	13	.236
Road	134	39	2	15	.291	RHP	218	62	6	30	.284
First Half	222	64	6	28	.288	Sc Pos	90	19	1	30	.211
Scnd Half	85	19	3	15	.224	Clutch	53	19	2	9	.358

2003 Season

Ruben Sierra kept his career going last year by hooking on with the Rangers as a reserve. In an unlikely turn of events, he then was traded in June to the Yankees, who had soured on him back in 1996. This time, he hit well for New York for a few weeks, but slumped in the second half and saw his playing time dwindle.

Hitting, Baserunning & Defense

The switch-hitting Sierra was a better hitter from the right side for most of his career, but he now sees most of his at-bats from the left side and is more effective from that side. Over the last three years, he's shown an odd inability to produce with men on base, especially in scoring position. His usefulness in the outfield is limited, as he has barely adequate range in left or right. He no longer throws well and has had only two assists in 137 games in the outfield over the last three years. He hasn't been a stolen-base threat since the early 1990s.

2004 Outlook

The 38-year-old Sierra was a free agent, but the Yankees re-signed him as an extra outfielder and bat off the bench.

Jeff Weaver

Position: SP
Bats: R **Throws:** R
Ht: 6' 5" **Wt:** 200

Opening Day Age: 27
Born: 8/22/76 in
Northridge, CA
ML Seasons: 5

Overall Statistics

	W	L	Pct.	ERA	G	GS	Sv	IP	H	BB	SO	HR	Avg
'03	7	9	.438	5.99	32	24	0	159.1	211	47	93	16	.320
Car.	51	63	.447	4.59	158	141	2	952.0	1020	271	627	104	.274

2003 Situational Stats

	W	L	ERA	Sv	IP		AB	H	HR	RBI	Avg
Home	4	4	5.47	0	75.2	LHB	383	131	11	62	.342
Road	3	5	6.45	0	83.2	RHB	276	80	5	38	.290
First Half	5	7	5.20	0	110.2	Sc Pos	181	59	5	80	.326
Scnd Half	2	2	7.77	0	48.2	Clutch	32	14	2	9	.438

2003 Season

The 2003 season couldn't have gone much worse for Jeff Weaver. He came out of spring training as the Yankees' fifth starter, but soon fell into a rut that he never was able to climb out of. He was dropped from the rotation in August and briefly sent to the minors. In September and in the playoffs, Weaver was the last man on the staff and seldom was used.

Pitching & Defense

It's a mystery how Weaver could put such good stuff to such poor use, although his tendency to let his frustration snowball may have something to do with it. He has a low-90s fastball that rides in on righthanded hitters, a hard slider and a two-seamer, and he throws strikes. Last year, he seemed to try too hard to throw strikes, and ended up leaving too many balls over the plate. Weaver fields his position adequately and gets the ball to the plate quickly enough to cut off the running game.

2004 Outlook

Weaver has two years and $15.5 million left on his contract, so it may be hard for the Yankees to find a taker. He has the talent to get back on track, but he may need a change of scenery in order to do so.

Gabe White

Position: RP
Bats: L **Throws:** L
Ht: 6' 2" **Wt:** 204

Opening Day Age: 32
Born: 11/20/71 in
Sebring, FL
ML Seasons: 9

Overall Statistics

	W	L	Pct.	ERA	G	GS	Sv	IP	H	BB	SO	HR	Avg
'03	5	1	.833	4.05	46	0	0	46.2	44	8	29	7	.251
Car.	33	23	.589	4.26	402	15	16	502.2	470	128	412	81	.247

2003 Situational Stats

	W	L	ERA	Sv	IP		AB	H	HR	RBI	Avg
Home	3	0	5.33	0	27.0	LHB	77	19	2	15	.247
Road	2	1	2.29	0	19.2	RHB	98	25	5	16	.255
First Half	3	0	3.93	0	34.1	Sc Pos	59	14	2	23	.237
Scnd Half	2	1	4.38	0	12.1	Clutch	90	18	3	8	.200

2003 Season

Lefthander Gabe White did a decent job as a middle reliever and setup man for the Reds before suffering a strained groin in late June. He missed two months, during which he was traded to the Yankees in a deadline deal. He came off the disabled list in late August and made something of a contribution during the final six weeks of the season. He held batters to a .182 average with New York.

Pitching & Defense

White comes right at hitters, working up in the zone with a fastball and changeup. The lack of a breaking ball makes him no more effective against lefthanded hitters than he is against righthanders. He can be susceptible to the longball but seldom gives out a free pass. He's at his best when he gets frequent work. He gets the ball to the plate quickly enough to keep the running game in check, and last year he committed only the first error of his major league career.

2004 Outlook

The Yankees declined their option on White, making him a free agent. He could be a capable setup man if he lands in a situation where he is able to get lots of work and isn't limited to a specialist role.

Other New York Yankees

Erick Almonte (Pos: SS, Age: 26, Bats: R)

	G	AB	R	H	D	T	HR	RBI	SB	BB	SO	Avg	OBP	Slg
'03	31	100	17	26	6	0	1	11	1	8	24	.260	.321	.350
Car.	39	104	17	28	7	0	1	11	3	8	25	.269	.327	.365

Almonte was a budding prospect a few years ago, but playing in the high minors behind Derek Jeter has to play with his mind. He got to play when Jeter was hurt in April, but then it was back to Columbus. 2004 Outlook: C

Randy Choate (Pos: LHP, Age: 28)

	W	L	Pct.	ERA	G	GS	Sv	IP	H	BB	SO	HR	Avg
'03	0	0	–	7.36	5	0	0	3.2	7	1	0	0	.467
Car.	3	2	.600	4.43	82	0	0	91.1	73	51	64	4	.221

While Choate has fared reasonably well at Triple-A Columbus the last two seasons, he's done little in New York. He missed a key chance in 2003. He's been dealt to Montreal in the Javier Vazquez deal. 2004 Outlook: C

Roger Clemens (Pos: RHP, Age: 41)

W	L	Pct.	ERA	G	GS	Sv	IP	H	BB	SO	HR	Avg
17	9	.654	3.91	33	33	0	211.2	199	58	190	24	.247
310	160	.660	3.19	607	606	0	4278.2	3677	1379	4099	321	.231

Not many pitchers, not matter how old they are, retire after a 17-9 season. But the Rocket says he's retiring, and he departs with 310 wins and 4,099 strikeouts. Good bye, Roger. Hello, Hall of Fame. 2004 Outlook: D

John Flaherty (Pos: C, Age: 36, Bats: R)

	G	AB	R	H	D	T	HR	RBI	SB	BB	SO	Avg	OBP	Slg
'03	40	105	16	28	8	0	4	14	0	4	19	.267	.297	.457
Car.	953	3118	298	796	162	3	72	368	10	164	463	.255	.293	.378

Flaherty's playing time has been on the slide, and he signed to back up Jorge Posada last spring. Flaherty was productive in his limited at-bats, posting a career high in slugging. 2004 Outlook: C

Charles Gipson (Pos: CF, Age: 31, Bats: R)

	G	AB	R	H	D	T	HR	RBI	SB	BB	SO	Avg	OBP	Slg
'03	18	10	3	2	0	0	0	2	2	1	2	.200	.273	.200
Car.	349	306	75	72	14	7	0	29	14	29	67	.235	.311	.327

Gipson's defensive game and speed on the bases have allowed him to stick in the majors, but the Yankees sent him out after getting picked off three times in the first half, once to end a loss to the Cubs. 2004 Outlook: C

Felix Heredia (Pos: LHP, Age: 28)

	W	L	Pct.	ERA	G	GS	Sv	IP	H	BB	SO	HR	Avg
'03	5	3	.625	2.69	69	0	1	87.0	74	33	45	10	.228
Car.	27	18	.600	4.27	461	2	6	417.0	403	211	324	40	.253

The Yankees were rifling through relievers last season, trying to find someone to hold onto all year. One of the few who arrived and stayed is Heredia, who posted a 1.20 ERA in 12 games and was re-signed to a two-year, $3.8 million pact in December. 2004 Outlook: B

Michel Hernandez (Pos: C, Age: 25, Bats: R)

	G	AB	R	H	D	T	HR	RBI	SB	BB	SO	Avg	OBP	Slg
'03	5	4	0	1	0	0	0	0	0	1	1	.250	.400	.250
Car.	5	4	0	1	0	0	0	0	0	1	1	.250	.400	.250

Hernandez enjoyed a solid season at Triple-A Columbus, batting .280 with a .367 OBP. The Yankees rewarded him with his first callup to the Bronx. He's not really in the team's long-term plans, however. 2004 Outlook: C

Chris Latham (Pos: CF, Age: 30, Bats: B)

	G	AB	R	H	D	T	HR	RBI	SB	BB	SO	Avg	OBP	Slg
	4	2	3	2	0	0	0	0	1	0	0	1.000	1.000	1.000
	110	213	34	43	5	1	3	19	9	23	85	.202	.280	.277

With a surprising spring, Latham made the Yankees and enjoyed a perfect season until he was designated for assignment in late April. He signed with the Yomiuri Giants and played in Japan. 2004 Outlook: C

Curtis Pride (Pos: RF, Age: 35, Bats: L)

	G	AB	R	H	D	T	HR	RBI	SB	BB	SO	Avg	OBP	Slg
'03	4	12	1	1	0	0	1	1	0	0	2	.083	.083	.333
Car.	353	718	119	182	33	12	19	77	28	79	188	.253	.332	.412

Pride continues to put together solid Triple-A seasons, and in July he surfaced in the majors for the first time since 2001. He didn't show much in three weeks and he was gone in a New York minute. 2004 Outlook: C

Bret Prinz (Pos: RHP, Age: 26)

	W	L	Pct.	ERA	G	GS	Sv	IP	H	BB	SO	HR	Avg
'03	0	0	–	12.00	3	0	0	3.0	7	4	3	1	.438
Car.	4	3	.571	4.71	69	0	9	57.1	63	33	40	6	.283

It was a difficult season for Prinz, who tore a groin muscle pitching on Opening Day. He was dealt by Arizona to New York for Raul Mondesi days after coming off the disabled list in July, and struggled. 2004 Outlook: C

Al Reyes (Pos: RHP, Age: 33)

	W	L	Pct.	ERA	G	GS	Sv	IP	H	BB	SO	HR	Avg
'03	0	0	–	3.18	13	0	0	17.0	13	9	9	1	.203
Car.	15	8	.652	4.06	220	0	3	270.2	229	142	255	33	.229

Reyes was recalled in June, when the Yankees were trying to stabilize their bullpen. Reyes was solid in all but a couple of outings, but he was shipped out when Armando Benitez was acquired. 2004 Outlook: C

Fernando Seguignol (Pos: 1B, Age: 29, Bats: B)

	G	AB	R	H	D	T	HR	RBI	SB	BB	SO	Avg	OBP	Slg
'03	5	7	0	1	0	0	0	0	0	1	3	.143	.250	.143
Car.	178	366	42	91	23	0	17	40	0	20	114	.249	.303	.451

Seguignol enjoyed a terrific Triple-A season at Columbus, batting .341 and slugging .624 with 28 homers. He got the September call, marking his first appearance in the bigs since 2001 with the Expos. 2004 Outlook: C

Luis Sojo (Pos: 1B, Age: 38, Bats: R)

	G	AB	R	H	D	T	HR	RBI	SB	BB	SO	Avg	OBP	Slg
'03	3	4	0	0	0	0	0	0	0	0	0	.000	.000	.000
Car.	848	2571	300	671	103	12	36	261	28	124	198	.261	.297	.352

Sojo made a brief comeback in September after Derek Jeter suffered a ribcage injury and the Yankees needed an infielder. Sojo announced his retirement in October, but if the Yankees asked. . . 2004 Outlook: D

Bubba Trammell (Pos: DH, Age: 32, Bats: R)

	G	AB	R	H	D	T	HR	RBI	SB	BB	SO	Avg	OBP	Slg
'03	22	55	4	11	5	0	0	5	0	6	10	.200	.279	.291
Car.	584	1798	243	469	96	7	82	285	10	210	325	.261	.339	.459

A potentially valuable part timer because of his power, Trammell played little and left the team without warning in June. The Yanks put him on the restricted list and terminated his contract. 2004 Outlook: C

Enrique Wilson (Pos: SS/3B, Age: 30, Bats: B)

	G	AB	R	H	D	T	HR	RBI	SB	BB	SO	Avg	OBP	Slg
'03	63	135	18	31	9	0	3	15	3	7	14	.230	.276	.363
Car.	447	1144	135	289	62	5	16	110	13	71	148	.253	.296	.358

Wilson seems to have found a niche as a Yankee reserve who fills in all over the infield. It doesn't seem to matter if he hits much, as the Yanks keep signing him, which they did again in December. 2004 Outlook: C

New York Yankees Minor League Prospects

Organization Overview:

The Yankees' system isn't what it was a few years ago, as the club has been dealing prospects steadily to stay atop the American League East all these years. Just in the last two years the Yankees have parted with Nick Johnson, Juan Rivera, Brandon Claussen, Ted Lilly, Jason Arnold, John-Ford Griffin and a host of lesser prospects. If it weren't for the international signings of Jose Contreras and Hideki Matsui, the Yankees wouldn't have a Rookie of the Year candidate to talk about. There isn't one in 2004 as well, though New York could get some help from righthanders Jorge DePaula, Scott Proctor and Ramon Ramirez. With all of the free-agent signings to bolster the bullpen, only one of them might make the Opening Day roster.

Danny Borrell

Position: P **Opening Day Age:** 25
Bats: L **Throws:** L **Born:** 1/24/79 in
Ht: 6' 3" **Wt:** 200 Lansdale, PA

Recent Statistics

	W	L	ERA	G	GS	Sv	IP	H	R	BB	SO	HR
2002 A Tampa	4	1	2.33	7	6	0	38.2	33	11	10	44	0
2002 AA Norwich	9	4	2.31	21	20	0	128.1	116	44	39	91	5
2003 AAA Columbus	4	2	2.93	10	10	0	55.1	55	24	22	30	4

A second-rounder in 2000, Borrell was a slugging first baseman and outfielder at Wake Forest, so he was more raw as a pitcher. Still, he moved quickly through the system, calling on a 90-MPH fastball that he worked effectively on both sides of the plate and less-advanced secondary pitches. The only thing that slowed his progress was shoulder pain that shut him down during the second half of the 2001 season. Shoulder trouble surfaced again in 2003. He was diagnosed with a torn labrum in June and underwent season-ending surgery. Before he was hurt, he showed a solid curveball and an improving changeup, and Borrell was able to pitch backwards successfully. He is expected to be fully healthy soon after the 2004 season begins.

Jorge DePaula

Position: P **Opening Day Age:** 25
Bats: R **Throws:** R **Born:** 11/10/78 in
Ht: 6' 1" **Wt:** 160 Sabana Grande, DR

Recent Statistics

	W	L	ERA	G	GS	Sv	IP	H	R	BB	SO	HR
2003 AAA Columbus	10	11	4.35	27	27	0	167.2	168	90	57	125	22
2003 AL New York	0	0	0.79	4	1	0	11.1	3	1	1	7	1

DePaula was acquired for Triple-A reliever Craig Dingman in April 2001, because Colorado wanted a pitcher who was closer to the majors. That sounds more like DePaula now. The righthander had gone 29-12 in his first two seasons with Yankee affiliates before find-ing the going a bit rougher at Triple-A Columbus in 2003. He features deceptive arm action on a low-90s fastball, and he mixes in a changeup and slider. His advanced changeup was better than his slider last summer, but DePaula lacks a classic out pitch. The Yankees liked his poise during his major league stints last year, when he often had impressive command of his fastball. All the Yankees' free-agent signings have diminished his chances of making the team this spring.

Rudy Guillen

Position: OF **Opening Day Age:** 20
Bats: R **Throws:** R **Born:** 11/23/83 in Santo
Ht: 6' 3" **Wt:** 186 Domingo, DR

Recent Statistics

	G	AB	R	H	D	T	HR	RBI	SB	BB	SO	Avg
2002 R Yankees	59	219	38	67	7	2	3	35	7	14	39	.306
2003 A Battle Creek	133	493	64	128	29	4	13	79	13	32	87	.260

After being signed by the Yankees in 2000, Guillen created a buzz in the Rookie-level Gulf Coast League in 2002. He is a power prospect with impressive speed and five-tool potential, and he put that talent on display in his North American debut, batting .306 with a .351 OBP in rookie ball. Guillen's high ceiling could fall if he doesn't pick up some plate discipline. Despite above-average bat speed, he tends to swing a bit wild from time to time, sometimes chasing pitches early in the count. He's still very young and could develop the discipline he will need. Guillen played center field at Class-A Battle Creek in 2003, though he may take his terrific arm to right as he fills out.

Drew Henson

Position: 3B **Opening Day Age:** 24
Bats: R **Throws:** R **Born:** 2/13/80 in San
Ht: 6' 5" **Wt:** 220 Diego, CA

Recent Statistics

	G	AB	R	H	D	T	HR	RBI	SB	BB	SO	Avg
2003 AAA Columbus	133	483	60	113	40	2	14	78	8	32	122	.234
2003 AL New York	5	8	2	1	0	0	0	0	0	0	2	.125

Drafted in 1998, Henson flirted with a football career at Michigan, playing baseball part-time until he signed a six-year, $17 million contract in 2001. Playing half-seasons and then jumping straight to Triple-A Columbus as a full-time player hasn't gone well for Henson. While his power potential is evident in batting practice, he struggles with confidence in game situations and does-n't hit breaking balls and offspeed stuff effectively. He can be an easy target for Triple-A hurlers, who can take advantage of a swing that gets long and his lack of plate discipline. Defensively, he has a strong arm and he's better at third base. But his offensive troubles are cast-ing doubts about his future in baseball.

Dioner Navarro

Position: C **Opening Day Age:** 20
Bats: B **Throws:** R **Born:** 2/9/84 in Caracas, VZ
Ht: 5' 10" **Wt:** 189

Recent Statistics

	G	AB	R	H	D	T	HR	RBI	SB	BB	SO	Avg
2002 A Tampa	1	2	1	1	0	0	0	0	0	0	0	.500
2002 A Greensboro	92	328	41	78	12	2	8	36	1	39	61	.238
2003 A Tampa	52	197	28	59	16	4	3	28	1	17	27	.299
2003 AA Trenton	58	208	28	71	15	0	4	37	2	18	26	.341

Not many teenage catchers hit .341 in Double-A ball, as Navarro did in a half-season at Trenton. Minnesota's Joe Mauer also hit .341 in a half season at New Britain but he's a year older. That's not to say that Navarro is a better prospect, but he's a quick and agile receiver with a strong and accurate arm. A so-so success rate throwing out baserunners in 2003 suggests his defensive game still is a bit inconsistent. At the plate, Navarro is a switch-hitter with the tools to hit for average in the majors, and he may generate more power as he matures. He hits better from the left side and gets a bit pull-conscious from the right side. For someone so young, Navarro has decent strike-zone judgment.

Scott Proctor

Position: P **Opening Day Age:** 27
Bats: R **Throws:** R **Born:** 1/2/77 in Stuart, FL
Ht: 6' 1" **Wt:** 198

Recent Statistics

	W	L	ERA	G	GS	Sv	IP	H	R	BB	SO	HR
2002 AA Jacksnville	7	9	3.51	26	25	0	133.1	111	63	85	131	10
2003 AA Jacksnville	1	2	1.00	17	0	0	27.0	20	6	7	24	0
2003 AAA Las Vegas	4	2	3.66	24	0	1	39.1	35	17	13	35	2
2003 AAA Columbus	2	0	1.42	10	0	0	19.0	13	3	3	26	2

Acquired from the Dodgers in last July's Robin Ventura trade, Proctor worked near the 90-MPH mark as a starter. A move to the bullpen in 2003 pushed his velocity into the high 90s, and his strikeout-walk ratio also enjoyed a surge. His slider is a solid second pitch, and Proctor displays good mound presence and a confident demeanor, key ingredients to a successful reliever. When he keeps the ball down in the zone consistently, he is lights out. After a dominating stretch at Triple-A Columbus after the trade, Proctor will battle Jorge DePaula and Ramon Ramirez for the final spot on the Yankees' pitching staff.

Ramon Ramirez

Position: P **Opening Day Age:** 22
Bats: R **Throws:** R **Born:** 8/31/81 in Dominican Republic
Ht: 5' 11" **Wt:** 170

Recent Statistics

	W	L	ERA	G	GS	Sv	IP	H	R	BB	SO	HR
2003 A Tampa	2	8	5.21	14	14	0	74.1	88	47	20	70	7
2003 AA Trenton	1	1	1.69	4	3	0	21.1	18	8	8	21	3
2003 AAA Columbus	0	1	4.50	2	1	0	6.0	5	5	1	5	1

Ramirez comes to the Yankees via Japan, signed last March for $275,000. He's not a big man for a righty, and when he arrived, he had delivery issues and was more of a thrower than a pitcher. The Yankees say he made the kind of progress in 2003 that is rarely seen in a single season. Throwing a 92-95 MPH fastball with an average changeup and a slider that is his best pitch, Ramirez struggled early at high Class-A Tampa, but began to pitch well at Double-A Trenton when he was promoted because of an injury there. He continued to improve through a stint at Triple-A Columbus and opened eyes with his progress during the Arizona Fall League. Ramirez probably will start 2004 at Columbus.

Bronson Sardinha

Position: OF **Opening Day Age:** 20
Bats: L **Throws:** R **Born:** 4/6/83 in Kahuku, HI
Ht: 6' 0" **Wt:** 190

Recent Statistics

	G	AB	R	H	D	T	HR	RBI	SB	BB	SO	Avg
2002 A Greensboro	93	342	49	90	13	0	12	44	15	34	78	.263
2002 A Staten Island	36	124	25	40	8	0	4	16	4	24	36	.323
2003 A Tampa	59	212	23	41	8	2	1	17	8	24	57	.193
2003 A Battle Creek	71	269	54	74	16	0	8	41	5	40	40	.275

The third Sardinha to be drafted as a pro, Bronson was a first-round pick in 2001. At 18, he was a Rookie-level Gulf Coast League All-Star. Sardinha has a sweet left-handed swing and a good approach at the plate, so it's hard to explain why he's had to drop to a lower level than his original assignment the last two springs before hitting well at his second destination. After his 2003 demotion to Class-A Battle Creek, he went back to an old batting stance he had used for years and his season turned around. Drafted as a shortstop, Sardinha moved to the outfield last season and may be moved to third base this spring.

Others to Watch

Second baseman **Robinson Cano** (21) has a quick bat, power potential and an innate ability to adjust to pitches with his hands. While he makes hard contact, Cano hasn't learned to lift the ball yet. He may start the year at Double-A Trenton, and a move to third base is possible. . . . Third baseman **Eric Duncan** (19) was a top performer in the Rookie-level Gulf Coast League last season. He's a pure hitter who made consistent contact and drove the ball to all fields. He was even better after a jump to short-season Staten Island, where he batted .373 with 11 extra-base hits in 14 games. . . After a breakout season in 2002, second baseman **Andy Phillips** (26) was lost 17 games into 2003. An elbow injury led to season-ending surgery. Phillips enjoyed a .287-28-87 season in the high minors in 2002, and he'll be ready for Triple-A Columbus this spring. . . . Finger blisters put **Chien-Ming Wang** (24) on the disabled list twice in 2003, but those were minor compared to the shoulder surgery that sidelined him for 2001 and part of 2002. He jumped from short-season Staten Island to Double-A Trenton this year, a major challenge for Wang, who throws four solid-average pitches with very good command. He was 7-6 (4.65) at Trenton, calling on a low-90s fastball, splitter, slider and changeup.

Network Associates Coliseum

Offense

Oakland had the best home record in the American League. Consistently winning at home has been a way of life for the Athletics. The team's offense in 2003, though lighter than in the past, was productive at the Net. The ball carries better there since center field was enclosed, and when the weather gets warm, the homers can fly out in bunches.

Defense

With manicured grass and a lot of foul ground, speed is an important asset to team defense in Oakland. The park has wide gaps in the outfield. With few rainouts at the Net, the ball moves quickly along the turf, and defenders slow to react can pay the price. Playing there late in the summer requires sunglasses, especially on the right side of the field, as the sun is blinding from late afternoon through sunset.

Who It Helps the Most

Depending upon whether there is heat or fog, a flyball can be a long out or a cheap homer, so both pitchers and hitters can take advantage of conditions. All that foul ground, however, helps pitchers, as many a foul out at the Net would be a foul ball at almost every other park.

Who It Hurts the Most

Because of all the foul territory, a disciplined hitter who likes to foul off pitchers can find himself back on the bench—instead of readying for another chance—if he gets under a pitch. Flyball pitchers, especially nibblers, can get slaughtered on warm afternoons and evenings.

Rookies & Newcomers

Bobby Crosby will be under a microscope as the man slated to replace Miguel Tejada. Two solid defenders, Mark Kotsay and Bobby Kielty, join an outfield that didn't produce in 2003. If the Athletics still need a power boost, they may look to Graham Koonce, who enjoyed a .277-34-115 season at Triple-A Sacramento. Rich Harden, who may stick in the 2004 rotation, was more successful at the Net than on the road during his 2003 debut.

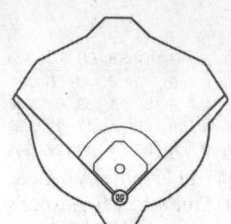

Dimensions: LF-330, LCF-362, CF-400, RCF-362, RF-330

Capacity: 43,662

Elevation: 25 feet

Surface: Grass

Foul Territory: Large

Park Factors

2003 Season

| | Home Games | | | Away Games | | | |
	Athletics	Opp	Total	Athletics	Opp	Total	Index
G	72	72	144	72	72	144	
Avg	.257	.226	.241	.253	.255	.254	95
AB	2378	2439	4817	2518	2366	4884	99
R	333	234	567	355	313	668	85
H	612	551	1163	636	604	1240	94
2B	141	112	253	141	106	247	104
3B	8	7	15	13	9	22	69
HR	75	57	132	84	57	141	95
BB	227	214	441	263	228	491	91
SO	380	472	852	416	434	850	102
E	36	55	91	57	38	95	96
E-Infield	33	47	80	46	34	80	100
LHB-Avg	.264	.224	.247	.252	.250	.251	98
LHB-HR	36	15	51	46	25	71	75
RHB-Avg	.251	.227	.237	.253	.258	.256	93
RHB-HR	39	42	81	38	32	70	114

2001-2003

| | Home Games | | | Away Games | | | |
	Athletics	Opp	Total	Athletics	Opp	Total	Index
G	216	216	432	216	216	432	
Avg	.259	.239	.249	.260	.261	.261	95
AB	7180	7448	14628	7628	7240	14868	98
R	1072	820	1892	1123	928	2051	92
H	1861	1779	3640	1985	1892	3877	94
2B	391	338	729	434	328	762	97
3B	30	25	55	36	37	73	77
HR	267	187	454	253	191	444	104
BB	817	594	1411	799	669	1468	98
SO	1265	1464	2729	1312	1341	2653	105
E	137	148	285	158	121	279	102
E-Infield	115	118	233	131	103	234	100
LHB-Avg	.272	.240	.258	.263	.256	.260	99
LHB-HR	143	62	205	141	79	220	97
RHB-Avg	.246	.238	.241	.257	.265	.261	92
RHB-HR	124	125	249	112	112	224	111

2003 Rankings (American League)

- Lowest run factor
- Lowest walk factor
- Second-lowest hit factor
- Second-lowest RHB batting-average factor
- Third-lowest LHB home-run factor

Ken Macha

Born: 9/29/50 in Monroeville, PA

Playing Experience: 1974-1981, Pit, Mon, Tor

Managerial Experience: 1 season

2003 Season

Sometimes you have to walk around the block to get to the house next door, which describes skipper Ken Macha's path to the helm of the Athletics. The team's former bench coach picked up where predecessor Art Howe left off, guiding his team to the postseason and first-round elimination. All in all, Macha did a remarkable job, making the best of less offense, going for defense and using his speed more than Howe. He also maintained an open door for his players, and personally conveyed changes and decisions to them before going public.

Offense

Macha successfully guided the Athletics despite not having a single outfielder who was a run producer. Macha did put his runners in motion a bit more often and tried more things at the plate than did Howe. Perhaps replacing hitting coach Thad Bosley with Dave Hudgens—Bosley's predecessor—suggests that Macha wanted a more mainstream approach to whacking the ball.

Pitching & Defense

With pitching coach Rick Peterson on hand to smooth the transition to the Macha administration, Oakland enjoyed another season of excellent pitching last year—pretty much by sticking with what has worked. The Athletics stress not giving away outs at the plate and in the field, and one thing that seriously improved under Macha was the team's defense. Ramon Hernandez emerged as an All-Star, Eric Chavez is a Gold Glover, and Miguel Tejada and Mark Ellis should be. With an improved Scott Hatteberg at first, Oakland arguably had the best defensive infield in the American League in 2003.

2004 Outlook

Macha will be under pressure to win an American League pennant soon. The Athletics need more production from their rebuilt outfield, and they need shortstop Bobby Crosby to play half as well as Miguel Tejada did in Oakland. Just based on the strength of its pitching, however, Oakland should stay a contender, even with the departure of Peterson to the Mets and Ted Lilly to Toronto.

Manager Statistics

Year	Team, Lg	W	L	Pct	GB	Finish
2003	Oakland, AL	96	66	.593	–	1st West
1 Season		96	66	.593	–	–

2003 Starting Pitchers by Days Rest

	<=3	4	5	6+
Athletics Starts	0	99	37	17
Athletics ERA	–	3.47	3.81	4.39
AL Avg Starts	2	79	50	22
AL ERA	3.19	4.64	4.57	4.98

2003 Situational Stats

	Ken Macha	AL Average
Hit & Run Success %	46.2	36.7
Stolen Base Success %	77.4	70.0
Platoon Pct.	56.7	61.7
Defensive Subs	17	23
High-Pitch Outings	4	5
Quick/Slow Hooks	20/11	19/16
Sacrifice Attempts	32	55

2003 Rankings (American League)

- 1st in stolen-base percentage and fewest caught stealings of second base (14)
- 2nd in 2+ pitching changes in low-scoring games (35)
- 3rd in hit-and-run success percentage, intentional walks (31) and saves with over 1 inning pitched (12)

Eric Chavez

2003 Season

Most ballplayers would be thrilled to have a season like the one Eric Chavez had in 2003, but for him it was no more than typical. He topped 100 RBI for the third consecutive season, and just missed belting 30 homers a third straight time as well. As in past years, Chavez surged over the second half. Even though he hit more homers before the break, his slugging mark was up almost 100 points over the second half, while his average and OBP increased by roughly 50 points.

Hitting

Blessed with quick hands and a developing eye, Chavez can hit for power, and he is moving in the direction of becoming a .300 hitter. As poor as his totals were against lefthanders in 2003, they still were an improvement over his 2002 numbers, when he batted just .209 against southpaws. It is notable that Chavez walked 62 times while striking out just 89 times, pushing that ratio to nearly one, a promising trend for a quality hitter.

Baserunning & Defense

A Gold Glove winner in 2001 and 2002, Chavez seemed even better last season, diving to his left and right, bare-handing balls and sliding on his knees into the dugout to grab pop fouls. He has a great arm, and if he can get close to the ball, he can pick it. He was awarded a third straight Gold Glove at season's end. On the basepaths, Chavez has very good speed and has become a smarter baserunner. He can swipe a bag, but the sign does not come often.

2004 Outlook

He has become a fixture at the hot corner in Oakland, although Chavez' contract runs only through this season. Could he be the next Oakland superstar to leave? It is interesting enough that it's a contract year for Chavez, but following three very similar seasons, he is poised to reach the next level. That could mean .300-30-100 or better.

Position: 3B
Bats: L **Throws:** R
Ht: 6' 1" **Wt:** 206

Opening Day Age: 26
Born: 12/7/77 in Los Angeles, CA
ML Seasons: 6
Pronunciation: shah-VEZ

Overall Statistics

	G	AB	R	H	D	T	HR	RBI	SB	BB	SO	Avg	OBP	Slg
'03	156	588	94	166	39	5	29	101	8	62	89	.282	.350	.514
Car.	744	2627	414	727	161	15	134	466	28	279	462	.277	.346	.502

Where He Hits the Ball

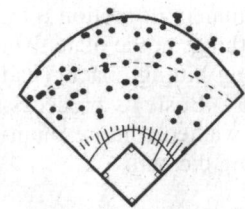
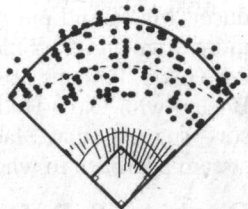

Vs. LHP   **Vs. RHP**

2003 Situational Stats

	AB	H	HR	RBI	Avg		AB	H	HR	RBI	Avg
Home	278	79	12	46	.284	LHP	191	42	9	29	.220
Road	310	87	17	55	.281	RHP	397	124	20	72	.312
First Half	323	83	17	50	.257	Sc Pos	141	42	3	62	.298
Scnd Half	265	83	12	51	.313	Clutch	81	20	3	10	.247

2003 Rankings (American League)

- 3rd in fielding percentage at third base (.971)
- Led the Athletics in batting average, home runs, total bases (302), caught stealing (3), GDPs (14), slugging percentage, HR frequency (20.3 ABs per HR), batting average vs. righthanded pitchers and batting average at home
- Led AL third basemen in home runs and RBI

Erubiel Durazo

2003 Season

After four seasons of having injuries and free-agent signings block his path to regular duty, Erubiel Durazo found his way to a full-time gig in Oakland. Since general manager Billy Beane had coveted the budding slugger for nearly all four of those years, the acquisition was considered a coup. Durazo responded by getting out of the blocks hot (.307-4-24 in April). After simmering down for four months, Durazo returned to form (.305-4-10 in September) as the Athletics pushed towards postseason play. Durazo did log a full season of play for the first time, after never totaling more than 222 at-bats in a season going into 2003.

Hitting

Durazo is a dangerous hitter with a good eye and serious power. In the past, facing southpaws had been a problem for him, but he was quite successful against them during his first year in the American League. Like many power hitters, he is streaky, and his on-base numbers both in clutch situations and with runners in scoring position have been good, though he walks more than hits in those situations.

Baserunning & Defense

Durazo is not much of a basestealer, but he has pretty good speed once he gets going and runs the bases very well. His defensive play isn't especially noteworthy, and Durazo was limited to DH duties in 2003, except when starter Scott Hatteberg was injured.

2004 Outlook

Durazo has a big year in his bat somewhere, and though his numbers fell short of both potential and extrapolated numbers from the past, he still had a pretty good first full season as a regular in 2003. Look for his totals to take a jump, especially his batting average and his output versus righthanders. If he can stay on track with the lefties, a monster year could be coming.

Position: DH/1B
Bats: L **Throws:** L
Ht: 6' 3" **Wt:** 240

Opening Day Age: 29
Born: 1/23/75 in Hermosillo, Mexico
ML Seasons: 5
Pronunciation: uh-ROO-bee-el du RAH zo

Overall Statistics

	G	AB	R	H	D	T	HR	RBI	SB	BB	SO	Avg	OBP	Slg
'03	154	537	92	139	29	0	21	77	1	100	105	.259	.374	.430
Car.	441	1285	238	347	67	4	68	226	3	237	300	.270	.383	.487

Where He Hits the Ball

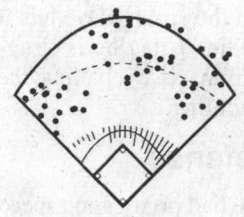 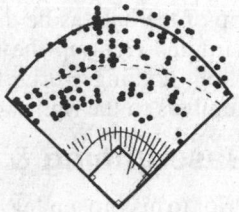

Vs. LHP   **Vs. RHP**

2003 Situational Stats

	AB	H	HR	RBI	Avg		AB	H	HR	RBI	Avg
Home	265	72	10	45	.272	LHP	173	49	7	27	.283
Road	272	67	11	32	.246	RHP	364	90	14	50	.247
First Half	304	84	10	46	.276	Sc Pos	119	35	2	49	.294
Scnd Half	233	55	11	31	.236	Clutch	80	26	5	15	.325

2003 Rankings (American League)

- 3rd in walks
- 5th in intentional walks (12) and lowest cleanup slugging percentage (.406)
- 6th in lowest batting average vs. righthanded pitchers
- 7th in errors at first base (6)
- 10th in most pitches seen per plate appearance (3.99)
- Led the Athletics in walks, intentional walks (12), times on base (241), strikeouts and on-base percentage

Jermaine Dye

2003 Season

As Jermaine Dye finished off his .252-24-86 season in 2002, it looked like the nasty broken leg he endured during the 2001 playoffs was history. The 2003 results were, needless to say, off the charts, only in the wrong direction. He tore cartilage in his right knee in late April, and later in the season Dye slammed into Bengie Molina and separated his shoulder. It was that kind of year.

Hitting

Dye's stats took such a dive in 2003 that it is hard to find a specific source of failure. His history as a free swinger probably didn't help as he struggled through the season. He has excellent power to the deep parts of the park, and when he gets on top of the ball, as he did in the spring, Dye hits it hard and right up the middle. When he is struggling, nothing works for him, as eyeballing the numbers to the right will confirm.

Baserunning & Defense

Prior to his broken leg, Dye had pretty good speed and could have nabbed double digits in swipes. Oakland, though, has not been a team to put runners in motion, and the injury has made him more tentative on the bases. In the field he has a very good glove, and even if he has lost a step, Dye gets a good jump. His arm is tremendous, and baserunners and opposing coaches know it.

2004 Outlook

With a promising career mired in questions at age 30, Dye needs to make an about face in 2004. With two years and a little more than $20 million remaining on his contract, the Athletics are looking for more production. General manager Billy Beane was looking to swap some salary, and he managed that by dealing Ted Lilly and Terrence Long. With Dye making $11 million a year, moving him as well could be difficult. If he stays and plays in Oakland's rebuilt outfield, Dye should rebound and be better than last year, but the big questions are how much better and for how long.

Position: RF
Bats: R **Throws:** R
Ht: 6' 5" **Wt:** 220

Opening Day Age: 30
Born: 1/28/74 in Vacaville, CA
ML Seasons: 8
Pronunciation: ger-MAIN

Overall Statistics

	G	AB	R	H	D	T	HR	RBI	SB	BB	SO	Avg	OBP	Slg
'03	65	221	28	38	6	0	4	20	1	25	42	.172	.261	.253
Car.	902	3286	478	896	184	13	138	531	19	297	644	.273	.335	.463

Where He Hits the Ball

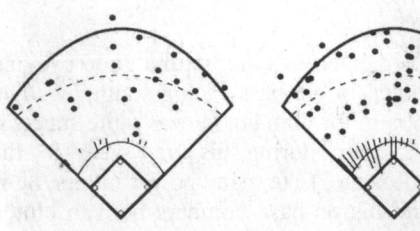

Vs. LHP   **Vs. RHP**

2003 Situational Stats

	AB	H	HR	RBI	Avg		AB	H	HR	RBI	Avg
Home	118	24	3	12	.203	LHP	50	13	2	5	.260
Road	103	14	1	8	.136	RHP	171	25	2	15	.146
First Half	150	24	2	12	.160	Sc Pos	56	10	0	15	.179
Scnd Half	71	14	2	8	.197	Clutch	35	8	1	5	.229

2003 Rankings (American League)

- 6th in most GDPs per GDP situation (19.3%)

Mark Ellis

2003 Season

A surprise in 2002, Mark Ellis developed into an excellent second basemen in 2003. Though his offensive totals were not spectacular, they were steady as he logged a first full season in the big leagues. Ellis also hit in just about every spot in the order, and though most of his at-bats were at leadoff, he never really settled into a role. Ellis did become part of one of the better double-play combos in baseball.

Hitting

Ellis has succeeded using the plate selectivity that the Athletics prefer. After tearing through the Royals' chain at Class-A Wilmington and Double-A Wichita in 2000, he found himself an Athletic playing at Triple-A Sacramento in 2001. He improved his bat speed enough in 2002 to merit the promotion to Oakland. It took Ellis a year to get the hang of Triple-A Pacific Coast League pitching, and it likely will take him at least that long to adjust to the majors. He does have good gap power. Plus, he can bunt, hit behind a runner or surprise with a homer.

Baserunning & Defense

Ellis has excellent speed and had stolen more than 20 bases in each of his three minor league seasons. Even though Oakland played more small ball under Ken Macha than Art Howe, it is unlikely that Ellis will steal 20 bases with Oakland. Still, he does have speed and runs the bases well. In the field, the converted shortstop was a regular highlight film of backward ball flips to Miguel Tejada and diving stops into the hole. He is a Gold Glover in the making.

2004 Outlook

Ellis will be relied upon to help stabilize Bobby Crosby, Oakland's heir apparent at shortstop, while helping out atop the order. He bounced around the batting order last season—and might fare similarly in 2004—but expect Ellis to improve his numbers, particularly his on-base percentage and OPS.

Position: 2B
Bats: R **Throws:** R
Ht: 5'11" **Wt:** 180

Opening Day Age: 26
Born: 6/6/77 in Rapid City, SD
ML Seasons: 2

Overall Statistics

	G	AB	R	H	D	T	HR	RBI	SB	BB	SO	Avg	OBP	Slg
'03	154	553	78	137	31	5	9	52	6	48	94	.248	.313	.371
Car.	252	898	136	231	47	9	15	87	10	92	148	.257	.331	.380

Where He Hits the Ball

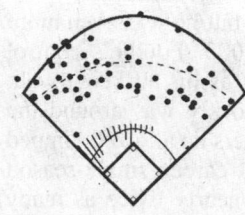 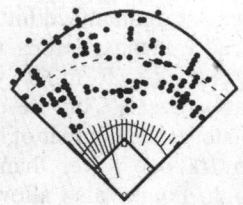

Vs. LHP   **Vs. RHP**

2003 Situational Stats

	AB	H	HR	RBI	Avg		AB	H	HR	RBI	Avg
Home	269	71	7	32	.264	LHP	152	33	2	13	.217
Road	284	66	2	20	.232	RHP	401	104	7	39	.259
First Half	309	79	5	26	.256	Sc Pos	112	32	2	40	.286
Scnd Half	244	58	4	26	.238	Clutch	78	25	2	11	.321

2003 Rankings (American League)

- 3rd in lowest percentage of swings on the first pitch (9.1)
- 4th in errors at second base (14)
- 5th in fielding percentage at second base (.982)
- 6th in lowest batting average on the road
- Led the Athletics in sacrifice bunts (9), most pitches seen per plate appearance (4.07) and bunts in play (12)

Oakland

219

Keith Foulke

2003 Season

Secure in knowing he not only would be the Oakland closer on Opening Day, but that in all likelihood he would stay in that role all season, Keith Foulke settled into his job in the spring and enjoyed his best season. Notching career highs in saves and ERA, and tying his best in appearances, Foulke did play vulture to Tim Hudson, earning five of his nine victories when Hudson took the ball.

Pitching

As a closer, it works for Foulke to rely on a good low-90s fastball and an even better changeup to get hitters out, as he rarely faces more than six hitters in an appearance. He generally is solid against righthanded hitters, but he was even more deadly against lefties in 2003. Foulke's control was back to form last year, as his strikeout-walk ratio reveals. And he obviously was around the plate, as the number of homers he allowed jumped to 10, one fewer than his career single-season high. Foulke also allowed nearly twice as many flyballs as groundballs, a decided change in his stats, so maybe the homers make sense.

Defense

Foulke picks his position well, and last year completed a fourth straight season without committing a miscue (that's 281 regular-season games, folks). He also participated in one double play. He doesn't hold runners particularly well, as nine of 12 would-be basestealers were successful in 2003.

2004 Outlook

Oakland must dig into its pocketbook to see if the money is there to retain Foulke's services. Foulke made $6 million in 2003, and that might be too much for the Oakland front office. He will make a nice addition to some bullpen, and again, if used appropriately as he was last year, will be among the top closers in baseball.

Position: RP
Bats: R **Throws:** R
Ht: 6' 0" **Wt:** 210

Opening Day Age: 31
Born: 10/19/72 in Ellsworth AFB, SD
ML Seasons: 7
Pronunciation: FOLK

Overall Statistics

	W	L	Pct.	ERA	G	GS	Sv	IP	H	BB	SO	HR	Avg
'03	9	1	.900	2.08	72	0	43	86.2	57	20	88	10	.184
Car.	28	25	.528	3.16	429	8	143	577.1	456	141	546	62	.215

2003 Pitching Profile

	Keith Foulke	AL Average
Overall Strike %	67.2	62.8
1st Pitch Strike %	66.1	58.7
Ratio	0.89	1.39
Strikeouts per 9 IP	9.14	6.11
Walks per 9 IP	2.08	3.16
Home Runs per 9 IP	1.04	1.11
Strikeout/Walk Ratio	4.40	1.93
Groundball/Flyball Ratio	0.50	1.18

2003 Situational Stats

	W	L	ERA	Sv	IP		AB	H	HR	RBI	Avg
Home	7	0	2.26	23	51.2	LHB	152	24	5	12	.158
Road	2	1	1.80	20	35.0	RHB	157	33	5	13	.210
First Half	7	1	2.68	24	50.1	Sc Pos	70	12	2	17	.171
Scnd Half	2	0	1.24	19	36.1	Clutch	220	39	7	20	.177

2003 Rankings (American League)

- 1st in saves, games finished (67) and relief wins (9)
- 2nd in lowest batting average allowed vs. lefthanded batters, save percentage (89.6) and fewest baserunners allowed per nine innings in relief (8.7)
- 3rd in relief innings (86.2)
- 9th in games pitched
- Led the Athletics in games pitched, saves, games finished (67), winning percentage, lowest batting average allowed vs. lefthanded batters, save percentage (89.6), first batter efficiency (.190), blown saves (5), relief ERA (2.08), relief wins (9), relief innings (86.2), lowest batting average allowed in relief (.184), fewest baserunners allowed per nine innings in relief (8.7) and most strikeouts per nine innings in relief (9.1)

Scott Hatteberg

2003 Season

In some ways, 2003 was a banner year for Scott Hatteberg. Firmly established as the starting first sacker in Oakland, he enjoyed career highs in games played, at-bats and runs. On the down side, his on-base and slugging numbers dipped significantly, and even though Hatteberg collected 54 more plate appearances last year over 2002, his RBI, hit and homer totals were just about the same.

Hitting

Hatteberg generally is patient, and he puts the ball in play up the middle of the field. He tends to hang in there against lefties, but last year Hatteberg hit righthanders with more power. He does hit well with runners in scoring position, as long as there are less than two outs. Hatteberg has a quick and often explosive bat, though, and is more than capable of delivering a walkoff homer.

Baserunning & Defense

A major leaguer since 1995, Hatteberg only appeared as a catcher until 2000, when he played one game at third. It wasn't until 2002 that he played his first big league game at first. That said, his defensive play has become a revelation, as he is reactive and aware when playing his spot. Hatteberg can pick and scoop with the best of them, and chances are he will improve. As a former backstop, speed never was part of his game; he has just one swipe over those nine seasons. Just as Hatteberg is a smart defensive player, he is equally alert and effective on the basepaths.

2004 Outlook

Hatteberg signed a two-year extension last year, which could keep him in Oakland through 2006, given the right set of circumstances. Naturally, the Athletics will look to him to better pace himself over 500 at-bats in 2004, and perhaps will even rest him on a more regular basis to keep him fresh. His defense will continue to flourish over that time, so all he needs to do is regulate the stick a little better.

Position: 1B/DH
Bats: L **Throws:** R
Ht: 6' 1" **Wt:** 210

Opening Day Age: 34
Born: 12/14/69 in Salem, OR
ML Seasons: 9
Pronunciation: HATT ch borg

Overall Statistics

	G	AB	R	H	D	T	HR	RBI	SB	BB	SO	Avg	OBP	Slg
'03	147	541	63	137	34	0	12	61	0	66	53	.253	.342	.383
Car.	737	2343	284	625	142	6	61	281	1	309	318	.267	.357	.411

Where He Hits the Ball

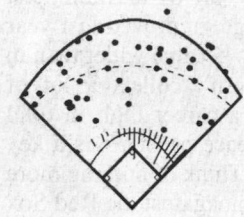 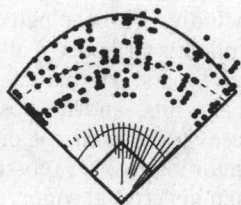

Vs. LHP   **Vs. RHP**

2003 Situational Stats

	AB	H	HR	RBI	Avg		AB	H	HR	RBI	Avg
Home	276	68	6	29	.246	LHP	149	38	2	15	.255
Road	265	69	6	32	.260	RHP	392	99	10	46	.253
First Half	324	84	7	42	.259	Sc Pos	126	39	3	44	.310
Scnd Half	217	53	5	19	.244	Clutch	83	30	3	23	.361

2003 Rankings (American League)

- 1st in highest percentage of pitches taken (67.1), highest percentage of swings put into play (60.5) and lowest percentage of swings on the first pitch (6.3)
- 3rd in lowest percentage of swings that missed (8.8), errors at first base (10) and lowest fielding percentage at first base (.992)
- Led the Athletics in GDPs (14), highest groundball-flyball ratio (1.3), highest percentage of pitches taken (67.1), lowest percentage of swings that missed (8.8), highest percentage of swings put into play (60.5), batting average with runners in scoring position, batting average in the clutch and lowest percentage of swings on the first pitch (6.3)

Ramon Hernandez

2003 Season

Ramon Hernandez raised some eyebrows when he earned the starting catcher job as a 23-year-old. That was four years ago, and following a disappointing 2002 season, offensive expectations for him dropped in 2003. Then Hernandez pulled off the big surprise, as he seemed to mature, right before our eyes, in every aspect of his game. He logged career highs in power numbers, played solid defense and directed the best pitching staff around to an American League West crown.

Hitting

Perhaps lowered expectations allowed Hernandez to relax a little more at the plate. Surely he hit the ball harder. Oddly, though, all of his numbers, including on-base percentage, improved last year while his strikeout-walk gap became wider than in past years. Hernandez doesn't collect a lot of cheap hits, and he posted a career high in total bases last summer. Confidence probably is a key factor in his 2003 rebound. Think of nothing more than his critical squeeze bunt against the Red Sox during the Division Series, a play brilliantly conceived and executed.

Baserunning & Defense

Hernandez is not going to win any land speed competitions, but he is a smart player who pays attention. As a result, he gets the job done on the bases. He threw out the fifth-most runners in the league last year (23), and handled the second-most chances of his career while committing just eight errors. Defensively, Hernandez has really stepped into his role, coaxing big pitches out of the Athletics' starters.

2004 Outlook

Hernandez goes into the third year of a four-year deal in 2004, but he'll complete the contract in San Diego. He was dealt with Terrence Long to the Padres for outfielder Mark Kotsay. San Diego gets the catcher it needs, and with Hernandez just approaching his prime, he could be a fixture there for years. He also could play a key role in developing the collection of young hurlers coming on the scene.

Position: C
Bats: R **Throws:** R
Ht: 6' 0" **Wt:** 210

Opening Day Age: 27
Born: 5/20/76 in Caracas, VZ
ML Seasons: 5
Pronunciation: ruh-MOWN

Overall Statistics

	G	AB	R	H	D	T	HR	RBI	SB	BB	SO	Avg	OBP	Slg
'03	140	483	70	132	24	1	21	78	0	33	79	.273	.331	.458
Car.	595	1894	241	480	95	1	60	263	3	169	286	.253	.322	.400

Where He Hits the Ball

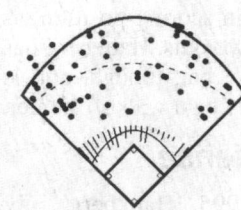
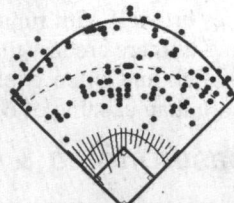

Vs. LHP   **Vs. RHP**

2003 Situational Stats

	AB	H	HR	RBI	Avg		AB	H	HR	RBI	Avg
Home	233	62	9	33	.266	LHP	149	31	6	13	.208
Road	250	70	12	45	.280	RHP	334	101	15	65	.302
First Half	275	72	11	40	.262	Sc Pos	128	34	6	57	.266
Scnd Half	208	60	10	38	.288	Clutch	81	20	2	16	.247

2003 Rankings (American League)

- 3rd in lowest percentage of runners caught stealing as a catcher (24.0)
- 4th in errors at catcher (8)
- 5th in lowest batting average vs. lefthanded pitchers
- Led the Athletics in hit by pitch (12), GDPs (14) and batting average with two strikes (.230)

Tim Hudson

2003 Season

Though Tim Hudson's won-lost mark might not show it, 2003 was his best season as a major league pitcher. He registered his lowest single-season ERA and posted a career high in innings, while holding hitters to a miniscule .223 average. But on April 22, off to a 2-1 start, Hudson absorbed a no-decision in a game that saw Oakland defeat Detroit, igniting a stretch through June 10 in which the righthander didn't get a decision in six of 10 starts. With just a little luck, a 20-win season would have capped his 2003 campaign.

Pitching

Hudson's focus on the mound is nearing legendary, as he brings his grit, along with a fastball that hits 92 MPH, and a great splitter. He basically has his way with hitters. Hudson also works a change and slider into the mix, but it is that splitter that makes the other pitches work so well, along with a consistent delivery that does not allow hitters to gauge a pitch upon release. Even so, Hudson just will not give in.

Defense

A serious groundball pitcher (with a 2.26 groundball-flyball ratio last season), Hudson handled 76 balls and made only two errors in 2003. He is quick to respond and usually makes the play. He has become very good at holding runners over the past two years, allowing just seven steals, and nailing another six would-be thieves in 2003.

2004 Outlook

With Hudson signed through the 2004 season, Oakland exercised its 2005 option on him as well—a smart move keeping one of the game's best starters in tow. As he is just entering his prime, Hudson should have a number of chances to win 20 games and make a run at a Cy Young trophy.

Position: SP
Bats: R **Throws:** R
Ht: 6' 1" **Wt:** 164

Opening Day Age: 28
Born: 7/14/75 in Columbus, GA
ML Seasons: 5

Overall Statistics

	W	L	Pct.	ERA	G	GS	Sv	IP	H	BB	SO	HR	Avg
'03	16	7	.696	2.70	34	34	0	240.0	197	61	162	15	.223
Car.	80	33	.708	3.26	156	156	0	1052.0	940	338	796	86	.239

2003 Pitching Profile

	Tim Hudson	AL Average
Overall Strike %	64.7	62.8
1st Pitch Strike %	60.3	58.7
Ratio	1.08	1.39
Strikeouts per 9 IP	6.08	6.11
Walks per 9 IP	2.29	3.16
Home Runs per 9 IP	0.56	1.11
Strikeout/Walk Ratio	2.66	1.93
Groundball/Flyball Ratio	2.26	1.18

2003 Situational Stats

	W	L	ERA	Sv	IP		AB	H	HR	RBI	Avg
Home	9	3	2.32	0	147.1	LHB	524	120	9	45	.229
Road	7	4	3.30	0	92.2	RHB	359	77	6	31	.214
First Half	7	3	2.71	0	143.0	Sc Pos	172	43	4	58	.250
Scnd Half	9	4	2.69	0	97.0	Clutch	85	19	2	7	.224

2003 Rankings (American League)

- 1st in shutouts (2) and lowest slugging percentage allowed (.308)
- 2nd in ERA and fewest home runs allowed per nine innings (.56)
- 3rd in innings pitched, lowest batting average allowed (.223), highest groundball-flyball ratio allowed (2.3) and lowest ERA at home
- 4th in batters faced (967), lowest on-base percentage allowed (.280) and lowest batting average allowed vs. righthanded batters
- Led the Athletics in ERA, wins, innings pitched, hits allowed, batters faced (967), hit batsmen (10), strikeouts, GDPs induced (23), lowest on-base percentage allowed (.280), highest groundball-flyball ratio allowed (2.3), lowest ERA on the road, most run support per nine innings (5.7), lowest batting average allowed with runners in scoring position and fewest home runs allowed per nine innings (.56)

Oakland

223

Terrence Long

Traded To PADRES

2003 Season

Terrence Long came out of the blocks hot, hitting five homers, scoring 15 runs and driving in 15 during April. He cooled off soon after, saw his consecutive-games streak end at 457 and registered a significant drop in production in numerous offensive categories. Perhaps the early-June departure of hitting coach Thad Bosley preyed upon the outfielder, who endured a disappointing season.

Hitting

The Athletics have been waiting for Long to develop into the hitter they hoped for when they traded for him in 1999. Unfortunately, he has struggled against righthanded pitchers, who have been far more successful against Long the last two seasons. He does have good power, especially to the gaps, but he also has a big swing and gets caught on his heels too often.

Baserunning & Defense

Long has very good speed, but like many of his teammates last season, he didn't get on base enough in crucial situations to be able to use it to much of an advantage. He did improve his stolen-base success rate to 80 percent in 2003, but he attempted just five steals. Long's defense did improve some with him playing mostly left field, but he still had four total errors, a lot for a part-time outfielder.

2004 Outlook

At season's end, Long ripped the communication skills of first-year manager Ken Macha, just a couple of weeks after he had complained about his playing time to the media. His ticket out of town came swiftly, as Long was dealt to San Diego, along with catcher Ramon Hernandez, in exchange for outfielder Mark Kotsay. Rumors were flying that the Padres might move Long elsewhere, but what is certain is that he will get another chance to follow through on all that promise.

Position: LF/RF
Bats: L **Throws:** L
Ht: 6' 1" **Wt:** 202

Opening Day Age: 28
Born: 2/29/76 in Montgomery, AL
ML Seasons: 5

Overall Statistics

	G	AB	R	H	D	T	HR	RBI	SB	BB	SO	Avg	OBP	Slg
'03	140	486	64	119	22	2	14	61	4	31	67	.245	.293	.385
Car.	605	2289	329	606	125	14	60	293	21	174	345	.265	.317	.410

Where He Hits the Ball

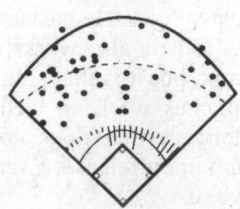 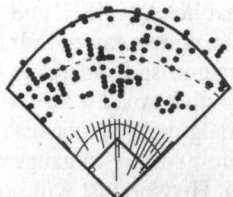

Vs. LHP   **Vs. RHP**

2003 Situational Stats

	AB	H	HR	RBI	Avg		AB	H	HR	RBI	Avg
Home	224	62	8	33	.277	LHP	140	33	2	16	.236
Road	262	57	6	28	.218	RHP	346	86	12	45	.249
First Half	291	73	10	39	.251	Sc Pos	113	33	3	41	.292
Scnd Half	195	46	4	22	.236	Clutch	91	24	2	11	.264

2003 Rankings (American League)

- 4th in lowest on-base percentage and lowest batting average on the road
- 5th in errors in right field (4)
- 7th in lowest batting average
- 8th in lowest percentage of swings on the first pitch (14.9)

Mark Mulder

2003 Season

For a second consecutive year, Mark Mulder had a terrific season interrupted by injury. In 2003, however, the impact on both Mulder and the Athletics was greater than a year earlier. The Athletics did finish the season with a division title, but the ride would have been easier for them had Mulder not spent the final six weeks on the disabled list with a stress fracture of the hip. Even so, Mulder had stellar totals. He would have been a likely 20-game winner and Cy Young Award candidate if he hadn't been hurt.

Pitching

As stylish a hurler as there is, Mulder pretty much can dominate any lineup when he is on, with an assortment that includes a moving low-90s fastball, slider, curve and changeup. Mulder is a master at disguising his delivery, so hitters usually don't know what pitch is on the way until it is too late. Add in his 6-foot-6 frame, and it is easy to see why he can be so overpowering. He has been injury-prone the last couple of seasons, but he bounces back well. Despite missing seven or so starts, Mulder still logged an impressive number of innings last year.

Defense

Mulder does everything with style, and fielding his position is just one of many things at which he excels. Primarily a groundball pitcher, Mulder has handled 91 chances successfully over the past two years without an error. He holds runners well, too, as half of the 20 potential basestealers were cut down trying to swipe a bag in 2003.

2004 Outlook

Mulder should be back in the fold come February, healthy and ready to take his spot alongside Tim Hudson and Barry Zito as one of the best starting trios in baseball. Word was that Mulder could have pitched in relief during the playoffs had Oakland made it another round, so he should be raring to go, in potential Cy Young form, when camp opens.

Position: SP
Bats: L **Throws:** L
Ht: 6' 6" **Wt:** 208

Opening Day Age: 26
Born: 8/5/77 in South Holland, IL
ML Seasons: 4

Overall Statistics

	W	L	Pct.	ERA	G	GS	Sv	IP	H	BB	SO	HR	Avg
'03	15	9	.625	3.13	26	26	0	186.2	180	40	128	15	.259
Car.	64	34	.653	3.77	117	117	0	777.1	767	215	528	74	.259

2003 Pitching Profile

	Mark Mulder	AL Average
Overall Strike %	64.4	62.8
1st Pitch Strike %	59.3	58.7
Ratio	1.18	1.39
Strikeouts per 9 IP	6.17	6.11
Walks per 9 IP	1.93	3.16
Home Runs per 9 IP	0.72	1.11
Strikeout/Walk Ratio	3.20	1.93
Groundball/Flyball Ratio	2.01	1.18

2003 Situational Stats

	W	L	ERA	Sv	IP		AB	H	HR	RBI	Avg
Home	10	2	2.18	0	103.0	LHB	119	30	3	7	.252
Road	5	7	4.30	0	83.2	RHB	577	150	12	57	.260
First Half	12	6	3.03	0	139.2	Sc Pos	151	40	3	48	.265
Scnd Half	3	3	3.45	0	47.0	Clutch	68	11	0	2	.162

2003 Rankings (American League)

- 1st in complete games (9), shutouts (2) and fielding percentage at pitcher (1.000)
- 2nd in runners caught stealing (10) and lowest ERA at home
- 3rd in fewest pitches thrown per batter (3.51)
- 4th in ERA, highest groundball-flyball ratio allowed (2.0) and fewest home runs allowed per nine innings (.72)
- 5th in fewest walks per nine innings (1.9)
- 9th in highest strikeout-walk ratio (3.2), lowest slugging percentage allowed (.386), lowest on-base percentage allowed (.300) and least run support per nine innings (4.7)
- Led the Athletics in complete games (9), shutouts (2), wild pitches (7), runners caught stealing (10), highest strikeout-walk ratio (3.2), lowest stolen-base percentage allowed (50.0), lowest ERA at home and fewest walks per nine innings (1.9)

Miguel Tejada

2003 Season

The American League's reigning MVP, Miguel Tejada, came to spring training under the contract cloud. Would the Athletics retain Tejada's pricey services, or sadly cut him loose, a la Jason Giambi? It quickly was determined that Tejada would not be in Oakland in 2004. That might have been a distraction in April, when he hit .161-4-13, but he turned it on after that, going .303-23-93 from May on, surging during the second half and completing his fourth straight 100-plus RBI season.

Hitting

On the surface it looks like Tejada's offensive numbers hit the skids in 2003, but in truth there are indicators that he may be able to move to yet a little higher offensive level than what he showed during his MVP year. He does have good power to all fields, has learned to shorten his swing in pressure situations and continues to hit well with runners on base. Tejada reduced his strikeouts to a career-low 65 in 2003, while walking a few more times. That suggests he was a lot more patient than his final on-base numbers might reflect.

Baserunning & Defense

Tejada has excellent speed, which benefits all aspects of his game. His savvy on the bases improved last year, and he was a perfect 10-for-10 in stolen bases. In the field, Tejada was nothing short of acrobatic, and with Eric Chavez, comprised what arguably was the best defensive left side in all of baseball.

2004 Outlook

It will be hard to see Tejada suit up with a club other than the Athletics, as they have had a relationship with him since he was a teenager. But that seems the likely course, and he probably will sign the lucrative deal that befits an MVP shortstop in his prime. It should not matter where he plays: Tejada will continue to perform and improve.

Position: SS
Bats: R **Throws:** R
Ht: 5' 9" **Wt:** 200

Opening Day Age: 27
Born: 5/25/76 in Bani, DR
ML Seasons: 7
Pronunciation: mee-GHEL tay-HA-duh

Overall Statistics

	G	AB	R	H	D	T	HR	RBI	SB	BB	SO	Avg	OBP	Slg
'03	162	636	98	177	42	0	27	106	10	53	65	.278	.336	.472
Car.	936	3584	574	968	191	11	156	604	49	287	542	.270	.331	.460

Where He Hits the Ball

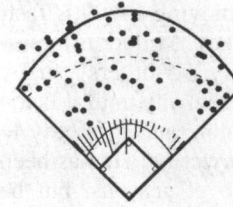 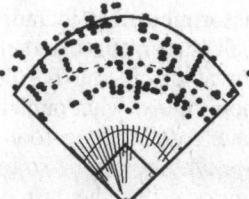

Vs. LHP   **Vs. RHP**

2003 Situational Stats

	AB	H	HR	RBI	Avg		AB	H	HR	RBI	Avg
Home	316	80	15	54	.253	LHP	167	45	8	25	.269
Road	320	97	12	52	.303	RHP	469	132	19	81	.281
First Half	375	92	15	56	.245	Sc Pos	153	44	9	78	.288
Scnd Half	261	85	12	50	.326	Clutch	87	19	2	9	.218

2003 Rankings (American League)

- 2nd in games played and errors at shortstop (21)
- 4th in lowest percentage of swings on the first pitch (10.2)
- 5th in cleanup slugging percentage (.544) and fielding percentage at shortstop (.972)
- Led the Athletics in at-bats, runs scored, hits, singles, doubles, RBI, sacrifice flies (8), stolen bases, pitches seen (2,695), plate appearances (703), games played, steals of third (4), cleanup slugging percentage (.544), and batting average on the road

Barry Zito

2003 Season

It would be easy to dismiss Barry Zito, looking at his 2003 totals on the heels of his Cy Young season in 2002. His ERA was up and his won-lost totals skewed. Yet, Zito pitched nearly the same number of innings each year, and allowed about the same number of hits and walks in both. Opposing hitters batted about the same, and Zito actually coughed up five more homers in 2002. So, other than the drop in strikeouts, what happened? Zito seemed to think too much, and that pulled him out of his game some of the time. He still got it back enough that most hurlers would be happy with his results.

Pitching

Oh, that wonderful curve that Zito can drop across the plate, freezing hitters in their place. Zito uses the curve, along with a high-80s fastball and a very good change, to totally confuse the opposition. When he is on, which is most of the time, he pretty much can put all three offerings anywhere he wants, anytime he wants. When he can't, the opposition still doesn't cash in very often.

Defense

The key to Zito's game is being in the moment, and when he succeeds, he is as ever present with his glove as he is on the mound. He reduced his number of errors to just one in 2003, two less than in 2002. Zito did lose ground on holding runners, though, as 13 of 20 basestealers were successful running against him.

2004 Outlook

Though 2003 hardly was an aberration, it was a good learning experience for Zito, who is just 25 and has posted some pretty solid numbers. What he learned was to go back to the basics that earned him the Cy Young Award in 2002. Watch the numbers get better in 2004 because of last year's lessons.

Position: SP
Bats: L **Throws:** L
Ht: 6' 4" **Wt:** 215

Opening Day Age: 25
Born: 5/13/78 in Las Vegas, NV
ML Seasons: 4
Pronunciation: ZEE-toe

Overall Statistics

	W	L	Pct.	ERA	G	GS	Sv	IP	H	BB	SO	HR	Avg
'03	14	12	.538	3.30	35	35	0	231.2	186	88	146	19	.219
Car.	61	29	.678	3.12	119	119	0	768.0	616	291	611	67	.219

2003 Pitching Profile

	Barry Zito	AL Average
Overall Strike %	60.9	62.8
1st Pitch Strike %	53.1	58.7
Ratio	1.18	1.39
Strikeouts per 9 IP	5.67	6.11
Walks per 9 IP	3.42	3.16
Home Runs per 9 IP	0.74	1.11
Strikeout/Walk Ratio	1.66	1.93
Groundball/Flyball Ratio	0.89	1.18

2003 Situational Stats

	W	L	ERA	Sv	IP		AB	H	HR	RBI	Avg
Home	7	5	3.03	0	98.0	LHB	197	44	5	29	.223
Road	7	7	3.50	0	133.2	RHB	652	142	14	62	.218
First Half	8	6	3.28	0	134.1	Sc Pos	160	46	5	70	.288
Scnd Half	6	6	3.33	0	97.1	Clutch	70	19	1	7	.271

2003 Rankings (American League)

- 1st in pitches thrown (3,747)
- 2nd in games started, walks allowed and lowest batting average allowed (.219)
- 3rd in lowest slugging percentage allowed (.324) and most pitches thrown per batter (3.92)
- 4th in complete games (4), innings pitched and lowest ERA at home
- 5th in batters faced (957), lowest batting average allowed vs. righthanded batters, fewest home runs allowed per nine innings (.74) and highest walks per nine innings (3.4)
- 6th in lowest groundball-flyball ratio allowed (0.9)
- Led the Athletics in losses, games started, walks allowed, pitches thrown (3,747), pick off throws (122) and lowest batting average allowed (.219)

Chad Bradford

Position: RP
Bats: R **Throws:** R
Ht: 6' 5" **Wt:** 203

Opening Day Age: 29
Born: 9/14/74 in
Jackson, MS
ML Seasons: 6

Overall Statistics

	W	L	Pct.	ERA	G	GS	Sv	IP	H	BB	SO	HR	Avg
'03	7	4	.636	3.04	72	0	2	77.0	67	30	62	7	.236
Car.	16	8	.667	3.23	226	0	6	237.0	230	63	172	16	.254

2003 Situational Stats

	W	L	ERA	Sv	IP		AB	H	HR	RBI	Avg
Home	3	2	2.86	2	44.0	LHB	95	31	5	17	.326
Road	4	2	3.27	0	33.0	RHB	189	36	2	16	.190
First Half	5	3	3.86	1	46.2	Sc Pos	85	22	1	24	.259
Scnd Half	2	1	1.78	1	30.1	Clutch	137	33	4	16	.241

2003 Season

Aside from a couple of bumpy periods during June and July, Chad Bradford turned in a second straight solid season in 2003, establishing himself as the setup man in the Athletics' pen. He bagged career highs in innings pitched and wins.

Pitching & Defense

It is Bradford's submarine delivery that adds the baffle to his repertoire. So even though his fastball arrives in the mid-80s at best, it sneaks up on hitters from that low delivery point. Bradford, who also has a good curve and changeup, often drops so low in his release that he scrapes his knuckles on the dirt of the mound. He does strike out nearly a hitter an inning, but otherwise Bradford is a groundball pitcher with nearly four times as many groundballs as flyballs. He fields his spot well and successfully holds runners.

2004 Outlook

The Athletics like Bradford, and vice versa, and it is likely he will stay put. He is durable, and other than during those periods when his fastball starts rising, he is effective and should continue to be so.

Eric Byrnes

Position: CF/LF
Bats: R **Throws:** R
Ht: 6' 2" **Wt:** 210

Opening Day Age: 28
Born: 2/16/76 in
Redwood City, CA
ML Seasons: 4
Pronunciation:
burns

Overall Statistics

	G	AB	R	H	D	T	HR	RBI	SB	BB	SO	Avg	OBP	Slg
'03	121	414	64	109	27	9	12	51	10	42	71	.263	.333	.459
Car.	240	556	102	144	32	11	18	67	16	50	95	.259	.326	.453

2003 Situational Stats

	AB	H	HR	RBI	Avg		AB	H	HR	RBI	Avg
Home	213	56	7	26	.263	LHP	147	42	6	18	.286
Road	201	53	5	25	.264	RHP	267	67	6	33	.251
First Half	301	90	11	42	.299	Sc Pos	82	23	6	40	.280
Scnd Half	113	19	1	9	.168	Clutch	69	21	4	18	.304

2003 Season

Eric Byrnes was among the last to know he made the Athletics' Opening Day roster last year, and he got a chance to play when Jermaine Dye was hurt. Byrnes singled in his first appearance after replacing Dye, and embarked on a 22-game hitting streak during May. On June 29, he hit for the cycle—with two doubles in a five-hit game in San Francisco. While Byrnes' performance leveled off, he still made a striking impression on fans and teammates with his all-out play.

Hitting, Baserunning & Defense

Byrnes has some power and speed, as his 20-homer/20-steal season at Triple-A Sacramento in 2001 reminds us, although hustle and resolve are what make his game go. Byrnes will stretch a single into a double at the cost of a limb, just as he will go parallel and risk a kidney to catch a sinking liner. It isn't that Byrnes doesn't have talent, but heart is what his game is about.

2004 Outlook

As well as Byrnes played in his first two months as a starter, his season revealed that he is better suited to 300-plus at-bats and a fourth-outfielder job. He probably will continue in that role with Oakland, as the Athletics retooled their outfield with Bobby Kielty and Mark Kotsay.

Jose Guillen

Position: RF/LF
Bats: R **Throws:** R
Ht: 5'11" **Wt:** 190

Opening Day Age: 27
Born: 5/17/76 in San Cristobal, DR
ML Seasons: 7
Pronunciation: GHEE-yen

Overall Statistics

	G	AB	R	H	D	T	HR	RBI	SB	BB	SO	Avg	OBP	Slg
'03	136	485	77	151	28	2	31	86	1	24	95	.311	.359	.569
Car.	750	2535	316	684	130	14	83	354	15	120	474	.270	.315	.430

2003 Situational Stats

	AB	H	HR	RBI	Avg		AB	H	HR	RBI	Avg
Home	226	68	14	37	.301	LHP	130	41	7	20	.315
Road	259	83	17	49	.320	RHP	355	110	24	66	.310
First Half	258	87	18	49	.337	Sc Pos	105	33	3	43	.314
Scnd Half	227	64	13	37	.282	Clutch	74	20	3	10	.270

2003 Season

Free-swinging Jose Guillen, who enjoyed a banner 2003, was Billy Beane's surprise stretch-run acquisition. Acquired at the trade deadline to spark a struggling outfield, Guillen's numbers dropped with his arrival in Oakland. After posting an on-base-plus-slugging of 1.014 with the Reds, his mark was .770 in 45 games with Oakland. A broken hamate bone in his left hand, with which Guillen played during the playoffs, may have hurt his production.

Hitting, Baserunning & Defense

Maybe it was because Oakland batters took a cumulative hit to their on-base percentage in 2003 that the temporary use of Guillen was acceptable. Though Guillen did clear the 30-homer mark last year, he was the same free swinger he had always been. He continues to be a butcher in the field, and his 12 errors last season suggest that isn't going to change. His terrific arm—he collected nine assists last year—sometimes offsets his bad glove. Guillen has decent speed but is not much of a basestealer.

2004 Outlook

Guillen's tenure in Oakland was destined to be brief, even if he had had good numbers. He probably will bag a nice deal somewhere after his 30-homer 2003, but it is unlikely he will deliver a big return on a long-term contract.

John Halama

Position: RP/SP
Bats: L **Throws:** L
Ht: 6' 5" **Wt:** 215

Opening Day Age: 32
Born: 2/22/72 in Brooklyn, NY
ML Seasons: 6
Pronunciation: ha LA mu

Overall Statistics

	W	L	Pct.	ERA	G	GS	Sv	IP	H	BB	SO	HR	Avg
'03	3	5	.375	4.22	35	13	0	108.2	117	36	51	18	.268
Car.	45	37	.549	4.49	171	100	0	698.0	797	220	384	84	.289

2003 Situational Stats

	W	L	ERA	Sv	IP		AB	H	HR	RBI	Avg
Home	3	1	3.18	0	62.1	LHB	112	24	4	14	.214
Road	0	4	5.63	0	46.1	RHB	324	93	14	44	.287
First Half	2	4	4.12	0	74.1	Sc Pos	106	27	5	42	.255
Scnd Half	1	1	4.46	0	34.1	Clutch	11	3	1	1	.273

2003 Season

Despite a wretched spring, John Halama earned the No. 5 starter job in Oakland's rotation. Unfortunately, the spring numbers were pretty much a harbinger of the year to come. His ERA jumped a half-run from the previous year, and his strikeout-walk ratio was among his worst. By mid-summer, he was replaced in the rotation.

Pitching & Defense

Halama is one of those guys who needs pinpoint control to be successful, and he has it less often than not. With a fastball in the high 80s, he needs the working kit bag of breaking balls that dart in all directions as well. Yet too often he is too fine, as his 18 homers allowed over 108.2 innings last year show. Halama does coax a lot of grounders. He fields his share of them, booting few. He also has an excellent move to first and holds runners well.

2004 Outlook

Halama made the postseason squad, but his last appearance with Oakland came during the regular season. He joins his former manager, Lou Piniella, after signing a one-year deal for $600,000 with the Devil Rays in November. There are doubts he'll ever be more than a Triple-A hurler, but he'll compete for a job in the Tampa Bay rotation this spring.

Oakland

Rich Harden

Position: SP
Bats: L **Throws:** R
Ht: 6' 1" **Wt:** 180

Opening Day Age: 22
Born: 11/30/81 in Victoria, BC, Canada
ML Seasons: 1

Overall Statistics

	W	L	Pct.	ERA	G	GS	Sv	IP	H	BB	SO	HR	Avg
'03	5	4	.556	4.46	15	13	0	74.2	72	40	67	5	.259
Car.	5	4	.556	4.46	15	13	0	74.2	72	40	67	5	.259

2003 Situational Stats

	W	L	ERA	Sv	IP		AB	H	HR	RBI	Avg
Home	3	1	3.86	0	35.0	LHB	166	45	4	24	.271
Road	2	3	4.99	0	39.2	RHB	112	27	1	9	.241
First Half	0	0	–	0	0.0	Sc Pos	71	12	2	25	.169
Scnd Half	5	4	4.46	0	74.2	Clutch	12	1	0	1	.083

2003 Season

Last summer, Rich Harden arrived in Oakland at just the right time. After blistering through Double-A Midland (2-0, 0.00 ERA), and then conquering Triple-A Sacramento (9-4, 3.15), he was recalled when Oakland needed a dependable fifth starter. Harden responded well, getting a no-decision in shutting down the Royals on July 21, then winning three starts in row before struggling off and on the remainder of the year.

Pitching & Defense

Harden is a big guy who throws a hard, rising fast-ball that clocks near 96 MPH. He also drops in a change and curve to round things out, but it is the high heat that is his bread and butter. As a rookie, he tended to overthrow the heater when tired. He still is learning to mix his pitches and disguise them better. With his size, he is neither quick off the mound nor to first base with a pickoff move.

2004 Outlook

Harden could have used more time in the minors, rather than take his lumps with a major league contender. Yet, Oakland seems committed to having him in the 2004 rotation. That looks more certain after Ted Lilly was dealt in November. Given a few years to gain better command, Harden should become a very good big league hurler.

Ted Lilly

Position: SP
Bats: L **Throws:** L
Ht: 6' 1" **Wt:** 190

Opening Day Age: 28
Born: 1/4/76 in Lamita, CA
ML Seasons: 5
Pronunciation: LILL-ee

Overall Statistics

	W	L	Pct.	ERA	G	GS	Sv	IP	H	BB	SO	HR	Avg
'03	12	10	.545	4.34	32	31	0	178.1	179	58	147	24	.255
Car.	22	24	.478	4.68	96	71	0	430.2	423	154	375	67	.252

2003 Situational Stats

	W	L	ERA	Sv	IP		AB	H	HR	RBI	Avg
Home	7	5	3.95	0	86.2	LHB	162	38	2	11	.235
Road	5	5	4.71	0	91.2	RHB	541	141	22	71	.261
First Half	5	7	4.96	0	105.1	Sc Pos	165	46	4	57	.279
Scnd Half	7	3	3.45	0	73.0	Clutch	30	6	1	4	.200

2003 Season

Following a sloppy first half, Ted Lilly stepped up to the mound, so to speak, picking up the slack after Mark Mulder was lost for the year. Lilly went 6-1 from August 20 through the end of the season, helping Oakland to a second straight American League West crown, while registering personal career highs across the board.

Pitching & Defense

Lilly relies a lot on control, but he gained enough command by the end of last season to log a very good 147 whiffs. He throws a fastball that just kisses 90 MPH, along with a good curve and very good change. Despite being a southpaw, Lilly is victimized frequently by baserunners because of a slow move to the plate. He throws a lot more fly-outs than groundouts, but fields his spot well when grounders come his way.

2004 Outlook

With his strong second half, Lilly may be realizing the talent that the Dodgers, Expos, Yankees and Athletics have seen in him. The Blue Jays may reap the benefits, acquiring him for outfielder Bobby Kielty on November 18. Lilly, who joins a rebuilt Toronto rotation, may be on the verge of becoming a premier AL starter.

Billy McMillon

Position: LF
Bats: L **Throws:** L
Ht: 5'11" **Wt:** 195

Opening Day Age: 32
Born: 11/17/71 in
Otero, NM
ML Seasons: 5

Overall Statistics

	G	AB	R	H	D	T	HR	RBI	SB	BB	SO	Avg	OBP	Slg
'03	66	153	15	41	11	0	6	26	0	19	36	.268	.354	.458
Car.	217	509	56	132	31	3	13	82	4	56	118	.259	.333	.409

2003 Situational Stats

	AB	H	HR	RBI	Avg		AB	H	HR	RBI	Avg
Home	69	17	2	7	.246	LHP	17	2	1	1	.118
Road	84	24	4	19	.286	RHP	136	39	5	25	.287
First Half	53	15	1	4	.283	Sc Pos	38	12	2	22	.316
Scnd Half	100	26	5	22	.260	Clutch	29	10	1	6	.345

2003 Season

For a 31-year-old who started the season at Triple-A Sacramento and never had played more than 46 games in a big league season, Billy McMillon blossomed last year. It wasn't a stunning emergence of major proportions, but McMillon supplied excellent power as a lefty bat off the bench. He was adept at getting on as a pinch-hitter, batting .385 with seven RBI in 26 at-bats.

Hitting, Baserunning & Defense

McMillon was solid against righthanders last season. He has good gap power and can turn on a pitch, as his 17 extra-base hits in 153 at-bats indicate. He was great off the bench and with runners in scoring position in 2003. He has decent speed, but is less than spectacular on defense and possesses an average arm at best. McMillion is not much of a threat to steal, nor is he called on to pinch-run.

2004 Outlook

Despite his success in a limited role, McMillon probably is considered expendable. If another team should pick him up, he would take on the same type of limited role he had in Oakland. A repeat of his 2003 season, with McMillon starting the year in the minors and getting a big league chance as a reserve player, is possible.

Jim Mecir

Position: RP
Bats: B **Throws:** R
Ht: 6' 1" **Wt:** 230

Opening Day Age: 33
Born: 5/16/70 in
Queens, NY
ML Seasons: 9
Pronunciation:
mah SEAR

Overall Statistics

	W	L	Pct.	ERA	G	GS	Sv	IP	H	BB	SO	HR	Avg
'03	2	3	.400	5.59	41	0	1	37.0	40	16	25	4	.280
Car.	28	26	.519	3.86	357	0	10	436.0	398	189	367	34	.245

2003 Situational Stats

	W	L	ERA	Sv	IP		AB	H	HR	RBI	Avg
Home	1	1	5.74	0	15.2	LHB	61	19	3	11	.311
Road	1	2	5.48	1	21.1	RHB	82	21	1	7	.256
First Half	2	1	3.60	0	25.0	Sc Pos	35	7	1	14	.200
Scnd Half	0	2	9.75	1	12.0	Clutch	58	16	1	10	.276

2003 Season

Because of shoulder and knee troubles, Jim Mecir has posted erratic numbers over the past three seasons. In 2003, he pitched just 37 innings, his fewest since 1999, and struggled with his control during most of them. He must be looking forward to 2004 after posting some of his worst ERA and strikeout-walk numbers ever. Those stats probably hurt as much as his arms and legs.

Pitching & Defense

Mecir lives by a screwball, and when it is biting, he eliminates all of the lefty righty advantages the hitter has. He also throws a fastball in the low 90s and tosses in a slider, but very little that he threw last season fooled hitters. Mecir does not hold runners well, and due to those shaky knees, he is not that quick off the mound. He is, however, very surehanded when he does get to the ball, committing just one error since 1995.

2004 Outlook

Mecir is in the final season of a four-year deal. Based upon his past inconsistencies, not to mention his injury vulnerability, it is probably his final season in Oakland. A full year of solid pitching could change that, but it would have to be a very productive and healthy year.

Ricardo Rincon

Position: RP
Bats: L **Throws:** L
Ht: 5' 9" **Wt:** 190

Opening Day Age: 33
Born: 4/13/70 in
Veracruz, Mexico
ML Seasons: 7
Pronunciation:
rin-CONE

Overall Statistics

	W	L	Pct.	ERA	G	GS	Sv	IP	H	BB	SO	HR	Avg
'03	8	4	.667	3.25	64	0	0	55.1	45	32	40	4	.230
Car.	19	22	.463	3.42	418	0	21	355.0	295	154	324	29	.227

2003 Situational Stats

	W	L	ERA	Sv	IP		AB	H	HR	RBI	Avg
Home	4	1	2.48	0	29.0	LHB	80	16	1	6	.200
Road	4	3	4.10	0	26.1	RHB	116	29	3	16	.250
First Half	5	3	4.22	0	32.0	Sc Pos	52	11	1	18	.212
Scnd Half	3	1	1.93	0	23.1	Clutch	106	23	4	13	.217

2003 Season

During his first full season in Oakland, Ricardo Rincon returned to form, handling the situational lefty bullpen role with finesse and logging his third straight season of 60 or more appearances. Rincon did struggle with his command, even though he lowered his ERA in 2003.

Pitching & Defense

Rincon's effectiveness is rooted in a decent low-90s fastball that bottoms out at the last moment, and a good hard slider. He usually has displayed good control, and he still dominates lefthanded hitters. He allowed four stolen bases to seven would-be thieves last year. Rincon fields his position successfully. He enjoyed an error-free summer for a second straight season in 2003.

2004 Outlook

Rincon was a contributor with Oakland last summer, winning eight games and getting stingier as the season wore on. He also blew his only three save opportunities. He was a free agent at season's end, and it's possible he could land in Oakland again. Wherever he takes the mound in 2004, Rincon should deliver numbers pretty close to those of the past three years.

Chris Singleton

Position: CF
Bats: L **Throws:** L
Ht: 6' 2" **Wt:** 217

Opening Day Age: 31
Born: 8/15/72 in
Martinez, CA
ML Seasons: 5

Overall Statistics

	G	AB	R	H	D	T	HR	RBI	SB	BB	SO	Avg	OBP	Slg
'03	120	306	38	75	24	1	1	36	7	26	55	.245	.301	.340
Car.	676	2171	317	593	128	23	45	265	81	124	329	.273	.311	.415

2003 Situational Stats

	AB	H	HR	RBI	Avg		AB	H	HR	RBI	Avg
Home	142	35	0	16	.246	LHP	48	8	0	6	.167
Road	164	40	1	20	.244	RHP	258	67	1	30	.260
First Half	183	51	1	21	.279	Sc Pos	78	19	0	32	.244
Scnd Half	123	24	0	15	.195	Clutch	48	16	0	6	.333

2003 Season

It is hard to figure what the Athletics were looking for when they signed Chris Singleton to a contract in December 2002. Singleton's low on-base numbers didn't fit the Athletics' mold, and his bat was no better in 2003. His defense, which might have been what Billy Beane was after, also proved suspect. It was a tough year for the veteran Singleton.

Hitting, Baserunning & Defense

Singleton has shown that he can hit for a better average with more power than he displayed in 2003, but his basic approach to hitting is hacking. He gets a lot of swings, yet generates too many flyouts to get the full benefit of his speed. Singleton is a good basestealer, so again, his tenure with Oakland seemed strange from the start. His career low of seven steals confirms that fact. In a limited 2003 role, Singleton committed a career-high six errors in a career-low 194 chances.

2004 Outlook

Although the Athletics had an option to retain Singleton's services for 2004, they declined it and made the outfielder a free agent. He offers little in the way of offense to merit much of a deal or role. He will be a fourth outfielder somewhere, but he should not be an expensive one.

Other Oakland Athletics

Micah Bowie (Pos: LHP, Age: 29)

	W	L	Pct.	ERA	G	GS	Sv	IP	H	BB	SO	HR	Avg
'03	0	1	.000	7.56	6	0	0	8.1	13	2	4	1	.361
Car.	4	8	.333	8.45	33	11	0	71.1	106	44	53	11	.348

Bowie presses on as he approaches age 30. He surfaced in Oakland again for a second straight season, but two stints on the disabled list for a sore elbow limited him to just 14.1 innings at all levels. 2004 Outlook: C

Mike Edwards (Pos: LF, Age: 27, Bats: R)

	G	AB	R	H	D	T	HR	RBI	SB	BB	SO	Avg	OBP	Slg
'03	4	4	0	1	0	0	0	0	0	2	1	.250	.500	.250
Car.	4	4	0	1	0	0	0	0	0	2	1	.250	.500	.250

Edwards started the annual ritual of changing organizations and Triple-A clubs in 2001, but after a .298-14-95 season at Sacramento, Edwards got his first big league cup of coffee in September. 2004 Outlook: C

Jeremy Fikac (Pos: RHP, Age: 28)

	W	L	Pct.	ERA	G	GS	Sv	IP	H	BB	SO	HR	Avg
'03	0	1	.000	4.50	14	0	0	16.0	14	11	9	4	.246
Car.	6	8	.429	4.37	102	0	0	111.1	103	50	94	19	.242

Fikac has been terrific in the high minors, and he pitched effectively in spring training and made the A's. But a run of free passes in April and May led to a summer in Sacramento, where he pitched well. 2004 Outlook: C

Ron Gant (Pos: LF, Age: 39, Bats: R)

	G	AB	R	H	D	T	HR	RBI	SB	BB	SO	Avg	OBP	Slg
	17	41	4	6	0	0	1	4	0	2	9	.146	.182	.220
	1832	6410	1080	1651	302	50	321	1008	243	770	1411	.256	.336	.468

Gant started his 16th big league season with Oakland, but he struggled and the A's released him in early June. The one-time slugger departs with 321 career homers and 1,008 RBI. 2004 Outlook: D

Esteban German (Pos: 2B, Age: 26, Bats: R)

	G	AB	R	H	D	T	HR	RBI	SB	BB	SO	Avg	OBP	Slg
'03	5	4	0	1	0	0	0	1	0	0	1	.250	.250	.250
Car.	14	39	4	8	0	0	0	1	1	4	12	.205	.295	.205

German seems like a perfect candidate for Oakland, never having posted an OBP below .379 in the high minors, but his defensive shortcomings and a lack of success in limited chances has stalled his career. 2004 Outlook: C

Jason Grabowski (Pos: RF, Age: 27, Bats: L)

	G	AB	R	H	D	T	HR	RBI	SB	BB	SO	Avg	OBP	Slg
'03	8	8	0	0	0	0	0	0	0	1	5	.000	.111	.000
Car.	12	16	3	3	1	1	0	1	0	4	6	.188	.350	.375

Grabowski is a utility player who has posted good OBPs in the minors. A year ago, his prospects looked good after going 3-for-8 with a double and triple in Oakland. Last year he was 0-for-8 with five Ks. 2004 Outlook: C

Chad Harville (Pos: RHP, Age: 27)

	W	L	Pct.	ERA	G	GS	Sv	IP	H	BB	SO	HR	Avg
'03	1	0	1.000	5.82	21	0	1	21.2	25	17	18	3	.294
Car.	1	2	.333	5.77	39	0	1	39.0	45	27	35	5	.292

Harville was designated the A's closer of the future years ago, but numerous injuries have sidetracked his career in recent seasons. He's learned new pitches to enhance his chances, and maybe his time is now. 2004 Outlook: C

Mark Johnson (Pos: C, Age: 28, Bats: L)

	G	AB	R	H	D	T	HR	RBI	SB	BB	SO	Avg	OBP	Slg
'03	13	27	3	3	1	0	0	3	0	3	4	.111	.219	.148
Car.	315	906	113	198	37	4	16	79	8	120	193	.219	.314	.321

Johnson did little with the one chance he got with the White Sox in 2002, and he moved to Oakland in last winter's Billy Koch deal. He played even less there and signed a minor league deal with Milwaukee. 2004 Outlook: C

Adam Melhuse (Pos: C, Age: 32, Bats: B)

	G	AB	R	H	D	T	HR	RBI	SB	BB	SO	Avg	OBP	Slg
'03	40	77	13	23	7	0	5	14	0	9	19	.299	.372	.584
Car.	104	172	21	40	9	1	6	26	1	18	43	.233	.302	.401

Melhuse came over from Colorado as a minor league free agent a year ago, and he posted solid numbers in limited at-bats. The Ramon Hernandez trade opens a door, but the A's probably will sign a veteran catcher. 2004 Outlook: C

Frank Menechino (Pos: 2B/3B, Age: 33, Bats: R)

	G	AB	R	H	D	T	HR	RBI	SB	BB	SO	Avg	OBP	Slg
'03	13	83	10	16	0	0	2	9	0	19	16	.193	.364	.265
Car.	295	840	145	196	38	3	23	110	3	138	194	.233	.354	.368

Purged with others in May 2002, when a talented Oakland club struggled early on, Menechino resurfaced with the Athletics in 2003 and spent the year there. But he didn't hit enough to escape utility duty. 2004 Outlook: C

Mike Neu (Pos: RHP, Age: 26)

	W	L	Pct.	ERA	G	GS	Sv	IP	H	BB	SO	HR	Avg
'03	0	0	–	3.64	32	0	1	42.0	43	26	20	2	.261
Car.	0	0	–	3.64	32	0	1	42.0	43	26	20	2	.261

A Rule 5 pickup from the Reds, Neu enjoyed a decent spring and stuck on the A's roster all season. His numbers were decent in the high minors in 2002, and Neu may stick again this summer. 2004 Outlook: C

Steve Sparks (Pos: RHP, Age: 38)

	W	L	Pct.	ERA	G	GS	Sv	IP	H	BB	SO	HR	Avg
'03	0	6	.000	4.88	51	0	2	107.0	114	37	54	13	.277
Car.	56	69	.448	4.77	241	164	3	1199.0	1312	475	601	136	.279

The knuckleballer enjoyed a career year with Detroit in 2001, going 14-9 with a 3.65 ERA. Last season, after starting 0-6 as a reliever with the Tigers, he was released and signed by Oakland. He became a free agent in October. 2004 Outlook: C

Oakland Athletics Minor League Prospects

Organization Overview:

The Oakland system isn't as deep as it was a few years ago, but that has more to do with the various trades that general manager Billy Beane has executed to fill holes. Depending on the farm system to stock the Athletics' core players, as well as to acquire players in the heat of pennant races, is doubly demanding on the talent evaluators who keep the system stocked. While several key people have left the organization, Beane and farm director Keith Lieppman remain, and the Athletics seem to keep a steady stream of prospects coming. Eric Byrnes and Rich Harden stepped up in 2003, and the new season should mark the emergence of Bobby Crosby and Justin Duchscherer.

Joe Blanton

Position: P
Opening Day Age: 23
Bats: R **Throws:** R
Born: 12/11/80 in
Ht: 6' 3" **Wt:** 225
Bowling Green, KY

Recent Statistics

	W	L	ERA	G	GS	Sv	IP	H	R	BB	SO	HR
2002 A Vancouver	1	1	3.14	4	2	0	14.1	11	5	2	15	0
2002 A Modesto	0	1	7.50	2	1	0	6.0	8	6	6	6	1
2003 A Kane County	8	7	2.57	21	21	0	133.0	110	47	19	144	6
2003 AA Midland	3	1	1.26	7	5	1	35.2	21	6	7	30	1

Blanton was taken 24th overall in 2002 after four years at Kentucky. His superb command sparked his dominating season at Class-A Kane County in 2003. He threw strikes with all four of his pitches—a mid-90s fastball, tight slider, knee-buckling curve and change-up. His slider was a terrific pitch for him. The Athletics have worked on his maximum-effort delivery, though Blanton's motion doesn't seem to compromise his command. Refining a changeup should keep him on track as a starter, and he could be pitching at Triple-A Sacramento in the spring. With better hitters in his future, Blanton needs to work on the mental aspects of the game, including the sequencing of his pitches.

Freddie Bynum

Position: 2B
Opening Day Age: 24
Bats: L **Throws:** R
Born: 3/15/80 in Wilson,
Ht: 6' 1" **Wt:** 175
NC

Recent Statistics

	G	AB	R	H	D	T	HR	RBI	SB	BB	SO	Avg
2002 A Visalia	135	539	83	165	26	5	3	56	41	64	116	.306
2003 AA Midland	132	510	84	134	18	9	5	58	22	56	135	.263

The raw but talented Bynum, drafted in 2000, began to elevate his game during his second season of high Class-A ball in 2002. He has the tools to be a talented middle infielder and leadoff hitter. Bynum has speed, range and a strong arm defensively, as well as a line-drive stroke that drives the ball to all fields. At Visalia

in 2002, he notably improved his plate discipline and his ability to get on base. While Bynum did many things well in his first taste of Double-A ball in 2003, he hasn't completely locked into the mind frame of a leadoff hitter. He needs to cut down on his strikeouts, which more than doubled his walks at Midland. Bynum got an occasional look in center field last season.

Bobby Crosby

Position: SS
Opening Day Age: 24
Bats: R **Throws:** R
Born: 1/12/80 in
Ht: 6' 3" **Wt:** 195
Lakewood, CA

Recent Statistics

	G	AB	R	H	D	T	HR	RBI	SB	BB	SO	Avg
2003 AAA Sac'mento	127	465	86	143	32	6	22	90	24	63	110	.308
2003 AL Oakland	11	12	1	0	0	0	0	0	0	1	5	.000

With solid baseball instincts, Crosby, a 2001 draft pick, has advanced quickly and is in line to replace Miguel Tejada if the shortstop departs Oakland. Crosby has hit for average, and in 2002 he showed more power by getting more extension on his swing, keeping the bat barrel in the zone longer and getting more loft. While Crosby's pitch selection improved in 2003, he needed to further tweak his swing with help from Triple-A Sacramento coach Roy White. After getting himself out too often early in the year, Crosby learned to stay back longer and his homers and total bases spiked upward. Defensively he's not flashy and lacks range, but he makes the routine plays with good positioning, reading balls well off the bat, getting his feet in motion quickly and exhibiting a strong arm.

Justin Duchscherer

Position: P
Opening Day Age: 26
Bats: R **Throws:** R
Born: 11/19/77 in
Ht: 6' 3" **Wt:** 190
Aberdeen, SD

Recent Statistics

	W	L	ERA	G	GS	Sv	IP	H	R	BB	SO	HR
2003 AAA Sac'mento	14	2	3.25	24	23	0	155.0	151	59	18	117	12
2003 AL Oakland	1	1	3.31	4	3	0	16.1	17	7	3	15	1

The 6-foot-3 Duchscherer lacks a big-time fastball, but he has good command of a knee-locking curveball. Plus, he changes speeds effectively and mixes in a cutter and changeup. Duchscherer throws lots of strikes and calls on his entire arsenal in any count. He confidently will pitch backwards, often starting a hitter with a changeup or a curve that hitters have trouble recognizing. His 2003 season was much better than his 2002, because Duchscherer mastered the air space around the plate and was free of back problems that had plagued him in recent years. An offseason conditioning program seems to have silenced his back ailment. Duchscherer competes for an A's rotation spot in 2004.

Dan Johnson

Position: 1B
Bats: L **Throws:** R
Ht: 6' 1" **Wt:** 215

Opening Day Age: 24
Born: 8/10/79 in Coon Rapids, MN

Recent Statistics

	G	AB	R	H	D	T	HR	RBI	SB	BB	SO	Avg
2002 A Modesto	126	426	56	125	23	1	21	85	4	57	87	.293
2003 AA Midland	139	538	90	156	26	4	27	114	7	68	82	.290
2003 AAA Sac'mento	1	4	0	1	1	0	0	0	0	0	0	.250

A 2001 seventh-round pick, Johnson has been a regular in the Athletics' offseason conditioning program, getting stronger and staying in excellent shape. The home runs began to accumulate during a red-hot surge late in the 2002 season at high Class-A Modesto. One of the more consistent hitters in the system, Johnson is very strong and among the best at centering the ball on the bat and driving it. He solid strike-zone judgment was better in 2003, which means he doesn't offer at as many breaking balls off the plate, but he needs more work hitting breaking stuff. His defensive game continues to improve. At best he's an adequate first baseman.

John Rheinecker

Position: P
Bats: L **Throws:** L
Ht: 6' 2" **Wt:** 215

Opening Day Age: 24
Born: 5/29/79 in Waterloo, IL

Recent Statistics

	W	L	ERA	G	GS	Sv	IP	H	R	BB	SO	HR
2002 A Visalia	3	0	2.31	9	9	0	50.2	41	16	10	62	2
2002 AA Midland	7	7	3.38	20	20	0	128.0	137	63	24	100	7
2003 AA Midland	9	6	4.74	23	23	0	142.1	186	90	32	89	13
2003 AAA Sac'mento	2	0	3.79	6	6	0	38.0	47	19	12	26	1

A 2001 first-rounder, Rheinecker has advanced quickly through the system, calling on a low-90s fastball and two solid breaking pitches. His curve ranks among the best in the system. Last spring, Rheinecker experimented with a two-seamer that he hoped to throw to righthanded hitters. Initially it wasn't very effective and he got away from his usual mix, so Rheinecker struggled. Later in the summer his arsenal was back on track, and he moved up to Triple-A Sacramento. His fastball command suffered in 2003, and Rheinecker needs to refine the sequence of his pitches. He sometimes works too deep into counts, which translates into shorter outings.

Michael Rouse

Position: SS
Bats: L **Throws:** R
Ht: 6' 0" **Wt:** 185

Opening Day Age: 23
Born: 4/25/80 in San Jose, CA

Recent Statistics

	G	AB	R	H	D	T	HR	RBI	SB	BB	SO	Avg
2002 AA Tennessee	71	231	35	60	11	0	9	43	7	29	47	.260
2003 AA Midland	130	457	75	137	33	3	3	53	7	63	83	.300
2003 AAA Sac'mento	2	7	2	3	0	0	0	1	0	0	0	.429

Rouse was an oft-injured and little-known collegian until he was a catalyst to Cal State-Fullerton's College World Series appearance in 2001. Toronto drafted him and Rouse enjoyed a promising debut at high Class-A Dunedin, swinging the bat and adjusting to pitchers well. He's a good situational hitter, a guy who successfully does the little things. After a solid Double-A season in 2002, disrupted by a broken hamate bone in his wrist, Rouse was traded to Oakland for Cory Lidle in November. At Double-A Midland last summer, Rouse hit for a much better average and increased his walk rate. Defensively, he's a grinder at shortstop, a blue-collar guy who doesn't impress with flash and style.

Mike Wood

Position: P
Bats: R **Throws:** R
Ht: 6' 3" **Wt:** 180

Opening Day Age: 23
Born: 4/26/80 in West Palm Beach, FL

Recent Statistics

	W	L	ERA	G	GS	Sv	IP	H	R	BB	SO	HR
2003 AAA Sac'mento	9	3	3.05	16	16	0	91.1	87	34	23	59	5
2003 AL Oakland	2	1	10.54	7	1	0	13.2	24	17	7	15	1

A 2001 pick, Wood works with a sinker-slider combo that draws comparisons to Tim Hudson's, but Wood throws his hard-sinking fastball at 86-88 MPH. Getting hitters out with it at higher levels will be a challenge, but it didn't stop Wood from going 14-6 at two levels in 2002 and succeeding at Triple-A Sacramento in 2003. It didn't seem to matter that Wood missed nearly two months early in the season with a strained elbow. Or that he was working in the Pacific Coast League. Wood, who also mixes in a splitter and changeup, sometimes struggles to retire hitters after the second time through the order. He may be in line for relief work. Either way, command and pitch movement will remain critical to Wood's success.

Others to Watch

Catcher **Jeremy Brown** (24) enjoyed an impressive debut in 2002 after his selection in the June draft, reaching high Class-A Visalia and batting .310 there. He was off to a good start at Double-A Midland, with a .275 average and .388 OBP, when he stretched thumb ligaments in June and missed the rest of the season. . . First baseman **Graham Koonce** (28) is a late bloomer, a 1993 60th-round pick who has bounced around. A super-selective hitter with terrific power, his patience often was interpreted as being too passive. A minor league Rule 5 pickup by Oakland two years ago, Koonce led the minors in homers in 2003 and claimed MVP honors in the Triple-A Pacific Coast League with a .277-34-115 season. . . Outfielder **Jason Perry** (23) was an advanced hitter drafted by Toronto in 2002. Using a short, strong stroke, Perry reached high Class-A Dunedin in his debut season. He was dealt to Oakland last June, and he batted .305 with good on-base ability between two high Class-A stops in 2003. . . Drafted last June, shortstop **Omar Quintanilla** (22) is a hard worker who lacks big-time tools. But he can hit. He is intelligent and makes adjustments with a quick, line-drive stroke that produced a .358 average between short-season Vancouver and high Class-A Modesto.

Safeco Field

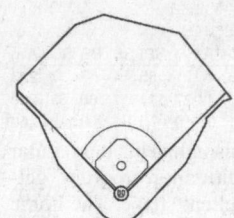

Offense

Safeco Field did not depress scoring in 2003 to quite the extent it had in the previous two years, but it remains one of the most extreme pitchers' parks in baseball. Since the park opened, hitters have complained that glare in the center-field "batter's eye"—particularly in the afternoon, or when the roof is open—made it difficult to pick up pitches. At last year's All-Star break, the wall behind center field was painted black in an effort to remedy the situation, and hitters said it helped. The cool, heavy air keeps the ball from carrying, especially to left field.

Defense

With its deep alleys, Safeco requires outfielders to cover a lot of ground, especially the center fielder. Pitchers know they have more margin for error when they pitch up in the zone, and young hurlers have an easier time building confidence because blowouts are so rare. Teams tend to run more here, so it helps to have a catcher with a good arm.

Who It Helps the Most

It's hard to find a pitcher who hasn't been helped by Safeco. Both Gil Meche and Joel Pineiro have been terrific here. Kazuhiro Sasaki has been especially tough here as well. Bret Boone is one of the few righthanded hitters who hasn't been hurt much, since he has such good opposite-field power.

Who It Hurts the Most

Mike Cameron, who has a slight vision problem, has been far less productive at Safeco. Ben Davis has fared miserably in his home games as a Mariner, while Dan Wilson's and John Olerud's numbers also have suffered.

Rookies & Newcomers

Jamal Strong is a pure contact hitter, so the wide-open spaces in the outfield actually may be to his liking. Chris Snelling, who has more power, probably will be hurt more. The majority of the Mariners' most advanced prospects are pitchers, and whichever ones come up likely will be helped by their home park.

Dimensions: LF-331, LCF-390, CF-405, RCF-387, RF-327

Capacity: 47,447

Elevation: -2 feet

Surface: Grass

Foul Territory: Average

Park Factors

2003 Season

	Home Games			Away Games			
	Mariners	Opp	Total	Mariners	Opp	Total	Index
G	72	72	144	72	72	144	
Avg	.271	.235	.253	.275	.265	.270	93
AB	2387	2437	4824	2570	2411	4981	97
R	370	271	641	355	315	670	96
H	646	573	1219	708	639	1347	90
2B	109	84	193	153	116	269	74
3B	16	10	26	15	4	19	141
HR	64	81	145	66	78	144	104
BB	278	208	486	245	209	454	111
SO	422	455	877	462	429	891	102
E	28	45	73	34	33	67	109
E-Infield	21	39	60	31	25	56	107
LHB-Avg	.269	.247	.257	.277	.277	.277	93
LHB-HR	26	50	76	16	47	63	124
RHB-Avg	.272	.224	.249	.274	.252	.264	94
RHB-HR	38	31	69	50	31	81	88

2001-2003

	Home Games			Away Games			
	Mariners	Opp	Total	Mariners	Opp	Total	Index
G	216	216	432	216	216	432	
Avg	.274	.238	.256	.285	.260	.273	94
AB	7192	7399	14591	7763	7283	15046	97
R	1092	830	1922	1179	974	2153	89
H	1969	1764	3733	2214	1892	4106	91
2B	352	322	674	444	382	826	84
3B	46	19	65	44	31	75	89
HR	185	214	399	217	251	468	88
BB	863	617	1480	779	622	1401	109
SO	1279	1424	2703	1368	1337	2705	103
E	95	162	257	114	149	263	98
E-Infield	77	138	215	94	129	223	96
LHB-Avg	.280	.248	.264	.294	.273	.284	93
LHB-HR	69	122	191	72	121	193	102
RHB-Avg	.268	.229	.249	.278	.248	.263	94
RHB-HR	116	92	208	145	130	275	78

2003 Rankings (American League)

- Highest walk factor
- Third-highest triple factor
- Lowest batting-average factor
- Lowest hit factor
- Lowest double factor
- Second-lowest LHB batting-average factor
- Third-lowest RHB batting-average factor

Bob Melvin

2003 Season

It's hard to criticize a first-year manager whose team won 93 games, but Bob Melvin's 2003 Mariners seemed like they were on the way to doing so much more. They were one of the best teams in baseball during the first half, but over the last two months of the season they lost first the division lead and then the lead in the wild card race. Whether it was Melvin's fault or not, he seemed powerless to stop the slide. In a way, however, he was a victim of the expectations generated by his team's first-half success.

Offense

Melvin tended to manage for today's game, putting his best lineup on the field whenever possible. This meant that the regulars rarely got a day off, and some of the bench players had trouble getting enough at-bats to stay fresh. He seldom pinch-hit. To be fair, all of this was, to a certain extent, dictated by his lack of firepower on the bench. He generally preferred the stolen base to the sacrifice, especially early in innings, and didn't ask the bottom third of the order to bunt runners over as often as they had in the past.

Pitching & Defense

Melvin often let his starters pitch deep into games, and perhaps as a result, youngsters Joel Pineiro and Gil Meche struggled late in the year. With only one lefthander in the bullpen, he tended to juggle relievers inning-by-inning instead of batter-by-batter. To his credit, he got excellent work out of a bullpen that was in a constant state of flux.

2004 Outlook

The Mariners' organization is at something of a crossroads, and the path it chooses largely will determine what the expectations will be for Melvin's Mariners this year. The skipper will work with a new general manager, Bill Bavasi, and it appears the team will spend money to replace key departures. With new faces coming on board, Melvin may have a greater chance to put his stamp on the club.

Born: 10/28/61 in Palo Alto, CA

Playing Experience: 1985-1994, Det, SF, Bal, KC, Bos, CWS, NYY

Managerial Experience: 1 season

Manager Statistics

Year	Team, Lg	W	L	Pct	GB	Finish
2003	Seattle, AL	93	69	.574	3.0	2nd West
1 Season		93	69	.574	–	–

2003 Starting Pitchers by Days Rest

	<=3	4	5	6+
Mariners Starts	2	78	65	12
Mariners ERA	3.00	3.77	3.62	5.11
AL Avg Starts	2	79	50	22
AL ERA	3.19	4.64	4.57	4.98

2003 Situational Stats

	Bob Melvin	AL Average
Hit & Run Success %	50.0	36.7
Stolen Base Success %	74.5	70.0
Platoon Pct.	62.2	61.7
Defensive Subs	28	23
High-Pitch Outings	7	5
Quick/Slow Hooks	10/11	19/16
Sacrifice Attempts	47	55

2003 Rankings (American League)

- 1st in steals of third base (19), hit-and-run success percentage and 2+ pitching changes in low-scoring games (36)
- 2nd in double steals (6)

Bret Boone

2003 Season

Bret Boone followed up his excellent second half of 2002 with an equally strong first half in 2003. At midseason he was a potential MVP candidate for the first-place Mariners, but he cooled off after the break. His bat didn't fully come back to life until mid-September, by which time the Mariners already had lost the inside track on a playoff spot. It was a fine season for him nonetheless, as he put up strong numbers at the No. 3 spot in the order and played his usual Gold Glove-caliber defense.

Hitting

Boone is a very good opposite-field hitter, and what's made the difference the last few years is that he's become strong enough to reach the seats in right-center. He's still dangerous inside, especially down and in, but isn't able to generate quite the same power when he isn't able to extend his arms. When he's ahead in the count he muscles up and looks to drive the ball. He can stay locked in for weeks or even months at a time, but he just an easily can fall into a rut that will last just as long. Last year he showed better patience at the plate, drawing a career-high 68 walks.

Baserunning & Defense

Boone is one of the best defensive second basemen in the game, and he picked up his third career Gold Glove Award last year. His strong throwing arm allows him to set up deep and get to more balls. He has excellent hands and catches everything he gets to, and his double-play pivot is flawless. Over the last two years, Boone has run more often and has picked his spots quite well, despite unremarkable speed. He's aggressive in going after the extra base and usually makes good gambles on the basepaths.

2004 Outlook

No matter how extensive the Mariners' offseason makeover may be, Boone will remain one of their central players on both offense and defense. He's signed through next season with a club option for 2005.

Position: 2B
Bats: R **Throws:** R
Ht: 5'10" **Wt:** 190

Opening Day Age: 34
Born: 4/6/69 in El Cajon, CA
ML Seasons: 12

Overall Statistics

G	AB	R	H	D	T	HR	RBI	SB	BB	SO	Avg	OBP	Slg
159	622	111	183	35	5	35	117	16	68	125	.294	.366	.535
1544	5764	820	1554	321	25	221	901	80	468	1095	.270	.328	.449

Where He Hits the Ball

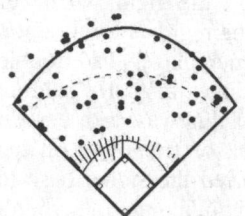 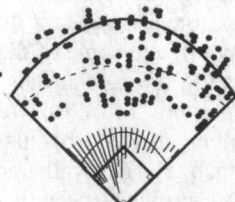

Vs. LHP   **Vs. RHP**

2003 Situational Stats

	AB	H	HR	RBI	Avg		AB	H	HR	RBI	Avg
Home	302	90	16	58	.298	LHP	167	43	8	35	.257
Road	320	93	19	59	.291	RHP	455	140	27	82	.308
First Half	364	114	24	76	.313	Sc Pos	183	54	10	83	.295
Scnd Half	258	69	11	41	.267	Clutch	82	21	5	10	.256

2003 Rankings (American League)

- 2nd in fielding percentage at second base (.990)
- 3rd in RBI
- 6th in pitches seen (2,770)
- 7th in runs scored and times on base (258)
- 8th in home runs, strikeouts and plate appearances (705)
- 9th in total bases (333)
- Led the Mariners in home runs, runs scored, total bases (333), RBI, sacrifice flies (7), times on base (258), pitches seen (2,770), games played, slugging percentage, HR frequency (17.8 ABs per HR), stolen-base percentage (84.2), and batting average vs. righthanded pitchers
- Led AL second basemen in RBI

Mike Cameron

2003 Season

Mike Cameron was on target for one of his better seasons when he pulled a groin muscle in mid-August. He returned a few days later but hit under .200 over the final six weeks of the season, contributing to the team's late-season decline in the standings. It was a good year overall, however, especially on defense, where he always shines.

Position: CF
Bats: R **Throws:** R
Ht: 6' 2" **Wt:** 200

Opening Day Age: 31
Born: 1/8/73 in LaGrange, GA
ML Seasons: 9

Hitting

It's easy to underestimate Cameron's offensive impact because his two major weaknesses—his low average and high strikeout totals—are so visible. Between his power, ability to draw walks and baserunning skills, he contributes in a variety of ways. Cameron doesn't hit for a high enough average to bat at the top of the order, but he has enough power to be a useful run producer. Safeco has held down his power numbers, since his power mainly is to straightaway center and left-center. He strikes out a lot—he cut his strikeouts by 39 last year but still nearly led the American League—but also works deep counts and draws a good number of walks. Streakiness seems to be an unavoidable part of his game.

Baserunning & Defense

When it comes to the game's top defensive center fielders, Cameron deserves to be mentioned in the same breath as Torii Hunter and Andruw Jones. He gets excellent jumps, covers a vast amount of territory and pulls more home runs back into the park than just about anyone. He caught more balls last year than any major league outfielder, and no one else was even close. The end result was the second Gold Glove of his career. His throwing arm also is above-average. He runs very well and is a good basestealer, except when a southpaw is on the mound.

2004 Outlook

Cameron is a free agent and it would be a surprise if he elected to return to Seattle, since his inability to hit at Safeco Field has been an ongoing source of frustration. In a park that rewards rather than blunts his power, he easily could put up the best numbers of his career.

Overall Statistics

	G	AB	R	H	D	T	HR	RBI	SB	BB	SO	Avg	OBP	Slg
'03	147	534	74	135	31	5	18	76	17	70	137	.253	.344	.431
Car.	1052	3528	567	882	185	36	131	510	194	472	970	.250	.343	.434

Where He Hits the Ball

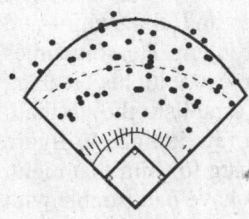
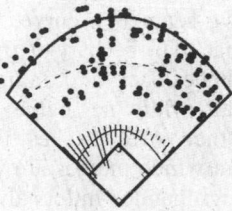

Vs. LHP   **Vs. RHP**

2003 Situational Stats

	AB	H	HR	RBI	Avg		AB	H	HR	RBI	Avg
Home	247	58	11	39	.235	LHP	147	42	4	22	.286
Road	287	77	7	37	.268	RHP	387	93	14	54	.240
First Half	314	85	13	56	.271	Sc Pos	147	43	6	59	.293
Scnd Half	220	50	5	20	.227	Clutch	69	17	4	13	.246

2003 Rankings (American League)

- 2nd in strikeouts
- 3rd in fielding percentage in center field (.992) and lowest batting average vs. righthanded pitchers
- 5th in errors in center field (4)
- Led the Mariners in strikeouts

Freddy Garcia

2003 Season

It was one of the most inconsistent seasons by a pitcher in recent memory. Freddy Garcia, counted on to be the ace of the Mariners' staff, pitched like an ace for weeks at a time, but also went through stretches where he got hammered regularly. He bounced back and forth between the two extremes so often that it was impossible to know what to expect from him on any given day. Understandably, the situation produced frustration all around, not the least of which from Garcia himself, whose maturity had been questioned in the past.

Pitching

Garcia has many weapons—a low-90s fastball, a two-seamer, a curve, slider and changeup—and that may be part of the problem. He sometimes pitches backward, falling in love with his breaking ball while neglecting to establish the fastball. Other times it takes him a few innings to figure out which pitches are working for him that night. Righthanded hitters always have had trouble with him, and continued to last year, even when he was struggling. Big and strong, he has good stamina and tends to settle down if he can ride out the bumps early on. He's been remarkably durable and hasn't suffered a major arm injury in his big league career.

Defense

Garcia used to be vulnerable to the stolen base, but he has developed a pretty good pickoff move and has become quite hard to run on. He yielded just six stolen bases in 2003. He's otherwise capable in the field, and moves fairly well for a man his size.

2004 Outlook

The Mariners may have reached the end of their rope with Garcia. He is eligible for arbitration, and they may decide that he is not worth the salary he'll be able to command. There were trade whispers at times last season, and he could be dealt before the start of 2004. As Seattle knows all too well, Garcia remains capable of putting together a big season, but is equally capable of falling well short of expectations.

Position: SP
Bats: R **Throws:** R
Ht: 6' 4" **Wt:** 240

Opening Day Age: 27
Born: 6/10/76 in Caracas, VZ
ML Seasons: 5

Overall Statistics

	W	L	Pct.	ERA	G	GS	Sv	IP	H	BB	SO	HR	Avg
'03	12	14	.462	4.51	33	33	0	201.1	196	71	144	31	.255
Car.	72	43	.626	3.97	155	154	0	989.1	939	357	737	111	.249

2003 Pitching Profile

	Freddy Garcia	AL Average
Overall Strike %	60.8	62.8
1st Pitch Strike %	59.5	58.7
Ratio	1.33	1.39
Strikeouts per 9 IP	6.44	6.11
Walks per 9 IP	3.17	3.16
Home Runs per 9 IP	1.39	1.11
Strikeout/Walk Ratio	2.03	1.93
Groundball/Flyball Ratio	1.04	1.18

2003 Situational Stats

	W	L	ERA	Sv	IP		AB	H	HR	RBI	Avg
Home	6	7	4.17	0	99.1	LHB	420	118	23	69	.281
Road	6	7	4.85	0	102.0	RHB	350	78	8	27	.223
First Half	9	8	4.41	0	122.1	Sc Pos	147	34	5	61	.231
Scnd Half	3	6	4.67	0	79.0	Clutch	59	18	1	3	.305

2003 Rankings (American League)

- 3rd in wild pitches (11)
- 4th in most pitches thrown per batter (3.90)
- 5th in home runs allowed
- 6th in most home runs allowed per nine innings (1.39)
- 7th in losses and lowest batting average allowed vs. righthanded batters
- 8th in games started, walks allowed and hit batsmen (11)
- 9th in lowest stolen-base percentage allowed (46.2) and highest walks per nine innings (3.2)
- 10th in lowest batting average allowed with runners in scoring position
- Led the Mariners in losses, games started, hit batsmen (11), wild pitches (11), runners caught stealing (7), lowest stolen-base percentage allowed (46.2) and most strikeouts per nine innings (6.4)

Carlos Guillen

2003 Season

Carlos Guillen was in the midst of a solid season when injuries struck, as they had so often in past seasons. He missed most of July with a groin pull and most of August with an unusual ailment, pelvic inflammation. By the time he returned, Rey Sanchez had been acquired to play shortstop, but there was a hole at third, so Guillen was plugged in there. He was surprisingly competent at the hot corner and was more or less the regular the rest of the way.

Hitting

The switch-hitting Guillen is equally adept from either side of the plate, although he shows better patience from the left side. A spray-hitter, he stays within himself and isn't much of an extra-base threat. He had spent most of his career batting in the lower third of the order, until last year, when he saw considerable time in the No. 2 spot and reached base often enough to help in that spot. There's no guarantee a slump won't drop him back down to the bottom of the lineup card, however. The Mariners sometimes call on him to bunt runners over rather than try to drive them in.

Baserunning & Defense

Guillen's glovework is similar to his offense: consistent and reliable, though rarely attention-grabbing. His savvy positioning and a good first step give him ample range at short, and he has more than enough arm for the position. In his time at third, he was impressive and looked surprisingly comfortable, even charging bunts. He looked much surer of himself than he had when he played some third base for Seattle back in 2000. He has decent speed but is not much of a threat to run.

2004 Outlook

With Sanchez expected to depart as a free agent, Guillen likely will move back to his natural position. If the Mariners sign a shortstop, he may stick at third. His goal will remain to avoid the injuries that have eaten into his playing time throughout his career.

Position: SS/3B
Bats: B **Throws:** R
Ht: 6' 1" **Wt:** 205

Opening Day Age: 28
Born: 9/30/75 in Maracay, VZ
ML Seasons: 6
Pronunciation: GEY-un

Overall Statistics

	G	AB	R	H	D	T	HR	RBI	SB	BB	SO	Avg	OBP	Slg
'03	109	388	63	107	19	3	7	52	4	52	64	.276	.359	.394
Car.	488	1665	264	439	80	16	29	211	15	183	312	.264	.335	.383

Where He Hits the Ball

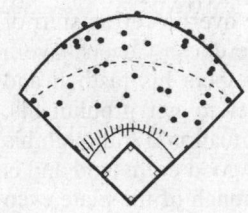 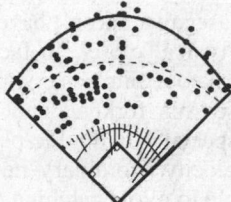

Vs. LHP   **Vs. RHP**

2003 Situational Stats

	AB	H	HR	RBI	Avg		AB	H	HR	RBI	Avg
Home	196	51	4	25	.260	LHP	113	30	2	15	.265
Road	192	56	3	27	.292	RHP	275	77	5	37	.280
First Half	251	71	4	27	.283	Sc Pos	96	27	2	44	.281
Scnd Half	137	36	3	25	.263	Clutch	45	10	0	6	.222

2003 Rankings (American League)

- Did not rank near the top or bottom in any category

Shigetoshi Hasegawa

2003 Season

Shigetoshi Hasegawa became the Mariners' closer in July after a series of unlikely developments. One of those developments was his near-spotless performance over the first half, while the other was a series of injuries that took several of the more-qualified closer candidates out of the equation. Hasegawa's improbable run continued as he converted his first 14 save opportunities and took a sub-1.00 ERA into September. He faltered during the final weeks of the season but still finished with the lowest ERA of any American League reliever. He also stranded 25 of the 30 runners he inherited.

Pitching

Hasegawa doesn't have the overpowering stuff of a typical closer. In fact, he doesn't even have a strikeout pitch. He simply spots his fastball and uses his forkball and slider to get groundballs, especially in double-play situations. Although his velocity is ordinary, he has good command and is able to avoid catching too much of the plate even when he's behind in the count. Lefthanded hitters find him just as tough to solve as righties do. Hasegawa isn't as sharp when used on consecutive days, but he remains effective for more than an inning at a time. The key to his emergence last season was a sudden knack for completely shutting down opponents whenever runners reached base. He never had shown such ability before, and it's hard to expect it to continue.

Defense

Hasegawa is a reliable fielder in every respect. He fields comebackers capably, never throws the ball away and cuts off the running game with a compact stretch delivery. He hasn't allowed a stolen base since May 12, 2001.

2004 Outlook

A free agent, the 35-year-old Hasegawa wasn't certain to find a team that would make him its closer, even given his success in that role last season. He has a track record as a capable setup man, and the reliever agreed to return to Seattle, signing a two-year, $6.3 million deal to stay.

Position: RP
Bats: R **Throws:** R
Ht: 5'11" **Wt:** 180

Opening Day Age: 35
Born: 8/1/68 in Kobe, Japan
ML Seasons: 7
Pronunciation:
shig-eh-toe-shi hoss-eh-gawa
Nickname: Shiggy

Overall Statistics

	W	L	Pct.	ERA	G	GS	Sv	IP	H	BB	SO	HR	Avg
'03	2	4	.333	1.48	63	0	16	73.0	62	18	32	5	.235
Car.	40	34	.541	3.47	403	8	33	585.2	558	218	371	67	.256

2003 Pitching Profile

	Shigetoshi Hasegawa	AL Average
Overall Strike %	59.8	62.8
1st Pitch Strike %	59.2	58.7
Ratio	1.10	1.39
Strikeouts per 9 IP	3.95	6.11
Walks per 9 IP	2.22	3.16
Home Runs per 9 IP	0.62	1.11
Strikeout/Walk Ratio	1.78	1.93
Groundball/Flyball Ratio	1.47	1.18

2003 Situational Stats

	W	L	ERA	Sv	IP		AB	H	HR	RBI	Avg
Home	0	2	0.97	8	37.0	LHB	142	35	2	10	.246
Road	2	2	2.00	8	36.0	RHB	122	27	3	6	.221
First Half	1	0	0.77	5	46.2	Sc Pos	56	11	1	12	.196
Scnd Half	1	4	2.73	11	26.1	Clutch	141	30	2	9	.213

2003 Rankings (American League)

- 1st in most GDPs induced per GDP situation (25.0%)
- 3rd in lowest percentage of inherited runners scored (16.7) and fewest strikeouts per nine innings in relief (3.9)
- Led the Mariners in saves, games finished (36), save percentage (94.1), lowest percentage of inherited runners scored (16.7), relief ERA (1.48) and relief losses (4)

Edgar Martinez

2003 Season

Edgar Martinez was in the midst of a typical Edgar Martinez season—one which would have been one of the best seasons ever for a 40-year-old—when he broke his left big toe in late August. Incredibly, he continued to play; less incredibly, his production fell off badly, as he batted only .238 with two home runs in his last 101 at-bats as the Mariners lost their hold on a playoff spot. He finished with fine numbers, but it was a disheartening finish to what at the time could have been his final season.

Hitting

There is no sure way to get Martinez out—even waiting for him to grow old hasn't seemed to have worked. A thinking man's hitter, he almost always looks over several pitches before picking one to attack. He saw more pitches per plate appearance last year than any other hitter in the American League, and he went to a three-ball count in nearly a third of his plate appearances. When ahead in the count, he will look for a certain pitch in a certain location, and will let just about anything else pass. He isn't afraid to go after a pitch on the outer half of the plate, since he can drive the ball to right field as effortlessly as to left.

Baserunning & Defense

Martinez is so prone to muscle pulls in his legs, and his bat is so irreplaceable, that the Mariners virtually refuse to use him in the field (he's done nothing but DH since 2001). He also is strictly a station-to-station baserunner, although he's still capable of getting up a decent head of steam when absolutely necessary.

2004 Outlook

For most of last season, Martinez gave every indication that 2003 would be his final year. Late in the season, however, he left open the possibility of returning in 2004. It didn't take long for Martinez to make a final decision, agreeing to a one-year deal in early November. If he is healthy enough to play, he'll hit. The only question is how much he'll play.

Position: DH
Bats: R **Throws:** R
Ht: 5'11" **Wt:** 204

Opening Day Age: 41
Born: 1/2/63 in New York, NY
ML Seasons: 17

Overall Statistics

G	AB	R	H	D	T	HR	RBI	SB	BB	SO	Avg	OBP	Slg
145	497	72	146	25	0	24	98	0	92	95	.294	.406	.489
1914	6727	1174	2119	491	15	297	1198	48	1225	1095	.315	.423	.525

Where He Hits the Ball

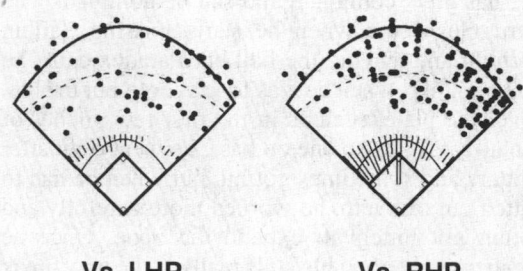

Vs. LHP   **Vs. RHP**

2003 Situational Stats

	AB	H	HR	RBI	Avg		AB	H	HR	RBI	Avg
Home	246	61	8	43	.248	LHP	123	37	8	32	.301
Road	251	85	16	55	.339	RHP	374	109	16	66	.291
First Half	280	85	19	64	.304	Sc Pos	142	50	8	75	.352
Scnd Half	217	61	5	34	.281	Clutch	65	20	1	5	.308

2003 Rankings (American League)

- 1st in most pitches seen per plate appearance (4.32) and batting average on the road
- 2nd in highest percentage of pitches taken (65.0)
- 3rd in batting average with runners in scoring position
- 4th in on-base percentage
- Led the Mariners in sacrifice flies (7), walks, intentional walks (7), on-base percentage, most pitches seen per plate appearance (4.32), highest percentage of pitches taken (65.0), batting average with runners in scoring position, cleanup slugging percentage (.486), batting average on the road and lowest percentage of swings on the first pitch (13.5)

Gil Meche

2003 Season

After having spent most of the last two years battling shoulder injuries and pitching in the minors, Gil Meche was one of the biggest surprises of 2003, opening the season by winning 10 of his first 13 decisions. He was unable to sustain his pace, however, and endured a brutal second half in which he rarely pitched effectively. Still, the best news may have been that he finally managed to get through an entire campaign without an arm injury.

Pitching

Meche has a fastball in the mid-90s and a nasty curve, plus a slider and a changeup. When he's on, he has great command and can be dominant. The struggles come when he starts missing, falling behind and leaving the ball up. Paradoxically, he also got hurt when he was too eager to put the ball over the plate, such as in the first few pitches of an at-bat. With no one on base, he went right after hitters and sometimes got hit, but when he had to pitch out of a jam, he worked more carefully and often got hitters to expand the zone. Once he realizes how good his stuff really is, he may break through to the next level. He still must prove he has the stamina to be a starter—besides his second-half drop-off, he also tended to lose effectiveness after he reached the 60-pitch mark.

Defense

Meche rarely hurts himself with the glove and has committed just one error in his big league career. He doesn't have much of a pickoff move, so he rarely throws over, but he keeps the running game well in hand by shortening up his delivery.

2004 Outlook

Before Meche hurt his shoulder in 2000, he was one of the more promising young pitchers in the game. Now it seems he's back on track to becoming the pitcher that was once envisioned. At age 25, he may be coming into his own. The possibility of re-injury remains, but if he stays healthy he certainly is capable of having a big year.

Position: SP
Bats: R **Throws:** R
Ht: 6' 3" **Wt:** 200

Opening Day Age: 25
Born: 9/8/78 in Lafayette, LA
ML Seasons: 3
Pronunciation: MESH

Overall Statistics

	W	L	Pct.	ERA	G	GS	Sv	IP	H	BB	SO	HR	Avg
'03	15	13	.536	4.59	32	32	0	186.1	187	63	130	30	.263
Car.	27	21	.563	4.43	63	62	0	357.2	335	160	237	46	.252

2003 Pitching Profile

	Gil Meche	AL Average
Overall Strike %	61.6	62.8
1st Pitch Strike %	54.3	58.7
Ratio	1.34	1.39
Strikeouts per 9 IP	6.28	6.11
Walks per 9 IP	3.04	3.16
Home Runs per 9 IP	1.45	1.11
Strikeout/Walk Ratio	2.06	1.93
Groundball/Flyball Ratio	0.92	1.18

2003 Situational Stats

	W	L	ERA	Sv	IP		AB	H	HR	RBI	Avg
Home	8	5	3.31	0	87.0	LHB	385	106	17	38	.275
Road	7	8	5.71	0	99.1	RHB	326	81	13	41	.248
First Half	10	5	3.61	0	112.1	Sc Pos	140	30	3	43	.214
Scnd Half	5	8	6.08	0	74.0	Clutch	31	11	1	2	.355

2003 Rankings (American League)

- 3rd in most home runs allowed per nine innings (1.45)
- 5th in most pitches thrown per batter (3.90) and highest ERA on the road
- 8th in home runs allowed and lowest batting average allowed with runners in scoring position
- 9th in lowest groundball-flyball ratio allowed (0.9)
- 10th in losses, lowest ERA at home and most run support per nine innings (6.0)
- Led the Mariners in highest strikeout-walk ratio (2.1) and lowest batting average allowed with runners in scoring position

Jamie Moyer

2003 Season

At age 40, ageless lefthander Jamie Moyer enjoyed perhaps the best season of his 17-year major league career. He won a personal-best 21 games, had the lowest ERA of his career and became only the fifth pitcher in modern history to post a 20 win season in his forties. Late in the season, Moyer's stellar pitching helped keep Seattle in the wild-card race until the season's final days.

Pitching

Moyer's fastball rarely gets past the mid-80s, but he adds several "virtual" miles per hour to it by mixing it with one of the game's best changeups, which he'll throw at any point in the count. He also throws a slow curve to lefthanded hitters, and a cutter to move righthanded hitters off the plate and set up the changeup. His ability to paint the black enables him to work ahead in the count and force hitters to chase changeups off the corner. His reliance on location and changing speeds, rather than throwing breaking balls, helps make him one of the rare southpaws who's more effective against righthanded hitters. And although he's anything from overpowering, he isn't afraid to work up in the zone.

Defense

Moyer has a good pickoff move and isn't afraid to use it. He is tough to run on, although he sometimes neglects to hold runners on second—he gave up four steals of third base—but baserunners trying to steal second were successful on only seven of 13 attempts. Like Greg Maddux, Moyer finishes his delivery in good position to field, and he is an active and capable member of his infield defense. He's in good shape and moves as well as ever.

2004 Outlook

When will Moyer begin to show his age? He's defied the normal aging process thus far, so it's hard to say. The time may be coming when he won't be able to throw quite as many innings, but in a big park with fast outfielders behind him, he'll likely remain effective a while longer.

Position: SP
Bats: L **Throws:** L
Ht: 6' 0" **Wt:** 175

Opening Day Age: 41
Born: 11/18/62 in Sellersville, PA
ML Seasons: 17

Overall Statistics

W	L	Pct.	ERA	G	GS	Sv	IP	H	BB	SO	HR	Avg
21	7	.750	3.27	33	33	0	215.0	199	66	129	19	.246
185	132	.584	4.07	472	420	0	2737.2	2785	780	1657	314	.264

2003 Pitching Profile

	Jamie Moyer	AL Average
Overall Strike %	62.0	62.8
1st Pitch Strike %	58.4	58.7
Ratio	1.23	1.39
Strikeouts per 9 IP	5.40	6.11
Walks per 9 IP	2.76	3.16
Home Runs per 9 IP	0.80	1.11
Strikeout/Walk Ratio	1.95	1.93
Groundball/Flyball Ratio	0.85	1.18

2003 Situational Stats

	W	L	ERA	Sv	IP		AB	H	HR	RBI	Avg
Home	12	2	3.24	0	102.2	LHB	247	68	7	29	.275
Road	9	5	3.28	0	112.1	RHB	563	131	12	49	.233
First Half	12	5	3.02	0	122.1	Sc Pos	168	42	6	62	.250
Scnd Half	9	2	3.59	0	92.2	Clutch	48	16	0	3	.333

2003 Rankings (American League)

- 2nd in wins
- 4th in winning percentage and lowest ground ball-flyball ratio allowed (0.8)
- 6th in ERA, lowest slugging percentage allowed (.367) and most pitches thrown per batter (3.84)
- 7th in lowest ERA on the road
- 8th in games started, innings pitched, batters faced (897) and fewest home runs allowed per nine innings (.80)
- 9th in pitches thrown (3,448), lowest batting average allowed (.246) and lowest ERA at home
- 10th in pickoff throws (109)
- Led the Mariners in ERA, wins, games started, innings pitched, hits allowed, batters faced (897), stolen bases allowed (11), winning percentage, lowest on-base percentage allowed (.307), lowest ERA at home and fewest home runs allowed per nine innings (.80)

Seattle

John Olerud

2003 Season

It finally happened: John Olerud had an off year. A strained right hamstring suffered in early July might have had something to do with it, although Olerud—characteristically—played through it and never complained. Still, his struggles at the plate in the second half had a lot to do with the Mariners' offensive problems and their resulting decline in the standings. By the time Olerud got his bat going, too much ground already had been lost.

Hitting

Olerud is a line-drive hitter who covers the entire plate with his smooth lefthanded swing. He hits the ball where it's pitched and stays back well on breaking balls. It sounds strange to say, but Olerud is one of the best contact hitters in baseball—when he goes after a pitch, he rarely misses it. One of his greatest assets is his batting eye, which enables him to draw a good number of walks and work himself into hitters' counts. Lefthanders can give him trouble, and he sometimes was given a day off against them last year before Greg Colbrunn got hurt.

Baserunning & Defense

Olerud is one of the best defensive first basemen in the majors, and was rewarded with his third Gold Glove last year. He isn't flashy, so his reputation has taken a while to catch up. He simply makes all the plays and makes them look easy. Few are better at scooping low throws, and he catches every foul pop that can be caught. He doesn't have the speed to be any sort of factor on the bases, but he knows his limitations and hardly ever makes a poor gamble.

2004 Outlook

Olerud has a year left on his contract. The Mariners have not gone into a rebuilding stage, so he is likely to remain for that final season as long as the Mariners compete. With Olerud coming off a subpar season, the Mariners are looking for a return to his usual levels of production.

Position: 1B
Bats: L **Throws:** L
Ht: 6' 5" **Wt:** 225

Opening Day Age: 35
Born: 8/5/68 in Seattle, WA
ML Seasons: 15
Pronunciation: OLE-le-RUDE

Overall Statistics

G	AB	R	H	D	T	HR	RBI	SB	BB	SO	Avg	OBP	Slg
152	539	64	145	35	0	10	83	0	84	67	.269	.372	.390
2020	6994	1076	2079	473	12	239	1145	11	1198	935	.297	.402	.471

Where He Hits the Ball

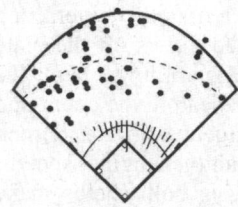 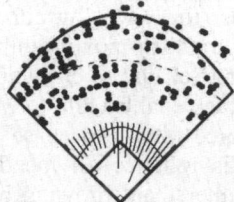

Vs. LHP   **Vs. RHP**

2003 Situational Stats

	AB	H	HR	RBI	Avg		AB	H	HR	RBI	Avg
Home	261	75	8	50	.287	LHP	155	37	0	23	.239
Road	278	70	2	33	.252	RHP	384	108	10	60	.281
First Half	293	81	4	40	.276	Sc Pos	149	43	5	73	.289
Scnd Half	246	64	6	43	.260	Clutch	71	19	0	8	.268

2003 Rankings (American League)

- 3rd in highest percentage of swings put into play (53.6) and fielding percentage at first base (.998)
- 4th in highest percentage of pitches taken (64.2)
- 6th in GDPs (20)
- 7th in lowest percentage of swings that missed (11.0) and lowest percentage of swings on the first pitch (14.8)
- 9th in walks
- Led the Mariners in intentional walks (7), GDPs (20), lowest percentage of swings that missed (11.0) and highest percentage of swings put into play (53.6)

Joel Pineiro

2003 Season

As young pitchers sometimes do, Joel Pineiro showed flashes of brilliance along with some inconsistency last year. After finding mixed success over the first two months of the season, he became one of the hottest starters in baseball in June and July. Heading into August, it looked like he might have a shot at a 20-win season. Suddenly, he went into a mysterious funk, dropping five straight starts. Overall, it still was a creditable season for the youngster, who was only 24 and was in his first full season in the rotation. His ERA was more than a half-run higher than in 2002, but that was misleading—he actually pitched better than he had the year before.

Pitching

Pineiro doesn't have jaw-dropping stuff, but he has a number of weapons and locates them well. He works off a low-90s fastball and a two-seamer. Depending on what's working on a given night, he'll mix in sliders, changeups and overhand curves. His patterns never are predictable. Coming into the 2002 season, his stamina was untested, but his problems last year wound up being of the opposite type—first-inning troubles dogged him time and again in 2003. If he made it through the early innings, he often cruised through the later frames. He actually threw more pitches per start than any hurler in the American League, despite his youth and decidedly non-workhorse-like build.

Defense

Basestealers seemed to have an easier time reading Pineiro in the second half, but he did a decent job against the running game overall, especially for someone with a high leg kick and without much of a pickoff move. He's a decent fielder and is athletic enough to make all the plays. He made just one error in 45 total chances in 2003.

2004 Outlook

It won't take much more development for Pineiro to become a potential ace of the rotation. He doesn't quite have a No. 1 starter's stuff, though, so it's anything but certain that he'll be able to take that next step. Still, he is one of the better young starters in baseball, period.

Position: SP
Bats: R **Throws:** R
Ht: 6' 1" **Wt:** 200

Opening Day Age: 25
Born: 9/25/78 in Rio Padres, PR
ML Seasons: 4

Overall Statistics

	W	L	Pct.	ERA	G	GS	Sv	IP	H	BB	SO	HR	Avg
'03	16	11	.593	3.78	32	32	0	211.2	192	76	151	19	.241
Car.	37	20	.649	3.38	94	72	0	500.2	456	164	353	48	.243

2003 Pitching Profile

	Joel Pineiro	AL Average
Overall Strike %	63.2	62.8
1st Pitch Strike %	60.9	58.7
Ratio	1.27	1.39
Strikeouts per 9 IP	6.42	6.11
Walks per 9 IP	3.23	3.16
Home Runs per 9 IP	0.81	1.11
Strikeout/Walk Ratio	1.99	1.93
Groundball/Flyball Ratio	1.26	1.18

2003 Situational Stats

	W	L	ERA	Sv	IP		AB	H	HR	RBI	Avg
Home	10	7	3.35	0	115.2	LHB	441	103	11	53	.234
Road	6	4	4.31	0	96.0	RHB	355	89	8	35	.251
First Half	11	5	3.28	0	129.0	Sc Pos	181	48	2	63	.265
Scnd Half	5	6	4.57	0	82.2	Clutch	26	6	0	1	.231

2003 Rankings (American League)

- 1st in shutouts (2)
- 2nd in most pitches thrown per batter (3.93)
- 5th in walks allowed and lowest slugging percentage allowed (.359)
- 6th in highest walks per nine innings (3.2)
- 7th in complete games (3), pitches thrown (3,497), lowest batting average allowed (.241) and highest stolen-base percentage allowed (84.6)
- 8th in wins
- Led the Mariners in complete games (3), shutouts (2), walks allowed, strikeouts, pitches thrown (3,497), stolen bases allowed (11), lowest batting average allowed (.241), lowest slugging percentage allowed (.359), highest groundball-flyball ratio allowed (1.3) and most run support per nine innings (6.0)

Ichiro Suzuki

2003 Season

For both Ichiro Suzuki and the Mariners, it was a good season until the final six weeks. Ichiro was hitting .342 through August 16 but hit just .220 the rest of the way. The slump came at the worst possible time, and he later admitted he'd been feeling the pressure keenly as he struggled and the team's playoff hopes slowly died. Nonetheless, it was another fine season on the whole, as he was a steady leadoff man for most of the year and excelled in the field from start to finish.

Hitting

Ichiro's bat control is becoming legendary. He can wait until the last instant before flipping the ball through a hole in the defense, like a tennis player backhanding a volley. He does this as almost an afterthought on his way out of the box, and seemingly is a step down the line before he completes his swing. This, combined with his terrific speed, makes for many infield hits and very few ground-balls that are considered routine. He will stay back and drive the ball on occasion, and did so a bit less infrequently last year. He still hits mostly groundballs. He seldom walks—not because he's recklessly aggressive, but because he puts the ball in play so often when he does swing.

Baserunning & Defense

With the speed and range for center field and the arm for right field, Ichiro is the best defensive corner outfielder in the majors. Not surprisingly, he won his third Gold Glove in as many years in the bigs. How good is his throwing arm? No one runs on him, and yet he *still* led American League right fielders in assists. He also is a top basestealer who can swipe second or third and rarely gets thrown out.

2004 Outlook

Ichiro is arbitration-eligible for the first time, and he may be in a position to extract a long-term deal from the Mariners. If no agreement is reached, the issue could become a distraction this season; there's little else that could slow him down.

Position: RF
Bats: L **Throws:** R
Ht: 5' 9" **Wt:** 172

Opening Day Age: 30
Born: 10/22/73 in Kasugai, Japan
ML Seasons: 3
Pronunciation: ee-chee-row

Overall Statistics

	G	AB	R	H	D	T	HR	RBI	SB	BB	SO	Avg	OBP	Slg
'03	159	679	111	212	29	8	13	62	34	36	69	.312	.352	.436
Car.	473	2018	349	662	90	24	29	182	121	134	184	.328	.374	.440

Where He Hits the Ball

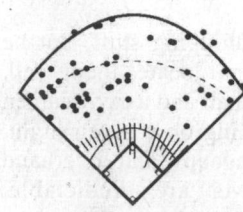 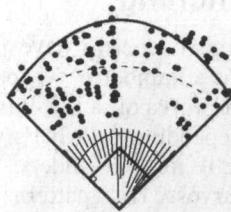

Vs. LHP   **Vs. RHP**

2003 Situational Stats

	AB	H	HR	RBI	Avg		AB	H	HR	RBI	Avg
Home	329	103	8	35	.313	LHP	209	75	0	17	.359
Road	350	109	5	27	.311	RHP	470	137	13	45	.291
First Half	389	137	8	28	.352	Sc Pos	105	36	3	47	.343
Scnd Half	290	75	5	34	.259	Clutch	77	22	1	7	.286

2003 Rankings (American League)

- 1st in singles, steals of third (12) and fielding percentage in right field (.994)
- 2nd in at-bats, hits and fewest GDPs per GDP situation (3.1%)
- 3rd in plate appearances (725) and batting average vs. lefthanded pitchers
- Led the Mariners in batting average, at-bats, runs scored, hits, singles, triples, stolen bases, caught stealing (8), intentional walks (7), plate appearances (725), games played, highest groundball-flyball ratio (1.8), bunts in play (22), steals of third (12), fewest GDPs per GDP situation (3.1%), batting average with the bases loaded (.600), batting average vs. lefthanded pitchers, on-base percentage for a leadoff hitter (.352)

Randy Winn

2003 Season

Coming off his best season, Randy Winn was traded from Tampa Bay to Seattle in October 2002 as compensation for manager Lou Piniella, then virtually duplicated his 2002 performance. That doesn't mean there weren't bumps along the way, however. He had a subpar first half amid rumors that the Mariners were looking to add a bat and it seemed a given that Winn would be the one bumped to the bench when a deal was struck. A deal never came, though, and Winn went on to enjoy an excellent second half.

Hitting

Winn no longer is the pure slap-hitter he was when he first came up. He still hits the ball on the ground a lot and uses his speed to reach base, but he also has learned to drive the ball at times. He's a better hitter from the right side of the plate. He can bunt for a hit or a sacrifice. Winn doesn't have the patience or strike-zone judgment to be an ideal leadoff hitter, but he is a good fit in the second slot in the order. And while he isn't what anyone would call an RBI man, he does have a knack for finding holes when runners are on base.

Baserunning & Defense

Below-average reads prevent Winn from being a good defensive center fielder, but his pure speed helps him make up for errors in judgment, and the overall package is better than average for a left fielder. He compensates for a weak throwing arm by charging balls well and always being in a good position to throw. Baserunners test him, but he's rung up as many as 13 assists in a season. Winn has become an excellent percentage basestealer and is a threat to steal even when he's on second.

2004 Outlook

Winn was arbitration-eligible at season's end, so there was a chance the Mariners would non-tender him and opt for a more traditional hitter for left field. Now Winn looks destined for center after the Mariners signed Raul Ibanez to play left and didn't offer salary arbitration to center fielder Mike Cameron. In mid-December, Winn was signed to a two-year contract that gives him an option to return for 2006.

Position: LF/CF
Bats: B **Throws:** R
Ht: 6' 2" **Wt:** 197

Opening Day Age: 29
Born: 6/9/74 in Los Angeles, CA
ML Seasons: 6

Overall Statistics

	G	AB	R	H	D	T	HR	RBI	SB	BB	SO	Avg	OBP	Slg
'03	157	600	103	177	37	4	11	75	23	41	108	.295	.346	.425
Car.	676	2436	367	690	131	32	35	257	103	206	455	.283	.343	.406

Where He Hits the Ball

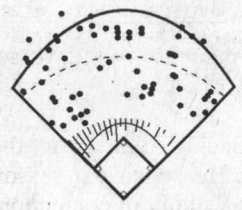 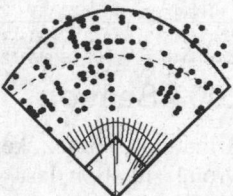

Vs. LHP   Vs. RHP

2003 Situational Stats

	AB	H	HR	RBI	Avg		AB	H	HR	RBI	Avg
Home	285	81	6	37	.284	LHP	169	53	3	16	.314
Road	315	96	5	38	.305	RHP	431	124	8	59	.288
First Half	339	91	2	32	.268	Sc Pos	169	59	6	66	.349
Scnd Half	261	86	9	43	.330	Clutch	75	19	2	12	.253

2003 Rankings (American League)

- 3rd in fielding percentage in left field (.990)
- 4th in batting average with runners in scoring position
- 6th in singles and steals of third (5)
- Led the Mariners in doubles, sacrifice bunts (6) and hit by pitch (8)

Armando Benitez

Position: RP
Bats: R **Throws:** R
Ht: 6' 4" **Wt:** 229

Opening Day Age: 31
Born: 11/3/72 in Ramon Santana, DR
ML Seasons: 10
Pronunciation: buh-NEE-tezz

Overall Statistics

	W	L	Pct.	ERA	G	GS	Sv	IP	H	BB	SO	HR	Avg
'03	4	4	.500	2.96	69	0	21	73.0	59	41	75	6	.218
Car.	30	31	.492	3.03	564	0	197	584.1	392	314	764	67	.188

2003 Situational Stats

	W	L	ERA	Sv	IP		AB	H	HR	RBI	Avg
Home	3	2	3.54	13	40.2	LHB	140	30	5	23	.214
Road	1	2	2.23	8	32.1	RHB	131	29	1	8	.221
First Half	3	3	3.10	21	49.1	Sc Pos	89	17	4	27	.191
Scnd Half	1	1	2.66	0	23.2	Clutch	165	41	4	24	.248

2003 Season

Armando Benitez kept finding himself in the wrong situation last year. He began the season with the Mets, who quickly fell out of contention. After struggling early, he rebounded and made the All-Star team, but the Mets shed his salary by dealing him to the Yankees in July. He served as a setup man for them for three weeks, and then was traded to Seattle, where he pitched decently at first but soon got buried.

Pitching & Defense

Benitez complements a high-90s fastball with a hard splitter and short slider. When he's able to throw enough strikes to keep batters swinging, he can be tough to hit, but his command can waver. He's noticeably less sharp when asked to work on consecutive days. With no weapons to combat the running game, he's especially easy to run on—opposing basestealers were 10 of 11 against him in 2003. He isn't very mobile in the field, either.

2004 Outlook

Benitez' demotion from closer to setup man last season probably will be short-lived. Despite his memorable big-game blowups, he's been a capable closer over the course of several seasons. Now a free agent, he almost certainly will be closing games for some team again this year.

Jeff Cirillo

Position: 3B
Bats: R **Throws:** R
Ht: 6' 1" **Wt:** 200

Opening Day Age: 34
Born: 9/23/69 in Pasadena, CA
ML Seasons: 10
Pronunciation: suh-RILL-oh

Overall Statistics

	G	AB	R	H	D	T	HR	RBI	SB	BB	SO	Avg	OBP	Slg
'03	87	258	24	53	11	0	2	23	1	24	32	.205	.284	.271
Car.	1317	4680	702	1398	296	19	102	647	56	495	606	.299	.369	.435

2003 Situational Stats

	AB	H	HR	RBI	Avg		AB	H	HR	RBI	Avg
Home	123	22	1	8	.179	LHP	88	20	1	6	.227
Road	135	31	1	15	.230	RHP	170	33	1	17	.194
First Half	239	52	2	22	.218	Sc Pos	71	18	0	18	.254
Scnd Half	19	1	0	1	.053	Clutch	25	2	0	2	.080

2003 Season

The nightmare deepened for Jeff Cirillo in 2003. His first year in Seattle had been disappointing, but last year was immeasurably worse. He got off to a frigid start, lost his job in mid-July, and hardly played the rest of the year. He posted career lows in all three major hitting-percentage categories, and barely finished above the Mendoza line.

Hitting, Baserunning & Defense

Once a high-average line-drive hitter, Cirillo has become completely lost at the plate, rarely driving the ball with any authority. One thing that remains strong is Cirillo's defense. He has a very strong arm and can throw off-balance or from behind the bag. He may have lost a step laterally, but his range is still decent, and he still charges bunts very well. He no longer has enough speed to run much, and his opportunities to do so have become increasingly limited.

2004 Outlook

It's clear Cirillo's days in Seattle are over. He has two years and $15 million left on his contract, so the Mariners would have to eat part of it in order to find a taker. Even in the right situation, it's very much an open question whether he still has the offensive skills to be a regular.

Ben Davis

Position: C
Bats: B **Throws:** R
Ht: 6' 4" **Wt:** 225

Opening Day Age: 27
Born: 3/10/77 in
Chester, PA
ML Seasons: 6

Overall Statistics

	G	AB	R	H	D	T	HR	RBI	SB	BB	SO	Avg	OBP	Slg
'03	80	246	25	58	18	0	6	42	0	18	61	.236	.284	.382
Car.	418	1319	146	318	68	2	32	186	8	141	336	.241	.313	.368

2003 Situational Stats

	AB	H	HR	RBI	Avg			AB	H	HR	RBI	Avg
Home	105	23	2	16	.219	LHP	57	16	3	12	.281
Road	141	35	4	26	.248	RHP	189	42	3	30	.222
First Half	153	45	5	32	.294	Sc Pos	67	20	1	34	.299
Scnd Half	93	13	1	10	.140	Clutch	35	8	2	8	.229

2003 Season

After coming to camp 30 pounds heavier and noticeably stronger in his upper body, Ben Davis continued to split time with Dan Wilson behind the plate. At first, the added bulk seemed to help, as Davis took a .300 average into mid-July. After the All-Star break, however, his production nose-dived, and he ended up with numbers worse than the season before.

Hitting, Baserunning & Defense

The switch-hitting Davis is a good fastball hitter who does his best hitting early in the count. He can be set up or induced to expand the zone when he falls behind. He seems to have slightly better power from the right side. His strong throwing arm is his best asset behind the plate, and he nabbed a respectable 31.9 percent of would-be basestealers last year. Davis still is refining his pitch-blocking skills. He's a below-average runner by any standard.

2004 Outlook

This season may be Wilson's last in Seattle, so it's time for Davis to assert himself if he's to take over the full-time job. Davis had been expected to make some progress toward that end last year, but his brutal second half raised some doubts.

Ryan Franklin

Position: SP
Bats: R **Throws:** R
Ht: 6' 3" **Wt:** 180

Opening Day Age: 31
Born: 3/5/73 in Fort
Smith, AR
ML Seasons: 4

Overall Statistics

	W	L	Pct.	ERA	G	GS	Sv	IP	H	BB	SO	HR	Avg
'03	11	13	.458	3.57	32	32	0	212.0	199	61	99	34	.251
Car.	23	19	.548	3.73	117	44	0	420.1	402	115	230	63	.252

2003 Situational Stats

	W	L	ERA	Sv	IP			AB	H	HR	RBI	Avg
Home	6	7	3.83	0	122.1	LHB	408	109	23	57	.267
Road	5	6	3.21	0	89.2	RHB	386	90	11	33	.233
First Half	6	8	3.75	0	117.2	Sc Pos	145	35	6	54	.241
Scnd Half	5	5	3.34	0	94.1	Clutch	34	9	1	2	.265

2003 Season

Ryan Franklin's first full season in the starting rotation was a success. Though he was perhaps the least-heralded member of the Mariners' starting staff, he wound up being its most effective and consistent member besides Jamie Moyer. Franklin got little run support at times and deserved a better won-lost record—his 3.57 ERA was ninth-best in the American League among qualifiers.

Pitching & Defense

Franklin has one of the most varied repertoires in the majors. He works primarily with a fastball, curveball, slider and changeup, and also can throw a splitter. He added a sinker this season, and began to work on a cutter. His velocity is average at best, so he must rely on command and deception instead. A flyball pitcher, he can be susceptible to the longball, especially against lefthanded hitters. He's a reliable fielder and cuts off the running game well with a quick pickoff move (that he uses a lot) and a compact delivery.

2004 Outlook

It's hard to imagine how Franklin could get any more out of his ability, and the Mariners rewarded him with a two-year contract. He may remain a solid mid-rotation starter, but he will do well just to maintain the levels he established last year.

Seattle

Julio Mateo

Position: RP
Bats: R **Throws:** R
Ht: 6' 0" **Wt:** 177

Opening Day Age: 26
Born: 8/2/77 in Bani, DR
ML Seasons: 2

Overall Statistics

	W	L	Pct.	ERA	G	GS	Sv	IP	H	BB	SO	HR	Avg
'03	4	0	1.000	3.15	50	0	1	85.2	69	13	71	14	.220
Car.	4	0	1.000	3.38	62	0	1	106.2	89	25	86	16	.225

2003 Situational Stats

	W	L	ERA	Sv	IP		AB	H	HR	RBI	Avg
Home	2	0	3.61	1	42.1	LHB	168	37	8	22	.220
Road	2	0	2.70	0	43.1	RHB	146	32	6	12	.219
First Half	1	0	3.46	0	41.2	Sc Pos	62	13	3	20	.210
Scnd Half	3	0	2.86	1	44.0	Clutch	25	7	2	2	.280

2003 Season

Julio Mateo's first full season was surprisingly good. He was effective despite being used in a variety of roles, pitching long and middle relief, and even in a setup role when needed. He was one of the most important members of the bullpen in July and August. From June 1 on, he logged 50 strikeouts against just four unintentional walks.

Pitching & Defense

Mateo has a deep repertoire for a reliever, with a low-90s fastball, a hard slider, two-seamer and splitter. The latter two pitches give him weapons to keep lefthanded hitters in check. He throws strikes but works up in the zone and can be taken deep. Being used inconsistently didn't seem to affect him. He has the arm to pitch on consecutive days or to work several innings at a time. One thing he doesn't do is help himself with the glove, as he doesn't reach many balls. He also does little to deter basestealers, who stole successfully in all nine attempts against him.

2004 Outlook

Mateo is the type of pitcher who is most useful when he isn't overexposed. Being the all-purpose innings sponge of the bullpen served him well, and he may continue to be useful in that role.

Arthur Rhodes

Position: RP
Bats: L **Throws:** L
Ht: 6' 2" **Wt:** 212

Opening Day Age: 34
Born: 10/24/69 in Waco, TX
ML Seasons: 13

Overall Statistics

	W	L	Pct.	ERA	G	GS	Sv	IP	H	BB	SO	HR	Avg
'03	3	3	.500	4.17	67	0	3	54.0	53	18	48	4	.256
Car.	69	51	.575	4.33	514	61	17	883.1	770	388	868	98	.235

2003 Situational Stats

	W	L	ERA	Sv	IP		AB	H	HR	RBI	Avg
Home	1	1	5.02	3	28.2	LHB	104	28	2	9	.269
Road	2	2	3.20	0	25.1	RHB	103	25	2	19	.243
First Half	1	1	3.82	3	37.2	Sc Pos	64	16	2	23	.250
Scnd Half	2	2	4.96	0	16.1	Clutch	106	28	3	15	.264

2003 Season

Arthur Rhodes continued to be one of the American League's most effective and frequently used relievers for the first half of 2003. He sprained his right ankle in late July though, and while he didn't miss any time, it affected him for most of the second half. His velocity and effectiveness waned, and he was bumped down a few notches on the bullpen totem pole. His 48 punchouts represented his lowest total since 1994.

Pitching & Defense

When Rhodes is right, he starts hitters with hard fastballs and finishes them with hard sliders. He also has a curve and change, but doesn't need to go to them much. He has the stuff to attack hitters, get ahead in the count and put them away. Batters from either side of the plate find him equally tough. He's one of the toughest short relievers to run on—only four bases have been stolen off him in the last four years. He isn't especially mobile, but he's quite surehanded.

2004 Outlook

A free agent, Rhodes is too good to be pigeon-holed as a lefty specialist. He'll likely find a team willing to make him the closer or co-closer, and he's quite capable of thriving in that type of role.

Rey Sanchez

Position: SS/2B
Bats: R **Throws:** R
Ht: 5' 9" **Wt:** 170

Opening Day Age: 36
Born: 10/5/67 in Rio Piedras, PR
ML Seasons: 13
Pronunciation: RAY SAN-chezz

Overall Statistics

	G	AB	R	H	D	T	HR	RBI	SB	BB	SO	Avg	OBP	Slg
'03	102	344	33	86	8	2	0	23	2	16	39	.250	.285	.285
Car.	1376	4522	519	1235	178	29	13	361	55	215	477	.273	.309	.334

2003 Situational Stats

	AB	H	HR	RBI	Avg		AB	H	HR	RBI	Avg
Home	170	40	0	18	.235	LHP	89	26	0	5	.292
Road	174	46	0	5	.264	RHP	255	60	0	18	.235
First Half	164	34	0	11	.207	Sc Pos	87	20	0	23	.230
Scnd Half	180	52	0	12	.289	Clutch	52	12	0	3	.231

2003 Season

Signed as a free agent to play shortstop for the Mets until Jose Reyes was ready, Rey Sanchez failed to hit and went down in early May with a sprained thumb that sidelined him for most of the next two months. Sanchez returned in July, and at the end of the month he was dealt to Seattle, where he took over at shortstop for the rest of the year. He hit well in August (.347) but slumped in September (.229).

Hitting, Baserunning & Defense

Though he generally hits for a decent average, Sanchez has little offensive value, as his complete lack of power and inability to work walks limit him to the lower third of the order. He has good first-step quickness but lacks the speed to be much of a factor on the bases. He has just four steals in seven attempts over the past two years. It's his fielding skills that keep Sanchez around. He's the complete package at short, with very good range, a strong arm and incredibly soft hands, and he's just as good at second base.

2004 Outlook

A free agent, Sanchez will try to land another one-year deal from a team looking for a short-term stopgap, as he did last winter.

Kazuhiro Sasaki

Position: RP
Bats: R **Throws:** R
Ht: 6' 4" **Wt:** 220

Opening Day Age: 36
Born: 2/22/68 in Sendai, Japan
ML Seasons: 4
Pronunciation: kaz-oo-hero sa-sa-key
Nickname: Daimajin

Overall Statistics

	W	L	Pct.	ERA	G	GS	Sv	IP	H	BB	SO	HR	Avg
'03	1	2	.333	4.05	35	0	10	33.1	31	15	29	2	.238
Car.	7	16	.304	3.14	228	0	129	223.1	165	77	242	24	.200

2003 Situational Stats

	W	L	ERA	Sv	IP		AB	H	HR	RBI	Avg
Home	1	0	3.00	3	15.0	LHB	68	16	1	8	.235
Road	0	2	4.91	7	18.1	RHB	62	15	1	8	.242
First Half	1	1	4.12	10	19.2	Sc Pos	32	8	1	15	.250
Scnd Half	0	1	3.95	0	13.2	Clutch	62	18	1	7	.290

2003 Season

A series of injuries ruined Kazuhiro Sasaki's 2003 season, and by the end he'd even been displaced from his customary role as closer. He missed time early in the year with back problems, and then was sidelined from mid-June to mid-August with cracked ribs. After returning late in the year, he was used only in middle relief and rarely saw action in important situations. It was a big comedown for the Mariners' highest-paid player.

Pitching & Defense

A healthy Sasaki sets up his out pitch, a terrific hard splitter, with a low-90s fastball and an occasional curveball. His velocity is key, since he must be able to get ahead with the fastball in order to make hitters chase his splitter. As a strikeout/flyball pitcher, he rarely catches anything himself besides the catcher's return throws. He does a decent job of holding runners, though basestealers who do chose to run on him almost always are successful.

2004 Outlook

Sasaki will be 36 on Opening Day, but he still has more than enough left to reclaim his job as the closer and run with it. It all will depend on his health. As long as he's able to throw hard enough to set up his splitter, he ought to remain effective.

Seattle

Rafael Soriano

Position: RP
Bats: R **Throws:** R
Ht: 6' 1" **Wt:** 175

Opening Day Age: 24
Born: 12/19/79 in San Jose, DR
ML Seasons: 2

Overall Statistics

	W	L	Pct.	ERA	G	GS	Sv	IP	H	BB	SO	HR	Avg
'03	3	0	1.000	1.53	40	0	1	53.0	30	12	68	2	.162
Car.	3	3	.500	2.96	50	8	2	100.1	75	28	100	10	.203

2003 Situational Stats

	W	L	ERA	Sv	IP		AB	H	HR	RBI	Avg
Home	1	0	1.27	1	28.1	LHB	94	18	1	6	.191
Road	2	0	1.82	0	24.2	RHB	91	12	1	3	.132
First Half	1	0	2.63	0	13.2	Sc Pos	36	4	0	6	.111
Scnd Half	2	0	1.14	1	39.1	Clutch	59	11	1	4	.186

2003 Season

The Mariners' biggest find of the season was Rafael Soriano. He'd missed most of the second half of 2002 with a strained shoulder, and failed to make the team out of camp in 2003. He spent a couple of weeks with the big club in late April and early May, was recalled in mid-June and went on to become perhaps the most effective reliever in the majors over the second half. By mid-August, he'd established himself as the Mariners' top setup man.

Pitching & Defense

With a lively mid-90s fastball and a hard slider, Soriano has the stuff to throw the ball past hitters, and he does. Command had held him back in the past, but he made great strides last year. Pitching relief seemed to suit him perfectly, as he could go full-throttle for an inning at a time and leave his work-in-progress changeup in his back pocket. He is reputed to be a capable fielder, although actual trials have been rare. He ignores baserunners and gets the out at the plate.

2004 Outlook

Soriano is expected to assume a larger role as soon as possible. He could join the rotation if a spot opens up, or serve as the closer if needed. Either way, there's no limit on what he might do.

Dan Wilson

Position: C
Bats: R **Throws:** R
Ht: 6' 3" **Wt:** 215

Opening Day Age: 35
Born: 3/25/69 in Barrington, IL
ML Seasons: 12

Overall Statistics

	G	AB	R	H	D	T	HR	RBI	SB	BB	SO	Avg	OBP	Slg
'03	96	316	32	76	15	2	4	43	0	15	52	.241	.272	.339
Car.	1185	3840	416	1012	198	13	86	484	23	254	696	.264	.310	.389

2003 Situational Stats

	AB	H	HR	RBI	Avg		AB	H	HR	RBI	Avg
Home	167	38	1	21	.228	LHP	106	28	2	20	.264
Road	149	38	3	22	.255	RHP	210	48	2	23	.229
First Half	174	42	1	25	.241	Sc Pos	98	25	1	38	.255
Scnd Half	142	34	3	18	.239	Clutch	31	3	0	6	.097

2003 Season

Dan Wilson's offensive numbers fell off last year but, as always, he made his most significant contributions behind the plate. Wilson started whenever Jamie Moyer pitched, and split time with Ben Davis in all other games. Partly due to Moyer's success, the staff ERA with Wilson behind the plate was just 3.79.

Hitting, Baserunning & Defense

A somewhat defensive hitter, Wilson takes a short stroke, sprays the ball and rarely shows extra-base power. He can bunt a runner over when necessary, although last year he wasn't asked to give himself up as often as he had been in the past. His subpar strike-zone judgment prevents him from drawing many walks or working his way into hitters' counts. He remains one of the best all-around defensive catchers in the majors. He's terrific at blocking pitches, his throwing arm is unfailingly accurate and his pitch-calling skills are respected. He runs better than many catchers but seldom takes chances on the bases.

2004 Outlook

Wilson is signed through 2004. Look for him to cede an increasing share of the catching duties to Davis, perhaps even loosening up his status as the first-stringer. His average could bounce back somewhat.

Other Seattle Mariners

Willie Bloomquist (Pos: 3B/SS, Age: 26, Bats: R)

	G	AB	R	H	D	T	HR	RBI	SB	BB	SO	Avg	OBP	Slg
'03	89	196	30	49	7	2	1	14	4	19	39	.250	.317	.321
Car.	101	229	41	64	11	2	1	21	7	24	41	.279	.348	.358

Bloomquist wasn't able to approach his .455 average in 33 at-bats with Seattle in 2002. But he stayed in the majors for all of 2003 and played all four infield spots and the outfield adequately. 2004 Outlook: C

Pat Borders (Pos: C, Age: 40, Bats: R)

	G	AB	R	H	D	T	HR	RBI	SB	BB	SO	Avg	OBP	Slg
'03	12	14	1	2	1	0	0	1	0	1	5	.143	.200	.214
Car.	1022	3070	268	786	157	12	67	329	6	150	513	.256	.291	.380

Borders is a 40-year-old catcher with just 58 big league at-bats over the last four seasons. Yet, he keeps plugging away at Triple-A. Now he's been encouraged by batting .314 and slugging .536 at Tacoma. 2004 Outlook: C

Giovanni Carrara (Pos: RHP, Age: 36)

	W	L	Pct.	ERA	G	GS	Sv	IP	H	BB	SO	HR	Avg
'03	2	0	1.000	6.83	23	0	0	29.0	40	14	13	6	.333
Car.	17	11	.607	5.31	174	18	1	315.1	349	137	209	62	.282

After two decent seasons in Los Angeles, Carrara came to Seattle and saw his ERA double over half a season before a demotion to Triple-A Tacoma. He was better there, but didn't return in September. 2004 Outlook: C

Greg Colbrunn (Pos: 1B, Age: 34, Bats: R)

	G	AB	R	H	D	T	HR	RBI	SB	BB	SO	Avg	OBP	Slg
'03	22	58	7	16	1	1	3	7	0	4	16	.276	.323	.483
Car.	972	2742	336	798	155	12	98	421	29	169	439	.291	.340	.464

In the five seasons prior to 2003, Colbrunn has batted .315 and slugged .526. He's been especially tough against lefties lately, but an abdominal strain and a pair of wrist surgeries compromised 2003. 2004 Outlook: B

Aaron Looper (Pos: RHP, Age: 27)

	W	L	Pct.	ERA	G	GS	Sv	IP	H	BB	SO	HR	Avg
'03	0	0	—	5.14	6	0	0	7.0	7	2	6	1	.269
Car.	0	0	—	5.14	6	0	0	7.0	7	2	6	1	.269

A cousin to the Marlins' reliever, Looper has been solid himself as a reliever in the high minors the last two seasons. He's not the hard thrower his cousin is, though he could help in Seattle. 2004 Outlook: C

John Mabry (Pos: RF/DH, Age: 33, Bats: L)

	G	AB	R	H	D	T	HR	RBI	SB	BB	SO	Avg	OBP	Slg
'03	64	104	12	22	6	0	3	16	0	15	21	.212	.328	.356
Car.	988	2679	304	721	148	4	69	344	7	210	524	.269	.325	.405

Mabry seemed to rekindle his career as a part-time player in 2002, but a shoulder injury compromised the middle months of his season. He was batting .159 on August 13, but hit .314 down the stretch. 2004 Outlook: C

Mark McLemore (Pos: SS/3B/LF, Age: 39, Bats: B)

	G	AB	R	H	D	T	HR	RBI	SB	BB	SO	Avg	OBP	Slg
'03	99	309	34	72	15	2	2	37	5	38	71	.233	.318	.314
Car.	1755	5942	914	1540	241	47	51	594	272	834	950	.259	.349	.341

McLemore's on-base percentage dropped below .350 for the first time since 1997, though he still managed to play all over the field and batted .264 with a .350 OBP in the second half. He's not dead yet. 2004 Outlook: B

Chad Meyers (Pos: DH, Age: 28, Bats: R)

	G	AB	R	H	D	T	HR	RBI	SB	BB	SO	Avg	OBP	Slg
'03	9	1	1	0	0	0	0	0	1	0	0	.000	.000	.000
Car.	106	212	27	44	11	0	0	9	6	14	43	.208	.281	.259

Meyers has enjoyed solid Triple-A seasons in odd-numbered years of late, and his .300 average and .361 OBP at Triple-A Tacoma earned him his first recall since 2001. He did little to aid his 2004 cause. 2004 Outlook: C

Brian Sweeney (Pos: RHP, Age: 29)

	W	L	Pct.	ERA	G	GS	Sv	IP	H	BB	SO	HR	Avg
'03	0	0	—	1.93	5	0	0	9.1	7	1	7	0	.212
Car.	0	0	—	1.93	5	0	0	9.1	7	1	7	0	.212

A 29-year-old Sweeney, in the midst of his second season at Triple-A Tacoma, got the call when a depleted Seattle pen needed some help in August. He was better than anticipated in his debut. 2004 Outlook: C

Luis Ugueto (Pos: 2B, Age: 25, Bats: B)

	G	AB	R	H	D	T	HR	RBI	SB	BB	SO	Avg	OBP	Slg
'03	12	5	4	1	0	0	0	1	2	1	0	.200	.333	.200
Car.	74	28	23	6	0	0	1	2	10	3	8	.214	.290	.321

A Rule 5 pickup from Florida who spent 2002 in Seattle, Ugueto split most of 2003 between Double-A and Triple-A ball. He could land at short in Seattle if he learns how to get on base more frequently. 2004 Outlook: C

Matt White (Pos: LHP, Age: 26)

	W	L	Pct.	ERA	G	GS	Sv	IP	H	BB	SO	HR	Avg
'03	0	1	.000	22.24	6	0	0	5.2	13	5	0	3	.481
Car.	0	1	.000	22.24	6	0	0	5.2	13	5	0	3	.481

After a so-so Double-A season in the Cleveland system in 2002, White was a Rule 5 pick by Boston in December and traded to Seattle in June. Returned to Cleveland in July, he was solid at Triple-A Buffalo. 2004 Outlook: C

Seattle

Seattle Mariners Minor League Prospects

Organization Overview:

Prior to last season, a string of injuries to top pitching prospects took its toll on the Seattle system, but the emergence of Gil Meche, Rafael Soriano and Julio Mateo in the majors and Travis Blackley, Clint Nageotte and Aaron Taylor in the minors has softened the blow. Blackley, Nageotte, Rett Johnson and Bobby Madritsch at Double-A San Antonio anchored one of the best minor league rotations of 2003. Most of Seattle's key signings have come out of Australia and the Orient, but the club's next star may be Venezuelan Jose Lopez, who at 19 played behind that San Antonio staff. Others who soon may help in Seattle include out-fielders Chris Snelling and Jamal Strong.

Travis Blackley

Position: P **Opening Day Age:** 21
Bats: L **Throws:** L **Born:** 11/4/82 in
Ht: 6' 3" **Wt:** 190 Cheltenham, Australia

Recent Statistics

	W	L	ERA	G	GS	Sv	IP	H	R	BB	SO	HR
2002 A San Berndno	5	9	3.49	21	20	0	121.1	102	52	44	152	11
2003 AA San Antonio	17	3	2.61	27	27	0	162.1	125	55	62	144	11

The Australian lefty went unnoticed until Seattle scouts saw him square off against South Korea's Shin-Soo Choo in the World Junior Championship in 2000. The Mariners signed both of them, Choo as an outfielder. Blackley impressed at short-season Everett in 2001 before suffering a small fracture in his throwing elbow during instructional league. He made a remarkable recovery and fanned 152 in 121.1 innings at high Class-A San Bernardino in 2002, calling on a high-80s fast-ball, an excellent curve and a changeup that was his best pitch. Blackley's command was his biggest asset in an outstanding season at Double-A San Antonio in 2003. His breaking stuff was inconsistent early on, yet he won with his command of his fastball and change. He doesn't overpower hitters.

Shin-Soo Choo

Position: OF **Opening Day Age:** 21
Bats: L **Throws:** L **Born:** 7/13/82 in Pusan,
Ht: 5' 11" **Wt:** 178 South Korea

Recent Statistics

	G	AB	R	H	D	T	HR	RBI	SB	BB	SO	Avg
2002 A Wisconsin	119	420	69	127	24	8	6	48	34	70	98	.302
2002 A San Berndno	11	39	14	12	5	1	1	9	3	9	9	.308
2003 A Inland Empi	110	412	62	118	18	13	9	55	18	44	84	.286

Signed in August 2000, Choo led the Rookie-level Arizona League in runs, triples and walks in 2001. He successfully jumped to full-season ball and played in the Futures Game in 2002. Choo broke a bone in his right foot last July at high Class-A Inland Empire and

missed three weeks. While he failed to bat .300 for the first time as a pro, he still displayed his quick, line-drive stroke and the advanced plate discipline that has generated a .401 OBP in the minors. He still is learning to adjust to offspeed stuff and worked hard at his plate coverage in 2003. He isn't generating many homers, but the Mariners think a power surge is coming. His power potential is more critical if Choo, with a plus arm and good instincts, doesn't succeed as a center fielder.

Felix Hernandez

Position: P **Opening Day Age:** 17
Bats: R **Throws:** R **Born:** 4/8/86 in Valencia,
Ht: 6' 3" **Wt:** 170 VZ

Recent Statistics

	W	L	ERA	G	GS	Sv	IP	H	R	BB	SO	HR
2003 A Everett	7	2	2.29	11	7	0	55.0	43	17	24	73	2
2003 A Wisconsin	0	0	1.93	2	2	0	14.0	9	4	3	18	1

Signed late in 2002, Hernandez made an impressive debut against older college talent in the Rookie-level Northwest League. He dominated with an overpowering mid-90s fastball, a solid curveball and command beyond his years. Hernandez was able to move his fastball all over the strike zone and get hitters to climb the ladder. His curve and changeup also are advanced for his age. Only a late-season promotion to Class-A Wisconsin kept Hernandez from qualifying among Northwest League leaders in wins, ERA and strikeouts. Hernandez looks like a fast-track candidate, someone who may develop into a No. 1 or 2 starter.

Jose Lopez

Position: SS **Opening Day Age:** 20
Bats: R **Throws:** R **Born:** 11/24/83 in
Ht: 6' 2" **Wt:** 170 Anzoategui, VZ

Recent Statistics

	G	AB	R	H	D	T	HR	RBI	SB	BB	SO	Avg
2002 A San Berndno	123	522	82	169	39	5	8	60	31	27	45	.324
2003 AA San Antonio	132	538	82	139	35	2	13	69	18	27	56	.258

Signed in 2000, Lopez was the youngest player in the Rookie-level Northwest League during his 2001 debut, and the teenager was the youngest player in the Double-A Texas League last summer. Yet, Lopez ranks among the best at his position with soft hands, good range, strong arm and instincts rarely seen in someone so young. A growth on a bone in his right foot led to January surgery. Despite a brief spring training, Lopez started quickly and held his own at Double-A San Antonio in 2003. The higher level exposed his free-swinging ways and a need to be more patient. Lopez began learning how pitchers work him, and he started laying off breaking pitches late in the year. When Lopez makes contact, the ball often finds the center of his bat and jumps off it.

Clint Nageotte

Position: P   **Opening Day Age:** 23
Bats: R **Throws:** R   **Born:** 10/25/80 in
Ht: 6' 4" **Wt:** 200   Parma, OH

Recent Statistics

	W	L	ERA	G	GS	Sv	IP	H	R	BB	SO	HR
2002 A San Berndno	9	6	4.54	29	29	0	164.2	153	101	68	214	10
2003 AA San Antonio	11	7	3.10	27	27	0	154.0	127	60	67	157	6

A 1999 first-rounder, Nageotte has averaged well more than a strikeout an inning and led the minors with 214 in the high Class-A California League in 2002. The key to his success is a low 90s fastball and a paralyzing slider that he throws so frequently that some scouts wonder about his long-term health. While Nageotte's slider is his out pitch, the Mariners want him to trust his fastball more, which should lower his pitch counts as he focuses less on strikeouts. His changeup is a work in progress, and he lacks confidence in it. Getting it in order and improving the command of his fastball would take his game to the next level.

Chris Snelling

Position: OF   **Opening Day Age:** 22
Bats: L **Throws:** L   **Born:** 12/3/81 in North
Ht: 5' 10" **Wt:** 165   Miami, FL

Recent Statistics

	G	AB	R	H	D	T	HR	RBI	SB	BB	SO	Avg
2002 AA San Antonio	23	89	10	29	9	2	1	12	5	12	11	.326
2002 AL Seattle	8	27	2	4	0	0	1	3	0	2	4	.148
2003 AA San Antonio	47	186	24	62	12	2	3	25	1	8	30	.333
2003 AAA Tacoma	18	67	11	18	2	0	3	10	1	5	12	.269

Only injuries have slowed Snelling since signing out of Australia in 1999. He won a batting title at high Class-A San Bernardino in 2001, despite a stress fracture in his right ankle. In fact, Snelling has batted .300 in every pro season, and he hit .316 in the high minors in 2003. Snelling broke his thumb in spring training in 2002, yet enjoyed a solid Double-A season before tearing the ACL in his left knee and having surgery that summer, eight games into his big league career. His 2003 season ended with torn meniscus in the same knee. If he can tone down his all-or-nothing style enough to stay healthy, Snelling has the skills and instincts to hit for average, show some pop and draw walks, plus play solidly in the outfield with enough arm to play in right.

Jamal Strong

Position: OF   **Opening Day Age:** 25
Bats: R **Throws:** R   **Born:** 8/5/78 in
Ht: 5' 10" **Wt:** 180   Pasadena, CA

Recent Statistics

	G	AB	R	H	D	T	HR	RBI	SB	BB	SO	Avg
2003 R Mariners	2	7	5	5	0	1	0	4	3	3	1	.714
2003 AAA Tacoma	56	210	38	64	6	1	2	19	26	25	38	.305
2003 AL Seattle	12	2	2	0	0	0	0	0	0	0	0	.000

Drafted in 2000, Strong is all about little-ball skills. He has a career .406 OBP and an average of 54 steals a year in the minors. Strong separated a shoulder sliding in a spring training game, which was expected to end his 2003 season, but he returned to post a .390 OBP at Triple-A Tacoma. Strong's strike-zone judgment improved at Tacoma, and that remains a key to his success. He's as fast as nearly anyone in the game, and he covers plenty of turf in the outfield. His arm is not an asset, though he may have improved his throwing enough to play center field in the majors. While little ball is his ticket, showing more pop and handling hard stuff in on his hands will advance his game.

Aaron Taylor

Position: P   **Opening Day Age:** 26
Bats: R **Throws:** R   **Born:** 8/20/77 in
Ht: 6' 7" **Wt:** 245   Valdosta, GA

Recent Statistics

	W	L	ERA	G	GS	Sv	IP	H	R	BB	SO	HR
2003 AAA Tacoma	1	3	2.45	33	0	16	40.1	30	11	13	34	3
2003 AL Seattle	0	0	8.53	10	0	0	12.2	17	12	6	9	0

Taylor came to the Mariners via Atlanta in the Rule 5 draft in 1999. He struggled in 2000 and quit baseball briefly the next spring before starting a rapid rise through the system with a solid 2001 season at Class-A Wisconsin. The 6-foot-7 Taylor, who works in relief, is intimidating with a mid-90s fastball that he mixes with a split-finger pitch and slider to keep hitters from sitting on the heat. He's nasty when his secondary pitches are working. Some tinkering to them and better command of his fastball are critical to how far Taylor goes in the majors. He could become a big league closer. In September, Taylor underwent minor shoulder surgery that may sideline him a bit beyond Opening Day.

Others to Watch

Seattle's first big international signing in 1998, righthander **Cha Baek** (23) underwent Tommy John surgery in 2001 and needed 18 months to recover. His solid command and low-90s velocity were nearly restored after an 8-4 season (3.12 ERA) at high Class-A Inland Empire and Double-A San Antonio. . . Calling on a low-90s fastball and high-80s slider, righthander **Rett Johnson** (24) has stormed through three levels in two seasons. After a bout of spring wildness was corrected with a shortened delivery, Johnson went 11-4 (2.63 ERA) between Double-A San Antonio and Triple-A Tacoma in 2003. . . After two lackluster Class-A seasons, third baseman **Justin Leone** (27) emerged with a .288-21-92 campaign and Double-A Texas League MVP honors. Small adjustments to get his bat head moving forward for a little extra drive paid off, and he's a very good third baseman with good range and strong arm. . . After three seasons as a starter, righthander **J.J. Putz** (27) moved to the pen at Triple-A Tacoma in 2003. He saved 11 games and posted a 2.51 ERA in the PCL, but needs to fine-tune his secondary pitches to be effective in Seattle.

Tropicana Field

Offense

Even though the Devil Rays largely have had impotent teams during their six seasons, the overall numbers show Tropicana Field to be one of the least accommodating American League parks in terms of home runs. The number of doubles also is not extraordinary, though there are an excessive amount of triples due to the deep gaps, oddly angled walls and asymmetrical design.

Defense

The Rays finally acknowledged that the best way to cover their large turf field is with athletic speedy defenders. The unusual combination of FieldTurf infield and all-dirt basepaths can be tricky, and the 97 infield errors at the Trop matched Jacobs Field for the most in the AL in intraleague games. There is no question that the outfield is tricky, with balls caroming off the catwalks and being lost in the scattered lights and against the off-white roof.

Who It Helps the Most

Carl Crawford found the roomy dimensions to his liking, hitting 71 points better and all five homers at home. Damian Rolls also takes advantage of the gaps. Righthanded reliever Travis Harper benefits from the dimensions, with a 2-0 record and 2.27 ERA at home and a 2-8, 5.36 mark on the road.

Who It Hurts the Most

The Rays' righthanded hitters didn't have much success, with Rocco Baldelli hitting only two of his 11 homers at home, Toby Hall only four of his 12 and Julio Lugo five of his 15. Second baseman Marlon Anderson, a lefthander who should benefit from the speedy surface, struggled at home. Jeremi Gonzalez had a much higher ERA at home.

Rookies & Newcomers

As fast as Crawford and Baldelli are, the Rays may have an even faster outfielder in Joey Gathright, who could arrive in 2004. So too could silky smooth shortstop B.J. Upton, who will need to adjust quickly to the fast surface. New first baseman Tino Martinez may not find his new home park any more homer-friendly than his old one.

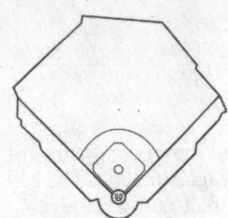

Dimensions: LF-315, LCF-370, CF-404, RCF-370, RF-322

Capacity: 43,772

Elevation: 15 feet

Surface: Turf

Foul Territory: Average

Park Factors

2003 Season

	Home Games			Away Games			
	Devil Rays	Opp	Total	Devil Rays	Opp	Total	Index
G	72	72	144	72	72	144	
Avg	.269	.259	.264	.266	.274	.270	98
AB	2486	2533	5019	2570	2391	4961	101
R	319	370	689	331	391	722	95
H	669	655	1324	684	656	1340	99
2B	133	136	269	128	147	275	97
3B	17	13	30	15	12	27	110
HR	53	86	139	76	93	169	81
BB	195	275	470	165	289	454	102
SO	450	420	870	450	364	814	106
E	51	57	108	40	41	81	133
E-Infield	42	55	97	31	39	70	139
LHB-Avg	.274	.255	.265	.277	.269	.273	97
LHB-HR	35	35	70	37	44	81	86
RHB-Avg	.263	.262	.262	.254	.280	.267	98
RHB-HR	18	51	69	39	49	88	77

2001-2003

	Home Games			Away Games			
	Devil Rays	Opp	Total	Devil Rays	Opp	Total	Index
G	216	216	432	215	215	430	
Avg	.267	.266	.267	.252	.281	.266	100
AB	7411	7666	15077	7495	7164	14659	102
R	933	1164	2097	905	1220	2125	98
H	1977	2042	4019	1891	2011	3902	103
2B	415	438	853	377	429	806	103
3B	45	42	87	32	30	62	136
HR	157	262	419	193	296	489	83
BB	607	799	1406	564	845	1409	97
SO	1413	1368	2781	1460	1150	2610	104
E	149	139	288	168	126	294	98
E-Infield	129	127	256	137	112	249	102
LHB-Avg	.272	.272	.272	.266	.285	.275	99
LHB-HR	90	121	211	93	132	225	91
RHB-Avg	.262	.262	.262	.239	.277	.258	101
RHB-HR	67	141	208	100	164	264	77

2003 Rankings (American League)

- Highest error factor
- Highest infield-error factor
- Third-highest strikeout factor
- Second-lowest home-run factor
- Second-lowest RHB home-run factor

Lou Piniella

2003 Season

Lou Piniella knew the 2003 season was going to be unlike any he had experienced, and the 99 losses made it official. But as hard as the losing was to take, he said the season was a success because the Rays were able to thoroughly evaluate what they had in the organization. The emergence of Aubrey Huff and Carl Crawford as future All-Stars, and the impressive debuts of Rocco Baldelli and Doug Waechter, gave Piniella even more reason for optimism.

Offense

Piniella likes to make things happen, so it wasn't a surprise that the Rays led the American League with 142 stolen bases, had the second-best success rate for hit-and-runs in the majors (47.8 percent) and grounded into an AL-low 108 double plays. Given their lack of power, he didn't have any choice but to rely on speed, but his preference would be to have a few sluggers in the middle of the lineup. Piniella likes to mix right- and left-handed hitters throughout the lineup, and the Rays went into the offseason looking for a veteran righthanded bat to use in the cleanup spot.

Pitching & Defense

Piniella was more tolerant than expected with the young Tampa Bay pitching staff, but he made it clear his patience was tested by pitchers who didn't throw strikes. Pitching coach Chris Bosio resigned for personal reasons after the season, so the Rays turned to a familiar face, naming minor league pitching coordinator Chuck Hernandez to the job. Piniella likes to put a good defensive team on the field, though the likely loss of first baseman Travis Lee will make that a bigger challenge in 2004.

2004 Outlook

Piniella said what got him through the 2003 season was the promise of 2004 and beyond. With the continued development of young players and the expected influx of several veterans thanks to a modest payroll increase, he expects better things ahead. For the Rays, a .500 record would be a monumental success.

Born: 8/28/43 in Tampa, FL

Playing Experience: 1964-1984, Bal, Cle, KC, NYY

Managerial Experience: 17 seasons

Manager Statistics

Year	Team, Lg	W	L	Pct	GB	Finish
2003	Tampa Bay, AL	63	99	.389	38.0	5th East
17 Seasons		1382	1234	.528	–	–

2003 Starting Pitchers by Days Rest

	<=3	4	5	6+
Devil Rays Starts	3	77	38	30
Devil Rays ERA	2.89	5.99	5.09	4.86
AL Avg Starts	2	79	50	22
AL ERA	3.19	4.64	4.57	4.98

2003 Situational Stats

	Lou Piniella	AL Average
Hit & Run Success %	47.8	36.7
Stolen Base Success %	77.2	70.0
Platoon Pct.	60.1	61.7
Defensive Subs	15	23
High-Pitch Outings	9	5
Quick/Slow Hooks	23/19	19/16
Sacrifice Attempts	55	55

2003 Rankings (American League)

- 1st in steals of second base (122), steals of third base (19) and pinch-hitters used (159)
- 2nd in stolen base attempts (184), stolen-base percentage and hit-and-run success percentage
- 3rd in steals of home plate (1), hit-and-run attempts (92), slow hooks, starts with over 120 pitches (9) and starts on three days rest

Marlon Anderson

2003 Season

After being non-tendered by Philadelphia, Marlon Anderson found a home—and a starting job—with the Devil Rays. Anderson took advantage of the opportunity to at least partially reverse an offensive slide. He finished with a career-high 67 RBI while raising his average to .270 and cutting down considerably on his strikeouts. His six homers and 27 doubles, however, were his fewest for a full major league season since 1999.

Hitting

Anderson is a free swinger who doesn't do a lot of little things at the plate that middle infielders usually do. Instead, he plays more of a "big" game, trying to hit the ball into the gaps. He doesn't really fit the mold of a top-of-the-order hitter, but isn't really an RBI guy either. He hit .140 in the leadoff spot and .417 in the No. 9 hole last season, with everything else in-between. Anderson did make significant improvement against left-handers, raising his average nearly 100 points to .315.

Baserunning & Defense

Anderson has good speed, and manager Lou Piniella put it to good use. Anderson stole a career-high 19 bases last year and produced the second-best stolen-base success rate in the AL at 86.4 percent. While he may not be the most instinctive baserunner, he gets around the bases quickly. Anderson's defense is not what would be considered fundamentally sound. While his speed and quickness allow him to get to a lot of balls, his footwork is not smooth and his throwing motion is unorthodox, to put it politely. Add in an average-at-best arm and it is not surprising that he ranked third among AL second basemen with 15 errors.

2004 Outlook

For what the Devil Rays expected, and for what they paid ($600,000), Anderson did a good job. But that apparently was not enough to guarantee his return. The Rays went into the offseason seeking to upgrade the offensive production of the infield. Anderson showed enough offensively to be a starter somewhere, but his options are going to be limited if Tampa does not bring him back.

Position: 2B
Bats: L **Throws:** R
Ht: 5'11" **Wt:** 200

Opening Day Age: 30
Born: 1/6/74 in Montgomery, AL
ML Seasons: 6

Overall Statistics

	G	AB	R	H	D	T	HR	RBI	SB	BB	SO	Avg	OBP	Slg
'03	145	482	59	130	27	3	6	67	19	41	60	.270	.328	.376
Car.	624	2200	254	587	124	16	32	249	49	155	294	.267	.316	.381

Where He Hits the Ball

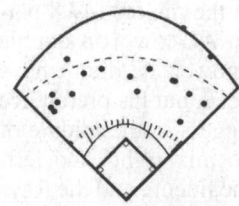
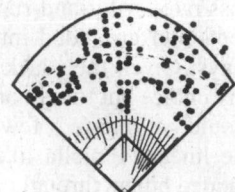

Vs. LHP   **Vs. RHP**

2003 Situational Stats

	AB	H	HR	RBI	Avg		AB	H	HR	RBI	Avg
Home	248	57	2	33	.230	LHP	73	23	2	15	.315
Road	234	73	4	34	.312	RHP	409	107	4	52	.262
First Half	275	72	4	43	.262	Sc Pos	126	43	3	62	.341
Scnd Half	207	58	2	24	.280	Clutch	98	27	2	22	.276

2003 Rankings (American League)

- 1st in lowest fielding percentage at second base (.973)
- 2nd in stolen-base percentage (86.4)
- 3rd in errors at second base (15)
- 6th in lowest HR frequency (80.3 ABs per HR) and lowest batting average at home
- 8th in lowest slugging percentage
- 9th in batting average on the road
- 10th in batting average with runners in scoring position
- Led the Devil Rays in stolen-base percentage (86.4) and batting average with runners in scoring position

Rocco Baldelli

2003 Season

Rocco Baldelli led all rookies with 184 hits in a season that ranks as one of the best all-around debuts in history. Pretty good for a 21-year-old who spent most of the previous year at high Class-A Bakersfield. Baldelli excelled at nearly every facet of the game, leading the American League with 14 outfield assists from center field and ranking among the league leaders in hits, triples and stolen bases.

Hitting

Baldelli is a free swinger who was learning on the job. Quick hands and deceptive strength make him a good hitter, blazing speed makes him even more dangerous, and a tremendous knowledge of the game and desire to improve should make him a superstar. He will hit more homers as he gets stronger and his average will increase when he better learns the strike zone. He also needs to be more comfortable using the whole field. The Rays were forced to hit him in the No. 3 and 4 spots, cutting down his opportunities to bunt, which could be a bigger part of his offensive game.

Baserunning & Defense

According to several scouts, Baldelli is the fastest righthanded batter in the league. He is an instinctive player who does a lot of little things well, such as running the bases and knowing how to adjust his slide. His speed alone makes him a threat to score from first on any ball hit in a gap. Similarly, he is a strong defensive player because of his speed, jumping ability and willingness to dive for balls. His arm is not that strong, but he compensates with smart positioning and a quick release.

2004 Outlook

As good as Baldelli was in 2003, it only makes sense that he will be better in 2004. If the Rays add a proven hitter or two to their lineup, he likely will settle into the No. 2 spot in the order, where he should be able to boost his average to .300. There is some talk of moving him to right field, but he'll most likely stay in center.

Position: CF
Bats: R **Throws:** R
Ht: 6' 4" **Wt:** 190

Opening Day Age: 22
Born: 9/25/81 in Woonsocket, RI
ML Seasons: 1

Overall Statistics

	G	AB	R	H	D	T	HR	RBI	SB	BB	SO	Avg	OBP	Slg
'03	156	637	89	184	32	8	11	78	27	30	128	.289	.326	.416
Car.	156	637	89	184	32	8	11	78	27	30	128	.289	.326	.416

Where He Hits the Ball

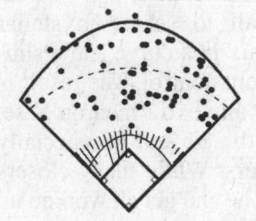
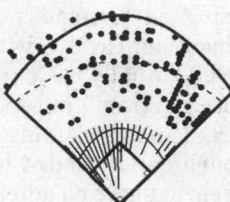

Vs. LHP **Vs. RHP**

2003 Situational Stats

	AB	H	HR	RBI	Avg		AB	H	HR	RBI	Avg
Home	305	91	2	36	.298	LHP	188	56	4	21	.298
Road	332	93	9	42	.280	RHP	449	128	7	57	.285
First Half	359	109	6	43	.304	Sc Pos	163	44	1	65	.270
Scnd Half	278	75	5	35	.270	Clutch	112	30	0	11	.268

2003 Rankings (American League)

- 1st in lowest cleanup slugging percentage (.358)
- 2nd in caught stealing (10), batting average with the bases loaded (.600), batting average among rookies, errors in center field (5) and lowest fielding percentage in center field (.989)
- 3rd in RBI among rookies
- 4th in singles
- 6th in strikeouts
- Led the Devil Rays in at-bats, caught stealing (10), hit by pitch (8), strikeouts and batting average with the bases loaded (.600)

Lance Carter

2003 Season

Lance Carter's accomplishments in his rookie season got lost in the attention showered on team-mate Rocco Baldelli, but Carter had an impressive year as well. He ranked seventh in the American League with 26 saves, and his combination of 33 saves plus wins gave him a hand in 52.3 percent of Tampa's total victories (63). Carter also was a surprise All-Star selection. He made a team-high 62 appearances, ranked second on the Rays' staff with seven wins and finished with the ninth-highest rookie saves total in history.

Pitching

Carter is not the prototypical hard-throwing closer. Instead, he succeeds with control and finesse, using an average fastball to set up a stellar changeup. He also will mix in a curve and a slider and usually has excellent control. The result is that he doesn't put too many extra men on base, gets most of his outs in the air and is especially tough on lefthanded batters. While many closers seem to thrive on adrenaline and get all worked up on the mound, Carter is the opposite, keeping calm in even the toughest situations and shaking off tough losses with no problem.

Defense

Carter is a heady player who keeps his cool on the mound, allowing him to field his position well and keep decent tabs on baserunners. Because Carter missed so much time due to injuries (two Tommy John surgeries) and spent so much time in the minors, he is willing to put in the time to do all the little things right and is a true professional.

2004 Outlook

The Rays went into the offseason saying they were looking for a proven late-inning reliever, so there is a chance Carter may be bumped out of the closer's role. But he won't go far, because pitchers with his control and sense of calm in late-inning situations are hard to find. At worst, Carter should end up as a late-inning setup man.

Position: RP
Bats: R **Throws:** R
Ht: 6' 1" **Wt:** 190

Opening Day Age: 29
Born: 12/18/74 in Bradenton, FL
ML Seasons: 3

Overall Statistics

	W	L	Pct.	ERA	G	GS	Sv	IP	H	BB	SO	HR	Avg
'03	7	5	.583	4.33	62	0	26	79.0	72	19	47	12	.242
Car.	9	6	.600	3.78	76	0	28	104.2	90	27	64	16	.231

2003 Pitching Profile

	Lance Carter	AL Average
Overall Strike %	62.7	62.8
1st Pitch Strike %	56.6	58.7
Ratio	1.15	1.39
Strikeouts per 9 IP	5.35	6.11
Walks per 9 IP	2.16	3.16
Home Runs per 9 IP	1.37	1.11
Strikeout/Walk Ratio	2.47	1.93
Groundball/Flyball Ratio	0.69	1.18

2003 Situational Stats

	W	L	ERA	Sv	IP		AB	H	HR	RBI	Avg
Home	4	2	3.83	17	42.1	LHB	162	36	5	23	.222
Road	3	3	4.91	9	36.2	RHB	136	36	7	18	.265
First Half	5	3	4.05	15	46.2	Sc Pos	60	15	3	29	.250
Scnd Half	2	2	4.73	11	32.1	Clutch	207	50	8	33	.242

2003 Rankings (American League)

- 4th in lowest save percentage (78.8)
- 5th in games finished (55), blown saves (7) and relief wins (7)
- 7th in saves
- Led the Devil Rays in games pitched, saves, games finished (55), winning percentage, save percentage (78.8), blown saves (7), relief wins (7), lowest batting average allowed in relief (.242) and fewest baserunners allowed per nine innings in relief (10.8)

Carl Crawford

2003 Season

Carl Crawford made pretty big news by stealing 55 bases. But it was what he did to get on base, specifically hitting .306 over the final 80 games, along with his development as a leadoff hitter, that generated more excitement within the organization. Crawford had three hitting streaks of 10 or more games, and he came through when it mattered, hitting .309 with runners in scoring position and a team-best .316 with men in scoring position and two outs.

Hitting

Crawford is a tremendous athlete, and the Rays are refining his skills to make him a successful major leaguer. A midseason adjustment by hitting coach Lee Elia to open up Crawford's stance allowed him to take better swings, make contact on a more consistent basis and make better use of his electrifying speed by hitting the ball on a line or on the ground. Crawford still is prone to stretches where he chases pitches off the plate and gets himself out, though with less frequency than before. He also is improving as a bunter.

Baserunning & Defense

Crawford is so fast that defenses have to adjust to him, creating holes for other Rays to take advantage of. He should produce even more triples as he improves his turn at second base, and he will pile up even more stolen bases as he learns pitchers and improves his jumps. The same athleticism that enables Crawford to be an offensive force gives him the ability to be a plus defensive player. He covers vast amounts of ground in left field and throws well.

2004 Outlook

In manager Lou Piniella's opinion, Crawford has the ability to add a Gold Glove and a batting title to what could be a series of stolen-base crowns. If Crawford can continue the improvement he showed in the second half of 2003, a .300-10-75 showing would be a reasonable goal for 2004, along with 60 stolen bases. There is a chance the Rays could shift Crawford to center field and move Rocco Baldelli to right.

Position: LF/CF
Bats: L **Throws:** L
Ht: 6' 2" **Wt:** 219

Opening Day Age: 22
Born: 8/5/81 in Houston, TX
ML Seasons: 2

Overall Statistics

	G	AB	R	H	D	T	HR	RBI	SB	BB	SO	Avg	OBP	Slg
'03	151	630	80	177	18	9	5	54	55	26	102	.281	.309	.362
Car.	214	889	103	244	29	15	7	84	64	35	143	.274	.304	.364

Where He Hits the Ball

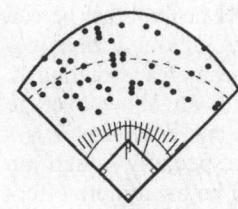 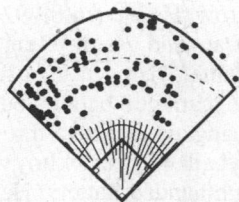

Vs. LHP	Vs. RHP

2003 Situational Stats

	AB	H	HR	RBI	Avg		AB	H	HR	RBI	Avg
Home	295	94	5	36	.319	LHP	179	47	0	12	.263
Road	335	83	0	18	.248	RHP	451	130	5	42	.288
First Half	340	91	2	30	.268	Sc Pos	139	43	3	52	.309
Scnd Half	290	86	3	24	.297	Clutch	109	25	2	10	.229

2003 Rankings (American League)

- 1st in stolen bases
- 2nd in caught stealing (10), steals of third (9), fielding percentage in left field (.991) and lowest on-base percentage for a leadoff hitter (.310)
- 3rd in singles and lowest slugging percentage
- 4th in triples, stolen-base percentage (84.6) and lowest HR frequency (126.0 ABs per HR)
- 6th in highest groundball-flyball ratio (2.1)
- Led the Devil Rays in singles, triples, stolen bases, caught stealing (10), highest ground ball-flyball ratio (2.1), steals of third (9), fewest GDPs per GDP situation (4.8%), on-base percentage for a leadoff hitter (.310), and batting average at home

Jeremi Gonzalez

2003 Season

Just getting to the mound in a Devil Rays uniform was a victory for Jeremi Gonzalez, who had not pitched in the big leagues in nearly five years due to three surgeries and a variety of injuries. He ended up being the Rays' most consistent pitcher, with a team-high 16 quality starts. He allowed three runs or fewer in 17 starts and five hits or fewer in 15 outings, but enjoyed the lowest run support (3.91 runs per game) of any American League East starter.

Pitching

The difference between Gonzalez now and the Gonzalez who was with the Cubs in 1997-98 is that this one knows how to pitch rather than just throw. He has an 89-92 MPH fastball that he can locate and use different ways, sinking it as a two-seamer, rising it as a four-seamer and cutting it. He can get batters out with an above-average changeup and also throws a curve. Gonzalez is a flyball pitcher who was especially tough on righthanded batters. He will be even more effective if he can cut down on his pitch counts, and he could stand to do a better job keeping his emotions in check on the mound.

Defense

Gonzalez is an experienced veteran who knows how to make the necessary plays. He fields his position well, making only one error last year, and he does a decent job holding on runners. He registered five pickoffs in 2003, and now has 14 pickoffs in three big league seasons.

2004 Outlook

Gonzalez was a true find for the Rays in 2003, perhaps the best six-year free agent signing in the game. He was the Rays' de facto No. 1 starter by the middle of the season and could assume a similar role in 2004. Gonzalez, who is arbitration eligible, won't be a surprise to anybody this coming season, but he should be better too, having seen the new hitters, learned the new umpires and adjusted to the new ballparks. The Rays are hoping for big things.

Position: SP
Bats: R **Throws:** R
Ht: 6' 0" **Wt:** 220

Opening Day Age: 29
Born: 1/8/75 in Maracaibo, VZ
ML Seasons: 3

Overall Statistics

	W	L	Pct.	ERA	G	GS	Sv	IP	H	BB	SO	HR	Avg
'03	6	11	.353	3.91	25	25	0	156.1	131	69	97	18	.228
Car.	24	27	.471	4.41	68	68	0	410.1	381	179	260	47	.246

2003 Pitching Profile

	Jeremi Gonzalez	AL Average
Overall Strike %	60.5	62.8
1st Pitch Strike %	55.6	58.7
Ratio	1.28	1.39
Strikeouts per 9 IP	5.58	6.11
Walks per 9 IP	3.97	3.16
Home Runs per 9 IP	1.04	1.11
Strikeout/Walk Ratio	1.41	1.93
Groundball/Flyball Ratio	0.67	1.18

2003 Situational Stats

	W	L	ERA	Sv	IP		AB	H	HR	RBI	Avg
Home	3	7	4.90	0	71.2	LHB	293	69	9	31	.235
Road	3	4	3.08	0	84.2	RHB	282	62	9	31	.220
First Half	3	4	4.11	0	65.2	Sc Pos	129	27	3	40	.209
Scnd Half	3	7	3.77	0	90.2	Clutch	34	5	1	1	.147

2003 Rankings (American League)

- 2nd in hit batsmen (12)
- 5th in lowest ERA on the road and lowest batting average allowed with runners in scoring position
- 6th in lowest batting average allowed vs. righthanded batters
- 7th in balks (2)
- 8th in lowest winning percentage
- Led the Devil Rays in ERA, complete games (2), pickoff throws (100), lowest batting average allowed (.228), lowest on-base percentage allowed (.319) and lowest ERA on the road

Toby Hall

Position: C
Bats: R **Throws:** R
Ht: 6' 3" **Wt:** 240

Opening Day Age: 28
Born: 10/21/75 in Tacoma, WA
ML Seasons: 4

2003 Season

Toby Hall had a successful season if for no other reason than for the first time in his career he didn't spend any time in the minors. He ranked as the top catcher in the American League in terms of throwing out potential basestealers and would have been the toughest batter in the AL to strike out if he had made four more plate appearances. His .253 average was the lowest of his three big league seasons, but his 12 homers and 47 RBI were his most.

Hitting

Hall is successful by being selective at the plate and hitting the ball hard. He gets away from that on occasion and falls into ruts where he chases bad pitches, especially breaking balls outside the zone. A more common problem is that he tends to be so protective of the strike zone that he makes weak outs where he might be better off taking aggressive swings at the ball and adding an occasional strikeout to his total. He doesn't walk much, either.

Baserunning & Defense

Hall made significant improvement in his throwing during the 2002 season and carried that over to 2003. He threw out 31 of 75 potential basestealers for a 41.3 percentage. He has gotten better, but still could stand to make further improvement in pitch-blocking and increasing his mobility around the plate. The bigger issue in 2003 had to do with pitch-calling and learning to accept the high amount of responsibility that manager Lou Piniella places on his catcher. As a baserunner, Hall is a typical catcher.

2004 Outlook

Hall showed enough production at the plate, and enough improvement behind it, to keep the Rays from needing to look for another catcher. He may not develop into the middle-of-the-order power hitter they were hoping for, but if he keeps his defense at such a high standard, a .270 average and 15-20 home runs probably will be good enough. This is a big year since Hall will be arbitration-eligible going into 2005.

Overall Statistics

	G	AB	R	H	D	T	HR	RBI	SB	BB	SO	Avg	OBP	Slg
'03	130	463	50	117	23	0	12	47	0	23	40	.253	.295	.380
Car.	268	993	116	260	58	1	23	120	2	45	83	.262	.299	.392

Where He Hits the Ball

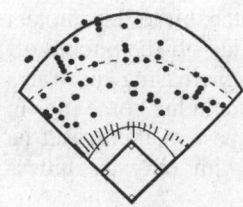
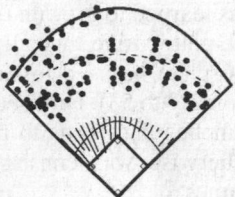

Vs. LHP   **Vs. RHP**

2003 Situational Stats

	AB	H	HR	RBI	Avg		AB	H	HR	RBI	Avg
Home	218	56	4	18	.257	LHP	150	38	3	11	.253
Road	245	61	8	29	.249	RHP	313	79	9	36	.252
First Half	254	67	7	27	.264	Sc Pos	127	31	2	33	.244
Scnd Half	209	50	5	20	.239	Clutch	85	24	2	9	.282

2003 Rankings (American League)

- 1st in errors at catcher (9) and highest percentage of runners caught stealing as a catcher (41.3)
- Led the Devil Rays in lowest percentage of swings that missed (11.4)

Aubrey Huff

2003 Season

Aubrey Huff went from being a good young player with potential to a legitimate star, posting the best offensive season in Devil Rays' history and ranking among the best in either league. Pretty good for a guy playing his first full season in the big leagues. Huff set team records for average, RBI, doubles, extra-base hits, total bases, and runs while tying the record with 34 homers. He did all this while playing 162 games, most of them in the unfamiliar position of right field.

Hitting

Huff is described as a professional hitter, as much because of what he does as how easy he makes it look with powerful strokes and a sweet swing. He has learned to go with the pitch, hit lefties, protect the plate, drive the ball and lay off the pitches off the plate he used to chase (increasing his walks from 37 to 53). Huff seems to hit his home runs in bunches and tends to pull most of them. But he otherwise was consistent, with only 37 hitless games.

Baserunning & Defense

Huff opened the 2003 season at third base but was moved after three errors in the first five games. He ended up in the outfield and adapted well, making most of the routine plays and flashing a better-than-expected arm. He also made at 20 starts at first, which probably is his most natural position. Huff isn't particularly fast and doesn't take many chances, but he runs the bases well and can score from second on most hits.

2004 Outlook

Huff had a spectacular season without much experience or protection around him in the Tampa Bay lineup. A bit more of both should help him perform at an even higher level. Huff could stay in right field, move to left or first, or end up the DH. What won't change is that he'll be right in the middle of the Rays' lineup, trying to improve on a season in which he established himself as a big-time player.

Position: RF/DH/1B
Bats: L **Throws:** R
Ht: 6' 4" **Wt:** 231

Opening Day Age: 27
Born: 12/20/76 in Marion, OH
ML Seasons: 4

Overall Statistics

	G	AB	R	H	D	T	HR	RBI	SB	BB	SO	Avg	OBP	Slg
'03	162	636	91	198	47	3	34	107	2	53	80	.311	.367	.555
Car.	425	1623	212	477	104	4	69	225	7	118	225	.294	.343	.490

Where He Hits the Ball

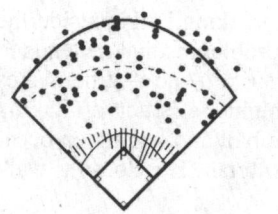 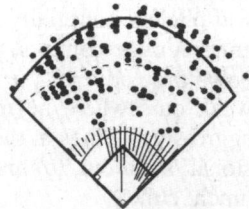

Vs. LHP	Vs. RHP

2003 Situational Stats

	AB	H	HR	RBI	Avg		AB	H	HR	RBI	Avg
Home	311	94	15	53	.302	LHP	220	70	7	29	.318
Road	325	104	19	54	.320	RHP	416	128	27	78	.308
First Half	358	109	17	50	.304	Sc Pos	148	44	8	70	.297
Scnd Half	278	89	17	57	.320	Clutch	96	34	4	15	.354

2003 Rankings (American League)

- 1st in errors in right field (6)
- 2nd in games played
- 3rd in doubles and intentional walks (17)
- 4th in total bases (353) and batting average with two strikes (.259)
- Led the Devil Rays in batting average, home runs, runs scored, hits, doubles, RBI, sacrifice flies (9), hit by pitch (8), times on base (259), GDPs (19), pitches seen (2,478), plate appearances (706), slugging percentage, on-base percentage, HR frequency (18.7 ABs per HR), highest percentage of swings put into play (48.8), batting average in the clutch, cleanup slugging percentage (.498) and batting average on the road

Joe Kennedy

Position: SP/RP
Bats: R **Throws:** L
Ht: 6' 4" **Wt:** 237

Opening Day Age: 24
Born: 5/24/79 in La Mesa, CA
ML Seasons: 3

2003 Season

Joe Kennedy had a lost season—he lost his job at the front end of the Devil Rays' rotation and lost his place among the most promising young left-handers in the game. Kennedy was the Rays' Opening Day starter but finished the year in middle relief after losing 12 games while winning only three, missing six weeks due to left shoulder inflammation but saying his arm wasn't hurt, and generally posting some of the worst numbers of any starter in the majors. When he went on the disabled list June 1, Kennedy had allowed the most hits and earned runs in the American League.

Pitching

Kennedy insisted he wasn't doing anything different or wrong from what worked in 2002, but the results were stunningly different. He didn't have the same velocity on or command of his fastball, nor did it have much consistent movement. Worse, his once dominating 12-to-6 curveball, which he uses as his strikeout pitch, often was flat and didn't fool too many people. The Rays tried moving Kennedy to different spots on the rubber, but he wasn't comfortable with the changes given his somewhat funky across-the-body delivery. Scouts wondered if his arm was hurting more than he let on.

Defense

Kennedy *did* improve his defense in 2003. After making 10 errors in 2002, he made only one miscue last season. The difference wasn't the result of a dramatic improvement, just a matter of slowing down and taking his time. Kennedy has a tremendous pickoff move when he works at it and can use that to his advantage.

2004 Outlook

The subject of numerous trade rumors during the 2003 season, Kennedy's future is unsettled. He would like to return to the rotation and the Rays could use the help. But manager Lou Piniella mentioned on several occasions that he liked what he saw from Kennedy in relief, especially his ability to pitch two or three innings at a time. The Rays could be proactive before Kennedy becomes arbitration eligible and trade him before or during the season.

Overall Statistics

	W	L	Pct.	ERA	G	GS	Sv	IP	H	BB	SO	HR	Avg
'03	3	12	.200	6.13	32	22	1	133.2	167	47	77	19	.303
Car.	18	31	.367	4.98	82	72	1	448.0	493	136	264	58	.279

2003 Pitching Profile

	Joe Kennedy	AL Average
Overall Strike %	63.1	62.8
1st Pitch Strike %	58.6	58.7
Ratio	1.60	1.39
Strikeouts per 9 IP	5.18	6.11
Walks per 9 IP	3.16	3.16
Home Runs per 9 IP	1.28	1.11
Strikeout/Walk Ratio	1.64	1.93
Groundball/Flyball Ratio	1.09	1.18

2003 Situational Stats

	W	L	ERA	Sv	IP		AB	H	HR	RBI	Avg
Home	1	7	6.53	1	71.2	LHB	126	29	3	19	.230
Road	2	5	5.66	0	62.0	RHB	426	138	16	78	.324
First Half	3	5	5.60	0	72.1	Sc Pos	151	53	4	72	.351
Scnd Half	0	7	6.75	1	61.1	Clutch	43	7	1	6	.163

2003 Rankings (American League)

- 1st in lowest winning percentage and highest batting average allowed with runners in scoring position
- 4th in highest batting average allowed vs. righthanded batters
- 8th in hit batsmen (11)
- Led the Devil Rays in losses, hits allowed, highest strikeout-walk ratio (1.6) and fewest walks per nine innings (3.2)

Travis Lee

2003 Season

After signing with the Devil Rays in February when he had no other alternatives, Travis Lee had a very productive season. He was dazzling on defense, saving the Rays' erratic infielders from throwing errors on almost a nightly basis and making a handful of highlight-reel plays of his own. He missed two weeks due to a strained right oblique in April but still ranked second on the team in doubles, home runs, extra-base hits and on-base percentage.

Hitting

Lee is not a classic slugging first baseman, but he showed signs of providing enough offense to fit in well with a team that can get homers from elsewhere in the lineup. He has power, as evidenced by his batting practice displays, but tends to be more of a line-drive and gap hitter. Lee shows good plate discipline and has learned to use the count to his advantage, but he isn't much of a two-strike hitter. His laid-back attitude creates the perception of a lack of intensity, which can be troubling to some.

Baserunning & Defense

Lee is one of the few players in today's game who is known more for his defensive skills, and the attention is warranted. His ability to anticipate bad throws and put himself in position to react and scoop the ball is extraordinary. He is nimble enough to make diving stops and run down foul balls, frustrating opposing hitters on a regular basis. Lee isn't going to run as much as he did early in his career, but he is quick enough to steal a base in the right situation and does a good job of getting around the bases.

2004 Outlook

When the Rays and Lee both declined his mutual option, and the team didn't offer him salary arbitration, it marked the end of a one-year relationship. Lee is looking for a multiyear deal and possibly the chance to return to the West Coast, while the Rays are seeking to add more power to their lineup. The club traded for Tino Martinez in late November.

Position: 1B
Bats: L **Throws:** L
Ht: 6' 3" **Wt:** 225

Opening Day Age: 28
Born: 5/26/75 in San Diego, CA
ML Seasons: 6

Overall Statistics

	G	AB	R	H	D	T	HR	RBI	SB	BB	SO	Avg	OBP	Slg
'03	145	542	75	149	37	3	19	70	6	64	97	.275	.348	.459
Car.	849	2974	386	769	157	12	92	406	47	379	562	.259	.341	.412

Where He Hits the Ball

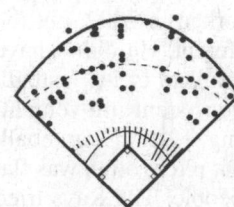

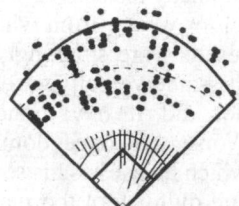

Vs. LHP   **Vs. RHP**

2003 Situational Stats

	AB	H	HR	RBI	Avg		AB	H	HR	RBI	Avg
Home	263	68	9	29	.259	LHP	193	55	3	25	.285
Road	279	81	10	41	.290	RHP	349	94	16	45	.269
First Half	291	77	7	30	.265	Sc Pos	136	32	5	46	.235
Scnd Half	251	72	12	40	.287	Clutch	101	30	3	13	.297

2003 Rankings (American League)

- 2nd in fielding percentage at first base (.998)
- 3rd in lowest cleanup slugging percentage (.380)
- 5th in lowest batting average with the bases loaded (.077)
- Led the Devil Rays in walks

Julio Lugo

2003 Season

Having been released by the Astros after being arrested on a domestic assault charge, Julio Lugo signed with the Devil Rays in May and not only salvaged his season with a strong performance, but may have resurrected his career. Lugo started 116 of 117 games at shortstop for Tampa and finished with a career-high 15 home runs and 55 RBI. He got better as the season went on, and after he was acquitted of the charges during an All-Star break trial, he hit .304 over his final 67 games.

Hitting

Lugo is something of a hybrid hitter in that he'll use his above-average speed and bunting ability to get on base while also swinging for the fences at times. The result is a higher strikeout total and a lower on-base percentage than expected. He has excellent bat speed and tries to catch up to just about any fastball. He is best when he sprays the ball around the field, though he lacks patience and selectivity can be a problem. His strong finish showed he has pretty good pop in his bat, but there is concern that he will become power hungry and get away from the small-ball tactics that are integral to his success.

Baserunning & Defense

Lugo's aggressive style carries over to the bases, where he tends to take wide turns and occasional chances. He stole only 12 bases last year but has the speed to double that. Lugo has quick feet, an athletic body and good instincts, which help make up for the lack of an overly strong arm. He is the type of player who makes mistakes on routine plays, usually on throws, but then makes a spectacular play look easy.

2004 Outlook

The Rays liked what they saw from Lugo and picked up his $1.75 million option for 2004. They aren't sure, however, whether they are going to leave him at shortstop or move him to second and acquire another shortstop. Either way, Lugo has a chance to re-establish himself as a valuable everyday starter with another solid season.

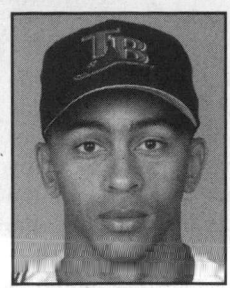

Position: SS
Bats: R **Throws:** R
Ht: 6' 1" **Wt:** 170

Opening Day Age: 28
Born: 11/16/75 in Barahona, DR
ML Seasons: 4
Pronunciation: loo-GO

Overall Statistics

	G	AB	R	H	D	T	HR	RBI	SB	BB	SO	Avg	OBP	Slg
'03	139	498	64	135	16	4	15	55	12	44	100	.271	.333	.410
Car.	483	1753	280	473	73	13	43	167	55	155	383	.270	.332	.400

Where He Hits the Ball

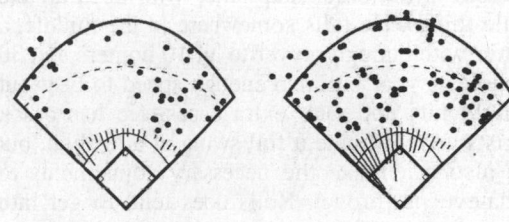

Vs. LHP   **Vs. RHP**

2003 Situational Stats

	AB	H	HR	RBI	Avg		AB	H	HR	RBI	Avg
Home	232	66	5	27	.284	LHP	146	35	5	12	.240
Road	266	69	10	28	.259	RHP	352	100	10	43	.284
First Half	241	58	3	18	.241	Sc Pos	123	35	4	43	.285
Scnd Half	257	77	12	37	.300	Clutch	80	18	3	10	.225

2003 Rankings (American League)

- 4th in lowest fielding percentage at shortstop (.970)
- 5th in errors at shortstop (17)
- 6th in bunts in play (22)
- Led the Devil Rays in sacrifice bunts (7), most pitches seen per plate appearance (3.88), bunts in play (22) and highest percentage of pitches taken (57.7)

Tampa Bay

269

Damian Rolls

2003 Season

Damian Rolls experienced a series of firsts during the 2003 season, including his first chance to play every day at the same position in the major leagues. Given the third-base job almost by default in mid-June, he made the most of the opportunity. Rolls, who began the season in the outfield and was scheduled to be a super-utility type until fracturing the tip of his right thumb in late April and missing a month, seemed to tire as the season went on, however.

Hitting

Rolls isn't a prototypical third baseman who hits a lot of home runs, nor is he a prototypical top- or bottom-of-the-order slap-hitter who does all the little things. He falls somewhere in the middle, a hitter with enough power to hit 10 homers and 30 doubles a year but also enough speed to beat out infield hits and take extra bases. He has quick wrists and will take a full swing at a fastball, but he also can make the necessary adjustments to whatever is thrown. Rolls does tend to get into ruts where he chases pitches off the plate and gets himself out.

Baserunning & Defense

Rolls is athletic and fast. He was a first-round pick of the Dodgers in 1996 as a third baseman and went through shoulder surgery, the expansion draft, rehab and a series of position changes before getting the chance to play third regularly. He was good, but with more work should be better. What he lacks in a strong arm he makes up for with desire, effort and anticipation.

2004 Outlook

Rolls again may end up as the regular third baseman if the Rays can't find anyone bigger, faster, stronger or better. They know he can do the job if necessary. But if the Rays find a third baseman, Rolls will be a super utilityman, in a role much like the one manager Lou Piniella fashioned for Mark McLemore in Seattle, with the ability to play any of seven positions, pinch-hit and/or pinch-run.

Position: 3B/RF
Bats: R **Throws:** R
Ht: 6' 2" **Wt:** 215

Opening Day Age: 26
Born: 9/15/77 in Manhattan, KS
ML Seasons: 4

Overall Statistics

	G	AB	R	H	D	T	HR	RBI	SB	BB	SO	Avg	OBP	Slg
'03	107	373	43	95	20	0	7	46	11	19	84	.255	.301	.365
Car.	213	702	91	184	37	2	9	64	25	32	148	.262	.302	.359

Where He Hits the Ball

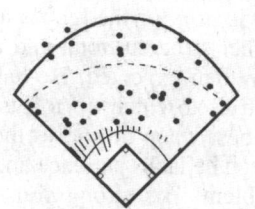
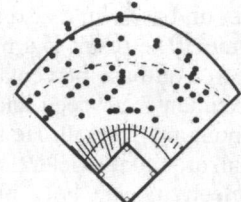

Vs. LHP   **Vs. RHP**

2003 Situational Stats

	AB	H	HR	RBI	Avg		AB	H	HR	RBI	Avg
Home	192	53	4	25	.276	LHP	121	33	3	11	.273
Road	181	42	3	21	.232	RHP	252	62	4	35	.246
First Half	138	35	4	18	.254	Sc Pos	92	27	3	38	.293
Scnd Half	235	60	3	28	.255	Clutch	67	15	0	5	.224

2003 Rankings (American League)

- 10th in batting average with the bases loaded (.455)
- Led the Devil Rays in lowest percentage of swings on the first pitch (25.2)

Victor Zambrano

2003 Season

Victor Zambrano's 2003 season clearly was a matter of perspective. His 12 wins, 188.1 innings, .237 opponents average, four victories during the team's five-win June, a complete game against Oakland on September 7 and a memorable duel with Roger Clemens made it a success. His American League high 106 walks, 20 hit batters and 15 wild pitches.

Pitching

Zambrano has great stuff, as good anyone's on the Rays' staff and among some of the best in the league. The problem Tampa Bay has had for years is trying to get him to trust it. Zambrano tends to nibble at the corners and get himself in trouble by falling behind in counts, then having to come in with a fastball over the plate. When he pitches aggressively, using his 92-95 MPH sinking fastball to set up an excellent changeup, he can be dominating. Zambrano occasionally will mix in a nasty slider, but there is enough movement on his fastball and deception to his changeup that he can rely on just those two offerings and still be successful as a starter.

Defense

Zambrano is a converted infielder who fields his position well. He tends to let down after a bad pitch and that can sometimes effect his concentration on the mound. He does a decent job holding on runners, but could do better in that area.

2004 Outlook

The first thing the Rays seemed to establish in 2003 is that Zambrano is a starter rather than a reliever. The second was that at times he can be very successful. The challenge for 2004 is to continue that development. Zambrano won 11 games as a starter for a 99-loss team, despite spending two weeks in the minors and another couple weeks in the bullpen. So 15-18 wins would seem a reasonable goal for 2004. The addition of a veteran or two to the rotation, pushing him down to the No. 3 slot, would help.

Position: SP
Bats: R **Throws:** R
Ht: 6' 0" **Wt:** 203

Opening Day Age: 28
Born: 8/6/75 in Los Teques, VZ
ML Seasons: 3

Overall Statistics

	W	L	Pct.	ERA	G	GS	Sv	IP	H	BB	SO	HR	Avg
'03	12	10	.545	4.21	34	28	0	188.1	165	106	132	21	.237
Car.	26	20	.565	4.48	112	39	3	353.2	323	192	263	42	.245

2003 Pitching Profile

	Victor Zambrano	AL Average
Overall Strike %	57.2	62.8
1st Pitch Strike %	52.0	58.7
Ratio	1.44	1.39
Strikeouts per 9 IP	6.31	6.11
Walks per 9 IP	5.07	3.16
Home Runs per 9 IP	1.00	1.11
Strikeout/Walk Ratio	1.25	1.93
Groundball/Flyball Ratio	1.31	1.18

2003 Situational Stats

	W	L	ERA	Sv	IP		AB	H	HR	RBI	Avg
Home	7	4	3.56	0	93.2	LHB	372	98	11	49	.263
Road	5	6	4.85	0	94.2	RHB	325	67	10	40	.206
First Half	6	4	3.84	0	100.2	Sc Pos	201	43	4	64	.214
Scnd Half	6	6	4.62	0	87.2	Clutch	53	10	3	3	.189

2003 Rankings (American League)

- 1st in walks allowed, hit batsmen (20), wild pitches (15) and highest walks per nine innings (5.1)
- 2nd in lowest strikeout-walk ratio (1.2)
- 3rd in balks (3) and lowest batting average allowed vs. righthanded batters
- 4th in highest stolen-base percentage allowed (88.9)
- Led the Devil Rays in wins, games started, innings pitched, batters faced (836), home runs allowed, walks allowed, hit batsmen (20), strikeouts, wild pitches (15), balks (3), pitches thrown (3,137), stolen bases allowed (16), GDPs induced (15), lowest slugging percentage allowed (.392), highest ground ball-flyball ratio allowed (1.3), lowest ERA at home, lowest batting average allowed vs. righthanded batters and most strikeouts per nine innings (6.3)

Tampa Bay

Brandon Backe

Position: RP
Bats: R **Throws:** R
Ht: 6' 0" **Wt:** 188

Opening Day Age: 25
Born: 4/5/78 in
Galveston, TX
ML Seasons: 2
Pronunciation:
back-EE

Overall Statistics

	W	L	Pct.	ERA	G	GS	Sv	IP	H	BB	SO	HR	Avg
'03	1	1	.500	5.44	28	0	0	44.2	40	25	36	6	.247
Car.	1	1	.500	5.77	37	0	0	57.2	55	32	42	9	.257

2003 Situational Stats

	W	L	ERA	Sv	IP		AB	H	HR	RBI	Avg
Home	0	1	6.87	0	18.1	LHB	53	16	2	7	.302
Road	1	0	4.44	0	26.1	RHB	109	24	4	18	.220
First Half	0	0	3.77	0	14.1	Sc Pos	42	9	2	18	.214
Scnd Half	1	1	6.23	0	30.1	Clutch	22	5	0	3	.227

2003 Season

A converted outfielder, Brandon Backe struggled the first time the Devil Rays called him up in mid-May, but he came back in mid-June and did well enough to stick for the rest of the season. He was used mostly as a middle reliever and was most effective during a month-long stretch from July 22-August 21, posting a 1.45 ERA in nine games.

Pitching & Defense

Backe got to the major leagues because of his ability to throw strikes. Unlike most young relievers who make their living with a blazing fastball, he has a curveball that can be his No. 1 pitch and allows him to dominate righthanded batters. He also can throw a sinking fastball, slider and changeup. Backe is a tremendous athlete and does an extremely good job fielding his position and covering the bases.

2004 Outlook

Backe has been a starter in the minor leagues, but his role with the big league team will be in middle relief. Manager Lou Piniella likes the idea of having different style pitchers in the bullpen, and Backe fits that role because of his ability to rely on a strong breaking ball. He was rushed to the majors and needs innings, however, to gain better command of his fastball.

Jesus Colome

Position: RP
Bats: R **Throws:** R
Ht: 6' 4" **Wt:** 205

Opening Day Age: 26
Born: 12/23/77 in San
Pedro de Macoris, DR
ML Seasons: 3
Pronunciation:
hay-soos cal-um-ay

Overall Statistics

	W	L	Pct.	ERA	G	GS	Sv	IP	H	BB	SO	HR	Avg
'03	3	7	.300	4.50	54	0	2	74.0	69	46	69	9	.247
Car.	7	17	.292	5.10	116	0	2	164.0	162	104	133	23	.261

2003 Situational Stats

	W	L	ERA	Sv	IP		AB	H	HR	RBI	Avg
Home	2	3	4.62	0	39.0	LHB	119	26	4	14	.218
Road	1	4	4.37	2	35.0	RHB	160	43	5	31	.269
First Half	2	5	4.71	0	49.2	Sc Pos	89	18	2	36	.202
Scnd Half	1	2	4.07	2	24.1	Clutch	118	32	5	25	.271

2003 Season

There was an offseason car accident and a rough first couple weeks, and there was an injury that kept him from pitching the final month. But for most of the time in between, Jesus Colome showed the Devil Rays how good a reliever he can be, posting a 2.84 ERA over a 17-game span. Colome picked up a pair of saves but did most of his work as a setup man, and the Rays kept him busy.

Pitching & Defense

Colome throws hard, but the Rays knew his 98-MPH fastball wasn't enough for him to succeed in the big leagues. The breakthrough came when he learned to throw—and to trust—both his slider and changeup. The process is ongoing, but he made significant strides in 2003. Colome is not an instinctive defensive player and needs to improve his ability to hold runners and to make pickoff throws.

2004 Outlook

Colome has been considered a future closer since the Rays got him, but he has yet to show he can handle the responsibility of that role. Until then, he likely will continue to be used in a sctup role. The Rays will be ecstatic if he improves as much from 2003 to 2004 as he did from '02 to '03.

Ben Grieve

Position: DH/RF
Bats: L **Throws:** R
Ht: 6' 4" **Wt:** 216

Opening Day Age: 27
Born: 5/4/76 in Arlington, TX
ML Seasons: 7
Pronunciation:
greev

Overall Statistics

	G	AB	R	H	D	T	HR	RBI	SB	BB	SO	Avg	OBP	Slg
'03	55	165	28	38	7	0	4	17	0	32	41	.230	.371	.345
Car.	830	2945	440	794	175	5	110	456	24	422	707	.270	.368	.444

2003 Situational Stats

	AB	H	HR	RBI	Avg			AB	H	HR	RBI	Avg
Home	98	25	2	11	.255	LHP		53	11	0	7	.208
Road	67	13	2	6	.194	RHP		112	27	4	10	.241
First Half	161	37	4	17	.230	Sc Pos		47	7	1	14	.149
Scnd Half	4	1	0	0	.250	Clutch		28	4	0	3	.143

2003 Season

Ben Grieve's 2003 season was more about what happened to him off the field than what he accomplished on it. Two odd medical conditions, both requiring surgery, limited him to 55 games. He had one operation to find the source of a left thumb infection in May, and then underwent season-ending surgery in July to remove a portion of his right rib that was causing an impingement that may have led to blood clots.

Hitting, Baserunning & Defense

Health problems aside, Grieve's once-feared bat has slowed and he has become overly passive and picky at the plate. Despite the struggles, hitting still is what Grieve does best. He has little speed on the bases and is a lackadaisical defensive outfielder with a below-average arm. He should be a prime supporter to keep the DH rule in play as long as possible.

2004 Outlook

Grieve's contract expired at the end of the season and for their $12 million over three years, the Rays got a .254 average, 34 home runs and 153 RBI in 345 games. He was expected to recover from the surgery in time to be ready for spring training, and will have to prove to some AL team that his once-promising career is not over.

Travis Harper

Position: RP
Bats: R **Throws:** R
Ht: 6' 4" **Wt:** 192

Opening Day Age: 27
Born: 5/21/76 in Harrisonburg, VA
ML Seasons: 4

Overall Statistics

	W	L	Pct.	ERA	G	GS	Sv	IP	H	BB	SO	HR	Avg
'03	4	8	.333	3.77	61	0	1	93.0	86	31	64	9	.252
Car.	10	21	.323	4.71	106	14	2	217.2	232	76	140	33	.274

2003 Situational Stats

	W	L	ERA	Sv	IP			AB	H	HR	RBI	Avg
Home	2	0	2.27	1	47.2	LHB		157	45	4	23	.287
Road	2	8	5.36	0	45.1	RHB		184	41	5	19	.223
First Half	1	5	3.26	0	60.2	Sc Pos		80	21	1	30	.263
Scnd Half	3	3	4.73	1	32.1	Clutch		156	44	4	21	.282

2003 Season

Travis Harper was a versatile and valuable member of the Rays' bullpen, pitching in a career-high 61 games while throwing 93 innings, second only to Steve Sparks among AL relievers. He was most effective when used in short, middle-relief stints, usually two innings or fewer. He clearly was tired by the end of the season, however, with a rough final month that raised his ERA nearly half a run.

Pitching & Defense

Harper uses his full repertoire to succeed. His fastball usually sits in the low 90s, and he can mix in a sharp-breaking curve, a changeup that he started throwing with a split-finger grip late in the season and a solid two-seamer that might be his best pitch. It would further help him to add a slider or a cutter to provide another look. Harper is a groundball pitcher who fields his position well and does a good job holding runners on.

2004 Outlook

Harper seemed to prove two things in 2003 during his first full major league season: he can do well as a setup man but doesn't do well in the late innings. He also was much more effective with two day's rest than pitching back-to-back days. His role in 2004 should be clear.

Tampa Bay

Seth McClung

Position: RP
Bats: L **Throws:** R
Ht: 6' 6" **Wt:** 235

Opening Day Age: 23
Born: 2/7/81 in
Lewisburg, WV
ML Seasons: 1

Overall Statistics

	W	L	Pct.	ERA	G	GS	Sv	IP	H	BB	SO	HR	Avg
'03	4	1	.800	5.35	12	5	0	38.2	33	25	25	6	.241
Car.	4	1	.800	5.35	12	5	0	38.2	33	25	25	6	.241

2003 Situational Stats

	W	L	ERA	Sv	IP			AB	H	HR	RBI	Avg
Home	3	0	3.15	0	20.0		LHB	64	18	2	8	.281
Road	1	1	7.71	0	18.2		RHB	73	15	4	10	.205
First Half	4	1	5.35	0	38.2		Sc Pos	24	7	2	12	.292
Scnd Half	0	0	—	0	0.0		Clutch	16	5	1	1	.313

2003 Season

Seth McClung made the jump from Double-A to earn a spot in the bullpen and had moved impressively into the rotation when he suffered an elbow injury during a May 22 start. After rest and rehabilitation didn't help, he underwent Tommy John surgery on June 26 and was lost for the season. His four wins still tied for fifth most on the team.

Pitching & Defense

McClung is a classic power pitcher, with a fastball that was routinely measured in the high 90s and has hit 100 MPH, an above-average hard curveball and an improving changeup. He is smart and hard-working, which enables him to make the most of his ability and limit his mistakes. Despite his size, McClung is a good athlete—he played seven sports in high school—who can field his position well and cover plenty of ground.

2004 Outlook

McClung was recovering at or ahead of schedule and is expected to be pitching at some point during the middle of the 2004 season. He hopes to be throwing during spring training and be pitching in games, at least on a minor league rehab assignment, sometime in May. The Rays likely will be cautious with him initially, using him in limited roles out of the bullpen.

Rey Ordonez

Position: SS
Bats: R **Throws:** R
Ht: 5' 9" **Wt:** 159

Opening Day Age: 33
Born: 1/11/71 in
Havana, Cuba
ML Seasons: 8
Pronunciation:
RAY or-DOAN-yez

Overall Statistics

	G	AB	R	H	D	T	HR	RBI	SB	BB	SO	Avg	OBP	Slg
'03	34	117	14	37	11	0	3	22	0	2	12	.316	.328	.487
Car.	950	3054	289	757	126	17	11	282	28	189	325	.248	.291	.311

2003 Situational Stats

	AB	H	HR	RBI	Avg			AB	H	HR	RBI	Avg
Home	66	21	1	15	.318		LHP	26	8	0	6	.308
Road	51	16	2	7	.314		RHP	91	29	3	16	.319
First Half	117	37	3	22	.316		Sc Pos	25	7	1	15	.280
Scnd Half	0	0	0	0	—		Clutch	30	5	1	3	.167

2003 Season

Rey Ordonez was Tampa Bay's primary offseason acquisition and it looked like quite a deal when he got off to a great start. But he injured his left knee diving for a ball in a May 8 game. He spent more than a month trying rest and rehabilitation, but he was unable to play without pain and underwent season-ending surgery on June 30 to repair a torn ligament.

Hitting, Baserunning & Defense

All the bad things the Rays had heard about Ordonez' hitting style disappeared once the season started. He did not routinely chase horribly bad pitches, get himself out all the time or show lapses in concentration. He *did* come up with clutch hits and drive the ball into the gaps when needed. Ordonez' defensive abilities are unparalleled, and he showed no trouble adjusting to the tricky turf/dirt infield at Tropicana Field. He has a quick first step and runs the bases well but is not much of a threat to steal.

2004 Outlook

Ordonez is hoping to be ready for spring training, but he was several weeks behind schedule in resuming baseball activities going into the winter. He is a free agent, but is likely to find the market slow since he is coming off the surgery.

Antonio Perez

Position: 2B
Bats: R **Throws:** R
Ht: 5'11" **Wt:** 170

Opening Day Age: 24
Born: 1/26/80 in Bani, DR
ML Seasons: 1

Overall Statistics

	G	AB	R	H	D	T	HR	RBI	SB	BB	SO	Avg	OBP	Slg
'03	48	125	19	31	6	1	2	12	4	18	34	.248	.345	.360
Car.	48	125	19	31	6	1	2	12	4	18	34	.248	.345	.360

2003 Situational Stats

	AB	H	HR	RBI	Avg		AB	H	HR	RBI	Avg
Home	58	14	0	3	.241	LHP	59	14	0	2	.237
Road	67	17	2	9	.254	RHP	66	17	2	10	.258
First Half	35	11	1	2	.314	Sc Pos	25	8	1	10	.320
Scnd Half	90	20	1	10	.222	Clutch	17	3	0	1	.176

2003 Season

Antonio Perez came to the Devil Rays from Seattle as part of the deal that landed manager Lou Piniella. The first time he was called up in May he didn't appear ready to play in the majors, but when the Rays brought him back in late June, after a hot streak at Triple-A Durham, he looked like a major league player. He hit .319 in July, including four three-hit games and one five-RBI performance.

Hitting, Baserunning & Defense

Perez has an aggressive hitting style that needs to be refined as he learns the strike zone. During his hot streak, he was swinging at strikes. But once opponents found out he would chase pitches off the plate, they forced him to swing at bad pitches, and then at worse pitches, cutting down his confidence. Perez came up as a shortstop but seems more suited to second base, especially because of his limited arm strength. He has decent speed but a lack of concentration contributed to several baserunning mistakes late in the season.

2004 Outlook

The Rays were encouraged during Perez' hot July. But his immense late-season struggles and bad baserunning decisions appear to have set him back. If they land a veteran infielder, he likely will open the season at Triple-A Durham.

Jared Sandberg

Position: 3B
Bats: R **Throws:** R
Ht: 6' 3" **Wt:** 226

Opening Day Age: 26
Born: 3/2/78 in Olympia, WA
ML Seasons: 3

Overall Statistics

	G	AB	R	H	D	T	HR	RBI	SB	BB	SO	Avg	OBP	Slg
'03	55	136	15	29	10	1	6	23	0	16	52	.213	.305	.434
Car.	196	630	83	139	38	2	25	92	4	65	236	.221	.297	.406

2003 Situational Stats

	AB	H	HR	RBI	Avg		AB	H	HR	RBI	Avg
Home	48	7	0	3	.146	LHP	67	14	2	8	.209
Road	88	22	6	20	.250	RHP	69	15	4	15	.217
First Half	59	14	2	13	.237	Sc Pos	37	8	1	13	.216
Scnd Half	77	15	4	10	.195	Clutch	25	4	0	2	.160

2003 Season

Jared Sandberg opened the season in the minors, was called up May 13 and homered that night, then went on to hit .237 with two homers and 13 RBI in 23 games with the Rays. He went back to the minors for six weeks, then rejoined the Rays for good in late July, but never got in a good groove. He struck out 52 times in 136 at-bats in the big leagues, and 95 more times in 272 minor league at-bats.

Hitting, Baserunning & Defense

The nephew of former Cubs great Ryne Sandberg, Jared has loads of power. But he tends to get into trouble when he tries to pull too many pitches and because he swings and misses too often. What Sandberg gives away at the plate, he tends to make up for in the field with soft hands and a strong arm. He doesn't have much speed but runs the bases intelligently.

2004 Outlook

One of the Rays' biggest needs over the last two seasons has been for a righthanded power hitter, and Sandberg has been unable to take advantage of the opportunity. He likely is headed back to the minors, where he will have to show that he can cut down on his strikeouts.

Jorge Sosa

Position: SP/RP
Bats: B **Throws:** R
Ht: 6' 2" **Wt:** 170

Opening Day Age: 26
Born: 4/28/77 in Santo Domingo, DR
ML Seasons: 2
Pronunciation: hor-hey

Overall Statistics

	W	L	Pct.	ERA	G	GS	Sv	IP	H	BB	SO	HR	Avg
'03	5	12	.294	4.62	29	19	0	128.2	137	60	72	14	.278
Car.	7	19	.269	5.01	60	33	0	228.0	225	114	120	30	.260

2003 Situational Stats

	W	L	ERA	Sv	IP		AB	H	HR	RBI	Avg
Home	3	7	4.38	0	72.0	LHB	248	78	7	38	.315
Road	2	5	4.92	0	56.2	RHB	245	59	7	34	.241
First Half	2	7	4.70	0	59.1	Sc Pos	136	42	2	53	.309
Scnd Half	3	5	4.54	0	69.1	Clutch	45	10	2	4	.222

2003 Season

The conversion of Jorge Sosa from outfielder to pitcher is complete. Now the Devil Rays have to determine what kind of pitcher he is. He started 19 games, going 5-11 with a 4.76 ERA, and made 10 relief appearances, going 0-1 with a 4.01 ERA. When he was good, he was very good, highlighted by a four-hit complete-game 1-0 shutout of Seattle on September 4, but consistency was a major problem.

Pitching & Defense

Sosa can throw as hard as anyone the Rays have, regularly working in the 97-98 MPH range if he wants to. Tampa spent much of 2003 addressing two issues: getting Sosa to throw harder in the first inning of his starts and getting him to not throw so hard in the later innings. When he was at his best, he keeps his fastball in the mid-90s and mixes in a changeup and a slider. Sosa is not a smooth defensive player.

2004 Outlook

Sosa was used in a variety of roles in 2003, and that is not likely to change unless he unexpectedly wins a spot in the rotation during spring training. Until he refines his offspeed pitches and has more control of his fastball, he seems slated for a long-relief/swing role.

Doug Waechter

Position: SP
Bats: R **Throws:** R
Ht: 6' 4" **Wt:** 209

Opening Day Age: 23
Born: 1/28/81 in St. Petersburg, FL
ML Seasons: 1
Nickname: WECK-ter

Overall Statistics

	W	L	Pct.	ERA	G	GS	Sv	IP	H	BB	SO	HR	Avg
'03	3	2	.600	3.31	6	5	0	35.1	29	15	29	4	.225
Car.	3	2	.600	3.31	6	5	0	35.1	29	15	29	4	.225

2003 Situational Stats

	W	L	ERA	Sv	IP		AB	H	HR	RBI	Avg
Home	2	1	2.45	0	22.0	LHB	66	12	1	1	.182
Road	1	1	4.73	0	13.1	RHB	63	17	3	10	.270
First Half	0	0	—	0	0.0	Sc Pos	24	5	1	6	.208
Scnd Half	3	2	3.31	0	35.1	Clutch	7	3	0	0	.429

2003 Season

Doug Waechter worked his way from Double-A Orlando to Triple-A Durham to the major leagues, and he did a solid job with the parent club. He picked up a win in relief in his debut August 27 at Seattle, then threw a two-hit, complete-game shutout on September 3 in his first major league start to beat the Mariners in front of the hometown crowd.

Pitching & Defense

Waechter's smooth mechanics produce a sneaky low-90s fastball that is his primary pitch, and he supplements that with a plus slider and changeup. As good as his stuff is, and it is very good when he locates his fastball, his toughness, maturity and determination are also key factors in his success. Waechter is a tremendous athlete who will do whatever it takes defensively to make plays. One area where he could use some work is in holding runners, specifically with his slide-step delivery.

2004 Outlook

Waechter was impressive enough in his six appearances that manager Lou Piniella has him penciled in for a spot in the rotation. The Rays eventually see Waechter as a power-pitching, 200-inning workhorse who could be at least a No. 2 or 3 starter for years to come.

Other Tampa Bay Devil Rays

Rob Bell (Pos: RHP, **Age:** 27)

	W	L	Pct.	ERA	G	GS	Sv	IP	H	BB	SO	HR	Avg
'03	5	4	.556	5.52	19	18	0	101.0	103	39	44	15	.263
Car.	21	25	.457	5.86	89	86	0	485.0	522	211	323	95	.275

The enigmatic Bell continued his career pattern, dropping subtle hints of brilliance. He was 0-2 in his first four starts for the Devil Rays, before finishing the season by winning five of his last seven decisions. 2004 Outlook: C

Matt Diaz (Pos: LF, **Age:** 26, **Bats:** R)

	G	AB	R	H	D	T	HR	RBI	SB	BB	SO	Avg	OBP	Slg
'03	4	9	2	1	0	0	0	0	0	1	3	.111	.200	.111
Car.	4	9	2	1	0	0	0	0	0	1	3	.111	.200	.111

It's hard to deem Diaz a prospect at this point, but his .325 average at Durham was difficult for the Rays to ignore when they called him up in July. He went 1-for-9 during his 11 days with Tampa. 2004 Outlook: C

Damion Easley (Pos: 3B, **Age:** 34, **Bats:** R)

	G	AB	R	H	D	T	HR	RBI	SB	BB	SO	Avg	OBP	Slg
'03	36	107	8	20	3	1	1	7	0	2	18	.187	.202	.262
Car.	1227	4296	591	1086	226	22	120	513	105	401	749	.253	.329	.399

The Devil Rays released Easley in June. The veteran hit .187 with one home run and seven RBI for Tampa Bay. It has been a downward spiral for Easley after hitting 27 homers with 100 RBI in 1998. 2004 Outlook: C

Felix Escalona (Pos: SS, **Age:** 25, **Bats:** R)

	G	AB	R	H	D	T	HR	RBI	SB	BB	SO	Avg	OBP	Slg
'03	10	27	2	5	2	0	0	2	1	2	6	.185	.241	.259
Car.	69	184	19	39	10	2	0	11	8	5	50	.212	.259	.288

Escalona was Tampa Bay's regular shortstop for about a week in May. The Orioles claimed him off waivers later that month and he underwent knee surgery three weeks later. 2004 Outlook: C

Jeff Liefer (Pos: 1B, **Age:** 29, **Bats:** L)

	G	AB	R	H	D	T	HR	RBI	SB	BB	SO	Avg	OBP	Slg
'03	44	113	10	20	4	0	4	21	0	6	39	.177	.217	.319
Car.	253	695	82	162	32	1	29	100	2	53	200	.233	.287	.407

Tampa Bay claimed Liefer from the Expos in June after Montreal had acquired him in the Bartolo Colon trade. He has done little since clubbing 18 home runs in 2001. 2004 Outlook: C

George Lombard (Pos: RF, **Age:** 28, **Bats:** L)

	G	AB	R	H	D	T	HR	RBI	SB	BB	SO	Avg	OBP	Slg
'03	13	37	8	8	1	0	1	4	1	0	6	.216	.237	.324
Car.	124	329	53	74	12	3	7	20	21	22	101	.225	.279	.343

Lombard was coming off a 2002 in which he played in a career-high 72 games for Detroit when the Devil Rays got him on a waiver claim in March 2003. He hit .348 in April, but was 0-for-14 in May. 2004 Outlook: C

Mark Malaska (Pos: LHP, **Age:** 26)

	W	L	Pct.	ERA	G	GS	Sv	IP	H	BB	SO	HR	Avg
'03	2	1	.667	2.81	22	0	0	16.0	13	12	17	0	.232
Car.	2	1	.667	2.81	22	0	0	16.0	13	12	17	0	.232

Malaska had a 2-2 record and a 3.19 ERA with one save between Double-A Orlando and Triple-A Durham, but he was 0-for-3 in save opportunities after the Devil Rays purchased his contract in July. The Red Sox claimed him off waivers in December. 2004 Outlook: C

Al Martin (Pos: DH, **Age:** 36, **Bats:** L)

	G	AB	R	H	D	T	HR	RBI	SB	BB	SO	Avg	OBP	Slg
'03	100	238	19	60	12	2	3	26	2	17	51	.252	.306	.357
Car.	1232	4242	664	1172	220	48	132	485	173	390	879	.276	.339	.444

Tampa Bay picked up Martin when he was released by the Marlins last spring. He was out of baseball in 2002 after struggling with the Mariners in 2001. He was limited to DH duties with the Rays. 2004 Outlook: C

Jim Parque (Pos: LHP, **Age:** 28)

	W	L	Pct.	ERA	G	GS	Sv	IP	H	BB	SO	HR	Avg
'03	1	1	.500	11.94	5	5	0	17.1	27	16	8	2	.351
Car.	31	34	.477	5.42	103	97	0	544.1	650	241	335	78	.297

Parque went to the disabled list once before he was demoted in May. The lefty was considering retirement, but reported and went 5-7 with a 4.08 ERA for Durham. He was released in September. 2004 Outlook: C

Steve Parris (Pos: RHP, **Age:** 36)

	W	L	Pct.	ERA	G	GS	Sv	IP	H	BB	SO	HR	Avg
'03	0	3	.000	6.18	10	7	0	43.2	60	13	14	12	.328
Car.	44	49	.473	4.75	139	129	0	753.1	846	288	479	114	.286

Parris got a spot in the Tampa rotation out of spring training, but had a career-high 6.25 ERA in seven starts before going on the disabled list with shoulder tendinitis. The club released him in June. 2004 Outlook: C

Adam Piatt (Pos: LF/RF, **Age:** 28, **Bats:** R)

	G	AB	R	H	D	T	HR	RBI	SB	BB	SO	Avg	OBP	Slg
'03	61	132	11	30	13	0	6	18	1	9	46	.227	.273	.462
Car.	212	521	62	129	31	6	16	65	3	57	149	.248	.323	.422

It looked like Piatt finally would get a chance to play when Tampa Bay claimed him off waivers from Oakland in August. He logged just 14 games, however, and was released in November. 2004 Outlook: C

Carlos Reyes (Pos: RHP, **Age:** 34)

	W	L	Pct.	ERA	G	GS	Sv	IP	H	BB	SO	HR	Avg
'03	0	3	.000	5.22	10	3	0	39.2	40	5	13	10	.265
Car.	20	36	.357	4.66	293	29	4	558.0	576	220	360	86	.268

The Devil Rays sent Reyes outright to Triple-A Durham in October, but he opted for free agency instead. The hurler had a 5.22 ERA in 10 games in his first appearance in the majors since 2000 with San Diego. 2004 Outlook: C

John Rocker (**Pos**: LHP, **Age**: 29)

	W	L	Pct.	ERA	G	GS	Sv	IP	H	BB	SO	HR	Avg
'03	0	0	–	9.00	2	0	0	1.0	2	3	0	0	.500
Car.	13	22	.371	3.42	280	0	88	255.1	200	164	332	23	.213

The former Braves closer had a 9.15 ERA in 17 games for Orlando and a 9.00 ERA in two games up with Tampa. The Rays released Rocker from Double-A in June. He underwent rotator cuff surgery in September. 2004 Outlook: C

Bobby Seay (**Pos**: LHP, **Age**: 25)

	W	L	Pct.	ERA	G	GS	Sv	IP	H	BB	SO	HR	Avg
'03	0	0	–	3.00	12	0	0	9.0	7	6	5	0	.226
Car.	1	1	.500	4.91	24	0	0	22.0	20	11	17	3	.247

Seay made his first appearance in the big leagues since 2001, but he had to be shut down for about a month and a half when he experienced soreness in the back of his shoulder in April. 2004 Outlook: C

Terry Shumpert (**Pos**: 2B/3B/DH, **Age**: 37, **Bats**: R)

	G	AB	R	H	D	T	HR	RBI	SB	BB	SO	Avg	OBP	Slg
'03	59	84	14	16	5	2	2	7	1	10	17	.190	.289	.369
Car.	854	1969	295	497	109	26	49	223	85	166	369	.252	.315	.409

Shumpert signed with Tampa Bay immediately following his release from the Dodgers in March. He had spent five seasons with Colorado. He played in 59 games, his fewest since 1998, and became a free agent. 2004 Outlook: C

Jason Smith (**Pos**: 3B, **Age**: 26, **Bats**: L)

	G	AB	R	H	D	T	HR	RBI	SB	BB	SO	Avg	OBP	Slg
'03	1	4	0	1	0	0	0	0	0	0	0	.250	.250	.250
Car.	29	70	9	14	1	2	1	6	3	2	25	.200	.222	.314

Smith played in one game during his four days with the Rays in June, going 1-for-4 and making two errors at third base. He hit .285 with 15 home runs and 71 RBI in 130 games at Triple-A Durham, and the Tigers signed him to a minor league deal in December. 2004 Outlook: C

Chris Truby (**Pos**: 3B, **Age**: 30, **Bats**: R)

	G	AB	R	H	D	T	HR	RBI	SB	BB	SO	Avg	OBP	Slg
'03	13	43	4	12	3	0	0	3	0	5	13	.279	.354	.349
Car.	263	819	78	189	42	9	23	107	5	38	205	.231	.269	.388

Truby caught on with his fourth organization in three seasons when he joined the Devil Rays last January. He hit .279 in 13 games before losing his spot, but that was after a 3-for-20 showing in May. 2004 Outlook: C

Jason Tyner (**Pos**: RF, **Age**: 26, **Bats**: L)

	G	AB	R	H	D	T	HR	RBI	SB	BB	SO	Avg	OBP	Slg
'03	46	90	12	25	7	0	0	6	2	10	12	.278	.350	.356
Car.	245	778	89	200	21	6	0	49	47	37	89	.257	.294	.299

Tyner was thought to be a fixture in the Tampa Bay outfield in 2001 when he batted .280 and was 31-for-37 in steals. He failed to make the D-Rays out of spring training, but hit .278 in 46 games in 2003. Texas claimed him off waivers in December. 2004 Outlook: C

Javier Valentin (**Pos**: C, **Age**: 28, **Bats**: B)

	G	AB	R	H	D	T	HR	RBI	SB	BB	SO	Avg	OBP	Slg
'03	49	135	13	30	7	1	3	15	0	5	31	.222	.254	.356
Car.	190	526	47	120	26	3	11	61	0	38	103	.228	.279	.352

After 10 years in Minnesota, Valentin was traded to the Brewers shortly after 2002 season. He was dealt again in March to the Devil Rays, where he hit just .222 with three home runs in 135 at-bats. 2004 Outlook: C

Mike Venafro (**Pos**: LHP, **Age**: 30)

	W	L	Pct.	ERA	G	GS	Sv	IP	H	BB	SO	HR	Avg
'03	1	0	1.000	4.74	24	0	0	19.0	24	3	9	1	.308
Car.	14	10	.583	4.11	283	0	5	240.2	250	88	123	14	.273

Venafro spent time with four organizations in 2003. He had a 3.45 ERA in April and May, but blew up for a 10.80 ERA in June and was released by the Rays. He signed with Kansas City after the season. 2004 Outlook: C

Tampa Bay Devil Rays Minor League Prospects

Organization Overview:

The Devil Rays struck out with tools-rich Louisiana prospect Toe Nash, but Tampa Bay scout Benny Latino, a Louisiana native, has plucked a couple of little-known plums from his home state. Speedster Joey Gathright and righthander Chad Gaudin were Latino finds, drafted in the 32nd and 34th rounds of the 2001 draft, and they are among the system's best prospects today. Not all of the system's best are from Louisiana, but more Tampa Bay talent than ever is on the fringe of helping out in the majors. Gaudin and lefthander Jon Switzer could land in the Rays' bullpen, and Dewon Brazelton could join the rotation if he can overcome his tendency to start slowly. Catcher Pete LaForest and outfielder Jonny Gomes may arrive to shore up the offense.

Dewon Brazelton

Position: P **Opening Day Age:** 23
Bats: R **Throws:** R **Born:** 6/16/80 in
Ht: 6' 4" **Wt:** 214 Tullahoma, TN

Recent Statistics

	W	L	ERA	G	GS	Sv	IP	H	R	BB	SO	HR
2003 AAA Durham	2	2	4.21	5	5	0	25.2	23	14	11	18	1
2003 A Bakersfield	1	5	5.26	9	9	0	49.2	62	33	19	42	4
2003 AA Orlando	2	0	2.53	2	2	0	10.2	8	6	8	5	0
2003 AL Tampa Bay	1	6	6.89	10	10	0	48.1	57	49	23	24	9

The third overall pick in 2001, Brazelton signed a major league contract in August and simply worked with Rays coaches on his mechanics and changeup, his best pitch. In early 2002, Brazelton struggled with command, reduced his windup at the behest of coaches and lacked a breaking ball, and pitching at Double-A Orlando didn't go well. After returning to the high-leg-kick delivery that he used in college, he finished strong. Brazelton's 2003 started with two minor leg injuries, costing him two weeks of prep time. He again had a rough first half, working with a newly overhauled motion, and again went back to his college delivery. He enjoyed a terrific Arizona Fall League, featuring an improved slider to go with his moving mid-90s fastball.

Joey Gathright

Position: OF **Opening Day Age:** 21
Bats: L **Throws:** R **Born:** 4/22/82 in
Ht: 5' 10" **Wt:** 175 Hattiesburg, MS

Recent Statistics

	G	AB	R	H	D	T	HR	RBI	SB	BB	SO	Avg
2002 A Chrlstn (SC)	59	208	30	55	1	0	0	14	22	21	36	.264
2003 A Bakersfield	89	340	65	110	6	3	0	23	57	41	54	.324
2003 AA Orlando	22	85	12	32	1	0	0	5	12	5	15	.376

One of the fastest guys in the game, Gathright, a 32nd-rounder in 2001, benefits from a hitting approach that best suits his game and promising plate patience. With a good knowledge of the strike zone, Gathright often chops the ball or bunts to reach base. While he hit .334 between two stops in 2003, he managed just 10 extra-base hits in 425 at-bats. He also stole 69 bases, though he steals more on raw speed than technique. His 2003 season ended a month early when he dove for a ball and dislocated his left shoulder. Whether he will hit enough at higher levels is a concern, but Gathright is effective slashing the ball through the middle or the other way.

Chad Gaudin

Position: P **Opening Day Age:** 21
Bats: R **Throws:** R **Born:** 3/24/83 in New
Ht: 5' 11" **Wt:** 165 Orleans, LA

Recent Statistics

	W	L	ERA	G	GS	Sv	IP	H	R	BB	SO	HR
2003 A Bakersfield	5	3	2.13	14	14	0	80.1	63	23	23	70	2
2003 AA Orlando	2	0	0.47	3	3	0	19.0	8	1	3	23	0
2003 AL Tampa Bay	2	0	3.60	15	3	0	40.0	37	18	16	23	4

Gaudin is a 34th-round pick in 2001, a 5-foot-11 righthander. Those are two attributes that seldom are associated with budding pitching prospects, but Gaudin has risen rapidly through the Rays' system in two seasons, spotting the ball effectively and calling on a moving 86-90 MPH fastball, late-biting slider and changeup. In 2003, he went 7-3 at two minor league stops with a 1.81 ERA in 17 starts. After tossing a seven-inning perfect game in his Double-A debut in July, he was in the majors in August, and he settled into the Tampa Bay pen. He was the youngest pitcher in the majors, and he will stick if he can solve more advanced hitters.

Josh Hamilton

Position: OF **Opening Day Age:** 22
Bats: L **Throws:** L **Born:** 5/21/81 in Raleigh,
Ht: 6' 4" **Wt:** 205 NC

Recent Statistics

	G	AB	R	H	D	T	HR	RBI	SB	BB	SO	Avg
2002 A Bakersfield	56	211	32	64	14	1	9	44	10	20	46	.303

Chosen first overall in 1999, Hamilton is a five-tool prospect whose development has been hindered by injuries and personal issues. A spring-training car accident in 2001 sparked back and leg ailments that led to a lost season. Three trips to the disabled list in 2002 ended with arthroscopic cleanups of his left shoulder and elbow that July. Hamilton has been productive offensively when healthy, and he has the tools to be a solid right fielder in the majors, but his big league arrival was expected by now. In 2003, Hamilton left camp during spring training and again in May, and soon after was granted a leave for personal reasons. That ended when Hamilton worked out with Triple-A Durham during the final week of the minor league season.

Pete LaForest

Position: C
Bats: L **Throws:** R
Ht: 6' 2" **Wt:** 208

Opening Day Age: 26
Born: 1/27/78 in Hull, Canada

Recent Statistics

	G	AB	R	H	D	T	HR	RBI	SB	BB	SO	Avg
2003 AA Orlando	21	72	9	18	8	0	3	15	0	16	17	.250
2003 AAA Durham	61	201	40	54	14	2	14	38	2	36	56	.269
2003 AL Tampa Bay	19	48	0	8	2	0	0	6	0	1	14	.167

A year ago LaForest missed his first big league spring training when visa complications grounded the Canadian native until the season was six weeks old. Still, he progressed through the high minors and reached Tampa Bay in September. It's not surprising that LaForest, an undrafted free agent signed in 1997, has hit so well. His bat prompted the Rays to make him a catcher three years ago. His progress *behind* the plate has been slower, though he has quick feet, an average arm and good game-calling skills. LaForest improved his defensive game with a lot of work during his spring downtime. He mostly needs to fine-tune his throwing mechanics, so that he's more consistent with his throws.

Jon Switzer

Position: P
Bats: L **Throws:** L
Ht: 6' 2" **Wt:** 191

Opening Day Age: 24
Born: 8/13/79 in Houston, TX

Recent Statistics

	W	L	ERA	G	GS	Sv	IP	H	R	BB	SO	HR
2003 AA Orlando	8	8	3.43	22	22	0	126.0	117	63	32	100	10
2003 AAA Durham	1	0	1.80	1	1	0	5.0	6	1	0	3	1
2003 AL Tampa Bay	0	0	7.45	5	0	0	9.2	13	8	3	7	2

A second-round pick in 2001, Switzer continued a steady climb with a solid season at Double-A Orlando, and moved to Triple-A Durham for the International League playoffs. He also spent time with the Rays in August and September. Rays manager Lou Piniella said Switzer's low-90s fastball and improved changeup were solid pitches. While his change was his third pitch at the start of the season, his solid slider was inconsistent during his big league stay. He went from short-season Class-A in 2001 to high Class-A Bakersfield without a hitch in 2002, and he exhibited better command of all of his pitches in 2003, moving them around the strike zone effectively. The Rays are light on lefties, especially in the pen, and Switzer could help out in 2004.

B.J. Upton

Position: SS
Bats: R **Throws:** R
Ht: 6' 2" **Wt:** 167

Opening Day Age: 19
Born: 8/21/84 in Chesapeake, VA

Recent Statistics

	G	AB	R	H	D	T	HR	RBI	SB	BB	SO	Avg
2003 A Chrlstn (SC)	101	384	70	116	22	6	7	46	38	57	80	.302
2003 AA Orlando	29	105	14	29	8	0	1	16	2	16	25	.276

The second overall pick in 2002, Upton has five-tool talent, and his package of tools, skills and baseball instincts makes him a fast-track candidate. Upton jumped from low-A ball to Double-A Orlando late in his debut season, and he continued to produce with the bat and show patience. His defensive game wasn't as far along, which was more apparent at Orlando. The Southern League is a lot of faster than the Sally League, as Upton found out, but his desire and makeup helped him adjust and prosper. His 56 errors weren't a major concern, as uneven play is common among young shortstops, especially a teenager who approaches his work aggressively. Upton probably will start at Orlando in 2004.

Others to Watch

Outfielder **Wes Bankston** (20) showed more of his five-tool potential in 2003 as one of the younger regulars in the Class-A Sally League. The righthanded hitter was bigger and stronger last summer, and posted 12 homers, 60 RBI and 53 walks in 103 games at Charleston (S.C.). . . Acquired from the Mexico City Tigers before the 2002 season, Mexico native **Gerardo Garcia** (24) advanced to Triple-A ball in his debut season. He's a savvy righthander who changes speeds well and works effectively with four pitches, including a pair of snappy breaking balls. He has the mid-90s heater and stuff to close, but he's a starter for now. Elbow and shoulder woes sidelined him for much of the 2003 season, but he went to Mexico to pitch winter ball and should be good to go in the spring. . . A 2001 pick, **Jonny Gomes** (23) displays a quick bat and tons of raw power. He led the Rookie-level Appy League with 16 homers in 2001, and drilled 30 more at high Class-A Bakersfield in 2002. While his raw numbers and hitting percentages were down at Double-A Orlando last summer, Gomes made consistent progress all year and dropped his strikeout rate en route to a cup of coffee with the Rays. . . A 2002 second-round pick with solid tools and a nice stroke, outfielder **Jason Pridie** (20) spent his first full season as a pro at Class-A Charleston as a teenager. He makes good contact and sprays the ball around. Still, his strikeouts are high and he needs to work more walks as a potential leadoff hitter. . . Righthander **Jason Standridge** (25) has a low-90s sinker and a sharp-breaking curve that is his out pitch. The former first-round pick from 1997 enjoyed a promising Triple-A debut (10-9, 3.12) in 2002, but he wasn't as effective in his second go-round at Durham (2-4, 4.50) last season. Poor command in the strike zone remains a critical issue for Standridge. . . The younger brother of Detroit's Dmitri Young, high school outfielder **Delmon Young** (18) was the first overall pick in 2003. The power prospect signed a major league contract in September, good for five years and roughly $6.2 million. Young spent two weeks in the instructional league and showed his promise as a hitter. He has a good feel for the strike zone and displays a good approach with the stick. He's a plus runner with a plus arm. Young is likely to debut at Class-A Charleston, where most of Tampa Bay's top-flight prospects have started.

The Ballpark in Arlington

Offense

The Ballpark in Arlington is the hitters' haven of the American League. Huge power alleys make it an inviting doubles park, while a short right-field porch invites lefthanded hitters to turn flyballs into homers. A lightning-quick infield often turns hard bouncers into hits, and there is not an abundance of foul ground, which means foul pops often are souvenirs instead of outs.

Defense

The Ballpark demands an intelligent, athletic center fielder to patrol huge gaps. But because it's an AL park, the player must also have some offensive skills. The infield is very quick because of hot, windy and dry Texas summers, also putting a premium on above-average defenders with good reactions and soft hands. The Rangers currently have plenty of those.

Who It Helps the Most

Lefthanded hitters with power love the short porch in right field, as well as the jet stream that catches flies in right center and turns them into extra bases. The Rangers have a cadre of young lefthanded hitters including third baseman Hank Blalock, first baseman Mark Teixeira (a switch-hitter) and outfielder Laynce Nix.

Who It Hurts the Most

Flyball pitchers often need therapy after extended exposure to The Ballpark. Chan Ho Park has been the poster child for that problem. Around all his DL assignments, Park is 6-6 with a 6.82 ERA at The Ballpark. GM John Hart and staff, after more than a year of thinking hard-throwing, high-strikeout pitchers were the answer, have reverted to the previous administration's tactic of looking for groundball hurlers who don't cause themselves extra problems with lots of walks.

Rookies & Newcomers

The Rangers will make a concerted effort to integrate more groundball-throwing lefties into the mix. Look for guys like Ben Kozlowski, Ryan Snare and A.J. Murray to get their shots if they are healthy. Lefthanded-hitting Brad Fullmer may like the short porch in right.

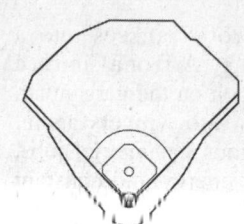

Dimensions: LF-332, LCF-390, CF-400, RCF-381, RF-325

Capacity: 49,115

Elevation: 551 feet

Surface: Grass

Foul Territory: Average

Park Factors

2003 Season

| | Home Games | | | Away Games | | | |
	Rangers	Opp	Total	Rangers	Opp	Total	Index
G	72	72	144	72	72	144	
Avg	.287	.287	.287	.244	.285	.264	109
AB	2465	2591	5056	2570	2439	5009	101
R	443	435	878	301	410	711	123
H	707	743	1450	626	694	1320	110
2B	125	168	293	119	138	257	113
3B	22	17	39	10	16	26	149
HR	129	92	221	89	89	178	123
BB	223	262	485	201	278	479	100
SO	450	480	930	486	425	911	101
E	39	49	88	50	45	95	93
E-Infield	31	40	71	42	37	79	90
LHB-Avg	.287	.288	.288	.238	.290	.267	108
LHB-HR	62	44	106	36	44	80	128
RHB-Avg	.287	.285	.286	.247	.279	.261	109
RHB-HR	67	48	115	53	45	98	118

2001-2003

| | Home Games | | | Away Games | | | |
	Rangers	Opp	Total	Rangers	Opp	Total	Index
G	217	217	434	214	214	428	
Avg	.283	.286	.285	.255	.280	.267	106
AB	7402	7853	15255	7632	7228	14860	101
R	1260	1302	2562	1016	1189	2205	115
H	2097	2248	4345	1948	2027	3975	108
2B	404	526	930	403	442	845	107
3B	50	61	111	26	52	78	139
HR	361	290	651	283	258	541	117
BB	736	810	1546	672	848	1520	99
SO	1350	1393	2743	1460	1250	2710	99
E	135	148	283	143	140	283	99
E-Infield	112	122	234	115	117	232	99
LHB-Avg	.284	.284	.284	.259	.287	.274	104
LHB-HR	149	137	286	110	121	231	116
RHB-Avg	.283	.288	.286	.253	.275	.263	109
RHB-HR	212	153	365	173	137	310	118

2003 Rankings (American League)

- Highest batting-average factor
- Highest RHB batting-average factor
- Second-highest run factor
- Second-highest hit factor
- Second-highest triple factor
- Second-highest home-run factor
- Second-highest LHB batting-average factor
- Third-highest double factor

Buck Showalter

2003 Season

After rebuilding the New York Yankees into a playoff team and molding Arizona into a contender, Buck Showalter took on the gargantuan task of turning the Rangers into winners again. Just like he had in his previous managerial jobs, Showalter displayed tireless energy and constant attention to detail. His efforts didn't translate into more wins in 2003, but that may only be a temporary situation.

Offense

Showalter likes to play National League-style ball, but he didn't have a team capable of playing small-ball for him. The offense was mostly station-to-station, and playing for one run was meaningless with a pitching staff that couldn't hold leads. Nonetheless, he did prove more aggressive than his predecessors, Jerry Narron and Johnny Oates. Showalter is well prepared for every eventuality. If the Rangers' pitching improves, his touch can be worth a few extra wins a season.

Pitching & Defense

Though he had a history of letting starting pitchers go deep into games with New York and Arizona, Showalter didn't have anywhere near the same patience with Texas hurlers. Rangers starters averaged just five innings per outing, leaving the bullpen to set a major league record for innings pitched. Relievers pitched 601.1 innings, two innings more than the 1977 Seattle Mariners. Showalter will have to adjust to getting by with a below-average staff. He loves "ballplayers," guys who do the right thing at the right time. He understands the value of defense at The Ballpark in Arlington.

2004 Outlook

Showalter has a foundation to work with, including an infield that might already be the AL's best, but he will struggle to turn the Rangers around until the team's pitching improves. He has endorsed the full-scale rebuilding plan on which the Rangers have embarked, and he has the energy and wherewithal to complete the project.

Born: 5/23/56 in DeFuniak, FL

Playing Experience: No major league playing experience

Managerial Experience: 8 seasons

Manager Statistics

Year	Team, Lg	W	L	Pct	GB	Finish
2003	Texas, AL	71	91	.438	25.0	4th West
8 Seasons		634	595	.516	–	–

2003 Starting Pitchers by Days Rest

	<=3	4	5	6+
Rangers Starts	3	82	31	31
Rangers ERA	2.25	6.05	6.61	5.50
AL Avg Starts	2	79	50	22
AL ERA	3.19	4.64	4.57	4.98

2003 Situational Stats

	Buck Showalter	AL Average
Hit & Run Success %	28.1	36.7
Stolen Base Success %	72.2	70.0
Platoon Pct.	61.0	61.7
Defensive Subs	33	23
High-Pitch Outings	4	5
Quick/Slow Hooks	26/16	19/16
Sacrifice Attempts	36	55

2003 Rankings (American League)

- 1st in relief appearances (494) and mid-inning pitching changes (237)
- 2nd in fewest caught stealings of third base (1), intentional walks (33), starting lineups used (133), quick hooks and first-batter platoon percentage
- 3rd in fewest caught stealings of second base (24), defensive substitutions, starts on three days rest and one-batter pitcher appearances (34)

Hank Blalock

2003 Season

After a washout rookie season in 2002, Hank Blalock returned to the majors and demonstrated the line-drive hitting capabilities that made him one of the hottest prospects in baseball. In 2002, Blalock tried to pull almost everything. In '03, he went back to using the whole field. As a result, he wound with 63 extra-base hits and was one homer shy of a 30-homer, 30-double season. And though it ended up not meaning anything, he decided who would have home-field advantage in the World Series with a big home run off Eric Gagne in the All-Star game.

Hitting

The only thing keeping Blalock from winning a batting title is his lack of success against left-handed pitching. He is only a career .183 hitter against lefties. Manager Buck Showalter shielded him from facing lefties for most of the season, but lifted the restrictions in September. Blalock hit only .229 for the month. He has a tendency to get too aggressive and can go whole games seeing only four or five pitches. When he does that, he gets himself out.

Baserunning & Defense

Though Blalock has carved out his reputation as a George Brett-type line-drive hitter, his defense should not be overlooked. He has a very strong arm and has shown above-average range. Even when he struggled in 2002, he didn't take his poor at-bats into the field. For somebody with precious little major league experience, Blalock is an extremely heady player. Though he has only average speed on the bases, he has very good instincts. Still, he won't be much of a threat to steal in his big league career.

2004 Outlook

Blalock's poor September took a bit, but not all, of the shine off an otherwise spectacular year. The Rangers expect him to be part of the foundation for their future success. If he can improve against lefties and keep himself strong for 150-plus games, he just might find himself in the thick of the 2004 batting race.

Position: 3B
Bats: L **Throws:** R
Ht: 6' 1" **Wt:** 192

Opening Day Age: 23
Born: 11/21/80 in San Diego, CA
ML Seasons: 2
Pronunciation: BLAY-lock

Overall Statistics

	G	AB	R	H	D	T	HR	RBI	SB	BB	SO	Avg	OBP	Slg
'03	143	567	89	170	33	3	29	90	2	44	97	.300	.350	.522
Car.	192	714	105	201	41	3	32	107	2	64	140	.282	.340	.482

Where He Hits the Ball

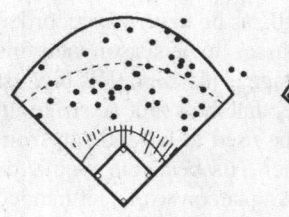
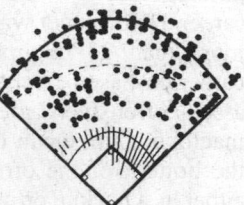

Vs. LHP   **Vs. RHP**

2003 Situational Stats

	AB	H	HR	RBI	Avg		AB	H	HR	RBI	Avg
Home	275	94	18	53	.342	LHP	139	29	3	11	.209
Road	292	76	11	37	.260	RHP	428	141	26	79	.329
First Half	313	101	14	48	.323	Sc Pos	138	38	8	62	.275
Scnd Half	254	69	15	42	.272	Clutch	67	15	1	10	.224

2003 Rankings (American League)

- 3rd in batting average vs. righthanded pitchers
- 4th in batting average at home
- 5th in fielding percentage at third base (.959)
- Led the Rangers in doubles, caught stealing (3), GDPs (16) and batting average vs. righthanded pitchers
- Led AL third basemen in home runs

Einar Diaz

2003 Season

The Rangers traded Travis Hafner to Cleveland for Einar Diaz as part of a four-player deal last winter, then put Diaz in the untenable position of being Ivan Rodriguez' replacement. While Texas certainly did not expect him to duplicate Pudge's offense, they were hoping Diaz' game-calling skills could help the pitching staff improve. It didn't. The staff ERA with Rodriguez behind the plate in 2002 was 5.20; with Diaz in 2003 it was 5.47.

Hitting

In an era of inflated offense, Diaz shows no significant offensive skills. He does not hit for power, with a homer every 94 at-bats for his career. He does not walk, as he never has recorded more than 23 free passes in a season and his career on-base percentage is just .306. His biggest assets offensively are that he's not a strikeout machine, and he can be used to hit-and-run from the bottom of the order. His best role would be either as a backup or in a platoon with a lefthanded hitter, though he batted only .253 against lefties last year.

Baserunning & Defense

When they acquired Diaz, the Rangers described him as a guy who plays "like his hair is on fire." That means he's energetic. He's a solid receiver, but he could not help the woeful pitching staff improve. He made eight errors and allowed four passed balls, not terrible numbers, but his offense essentially makes him a defensive specialist. He caught 22 of 71 runners (31.0 percent), better than in injury-plagued 2002, but still down from the mid-30s range that earned him his defensive reputation.

2004 Outlook

While Diaz is under contract for 2004, expect his playing time to slide if rookie Gerald Laird makes any progress at all. Laird already began to take playing time away from Diaz this past September. The Rangers are building for the future, and Laird, not Diaz, is part of that future.

Position: C
Bats: R **Throws:** R
Ht: 5'10" **Wt:** 195

Opening Day Age: 31
Born: 12/28/72 in Chiriqui, Panama
ML Seasons: 8
Pronunciation: EYE-nar
Nickname: The Dream

Overall Statistics

	G	AB	R	H	D	T	HR	RBI	SB	BB	SO	Avg	OBP	Slg
'03	101	334	30	86	14	1	4	35	3	9	32	.257	.294	.341
Car.	557	1789	199	463	104	5	19	174	19	80	177	.259	.306	.354

Where He Hits the Ball

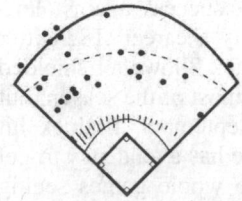 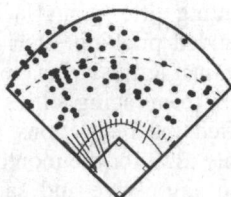

Vs. LHP   **Vs. RHP**

2003 Situational Stats

	AB	H	HR	RBI	Avg		AB	H	HR	RBI	Avg
Home	170	44	2	24	.259	LHP	79	20	1	11	.253
Road	164	42	2	11	.256	RHP	255	66	3	24	.259
First Half	218	57	2	21	.261	Sc Pos	92	23	1	31	.250
Scnd Half	116	29	2	14	.250	Clutch	41	12	0	2	.293

2003 Rankings (American League)

- 3rd in highest percentage of runners caught stealing as a catcher (31.0)
- 4th in errors at catcher (8) and most GDPs per GDP situation (20.0%)
- Led the Rangers in sacrifice bunts (4), bunts in play (11), lowest percentage of swings that missed (12.5), highest percentage of swings put into play (51.0) and batting average in the clutch

Juan Gonzalez

2003 Season

It was another tumultuous year in the soap opera that is Juan Gonzalez' star-crossed career. He vetoed one trade to Montreal, fired two agents and missed the last half of the season with what originally was diagnosed as a calf strain. When healthy, he averaged a homer every 13.6 at-bats and an RBI every 4.7 at-bats. But at just 34, there are concerns that he has wasted Hall of Fame talent.

Hitting

When healthy, Gonzalez showed no lingering effects of a hand injury that robbed him of some power in 2002. Unlike other power hitters, such as Barry Bonds and Jason Giambi, who gladly will take walks, Gonzalez can be pitched to. His long arms provide good plate coverage, but he never has been one to lay off breaking balls out of the zone. Never a big fan of a free pass in the first place, Gonzalez has regressed the last two years. His on-base percentage in 2002 and 2003 was a combined .327.

Baserunning & Defense

Don't expect Gonzalez to make diving catches; that's not his style. Perhaps because of his laconic approach to balls, hitters are willing to run on Gonzalez even though he has an outstanding arm. He played just 57 games in right field last year, but still posted 10 assists. Gonzalez won't steal bases, but his long strides on the basepaths makes him deceptively quick.

2004 Outlook

The Rangers made it clear they don't want Gonzalez back. For his part, Gonzalez has indicated he doesn't want to go to a National League club, perhaps out of fear of switching leagues. He'll almost certainly be playing somewhere in 2004 on a one-year deal with a low base and lots of incentives. That seems to be his best motivation. The last time he was on a one-year deal, with Cleveland in 2001, he hit .325 with 35 homers and 140 RBI. That he has turned down trades to contenders twice in the last three years only raised more questions about his desire.

Texas

Position: RF/DH
Bats: R **Throws:** R
Ht: 6' 3" **Wt:** 220

Opening Day Age: 34
Born: 10/16/69 in Vega Baja, PR
ML Seasons: 15
Nickname: Igor

Overall Statistics

G	AB	R	H	D	T	HR	RBI	SB	BB	SO	Avg	OBP	Slg
82	327	49	96	17	1	24	70	1	14	73	.294	.329	.572
1655	6428	1044	1901	384	24	429	1387	26	448	1254	.296	.344	.563

Where He Hits the Ball

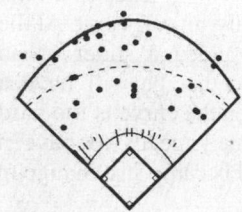 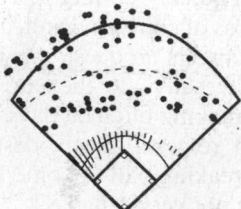

Vs. LHP	Vs. RHP

2003 Situational Stats

	AB	H	HR	RBI	Avg		AB	H	HR	RBI	Avg
Home	157	46	11	30	.293	LHP	99	27	4	8	.273
Road	170	50	13	40	.294	RHP	228	69	20	62	.303
First Half	319	92	23	66	.288	Sc Pos	90	23	10	50	.256
Scnd Half	8	4	1	4	.500	Clutch	42	11	2	7	.262

2003 Rankings (American League)

- Led the Rangers in batting average on the road

Colby Lewis

2003 Season

Colby Lewis had a strong start and a solid finish to the season, but in between was inadequate due to a total lack of command. The Rangers grew so frustrated with their top young pitcher that they sent him back to the minors for six weeks in the middle of last year. Perhaps no stat better sums up Lewis' campaign than this: In 26 starts, he averaged just shy of five innings per outing. That won't qualify as quality in anyone's league.

Pitching

Lewis has an explosive 92-95 MPH fastball and a wicked curve. Problem is, he has too much late movement on the fastball and has yet to learn how to quickly correct it. The problem leads to a total loss of command and, usually, an early exit. At the Rangers' request, he has added a slider as an alternative to the curve so that he will have a breaking pitch on days when the curve is too hard to rein in. Lewis desperately needs to have a breaking ball of some kind because his changeup is not very reliable.

Defense

Lewis often looks like the kid who went through a big summer growth spurt. His body doesn't always seem to fit his actions. He had trouble getting to groundballs between the mound and first base. He also found himself in the wrong place too often defensively last year. One of the Rangers' big offseason projects was to get him on a conditioning plan that would improve his stamina on the mound and his reactions on defense. He is, however, very cognizant of runners.

2004 Outlook

Lewis will get every possible chance to make the rotation in 2004, and every possible chance to stay in it for the entire season. The Rangers are hopeful that the September streak is a sign that their lessons are beginning to sink in. Throw in another winter of working with the slider along with better conditioning, and the organization hopes he can make a big jump. If not, there already has been some talk that he might make an effective closer.

Position: SP
Bats: R **Throws:** R
Ht: 6' 4" **Wt:** 230

Opening Day Age: 24
Born: 8/2/79 in Bakersfield, CA
ML Seasons: 2

Overall Statistics

	W	L	Pct.	ERA	G	GS	Sv	IP	H	BB	SO	HR	Avg
'03	10	9	.526	7.30	26	26	0	127.0	163	70	88	23	.317
Car.	11	12	.478	7.08	41	30	0	161.1	205	96	116	27	.314

2003 Pitching Profile

	Colby Lewis	AL Average
Overall Strike %	60.5	62.8
1st Pitch Strike %	55.5	58.7
Ratio	1.83	1.39
Strikeouts per 9 IP	6.24	6.11
Walks per 9 IP	4.96	3.16
Home Runs per 9 IP	1.63	1.11
Strikeout/Walk Ratio	1.26	1.93
Groundball/Flyball Ratio	1.19	1.18

2003 Situational Stats

	W	L	ERA	Sv	IP		AB	H	HR	RBI	Avg
Home	6	3	6.88	0	68.0	LHB	285	91	12	41	.319
Road	4	6	7.78	0	59.0	RHB	230	72	11	48	.313
First Half	4	5	8.66	0	61.1	Sc Pos	138	44	5	60	.319
Scnd Half	6	4	6.03	0	65.2	Clutch	4	1	0	0	.250

2003 Rankings (American League)

- 1st in wins among rookies
- 3rd in losses among rookies
- 7th in highest batting average allowed with runners in scoring position
- 10th in walks allowed and highest batting average allowed vs. righthanded batters
- Led the Rangers in walks allowed, runners caught stealing (6) and most run support per nine innings (7.1)

Kevin Mench

2003 Season

In the end, the Rangers were frustrated by Kevin Mench. Mench was hit by a pitch just before the All-Star break and suffered a broken bone in his left wrist. The injury limited him to just 125 at-bats. He did not play in the second half, prompting Texas officials to encourage him to go to winter ball to get more experience, but, initially at least, Mench balked at the idea. The Rangers were openly unhappy about that decision.

Hitting

Mench left a lot of questions to be answered in his sophomore campaign. He hit only .192 with no home runs in September 2002, which raised concerns about his durability and his ability to make adjustments to major league pitching. Mench is a pull hitter, but as a corner outfielder he must generate power consistently to hold his spot. When the homer drought lasted into June, it did nothing to erase questions about his power, though he did hit for average. The wrist injury, however, prevented the Rangers from finding out how he would respond to the rigors of a full season.

Baserunning & Defense

Though he's built like Pete Incaviglia, barrel-chested and stout, Mench runs surprisingly well. He's not going to steal many bases, but he can go from first to third on a single. He must concentrate, however, as he's made too many blooper-reel plays on the bases and in the field for a player with little more than one year of experience. Mench has the range to roam the generous left-field area at The Ballpark, but he's never going to win a Gold Glove.

2004 Outlook

Mench went into the winter as the favorite to start in left field in 2004, but his boycott of winter ball tested the Rangers' patience. He may not get as long a rope as somebody who has followed all of the club's "suggestions." Mench also could be trade bait. Wherever he plays, he will have to resolve the stamina and power issues.

Position: LF
Bats: R **Throws:** R
Ht: 6' 0" **Wt:** 230

Opening Day Age: 26
Born: 1/7/78 in Wilmington, DE
ML Seasons: 2

Overall Statistics

	G	AB	R	H	D	T	HR	RBI	SB	BB	SO	Avg	OBP	Slg
'03	38	125	15	40	12	0	2	11	1	10	17	.320	.381	.464
Car.	148	491	67	135	32	2	17	71	2	41	100	.275	.341	.452

Where He Hits the Ball

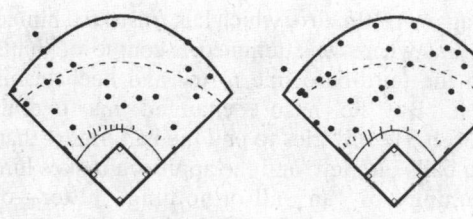

Vs. LHP   **Vs. RHP**

2003 Situational Stats

	AB	H	HR	RBI	Avg		AB	H	HR	RBI	Avg
Home	73	23	1	4	.315	LHP	52	18	1	2	.346
Road	52	17	1	7	.327	RHP	73	22	1	9	.301
First Half	125	40	2	11	.320	Sc Pos	21	7	1	8	.333
Scnd Half	0	0	0	0	—	Clutch	16	4	0	0	.250

2003 Rankings (American League)

- Did not rank near the top or bottom in any category

Rafael Palmeiro

2003 Season

The best word to describe Rafael Palmeiro would be consistency. He is the model of it. In 2003, he put together his ninth consecutive season with at least 38 home runs and 104 RBI, and pushed into the 500 homer club. He also played in more than 150 games for the ninth consecutive campaign. But Palmeiro's role with the Rangers changed from everyday first baseman to DH with the emergence of rookie Mark Teixeira.

Hitting

Palmeiro's average has dropped markedly over the past few years, partly because he can't single through the right side anymore. Virtually every club in the league employs a Ted Williams-like shift against Palmeiro, which has frustrated him to the point where he attempted a couple of bunts down the third-base line to try and keep teams honest. But he hasn't changed his overall approach. He still tries to pull the ball, rather than dump balls into left, and the approach makes him something of an all-or-nothing hitter—of Palmeiro's 146 hits in 2003, 123 either were singles (85) or homers (38).

Baserunning & Defense

Balky knees and advancing age have conspired to turn Palmeiro from Gold Glove-winner into a full-time DH. He played only 55 games at first in 2003, down from 97 in 2002, and that trend is likely to continue as he enters his 40th year. He still handles balls he can get to well and throws adequately for a first baseman, but his range is below average. He is a base-at-a-time runner.

2004 Outlook

Palmeiro is a free agent and it looks like another five-year stint with the Rangers will come to a close. He'd like a shot to play first base regularly, which won't happen in Texas, and he's not likely to accept the steep hometown discount the Rangers will bank on. He turned down a trade to the contending Chicago Cubs in August, which may leave some clubs wondering if he's more comfortable with a loser.

Position: DH/1B
Bats: L **Throws:** L
Ht: 6' 0" **Wt:** 190

Opening Day Age: 39
Born: 9/24/64 in Havana, Cuba
ML Seasons: 18
Pronunciation: pahl-MARE-oh
Nickname: Raffy

Overall Statistics

G	AB	R	H	D	T	HR	RBI	SB	BB	SO	Avg	OBP	Slg
154	561	92	146	21	2	38	112	2	84	77	.260	.359	.508
2567	9553	1548	2780	543	38	528	1687	93	1224	1244	.291	.373	.522

Where He Hits the Ball

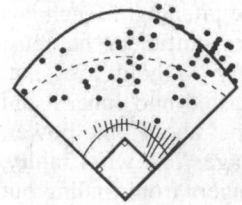 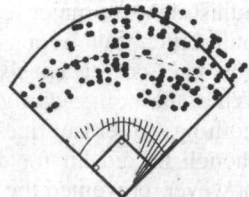

Vs. LHP   **Vs. RHP**

2003 Situational Stats

	AB	H	HR	RBI	Avg		AB	H	HR	RBI	Avg
Home	278	78	21	59	.281	LHP	170	48	15	43	.282
Road	283	68	17	53	.240	RHP	391	98	23	69	.251
First Half	313	77	21	55	.246	Sc Pos	147	46	11	78	.313
Scnd Half	248	69	17	57	.278	Clutch	69	18	4	10	.261

2003 Rankings (American League)

- 5th in home runs
- 6th in HR frequency (14.8 ABs per HR)
- 7th in RBI, most pitches seen per plate appearance (4.07), lowest groundball-flyball ratio (0.7) and lowest batting average on the road
- 9th in walks and pitches seen (2,665)
- 10th in batting average with the bases loaded (.455) and lowest batting average vs. righthanded pitchers
- Led the Rangers in most pitches seen per plate appearance (4.07), highest percentage of pitches taken (60.2), cleanup slugging percentage (.509) and lowest percentage of swings on the first pitch (18.6)

2003 Season

Some would say that 2003 was a subpar season for Alex Rodriguez. His 47 homers, 118 RBI and .298 average represented his lowest totals since joining Texas prior to the 2001 season. That said, A-Rod still put together his sixth consecutive season with at least 40 homers and 110 RBI. He became the second-youngest player in major league history to reach 300 career home runs. And, perhaps most importantly, he became just the second player ever to win a league MVP Award while playing for a last-place club (the Cubs' Andre Dawson in 1987 was the other).

Hitting

Rodriguez struggled with a herniated disc in his neck early in the year, but he got off to a hot start nonetheless, hitting .363 in April. Still, he didn't fully recover until the Rangers' season was irretrievably broken. Rodriguez still gets a bit too anxious to do great things with every at-bat, as evidenced by his pedestrian .276 average with runners in scoring position. Pitchers are willing to take their chances against him in key situations because he's averaged a strikeout every 4.8 at-bats the last four seasons.

Baserunning & Defense

A year after winning his first Gold Glove, Rodriguez did the unimaginable. He got better. In 158 starts at short last year, Rodriguez made only eight errors en route to his second Gold Glove. He and second baseman Michael Young may be the best double-play combo in the league, which will be a huge asset to Texas if it ever gets a cadre of groundball pitchers. As a baserunner, A-Rod probably never again will be a 40-40 player, but he's a smart runner who rarely makes mistakes.

2004 Outlook

There is no reason to think Rodriguez won't continue at an MVP pace, even as the Rangers get younger around him. His biggest hurdle may be to remain focused on the field and not worry about personnel moves made by the front office. Another challenge: with Rafael Palmeiro likely headed elsewhere, Rodriguez may have less protection behind him in the lineup than at any point in his career.

Position: SS
Bats: R **Throws:** R
Ht: 6' 3" **Wt:** 210

Opening Day Age: 28
Born: 7/27/75 in New York, NY
ML Seasons: 10
Pronunciation: rod-REE-guez
Nickname: A-Rod

Overall Statistics

G	AB	R	H	D	T	HR	RBI	SB	BB	SO	Avg	OBP	Slg
161	607	124	181	30	6	47	118	17	87	126	.298	.396	.600
1275	4989	1009	1535	285	22	345	990	177	559	995	.308	.382	.581

Where He Hits the Ball

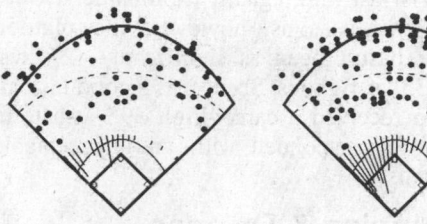

Vs. LHP   **Vs. RHP**

2003 Situational Stats

	AB	H	HR	RBI	Avg		AB	H	HR	RBI	Avg
Home	309	97	26	71	.314	LHP	187	57	16	37	.305
Road	298	84	21	47	.282	RHP	420	124	31	81	.295
First Half	355	101	22	60	.285	Sc Pos	145	40	8	63	.276
Scnd Half	252	80	25	58	.317	Clutch	73	19	9	23	.260

2003 Rankings (American League)

- 1st in home runs, runs scored, slugging percentage, HR frequency (12.9 ABs per HR) and fielding percentage at shortstop (.989)
- 2nd in total bases (364) and RBI
- 3rd in stolen-base percentage (85.0)
- 4th in times on base (283) and games played
- Led the Rangers in home runs, runs scored, total bases (364), RBI, stolen bases, caught stealing (3), walks, intentional walks (10), hit by pitch (15), times on base (283), strikeouts, GDPs (16), plate appearances (715), games played, slugging percentage, on-base percentage, HR frequency (12.9 ABs per HR) and batting average with the bases loaded (.571)
- Led AL shortstops in home runs and RBI

Shane Spencer

2003 Season

Shane Spencer came to the Rangers as a toss-in to a midseason deal that brought injured righthanded pitcher Ricardo Rodriguez from Cleveland. The deal allowed the Rangers to consider Spencer for their 2004 outfield rotation. After watching him hit .227 in 55 games, Texas brass apparently decided it could fill a backup outfield spot for a cheaper price and made him a free agent at season's end.

Hitting

Spencer is of most use to a team to spell a lefthanded hitter from facing tough southpaws. He has a career .303 average against lefties, while his mark is just .237 against righthanders. Over the past two seasons, however, the platoon difference hasn't been as significant—.274 vs. lefties, .235 vs. righties. Spencer is s good fastball hitter who received a career-high 395 at-bats in 2003, but he responded with an unacceptable 92 strikeouts.

Baserunning & Defense

Spencer's defensive liabilities, which include a slightly below-average arm and only adequate range, could be overlooked if he was a significant run producer. So, clubs must ask themselves if the potential pop in his bat is worth having a backup outfielder whose defense is just short. He made three errors in 188 chances last year (.984), splitting time between the corner outfield spots. He is conservative on the basepaths, but doesn't clog things up.

2004 Outlook

Spencer seems to have carved a career for himself with a charmed September for the Yankees in 1998, when he hit .421 with eight homers and 21 RBI in just 14 games. Take that magical month away, and Spencer is a career .256 hitter who strikes out once every 4.6 at-bats. His home-run ratio isn't enough to outweigh the other strikes against him. The Rangers released Spencer in October, and he will to have to prove himself all over again in 2004. He will shop for a minor league contract that offers a chance at a backup spot in spring training.

Position: LF/RF/1B
Bats: R **Throws:** R
Ht: 6' 0" **Wt:** 225

Opening Day Age: 32
Born: 2/20/72 in Key West, FL
ML Seasons: 6

Overall Statistics

	G	AB	R	H	D	T	HR	RBI	SB	BB	SO	Avg	OBP	Slg
'03	119	395	39	99	20	0	12	49	2	45	92	.251	.328	.392
Car.	464	1486	187	386	74	7	55	216	7	139	320	.260	.325	.430

Where He Hits the Ball

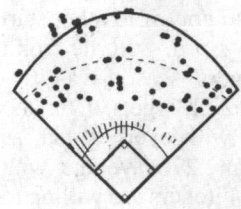
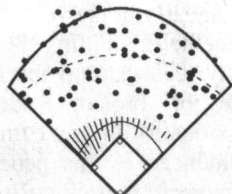

Vs. LHP   **Vs. RHP**

2003 Situational Stats

	AB	H	HR	RBI	Avg		AB	H	HR	RBI	Avg
Home	184	56	5	27	.304	LHP	166	46	7	26	.277
Road	211	43	7	22	.204	RHP	229	53	5	23	.231
First Half	206	56	7	25	.272	Sc Pos	103	27	3	36	.262
Scnd Half	189	43	5	24	.228	Clutch	62	14	2	5	.226

2003 Rankings (American League)

- Did not rank near the top or bottom in any category

Mark Teixeira

2003 Season

After just 86 minor league games, Mark Teixeira jumped to the majors. He overcame an awful first month, a position switch and a sometimes frosty attitude from veteran Rafael Palmeiro, whom he replaced at first base. By the end of 2003, Teixeira had improved as much as any rookie in the league. His 26 homers were the second-most ever for a Texas rookie (Pete Incaviglia had 30 in 1986).

Hitting

The switch-hitting Teixeira still has a ways to go when it comes to hitting righthanded pitching. He batted 50 points lower against righties than against lefties in 2003. That said, the Rangers were impressed enough by his power that he ended up with more at-bats in the No. 5 spot than anywhere else in the lineup. He hit only .218 in 206 at-bats there, however, so asking him to be a threat in the heart of the order in the absence of Rafael Palmeiro simply may be asking for too much too soon.

Baserunning & Defense

A month into the season, when it became clear Hank Blalock could hold down third base, the Rangers asked Teixeira to move to first. He proved incredibly adept at it. He was as good as just about any first baseman in the league at stopping groundballs and wasn't afraid to make throws. Though he made 12 errors last season, seven of miscues came in 15 games at third. It's not a stretch to think he could have Gold Glove in his future. On the bases, he will be a typical corner infielder; in other words, he won't scare anybody with his speed.

2004 Outlook

Teixeira will have a place in the Texas lineup for 2004 and beyond. The question is where. The Rangers have discussed the possibility of eventually moving him to the outfield when prospect Adrian Gonzalez, who may be even better than Teixeira defensively, is ready. Whether in 2004 or later, he's going to be counted on as a middle-of-the-order hitter, so he'll have to figure out righties.

Position: 1B/3B/LF/RF
Bats: B **Throws:** R
Ht: 6' 2" **Wt:** 215

Opening Day Age: 23
Born: 4/11/80 in Severna Park, MD
ML Seasons: 1
Pronunciation: tuh-SHARE-uh

Texas

Overall Statistics

	G	AB	R	H	D	T	HR	RBI	SB	BB	SO	Avg	OBP	Slg
'03	146	529	66	137	29	5	26	84	1	44	120	.259	.331	.480
Car.	146	529	66	137	29	5	26	84	1	44	120	.259	.331	.480

Where He Hits the Ball

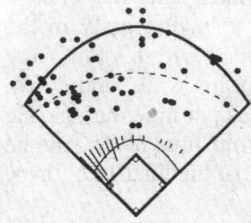 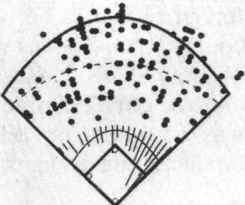

Vs. LHP	Vs. RHP

2003 Situational Stats

	AB	H	HR	RBI	Avg		AB	H	HR	RBI	Avg
Home	275	82	19	66	.298	LHP	173	51	11	32	.295
Road	254	55	7	18	.217	RHP	356	86	15	52	.242
First Half	260	66	14	43	.254	Sc Pos	141	37	6	57	.262
Scnd Half	269	71	12	41	.264	Clutch	70	15	2	6	.214

2003 Rankings (American League)

- 1st in home runs among rookies
- 2nd in RBI among rookies
- 3rd in lowest batting average on the road
- 4th in lowest batting average vs. righthanded pitchers
- 5th in fielding percentage at first base (.996)

John Thomson

2003 Season

Finding players who are up to the daunting task of pitching at The Ballpark in Arlington is a delicate matter. John Thomson proved up to the challenge. After spending the first part of his career pitching his home games in Coors Field, Thomson showed he understood the lessons he learned in Colorado. He kept the ball down, kept the Rangers in games and ended up crossing the 200-inning threshold for the first time in his career.

Pitching

Thomson flourished while working with first-year pitching coach Orel Hershiser. Hershiser emphasized using the changeup more, and the combination of a hard sinker and the change forced hitters to be ready to swing early in the count. Thomson was rewarded with his fair share of groundballs. He also kept his walk total down, allowed only 2.03 free passes per nine innings. He was 9-5 with a 3.89 ERA from June 30 on, and he produced quality starts in 12 of his final 18 outings.

Defense

Because he is a groundball pitcher, Thomson better be ready to field balls hit back through the box, and he generally is in a good position to do so. Though he's not a Gold Glover by any means, his defense is improving and he is more athletic than you'd expect for someone with his lanky build. He doesn't have much in his arsenal to slow down the running game, and his next pickoff will be just the second of his six-year big league career.

2004 Outlook

A free agent, Thomson picked a good time for the best season of his career. He eats innings and throws strikes, like Rick Helling once did for Texas, which may make Thomson worth more to the Rangers than other clubs. The Rangers went into the offseason hoping to re-sign him, but the Braves stepped up with a two-year, $7 million deal in December, two days after parting ways with former ace Greg Maddux. While Thomson might have been the No. 1 starter with Texas, the righthander slots behind Russ Ortiz and Mike Hampton in an evolving Atlanta rotation.

Position: SP
Bats: R **Throws:** R
Ht: 6' 3" **Wt:** 190

Opening Day Age: 30
Born: 10/1/73 in Vicksburg, MS
ML Seasons: 6
Pronunciation: TOM-son
Nickname: Red

Overall Statistics

	W	L	Pct.	ERA	G	GS	Sv	IP	H	BB	SO	HR	Avg
'03	13	14	.481	4.85	35	35	0	217.0	234	49	136	27	.276
Car.	42	63	.400	4.93	146	145	0	882.1	971	254	557	117	.281

2003 Pitching Profile

	John Thomson	AL Average
Overall Strike %	64.7	62.8
1st Pitch Strike %	59.5	58.7
Ratio	1.30	1.39
Strikeouts per 9 IP	5.64	6.11
Walks per 9 IP	2.03	3.16
Home Runs per 9 IP	1.12	1.11
Strikeout/Walk Ratio	2.78	1.93
Groundball/Flyball Ratio	1.35	1.18

2003 Situational Stats

	W	L	ERA	Sv	IP		AB	H	HR	RBI	Avg
Home	6	6	5.05	0	101.2	LHB	455	128	13	54	.281
Road	7	8	4.68	0	115.1	RHB	393	106	14	56	.270
First Half	6	9	5.43	0	117.2	Sc Pos	164	51	4	74	.311
Scnd Half	7	5	4.17	0	99.1	Clutch	39	13	5	12	.333

2003 Rankings (American League)

- 2nd in games started
- 5th in GDPs induced (24)
- 6th in hits allowed and highest ERA
- 7th in losses, complete games (3), innings pitched and batters faced (910)
- 8th in fewest walks per nine innings (2.0)
- 10th in highest ERA at home
- Led the Rangers in ERA, wins, losses, games started, complete games (3), innings pitched, hits allowed, batters faced (910), home runs allowed, strikeouts, pitches thrown (3,339), stolen bases allowed (13), GDPs induced (24), highest strikeout-walk ratio (2.8), lowest slugging percentage allowed (.443), lowest on-base percentage allowed (.316), highest groundball-flyball ratio allowed (1.4), lowest ERA on the road, fewest home runs allowed per nine innings (1.12), and fewest walks per nine innings (2.0)

Ismael Valdes

2003 Season

After getting decent value from a one-year deal in 2002, the Rangers brought Ismael Valdes back for 2003. This time, Texas failed to get the same return on its investment. Valdes was 5-2 with a 4.98 ERA through May, but he went just 3-6 with a 6.78 ERA the rest of the season. The Rangers shelved him after September 2 so that they could take a closer look at young pitchers who may figure into their future. Valdes also took two tours of the DL, upping his total to five stints on the injured list since 2000.

Pitching

Though Valdes didn't turn 30 until last August, the days of his electric sinking fastball are long gone. He now gets by with his sinker, which barely touches 90 MPH. He also throws strikes, works quickly, and is not apt to hurt himself by giving up lots of walks. Valdes induced more grounders in 2003—1.22 for every flyball—and that helped to keep his numbers from getting even uglier, as his teammates turned 16 double plays behind him.

Defense

Usually, Valdes is an average defender who gets the most from his skills, but 2003 was an exception. He had a terrible year in the field, committing four errors in 29 chances for an .862 fielding percentage. His fast pace on the mound and willingness to repeatedly throw to first keeps stolen-base totals down. Once able to catch a runner napping, he has just one pickoff to his credit during the past two seasons.

2004 Outlook

Valdes has gone from rising star to ultimate vagabond. Since leaving Los Angeles after the 1999 campaign, he has pitched for five teams in four years, and he's almost certain to move on to No. 6 in 2004 after the Rangers failed to offer him salary arbitration in December. He has not reached double figures in victories in a season since 1998, so the free agent may have to settle for a minor league contract with the chance to prove himself in spring training.

Position: SP
Bats: R **Throws:** R
Ht: 6' 4" **Wt:** 225

Opening Day Age: 30
Born: 8/21/73 in Ciudad Victoria, Mexico
ML Seasons: 10
Pronunciation: ees-mah-ALE val-DEZ
Nickname: Rocket

Overall Statistics

	W	L	Pct.	ERA	G	GS	Sv	IP	H	BB	SO	HR	Avg
'03	8	8	.500	6.10	22	22	0	115.0	148	29	47	23	.318
Car.	88	94	.484	3.93	277	250	1	1606.2	1606	452	1079	195	.260

2003 Pitching Profile

	Ismael Valdes	AL Average
Overall Strike %	63.1	62.8
1st Pitch Strike %	62.1	58.7
Ratio	1.54	1.39
Strikeouts per 9 IP	3.68	6.11
Walks per 9 IP	2.27	3.16
Home Runs per 9 IP	1.80	1.11
Strikeout/Walk Ratio	1.62	1.93
Groundball/Flyball Ratio	1.22	1.18

2003 Situational Stats

	W	L	ERA	Sv	IP		AB	H	HR	RBI	Avg
Home	5	4	7.32	0	55.1	LHB	223	63	8	33	.283
Road	3	4	4.98	0	59.2	RHB	243	85	15	46	.350
First Half	7	6	6.22	0	85.1	Sc Pos	99	32	5	52	.323
Scnd Half	1	2	5.76	0	29.2	Clutch	11	1	0	0	.001

2003 Rankings (American League)

- 2nd in highest batting average allowed vs. righthanded batters
- 3rd in errors at pitcher (4)
- 5th in pickoff throws (135)
- Led the Rangers in pickoff throws (135) and fewest pitches thrown per batter (3.58)

Michael Young

2003 Season

Michael Young had a breakout year in 2003, jumping from the ranks of spectacular defensive player with suspect offensive skills to become one of the top second basemen in the league. Young came to camp with 20 extra pounds on his frame from an offseason workout plan, then proceeded to play like he had something to prove to those in management who thought he might not hit enough to warrant an everyday spot in the lineup. He finished the season with an exclamation point—a .343 September average.

Hitting

Young nearly had a quadruple-double in 2003, with double figures in homers (14), doubles (33), stolen bases (13) and triples (9). If he develops a bit more patience at the plate, he could become an elite leadoff man. He took only 36 walks in more than 700 plate appearances last year. That's a figure that will have to improve to keep him atop the lineup.

Baserunning & Defense

When you look at it from both an offensive and defensive perspective, Young and Alex Rodriguez formed the best double-play combination in the American League last year. Along with corner infielders Mark Teixeira and Hank Blalock, this group may coalesce into the best purely defensive infield in the league. Young has such a strong arm from second that there has been talk in the past about moving him to center field. The only reason he has not won consecutive Gold Gloves is because Bret Boone plays in the same league. But Young certainly is Boone's equal in the field. Young's speed is above average, and he was successful on 13 of his 15 stolen-base attempts last year.

2004 Outlook

The foundation for the Rangers' future success lies with their talented infield, and Young may be the most significant figure in the group. He is the bridge between the veterans like Rodriguez and the true youngsters. In the past, he's been dogged by questions about whether he'd ever hit enough. For 2004, the question will be: Can he repeat it?

Position: 2B
Bats: R **Throws:** R
Ht: 6' 1" **Wt:** 190

Opening Day Age: 27
Born: 10/19/76 in Covina, CA
ML Seasons: 4

Overall Statistics

	G	AB	R	H	D	T	HR	RBI	SB	BB	SO	Avg	OBP	Slg
'03	160	666	106	204	33	9	14	72	13	36	103	.306	.339	.446
Car.	424	1627	240	450	77	21	34	183	22	103	307	.277	.318	.412

Where He Hits the Ball

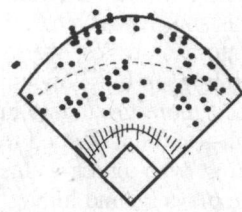
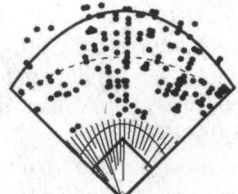

Vs. LHP   **Vs. RHP**

2003 Situational Stats

	AB	H	HR	RBI	Avg		AB	H	HR	RBI	Avg
Home	323	114	9	34	.353	LHP	198	61	5	23	.308
Road	343	90	5	38	.262	RHP	468	143	9	49	.306
First Half	365	117	9	42	.321	Sc Pos	126	42	5	58	.333
Scnd Half	301	87	5	30	.289	Clutch	80	14	0	3	.175

2003 Rankings (American League)

- 2nd in singles and batting average at home
- 3rd in hits and fielding percentage at second base (.987)
- 4th in at-bats and triples
- 5th in pitches seen (2,788)
- 6th in plate appearances (713) and batting average with two strikes (.257)
- 7th in errors at second base (10)
- Led the Rangers in batting average, at-bats, hits, singles, doubles, triples, sacrifice flies (7), pitches seen (2,788), highest groundball-flyball ratio (1.4), stolen-base percentage (86.7), batting average vs. lefthanded pitchers, batting average at home and batting average with two strikes (.257)
- Led AL second basemen in batting average

Joaquin Benoit

Position: SP
Bats: R **Throws:** R
Ht: 6' 3" **Wt:** 205

Opening Day Age: 26
Born: 7/26/77 in Santiago, DR
ML Seasons: 3
Pronunciation: wah-KEEN

Overall Statistics

	W	L	Pct.	ERA	G	GS	Sv	IP	H	BB	SO	HR	Avg
'03	8	5	.615	5.49	25	17	0	105.0	99	51	87	23	.246
Car.	12	10	.545	5.55	43	31	1	194.2	198	112	150	32	.261

2003 Situational Stats

	W	L	ERA	Sv	IP		AB	H	HR	RBI	Avg
Home	5	2	5.30	0	54.1	LHB	212	47	13	34	.222
Road	3	3	5.68	0	50.2	RHB	191	52	10	30	.272
First Half	4	4	5.24	0	56.2	Sc Pos	77	20	2	36	.260
Scnd Half	4	1	5.77	0	48.1	Clutch	7	1	0	0	.143

2003 Season

Joaquin Benoit did nothing to erase the stigma of being an enigma that arose in 2002. In nine of his 17 starts, he allowed three or more walks and was 1-4 with a 7.68 ERA. In his other eight starts, he was 4-1 with a 3.68 ERA. At times, the Rangers thought he was on the verge of joining their rotation for good, at others they thought he would be best suited as a reliever.

Pitching & Defense

When he's got his command, Benoit's sinking 92-MPH fastball and an outstanding changeup make him a formidable starter. He still hasn't developed a consistent breaking ball, eschewing a slider last year for an occasional curve. One aspect that may lead to his inconsistency is his constant tinkering with his delivery. Though not terribly athletic at fielding his position, Benoit does pay good attention to runners.

2004 Outlook

Though Benoit will be out of options in the spring, he's made only 31 major league starts. So it's fair to say he hasn't had a legitimate chance to prove himself. With the Rangers in rebuilding mode, he's likely to get a longer look than the past two years, but this will be his last shot with Texas.

Francisco Cordero

Position: RP
Bats: R **Throws:** R
Ht: 6' 2" **Wt:** 200

Opening Day Age: 28
Born: 5/11/75 in Santo Domingo, DR
ML Seasons: 5
Pronunciation: cor-DAIR-oh
Nickname: Coco

Overall Statistics

	W	L	Pct.	ERA	G	GS	Sv	IP	H	BB	SO	HR	Avg
'03	5	8	.385	2.94	73	0	15	82.2	70	38	90	4	.230
Car.	10	13	.435	3.57	191	0	25	226.2	212	119	200	19	.250

2003 Situational Stats

	W	L	ERA	Sv	IP		AB	H	HR	RBI	Avg
Home	5	2	2.43	9	40.2	LHB	148	35	1	13	.236
Road	0	6	3.43	6	42.0	RHB	157	35	3	26	.223
First Half	3	6	3.33	2	51.1	Sc Pos	86	24	0	34	.279
Scnd Half	2	2	2.30	13	31.1	Clutch	219	52	3	33	.237

2003 Season

After an impressive run in the closer's role in the second half of 2002, Francisco Cordero moved back to setting up for Ugueth Urbina for the first half of the 2003 season. He regained the closer's role when Urbina was dealt to Florida, and though he tied for the American League lead in blown saves (10), Cordero was 13-for-17 with a 2.23 ERA after taking over as the closer.

Pitching & Defense

Cordero's transition from thrower to pitcher continues. He used to fall in love with his straight 98-MPH fastball, and would take a beating with it. In 2002, he made serious progress with a slider, and that progress continued in 2003. At about 10 MPH slower than the fastball, the slider can serve as a very effective second pitch. He also unveiled a genuine change. Cordero does a fine job of controlling the running game, and his defense is good.

2004 Outlook

With Jeff Zimmerman's status iffy at best, Cordero may be given another shot at the closer's spot. His success—and ultimately his role—will be determined by his ability to throw strikes. If Cordero doesn't do that early on, the Rangers are bound to start looking elsewhere.

R.A. Dickey

Position: RP/SP
Bats: R **Throws:** R
Ht: 6' 3" **Wt:** 205

Opening Day Age: 29
Born: 10/29/74 in
Nashville, TN
ML Seasons: 2

Overall Statistics

	W	L	Pct.	ERA	G	GS	Sv	IP	H	BB	SO	HR	Avg
'03	9	8	.529	5.09	38	13	1	116.2	135	38	94	16	.292
Car.	9	9	.500	5.25	42	13	1	128.2	148	45	98	19	.291

2003 Situational Stats

	W	L	ERA	Sv	IP		AB	H	HR	RBI	Avg
Home	6	3	4.95	0	60.0	LHB	251	70	11	31	.279
Road	3	5	5.24	1	56.2	RHB	212	65	5	34	.307
First Half	4	4	5.00	0	45.0	Sc Pos	140	35	4	49	.250
Scnd Half	5	4	5.15	1	71.2	Clutch	40	10	1	3	.250

2003 Season

For the first six years of his pro career, the most significant fact about R.A. Dickey may have been that he was born without a ligament in his right elbow. But the former first-round pick created a new reputation in 2003, that of a hard-working overachiever. His nine wins tied for second among AL rookies, and John Thomson was the only Rangers starter who was more effective.

Pitching & Defense

Despite the lack of the ligament, Dickey has built his fastball up to the 90-91 MPH range. But what really makes him effective is "The Thing," a hybrid knuckle-curve/splitter that he can make move like a slider. He thinks pitching sequences through, pays attention to runners and is in the right place when things are going on around him. He is an excellent fielder, who can help himself with defense.

2004 Outlook

The motto for the rebuilt Rangers' pitching staff is to pitch to contact. Dickey might be the poster child for that. Couple that with his selfless work ethic, he earned the respect, admiration and loyalty of manager Buck Showalter, who went so far as to say that, if he had anything to do with it, Dickey would have a spot for 2004.

Aaron Fultz

Position: RP
Bats: L **Throws:** L
Ht: 6' 0" **Wt:** 200

Opening Day Age: 30
Born: 9/4/73 in
Memphis, TN
ML Seasons: 4

Overall Statistics

	W	L	Pct.	ERA	G	GS	Sv	IP	H	BB	SO	HR	Avg
'03	1	3	.250	5.21	64	0	0	67.1	75	27	53	9	.287
Car.	11	8	.579	4.81	231	0	2	249.0	259	95	213	30	.274

2003 Situational Stats

	W	L	ERA	Sv	IP		AB	H	HR	RBI	Avg
Home	1	0	6.08	0	37.0	LHB	119	26	2	13	.218
Road	0	3	4.15	0	30.1	RHB	142	49	7	28	.345
First Half	1	1	4.61	0	41.0	Sc Pos	70	24	1	32	.343
Scnd Half	0	2	6.15	0	26.1	Clutch	87	22	6	15	.253

2003 Season

Aaron Fultz' entire 2003 season was changed by a silly batting practice injury in which he ran into the outfield wall while shagging flies. At the time he suffered the bruised shoulder in late June, he was the most-trusted lefty in the Rangers' bullpen. He came back after only two weeks on the DL, but was never the same, compiling a 7.48 ERA in his final 27 appearances.

Pitching & Defense

Before the injury, Fultz was a legitimate three-pitch guy who was successful because he used his upper-80s fastball, curve and change without falling into patterns. While the fastball is a bit below average, the curve and change are solid pitches, so long as he's got command. He lost that with the injury. He holds runners well and is an average fielder.

2004 Outlook

Disappointed in Fultz' finish, the Rangers made him a free agent at the end of the season, but he could come back for less money. If he can prove the shoulder injury is behind him, he could be an effective addition to the left side of someone's bullpen. He is only 30, still a relative adolescent by the standards of major league lefty relievers.

Ron Mahay

Position: RP
Bats: L **Throws:** L
Ht: 6' 2" **Wt:** 190

Opening Day Age: 32
Born: 6/28/71 in
Crestwood, IL
ML Seasons: 7

Overall Statistics

	W	L	Pct.	ERA	G	GS	Sv	IP	H	BB	SO	HR	Avg
'03	3	3	.500	3.18	35	0	0	45.1	33	20	38	3	.195
Car.	12	5	.706	4.21	149	3	2	192.1	170	97	159	30	.234

2003 Situational Stats

	W	L	ERA	Sv	IP		AB	H	HR	RBI	Avg
Home	0	1	2.70	0	23.1	LHB	53	11	1	8	.208
Road	3	2	3.68	0	22.0	RHB	116	22	2	11	.190
First Half	0	0	0.00	0	10.1	Sc Pos	48	9	2	16	.188
Scnd Half	3	3	4.11	0	35.0	Clutch	74	14	0	10	.189

2003 Season

Signed to a minor league contract in November 2002, Ron Mahay didn't return to the majors until the end of June, but he quickly became the team's most-trusted lefty. A career high in both appearances and innings seemed to catch up with him, however, as his sub-2.00 ERA ballooned to 3.18 because he allowed 10 runs in 10.1 innings in September.

Pitching & Defense

The 2003 campaign would have been an unmitigated success for Mahay had it not been for the September collapse. A loss of control was the biggest problem. He allowed eight walks and struck out just four in September. He gave the Rangers encouragement that he could be a versatile middle reliever. He went two or more innings nine times and actually held righthanders to a lower average than lefties. Mahay was an outfielder before he was a pitcher and is a good athlete for his position.

2004 Outlook

Despite the September collapse, Mahay was impressive enough to earn a contract for the 2004 season. With the Rangers in full-scale rebuilding mode, he'll get a decent opportunity. But if he can't build up his stamina to last through the year, he'll be of little use to anybody down the stretch.

Laynce Nix

Position: RF/CF
Bats: L **Throws:** L
Ht: 6' 0" **Wt:** 190

Opening Day Age: 23
Born: 10/30/80 in
Houston, TX
ML Seasons: 1

Overall Statistics

	G	AB	R	H	D	T	HR	RBI	SB	BB	SO	Avg	OBP	Slg
'03	53	184	25	47	10	0	8	30	3	9	53	.255	.289	.440
Car.	53	184	25	47	10	0	8	30	3	9	53	.255	.289	.440

2003 Situational Stats

	AB	H	HR	RBI	Avg		AB	H	HR	RBI	Avg
Home	94	30	7	25	.319	LHP	20	3	1	3	.150
Road	90	17	1	5	.189	RHP	164	44	7	27	.268
First Half	12	2	0	1	.167	Sc Pos	51	13	4	23	.255
Scnd Half	172	45	8	29	.262	Clutch	27	4	0	3	.148

2003 Season

Laynce Nix was the Rangers' Minor League Player of the Year in 2002. By the end of 2003, he already was in the majors with a pretty strong toe-hold. Nix' hard-nosed, all-out style of play wowed manager Buck Showalter in spring training. Once in the majors, his style reminded Texas fans of a young Rusty Greer.

Hitting, Baserunning & Defense

Perhaps the thing that most impressed the Rangers was Nix' confidence. He never looked over-matched even when he struggled at the plate. But all the confidence in the world can't make up for experience, which he lacks against lefties. Nix gives all-out effort in the outfield, but did make five errors in 136 chances, most of them bobbles from overrunning balls. He's a smart and effective runner, who has been caught just three times in 32 steal attempts dating back to Class-A last year.

2004 Outlook

There is some sentiment to give Nix a longer look in center, but he appears best suited to be a corner outfielder with above-average range. His biggest obstacles will be cutting down on strikeouts and learning to hit lefties. Both issues are liable to take more than one year to overcome, but the Rangers can afford to have patience.

Chan Ho Park

Position: SP
Bats: R **Throws:** R
Ht: 6' 2" **Wt:** 204

Opening Day Age: 30
Born: 6/30/73 in Kong
Ju City, South Korea
ML Seasons: 10

Overall Statistics

	W	L	Pct.	ERA	G	GS	Sv	IP	H	BB	SO	HR	Avg
'03	1	3	.250	7.58	7	7	0	29.2	34	25	16	5	.306
Car.	90	65	.581	4.09	253	208	0	1359.0	1189	663	1235	149	.237

2003 Situational Stats

	W	L	ERA	Sv	IP		AB	H	HR	RBI	Avg
Home	0	2	6.75	0	20.0	LHB	60	22	3	15	.367
Road	1	1	9.31	0	9.2	RHB	51	12	2	7	.235
First Half	1	3	7.58	0	29.2	Sc Pos	40	12	1	16	.300
Scnd Half	0	0	–	0	0.0	Clutch	0	0	0	0	–

2003 Season

If things don't change quickly, Chan Ho Park may go down as the biggest free-agent bust of all time. The Rangers spent $13 million more on him in 2003 and got double the number of DL assignments (two) than wins (one). His problem was diagnosed as a weak lower back. He spent the rest of the season trying to strengthen it, but never made it back to the active roster.

Pitching & Defense

Park had a 95-MPH fastball before he came to Texas, but that has not been seen in two years with the Rangers. In addition, Park is a moderate fly-ball pitcher, which was fine in pitcher-friendly Dodger Stadium, but it's a death-knell at The Ballpark. His array of hamstring and back injuries the last two years makes him a suspect defensive player, but he does a good job of controlling the running game when he's on the mound.

2004 Outlook

Park actually may be of more value to the Rangers hurt than healthy. At least if he stays on the DL, the Rangers can recoup some of his contract through insurance claims. Texas tried removing the pressure of being the staff ace for 2003 and that didn't work; they have virtually no expectations for 2004.

Jay Powell

Position: RP
Bats: R **Throws:** R
Ht: 6' 4" **Wt:** 225

Opening Day Age: 32
Born: 1/9/72 in
Meridian, MS
ML Seasons: 9

Overall Statistics

	W	L	Pct.	ERA	G	GS	Sv	IP	H	BB	SO	HR	Avg
'03	3	0	1.000	7.82	51	0	0	58.2	75	34	40	7	.319
Car.	35	22	.614	4.23	484	0	22	515.0	518	257	405	39	.262

2003 Situational Stats

	W	L	ERA	Sv	IP		AB	H	HR	RBI	Avg
Home	2	0	9.00	0	31.0	LHB	94	24	3	28	.255
Road	1	0	6.51	0	27.2	RHB	141	51	4	33	.362
First Half	2	0	8.42	0	36.1	Sc Pos	90	31	4	54	.344
Scnd Half	1	0	6.85	0	22.1	Clutch	7	0	0	0	.000

2003 Season

In each of his first two seasons with Texas, Jay Powell has been beset by strange spring-training maladies that have affected his performance well into the season. In 2002, it was a finger ligament injury. In 2003, it was vertigo-like symptoms. Powell allowed 12 runs in his first 6.1 innings and never got on any kind of significant roll.

Pitching & Defense

Powell's sinking fastball, once devastating at 92-94 MPH, is no longer there, replaced by a more hittable 90-91 MPH version. Thus, he has started experimenting with sidearm delivery. He got only mixed results from the new look, and he went into the offseason uncertain if he'd try to keep the new delivery, incorporate it into his traditional repertoire or junk it completely. Powell has committed one error in 49 chances dating back to the start of the 2000 season. He does a decent job of holding runners.

2004 Outlook

Powell is in the last year of a three-year, $9 million contract and, because of those circumstances, his margin for error is small. The Rangers didn't trust him in tight situations in 2003, so he'll have a long way to go to prove that he can handle a bigger role for 2004.

Erasmo Ramirez

Position: RP
Bats: L **Throws:** L
Ht: 6' 0" **Wt:** 180

Opening Day Age: 27
Born: 4/29/76 in Santa Ana, CA
ML Seasons: 1

Overall Statistics

	W	L	Pct.	ERA	G	GS	Sv	IP	H	BB	SO	HR	Avg
'03	3	1	.750	3.86	34	0	0	49.0	46	9	28	4	.251
Car.	3	1	.750	3.86	34	0	0	49.0	46	9	28	4	.251

2003 Situational Stats

	W	L	ERA	Sv	IP		AB	H	HR	RBI	Avg
Home	3	0	3.86	0	23.1	LHB	64	16	2	11	.250
Road	0	1	3.86	0	25.2	RHB	119	30	2	9	.252
First Half	0	0	6.52	0	9.2	Sc Pos	38	14	3	19	.368
Scnd Half	3	1	3.20	0	39.1	Clutch	40	13	0	3	.325

2003 Season

A throw-in for Andres Galarraga two years ago, Erasmo Ramirez came from nowhere to reach the majors in 2003. He proceeded to be durable and, most importantly, effective. He allowed only four of 17 inherited runners to score, partly because he was the best member of the bullpen at coming in and throwing strikes.

Pitching & Defense

Ramirez gets by almost exclusively with a below-hitting-speed changeup the Rangers have fondly come to call "The Crippler." He can throw the change at several speeds and can slow it down to the mid 60s if need be. Added to that is a funky sidearm motion in which he keeps the ball well-hidden. The arm angle allows Ramirez to get a decent number of groundball outs from his below-average fastball. He pays attention to runners and almost always is in the proper place defensively.

2004 Outlook

Ramirez, Ron Mahay and Brian Shouse may be fighting for two spots in the Rangers' bullpen. Ramirez pitched well enough in his first major league season that he'll get a shot somewhere. Wherever he lands, he'll likely have to prove he can pitch on consecutive days—something he was asked to do only three times in 2003.

Brian Shouse

Position: RP
Bats: L **Throws:** L
Ht: 5'11" **Wt:** 180

Opening Day Age: 35
Born: 9/26/68 in Effingham, IL
ML Seasons: 4

Overall Statistics

	W	L	Pct.	ERA	G	GS	Sv	IP	H	BB	SO	HR	Avg
'03	0	1	.000	3.10	62	0	1	61.0	62	14	40	1	.267
Car.	0	2	.000	4.11	98	0	1	87.2	93	29	59	7	.273

2003 Situational Stats

	W	L	ERA	Sv	IP		AB	H	HR	RBI	Avg
Home	0	0	4.24	0	34.0	LHB	133	26	1	18	.195
Road	0	1	1.67	1	27.0	RHB	99	36	0	10	.364
First Half	0	1	3.79	0	40.1	Sc Pos	77	19	0	25	.247
Scnd Half	0	0	1.74	1	20.2	Clutch	48	15	0	2	.313

2003 Season

With his eighth different organization, sinkballer Brian Shouse finally got a chance to pitch regularly, and produced unexpected results. Of the four lefties in the Rangers' bullpen, Shouse was the most consistent. After 98 career major league appearances, however, he still is searching for his first win.

Pitching & Defense

Shouse's delivery produces lots of groundballs, essential to success at The Ballpark in Arlington. He ranked 11th in the majors in groundball-flyball ratio (2.92) among pitchers who faced at least 150 batters. Shouse pitched as much as 3.1 innings in a game, but his long-term place probably is as a specialist against lefthanded hitters. One of every 10 batters hit a ball at Shouse in 2003, and he reacted well with six putouts and 18 assists. He also started a double play and has not committed an error in 33 career chances.

2004 Outlook

Managers who toiled forever as players in the minors don't forget their brethren, and perhaps that's why Buck Showalter developed such a fondness and trust for Shouse. Though he'll start the season at age 35, Shouse will get a long look in the Rangers' bullpen, and he'll also get the chance to make—and recover from—a few mistakes.

Other Texas Rangers

Alan Benes (Pos: RHP, Age: 32)

	W	L	Pct.	ERA	G	GS	Sv	IP	H	BB	SO	HR	Avg
'03	0	3	.000	8.10	7	4	1	23.1	37	14	20	2	.370
Car.	29	28	.509	4.59	115	70	1	494.0	493	220	401	59	.263

Benes was top-flight prospect until shoulder troubles began in 1997. He still struggles with walks and homers at the Triple-A level, and he bounced from the Cubs to the Rangers and back to the Cubs. 2004 Outlook: C

Mickey Callaway (Pos: RHP, Age: 28)

	W	L	Pct.	ERA	G	GS	Sv	IP	H	BB	SO	HR	Avg
'03	1	7	.125	6.68	23	7	0	60.2	84	24	41	7	.335
Car.	4	10	.286	6.11	36	17	0	119.1	148	51	77	15	.305

Callaway has been solid as a Triple-A swingman since 2001, going 23-9 with a 2.47 ERA in 258.2 innings. Only in 2002 was he effective in the majors, with a 2-1 mark (4.19 ERA) in six starts with Anaheim. 2004 Outlook: C

Ryan Christenson (Pos: CF, Age: 30, Bats: R)

	G	AB	R	H	D	T	HR	RBI	SB	BB	SO	Avg	OBP	Slg
'03	60	165	22	29	7	0	2	16	2	15	44	.176	.255	.255
Car.	452	998	159	222	48	5	16	102	16	114	256	.222	.303	.329

Christenson hit .313 with a .400 OBP at Triple-A Oklahoma in 2003, but getting anywhere near the Mendoza line with Milwaukee in 2002 (.155) and Texas in 2003 was tough. His chances may be drying up, though the Marlins will give him a shot this spring. 2004 Outlook: C

Ryan Drese (Pos: RHP, Age: 27)

	W	L	Pct.	ERA	G	GS	Sv	IP	H	BB	SO	HR	Avg
'03	2	4	.333	6.85	11	8	0	46.0	61	24	26	8	.314
Car.	13	15	.464	6.10	46	38	0	220.0	269	101	152	25	.305

Drese's diverse arsenal worked well at Triple-A Buffalo in 2001-02 (6-1, 3.38 ERA), but it hasn't with Cleveland, Texas or Triple-A Oklahoma, his main stop since moving to Texas with Einar Diaz in 2002. 2004 Outlook: C

Robert Ellis (Pos: RHP, Age: 33)

	W	L	Pct.	ERA	G	GS	Sv	IP	H	BB	SO	HR	Avg
'03	1	1	.500	8.35	4	4	0	18.1	26	10	8	7	.342
Car.	7	7	.500	6.03	29	21	0	118.0	138	48	54	20	.296

His numbers have been on the slide at the Triple-A level the last three seasons, but Ellis has managed callups by Arizona, Los Angeles and Texas. It hasn't been pretty during his brief major league stays. 2004 Outlook: C

Todd Greene (Pos: C, Age: 32, Bats: R)

	G	AB	R	H	D	T	HR	RBI	SB	BB	SO	Avg	OBP	Slg
'03	62	205	25	47	10	1	10	20	0	2	47	.229	.243	.434
Car.	362	1093	132	264	52	1	52	142	5	37	228	.242	.270	.434

Greene has slugged .486 with 20 homers in 317 at-bats with Texas the last two seasons, but his poor batting average, abysmal strikeout-walk rate and weak arm behind the plate counter his power production. 2004 Outlook: C

Jason Jones (Pos: LF/RF, Age: 27, Bats: B)

	G	AB	R	H	D	T	HR	RBI	SB	BB	SO	Avg	OBP	Slg
'03	40	107	11	23	6	0	3	11	0	10	21	.215	.298	.355
Car.	40	107	11	23	6	0	3	11	0	10	21	.215	.298	.355

Jones signed as a pro when he already was 22, but he's hit .289 and drawn walks while climbing the ladder over five seasons. The door may soon close, and he didn't bust through it with Texas in 2003. 2004 Outlook: C

Chad Kreuter (Pos: C, Age: 39, Bats: B)

	G	AB	R	H	D	T	HR	RBI	SB	BB	SO	Avg	OBP	Slg
'03	7	18	0	2	1	0	0	0	0	3	2	.111	.238	.167
Car.	944	2505	289	593	123	8	54	274	5	361	593	.237	.335	.357

Kreuter, who was signed because of his work with Chan Ho Park in Los Angeles, was cut loose in early May and never signed on with another team. It's likely we've seen the last of Kreuter. 2004 Outlook: C

Mike Lamb (Pos: 1B, Age: 28, Bats: L)

	G	AB	R	H	D	T	HR	RBI	SB	BB	SO	Avg	OBP	Slg
'03	28	38	3	5	0	0	0	2	1	2	7	.132	.190	.132
Car.	357	1129	164	318	56	2	19	117	3	83	142	.282	.336	.385

With his decent batting average and an ability to draw a walk, the third baseman might forge a career as a part-time player. That won't happen in a system with budding stars Hank Blalock and Mark Teixeira. 2004 Outlook: C

Tony Mounce (Pos: LHP, Age: 29)

	W	L	Pct.	ERA	G	GS	Sv	IP	H	BB	SO	HR	Avg
'03	1	5	.167	7.11	11	11	0	50.2	65	25	30	9	.317
Car.	1	5	.167	7.11	11	11	0	50.2	65	25	30	9	.317

A former Astros prospect who got off to a great start in the mid-1990s, Mounce struggled in the high minors and underwent Tommy John surgery in 2001. He's been better since, but now he's off to Japan. 2004 Outlook: D

C.J. Nitkowski (Pos: LHP, Age: 31)

	W	L	Pct.	ERA	G	GS	Sv	IP	H	BB	SO	HR	Avg
'03	0	0	—	7.45	6	0	0	9.2	17	8	5	0	.415
Car.	16	31	.340	5.33	288	44	3	442.2	474	245	319	53	.277

Nitkowski is another lefthander with nine lives. He's been released twice and signed to five minor league contracts since December 2001. His sixth such pact comes with Atlanta, despite a 5.33 career ERA. 2004 Outlook: C

Herbert Perry (Pos: 1B, Age: 34, Bats: R)

	G	AB	R	H	D	T	HR	RBI	SB	BB	SO	Avg	OBP	Slg
'03	11	24	1	4	1	0	0	2	0	0	3	.167	.167	.208
Car.	480	1562	228	431	100	5	50	229	12	114	272	.276	.337	.442

Injuries struck early in the 2003 campaign, and by May Perry was out for the year with a torn labrum and rotator cuff. After June surgery came word both knees needed surgery when his shoulder was ready for crutches. 2004 Outlook: B

Mario Ramos (Pos: LHP, Age: 26)

	W	L	Pct.	ERA	G	GS	Sv	IP	H	BB	SO	HR	Avg
'03	1	1	.500	6.23	3	3	0	13.0	11	13	8	3	.224
Car.	1	1	.500	6.23	3	3	0	13.0	11	13	8	3	.224

Ramos had been a promising finesse guy with excellent control, but his stuff hasn't fooled hitters at Triple-A Oklahoma the last two seasons. The former A's prospect was claimed off waivers by Oakland in November, and he'll try to get back on track with his original organization. 2004 Outlook: C

Donnie Sadler (Pos: 3B/SS/LF/CF, Age: 28, Bats: R)

	G	AB	R	H	D	T	HR	RBI	SB	BB	SO	Avg	OBP	Slg
'03	77	131	27	26	5	2	1	5	4	13	34	.198	.277	.290
Car.	399	744	124	152	27	8	6	46	25	54	156	.204	.265	.286

A former Red Sox prospect with good speed when he was drafted nearly a decade ago, the utilityman has failed to hit above the Mendoza line in 414 at-bats over the last three seasons. Arizona signed him to a minor league deal in November. 2004 Outlook: C

Victor Santos (Pos: RHP, Age: 27)

	W	L	Pct.	ERA	G	GS	Sv	IP	H	BB	SO	HR	Avg
'03	0	2	.000	7.01	8	4	0	25.2	29	16	15	5	.299
Car.	2	8	.200	5.48	65	13	0	128.0	132	87	92	17	.269

Santos enjoyed the best of his three Triple-A seasons in 2003, going 5-4 with a 3.41 ERA in 20 games (16 starts). His improved numbers didn't follow him to Texas, but the Brewers will give him another shot. 2004 Outlook: C

Marcus Thames (Pos: RF, Age: 27, Bats: R)

	G	AB	R	H	D	T	HR	RBI	SB	BB	SO	Avg	OBP	Slg
'03	30	70	10	15	2	0	1	4	0	8	18	.205	.298	.274
Cur.	37	90	14	18	3	0	2	6	0	8	22	.209	.293	.314

The former Yankee prospect hasn't enjoyed a noteworthy season since a .321-31-97 campaign at Double-A Norwich in 2001. He was dealt to Texas for Ruben Sierra in June, but the Rangers cut him loose in October and the Tigers signed him in December. 2004 Outlook: C

Texas Rangers Minor League Prospects

Organization Overview:

Five Rangers affiliates made the postseason in 2003, the most ever for the franchise, suggesting that the resurgence the organization saw real signs of in 2002 was in full bloom. The lone team not to make the playoffs was Triple-A Oklahoma. The bright spots were at the lower levels. For the first time in several seasons, the Rangers didn't lose draft picks because of frivolous free-agent signings. Assistant GM Grady Fuson, lured from Oakland to restock the farm system, got good initial results from his first full draft. The key may be second-rounder 1B-OF Vince Sinisi from Rice, who likely would have been a first-rounder if not represented by Scott Boras.

Juan Dominguez

Position: P	**Opening Day Age:** 21
Bats: R **Throws:** R	**Born:** 8/7/82 in
Ht: 6' 2" **Wt:** 180	Ensanchez Ramirez, DR

Recent Statistics

	W	L	ERA	G	GS	Sv	IP	H	R	BB	SO	HR
2003 A Stockton	4	0	2.84	16	9	1	63.1	55	27	16	72	3
2003 AAA Oklahoma	1	0	3.50	3	3	0	18.0	15	7	3	14	1
2003 AA Frisco	5	0	2.60	9	9	0	55.1	35	17	21	54	2
2003 AL Texas	0	2	7.16	6	3	0	16.1	16	14	12	13	5

In an organization starved for pitching prospects, Dominguez was *the* breakthrough prospect in 2003. He did it with an electric fastball and a well-disguised change. When he came to the majors in August, however, his lack of a breaking ball was badly exposed and he was sent back after three unsuccessful starts. The team did call him back in September to work with pitching coach Orel Hershiser and bullpen coach Mark Connor on the breaking ball. The Rangers also grew concerned about his long-term health late in the season, since Dominguez' 153-inning total was more than double that of any of his three previous campaigns. That is partly why he did not go to the Arizona Fall League.

Reynaldo Garcia

Position: P	**Opening Day Age:** 29
Bats: R **Throws:** R	**Born:** 4/15/74 in Mayua,
Ht: 6' 3" **Wt:** 170	DR

Recent Statistics

	W	L	ERA	G	GS	Sv	IP	H	R	BB	SO	HR
2003 AAA Oklahoma	4	3	3.69	39	3	9	61.0	64	27	19	64	3
2003 AL Texas	0	0	9.00	17	0	0	18.0	19	18	14	15	6

According to the Rangers, Garcia has a devastating splitter to go along with a mid-90s fastball, but he hasn't shown it in parts of two seasons with the parent club. He has allowed 15 walks and compiled an 11.25 ERA in 20 major league games. He also has allowed nine homers in 20 major league innings. Perhaps at least some of his control issues can be explained by a vision problem in one of his eyes. Nonetheless, if he learns the strike zone and manages to keep the ball down, he could be an effective middle or setup reliever. With the Rangers in full rebuilding mode, he should get more chances.

Rosman Garcia

Position: P	**Opening Day Age:** 25
Bats: R **Throws:** R	**Born:** 1/3/79 in Maracay,
Ht: 6' 2" **Wt:** 160	VZ

Recent Statistics

	W	L	ERA	G	GS	Sv	IP	H	R	BB	SO	HR
2003 AAA Oklahoma	0	0	0.55	14	0	10	16.1	8	1	5	12	0
2003 AL Texas	1	2	6.02	46	0	0	46.1	63	33	23	25	4

At one point in the season, Garcia was the Rangers' best reliever, but a stretch in which he retired only three of 24 batters completely shook his confidence. He displayed awful body language on the mound and showed no real ability to make adjustments once hitters had adjusted to him. In the final three months of the season, he allowed 17 earned runs in 21 innings. Just as disheartening was the fact that he allowed 16 walks in those 21 innings, after allowing just seven free passes in his first 25.1 frames. He could not be trusted in tight situations, as he allowed 14 of 25 inherited runners to score.

Adrian Gonzalez

Position: 1B	**Opening Day Age:** 21
Bats: L **Throws:** L	**Born:** 5/8/82 in San
Ht: 6' 2" **Wt:** 190	Diego, CA

Recent Statistics

	G	AB	R	H	D	T	HR	RBI	SB	BB	SO	Avg
2002 AA Portland	138	508	70	135	34	1	17	96	6	54	112	.266
2003 AAA Albuquerque	39	139	17	30	5	1	1	18	1	14	25	.216
2003 AA Carolina	36	137	15	42	9	1	1	16	1	14	25	.307
2003 AA Frisco	45	173	16	49	6	2	3	17	0	11	27	.283

Gonzalez was the crown jewel of the package the Rangers extracted from Florida for closer Ugueth Urbina last summer. The top overall pick in the 2000 draft, Gonzalez reminds some people of a young Rafael Palmeiro—a .300-hitting line-drive type who fields his position with excellence. But Palmeiro's home-run potential was more evident nearly 20 years ago than Gonzalez' is now. Five home runs in 449 minor league at-bats last year simply doesn't translate to proper power for a corner infielder, particularly a lefthanded hitter at The Ballpark in Arlington. Nonetheless, if Gonzalez does start to show more power in 2004, he could push current first baseman Mark Teixeira to the outfield.

Gerald Laird

Position: C
Bats: R **Throws:** R
Ht: 6' 2" **Wt:** 195

Opening Day Age: 24
Born: 11/13/79 in
Westminster, CA

Recent Statistics

	G	AB	R	H	D	T	HR	RBI	SB	BB	SO	Avg
2003 AAA Oklahoma	99	338	50	88	20	5	9	42	9	37	61	.260
2003 AL Texas	19	44	9	12	2	1	1	4	0	5	11	.273

When the Rangers traded former top pick Carlos Pena to Oakland, lefty Mario Ramos was expected to be the prime catch. Laird, however, passed him in 2003 and may be Texas' regular catcher for 2004. Laird got a long look in September and already appears to be the equal of Einar Diaz offensively, but that isn't saying much. What does give the Rangers encouragement is that Laird is making adjustments at the plate, and he also shows no fear. He does have to improve as a receiver, as he seemed to have trouble simply holding on to balls. He flashed a better-than-expected arm, throwing out three of seven attempted basestealers for the parent club last year.

A.J. Murray

Position: P
Bats: L **Throws:** L
Ht: 6' 3" **Wt:** 180

Opening Day Age: 22
Born: 3/17/82 in Vernal,
UT

Recent Statistics

	W	L	ERA	G	GS	Sv	IP	H	R	BB	SO	HR
2002 A Savannah	5	3	2.87	14	8	0	62.2	63	22	14	51	0
2002 A Charlotte	3	3	3.02	19	14	2	83.1	77	31	20	68	4
2003 AA Frisco	10	4	3.63	27	25	0	144.0	134	68	63	90	13

The Rangers have a slew of southpaws approaching Texas, and Murray may be the closest to helping out after going 10-4 with a 3.63 ERA in the Double-A Texas League. A 19th-round pick in 2000, Murray is a typical finesse lefty. He throws an 86-88 MPH fastball, an advanced changeup and an effective slider. The left-hander has been able to spot the slider and changeup low in the strike zone. Getting opposing hitters off balance and chasing his secondary pitches has been a big part of his success as he has climbed through the system. Throwing the slider for strikes will remain critical to getting more advanced hitters out, and keeping all of his offerings low in the zone is his ticket to the majors.

Ramon Nivar

Position: 2B
Bats: B **Throws:** R
Ht: 5' 10" **Wt:** 170

Opening Day Age: 24
Born: 2/22/80 in San
Cristobal, DR

Recent Statistics

	G	AB	R	H	D	T	HR	RBI	SB	BB	SO	Avg
2003 AA Frisco	79	317	53	110	17	4	4	37	9	20	23	.347
2003 AAA Oklahoma	23	89	11	30	2	2	2	12	6	5	5	.337
2003 AL Texas	28	90	9	19	1	2	0	7	4	4	10	.211

Along with a slew of other Latin players, Nivar saw both his age and name change before the 2003 season.

He also made a position change, moving from second base to center. Though he has lightning speed and a strong work ethic, he's got a long way to go to be a major league center fielder. He doesn't yet get good reads on balls and often makes improper throws, and his instincts on the bases aren't refined. But 2003 was a breakthrough year for him, which continued into the Arizona Fall League, where he batted .381 before leaving to attend the birth of his first child. With more defensive work and a smidgeon of plate discipline, Nivar could be a prototypical speedy, leadoff-hitting center fielder.

Ricardo Rodriguez

Position: P
Bats: R **Throws:** R
Ht: 6' 3" **Wt:** 190

Opening Day Age: 25
Born: 5/21/78 in Manga,
DR

Recent Statistics

	W	L	ERA	G	GS	Sv	IP	H	R	BB	SO	HR
2003 AAA Buffalo	0	1	4.32	2	2	0	8.1	6	4	3	7	2
2003 AL Cleveland	3	9	5.73	15	15	0	81.2	89	57	28	41	16

Rodriguez did not pitch for the Rangers after being obtained from Cleveland in a trade for Ryan Ludwick. A hip injury eventually required surgery, but the club is confident he'll be ready for the start of 2004. Rodriguez did not have much success in Cleveland, but the Rangers think his groundball tendencies can make him a good fit for The Ballpark. The balls that did not get hit on the ground, however, could cause trouble for Rodriguez in his home park. He allowed 16 homers in 81.2 major league innings last year, and The Ballpark is known as a homer haven.

Others to Watch

Texas will put a strong emphasis on on-base percentage in the future, making outfielder-first baseman **Jason Botts** (23) and infielder **Jason Bourgeois** (22) valuable. Bourgeois made the jump to Double-A in the second half of the season, then spent most of the Arizona Fall League with a .400 on-base percentage. Botts posted a .382 on-base percentage at Class-A and Double-A ball last year, while hitting a combined .294 with 13 homers and 18 steals. . . The Rangers got encouraging news about talented but oft-injured righthander **Jovanny Cedeno** (24), who pitched a total of just 14.2 innings in 2001-02 because of shoulder problems. Cedeno returned to go 4-0 with a 1.93 ERA and 34 strikeouts in 32.2 innings at the lower levels of the system. . . First baseman **Jason Hart** (26), who has power potential but has not mastered Triple-A pitching, could be had for a song since the organization is deep at the position. . . The Rangers hope to develop a few lefty starters, including **Ben Kozlowski** (23), acquired from the Braves two years ago, **Ryan Snare** (25), obtained from Florida in the Ugueth Urbina deal last July, and **C.J. Wilson** (23). Snare has the best chance to get a look in 2004, as Kozlowski underwent Tommy John surgery in June and Wilson followed him in August.

SkyDome

Offense

When the roof is open, balls carry, especially to right-center field. The airflow can knock down balls to left-center. When the roof is closed, it's true to all fields. The stadium is hitter-friendly, producing doubles galore due to the artificial turf. All hitters averaged .282 last season, and the 11.1 total runs per game ranked fifth in the majors. At .465, Blue Jays hitters slugged 20 points higher at home than on the road in 2003.

Defense

The dimensions are standard down both lines and into the alleys, and there are no tricks or gimmicks built into the field. From the alleys to center field is very expansive, and it helps to have good defenders with impressive speed in the outfield.

Who It Helps the Most

Contact hitters who put the ball on the ground and line-drive hitters can prosper and look to take the extra base at SkyDome. Frank Catalanotto and Vernon Wells enjoy the home park. The hitting percentages of both Carlos Delgado and Eric Hinske are better across the board at SkyDome. Ace Roy Halladay, though he induces a lot of grounders, has often fared better at home than on the road. Cliff Pollitte, homer-prone on the road, was far more effective at SkyDome in 2003. So was Jason Kershner.

Who It Hurts the Most

Sinkerball and finesse pitchers in search of groundouts on the SkyDome turf can struggle. In 2003, starter Mark Hendrickson gave up more hits per inning and posted a 7.67 home ERA that nearly was double his road mark. Relief pitcher Trever Miller was hurt by the longball at home and recorded a 5.28 ERA that was a run-and-a-half worse than his road ERA. The place doesn't seem to hurt Jays hitters.

Rookies & Newcomers

New arrival Ted Lilly has been very hittable and homer-prone in five games at SkyDome, posting an 8.36 ERA. Young righthander Josh Towers thrived at SkyDome in 2003, going 5-1 with a 3.92 ERA. Outfielder Reed Johnson hit well everywhere.

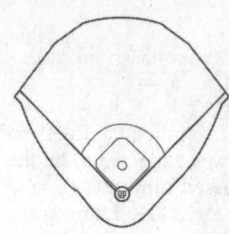

Dimensions: LF-328, LCF-375, CF-400, RCF-375, RF-328

Capacity: 50,516

Elevation: 300 feet

Surface: Turf

Foul Territory: Large

Park Factors

2003 Season

	Home Games			Away Games			
	Blue Jays	Opp	Total	Blue Jays	Opp	Total	Index
G	72	72	144	72	72	144	
Avg	.283	.282	.282	.273	.265	.269	105
AB	2471	2608	5079	2568	2429	4997	102
R	406	404	810	386	320	706	115
H	699	735	1434	701	643	1344	107
2B	182	157	339	151	112	263	127
3B	14	17	31	13	17	30	102
HR	76	99	175	81	68	149	116
BB	255	218	473	236	210	446	104
SO	461	486	947	521	382	903	103
E	44	46	90	57	42	99	91
E-Infield	39	36	75	49	34	83	90
LHB-Avg	.294	.273	.283	.271	.249	.260	109
LHB-HR	42	40	82	37	24	61	135
RHB-Avg	.275	.290	.282	.275	.280	.277	102
RHB-HR	34	59	93	44	44	88	103

2001-2003

	Home Games			Away Games			
	Blue Jays	Opp	Total	Blue Jays	Opp	Total	Index
G	216	216	432	215	215	430	
Avg	.273	.274	.273	.262	.272	.267	102
AB	7362	7693	15055	7665	7326	14991	100
R	1124	1136	2260	1091	1009	2100	107
H	2008	2105	4113	2008	1990	3998	102
2B	453	481	934	400	379	779	119
3B	43	40	83	47	41	88	94
HR	252	253	505	252	222	474	106
BB	699	703	1402	663	685	1348	104
SO	1421	1420	2841	1565	1268	2833	100
E	134	143	277	154	127	281	98
E-Infield	121	114	235	129	101	230	102
LHB-Avg	.267	.279	.274	.269	.277	.273	100
LHB-HR	122	120	242	128	101	229	108
RHB-Avg	.276	.268	.273	.257	.266	.261	104
RHB-HR	130	133	263	124	121	245	105

2003 Rankings (American League)

- Highest double factor
- Highest LHB batting-average factor
- Highest LHB home-run factor
- Third-highest run factor
- Third-highest home-run factor

Carlos Tosca

2003 Season

Following a poor start, the Blue Jays rebounded to challenge Boston and New York for the AL East lead prior to the All-Star break. The team couldn't decide whether to go for it or to get on with trading high-salaried players. The club elected to do nothing and fell out of contention in July.

Offense

In concert with general manager J.P. Ricciardi, Tosca preaches the Oakland philosophy of combining high on-base percentage with the big hit. The team ranked near the top of the American League in most offensive categories, but making consistent contact was a problem. Only Detroit recorded more strikeouts than the Jays. Ricciardi and Tosca treat the stolen base and sacrifice bunt like sour milk. The club ranked last among AL teams with 37 steals. The Jays also eschewed the hit-and-run, despite a favorable 43-percent success rate in 49 attempts. Tosca used 128 pinch-hitters, the second most in the AL, primarily in platoon situations. They delivered a .231 average without a homer.

Pitching & Defense

Losing Justin Miller to shoulder surgery and the failure of Cory Lidle and other Ricciardi acquisitions forced Tosca to tinker with the rotation and bullpen. Kelvim Escobar moved from relief to a starting role in May, but his successor as closer, Cliff Politte, blew six of 18 save chances before Tosca turned to rookie Aquilino Lopez. Middle relief hurt the club all season, and Tosca was criticized for his rigid left-versus-left, right-versus-right style with his young pen. Tosca leans heavily on the pitchout, leading AL managers with 49 and catching 12 runners trying to steal. The Jays' defense, which ranked 12th in the league in fielding percentage, was plagued by a leaky left side of the infield. Third baseman Eric Hinske and shortstop Chris Woodward struggled in their second seasons.

2004 Outlook

Tosca has a good rapport with his players and has their respect. The bullpen woes need to be resolved. It may be time to inject a little more Jack McKeon-esque flexibility into his approach.

Born: 9/29/53 in Pinar del Rio, Cuba

Playing Experience: No major league playing experience

Managerial Experience: 2 seasons

Manager Statistics

Year	Team, Lg	W	L	Pct	GB	Finish
2003	Toronto, AL	86	76	.531	15.0	3rd East
2 Seasons		144	127	.531	–	–

2003 Starting Pitchers by Days Rest

	<=3	4	5	6+
Blue Jays Starts	4	102	30	17
Blue Jays ERA	2.59	4.76	4.58	4.53
AL Avg Starts	2	79	50	22
AL ERA	3.19	4.64	4.57	4.98

2003 Situational Stats

	Carlos Tosca	AL Average
Hit & Run Success %	42.9	36.7
Stolen Base Success %	59.7	70.0
Platoon Pct.	60.1	61.7
Defensive Subs	22	23
High-Pitch Outings	4	5
Quick/Slow Hooks	20/24	19/16
Sacrifice Attempts	14	55

2003 Rankings (American League)

- 1st in pitchouts (49), pitchouts with a runner moving (12), slow hooks, mid-inning pitching changes (237) and saves with over 1 inning pitched (14)
- 2nd in fewest caught stealings of second base (20), sacrifice-bunt percentage (85.7%), pinch-hitters used (128), starts on three days rest and one-batter pitcher appearances (46)
- 3rd in relief appearances (444) and first-batter platoon percentage

Frank Catalanotto

2003 Season

After three years each with both Texas and Detroit, the versatile Frank Catalanotto started 115 games for Toronto and reached career highs in at-bats, runs, doubles, homers, RBI, extra-base hits, total bases and strikeouts. After a 5-for-5 performance on July 9 against Boston, Catalanotto slumped, going 9-for-62 (.145) through August 3. At that time, he saw an eye doctor and was fitted for new contacts. He batted .412 in August, but during the month and through September, Catalanotto played less as the Jays tested young players. For the season, he ranked among the best in the American League with a .344 average with runners in scoring position.

Hitting

Catalanotto is an aggressive gap hitter, and the numbers from last season epitomize a career-long preference for batting at the top of the order and hitting early in the count. In 438 combined at-bats in the leadoff and No. 2 positions, Catalanotto averaged .308 with 13 homers. Otherwise, he hit .216. He was a master at hunting for the first-pitch fastball, hitting .453 with an 0-0 count in 2003. He's a good situational hitter, willing to give himself up to move a runner. Over his career, Catalanotto has a history of hitting better with runners on base and in scoring position, as well as with the sacks full.

Baserunning & Defense

Catalanotto has slightly above-average speed, which has allowed him to reach double figures in stolen bases once in his career—with Texas in 2001—but he attempted just four steals last summer. Defensively, he can play left and right field as well as first and second base, though shoulder surgery in 1997 has made his arm far more suitable to left.

2004 Outlook

Signed to a one-year, $2.3 million deal for 2004, Catalanotto is likely to play left field and bat leadoff. Modest power, impatience at the plate and struggles against lefties make him better suited to platoon duty. Catalanotto has undergone two laser vision correction procedures and may need another. That's a possibility during the offseason.

Position: LF/RF/DH
Bats: L **Throws:** R
Ht: 5'11" **Wt:** 195

Opening Day Age: 29
Born: 4/27/74 in Smithtown, NY
ML Seasons: 7
Pronunciation: ca-tal-a-NAH-tow

Overall Statistics

	G	AB	R	H	D	T	HR	RBI	SB	BB	SO	Avg	OBP	Slg
'03	133	489	83	146	34	6	13	59	2	35	62	.299	.351	.472
Car.	639	1971	323	585	128	21	54	241	38	162	275	.297	.359	.465

Where He Hits the Ball

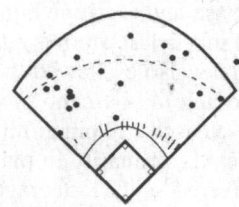 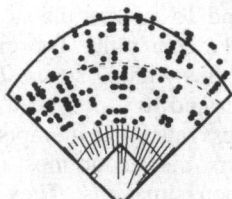

Vs. LHP   **Vs. RHP**

2003 Situational Stats

	AB	H	HR	RBI	Avg		AB	H	HR	RBI	Avg
Home	237	74	7	30	.312	LHP	68	12	1	6	.176
Road	252	72	6	29	.286	RHP	421	134	12	53	.318
First Half	349	107	8	45	.307	Sc Pos	96	33	4	44	.344
Scnd Half	140	39	5	14	.279	Clutch	50	11	0	6	.220

2003 Rankings (American League)

- 6th in batting average vs. righthanded pitchers
- 8th in batting average with runners in scoring position
- 10th in batting average with two strikes (.243)
- Led the Blue Jays in triples, lowest percentage of swings that missed (11.5), batting average with the bases loaded (.667), batting average vs. righthanded pitchers and batting average with two strikes (.243)

Carlos Delgado

2003 Season

In arguably his finest all-round season, Carlos Delgado ranked first among American League hitters in RBI and on-base-plus-slugging (1.019). He finished second in walks, homers, on-base percentage, slugging and the AL Most Valuable Player vote at season's end. By the All-Star break, Delgado had 28 homers and 97 RBI, which positioned him to challenge for the all-time RBI record. But his power production declined in the second half. Between July 8 and September 20, Delgado hit just seven homers, with four of them coming on September 25. He became the 15th player in major league history to hit four homers in a single game.

Hitting

Toward the end of 2002, Delgado corrected a mechanical fault that had him leaning on his front foot too early in his swing. With his balance perfected, Delgado went on a three-month tear to start the 2003 season. The lefthanded hitter has enormous power to both alleys, allowing him to average 39.5 homers and 123.5 RBI a year over the last six seasons. Delgado also shows patience in search of his pitch, having drawn more than 100 walks in each of the last four seasons. A number of teams use an infield shift to the right side. Some pitchers try to work him high and tight, while others try to make him hit the low-and-outside breaking ball to left field.

Baserunning & Defense

On the bases, Delgado runs conservatively but smartly. His first few steps aren't quick, but once up to speed he gets around well for a big man. His fielding at first base improves in annual increments. He'll make the occasional spectacular play to his left and is solid to his right. His arm strength is adequate for his position.

2004 Outlook

To start the season, Delgado will bat fourth in the lineup for the Blue Jays. He is entering the last year of a four-year, $68 million contract. The Jays have expressed interest in re-upping, but if talks fall through, the club could be asking him to waive a no-trade clause.

Position: 1B/DH
Bats: L **Throws:** R
Ht: 6' 3" **Wt:** 230

Opening Day Age: 31
Born: 6/25/72 in Aguadilla, PR
ML Seasons: 11
Pronunciation: del-GAH-doh

Overall Statistics

G	AB	R	H	D	T	HR	RBI	SB	BB	SO	Avg	OBP	Slg
161	570	117	172	38	1	42	145	0	109	137	.302	.426	.593
1295	4550	815	1290	317	11	304	959	9	758	1127	.284	.395	.558

Where He Hits the Ball

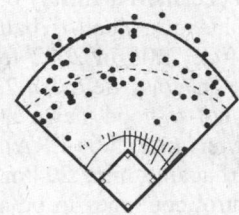 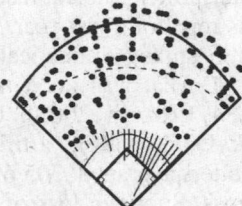

Vs. LHP   **Vs. RHP**

2003 Situational Stats

	AB	H	HR	RBI	Avg		AB	H	HR	RBI	Avg
Home	285	96	24	83	.337	LHP	183	52	7	46	.284
Road	285	76	18	62	.267	RHP	387	120	35	99	.310
First Half	345	108	28	97	.313	Sc Pos	157	56	11	101	.357
Scnd Half	225	64	14	48	.284	Clutch	57	20	5	14	.351

2003 Rankings (American League)

- 1st in RBI, times on base (300) and cleanup slugging percentage (.593)
- 2nd in home runs, walks, intentional walks (23), strikeouts, slugging percentage, on-base percentage and batting average with runners in scoring position
- 3rd in hit by pitch (19) and errors at first base (10)
- Led the Blue Jays in times on base (300), strikeouts, pitches seen (2,807), games played, on-base percentage, HR frequency (13.6 ABs per HR) (7.0%)
- Led AL first basemen in batting average, home runs and RBI

Kelvim Escobar

Signed By ANGELS

Position: SP/RP
Bats: R **Throws:** R
Ht: 6' 1" **Wt:** 210

Opening Day Age: 27
Born: 4/11/76 in La Guaria, VZ
ML Seasons: 7

2003 Season

After several seasons of moving Kelvim Escobar in and out of the bullpen, the Blue Jays had decided to establish the hard-throwing righthander as a closer. But a 7.79 ERA in 15 appearances forced a change in strategy, ultimately for the better. In late May, Escobar became a starter and went 12-8 with a 3.92 ERA in 26 outings. He compiled an 8-3 record in 14 starts after the All-Star break, and for the season, he posted a career-high 159 strikeouts.

Pitching

Escobar throws a four-seam fastball that tops out at 97 MPH, a two-seamer, changeup, curve, cutter and splitter. The cut fastball became a mainstay of his repertoire last year, and his groundball-flyball ratio spiked dramatically, from 1.03 in 2002 to 1.54. That was good news on grass fields (8-2, 2.84 ERA in 2003), but not-so-good news at SkyDome with its artificial turf (5-7, 5.64 ERA). Batters averaged .305 on turf against him, .224 on grass. Sporadic loss of control continues to be a problem. When he gets ahead in the count, though, Escobar often is dominant. After he fell behind 1-0 in the count last season, batters averaged .301 in 279 at-bats.

Defense

Not only is Escobar durable—he hasn't been on the disabled list since 1998—he's also very agile and athletic. Escobar moves quickly off the mound to recover short grounders or bunts. He also covers first base easily. With just an average move to first, he has been prone to stolen bases. The righthander allowed 24 steals in 26 attempts last summer, and over his career basestealers have an 83-percent success rate against him.

2004 Outlook

After making the conversion to starting pitcher, Escobar tended to tire in the 76-90 pitch range, then picked up steam again. This offseason he will be able to train for a rotation role. Toronto offered the free agent a two-year contract, but Escobar was looking for a three-year deal and got it from the Angels. The package reportedly is worth $18.75 million.

Overall Statistics

	W	L	Pct.	ERA	G	GS	Sv	IP	H	BB	SO	HR	Avg
'03	13	9	.591	4.29	41	26	4	180.1	189	78	159	15	.270
Car.	58	55	.513	4.58	301	101	58	849.0	846	394	744	84	.259

2003 Pitching Profile

	Kelvim Escobar	AL Average
Overall Strike %	62.4	62.8
1st Pitch Strike %	55.8	58.7
Ratio	1.48	1.39
Strikeouts per 9 IP	7.94	6.11
Walks per 9 IP	3.89	3.16
Home Runs per 9 IP	0.75	1.11
Strikeout/Walk Ratio	2.04	1.93
Groundball/Flyball Ratio	1.54	1.18

2003 Situational Stats

	W	L	ERA	Sv	IP		AB	H	HR	RBI	Avg
Home	5	7	5.64	1	95.2	LHB	356	83	8	45	.233
Road	8	2	2.76	3	84.2	RHB	344	106	7	39	.308
First Half	5	6	4.72	4	87.2	Sc Pos	183	48	7	72	.262
Scnd Half	8	3	3.88	0	92.2	Clutch	52	14	2	8	.269

2003 Rankings (American League)

- 2nd in highest ERA at home and highest walks per nine innings (3.9)
- 3rd in stolen bases allowed (24) and highest stolen-base percentage allowed (92.3)
- 4th in walks allowed and lowest ERA on the road
- 5th in most strikeouts per nine innings (7.9)
- 6th in wild pitches (9), fewest home runs allowed per nine innings (.75) and highest on-base percentage allowed (.348)
- Led the Blue Jays in walks allowed, hit batsmen (9), wild pitches (9), pickoff throws (48), stolen bases allowed (24), lowest slugging percentage allowed (.384), lowest ERA on the road, fewest home runs allowed per nine innings (.75), and most strikeouts per nine innings (7.9)

Roy Halladay

2003 Season

Both an All-Star and 20-game winner for the first time, Roy Halladay dominated hitters almost the entire season and claimed his first Cy Young Award. From May 1 through the end of July, the righthander won 15 straight decisions without a loss and posted a 2.84 ERA. In those 15 victories, he limited opponents to two earned runs or less in 12 of them. After taking three losses in a four-game stretch in August, Halladay rebounded in September by going 5-1 with a 1.41 ERA—a run that included three consecutive shutouts between September 6 and 17. The league leader in innings, Halladay finished tied for first among American League pitchers in complete games (nine) and third in strikeouts (204).

Pitching

Halladay throws a four-seam fastball that reaches 97 MPH with late sinking action, a cutter that arrives at 89-92 MPH, a drop-dead curve that starts inside at shoulder height against righthanders and winds up at the knees over the outside black, plus a splitter. In short, his stuff is nasty. His approach is unfailingly aggressive, his mound demeanor just on the calm side of glowering. He gets ahead in the count with strike-zone mastery of all his pitches. Two years ago, his career strikeout-walk ratio barely exceeded 1.5:1. Last season, it was almost 6.5:1. The sinking action on his pitches resulted in 2.7 grounders for every fly-out— that is, when hitters managed to make contact.

Defense

With an average move to first, and not an especially quick delivery to the plate, Halladay has allowed more than 20 stolen bases the last two seasons. But with a basketball forward's agility, the 6-foot-6 righthander fields the ball well to both sides of the mound and easily covers first base.

2004 Outlook

Now firmly established as the ace of the Toronto rotation, Halladay earned $3.8 million last season and the team is looking to sign him to a long-term deal. He remains under the Blue Jays' control for two more seasons, but the Jays would like to get something done.

Position: SP
Bats: R **Throws:** R
Ht: 6' 6" **Wt:** 230

Opening Day Age: 26
Born: 5/14/77 in Denver, CO
ML Seasons: 6
Pronunciation: HAL-luh-day

Overall Statistics

	W	L	Pct.	ERA	G	GS	Sv	IP	H	BB	SO	HR	Avg
'03	22	7	.759	3.25	36	36	0	266.0	253	32	204	26	.247
Car.	59	31	.656	3.84	144	119	1	841.2	845	242	607	74	.258

2003 Pitching Profile

	Roy Halladay	AL Average
Overall Strike %	68.6	62.8
1st Pitch Strike %	63.4	58.7
Ratio	1.07	1.39
Strikeouts per 9 IP	6.90	6.11
Walks per 9 IP	1.08	3.16
Home Runs per 9 IP	0.88	1.11
Strikeout/Walk Ratio	6.38	1.93
Groundball/Flyball Ratio	2.70	1.18

2003 Situational Stats

	W	L	ERA	Sv	IP		AB	H	HR	RBI	Avg
Home	10	2	3.21	0	126.1	LHB	610	160	17	69	.262
Road	12	5	3.29	0	139.2	RHB	415	93	9	35	.224
First Half	13	2	3.41	0	153.0	Sc Pos	222	58	5	76	.261
Scnd Half	9	5	3.03	0	113.0	Clutch	114	28	2	9	.246

2003 Rankings (American League)

- 1st in wins, games started, complete games (9), shutouts (2), innings pitched, hits allowed, batters faced (1,071) and highest strikeout-walk ratio (6.4)
- 2nd in pitches thrown (3,630), highest groundball-flyball ratio allowed (2.7), fewest pitches thrown per batter (3.39) and fewest walks per nine innings (1.1)
- 3rd in strikeouts, winning percentage and lowest on-base percentage allowed (.275)
- Led the Blue Jays in ERA, batters faced (1,071), home runs allowed, hit batsmen (9), strikeouts, GDPs induced (23), lowest batting average allowed (.247), lowest on-base percentage allowed (.275), fewest pitches thrown per batter (3.39), lowest ERA at home, and fewest walks per nine innings (1.1)

Mark Hendrickson

2003 Season

In his first full season as a major league starter, Mark Hendrickson logged 5.3 innings per outing over his 30 starts. He had been moving away from starting in recent minor league seasons, but with a couple of solid August wins over Seattle, he showed more promise as a starter toward the end of the season. He won three of his final four decisions, holding the Devil Rays and Mariners to two earned runs in each victory.

Pitching

Long and lanky like Randy Johnson, Hendrickson's fastball generally travels to the plate in the high 80s. He doesn't overpower anyone and lacks an out pitch versus righthanders, who feasted off him in 2003. While he has a decent changeup, his sinker and cut slider don't serve him well on SkyDome's artificial turf. Opposing hitters averaged .338 there. Because hitters generally make contact, Hendrickson can't afford to issue walks, and he may have pressed to get ahead in the count last year. When opponents put the first pitch in play, they batted .363.

Defense

Despite his large size, Hendrickson is very athletic, which is what inspired former Jays scouting director Tim Wilken to draft the former NBA veteran. Consequently, Hendrickson is very agile with quick hands coming off the mound. He fields his position very well. He's not as effective controlling the running game. Baserunners stole 20 bases with Hendrickson on the mound in 2003, although he did execute three pickoffs.

2004 Outlook

While he turns 30 this summer, Hendrickson's arm is relatively young after spending four seasons in the NBA and pitching limited innings during those years. Although Hendrickson probably would be effective in the long term as a situational reliever against lefthanded hitters, the Jays' plan is to continue using him as a starter.

Position: SP
Bats: L **Throws:** L
Ht: 6' 9" **Wt:** 230

Opening Day Age: 29
Born: 6/23/74 in Mount Vernon, WA
ML Seasons: 2

Overall Statistics

	W	L	Pct.	ERA	G	GS	Sv	IP	H	BB	SO	HR	Avg
'03	9	9	.500	5.51	30	30	0	158.1	207	40	76	24	.317
Car.	12	9	.571	4.94	46	34	0	195.0	232	52	97	25	.298

2003 Pitching Profile

	Mark Hendrickson	AL Average
Overall Strike %	64.3	62.8
1st Pitch Strike %	54.7	58.7
Ratio	1.56	1.39
Strikeouts per 9 IP	4.32	6.11
Walks per 9 IP	2.27	3.16
Home Runs per 9 IP	1.36	1.11
Strikeout/Walk Ratio	1.90	1.93
Groundball/Flyball Ratio	1.31	1.18

2003 Situational Stats

	W	L	ERA	Sv	IP		AB	H	HR	RBI	Avg
Home	4	5	7.67	0	61.0	LHB	167	45	1	18	.269
Road	5	4	4.16	0	97.1	RHB	487	162	23	83	.333
First Half	5	6	5.55	0	94.0	Sc Pos	165	53	5	75	.321
Scnd Half	4	3	5.46	0	64.1	Clutch	14	5	0	3	.357

2003 Rankings (American League)

- 2nd in wins among rookies
- 3rd in losses among rookies and highest batting average allowed vs. righthanded batters
- 6th in highest batting average allowed with runners in scoring position
- 7th in runners caught stealing (8)
- 8th in stolen bases allowed (20)
- Led the Blue Jays in runners caught stealing (8), lowest stolen-base percentage allowed (71.4) and most run support per nine innings (6.7)

Eric Hinske

Position: 3B
Bats: L **Throws:** R
Ht: 6' 2" **Wt:** 225

Opening Day Age: 26
Born: 8/5/77 in Menasha, WI
ML Seasons: 2
Pronunciation: hin-SKEE

2003 Season

Struggling out of the gate in his sophomore season, Eric Hinske left spring training hurt and had just two homers and a .232 batting average before going on the disabled list May 24 with a broken hand. He returned to the lineup four weeks later and continued to struggle for much of the summer until a modest surge in September. His dozen homers amounted to half his 2002 output, though he played 27 fewer games in 2003. Hinske still showed power potential with 45 doubles. Despite missing a month, he topped all AL third basemen with 22 errors.

Hitting

General manager J.P. Ricciardi acquired Hinske from Oakland because he worked deep into the count, produced a respectable on-base percentage and still hit for power. The formula worked in his Rookie of the Year season, as he drew 77 walks, hit 24 homers and drove in 84 runs. American League pitchers adjusted. Hinske prefers low fastballs, middle-away. So the book on him is to get ahead in the count and retire him with high fastballs or offspeed stuff out of the zone. In 2003, Hinske hit .202 after falling behind 0-1 in the count. While he saw slightly more pitches per plate appearance last summer, his hitting percentages plummeted.

Baserunning & Defense

Hinske has above-average speed and good instincts. He has swiped 25 bases in two seasons for a team that doesn't steal. He's improved his range defensively and uses quick feet to turn slow rollers into routine outs. But he came into the league with a reputation for defensive inconsistency, and he regressed from his rookie season. His fielding percentage slipped from .946 in 2002 to a poor .930 last season.

2004 Outlook

Ricciardi signed Hinske to a five-year, $14.75 million contract after his rookie campaign. Will 2003 prove to be an injury-induced sophomore slump, or a sign of more tumbling to come? More than likely, Hinske's bat will rebound, especially in the power department. His defense may be another matter, but he'll be starting at third base.

Overall Statistics

	G	AB	R	H	D	T	HR	RBI	SB	BB	SO	Avg	OBP	Slg
'03	124	449	74	109	45	3	12	63	12	59	104	.243	.329	.437
Car.	275	1015	173	267	83	5	36	147	25	136	242	.263	.349	.461

Where He Hits the Ball

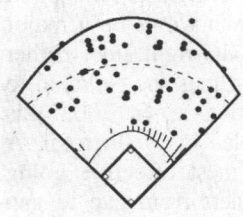
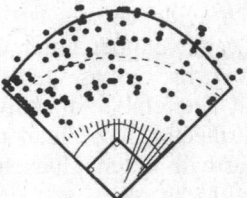

Vs. LHP   **Vs. RHP**

2003 Situational Stats

	AB	H	HR	RBI	Avg		AB	H	HR	RBI	Avg
Home	219	52	4	24	.237	LHP	133	34	2	26	.256
Road	230	57	8	39	.248	RHP	316	75	10	37	.237
First Half	219	52	6	32	.237	Sc Pos	114	31	3	49	.272
Scnd Half	230	57	6	31	.248	Clutch	58	16	1	6	.276

2003 Rankings (American League)

- 1st in errors at third base (22) and lowest fielding percentage at third base (.930)
- 5th in doubles, most pitches seen per plate appearance (4.08), lowest batting average and lowest percentage of swings put into play (37.3)
- Led the Blue Jays in stolen bases, stolen-base percentage (85.7), most pitches seen per plate appearance (4.08) and steals of third (2)

Orlando Hudson

2003 Season

Defensively, Orlando Hudson established himself as a reliable second baseman who could become a standout at the position. Offensively, the switch-hitter batted primarily in the seventh and eighth holes in the batting order, faring very well against righthanders while batting .160 and slugging .190 against versus lefties. After a promising start at the plate, carrying a .294 average and .431 slugging mark through June, he struggled through a streaky July and August that included an eight-game hit streak and 14 straight hitless at-bats. It wasn't a productive second half.

Hitting

While Hudson hits liners to all fields, at this point the evidence suggests Hudson won't be a major League-caliber hitter from the right side. Either way, his on-base percentage must be elevated to fit the club's offensive strategy. In 2003, his strikeouts more than doubled his walk total. A fastball hitter, Hudson is most effective going with the pitch, spraying liners from gap to gap rather than attempting to pull the ball. Pitchers will dare him to hit the breaking stuff until he proves capable.

Baserunning & Defense

Hudson shows a steady glove and outstanding range at second base, particularly chasing pop flies down the right-field line and grounders into the hole. He'll also flag down grounders to his backhand side, behind second base. Formerly a Double-A third baseman, he's well equipped to turn the double play with a strong arm and quick feet. After making some costly blunders on the basepaths in his rookie season, Hudson settled down in 2003. His speed translates to basestealing potential, but the club doesn't emphasize the stolen base.

2004 Outlook

For now, Hudson's got a lock on the starting job at second base. Ideally he would hit leadoff or in the No. 2 hole, but he won't make the jump until showing more patience and consistent contact. In fact, without improvement in these areas, one day his job will be on the line.

Position: 2B
Bats: B **Throws:** R
Ht: 6' 0" **Wt:** 185

Opening Day Age: 26
Born: 12/12/77 in Darlington, SC
ML Seasons: 2

Overall Statistics

	G	AB	R	H	D	T	HR	RBI	SB	BB	SO	Avg	OBP	Slg
'03	142	474	54	127	21	6	9	57	5	39	87	.268	.328	.395
Car.	196	666	74	180	31	11	13	80	5	50	114	.270	.326	.408

Where He Hits the Ball

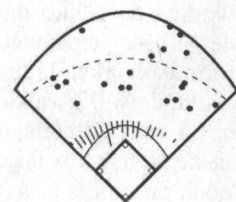
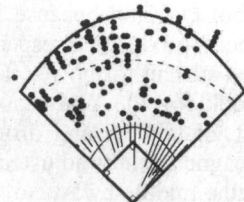

Vs. LHP	Vs. RHP

2003 Situational Stats

	AB	H	HR	RBI	Avg		AB	H	HR	RBI	Avg
Home	221	62	5	22	.281	LHP	100	16	0	4	.160
Road	253	65	4	35	.257	RHP	374	111	9	53	.297
First Half	284	80	5	36	.282	Sc Pos	125	38	1	45	.304
Scnd Half	190	47	4	21	.247	Clutch	54	12	0	1	.222

2003 Rankings (American League)

- 4th in fielding percentage at second base (.984)
- 5th in errors at second base (12)
- Led the Blue Jays in triples and caught stealing (4)

Bobby Kielty

2003 Season

Toronto traded left fielder Shannon Stewart and a player to be named for Bobby Kielty in mid-July. At the time, Minnesota had lost 22 of 28 games and Kielty was playing part-time. Stewart took over the leadoff slot and propelled the Twins into the playoffs. Kielty hit .233 with four homers in 61 games for Toronto. Overall, he averaged just .244, but Toronto general manager J.P. Ricciardi traded for his on-base percentage, which fell from .405 in 2002 to .358 last summer. Still, he ranked 15th in the American League in walks.

Hitting

A switch-hitter, Kielty has displayed patience, knowledge of the strike zone, power potential from both sides and an ability to get on base. A good fastball hitter, he's disciplined enough to lay off breaking balls. He fared better from the left side in his 2002 full-season debut, but was markedly better from the right side in 2003, which explains his dropoff in production. He batted .303 with a .417 OBP against righthanders in 2002.

Baserunning & Defense

Scrappy and versatile, Kielty is a solid, all-around player who can play all three outfield positions and first base. He has enough speed to handle center field, as well as the strong and accurate arm that is needed in right. Smart and aggressive on the basepaths, Kielty will take the extra base. Yet, he's never stolen many bases.

2004 Outlook

Why trade Stewart, a career .300 hitter, for Kielty? Stewart, a career-long Jay earning $6.2 million, was on the verge of free agency, though he wanted to stay in Toronto. Kielty, described as a blossoming Stewart type by Ricciardi, was making $325,000 in his third season. Despite the savings, the general manager wasted little time in moving Kielty to fill another need. In mid-November, Ricciardi dealt Kielty and a minor leaguer to be named to Oakland for lefthanded starter Ted Lilly. Kielty joins an outfield mix in Oakland that includes Jermaine Dye, Eric Byrnes and Mark Kotsay.

Position: RF/DH
Bats: B **Throws:** R
Ht: 6' 1" **Wt:** 225

Opening Day Age: 27
Born: 8/5/76 in Fontana, CA
ML Seasons: 3
Pronunciation: kell-tee

Overall Statistics

	G	AB	R	H	D	T	HR	RBI	SB	BB	SO	Avg	OBP	Slg
'03	137	427	71	104	26	1	13	57	8	71	92	.244	.358	.400
Car.	286	820	128	214	48	4	27	117	15	131	183	.261	.367	.428

Where He Hits the Ball

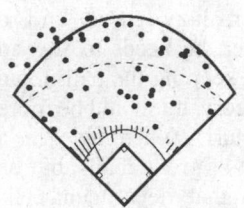
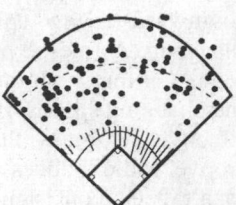

Vs. LHP	Vs. RHP

2003 Situational Stats

	AB	H	HR	RBI	Avg		AB	H	HR	RBI	Avg
Home	225	50	6	30	.222	LHP	140	42	8	27	.300
Road	202	54	7	27	.267	RHP	287	62	5	30	.216
First Half	238	60	9	32	.252	Sc Pos	109	31	3	45	.284
Scnd Half	189	44	4	25	.233	Clutch	55	12	3	15	.218

2003 Rankings (American League)

- 3rd in lowest batting average at home (.222)
- 6th in lowest batting average (.244)
- 9th in highest percentage of pitches taken (61.7)
- Led the Blue Jays in highest percentage of pitches taken (61.6)

Toronto

Cory Lidle

Position: SP
Bats: R **Throws:** R
Ht: 5'11" **Wt:** 192

Opening Day Age: 32
Born: 3/22/72 in Hollywood, CA
ML Seasons: 6
Pronunciation: LIE-dell

2003 Season

A year ago, the Jays picked up Corey Lidle in an offseason trade with Oakland. Through May it looked like a good move, with Lidle's 8-3 mark inspiring talk of an All-Star appearance. It was all downhill from there, as the righthander was 4-12 with a 6.87 ERA the rest of the way. By then, the Blue Jays were trying to unload Lidle via trade, but his midseason slump dampened interest. A groin strain in August put him on the disabled list for two weeks and he lost 11 of his final 13 decisions. He didn't help himself much, allowing hitters to bat .305 with runners in scoring position.

Pitching

Lidle's repertoire includes a sinking fastball, downward-tailing splitter, lazy curve and a changeup. A finesse pitcher, he needs to stay in control of the situation by keeping the ball down and changing speeds. In theory, he should be more effective on grass than turf. When he's in a groove, Lidle induces a lot of groundballs, but he hasn't been consistent in that department. His groundball-flyball ratio has ranged from 2.76 to 1.42. Because he depends on getting ahead in the count, batters look for his first pitch. They averaged .379 when they put his first pitch in play last year.

Defense

Lidle fields his position capably, managing to handle a fair number of balls hit in his direction. His move to first does little to stunt the running game. Basestealers were successful in 16 of 22 attempts against Lidle in 2003, and they enjoy a 66-percent success rate against him over his career.

2004 Outlook

Lidle made $5.65 million in the final year of his contract. The Jays didn't get much for their money and were unlikely to re-sign him, as they moved quickly to acquire Pat Hentgen and Ted Lilly early in the offseason. He'll be a No. 4-type pitcher in someone's rotation.

Overall Statistics

	W	L	Pct.	ERA	G	GS	Sv	IP	H	BB	SO	HR	Avg
'03	12	15	.444	5.75	31	31	0	192.2	216	60	112	24	.282
Car.	45	39	.536	4.42	181	104	2	756.0	785	197	461	84	.268

2003 Pitching Profile

	Cory Lidle	AL Average
Overall Strike %	62.8	62.8
1st Pitch Strike %	59.4	58.7
Ratio	1.43	1.39
Strikeouts per 9 IP	5.23	6.11
Walks per 9 IP	2.80	3.16
Home Runs per 9 IP	1.12	1.11
Strikeout/Walk Ratio	1.87	1.93
Groundball/Flyball Ratio	1.68	1.18

2003 Situational Stats

	W	L	ERA	Sv	IP		AB	H	HR	RBI	Avg
Home	4	9	5.84	0	101.2	LHB	427	113	11	61	.265
Road	8	6	5.64	0	91.0	RHB	338	103	13	55	.305
First Half	10	8	5.96	0	125.1	Sc Pos	187	57	7	89	.305
Scnd Half	2	7	5.35	0	67.1	Clutch	28	7	0	3	.250

2003 Rankings (American League)

- 1st in fielding percentage at pitcher (1.000), highest ERA and highest ERA at home
- 3rd in highest slugging percentage allowed (.467)
- 4th in fewest pitches thrown per batter (3.52)
- 5th in losses
- 6th in wild pitches (9) and highest ERA on the road
- 7th in highest groundball-flyball ratio allowed (1.7)
- 9th in highest batting average allowed (.282)
- 10th in stolen bases allowed (16)
- Led the Blue Jays in losses and wild pitches (9)

Josh Phelps

2003 Season

Josh Phelps didn't get as many at-bats as anticipated following a promising 2002 campaign in which he hit .309 with 15 homers and 58 RBI in 74 games. He didn't fare nearly as well against righthanded pitching last summer, and his high strikeout total discouraged a team stressing on-base percentage. Used primarily as a designated hitter, Phelps received only 67 at-bats in June and July, and hit .125 in the latter month. After fanning 61 times in 195 at-bats during April and May, he rebounded to bat .288 with nine homers, 31 RBI and a lower strikeout rate over the final two months.

Hitting

Keeping his swing tight and compact makes Phelps very dangerous, a power threat with 100-RBI potential. When overswinging, though, he is prone to the strikeout, which he recorded once in every 3.44 at-bats in 2003. His strength is up the middle and to the right-center power alley. Therefore, he looks for fastballs middle-out, and pitchers react by teasing him up and away before busting him inside. If his 2003 tendency plays out, he'll hit for a higher average against lefthanders and shows a bit more power against righties. Phelps likes the first-pitch fastball; in two seasons he has batted .411 when he puts the first pitch in play.

Baserunning & Defense

Phelps has minor league experience as a catcher, outfielder and first baseman. Originally, it appeared his future was behind the plate, but he's had elbow trouble and his footwork limited his success as a catcher. With a lack of range elsewhere in the field, Phelps appears best suited to a DH role. On the bases, Phelps runs well for his size but is slow off the mark.

2004 Outlook

Potentially, Phelps could fill the No. 5 hole in the Jays' batting order behind Carlos Delgado. As long as he can build on his first two extended looks in the big leagues, he should receive more at-bats in 2004 as the designated hitter, with occasional time at first spelling Delgado. Phelps also is viewed as an emergency third catcher.

Position: DH
Bats: R **Throws:** R
Ht: 6' 3" **Wt:** 220

Opening Day Age: 25
Born: 5/12/78 in Anchorage, AK
ML Seasons: 4

Overall Statistics

	G	AB	R	H	D	T	HR	RBI	SB	BB	SO	Avg	OBP	Slg
'03	119	396	57	106	18	1	20	66	1	39	115	.268	.358	.470
Car.	202	674	101	188	38	2	35	125	2	60	203	.279	.355	.497

Where He Hits the Ball

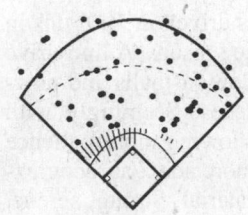 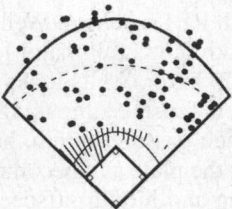

Vs. LHP   **Vs. RHP**

2003 Situational Stats

	AB	H	HR	RBI	Avg		AB	H	HR	RBI	Avg
Home	194	54	11	38	.278	LHP	145	46	7	20	.317
Road	202	52	9	28	.257	RHP	251	60	13	46	.239
First Half	252	66	10	32	.262	Sc Pos	118	33	6	48	.280
Scnd Half	144	40	10	34	.278	Clutch	38	11	3	11	.289

2003 Rankings (American League)

- 1st in highest percentage of swings that missed (31.8) and lowest percentage of swings put into play (35.0)
- 5th in hit by pitch (17)

Vernon Wells

2003 Season

In his second full season, Vernon Wells quietly played a Gold Glove-caliber center field and posted MVP-type offensive stats, highlighted by a major league-leading 215 hits, along with 33 homers, a .550 slugging percentage and an American League-best 373 total bases. The emerging star was more consistent than he was in 2002, his first full season as a major league regular, and he finished strong, batting .344 in August and September. Wells hit .340 when leading off an inning, .324 in close-and-late situations and .329 with runners in scoring position and two out. In short, a thoroughly outstanding season.

Hitting

An RBI machine, Wells has driven in 100 runs in both of his full major league seasons. A line-drive gap hitter, Wells looks for low fastballs and powders mistake breaking pitches. Seemingly with each passing month, he's showing more patience at the plate and becoming more adept at recognizing and hitting offspeed material. Strong, serene, cerebral and very disciplined, he studies pitchers by routine. In 2002, Wells hit .248 against pitchers during his first at-bat in a game, and improved as the game progressed. With an enhanced knowledge of AL pitchers, he averaged .336 in his first at-bats against pitchers last season.

Baserunning & Defense

A quick jump, gliding stride and good range allow Wells to track down balls hit into the gaps and over his head. What become highlight-video catches by ordinary center fielders, Wells turns into the routine. With above-average speed, Wells could develop into a 20-steal type if the Blue Jays encouraged stealing. He's a smart runner on the basepaths, taking the extra base when given.

2004 Outlook

Wells signed a five-year, $14.5 million contract prior to the 2003 season, a move he may come to regret as his star rises. He'll play center field on a daily basis and hit third in the Jays' batting order.

Position: CF
Bats: R **Throws:** R
Ht: 6' 1" **Wt:** 225

Opening Day Age: 25
Born: 12/8/78 in Shreveport, LA
ML Seasons: 5

Overall Statistics

	G	AB	R	H	D	T	HR	RBI	SB	BB	SO	Avg	OBP	Slg
'03	161	678	118	215	49	5	33	117	4	42	80	.317	.359	.550
Car.	377	1472	227	435	96	9	58	231	19	78	198	.296	.332	.491

Where He Hits the Ball

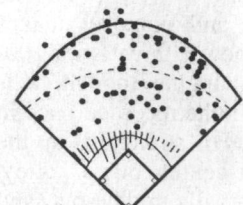 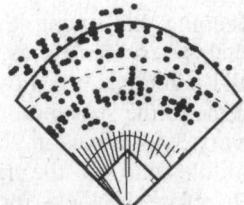

Vs. LHP   **Vs. RHP**

2003 Situational Stats

	AB	H	HR	RBI	Avg		AB	H	HR	RBI	Avg
Home	335	102	13	57	.304	LHP	173	60	4	26	.347
Road	343	113	20	60	.329	RHP	505	155	29	91	.307
First Half	405	121	23	84	.299	Sc Pos	187	58	9	80	.310
Scnd Half	273	94	10	33	.344	Clutch	74	24	5	17	.324

2003 Rankings (American League)

- 1st in hits, doubles, total bases (373) and plate appearances (735)
- 3rd in at-bats, runs scored, RBI and lowest fielding percentage in center field (.990)
- 4th in batting average, GDPs (21), games played and batting average on the road
- Led the Blue Jays in batting average, at-bats, runs scored, hits, singles, doubles, total bases (373), sacrifice flies (8), GDPs (21), plate appearances (735), games played, highest percentage of swings put into play (49.3), and steals of third (2)
- Led AL center fielders in batting average, home runs and RBI

Chris Woodward

2003 Season

After failing to make progress as a hitter and performing inconsistently as the Jays' shortstop, Chris Woodward lost his starting job to Mike Bordick in late July. Woodward started just 18 times after August 1 and sat on the bench through most of September with the club out of the playoff race. The Blue Jays stress on-base percentage and Woodward sinned by incurring nearly three times as many strikeouts as walks and posting a .316 OBP that was a dropoff from 2002. He had committed 17 errors when he was benched, which proved to be his final total and the fifth highest (tied) among American League shortstops.

Hitting

A 54th-round draft selection, Woodward overcame long odds by graduating to a starting position in 2002. He's fit, wiry and athletic with strong hands, contributing to above-average bat speed, which can produce surprising pop. Nonetheless, he can be overpowered up in the strike zone and is vulnerable to breaking stuff low and away. The book on Woodward still is being written. In 2002, he struggled against lefties, hitting .149, whereas last season he averaged .307 vs. lefties with 13 extra-base hits in 101 at-bats. Conversely, against righthanders, his on-base percentage (.298) and slugging percentage (.359) dropped significantly.

Baserunning & Defense

While getting on base enough is a concern, Woodward is a smart, fundamentally sound runner with good speed when he reaches. He is not a basestealer. Defensively, his range is not a strength, but he has an adequate arm and turns the double play crisply. Errors on routine grounders plagued him in 2003, and that's a matter he'll have to address to return to starting duties.

2004 Outlook

With Bordick announcing his retirement, Woodward has a lock on the starting job at short and likely will bat eighth or ninth in the order, barring an offseason acquisition. Toronto has two standout shortstop prospects, Russ Adams and Aaron Hill, but neither is expected to be ready before 2005.

Position: SS
Bats: R **Throws:** R
Ht: 6' 0"   **Wt:** 185

Opening Day Age: 27
Born: 6/27/76 in Covina, CA
ML Seasons: 5
Nickname: Woody

Toronto

Overall Statistics

	G	AB	R	H	D	T	HR	RBI	SB	BB	SO	Avg	OBP	Slg
'03	104	349	49	91	22	2	7	45	1	28	72	.261	.316	.395
Car.	282	854	123	214	46	8	25	111	5	67	192	.251	.305	.411

Where He Hits the Ball

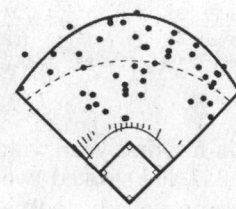

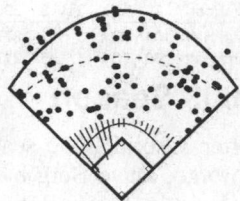

Vs. LHP   **Vs. RHP**

2003 Situational Stats

	AB	H	HR	RBI	Avg		AB	H	HR	RBI	Avg
Home	172	47	4	24	.273	LHP	101	31	2	16	.307
Road	177	44	3	21	.249	RHP	248	60	5	29	.242
First Half	265	71	6	34	.268	Sc Pos	102	26	0	31	.255
Scnd Half	84	20	1	11	.238	Clutch	40	10	1	3	.250

2003 Rankings (American League)

- 1st in lowest batting average with the bases loaded (.000)
- 5th in errors at shortstop (17)

Dave Berg

Position: 2B/3B
Bats: R **Throws:** R
Ht: 5'11" **Wt:** 185

Opening Day Age: 33
Born: 9/3/70 in
Roseville, CA
ML Seasons: 6

Overall Statistics

	G	AB	R	H	D	T	HR	RBI	SB	BB	SO	Avg	OBP	Slg
'03	61	161	26	41	6	1	4	18	0	11	34	.255	.301	.379
Car.	524	1446	177	391	87	6	18	140	8	129	281	.270	.333	.376

2003 Situational Stats

	AB	H	HR	RBI	Avg		AB	H	HR	RBI	Avg
Home	82	23	2	10	.280	LHP	79	24	3	14	.304
Road	79	18	2	8	.228	RHP	82	17	1	4	.207
First Half	101	28	3	13	.277	Sc Pos	44	8	1	12	.182
Scnd Half	60	13	1	5	.217	Clutch	19	1	0	1	.053

2003 Season

After a solid 2002 season in his first year with Toronto, Dave Berg batted .357 and stroked two homers in April. But his season quickly took a downturn. Berg began experiencing dizzy spells, and then he began suffering extreme fatigue after fielding no more than a dozen grounders. He missed all of July because of the strange malady, which no one ever was able to diagnose. He wasn't very productive the rest of the season, though he managed to hit another homer in August to tie his single-season career high of four.

Hitting, Baserunning & Defense

Berg is an aggressive slap hitter who generally enjoys more success against lefthanded pitchers. A selfless, adept situational hitter, committed to advancing runners, he'll take fastballs up the middle and to the opposite field. As long as he is healthy, Berg could play a long time, as he's become an extremely versatile player, able to handle first, second and third base, left and right field.

2004 Outlook

A healthy Berg should continue in a utility role or as a platoon player. The Jays have him under contract for 2004, so he'll be back to battle for playing time with players who are mostly much younger than he is.

Reed Johnson

Position: RF/LF
Bats: R **Throws:** R
Ht: 5'10" **Wt:** 180

Opening Day Age: 27
Born: 12/8/76 in
Riverside, CA
ML Seasons: 1

Overall Statistics

	G	AB	R	H	D	T	HR	RBI	SB	BB	SO	Avg	OBP	Slg
'03	114	412	79	121	21	2	10	52	5	20	67	.294	.353	.427
Car.	114	412	79	121	21	2	10	52	5	20	67	.294	.353	.427

2003 Situational Stats

	AB	H	HR	RBI	Avg		AB	H	HR	RBI	Avg
Home	199	55	6	29	.276	LHP	122	40	5	17	.328
Road	213	66	4	23	.310	RHP	290	81	5	35	.279
First Half	179	56	6	24	.313	Sc Pos	89	29	1	41	.326
Scnd Half	233	65	4	28	.279	Clutch	48	9	1	5	.188

2003 Season

Having been dropped from the 40-man roster the previous winter, Reed Johnson came out of nowhere to stake a claim to the Jays' leadoff spot. His rookie highlights included a 10th-inning walk-off homer versus the Cubs on June 15 and a 20-game hitting streak that began in late August. He struggled in mid-August, but then rebounded over the last five weeks of the season.

Hitting, Baserunning & Defense

Johnson is an aggressive gap hitter who has modest punch, but he can take pitches the other way. He needs to be more patient and draw more walks if he is going to succeed as a leadoff hitter. In his rookie season he fared poorly when falling behind in the count, indicating vulnerability to offspeed pitches. A good runner with basestealing potential, Johnson covers the gaps very well in the outfield and features a strong and accurate arm. Johnson can play either left or right field.

2004 Outlook

With the trade of Bobby Kielty to Oakland, Johnson should claim a starting corner-outfield job and hit first in the batting order. That is, if second baseman Orlando Hudson fails to claim the leadoff role in spring training. Johnson has an opportunity to become a franchise building block.

Jason Kershner

Position: RP
Bats: L **Throws:** L
Ht: 6' 2" **Wt:** 165

Opening Day Age: 27
Born: 12/19/76 in Scottsdale, AZ
ML Seasons: ?

Overall Statistics

	W	L	Pct.	ERA	G	GS	Sv	IP	H	BB	SO	HR	Avg
'03	3	3	.500	3.17	40	0	0	54.0	43	15	32	5	.217
Car.	3	4	.429	3.69	65	0	1	78.0	63	29	50	8	.218

2003 Situational Stats

	W	L	ERA	Sv	IP		AB	H	HR	RBI	Avg
Home	2	0	2.36	0	34.1	LHB	90	16	2	5	.178
Road	1	3	4.58	0	19.2	RHB	108	27	3	14	.250
First Half	0	1	3.24	0	16.2	Sc Pos	44	9	1	15	.205
Scnd Half	3	2	3.13	0	37.1	Clutch	52	14	2	7	.269

2003 Season

A 12th-round pick by the Phillies in 1995, and a Blue Jays waiver pickup from San Diego in August 2002, Jason Kershner appears to be a late bloomer. After struggling in Toronto in April, he excelled with Triple-A Syracuse in May and June, going 6-1 with a 2.36 ERA and just nine walks in 45.2 innings. He returned to Toronto and was more successful. For the season, Kershner held opponents to a .217 batting average.

Pitching & Defense

Kershner uses a fastball, change, screwball and a breaking ball that moves in on lefthanded hitters and successfully induces grounders. While his stuff is average, his repertoire makes him extraordinarily tough against lefthanded hitters. Kershner held them to .229 on-base percentage and four extra-base hits in 90 at-bats last season. Plus, the Jays learned he could be used effectively against righthanded hitters. Kershner also holds runners extremely well.

2004 Outlook

Kershner has become a regular member of Toronto's bullpen, with a chance to move into late-inning situations. His ability to bounce back and pitch on consecutive days is less certain, as his numbers have been better after two days' rest.

Aquilino Lopez

Position: RP
Bats: R **Throws:** R
Ht: 6' 3" **Wt:** 165

Opening Day Age: 28
Born: 4/21/75 in Villa Altagracia, DR
ML Seasons: 1
Pronunciation: aquil-LEENO

Overall Statistics

	W	L	Pct.	ERA	G	GS	Sv	IP	H	BB	SO	HR	Avg
'03	1	3	.250	3.42	72	0	14	73.2	58	34	64	5	.212
Car.	1	3	.250	3.42	72	0	14	73.2	58	34	64	5	.212

2003 Situational Stats

	W	L	ERA	Sv	IP		AB	H	HR	RBI	Avg
Home	1	0	2.38	7	41.2	LHB	112	28	4	16	.250
Road	0	3	4.78	7	32.0	RHB	161	30	1	15	.186
First Half	1	2	4.18	2	47.1	Sc Pos	73	12	1	24	.164
Scnd Half	0	1	2.05	12	26.1	Clutch	120	20	0	11	.167

2003 Season

A Rule 5 draftee from the Seattle organization, Aquilino Lopez moved from middle relief to setup man to closer by season's end. The lean righthander saved 14 games in 16 chances, including all 12 after the All-Star break. Despite his slight frame, Lopez proved durable and held hitters to a .212 batting average, striking out 7.82 hitters for every nine innings.

Pitching & Defense

Lopez relies on a slider to complement a low-90s fastball and changeup. He works aggressively, throws strikes and shows no fear of major league hitters. Lopez is learning to throw a splitter, which he needs to become more effective against lefties. As young as he is, the righthander was able to put away hitters after recording two strikes. He limited hitters to a .109 average on two-strike counts. He was nearly as stingy when the opposition put runners in scoring position. Nimble off the mound, Lopez fields his position adequately. Basestealers were a perfect 7-for-7 against him in 2003.

2004 Outlook

His role will be determined by Toronto's offseason moves. Lopez may start the new year as the Jays' closer. Or he may serve as a primary setup man if the club pursues a closer during the offseason.

Justin Miller

Position: SP
Bats: R **Throws:** R
Ht: 6' 2" **Wt:** 209

Opening Day Age: 26
Born: 8/27/77 in
Torrance, CA
ML Seasons: 1

Overall Statistics

	W	L	Pct.	ERA	G	GS	Sv	IP	H	BB	SO	HR	Avg
'03					Did Not Play								
Car.	9	5	.643	5.54	25	18	0	102.1	103	66	68	12	.268

2003 Situational Stats

	W	L	ERA	Sv	IP		AB	H	HR	RBI	Avg
Home	–	–	–	–	–	LHB	–	–	–	–	.–
Road	–	–	–	–	–	RHB	–	–	–	–	–
First Half	–	–	–	–	–	Sc Pos	–	–	–	–	–
Scnd Half	–	–	–	–	–	Clutch	–	–	–	–	–

2003 Season

A shoulder injury incurred by Justin Miller while lifting weights prior to the start of spring training required surgery, causing him to miss the entire year except for one appearance for high Class-A Dunedin. It was a disappointment to lose a young pitcher who debuted with nine wins in 2002. His ERA and walk rate weren't pretty during his rookie season, but he had improved and become more consistent late in the year.

Pitching & Defense

Prior to surgery, Miller showed mean stuff highlighted by late downward movement on his two-seam fastball. The pitch can induce a lot of grounders. His slider is another strong offering, but he lacks an out pitch for lefthanded hitters and sometimes gets into trouble in the first inning. Miller tends to get stronger as he moves deeper into games.

2004 Outlook

Acquired from Oakland with Eric Hinske in a December 2001 trade for Billy Koch, Miller had been penciled into the rotation last year. The club's thirst for pitching hasn't been quenched. If he's healthy, he may find work in the rebuilt Toronto rotation. After missing a year, he may need to start the season at Triple-A Syracuse.

Trever Miller

Position: RP
Bats: R **Throws:** L
Ht: 6' 4" **Wt:** 195

Opening Day Age: 30
Born: 5/29/73 in
Louisville, KY
ML Seasons: 5

Overall Statistics

	W	L	Pct.	ERA	G	GS	Sv	IP	H	BB	SO	HR	Avg
'03	2	2	.500	4.61	79	0	4	52.2	46	28	44	7	.231
Car.	7	8	.467	5.20	184	5	6	188.2	216	98	130	23	.286

2003 Situational Stats

	W	L	ERA	Sv	IP		AB	H	HR	RBI	Avg
Home	2	2	5.28	2	30.2	LHB	106	24	6	16	.226
Road	0	0	3.68	2	22.0	RHB	93	22	1	9	.237
First Half	1	1	5.01	0	32.1	Sc Pos	60	9	1	17	.150
Scnd Half	1	1	3.98	4	20.1	Clutch	83	17	2	11	.205

2003 Season

Lefthander Trever Miller played for four teams over four seasons between 1996 and 2000 before settling into Toronto last summer. He made a Dan Plesac-like 79 appearances, which was a career high and tops in the American League. His ERA dropped by more than a run in the second half, and he stranded 21 of his last 23 inherited runners. The hard-throwing lefty spiked his strikeouts per nine innings by posting a career-high 7.52 in 2003.

Pitching & Defense

While used most often to retire lefthanded hitters, Miller also was tough on righthanders after being torched by them early in his career. In fact, of the 12 extra-base hits allowed by Miller last year, righthanded hitters had just three of them, including only one homer. While he wasn't hurt by grounders on SkyDome's artificial turf, Miller was victimized by the longball at home.

2004 Outlook

Only once previously in his career had Miller pitched as effectively as he did in 2003—for Houston in 1998—and that was in fewer than half the games. With his improvement over the second half, Miller should work in middle-to-late relief. Look for him to be a workhorse in Toronto's pen, recording plenty of holds and the occasional save.

Greg Myers

Position: C/DH
Bats: L **Throws:** R
Ht: 6' 2" **Wt:** 225

Opening Day Age: 37
Born: 4/14/66 in
Riverside, CA
ML Seasons: 16

Overall Statistics

	G	AB	R	H	D	T	HR	RBI	SB	BB	SO	Avg	OBP	Slg
'03	121	329	51	101	19	0	15	52	0	37	57	.307	.374	.502
Car.	1094	3012	333	771	148	7	87	394	3	265	534	.256	.314	.396

2003 Situational Stats

	AB	H	HR	RBI	Avg		AB	H	HR	RBI	Avg
Home	161	45	8	23	.280	LHP	42	14	0	6	.333
Road	168	56	7	29	.333	RHP	287	87	15	46	.303
First Half	198	68	10	36	.343	Sc Pos	99	29	3	38	.293
Scnd Half	131	33	5	16	.252	Clutch	44	5	2	5	.114

2003 Season

After the Athletics declined a $1.1 million option for 2003, Greg Myers returned to his original team for $800,000 and enjoyed an amazing season for the Blue Jays. With the bat, he achieved the 100-hit mark for the first time in 16 seasons and posted career highs across the board. Myers enjoyed an especially hot first half, but he slid to a more typical second half as the Jays experimented with catcher-of-the-future Kevin Cash.

Hitting, Baserunning & Defense

Behind the plate, the journeyman catcher provides a young staff exactly what it needs—a solid defensive player with a strong arm and thorough knowledge of hitters and pitchers. Myers stays durable by keeping his body strong and lean. Traditionally Myers has been kept out of the lineup against lefties, but he hit .333 against them last season. Through 3,000 at-bats, he has become patient at the plate, waiting for fastballs or mistake breaking balls that he can pull or drive into the alleys. Myers is extraordinarily slow on the basepaths.

2004 Outlook

Toronto re-signed Myers to a one-year, $900,000 contract as a backup to Kevin Cash. If the weak-hitting Cash falters, look for Myers to get the bulk of the work behind the plate.

Cliff Politte

Position: RP
Bats: R **Throws:** R
Ht: 5'11" **Wt:** 185

Opening Day Age: 30
Born: 2/27/74 in St. Louis, MO
ML Seasons: 6
Pronunciation: po-LEET

Overall Statistics

	W	L	Pct.	ERA	G	GS	Sv	IP	H	BB	SO	HR	Avg
'03	1	5	.167	5.66	54	0	12	49.1	52	17	40	11	.269
Car.	13	17	.433	4.52	178	16	13	262.2	252	113	222	34	.253

2003 Situational Stats

	W	L	ERA	Sv	IP		AB	H	HR	RBI	Avg
Home	1	1	2.77	4	26.0	LHB	101	29	3	17	.287
Road	0	4	8.87	8	23.1	RHB	92	23	8	21	.250
First Half	1	5	6.42	11	33.2	Sc Pos	55	17	4	30	.309
Scnd Half	0	0	4.02	1	15.2	Clutch	92	26	7	23	.283

2003 Season

Following a 2002 campaign in which he was difficult to hit after joining the Jays via a trade, Cliff Politte was anointed the Jays' closer to start 2003. He saved nine games in 10 chances in May, but started coughing up runs in the middle of the month, posted a 13.03 ERA in June and lost the closer job to rookie Aquilino Lopez near midseason. He missed most of July with a shoulder strain, and finished the season with 12 saves and six blown saves.

Pitching & Defense

Last summer, Politte lost several MPH on his fastball, which is his best pitch. It was down considerably from 96 MPH, a radar reading that was routine in 2002. The righthander also mixes a change-up and a two-seamer with his out pitch, a hard, tight slider. He's very quick to the plate with a simple delivery, which should make him difficult to run on, but baserunners steal the occasional base. He fields his position adequately, though he's handled few chances in recent seasons.

2004 Outlook

Whether Politte regains his powerful fastball will determine his role and effectiveness in 2004. With it, he sets up or even closes. Without it, he's no more than a sixth- or seventh-inning guy.

Jayson Werth

Position: RF
Bats: R **Throws:** R
Ht: 6' 5" **Wt:** 215

Opening Day Age: 24
Born: 5/20/79 in Springfield, IL
ML Seasons: 2

Overall Statistics

	G	AB	R	H	D	T	HR	RBI	SB	BB	SO	Avg	OBP	Slg
'03	26	48	7	10	4	0	2	10	1	3	22	.208	.255	.417
Car.	41	94	11	22	6	1	2	16	2	9	33	.234	.298	.383

2003 Situational Stats

	AB	H	HR	RBI	Avg		AB	H	HR	RBI	Avg
Home	16	2	0	5	.125	LHP	18	1	0	4	.056
Road	32	8	2	5	.250	RHP	30	9	2	6	.300
First Half	41	9	2	9	.220	Sc Pos	19	5	1	9	.263
Scnd Half	7	1	0	1	.143	Clutch	3	0	0	0	.000

2003 Season

Jayson Werth injured his wrist taking batting practice in early March and lost valuable time to prepare for the season. The wrist hampered him into the season, and he was recalled by Toronto to fill needs because of injury, rather than when he was ready. Werth batted .237 in 64 games at Triple-A Syracuse, and he fared worse in Toronto. It wasn't the kind of season Werth anticipated.

Hitting, Baserunning & Defense

Despite his 6-foot-5 frame, Werth has been a contact hitter who didn't start tapping into his power until 2001 in Double-A ball. His power trend was slowed by his injured wrist last season. His plate discipline is promising, but he also struggles with a swing that sometimes gets long, and the strikeouts will mount. Werth was drafted as a catcher, but he's so athletic, has a good arm and runs well enough that he has made a seamless transition to the outfield. He's posted double-digit steals in Triple-A ball in 2002, so he can steal a base.

2004 Outlook

A healthier spring could mean better things for Werth. With Bobby Kielty traded to Oakland, the outfield shapes up as Reed Johnson, Vernon Wells and Frank Catalanotto as starters. Werth is in line for the fourth-outfielder spot.

Tom Wilson

Position: C/1B
Bats: R **Throws:** R
Ht: 6' 3" **Wt:** 220

Opening Day Age: 33
Born: 12/19/70 in Fullerton, CA
ML Seasons: 3

Overall Statistics

	G	AB	R	H	D	T	HR	RBI	SB	BB	SO	Avg	OBP	Slg
'03	96	256	37	66	19	0	5	35	0	28	80	.258	.331	.391
Car.	201	542	74	138	29	0	15	76	0	57	164	.255	.330	.391

2003 Situational Stats

	AB	H	HR	RBI	Avg		AB	H	HR	RBI	Avg
Home	131	35	2	14	.267	LHP	107	32	1	9	.299
Road	125	31	3	21	.248	RHP	149	34	4	26	.228
First Half	173	50	5	24	.289	Sc Pos	76	17	0	28	.224
Scnd Half	83	16	0	11	.193	Clutch	34	5	1	9	.147

2003 Season

A journeyman minor leaguer who made his big league debut with Oakland at age 30, Wilson has appeared in 96 games in each of the past two seasons with the Blue Jays. He bridged a gap to catching prospect Kevin Cash, who assumed the starting role late in the second half. After a solid start before the All-Star break, Wilson endured a career-high 17 at-bat hitless streak and a dramatic drop in performance after the break.

Hitting, Baserunning & Defense

Defensively, Wilson is very dependable and surehanded behind the plate, and he is accustomed to working with young pitchers. He has no more than an average arm. Wilson also has played first base and in the outfield. At the plate, Wilson fares much better against southpaws, posting career hitting percentages that are nearly 100 points higher than against righthanders. He can be overpowered with high fastballs. He showed potential as a pinch-hitter with a .438 average last season in 16 at-bats. Like many catchers, he is molasses on the basepaths.

2004 Outlook

With Cash in line to start, there may not be a place on the major league roster for Wilson. And with Greg Myers re-signed, Wilson's destination may be Triple-A Syracuse.

Other Toronto Blue Jays

Juan Acevedo (**Pos**: RHP, **Age**: 33)

	W	L	Pct.	ERA	G	GS	Sv	IP	H	BB	SO	HR	Avg
'03	1	5	.167	6.57	39	0	6	38.1	52	18	28	6	.319
Car.	28	40	.412	4.33	367	34	53	570.0	597	226	350	72	.274

Acevedo posted 28 saves and a 2.65 ERA for Detroit in 2002, priced himself out of town and struggled in the Yankees' pen last spring. By early August the Jays had cut him, too. The Pirates signed him in December. 2004 Outlook: C

Mike Bordick (**Pos**: SS/2B/3B, **Age**: 38, **Bats**: R)

	G	AB	R	H	D	T	HR	RBI	SB	BB	SO	Avg	OBP	Slg
'03	102	343	39	94	18	2	5	54	3	33	60	.274	.340	.382
Car.	1720	5770	676	1500	257	30	91	626	96	500	800	.260	.323	.362

In his first game with the Jays, Bordick's record errorless streak ended at 544 chances and 110 games. Still, it was a solid final season in the majors for Bordick, whose last hit gave him exactly 1,500 for his career. The defensive whiz has announced his retirement. 2004 Outlook: D

Brian Bowles (**Pos**: RHP, **Age**: 27)

	W	L	Pct.	ERA	G	GS	Sv	IP	H	BB	SO	HR	Avg
'03	0	0	—	2.57	5	0	0	7.0	8	2	2	1	.267
Car.	2	1	.667	3.23	24	0	0	30.2	25	17	25	1	.217

Bowles has been a fairly decent reliever at the Triple-A level the last three seasons, but his walk rate there stands in the way of major league success. Better control in the spring could go a long way. 2004 Outlook: C

Howie Clark (**Pos**: 3B, **Age**: 30, **Bats**: L)

	G	AB	R	H	D	T	HR	RBI	SB	BB	SO	Avg	OBP	Slg
'03	38	70	9	25	3	1	0	7	0	3	6	.357	.400	.429
Car.	52	123	12	41	8	1	0	11	0	6	12	.333	.383	.415

For a second straight season, Clark got a cup of coffee in the majors and made excellent contact, posting better hitting percentages than he did in Triple-A ball. He played all over the field for the Jays. 2004 Outlook: C

Doug Creek (**Pos**: LHP, **Age**: 35)

	W	L	Pct.	ERA	G	GS	Sv	IP	H	BB	SO	HR	Avg
'03	0	0	—	3.29	21	0	0	13.2	14	12	11	2	.264
Car.	7	14	.333	5.19	259	3	1	267.0	236	192	274	42	.238

Despite a respectable ERA, Creek continued to allow far too many baserunners to reach before an elbow problem arose in May. In June, he had Tommy John surgery and may be out until the second half. 2004 Outlook: C

Ken Huckaby (**Pos**: C, **Age**: 33, **Bats**: R)

	G	AB	R	H	D	T	HR	RBI	SB	BB	SO	Avg	OBP	Slg
'03	5	11	1	2	1	0	0	2	0	0	2	.182	.182	.273
Car.	94	285	30	69	7	1	3	24	0	9	47	.242	.265	.305

A 31-year-old rookie in 2002, Huckaby was valuable as a catcher who could help out until prospects Kevin Cash and Guillermo Quiroz arrive. After a slow 2003 start, he went to Syracuse and wasn't a factor. Texas signed him in November. 2004 Outlook: C

Doug Linton (**Pos**: RHP, **Age**: 39)

	W	L	Pct.	ERA	G	GS	Sv	IP	H	BB	SO	HR	Avg
'03	0	0	—	3.00	7	0	0	9.0	7	4	7	2	.226
Car.	17	20	.459	5.78	112	35	0	305.1	360	125	206	50	.294

Linton hadn't been seen in the majors since 1999, but he made the Jays in the spring, went to the minors in mid-April and turned in his poorest Triple-A season of the last three years. 2004 Outlook: C

Dan Reichert (**Pos**: RHP, **Age**: 27)

	W	L	Pct.	ERA	G	GS	Sv	IP	H	BB	SO	HR	Avg
'03	0	0	—	6.06	15	0	0	16.1	28	8	13	2	.389
Car.	21	25	.457	5.55	124	51	2	395.1	441	223	240	43	.290

The former Royals prospect pitched well in Tampa Bay's camp, but he was cut to save money. He signed with the Jays and came up a couple of times, but he doesn't appear to be in Toronto's long-term plans. 2004 Outlook: C

Scott Service (**Pos**: RHP, **Age**: 37)

	W	L	Pct.	ERA	G	GS	Sv	IP	H	BB	SO	HR	Avg
'03	0	2	.000	4.72	33	0	1	34.1	38	8	35	4	.281
Car.	19	21	.475	4.89	317	1	16	396.0	411	172	396	51	.271

Service surfaced in the majors for the first time since 2000 after pitching well in Triple-A ball in both 2002 and '03. At age 37, his major league return is likely to be brief. 2004 Outlook: C

Tanyon Sturtze (**Pos**: RHP, **Age**: 33)

	W	L	Pct.	ERA	G	GS	Sv	IP	H	BB	SO	HR	Avg
'03	7	6	.538	5.94	40	8	0	89.1	107	43	54	14	.296
Car.	29	39	.426	5.20	159	80	1	628.2	717	266	372	88	.291

Sturtze lost 18 games for the Rays in 2002, before anyone gave much thought to Mike Maroth. Still, the starter-turned-reliever posted a higher walk rate and ERA in the rebuilding Jays' pen in '03. 2004 Outlook: C

Jeff Tam (**Pos**: RHP, **Age**: 33)

	W	L	Pct.	ERA	G	GS	Sv	IP	H	BB	SO	HR	Avg
'03	0	4	.000	5.64	44	0	1	44.2	58	25	26	5	.314
Car.	7	14	.333	3.91	251	0	7	271.1	289	98	146	18	.277

Tam made the Jays' roster out of spring training, but he never pitched that effectively and was sent to Triple-A Syracuse in July. While he pitched well there, the Jays released him in September. 2004 Outlook: C

Corey Thurman (**Pos**: RHP, **Age**: 25)

	W	L	Pct.	ERA	G	GS	Sv	IP	H	BB	SO	HR	Avg
'03	1	1	.500	6.46	6	3	0	15.1	21	9	11	3	.313
Car.	3	4	.429	4.75	49	4	0	83.1	86	54	67	14	.261

The Jays played musical chairs with their rotation, and Thurman got his chance in August and struggled. He added a slider in 2003, as he needed a breaking pitch, and he'll be competing for a starting job this year. 2004 Outlook: C

Josh Towers (Pos: RHP, **Age**: 27)

	W	L	Pct.	ERA	G	GS	Sv	IP	H	BB	SO	HR	Avg
'03	8	1	.889	4.48	14	8	1	64.1	67	7	42	15	.266
Car.	16	14	.533	4.89	43	31	1	232.0	274	28	113	47	.297

Towers is a soft-tosser who climbed through the Orioles' system with good command of four pitches, but he struggled in Baltimore. A 4-0 September (3.06 ERA) against weak teams puts him in the Jays' mix. 2004 Outlook: C

Pete Walker (Pos: RHP, **Age**: 34)

	W	L	Pct.	ERA	G	GS	Sv	IP	H	BB	SO	HR	Avg
'03	2	2	.500	4.88	23	7	0	55.1	59	24	29	11	.277
Car.	13	7	.650	4.71	80	27	1	225.1	244	87	121	33	.280

Toronto acquired a 33-year-old Walker off waivers in May 2002, and he put himself in the Jays' plans with a 10-5 (4.33) season. Shoulder and knee problems derailed his 2003 season. He'll try again in '04. 2004 Outlook: C

John Wasdin (Pos: RHP, **Age**: 31)

	W	L	Pct.	ERA	G	GS	Sv	IP	H	BB	SO	HR	Avg
'03	0	1	.000	23.40	3	2	0	5.0	16	4	5	2	.533
Car.	31	30	.508	5.22	261	44	3	603.0	649	188	421	101	.274

In his first 2003 start, Wasdin worked a perfect game for Triple-A Nashville and set a team record with 15 strikeouts. He enjoyed a solid minor league season, but it didn't carry over to Toronto. The Rangers inked him to a minor league deal in October. 2004 Outlook: C

Toronto Blue Jays Minor League Prospects

Organization Overview:

The new regime under general manager J.P. Ricciardi has moved out the dead wood in the majors, filled some key spots in the Toronto lineup with young players, and stocked the system with college talent in the last couple of drafts. A host of talent is moving closer to Toronto. That includes Jason Arnold and John-Ford Griffin, who were acquired in trades, and Russ Adams and David Bush, two college players drafted in 2002. Perhaps most impressive are the power prospects in the outfield—Griffin, Gabe Gross and Alexis Rios—who were together at Double-A New Haven in 2003. And soon top pitching prospect Dustin McGowan and Yankees castoff Arnold will be ready to join the Jays' rotation.

Jason Arnold

Position: P
Bats: R **Throws:** R
Ht: 6' 3" **Wt:** 210

Opening Day Age: 24
Born: 5/2/79 in Melbourne, FL

Recent Statistics

	W	L	ERA	G	GS	Sv	IP	H	R	BB	SO	HR
2002 A Tampa	7	1	2.48	13	13	0	80.0	64	27	22	83	2
2002 AA Norwich	1	2	4.15	3	3	0	17.1	17	14	5	18	1
2002 AA Midland	5	1	2.33	10	10	0	58.0	42	22	24	53	2
2003 A New Haven	3	1	1.53	6	6	0	35.1	18	7	11	33	2
2003 AAA Syracuse	4	8	4.33	21	20	0	120.2	121	69	46	82	16

A 2001 pick by the Yankees, Arnold was dealt to Oakland the following summer in a three-team trade, and in December 2002, he was sent to Toronto in a four-team deal that moved Felipe Lopez to Cincinnati. He has succeeded with a deceptive motion, a 90-MPH fastball, a pair of palmballs and an advanced sense of setting up hitters. He limited them to a .153 average at Double-A New Haven before a jump to Triple-A Syracuse, where the going was rougher. Arnold lacks a dominating pitch and his velocity was down last summer, which can hurt a fastball-changeup guy, but his offspeed stuff was very good. More time in Syracuse is likely in 2004.

Kevin Cash

Position: C
Bats: R **Throws:** R
Ht: 6' 0" **Wt:** 185

Opening Day Age: 26
Born: 12/6/77 in Tampa, FL

Recent Statistics

	G	AB	R	H	D	T	HR	RBI	SB	BB	SO	Avg
2003 AAA Syracuse	93	326	37	88	28	2	8	37	1	29	81	.270
2003 AL Toronto	34	106	10	15	3	0	1	8	0	4	22	.142

Serving as an emergency fill-in at catcher in a Cape Cod League game in 1999 led to a contract and a catching career for the undrafted Cash. Now he's the best defensive catcher in the Toronto system, with excellent receiving skills, a terrific arm and improving game-calling skills. With his best tool, Cash threw out 50 per-cent of baserunners trying to steal at Triple-A Syracuse in 2003. Cash was a better hitter in his second go-round at Syracuse. Asked by the Jays to be more disciplined at the plate, Cash initially struggled, falling behind in the count by taking too many pitches, but he learned to be more patient without compromising his aggressiveness.

Vinnie Chulk

Position: P
Bats: R **Throws:** R
Ht: 6' 2" **Wt:** 195

Opening Day Age: 25
Born: 12/19/78 in Miami, FL

Recent Statistics

	W	L	ERA	G	GS	Sv	IP	H	R	BB	SO	HR
2003 AAA Syracuse	8	10	4.22	23	21	0	119.1	118	70	46	90	14
2003 AL Toronto	0	0	5.06	3	0	0	5.1	6	3	3	2	0

Drafted in 2000, Chulk quickly showed he could throw his pitches—fastball, slider, changeup and slurvy curveball—from three different arm slots. He favors a three-quarters slot that adds sink to his 92-94 MPH fastball. After a terrific 2002 at Double-A Tennessee, Chulk experienced a slight drop in velocity to start 2003 and wasn't as effective. His performance was better after missing four weeks with an elbow spur. Chulk credits Syracuse pitching coach Tom Filer for his second-half improvement. He learned how to attack hitters and use his improved changeup more effectively. The Jays believe Chulk may be better suited to the bullpen. He needs to work on his pitch location to reduce the number of mistake pitches he throws.

John-Ford Griffin

Position: OF
Bats: L **Throws:** L
Ht: 6' 2" **Wt:** 195

Opening Day Age: 24
Born: 11/19/79 in Sarasota, FL

Recent Statistics

	G	AB	R	H	D	T	HR	RBI	SB	BB	SO	Avg
2002 A Tampa	65	255	32	68	16	1	3	31	1	29	45	.267
2002 AA Norwich	18	67	17	22	3	0	5	10	0	8	13	.328
2002 AA Midland	2	7	0	1	0	0	0	0	0	0	3	.143
2003 AA New Haven	104	373	48	104	23	3	13	75	2	49	85	.279

A 23rd overall pick in 2001, Griffin also took the New York-Oakland route to Toronto. He went from the Yankees to Oakland in the three-team Jeff Weaver deal and moved to Toronto in January 2003. Griffin has advanced quickly with his sweet swing, terrific bat speed and his ability to make rapid adjustments at the plate. He suffered a stress fracture in his foot late in the 2003 season. Prior to the injury, he enjoyed a successful Double-A campaign in which he shortened his stroke, yet still showed more power. Griffin also showed more plate discipline. His defensive game is more consistent, but still needs work. A below-average arm limits him to left field or first base.

Gabe Gross

Position: OF   **Opening Day Age:** 24
Bats: L **Throws:** R   **Born:** 10/21/79 in
Ht: 6' 3" **Wt:** 209   Baltimore, MD

Recent Statistics

	G	AB	R	H	D	T	HR	RBI	SB	BB	SO	Avg
2002 AA Tennessee	112	403	57	96	17	5	10	54	8	53	71	.238
2003 AA New Haven	84	310	52	99	23	3	7	51	3	52	53	.319
2003 AAA Syracuse	53	182	22	48	16	2	5	23	1	31	56	.264

Drafted 15th overall in 2001, Gross adjusted quickly to the wood bat and batted .302 with a .426 OBP in his 2001debut at high Class-A Dunedin. He struggled at Double-A Tennessee in 2002. He maintained his solid strike-zone judgment, but didn't enjoy much payoff at the end of at-bats. Gross was more aggressive and successful with the count in his favor in 2003. He doesn't always drive the ball authoritatively, but he shows pop the other way and power potential. He runs and throws well in the field, but he's still learning to get better jumps and take better routes.

Dustin McGowan

Position: P   **Opening Day Age:** 22
Bats: R **Throws:** R   **Born:** 3/24/82 in
Ht: 6' 3" **Wt:** 190   Savannah, GA

Recent Statistics

	W	L	ERA	G	GS	Sv	IP	H	R	BB	SO	HR
2002 A Chrlstn (WV)	11	10	4.19	28	28	0	148.1	143	77	59	163	10
2003 A Dunedin	5	6	2.85	14	14	0	75.2	62	29	25	66	1
2003 AA New Haven	7	0	3.17	14	14	0	76.2	78	28	19	72	1

A first-rounder in 2000, McGowan has a great pitcher's body, a plus arm and power stuff. He was downright wild in his first two pro seasons, and inconsistent command and delivery remained issues in 2002. His fastball command improved late in 2002, setting the stage for his breakout in 2003. McGowan was stellar at both high Class-A Dunedin and Double-A New Haven, combining for a 12-6 record and 3.01 ERA. He exhibited better command and poise, hitting his spots and pitching inside effectively. He also applied what he was learning about setting up hitters. McGowan refined his slider, which was an out pitch for him. Both his 95-96 MPH fastball and sinker had good life, and he showed good arm action on his changeup.

Guillermo Quiroz

Position: C   **Opening Day Age:** 22
Bats: R **Throws:** R   **Born:** 11/29/81 in
Ht: 6' 1" **Wt:** 195   Maracaibo, VZ

Recent Statistics

	G	AB	R	H	D	T	HR	RBI	SB	BB	SO	Avg
2002 A Dunedin	111	411	50	107	28	1	12	68	1	35	91	.260
2002 AAA Syracuse	13	45	7	10	4	0	1	6	0	3	14	.222
2003 AA New Haven	108	369	63	104	27	0	20	79	0	45	83	.282

Signed in 1998, Quiroz quickly showed his athleticism and agility behind the plate. His receiving skills and his handling of pitchers are impressive, and with his plus-plus arm he threw out 44 percent of baserunners trying to steal at Double-A New Haven in 2003. His bat had been far behind his glove, but some plate patience and power began to emerge in 2002 before he broke through with a big 2003 at New Haven. He had a better approach to breaking balls and started to hit the ball hard the other way. He's had summers with a few good months, but last year he hit well all season long and posted career-best hitting percentages. He suffered a collapsed lung near the end of the season and missed the first round of the Eastern League playoffs.

Alexis Rios

Position: OF   **Opening Day Age:** 23
Bats: R **Throws:** R   **Born:** 2/18/81 in Coffee,
Ht: 6' 5" **Wt:** 178   AL

Recent Statistics

	G	AB	R	H	D	T	HR	RBI	SB	BB	SO	Avg
2002 A Dunedin	111	456	60	139	22	8	3	61	14	27	55	.305
2003 AA New Haven	127	514	86	181	32	11	11	82	11	39	85	.352

The Jays took heat for drafting Rios as a less-costly first-rounder in 1999, but today they view him as a potential star with five-tool talent. The wiry 6-foot-5 Rios connects with a short, quick stroke that promises more power. Last summer that stroke produced a Double-A Eastern League batting title and MVP honors. Rios solidified his approach at the plate at New Haven. He improved at hitting breaking balls, and he now successfully drives the ball the other way. He might have hit more homers with New Haven, but it's a long poke to left and center fields to drive the ball out of his home park. Defensively, Rios is sound with above-average speed and arm strength, and at his current size he can play all three spots.

Others to Watch

The Jays' first-rounder in 2002, shortstop **Russ Adams** (23) successfully handled playing a demanding position well up the developmental ladder in his first full season as a pro. The budding leadoff hitter posted a .365 OBP between high Class-A Dunedin and Double-A New Haven. . . The Jays' second pick in 2002, righthander **David Bush** (24) followed Adams on a rapid rise to Double-A New Haven. He was a dominating closer at short-season Auburn in 2002, featuring a low-90s fastball and mid-80s slider, and he went 14-6 (2.79) as a starter between Dunedin and New Haven in 2003. . . After a less-than-stellar senior season at the University of Richmond, first baseman **Vito Chiaravalloti** (23), a 15th-round pick last summer, took it to the short-season New York-Penn League. He won the Triple Crown with a .351-12-67 campaign and led the circuit in all three hitting percentages. He's a deep-count hitter with quick hands and an efficient swing.

National League Players

Bank One Ballpark

Offense

The combination of the majors' second-highest altitude plus warm air makes Bank One Ballpark a good hitters' park. The ball carries better with the roof open, because that raises the temperature. The roof is typically closed—and the park air-conditioned—from sometime in May or early June through late September. Even then, the fences are reachable from gap to line, especially in left field. Center field is spacious.

Defense

A good center fielder is key, since there is a large area to cover and the potential of tricky caroms off the overhangs. The corner outfielders, especially in left, will have chances to take home runs away. The dirt plays true, but later in the season—as the roof is closed more and less sunlight reaches the grass—the sod will get loose and can come out in large divots in the outfield.

Who It Helps the Most

Shea Hillenbrand, a line-drive hitter, now has balls leave the park instead of hitting Boston's Green Monster. Historically Steve Finley has been better at BOB than on the road. Almost all pitchers' ERAs go up at BOB, but groundball pitchers Brandon Webb and Elmer Dessens should be less affected, at least in theory. Dessens had a significantly better ERA at home in 2003.

Who It Hurts the Most

Webb posted a 3.43 home ERA that was more than a run worse than his road mark (2.27), and he gave up more than twice as many doubles in roughly the same number of innings. Luis Gonzalez struggled at home last year, but did not have such wide splits in previous seasons.

Rookies & Newcomers

Richie Sexson has enjoyed hitting at BOB, batting .378 with six homers, 16 RBI and an .867 slugging mark in 12 games. John Patterson, a fly-ball pitcher, would seem to be hurt by Bank One Ballpark. The same could be true for Casey Fossum, the lefty acquired from Boston, who was a severe flyball pitcher in 2003.

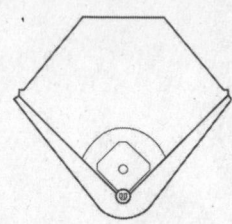

Dimensions: LF-330, LCF-374, CF-407, RCF-374, RF-334

Capacity: 49,033

Elevation: 1090 feet

Surface: Grass

Foul Territory: Average

Park Factors

2003 Season

	Home Games Dbacks	Opp	Total	Away Games Dbacks	Opp	Total	Index
G	75	75	150	72	72	144	
Avg	.273	.253	.263	.247	.244	.245	107
AB	2521	2608	5129	2514	2383	4897	101
R	365	349	714	264	280	544	126
H	689	659	1348	620	582	1202	108
2B	150	144	294	113	100	213	132
3B	27	15	42	16	7	23	174
HR	73	79	152	69	65	134	108
BB	276	241	517	217	239	456	108
SO	448	605	1053	479	578	1057	95
E	44	41	85	52	44	96	85
E-Infield	33	37	70	45	36	81	83
LHB-Avg	.281	.288	.284	.256	.245	.251	113
LHB-HR	32	38	70	40	25	65	104
RHB-Avg	.265	.230	.244	.236	.244	.240	102
RHB-HR	41	41	82	29	40	69	113

2001-2003

	Home Games Dbacks	Opp	Total	Away Games Dbacks	Opp	Total	Index
G	222	222	444	216	216	432	
Avg	.280	.253	.266	.249	.242	.246	108
AB	7453	7762	15215	7577	7103	14680	101
R	1188	1011	2199	933	833	1766	121
H	2088	1963	4051	1889	1716	3605	109
2B	416	385	801	357	297	654	118
3B	69	51	120	47	21	68	170
HR	254	265	519	228	198	426	118
BB	875	647	1522	746	640	1386	106
SO	1325	1817	3142	1470	1712	3182	95
E	126	136	262	128	147	275	93
E-Infield	109	112	221	113	126	239	90
LHB-Avg	.290	.273	.283	.262	.252	.258	110
LHB-HR	128	110	238	132	82	214	110
RHB-Avg	.269	.242	.253	.234	.235	.235	108
RHB-HR	126	155	281	96	116	212	125

2003 Rankings (National League)

- Highest LHB batting-average factor
- Second-highest run factor
- Second-highest double factor
- Second-highest walk factor
- Third-highest batting-average factor
- Third-highest hit factor
- Third-highest triple factor
- Second-lowest infield-error factor

Bob Brenly

2003 Season

Having gone to the playoffs in each of Bob Brenly's first two seasons, the Diamondbacks picked up his $1 million option for 2004 just before last season opened. When injuries struck over the first half of the season, Brenly won praise for keeping the club in the race with a group of youngsters known as the "Baby 'Backs." Arizona was still in the hunt in mid-August, but then faded to finish third in the NL West.

Offense

Brenly moves players in and out and up and down daily, depending on matchups and who is hot or cold. He plays the "hot hand" often, leaving a player in the lineup if he plays well. Brenly has good timing in calling for the hit-and-run and would likely steal more often if he had a roster with more speed. With a lack of power, manufacturing runs will be emphasized this year.

Pitching & Defense

The "hot hand" also applies to pitchers, and those who are on a roll in relief will be used frequently. This can lead to some troubling usage patterns, with relievers working three or more days in a row. Brenly will stay with his top two starters (Randy Johnson and Brandon Webb) for long pitch counts and skip a starter to keep them pitching every fifth day. On occasion Brenly will use his closer for more than three outs, but prefers to have him start the ninth inning.

2004 Outlook

Management was upset with the team's poor fundamentals in 2003 (sloppy defense, bad baserunning), which resulted in a shakeup of the coaching staff. That seemed to send a message that Brenly is on the hot seat. The team could not afford to eat his $1 million salary, but a slow start or continued dissatisfaction from management (or inside the clubhouse) could lead to a midseason change.

Born: 2/25/54 in Coshocton, OH

Playing Experience: 1981-1989, SF, Tor

Managerial Experience: 3 seasons

Manager Statistics

Year	Team, Lg	W	L	Pct	GB	Finish
2003	Arizona, NL	84	78	.519	16.5	3rd West
3 Seasons		274	212	.564	–	–

2003 Starting Pitchers by Days Rest

	<=3	4	5	6+
Diamondbacks Starts	1	100	20	30
Diamondbacks ERA	–	3.78	4.47	3.79
NL Avg Starts	2	84	43	23
NL ERA	5.00	4.23	4.42	4.68

2003 Situational Stats

	Bob Brenly	NL Average
Hit & Run Success %	32.3	32.7
Stolen Base Success %	66.7	68.9
Platoon Pct.	62.0	52.0
Defensive Subs	10	19
High-Pitch Outings	7	8
Quick/Slow Hooks	19/6	20/12
Sacrifice Attempts	92	93

2003 Rankings (National League)

- 1st in starting lineups used (145)
- 2nd in pitchouts (47), pitchouts with a runner moving (9) and intentional walks (43)
- 3rd in one-batter pitcher appearances (49)

Arizona

Miguel Batista

2003 Season

Miguel Batista was passed over for the Diamondbacks' rotation in spring training but was soon in a starting role when Oscar Villarreal was deemed more suitable for relief. With the injuries to Curt Schilling and Randy Johnson, Batista led the staff in innings pitched, tied for the lead in wins and was in the NL's top 10 in ERA until late in the season. Fatigue seemed to catch up to him late in the year, and he posted a 5.76 ERA in his final eight starts.

Pitching

With good movement on all his pitches, Batista can be hard to hit, but he also can struggle with the strike zone. His four-seam fastball can hit 94 MPH and bores in on a righthanded hitter. He throws an 86-88 MPH slider to righthanders and has a curve and split-finger pitch. But at times he gets away from offspeed stuff and relies too much on his fastball and cut fastball. He's a groundball pitcher and difficult to go deep against.

Defense & Hitting

Batista fields the ball well but sometimes struggles with quick decisions, such as which base to throw to. He uses a slide step delivery with men on base, making it harder to steal against him. At the plate, Batista overswings and thus makes little contact—although he will occasionally hit a ball far.

2004 Outlook

Arizona declined a $5 million option on Batista but was attempting to re-sign him to a less costly deal. Batista hit the free-agent market at the peak of his career, and had one of the lower 2003 ERAs among available starters. During the winter meetings, the righthander agreed to a three-year, $13.1 million contract with the Blue Jays. He joins a rebuilt Toronto rotation that now includes ace Roy Halladay and recent arrivals Pat Hentgen and Ted Lilly.

Position: SP
Bats: R **Throws:** R
Ht: 6' 1" **Wt:** 197

Opening Day Age: 33
Born: 2/19/71 in Santo Domingo, DR
ML Seasons: 9
Pronunciation: bah-TEESE-tah

Overall Statistics

	W	L	Pct.	ERA	G	GS	Sv	IP	H	BB	SO	HR	Avg
'03	10	9	.526	3.54	36	29	0	193.1	197	60	142	13	.267
Car.	42	50	.457	4.39	254	121	1	902.0	903	384	602	84	.264

2003 Pitching Profile

	Miguel Batista	NL Average
Overall Strike %	63.7	62.4
1st Pitch Strike %	61.6	58.4
Ratio	1.33	1.38
Strikeouts per 9 IP	6.61	6.65
Walks per 9 IP	2.79	3.42
Home Runs per 9 IP	0.61	1.05
Strikeout/Walk Ratio	2.37	1.94
Groundball/Flyball Ratio	2.04	1.29

2003 Situational Stats

	W	L	ERA	Sv	IP		AB	H	HR	RBI	Avg
Home	6	2	3.87	0	88.1	LHB	347	103	6	40	.297
Road	4	7	3.26	0	105.0	RHB	390	94	7	42	.241
First Half	6	4	3.00	0	108.0	Sc Pos	186	48	4	63	.258
Scnd Half	4	5	4.22	0	85.1	Clutch	39	9	0	5	.231

2003 Rankings (National League)

- 4th in fewest home runs allowed per nine innings (.61)
- 5th in highest groundball-flyball ratio allowed (2.0)
- 6th in fewest pitches thrown per batter (3.51)
- 7th in runners caught stealing (8)
- 8th in lowest stolen-base percentage allowed (50.0)
- 10th in GDPs induced (22), lowest ERA on the road, errors at pitcher (3) and lowest fielding percentage at pitcher (.932)
- Led the Diamondbacks in wins, losses, innings pitched, batters faced (822), pickoff throws (103), runners caught stealing (8), GDPs induced (22), lowest stolen-base percentage allowed (50.0) and fewest pitches thrown per batter (3.51)

Alex Cintron

2003 Season

Alex Cintron was one of the Diamondbacks' final cuts in spring training, losing out to Carlos Baerga in the competition for a backup infield spot. But in early May, with Tony Womack struggling and Craig Counsell out with a thumb injury, Cintron was recalled from Triple-A Tucson, where he was batting .393. When Womack suffered a knee injury in late June, Cintron took over as the every-day shortstop and never looked back. He finished the season playing like a legitimate star, batting .341 in August and September while committing only one error in his final 31 games.

Hitting

Stronger than when he first came up, Cintron no longer has the bat knocked out of his hands by a good fastball. He has power from both sides of the plate and is an especially potent hitter early in the count. While a fine hitter from either side of the plate, he's much more dangerous from the right side. He seldom draws a walk, but he also doesn't strike out very often. With his pop and ability to handle the bat, he was especially effective as a No. 2 hitter last year.

Baserunning & Defense

Cintron has average range but an above-average arm at shortstop. He is athletic for his size and, with his height, can go up to spear grounders. Cintron has good instincts and good hands. He has the speed to leg out triples and doubles but has to develop his stolen-base skills.

2004 Outlook

Cintron proved last year that, at the very least, he can be an everyday shortstop who contributes offensively. And if he keeps playing like he did late in the year, his upside could be a good deal higher than that. He will be one of the corner-stones as the Diamondbacks continue to make the transition to a younger, homegrown team.

Position: SS/3B
Bats: B **Throws:** R
Ht: 6' 2" **Wt:** 199

Opening Day Age: 25
Born: 12/17/78 in Humacao, PR
ML Seasons: 3
Pronunciation: SIN-tron

Overall Statistics

	G	AB	R	H	D	T	HR	RBI	SB	BB	SO	Avg	OBP	Slg
'03	117	448	70	142	26	6	13	51	2	29	33	.317	.359	.489
Car.	163	530	81	160	32	7	13	55	2	41	46	.302	.352	.462

Where He Hits the Ball

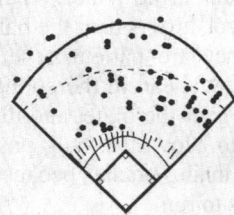
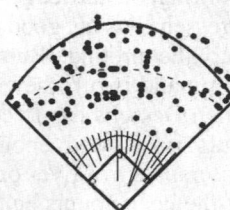

Vs. LHP   **Vs. RHP**

2003 Situational Stats

	AB	H	HR	RBI	Avg		AB	H	HR	RBI	Avg
Home	198	68	6	27	.343	LHP	137	50	5	19	.365
Road	250	74	7	24	.296	RHP	311	92	8	32	.296
First Half	200	60	7	26	.300	Sc Pos	106	33	2	37	.311
Scnd Half	248	82	6	25	.331	Clutch	82	25	3	9	.305

2003 Rankings (National League)

- 6th in batting average vs. lefthanded pitchers
- 8th in batting average with two strikes (.275)
- 9th in triples
- Led the Diamondbacks in batting average, highest percentage of swings put into play (51.6), batting average vs. lefthanded pitchers, batting average at home and batting average with two strikes (.275)

Elmer Dessens

2003 Season

Acquired from Cincinnati in a four-team deal that sent Erubiel Durazo to Oakland, Elmer Dessens was trumpeted as the No. 3 starter the team had always sought. And while Dessens led the team in starts, over the second half he was treated as the No. 5 starter—his turn skipped whenever there was an off day in the schedule. After winning three games in April, Dessens posted only one win in each month the rest of the way. He finished the year with a hideous 7.40 ERA in September.

Pitching

Dessens throws a 90-93 MPH sinking fastball, a cut fastball and a slider, and is best when he is working on the edges of the strike zone. When Dressens has his good control, hitters beat the ball into the ground. But if they are patient or his command is off, they can get ahead in the count. Then Dessens has to come over the plate, and his stuff isn't good enough to blow the ball past hitters. He is a five- or six-inning pitcher because of the deep counts he tends to run.

Defense & Hitting

Dessens is a good hitter for a pitcher and a very good bunter. He can even hit an occasional gapper. He also fields his position well, an important attribute for a groundball pitcher. His slide step delivery makes him tough to run on.

2004 Outlook

Dessens vowed to work on his stamina during the offseason so he could go deeper into games. But with his style, he needs to nibble and thus can get to 100 pitches pretty quickly. Dessens is signed for $4 million this year (with a 2005 option). Ideally he should fall to the back end of Arizona's rotation, where he would be a decent fit, but with the Curt Schilling trade, Dessens currently slots behind Randy Johnson and Brandon Webb. If the Diamondbacks complete the rotation with youngsters, Dessens may be slotted higher than he should be.

Position: SP
Bats: R **Throws:** R
Ht: 5'10" **Wt:** 198

Opening Day Age: 33
Born: 1/13/71 in Hermosillo, Mexico
ML Seasons: 7
Pronunciation: duh-SENZ

Overall Statistics

	W	L	Pct.	ERA	G	GS	Sv	IP	H	BB	SO	HR	Avg
'03	8	8	.500	5.07	34	30	0	175.2	212	57	113	22	.299
Car.	38	43	.469	4.46	199	118	1	809.0	908	234	477	100	.287

2003 Pitching Profile

	Elmer Dessens	NL Average
Overall Strike %	61.4	62.4
1st Pitch Strike %	59.6	58.4
Ratio	1.53	1.38
Strikeouts per 9 IP	5.79	6.65
Walks per 9 IP	2.92	3.42
Home Runs per 9 IP	1.13	1.05
Strikeout/Walk Ratio	1.98	1.94
Groundball/Flyball Ratio	1.60	1.29

2003 Situational Stats

	W	L	ERA	Sv	IP		AB	H	HR	RBI	Avg
Home	6	4	4.47	0	94.2	LHB	332	121	12	50	.364
Road	2	4	5.78	0	81.0	RHB	376	91	10	49	.242
First Half	5	6	5.13	0	112.1	Sc Pos	170	50	2	67	.294
Scnd Half	3	2	4.97	0	63.1	Clutch	24	9	1	4	.375

2003 Rankings (National League)

- 1st in fielding percentage at pitcher (1.000)
- 2nd in highest batting average allowed (.299), highest ERA on the road and highest batting average allowed vs. lefthanded batters
- 5th in balks (2), highest on-base percentage allowed (.354) and highest ERA at home
- 7th in hits allowed and highest ERA
- 8th in highest slugging percentage allowed (.459)
- Led the Diamondbacks in sacrifice bunts (10), games started, hits allowed, home runs allowed, balks (2) and pitches thrown (2,905)

Steve Finley

Position: CF
Bats: L **Throws:** L
Ht: 6' 2" **Wt:** 194

Opening Day Age: 39
Born: 3/12/65 in Union City, TN
ML Seasons: 15

2003 Season

Steve Finley got off to his typical slow start and then wound up with his typical final statistics. He was hottest in June and July, then went through another slump in August before finishing solidly. With no one else on the roster well-suited to hitting first, Finley batted leadoff for most of the final month. Finley became the oldest player in the past 30 years, other than Otis Nixon in 1997-98, to play 100 or more games in center field. He also was the oldest player to lead his league in triples since Tommy Henrich in 1948.

Hitting

Finley always has been a streak hitter, with prolonged hot and cold spells. He is no longer the 30-homer-a-year guy he was a few seasons ago, but he's still capable of hitting 20-plus, as he did in 2002-03. Unlike many lefthanded hitters, he feasts on high fastballs. Finley is basically a pull hitter, especially on groundballs. When he hits a ball in the gap, he has the speed to leg out extra-base hits.

Baserunning & Defense

Despite his age, Finley is still an above-average outfielder, although not quite as good as his Gold Glove form of earlier years. He gets good jumps and thus runs down balls without flashy dives. His arm strength is average but his accuracy is above average. Finley still can steal bases when asked to and was 4-for-4 on steal attempts when used in the leadoff spot in 2003.

2004 Outlook

Finley has another year on his contract and has full no-trade protection. He figures to be Arizona's regular center fielder, and his dedication to fitness should keep his age from being an issue. Manager Bob Brenly has said if no other options present themselves, Finley could go into the season as the Diamondbacks' leadoff hitter.

Overall Statistics

G	AB	R	H	D	T	HR	RBI	SB	BB	SO	Avg	OBP	Slg
147	516	82	148	24	10	22	70	15	57	94	.287	.363	.500
2127	7843	1235	2166	377	108	249	977	296	703	1087	.276	.337	.447

Where He Hits the Ball

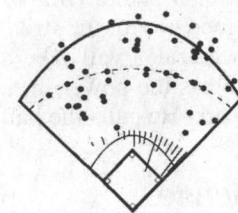
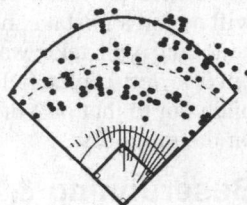

Vs. LHP   **Vs. RHP**

2003 Situational Stats

	AB	H	HR	RBI	Avg		AB	H	HR	RBI	Avg
Home	249	74	10	36	.297	LHP	163	40	7	25	.245
Road	267	74	12	34	.277	RHP	353	108	15	45	.306
First Half	289	89	15	47	.308	Sc Pos	130	33	9	51	.254
Scnd Half	227	59	7	23	.260	Clutch	107	34	5	12	.318

2003 Rankings (National League)

- 1st in triples
- 3rd in errors in center field (5) and lowest fielding percentage in center field (.982)
- 5th in lowest stolen-base percentage (65.2)
- 6th in lowest percentage of swings on the first pitch (16.8)
- Led the Diamondbacks in triples, stolen bases, caught stealing (8), fewest GDPs per GDP situation (6.4%) and on-base percentage for a leadoff hitter (.373)

Arizona

Luis Gonzalez

2003 Season

While the team's offensive problems made it seem that Luis Gonzalez had an off year, he actually improved in virtually every category from 2002. He came within one of his career high in doubles, had more than 100 RBI for the fifth straight season and cut down on his strikeouts. Overall it was a more than satisfactory fifth season in Arizona for Gonzalez, who has had more hits since 1999 than any National League player except for Todd Helton.

Hitting

More than in the past, Gonzalez is susceptible to lefthanders' breaking balls. He is also more vulnerable to inside pitches than before. But he will pound a mistake, has a good eye for the strike zone and will take walks. Gonzalez will take a pitch to left-center field and has the power hit a pitch out to that part of the park. He pulls the ball on the ground.

Baserunning & Defense

Gonzalez plays a deep left field, enabling him to go back on balls and sometimes take home runs away at Bank One Ballpark' short fence. The downside is that loopers will sometimes drop in front of him. An MRI after last season revealed a partially torn ligament in Gonzalez' right elbow, so his throwing—which improved some in the middle of last season—again might be a major liability. He is a smart baserunner with average speed, but not much of a threat to steal.

2004 Outlook

This season begins Gonzalez' three-year, $30 million contract extension, and he has trade-veto power. There is some nervousness about his elbow, since he could potentially face season-ending surgery if the ligament doesn't heal. If healthy he will be counted on again as a middle-of-the-order hitter, though he needs a true power bat behind him so he doesn't have to press for RBIs, especially against lefthanded pitchers.

Position: LF
Bats: L **Throws:** R
Ht: 6' 2" **Wt:** 200

Opening Day Age: 36
Born: 9/3/67 in Tampa, FL
ML Seasons: 14

Overall Statistics

G	AB	R	H	D	T	HR	RBI	SB	BB	SO	Avg	OBP	Slg
156	579	92	176	46	4	26	104	5	94	67	.304	.402	.532
1903	6808	1060	1959	430	58	275	1124	115	843	913	.288	.370	.489

Where He Hits the Ball

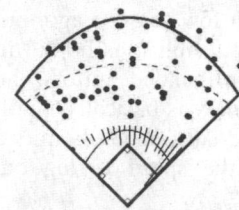
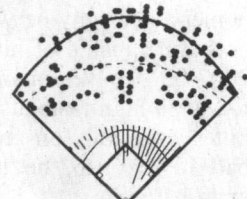

Vs. LHP   **Vs. RHP**

2003 Situational Stats

	AB	H	HR	RBI	Avg		AB	H	HR	RBI	Avg
Home	284	75	6	43	.264	LHP	220	49	8	30	.223
Road	295	101	20	61	.342	RHP	359	127	18	74	.354
First Half	352	109	18	67	.310	Sc Pos	148	50	5	70	.338
Scnd Half	227	67	8	37	.295	Clutch	93	29	4	19	.312

2003 Rankings (National League)

- 1st in batting average vs. righthanded pitchers
- 2nd in batting average on the road
- 3rd in lowest batting average vs. lefthanded pitchers
- 4th in intentional walks (17) and lowest percentage of swings on the first pitch (15.9)
- 5th in fielding percentage in left field (.989)
- Led the Diamondbacks in home runs, at-bats, runs scored, hits, singles, doubles, total bases (308), RBI, walks, intentional walks (17), times on base (273), GDPs (19), pitches seen (2,644), plate appearances (679), games played, slugging percentage, on-base percentage, batting average vs. righthanded pitchers and batting average on the road
- Led NL left fielders in RBI

Shea Hillenbrand

2003 Season

With Arizona in need of offense in late May, it sent righthander Byung-Hyun Kim to Boston for Shea Hillenbrand, a local product who was installed as the team's third baseman (Matt Williams was designated for assignment). After missing three weeks with an oblique muscle strain, Hillenbrand shifted to first base when Lyle Overbay was sent down, and spent most of the rest of the season at that position. He proved to be a very streaky hitter, but wound up with 17 homers and 59 RBI in 85 games with the Diamondbacks—about what they were expecting when they traded for him.

Hitting

Hillenbrand has a level, short swing, meaning he can hit flat strikes and mistake pitches. He is mostly a gap hitter, but the move to Bank One Ballpark helped his home-run numbers. Hillenbrand makes good contact but doesn't draw many walks. His career rate of one walk every 28 plate appearances is the second-worst figure among active players (minimum 1,500 PA).

Baserunning & Defense

Although Hillenbrand has good hands, his bad footwork leads to errors and throwing problems. Having changed positions throughout his professional career, he has not come close to mastering any position. Hillenbrand may never be nimble, but with improved footwork he might be capable at third base. He is an average runner but no threat to steal.

2004 Outlook

Hillenbrand has a strong work ethic, which may help him become an average defender at first or third. His role has been solidified with Arizona's acquisition of first baseman Richie Sexson from Milwaukee on December 1. Hillenbrand's salary starts to climb rapidly beginning this year because of arbitration. That could tempt the Diamondbacks to trade him; if he stays, he will spend a majority of the 2004 season at third base.

Position: 1B/3B
Bats: R **Throws:** R
Ht: 6' 1" **Wt:** 211

Opening Day Age: 28
Born: 7/27/75 in Mesa, AZ
ML Seasons: 3
Pronunciation: SHAY

Overall Statistics

	G	AB	R	H	D	T	HR	RBI	SB	BB	SO	Avg	OBP	Slg
'03	134	515	60	144	35	1	20	97	1	24	70	.280	.314	.468
Car.	429	1617	206	453	98	7	50	229	8	62	226	.280	.314	.442

Where He Hits the Ball

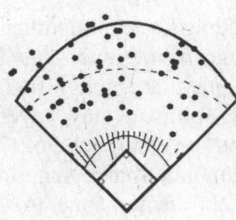
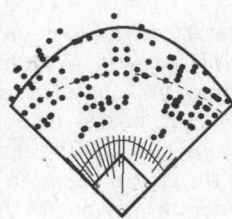

Vs. LHP	Vs. RHP

2003 Situational Stats

	AB	H	HR	RBI	Avg		AB	H	HR	RBI	Avg
Home	243	68	11	57	.280	LHP	161	48	6	32	.298
Road	272	76	9	40	.279	RHP	354	96	14	65	.271
First Half	269	85	9	59	.316	Sc Pos	154	44	5	75	.286
Scnd Half	246	59	11	38	.240	Clutch	82	24	0	10	.293

2003 Rankings (National League)

- 9th in lowest cleanup slugging percentage (.506)
- Led the Diamondbacks in sacrifice flies (5) and HR frequency (19.4 ABs per HR)

Arizona

Randy Johnson

2003 Season

After securing a career-high 24 wins and receiving his fourth straight National League Cy Young Award in 2002, Randy Johnson went through one of the toughest seasons of his career in 2003. After missing 12 weeks while recovering from arthroscopic surgery to remove cartilage from his right knee, Johnson never reached the form of his previous four seasons. He suffered through his first losing season since 1992 and posted his highest ERA since his rookie season of 1989. Johnson never won more than two decisions in a row, but in his final four outings, he was 2-1 with a 2.17 ERA.

Pitching

The stability of Johnson's landing knee is important to his delivery. With his large frame, even small errors in Johnson's mechanics are magnified, resulting in loss of control. Johnson may never throw 98-100 MPH again, but he can reach 96-97 at times. He needs to regain his sharp, snappy slider, which breaks from the strike zone to a righthanded hitter's shoetops. If his arm drops, his slider spins and is easily hit. Johnson also uses a split-finger pitch as a changeup, sometimes 10-20 pitches a game.

Defense & Hitting

Switching to a heavy bat borrowed from Raul Mondesi over his final three games last year, Johnson hit his first career homer and went 4-for-8. Perhaps that improvement will continue. Johnson is an awkward fielder who will settle for the easy out on a ball he gets to. He has only a token pickoff move and can be run on easily.

2004 Outlook

Johnson knows his knee will need constant maintenance and plans to get more lubricating injections before spring training begins. His motivation should be as high as ever after last year, and he needs to re-establish his intimidating persona. Johnson begins a two-year, $33 million extension this season and has a full no-trade clause.

Position: SP
Bats: R **Throws:** L
Ht: 6'10" **Wt:** 231

Opening Day Age: 40
Born: 9/10/63 in Walnut Creek, CA
ML Seasons: 16
Nickname: Big Unit

Overall Statistics

W	L	Pct.	ERA	G	GS	Sv	IP	H	BB	SO	HR	Avg
6	8	.429	4.26	18	18	0	114.0	125	27	125	16	.280
230	114	.669	3.10	454	444	2	3122.1	2435	1258	3871	283	.215

2003 Pitching Profile

	Randy Johnson	NL Average
Overall Strike %	66.8	62.4
1st Pitch Strike %	62.6	58.4
Ratio	1.33	1.38
Strikeouts per 9 IP	9.87	6.65
Walks per 9 IP	2.13	3.42
Home Runs per 9 IP	1.26	1.05
Strikeout/Walk Ratio	4.63	1.94
Groundball/Flyball Ratio	1.39	1.29

2003 Situational Stats

	W	L	ERA	Sv	IP		AB	H	HR	RBI	Avg
Home	4	5	4.37	0	68.0	LHB	66	20	3	9	.303
Road	2	3	4.11	0	46.0	RHB	380	105	13	47	.276
First Half	1	2	6.94	0	23.1	Sc Pos	123	36	3	41	.293
Scnd Half	5	6	3.57	0	90.2	Clutch	13	2	1	1	.154

2003 Rankings (National League)

- Led the Diamondbacks in stolen bases allowed (13)

Matt Mantei

2003 Season

After spending 2002 working his way back from reconstructive elbow surgery, Matt Mantei got his closer's job back last year (Byung-Hyun Kim was moved to the rotation and eventually traded). Although Mantei missed a month with shoulder trouble, and pitched through the problem the final three months of the season, he had in many regards the best year of his career. His 29 saves were the second most in his career, and from July 1 to the end of the season, Mantei was 22-for-23 in save opportunities while posting a 1.42 ERA with a minuscule opponents' batting average of only .150.

Pitching

Once just a hard thrower, Mantei has added a curve and slider to his 96-97 MPH fastball. Hitters, gearing up for the hard stuff, almost always will take the breaking pitches. But because Mantei can throw them for strikes, he will use the curve and slider (89-90 MPH) with a two-strike count for a called strikeout.

Defense & Hitting

As a closer, Mantei rarely bats. His delivery doesn't usually leave him in good position to field the ball, but he can handle comebackers fine. He is relatively easy to steal on, but is seldom in a situation where opposing runners will risk a steal attempt.

2004 Outlook

Because Mantei has such a violent delivery, and because he brings the ball back with his wrist facing the pitcher, he will always be susceptible to injury. But when healthy, he can be considered an elite closer, more so than ever since he now has a second and third pitch to go with his fastball. Mantei exercised a $7 million player option for 2004 but would be tempting for budget-conscious Arizona to trade, since Jose Valverde and prospect Brian Bruney are closers in waiting.

Position: RP
Bats: R **Throws:** R
Ht: 6' 1" **Wt:** 198

Opening Day Age: 30
Born: 7/7/73 in Tampa, FL
ML Seasons: 8
Pronunciation: MAN-tie

Overall Statistics

	W	L	Pct.	ERA	G	GS	Sv	IP	H	BB	SO	HR	Avg
'03	5	4	.556	2.62	50	0	29	55.0	37	18	68	6	.191
Car.	13	15	.464	3.56	269	0	89	285.2	209	170	361	24	.204

2003 Pitching Profile

	Matt Mantei	NL Average
Overall Strike %	64.7	62.4
1st Pitch Strike %	58.2	58.4
Ratio	1.00	1.38
Strikeouts per 9 IP	11.13	6.65
Walks per 9 IP	2.95	3.42
Home Runs per 9 IP	0.98	1.05
Strikeout/Walk Ratio	3.78	1.94
Groundball/Flyball Ratio	0.77	1.29

2003 Situational Stats

	W	L	ERA	Sv	IP		AB	H	HR	RBI	Avg
Home	3	2	2.86	14	28.1	LHB	84	13	4	6	.155
Road	2	2	2.36	15	26.2	RHB	110	24	2	8	.218
First Half	4	3	3.62	10	27.1	Sc Pos	34	3	1	9	.088
Scnd Half	1	1	1.63	19	27.2	Clutch	140	24	5	13	.171

2003 Rankings (National League)

- 3rd in most strikeouts per nine innings in relief (11.1) and fewest GDPs induced per GDP situation (2.9%)
- 6th in save percentage (90.6)
- 7th in saves
- 9th in fewest baserunners allowed per nine innings in relief (9.3)
- Led the Diamondbacks in saves, games finished (44), lowest batting average allowed vs. lefthanded batters and save percentage (90.6)

Raul Mondesi

2003 Season

Raul Mondesi began the 2003 season with the Yankees, but after he took exception to being removed for a pinch-hitter and left Fenway Park in mid game, New York gladly traded him to Arizona. The Diamondbacks were desperate for offense as the trade deadline approached and installed Mondesi as their regular right fielder. The veteran responded, hitting .302 in 45 games for the Diamondbacks. He finished the year strongly, with four homers and 11 RBI in his final eight games.

Hitting

Mondesi is a dead fastball hitter. He is susceptible to sliders from righthanders and pitchers who change speeds well. His power isn't what it once was but he is capable of hitting 20 home runs. Mondesi's RBI totals are low because he can be pitched to with men in scoring position. In those situations, he chases pitches out of the strike zone and gets himself out.

Baserunning & Defense

Long known for his strong throwing arm, Mondesi still has a gun. But he has a tendency to rush throws and thus be off line. While Mondesi has decent speed, he at times will attempt to steal in ill-advised situations, perhaps cutting short a rally. While he stole 22 bases for the year, he was only 5-for-9 after joining the Diamondbacks.

2004 Outlook

After failing to make the playoffs, Arizona isn't expected to re-sign Mondesi for 2004. Despite his decent performance for the Diamondbacks, his next contract will be closer to $1 million than the $13 million-per-year deal he just finished. Mondesi, who had run-ins with managers in his previous three stops, pleased the Diamondbacks with his behavior. Perhaps a one-year deal somewhere would give Mondesi motivation, and some team could get a Reggie Sanders-type payoff.

Position: RF
Bats: R **Throws:** R
Ht: 5'11" **Wt:** 230

Opening Day Age: 33
Born: 3/12/71 in San Cristobal, DR
ML Seasons: 11
Pronunciation: MON-de-see

Overall Statistics

G	AB	R	H	D	T	HR	RBI	SB	BB	SO	Avg	OBP	Slg
143	523	83	142	31	4	24	71	22	56	97	.272	.343	.484
1450	5539	882	1527	303	48	264	828	229	450	1064	.276	.333	.491

Where He Hits the Ball

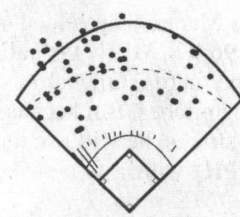
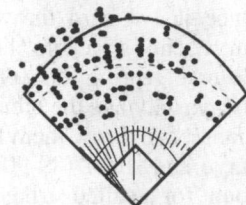

Vs. LHP   **Vs. RHP**

2003 Situational Stats

	AB	H	HR	RBI	Avg		AB	H	HR	RBI	Avg
Home	269	79	14	43	.294	LHP	122	32	5	18	.262
Road	254	63	10	28	.248	RHP	401	110	19	53	.274
First Half	329	85	14	44	.258	Sc Pos	151	23	4	41	.152
Scnd Half	194	57	10	27	.294	Clutch	75	21	4	14	.280

2003 Rankings (National League)

- Led the Diamondbacks in cleanup slugging percentage (.600)

Curt Schilling

2003 Season

Curt Schilling missed two weeks in April and May due to an appendectomy. Then he missed another six weeks, including all of June, when San Diego's Sean Burroughs hit a liner off his right hand and broke two bones. Otherwise—despite his win-loss record –Schilling was his usual self. He was 4-0 in six starts when the Diamondbacks scored more than three runs for him, but the Diamondbacks scored fewer than three runs with Schilling on the mound in 14 of his starts, including nine straight at one point.

Pitching

Schilling will throw 92-93 MPH through much of the game, but can dial it up to 95-97 MPH when he needs to in a key count or big situation. He will try to get ahead of the hitter and then—more so than ever—use a tumbling split-finger pitch to get a strikeout. Schilling also likes to use the up-and-away four-seam fastball to get hitters out, but perhaps because of QuesTec-influenced umpiring, he did not get the pitch called for him last year. He also will throw a handful of big, slow curveballs a game, usually trying to get a called strike.

Defense & Hitting

With a quick delivery to the plate, Schilling is good at keeping runners from stealing. He is an average hitter and fielder for a pitcher and a decent bunter—better in all three phases than he showed last year.

2004 Outlook

In the final season of a three-year extension he received when he was traded to Arizona, Schilling is scheduled to make $12 million in 2004. With the Diamondbacks facing a budget crunch, he waived his no-trade clause and accepted a late-November trade to Boston. Schilling was dealt for Brandon Lyon, Casey Fossum and minor leaguers Michael Goss and Jorge De La Rosa. To get the deal done, the righthander and the Red Sox worked out a two-year extension for a reported $25.5 million, which would carry through the 2006 season. Schilling will be part of a trio of righthanded aces that includes Pedro Martinez and Derek Lowe.

Position: SP
Bats: R **Throws:** R
Ht: 6' 5" **Wt:** 235

Opening Day Age: 37
Born: 11/14/66 in Anchorage, AK
ML Seasons: 16
Pronunciation: SHILL-ing

Overall Statistics

W	L	Pct.	ERA	G	GS	Sv	IP	H	BB	SO	HR	Avg
8	9	.471	2.95	24	24	0	168.0	144	32	194	17	.230
163	117	.582	3.33	450	338	13	2586.0	2286	603	2542	263	.236

2003 Pitching Profile

	Curt Schilling	NL Average
Overall Strike %	69.6	62.4
1st Pitch Strike %	68.6	58.4
Ratio	1.05	1.38
Strikeouts per 9 IP	10.39	6.65
Walks per 9 IP	1.71	3.42
Home Runs per 9 IP	0.91	1.05
Strikeout/Walk Ratio	6.06	1.94
Groundball/Flyball Ratio	1.05	1.29

2003 Situational Stats

	W	L	ERA	Sv	IP		AB	H	HR	RBI	Avg
Home	1	6	3.69	0	85.1	LHB	278	71	7	26	.255
Road	7	3	2.18	0	82.2	RHB	348	73	10	28	.210
First Half	4	4	3.27	0	77.0	Sc Pos	127	29	6	40	.228
Scnd Half	4	5	2.67	0	91.0	Clutch	45	10	1	5	.222

2003 Rankings (National League)

- 1st in highest strikeout-walk ratio (6.1), errors at pitcher (5) and lowest fielding percentage at pitcher (.808)
- 2nd in lowest on-base percentage allowed (.270), lowest ERA on the road, fewest walks per nine innings (1.7) and least run support per nine innings (3.8)
- 3rd in most strikeouts per nine innings (10.4)
- 4th in shutouts (2)
- 5th in ERA and strikeouts
- 7th in complete games (3)
- Led the Diamondbacks in losses, complete games (3), shutouts (2), strikeouts, highest strikeout-walk ratio (6.1), lowest on-base percentage allowed (.270), lowest stolen-base percentage allowed (50.0), most strikeouts per nine innings (10.4), and fewest walks per nine innings (1.7)

Junior Spivey

Traded To BREWERS

2003 Season

Junior Spivey was the Diamondbacks' second baseman and No. 3 hitter on Opening Day, but he was hitting just .255 when he suffered a torn ligament is his left ankle in mid-June. After missing a month, Spivey returned to split time with rookie Matt Kata. He never again got his average better than .266 and finished the season striking out in 16 of his final 45 at-bats. It was a big comedown for a player who had batted .301 and made the National League All-Star team in 2002.

Hitting

Spivey is a mistake hitter with the power to hit 15-20 homers a year. But he often tries too hard to play the role of slugger, resulting in overswinging and strikeouts. He is best when he attempts to hit the ball to right-center and the middle of the field instead of pulling it; then his power comes naturally. Spivey always has had success against lefthanded pitching.

Baserunning & Defense

In the field, Spivey has excellent range—especially on balls hit in the air—and a strong arm. But his hands are stiff, making it hard for him to turn a double play as quickly as most top second basemen. At times he will rush his throws, resulting in errors. Spivey has great speed but has yet to develop into a consistent basestealing threat.

2004 Outlook

Spivey hasn't been the same player since the first half of 2002, when he was hitting .328 with 46 RBI at the All-Star break. If he returns to a shorter swing, he could recover his success. Meanwhile, Kata's development has made Spivey and his sizeable contract ($2,367,500 for 2004) expendable, and the Diamondbacks traded him, fellow infielder Craig Counsell, first baseman Lyle Overbay, catcher Chad Moeller and left-handers Chris Capuano and Jorge De La Rosa to Milwaukee for Richie Sexson and two minor leaguers, lefty Shane Nance and a player to be named. Spivey is likely to take over at second base in Milwaukee if his contract isn't moved elsewhere by the Brewers' front office.

Position: 2B
Bats: R **Throws:** R
Ht: 6' 0" **Wt:** 201

Opening Day Age: 29
Born: 1/28/75 in Oklahoma City, OK
ML Seasons: 3
Pronunciation: spy-VEE

Overall Statistics

	G	AB	R	H	D	T	HR	RBI	SB	BB	SO	Avg	OBP	Slg
'03	106	365	52	93	22	2	13	50	4	33	95	.255	.326	.433
Car.	321	1066	188	297	62	11	34	149	18	121	242	.279	.363	.453

Where He Hits the Ball

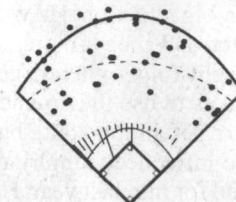 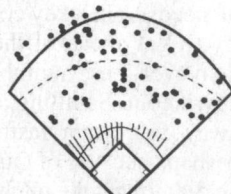

Vs. LHP   **Vs. RHP**

2003 Situational Stats

	AB	H	HR	RBI	Avg		AB	H	HR	RBI	Avg
Home	204	60	10	31	.294	LHP	125	36	5	19	.288
Road	161	33	3	19	.205	RHP	240	57	8	31	.238
First Half	204	52	9	30	.255	Sc Pos	90	23	4	34	.256
Scnd Half	161	41	4	20	.255	Clutch	73	15	1	8	.205

2003 Rankings (National League)

- 8th in errors at second base (8)
- Led the Diamondbacks in hit by pitch (7), strikeouts and batting average with the bases loaded (.429)

Brandon Webb

2003 Season

Brandon Webb impressed Diamondbacks manager Bob Brenly in spring training, but was not called up until Randy Johnson went on the disabled list in late April. Webb struck out 10 in seven shutout innings in his first major league start against the Mets on April 27, was sent down after the game when Johnson was activated, and returned for good May 1 when Johnson went down again. Webb proceeded to make a strong case for Rookie of the Year honors, with 21 quality starts (out of 28), while leading all rookie pitchers with 172 strikeouts. He was only 3-7 after the All-Star break, but lack of run support was a major factor.

Pitching

Webb's sinker is so good that hitters have trouble with it when they know it's coming. He throws the pitch 88-91 MPH with live, late action that makes it difficult for hitters to elevate the ball. Although Webb throws his sinkers 70 percent of the time or more—he does not use a four-seam fastball—he also has two other above-average pitches from his over-the-top delivery: a straight changeup he will throw to lefthanded and righthanded hitters, and a curve.

Defense & Hitting

With a relatively quick delivery to the plate, Webb holds runners well. He also fields his position adeptly, a necessity considering how many grounders he gives up. Webb is not a good hitter but is a capable bunter.

2004 Outlook

Besides his stuff, Webb showed excellent poise in his first season in the majors. There is no reason to believe his success will not continue, and he seems to have a durable build. Webb's emergence as a top-of-the-rotation pitcher allowed Arizona to trim its budget by trading righthanded ace Curt Schilling to Boston.

Position: SP
Bats: R **Throws:** R
Ht: 6' 2" **Wt:** 228

Opening Day Age: 24
Born: 5/9/79 in Ashland, KY
ML Seasons: 1

Overall Statistics

	W	L	Pct.	ERA	G	GS	Sv	IP	H	BB	SO	HR	Avg
'03	10	9	.526	2.84	29	28	0	180.2	140	68	172	12	.212
Car.	10	9	.526	2.84	29	28	0	180.2	140	68	172	12	.212

2003 Pitching Profile

	Brandon Webb	NL Average
Overall Strike %	62.3	62.4
1st Pitch Strike %	59.6	58.4
Ratio	1.15	1.38
Strikeouts per 9 IP	8.57	6.65
Walks per 9 IP	3.39	3.42
Home Runs per 9 IP	0.60	1.05
Strikeout/Walk Ratio	2.53	1.94
Groundball/Flyball Ratio	3.44	1.29

2003 Situational Stats

	W	L	ERA	Sv	IP		AB	H	HR	RBI	Avg
Home	5	4	3.43	0	89.1	LHB	335	86	10	35	.257
Road	5	5	2.27	0	91.1	RHB	324	54	2	20	.167
First Half	7	2	2.41	0	97.0	Sc Pos	161	33	2	38	.205
Scnd Half	3	7	3.33	0	83.2	Clutch	30	4	1	1	.133

2003 Rankings (National League)

- 1st in lowest slugging percentage allowed (.307), highest groundball-flyball ratio allowed (3.4) and ERA among rookies
- 2nd in lowest batting average allowed vs. righthanded batters and losses among rookies
- 3rd in lowest batting average allowed (.212), lowest ERA on the road and fewest home runs allowed per nine innings (.60)
- 4th in ERA, hit batsmen (13) and wins among rookies
- 6th in most strikeouts per nine innings (8.6)
- Led the Diamondbacks in wins, losses, walks allowed, hit batsmen (13), wild pitches (9), lowest batting average allowed (.212), lowest slugging percentage allowed (.307), highest groundball-flyball ratio allowed (3.4), lowest ERA at home, lowest batting average allowed vs. righthanded batters and lowest batting average allowed with runners in scoring position

Arizona

Rod Barajas

Position: C
Bats: R **Throws:** R
Ht: 6' 2" **Wt:** 220

Opening Day Age: 28
Born: 9/5/75 in Ontario, CA
ML Seasons: 5
Pronunciation: bar-AH-hoss

Overall Statistics

	G	AB	R	H	D	T	HR	RBI	SB	BB	SO	Avg	OBP	Slg
'03	80	220	19	48	15	0	3	28	0	14	43	.218	.265	.327
Car.	211	509	44	108	29	0	11	66	1	29	99	.212	.257	.334

2003 Situational Stats

	AB	H	HR	RBI	Avg		AB	H	HR	RBI	Avg
Home	106	24	3	16	.226	LHP	41	10	1	6	.244
Road	114	24	0	12	.211	RHP	179	38	2	22	.212
First Half	134	31	2	20	.231	Sc Pos	53	17	0	24	.321
Scnd Half	86	17	1	8	.198	Clutch	44	13	2	6	.295

2003 Season

Rod Barajas began the year sharing catching duties with Chad Moeller, and as Curt Schilling's designated catcher. Barajas missed most of July with tendinitis in his left wrist and split time over the last two months with rookie Robby Hammock. His modest .218 average was about on par with the rest of his career, but Barajas did hit well in clutch situations.

Hitting, Baserunning & Defense

Basically a dead pull hitter, Barajas looks for pitches from the middle in. He can be pitched to on the outer third of the plate, but miss inside and he can hit a home run or hook a double into the corner. He can hit a slow breaking ball but can be retired on sharper ones. A good defender, Barajas has a quick release and strong arm behind the plate. He is also adept at blocking pitches in the dirt. He is a slow runner.

2004 Outlook

Questions about Hammock's durability should continue to give Barajas 70-80 games behind the plate. His defensive ability and occasional power make him a valuable piece if not a front-liner.

Danny Bautista

Position: RF/CF
Bats: R **Throws:** R
Ht: 5'11" **Wt:** 225

Opening Day Age: 31
Born: 5/24/72 in Santo Domingo, DR
ML Seasons: 11
Pronunciation: BAW-tee-sta

Overall Statistics

	G	AB	R	H	D	T	HR	RBI	SB	BB	SO	Avg	OBP	Slg
'03	88	284	29	78	16	3	4	36	3	21	50	.275	.330	.394
Car.	754	1978	253	531	94	18	51	254	31	114	343	.268	.310	.412

2003 Situational Stats

	AB	H	HR	RBI	Avg		AB	H	HR	RBI	Avg
Home	142	34	2	21	.239	LHP	101	27	1	11	.267
Road	142	44	2	15	.310	RHP	183	51	3	25	.279
First Half	173	45	1	18	.260	Sc Pos	84	21	2	31	.250
Scnd Half	111	33	3	18	.297	Clutch	55	18	1	10	.327

2003 Season

After Danny Bautista missed all but six weeks of the 2002 season due to a shoulder injury, the Diamondbacks were excited about his return to the lineup. Bautista was Arizona's Opening Day right fielder, but a hamstring injury cost him a month (late June to late July) and his lack of production eventually led the team to acquire Raul Mondesi to play right.

Hitting, Baserunning & Defense

Bautista hits fastballs over the plate, where he can extend his arms. While he has a powerful bat, Bautista's swing has a downward plane, creating backspin liners instead of home runs. The way to attack him is hard in and with sliders away. Bautista has a strong arm, but often misses cutoff men. He can play all three outfield positions and has good speed when healthy.

2004 Outlook

With one season (at $4 million) remaining on the three-year, $9 million contract Bautista signed after his strong 2001 postseason, Bautista again will be counted on as Arizona's right fielder. But he is not really a middle-of-the-order hitter and should not be counted on for home runs.

Craig Counsell

Traded To BREWERS

Position: 3B/SS/2B
Bats: L **Throws:** R
Ht: 6' 0" **Wt:** 184

Opening Day Age: 33
Born: 8/21/70 in South Bend, IN
ML Seasons: 8
Nickname: Rudy

Overall Statistics

	G	AB	R	H	D	T	HR	RBI	SB	BB	SO	Avg	OBP	Slg
'03	89	303	40	71	6	3	3	21	11	41	32	.234	.328	.304
Car.	658	2023	289	539	93	15	16	188	32	251	266	.266	.349	.351

2003 Situational Stats

	AB	H	HR	RBI	Avg		AB	H	HR	RBI	Avg
Home	142	34	3	12	.239	LHP	73	16	1	8	.219
Road	161	37	0	9	.230	RHP	230	55	2	13	.239
First Half	142	38	3	15	.268	Sc Pos	64	12	0	17	.188
Scnd Half	161	33	0	6	.205	Clutch	51	16	0	2	.314

2003 Season

After a neck injury and fusion surgery cut his 2002 season short, Craig Counsell returned to his utility role. He missed two months because of a torn thumb ligament and played mostly third base (when he did play) over the second half of the season, after Alex Cintron took over as shortstop. He finished the year with a .234 batting average, by far his worst since joining the Diamondbacks in 2000.

Hitting, Baserunning & Defense

Counsell has little power and is best when he hits the ball to left-center. He is a good bunter and can play hit-and-run. On the bases and in the field he is fundamentally sound, with good hands on defense and the ability to play anywhere in the infield. Counsell has enough speed to steal a base.

2004 Outlook

Counsell is best suited to a reserve role because of his versatility and offensive limitations, but he'll compete for regular duty in a Milwaukee infield that lacks tested veterans. He was dealt to Milwaukee with infielder Junior Spivey, first baseman Lyle Overbay, catcher Chad Moeller and lefthanders Chris Capuano and Jorge de la Rosa for Richie Sexson and two minor leaguers, lefty Shane Nance and a player to be named.

Robby Hammock

Position: C/3B/RF
Bats: R **Throws:** R
Ht: 5'11" **Wt:** 180

Opening Day Age: 26
Born: 5/13/77 in Macon, GA
ML Seasons: 1
Pronunciation: HAM-uk

Overall Statistics

	G	AB	R	H	D	T	HR	RBI	SB	BB	SO	Avg	OBP	Slg
'03	65	195	30	55	10	2	8	28	3	17	44	.282	.343	.477
Car.	65	195	30	55	10	2	8	28	3	17	44	.282	.343	.477

2003 Situational Stats

	AB	H	HR	RBI	Avg		AB	H	HR	RBI	Avg
Home	104	34	5	20	.327	LHP	78	24	2	10	.308
Road	91	21	3	8	.231	RHP	117	31	6	18	.265
First Half	103	29	5	18	.282	Sc Pos	47	13	2	20	.277
Scnd Half	92	26	3	10	.283	Clutch	29	8	1	3	.276

2003 Season

Versatile rookie Robby Hammock was called up four times by the Diamondbacks last year, playing part-time at third base in June and then getting to stay with the big club from August 6 through the end of the season. He made 28 starts at catcher—splitting time with Rod Barajas down the stretch—11 at third base and nine in right field. He was an effective player wherever he was used, though he was a somewhat streaky hitter.

Hitting, Baserunning & Defense

Hammock is a good fastball hitter but at times looks bad on breaking pitches. He has good power. Behind the plate he is a good receiver with a quick release that enables him to throw out basestealers. He is also a capable outfielder and third baseman and can play first as well. Hammock is an average baserunner.

2004 Outlook

His versatility and low salary will likely earn Hammock a spot on the Diamondbacks' roster this year. His relatively slight build makes it hard to envision him as an every-day catcher, but if he hits he can maintain a spot in the lineup by catching part-time and rotating at other positions.

Matt Kata

Position: 2B/3B
Bats: B **Throws:** R
Ht: 6' 1" **Wt:** 185

Opening Day Age: 26
Born: 3/14/78 in Avon Lakes, OH
ML Seasons: 1
Pronunciation: KATE-a

Overall Statistics

	G	AB	R	H	D	T	HR	RBI	SB	BB	SO	Avg	OBP	Slg
'03	78	288	42	74	16	5	7	29	3	25	53	.257	.315	.420
Car.	78	288	42	74	16	5	7	29	3	25	53	.257	.315	.420

2003 Situational Stats

	AB	H	HR	RBI	Avg		AB	H	HR	RBI	Avg
Home	137	36	3	13	.263	LHP	97	29	4	15	.299
Road	151	38	4	16	.252	RHP	191	45	3	14	.236
First Half	96	33	5	11	.344	Sc Pos	43	16	1	22	.372
Scnd Half	192	41	2	18	.214	Clutch	46	12	2	7	.261

2003 Season

The Diamondbacks called up Matt Kata in mid-June when Junior Spivey suffered a sprained ankle. Playing second base, Kata was a sparkplug in the team's 12-game winning streak later that month. When Spivey returned and Shea Hillenbrand moved to first base, Kata split time between third base and second and even played a few games at shortstop.

Hitting, Baserunning & Defense

The switch-hitting Kata, who is a better hitter righthanded, can be pitched to with breaking balls and by changing speeds. He has decent power for a middle infielder. Kata is a hard-nosed player who is very good at second base and capable at shortstop and third. He has enough speed to steal bases on occasion.

2004 Outlook

An MRI after the season ended revealed a stress fracture in Kata's left hip, but he should be fine by spring training. He projects as a utility player on a good team, but with both Craig Counsell and Junior Spivey sent to Milwaukee in the Richie Sexson trade, Kata is in line to start at second base.

Mike Koplove

Position: RP
Bats: R **Throws:** R
Ht: 5'10" **Wt:** 178

Opening Day Age: 27
Born: 8/30/76 in Philadelphia, PA
ML Seasons: 3
Pronunciation: COP-luv

Overall Statistics

	W	L	Pct.	ERA	G	GS	Sv	IP	H	BB	SO	HR	Avg
'03	3	0	1.000	2.15	31	0	0	37.2	31	10	27	3	.225
Car.	9	2	.818	2.96	95	0	0	109.1	86	42	87	6	.217

2003 Situational Stats

	W	L	ERA	Sv	IP		AB	H	HR	RBI	Avg
Home	1	0	3.79	0	19.0	LHB	58	13	2	4	.224
Road	2	0	0.48	0	18.2	RHB	80	18	1	6	.225
First Half	3	0	2.15	0	37.2	Sc Pos	30	3	0	6	.100
Scnd Half	0	0	—	0	0.0	Clutch	87	18	1	6	.207

2003 Season

Mike Koplove made the Diamondbacks' roster out of spring training and pitched in 27 of Arizona's first 52 games. But after working three straight days in late May, he went on the disabled list with shoulder tendinitis. Upon his return, he pitched four times in five days and then went back on the DL for good. Koplove had surgery in September to repair two tears in his labrum.

Pitching, Defense & Hitting

With his sidearm delivery, the ability to hit 92 MPH and a good changeup, Koplove can be difficult to hit, especially for righthanders. He has a curve and slider and can vary his arm angle to keep hitters off-balance. He can set up or be a long man. A former college shortstop, Koplove is an excellent fielder and tough to steal on.

2004 Outlook

Koplove should be fully recovered from his surgery by spring training and will have a good chance, based on past success, to earn a spot in the bullpen. But he will have to work harder in the weight room to strengthen his shoulder and take stress off his labrum in order to stay healthy.

Lyle Overbay

Traded To BREWERS

Position: 1B
Bats: L **Throws:** L
Ht: 6' 2" **Wt:** 222

Opening Day Age: 27
Born: 1/28/77 in Centralia, WA
ML Seasons: 3

Overall Statistics

	G	AB	R	H	D	T	HR	RBI	SB	BB	SO	Avg	OBP	Slg
'03	86	254	23	70	20	0	4	28	1	35	67	.276	.365	.402
Car.	98	266	23	72	20	0	4	29	1	35	73	.271	.357	.391

2003 Situational Stats

	AB	H	HR	RBI	Avg		AB	H	HR	RBI	Avg
Home	129	35	2	13	.271	LHP	86	25	0	9	.291
Road	125	35	2	15	.280	RHP	168	45	4	19	.268
First Half	220	61	4	24	.277	Sc Pos	70	18	0	21	.257
Scnd Half	34	9	0	4	.265	Clutch	51	11	1	3	.216

2003 Season

With Erubiel Durazo traded and Mark Grace relegated to a backup role in his final season, rookie Lyle Overbay was handed the Diamondbacks' first-base job before the season began. He was sent down July 23; at the time he was hitting .273 but had just 25 RBI in 227 at-bats. Overbay returned as a September callup, making six starts.

Hitting, Baserunning & Defense

Overbay has a flat swing, enabling him to spray the ball around but not allowing him to hit many home runs. He tends to look for a good pitch, thus working the count, but sometimes getting behind and striking out. Considering Overbay did not play first base until after he was drafted, he handles the position well, with good hands and average range. He is a slow runner.

2004 Outlook

Overbay's window of opportunity in Arizona closed quickly, as the club included him in a nine-player December trade with Milwaukee that netted first baseman Richie Sexson. Overbay will get a longer look with the rebuilding Brewers, and Miller Park should be an inviting place to get his career on track.

John Patterson

Position: SP/RP
Bats: R **Throws:** R
Ht: 6' 5" **Wt:** 208

Opening Day Age: 26
Born: 1/30/78 in Orange, TX
ML Seasons: 2

Overall Statistics

	W	L	Pct.	ERA	G	GS	Sv	IP	H	BB	SO	HR	Avg
'03	1	4	.200	6.05	16	8	1	55.0	61	30	43	7	.281
Car.	3	4	.429	5.04	23	13	1	85.2	88	37	74	14	.265

2003 Situational Stats

	W	L	ERA	Sv	IP		AB	H	HR	RBI	Avg
Home	1	1	6.35	0	22.2	LHB	89	25	2	7	.281
Road	0	3	5.85	1	32.1	RHB	128	36	5	28	.281
First Half	1	4	6.91	0	41.2	Sc Pos	60	17	1	25	.283
Scnd Half	0	0	3.38	1	13.1	Clutch	19	3	0	0	.158

2003 Season

John Patterson came to spring training as the Diamondbacks' presumed No. 5 starter but lost the spot to Oscar Villarreal. When Villarreal was made a full-time reliever, Patterson was called up for one start, but was sent back down after losing. He made seven starts in midseason during the rash of pitching injuries but struggled. Returning in September, he pitched well in long relief.

Pitching, Defense & Hitting

Patterson threw in the mid-90s before reconstructive elbow surgery in 2000. Now he tops out at about 92-93 MPH. He still has a sharp, 12-to-6 curve he can throw for strikes or bounce in the dirt when looking for a swinging strike, but his split-finger is a work in progress. He never has done much with the bat and is easy to run on.

2004 Outlook

Once considered the team's top pitching prospect, Patterson will compete against Andrew Good and Edgar Gonzalez for the two rotation spots vacated by Miguel Batista and Curt Schilling. Patterson, another year removed from his Tommy John surgery, still could emerge with one of the openings.

Arizona

Jose Valverde

Position: RP
Bats: R **Throws:** R
Ht: 6' 4" **Wt:** 254

Opening Day Age: 24
Born: 7/24/79 in San Pedro de Macoris, DR
ML Seasons: 1
Pronunciation: val-VARE-day

Overall Statistics

	W	L	Pct.	ERA	G	GS	Sv	IP	H	BB	SO	HR	Avg
'03	2	1	.667	2.15	54	0	10	50.1	24	26	71	4	.137
Car.	2	1	.667	2.15	54	0	10	50.1	24	26	71	4	.137

2003 Situational Stats

	W	L	ERA	Sv	IP		AB	H	HR	RBI	Avg
Home	2	1	1.04	5	26.0	LHB	77	13	2	7	.169
Road	0	0	3.33	5	24.1	RHB	98	11	2	11	.112
First Half	1	0	1.00	9	18.0	Sc Pos	60	11	2	16	.183
Scnd Half	1	1	2.78	1	32.1	Clutch	88	10	1	7	.114

2003 Season

Jose Valverde was called up June 1, when closer Matt Mantei went on the disabled list, and was an immediate success. He went 9-for-9 in save chances while Mantei was out, pitched very well in a setup role after Mantei's return, and held opposing hitters to a minuscule .137 average for the season—second only to Eric Gagne among major league relievers.

Pitching, Defense & Hitting

Valverde has a funky, short-arm delivery that hides the ball from hitters. He throws 93-94 MPH with a slider. His split-finger pitch improved last year and can be a strikeout pitch, but he does not throw it for strikes often. Valverde was a closer through his minor league career and has little experience as a hitter. Holding runners is a problem for him.

2004 Outlook

As the closer-in-waiting, Valverde can set up Mantei and then take over if Mantei is traded or suffers an injury. But there also should be health concerns with Valverde because of his untraditional delivery that would seem to put strain on his elbow. On the positive side, Valverde has shown poise and maturity that was not always there when he pitched in the minors.

Oscar Villarreal

Position: RP
Bats: L **Throws:** R
Ht: 6' 0" **Wt:** 177

Opening Day Age: 22
Born: 11/22/81 in Nuevo Leon, Mexico
ML Seasons: 1
Pronunciation: VEE-yuh-ray-al

Overall Statistics

	W	L	Pct.	ERA	G	GS	Sv	IP	H	BB	SO	HR	Avg
'03	10	7	.588	2.57	86	1	0	98.0	80	46	80	6	.222
Car.	10	7	.588	2.57	86	1	0	98.0	80	46	80	6	.222

2003 Situational Stats

	W	L	ERA	Sv	IP		AB	H	HR	RBI	Avg
Home	4	3	3.25	0	44.1	LHB	135	34	4	16	.252
Road	6	4	2.01	0	53.2	RHB	226	46	2	22	.204
First Half	6	4	2.75	0	55.2	Sc Pos	112	28	2	33	.250
Scnd Half	4	3	2.34	0	42.1	Clutch	174	35	3	15	.201

2003 Season

An afterthought when spring training opened, Oscar Villarreal pitched himself into the the fifth starter's spot by the time the Diamondbacks broke camp. After one start, he was assigned full-time to the bullpen. A starting pitcher throughout his minor league career, Villarreal thrived in his new role. He was second in the NL in appearances—pitching 18 times in August alone—and tied for the team lead in wins.

Pitching, Defense & Hitting

From his three-quarters delivery, Villarreal can hit 93 MPH. His best pitches are a sinker and a slider. He hides the ball well from the hitter, especially righthanders, but has to pitch down in the strike zone. Villarreal is a below-average fielder and not much of a hitter.

2004 Outlook

The frequent use of Villarreal last year concerned many in the organization, but he generally showed no ill effects. It will be interesting to see if any problems crop up this year and whether his usage continues in the same pattern. Villarreal has proven he can be an effective setup man and he probably could be an effective starter. He may get that chance with the departures of Curt Schilling and Miguel Batista.

Other Arizona Diamondbacks

Carlos Baerga (Pos: 1B/2B, **Age**: 35, **Bats**: B)

	G	AB	R	H	D	T	HR	RBI	SB	BB	SO	Avg	OBP	Slg
'03	105	207	31	71	13	0	4	39	1	18	20	.343	.396	.464
Car.	1458	5196	707	1523	270	17	130	744	59	278	551	.293	.333	.427

Baerga has resurrected his career in Arizona. He went a steady 19-for-55 (.345) off the bench last year, collecting the second-most pinch-hits in baseball while playing three positions in the infield. 2004 Outlook: B

Ricky Bottalico (Pos: RHP, Age: 34)

	W	L	Pct.	ERA	G	GS	Sv	IP	H	BB	SO	HR	Avg
'03	1	0	1.000	5.40	2	0	0	1.2	3	2	2	0	.375
Car.	28	38	.424	4.03	462	0	114	517.2	464	263	485	61	.241

Bottalico is fighting his way back to the majors since he suffered a torn labrum in June 2002. Though he saved 34 games in back-to-back years in the mid-90s, the 34-year-old now is a journeyman reliever. 2004 Outlook: C

Mark Grace (Pos: 1B, **Age**: 39, **Bats**: L)

G	AB	R	H	D	T	HR	RBI	SB	BB	SO	Avg	OBP	Slg
66	135	13	27	5	0	3	16	0	16	15	.200	.279	.304
2245	8065	1179	2445	511	45	173	1146	70	1075	642	.303	.383	.442

Grace ended his career with a .303 lifetime batting average to go along with 511 doubles. He now will take his considerable wit and charm into the Diamondbacks' broadcast booth. 2004 Outlook: D

Felix Jose (Pos: RF, **Age**: 38, **Bats**: B)

	G	AB	R	H	D	T	HR	RBI	SB	BB	SO	Avg	OBP	Slg
'03	18	18	1	6	1	0	1	6	0	6	3	.333	.500	.556
Car.	747	2527	322	708	135	14	54	324	102	203	507	.280	.334	.409

Jose has been playing professional baseball since 1984 and has received a handful of at-bats from the Diamondbacks in each of the past two seasons. He comes off the bench ready to hit, but that's about it. 2004 Outlook: C

Quinton McCracken (Pos: RF/CF, **Age**: 33, **Bats**: B)

	G	AB	R	H	D	T	HR	RBI	SB	BB	SO	Avg	OBP	Slg
'03	115	203	17	46	5	2	0	18	5	15	34	.227	.276	.271
Car.	746	2018	305	565	102	27	17	216	80	187	374	.280	.341	.383

After hitting .309 in 2002, McCracken struggled at the plate last year. However, he brings enough tools to the park to be helpful as a No. 5 outfielder, and he can play all three spots. 2004 Outlook: C

Chad Moeller (Pos: C, **Age**: 29, **Bats**: R)

	G	AB	R	H	D	T	HR	RBI	SB	BB	SO	Avg	OBP	Slg
'03	78	239	29	64	17	1	7	29	1	23	59	.268	.335	.435
Car.	188	528	60	134	31	4	11	56	2	55	127	.254	.325	.390

Moeller split most of Arizona's catching duties with Rod Barajas last year. Though he threw out only 23.1 percent of opposing basestealers, Moeller can be quite dangerous when he has a bat in his hand. He was traded to the Brewers in December as part of the Richie Sexson deal, and Moeller could battle for the starting duties behind the plate in Milwaukee. 2004 Outlook: B

Mike Myers (Pos: LHP, **Age**: 34)

	W	L	Pct.	ERA	G	GS	Sv	IP	H	BB	SO	HR	Avg
'03	0	1	.000	5.70	64	0	0	36.1	38	21	21	4	.262
Car.	12	20	.375	4.37	609	0	14	376.2	362	187	327	41	.256

The sidewinding southpaw has held opposing lefties to a .209 batting average, but Myers' ERA has risen in each of the past four years. He has pitched just 376.2 innings in 609 career appearances. 2004 Outlook: C

Eddie Oropesa (Pos: LHP, Age: 32)

	W	L	Pct.	ERA	G	GS	Sv	IP	H	BB	SO	HR	Avg
'03	3	3	.500	5.82	47	0	0	38.2	38	27	39	3	.257
Car.	6	3	.667	6.94	109	0	0	83.0	93	59	72	10	.283

Oropesa has split his time between the majors and minors in each of the last three seasons. Since he held opposing lefties to a .206 average last year, he probably will find a bullpen job somewhere. 2004 Outlook: C

Brady Raggio (Pos: RHP, **Age**: 31)

	W	L	Pct.	ERA	G	GS	Sv	IP	H	BB	SO	HR	Avg
'03	0	0	–	6.48	10	0	1	8.1	9	6	8	1	.290
Car.	2	3	.400	8.10	29	5	1	46.2	75	25	32	3	.375

Before he made 10 appearances for Arizona last year, Raggio had not pitched in the majors since 1998. The 31-year-old had a 4-1 strikeout-walk ratio in Triple-A in 2003, so he might get another shot in the bigs. 2004 Outlook: C

Stephen Randolph (Pos: LHP, **Age**: 29)

	W	L	Pct.	ERA	G	GS	Sv	IP	H	BB	SO	HR	Avg
'03	8	1	.889	4.05	50	0	0	60.0	50	43	50	7	.226
Car.	8	1	.889	4.05	50	0	0	60.0	50	43	50	7	.226

After pitching for Triple-A Tucson in every season since 1998, Randolph finally made it to the bigs. He held opponents to a .226 batting average and could play a bigger role this year. 2004 Outlook: C

Dennys Reyes (Pos: LHP, **Age**: 26)

	W	L	Pct.	ERA	G	GS	Sv	IP	H	BB	SO	HR	Avg
'03	0	0	–	10.66	15	0	0	12.2	15	10	16	2	.300
Car.	15	21	.417	4.77	268	27	2	368.0	373	223	348	34	.260

Signed by Kansas City after last season, Reyes has been with six organizations since 2001. Though he has good stuff, his ERA has risen in each of the last five seasons. KC might give him a chance to start. 2004 Outlook: C

Matt Williams (Pos: 3B, **Age**: 38, **Bats**: R)

G	AB	R	H	D	T	HR	RBI	SB	BB	SO	Avg	OBP	Slg
44	134	17	33	9	0	4	16	0	16	26	.246	.327	.403
1866	7000	997	1878	338	35	378	1218	53	469	1363	.268	.317	.489

In his prime, Williams was one of the most-feared power hitters in the game, and he was just as adept in the field. Now retired, he can reflect on what might have been had the 1994 strike not occurred. 2004 Outlook: D

Arizona Diamondbacks Minor League Prospects

Organization Overview:

The Diamondbacks knew all along their farm system would need to produce once their veterans moved on and deferred payments to those players piled up. It wasn't supposed to happen as soon as 2003, but because of injuries it became necessary, and the organization acquitted itself well. Andrew Good, Robby Hammock, Matt Kata, Jose Valverde and Oscar Villarreal all made contributions despite not being expected to play in the majors when spring training opened. There are more players on the way, which is important, since the team will get younger and younger in the near future. Arizona is aiming for an $80 million payroll this year and just $55 million in 2005, when the team could be nearly all homegrown other than Randy Johnson and Luis Gonzalez. Arizona's top prospects include some promising pitchers and a number of players with offensive potential but defensive questions.

Brian Bruney

Position: P
Bats: R **Throws:** R
Ht: 6' 3" **Wt:** 220

Opening Day Age: 22
Born: 2/17/82 in Astoria, OR

Recent Statistics

	W	L	ERA	G	GS	Sv	IP	H	R	BB	SO	HR
2002 A South Bend	4	3	1.68	37	0	10	48.1	37	15	17	54	1
2002 AA El Paso	0	2	2.92	10	0	0	12.1	11	5	4	14	1
2003 AA El Paso	0	2	2.59	28	0	14	31.1	29	17	13	28	1
2003 AAA Tucson	3	1	2.81	32	0	12	32.0	24	12	18	32	0

Bruney worked on improving his slider last year at Double-A El Paso and got to the point he could use it as an out pitch, earning him a promotion to Triple-A Tucson. But his best pitch is still his fastball, which touches 96 MPH and is consistently 93-94 MPH. Bruney also has a closer's makeup, with the ability to not let a bad outing carry over and to not let hitters know when he isn't at his best. Arizona toyed with calling up Bruney at times last year, but he probably could use more time at Tucson to work on his slider and changeup. He could supplant Jose Valverde as the team's closer of the future.

Edgar Gonzalez

Position: P
Bats: R **Throws:** R
Ht: 6' 2" **Wt:** 215

Opening Day Age: 21
Born: 2/23/83 in Monterrey, Mexico

Recent Statistics

	W	L	ERA	G	GS	Sv	IP	H	R	BB	SO	HR
2003 AA El Paso	2	2	3.50	6	6	0	36.0	40	18	11	30	1
2003 AAA Tucson	8	7	3.75	20	19	0	129.2	126	65	28	69	4
2003 NL Arizona	2	1	4.91	9	2	0	18.1	28	10	7	14	3

When the Diamondbacks called up Gonzalez for two emergency starts in June, he was the youngest player in the majors and became the youngest pitcher to win a major league game in nearly six years. Gonzalez has the poise and feel for pitching of an older player. He will spend most of the game throwing his fastball 89-91 MPH, but in a key spot or against a better hitter, he will dial it up to 94 MPH. He also has a very good slider and a sinking changeup. With both Miguel Batista and Curt Schilling gone, Gonzalez will be in a group of youngsters fighting for a rotation spot this year.

Andrew Good

Position: P
Bats: R **Throws:** R
Ht: 6' 2" **Wt:** 209

Opening Day Age: 24
Born: 9/19/79 in San Diego, CA

Recent Statistics

	W	L	ERA	G	GS	Sv	IP	H	R	BB	SO	HR
2003 AAA Tucson	4	4	5.00	11	11	0	63.0	78	36	13	45	12
2003 NL Arizona	4	2	5.29	16	10	0	66.1	74	42	16	42	15

In two callups last year, Good made 16 appearances, 10 of those starts. After pitching four times in 11 days in July, his ERA rose from 4.67 to 5.29. He was not recalled in September and was scratched from the Arizona Fall League because of elbow tendinitis. Good's best pitch is a changeup, and he has to be precise with his relatively straight 89-MPH fastball to be effective. He also throws a curveball. An intelligent pitcher, Good is able to succeed with his stuff, but he projects as a No. 4 or 5 starter. Because of his history of elbow trouble—he is another Tommy John surgery survivor—he is not suited to relief.

Mike Gosling

Position: P
Bats: L **Throws:** L
Ht: 6' 2" **Wt:** 210

Opening Day Age: 23
Born: 9/23/80 in Madison, WI

Recent Statistics

	W	L	ERA	G	GS	Sv	IP	H	R	BB	SO	HR
2002 AA El Paso	14	5	3.13	27	27	0	166.2	149	66	62	115	7
2003 AAA Tucson	9	12	5.61	26	26	0	136.1	190	106	56	89	13

Surgery to repair a left shoulder injury that bothered Gosling all last year likely will keep him from being a candidate for the Opening Day rotation. He underwent a procedure in late September to repair a torn labrum, an injury that originally was thought to be tendinitis. A second-round pick from Stanford in 2001, Gosling never looked right last year with Triple-A Tucson, and he admitted after the season that he compensated for the pain by limiting his throwing between starts. If he returns to form, he can be expected to throw 91-92 MPH with a power slider and a good feel for his changeup. His intelligence, poise and maturity, along with his good stuff, projects Gosling as a middle-of-the-rotation starter.

Scott Hairston

Position: 2B
Bats: R **Throws:** R
Ht: 6' 1" **Wt:** 188

Opening Day Age: 23
Born: 5/25/80 in Fort Worth, TX

Recent Statistics

	G	AB	R	H	D	T	HR	RBI	SB	BB	SO	Avg
2002 A South Bend	109	394	79	131	35	4	16	72	9	58	74	.332
2002 A Lancaster	18	79	20	32	11	1	6	26	1	6	16	.405
2003 AA El Paso	88	337	53	93	21	7	10	47	6	30	80	.276
2003 AAA Tucson	1	0	0	0	0	0	0	1	0	0	0	—

A strong showing in the Arizona Fall League helped Hairston—the brother of Baltimore's Jerry Hairston Jr.—make up for missing much of last season with back trouble. Other than his back, the only question about Hairston is a position. He can be an impact hitter, with good bat speed, plate discipline and excellent pitch recognition. He has above-average speed, but has yet to develop into a stolen-base threat. At second base, Hairston is mechanical. He tends to try to make all his throws from the same arm angle, rather than adjust on plays in either direction or in front of him. He is slow turning double plays. Hairston could end up in left field, or perhaps third base.

Sergio Santos

Position: SS
Bats: R **Throws:** R
Ht: 6' 3" **Wt:** 190

Opening Day Age: 20
Born: 7/4/83 in Hacienda Heights, CA

Recent Statistics

	G	AB	R	H	D	T	HR	RBI	SB	BB	SO	Avg
2002 R Missoula	54	202	38	55	19	2	9	37	6	29	49	.272
2003 A Lancaster	93	341	55	98	13	2	8	49	5	41	64	.287
2003 AA El Paso	37	107	10	06	7	1	2	16	0	8	25	.255

A little more than a year after finishing high school, Santos was in the Double-A Texas League and then played in the Arizona Fall League. Arizona's first-round pick in 2002, Santos has a potential impact bat, but he may not last in the middle infield. He has the arm and hands to play shortstop, but is deliberate and his range is lacking. He projects as a third baseman. Santos has an enthusiasm for the game and his offense will improve as he learns to adjust to pitchers. He has excellent power and good bat speed.

Luis Terrero

Position: OF
Bats: B **Throws:** R
Ht: 6' 1" **Wt:** 206

Opening Day Age: 23
Born: 5/18/80 in Barahona, DR

Recent Statistics

	G	AB	R	H	D	T	HR	RBI	SB	BB	SO	Avg
2003 AAA Tucson	118	467	83	134	20	15	3	46	23	31	103	.287
2003 NL Arizona	5	4	0	1	0	0	0	0	0	0	1	.250

Terrero has a chance to be a five-tool player, with perhaps the biggest question being his makeup. He was benched at times last year for lack of hustle or attitude and has had trouble getting along with teammates. But he is a legitimate center fielder with good speed and a very strong arm. Terrero has power in his bat but has yet to show it much in games. His tendency to strike out also keeps his average and homer totals down. Despite his speed, he has yet to learn to be an efficient bases-stealer or good baserunner. Injuries have cut into Terrero's playing time the past few years, so he could use more time in the minors. However, he could arrive in the majors to stay this year, and will be counted on when Steve Finley's contract expires after this season.

Chad Tracy

Position: 3B
Bats: L **Throws:** R
Ht: 6' 2" **Wt:** 200

Opening Day Age: 23
Born: 5/22/80 in Charlotte, NC

Recent Statistics

	G	AB	R	H	D	T	HR	RBI	SB	BB	SO	Avg
2002 AA El Paso	129	514	80	177	39	5	8	74	2	38	51	.344
2003 AAA Tucson	133	522	91	169	31	4	10	80	0	41	52	.324

In two-plus minor league seasons, Tracy has a .333 career average, with 82 doubles and just 127 strikeouts in 1,287 at-bats. He has a flat swing, tending not to elevate the ball for home runs. A gap hitter now, he could develop decent power in the majors. A first baseman in college (East Carolina), Tracy has improved his play at third base—his arm is just fine—and could be considered adequate. While Tracy probably is ready to hit in the majors, the Diamondbacks seem committed to Shea Hillenbrand at third base, which leaves Tracy either stuck or trade bait.

Others to Watch

Righthander **Casey Daigle** (22) is 6-foot-6 with an ideal pitcher's body, but he has yet to establish consistency. He can hit 92-93 MPH, while pitching primarily at 89-91 MPH, and has shown he can have a plus curve and slider. But the quality of his pitches, as well as his command, tend to come and go. On the 40-man roster for the first time, now is his chance to step forward. . . Outfielder **Conor Jackson** (21), Arizona's first first-round pick last year, set a modern-day short-season Northwest League record with 35 doubles. As he learns to hit with more backspin, those doubles could become homers. Jackson also has a very good eye for the strike zone. He is making the adjustment to the outfield from playing corner infield in college. . . **Josh Kroeger** (21) is a good athlete who can play all three outfield positions and has a good arm. He has a classic lefthanded swing and reached Double-A last year before his 21st birthday. . . Six-foot-7 righthander **Dustin Nippert** (22) has good mechanics and throws on a downward plane. He had an encouraging Arizona Fall League. . . Righthander **Adriano Rosario** (18) has hit 99 MPH on the radar gun and pitches consistently at 94-95 MPH. He also has a very good slider and mound presence. Although he doesn't turn 19 until May, he could be in Double-A this year.

Ted Turner Field

Offense

Considered a pitchers' park since opening in 1997, Turner Field actually is a fairly neutral offensive facility. Both the Braves and their opponents have hit more home runs on the road than at Turner in recent years, but the difference is not huge. The park produces an average number of triples, but not as many doubles. Lefthanded hitters tend to fare well at Turner, particularly in the singles department, due to the large amount of real estate in right field.

Defense

Flyballs that carry for home runs during the summer months at Turner tend to become long outs early in the season due to the winds that blow through the opening in center field. A superb center fielder with plus speed and instincts and an above-average right fielder with a strong arm are required at Turner. Atlanta has fared well at those two positions in recent years with Andruw Jones and Gary Sheffield.

Who It Helps the Most

Russ Ortiz thrived in his new surroundings in 2003. Javy Lopez had the best season ever for a righthanded hitter at Turner Field last year. The catcher batted .376 at home, compared to .290 on the road, and 26 of his 43 home runs came at The Ted.

Who It Hurts the Most

Righthanded hitters Marcus Giles and Vinny Castilla have both fared better away from home than they have at Turner. Lefthanded hitter Robert Fick hit 42 points higher on the road, with only four of his 11 homers coming at Turner.

Rookies & Newcomers

First baseman Adam LaRoche, the possessor of a sweet lefthanded swing that produces line drives, should find his comfort zone quickly at Turner Field with the spacious right field. LaRoche also is a superb defensive player, a fact that should ingratiate him to Cox' managing style.

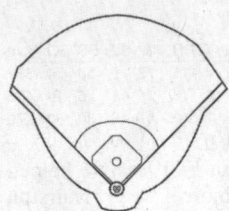

Dimensions: LF-335, LCF-380, CF-401, RCF-390, RF-330

Capacity: 50,091

Elevation: 1050 feet

Surface: Grass

Foul Territory: Average

Park Factors

2003 Season

	Home Games Braves	Opp	Total	Away Games Braves	Opp	Total	Index
G	75	75	150	69	69	138	
Avg	.286	.249	.267	.286	.271	.279	96
AB	2530	2586	5116	2517	2357	4874	97
R	392	340	732	418	336	754	89
H	723	643	1366	720	639	1359	92
2B	138	122	260	153	150	303	82
3B	15	11	26	14	10	24	103
HR	101	64	165	104	72	176	89
BB	254	264	518	226	231	457	108
SO	413	443	856	432	432	864	94
E	58	54	112	53	43	96	107
E-Infield	46	41	87	49	37	86	93
LHB-Avg	.285	.245	.263	.273	.250	.261	101
LHB-HR	23	19	42	20	24	44	89
RHB-Avg	.286	.251	.269	.292	.282	.288	94
RHB-HR	78	45	123	84	48	132	90

2001-2003

	Home Games Braves	Opp	Total	Away Games Braves	Opp	Total	Index
G	219	219	438	212	212	424	
Avg	.270	.249	.259	.264	.253	.259	100
AB	7275	7533	14808	7512	7083	14595	98
R	1027	899	1926	1034	854	1888	99
H	1965	1877	3842	1985	1794	3779	98
2B	373	335	708	392	344	736	95
3B	38	29	67	34	39	73	90
HR	254	190	444	249	194	443	99
BB	687	734	1421	715	697	1412	99
SO	1287	1394	2681	1418	1397	2815	94
E	161	155	316	140	136	276	111
E-Infield	139	127	266	120	109	229	112
LHB-Avg	.264	.258	.261	.265	.245	.255	102
LHB-HR	68	72	140	62	65	127	108
RHB-Avg	.274	.244	.259	.264	.258	.261	99
RHB-HR	186	118	304	187	129	316	95

2003 Rankings (National League)

- Third-highest walk factor
- Second-lowest double factor
- Second-lowest RHB batting-average factor
- Third-lowest hit factor

Bobby Cox

2003 Season

Bobby Cox continued to make history in 2003. He guided the Braves to their 12th straight division title, the longest string in the history of professional sports, and notched 100 wins in a season for the sixth time. Cox also maintained his reputation as a difficult skipper for the arbiters with nine ejections, the second-highest total in the big leagues. Only former White Sox manager Jerry Manuel, who received the heave-ho 10 times, was asked to leave more often.

Offense

Cox usually eschews the hit-and-run and stolen base, preferring to wait for the big hit. His philosophy dovetailed perfectly with his 2003 team, which set numerous club hitting records. He is a firm believer in platooning to get the most advantageous matchups. Cox usually relies on the experience of veterans in key situations, but he's begun to give rookies more opportunities to prove themselves.

Pitching & Defense

Atlanta has hung its hat on pitching and defense since beginning its current division-winning streak in 1991. The results changed last year, when the Braves ranked ninth in ERA in the National League. Cox goes to the bullpen extensively and is a firm believer in using relievers for specific roles, even if it means employing them for only one batter. Cox also demands stellar defensive efforts; he will keep a struggling bat in the lineup provided the player is contributing with his glove.

2004 Outlook

Cox received as much criticism as anyone for the Braves' latest early exit from the playoffs, but GM John Schuerholz made it clear Cox was not going anywhere. Only Connie Mack, John McGraw, Walter Alston and Tommy Lasorda have had more wins with one team than Cox' 1,551 triumphs with the Braves. With 102 victories in 2004, Cox would tie Leo Durocher for eighth on the all-time list for managerial wins.

Born: 5/21/41 in Tulsa, OK

Playing Experience: 1968-1969, NYY

Managerial Experience: 22 seasons

Manager Statistics

Year	Team, Lg	W	L	Pct	GB	Finish
2003	Atlanta, NL	101	61	.623	–	1st East
22 Seasons		1906	1465	.565	–	–

2003 Starting Pitchers by Days Rest

	<=3	4	5	6+
Braves Starts	7	107	22	19
Braves ERA	5.70	4.11	4.15	4.11
NL Avg Starts	2	84	43	23
NL ERA	5.00	4.23	4.42	4.68

2003 Situational Stats

	Bobby Cox	NL Average
Hit & Run Success %	33.3	32.7
Stolen Base Success %	75.6	68.9
Platoon Pct.	49.2	52.0
Defensive Subs	18	19
High-Pitch Outings	5	8
Quick/Slow Hooks	19/13	20/12
Sacrifice Attempts	87	93

2003 Rankings (National League)

- 1st in stolen-base percentage and fewest caught stealings of second base (17)
- 2nd in pitchouts (47), intentional walks (43) and starts on three days rest
- 3rd in relief appearances (489) and saves with over 1 inning pitched (10)

Vinny Castilla

Position: 3B
Bats: R **Throws:** R
Ht: 6' 1" **Wt:** 205

Opening Day Age: 36
Born: 7/4/67 in Oaxaca, Mexico
ML Seasons: 13
Pronunciation: cas-TEE-yah

2003 Season

Vinny Castilla bounced back from a dismal 2002 campaign to have a respectable second season with the Braves. Castilla increased his numbers in virtually every offensive category in one fewer at-bat. The Mexican native improved as the season progressed, hitting .314 with 10 home runs and 41 RBI in his final 65 games.

Hitting

Castilla continues to possess decent power, even though there are occasions when his bat speed could be timed with a sundial. He has frequent problems getting his hands through the strike zone, though he can find a rhythm and be productive for short stretches. He remains one of the least patient hitters in the game, and veteran pitchers use his overaggressive ways against him. Castilla did a better job of using the entire field last year, but he still tries to pull too many pitches.

Baserunning & Defense

After committing just six errors at third base in 2002, Castilla's miscues more than tripled last year. Part of his problem was an inexperienced Robert Fick manning first base, causing several throws in the dirt to become errors. Castilla uses his experience to place himself properly for each batter. His hands remain soft, and his arm is accurate on throws to second and first base. Castilla never has had any more than average speed, and his baserunning skills force him to take one bag at a time.

2004 Outlook

Castilla showed last season that he has a couple more years left in both his bat and glove. He entered the offseason as a free agent, and it was thought he might return to Atlanta on a short-term deal, fueled by manager Bobby Cox' appreciation of Castilla's defense. That didn't come to pass, as Castilla signed a one-year deal in December to return to Colorado in 2004. Castilla enjoyed his best big league seasons with the Rockies several years ago, though at his current age it's unlikely he will be reaching the 40-homer plateau again.

Overall Statistics

	G	AB	R	H	D	T	HR	RBI	SB	BB	SO	Avg	OBP	Slg
'03	147	542	65	150	28	3	22	76	1	26	86	.277	.310	.461
Car.	1477	5470	730	1538	260	24	268	881	29	320	825	.281	.323	.484

Where He Hits the Ball

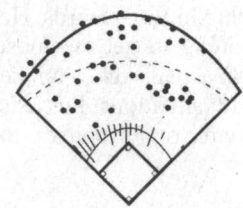

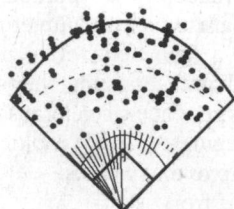

Vs. LHP   **Vs. RHP**

2003 Situational Stats

	AB	H	HR	RBI	Avg		AB	H	HR	RBI	Avg
Home	246	69	6	30	.280	LHP	124	36	5	17	.290
Road	296	81	16	46	.274	RHP	418	114	17	59	.273
First Half	321	87	15	48	.271	Sc Pos	131	37	4	48	.282
Scnd Half	221	63	7	28	.285	Clutch	70	18	2	7	.257

2003 Rankings (National League)

- 1st in lowest percentage of pitches taken (43.9) and highest percentage of swings on the first pitch (50.3)
- 2nd in errors at third base (19) and fewest pitches seen per plate appearance (3.27)
- 3rd in lowest fielding percentage at third base (.955)
- 5th in GDPs (22)
- Led the Braves in GDPs (22)

Robert Fick

2003 Season

After manning right field for the Tigers in 2002, Robert Fick was non-tendered and signed with Atlanta prior to last season. Fick became the Braves' starting first baseman against righthanded pitching in a platoon with Julio Franco and surpassed his previous career-best in RBI by 17. While he endured some nasty slumps, he performed well in clutch situations.

Hitting

Fick discovered how difficult hitting home runs at Turner Field can be. After hitting 36 round-trippers the previous two years with Detroit, Fick's quick, compact swing from the left side produced just 11 homers last year, including only one after July 27. The drought seemed to frustrate Fick, who has a tendency to fall into prolonged slumps. When he's in his rhythm, he uses the entire field and makes consistent contact. His knowledge of the strike zone continues to improve, with Fick cutting his whiffs nearly in half from 2002 to 2003.

Baserunning & Defense

Fick did a respectable job at first base after playing right field in 2002. While his footwork and his range leave something to be desired, he has good hands, catches most everything he reaches and was not a liability for the Braves, despite his 14 errors. As a right fielder, he showed a strong arm after being erratic in the throwing department as a minor league catcher. Though he does not clog the bases, Fick does not run well and shows little quickness in getting jumps or reading balls off the bat.

2004 Outlook

Known for his abrasive personality in Detroit, Fick was a model citizen in Atlanta before unraveling in Game 4 of the National League Division Series, when he deliberately chopped Eric Karros' arm on a play at first base and cursed reporters afterwards. The Braves released him after the season, so look for Fick to land elsewhere and be a useful platoon player.

Position: 1B
Bats: L **Throws:** R
Ht: 6' 1" **Wt:** 205

Opening Day Age: 30
Born: 3/15/74 in Torrance, CA
ML Seasons: 6

Overall Statistics

	G	AB	R	H	D	T	HR	RBI	SB	BB	SO	Avg	OBP	Slg
'03	126	409	52	110	26	1	11	80	1	42	47	.269	.335	.418
Car.	486	1592	210	427	91	7	56	243	5	158	251	.268	.336	.440

Where He Hits the Ball

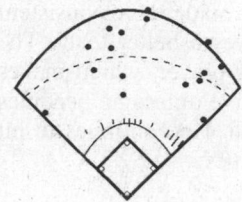 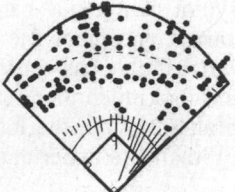

Vs. LHP   **Vs. RHP**

2003 Situational Stats

	AB	H	HR	RBI	Avg		AB	H	HR	RBI	Avg
Home	183	45	4	37	.246	LHP	52	7	2	8	.135
Road	226	65	7	43	.288	RHP	357	103	9	72	.289
First Half	243	72	8	51	.296	Sc Pos	117	40	8	71	.342
Scnd Half	166	38	3	29	.229	Clutch	55	18	2	14	.327

2003 Rankings (National League)

- 1st in errors at first base (14) and lowest fielding percentage at first base (.987)
- 7th in sacrifice flies (7)
- 10th in batting average with runners in scoring position
- Led the Braves in most pitches seen per plate appearance (3.91)

Atlanta

Rafael Furcal

2003 Season

After two mediocre seasons, Rafael Furcal bounced back with a stellar effort last year. He got off to a great start, slumped a bit in June and July, then regained his groove to set career highs in hits, runs, doubles, triples, home runs and RBI while setting the table for the most potent offense in the National League. Furcal also entered the record books in August when he executed the 11th regular-season unassisted triple play in major league history.

Hitting

At the behest of hitting coach Terry Pendleton, Furcal cut down on his swing at midseason and focused his efforts simply on trying to get on base. By not swinging as hard, he made more consistent contact and made the Braves a better team. The switch-hitter has surprising power, which makes him that much more effective unless he becomes infatuated with the longball. He continues to hit righthanders better than lefties.

Baserunning & Defense

Furcal may have the strongest arm among major league infielders. He struggles with the accuracy of his throws on occasion, particularly when he's trying to make the spectacular play. His defense also suffers when he relies on his arm strength and allows balls to get into his body instead of being aggressive and charging the grounders. Furcal's speed is exceptional; he hit into only one double play in 664 at-bats. He also has become more effective in reading pitchers, enabling him to steal 25 bases in 27 attempts last season.

2004 Outlook

The Braves wondered a year ago if Furcal was the long-term answer at shortstop. He answered that question positively for the second time in his career by emerging as one of the most prolific leadoff hitters in the game. With some additional defensive consistency, Furcal should add to last year's selection to the NL All-Star team.

Position: SS
Bats: B **Throws:** R
Ht: 5'10" **Wt:** 165

Opening Day Age: 26
Born: 10/24/77 in Loma de Cabrera, DR
ML Seasons: 4
Pronunciation: fur-CALL

Overall Statistics

	G	AB	R	H	D	T	HR	RBI	SB	BB	SO	Avg	OBP	Slg
'03	156	664	130	194	35	10	15	61	25	60	76	.292	.352	.443
Car.	520	2079	351	592	105	22	31	175	114	200	326	.285	.348	.401

Where He Hits the Ball

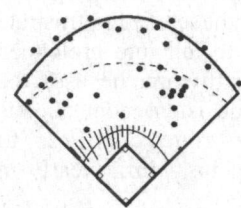 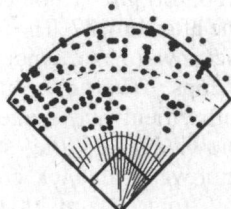

Vs. LHP   **Vs. RHP**

2003 Situational Stats

	AB	H	HR	RBI	Avg		AB	H	HR	RBI	Avg
Home	318	96	4	23	.302	LHP	154	38	5	18	.247
Road	346	98	11	38	.283	RHP	510	156	10	43	.306
First Half	387	109	13	38	.282	Sc Pos	124	38	1	46	.306
Scnd Half	277	85	2	23	.307	Clutch	74	21	3	8	.284

2003 Rankings (National League)

- 1st in triples, stolen-base percentage (92.6), fewest GDPs per GDP situation (1.4%), errors at shortstop (31) and lowest fielding percentage at shortstop (.959)
- 2nd in at-bats and plate appearances (734)
- 3rd in runs scored and pitches seen (2,845)
- 4th in hits
- Led the Braves in at-bats, runs scored, hits, singles, triples, stolen bases, pitches seen (2,845), plate appearances (734), games played, highest groundball-flyball ratio (1.6), stolen-base percentage (92.6), bunts in play (20), lowest percentage of swings that missed (10.8), steals of third (3), fewest GDPs per GDP situation (1.4%) and on-base percentage for a leadoff hitter (.353)

Marcus Giles

2003 Season

After losing his starting job at the keystone in 2002 while battling an ankle injury and the death of his infant daughter, Marcus Giles put those difficulties behind him to reclaim his spot as a cornerstone in the Atlanta lineup. Giles exceeded expectations by setting the modern franchise record for doubles in a season while improving his batting average by a whopping 86 points.

Hitting

A prolific hitter in the minors, Giles has made some adjustments to the big leagues in the last year to emerge as one of the most effective No. 2 hitters in the game. He made his once-huge swing more compact, became more disciplined in his pitch selection, and realized the advantage of going with pitches by driving them to right field. He hits with power against both righties and lefties.

Baserunning & Defense

Giles lost 10 pounds prior to last season, enabling him to gain at least a step in the field and another step on the basepaths. He also added some quickness, which allowed him to turn double plays more efficiently and display more range than anyone in the organization thought possible. His arm strength is decent and the accuracy of his throws is good at second base. Giles is an aggressive baserunner who is not afraid to take the extra base. He also has learned to read the deliveries of pitchers, enabling him to rank third on the team in stolen bases.

2004 Outlook

Named a starter in last year's All-Star Game, Giles could not answer the bell after suffering a mild concussion due to a collision with the Cubs' Mark Prior. After missing three games, Giles bounced back and hit .349 following the injury. Playing second and hitting second as well as he does, Giles will not be known as Brian Giles' little brother much longer.

Position: 2B
Bats: R **Throws:** R
Ht: 5' 8" **Wt:** 180

Opening Day Age: 25
Born: 5/18/78 in San Diego, CA
ML Seasons: 3
Pronunciation: JYLES

Overall Statistics

	G	AB	R	H	D	T	HR	RBI	SB	BB	SO	Avg	OBP	Slg
'03	145	551	101	174	49	2	21	69	14	59	80	.316	.390	.526
Car.	281	1008	164	287	69	5	38	123	17	112	158	.285	.362	.476

Where He Hits the Ball

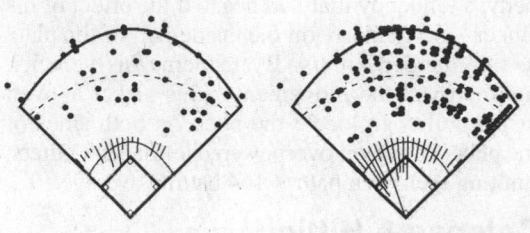

Vs. LHP **Vs. RHP**

2003 Situational Stats

	AB	H	HR	RBI	Avg		AB	H	HR	RBI	Avg
Home	282	82	9	29	.291	LHP	127	36	8	20	.283
Road	269	92	12	40	.342	RHP	424	138	13	49	.325
First Half	313	91	8	37	.291	Sc Pos	118	34	3	44	.288
Scnd Half	238	83	13	32	.349	Clutch	70	22	3	12	.314

2003 Rankings (National League)

- 2nd in doubles
- 3rd in batting average on the road
- 4th in errors at second base (14) and lowest fielding percentage at second base (.982)
- Led the Braves in doubles, sacrifice bunts (10), caught stealing (4) and hit by pitch (11)

Atlanta

Mike Hampton

2003 Season

Mike Hampton escaped the horrifying thin air in Denver, landing in Atlanta via a complicated three-team deal with Florida. After getting off to a slow start, he overcame a strained left groin and looked like the Hampton of old after the All-Star break. He won nine straight decisions while going 11-3 with a 3.26 ERA in his final 17 starts.

Pitching

Hampton benefited from the insight he garnered from Atlanta pitching coach Leo Mazzone, who got the lefthander to make some mechanical adjustments. Mazzone convinced Hampton to slow his delivery and stop throwing across his body, a tendency that had negated the effect of his sinker—particularly on the inside part of the plate to righthanded hitters. By reducing his velocity, he improved the movement of his sinker as well as his ability to locate the pitch on both sides of the plate. Hampton overpowered lefthanded hitters, limiting them to a paltry .164 batting average.

Defense & Hitting

Hampton helps himself as much as any pitcher in the game. He won his first Gold Glove last year, the first NL pitcher *not* named Greg Maddux to win the award since 1989. Due to his sinker, he gets an above-average number of balls hit back to the mound. He has soft hands, excellent range and is not afraid to nail the lead runner when opponents attempt a sacrifice bunt. Hampton rarely throws over to first base, relying instead on his quick portside delivery to hold runners. At the plate, he is one of the league's best hitting pitchers. He dropped down nine sacrifice bunts in addition to recording 11 hits, two home runs and eight RBI last year.

2004 Outlook

If Hampton can maintain his confidence and rhythm, he has a chance to resume his role as a consistent 15-game winner. He is signed with the Braves through the 2008 season and is expected to remain one of the team's top three starters for the foreseeable future.

Position: SP
Bats: R **Throws:** L
Ht: 5'10" **Wt:** 180

Opening Day Age: 31
Born: 9/9/72 in Brooksville, FL
ML Seasons: 11

Overall Statistics

	W	L	Pct.	ERA	G	GS	Sv	IP	H	BB	SO	HR	Avg
'03	14	8	.636	3.84	31	31	0	190.0	186	78	110	14	.255
Car.	120	89	.574	3.96	334	280	1	1832.1	1884	743	1158	157	.269

2003 Pitching Profile

	Mike Hampton	NL Average
Overall Strike %	62.7	62.4
1st Pitch Strike %	57.0	58.4
Ratio	1.39	1.38
Strikeouts per 9 IP	5.21	6.65
Walks per 9 IP	3.69	3.42
Home Runs per 9 IP	0.66	1.05
Strikeout/Walk Ratio	1.41	1.94
Groundball/Flyball Ratio	1.95	1.29

2003 Situational Stats

	W	L	ERA	Sv	IP		AB	H	HR	RBI	Avg
Home	7	4	3.26	0	99.1	LHB	146	24	3	9	.164
Road	7	4	4.47	0	90.2	RHB	583	162	11	65	.278
First Half	5	5	4.85	0	91.0	Sc Pos	200	53	1	57	.265
Scnd Half	9	3	2.91	0	99.0	Clutch	33	7	0	2	.212

2003 Rankings (National League)

- 2nd in lowest stolen-base percentage allowed (33.3)
- 3rd in lowest batting average allowed vs. lefthanded batters
- 5th in lowest strikeout-walk ratio (1.4)
- 7th in highest groundball-flyball ratio allowed (2.0) and fewest home runs allowed per nine innings (.66)
- 9th in most run support per nine innings (5.6)
- 10th in wild pitches (10) and winning percentage
- Led the Braves in wild pitches (10), highest groundball-flyball ratio allowed (2.0), lowest stolen-base percentage allowed (33.3), lowest ERA at home, lowest batting average allowed vs. lefthanded batters, and fewest home runs allowed per nine innings (.66)

Andruw Jones

2003 Season

Despite playing with a strained oblique muscle for most of the summer, Andruw Jones had one of his most productive seasons in 2003. He established his career-best in RBI, equaled his career-high in home runs and eclipsed the 30 homer mark for the fourth straight season. He also earned his sixth straight Gold Glove Award.

Hitting

Jones is a dangerous hitter who could reach another level of production if he maintained a little more consistency and focus. He showed better plate coverage last year, yet he continued to strike out too often. And after showing more patience with a career-high 83 walks in 2002, he drew only 53 free passes last season. He still has holes in his swing and remains susceptible to chasing sinkers, as well as breaking balls down and away. Jones is an excellent bad-pitch hitter. Balls jump off his bat, and he can turn on any fastball.

Baserunning & Defense

Jones arguably is the majors' best defensive center fielder in at least three decades. No one gets a better jump on balls hit to the middle garden than Jones, allowing him to cover more ground than any outfielder in the game. His first step and fly-ball judgment saves Braves pitchers numerous doubles and triples. His arm is one of baseball's strongest and most accurate, so much so that few teams are willing to test him. Jones' above-average speed does not translate into exceptional baserunning. He swiped just four bases in seven attempts last year and is prone to making mental mistakes on the basepaths.

2004 Outlook

No one should be surprised if Jones surpasses 40 home runs and 125 RBI in a season sometime soon. Then again, the Braves have been awaiting an outburst for a few years. He nevertheless remains one of the premier all-around center fielders in the game, and he can dominate when at his best.

Position: CF
Bats: R **Throws:** R
Ht: 6' 1"   **Wt:** 210

Opening Day Age: 26
Born: 4/23/77 in Willemstad, Curacao
ML Seasons: 8

Overall Statistics

	G	AB	R	H	D	T	HR	RBI	SB	BB	SO	Avg	OBP	Slg
'03	156	595	101	165	28	2	36	116	4	53	125	.277	.338	.513
Car.	1137	4115	675	1105	216	25	221	675	118	430	870	.269	.341	.494

Where He Hits the Ball

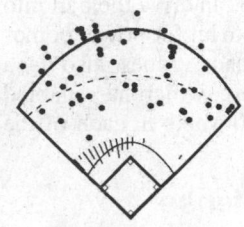 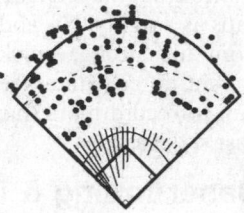

Vs. LHP   **Vs. RHP**

2003 Situational Stats

	AB	H	HR	RBI	Avg		AB	H	HR	RBI	Avg
Home	277	78	16	54	.282	LHP	131	34	11	27	.260
Road	318	87	20	62	.274	RHP	464	131	25	89	.282
First Half	343	96	23	64	.280	Sc Pos	195	53	8	74	.272
Scnd Half	252	69	13	52	.274	Clutch	82	22	5	16	.268

2003 Rankings (National League)

- 2nd in highest percentage of swings on the first pitch (42.6)
- 3rd in fielding percentage in center field (.993)
- 5th in lowest percentage of pitches taken (48.7)
- 7th in RBI
- 8th in errors in center field (3) and highest percentage of swings that missed (28.4)
- 10th in home runs
- Led the Braves in strikeouts and games played

Atlanta

Chipper Jones

2003 Season

Despite driving in 100 runs for the eighth straight season—becoming only the 12th player in major league history to accomplish the feat—Chipper Jones rated his 2003 campaign as "possibly the worst of my career." Although Jones' .305 batting average was his lowest since 1997, the Braves had no complaints about the left fielder's output. He surpassed the 900 RBI plateau in his career and now ranks fourth in modern franchise history.

Hitting

Jones has become one of the top switch-hitters in the game by improving from the right side of the plate in recent years. While most of his power comes from the left side, he can drive the ball into gaps as a righty. His ability to hit for power comes from his strong, quick hands. Jones also is a patient hitter with a keen eye, which has enabled him to record more than 90 walks in each of the past six seasons.

Baserunning & Defense

In his second season as a left fielder, Jones displayed better range by getting quicker jumps on balls off the bat. He led Atlanta's outfielders in assists for the second straight year with his accurate arm, and improved his routes on flyballs. Jones may have lost a half-step in the past year or two, stealing just two bases in 2003 after swiping as many as 25 earlier in his career. Even so, he continues to be a smart and aggressive baserunner with as much ability and athleticism as any cleanup hitter in the major leagues.

2004 Outlook

There are some members of the Atlanta organization who believe Jones will wind up at first base. In the meantime, the former third baseman is expected to remain in left field, while continuing to provide some of the steadiest production in the game as the heart and soul of the Braves' batting order.

Position: LF
Bats: B **Throws:** R
Ht: 6' 4" **Wt:** 220

Opening Day Age: 31
Born: 4/24/72 in DeLand, FL
ML Seasons: 10

Overall Statistics

	G	AB	R	H	D	T	HR	RBI	SB	BB	SO	Avg	OBP	Slg
'03	153	555	103	169	33	2	27	106	2	94	83	.305	.402	.517
Car.	1405	5144	966	1588	305	26	280	943	116	853	781	.309	.404	.541

Where He Hits the Ball

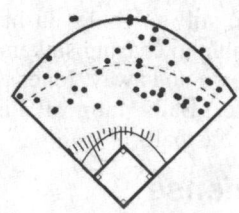 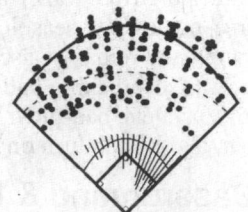

Vs. LHP   **Vs. RHP**

2003 Situational Stats

	AB	H	HR	RBI	Avg		AB	H	HR	RBI	Avg
Home	273	85	16	60	.311	LHP	121	37	2	18	.306
Road	282	84	11	46	.298	RHP	434	132	25	88	.304
First Half	318	92	17	57	.289	Sc Pos	165	54	6	79	.327
Scnd Half	237	77	10	49	.325	Clutch	69	21	4	9	.304

2003 Rankings (National League)

- 1st in lowest fielding percentage in left field (.968)
- 2nd in errors in left field (7)
- 7th in intentional walks (13)
- 9th in runs scored, RBI and on-base percentage
- 10th in walks
- Led the Braves in walks, intentional walks (13) and cleanup slugging percentage (.513)
- Led NL left fielders in RBI

Javy Lopez

2003 Season

After two disappointing seasons, Javy Lopez lost 35 pounds and put together the best offensive campaign of his career in 2003, the final year of his contract. He broke Todd Hundley's record for home runs in a season by a catcher and joined Mike Piazza and Roy Campanella as the only receivers in major league history to hit higher than .300 with at least 40 homers and 100 RBI in a single season.

Hitting

Lopez has had solid pop in his bat throughout his career, but his home-run production last year was a surprise since he had hit more than 24 homers just once. Long prone to free swinging and trying overzealously to pull pitches, Lopez became more conscious of keeping his head down and his lead shoulder closed. He also scaled back on looking for the first-pitch fastball, which helped him reduce the number of bad pitches he swung at early in the count. The result was more consistent and much harder contact.

Baserunning & Defense

Lopez is a much better defensive catcher than he was early in his career. Though no Ivan Rodriguez, his throwing has improved, particularly the quickness of his release and his overall accuracy. However, he will try to backhand pitches in the dirt instead of blocking them, resulting in wild pitches and passed balls. There also are concerns about Lopez' back. Combine that with his suspect game-calling abilities—which have long been criticized by scouts—and Lopez could be headed for first base, a move he would welcome, at least on a part-time basis.

2004 Outlook

Lopez is expected to receive significant interest on the free-agent market after his stellar offensive output last summer. A Brave throughout his career, he is almost certain to be playing elsewhere in 2004 after the Braves didn't offer him salary arbitration.

Position: C
Bats: R **Throws:** R
Ht: 6' 3" **Wt:** 215

Opening Day Age: 33
Born: 11/5/70 in Ponce, PR
ML Seasons: 12
Pronunciation: HAH-vee LOE-pezz

Overall Statistics

	G	AB	R	H	D	T	HR	RBI	SB	BB	SO	Avg	OBP	Slg
'03	129	457	89	150	29	3	43	109	0	33	90	.328	.378	.687
Car.	1156	4003	508	1148	190	14	214	694	8	271	728	.287	.337	.502

Where He Hits the Ball

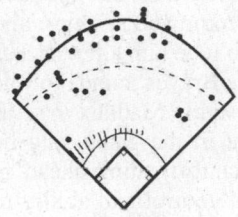
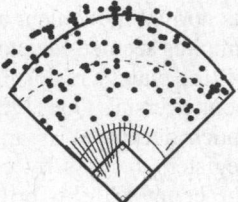

Vs. LHP	Vs. RHP

2003 Situational Stats

	AB	H	HR	RBI	Avg		AB	H	HR	RBI	Avg
Home	205	77	26	59	.376	LHP	110	37	11	30	.336
Road	252	73	17	50	.290	RHP	347	113	32	79	.326
First Half	261	80	23	52	.307	Sc Pos	117	40	11	69	.342
Scnd Half	196	70	20	57	.357	Clutch	72	23	10	23	.319

2003 Rankings (National League)

- 3rd in highest percentage of runners caught stealing as a catcher (27.8)
- 4th in home runs
- Led the Braves in home runs, slugging percentage, HR frequency (10.6 ABs per HR) and batting average at home
- Led NL catchers in home runs and RBI

Greg Maddux

2003 Season

After losing his first three starts for the first time in his major league career, Greg Maddux recovered to become the first pitcher in major league annals to record 16 straight seasons with at least 15 victories, and the first since Bob Gibson to register 13 consecutive winning campaigns. He concluded 2003 with 289 career triumphs, good for 22nd on the all-time charts.

Pitching

After struggling early in the year to find the consistent feel for his pitches, Maddux rediscovered his groove at midseason and continued to confound hitters with his ability to dominate without overpowering stuff. His fastball did not have its normal movement and command at times, and umpires seemed reluctant to give him a few inches off the plate, a result (in the Braves' minds) of the controversial QuesTec system. Maddux has as much deception as anyone in the game, and he registers success by constantly getting ahead in the count with his brilliant control and ability to change speeds. He also gets more from less— Maddux has thrown fewer pitches per inning than any starter over the past two years.

Defense & Hitting

Though he failed to win a Gold Glove last year, Maddux has great hands, instincts and quickness in fielding the ball. His weakness continues to be holding runners on base, a fact exacerbated by his focus on the hitter and a nonchalant attitude regarding the baserunner. The ultra-competitive Maddux continues to be a decent hitter and effective bunter.

2004 Outlook

Though his 3.96 ERA in 2003 was his highest since 1987, there's no reason to think that Maddux won't become the 21st member of the 300-win club this year. The only question is where the free agent will accomplish the feat. It's highly unlikely to be Atlanta after the Braves didn't offer him salary arbitration. Maddux says he wants to pitch as many as four more seasons. At his current rate, that might be achievable.

Position: SP
Bats: R **Throws:** R
Ht: 6' 0" **Wt:** 185

Opening Day Age: 37
Born: 4/14/66 in San Angelo, TX
ML Seasons: 18
Pronunciation: MADD-ucks

Overall Statistics

W	L	Pct.	ERA	G	GS	Sv	IP	H	BB	SO	HR	Avg
16	11	.593	3.96	36	36	0	218.1	225	33	124	24	.268
289	163	.639	2.89	575	571	0	3968.2	3625	838	2765	234	.244

2003 Pitching Profile

	Greg Maddux	NL Average
Overall Strike %	66.0	62.4
1st Pitch Strike %	61.8	58.4
Ratio	1.18	1.38
Strikeouts per 9 IP	5.11	6.65
Walks per 9 IP	1.36	3.42
Home Runs per 9 IP	0.99	1.05
Strikeout/Walk Ratio	3.76	1.94
Groundball/Flyball Ratio	1.84	1.29

2003 Situational Stats

	W	L	ERA	Sv	IP		AB	H	HR	RBI	Avg
Home	9	7	3.41	0	118.2	LHB	391	106	9	40	.271
Road	7	4	4.61	0	99.2	RHB	450	119	15	64	.264
First Half	7	8	4.63	0	126.1	Sc Pos	201	56	5	74	.279
Scnd Half	9	3	3.03	0	92.0	Clutch	51	12	2	5	.235

2003 Rankings (National League)
- 1st in games started, fewest pitches thrown per batter (3.26) and fewest walks per nine innings (1.4)
- 2nd in stolen bases allowed (26)
- 3rd in pickoff throws (163)
- 4th in hits allowed
- 5th in wins and highest strikeout-walk ratio (3.8)
- 6th in innings pitched
- 7th in runners caught stealing (8)
- 8th in lowest on-base percentage allowed (.299)
- Led the Braves in losses, games started, innings pitched, hits allowed, home runs allowed, hit batsmen (8), pickoff throws (163), stolen bases allowed (26), runners caught stealing (8), highest strikeout-walk ratio (3.8), lowest on-base percentage allowed (.299), fewest pitches thrown per batter (3.26) and fewest walks per nine innings (1.4)

Russ Ortiz

Position: SP
Bats: R **Throws:** R
Ht: 6' 1" **Wt:** 208

Opening Day Age: 29
Born: 6/5/74 in Encino, CA
ML Seasons: 6
Pronunciation: OR-teez

2003 Season

A successful pitcher in San Francisco for four years, Russ Ortiz took the next step in his career after joining the Braves in an offseason trade last year. Winning a circuit-high 21 victories, Ortiz notched a 14-3 record in his final 19 starts.

Pitching

Ortiz is one of the few pitchers who can get by with working up in the strike zone. He does not have a signature pitch, and his stuff will not blow hitters away, despite a fastball in the 92-94 MPH range and a hard-breaking curveball. Not unlike the pitcher he replaced in the Atlanta rotation—Tom Glavine—Ortiz is stubborn and calculating on the mound. He never gives in to hitters and will risk a walk instead of giving hitters what they're looking for. That philosophy led to Ortiz leading the league in walks and ranking among the leaders in pitches per start. He remains a workhorse, having gone at least six innings in 132 of his 178 career starts.

Defense & Hitting

Ortiz has quick reflexes, soft hands, and he does a good job of covering first base. He is willing to gamble and nail the lead runner, enabling him to start five double plays last year. Offensively, Ortiz has emerged as one of the premier hitters among pitchers. He batted .257 last year with two home runs and 10 RBI. His bunting is not as effective as his swing, yet he still dropped down six sacrifices in 2003. After controlling the running game effectively in 2001-02, he was one of the easier pitchers to steal on in 2003.

2004 Outlook

Ortiz may not be a quintessential No. 1 starter, but he does an excellent job of keeping his team in the game. The Braves, who exercised their 2004 option on Ortiz' contract, will be counting on an encore performance from him in their quest for a 13th straight division flag.

Overall Statistics

	W	L	Pct.	ERA	G	GS	Sv	IP	H	BB	SO	HR	Avg
'03	21	7	.750	3.81	34	34	0	212.1	177	102	149	17	.223
Car.	88	51	.633	3.97	188	178	0	1137.0	1026	570	861	108	.242

2003 Pitching Profile

	Russ Ortiz	NL Average
Overall Strike %	58.9	62.4
1st Pitch Strike %	52.6	58.4
Ratio	1.31	1.38
Strikeouts per 9 IP	6.32	6.65
Walks per 9 IP	4.32	3.42
Home Runs per 9 IP	0.72	1.05
Strikeout/Walk Ratio	1.46	1.94
Groundball/Flyball Ratio	1.07	1.29

2003 Situational Stats

	W	L	ERA	Sv	IP		AB	H	HR	RBI	Avg
Home	14	3	3.53	0	119.2	LHB	366	97	7	41	.265
Road	7	4	4.18	0	92.2	RHB	427	80	10	45	.187
First Half	12	4	3.51	0	128.1	Sc Pos	193	50	7	72	.259
Scnd Half	9	3	4.29	0	84.0	Clutch	41	10	1	1	.244

2003 Rankings (National League)

- 1st in wins and walks allowed
- 2nd in winning percentage
- 3rd in games started and lowest batting average allowed vs. righthanded batters
- 4th in pitches thrown (3,569), lowest batting average allowed (.223), most run support per nine innings (6.5) and highest walks per nine innings (4.3)
- 5th in stolen bases allowed (22)
- 6th in batters faced (912) and lowest slugging percentage allowed (.347)
- Led the Braves in ERA, wins, batters faced (912), walks allowed, strikeouts, pitches thrown (3,569), winning percentage, lowest batting average allowed (.223), lowest slugging percentage allowed (.347), lowest batting average allowed vs. righthanded batters, most run support per nine innings (6.5) and most strikeouts per nine innings (6.3)

Gary Sheffield

2003 Season

Gary Sheffield deserves as much credit as anyone for the Braves establishing the best all-around offensive season in franchise history. Sheffield broke Hank Aaron's Atlanta mark for RBI in a season. He had three hitting streaks of at least 12 games, including a career-best 24-game stretch from July 26 through August 20. The lone negative occurred in October, when Sheffield endured another postseason to forget, going 2-for-14 against the Cubs in the National League Division Series.

Hitting

Sheffield owns a near-perfect line-drive swing and quick, powerful hands and wrists that allow him to drive the ball to all fields. His bat speed remains among the fastest in the game. He has an exceptional eye at the plate, along with the patience to wait for his pitch. Many scouts consider Sheffield to be the game's best 0-2 hitter. His most valuable attribute may be his consistency. He has hit higher than .300 for six straight seasons and has reached the century mark in RBI in four of the last five years.

Baserunning & Defense

Sheffield is a pure five-tool talent. He has one of the game's stronger arms in right field and rarely makes a physical or mental mistake on defense. He does an outstanding job of cutting balls off in the gap, and he displayed more mobility last season after undergoing surgery in December 2002 to detach some nerve endings from both knees. Sheffield is a good baserunner who last season became only the 17th player in history to steal 200 bases while hitting at least 300 home runs in a career.

2004 Outlook

A free agent, Sheffield is one of the few players teams considered lining up for this offseason. When healthy, he remains one of the most effective and dangerous performers in the game. Chances are he will sign the last lucrative long-term contract of his career.

Position: RF
Bats: R **Throws:** R
Ht: 6' 0" **Wt:** 205

Opening Day Age: 35
Born: 11/18/68 in Tampa, FL
ML Seasons: 16

Overall Statistics

G	AB	R	H	D	T	HR	RBI	SB	BB	SO	Avg	OBP	Slg
155	576	126	190	37	2	39	132	18	86	55	.330	.419	.604
1882	6729	1190	2009	356	23	379	1232	200	1110	796	.299	.401	.527

Where He Hits the Ball

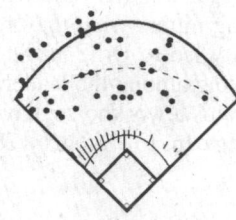 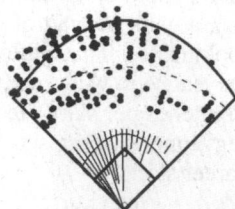

Vs. LHP **Vs. RHP**

2003 Situational Stats

	AB	H	HR	RBI	Avg		AB	H	HR	RBI	Avg
Home	290	92	20	64	.317	LHP	123	42	10	32	.341
Road	286	98	19	68	.343	RHP	453	148	29	100	.327
First Half	324	106	22	70	.327	Sc Pos	153	58	7	92	.379
Scnd Half	252	84	17	62	.333	Clutch	71	25	4	17	.352

2003 Rankings (National League)

- 1st in batting average on the road
- 2nd in RBI
- 3rd in total bases (348) and batting average with runners in scoring position
- 4th in runs scored, times on base (284), stolen-base percentage (81.8) and fielding percentage in right field (.986)
- 5th in batting average, sacrifice flies (8), slugging percentage and lowest percentage of swings on the first pitch (16.0)
- Led the Braves in batting average, total bases (348), RBI, sacrifice flies (8), caught stealing (4), times on base (284), on-base percentage, highest percentage of pitches taken (60.8)

John Smoltz

2003 Season

A trip to the disabled list with elbow tendinitis for a month in August and early September was the lone complication John Smoltz encountered in an otherwise near-perfect season. Prior to that, Smoltz was on a record pace with 44 saves through August 23. He returned in time to pitch in the postseason, and finished the campaign by joining the Dodgers' Eric Gagne as the only relievers ever to post 100 or more saves in a two-year period.

Pitching

Smoltz is close to unhittable when healthy. He dominates opposing hitters with his 96-98 MPH fastball and a slider in the 88-90 MPH range. His heater has exceptional movement and is hard enough for him to get away with leaving the pitch up in the strike zone. His slider is one of the nastiest pitches in the game. It resembles his fastball before taking a late, darting dive, resulting in countless half-swings and complete misses. Smoltz did not throw his split-finger fastball as much last year as he did in 2002 due to the effect the pitch has on his arm. On rare occasions he also throws a changeup and knuckleball.

Defense & Hitting

No one competes harder than Smoltz, regardless of the activity. He expects perfection in everything he attempts, including hitting and fielding. His glovework is consistent, with Smoltz displaying soft hands and excellent all-around athleticism. He also holds runners effectively.

2004 Outlook

Smoltz began the offseason by having surgery for the fourth time on his right elbow, this time to remove painful scar tissue. Smoltz said that would be the final time he underwent the knife to salvage his baseball career. He continues to politic to return to the starting rotation, but the Braves feel he is most valuable as one of the two best closers in the game.

Position: RP
Bats: R **Throws:** R
Ht: 6' 3" **Wt:** 220

Opening Day Age: 36
Born: 5/15/67 in Warren, MI
ML Seasons: 15

Overall Statistics

W	L	Pct.	ERA	G	GS	Sv	IP	H	BB	SO	HR	Avg
0	2	.000	1.12	62	0	45	64.1	48	8	73	2	.204
163	120	.576	3.29	529	361	110	2618.0	2252	816	2313	208	.232

2003 Pitching Profile

	John Smoltz	NL Average
Overall Strike %	72.7	62.4
1st Pitch Strike %	71.2	58.4
Ratio	0.87	1.38
Strikeouts per 9 IP	10.21	6.65
Walks per 9 IP	1.12	3.42
Home Runs per 9 IP	0.28	1.05
Strikeout/Walk Ratio	9.13	1.94
Groundball/Flyball Ratio	1.23	1.29

2003 Situational Stats

	W	L	ERA	Sv	IP		AB	H	HR	RBI	Avg
Home	0	0	0.48	27	37.1	LHB	111	21	0	6	.189
Road	0	2	2.00	18	27.0	RHB	124	27	2	10	.218
First Half	0	1	0.95	34	47.1	Sc Pos	46	7	0	10	.152
Scnd Half	0	1	1.59	11	17.0	Clutch	162	33	1	14	.204

2003 Rankings (National League)

- 2nd in saves and fewest baserunners allowed per nine innings in relief (7.8)
- 4th in save percentage (91.8)
- Led the Braves in saves, games finished (55), save percentage (91.8), blown saves (4), relief ERA (1.12), relief innings (64.1), lowest batting average allowed in relief (.204), fewest baserunners allowed per nine innings in relief (7.8), and most strikeouts per nine innings in relief (10.2)

Jung Bong

Position: RP
Bats: L **Throws:** L
Ht: 6' 3" **Wt:** 175

Opening Day Age: 23
Born: 7/15/80 in Seoul, South Korea
ML Seasons: 2

Overall Statistics

	W	L	Pct.	ERA	G	GS	Sv	IP	H	BB	SO	HR	Avg
'03	6	2	.750	5.05	44	0	1	57.0	56	31	47	8	.267
Car.	6	3	.667	5.29	45	1	1	63.0	64	33	51	8	.272

2003 Situational Stats

	W	L	ERA	Sv	IP		AB	H	HR	RBI	Avg
Home	2	0	6.33	1	27.0	LHB	72	19	4	15	.264
Road	4	2	3.90	0	30.0	RHB	138	37	4	20	.268
First Half	6	1	3.83	1	47.0	Sc Pos	66	18	3	29	.273
Scnd Half	0	1	10.80	0	10.0	Clutch	57	12	2	7	.211

2003 Season

Primarily a starter during his five seasons in the minors, Jung Bong worked in relief throughout his rookie season. He was effective early in the year but then struggled, posting a 9.18 ERA after July 1.

Pitching, Defense & Hitting

A native of South Korea, Bong throws one of the best changeups in the National League. His fastball sits at 91-92 MPH and touches 94 MPH on occasion, but he does not always have command of the pitch. Though he has shown solid improvement with his curveball over the past three seasons, he lacks the confidence to throw it often enough to keep hitters off-balance. The Braves have worked with Bong on becoming more aggressive on the mound. An excellent athlete who was considered a premier hitting prospect prior to signing, Bong fields his position very well and holds runners effectively.

2004 Outlook

While he is expected to remain in the Atlanta bullpen this year, Bong could be considered for a job in the rotation when he starts using all three of his pitches more consistently. He also could get more seasoning in Triple-A.

Mark DeRosa

Position: 2B/3B/SS
Bats: R **Throws:** R
Ht: 6' 1" **Wt:** 205

Opening Day Age: 29
Born: 2/26/75 in Passaic, NJ
ML Seasons: 6

Overall Statistics

	G	AB	R	H	D	T	HR	RBI	SB	BB	SO	Avg	OBP	Slg
'03	103	266	40	70	14	0	6	22	1	16	49	.263	.316	.383
Car.	275	666	102	185	32	2	14	68	5	42	96	.278	.330	.395

2003 Situational Stats

	AB	H	HR	RBI	Avg		AB	H	HR	RBI	Avg
Home	127	33	3	9	.260	LHP	83	23	3	12	.277
Road	139	37	3	13	.266	RHP	183	47	3	10	.257
First Half	136	31	4	12	.228	Sc Pos	56	12	0	14	.214
Scnd Half	130	39	2	10	.300	Clutch	37	8	1	5	.216

2003 Season

Last year could be deemed a disappointment for Mark DeRosa, if for no other reason than his lack of opportunity. With Marcus Giles retaking second base and Vinny Castilla maintaining a consistent glove at third, DeRosa played a reserve role at all four infield positions after entering spring training as a potential starter. He finished the season on a tear, batting .364 average in his final 21 games.

Hitting, Baserunning & Defense

DeRosa was uncharacteristically overaggressive at times last year, leading to more strikeouts than usual for him. He makes solid contact, has surprising power, and routinely drives pitches into the gaps. He draws walks only infrequently. DeRosa runs well and will take the extra base. A shortstop throughout his days in the minors, he has above-average range with soft hands and a strong and accurate arm.

2004 Outlook

DeRosa's best chance to start would come if the Braves opt against re-signing Castilla or another free-agent third baseman. Castilla has departed for Colorado, so DeRosa may be closer to starting at third for Atlanta. If the Braves sign another third baseman, DeRosa would play a utility role and probably would post numbers similar to his 2003 output.

Julio Franco

Position: 1B
Bats: R **Throws:** R
Ht: 6' 1" **Wt:** 188

Opening Day Age: 42
Born: 8/23/61 in San Pedro de Macoris, DR
ML Seasons: 19

Overall Statistics

G	AB	R	H	D	T	HR	RBI	SB	BB	SO	Avg	OBP	Slg
103	197	28	58	12	2	5	31	0	25	43	.294	.372	.452
2144	7869	1196	2358	364	50	155	1053	265	827	1144	.300	.366	.418

2003 Situational Stats

	AB	H	HR	RBI	Avg		AB	H	HR	RBI	Avg
Home	90	22	1	14	.244	LHP	94	33	3	19	.351
Road	107	36	4	17	.336	RHP	103	25	2	12	.243
First Half	126	39	2	19	.310	Sc Pos	56	19	0	23	.339
Scnd Half	71	19	3	12	.268	Clutch	39	9	0	2	.231

2003 Season

Julio Franco's activity diminished in 2003 due to the presence of Robert Fick and a fractured left middle finger that cost him the last two weeks of August. He produced when given the opportunity, driving in 31 runs, his highest total as a major leaguer since 1997. The Braves were 26-12 in Franco's starts at first base.

Hitting, Baserunning & Defense

Franco's swing may be unorthodox, with his hands wrapped across the top of his head and his knees knocking together, but the results remain impressive. He continues to feast on lefthanded pitching, hitting .369 against southpaws in his three seasons with the Braves. A frequent late-inning defensive replacement, Franco has soft, steady hands, committing just one error in 2003, and moves well around the first-base bag. He also is a good and smart baserunner.

2004 Outlook

Franco may be in his early 40s, but his production on the bench is too potent for the Braves to look elsewhere for help. While Atlanta is expected to search for a full-time first baseman, Franco should return to the Braves, punishing lefties while providing a constant stick and glove off the pines.

Kevin Gryboski

Position: RP
Bats: R **Throws:** R
Ht: 6' 5" **Wt:** 235

Opening Day Age: 30
Born: 11/15/73 in Wilkes-Barre, PA
ML Seasons: 2
Pronunciation: gri-BUS-ski

Overall Statistics

	W	L	Pct.	ERA	G	GS	Sv	IP	H	BB	SO	HR	Avg
'03	6	4	.600	3.86	64	0	0	44.1	44	23	32	3	.272
Car.	8	5	.615	3.66	121	0	0	96.0	94	60	65	9	.263

2003 Situational Stats

	W	L	ERA	Sv	IP		AB	H	HR	RBI	Avg
Home	4	0	3.97	0	22.2	LHB	44	10	0	5	.227
Road	2	4	3.74	0	21.2	RHB	118	34	3	24	.288
First Half	5	3	4.70	0	30.2	Sc Pos	67	17	0	23	.254
Scnd Half	1	1	1.98	0	13.2	Clutch	60	20	1	11	.333

2003 Season

Kevin Gryboski continues to be a consistent workhorse in the Atlanta bullpen. He got off to a rough start last season before posting a 2.35 ERA in his final 46 contests. He was on pace to rank among the league leaders in appearances before right shoulder tendinitis sidelined him for three-plus weeks beginning in late August.

Pitching, Defense & Hitting

Gryboski is a favorite of manager Bobby Cox due to his ability to work out of trouble by stranding runners and inducing double plays. The righthander's best pitch is a heavy, sinking fastball. With his ability to run the ball low and inside, Gryboski is particularly tough on lefthanded hitters. He struggles on occasion with his control, but has the confidence and guile to work out of trouble and succeed. He has improved at holding runners.

2004 Outlook

After spending more than seven years as a minor league journeyman, Gryboski has found a home in the Atlanta bullpen. As one of the younger members of the Braves' relief corps, Gryboski should again be a vital part of the team's situational pitching approach during the late innings of games.

Roberto Hernandez

Position: RP
Bats: R **Throws:** R
Ht: 6' 4" **Wt:** 250

Opening Day Age: 39
Born: 11/11/64 in
Santurce, PR
ML Seasons: 13

Overall Statistics

	W	L	Pct.	ERA	G	GS	Sv	IP	H	BB	SO	HR	Avg
'03	5	3	.625	4.35	66	0	0	60.0	61	43	45	10	.263
Car.	53	54	.495	3.30	762	3	320	835.0	759	348	761	72	.241

2003 Situational Stats

	W	L	ERA	Sv	IP		AB	H	HR	RBI	Avg
Home	4	1	5.61	0	25.2	LHB	105	26	5	20	.248
Road	1	2	3.41	0	34.1	RHB	127	35	5	21	.276
First Half	5	2	4.28	0	40.0	Sc Pos	61	18	3	29	.295
Scnd Half	0	1	4.50	0	20.0	Clutch	111	27	7	25	.243

2003 Season

Roberto Hernandez was closer John Smoltz' righthanded setup man before spending time on the disabled list in June with a strained right abdominal muscle and in August with a strained left hamstring. When healthy, Hernandez did an excellent job, ranking among the National League leaders with 19 holds.

Pitching, Defense & Hitting

When he had the feel for his fastball and splitter last year, Hernandez was close to unhittable. On other occasions, he had difficulty getting his rhythm and finding the strike zone after entering the game, which opened the door for trouble. A former closer, Hernandez still overpowers hitters with his upper-90s fastball and is not afraid to challenge anyone. Hernandez is a below-average fielder who is not quick off the mound. He is so-so at holding runners, and seldom bats.

2004 Outlook

The Braves entered the offseason interested in retaining Hernandez' services. He loves the challenge of closing games, but showed last year that he can be an effective pitcher in a setup role. The 39-year-old may resume setup work in 2004, though not with Atlanta after the Braves didn't offer him salary arbitration.

Trey Hodges

Position: RP
Bats: R **Throws:** R
Ht: 6' 3" **Wt:** 187

Opening Day Age: 25
Born: 6/29/78 in
Houston, TX
ML Seasons: 2

Overall Statistics

	W	L	Pct.	ERA	G	GS	Sv	IP	H	BB	SO	HR	Avg
'03	3	3	.500	4.66	52	1	0	65.2	69	31	66	11	.268
Car.	5	3	.625	4.77	56	1	0	77.1	85	33	72	13	.281

2003 Situational Stats

	W	L	ERA	Sv	IP		AB	H	HR	RBI	Avg
Home	2	1	5.00	0	36.0	LHB	104	28	6	22	.269
Road	1	2	4.25	0	29.2	RHB	153	41	5	26	.268
First Half	3	0	3.38	0	45.1	Sc Pos	76	22	4	38	.289
Scnd Half	0	3	7.52	0	20.1	Clutch	55	13	4	8	.236

2003 Season

In his first full year in the major leagues, Trey Hodges got off to a great start, posting a 1.64 ERA in his first 23 outings. But the righthander went 0-3 with a 7.71 ERA in 29 games the rest of the way. In fairness, Hodges was battling a strained right elbow muscle that sidelined him for more than two weeks in July and August.

Pitching, Defense & Hitting

The winner of 30 minor league games as a starter in 2001 and 2002, Hodges relies on a plus slider that he will throw at any time in the count. He also possesses good command of his sneaky 89-91 MPH fastball. His changeup was a work in progress in the minors, and he does not have total confidence in it at this point in his career. A decent athlete, Hodges fields his position well. He is a capable bunter at bat but so-so at holding runners.

2004 Outlook

Though Hodges feels more comfortable in the rotation, his role in Atlanta is expected to remain in the bullpen. To land a spot, he'll need to show he's healthy and flash more of the form he displayed early last season.

Ray King

Position: RP
Bats: L **Throws:** L
Ht: 6' 1" **Wt:** 247

Opening Day Age: 30
Born: 1/15/74 in
Chicago, IL
ML Seasons: 5

Overall Statistics

	W	L	Pct.	ERA	G	GS	Sv	IP	H	BB	SO	HR	Avg
'03	3	4	.429	3.51	80	0	0	59.0	46	27	43	3	.213
Car.	9	12	.429	3.22	284	0	1	218.1	185	96	166	16	.232

2003 Situational Stats

	W	L	ERA	Sv	IP		AB	H	HR	RBI	Avg
Home	3	0	3.06	0	32.1	LHB	95	19	1	11	.200
Road	0	4	4.05	0	26.2	RHB	121	27	2	25	.223
First Half	2	0	2.04	0	35.1	Sc Pos	62	21	1	33	.339
Scnd Half	1	4	5.70	0	23.2	Clutch	92	15	2	16	.163

2003 Season

Ray King was one of busiest pitchers in baseball last year, falling one appearance shy of tying the Braves franchise record for games pitched in a season. Serving as the Braves' lefthanded setup man, King limited first batters to a .169 batting average, and had 14 straight shutout appearances from June 3 through July 2.

Pitching, Defense & Hitting

King is rubber-armed reliever who is effective against batters from both sides of the plate. He features a sweeping slider and a fastball in the 88-90 MPH range. He mixes in a splitter to righthanded hitters, and does an outstanding job of keeping all of his pitches down in the strike zone. King has only average hands as a defender. As a lefty, he is able to freeze baserunners at first with a slight hesitation in his delivery. His job description does not include hitting.

2004 Outlook

King proved to be the perfect fit in the Atlanta bullpen. He becomes more effective the more he pitches, which makes him invaluable during the latter days of the pennant race. If he doesn't return to Atlanta, it primarily will be for money reasons.

Kent Mercker

Position: RP
Bats: L **Throws:** L
Ht: 6' 2" **Wt:** 200

Opening Day Age: 36
Born: 2/1/68 in Dublin, OH
ML Seasons: 14

Overall Statistics

	W	L	Pct.	ERA	G	GS	Sv	IP	H	BB	SO	HR	Avg
'03	0	2	.000	1.95	67	0	1	55.1	46	32	48	6	.227
Car.	66	64	.508	4.27	491	150	20	1168.2	1163	542	798	135	.261

2003 Situational Stats

	W	L	ERA	Sv	IP		AB	H	HR	RBI	Avg
Home	0	1	2.08	1	30.1	LHB	81	18	1	14	.222
Road	0	1	1.80	0	25.0	RHB	122	28	5	12	.230
First Half	0	1	2.36	0	26.2	Sc Pos	65	10	0	20	.154
Scnd Half	0	1	1.57	1	28.2	Clutch	54	16	2	9	.296

2003 Season

Former Brave Kent Mercker came home to Atlanta on August 12 and was a solid lefthanded setup man down the stretch. He opened last year with Cincinnati, and after returning to action in early July after a 15-day stint on the disabled list with a sprained lower back, Mercker posted a 1.52 ERA in his last 31 games.

Pitching, Defense & Hitting

A former starter, Mercker has a decent repertoire, including a 90-MPH fastball that he cuts and sinks along with a curveball and changeup. While his control always has been shaky, Mercker is a good competitor and is willing to take the mound in any situation. A mediocre fielder, he does a decent job of holding runners with his lefthanded delivery. He was an average hitter early in his career but rarely wields a bat nowadays.

2004 Outlook

Mercker continued to battle an aching back late in the 2003 season and during the playoffs, limiting his availability. If he can remain healthy, he will have little difficulty finding a bullpen role as a situational pitcher late in contests. He won't be pitching in Atlanta after the Braves didn't offer him salary arbitration.

Atlanta

Horacio Ramirez

Position: SP
Bats: L **Throws:** L
Ht: 6' 1" **Wt:** 170

Opening Day Age: 24
Born: 11/24/79 in
Carson, CA
ML Seasons: 1

Overall Statistics

	W	L	Pct.	ERA	G	GS	Sv	IP	H	BB	SO	HR	Avg
'03	12	4	.750	4.00	29	29	0	182.1	181	72	100	21	.263
Car.	12	4	.750	4.00	29	29	0	182.1	181	72	100	21	.263

2003 Situational Stats

	W	L	ERA	Sv	IP		AB	H	HR	RBI	Avg
Home	4	2	3.75	0	74.1	LHB	141	29	2	12	.206
Road	8	2	4.17	0	108.0	RHB	547	152	19	66	.278
First Half	8	3	4.00	0	99.0	Sc Pos	177	42	4	56	.237
Scnd Half	4	1	4.00	0	83.1	Clutch	34	7	3	4	.206

2003 Season

After undergoing Tommy John elbow surgery in 2001, Horacio Ramirez worked his way back into shape at Double-A Greenville in 2002 before surprising the masses to earn the fifth starter's job in Atlanta last year. The lefthander responded with 12 wins, tying for the second-most ever by an Atlanta rookie.

Pitching, Defense & Hitting

Ramirez is a purebred product of the Atlanta farm system. He mirrors the organizational philosophy for southpaws by throwing mostly sinkers and changeups down and on the outside part of the plate. His fastball resides in the low 90s, and his natural cut fastball has a sharp break when his mechanics are in sync. He does not hold runners well for a lefty, but at bat he can help himself with a bunt.

2004 Outlook

While Ramirez pitched well for most of last season, he was aided by the 6.0 runs per nine innings he received from the offense. The Braves believe he will learn from his mistakes and will improve with additional experience and arm strength, which should enable him to maintain a hold on a spot in the lower half of the Atlanta rotation.

Shane Reynolds

Position: SP
Bats: R **Throws:** R
Ht: 6' 3" **Wt:** 215

Opening Day Age: 36
Born: 3/26/68 in
Bastrop, LA
ML Seasons: 12

Overall Statistics

	W	L	Pct.	ERA	G	GS	Sv	IP	H	BB	SO	HR	Avg
'03	11	9	.550	5.43	30	29	0	167.1	191	59	94	20	.293
Car.	114	95	.545	4.09	304	277	0	1789.2	1929	417	1403	191	.275

2003 Situational Stats

	W	L	ERA	Sv	IP		AB	H	HR	RBI	Avg
Home	4	7	6.90	0	75.2	LHB	264	67	4	28	.254
Road	7	2	4.22	0	91.2	RHB	387	124	16	63	.320
First Half	7	4	5.46	0	94.0	Sc Pos	125	41	8	69	.328
Scnd Half	4	5	5.40	0	73.1	Clutch	18	5	0	3	.278

2003 Season

After missing the second half of the 2002 season following surgery to repair a pinched nerve in his lower back, Shane Reynolds was released by the Astros on March 27, then signed with the Braves on April 10. Atlanta won 10 of Reynolds' first 11 starts, but he was often hit hard thereafter and posted only one victory after August 15.

Pitching, Defense & Hitting

With his fastball now rarely topping 85 MPH, Reynolds had begun to throw everything away, but the Braves convinced him to start working inside more often. The key to his success is pinpoint command; when he's off, it's batting practice for the opponent. He also throws a split-finger fastball in the upper 70s and a decent curve. While he fields his position well, Reynolds is only average at holding runners. He is a good bunter and has above-average power for a pitcher.

2004 Outlook

Reynolds was not effective down the stretch and won't be returning to Atlanta, as the Braves didn't offer him salary arbitration. With his inconsistency and declining stuff, the cerebral Reynolds will not be in great demand this winter, but should be able to land a job.

Other Atlanta Braves

Henry Blanco (Pos: C, Age: 32, Bats: R)

	G	AB	R	H	D	T	HR	RBI	SB	BB	SO	Avg	OBP	Slg
'03	55	151	11	30	8	0	1	13	0	10	21	.199	.252	.272
Car.	424	1238	121	271	71	7	27	126	4	134	243	.219	.295	.353

Blanco had the lowest average of his six-year career, hitting below .200, and was sent outright to Triple-A in October. He declined the assignment and became a free agent. 2004 Outlook: C

Darren Bragg (Pos: RF/LF/CF, Age: 34, Bats: L)

	G	AB	R	H	D	T	HR	RBI	SB	BB	SO	Avg	OBP	Slg
'03	104	162	21	39	5	1	0	9	2	13	38	.241	.305	.284
Car.	869	2360	328	608	142	13	42	251	55	294	539	.258	.343	.382

The lefthanded-hitting Bragg batted .292 versus southpaws and .219 against righties as a reserve. He had a hot July (11-for-22) after starting the season 13-for-85 (.153). 2004 Outlook: C

Will Cunnane (Pos: RHP, Age: 29)

	W	L	Pct.	ERA	G	GS	Sv	IP	H	BB	SO	HR	Avg
'03	2	2	.500	2.70	20	0	3	20.0	14	6	20	2	.189
Car.	12	11	.522	5.16	175	12	3	261.2	294	124	223	35	.286

Cunnane was released by the Cubs in December 2002. He was called up in August by Atlanta, where he notched three saves in four days during September while filling in for John Smoltz. 2004 Outlook: B

Joe Dawley (Pos: RHP, Age: 32)

	W	L	Pct.	ERA	G	GS	Sv	IP	H	BB	SO	HR	Avg
'03	0	0	—	18.00	5	0	0	7.0	15	3	8	3	.405
Car.	0	0	—	17.18	6	0	0	7.1	15	3	9	3	.395

Dawley served brief stints with the Braves the last two years. The 32-year-old had a 3.34 ERA at Triple-A Richmond and signed with the Royals after the season. 2004 Outlook: B

Matt Franco (Pos: 1B, Age: 34, Bats: L)

	G	AB	R	H	D	T	HR	RBI	SB	BB	SO	Avg	OBP	Slg
'03	112	134	11	33	5	0	3	15	0	11	26	.246	.299	.351
Car.	661	977	110	261	43	6	22	117	2	124	158	.267	.349	.391

Franco has become a pinch-hitting specialist, as 78 of his 134 at-bats came off the bench. He hit better than .300 (3-for-9) versus lefthanders for the second straight season. 2004 Outlook: C

Jesse Garcia (Pos: 2B, Age: 30, Bats: R)

	G	AB	R	H	D	T	HR	RBI	SB	BB	SO	Avg	OBP	Slg
'03	13	10	6	4	0	1	0	2	0	0	1	.400	.400	.600
Car.	105	122	23	24	1	1	2	9	6	4	21	.197	.222	.270

Injuries made the Braves keep 12 pitchers out of spring training, costing Garcia a roster spot. He went 4-for-10 (.400) as the Braves' sixth infielder in September. 2004 Outlook: B

Mike Hessman (Pos: LF, Age: 26, Bats: R)

	G	AB	R	H	D	T	HR	RBI	SB	BB	SO	Avg	OBP	Slg
'03	19	21	2	6	2	0	2	3	0	5	6	.286	.423	.667
Car.	19	21	2	6	2	0	2	3	0	5	6	.286	.423	.667

Hessman moved from third to first base with Wilson Betemit's presence at Triple-A Richmond. He was recalled in August after missing time in May with an ankle sprain and July with a sore back. 2004 Outlook: C

Darren Holmes (Pos: RHP, Age: 37)

	W	L	Pct.	ERA	G	GS	Sv	IP	H	BB	SO	HR	Avg
'03	1	2	.333	4.29	48	0	0	42.0	47	11	46	5	.280
Car.	35	33	.515	4.25	557	6	59	680.0	709	256	581	63	.269

After emerging in the Atlanta bullpen with an 1.81 ERA in 2002, Holmes endured an injury plagued 2003. He finally had surgery to repair a rotator cuff after the season and may be ready by spring training. 2004 Outlook: C

Jason Marquis (Pos: RHP, Age: 25)

	W	L	Pct.	ERA	G	GS	Sv	IP	H	BB	SO	HR	Avg
'03	0	0	—	5.53	21	2	1	40.2	43	18	19	3	.270
Car.	14	15	.483	4.45	96	40	1	307.2	306	138	218	40	.260

Marquis wasn't happy when he was optioned after a rough early April. He pitched in three games in June before going down again, but was back in July with one save and a 5.40 ERA in 15 games. 2004 Outlook: B

Jaret Wright (Pos: RHP, Age: 28)

	W	L	Pct.	ERA	G	GS	Sv	IP	H	BB	SO	HR	Avg
'03	2	5	.286	7.35	50	0	2	56.1	76	31	50	9	.332
Car.	37	37	.500	5.68	148	96	2	572.0	628	299	410	69	.282

Wright was a force for Atlanta down the stretch and into the playoffs. He surrendered just two runs in 13 innings after the Braves claimed him off waivers from the Padres in August. Atlanta signed him for 2004 in early December. 2004 Outlook: B

Atlanta Braves Minor League Prospects

Organization Overview:

While other organizations are relying on statistical formulas when signing players, the Braves remain true to their pure scouting roots, with drafts centering on high school players—especially pitchers. Scouting director Roy Clark has done a magnificent job of building impressive depth in the Atlanta farm system over the past four drafts. The result is not only a solid corps of young hurlers, but top prospects who could enable Atlanta to field a starting lineup consisting solely of homegrown players in the near future. Nowhere is the organization deeper than catcher, once considered the weak link, with prospects Brian McCann, Jarrod Saltalamacchia and Brayan Pena honing their skills in the lower minors.

Wilson Betemit

Position: 3B

Bats: B **Throws:** R

Ht: 6' 2" **Wt:** 190

Opening Day Age: 22

Born: 11/2/81 in Santo Domingo, DR

Recent Statistics

	G	AB	R	H	D	T	HR	RBI	SB	BB	SO	Avg
2002 R Braves	7	19	2	5	4	0	0	2	1	5	2	.263
2002 AAA Richmond	93	343	43	84	17	1	8	34	8	34	82	.245
2003 AAA Richmond	127	478	55	125	23	13	8	65	8	38	115	.262

The Braves thought Betemit might reside in Atlanta's everyday lineup by now, but two difficult seasons at the Triple-A level have slowed his progress. A switch-hitter, Betemit has a line-drive stroke from both sides of the plate. His power and strength are becoming more obvious as his body matures, although he has yet to display those traits in game situations. He possesses a live body with easy actions and the strongest throwing arm of any infielder in the Atlanta farm system. He moved from shortstop to third base last season and tends to struggle defensively when he becomes lackadaisical on routine plays. The Braves believe Betemit could blossom this year, possibly as soon as spring training.

Jeff Francoeur

Position: OF

Bats: R **Throws:** R

Ht: 6' 4" **Wt:** 205

Opening Day Age: 20

Born: 1/8/84 in Atlanta, GA

Recent Statistics

	G	AB	R	H	D	T	HR	RBI	SB	BB	SO	Avg
2002 R Danville	38	147	31	48	12	1	8	31	8	15	34	.327
2003 A Rome	134	524	78	147	26	9	14	68	14	30	68	.281

Francoeur is a pure five-tool talent with an incredible makeup who reminds many scouts of former Brave Dale Murphy. One of the best pure athletes in the 2002 draft, Francoeur bypassed a scholarship to play defensive back at Clemson to pursue baseball. His baseball instincts are uncanny, and his speed allows him to cover the outfield and basepaths as rapidly as anyone in the organization. His arm strength is good enough to handle right field in the major leagues. Despite being less than two years removed from high school, he has excellent strike-zone judgment. He drives the ball into the gaps and should develop into a middle-of-the-lineup run producer. The Braves feel Francoeur is on the verge of jumping on the fast track to the major leagues.

Ryan Langerhans

Position: OF

Bats: L **Throws:** L

Ht: 6' 3" **Wt:** 195

Opening Day Age: 24

Born: 2/20/80 in San Antonio, TX

Recent Statistics

	G	AB	R	H	D	T	HR	RBI	SB	BB	SO	Avg
2003 AA Greenville	94	336	42	85	23	2	6	38	10	46	85	.253
2003 AAA Richmond	38	132	13	37	10	2	4	11	2	11	29	.280
2003 NL Atlanta	16	15	2	4	0	0	0	0	0	0	6	.267

There have been mixed emotions within the Atlanta organization regarding the long-term potential of Langerhans. Through perseverance, however, the former third-round draft pick is on the verge of earning a reserve spot in the outfield. Langerhans runs well and possesses a strong arm and the organization's best glovework, which enables him to handle any of the three outfield positions with ease. He also drives the ball to the gaps with consistency, and should hit for decent power once his body fully matures. If he can put the bat on the ball more consistently, particularly against lefthanded pitching, Langerhans could be Atlanta's fourth outfielder as soon as this season.

Adam Laroche

Position: 1B

Bats: L **Throws:** L

Ht: 6' 3" **Wt:** 180

Opening Day Age: 24

Born: 11/6/79 in Orange County, CA

Recent Statistics

	G	AB	R	H	D	T	HR	RBI	SB	BB	SO	Avg
2002 A Myrtle Beach	69	250	30	84	17	0	9	53	0	27	37	.336
2002 AA Greenville	45	173	17	50	9	0	4	19	1	19	38	.289
2003 AA Greenville	61	219	42	62	12	1	12	37	1	34	53	.283
2003 AAA Richmond	72	264	33	78	21	0	8	35	1	27	58	.295

LaRoche showed the Braves last year between the Triple-A and Double-A ranks that he has enough power to play first base in the major leagues. The son of former major league pitcher Dave LaRoche has a wide-open stance and a sweet line-drive stroke that he uses to drive pitches to the gaps. He also was tabbed the best defensive first baseman in both the Triple-A International and Double-A Southern leagues, and the Braves believe he could become a perennial Gold Glove candidate. With his all-around skills and all-out hustle on the field, LaRoche is a leading candidate to earn significant activity in Atlanta this year.

Andy Marte

Position: 3B
Bats: R **Throws:** R
Ht: 6' 1" **Wt:** 185

Opening Day Age: 20
Born: 10/21/83 in Villa Tapia, DR

Recent Statistics

	G	AB	R	H	D	T	HR	RBI	SB	BB	SO	Avg
2002 A Macon	126	488	69	137	32	4	21	105	2	41	114	.281
2003 A Myrtle Beach	130	463	69	132	35	1	16	63	5	67	109	.285

No one is making a more rapid climb through the Atlanta organization than Marte. In his first two full seasons of pro ball, he has earned All-Star recognition at third base while torturing pitchers with his amazing pitch recognition. He can make adjustments from one pitch to the next, and he hits the ball as hard as anyone in the Braves' system. His defensive skills are equally exceptional, with Marte possessing soft hands, a strong arm, good range and solid all-around athleticism. His lone average tool is his speed. His even-keel demeanor could land him in Atlanta as quickly as late 2004.

Bubba Nelson

Position: P
Bats: R **Throws:** R
Ht: 6' 2" **Wt:** 200

Opening Day Age: 22
Born: 8/26/81 in Clinton, MD

Recent Statistics

	W	L	ERA	G	GS	Sv	IP	H	R	BB	SO	HR
2002 R Braves	0	0	0.00	3	3	0	5.0	1	0	1	7	0
2002 A Myrtle Beach	11	5	1.72	23	23	0	135.2	98	37	44	105	4
2003 AA Greenville	8	10	3.18	23	20	0	119.0	106	47	45	77	7
2003 AAA Richmond	0	1	1.88	11	0	0	14.1	10	3	5	7	1

Most organizations would be pushing Nelson into their major league rotation. The Braves will make room for the righthander, but they want to be certain not to rush their second-round draft pick from 2000. After leading the minors with a 1.66 ERA while holding hitters to a .197 batting average in 2002, Nelson made impressive adjustments at the Double-A level last season before pitching in Triple-A during August. Nelson coerces groundballs with a 92-94 MPH fastball that has heavy sinking action. He will throw his plus curveball at any time in the count, and his hard slider can be unhittable for righthanded batters. The Braves want Nelson to continue to improve his changeup.

Andy Pratt

Position: P
Bats: L **Throws:** L
Ht: 5' 11" **Wt:** 185

Opening Day Age: 24
Born: 8/27/79 in Mesa, AZ

Recent Statistics

	W	L	ERA	G	GS	Sv	IP	H	R	BB	SO	HR
2002 AA Greenville	4	9	4.26	20	18	0	93.0	92	54	44	67	5
2002 AAA Richmond	4	2	3.10	6	6	0	40.2	35	15	9	36	2
2002 NL Atlanta	0	0	6.75	1	0	0	1.1	1	1	4	1	0
2003 AAA Richmond	7	10	3.40	28	27	0	156.0	146	77	77	161	10

Pratt was acquired from the Rangers for Ben Kozlowski during the first week of the 2002 campaign, and has made significant strides in his development since joining the Braves. His stuff is electric with impressive movement. He throws his fastball in the 92-93 MPH range and mixes the high-movement pitch with a plus cutter, a sharp curveball and a decent changeup. Pratt can be overpowering, as evidenced by his International League-best 161 strikeouts last year. Not unlike many lefthanders, control can be a problem for Pratt. The southpaw needs only minor fine-tuning in order to become a mainstay at the major league level.

Adam Wainwright

Position: P
Bats: R **Throws:** R
Ht: 6' 6" **Wt:** 205

Opening Day Age: 22
Born: 8/30/81 in Brunswick, GA

Recent Statistics

	W	L	ERA	G	GS	Sv	IP	H	R	BB	SO	HR
2002 A Myrtle Beach	9	6	3.31	28	28	0	163.1	149	67	66	167	7
2003 AA Greenville	10	8	3.37	27	27	0	149.2	133	59	37	128	9

Atlanta's first-round draft pick in 2000, Wainwright has made the adjustments at every level and shown signs of becoming a workhorse. While throwing at least 149 innings in each of the last three seasons, his fastball continues to reside in the 88-92 MPH range with good movement. Wainwright also throws a sharp-breaking curveball with excellent command and a solid change-up. The Braves were further impressed last season when he overcame five straight losses in as many outings before finishing with a 5-1 record in his last seven starts. He concluded the campaign ranked 10th in the Double-A Southern League in ERA. Wainwright and Bubba Nelson are on the same timetable for the major leagues, and could get their first tastes of Atlanta at some point in 2004.

Others to Watch

The Braves acquired catcher **Johnny Estrada** (27) prior to last season from Philadelphia in exchange for pitcher Kevin Millwood. The offensive oriented receiver did a respectable job of handling the Triple-A Richmond pitching staff. The Atlanta front office believes Estrada can replace Javy Lopez as the starter behind the plate this year. . . Shortstop **Kelly Johnson** (22) made some adjustments at the plate last year at Double-A Greenville, including spreading out more and working counts, and again showed the promise that he could be a good contact hitter with decent power at the major league level. Currently a shortstop, Johnson could land at third base or one of the outfield corners. . . **Macay McBride** (21) led the high Class-A Carolina League in strikeouts and innings pitched last year. The Braves consider him to be the most competitive pitcher in the organization, and he mixes his low-90s fastball, sharp slider and plus change-up with precision. . . **Dan Meyer** (22) may prove to be the steal of the 2002 draft, taken 34th overall by the Braves. Meyer has an 89-92 MPH fastball, a plus straight changeup and a hard slider that has shown steady development over the past two seasons.

Atlanta

Wrigley Field

Offense

Wrigley may not be quite the hitters' haven it used to be, but the short alleys provide an inviting target for hitters who don't pull the ball exclusively. In particular, the left-field bleachers can boost the home run totals of a righthanded flyball hitter. The small foul territory also helps the hitters. How the park plays changes with the weather. When it's cold early in the year, or when a cool wind blows in off the lake, it can be a pitchers' park. In midsummer, with a breeze blowing out, it can inflate scoring.

Defense

The park has become surprisingly neutral over the last several seasons, and some suspect that the mound may have been built up to help the Cubs' hard-throwing pitchers. The long infield grass slows down grounders and keeps many from going through for base hits.

Who It Helps the Most

Two line-drive hitters, Mark Grudzielanek and Ramon Martinez, hit well here last year, although neither fits the image of the type of hitter likely to be helped by the park. With pitchers, it seems to help to keep the ball out of play. Kyle Farnsworth certainly does that, and seems to pitch better here.

Who It Hurts the Most

Corey Patterson gets the ball in the air, but tends to pull it too much, hitting to the biggest part of the park rather than the alleys. He hasn't been hurt much, but he's the type of hitter who ought to be able to take better advantage.

Rookies & Newcomers

Aramis Ramirez, whose power is from left- to right-center, should be able to take advantage of the short alleys. A more recent acquisition, Derrek Lee, is moving from a park—Pro Player Stadium—that blunted his alley power, into Wrigley Field, which should reward it. He could enjoy a noticeable bump across the board. Hard-throwing Frank Beltran might be a good fit, but he'll need to get his feet on the ground first.

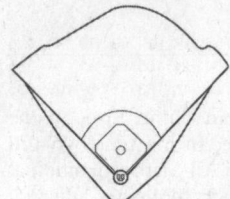

Dimensions: LF-355, LCF-368, CF-400, RCF-368, RF-353

Capacity: 39,241

Elevation: 595 feet

Surface: Grass

Foul Territory: Small

Park Factors

2003 Season

| | Home Games | | | Away Games | | | |
	Cubs	Opp	Total	Cubs	Opp	Total	Index
G	72	72	144	69	69	138	
Avg	.255	.236	.245	.261	.238	.250	98
AB	2392	2464	4856	2405	2261	4666	100
R	306	305	611	333	285	618	95
H	610	581	1191	627	538	1165	98
2B	126	106	232	136	104	240	93
3B	8	9	17	11	8	19	86
HR	79	60	139	78	62	140	95
BB	241	283	524	202	241	443	114
SO	560	664	1224	478	577	1055	111
E	51	52	103	48	47	95	104
E-Infield	44	39	83	38	41	79	101
LHB-Avg	.241	.238	.239	.261	.238	.249	96
LHB-HR	14	23	37	22	27	49	74
RHB-Avg	.261	.234	.248	.261	.238	.250	99
RHB-HR	65	37	102	56	35	91	107

2001-2003

| | Home Games | | | Away Games | | | |
	Cubs	Opp	Total	Cubs	Opp	Total	Index
G	219	219	438	219	219	438	
Avg	.253	.237	.245	.255	.256	.255	96
AB	7192	7464	14656	7596	7246	14842	99
R	964	935	1899	1014	988	2002	95
H	1819	1772	3591	1935	1855	3790	95
2B	343	348	691	395	369	764	92
3B	36	26	62	42	44	86	73
HR	250	222	472	261	204	465	103
BB	792	794	1586	714	787	1501	107
SO	1618	1984	3602	1572	1722	3294	111
E	144	151	295	155	148	303	97
E-Infield	120	127	247	129	127	256	96
LHB-Avg	.245	.241	.243	.243	.270	.256	95
LHB-HR	82	84	166	101	100	201	82
RHB-Avg	.258	.235	.246	.262	.246	.255	97
RHB-HR	168	138	306	160	104	264	118

2003 Rankings (National League)

- Highest walk factor
- Second-highest strikeout factor
- Lowest LHB home-run factor

Dusty Baker

2003 Season

It isn't often that a manager takes over a 95-game loser and gets them within a couple innings of a World Series berth. But people have come to expect that sort of thing from Dusty Baker. Last season, Baker struck the right balance at two positions, first base and second base, where a talented youngster was competing with an established veteran; he found a more appropriate offensive role for Corey Patterson, which helped the youngster develop dramatically; and he sorted out a confused bullpen and found an effective closer in someone few had considered.

Offense

More psychologist than tactician, Baker gets the most out of his players not by crafting complex strategies, but simply by creating a positive, low-pressure atmosphere. He seems to have a sixth sense about when a player needs a day off or a word of encouragement. When he alters the batting order or makes a substitution, it often has more to do with these considerations than with who the opposing pitcher happens to be. He's conventional in calling for the bunt, the steal and other one-run strategies.

Pitching & Defense

Baker is well-known for his willingness to leave an effective starter on the mound as long as possible—maybe a little *too* long at times, say critics of Baker's managing in last year's NLCS. To be fair, Baker has been careful in the past with guys who needed a shorter leash, such as Kirk Rueter. He did a good job of assigning roles in the bullpen, and once he found a combination that worked, he stuck with it.

2004 Outlook

After last year's near-pennant, there will be pressure for the Cubs to return to the playoffs. Baker seems to be the perfect manager to deflect that pressure and keep the club focused. The club's core talent remains, and Baker ought to be able to make it translate into a contender once again.

Born: 6/15/49 in Riverside, CA

Playing Experience: 1968-1986, Atl, LA, SF, Oak

Managerial Experience: 11 seasons

Manager Statistics

Year	Team, Lg	W	L	Pct	GB	Finish
2003	Chicago, NL	88	74	.543	–	1st Central
11 Seasons		928	789	.540	–	–

2003 Starting Pitchers by Days Rest

	<=3	4	5	6+
Cubs Starts	0	80	57	18
Cubs ERA	–	3.65	3.56	3.58
NL Avg Starts	2	84	43	23
NL ERA	5.00	4.23	4.42	4.68

2003 Situational Stats

	Dusty Baker	NL Average
Hit & Run Success %	31.7	32.7
Stolen Base Success %	70.2	68.9
Platoon Pct.	47.7	52.0
Defensive Subs	18	19
High-Pitch Outings	26	8
Quick/Slow Hooks	10/16	20/12
Sacrifice Attempts	97	93

2003 Rankings (National League)

- 1st in sacrifice-bunt percentage (85.6%), starts with over 120 pitches (26), starts with over 140 pitches (1) and first-batter platoon percentage
- 2nd in fewest caught stealings of third base (1)
- 3rd in slow hooks

Moises Alou

2003 Season

Moises Alou's second season with the Cubs was better than the first, though he didn't come close to returning to the heights he'd reached with the Astros. Alou worked hard to avoid the leg injuries that had slowed him the year before, and played in more games than he had in five years, but still seemed to wear down over the last two months of the season. He rebounded to enjoy a strong postseason despite playing through a partially torn ligament in his left thumb.

Hitting

Alou uses his strong wrists and forearms to generate a short, quick stroke that can catch up with just about anyone's fastball. He covers the plate well and uses the whole field, an approach that serves him especially well when protecting the plate with two strikes. His career average against lefties—.328—is among the best in the game. Batting cleanup, Alou's job is to protect Sammy Sosa. The respect pitchers have for him was reflected in Sosa's walk total. In 2002, when Alou was hobbled, Sosa was walked more than 100 times, but last year, with a healthier Alou, Sosa's walks dropped by 40 percent.

Baserunning & Defense

With a history of leg problems, Alou no longer runs aggressively, though his speed is still a tick above average. His age began to show in the field last year, as he tied his career high with six errors and registered only four assists. His average range is less of a liability in Wrigley than other parks.

2004 Outlook

Alou is going into the final year of his contract, and the Cubs will need him to match what he did last year if they are to contend as expected. Alou is getting up in years, but his bat is as quick as it's ever been, so he should be able to come through.

Position: LF
Bats: R **Throws:** R
Ht: 6' 3" **Wt:** 220

Opening Day Age: 37
Born: 7/3/66 in Atlanta, GA
ML Seasons: 12
Pronunciation: MOY-zes ah-LOO

Overall Statistics

	G	AB	R	H	D	T	HR	RBI	SB	BB	SO	Avg	OBP	Slg
'03	151	565	83	158	35	1	22	91	3	63	67	.280	.357	.462
Car.	1464	5287	829	1588	318	31	239	986	92	556	706	.300	.367	.508

Where He Hits the Ball

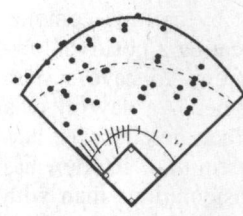 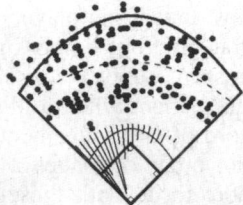

Vs. LHP   **Vs. RHP**

2003 Situational Stats

	AB	H	HR	RBI	Avg		AB	H	HR	RBI	Avg
Home	274	77	14	42	.281	LHP	127	44	6	28	.346
Road	291	81	8	49	.278	RHP	438	114	16	63	.260
First Half	347	102	14	56	.294	Sc Pos	163	50	6	69	.307
Scnd Half	218	56	8	35	.257	Clutch	91	23	2	11	.253

2003 Rankings (National League)

- 2nd in lowest fielding percentage in left field (.972)
- 3rd in errors in left field (6)
- 6th in highest percentage of swings on the first pitch (38.0)
- 7th in lowest cleanup slugging percentage (.491)
- 9th in batting average vs. lefthanded pitchers
- Led the Cubs in at-bats, hits, walks, times on base (228) and plate appearances (638)

Joe Borowski

2003 Season

For the second year in a row, Joe Borowski was one of the Cubs' biggest surprises—except this time, he was an even bigger surprise. When Antonio Alfonseca was injured in April, Borowski became the closer almost by default. He converted 33 saves in 37 chances, and was especially tough down the stretch, allowing only one earned run in his last 19 appearances. He also stranded 19 of the 21 runners he inherited.

Pitching

Borowski's repertoire is more like a starter's than a closer's. He doesn't throw especially hard, but has good command of a decent low-90s fastball, slider and changeup. Hitters from either side of the plate find him equally tough, but his raw stuff isn't dominant, and he can be hit when he leaves one over the plate. He's able to work on successive days but is at his strongest when he's given a couple of days off between appearances. He gives up a fair number of flyballs, but most of them stayed in the park last year. Since he pitched mostly in a setup role before last year, he's comfortable working more than one inning at a time.

Defense & Hitting

Borowski is a capable fielder. He has a so-so pick-off move and throws over to first a lot. But when he delivers to the plate, he's helpless to stop the running game. He has very little experience as a hitter.

2004 Outlook

Heading into the offseason after the 2003 campaign, Borowski seemed to have a firm grip on the closer's job. While there's no reason to think Borowski can't continue to be an effective closer, securing results that are more impressive than his stuff, the signing of LaTroy Hawkins almost certainly will bump him to a setup role. That's regardless of whatever pronouncements are made heading into camp. Borowski's abilities may be better suited to pitch the eighth than the ninth.

Position: RP
Bats: R **Throws:** R
Ht: 6' 2" **Wt:** 225

Opening Day Age: 32
Born: 5/4/71 in Bayonne, NJ
ML Seasons: 7
Pronunciation: bor-OW-ski

Overall Statistics

	W	L	Pct.	ERA	G	GS	Sv	IP	H	BB	SO	HR	Avg
'03	2	2	.500	2.63	68	0	33	68.1	53	19	66	5	.207
Car.	11	14	.440	3.41	199	1	35	234.2	221	92	197	22	.250

2003 Pitching Profile

	Joe Borowski	NL Average
Overall Strike %	65.5	62.4
1st Pitch Strike %	64.4	58.4
Ratio	1.05	1.38
Strikeouts per 9 IP	8.69	6.65
Walks per 9 IP	2.50	3.42
Home Runs per 9 IP	0.66	1.05
Strikeout/Walk Ratio	3.47	1.94
Groundball/Flyball Ratio	1.11	1.29

2003 Situational Stats

	W	L	ERA	Sv	IP		AB	H	HR	RBI	Avg
Home	2	2	3.72	15	36.1	LHB	104	22	4	12	.212
Road	0	0	1.41	18	32.0	RHB	152	31	1	13	.204
First Half	1	1	2.68	17	43.2	Sc Pos	67	11	1	20	.164
Scnd Half	1	1	2.55	16	24.2	Clutch	154	30	3	15	.195

2003 Rankings (National League)
- 5th in games finished (59)
- 6th in saves
- 7th in save percentage (89.2)
- 10th in fewest baserunners allowed per nine innings in relief (9.6)
- Led the Cubs in saves, games finished (59), save percentage (89.2), lowest percentage of inherited runners scored (9.5), blown saves (4), relief ERA (2.63) and fewest baserunners allowed per nine innings in relief (9.6)

Matt Clement

Position: SP
Bats: R **Throws:** R
Ht: 6' 3" **Wt:** 210

Opening Day Age: 29
Born: 8/12/74 in Butler, PA
ML Seasons: 6
Pronunciation: klah-MENT

2003 Season

Matt Clement's slow journey toward harnessing his stuff continued last year. The raw numbers may suggest he took a half-step back, but he pitched better than his ERA showed, and actually was nearly as effective as he'd been the year before. Perceptions were affected by his occasional bad outings, which admittedly occurred more frequently than they ought to for someone with his stuff. All in all, though, he pitched nearly as well as teammates Kerry Wood and Carlos Zambrano.

Pitching

Clement's pitches have terrific natural movement, which helps explain why it's taken him so long to learn how to put them where he wants to. Over the last two years, he's begun to throw enough strikes to tip the balance in his favor. Along with a sinking fastball in the low 90s and a terrific hard slider, he mixes in a few four-seamers and changeups. When he's on, he gets strikeouts, groundballs and little else. Clement's maturation also is reflected in his improved stamina, and his ability to keep his emotions in check when things don't go his way.

Defense & Hitting

Clement isn't comfortable throwing over to first, so he simply tries to look runners back and get the ball to the plate as quickly as he can. It works, as he's very tough to run on. He commits to many errors, and he'll bounce a throw from time to time. Hitting used to be a major weakness, but he had his best year yet in 2003.

2004 Outlook

For years, people have wondered what Clement might be able to do if he ever put it all together. He still has some kinks to iron out, but if he can improve his command a bit more and become a little more consistent, he might get there. And even if he doesn't, he's already a fine pitcher.

Overall Statistics

	W	L	Pct.	ERA	G	GS	Sv	IP	H	BB	SO	HR	Avg
'03	14	12	.538	4.11	32	32	0	201.2	169	79	171	22	.227
Car.	60	62	.492	4.46	164	162	0	975.1	902	467	838	95	.246

2003 Pitching Profile

	Matt Clement	NL Average
Overall Strike %	62.6	62.4
1st Pitch Strike %	58.9	58.4
Ratio	1.23	1.38
Strikeouts per 9 IP	7.63	6.65
Walks per 9 IP	3.53	3.42
Home Runs per 9 IP	0.98	1.05
Strikeout/Walk Ratio	2.16	1.94
Groundball/Flyball Ratio	2.04	1.29

2003 Situational Stats

	W	L	ERA	Sv	IP		AB	H	HR	RBI	Avg
Home	10	5	3.10	0	116.0	LHB	358	88	12	45	.246
Road	4	7	5.46	0	85.2	RHB	388	81	10	41	.209
First Half	7	7	4.39	0	112.2	Sc Pos	163	44	5	61	.270
Scnd Half	7	5	3.74	0	89.0	Clutch	39	8	2	3	.205

2003 Rankings (National League)

- 1st in wild pitches (13)
- 3rd in hit batsmen (14) and errors at pitcher (4)
- 4th in highest groundball-flyball ratio allowed (2.0) and lowest fielding percentage at pitcher (.915)
- 6th in lowest batting average allowed (.227) and highest ERA on the road
- 8th in lowest batting average allowed vs. righthanded batters
- 9th in least run support per nine innings (4.2)
- 10th in lowest slugging percentage allowed (.362) and most strikeouts per nine innings (7.6)
- Led the Cubs in losses, games started, wild pitches (13) and fewest pitches thrown per batter (3.70)

Alex Gonzalez

2003 Season

If not for the intervention of one particularly unfortunate Cubs fan, Alex Gonzalez likely would be vilified as the man whose crucial error helped cost the Cubs their first World Series berth in almost 60 years. Otherwise, it was a typical season for the hypnotically consistent shortstop, Gonzalez began the year as the No. 2 hitter, hit a few big extra-inning home runs in May, but slumped and was dropped to the bottom of the order.

Hitting

Gonzalez is a low-average hitter who is capable of hitting for power when he gets something to pull, especially a fastball on the inner half of the plate. It's a wonder he ever gets one, considering his oft-demonstrated willingness to chase breaking balls off the outside corner. He's a reactive hitter, and doesn't look to drive the ball on hitters' counts. Lacking both the on-base ability to be an asset near the top of the order and the power to hit in an RBI spot, he has no clear offensive role.

Baserunning & Defense

Gonzalez is one of the game's best shortstops, lacking only the flash that would bring him more attention. He has soft hands, very good range, and a powerful enough arm to make plays from the hole. In his second year after moving from artificial turf to natural grass, he cut his errors by doing a better job of anticipating the hops. While he runs well, he doesn't take many risks on the bases.

2004 Outlook

Gonzalez is signed through the end of this year, and it safely can be said that the Cubs know exactly what to expect from him. The time has long since passed for hoping he might close the holes in his offensive game, but the Cubs can live with that, especially if they can find someone else to bat second.

Position: SS
Bats: R **Throws:** R
Ht: 6' 0" **Wt:** 200

Opening Day Age: 30
Born: 4/8/73 in Miami, FL
ML Seasons: 10

Overall Statistics

G	AB	R	H	D	T	HR	RBI	SB	BB	SO	Avg	OBP	Slg
152	536	71	122	37	0	20	59	3	47	123	.228	.295	.409
1184	4307	536	1047	236	25	121	470	93	350	1017	.243	.304	.394

Where He Hits the Ball

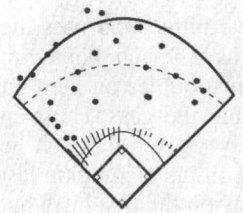
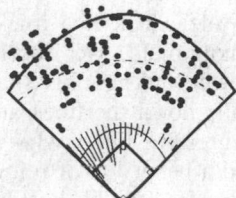

Vs. LHP   **Vs. RHP**

2003 Situational Stats

	AB	H	HR	RBI	Avg		AB	H	HR	RBI	Avg
Home	261	57	11	29	.218	LHP	123	28	3	11	.228
Road	275	65	9	30	.236	RHP	413	94	17	48	.228
First Half	344	85	12	36	.247	Sc Pos	105	22	4	34	.210
Scnd Half	192	37	8	23	.193	Clutch	73	13	4	9	.178

2003 Rankings (National League)

- 1st in fielding percentage at shortstop (.984)
- 3rd in lowest batting average
- 4th in lowest batting average at home
- 6th in lowest on-base percentage, lowest batting average with the bases loaded (.100), lowest batting average vs. lefthanded pitchers, lowest batting average vs. righthanded pitchers and lowest batting average with two strikes (.131)
- 7th in lowest batting average on the road
- Led the Cubs in GDPs (17) and games played
- Led NL shortstops in home runs

Mark Grudzielanek

2003 Season

The Cubs didn't expect much from Mark Grudzielanek when they obtained him from the Dodgers in a swap of burdensome contracts, but he met every challenge and enjoyed his best season in four years. First, he beat out youngster Bobby Hill for the second-base job coming out of camp. He established himself as their leadoff hitter, and then dropped to second when Kenny Lofton was acquired. Next to Lofton, Grudzielanek had the team's highest batting average and on-base percentage. The only negative was that he missed most of August with a broken right hand.

Hitting

Grudzielanek is a line-drive hitter who uses the whole field. He doesn't have much home-run power, but gets his share of doubles on hard-hit balls down the lines and into the gaps. He is an aggressive hitter who rarely walks, although he did a better job of reigning in his aggression last year. He does his best hitting on the first pitch but does a good job of protecting the plate with two strikes. He's able to bunt a runner over when asked.

Baserunning & Defense

The long grass at Wrigley kept Grudzielanek's lack of range from being as much of a liability as it might have been. He's an otherwise above-average second baseman with a strong arm and a good double-play pivot. He still runs fairly well but has been known to run into outs at times.

2004 Outlook

A free agent, Grudzielanek wound up back with the Cubs, who have few internal options for the second base spot. Signed to a one-year deal, he can't be expected to hit like he did last year. More likely, he'll fall back to his usual levels, something that could put him in jeopardy of being bumped down to the lower third of the batting order.

Position: 2B
Bats: R **Throws:** R
Ht: 6' 1" **Wt:** 190

Opening Day Age: 33
Born: 6/30/70 in Milwaukee, WI
ML Seasons: 9
Pronunciation: grud-zuh-LAN-nick

Overall Statistics

	G	AB	R	H	D	T	HR	RBI	SB	BB	SO	Avg	OBP	Slg
'03	121	481	73	151	38	1	3	38	6	30	64	.314	.366	.416
Car.	1218	4825	649	1377	261	25	60	420	116	245	661	.285	.329	.387

Where He Hits the Ball

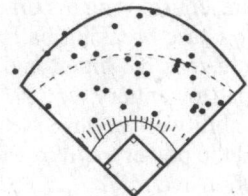
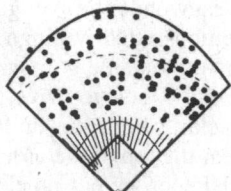

Vs. LHP   **Vs. RHP**

2003 Situational Stats

	AB	H	HR	RBI	Avg		AB	H	HR	RBI	Avg
Home	230	79	2	22	.343	LHP	100	36	0	4	.360
Road	251	72	1	16	.287	RHP	381	115	3	34	.302
First Half	339	103	2	19	.304	Sc Pos	100	31	1	36	.310
Scnd Half	142	48	1	19	.338	Clutch	67	19	0	7	.284

2003 Rankings (National League)

- 3rd in fielding percentage at second base (.986) and lowest HR frequency (160.3 ABs per HR)
- 6th in batting average at home
- Led the Cubs in batting average, singles, doubles, hit by pitch (11), on-base percentage, highest groundball-flyball ratio (1.9), batting average with runners in scoring position, batting average vs. righthanded pitchers, batting average at home and batting average on the road
- Led NL second basemen in batting average

Kenny Lofton

2003 Season

Forced to prove his worth all over again in 2003, Kenny Lofton made his point convincingly. A free agent coming off a couple of unremarkable seasons, a bargain-basement deal with the Pirates was all he could attract. He performed well for Pittsburgh, then played like the Kenny Lofton of old after being traded to the Cubs with Aramis Ramirez in late July. With Lofton's spark, the Cubs, who were 50-49 before the trade, went 38-25 the rest of the way and made the playoffs.

Hitting

Lofton has two distinctly different swings. Against a low pitch or an offspeed pitch, he'll stay back and flick the ball over the infield. If he gets a high fastball, especially one on the inner half of the plate, he can turn and drive it with authority. The threat of a bunt is always there. Lofton will wait out a walk, although he wasn't as patient last year as he had been in the past. Any nagging injuries that affects his speed will affect his whole game, so he tends to be at his best when given days off regularly.

Baserunning & Defense

It's been years since Lofton ran at will, but he's still capable of stealing second or third as the situation requires. His speed was more evident last year than it had been in the previous couple of years, when leg injuries had slowed him a step. His range in center remains above-average. Lofton's only weakness on defense is a poor throwing arm, something he partly makes up for by getting to the ball quickly.

2004 Outlook

Lofton is back where he was last winter, a free agent in a buyer's market. He remains a fine center fielder and leadoff hitter, and will find a place to play, even if he fails to get the kind of contract he feels he deserves.

Position: CF
Bats: L **Throws:** L
Ht: 6' 0" **Wt:** 180

Opening Day Age: 36
Born: 5/31/67 in East Chicago, IN
ML Seasons: 13

Overall Statistics

G	AB	R	H	D	T	HR	RBI	SB	BB	SO	Avg	OBP	Slg
140	547	97	162	32	8	12	46	30	46	51	.296	.352	.450
1645	6518	1245	1943	318	86	115	648	538	781	855	.298	.373	.426

Where He Hits the Ball

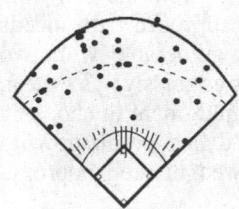 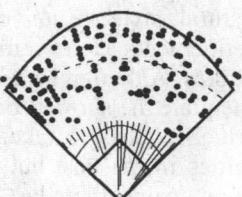

Vs. LHP	Vs. RHP

2003 Situational Stats

	AB	H	HR	RBI	Avg		AB	H	HR	RBI	Avg
Home	287	83	5	20	.289	LHP	135	33	1	11	.244
Road	260	79	7	26	.304	RHP	412	129	11	35	.313
First Half	318	90	9	26	.283	Sc Pos	116	28	1	31	.241
Scnd Half	229	72	3	20	.314	Clutch	86	17	0	7	.198

2003 Rankings (National League)

- 3rd in triples (8)
- 4th in lowest batting average with the bases loaded (.083)
- 5th in stolen bases (30), steals of third (5), fielding percentage in center field (.991) and fewest pitches seen per plate appearance (3.42)
- 6th in lowest percentage of swings that missed (9.0) and highest percentage of swings put into play (54.4)
- 7th in stolen-base percentage (76.9)
- 8th in caught stealing (9) and errors in center field (3)
- Led the Cubs in steals of third (2), on-base percentage for a leadoff hitter (.384) and batting average with two strikes (.268)

Corey Patterson

2003 Season

What was shaping up as a breakout season for Corey Patterson ended abruptly when he tore cartilage and a ligament in his left knee just before the All-Star break. At the time, Patterson was on pace to drive in more than 100 runs and finally was fulfilling the big expectations that had followed him since 1999.

Hitting

After batting mostly first or second in his first two years, Patterson was moved down to sixth last year, then third. The change released him from the pressure to do something he wasn't good at—work the count and get on base—and allowed him to be aggressive and look to drive the ball—his natural style. Patterson's approach still needs refinement, as he remains vulnerable with two strikes. Although he was as aggressive as ever at the plate, he showed better judgment in choosing which pitches to take. He'd had problems with lefties in the past but showed marked improvement against them last year.

Baserunning & Defense

While Patterson may have been miscast as a lead-off man, his compact build, speed and quickness make it easy to understand why he had been seen that way. He's a capable basestealer, and might steal 30 bases annually if he's able to learn to read lefthanders' moves. He shows good range and a strong throwing arm in center field, and with more experience he might become one of the game's best defensive center fielders.

2004 Outlook

Patterson is expected to make a full recovery and start the season on time. The bigger question may be whether he can put together a full season like the first half of last year. There may be more peaks and valleys to come; it's still feared that pitchers may find new ways to exploit his aggressiveness. On the other hand, he's only 24, with plenty of time to grow.

Position: CF
Bats: L **Throws:** R
Ht: 5' 9" **Wt:** 180

Opening Day Age: 24
Born: 8/13/79 in Atlanta, GA
ML Seasons: 4

Overall Statistics

	G	AB	R	H	D	T	HR	RBI	SB	BB	SO	Avg	OBP	Slg
'03	83	329	49	98	17	7	13	55	16	15	77	.298	.329	.511
Car.	306	1094	155	284	51	12	33	125	39	43	266	.260	.293	.419

Where He Hits the Ball

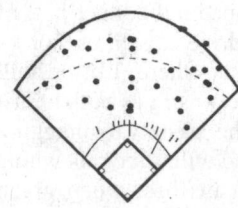 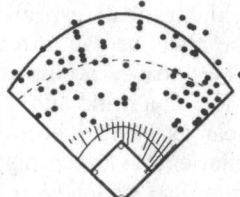

Vs. LHP   **Vs. RHP**

2003 Situational Stats

	AB	H	HR	RBI	Avg		AB	H	HR	RBI	Avg
Home	147	46	7	24	.313	LHP	90	26	4	22	.289
Road	182	52	6	31	.286	RHP	239	72	9	33	.301
First Half	329	98	13	55	.298	Sc Pos	93	28	3	39	.301
Scnd Half	0	0	0	0	–	Clutch	53	16	1	6	.302

2003 Rankings (National League)

- 5th in triples
- 7th in errors in center field (4)
- 9th in stolen-base percentage (76.2)
- Led the Cubs in triples and caught stealing (5)

Mark Prior

Position: SP
Bats: R **Throws:** R
Ht: 6' 5" **Wt:** 230

Opening Day Age: 23
Born: 9/7/80 in San Diego, CA
ML Seasons: 2

2003 Season

The only blemish on Mark Prior's 2003 regular season was that he missed a few starts after suffering a bruised right shoulder in a basepath collision in July. When Prior returned, he was better than ever, going 10-1 with a 1.52 ERA through the end of the regular season. The missed starts cost Prior a 20-win season and might have cost him the National League Cy Young award as well, as he ultimately finished third in the balloting. Prior continued to shine in the playoffs until Game 6 of the NLCS, when he finally wore down after taking a 3-0 leading into the eighth inning.

Pitching

No pitcher in baseball has Prior's combination of great stuff and great command. He has a fastball in the low to mid-90s and a hard curveball. He'll also mix in an occasional changeup. He seemingly can put each pitch right where he wants it, usually on the black. As a rookie in 2002, Prior sometimes was overly cautious, but last year he came right at hitters and did a better job of economizing on his pitches. He also showed better stamina, consistently maintaining his effectiveness into the late innings. The only time batters seem to have any luck against him is when he starts them off with a fastball that catches too much of the plate.

Defense & Hitting

As if Prior's pitching weren't enough, he just may be the best-hitting pitcher in baseball. He even was used as a pinch-hitter twice. A fine all-around athlete, Prior fields his position adeptly and improved at holding runners last year.

2004 Outlook

How much better can Prior get? He's only 23 this year, so it's hard to imagine he's already hit his peak. That's a scary thought for a pitcher who already looks like a perennial Cy Young Award candidate.

Overall Statistics

	W	L	Pct.	ERA	G	GS	Sv	IP	H	BB	SO	HR	Avg
'03	18	6	.750	2.43	30	30	0	211.1	183	50	245	15	.231
Car.	24	12	.667	2.74	49	49	0	328.0	281	88	392	29	.229

2003 Pitching Profile

	Mark Prior	NL Average
Overall Strike %	66.8	62.4
1st Pitch Strike %	64.8	58.4
Ratio	1.10	1.38
Strikeouts per 9 IP	10.43	6.65
Walks per 9 IP	2.13	3.42
Home Runs per 9 IP	0.64	1.05
Strikeout/Walk Ratio	4.90	1.94
Groundball/Flyball Ratio	1.12	1.29

2003 Situational Stats

	W	L	ERA	Sv	IP		AB	H	HR	RBI	Avg
Home	7	3	2.85	0	94.2	LHB	362	87	6	29	.240
Road	11	3	2.08	0	116.2	RHB	431	96	9	35	.223
First Half	8	5	3.01	0	128.2	Sc Pos	180	33	3	43	.183
Scnd Half	10	1	1.52	0	82.2	Clutch	81	19	1	6	.235

2003 Rankings (National League)

- 1st in lowest ERA on the road
- 2nd in wins, strikeouts, winning percentage, highest strikeout-walk ratio (4.9), most strikeouts per nine innings (10.4) and lowest fielding percentage at pitcher (.870)
- 3rd in ERA
- 4th in runners caught stealing (9) and lowest on-base percentage allowed (.283)
- 5th in lowest ERA at home, lowest batting average allowed with runners in scoring position and most pitches thrown per batter (3.94)
- Led the Cubs in ERA, wins, runners caught stealing (9), winning percentage, highest strikeout-walk ratio (4.9), lowest on-base percentage allowed (.283), lowest ERA at home, lowest ERA on the road and fewest walks per nine innings (2.1)

Chicago (NL)

Aramis Ramirez

2003 Season

Aramis Ramirez suffered through a miserable 2002 season with the Pirates, then began 2003 ice-cold, hitting .219 with one home run over his first 41 games. A bum ankle had been to blame in 2002, but this time there was no excuse. He pulled out of the skid all at once, driving in runs the way he had in his 112-RBI season of 2001. The Cubs traded for him in mid-July, and he did the same for them, hitting 15 homers in only 63 games while plugging a big hole at third base.

Hitting

Ramirez is a big, strong guy who generates the most power when he's able to get his arms extended. He can drive just about anything on the outer half of the plate and has good opposite-field power. He's most susceptible to pitches in on his hands and hard sinkers down and in. For a power hitter, he is an adequate two-strike hitter, but his plate patience is below-average.

Baserunning & Defense

Ramirez led major league third basemen in errors with 33, a full 50 percent more than anyone else at the position. Many of his errors result from poor footwork (either in approaching the ball or setting to throw), so it's hoped he can improve with experience. He has decent hands and a strong throwing arm, but his range is poor. Ramirez has very little speed and grounds into a lot of double plays for someone who hits relatively few groundballs.

2004 Outlook

Ramirez has put up impressive power numbers in the last two seasons he's been healthy, and is young enough to give hope that the best may be yet to come. In order to avoid becoming a one-dimensional slugging first baseman, though, he must show some improvement at the hot corner, soon.

Position: 3B
Bats: R **Throws:** R
Ht: 6' 1" **Wt:** 212

Opening Day Age: 25
Born: 6/25/78 in Santo Domingo, DR
ML Seasons: 6
Pronunciation: ah-RAH-mis

Overall Statistics

	G	AB	R	H	D	T	HR	RBI	SB	BB	SO	Avg	OBP	Slg
'03	159	607	75	165	32	2	27	106	2	42	99	.272	.324	.465
Car.	622	2293	253	602	124	6	91	355	9	145	411	.263	.312	.441

Where He Hits the Ball

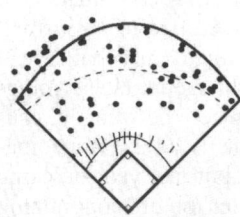 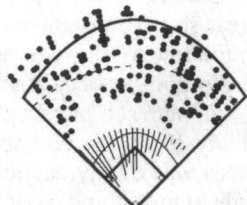

Vs. LHP　　　　**Vs. RHP**

2003 Situational Stats

	AB	H	HR	RBI	Avg		AB	H	HR	RBI	Avg
Home	308	81	10	44	.263	LHP	137	39	10	28	.285
Road	299	84	17	62	.281	RHP	470	126	17	78	.268
First Half	354	98	11	62	.277	Sc Pos	153	43	7	74	.281
Scnd Half	253	67	16	44	.265	Clutch	84	18	1	8	.214

2003 Rankings (National League)

- 1st in sacrifice flies (11), errors at third base (33) and lowest fielding percentage at third base (.929)
- 3rd in lowest percentage of pitches taken (47.9)
- 4th in lowest cleanup slugging percentage (.457)
- 6th in GDPs (21)
- 7th in at-bats (607) and games played (159)
- 8th in lowest groundball-flyball ratio (0.8)
- 9th in RBI (106)
- Led NL third basemen in RBI (106)

Sammy Sosa

2003 Season

Sammy Sosa suffered through more adversity during the first half of 2003 than he had in years. A frightening beaning in April left him with a cracked helmet, though he wasn't seriously hurt. Toe surgery cost him half of May, and he was suspended for a week in June for using a corked bat. He returned with a vengeance, hitting 22 home runs in his next 47 games. The longballs kept coming but his average sank as the Cubs battled for a playoff spot in September.

Hitting

Though Sosa's career turned the corner when he learned to be more patient at the plate, he remains a hacker at heart. His eyes light up on first-pitch fastballs, and he will take a rip at a 3-0 pitch if it's to his liking. He chooses not to shorten up with two strikes, retaining his power but leaving himself vulnerable to breaking balls down and out of the strike zone. Working him away can be dangerous, though, since he can put a charge into just about any pitch he can reach; his opposite-field power is among the best in the game.

Baserunning & Defense

Bigger and bulkier than he was in his twenties, Sosa no longer has the quickness to steal bases. He has above-average speed and isn't as prone to basepath blunders as he used to be. He has decent range and is generally reliable afield, although his arm isn't as strong as it used to be.

2004 Outlook

While Sosa remains capable of hitting home runs in bunches, he will be 35 years old this year and no longer is the perennial MVP candidate he was at his peak. He's slowly growing more one-dimensional, and one day his status as the Cubs' central offensive player will be challenged, but that day seems to be at least a couple of years away. After bypassing a chance to become a free agent in the fall, Sosa has two years remaining on his contract with the Cubs.

Position: RF
Bats: R **Throws:** R
Ht: 6' 0" **Wt:** 220

Opening Day Age: 35
Born: 11/12/68 in San Pedro de Macoris, DR
ML Seasons: 15

Overall Statistics

G	AB	R	H	D	T	HR	RBI	SB	BB	SO	Avg	OBP	Slg
137	517	99	144	22	0	40	103	0	62	143	.279	.358	.553
2012	7543	1314	2099	319	43	539	1450	233	800	1977	.278	.349	.546

Where He Hits the Ball

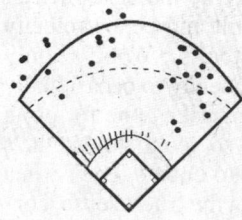
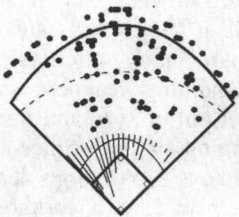

Vs. LHP   Vs. RHP

2003 Situational Stats

	AB	H	HR	RBI	Avg		AB	H	HR	RBI	Avg
Home	283	80	19	55	.283	LHP	105	35	7	14	.333
Road	234	64	21	48	.274	RHP	412	109	33	89	.265
First Half	260	81	18	51	.312	Sc Pos	141	40	10	61	.284
Scnd Half	257	63	22	52	.245	Clutch	70	17	5	12	.243

2003 Rankings (National League)

- 2nd in lowest fielding percentage in right field (.977)
- 3rd in highest percentage of swings that missed (32.6)
- 4th in HR frequency (12.9 ABs per HR) and errors in right field (5)
- 5th in strikeouts
- 6th in home runs
- Led the Cubs in home runs, runs scored, total bases (286), RBI, intentional walks (9), strikeouts, pitches seen (2,363), slugging percentage, HR frequency (12.9 ABs per HR), most pitches seen per plate appearance (4.01), and cleanup slugging percentage (.500)
- Led NL right fielders in home runs

Kerry Wood

2003 Season

It was perhaps Kerry Wood's finest season—he had 22 quality starts and led the majors in strike-outs—but it was overshadowed by how it all ended. Wood's inability to hold the lead in the final game of the NLCS led to a crushing loss and added another chapter to the Cubs' angst-filled history.

Pitching

Wood is one of the hardest throwers in baseball; in fact, having shelved his changeup, he throws just about everything hard. His fastball runs in the mid- to high-90s, and when it comes in above thigh-high few can get on top of it. His curve is a hard downer. His slider may be his best pitch of all; it has good downward tilt and better velocity than many pitchers' fastballs. Wood's only remaining weakness is a tendency to occasionally get out of sync and lose the strike zone for or an inning or two. Since he's so tough to hit, he's always prone to go deep into counts, even when he's on. He is a workhorse in the truest sense, consistently working deep into games and getting stronger as the game goes on.

Defense & Hitting

Wood's home run in the NLCS was no fluke—he has better power than just about any major league pitcher. He made great strides last year with his slide step and pickoff move, and allowed only one stolen base over the last four months of the season. He's a fine fielder, and handles a lot of plays for someone who allows the ball to be put into play so infrequently.

2004 Outlook

Absent injury, the only thing that could stop Wood, it seems, would be the lingering effects of last year's playoff loss. Needless to say, that doesn't seem likely. When listing this year's National League Cy Young Award candidates, Wood's name has to be one of the first to come to mind.

Position: SP
Bats: R **Throws:** R
Ht: 6' 5" **Wt:** 225

Opening Day Age: 26
Born: 6/16/77 in Irving, TX
ML Seasons: 5

Overall Statistics

	W	L	Pct.	ERA	G	GS	Sv	IP	H	BB	SO	HR	Avg
'03	14	11	.560	3.20	32	32	0	211.0	152	100	266	24	.203
Car.	59	41	.590	3.62	142	142	0	902.2	677	461	1065	93	.209

2003 Pitching Profile

	Kerry Wood	NL Average
Overall Strike %	60.9	62.4
1st Pitch Strike %	55.2	58.4
Ratio	1.19	1.38
Strikeouts per 9 IP	11.35	6.65
Walks per 9 IP	4.27	3.42
Home Runs per 9 IP	1.02	1.05
Strikeout/Walk Ratio	2.66	1.94
Groundball/Flyball Ratio	1.06	1.29

2003 Situational Stats

	W	L	ERA	Sv	IP		AB	H	HR	RBI	Avg
Home	6	8	3.56	0	116.1	LHB	313	62	10	30	.198
Road	8	3	2.76	0	94.2	RHB	436	90	14	38	.206
First Half	9	6	3.19	0	127.0	Sc Pos	159	25	3	43	.157
Scnd Half	5	5	3.21	0	84.0	Clutch	69	6	1	1	.087

2003 Rankings (National League)

- 1st in hit batsmen (21), strikeouts, lowest batting average allowed with runners in scoring position and most strikeouts per nine innings (11.3)
- 2nd in lowest batting average allowed (.203) and most pitches thrown per batter (4.00)
- 3rd in walks allowed
- 4th in shutouts (2)
- 5th in complete games (4), pitches thrown (3,545), lowest slugging percentage allowed (.344), lowest stolen-base percentage allowed (38.5) and highest walks per nine innings (4.3)
- Led the Cubs in games started, complete games (4), shutouts (2), home runs allowed, walks allowed, hit batsmen (21), strikeouts, pitches thrown (3,545), lowest batting average allowed (.203), lowest batting average allowed with runners in scoring position, and most strikeouts per nine innings (11.3)

Carlos Zambrano

2003 Season

Young Carlos Zambrano moved into the Cubs' rotation in the second half of 2002 and pitched quite creditably. Entering 2003, the question was whether he'd be able to do as well over an entire season. Question answered: Zambrano was more effective overall, pitching deeper into games and remaining effective right through the end of the season, although he was hit hard in three postseason starts. He would have received more acclaim as one of the best young pitchers in the league if he hadn't been the third-best starter on his own staff.

Pitching

Zambrano relies heavily on a terrific late-moving two-seamer that he throws in the low 90s. As with teammate Matt Clement, hitters can do little but strike out or beat the ball into the ground when Zambrano has his control. He also throws a straight four-seamer, a slider and a hard splitter. It's tough to get the ball in the air against him, and even tougher to get it out of the park. His main weakness is the base on balls, since his pitches have so much movement that he sometimes misses more than he wants to. He showed excellent stamina last year, especially for someone in his early 20s.

Defense & Hitting

Zambrano flags down a lot of the balls hit back through the box, but made a few wild throws last year. He's tough to run against, and few baserunners even try to steal off him. His hitting was a major surprise as he batted .240 with seven extra-base hits. He isn't much of a bunter, though.

2004 Outlook

If Zambrano continues to refine his command, he could be a big winner. There's always a risk when a youngster throws as many pitches as he did last year, but he may be one who can handle it, since he showed no ill effects.

Position: SP
Bats: B **Throws:** R
Ht: 6' 5" **Wt:** 245

Opening Day Age: 22
Born: 6/1/81 in Puerto Cabello, VZ
ML Seasons: 3
Pronunciation: zam-BRAH-no

Overall Statistics

	W	L	Pct.	ERA	G	GS	Sv	IP	H	BB	SO	HR	Avg
'03	13	11	.542	3.11	32	32	0	214.0	188	94	168	9	.239
Car.	18	21	.462	3.57	70	49	0	330.0	293	165	265	20	.241

2003 Pitching Profile

	Carlos Zambrano	NL Average
Overall Strike %	61.0	62.4
1st Pitch Strike %	56.1	58.4
Ratio	1.32	1.38
Strikeouts per 9 IP	7.07	6.65
Walks per 9 IP	3.95	3.42
Home Runs per 9 IP	0.38	1.05
Strikeout/Walk Ratio	1.79	1.94
Groundball/Flyball Ratio	2.28	1.29

2003 Situational Stats

	W	L	ERA	Sv	IP		AB	H	HR	RBI	Avg
Home	5	6	3.00	0	105.0	LHB	314	77	5	28	.245
Road	8	5	3.22	0	109.0	RHB	472	111	4	44	.235
First Half	6	8	3.58	0	120.2	Sc Pos	185	45	3	63	.243
Scnd Half	7	3	2.51	0	93.1	Clutch	70	16	2	5	.229

2003 Rankings (National League)

- 1st in fewest home runs allowed per nine innings (.38)
- 3rd in highest groundball-flyball ratio allowed (2.3) and errors at pitcher (4)
- 4th in GDPs induced (24), lowest slugging percentage allowed (.331) and lowest stolen-base percentage allowed (37.5)
- 5th in walks allowed
- Led the Cubs in games started, innings pitched, hits allowed, batters faced (907), pickoff throws (69), lowest slugging percentage allowed (.331), highest ground ball-flyball ratio allowed (2.3), lowest stolen-base percentage allowed (37.5), and fewest home runs allowed per nine innings (.38)

Hee Seop Choi

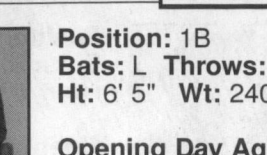

Traded To MARLINS

Position: 1B
Bats: L **Throws:** L
Ht: 6' 5" **Wt:** 240

Opening Day Age: 25
Born: 3/16/79 in Chun-Nam, South Korea
ML Seasons: 2
Pronunciation: hee sop choy

Overall Statistics

	G	AB	R	H	D	T	HR	RBI	SB	BB	SO	Avg	OBP	Slg
'03	80	202	31	44	17	0	8	28	1	37	71	.218	.350	.421
Car.	104	252	37	53	18	0	10	32	1	44	86	.210	.337	.401

2003 Situational Stats

	AB	H	HR	RBI	Avg		AB	H	HR	RBI	Avg
Home	109	23	5	14	.211	LHP	17	1	0	1	.059
Road	93	21	3	14	.226	RHP	185	43	8	27	.232
First Half	159	38	7	23	.239	Sc Pos	47	8	3	19	.170
Scnd Half	43	6	1	5	.140	Clutch	34	2	0	1	.059

2003 Season

Through June 6, Hee Seop Choi was enjoying a fairly successful rookie season. Platooning at first base, he was hitting below .250, but displaying good power and drawing a lot of walks. The next day, however, Choi collided with pitcher Kerry Wood while chasing a pop fly, hitting his head on the ground and suffering a concussion. He missed three weeks, and when he returned, struggled and lost his job.

Hitting, Baserunning & Defense

Choi has power to all fields and gets good lift on the ball. He has good strike-zone judgment but swings through a lot of pitches. He saw very few southpaws last year, but handled them consistently well in the minors. Choi moves fairly well for someone his size. Defensively, he appears to already have smoothed out many of the rough edges and is a solid fielding first baseman.

2004 Outlook

The pressure of the 2003 pennant race kept Choi from playing much after his injury, but he now goes to Florida, where the first-base job is wide open and he could get most of the 2004 playing time. Traded for Derrek Lee in November, Choi should provide enough power and walks to be a useful contributor.

Juan Cruz

Position: RP
Bats: R **Throws:** R
Ht: 6' 2" **Wt:** 165

Opening Day Age: 25
Born: 10/15/78 in Bonao, DR
ML Seasons: 3

Overall Statistics

	W	L	Pct.	ERA	G	GS	Sv	IP	H	BB	SO	HR	Avg
'03	2	7	.222	6.05	25	6	0	61.0	66	28	65	7	.275
Car.	8	19	.296	4.43	78	23	1	203.0	190	104	185	22	.252

2003 Situational Stats

	W	L	ERA	Sv	IP		AB	H	HR	RBI	Avg
Home	0	3	7.85	0	28.2	LHB	89	26	2	13	.292
Road	2	4	4.45	0	32.1	RHB	151	40	5	24	.265
First Half	1	3	6.92	0	26.0	Sc Pos	65	19	1	30	.292
Scnd Half	1	4	5.40	0	35.0	Clutch	43	10	3	7	.233

2003 Season

Young righthander Juan Cruz pitched well as a reliever for the Cubs over the second half of 2002, but got buried as a long man in early 2003. He bounced up and down between Chicago and Triple-A Iowa, but he never did find a role on the Cubs' pitching staff.

Pitching, Defense & Hitting

Cruz has a pitcher's arm and a shortstop's body. He throws in the mid-90s with a sinker and a changeup, but lacks stamina. Walks can be a problem. His future may lie in the bullpen, but on the other hand, he's been a consistently effective starter in the minors. Though Cruz has been a good hitter and fielder in the minors, he hasn't performed well in either capacity in the majors. He has shown improvement in controlling the running game, though.

2004 Outlook

The outlook for Cruz is the same as it's been for the past couple of years: this could be the year that he grabs a rotation spot or bullpen job and runs with it, or his struggles to establish a niche for himself could continue.

Shawn Estes

Position: SP
Bats: R **Throws:** L
Ht: 6' 2" **Wt:** 200

Opening Day Age: 31
Born: 2/18/73 in San Bernardino, CA
ML Seasons: 9
Pronunciation: ES tus
Nickname: Buck

Overall Statistics

	W	L	Pct.	ERA	G	GS	Sv	IP	H	BB	SO	HR	Avg
'03	8	11	.421	5.73	29	28	0	152.1	182	83	103	20	.305
Car.	77	73	.513	4.53	218	217	0	1303.0	1298	687	1007	107	.265

2003 Situational Stats

	W	L	ERA	Sv	IP		AB	H	HR	RBI	Avg
Home	3	6	5.90	0	76.1	LHB	116	32	4	19	.276
Road	5	5	5.57	0	76.0	RHB	481	150	16	80	.312
First Half	6	8	5.74	0	105.0	Sc Pos	158	51	3	73	.323
Scnd Half	2	3	5.70	0	47.1	Clutch	13	5	1	5	.385

2003 Season

Shawn Estes' once-promising career continued to spiral downward in 2003. Signed to be the Cubs' fifth starter, he was incapable of holding even that role. Manager Dusty Baker showed remarkable restraint as Estes ran hot-and-cold—mostly the latter—for much of the season, but finally yielded to reality and dropped Estes from the rotation in early September.

Pitching, Defense & Hitting

Inconsistent command is Estes' Achilles heel. He tries to get ahead with a high-80s fastball, a cutter and a changeup, but too often he either misses or catches too much of the plate. His big overhand curve can be a strikeout pitch if he's able to get ahead and make hitters chase it. When he's on, he works inside to righthanded hitters and gets groundballs. He has a decent pickoff move, and holds runners fairly well by using a slide step and varying his delivery. After two poor years at the plate, he rebounded last year.

2004 Outlook

Estes is a free agent and may have a hard time getting his career going again. Another rotation spot may be hard to come by, and he isn't particularly well-suited to relief work.

Kyle Farnsworth

Position: RP
Bats: R **Throws:** R
Ht: 6' 4" **Wt:** 235

Opening Day Age: 27
Born: 4/14/76 in Wichita, KS
ML Seasons: 5

Overall Statistics

	W	L	Pct.	ERA	G	GS	Sv	IP	H	BB	SO	HR	Avg
'03	3	2	.600	3.30	77	0	0	76.1	53	36	92	6	.196
Car.	18	32	.360	4.78	271	26	4	412.0	401	191	389	65	.253

2003 Situational Stats

	W	L	ERA	Sv	IP		AB	H	HR	RBI	Avg
Home	1	0	1.79	0	40.1	LHB	90	17	1	8	.189
Road	2	2	5.00	0	36.0	RHB	181	36	5	19	.199
First Half	3	0	2.60	0	45.0	Sc Pos	69	13	1	20	.188
Scnd Half	0	2	4.31	0	31.1	Clutch	101	22	3	13	.218

2003 Season

In 2001, Kyle Farnsworth suddenly developed into a dominant setup man. In 2002, he just as suddenly reverted to complete ineffectiveness. In 2003, he snapped right back to his 2001 form. The main difference was maturity, something that had been lacking both on and off the field in 2002.

Pitching, Defense & Hitting

Farnsworth's outstanding fastball is regularly clocked in the high 90s. It's dead straight, though, so complementing it always has been crucial. In 2001, he used a hard splitter to great effect, but he seems to have lost confidence in it. He now uses a hard curve as his second pitch. He can get hurt on first-pitch fastballs, but he's deadly after he gets ahead. Farnsworth's fielding has improved from brutal to adequate, although he's still easy to run on. He can't hit, but he can help himself with a bunt.

2004 Outlook

Farnsworth has been this good before and failed to sustain it, but it seems unlikely he'll regress to his 2002 form again. If he comes up with another pitch, he could become a closer down the road. At worst, he should remain a very capable setup man.

Chicago (NL)

Eric Karros

Position: 1B
Bats: R **Throws:** R
Ht: 6' 4" **Wt:** 220

Opening Day Age: 36
Born: 11/4/67 in Hackensack, NJ
ML Seasons: 13
Pronunciation: CARE-ose

Overall Statistics

	G	AB	R	H	D	T	HR	RBI	SB	BB	SO	Avg	OBP	Slg
'03	114	336	37	96	16	1	12	40	1	28	46	.286	.340	.446
Car.	1715	6338	789	1704	318	11	282	1016	58	545	1151	.269	.326	.456

2003 Situational Stats

	AB	H	HR	RBI	Avg		AB	H	HR	RBI	Avg
Home	165	51	7	24	.309	LHP	112	41	3	10	.366
Road	171	45	5	16	.263	RHP	224	55	9	30	.246
First Half	195	63	8	21	.323	Sc Pos	81	21	2	28	.259
Scnd Half	141	33	4	19	.234	Clutch	57	16	2	8	.281

2003 Season

Eric Karros made a surprisingly painless adjustment to a smaller role last year. For the first two months of the season, he platooned with rookie Hee Seop Choi and was more productive than he'd been in two years. When Choi got hurt in June, Karros took over full-time and kept hitting. He slumped late in the season and lost at-bats to mid-August acquisition Randall Simon, but still finished with better numbers than expected.

Hitting, Baserunning & Defense

As Karros' power has waned, he's adopted a more contact-oriented approach in order to keep his average up. Only when he pulls the ball is he a home-run threat. He no longer is productive enough against righthanded pitchers to play every day, but remains dangerous against lefties. He's slumped in the second half during each of the last four seasons. Karros has very little speed, but is a good defensive first baseman.

2004 Outlook

The Cubs declined their option on Karros, making him a free agent. He could do well as part of a first-base platoon, but it may be hard for him to find a team that needs him, as righthanded-hitting first basemen hardly are a scarce commodity.

Ramon Martinez

Position: 2B/3B/SS
Bats: R **Throws:** R
Ht: 6' 1" **Wt:** 195

Opening Day Age: 31
Born: 10/10/72 in Philadelphia, PA
ML Seasons: 6

Overall Statistics

	G	AB	R	H	D	T	HR	RBI	SB	BB	SO	Avg	OBP	Slg
'03	108	293	30	83	16	1	3	34	0	24	50	.283	.333	.375
Car.	476	1217	159	332	64	8	23	140	7	109	169	.273	.334	.395

2003 Situational Stats

	AB	H	HR	RBI	Avg		AB	H	HR	RBI	Avg
Home	139	44	3	19	.317	LHP	81	28	2	14	.346
Road	154	39	0	15	.253	RHP	212	55	1	20	.259
First Half	164	47	3	23	.287	Sc Pos	73	18	0	25	.247
Scnd Half	129	36	0	11	.279	Clutch	52	16	1	3	.308

2003 Season

As he had been for the Giants in past seasons, Ramon Martinez was a valuable reserve for the Cubs in 2003, filling in at second base, third base and shortstop while holding his own at the plate. At different points in the season there were questions at both second and third, but Martinez' presence provided a safety net.

Hitting, Baserunning & Defense

Martinez is a good contact hitter with occasional doubles power, and has been surprisingly productive against lefties over the course of his career. One thing he hasn't done well is pinch-hit. He has average speed, and occasional hamstring problems have limited his aggressiveness on the bases. His biggest asset is his ability to play competently all over the infield. Martinez is a steady, surehanded fielder with enough range to play shortstop and enough arm to get by at third.

2004 Outlook

Martinez may be no worse than some infielders with full-time jobs, but his versatility makes him more valuable as a reserve. He may be used to plug a temporary hole, but if a long-term solution is needed, the Cubs likely will look elsewhere.

Damian Miller

Position: C
Bats: R **Throws:** R
Ht: 6' 3" **Wt:** 220

Opening Day Age: 34
Born: 10/13/69 in La Crosse, WI
ML Seasons: 7

Overall Statistics

	G	AB	R	H	D	T	HR	RBI	SB	BB	SO	Avg	OBP	Slg
'03	114	352	34	82	19	1	9	36	1	39	91	.233	.310	.369
Car.	606	1883	219	494	118	3	59	243	4	180	466	.262	.329	.422

2003 Situational Stats

	AB	H	HR	RBI	Avg		AB	H	HR	RBI	Avg
Home	182	45	6	23	.247	LHP	109	27	0	9	.248
Road	170	37	3	13	.218	RHP	243	55	9	27	.226
First Half	217	51	6	26	.235	Sc Pos	76	17	2	27	.224
Scnd Half	135	31	3	10	.230	Clutch	55	14	1	1	.255

2003 Season

The Cubs traded for Damian Miller before the 2003 season, and he wound up handling the bulk of their catching chores. While he ending up having a sub-par season at the plate, Miller made a solid contribution defensively. His pitch-blocking skills were especially appreciated by a staff full of pitchers with hard breaking balls.

Hitting, Baserunning & Defense

Miller has occasional extra-base power, but is mostly content to hit the ball where it's pitched—usually to right field, since pitchers tend to work him away. Last year, he showed he could lay down a sacrifice when asked, and he draws a fair number of walks for a bottom-of-the-order hitter. He doesn't run well and has trouble staying out of the double play. Miller earns his keep on defense. He's a quality receiver with an accurate arm and a quick release, and was able to prevent a lot of potential wild pitches from going to the backstop last year.

2004 Outlook

The Cubs expect to see more of the same from Miller in 2004. His bat might rebound a bit, but not enough to ever thrust him into a more prominent offensive role.

Mike Remlinger

Position: RP
Bats: L **Throws:** L
Ht: 6' 1" **Wt:** 215

Opening Day Age: 38
Born: 3/23/66 in Middletown, NY
ML Seasons: 11
Pronunciation: REM-lin-jurr

Overall Statistics

	W	L	Pct.	ERA	G	GS	Sv	IP	H	BB	SO	HR	Avg
'03	6	5	.545	3.65	73	0	0	69.0	54	39	83	11	.211
Car.	50	46	.521	3.78	512	59	16	780.1	678	388	765	91	.235

2003 Situational Stats

	W	L	ERA	Sv	IP		AB	H	HR	RBI	Avg
Home	4	2	3.86	0	35.0	LHB	95	25	5	16	.263
Road	2	3	3.44	0	34.0	RHB	161	29	6	17	.180
First Half	5	3	4.50	0	40.0	Sc Pos	68	14	2	21	.206
Scnd Half	1	2	2.48	0	29.0	Clutch	101	15	3	8	.149

2003 Season

The Cubs signed Mike Remlinger prior to the 2003 season to be the top lefthander out of their bullpen. Working in a setup role, he had an up-and-down first half, showing an uncharacteristic lack of command at times, and leaving too many pitches up at other times. Remlinger came on in the second half, though, posting a 1.59 ERA over the final five weeks of the season.

Pitching, Defense & Hitting

Remlinger comes with a low-90s fastball, a slider and a changeup. He's one of the few lefthanded relievers in baseball who is consistently more effective against righthanded hitters. He has a resilient arm, thriving on frequent work, and maintains his effectiveness for more than an inning at a time. With a good pickoff move and a compact stretch delivery, he's tough to run on. He's otherwise unremarkable in the field, and is a very poor hitter.

2004 Outlook

Lefthanded relievers fall into two classes: specialists, and everyone else. Among the latter class, Remlinger is one of the best in the game, and is secure in his role. Though he'll turn 38 this spring, he seems to have plenty left in the tank.

Randall Simon

Position: 1B
Bats: L **Throws:** L
Ht: 6' 0" **Wt:** 240

Opening Day Age: 28
Born: 5/26/75 in
Willemstad, Curacao
ML Seasons: 6

Overall Statistics

	G	AB	R	H	D	T	HR	RBI	SB	BB	SO	Avg	OBP	Slg
'03	124	410	47	113	17	0	16	72	0	16	37	.276	.309	.434
Car.	445	1396	156	414	65	3	46	221	2	62	123	.297	.328	.446

2003 Situational Stats

	AB	H	HR	RBI	Avg		AB	H	HR	RBI	Avg
Home	172	45	4	20	.262	LHP	52	14	2	10	.269
Road	238	68	12	52	.286	RHP	358	99	14	62	.277
First Half	232	64	7	40	.276	Sc Pos	120	38	9	59	.317
Scnd Half	178	49	9	32	.275	Clutch	70	19	2	9	.271

2003 Season

Like Kenny Lofton, Randall Simon signed a free-agent deal with Pittsburgh last winter and hit fairly well for them. In July, Simon was involved in a bizarre incident at Miller Park in which he hit a sausage mascot with a bat. Later that month, he was traded to the Cubs, where he split time at first base and made important contributions down the stretch.

Hitting, Baserunning & Defense

Simon is possibly the most impatient hitter in the majors. Pitchers, predictably, feed him junk, and he somehow manages to put it in play, often with a charge in it. He hits a lot of groundballs, but has good power to all fields when he gets the ball in the air. Simon has limited experience against lefties and hasn't done much against them. The man is not built for speed—he runs the bases station-to-station and has little lateral range at first base. He has pretty good hands, though, and was credited with saving quite a few bad throws.

2004 Outlook

The Cubs' acquisition of Derrek Lee means that Simon likely will be non-tendered and allowed to become a free agent. Look for him to latch on with a team in need of an inexpensive first baseman.

Tony Womack

Position: SS/2B
Bats: L **Throws:** R
Ht: 5' 9" **Wt:** 168

Opening Day Age: 34
Born: 9/25/69 in
Danville, VA
ML Seasons: 10
Pronunciation:
WO-mack

Overall Statistics

	G	AB	R	H	D	T	HR	RBI	SB	BB	SO	Avg	OBP	Slg
'03	103	349	43	79	14	4	2	22	13	9	47	.226	.251	.307
Car.	1022	4013	595	1083	157	55	30	310	309	252	533	.270	.315	.359

2003 Situational Stats

	AB	H	HR	RBI	Avg		AB	H	HR	RBI	Avg
Home	171	47	2	13	.275	LHP	56	15	0	6	.268
Road	178	32	0	9	.180	RHP	293	64	2	16	.218
First Half	219	52	2	15	.237	Sc Pos	85	20	0	20	.235
Scnd Half	130	27	0	7	.208	Clutch	57	14	0	3	.246

2003 Season

It seemed everything that could go wrong, did go wrong for Tony Womack in 2003. A slow start led to him being dropped from Arizona's leadoff spot in mid-April. Then, a sprained knee put him out of action in late June. When he returned, he was dealt to Colorado, where he also failed to hit. Sent to the Cubs a month later, he suffered several more injuries, the final one being an elbow injury that kept him off the postseason roster and required Tommy John surgery.

Hitting, Baserunning & Defense

Womack is a slap-and-dash hitter who rarely pulls the ball or hits it with authority. He seldom walks, so he's far from an ideal leadoff man. He has very good speed, but has not used it as well on the basepaths in recent years. At shortstop, his arm—even before surgery—was adequate at best. He also can get by at second base and the outfield.

2004 Outlook

Now a free agent, Womack probably won't be ready to start the 2004 season on time, and may have to go to the minors to play his way back into shape. He may land a bench role somewhere.

Other Chicago Cubs

Antonio Alfonseca (Pos: RHP, Age: 31)

	W	L	Pct.	ERA	G	GS	Sv	IP	H	BB	SO	HR	Avg
'03	3	1	.750	5.83	60	0	0	66.1	76	27	51	7	.290
Car.	23	30	.434	4.11	400	0	121	446.1	489	174	310	42	.282

Slated to begin the year as the Cubs' closer, Alfonseca strained his hamstring and missed the first month of the season. Journeyman Joe Borowski claimed the job in Alfonseca's absence. 2004 Outlook: B

Paul Bako (Pos: C, Age: 31, Bats: L)

	G	AB	R	H	D	T	HR	RBI	SB	BB	SO	Avg	OBP	Slg
'03	70	188	19	43	13	3	0	17	0	22	47	.229	.311	.330
Car.	468	1300	119	315	67	8	13	119	3	138	330	.242	.314	.336

Acquired from Milwaukee in an offseason trade, Bako spent the 2003 season as a backup to Damian Miller. He hit .190 before the All-Star break, but turned it around in the second half, batting .273. 2004 Outlook: C

Doug Glanville (Pos: CF, Age: 33, Bats: R)

	G	AB	R	H	D	T	HR	RBI	SB	BB	SO	Avg	OBP	Slg
'03	80	246	24	65	5	0	5	16	4	8	29	.264	.286	.346
Car.	1028	3802	532	1066	165	31	57	319	160	200	481	.280	.318	.385

Glanville began last season with the Rangers, but injured his hamstring and lost his starting job after a stint on the disabled list. He later was acquired by the Cubs and was limited to backup duty in Chicago. 2004 Outlook: C

Tom Goodwin (Pos: CF/LF/RF, Age: 35, Bats: L)

	G	AB	R	H	D	T	HR	RBI	SB	BB	SO	Avg	OBP	Slg
'03	87	171	26	49	10	0	1	12	19	11	33	.287	.328	.363
Car.	1211	3741	625	1008	117	39	24	281	364	357	638	.269	.334	.341

Dusty Baker primarily used Goodwin off the bench in 2003, taking advantage of the outfielder's speed. Goodwin got just 171 at-bats, but hit .287 and swiped 19 bases in 87 games, so the Cubs re-signed him in December. 2004 Outlook: B

Mark Guthrie (Pos: LHP, Age: 38)

	W	L	Pct.	ERA	G	GS	Sv	IP	H	BB	SO	HR	Avg
'03	2	3	.400	2.74	65	0	0	42.2	40	22	24	6	.260
Car.	51	54	.486	4.05	765	43	14	978.2	989	381	778	101	.266

Guthrie has posted solid numbers each of the past two seasons, but age might catch up with him soon. Solid lefthanded relievers are coveted in the majors, so Guthrie should have a job in some major league town next season. 2004 Outlook: B

Trenidad Hubbard (Pos: CF, Age: 37, Bats: R)

	G	AB	R	H	D	T	HR	RBI	SB	BB	SO	Avg	OBP	Slg
'03	10	16	2	4	1	0	0	2	1	4	3	.250	.429	.313
Car.	476	762	124	196	33	7	16	72	33	83	166	.257	.333	.382

Hubbard turns 38 in May, so a return to the majors is unlikely. Despite his age, the outfielder still has good speed and a keen eye at the plate. However, he doesn't pack enough punch with his bat. 2004 Outlook: C

Sergio Mitre (Pos: RHP, Age: 23)

	W	L	Pct.	ERA	G	GS	Sv	IP	H	BB	SO	HR	Avg
'03	0	1	.000	8.31	3	2	0	8.2	15	4	3	1	.395
Car.	0	1	.000	8.31	3	2	0	8.2	15	4	3	1	.395

Mitre saw a couple of spot starts for Chicago last season, but spent most of the year in Double-A. With limited room in the Cubs' starting rotation, he likely will spend most of 2004 with Triple-A Iowa. 2004 Outlook: C

Troy O'Leary (Pos: LF/RF, Age: 34, Bats: L)

	G	AB	R	H	D	T	HR	RBI	SB	BB	SO	Avg	OBP	Slg
'03	93	174	18	38	9	0	5	28	3	14	31	.218	.275	.356
Car.	1198	4010	547	1100	234	40	127	591	17	334	661	.274	.332	.448

The power O'Leary possessed while a member of the Boston Red Sox in the late 1990s seemed to have disappeared over the past two seasons. His days of being in the lineup on a daily basis likely are over. 2004 Outlook: C

Augie Ojeda (Pos: SS, Age: 29, Bats: B)

	G	AB	R	H	D	T	HR	RBI	SB	BB	SO	Avg	OBP	Slg
'03	12	25	2	3	0	0	0	0	0	1	5	.120	.185	.120
Car.	148	316	32	62	12	2	3	24	2	28	39	.196	.267	.275

Despite recording just three hits in 25 at-bats with Chicago in 2003, Ojeda remains a fan favorite at Wrigley Field. His versatility and solid glove persuaded the Twins to grab him off waivers in November. 2004 Outlook: C

Josh Paul (Pos: C, Age: 28, Bats: R)

	G	AB	R	H	D	T	HR	RBI	SB	BB	SO	Avg	OBP	Slg
'03	16	23	6	6	0	0	0	4	0	3	6	.261	.346	.261
Car.	148	355	54	92	19	2	4	42	9	30	74	.259	.318	.358

Paul began the 2003 season on the south side, but refused an outright assignment by the White Sox and became a free agent. He then signed with the Cubs and appeared in 47 games with Triple-A Iowa before being released at the end of October. 2004 Outlook: C

Felix Sanchez (Pos: LHP, Age: 22)

	W	L	Pct.	ERA	G	GS	Sv	IP	H	BB	SO	HR	Avg
'03	0	0	—	10.80	3	0	0	1.2	2	3	2	1	.333
Car.	0	0	—	10.80	3	0	0	1.2	2	3	2	1	.333

Sanchez spent most of 2003 in Double-A, posting a 3.23 ERA in 30 appearances, including eight starts. He struggled in three outings with Chicago, so another year in the minor leagues is likely. 2004 Outlook: C

Dave Veres (Pos: RHP, Age: 37)

	W	L	Pct.	ERA	G	GS	Sv	IP	H	BB	SO	HR	Avg
'03	2	1	.667	4.68	31	0	1	32.2	36	5	26	4	.290
Car.	36	35	.507	3.44	605	0	95	694.0	661	257	617	78	.253

Veres had two stints on the DL in 2003, both due to shoulder tendinitis. He struggled on the road with the Cubs, posting an 8.79 ERA, compared to a 1.47 ERA at the friendly confines of Wrigley Field. 2004 Outlook: B

Chicago Cubs Minor League Prospects

Organization Overview:

The Cubs' surge to the NLCS was punctuated by the emergence of Mark Prior as one of baseball's top aces. Carlos Zambrano likewise enjoyed a breakout season, and Corey Patterson was on the same path before going down with a torn ACL in July. All are products of a thriving Cubs minor league system, and the bad news for National League Central rivals is that there is more to come. The Cubs are stacked with a plethora of strong young arms, led by Angel Guzman and Andy Sisco, and Felix Pie is on the fast track to finding a home in the Wrigley Field pasture. Sisco and Pie head a core group of Lansing Lugnuts that swept seven games on their way to the Class-A Midwest League championship. The Cubs hope that familiarity with success will translate to higher levels.

Francis Beltran

Position: P
Bats: R **Throws:** R
Ht: 6' 5" **Wt:** 230

Opening Day Age: 24
Born: 11/29/79 in Santo
Domingo, DR

Recent Statistics

	W	L	ERA	G	GS	Sv	IP	H	R	BB	SO	HR
2002 AA West Tenn	2	2	2.59	39	0	23	41.2	28	14	19	43	2
2002 NL Chicago	0	0	7.50	11	0	0	12.0	14	11	16	11	2
2003 AAA Iowa	6	2	2.96	31	2	4	48.2	46	17	19	33	2

Beltran was one of several pitching prospects who suffered arm ailments last season, cutting short his season at Triple-A Iowa in July with bicep tendinitis. A pre-emptive shutdown hastened his recovery, and he was pitching well in the Dominican Winter League. Beltran can rev up his heater as high as 97 MPH with good movement, but he still needs to work on his control and command of his repertoire, which includes a slider and change. While it is likely that he'll pick up where he left off at Iowa (6-2, 2.96, four saves with 33 strikeouts in 48.2 innings), a midseason callup to bolster the Cubs' bullpen is not out of the question.

Angel Guzman

Position: P
Bats: R **Throws:** R
Ht: 6' 2" **Wt:** 180

Opening Day Age: 22
Born: 12/14/81 in
Caracas, VZ

Recent Statistics

	W	L	ERA	G	GS	Sv	IP	H	R	BB	SO	HR
2002 A Lansing	5	2	1.89	9	9	0	62.0	42	18	16	49	3
2002 A Daytona	6	2	2.39	16	15	0	94.0	99	34	33	74	2
2003 AA West Tenn	3	3	2.81	15	15	0	89.2	83	30	26	87	8

Of all the highly regarded pitching prospects in the Chicago Cubs' system, Guzman is perhaps most prepared to make an immediate contribution. The then-21-year-old opened eyes at spring training, and it seemed only a matter of time before he joined the parent club.

He appeared to be on his way, ringing up 87 strikeouts in 89.2 innings in the Double-A Southern League and displaying fine control with a curve, changeup and low-90s sinking fastball that induces plenty of groundouts. Unfortunately, a sore shoulder put him on the shelf in June, and he underwent arthroscopic surgery. The damage was minimal, however, and Guzman began throwing again by mid-November. If he is up to full strength by the time the bell rings in April, he could battle for a spot at the back end of the Chicago rotation with a repeat performance of his spring trial last year.

Brendan Harris

Position: 3B
Bats: R **Throws:** R
Ht: 6' 0" **Wt:** 180

Opening Day Age: 23
Born: 8/26/80 in
Queensbury, NY

Recent Statistics

	G	AB	R	H	D	T	HR	RBI	SB	BB	SO	Avg
2002 A Daytona	110	425	82	140	35	6	13	54	16	43	57	.329
2002 AA West Tenn	13	53	8	17	4	1	2	11	1	2	5	.321
2003 AA West Tenn	120	435	56	122	34	7	5	52	6	51	72	.280

After a banner 2002 campaign, Harris raised expectations as he spent a full year at Double-A West Tenn in 2003. His slugging fell by more than 100 points to .425, but if he can build on a year in which he lashed out 34 doubles and seven triples, Harris could have a future at second base. He has a good eye at the plate, and the fact that he also can handle duties at the hot corner could hasten a major league promotion after some exposure to Triple-A pitching. The Cubs are enamored with his hard-nosed style of play, a quality Dusty Baker cherishes.

Nic Jackson

Position: OF
Bats: L **Throws:** R
Ht: 6' 4" **Wt:** 205

Opening Day Age: 24
Born: 9/25/79 in
Richmond, VA

Recent Statistics

	G	AB	R	H	D	T	HR	RBI	SB	BB	SO	Avg
2002 AA West Tenn	32	131	18	38	9	1	3	20	8	6	23	.290
2003 AAA Iowa	125	458	56	116	19	4	11	44	17	35	102	.253

Jackson appeared to struggle against Triple-A competition, slugging just .384 while registering a 35-102 walk-strikeout ratio, but remember that he did miss the majority of the 2002 season at Double-A West Tenn. The fact that he showed steady improvement from month to month as the season progressed bodes well, but he will have to control the strike zone if he hopes to win a spot in the Cubs' outfield this year. If Jackson does put his package of speed and power together, which he flashed in high Class-A Daytona two years ago, he could offer a lefthanded stick off the Chicago bench and the versatility to handle any outfield position before the 2004 campaign is over.

David Kelton

Position: OF
Bats: R **Throws:** R
Ht: 6' 2" **Wt:** 205
Opening Day Age: 24
Born: 12/17/79 in Dothan, AL

Recent Statistics

	G	AB	R	H	D	T	HR	RBI	SB	BB	SO	Avg
2003 AAA Iowa	121	442	62	119	24	3	16	67	8	46	115	.269
2003 NL Chicago	10	12	1	2	1	0	0	1	0	0	5	.167

Now that the acquisition of Aramis Ramirez has answered the Cubs' perennial question at third, Kelton finally might ease into a comfort zone as a corner outfielder. The club even experimented with him in center when Corey Patterson went down, but Kelton's immediate major league future looks to be in a righthanded platoon role in left field and as a backup at first base. He got a taste of the big leagues last year, where he showed surprising speed on his first major league hit, an infield single. His power numbers were down in his first go-round at Triple-A, and he needs to cut down on his strikeouts to take full advantage of a short power stroke. If he can do that, he is capable of contributing at the major league level.

Felix Pie

Position: OF
Bats: L **Throws:** L
Ht: 6' 2" **Wt:** 165
Opening Day Age: 19
Born: 2/8/85 in La Romana, DR

Recent Statistics

	G	AB	R	H	D	T	HR	RBI	SB	BB	SO	Avg
2002 R Cubs	55	218	42	70	16	13	4	37	17	21	47	.321
2002 A Boise	2	8	1	1	0	0	0	1	0	1	1	.125
2003 A Lansing	124	505	72	144	22	9	4	47	19	41	98	.285

Pie is perhaps the most exciting prospect in the Cubs' farm system. He's just scratching the surface of his four-tool talent, with outstanding glove work at the forefront—he was named as the best defensive outfielder in the Class-A Midwest League in a poll of managers. He's starting to improve his plate discipline, and though Pie has yet to develop home-run power, management feels that will come in time. At this point, the organization just wants him to settle in and have fun, something he surely did during the playoffs, where he led the team with a .429 batting average. The Cubs' addition of Vince Coleman as minor league baserunning mentor should help Pie improve his technique, as he was successful only 19 times in 32 attempts last year.

Andy Sisco

Position: P
Bats: L **Throws:** L
Ht: 6' 9" **Wt:** 260
Opening Day Age: 21
Born: 1/13/83 in Sammamish, WA

Recent Statistics

	W	L	ERA	G	GS	Sv	IP	H	R	BB	SO	HR
2002 A Boise	7	2	2.43	14	14	0	77.2	51	23	39	101	3
2003 A Lansing	6	8	3.54	19	19	0	94.0	76	44	31	99	3

What's not to like about a 6-foot-9, 260-pound, 21-year-old lefty who throws strikes in the mid-90s? Sisco gets good movement with his four-pitch repertoire, which includes a splitter, curve and change in addition to the gas, although he needs some polish on his command. His progress suffered a hit when he sat out two months at Class-A Lansing with a broken hand—self-inflicted in a pique of frustration. He came back from his hiatus to register more than a strikeout per inning, holding the opposition to a .220 average. On a positive note, the hand incident was testament to his competitive spirit; he's proven to be a gamer in postseason starts.

Todd Wellemeyer

Position: P
Bats: R **Throws:** R
Ht: 6' 3" **Wt:** 195
Opening Day Age: 25
Born: 8/30/78 in Louisville, KY

Recent Statistics

	W	L	ERA	G	GS	Sv	IP	H	R	BB	SO	HR
2003 AA West Tenn	1	1	5.48	4	4	0	21.1	19	13	10	34	1
2003 AAA Iowa	5	5	5.18	13	12	0	66.0	68	39	33	56	7
2003 NL Chicago	1	1	6.51	15	0	1	27.2	25	22	19	30	5

Wellemeyer made a splash in his major league debut last May, striking out the first three MLB hitters he faced to earn a save in a 17-inning affair in Milwaukee. That also captured the hearts of the Wrigley Field faithful, as well as the trust of Dusty Baker, at least for a month. Two disastrous outings at the end of June sent him packing to Triple-A Iowa, where he struggled to regain his form. He is capable of dialing his fastball up to 95 MPH, has a good moving curve and is not afraid to throw his lively change in a pinch. A strong showing this spring could bring a return to the Cubs' pen.

Others to Watch

Chadd Blasko (23), an imposing 6-foot-7 righty with a low- to mid-90s sinking fastball, was a revelation in his first year of pro ball, going 10-5, 1.98 in the high Class-A Florida State League while striking out nearly one batter per inning. . . **Bobby Brownlie** (23), a late signee after the Cubs tabbed him in the first round of the 2002 draft, was shut down in July after logging 66 innings (5-4, 3.00, 59 Ks) at high Class-A Daytona, following a full schedule of winter ball. He returned in the instructional league this fall. . . The Cubs might have a keeper in outfielder **Jason Dubois** (25), who was nearly lost to the Blue Jays in a Rule 5 pickup last year. He hit .358-9-29 in 30 Arizona Fall League games to pick up MVP honors and earn a spot on the 40-man roster. . . Some Class-A Midwest League observers regard lefty **Justin Jones** (19) as hot a commodity as teammate Andy Sisco, after Jones registered a 2.28 ERA at Lansing and whiffed 11 per nine innings. . . Wherefore art thou, **Luis Montanez** (22)? The overall third choice of the 2000 draft logged more time at second base than shortstop at high Class-A Daytona, saw his numbers decline across the board during his second straight year with the same team, and may be facing a career crossroad.

Great American Ball Park

Offense

Cincinnati's good-looking new home quickly was recognized as one of baseball's new wave of launching pads. The ball flies out in both straight-away left and right, with the power alleys also quite reachable. The ball also travels to dead center, with the prevailing winds usually favoring hitters. The offensive theme is carried to the infield, which is kept hard.

Defense

The new infield was fairly true in limiting bad hops. Cincinnati's outfield speed easily handled the gaps of the new outfield configuration. There is slightly more foul ground to cover in the new park, which is one aid to pitchers, who better keep the ball down or watch some routine flyballs head for the bleachers.

Who It Helps the Most

So many Reds regulars were injured that it was difficult to get a feel for who might be aided by the new surroundings. However, players such as Adam Dunn and Ken Griffey Jr. hit substantially better at home than on the road, and Great American also should help the power numbers of flyball hitters such as Jason LaRue.

Who It Hurts the Most

It's pretty clear that Cincinnati's pitchers will need to adjust to allowing some cheap home runs at home. The reachable seats also could hurt some hitters if they fall in love with trying to hoist too many pitches. A case in point last year was Sean Casey, who was tempted by the right-field porch and tried to lift balls too frequently.

Rookies & Newcomers

The Reds' first season at GABP turned so sour that whatever extra revenue that might have been generated won't translate into extra spending on players. However, they at least have a core of young talents who could put up some big numbers in the new home, at least offensively. Any new pitcher better keep in mind that he is walking into a shooting gallery.

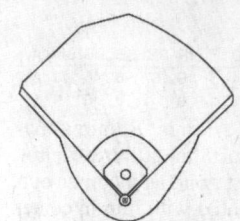

Dimensions: LF-328, LCF-379, CF-404, RCF-370, RF-325

Capacity: 42,263

Elevation: 550 feet

Surface: Grass

Foul Territory: Average

Park Factors

2003 Season

	Home Games			Away Games			
	Reds	Opp	Total	Reds	Opp	Total	Index
G	75	75	150	72	72	144	
Avg	.248	.271	.260	.242	.289	.265	98
AB	2505	2675	5180	2504	2481	4985	100
R	322	405	727	311	403	714	98
H	622	725	1347	607	716	1323	98
2B	117	154	271	105	151	256	102
3B	5	6	11	15	27	42	25
HR	88	110	198	69	84	153	125
BB	241	255	496	240	272	512	93
SO	586	449	1035	612	386	998	100
E	72	52	124	57	49	106	112
E-Infield	59	47	106	47	45	92	111
LHB-Avg	.255	.264	.260	.248	.283	.265	98
LHB-HR	39	39	78	32	35	67	116
RHB-Avg	.244	.275	.260	.239	.292	.266	98
RHB-HR	49	71	120	37	49	86	132

2001-2002 (Cinergy Field)

	Home Games			Away Games			
	Reds	Opp	Total	Reds	Opp	Total	Index
G	150	150	300	147	147	294	
Avg	.266	.279	.273	.254	.266	.260	105
AB	5047	5374	10421	5105	4936	10041	102
R	697	792	1489	654	681	1335	109
H	1342	1502	2844	1295	1312	2607	107
2B	318	319	637	238	266	504	122
3B	8	21	29	34	28	62	45
HR	159	201	360	166	133	299	116
BB	525	483	1008	451	506	957	101
SO	1021	936	1957	1156	852	2008	94
E	113	102	215	128	106	234	90
E-Infield	89	86	175	101	91	192	89
LHB-Avg	.287	.282	.284	.275	.274	.274	104
LHB-HR	73	87	160	87	70	157	100
RHB-Avg	.251	.278	.265	.237	.260	.249	107
RHB-HR	86	114	200	79	63	142	134

2003 Rankings (National League)

- Highest RHB home-run factor
- Third-highest home-run factor
- Third-highest error factor
- Lowest triple factor

Dave Miley

2003 Season

Dave Miley replaced Bob Boone in the last week of July, and though the team's won-loss record didn't miraculously turn around, Cincinnati held its own under the new skipper. A long-time manager and instructor in the Reds' minor league system, Miley was ahead of the learning curve in knowing many of the new players auditioned by Cincinnati in the season's final two months. As an experienced manager of young players, he immediately had a good rapport with the new faces populating the clubhouse.

Offense

It is difficult to judge Miley's big league managerial philosophy from such a small sampling of games. However, he wasn't afraid to press the action. He had a stream of new faces to watch and tried to plug people into optimum positions for success. Miley also arrived at a time when most of the established power was sidelined, so he was forced to manufacture runs more than he might with a healthy lineup.

Pitching & Defense

Miley tried his best to have his young starters last long enough to take something positive from each outing. He also could manage with eye toward developing pitchers, not just going for wins as if he were a contender. That meant often leaving pitchers in games beyond a point where they might normally have been hooked if the club were in the race. Miley also allowed his catchers to run the game without as much input from the dugout.

2004 Outlook

Cincinnati's ownership obviously is in the mode of rebuilding on the cheap, which meant it didn't go looking for a high-profile manager. The Reds seemed comfortable with the down-to-earth Miley, who has earned his dues during a long minor league career. New general manager Dan O'Brien, hired in October, didn't get much chance to evaluate Miley and pursued an exhaustive managerial search of his own. Still, at ownership's insistence, O'Brien took away Miley's interim title and signed him for 2004 with an option for 2005.

Born: 4/3/62 in Tampa, FL

Playing Experience: No major league playing experience

Managerial Experience: 1 season

Manager Statistics

Year	Team, Lg	W	L	Pct	GB	Finish
2003	Cincinnati, NL	22	35	.386	19.0	5th Central
1 Season		22	35	.386	–	–

2003 Starting Pitchers by Days Rest

	<=3	4	5	6+
Reds Starts	0	36	11	4
Reds ERA	–	4.85	5.10	5.23
NL Avg Starts	2	84	43	23
NL ERA	5.00	4.23	4.42	4.68

2003 Situational Stats

	Dave Miley	NL Average
Hit & Run Success %	35.7	32.7
Stolen Base Success %	63.0	68.9
Platoon Pct.	59.1	52.0
Defensive Subs	6	19
High-Pitch Outings	0	8
Quick/Slow Hooks	14/2	20/12
Sacrifice Attempts	25	93

2003 Rankings (National League)

- Did not rank near the top in any category

Russell Branyan

2003 Season

Russell Branyan had another season of intermittent opportunities in which he again produced mixed returns. He missed time early with after-effects of shoulder surgery and later was bothered by a persistent ankle injury. A majority of his playing time came in the second half of the season. He helped man third base after Aaron Boone's departure to the Yankees and also saw time in left field and at first base. Branyan had isolated bursts of his big-time power, but never found any type of consistent groove.

Hitting

Ever since Branyan was a prospect in the Cleveland organization, the question has been whether he ever would make consistent enough contact to warrant regular playing time and take advantage of his monster power. The question still remains. Branyan continues to strike out in more than a third of his at-bats, and remains extremely vulnerable to breaking balls and high fastballs. He can be crowded inside and his plate coverage never has been adequate on the outer half. Branyan is relatively competitive against left-handed pitching.

Baserunning & Defense

Branyan is just a mediocre baserunner with below-average speed, and is little threat to steal bases. He has worked to improve his third-base skills, particularly his throwing mechanics. His range is just average, but he has decent hands. He can handle the routine plays in left field and has improved his footwork at first, though he still looks crude at times at that position.

2004 Outlook

Branyan likely will get a chance to earn playing time at third, which is one of the Reds' many wide-open positions. His power potential continues to be a tease, and if he ever cut down on his strikeouts, he could be a breakout player. However, that's an "if" that has followed Branyan for years, and he remains an all-or-nothing player until proving otherwise.

Position: 3B/LF/1B
Bats: L **Throws:** R
Ht: 6' 3" **Wt:** 195

Opening Day Age: 28
Born: 12/19/75 in Warner Robins, GA
ML Seasons: 6
Pronunciation: BRAN-yen

Overall Statistics

	G	AB	R	H	D	T	HR	RBI	SB	BB	SO	Avg	OBP	Slg
'03	74	176	22	38	12	0	9	26	0	27	69	.216	.322	.438
Car.	400	1104	156	251	50	5	70	180	5	141	449	.227	.318	.472

Where He Hits the Ball

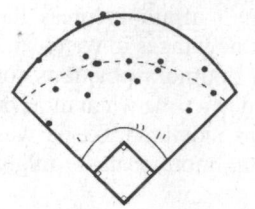 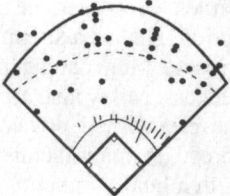

Vs. LHP   **Vs. RHP**

2003 Situational Stats

	AB	H	HR	RBI	Avg		AB	H	HR	RBI	Avg
Home	88	19	7	15	.216	LHP	44	11	2	9	.250
Road	88	19	2	11	.216	RHP	132	27	7	17	.205
First Half	48	11	2	6	.229	Sc Pos	47	9	3	18	.191
Scnd Half	128	27	7	20	.211	Clutch	40	10	2	6	.250

2003 Rankings (National League)

- Led the Reds in fewest GDPs per GDP situation (2.5%)

Sean Casey

2003 Season

Sean Casey came back from shoulder surgery to have a solid, if unspectacular, season as one of the few Cincinnati regulars to escape both injury and the club's second-half salary purge. Casey led the Reds in most major offensive categories other than home runs, driving in 80 runs for the fourth time in five years and missing a fourth .300 year by a handful of points.

Hitting

With a career average of .300, Casey obviously does a lot of things right. He fights off inside pitches and goes with pitches away to deposit many of his hits into left field. He makes consistent contact and does not pile up strikeouts. For most of his career, Casey has been able to handle lefthanded pitching, and he has always been very competitive in clutch situations. However, he also seems far too content with the status quo. He never has made any major adjustments to add power or pull the ball more frequently. And for such a good hitter, he can be handled far too easily by average fastballs on the inner half of the plate.

Baserunning & Defense

His below-average speed makes Casey a marginal threat on the bases, but he can pick his spots and does a good job of taking the extra base. Casey's defensive play has improved marginally each year. He never will have more than mediocre range, but he has upgraded his footwork, has good hands and also has improved the accuracy of his throws.

2004 Outlook

Signed through 2005 with a club option for 2006, Casey likely will stay in place amid the Reds' merry-go-around. He has remained the same solid player and solid citizen since arriving in Cincinnati. His lack of power remains the biggest knock against him, and he shows no sign of change in that area. However, there's nothing wrong with consistency, and if the team around him improves, Casey can be a good leader and run producer.

Position: 1B
Bats: L **Throws:** R
Ht: 6' 4" **Wt:** 225

Opening Day Age: 29
Born: 7/2/74 in Willingboro, NJ
MI Seasons: 7
Pronunciation: KAY-see

Overall Statistics

	G	AB	R	H	D	T	HR	RBI	SB	BB	SO	Avg	OBP	Slg
'03	147	573	71	167	19	3	14	80	4	51	58	.291	.350	.408
Car.	798	2917	413	875	180	9	85	448	11	294	383	.300	.369	.455

Where He Hits the Ball

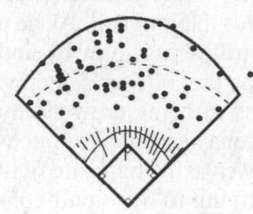
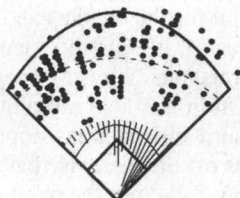

Vs. LHP   **Vs. RHP**

2003 Situational Stats

	AB	H	HR	RBI	Avg		AB	H	HR	RBI	Avg
Home	294	75	8	33	.255	LHP	181	58	4	22	.320
Road	279	92	6	47	.330	RHP	392	109	10	58	.278
First Half	343	104	10	48	.303	Sc Pos	137	46	4	65	.336
Scnd Half	230	63	4	32	.274	Clutch	95	34	2	13	.358

2003 Rankings (National League)

- 2nd in lowest cleanup slugging percentage (.416)
- 5th in fielding percentage at first base (.996)
- 6th in batting average in the clutch and batting average on the road
- 7th in singles and errors at first base (6)
- Led the Reds in at-bats, runs scored, hits, singles, triples, total bases (234), RBI, times on base (220), GDPs (19), pitches seen (2,264), plate appearances (629), games played, lowest percentage of swings that missed (10.7), batting average with runners in scoring position, batting average vs. lefthanded pitchers and batting average with two strikes (.275)

Adam Dunn

2003 Season

Already struggling through a long tailspin, Adam Dunn's season ended with an injury to his left thumb in early August. When he went down, Dunn was on his way to again challenging for the league strikeout lead and was in a power slump that had seen him hit only two home runs in the second half of the season.

Hitting

Dunn excites with his awesome power, but he has not yet made the adjustments to cut down on strikeouts and lift his average out of the doldrums. Though his patience and ability to wait out walks are admirable, his patience also can become a liability. He often will take too many pitches, waiting for the one he can lift for the longball. As a result, he lets too many strikes pass him by and thus puts himself more at the pitcher's mercy. Dunn has also not adjusted to being crowded by hard stuff, nor has stopped chasing offspeed pitches off the plate. He has power to the opposite field but falls into the habit of trying to be to pull-conscious.

Baserunning & Defense

One of Cincinnati's more memorable moments was Dunn running over Phillies catcher Mike Lieberthal on June 13 in a play that triggered a bench-clearing brawl between the teams. Dunn is an aggressive baserunner and a good basestealer for someone his size. His outfield play remains inconsistent, but his range has improved as he's learned how to position hitters better. His arm is of average strength and accuracy. He has played some first base, though not very well.

2004 Outlook

Dunn first needs a return to health, and then he needs to show signs of refining his strike-zone judgment. His sheer physical ability is eye-popping, but he is at a stage of his career where it's time to start adjusting to what pitchers are doing to him. Dunn is too good a talent to hit .215, and if he can ever start harnessing his skills, he can be an annual 40-homer threat.

Position: LF/1B
Bats: L **Throws:** R
Ht: 6' 6" **Wt:** 240

Opening Day Age: 24
Born: 11/9/79 in Houston, TX
ML Seasons: 3

Overall Statistics

	G	AB	R	H	D	T	HR	RBI	SB	BB	SO	Avg	OBP	Slg
'03	116	381	70	82	12	1	27	57	8	74	126	.215	.354	.465
Car.	340	1160	208	279	58	4	72	171	31	240	370	.241	.379	.484

Where He Hits the Ball

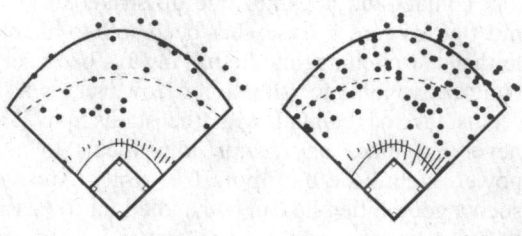

Vs. LHP   **Vs. RHP**

2003 Situational Stats

	AB	H	HR	RBI	Avg		AB	H	HR	RBI	Avg
Home	202	49	16	30	.243	LHP	119	24	9	25	.202
Road	179	33	11	27	.184	RHP	262	58	18	32	.221
First Half	287	58	25	48	.202	Sc Pos	94	16	7	32	.170
Scnd Half	94	24	2	9	.255	Clutch	60	10	3	11	.167

2003 Rankings (National League)

- 1st in errors in left field (9), lowest percentage of swings put into play (31.8) and lowest batting average with runners in scoring position
- 2nd in lowest batting average vs. lefthanded pitchers
- 6th in fewest GDPs per GDP situation (4.7%)
- 9th in steals of third (3) and lowest batting average with two strikes (.140)
- Led the Reds in home runs, sacrifice flies (4), walks, intentional walks (8), strikeouts, most pitches seen per plate appearance (4.33) and steals of third (3)

Danny Graves

2003 Season

The idea of making Danny Graves a starting pitcher made sense in theory. But in practice, it was a disaster, as he won only four of his 26 starts, two of those ironically being complete games. The experiment was shelved in the dying weeks of the season when Graves returned to the bullpen and had saves in two of his four relief outings.

Pitching

As a starter, Graves did not have the one out pitch to consistently put hitters away. Opponents often would lay off his heavy sinker and let it dive for balls, putting him behind in the count. His off-speed stuff remains marginal, with his slider too often hung over the plate, accounting for the high number of home runs and the whopping 92 extra-base hits he allowed last season. Graves also seemed to gradually lose the aggressiveness that made him so effective as a reliever, trying to nibble with his four-seamer and the slider instead of going after hitters with the sinker. He always had been willing to pitch inside, but he got away from that approach more as a starter.

Defense & Hitting

In his role as starter, Graves showed improvement in holding runners, something with which he got too much practice. He did not take advantage of his increased at-bats, however, managing to get on base only six times all season, all via singles. He also did not show much aptitude for laying down a bunt.

2004 Outlook

Cincinnati signed Graves to a three-year contract prior to the 2003 campaign, so the club is locked into his services. The Reds also damaged his trade value with what now looks to be a misguided attempt to convert him into a starting pitcher. As a reliever, Graves was a solid closer, and with Scott Williamson departed, it would seem likely that Graves will return to the bullpen, where he is a proven 30-save pitcher.

Position: SP
Bats: R **Throws:** R
Ht: 6' 0" **Wt:** 185

Opening Day Age: 30
Born: 8/7/73 in Saigon, Vietnam
ML Seasons: 8

Overall Statistics

	W	L	Pct.	ERA	G	GS	Sv	IP	H	BB	SO	HR	Avg
'03	4	15	.211	5.33	30	26	2	169.0	204	41	60	30	.298
Car.	39	36	.520	3.89	397	30	131	687.1	703	233	366	72	.268

2003 Pitching Profile

	Danny Graves	NL Average
Overall Strike %	64.1	62.4
1st Pitch Strike %	60.8	58.4
Ratio	1.45	1.38
Strikeouts per 9 IP	3.20	6.65
Walks per 9 IP	2.18	3.42
Home Runs per 9 IP	1.60	1.05
Strikeout/Walk Ratio	1.46	1.94
Groundball/Flyball Ratio	1.36	1.29

2003 Situational Stats

	W	L	ERA	Sv	IP		AB	H	HR	RBI	Avg
Home	1	5	6.03	1	71.2	LHB	293	87	11	43	.297
Road	3	10	4.81	1	97.1	RHB	391	117	19	57	.299
First Half	4	9	5.51	1	117.2	Sc Pos	176	52	9	69	.295
Scnd Half	0	6	4.91	1	51.1	Clutch	58	22	1	11	.379

2003 Rankings (National League)

- 1st in fielding percentage at pitcher (1.000), lowest winning percentage, highest slugging percentage allowed (.529) and fewest strikeouts per nine innings (3.2)
- 2nd in losses, fewest pitches thrown per batter (3.35) and most home runs allowed per nine innings (1.60)
- 3rd in highest ERA
- 4th in home runs allowed and highest batting average allowed (.298)
- 5th in least run support per nine innings (3.9)
- 8th in lowest strikeout-walk ratio (1.5)
- Led the Reds in losses, complete games (2), innings pitched, hits allowed, batters faced (741), home runs allowed, hit batsmen (7), stolen bases allowed (7), GDPs induced (17), fewest pitches thrown per batter (3.35), lowest batting average allowed with runners in scoring position and fewest walks per nine innings (2.2)

Ken Griffey Jr.

Position: CF
Bats: L **Throws:** L
Ht: 6' 3" **Wt:** 205

Opening Day Age: 34
Born: 11/21/69 in Donora, PA
ML Seasons: 15
Nickname: Junior, The Kid

2003 Season

The amazingly tragic return home of Ken Griffey Jr. continued its painful storyline with another injury-ravaged year with the Reds. Griffey suffered a dislocated shoulder barely a week into the 2003 campaign while attempting to make a diving catch, and did not return until mid-May. He then was lost for the season on July 17 when he ruptured a tendon in his right ankle, an injury that required surgery the following day. Before going down for good with the ankle injury, Griffey had not played well, hitting for an uncharacteristically low average and showing only occasional power.

Hitting

Griffey clearly has been trying to lift too many pitches, perhaps to compensate for what appears to be declining bat speed. In his prime seasons, he would crush pitches to all fields with a more level stroke that produced home runs in the course of hitting .300. Lately, Griffey appears to be trying for the longball, with the result being a longer swing that can be handled by average hard stuff and too often produces weakly hit grounders to the right side.

Baserunning & Defense

Long gone are the days when Griffey was a dangerous basestealer, and the ankle injury likely won't help in that regard. Opposing teams now disregard him as a threat. He remains a premier outfielder, though his range appears to have lost a step. It remains to be seen how August surgery to repair a torn labrum and partially torn rotator cuff in his right shoulder affects his arm strength.

2004 Outlook

No one knows what to expect from Griffey. Bad luck has much to do with his decline from superstar heights, but there are definite indications that his skills have begun to erode from injuries and inaction. Remember that last year Griffey came to spring training after a winter of his hardest conditioning in years, and he still got injured while at the same time showing only intermittent flashes of his brilliance. The Reds would deal him if anyone were interested, but until he shows otherwise, he is a risk no one is likely to take.

Overall Statistics

G	AB	R	H	D	T	HR	RBI	SB	BB	SO	Avg	OBP	Slg
53	166	34	41	12	1	13	26	1	27	44	.247	.370	.566
1914	7079	1271	2080	382	36	481	1384	177	940	1256	.294	.379	.562

Where He Hits the Ball

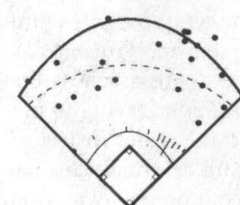 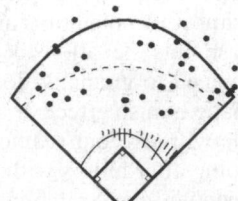

Vs. LHP   **Vs. RHP**

2003 Situational Stats

	AB	H	HR	RBI	Avg		AB	H	HR	RBI	Avg
Home	62	20	5	10	.323	LHP	56	14	4	7	.250
Road	104	21	8	16	.202	RHP	110	27	9	19	.245
First Half	163	40	13	26	.245	Sc Pos	44	5	1	10	.114
Scnd Half	3	1	0	0	.333	Clutch	30	6	3	7	.200

2003 Rankings (National League)

- Did not rank near the top or bottom in any category

Jimmy Haynes

2003 Season

In all his wisdom, departed Reds general manager Jim Bowden signed Jimmy Haynes to a two-year contract after Haynes' decent 2002 season. It proved to be another of Bowden's deal that was a dud. Haynes won only two of his 18 starts in 2003 before his season ended with back troubles. He averaged nearly two baserunners for every inning he pitched, and struck out fewer batters than he walked—not exactly a recipe for success.

Pitching

There's a good reason why Haynes is 23 games under .500 lifetime: He lacks the command of one reliable out pitch. When Haynes is effective, he is locating his 90-ish sinking fastball and then mixing in his split or change when he's in control of the count. However, he does not get ahead in counts consistently enough to avoid throwing far too many predictable fastballs, and those pitches simply are too hittable for him to survive. Haynes' penchant for getting behind has been blamed on mechanical problems with his release point and delivery. His staying power also is suspect, and he has worked just two complete games in 199 career starts, the second coming last season.

Defense & Hitting

Haynes does a competent job of holding runners and has developed a pickoff move that at least gives opponents something to think about. In fact, basestealers are barely above .500 on his watch during the past two seasons. Haynes fields his position adequately and can be at times useful when swinging the bat. He punched out six hits in 23 at-bats in 2003, good for a .261 batting average.

2004 Outlook

Stuck with his contract, the Reds will give Haynes the opportunity to revert back to being the competitive pitcher who won 15 games just two seasons ago. He still is young enough and possesses enough ability to get some mileage out of a career that never really has taken hold.

Position: SP
Bats: R **Throws:** R
Ht: 6' 4" **Wt:** 219

Opening Day Age: 31
Born: 9/5/72 in LaGrange, GA
ML Seasons: 9

Overall Statistics

	W	L	Pct.	ERA	G	GS	Sv	IP	H	BB	SO	HR	Avg
'03	2	12	.143	6.30	18	18	0	94.1	118	57	49	14	.311
Car.	63	86	.423	5.32	222	199	1	1185.2	1332	594	754	145	.288

2003 Pitching Profile

	Jimmy Haynes	NL Average
Overall Strike %	57.6	62.4
1st Pitch Strike %	52.3	58.4
Ratio	1.86	1.38
Strikeouts per 9 IP	4.67	6.65
Walks per 9 IP	5.44	3.42
Home Runs per 9 IP	1.34	1.05
Strikeout/Walk Ratio	0.86	1.94
Groundball/Flyball Ratio	1.30	1.29

2003 Situational Stats

	W	L	ERA	Sv	IP		AB	H	HR	RBI	Avg
Home	1	9	7.35	0	60.0	LHB	154	46	4	33	.299
Road	1	3	4.46	0	34.1	RHB	225	72	10	32	.320
First Half	2	9	5.29	0	80.0	Sc Pos	109	37	5	50	.339
Scnd Half	0	3	11.93	0	14.1	Clutch	6	3	0	0	.500

2003 Rankings (National League)

- 4th in highest batting average allowed vs. righthanded batters
- Led the Reds in sacrifice bunts (7), stolen bases allowed (7) and runners caught stealing (4)

D'Angelo Jimenez

2003 Season

It wouldn't be a normal season for D'Angelo Jimenez if he wasn't traded at midseason and then teased his new team into thinking he could be its answer at second base. For a third straight year, Jimenez was dealt during the season, and he gave the Reds 73 solid games. His combined numbers in Chicago and Cincinnati produced career highs in all his major offensive categories.

Hitting

Once a blue-chip prospect in the Yankees' organization, Jimenez has added some muscle over the last year and it helped produced his first real burst of power, the majority of which came from the switch-hitter's left side. However, Jimenez too often tried to jerk pitches instead of going with his strength, which is hitting line drives to all fields. When he isn't thinking longball, he can be an excellent early-count, fastball hitter. He can be fooled with offspeed stuff. He has decent patience but perhaps not enough to be an everyday leadoff hitter.

Baserunning & Defense

Though not a burner, Jimenez has quick first step and good instincts that combine to make him a basestealer not to be ignored. He also is aggressive about taking the extra base. At one point a highly touted shortstop as a minor leaguer, Jimenez no longer is not considered anything but a second baseman. His range is above average, but he is prone to careless errors and does not have the best hands. He also is erratic turning the double play.

2004 Outlook

Jimenez makes good first impressions and then wears out his welcome, largely through shaky defensive play and streakiness with the bat. However, he is at an age where he could begin to reach his potential. The emergence of a power stroke gives his game another dimension, and likely makes the Reds' second-base job his to lose as the season begins.

Position: 2B
Bats: B **Throws:** R
Ht: 6' 0" **Wt:** 195

Opening Day Age: 26
Born: 12/21/77 in Santo Domingo, DR
ML Seasons: 4
Pronunciation: he-MEN-ez

Overall Statistics

	G	AB	R	H	D	T	HR	RBI	SB	BB	SO	Avg	OBP	Slg
'03	146	561	69	153	24	7	14	57	11	66	89	.273	.349	.415
Car.	353	1318	178	354	60	14	21	138	19	158	234	.269	.346	.383

Where He Hits the Ball

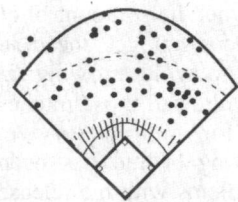 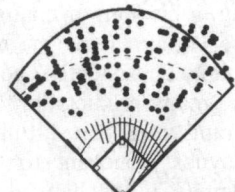

Vs. LHP   **Vs. RHP**

2003 Situational Stats

	AB	H	HR	RBI	Avg		AB	H	HR	RBI	Avg
Home	276	73	6	30	.264	LHP	154	42	2	12	.273
Road	285	80	8	27	.281	RHP	407	111	12	45	.273
First Half	294	77	7	26	.262	Sc Pos	112	28	2	41	.250
Scnd Half	267	76	7	31	.285	Clutch	92	30	3	11	.326

2003 Rankings (National League)

- 4th in batting average in the clutch (.377)
- Led the Reds in highest percentage of pitches taken (62.6), highest percentage of swings put into play (51.5), batting average in the clutch (.377), on-base percentage for a leadoff hitter (.380) and lowest percentage of swings on the first pitch (12.7)

Austin Kearns

2003 Season

A shoulder injury ended Austin Kearns' season in early July after he had worked through a slow start to begin producing like the budding star the Reds believe he can be. Kearns has missed more than 100 games in his first two seasons. Before his injury last year, however, he already had surpassed his home-run and RBI totals from his rookie season.

Hitting

Kearns has a quick bat and 30-plus home-run potential. However, his potential goes beyond power because he has the tools to be a complete hitter. He has extra-base pop to all fields and shows good pitch selection. He stands on the plate and can be jammed, but pitchers do not move him off the plate easily. Kearns is strong enough to fight off the hard stuff in and has the plate coverage to catch up with pitches away. For a young player, he is solid against breaking pitches. Like many Reds hitters, he might have been guilty of trying to pull too many pitches in the new homer-friendly Great American Ball Park.

Baserunning & Defense

Though his speed is average, Kearns is not to be ignored on the bases. He can steal in certain situations and reads balls well when he tries to take extra bases. Kearns can play any of the three outfield positions, though his range is best-suited for either left or right. He has a strong and accurate arm with a quick release that makes him someone against whom opposing baserunners are cautious when challenging.

2004 Outlook

Three straight seasons have been waylaid by injuries for Kearns. However, the Reds do not view him as fragile, but rather unlucky. He underwent surgery on his right shoulder in mid-August and expects to be over that hump when camp breaks. He is a big-time talent and a solid citizen, one of a handful of foundation players upon which Cincinnati's latest rebuilding effort depends. Give him an injury-free year, and he could be a 25-homer, 100-RBI key to the Reds' lineup.

Position: RF/CF
Bats: R **Throws:** R
Ht: 6' 3" **Wt:** 220

Opening Day Age: 23
Born: 5/20/80 in Lexington, KY
ML Seasons: ?

Overall Statistics

	G	AB	R	H	D	T	HR	RBI	SB	BB	SO	Avg	OBP	Slg
'03	82	292	39	77	11	0	15	58	5	41	68	.264	.364	.455
Car.	189	664	105	194	35	3	28	114	11	95	149	.292	.388	.480

Where He Hits the Ball

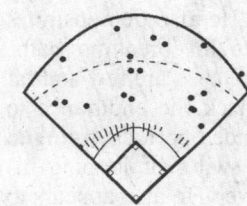 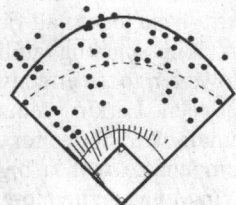

Vs. LHP   **Vs. RHP**

2003 Situational Stats

	AB	H	HR	RBI	Avg		AB	H	HR	RBI	Avg
Home	151	45	8	32	.298	LHP	79	21	I	8	.266
Road	141	32	7	26	.227	RHP	213	56	14	50	.263
First Half	292	77	15	58	.264	Sc Pos	86	27	5	45	.314
Scnd Half	0	0	0	0	–	Clutch	45	12	2	6	.267

2003 Rankings (National League)

- 5th in lowest cleanup slugging percentage (.459)
- 7th in lowest batting average with two strikes (.132)
- Led the Reds in highest groundball-flyball ratio (1.8), batting average with the bases loaded (.500) and cleanup slugging percentage (.459)

Cincinnati

Barry Larkin

2003 Season

Beginning in spring training with the lingering effects of toe surgery, Barry Larkin's streak of late-career injuries continued, as he finally was shut down in late August after three different trips to the disabled list with calf and finger injuries. A part-time player at this stage in his big league tenure even when healthy, Larkin never found any type of groove and ended his abbreviated campaign by matching a career low in home runs and just missing a career low with 18 RBI.

Hitting

When Larkin is able to remain healthy for a reasonable stretch of time, he still displays good bat speed and the ability hit hard stuff. He can spray extra-base hits to all fields. He also demonstrates his long-standing ability to hit breaking balls. However, those effective stretches are few and far between. Larkin seems to lack the endurance to remain in a groove for extended periods, trying to compensate with a bigger swing or looping his swing to generate more power. He also appears to be anxious at the plate, often biting at the first strike he sees rather than working deep counts as he did when he was a perennial .300 hitter.

Baserunning & Defense

Though he owns close to 400 stolen bases, Larkin no longer is a serious threat to steal. He remains an excellent baserunner, however, with outstanding instincts and the acceleration to take an extra base with consistency, provided of course he isn't hobbling with some kind of sprain or pull. Larkin's defensive skills at short have eroded in recent years. He rarely ranges deep in the hole, and his arm strength has deteriorated after a series of shoulder troubles.

2004 Outlook

After flirting with retirement, Larkin was brought back for another year when the Reds made a quick decision to offer him a new contract at the close of the 2003 season. What management can expect from him is uncertain. He has been a marginal player for the better part of the last three-plus years, and nothing suggests he will be anything more this season.

Position: SS
Bats: R **Throws:** R
Ht: 6' 0" **Wt:** 185

Opening Day Age: 39
Born: 4/28/64 in Cincinnati, OH
ML Seasons: 18

Overall Statistics

G	AB	R	H	D	T	HR	RBI	SB	BB	SO	Avg	OBP	Slg
70	241	39	68	16	1	2	18	2	22	32	.282	.345	.382
2069	7591	1274	2240	426	73	190	916	377	905	778	.295	.371	.446

Where He Hits the Ball

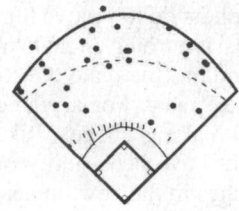
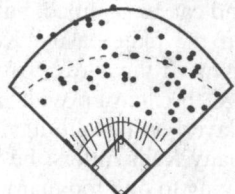

Vs. LHP   **Vs. RHP**

2003 Situational Stats

	AB	H	HR	RBI	Avg		AB	H	HR	RBI	Avg
Home	117	30	2	10	.256	LHP	60	12	0	3	.200
Road	124	38	0	8	.306	RHP	181	56	2	15	.309
First Half	167	47	1	15	.281	Sc Pos	40	13	0	15	.325
Scnd Half	74	21	1	3	.284	Clutch	53	16	1	10	.302

2003 Rankings (National League)

- Did not rank near the top or bottom in any category

Jason LaRue

Position: C
Bats: R **Throws:** R
Ht: 5'11" **Wt:** 200

Opening Day Age: 30
Born: 3/19/74 in Houston, TX
ML Seasons: 5
Pronunciation: la-ROO

2003 Season

For a third straight year, Jason LaRue was the Reds' regular catcher, and the club's new home ballpark helped him achieve a career high in home runs. He also just missed matching his best mark in runs batted in. Along the way, however, LaRue struggled to keep his average above .250, and he also turned in his worst season defensively.

Hitting

With his big swing and lack of ability to hit breaking pitches, LaRue won't ever be a high-average hitter. He has shown an inability to make any major adjustments at the plate. He has several holes in his swing that pitchers can take advantage of, including a vulnerability to inside hard stuff and a habit of chasing offspeed stuff out of the strike zone. LaRue has serious power, however, and he can crush mistake fastballs left down in the strike zone. In the Reds' new park, he has the strength to miss pitches and still send them to the wall. He is largely a pull-hitter when he gets the ball in the air. LaRue, like too many Reds hitters, strikes out far too often without working enough walks.

Baserunning & Defense

LaRue has above-average speed for a catcher and cannot be ignored as a possible basestealing threat. He has one of the better throwing arms among all major league catchers. However, LaRue was erratic with his release last year, making 11 errors. He also is inconsistent in his framing of pitches and is only fair in his ability to block pitches in the dirt.

2004 Outlook

The Reds have been disappointed in the progress of what, at one time, they believed was a solid group of catching prospects. As a result, LaRue's value to the organization has been increased. He has the power to be a 20-homer hitter if he could make consistent contact. He has not yet shown the ability to make the necessary adjustments, but LaRue still is a predictable asset on a team loaded with other question marks.

Overall Statistics

	G	AB	R	H	D	T	HR	RBI	SB	BB	SO	Avg	OBP	Slg
'03	118	379	52	87	23	1	16	50	3	33	111	.230	.321	.422
Car.	419	1284	157	303	71	4	48	167	11	103	385	.236	.315	.410

Where He Hits the Ball

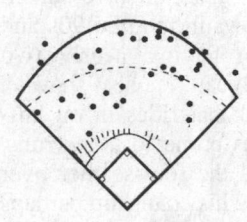
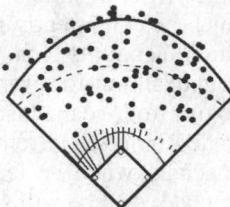

Vs. LHP **Vs. RHP**

2003 Situational Stats

	AB	H	HR	RBI	Avg		AB	H	HR	RBI	Avg
Home	207	50	12	35	.242	LHP	105	22	4	16	.210
Road	172	37	4	15	.215	RHP	274	65	12	34	.237
First Half	205	50	10	28	.244	Sc Pos	96	20	4	34	.208
Scnd Half	174	37	6	22	.213	Clutch	75	18	6	15	.240

2003 Rankings (National League)

- 1st in lowest fielding percentage at catcher (.984)
- 2nd in errors at catcher (11) and lowest percentage of swings put into play (32.2)
- 3rd in hit by pitch (20) and lowest batting average with the bases loaded (.071)
- 4th in highest percentage of swings that missed (32.2)
- 10th in lowest batting average with runners in scoring position
- Led the Reds in doubles, sacrifice flies (4) and hit by pitch (20)

Cincinnati

Chris Reitsma

2003 Season

In a season of so many disappointments in Cincinnati, one pleasant development was the solid transformation of Chris Reitsma from starter into reliever. He had success in a variety of bullpen roles, first as a strong setup man behind closer Scott Williamson. After Williamson was dealt away, Reitsma got a trial as closer, and for the season earned 12 saves in 18 opportunities. He led the Cincinnati staff in games finished.

Pitching

Reitsma seems to have found his niche in the bullpen. His lack of a reliable offspeed pitch was a liability as a starter. But in a relief role, Reitsma comes right at hitters with his explosive sinker, which he consistently throws in the mid-90s and which accounts for him having nearly two groundball out for every flyball. He also shows a moving four-seam fastball that rides in on left-handed hitters. He remains prone to home runs, especially when he leaves the four-seamer over the plate. And he will show his changeup perhaps too frequently. When Reitsma is leaning on his sinker, he is a very effective pitcher for four or five outs. His control has improved, both in terms of limiting his walks and also being ahead in the count.

Defense & Hitting

To hold runners, Reitsma often uses a slide step that does not appear to detract from his stuff. He has also quickened his delivery home, which makes him more difficult to run on than in the past. He gets off the mound well to make fielding plays. He is of little consequence as a hitter.

2004 Outlook

Cincinnati may have an emerging relief star in Reitsma, who is just learning how to fully adjust to coming out of the bullpen after being groomed as a starter throughout his professional career. He has the stuff and mentality to be a factor in the late innings, and he's at an age when he could be on the verge of stepping up to a high level as either a setup man or closer.

Position: RP
Bats: R **Throws:** R
Ht: 6' 5" **Wt:** 235

Opening Day Age: 26
Born: 12/31/77 in Minneapolis, MN
ML Seasons: 3
Pronunciation: REETS-muh

Overall Statistics

	W	L	Pct.	ERA	G	GS	Sv	IP	H	BB	SO	HR	Avg
'03	9	5	.643	4.29	57	3	12	84.0	92	19	53	14	.281
Car.	22	32	.407	4.52	125	53	12	404.1	445	113	233	54	.280

2003 Pitching Profile

	Chris Reitsma	NL Average
Overall Strike %	64.1	62.4
1st Pitch Strike %	55.0	58.4
Ratio	1.32	1.38
Strikeouts per 9 IP	5.68	6.65
Walks per 9 IP	2.04	3.42
Home Runs per 9 IP	1.50	1.05
Strikeout/Walk Ratio	2.79	1.94
Groundball/Flyball Ratio	1.79	1.29

2003 Situational Stats

	W	L	ERA	Sv	IP		AB	H	HR	RBI	Avg
Home	7	3	3.51	4	48.2	LHB	131	39	9	19	.298
Road	2	2	5.35	8	35.1	RHB	196	53	5	20	.270
First Half	7	2	4.56	0	49.1	Sc Pos	64	16	4	26	.250
Scnd Half	2	3	3.89	12	34.2	Clutch	163	41	7	22	.252

2003 Rankings (National League)

- 4th in relief wins (8)
- 5th in most GDPs induced per GDP situation (25.5%)
- 6th in blown saves (6)
- Led the Reds in wins, games pitched, games finished (36), winning percentage, most GDPs induced per GDP situation (25.5%), lowest percentage of inherited runners scored (23.8), blown saves (6), relief wins (8), relief losses (4) and fewest baserunners allowed per nine innings in relief (10.8)

Paul Wilson

2003 Season

For a second team in as many years, Paul Wilson pitched better than his final record might indicate. Wilson missed part of April with a back and hamstring problems he carried over from spring training, but once he joined the rotation, he was the Reds' most reliable starter. Wilson averaged six innings per start, with 17 of his 28 starts quality outings. He led the Cincinnati starting staff in innings pitched, but the Reds often played poorly behind him, with 11 of his runs allowed being unearned.

Pitching

Wilson does not have eye-popping stuff. He relies on a sinking fastball that rarely touches 90 MPH, an improved changeup and occasional slider or curve. He is a fine-line pitcher. None of his pitches are overpowering, so he must hit his spots and have good sink on his fastball to be successful. When he's off just a little, he gets hit hard. Wilson also is prone to nibbling when he gets into trouble, and that tendency not only makes him more hittable, but also accounts for too many walks at times.

Defense & Hitting

Though fairly slow in his delivery home and lacking a quality pickoff move, Wilson does a solid job of holding runners and limiting the running game. He occasionally uses a slide step to help limit stolen bases. Wilson also fields his position with good athletic skills. He is a work in progress as a hitter but showed signs of improvement in terms of making contact more frequently.

2004 Outlook

Wilson's stuff is that of a fourth or fifth starter for most clubs. On the Reds, however, he likely enters spring training as the No. 1 or 2 option in the rotation. That's Cincinnati's fault, not Wilson's. He's battled back from serious arm problems to become a very serviceable pitcher whose work ethic and eagerness to improve can make him a role model for what will be a young staff. And with better play behind him, he can win 12-14 games.

Position: SP
Bats: R **Throws:** R
Ht: 6' 5" **Wt:** 215

Opening Day Age: 31
Born: 3/28/73 in Orlando, FL
ML Seasons: 5

Overall Statistics

	W	L	Pct.	ERA	G	GS	Sv	IP	H	BB	SO	HR	Avg
'03	8	10	.444	4.64	28	28	0	166.2	190	50	93	24	.285
Car.	28	47	.373	4.81	132	115	0	711.2	769	256	472	90	.276

2003 Pitching Profile

	Paul Wilson	NL Average
Overall Strike %	63.4	62.4
1st Pitch Strike %	63.0	58.4
Ratio	1.44	1.38
Strikeouts per 9 IP	5.02	6.65
Walks per 9 IP	2.70	3.42
Home Runs per 9 IP	1.30	1.05
Strikeout/Walk Ratio	1.86	1.94
Groundball/Flyball Ratio	1.28	1.29

2003 Situational Stats

	W	L	ERA	Sv	IP		AB	H	HR	RBI	Avg
Home	4	5	3.42	0	97.1	LHB	269	78	12	36	.290
Road	4	5	6.36	0	69.1	RHB	397	112	12	54	.282
First Half	5	6	5.00	0	104.1	Sc Pos	158	47	4	62	.297
Scnd Half	3	4	4.04	0	62.1	Clutch	31	12	1	7	.387

2003 Rankings (National League)

- 7th in highest slugging percentage allowed (.462) and most home runs allowed per nine innings (1.30)
- 8th in fewest pitches thrown per batter (3.56) and fewest strikeouts per nine innings (5.0)
- 9th in highest batting average allowed (.285)
- 10th in highest ERA
- Led the Reds in ERA, games started, hit batsmen (7), strikeouts, pitches thrown (2,596), pickoff throws (42), runners caught stealing (4), GDPs induced (17), highest strikeout-walk ratio (1.9), lowest on-base percentage allowed (.342), and lowest ERA at home

Jose Acevedo

Position: SP
Bats: R **Throws:** R
Ht: 6' 0" **Wt:** 185

Opening Day Age: 26
Born: 12/18/77 in Santo Domingo, DR
ML Seasons: 3
Pronunciation: ah-ceh-VEE-doh

Overall Statistics

	W	L	Pct.	ERA	G	GS	Sv	IP	H	BB	SO	HR	Avg
'03	2	0	1.000	2.67	5	4	0	27.0	17	6	23	3	.183
Car.	11	9	.550	5.22	29	27	0	146.2	146	52	105	28	.261

2003 Situational Stats

	W	L	ERA	Sv	IP		AB	H	HR	RBI	Avg
Home	1	0	2.40	0	15.0	LHB	44	6	2	3	.136
Road	1	0	3.00	0	12.0	RHB	49	11	1	5	.224
First Half	0	0	—	0	0.0	Sc Pos	15	2	0	4	.133
Scnd Half	2	0	2.67	0	27.0	Clutch	3	0	0	0	.000

2003 Season

A left ankle injury and subsequent foot surgery curtailed what had been a promising stretch of pitching by Jose Acevedo. In his third stint with Cincinnati after a brief look in 2002 and a more extended trial in 2001, Acevedo won two of his four starts, including tossing one of the Reds' four complete games. Opponents hit only .183 against Acevedo in his abbreviated 2003 session with the parent club.

Pitching, Defense & Hitting

Acevedo has average velocity, but he demonstrates a good feel for pitching. His best offering probably is his changeup, but he has also added a cutter, which last year had developed into a good out pitch before he was sidelined. Acevedo has excellent control with all his pitches and usually is around the plate. A good athlete, he holds runners well and fields his position adequately—he has yet to make in error in 21 big league chances. He has limited experience with a bat in his hands.

2004 Outlook

If Acevedo is healthy—and he should be by spring—he likely is in the mix for what is basically a wide-open Reds rotation. He is not considered a top-of-the-rotation talent, but he could fill a spot nicely as a fourth or fifth starter.

Juan Castro

Position: 2B/3B/SS
Bats: R **Throws:** R
Ht: 5'11" **Wt:** 195

Opening Day Age: 31
Born: 6/20/72 in Los Mochis, Mexico
ML Seasons: 9
Pronunciation: KASS-tro

Overall Statistics

	G	AB	R	H	D	T	HR	RBI	SB	BB	SO	Avg	OBP	Slg
'03	113	320	28	81	14	1	9	33	2	18	58	.253	.290	.388
Car.	557	1300	124	288	54	7	20	103	3	85	245	.222	.267	.320

2003 Situational Stats

	AB	H	HR	RBI	Avg		AB	H	HR	RBI	Avg
Home	151	38	4	14	.252	LHP	88	17	0	2	.193
Road	169	43	5	19	.254	RHP	232	64	9	31	.276
First Half	182	45	5	15	.247	Sc Pos	70	21	3	26	.300
Scnd Half	138	36	4	18	.261	Clutch	50	7	1	5	.140

2003 Season

For the first time, Juan Castro showed some offensive promise. Aided by the friendly confines of Great American, his nine home runs were more than he had hit in any of his previous 12 pro seasons in the majors and minors. Castro also set a personal major league high in ribbies, while hitting more than 30 points above his current career average.

Hitting, Baserunning & Defense

Castro improved his bat speed by moving up on the plate and trying to pull more. He also added some muscle, which showed in his increase in power. He can be busted inside but is capable of turning on mistake fastballs. Castro has average speed and is not much of a basestealing threat. His greatest asset is his defensive versatility. He can play second, short or third competently, with second the best fit for his average range and throwing arm. He also turns the double play well from either short or second.

2004 Outlook

Though Castro's unexpected burst of power was a welcome development, he is not considered an option as an everyday player. However, if the new home-run pop is not a mirage, that, combined with Castro's defensive ability, make him a valuable man off the bench.

Ryan Dempster

Position: SP
Bats: R **Throws:** R
Ht: 6' 3" **Wt:** 215

Opening Day Age: 26
Born: 5/3/77 in Sechelt, BC, Canada
ML Seasons: 6

Overall Statistics

	W	L	Pct.	ERA	G	GS	Sv	IP	H	BB	SO	HR	Avg
'03	3	7	.300	6.54	22	20	0	115.2	134	70	84	14	.293
Car.	50	55	.476	5.01	161	156	0	964.0	1008	503	778	120	.273

2003 Situational Stats

	W	L	ERA	Sv	IP		AB	H	HR	RBI	Avg
Home	0	3	6.91	0	54.2	LHB	207	62	7	36	.300
Road	3	4	6.20	0	61.0	RHB	250	72	7	46	.288
First Half	3	6	6.55	0	99.0	Sc Pos	123	37	6	70	.301
Scnd Half	0	1	6.48	0	16.2	Clutch	28	8	0	3	.286

2003 Season

Ryan Dempster went backward in his latest effort to turn around his unfulfilled potential. He ended the season on the disabled list with inflamation in his pitching elbow. He won only three of his 20 starts, posted just seven quality starts and fashioned a career-worst 6.54 ERA.

Pitching, Defense & Hitting

No one questions Dempster's array of weapons, an arsenal that include a mid-90s fastball, hard slider and useful straight change. However, he has not been able to harness his stuff or maintain a consistent release point, which has meant an enormous amount of walks and total lack of command within in the strike zone. In fact, his 465 free passes since the start of the 1999 season are the second most in the major leagues behind Russ Ortiz (524). Dempster holds runners fairly well, but he struggled in the field last year and is of little help as a hitter.

2004 Outlook

A rare disappointment for Cincinnati's fine pitching coach, Don Gullett, Dempster underwent Tommy John surgery in early August and won't be ready to pitch until mid-2004. With too many other issues to settle, the Reds elected to cut Dempster loose after the season.

Aaron Harang

Position: SP
Bats: R **Throws:** R
Ht: 6' 7" **Wt:** 240

Opening Day Age: 25
Born: 5/9/78 in San Diego, CA
ML Seasons: 2
Pronunciation: ha-RANG

Overall Statistics

	W	L	Pct.	ERA	G	GS	Sv	IP	H	BB	SO	HR	Avg
'03	5	6	.455	5.31	16	15	0	76.1	89	19	42	11	.296
Car.	10	10	.500	5.06	32	30	0	154.2	167	64	106	18	.278

2003 Situational Stats

	W	L	ERA	Sv	IP		AB	H	HR	RBI	Avg
Home	2	5	6.02	0	40.1	LHB	158	43	7	27	.272
Road	3	1	4.50	0	36.0	RHB	143	46	4	17	.322
First Half	1	3	5.34	0	30.1	Sc Pos	68	22	3	30	.324
Scnd Half	4	3	5.28	0	46.0	Clutch	14	5	0	2	.357

2003 Season

Acquired in the deal that sent Jose Guillen to Oakland just prior to the trading deadline, Aaron Harang had some success over the last seven weeks with the Reds. Though he averaged only five innings per start in his nine outings with the Reds, his four victories actually tied him with Danny Graves for second among all Cincinnati starters for the entire season.

Pitching, Defense & Hitting

Harang throws a four-seamer with decent movement, though his velocity is not exceptional. He shows a slider and has worked on an improving change. He pitches too often up in the strike zone and that leads to home runs, especially with Cincinnati, where he was tagged for six longballs in just 46 innings. He is slow coming home and can be vulnerable to stolen bases—eight of 10 thieves were successful when Harang was on the mound last year. He has little experience as a hitter.

2004 Outlook

Harang is one of the key acquisitions among the Reds' many late-season moves. Though he is not considered top-of-the-rotation material, Cincinnati thinks he can be a useful part of the middle or back part of their starting staff, with the chance to develop into a 12-game winner.

Cincinnati

Tim Hummel

Position: 3B
Bats: R **Throws:** R
Ht: 6' 2" **Wt:** 195

Opening Day Age: 25
Born: 11/18/78 in Goshen, NY
ML Seasons: 1

Overall Statistics

	G	AB	R	H	D	T	HR	RBI	SB	BB	SO	Avg	OBP	Slg
'03	26	84	9	19	5	0	2	10	0	8	13	.226	.290	.357
Car.	26	84	9	19	5	0	2	10	0	8	13	.226	.290	.357

2003 Situational Stats

	AB	H	HR	RBI	Avg		AB	H	HR	RBI	Avg
Home	40	7	0	4	.175	LHP	27	7	2	4	.259
Road	44	12	2	6	.273	RHP	57	12	0	6	.211
First Half	0	0	0	0	—	Sc Pos	16	5	0	8	.313
Scnd Half	84	19	2	10	.226	Clutch	14	1	0	1	.071

2003 Season

Tim Hummel, obtained in late August from the White Sox' organization in the Scott Sullivan trade, once was mentioned as a possible heir to the second-base job in Chicago. He slipped down the Sox' organizational ladder, however, and finally got his first taste of the majors with a September look at third base for the Reds. He showed flashes of power and also the ability to hit lefthanded pitching.

Hitting, Baserunning & Defense

Hummel was considered a solid prospect with the White Sox until struggling in 2002. He has hit near .300 consistently during his minor league career and was able to make regular contact in the majors. Hummel can hit a fastball, though he still seems uncertain against offspeed pitches. He originally was a second baseman but the Reds looked at him at third, where he had throwing problems. Hummel has average speed and was only a moderate threat to steal in the minors.

2004 Outlook

Cincinnati looked at nearly 60 different players last season and Hummel was among the last. An 86 at-bat trial is not a good barometer for the future, but he appears to have shown enough to earn a long look as a possible utility-type player.

Brandon Larson

Position: 3B
Bats: R **Throws:** R
Ht: 6' 0" **Wt:** 210

Opening Day Age: 27
Born: 5/24/76 in San Angelo, TX
ML Seasons: 3

Overall Statistics

	G	AB	R	H	D	T	HR	RBI	SB	BB	SO	Avg	OBP	Slg
'03	32	89	6	9	1	0	1	9	2	13	31	.101	.212	.146
Car.	69	173	16	27	5	0	5	23	3	21	51	.156	.249	.272

2003 Situational Stats

	AB	H	HR	RBI	Avg		AB	H	HR	RBI	Avg
Home	44	3	0	4	.068	LHP	28	4	0	3	.143
Road	45	6	1	5	.133	RHP	61	5	1	6	.082
First Half	48	4	0	5	.083	Sc Pos	26	4	0	8	.154
Scnd Half	41	5	1	4	.122	Clutch	17	1	0	1	.059

2003 Season

Last winter, ex-GM Jim Bowden proclaimed Brandon Larson the Reds' third baseman and a star in the making. However, Larson spent time in the minors, was called up for brief and ineffective looks with the parent club and ended up back on the 60-day DL with a shoulder injury that required surgery in early September. He finished the year with all of nine major league hits.

Hitting, Baserunning & Defense

A first-round draft pick back in 1997, Larson has not put anything together outside of a strong Triple-A season two years ago. He appears to have fallen victim to much weight lifting, bulking up to where he may have adversely affected his bat speed. Last year, Larson was overpowered by average hard stuff and was prone to chase breaking balls. He is a good athlete with decent speed and the ability to play all four infield positions, plus left field.

2004 Outlook

The clock is ticking for Larson. He can't seem to stay healthy, and the 25 Triple-A home runs he hit in 2002 could end up being the pinnacle of his career. With a new front office in Cincinnati, Larson's status as a former top draft pick won't be enough to earn continued patience.

Felipe Lopez

Position: SS
Bats: B **Throws:** R
Ht: 6' 0" **Wt:** 185

Opening Day Age: 23
Born: 5/12/80 in Bayamon, PR
ML Seasons: 3

Overall Statistics

	G	AB	R	H	D	T	HR	RBI	SB	BB	SO	Avg	OBP	Slg
'03	59	197	28	42	7	2	2	13	8	28	59	.213	.313	.299
Car.	193	656	84	152	27	9	15	70	17	63	188	.232	.299	.369

2003 Situational Stats

	AB	H	HR	RBI	Avg		AB	H	HR	RBI	Avg
Home	95	20	0	5	.211	LHP	51	10	0	0	.196
Road	102	22	2	8	.216	RHP	146	32	2	13	.219
First Half	197	42	2	13	.213	Sc Pos	38	11	0	11	.289
Scnd Half	0	0	0	0	–	Clutch	33	6	1	4	.182

2003 Season

One of the Reds' infinite number of personnel mistakes was trying to rush Felipe Lopez into the everyday shortstop job. The talented but raw Lopez proved overmatched. Before finally being sent to the minors in June, he had struck out in nearly a third of his at-bats and had posted more errors than RBI.

Hitting, Baserunning & Defense

The switch-hitting Lopez has promising physical tools, including a quick bat and decent strength, but he cannot lay off high fastballs. He has little pitch-selection skill and looks helpless against breaking balls. Lopez has good speed and could develop into a solid basestealer. He also has a strong arm and fine range but may be better suited for third base, something many in Toronto believed before he was traded. His arm is very erratic at short, and he has crude footwork in the middle infield.

2004 Outlook

Lopez is another example of the failed science of departed GM Jim Bowden, who constantly acquired young "tools" players, most of whom unfortunately did not turn into good ballplayers. It's too soon to write off the talented Lopez, but to save his fragile confidence, the Reds might be best served by giving him more minor league seasoning.

Wily Mo Pena

Position: CF/RF
Bats: R **Throws:** R
Ht: 6' 3" **Wt:** 215

Opening Day Age: 22
Born: 1/23/82 in Laguna Salada, DR
ML Seasons: 2
Pronunciation:
will-ee moe PAIN-ya

Overall Statistics

	G	AB	R	H	D	T	HR	RBI	SB	BB	SO	Avg	OBP	Slg
'03	80	165	20	36	6	1	5	16	3	12	53	.218	.283	.358
Car.	93	183	21	40	6	1	6	17	3	12	64	.219	.278	.361

2003 Situational Stats

	AB	H	HR	RBI	Avg		AB	H	HR	RBI	Avg
Home	80	17	1	7	.213	LHP	54	11	2	5	.204
Road	85	19	4	9	.224	RHP	111	25	3	11	.225
First Half	35	3	0	2	.086	Sc Pos	40	7	1	9	.175
Scnd Half	130	33	5	14	.254	Clutch	24	6	1	4	.250

2003 Season

Another of former GM Jim Bowden's "tools" acquisitions, Wily Mo Pena got his first extended playing time toward the end of last season. Pena showed flashes of the big-time power that originally opened scouts' eyes. However, he had trouble making contact, striking out once in nearly every three at-bats.

Hitting, Baserunning & Defense

Pena has stupendous sheer power and can put on great shows in batting practice. However, with his big swing, he remains an all-or-nothing hitter. He is easy pickings for most major league pitchers, who can tie up him inside with fastballs or get him to flail at breaking stuff. He has good speed for a big man and can steal a base or two, but overall he lacks good instincts on the basepaths. Pena has decent range, a strong throwing arm and the physical tools to play any of the three outfield positions.

2004 Outlook

Many Reds personnel privately feel Pena remains overmatched against big league pitching. However, he still is only a baby in baseball years, so his prodigious skills cannot be dismissed. The prevailing thought right now is that he should spend a full season in the minors to get himself back on track.

John Riedling

Position: RP
Bats: R **Throws:** R
Ht: 5'11" **Wt:** 190

Opening Day Age: 28
Born: 8/29/75 in Fort Lauderdale, FL
ML Seasons: 4
Pronunciation: READ-ling

Overall Statistics

	W	L	Pct.	ERA	G	GS	Sv	IP	H	BB	SO	HR	Avg
'03	2	3	.400	4.90	55	8	1	101.0	107	47	65	7	.270
Car.	8	9	.471	3.75	130	8	3	196.2	179	95	136	11	.244

2003 Situational Stats

	W	L	ERA	Sv	IP		AB	H	HR	RBI	Avg
Home	1	2	5.24	0	46.1	LHB	159	39	2	27	.245
Road	1	1	4.61	1	54.2	RHB	238	68	5	34	.286
First Half	0	3	6.18	1	62.2	Sc Pos	114	37	4	51	.325
Scnd Half	2	0	2.82	0	38.1	Clutch	89	18	2	14	.202

2003 Season

One of the few Reds' pitchers to last all season with the club was John Riedling. Though mainly used in middle relief, he was pressed into service for the first eight major league starts of his career. He was one of only four Cincinnati pitchers to work more than 100 innings, while his 55 appearances ranked third on the club.

Pitching, Defense & Hitting

With a fastball in the mid-90s and hard splitter, Riedling's stuff is above average. He lacks an off-speed pitch, a deficiency that proved to be especially troublesome in his starts. His command also is uneven, both in terms of the number of walks he yields and the location of his strikes. His aggressive nature seems best-suited for the bullpen. Riedling won't hurt his cause in the field, but he is only fair at holding runners and is not much of a factor as a hitter, though he did produce four hits and a pair of RBI last year.

2004 Outlook

One thing about Riedling is that he is willing to take the ball and go after hitters. He may lack the consistency to warrant a look as the team's closer, but he should be a useful power arm somewhere in the middle of the Cincinnati bullpen.

Reggie Taylor

Position: CF/LF
Bats: L **Throws:** R
Ht: 6' 1" **Wt:** 178

Opening Day Age: 27
Born: 1/12/77 in Newberry, SC
ML Seasons: 4

Overall Statistics

	G	AB	R	H	D	T	HR	RBI	SB	BB	SO	Avg	OBP	Slg
'03	100	180	17	39	5	2	5	19	7	11	68	.217	.266	.350
Car.	249	485	60	113	20	6	14	57	19	26	156	.233	.275	.386

2003 Situational Stats

	AB	H	HR	RBI	Avg		AB	H	HR	RBI	Avg
Home	88	21	3	10	.239	LHP	30	5	2	5	.167
Road	92	18	2	9	.196	RHP	150	34	3	14	.227
First Half	102	22	2	10	.216	Sc Pos	50	8	1	12	.160
Scnd Half	78	17	3	9	.218	Clutch	51	5	0	4	.098

2003 Season

Before his season ended on the disabled list, Reggie Taylor was a spot-starter in the outfield and the Reds' busiest pinch-hitter. He had moments when he displayed some power and his good speed, but he struggled to get on base and fanned six times more often than he walked. Among Reds with at least 100 at-bats for the team in 2003, Taylor's .266 on-base percentage was dead last.

Hitting, Baserunning & Defense

Taylor strikes out far too much to be a solid major league hitter. He will chase high fastballs and is vulnerable to any offspeed pitch. He can show power, but only when he gets a low pitch over the plate. Taylor is an exceptional runner who was a perfect 7-for-7 in stolen bases last year. He has the range and skill to be a good defensive center fielder, though his arm is below average.

2004 Outlook

Like too many Reds, Taylor has loads of physical tools but lacks the consistency to be a productive member of the parent club. And also like too many Reds, he struggles with high strikeout totals. Taylor is at an age where it might be getting late for him to put it all together, and he appears to be in a fight to earn a backup job in 2004.

Other Cincinnati Reds

Jimmy Anderson (Pos: LHP, Age: 28)

	W	L	Pct.	ERA	G	GS	Sv	IP	H	BB	SO	HR	Avg
'03	1	5	.167	8.84	8	7	0	38.2	60	14	13	8	.359
Car.	25	47	.347	5.43	110	96	0	559.0	653	234	235	58	.295

Recent control problems have hindered Anderson's chances of retaining a starting job in the majors. Over the past three seasons, the lefthander has walked (160) more opponents than he has struck out (149). 2004 Outlook: C

Jeff Austin (Pos: RHP, Age: 27)

	W	L	Pct.	ERA	G	GS	Sv	IP	H	BB	SO	HR	Avg
'03	2	3	.400	8.58	7	7	0	28.1	28	21	22	9	.255
Car.	2	3	.400	6.75	38	7	0	65.1	69	41	55	13	.273

Austin was acquired from the Royals in March. His 2003 season was cut short by arthroscopic surgery on his pitching shoulder on July 29, but he is expected to be ready for spring training. 2004 Outlook: C

John Bale (Pos: LHP, Age: 29)

	W	L	Pct.	ERA	G	GS	Sv	IP	H	BB	SO	HR	Avg
'03	1	2	.333	4.47	10	9	0	46.1	50	12	37	7	.281
Car.	2	2	.500	4.69	27	9	0	78.2	75	34	68	11	.254

Bale spent spring training 2002 with the O's, was dealt to the Mets in exchange for Gary Matthews Jr. and finally ended up with the Reds. In 525 innings in the minors, he's fanned 572 and walked 194. He is headed to Japan for 2004. 2004 Outlook: D

Mark Budzinski (Pos: CF, Age: 30, Bats: L)

	G	AB	R	H	D	T	HR	RBI	SB	BB	SO	Avg	OBP	Slg
'03	4	7	0	0	0	0	0	0	0	0	4	.000	.000	.000
Car.	4	7	0	0	0	0	0	0	0	0	4	.000	.000	.000

Budzinski, who is approaching 1,000 games in the minors, made his major league debut with the Reds last season, going hitless in seven at-bats. The outfielder lacks power, however, and likely is past his prime, but the Phils signed him to a minor league deal. 2004 Outlook: C

Juan Cerros (Pos: RHP, Age: 27)

	W	L	Pct.	ERA	G	GS	Sv	IP	H	BB	SO	HR	Avg
'03	0	0	—	4.85	11	0	0	13.0	11	5	9	1	.224
Car.	0	0	—	4.85	11	0	0	13.0	11	5	9	1	.224

Cerros, who spent most of 2003 in the Mexican League, was yet another player to see his first major league action with the Reds last season. Another year in the minors is expected in 2004. 2004 Outlook: C

Jim Chamblee (Pos: 3B, Age: 28, Bats: R)

	G	AB	R	H	D	T	HR	RBI	SB	BB	SO	Avg	OBP	Slg
'03	2	2	0	0	0	0	0	0	0	0	2	.000	.000	.000
Car.	2	2	0	0	0	0	0	0	0	0	2	.000	.000	.000

Chamblee spent the bulk of 2003 in the minors, splitting the year between Double- and Triple-A. Although he improved his batting average, the third baseman saw a drop in his power numbers. 2004 Outlook: C

Seth Etherton (Pos: RHP, Age: 27)

	W	L	Pct.	ERA	G	GS	Sv	IP	H	BB	SO	HR	Avg
'03	2	4	.333	6.90	7	7	0	30.0	39	15	17	4	.322
Car.	7	5	.583	5.98	18	18	0	90.1	107	37	49	20	.292

Injuries have hampered Etherton's career. He missed the 2001 season and much of the 2002 campaign after undergoing shoulder surgery. Biceps, forearm and elbow issues forced him to miss time in 2003. 2004 Outlook: C

Ryan Freel (Pos: CF/2B, Age: 28, Bats: R)

	G	AB	R	H	D	T	HR	RBI	SB	BB	SO	Avg	OBP	Slg
'03	43	137	23	39	6	1	4	12	9	9	13	.285	.344	.431
Car.	52	159	24	45	7	1	4	15	11	10	17	.283	.343	.415

Freel filled in admirably for the banged-up Reds last season, batting .285 in 43 games. The utilityman committed just one error, despite playing four different positions. He could claim a bench job next year. 2004 Outlook: C

Josh Hall (Pos: RHP, Age: 23)

	W	L	Pct.	ERA	G	GS	Sv	IP	H	BB	SO	HR	Avg
'03	0	2	.000	6.57	6	5	0	24.2	33	15	18	4	.314
Car.	0	2	.000	6.57	6	5	0	24.2	33	15	18	4	.314

Hall spent most of 2003 with Double-A Chattanooga, posting a 3.47 ERA. He likely will not be ready for the start of the 2004 season after undergoing surgery to repair a torn labrum in his pitching shoulder. 2004 Outlook: C

Joey Hamilton (Pos: RHP, Age: 33)

	W	L	Pct.	ERA	G	GS	Sv	IP	H	BB	SO	HR	Avg
'03	0	0	—	12.66	3	0	0	10.2	21	5	7	3	.404
Car.	74	73	.503	4.44	242	209	1	1340.2	1408	493	894	130	.273

Hamilton spent spring training with the Cardinals, but was released prior to the start of the season. He re-signed with the Reds and went 8-3 with a 3.23 ERA in Triple-A. His days as a starter appear over, but he'll get another look with San Diego. 2004 Outlook: C

Josias Manzanillo (Pos: RHP, Age: 36)

	W	L	Pct.	ERA	G	GS	Sv	IP	H	BB	SO	HR	Avg
'03	0	0	.000	12.66	3	0	0	10.2	21	4	12	7	.389
Car.	10	12	.455	4.56	241	1	5	309.2	292	138	273	40	.251

Manzanillo had solid seasons with the Pirates in 2000 and 2001, but has been unable to return to that form since having bone chips removed from his pitching elbow in 2002. 2004 Outlook: C

Ruben Mateo (Pos: RF/CF, Age: 26, Bats: R)

	G	AB	R	H	D	T	HR	RBI	SB	BB	SO	Avg	OBP	Slg
'03	74	207	16	50	9	0	3	18	0	12	53	.242	.290	.329
Car.	244	750	93	193	40	3	18	75	10	41	163	.257	.309	.391

Mateo has posted solid numbers as a minor leaguer, but has yet to prove himself at the major league level, despite plenty of chances. His plate discipline could be the cause for his troubles. 2004 Outlook: C

Corky Miller (Pos: C, Age: 28, Bats: R)

	G	AB	R	H	D	T	HR	RBI	SB	BB	SO	Avg	OBP	Slg
'03	14	30	4	8	0	0	0	1	0	5	7	.267	.395	.267
Car.	70	193	18	46	12	0	6	23	1	18	43	.238	.323	.394

Miller is more skilled defensively than offensively, but his bat is starting to come around. The catcher had bone chips removed from his elbow after the season, but should be ready for spring training. 2004 Outlook: C

Phil Norton (Pos: LHP, Age: 28)

	W	L	Pct.	ERA	G	GS	Sv	IP	H	BB	SO	HR	Avg
'03	0	0	−	3.00	21	0	0	18.0	9	9	7	0	.155
Car.	0	1	.000	5.06	23	2	0	26.2	23	16	13	5	.235

Norton was solid in 17 relief appearances with the Reds after being called up in August. The lefthander, who was acquired from the Chicago Cubs earlier in the year, posted a 2.45 ERA in 14.2 innings. 2004 Outlook: C

Ray Olmedo (Pos: SS/2B, Age: 22, Bats: B)

	G	AB	R	H	D	T	HR	RBI	SB	BB	SO	Avg	OBP	Slg
'03	79	230	24	55	6	1	0	17	1	13	46	.239	.280	.274
Car.	79	230	24	55	6	1	0	17	1	13	46	.239	.280	.274

Due to numerous injuries, the Reds were forced to recall Olmedo last season, probably a year or two before he was ready. The infielder has a good glove, but lacks power and patience at the plate. 2004 Outlook: C

Scott Randall (Pos: RHP, Age: 28)

	W	L	Pct.	ERA	G	GS	Sv	IP	H	BB	SO	HR	Avg
'03	2	5	.286	6.51	15	2	0	27.2	34	11	25	1	.304
Car.	2	5	.286	6.51	15	2	0	27.2	34	11	25	1	.304

After bouncing around the minor leagues for eight seasons, Randall was called up by the Reds last August and appeared in 15 games. He won 18 straight decisions in the minors from 2002-03, but was released in November. 2004 Outlook: C

Brian Reith (Pos: RHP, Age: 26)

	W	L	Pct.	ERA	G	GS	Sv	IP	H	BB	SO	HR	Avg
'03	2	3	.400	4.11	42	1	1	61.1	61	36	39	8	.263
Car.	2	10	.167	5.58	51	9	1	101.2	117	52	61	21	.293

Reith posted a 1.96 ERA in 16 games with Triple-A Louisville, but spent most of 2003 in the Reds' pen. He had some minor control problems, walking 36 and allowing 61 hits in 61.1 innings. 2004 Outlook: C

Dane Sardinha (Pos: C, Age: 24, Bats: R)

	G	AB	R	H	D	T	HR	RBI	SB	BB	SO	Avg	OBP	Slg
'03	1	2	0	0	0	0	0	0	0	0	1	.000	.000	.000
Car.	1	2	0	0	0	0	0	0	0	0	1	.000	.000	.000

Sardinha batted .256 with little power in 72 games in Double-A last season. The young catcher still needs some work, especially offensively, meaning he likely will begin 2004 in Triple-A. 2004 Outlook: C

Dan Serafini (Pos: LHP, Age: 30)

	W	L	Pct.	ERA	G	GS	Sv	IP	H	BB	SO	HR	Avg
'03	1	3	.250	5.40	10	4	0	30.0	41	14	13	5	.336
Car.	15	16	.484	5.98	101	33	1	263.1	335	116	127	37	.315

After a two-year absence from the majors, Serafini posted a 5.40 ERA in 10 appearances with the Reds in 2003, including four starts. The former first-round draft pick has been unable to find his niche. 2004 Outlook: C

Eric Valent (Pos: RF, Age: 26, Bats: L)

	G	AB	R	H	D	T	HR	RBI	SB	BB	SO	Avg	OBP	Slg
'03	18	42	3	9	0	0	0	1	0	2	9	.214	.250	.214
Car.	47	93	7	15	2	0	0	2	0	6	23	.161	.220	.183

Valent struggled most of 2003, batting just .218 in 134 games in Triple-A, prompting the Phillies to trade the outfielder to the Reds in September. He likely will begin next season in the minors. 2004 Outlook: C

Joe Valentine (Pos: RHP, Age: 24)

	W	L	Pct.	ERA	G	GS	Sv	IP	H	BB	SO	HR	Avg
'03	0	0	−	18.00	2	0	0	2.0	5	1	1	1	.455
Car.	0	0	−	18.00	2	0	0	2.0	5	1	1	1	.455

The A's acquired Valentine from the White Sox last December before trading him to the Reds in July. The righthander has the potential to be a major league closer, but might need another year in the minors. 2004 Outlook: C

Todd Van Poppel (Pos: RHP, Age: 32)

	W	L	Pct.	ERA	G	GS	Sv	IP	H	BB	SO	HR	Avg
'03	3	1	.750	5.59	16	5	0	48.1	51	15	34	8	.263
Car.	36	46	.439	5.50	311	87	4	791.2	808	429	639	121	.265

Van Poppel was expected to serve as the Rangers' long reliever in 2003, but a strained groin forced him to miss the first month. He later was released and signed a minor league deal with the Reds. He re-upped with Cincy in December, agreeing to a minor league deal. 2004 Outlook: C

Mark Watson (Pos: LHP, Age: 30)

	W	L	Pct.	ERA	G	GS	Sv	IP	H	BB	SO	HR	Avg
'03	0	0	−	4.50	2	0	0	2.0	2	1	2	0	.250
Car.	1	1	.500	10.95	11	0	0	12.1	22	7	7	1	.386

Watson was 4-4 with a 4.36 ERA and four saves in 44 relief appearances with Triple-A Louisville in 2003. He was called up in August, but was placed on the disabled list shortly thereafter with a kidney ailment. 2004 Outlook: C

Cincinnati Reds Minor League Prospects

Organization Overview:

The Reds entered last season with some degree of optimism, fueled by a new ballpark and a club boasting a couple of emerging stars in Adam Dunn and Austin Kearns. But the 2003 Reds never really caught fire, and by late July, Cincinnati threw in the towel. General manager Jim Bowden was fired, as was manager Bob Boone, and the firesale commenced. To their credit, the Reds made pitching a focus, and they were able to swing deals that netted good arms. They struck paydirt with their first-round pick last June, as Ryan Wagner burst onto the scene in impressive fashion. They may not yet have the pitching to compete with the Cubs, but the Reds appear to be pointed in the right direction.

Bobby Basham

Position: P
Bats: R **Throws:** R
Ht: 6' 3" **Wt:** 205

Opening Day Age: 24
Born: 3/7/80 in Hardy, VA

Recent Statistics

	W	L	ERA	G	GS	Sv	IP	H	R	BB	SO	HR
2002 A Dayton	6	4	1.64	13	13	0	87.2	64	25	9	97	4
2003 AA Chattanooga	5	10	5.17	17	17	0	94.0	133	72	24	56	16
2003 A Potomac	0	1	2.70	1	1	0	6.2	5	3	1	1	0

Basham looked like a shooting rocket in 2002, when he dominated the Class-A Midwest League and was outstanding in the game that clinched the championship in the high Class-A California League. However, he didn't enjoy nearly the same level of success last season. Gone was the overwhelming command he had previously displayed. He simply didn't feature the consistency, location or crispness he had flashed in 2002. Basham delivers four pitches, with the slider serving as his best offering. He needs his changeup to play off a low-90s fastball. Mental fatigue may have been a problem as last season progressed, and it'll be interesting to see how Basham rebounds from last year's setbacks.

Matt Belisle

Position: P
Bats: R **Throws:** R
Ht: 6' 3" **Wt:** 195

Opening Day Age: 23
Born: 6/6/80 in McCallum, TX

Recent Statistics

	W	L	ERA	G	GS	Sv	IP	H	R	BB	SO	HR
2003 AA Greenville	6	8	3.52	21	21	0	125.1	128	59	42	94	5
2003 AAA Richmond	1	1	2.25	3	3	0	20.0	17	8	0	10	1
2003 AAA Louisville	1	3	3.81	4	4	0	26.0	31	15	5	15	2
2003 NL Cincinnati	1	1	5.19	6	0	0	8.2	10	5	2	6	1

After appearing as though his best seasons were well behind him, Kent Mercker helped the Reds as a situational lefty in 2003. But he may have made his biggest contribution when the Reds traded him to the Braves for Belisle last August. Cincinnati had good reports on

Belisle, who had been a second-round pick by Atlanta in 1998. His fastball features good sink and clocks in at around 90 MPH. He needs to keep the fastball down to be effective, but it's complemented by a decent curveball and changeup. Back problems have derailed his development in the past, but Belisle finally made his big league debut last September. A starter in the minors, he worked out of the bullpen with Cincinnati.

Brandon Claussen

Position: P
Bats: L **Throws:** L
Ht: 6' 2" **Wt:** 175

Opening Day Age: 24
Born: 5/1/79 in Rapid City, SD

Recent Statistics

	W	L	ERA	G	GS	Sv	IP	H	R	BB	SO	HR
2003 A Tampa	2	0	1.64	4	4	0	22.0	16	5	3	26	0
2003 AAA Columbus	2	1	2.75	11	11	0	68.2	53	28	18	39	4
2003 AAA Louisville	0	1	7.47	3	3	0	15.2	17	13	6	16	3
2003 AL New York	1	0	1.42	1	1	0	6.1	8	2	1	5	1

Claussen was part of the package the Reds received when they sent Aaron Boone to the Yankees last July. Prior to the trade, Claussen had made a fast recovery from Tommy John surgery, climbing to the majors and winning his only start for the Yankees in June. The Reds were a little concerned about the speed of his comeback, so with nothing left to prove in Triple-A, they ended his season early. His fastball was down a little bit after the surgery, but could come back to previous levels. His slider and changeup are effective, while his tremendous makeup, work ethic and drive will help him compete for a spot on the Reds' staff in '04.

Phil Dumatrait

Position: P
Bats: R **Throws:** L
Ht: 6' 2" **Wt:** 175

Opening Day Age: 22
Born: 7/12/81 in Bakersfield, CA

Recent Statistics

	W	L	ERA	G	GS	Sv	IP	H	R	BB	SO	HR
2002 A Augusta	8	5	2.77	22	22	0	120.1	109	44	47	108	5
2002 A Sarasota	0	2	3.86	4	4	0	14.0	10	9	15	16	0
2003 A Sarasota	7	5	3.02	21	20	1	104.1	74	41	59	74	4
2003 A Potomac	4	1	3.35	7	7	0	37.2	36	17	14	32	2

The Reds landed Dumatrait last July in the deal that shipped Scott Williamson to Boston. At the time of the trade, Dumatrait may have been that system's best pitching prospect. And he didn't do much to disappoint after moving into the Reds' organization. Dumatrait works with four solid pitches and demonstrates nice movement. His 88-91 MPH fastball has good life, he possesses good bite on his slider, and his changeup has sinking action. The Reds' rotation hasn't exactly been stacked with lefthanders in recent years, but Dumatrait is among a group of southpaws who one day may emerge in Cincinnati.

Edwin Encarnacion

Position: 3B   **Opening Day Age:** 21
Bats: R **Throws:** R **Born:** 1/7/83 in La
Ht: 6' 1" **Wt:** 175   Romana, DR

Recent Statistics

	G	AB	R	H	D	T	HR	RBI	SB	BB	SO	Avg
2002 A Dayton	136	518	80	146	32	4	17	73	25	40	108	.282
2003 A Potomac	58	215	40	69	15	1	6	29	7	24	32	.321
2003 AA Chattanooga	67	254	40	69	13	1	5	36	8	22	44	.272

After stroking 17 homers in the Class-A Midwest League while just a teenager in 2002, Encarnacion was bumped as high as Double-A last season. And while his home-run total declined a bit, he continued to flash the power potential that excites observers. He also improved both his walk and strikeout rates. The Reds want him to gain consistency at the plate and to focus on hitting to all fields. Brandon Larson has proven he can ravage Triple-A pitching, but he's clearly had trouble adjusting to the majors. The Reds don't seem to have many other third-base prospects in their system, so Encarnacion looks like he'll have an opportunity awaiting him in the not-too-distant future.

Ty Howington

Position: P   **Opening Day Age:** 23
Bats: B **Throws:** L **Born:** 11/4/80 in
Ht: 6' 4" **Wt:** 220   Vancouver, Washington

Recent Statistics

	W	L	ERA	G	GS	Sv	IP	H	R	BB	SO	HR
2002 AA Chattanooga	1	5	5.12	15	15	0	65.0	65	39	33	51	5
2002 A Stockton	1	1	3.09	2	2	0	11.2	7	6	4	9	1
2003 A Potomac	7	7	3.53	19	19	0	99.1	103	44	34	86	4
2003 AA Chattanooga	0	2	6.91	4	4	0	14.1	15	12	20	16	1

Howington began his professional career by hanging a 5-15 record in the Class-A Midwest League in 2000, and has since endured injuries and surgery. The left-hander boasts low-90s heat, and he's developed a good changeup. However, as the offspeed pitch has improved, he seems to have lost the feel for his curveball. He made another attempt at getting his sea legs at Double-A last year, but instead looked like the second coming of Rick Ankiel in four starts there. He needs to display consistent command, and show that his bout with wildness is not a long-term problem.

Dustin Moseley

Position: P   **Opening Day Age:** 22
Bats: R **Throws:** R **Born:** 12/26/81 in
Ht: 6' 3" **Wt:** 190   Texarkana, AR

Recent Statistics

	W	L	ERA	G	GS	Sv	IP	H	R	BB	SO	HR
2002 A Stockton	6	3	2.74	14	14	0	88.2	60	28	21	80	3
2002 AA Chattanooga	5	6	4.13	13	13	0	80.2	91	47	37	52	5
2003 AA Chattanooga	5	6	3.83	18	18	0	112.1	116	55	28	73	10
2003 AAA Louisville	2	3	2.70	8	8	0	50.0	46	19	14	27	5

Moseley has made fairly rapid progress through the Reds' system. A product of an Arkansas high school, he reached Triple-A last season at age 21. Command is a key factor in Moseley's success. He doesn't blow hitters away, and his mistakes often get punished. His fastball is only average, residing in the uppers 80s to 90 MPH. His curveball is a plus pitch, however, and he also utilizes a solid changeup. He needs to gain consistency with the offspeed pitch. Moseley pitched fairly well in eight starts at Triple-A last year, and he's likely headed back to that level when 2004 opens. But an audition in Cincinnati isn't out of the question at some point during the campaign.

Ryan Wagner

Position: P   **Opening Day Age:** 21
Bats: R **Throws:** R **Born:** 7/15/82 in
Ht: 6' 4" **Wt:** 210   Yoakum, TX

Recent Statistics

	W	L	ERA	G	GS	Sv	IP	H	R	BB	SO	HR
2003 AA Chattanooga	1	0	0.00	5	0	0	5.0	2	1	2	6	0
2003 AAA Louisville	0	1	4.50	4	0	0	4.0	5	2	0	4	0
2003 NL Cincinnati	2	0	1.66	17	0	0	21.2	13	4	12	25	2

Wagner went from college to the majors in the space of a couple months last summer. He had been nearly unhittable at the University of Houston, where he had produced an historic strikeout rate. The Reds selected him with the 14th overall pick in June, and after brief stops at Double-A and Triple-A, he was working in Cincinnati. While Wagner's low-90s fastball is a plus pitch, it's his slider that draws raves. He's a bit unusual in that he doesn't grip the laces on the pitch, but hitters have almost no chance when they chase it breaking out of the zone. Wagner should be a quality setup man this year, and he has the potential to be even more in the future.

Others to Watch

Second baseman **Will Bergolla** (21) stole 52 bases at high Class-A Potomac last season, but he needs to draw more walks to be truly effective at the top of a lineup. A solid fielder, he has the ability to help a club by playing shortstop, too. . . Righthander **Luke Hudson** (26) had surgery to repair his labrum last spring, but he should be pitching in games by the end of April. His mid-90s fastball and power curveball are so good that he's been described as a poor man's Mark Prior. He has a chance to make the Reds' rotation this season. . . Lefthander **Brian Shackelford** (27) hit 20 home runs at Double-A as recently as 2001. But the Royals began the conversion from position player to pitcher the next season, and he was traded to the Reds in the Jeff Austin deal last March. Shackelford is a longshot, but his slider is a late-biting strikeout pitch, and he might be valuable in a Brooks Kieschnick type of role. . . Outfielder **Stephen Smitherman** (25) has been a run producer with decent power in the minors, at least before he reached Triple-A. He must remember not to get pull-conscious.

Coors Field

Offense

No park is more rewarding to an offense than Coors Field. The Rockies averaged 6.38 runs per game at Coors Field in 2003 compared to 4.15 on the road. The irony is the pitching staff actually had a lower ERA (5.07) than on the road (5.35) for the first time in franchise history.

Defense

Coors Field puts plenty of pressure on defenses. Pitchers can't afford to have outs given away. There is a premium on having mobile outfielders who can throw, as runners constantly are looking to take the extra base. Outfielders have to get to balls quickly and make quick, accurate throws. Infielders have to have quick reactions because the grass is short due to growing problems in the semi-desert climate.

Who It Helps the Most

Obviously, hitters have fun at Coors. Even Charles Johnson hit .306 there. But pitchers who come to grips with the reality of the park do pretty well, too. Darren Oliver was 7-3 with a 4.50 ERA at Coors (6-8, 5.45 on the road), and Jason Jennings is 17-6 in his career at Coors.

Who It Hurts the Most

Pitchers in general don't like the place, and with reason. But the player who may be hurt the most is Todd Helton—at least in terms of how people evaluate him. There is a tendency to downgrade his stats because he plays 81 games a season at Coors. However, Helton has been solid on the road, too. And there is a strong belief that any great hitter will adapt to take advantage of what his park offers. Helton just happens to play in a park that offers plenty.

Rookies & Newcomers

Rene Reyes made his debut last July, and figures to be a backup outfielder or a possible platoon in left field, where he'll be required to cover lots of territory. Former Rockie Vinny Castilla, who was signed in December after a four-year absence, is a career .337 hitter at Coors. He has 118 homers and a .622 slugging mark there. He was a productive player as a Rockie.

Dimensions: LF-347, LCF-390, CF-415, RCF-375, RF-350

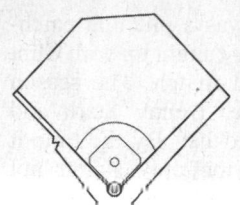

Capacity: 50,449

Elevation: 5280 feet

Surface: Grass

Foul Territory: Average

Park Factors

2003 Season

	Home Games			Away Games			
	Rockies	Opp	Total	Rockies	Opp	Total	Index
G	72	72	144	75	75	150	
Avg	.294	.288	.291	.236	.287	.261	112
AB	2450	2600	5050	2558	2485	5043	104
R	458	397	855	305	405	710	125
H	721	749	1470	603	712	1315	116
2B	169	142	311	137	150	287	108
3B	23	21	44	5	14	19	231
HR	98	104	202	74	77	151	134
BB	291	218	509	277	288	565	90
SO	439	416	855	608	360	968	88
E	48	54	102	59	53	112	95
E-Infield	40	42	82	50	46	96	89
LHB-Avg	.336	.301	.316	.247	.312	.285	111
LHB-HR	30	44	74	25	27	52	150
RHB-Avg	.277	.279	.278	.230	.267	.247	113
RHB-HR	68	60	128	49	50	99	125

2001-2003

	Home Games			Away Games			
	Rockies	Opp	Total	Rockies	Opp	Total	Index
G	219	219	438	222	222	444	
Avg	.314	.285	.299	.242	.271	.256	117
AB	7560	7809	15369	7624	7346	14970	104
R	1418	1303	2721	911	1109	2020	137
H	2375	2224	4599	1847	1991	3838	121
2B	491	458	949	369	432	801	115
3B	87	54	141	33	47	80	172
HR	299	349	648	210	243	453	139
BB	747	766	1513	733	807	1540	96
SO	1279	1335	2614	1672	1232	2904	88
E	145	160	305	144	144	288	107
E-Infield	114	122	236	121	127	248	96
LHB-Avg	.346	.289	.319	.265	.289	.276	115
LHB-HR	140	135	275	105	87	192	139
RHB-Avg	.291	.282	.287	.227	.260	.243	118
RHB-HR	159	214	373	105	156	261	139

2003 Rankings (National League)

- Highest batting-average factor
- Highest hit factor
- Highest home-run factor
- Highest LHB home-run factor
- Highest RHB batting-average factor
- Second-highest triple factor
- Lowest walk factor
- Lowest strikeout factor

Clint Hurdle

2003 Season

The Rockies' 2003 season was a pitching patch-work, and in August it finally caught up with Clint Hurdle's ability to mix and match. The season started with Denny Neagle, Denny Stark and Scott Elarton on the disabled list. By the time it ended, Darren Oliver was the only starter not sidelined by an injury or illness. Add in the fact that closer Jose Jimenez had imploded by midseason, and it is a bit surprising that the Rockies still were sitting above .500 as late as August 9. However, the Rockies, lost 30 of their final 44 games.

Offense

The Rockies were a three-man show—Todd Helton, Preston Wilson and Jay Payton. Hurdle got high marks for figuring out a way to get Larry Walker to play in 140 games for only the third time in 11 years, even if Walker had a subpar year. He also did a good job of finding the rest that allowed Charles Johnson to hit 20 home runs. However, Hurdle never could find the offensive answers at third, short and second. He took a major gamble in the spring, splitting the lefthanded bats of Helton and Walker with Wilson. Wilson paid off by leading the National League with 141 RBI.

Pitching & Defense

The pitching didn't always get much help from Colorado's middle infielders, who fared poorly in fielding percentage compared to their National League peers. Most of the Rockies' middle infielders from 2003 are now gone, and the club will have to sign some replacements.

2004 Outlook

Any team that has Helton-Wilson-Walker in the 3-4-5 spots in the lineup has a chance to get lucky. The key for Hurdle will be the pitching, and nobody is as vital in that area as Jason Jennings, who has the competitiveness and durability to be at the top of the rotation until a legitimate No. 1 steps up.

Born: 7/30/57 in Big Rapids, MI

Playing Experience: 1977-1987, KC, Cin, NYM, StL

Managerial Experience: 2 seasons

Manager Statistics

Year	Team, Lg	W	L	Pct	GB	Finish
2003	Colorado, NL	74	88	.457	26.5	4th West
2 Seasons		141	161	.467	–	–

2003 Starting Pitchers by Days Rest

	<=3	4	5	6+
Rockies Starts	1	71	62	15
Rockies ERA	4.50	4.58	6.06	8.61
NL Avg Starts	2	84	43	23
NL ERA	5.00	4.23	4.42	4.68

2003 Situational Stats

	Clint Hurdle	NL Average
Hit & Run Success %	22.9	32.7
Stolen Base Success %	63.0	68.9
Platoon Pct.	46.0	52.0
Defensive Subs	10	19
High-Pitch Outings	0	8
Quick/Slow Hooks	21/20	20/12
Sacrifice Attempts	86	93

2003 Rankings (National League)

- 2nd in slow hooks and relief appearances (500)

Shawn Chacon

2003 Season

Shawn Chacon's season had a great beginning. He became the first pitcher in Rockies history to win 11 games before the All-Star break, and only the second pitcher in franchise history to be selected to the All-Star team. However, he developed an inflammation in his right elbow that forced him to be scratched from a potential start in the All Star Game, and that eventually resulted in Chacon being placed on the disabled list. He tried to return but went out for the year on August 17.

Pitching

Chacon faced the challenge of having to make the team last spring and responded by becoming the Rockies' No. 1 pitcher when he was healthy. He has a fastball that's a steady 92-94 MPH and that he is able to spot effectively. He has a plus changeup. Most importantly, though, Chacon has a quality curveball which he throws with success at Coors Field. He doesn't know any better. He grew up in Greeley, about 50 miles north of Denver, and that's where he learned to throw the pitch, altitude notwithstanding. He also can throw a slider, but it's definitely a secondary pitch. He has begun to replace that pitch with a cutter that he runs in on the hands of lefthanded hitters.

Defense & Hitting

Chacon is an excellent athlete. Embarrassed by his poor performance at the plate as a rookie, he has worked hard to become a contributor with the bat, particularly in putting down a bunt. He moves well around the mound, can make the bunt play and will hold a runner to give the catcher a chance.

2004 Outlook

The big concern is health. With questions surrounding Chacon's durability and the Rockies needing a ninth-inning guy, manager Clint Hurdle has decided to turn to the righthander as his closer. With heat that approaches the mid-90s and a curveball that can be a strikeout pitch, Chacon could flourish in a role that will be less stressful on his elbow.

Position: SP
Bats: R **Throws:** R
Ht: 6' 3" **Wt:** 212

Opening Day Age: 26
Born: 12/23/77 in Anchorage, AK
ML Seasons: 3
Pronunciation: chah-CONE

Overall Statistics

	W	L	Pct.	ERA	G	GS	Sv	IP	H	BB	SO	HR	Avg
'03	11	8	.579	4.60	23	23	0	137.0	124	58	93	12	.243
Car.	22	29	.431	5.10	71	71	0	416.1	403	205	294	63	.255

2003 Pitching Profile

	Shawn Chacon	NL Average
Overall Strike %	60.9	62.4
1st Pitch Strike %	52.0	58.4
Ratio	1.33	1.38
Strikeouts per 9 IP	6.11	6.65
Walks per 9 IP	3.81	3.42
Home Runs per 9 IP	0.79	1.05
Strikeout/Walk Ratio	1.60	1.94
Groundball/Flyball Ratio	0.96	1.29

2003 Situational Stats

	W	L	ERA	Sv	IP		AB	H	HR	RBI	Avg
Home	7	3	4.38	0	74.0	LHB	272	69	6	29	.254
Road	4	5	4.86	0	63.0	RHB	239	55	6	36	.230
First Half	11	4	4.27	0	105.1	Sc Pos	126	31	3	49	.246
Scnd Half	0	4	5.68	0	31.2	Clutch	23	6	1	1	.261

2003 Rankings (National League)

- 6th in hit batsmen (12)
- Led the Rockies in ERA, hit batsmen (12), winning percentage, highest strikeout-walk ratio (1.6), lowest batting average allowed (.243), lowest slugging percentage allowed (.389), lowest on-base percentage allowed (.331), lowest ERA at home, lowest ERA on the road and most strikeouts per nine innings (6.1)

Aaron Cook

2003 Season

Aaron Cook was given a spot in the Rockies' rotation last March, but he couldn't keep it. The Rockies tried to jump start him with an 18-day trip to Triple-A Colorado Springs, but the struggles continued upon his return. As a result, Cook finished the season in the bullpen. It didn't make much difference. He had a 6.00 ERA in 16 starts, and a 6.08 ERA in 27 relief appearances.

Pitching

It's not a question of stuff. Cook has a Kevin Brown-type sinker. It has unbelievable action and is a solid 94-97 MPH. He has the makings of a decent changeup, at times experimenting with a split-finger pitch, which isn't really necessary. And he has a good hard slider. Cook has to believe in himself as much as those around him do. He gets in trouble when he tries to hurry and cuts himself up. Command in the strike zone is critical for him.

Defense & Hitting

Cook is athletic, but at times he can look lethargic. He can field his position, and he holds runners well. However, he will hurry his throws and get himself in trouble. He needs to take a deep breath every now and then. As a hitter Cook needs to work on his bat control, though he is improving in bunt situations.

2004 Outlook

The Rockies need to be patient with Cook. Remember, he spent five years at the Class-A level before everything clicked. In the next year, he went from Double-A to Triple-A to the big leagues. Now that he's had two years to acclimate himself, he should be ready to move forward. He's a sleeper who will be given every chance to prove he should be a starter. There's some talk that once he gets a strike-three pitch to go along with his sinker, he could wind up a closer.

Position: RP/SP
Bats: R **Throws:** R
Ht: 6' 3" **Wt:** 205

Opening Day Age: 25
Born: 2/8/79 in Ft. Campbell, KY
ML Seasons: 2

Overall Statistics

	W	L	Pct.	ERA	G	GS	Sv	IP	H	BB	SO	HR	Avg
'03	4	6	.400	6.02	43	16	0	124.0	160	57	43	8	.317
Car.	6	7	.462	5.69	52	21	0	159.2	201	70	57	12	.313

2003 Pitching Profile

	Aaron Cook	NL Average
Overall Strike %	60.2	62.4
1st Pitch Strike %	58.0	58.4
Ratio	1.75	1.38
Strikeouts per 9 IP	3.12	6.65
Walks per 9 IP	4.14	3.42
Home Runs per 9 IP	0.58	1.05
Strikeout/Walk Ratio	0.75	1.94
Groundball/Flyball Ratio	2.34	1.29

2003 Situational Stats

	W	L	ERA	Sv	IP		AB	H	HR	RBI	Avg
Home	4	0	6.49	0	61.0	LHB	219	75	6	44	.342
Road	0	6	5.57	0	63.0	RHB	285	85	2	32	.298
First Half	3	6	6.14	0	88.0	Sc Pos	145	49	4	65	.338
Scnd Half	1	0	5.75	0	36.0	Clutch	14	6	0	1	.429

2003 Rankings (National League)

- 2nd in highest batting average allowed with runners in scoring position
- 4th in highest batting average allowed vs. lefthanded batters
- 6th in pickoff throws (126)
- 10th in wild pitches (10) and highest batting average allowed vs. righthanded batters
- Led the Rockies in sacrifice bunts (6), wild pitches (10), most run support per nine innings (6.5), first batter efficiency (.115) and fewest home runs allowed per nine innings (.58)

Todd Helton

2003 Season

Todd Helton hasn't hit less than .315 or had fewer than 25 home runs or 97 RBI in any of his first six full big league seasons. Last year he played through a back problem that raised concerns in 2002, and finished second to Albert Pujols of St. Louis in the closest batting race in National League history. His .387 average against left-handers was the third highest by a lefthanded hitter since 1974.

Hitting

Helton is a complete hitter. He hits for average, he hits for power and he can hit any place he plays. Coors Field inflates his numbers some, but one thing about Helton is that he would adjust to his environment. He's a pleasure to watch with two strikes. He doesn't make concessions, but has such good command of the strike zone that he will work pitches. There's no real way to get him out. He has good plate coverage and likes to drive the ball to left-center. He's strong enough to hit the ball out of any part of the park, which allows him to react instead of guessing at pitches. With that football mentality, he hangs in.

Baserunning & Defense

An average runner, Helton isn't a basestealing threat. Don't be misled, however; he is a very good and aggressive baserunner. He will force doubles, a solid way to play at Coors Field. Helton, who has won two Gold Glove Awards, has made defense a key part of his workout prior to every game. He can look awkward on popups, but after struggling early in 2003 on that play, he put in overtime and regained his touch by midseason.

2004 Outlook

Helton is headed to the Hall of Fame. He's going to continue to be a big-time player. He has so much ability, but more than that he has a tremendous work ethic and carries a big-time desire to excel.

Position: 1B
Bats: L **Throws:** L
Ht: 6' 2" **Wt:** 204

Opening Day Age: 30
Born: 8/20/73 in Knoxville, TN
ML Seasons: 7

Colorado

Overall Statistics

	G	AB	R	H	D	T	HR	RBI	SB	BB	SO	Avg	OBP	Slg
'03	160	583	135	209	49	5	33	117	0	111	72	.358	.458	.630
Car.	981	3504	717	1182	279	20	219	740	27	540	470	.337	.425	.616

Where He Hits the Ball

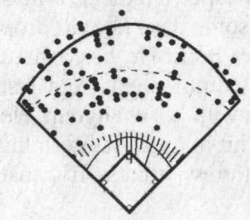 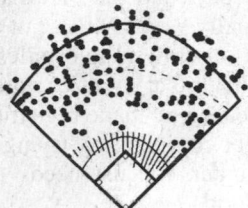

Vs. LHP   **Vs. RHP**

2003 Situational Stats

	AB	H	HR	RBI	Avg		AB	H	HR	RBI	Avg
Home	299	117	23	72	.391	LHP	199	77	10	49	.387
Road	284	92	10	45	.324	RHP	384	132	23	68	.344
First Half	358	125	21	78	.349	Sc Pos	133	55	7	78	.414
Scnd Half	225	84	12	39	.373	Clutch	60	20	4	9	.333

2003 Rankings (National League)

- 1st in times on base (322), batting average with runners in scoring position, batting average at home
- 2nd in batting average, runs scored, hits, doubles, total bases (367), walks, on-base percentage and errors at first base (11)
- 3rd in intentional walks (21), slugging percentage, batting average vs. lefthanded pitchers, batting average vs. righthanded pitchers and lowest fielding percentage at first base (.993)
- 4th in games played
- Led the Rockies in batting average, runs scored, hits, singles, doubles, , plate appearances (703), games played
- Led NL first basemen in batting average

Jason Jennings

2003 Season

Having won the National League Rookie of the Year in 2002 and claiming the Opening Day assignment in 2003, Jason Jennings suddenly saw his season dissolve. Even when ordinary, however, Jennings showed he can be a key member of a rotation. He missed the final two weeks of the season because of a viral infection, and lost more games than he won, but he had his second straight year with 32 starts and more than 180 innings.

Pitching

Jennings looked like he overreacted to his second year in the big leagues. He got himself in trouble pitching up in the strike zone last year. He doesn't need to do that. He has a super sinker. It's normally 91-92 MPH, but on some days he will drop it down a couple miles per hour. He has a hard slider that is an excellent complement. And last season he made big strides with his changeup. He got carried away trying to hit in and out. With his sinker, he just needs to throw strikes. It's that good.

Defense & Hitting

Jennings doesn't have an athletic-looking body, but he's a modern-day Rick Reuschel. He takes pride in being the complete package. He fields his position very well and reacts quickly to bunts or nubbers. He has a quick move to first, holding runners to give catchers a chance. And he can hit. A lefthanded hitter, Jennings is a converted catcher who hasn't neglected the opportunities he gets with his bat.

2004 Outlook

Jennings figures to get another Opening Day assignment in Colorado, but in truth he is a quality No. 3 starter. He doesn't let conditions bother him, he can win in Colorado (17-6 lifetime at Coors) and he is durable. He'll make his 30-plus starts and give the Rockies a chance to win most of them.

Position: SP
Bats: L **Throws:** R
Ht: 6' 2" **Wt:** 245

Opening Day Age: 25
Born: 7/17/78 in Dallas, TX
ML Seasons: 3

Overall Statistics

	W	L	Pct.	ERA	G	GS	Sv	IP	H	BB	SO	HR	Avg
'03	12	13	.480	5.11	32	32	0	181.1	212	88	119	20	.299
Car.	32	22	.593	4.79	71	71	0	406.0	455	177	272	48	.288

2003 Pitching Profile

	Jason Jennings	NL Average
Overall Strike %	59.0	62.4
1st Pitch Strike %	54.4	58.4
Ratio	1.65	1.38
Strikeouts per 9 IP	5.91	6.65
Walks per 9 IP	4.37	3.42
Home Runs per 9 IP	0.99	1.05
Strikeout/Walk Ratio	1.35	1.94
Groundball/Flyball Ratio	1.51	1.29

2003 Situational Stats

	W	L	ERA	Sv	IP		AB	H	HR	RBI	Avg
Home	8	1	4.64	0	66.0	LHB	378	122	9	58	.323
Road	4	12	5.38	0	115.1	RHB	332	90	11	49	.271
First Half	9	6	4.56	0	116.1	Sc Pos	211	59	7	89	.280
Scnd Half	3	7	6.09	0	65.0	Clutch	20	4	0	0	.200

2003 Rankings (National League)

- 1st in highest on-base percentage allowed (.377)
- 2nd in highest walks per nine innings (4.4)
- 3rd in lowest strikeout-walk ratio (1.4) and highest batting average allowed (.299)
- 5th in highest slugging percentage allowed (.466)
- 6th in losses and highest ERA
- 7th in hits allowed
- 8th in walks allowed and highest ERA on the road
- 10th in GDPs induced (22) and highest batting average allowed vs. lefthanded batters
- Led the Rockies in losses, games started, innings pitched, hits allowed, batters faced (820), walks allowed, strikeouts, pitches thrown (3,050), runners caught stealing (6), GDPs induced (22) and lowest stolen-base percentage allowed (60.0)

Jose Jimenez

2003 Season

In 2002, Jose Jimenez became the Rockies' all-time saves leader, and he currently sits at 102 saves for his career. But his work was shaky in 2003, and by midseason he had been dumped from the closer's role. He worked in long relief in the middle part of the season and then finished in the rotation, where he was 1-4 with a 4.31 ERA in seven starts. He allowed three or fewer runs in four of the starts.

Pitching

Jimenez has one of the true power sinkers in the game. The pitch, which he'll throw between 88-93 MPH, has major drop. He also has a decent slider, but he can get lazy with it. When he does, he leaves it up. If Jimenez is going to start, he needs another pitch or two. Right now everything he has is hard and down, so he doesn't change bat speed or eye level. He has experimented with a splitter, but hasn't gotten comfortable with it. Part of the problem with him starting would be the extended demands on his right shoulder. He has a violent delivery that could strain the shoulder with the way he flies open.

Defense & Hitting

Jimenez is lazy. He is a good athlete, which allows him to make some impressive defensive plays, but too often he bungles the routine play. He holds runners adequately, but hasn't concentrated on hitting in his short relief role.

2004 Outlook

With a $3.6 million salary in 2003, which meant the Rockies had to offer him nearly $3 million as a minimum salary in 2004, Jimenez was released. He received a lot of attention on the open market because of his versatility. His most serviceable role will be as a swingman, working long relief and stepping into the rotation on occasion. That could spur his focus and give him a chance for more success.

Position: RP
Bats: R **Throws:** R
Ht: 6' 3" **Wt:** 230

Opening Day Age: 30
Born: 7/7/73 in San Pedro de Macoris, DR
ML Seasons: 0
Pronunciation: he-MEN-ez

Overall Statistics

	W	L	Pct.	ERA	G	GS	Sv	IP	H	BB	SO	HR	Avg
'03	2	10	.167	5.22	63	7	20	101.2	137	32	45	7	.322
Car.	23	37	.383	4.66	298	38	102	485.0	527	172	298	40	.277

2003 Pitching Profile

	Jose Jimenez	NL Average
Overall Strike %	62.5	62.4
1st Pitch Strike %	57.6	58.4
Ratio	1.66	1.38
Strikeouts per 9 IP	3.98	6.65
Walks per 9 IP	2.83	3.42
Home Runs per 9 IP	0.62	1.05
Strikeout/Walk Ratio	1.41	1.94
Groundball/Flyball Ratio	2.57	1.29

2003 Situational Stats

	W	L	ERA	Sv	IP		AB	H	HR	RBI	Avg
Home	1	6	5.28	11	61.1	LHB	204	78	3	34	.382
Road	1	4	5.13	9	40.1	RHB	222	59	4	30	.266
First Half	0	5	6.70	19	44.1	Sc Pos	141	44	3	56	.312
Scnd Half	2	5	4.08	1	57.1	Clutch	121	39	2	24	.322

2003 Rankings (National League)

- 1st in highest batting average allowed vs. left handed batters
- 2nd in highest batting average allowed in relief (.323)
- 4th in most baserunners allowed per nine innings in relief (16.0)
- 5th in fewest strikeouts per nine innings in relief (4.5)
- 7th in highest batting average allowed with runners in scoring position and highest relief ERA (5.81)
- 8th in relief losses (6)
- 9th in save percentage (87.0)
- Led the Rockies in saves, games finished (40), highest groundball-flyball ratio allowed (2.6), save percentage (87.0), relief losses (6) and fewest walks per nine innings (2.8)

Charles Johnson

2003 Season

Charles Johnson came to the Rockies as part of a three-team trade that enabled Colorado to unload Mike Hampton. The Rockies allowed Johnson to regain his everyday role behind the plate. He responded with 20 home runs, the second-highest total of his career and the most ever by a Rockies catcher, and 61 RBI. However, he was pretty useless offensively away from Coors Field, hitting just .153 on the road.

Hitting

Offense is not why Johnson is on the team. He has a late trigger and two huge holes in his swing. He can be overpowered inside and will chase pitches low and away. His bat is slow enough that he's not going to catch up with a decent fastball. What he can do is hit a hanging breaking ball, and he is strong enough to drive the ball. He won't see many changeups because that's one pitch he will be right on.

Baserunning & Defense

Johnson is among the slowest players in the game. Fortunately, he knows what he can't do, and doesn't try to force issues. Defensively, Johnson still is adequate but not the Gold Glove receiver of his younger days. He throws decently and can block balls, but he wears down and he is not as fluid in the second half of the season. Don't look for Johnson to block the plate. He will set up upside the line to avoid a collision, and makes no bones about his desire to avoid an injury.

2004 Outlook

Johnson has the type of contract ($9 million this year) that pretty well assures the Rockies will give him the bulk of the catching time. This could be the final year, however, that Johnson's No. 1 status goes unchallenged. The Rockies are counting on J.D. Closser to be ready in 2005 after spending the 2004 season at Triple-A Colorado Springs.

Position: C
Bats: R **Throws:** R
Ht: 6' 3" **Wt:** 250

Opening Day Age: 32
Born: 7/20/71 in Fort Pierce, FL
ML Seasons: 10

Overall Statistics

	G	AB	R	H	D	T	HR	RBI	SB	BB	SO	Avg	OBP	Slg
'03	108	356	49	82	20	0	20	61	1	49	84	.230	.320	.455
Car.	1060	3485	418	859	187	4	154	518	4	417	895	.246	.328	.435

Where He Hits the Ball

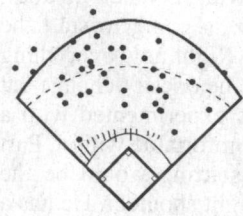 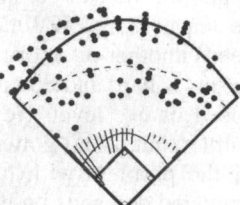

Vs. LHP   **Vs. RHP**

2003 Situational Stats

	AB	H	HR	RBI	Avg		AB	H	HR	RBI	Avg
Home	180	55	12	43	.306	LHP	96	24	2	10	.250
Road	176	27	8	18	.153	RHP	260	58	18	51	.223
First Half	224	51	11	42	.228	Sc Pos	106	19	3	35	.179
Scnd Half	132	31	9	19	.235	Clutch	40	6	2	5	.150

2003 Rankings (National League)

- 1st in lowest batting average with two strikes (.115)
- 2nd in lowest batting average with runners in scoring position
- 7th in sacrifice flies (7), fielding percentage at catcher (.993) and lowest batting average in the clutch
- Led the Rockies in sacrifice flies (7)

Darren Oliver

2003 Season

Darren Oliver has resurrected his career with the Rockies. Unwanted by any other team, Oliver got an invitation to spring training and a minimal contract from Colorado. He responded by leading the team with 13 wins, one shy of his career high, and not missing a start.

Pitching

Oliver doesn't overpower anybody, but he is not afraid to throw his 86-88 MPH fastball. He also has a cut fastball that he runs in on righthanded hitters. His main breaking pitch is a slider, but he will throw an occasional curveball. And he will change speeds. His command is good enough that hitters know what he's going to do, but he still gets away with it. When Oliver's command is off, however, he can get into trouble quickly. The strange thing is that as good as his command is coming inside, he is hesitant to pitch away to righthanded hitters. He could help himself by changing location and getting righthanded hitters off balance.

Defense & Hitting

The son of former big league first baseman Bob Oliver, Darren was a two-way player out of high school, but opted to pitch. He is comfortable at the plate, and takes a strong swing. He isn't real quick, but he stays calm on the mound, which allows him to field the slow rollers and bunts. Oliver can be a little long in his delivery, which basestealers take advantage of.

2004 Outlook

Oliver will have a rotation spot, but buyer beware. A year ago, Oliver was desperate and worked harder than at any time in his career. He even went to Puerto Rico to pitch and drum up interest. The end result was that he was in the best shape of his career when he showed up last spring. He's had success now, and there is a question as to whether that means he will lose his edge.

Position: SP
Bats: R **Throws:** L
Ht: 6' 2" **Wt:** 220

Opening Day Age: 33
Born: 10/6/70 in Kansas City, MO
ML Seasons: 11

Overall Statistics

	W	L	Pct.	ERA	G	GS	Sv	IP	H	BB	SO	HR	Avg
'03	13	11	.542	5.04	33	32	0	180.1	201	61	88	21	.284
Car.	84	76	.525	5.02	279	218	2	1334.1	1504	561	788	158	.287

2003 Pitching Profile

	Darren Oliver	NL Average
Overall Strike %	63.3	62.4
1st Pitch Strike %	58.0	58.4
Ratio	1.45	1.38
Strikeouts per 9 IP	4.39	6.65
Walks per 9 IP	3.04	3.42
Home Runs per 9 IP	1.05	1.05
Strikeout/Walk Ratio	1.44	1.94
Groundball/Flyball Ratio	1.36	1.29

2003 Situational Stats

	W	L	ERA	Sv	IP		AB	H	HR	RBI	Avg
Home	7	3	4.50	0	78.0	LHB	156	40	5	26	.256
Road	6	8	5.45	0	102.1	RHB	552	161	16	70	.292
First Half	7	5	4.67	0	106.0	Sc Pos	159	47	5	72	.296
Scnd Half	6	6	5.57	0	74.1	Clutch	14	7	0	4	.500

2003 Rankings (National League)

- 1st in fielding percentage at pitcher (1.000)
- 3rd in fewest strikeouts per nine innings (4.4)
- 5th in pickoff throws (127) and fewest pitches thrown per batter (3.50)
- 6th in most run support per nine innings (6.1) and lowest strikeout-walk ratio (1.4)
- 7th in highest ERA on the road
- 8th in highest ERA and highest on-base percentage allowed (.345)
- 10th in GDPs induced (22), highest batting average allowed (.284) and highest slugging percentage allowed (.455)
- Led the Rockies in wins, games started, home runs allowed, pickoff throws (127), stolen bases allowed (14), runners caught stealing (6), GDPs induced (22) and fewest pitches thrown per batter (3.50)

Jay Payton

Position: LF
Bats: R **Throws:** R
Ht: 5'10" **Wt:** 185

Opening Day Age: 31
Born: 11/22/72 in
Zanesville, OH
ML Seasons: 6

2003 Season

Jay Payton enjoyed the most active and productive season of his career, and it wasn't purely Coors Field. Obviously, there was a confidence factor from Coors that Payton parlayed into success. However, Payton hit .281 on the road, and hit 15 of his 28 home runs outside Coors. He enjoyed career highs in several offensive categories, including on-base percentage.

Hitting

Payton opened the season hitting second, but really came on strong when he was moved to the No. 6 slot in the order in the second half. Hitting down in the order allowed Payton to be aggressive, which he prefers. Payton is a line-drive hitter who is served well by the open gaps at Coors Field. He likes the fastball. When he goes into a funk, it's because the opposition is keeping him off-stride with offspeed and breaking pitches. He has the type of speed a manager would be tempted to put at the top of the order, but he doesn't work counts and doesn't steal bases.

Baserunning & Defense

Payton is the ideal left fielder for Coors Field, which has the biggest left field in baseball. He has the speed and range to play center, plus a decent arm. The questionable breaks that make him passable, at best, in center aren't as big of a problem in left. He is a heady player and understands the importance of hitting cutoff men. Payton can take the extra base, but despite above-average speed, he is a feeble basestealer. He doesn't have that feel for situations, and doesn't read pitchers well.

2004 Outlook

This is a critical season for Payton, who has a reputation for nagging injuries. If he can put together another healthy season, he finally could emerge as the quality player scouts anticipated, when he came out of Georgia Tech rated ahead of his teammates Jason Varitek and Nomar Garciaparra.

Overall Statistics

	G	AB	R	H	D	T	HR	RBI	SB	BB	SO	Avg	OBP	Slg
'03	157	600	93	181	32	5	28	89	6	43	77	.302	.354	.512
Car.	572	1924	272	559	93	14	69	245	23	121	249	.291	.337	.461

Where He Hits the Ball

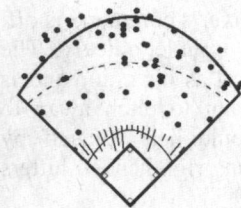 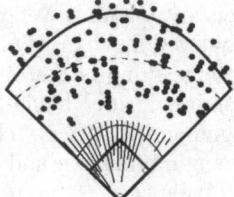

Vs. LHP　　　　**Vs. RHP**

2003 Situational Stats

	AB	H	HR	RBI	Avg		AB	H	HR	RBI	Avg
Home	298	96	13	50	.322	LHP	160	46	11	27	.288
Road	302	85	15	39	.281	RHP	440	135	17	62	.307
First Half	354	105	13	48	.297	Sc Pos	157	44	4	53	.280
Scnd Half	246	76	15	41	.309	Clutch	73	18	2	11	.247

2003 Rankings (National League)

- 1st in GDPs (27)
- 3rd in fielding percentage in left field (.990) and fewest pitches seen per plate appearance (3.35)
- 5th in batting average with two strikes (.281)
- Led the Rockies in at-bats, GDPs (27) and highest percentage of swings put into play (48.1)

Chris Stynes

2003 Season

Playing for his fourth team in four years, Chris Stynes had the most active year of his career. He reached career highs in a number of categories, and his 73 RBI were 33 more than his previous high. Signed by the Rockies to provide insurance at second base and third base, Stynes played so solidly at third that once shortstop Juan Uribe was healthy, the Rockies dealt Jose Hernandez, who was supposed to be the third baseman.

Hitting

Stynes is a dead fastball hitter. He likes the ball up and over the plate. He is not a home-run hitter, but is strong and will drive the ball into the gaps. However, he has too many holes in his swing to have extended success. He will chase breaking pitches and overswing on offspeed stuff. Like most of the Rockies' hitters, he struggled mightily away from Coors Field.

Baserunning & Defense

A full-speed player, Stynes is an average runner, but he makes up for his lack of true speed with his aggressiveness. He isn't much of a threat to steal bases but will take the extra base. He plays a solid third base. He has the quick reactions and hands. His arm is short, but he puts everything he has into his throws, and he does not have a scatter arm. His feet are slow at second base, but he will battle to do the job. He's not agile in turning the double play, but he will hang in.

2004 Outlook

Stynes is an extra player on a decent team. He's not a legitimate utility player, though, because he can't play shortstop and is adequate at best at second base. He will find himself back in a backup role after getting a chance to play third base on an everyday basis in 2003. He does bring an intensity to the bench that most teams can use.

Position: 3B
Bats: R **Throws:** R
Ht: 5'10" **Wt:** 205

Opening Day Age: 31
Born: 1/19/73 in Queens, NY
ML Seasons: 9

Overall Statistics

	G	AB	R	H	D	T	HR	RBI	SB	BB	SO	Avg	OBP	Slg
'03	138	443	71	113	31	3	11	73	3	48	76	.255	.335	.413
Car.	754	2164	335	605	108	9	50	249	49	182	285	.280	.340	.407

Where He Hits the Ball

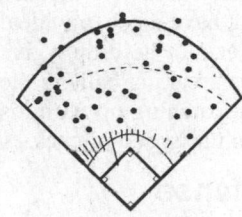 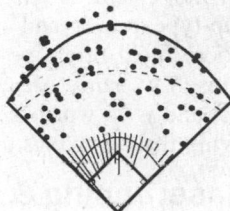

Vs. LHP   **Vs. RHP**

2003 Situational Stats

	AB	H	HR	RBI	Avg		AB	H	HR	RBI	Avg
Home	227	66	10	45	.291	LHP	134	38	2	22	.284
Road	216	47	1	28	.218	RHP	309	75	9	51	.243
First Half	263	74	8	52	.281	Sc Pos	113	31	2	58	.274
Scnd Half	180	39	3	21	.217	Clutch	58	16	2	21	.276

2003 Rankings (National League)

- 2nd in batting average with the bases loaded (.615) and fielding percentage at third base (.972)
- 10th in errors at third base (9)
- Led the Rockies in lowest percentage of swings on the first pitch (17.7)

Juan Uribe

2003 Season

Juan Uribe suffered a fractured fifth metatarsal in his right foot while running the bases during the exhibition season. With surgery required, he missed the first 58 games of the regular season. Once he was activated, he reaffirmed his hold on the Rockies' shortstop job. He wound up hitting .253 with 10 home runs in 87 games, showing the power potential that makes him so intriguing.

Hitting

For all the work the Rockies tried to do with his offensive approach, Uribe showed little progress. He has a two-piece swing that includes a stop when he brings the bat back. It disrupts his natural movement and slows the bat down. He has gap-type power and could have been an ideal Coors Field offensive player, but he didn't give himself a chance. He chases breaking balls in the dirt and is so worried about catching up with his swing that he swings through offspeed pitches.

Baserunning & Defense

Uribe has plus speed, but he's not a basestealer. He doesn't have a feel for that part of the game. He can, however, turn the speed into extra bases. He's a joy to watch running out a triple. In the field, he has impressive skills. His arm, range and hands are well above average. He makes the play in the hole look easy and is so athletic his double-play pivots are simplified. However, he makes too many lackadaisical errors. He has to show better concentration to move his game to the next level.

2004 Outlook

Feeling they weren't getting through to Uribe, the Rockies traded him to the White Sox for infielder Aaron Miles in December. The White Sox will find they have a player with the skills to play shortstop that few others have, and the natural ability makes it tough to not play him, even if he doesn't get better.

Position: SS/2B
Bats: R **Throws:** R
Ht: 5'11" **Wt:** 173

Opening Day Age: 24
Born: 7/22/79 in Bani, DR
ML Seasons: 3
Pronunciation: ohh-ree-bay

Overall Statistics

	G	AB	R	H	D	T	HR	RBI	SB	BB	SO	Avg	OBP	Slg
'03	87	316	45	80	19	3	10	33	7	17	60	.253	.297	.427
Car.	314	1155	146	298	59	21	24	135	19	59	235	.258	.298	.408

Where He Hits the Ball

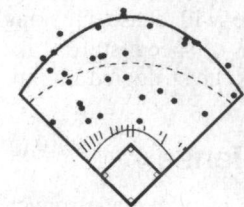 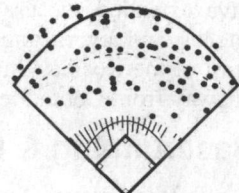

Vs. LHP   **Vs. RHP**

2003 Situational Stats

	AB	H	HR	RBI	Avg		AB	H	HR	RBI	Avg
Home	160	42	6	22	.263	LHP	83	25	2	7	.301
Road	156	38	4	11	.244	RHP	233	55	8	26	.236
First Half	160	40	5	17	.250	Sc Pos	69	19	2	21	.275
Scnd Half	156	40	5	16	.256	Clutch	38	5	0	2	.132

2003 Rankings (National League)

- 9th in fewest GDPs per GDP situation (5.4%)
- Led the Rockies in sacrifice bunts (6) and fewest GDPs per GDP situation (5.4%)

Larry Walker

2003 Season

Larry Walker used his no-trade clause to block a trade to Arizona, then talked about showing the Rockies they had a good thing. Things didn't work out. Although Walker played 140 games for only the second time in six years, his production was notably down. He did reach a career-high in walks, but failed to hit .300 for the first time in seven years.

Hitting

Walker has gone backwards. His bat is slow, his body is old. He doesn't show the desire to be the player he once was. In 2003, he didn't have the bat speed or quickness that was so key to his success. He gets himself out a lot, chasing pitches. He's not the zone-type hitter most good hitters are. He has survived in the past off his raw talents.

Baserunning & Defense

Walker has instincts on the bases and in the outfield that others can only dream about. He often trotted to first base last year, which cost him and the Rockies on close plays. Once he reached base, though, he showed he can still get an extra base, and he never tries to do too much. In right field, Walker does not track the ball as quickly as he used to. His arm is solid. What he lacks in carry he makes up for by never throwing to the wrong base and rarely overthrowing a cutoff man.

2004 Outlook

In October, Walker underwent surgery to repair a torn labrum in his left shoulder and a torn ligament in his right knee. He admitted he was embarrassed by the way he played last season, but will that provide him with motivation to bounce back? He did, for the first time, spend the winter working out with the Rockies' strength and conditioning coach, a sign that he may be taking his age and declining production seriously.

Position: RF
Bats: L **Throws:** R
Ht: 6' 3" **Wt:** 235

Opening Day Age: 37
Born: 12/1/66 in Maple Ridge, BC, Canada
ML Seasons: 15

Overall Statistics

G	AB	R	H	D	T	HR	RBI	SB	BB	SO	Avg	OBP	Slg
143	454	86	129	25	7	16	79	7	98	87	.284	.422	.476
1806	6334	1238	1992	435	57	351	1212	222	823	1110	.314	.400	.567

Where He Hits the Ball

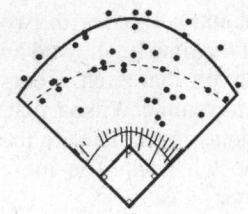
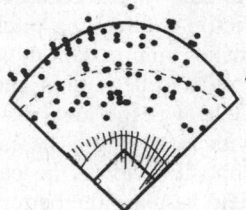

Vs. LHP   **Vs. RHP**

2003 Situational Stats

	AB	H	HR	RBI	Avg		AB	H	HR	RBI	Avg
Home	234	79	8	50	.338	LHP	156	50	4	32	.321
Road	220	50	8	29	.227	RHP	298	79	12	47	.265
First Half	292	86	9	54	.295	Sc Pos	134	41	3	63	.306
Sond Half	162	43	7	25	.265	Clutch	68	18	1	9	.265

2003 Rankings (National League)

- 5th in triples, on-base percentage, lowest batting average on the road and lowest fielding percentage in right field (.983)
- 6th in intentional walks (14) and errors in right field (4)
- Led the Rockies in triples, hit by pitch (11) and highest groundball-flyball ratio (1.8)

Preston Wilson

2003 Season

Acquired from Florida in the three-team deal that sent Mike Hampton to Atlanta, Preston Wilson had a breakthrough season in 2003. He led the National League with 141 RBI and earned an All-Star selection while also reaching career bests in home runs and average. He benefited from hitting between the lefthanded bats of Todd Helton and Larry Walker, particularly against righthanded pitchers, who challenged him rather than pitch to Walker.

Hitting

Wilson can hit a fastball a long way. The biggest difference in him last year was his plate patience. He still would get in ruts where he was an easy victim to breaking pitches, and not just with two strikes on him. But most of the time he showed an ability to be patient and lay off that pitch. Coors Field was the ideal place to remind Wilson that, with his strength, he can do as much damage the opposite way as he can to left field. The more field he uses, the better hitter he is.

Baserunning & Defense

Wilson will get some belated jumps, but he has the speed to outrun his mistakes, and at Coors Field he was able to put his physical abilities on display. He has a plus arm for a center fielder, and most likely will eventually wind up in right field. He is athletic and goes over the fence to make plays. Wilson has basestealing speed, but hitting between Helton and Walker, he has to be careful picking his spots.

2004 Outlook

Wilson has the physical tools to be a perennial All-Star. Putting together a second quality season in a row would go a long way toward helping him prove he has arrived. He should be better equipped to deal with the second-half physical demands of Colorado's altitude, having been through one full season at Coors Field.

Position: CF
Bats: R **Throws:** R
Ht: 6' 2" **Wt:** 213

Opening Day Age: 29
Born: 7/19/74 in Bamberg, SC
ML Seasons: 6

Overall Statistics

	G	AB	R	H	D	T	HR	RBI	SB	BB	SO	Avg	OBP	Slg
'03	155	600	94	169	43	1	36	141	14	54	139	.282	.343	.537
Car.	751	2716	412	724	153	12	140	472	102	255	750	.267	.335	.486

Where He Hits the Ball

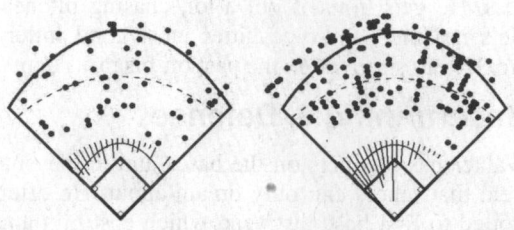

Vs. LHP	**Vs. RHP**

2003 Situational Stats

	AB	H	HR	RBI	Avg		AB	H	HR	RBI	Avg
Home	308	93	21	84	.302	LHP	179	49	5	25	.274
Road	292	76	15	57	.260	RHP	421	120	31	116	.285
First Half	374	115	23	91	.307	Sc Pos	207	65	15	110	.314
Scnd Half	226	54	13	50	.239	Clutch	66	16	3	13	.242

2003 Rankings (National League)

- 1st in RBI
- 2nd in errors in center field (7), lowest percentage of pitches taken (47.7) and lowest fielding percentage in center field (.980)
- 4th in GDPs (23)
- Led the Rockies in home runs, at-bats, RBI, stolen bases, caught stealing (7), strikeouts, HR frequency (16.7 ABs per HR), stolen-base percentage (66.7), steals of third (3) and cleanup slugging percentage (.539)
- Led NL center fielders in RBI

Mark Bellhorn

Position: 3B/2B
Bats: B **Throws:** R
Ht: 6' 1" **Wt:** 205

Opening Day Age: 29
Born: 8/23/74 in Boston, MA
ML Seasons: 6

Overall Statistics

	G	AB	R	H	D	T	HR	RBI	SB	BB	SO	Avg	OBP	Slg
'03	99	249	27	55	10	1	2	26	5	50	78	.221	.353	.293
Car.	371	1017	160	234	45	8	36	106	21	170	339	.230	.345	.396

2003 Situational Stats

	AB	H	HR	RBI	Avg		AB	H	HR	RBI	Avg
Home	130	30	1	17	.231	LHP	71	15	1	11	.211
Road	119	25	1	9	.210	RHP	178	40	1	15	.225
First Half	192	43	2	24	.224	Sc Pos	64	11	0	23	.172
Scnd Half	57	12	0	2	.211	Clutch	38	5	1	1	.132

2003 Season

Acquired from the Cubs in mid-June, Mark Bellhorn struggled to prove he could duplicate the 27-home run effort of 2002. He had only three extra-base hits, all doubles, in 110 at-bats with the Rockies and drove in just four runs. Given a chance off the bench, he was 3-for-22 as a pinch-hitter, but did have six walks.

Hitting, Baserunning & Defense

Bellhorn's weaknesses have been exposed: just keep the ball away from him and he won't come close. He is overmatched by sinkers and sliders. His only hope is when a pitcher tries to overpower him and gets the ball out over the plate. Bellhorn can play a lot of positions, but none well enough to be an everyday player. He doesn't have the quickness needed at third base nor the lateral movement to handle second. He also can fill in briefly at short, play first and left field. He has decent speed but isn't a steal threat.

2004 Outlook

Because he is a switch-hitter, because he has filled in at so many positions and because he did hit those 27 home runs in 2002, Bellhorn will get a long look in a utility role or as a part-time player at second base.

Ronnie Belliard

Position: 2B
Bats: R **Throws:** R
Ht: 5' 8" **Wt:** 197

Opening Day Age: 28
Born: 4/7/75 in Bronx, NY
ML Seasons: 6
Pronunciation: BELL-ee-yard

Overall Statistics

	G	AB	R	H	D	T	HR	RBI	SB	BB	SO	Avg	OBP	Slg
'03	116	447	73	124	31	2	8	50	7	49	71	.277	.351	.409
Car.	605	2133	316	567	133	18	38	224	25	248	325	.266	.343	.398

2003 Situational Stats

	AB	H	HR	RBI	Avg		AB	H	HR	RBI	Avg
Home	196	61	6	31	.311	LHP	113	39	4	20	.345
Road	251	63	2	19	.251	RHP	334	85	4	30	.254
First Half	258	77	2	24	.298	Sc Pos	98	31	2	41	.316
Scnd Half	189	47	6	26	.249	Clutch	49	9	1	4	.184

2003 Season

Ronnie Belliard went from a non-roster invitee to spring training with minimal chances of making the team to the Rockies' Opening Day second baseman. He started 105 games, and his .277 average and 50 RBI were his best in three years.

Hitting, Baserunning & Defense

Belliard is OK on an ordinary team. He's not going to make the team any better. He will have a few good at-bats when he focuses on driving the ball the other way to right-center. Then he becomes pull-conscious again. He's not big enough or strong enough to yank the ball on a consistent basis. Belliard has average speed, at best, and a roly-poly body. Too bad he refuses to get in shape. He has soft hands and a strong arm for a second baseman, but he gets lazy and tries to make routine plays spectacular, which leads to errors.

2004 Outlook

Released by the Rockies in November, Belliard's options are limited. He is a second baseman and nothing else. He'll find a role with a second-division team, and give them a capable player in the middle of the infield, but nothing close to what Milwaukee expected when it first brought Belliard to the big leagues.

Adam Bernero

Position: RP/SP
Bats: R **Throws:** R
Ht: 6' 4" **Wt:** 210

Opening Day Age: 27
Born: 11/28/76 in Los Gatos, CA
ML Seasons: 4
Pronunciation: bur-NAIR-o

Overall Statistics

	W	L	Pct.	ERA	G	GS	Sv	IP	H	BB	SO	HR	Avg
'03	1	14	.067	5.87	49	17	0	133.1	137	54	80	19	.267
Car.	5	22	.185	5.85	94	32	0	281.2	311	102	177	43	.283

2003 Situational Stats

	W	L	ERA	Sv	IP		AB	H	HR	RBI	Avg
Home	1	7	5.96	0	68.0	LHB	265	81	10	42	.306
Road	0	7	5.79	0	65.1	RHB	249	56	9	38	.225
First Half	1	12	6.08	0	100.2	Sc Pos	127	36	4	58	.283
Scnd Half	0	2	5.23	0	32.2	Clutch	44	13	2	9	.295

2003 Season

Adam Bernero was acquired from Detroit in a July trade for Ben Petrick. A starter with the Tigers, Bernero was moved into the bullpen with the Rockies. Initially, he did well, but his consistency disappeared and in his final 19 innings he allowed 17 earned runs. He retired only 19 of 32 first batters faced and allowed nine of 13 inherited runners to score.

Pitching, Defense & Hitting

Bernero needs to learn to use his fastball and pitch off it. He has a quality changeup and a split-finger fastball, but you can't survive without the fastball. He has average velocity, 90-91 MPH, and it is straight, but he can learn to hit locations and then come with the split or change and have hitters off balance. He has a clean delivery and lands in a good fielding position. He holds runners fairly well.

2004 Outlook

Bernero will be among a group of pitchers given a chance to claim a spot in the rotation. But until he refines his fastball and learns to make it his staple, he's going to find himself relegated to bullpen duty.

Brian Fuentes

Position: RP
Bats: L **Throws:** L
Ht: 6' 4" **Wt:** 220

Opening Day Age: 28
Born: 8/9/75 in Merced, CA
ML Seasons: 3
Pronunciation: foo-WHEN-tayz

Overall Statistics

	W	L	Pct.	ERA	G	GS	Sv	IP	H	BB	SO	HR	Avg
'03	3	3	.500	2.75	75	0	4	75.1	64	34	82	7	.231
Car.	6	4	.600	3.40	116	0	4	113.2	95	55	130	13	.231

2003 Situational Stats

	W	L	ERA	Sv	IP		AB	H	HR	RBI	Avg
Home	2	1	2.40	3	41.1	LHB	105	25	1	7	.238
Road	1	2	3.18	1	34.0	RHB	172	39	6	24	.227
First Half	2	0	3.22	2	44.2	Sc Pos	70	15	1	22	.214
Scnd Half	1	3	2.05	2	30.2	Clutch	113	26	2	7	.230

2003 Season

After basically making the team out of spring training because he is lefthanded and was out of options, Brian Fuentes became the mainstay in the Rockies' bullpen. He went through the month of August without allowing a run and even got a few save opportunities, converting four.

Pitching, Defense & Hitting

Fuentes describes his pitching style as trying to throw a frisbee. He comes from down under, but is not a true submariner. He has a little more giddy-up than most of the sidearmers, with a fastball that is steady in the low 90s. He can run the ball in on righthanded hitters, which allows him to stay in the game instead of being limited to lefthanded hitters only. In addition to the fastball that has a sinking action, he has a hard slider. Fuentes has a big delivery to the plate, but he does hold runners pretty well. He seldom swings the bat.

2004 Outlook

Fuentes has moved into a legitimate setup role with the ability to stay in a game and get a save. He has proven to be durable. Including time in the minors in 2002, he has reached 70 appearances in each of the last two seasons.

Javier Lopez

Position: RP
Bats: L **Throws:** L
Ht: 6' 4" **Wt:** 200

Opening Day Age: 26
Born: 7/11/77 in San Juan, PR
ML Seasons: 1

Overall Statistics

	W	L	Pct.	ERA	G	GS	Sv	IP	H	BB	SO	HR	Avg
'03	4	1	.800	3.70	75	0	1	58.1	58	12	40	5	.258
Car.	4	1	.800	3.70	75	0	1	58.1	58	12	40	5	.258

2003 Situational Stats

	W	L	ERA	Sv	IP		AB	H	HR	RBI	Avg
Home	3	0	1.71	0	31.2	LHB	116	29	2	15	.250
Road	1	1	6.08	1	26.2	RHB	109	29	3	6	.266
First Half	2	0	5.35	0	33.2	Sc Pos	62	13	1	16	.210
Scnd Half	2	1	1.46	1	24.2	Clutch	63	11	0	5	.175

2003 Season

Javier Lopez was one of the pleasant surprises in 2003. Left unprotected during the winter by Arizona and picked up by Boston, he was acquired by the Rockies in a late-spring trade. Making the jump from Double-A to the big leagues, Lopez appeared in a franchise rookie record 75 games and worked in some late-inning situations. He hit a rough spot in June, allowing nine runs in one inning over two appearances, but rebounded well, compiling a 1.46 post-All-Star ERA.

Pitching, Defense & Hitting

Lopez is a good situational lefthander. He's not afraid to throw strikes. His fastball will range from 81-85 MPH, but his funky submarine delivery makes it difficult for lefthanded hitters to pick up the ball. He has a soft slider that is his second pitch. He needs to work on his changeup, which is a distant third pitch. Lopez is a fine fielder and has an excellent pickoff move.

2004 Outlook

Lopez' role figures to grow. He will share setup duties and get a shot at an occasional save for a team that is reworking its bullpen. The more he pitches, the more success he has and the more confidence he develops.

Greg Norton

Position: 3B
Bats: B **Throws:** R
Ht: 6' 1" **Wt:** 200

Opening Day Age: 31
Born: 7/6/72 in San Leandro, CA
ML Seasons: 8
Nickname: Nawlon

Overall Statistics

	G	AB	R	H	D	T	HR	RBI	SB	BB	SO	Avg	OBP	Slg
'03	114	179	19	47	15	0	6	31	2	16	47	.263	.325	.447
Car.	681	1565	202	389	87	8	59	226	13	186	395	.249	.329	.427

2003 Situational Stats

	AB	H	HR	RBI	Avg		AB	H	HR	RBI	Avg
Home	93	28	2	20	.301	LHP	22	6	0	5	.273
Road	86	19	4	11	.221	RHP	157	41	6	26	.261
First Half	125	32	3	17	.256	Sc Pos	62	17	1	24	.274
Scnd Half	54	15	3	14	.278	Clutch	46	11	3	8	.239

2003 Season

Greg Norton has become one of the more useful extra men in baseball. He led the majors with 23 pinch-hits and 17 pinch-RBI last year, and finished with the league lead with four pinch-hit home runs.

Hitting, Baserunning & Defense

The switch-hitting Norton's power comes from the left side. He can hit good fastballs, which is why he is so good coming off the bench. However, he sometimes creates problems for himself by taking too many pitches. A below-average runner, Norton shows glimpses of being a decent third baseman. The more he thinks about defense, however, the more trouble he gets in. He doesn't set his feet well for throws, and he can get wild. He also crosses himself up in his initial step, which limits his range.

2004 Outlook

Norton will have a job. A switch-hitter who has proven he can pinch-hit is always of value. He mostly has played third base, but he can fill in at first base, and has expressed a desire to work more in the outfield to try and expand his opportunities to make an occasional start.

Steve Reed

Position: RP
Bats: R **Throws:** R
Ht: 6' 2" **Wt:** 212

Opening Day Age: 38
Born: 3/11/66 in Los
Angeles, CA
ML Seasons: 12

Overall Statistics

	W	L	Pct.	ERA	G	GS	Sv	IP	H	BB	SO	HR	Avg
'03	5	3	.625	3.27	67	0	0	63.1	59	26	39	9	.254
Car.	45	34	.570	3.50	738	0	18	772.0	698	257	577	95	.244

2003 Situational Stats

	W	L	ERA	Sv	IP			AB	H	HR	RBI	Avg
Home	4	1	3.24	0	33.1	LHB		99	37	7	19	.374
Road	1	2	3.30	0	30.0	RHB		133	22	2	10	.165
First Half	5	2	3.63	0	39.2	Sc Pos		77	14	3	20	.182
Scnd Half	0	1	2.66	0	23.2	Clutch		74	25	2	10	.338

2003 Season

At the age of 37, and in his 11th full season in the big leagues, Steve Reed reached 60-plus appearances for the 10th time. Reed never has been on the disabled list, but he did have a few extended rest periods in 2003 because of some soreness in his right triceps.

Pitching, Defense & Hitting

Reed is a luxury. He is a righthanded specialist. He is durable, but doesn't average an inning an appearance and struggles against lefthanded hitters. He is a sinker/slider pitcher with a submarine delivery that makes him extremely tough on righthanded hitters, but the movement of his pitches is in and down to lefties. He will hurry at times, and that leads to blowout innings. He has a quick move to first, which is important because he can take time to get the ball home. He gets off the mound quickly, and fields his position well.

2004 Outlook

After signing a one-year deal in December, Reed will return to Colorado as a righthanded specialist. He's going to get tough righthanded hitters out in clutch situations, but doesn't figure to get many opportunities to finish off games.

Justin Speier

Position: RP
Bats: R **Throws:** R
Ht: 6' 4" **Wt:** 205

Opening Day Age: 30
Born: 11/6/73 in Walnut
Creek, CA
ML Seasons: 6
Pronunciation:
SPY-er

Overall Statistics

	W	L	Pct.	ERA	G	GS	Sv	IP	H	BB	SO	HR	Avg
'03	3	1	.750	4.05	72	0	9	73.1	73	23	66	11	.257
Car.	19	10	.655	4.50	274	0	10	330.0	307	116	283	57	.245

2003 Situational Stats

	W	L	ERA	Sv	IP			AB	H	HR	RBI	Avg
Home	1	0	4.57	6	41.1	LHB		121	33	3	10	.273
Road	2	1	3.38	3	32.0	RHB		163	40	8	27	.245
First Half	2	1	3.19	5	48.0	Sc Pos		90	19	2	27	.211
Scnd Half	1	0	5.68	4	25.1	Clutch		135	28	4	20	.207

2003 Season

Justin Speier began the season in a setup role, then had a midseason opportunity as the closer when Jose Jimenez struggled. Speier wound up sharing the job with lefty Brian Fuentes. He appeared in a career-high 72 games and continued to be particularly effective pitching out of trouble. In his two and half seasons with the Rockies, Speier has allowed only 17 of 92 inherited runners to score.

Pitching, Defense & Hitting

Speier has legitimate strikeout stuff, but consistency still is a problem. His velocity will vary from a solid 93-95 MPH on some days to below 90 MPH on others. He has a hard slider, but he can get in trouble with that pitch because he gets floppy with his arm and it flattens out. His key pitch is a splitfinger fastball. When it is biting, he is unhittable. Speier is a fine fielder but has had some problems holding runners.

2004 Outlook

Speier will settle back into a setup role, which is where he is more comfortable. He has a tendency to get too excited when he is given the task of closing out a save.

Denny Stark

Position: SP
Bats: R **Throws:** R
Ht: 6' 2" **Wt:** 210

Opening Day Age: 29
Born: 10/27/74 in Edgerton, OH
ML Seasons: 4

Overall Statistics

	W	L	Pct.	ERA	G	GS	Sv	IP	H	BB	SO	HR	Avg
'03	3	3	.500	5.83	17	13	0	78.2	98	33	30	12	.305
Car.	15	8	.652	5.13	58	36	0	228.0	237	105	110	42	.266

2003 Situational Stats

	W	L	ERA	Sv	IP		AB	H	HR	RBI	Avg
Home	1	1	7.15	0	39.0	LHB	153	53	8	28	.346
Road	2	2	4.54	0	39.2	RHB	168	45	4	29	.268
First Half	0	0	3.94	0	16.0	Sc Pos	84	24	3	44	.286
Scnd Half	3	3	6.32	0	62.2	Clutch	1	0	0	0	.000

2003 Season

An impressive rookie in 2002, Denny Stark strained a muscle in his upper back during spring training and missed the first 84 games of the season. When he rejoined the Rockies, he went into the rotation, but struggled and by season's end was working in relief.

Pitching, Defense & Hitting

There's nothing pretty about Stark. Manager Clint Hurdle said he reminds you of the guy at the company picnic who keeps spilling food on his shirt, but by the end of the day he's won all the ribbons. His fastball is average and will touch 93 MPH at times, but he pitches up in the zone. His slider is flat and his changeup is average at best. What he does, though, is throw strikes, and there's enough deception in the delivery to give him an edge. He moves around the mound well but is so-so holding runners and was not a factor with the bat in 2003.

2004 Outlook

Stark will get a solid shot at regaining his spot in the rotation. The Rockies can overlook last year's struggles, and cling to the 11-4 season he had as a rookie in 2002, when he posted a 3.21 ERA at Coors Field.

Gregg Zaun

Position: C
Bats: B **Throws:** R
Ht: 5'10" **Wt:** 190

Opening Day Age: 32
Born: 4/14/71 in Glendale, CA
ML Seasons: 9
Pronunciation: ZAHN

Overall Statistics

	G	AB	R	H	D	T	HR	RBI	SB	BB	SO	Avg	OBP	Slg
'03	74	166	15	38	8	0	4	21	1	19	21	.229	.309	.349
Car.	579	1487	174	366	73	7	33	186	19	187	218	.246	.332	.371

2003 Situational Stats

	AB	H	HR	RBI	Avg		AB	H	HR	RBI	Avg
Home	79	17	1	9	.215	LHP	39	12	0	3	.308
Road	87	21	3	12	.241	RHP	127	26	4	18	.205
First Half	92	21	1	12	.228	Sc Pos	46	11	3	19	.239
Scnd Half	74	17	3	9	.230	Clutch	34	4	0	4	.118

2003 Season

Greg Zaun opened his season with Houston, but was released in mid-August and signed by the Rockies. A seldom-used backup to Brad Ausmus with the Astros, Zaun got into 15 games with the Rockies following his August 26 signing, catching three games a week so the staff could evaluate him as a backup for Charles Johnson this season.

Hitting, Baserunning & Defense

Zaun is an adequate backup with a little bit of offensive ability. His biggest value is leadership in the clubhouse and on the bench. He's hard-nosed. He can hit the fastball a little and is decent from both sides of the plate. However, he doesn't have the patience to handle breaking balls or offspeed pitches. He can control a pitching staff. He gets a game plan and makes sure the pitchers adhere to it. He moves pretty well on balls in the dirt and has an average arm.

2004 Outlook

Zaun is a backup catcher. Being a switch-hitter gives him a little extra value, but with most teams the key is being able to hit from the left side. At his age, he's not going to suddenly move into an everyday role.

Other Colorado Rockies

Luke Allen (**Pos**: RF, **Age**: 25, **Bats**: L)

	G	AB	R	H	D	T	HR	RBI	SB	BB	SO	Avg	OBP	Slg
'03	2	2	0	0	0	0	0	0	0	0	0	.000	.000	.000
Car.	8	9	2	1	1	0	0	0	0	2	3	.111	.273	.222

The former Dodgers farmhand has a .297 lifetime average in the minors and has the speed and pop to possibly earn a spot on the bench. 2004 Outlook: C

Brent Butler (**Pos**: 2B, **Age**: 26, **Bats**: R)

	G	AB	R	H	D	T	HR	RBI	SB	BB	SO	Avg	OBP	Slg
'03	37	90	13	19	3	1	1	4	1	7	13	.211	.276	.300
Car.	203	553	85	137	28	6	11	60	4	24	60	.248	.285	.380

Butler has spent parts of the last four seasons in Triple-A Colorado Springs. A lifetime .302 hitter in the minors, he is looking for his first full-time job in the bigs. He signed with the Cardinals in December. 2004 Outlook: C

Nelson Cruz (**Pos**: RHP, **Age**: 31)

	W	L	Pct.	ERA	G	GS	Sv	IP	H	BB	SO	HR	Avg
'03	3	5	.375	7.21	20	7	0	53.2	65	11	38	15	.301
Car.	15	23	.395	5.04	204	18	2	348.1	369	109	277	59	.272

Cruz has had shoulder problems in each of the last two years. His ERA has risen every season since he posted a 3.07 mark in 2000, and he has pitched for four different clubs in six seasons. 2004 Outlook: C

Scott Elarton (**Pos**: RHP, **Age**: 28)

	W	L	Pct.	ERA	G	GS	Sv	IP	H	BB	SO	HR	Avg
'03	4	4	.500	6.27	11	10	0	51.2	73	20	20	13	.329
Car.	36	27	.571	5.03	135	81	3	558.0	568	226	415	89	.262

After shoulder surgery wiped out his 2002 campaign, Elarton is trying to regain the form that allowed him to win 17 games for Houston in 2000. 2004 Outlook: C

Bobby Estalella (**Pos**: C, **Age**: 29, **Bats**: R)

	G	AB	R	H	D	T	HR	RBI	SB	BB	SO	Avg	OBP	Slg
'03	46	140	17	28	7	0	7	21	2	19	55	.200	.294	.400
Car.	298	877	123	190	49	5	46	143	6	127	279	.217	.316	.441

Right elbow surgery ended Estalella's season in August. While his lifetime average is just .217, he has 46 HR and 143 RBI in about two seasons' worth of at-bats (877). 2004 Outlook: C

Denny Neagle (**Pos**: LHP, **Age**: 35)

	W	L	Pct.	ERA	G	GS	Sv	IP	H	BB	SO	HR	Avg
'03	2	4	.333	7.90	7	7	0	35.1	47	12	21	12	.320
Car.	124	92	.574	4.24	392	286	3	1890.1	1887	594	1415	250	.260

Neagle's elbow kept him out of action until the middle of June. He made just seven starts before it flared up again and sent him back to the DL. 2004 Outlook: C

Pablo Ozuna (**Pos**: 2B, **Age**: 29, **Bats**: R)

	G	AB	R	H	D	T	HR	RBI	SB	BB	SO	Avg	OBP	Slg
'03	17	40	5	8	1	0	0	2	3	2	6	.200	.273	.225
Car.	65	111	11	29	4	2	0	5	5	3	11	.261	.297	.333

Ozuna is playing some outfield to enhance his versatility. He has a lifetime minor league average of .313 and once stole 62 bases in a season. 2004 Outlook: C

Kit Pellow (**Pos**: C, **Age**: 30, **Bats**: R)

	G	AB	R	H	D	T	HR	RBI	SB	BB	SO	Avg	OBP	Slg
'03	11	18	6	8	3	1	1	4	0	0	4	.444	.476	.889
Car.	40	81	12	23	4	1	2	9	1	9	25	.284	.372	.432

Pellow has averaged 26 home runs per year in his last six minor league seasons. He can play either infield corner and even catch a little, yet has just 81 major league at-bats under his belt. 2004 Outlook: C

Chris Richard (**Pos**: LF, **Age**: 29, **Bats**: L)

	G	AB	R	H	D	T	HR	RBI	SB	BB	SO	Avg	OBP	Slg
'03	19	27	3	6	1	1	1	3	0	3	6	.222	.300	.444
Car.	267	880	131	227	57	6	34	122	18	77	176	.258	.324	.452

Richard is two left shoulder surgeries removed from his breakout 2001 campaign with Baltimore. A career .227 hitter versus lefty pitching, his best shot probably is in a platoon situation. 2004 Outlook: C

Mandy Romero (**Pos**: C, **Age**: 36, **Bats**: B)

	G	AB	R	H	D	T	HR	RBI	SB	BB	SO	Avg	OBP	Slg
'03	3	7	2	3	1	0	0	0	0	0	1	.429	.556	.571
Car.	42	77	12	16	2	0	2	5	1	6	25	.208	.282	.312

Romero has been playing professionally since 1988 and has a .273 average in 4,223 minor league at-bats. However, he has compiled a total of 77 at-bats at the big league level. 2004 Outlook: C

Jesus Sanchez (**Pos**: LHP, **Age**: 29)

	W	L	Pct.	ERA	G	GS	Sv	IP	H	BB	SO	HR	Avg
'03	0	0	–	9.00	9	0	0	8.0	11	4	2	1	.324
Car.	23	32	.418	5.26	159	80	0	510.1	546	272	376	78	.279

After showing some promise as a starter for the Marlins in the late '90s, Sanchez has tossed just 16.1 major league innings in the last two years. He has a lifetime minor league ERA of 3.66. 2004 Outlook: C

Mark Sweeney (**Pos**: RF, **Age**: 34, **Bats**: L)

	G	AB	R	H	D	T	HR	RBI	SB	BB	SO	Avg	OBP	Slg
'03	67	97	13	25	9	0	2	14	0	9	27	.258	.321	.412
Car.	643	958	110	243	50	4	18	115	9	130	209	.254	.343	.371

Sweeney has a lifetime average of .311 in the minors, but more than one-third of his at-bats in the majors have been as a pinch-hitter. He has played for four different clubs in the last five seasons. 2004 Outlook: C

Greg Vaughn (**Pos**: LF, **Age**: 38, **Bats**: R)

	G	AB	R	H	D	T	HR	RBI	SB	BB	SO	Avg	OBP	Slg
	22	37	8	7	3	0	3	5	0	8	13	.189	.326	.514
	1731	6103	1017	1475	284	23	355	1072	121	865	1513	.242	.337	.470

Vaughn hit .302 with 12 homers in Triple-A last year, his first extended trip to the minors since 1989. In the majors, however, the 38-year-old has hit .167 over the last two seasons and probably is finished. 2004 Outlook: C

Colorado Rockies Minor League Prospects

Organization Overview:

The Rockies are confident that their minor league system has made major strides. So confident, in fact, that when the managing general partners announced a two-year contract extension for GM Dan O'Dowd, which carries through 2006, the key reason cited was the improvement of player development. It's going to be another year before the real impact is felt, however. Colorado always has emphasized pitching, and last year homegrown pitchers Jason Jennings, Aaron Cook, Chin-Hui Tsao, Shawn Chacon and Cory Vance all appeared in the big leagues. Now the organization has some position players on the way, too, including Clint Barmes, Matt Holliday, Garrett Atkins and Rene Reyes. For the first time, all four Rockies full-season teams had a winning record in 2003.

Garrett Atkins

Position: 3B
Bats: R **Throws:** R
Ht: 6' 3" **Wt:** 210

Opening Day Age: 24
Born: 12/12/79 in
Orange, CA

Recent Statistics

	G	AB	R	H	D	T	HR	RBI	SB	BB	SO	Avg
2003 AAA Col Sprngs	118	439	80	140	30	1	13	67	2	45	52	.319
2003 NL Colorado	25	69	6	11	2	0	0	4	0	3	14	.159

Atkins was a first baseman when he signed out of UCLA as a fifth-round draft pick in 2000. There's no room at Coors Field at first base so he was moved to third. It's a good thing Atkins can hit because his defense is marginal. He has slow feet that cause him problems with both fielding and throwing. The question is whether he has the inner drive to push himself to get better or whether he is convinced that if he hits enough he will get to play. Atkins also is not the big bat teams look for at the corner positions. He has more of a line-drive stroke, using the gaps and piling up doubles but not hitting home runs.

Clint Barmes

Position: SS
Bats: R **Throws:** R
Ht: 6' 1" **Wt:** 175

Opening Day Age: 25
Born: 3/6/79 in
Vincennes, IN

Recent Statistics

	G	AB	R	H	D	T	HR	RBI	SB	BB	SO	Avg
2003 AAA Col Sprngs	136	493	63	136	35	1	7	54	12	22	63	.276
2003 NL Colorado	12	25	2	8	2	0	0	2	0	0	10	.320

A 10th-round pick out of Indiana State in 2000, Barmes is a grinder who wins over his manager, coaches and teammates with his work ethic. He is one of those players who have to be seen on a regular basis to be appreciated, however. There's no real standout tool here, but he relies on instincts and winds up in the middle of good things. He has an ability to make contact and drives the ball in gaps. He doesn't really have the range or arm to play shortstop but gets the job done and will have to be pushed off the position. There is little doubt he can adjust to second base and could play third if he winds up in a utility role.

Matt Holliday

Position: OF
Bats: R **Throws:** R
Ht: 6' 4" **Wt:** 215

Opening Day Age: 24
Born: 1/10/00 in
Stillwater, OK

Recent Statistics

	G	AB	R	H	D	T	HR	RBI	SB	BB	SO	Avg
2002 AA Carolina	130	463	79	128	19	2	10	64	16	67	102	.276
2003 AA Tulsa	135	522	65	132	28	5	12	72	15	43	74	.253

The Rockies thought enough of Holliday coming out of high school—when he was ranked one of the top three prep quarterbacks in the country—they gave him a $745,000 bonus despite being drafted in the seventh round. Then two years ago, when the University of Tennessee and University of Miami made another run at him, the Rockies came up with a four-year, big league deal. Converted from third base, Holliday made major strides in the past year. He has legitimate power, although it hasn't shown up in games. The key is pitch recognition and selection, particularly early in the count. He is solid in left field, although he did play some center field in the Arizona Fall League. He was so impressive in the AFL that even though he wasn't invited to try out, he was added to the roster of Team USA for the Olympic qualifying tournament.

Matt Miller

Position: P
Bats: R **Throws:** R
Ht: 6' 3" **Wt:** 215

Opening Day Age: 32
Born: 11/23/71 in
Greenwood, MS

Recent Statistics

	W	L	ERA	G	GS	Sv	IP	H	R	BB	SO	HR
2003 AAA Col Sprngs	5	0	2.13	61	0	3	63.1	46	17	23	83	0
2003 NL Colorado	0	0	2.08	4	0	0	4.1	5	1	2	5	0

Signed as a six-year free agent prior to the 2003 season, Miller made his big league debut at the age of 31 last June. He only appeared in four games before returning to Triple-A Colorado Springs, where he had a 2.13 ERA in 61 appearances in a home ballpark that is more hitter friendly than Coors Field. There's nothing really eye-catching about Miller, but he has a submarine delivery that makes it very difficult for righthanded hitters to pick up the ball. The key is his ability to throw strikes and command his pitches. He figures to be a situational righthander, along the lines of the role Steve Reed filled for the Rockies in 2003.

Rene Reyes

Position: OF
Bats: B **Throws:** R
Ht: 5' 11" **Wt:** 213

Opening Day Age: 26
Born: 2/21/78 in
Margarita, VZ

Recent Statistics

	G	AB	R	H	D	T	HR	RBI	SB	BB	SO	Avg
2003 AAA Col Sprngs	98	370	60	127	23	3	6	50	12	22	56	.343
2003 NL Colorado	53	116	13	30	7	1	2	7	2	5	19	.259

Reyes is a skilled athlete, but motivation is a major question. A converted catcher, who at first moved to first base, he became an outfielder in 2001 and can play any of the three positions. He has a plus arm from left and center and a solid-average right-field arm. He is refining his jumps, particularly in left field. Reyes can hit, and has the type of approach that promises to eventually produce 20-plus home runs. He can be a bit unorthodox, but he consistently brings the head of the bat through the zone and makes solid contact. He also can steal bases, although he won't lead the big leagues like he has in the minors.

Chin-Hui Tsao

Position: P
Bats: R **Throws:** R
Ht: 6' 2" **Wt:** 177

Opening Day Age: 22
Born: 6/2/81 in
Hua-Lien, Taiwan

Recent Statistics

	W	L	ERA	G	GS	Sv	IP	H	R	BB	SO	HR
2003 AA Tulsa	11	4	2.46	18	18	0	113.1	88	34	26	125	7
2003 NL Colorado	3	3	6.02	9	8	0	43.1	48	30	20	29	11

Tsao represented the Rockies' first effort in the Asian market. The righthander from Taiwan received a $2.2 million bonus when he signed out of Taiwan in 1999. His career was slowed by reconstructive elbow surgery in 2001, but Tsao has regained his status as one of the elite pitching prospects in the game. He has a fastball with life that will sit in the mid-90s. His key pitch is a hard slider that has a sharp break. He has refined his changeup since coming back from surgery. He has a tendency to get lackadaisical because he overmatched talent at lower levels, which hurt him in his big league debut in 2003.

Cory Vance

Position: P
Bats: L **Throws:** L
Ht: 6' 1" **Wt:** 195

Opening Day Age: 24
Born: 6/29/79 in Dayton, OH

Recent Statistics

	W	L	ERA	G	GS	Sv	IP	H	R	BB	SO	HR
2003 AAA Col Sprngs	9	11	4.63	24	24	0	157.1	179	89	50	96	18
2003 NL Colorado	1	3	5.60	9	3	0	27.1	31	19	10	12	6

A fourth-round draft choice out of Georgia Tech in 2000, Vance has had to work to command a fastball that most often barely touches 90 MPH, but can occasionally hit 93. Without command of the fastball, he's not going to be able to pitch in the big leagues. He needs that pitch to set up a quality curveball and excellent change, which is vital for him to be effective against righthanded batters. He is a good athlete who moves around the mound well, and can negate an opponent's small-ball game. He needs to build stamina; after an 8-4 start at Triple-A Colorado Springs last year, he lost seven of his final nine decisions.

Jason Young

Position: P
Bats: R **Throws:** R
Ht: 6' 5" **Wt:** 210

Opening Day Age: 24
Born: 9/28/79 in
Oakland, CA

Recent Statistics

	W	L	ERA	G	GS	Sv	IP	H	R	BB	SO	HR
2003 AAA Col Sprngs	6	7	3.95	23	21	0	116.1	128	63	37	99	10
2003 NL Colorado	0	2	8.44	8	3	0	21.1	34	22	9	18	8

Young received a franchise record $2.75 million signing bonus after being a second-round pick out of Stanford in 2000. He didn't sign until late, making his pro debut in 2001. Young has a solid fastball that will sit in the low 90s, but it doesn't have a lot of movement. He has worked with both a curveball and slider, and has shown a quick mastery of the slider. He has an intellect for pitching, and is trying to develop some deception in his delivery with a little shoulder tilt to keep hitters from getting such a good view of his fastball. He still needs to gain upper-body strength, which could help with adding a little giddy-up to the fastball.

Others to Watch

Catcher **J.D. Closser** (24) put together a solid year in his second year at Double-A. He has a live bat and handles a pitching staff well, but he still needs to work on his throwing mechanics. The arm strength is there. . . Lefthanded pitcher **Jeff Francis** (23) was dominating in the second half in the high Class-A California League in 2003, showing an ability to mix his pitches and keep hitters off-balance with a low-90s fastball and excellent change. . . Righthander **Ubaldo Jimenez** (20) has a chance to come on in a hurry after making a late-season move from Class-A Asheville to high Class-A Visalia in 2003. He has a mid-90s fastball and hard-breaking curveball that buckles knees. . . **Ching-Lung Lo** (18) is out of the same high school in Taiwan as Tsao. The righthander is tall and skinny, still working to develop upper-body strength. He has a live arm and a nasty split-finger pitch that overmatches hitters. . . There's nothing about **Aaron Miles** (27) that excites scouts, but the little guy is a ballplayer. His game came together at Double-A Birmingham in 2002, when he was named Southern League MVP. Miles was traded from the White Sox in early December for Juan Uribe, and the Rockies hope to use him primarily at second base in 2004. . . Second baseman **Jayson Nix** (21) is a gamer. He hit in the top four spots in the lineup at high Class-A Visalia last year and tied for the minor league lead in doubles. He's a Bobby Grich type. . . **Ian Stewart** (18) was the Rockies' first-round selection last June. He has a tremendous power bat and shows the potential to become a quality third baseman.

Pro Player Stadium

Offense

In their offseason planning, the Marlins set out to construct a club that fit Pro Player Stadium better than recent editions had. Emphasizing contact hitters and speed merchants over strikeout-laden sluggers, the Marlins did set a franchise mark with a 53-28 (.654) home record compared to 38-43 (.469) on the road. However, most of that difference was due to the pitching staff: except for home runs, the Marlins' offense performed about the same at home and on the road.

Defense

The Marlins' pitching staff, helped by the fact that home runs are very hard to hit at Pro Player, posted a 3.17 ERA at home, nearly two runs better than its mark (4.98) on the road. Outfielders are challenged by the Teal Tower, a 26.5-foot-high out-of-town scoreboard, which causes more than its share of odd caroms. Right field is very spacious, forcing center fielder Juan Pierre to range far to his right and left into the gaps. Deep left-center features the Bermuda Triangle at 434 feet. The infield and outfield grass is among the fastest in the league, which caused late-season addition Jeff Conine some difficulties.

Who It Helps the Most

Miguel Cabrera, Luis Castillo, Pudge Rodriguez and Juan Pierre all thrived at Pro Player last year. Most of the Marlins' pitchers had much better ERAs at home than on the road, notably Carl Pavano, Mark Redman and Brad Penny.

Who It Hurts the Most

Most power hitters will see their home-run production suffer at Pro Player—especially righty swingers. Juan Encarnacion and Alex Gonzalez had better averages away from home last year.

Rookies & Newcomers

Setup man Chad Fox, who arrived in mid-August, allowed just one earned run in 11 regular-season outings at home. A first baseman with power potential, acquired from the Cubs in the Derrek Lee trade, Hee Seop Choi won't be helped by Pro Player Stadium's dimensions. But he has enough to focus on without thinking about the longball.

Dimensions: LF-330, LCF-385, CF-404, RCF-385, RF-345

Capacity: 36,331

Elevation: 10 feet

Surface: Grass

Foul Territory: Average

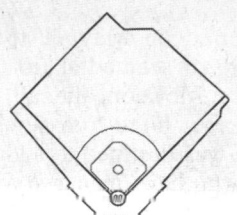

Park Factors

2003 Season

| | Home Games | | | Away Games | | | |
	Marlins	Opp	Total	Marlins	Opp	Total	Index
G	72	72	144	72	72	144	
Avg	.273	.240	.256	.259	.268	.263	97
AB	2403	2501	4904	2479	2369	4848	101
R	340	264	604	308	326	634	95
H	656	599	1255	641	636	1277	98
2B	113	122	235	145	145	290	80
3B	23	21	44	16	10	26	167
HR	64	45	109	74	63	137	79
BB	240	237	477	219	237	456	103
SO	425	571	996	451	451	902	109
E	33	46	79	41	56	97	81
E-Infield	28	37	65	37	48	85	76
LHB-Avg	.303	.231	.262	.260	.267	.263	100
LHB-HR	4	16	20	3	20	23	83
RHB-Avg	.260	.245	.253	.258	.269	.263	96
RHB-HR	60	29	89	71	43	114	79

2001-2003

| | Home Games | | | Away Games | | | |
	Marlins	Opp	Total	Marlins	Opp	Total	Index
G	215	215	430	217	217	434	
Avg	.268	.247	.257	.257	.272	.264	97
AB	7143	7442	14585	7537	7185	14722	100
R	994	890	1884	907	1086	1993	95
H	1915	1835	3750	1934	1957	3891	97
2B	375	380	755	416	407	823	93
3B	63	65	128	30	46	76	170
HR	199	170	369	216	223	439	85
BB	754	804	1558	642	813	1455	108
SO	1404	1691	3095	1508	1315	2823	111
E	117	132	249	145	154	299	84
E-Infield	93	108	201	124	130	254	80
LHB-Avg	.277	.247	.258	.260	.284	.275	94
LHB-HR	33	62	95	32	89	121	75
RHB-Avg	.265	.246	.257	.255	.264	.259	99
RHB-HR	166	108	274	184	134	318	89

2003 Rankings (National League)

- Lowest double factor
- Lowest home-run factor
- Lowest infield-error factor
- Second-lowest error factor
- Second-lowest RHB home-run factor

Jack McKeon

2003 Season

When Jack McKeon was hired on May 11 to replace the fired Jeff Torborg, it seemed at first like some sort of practical joke. McKeon, after all, was 72, the oldest manager ever hired to a new position. However, McKeon was destined to add his name to the list of men who have managed a World Series champion. He also pocketed the National League's Manager of the Year Award. McKeon wanted his young team to have fun, but he also pushed all the right psychological buttons to coax maximum performance from certain underachievers.

Offense

McKeon isn't afraid to tinker with his batting order, often dropping a slumping hitter a few spots until he gets going again. He doesn't use his bench much, preferring to ride the regulars until they drop. McKeon's resumé suggested he wasn't the right man for a speed-first lineup, but he adapted to the dual-leadoff man concept and gave Juan Pierre and Luis Castillo free rein at the top of the order. He became fond of the sacrifice bunt, especially with Castillo in the first inning.

Pitching & Defense

Torborg was fired in part because of the perception he was too hard on his starters, especially A.J. Burnett. However, McKeon probably was even more fearless with the demands he made on his young staff's arms—especially in the postseason. McKeon was willing to adjust bullpen roles as necessary, like dropping the slumping Braden Looper out of the closer role and moving veteran Ugueth Urbina into his place. McKeon rode the hot hand whenever possible with his bullpen.

2004 Outlook

Given a one-year extension after his World Series victory, McKeon failed to receive the multiple-year security most felt he deserved. With the Marlins planning only a modest payroll increase amid a spiraling salary structure, it's unclear how much this team will resemble the one McKeon led to the title. He will, however, move one year closer to passing Casey Stengel for second on the all-time list for oldest managers.

Born: 11/23/30 in South Amboy, NJ

Playing Experience: No major league playing experience

Managerial Experience: 13 seasons

Manager Statistics

Year	Team, Lg	W	L	Pct	GB	Finish
2003	Florida, NL	75	49	.605	10.0	2nd East
13 Seasons		845	782	.519	–	–

2003 Starting Pitchers by Days Rest

	<=3	4	5	6+
Marlins Starts	0	70	36	17
Marlins ERA	–	3.50	4.59	3.92
NL Avg Starts	2	84	43	23
NL ERA	5.00	4.23	4.42	4.68

2003 Situational Stats

	Jack McKeon	NL Average
Hit & Run Success %	42.0	32.7
Stolen Base Success %	62.7	68.9
Platoon Pct.	43.5	52.0
Defensive Subs	8	19
High-Pitch Outings	7	8
Quick/Slow Hooks	12/8	20/12
Sacrifice Attempts	92	93

2003 Rankings (National League)

- 1st in stolen base attempts (150)
- 2nd in steals of second base (85), sacrifice-bunt percentage (83.7%) and hit-and-run success percentage

Josh Beckett

2003 Season

When Josh Beckett went down with a sprained elbow ligament on May 7, few could have predicted the season would end with Beckett on the mound at Yankee Stadium, celebrating a five-hit shutout that clinched the World Series for the Marlins. Yet that's exactly what happened as Beckett, after a few years of false starts and injury scares and blister nightmares, put it all together. In the postseason, he took his intensity up another notch or five. A World Series MVP award was the result.

Pitching

After returning from an eight-week absence, Beckett was the Marlins' best pitcher in the second half. He noticeably slowed his delivery, an adjustment pitching coach Wayne Rosenthal made with several Marlins, and the change seemed to keep Beckett under control. His 93-97 MPH fastball often was overpowering and he had no trouble maintaining his stuff into the late innings. He began to get more called strikes with his big overhand curve, a pitch he showcased to great effect in the postseason. His fork-changeup was much improved as well and developed a nasty tail at the end. Extremely competitive, Beckett stopped beating himself up and finally started channeling that energy into making opponents look bad.

Defense & Hitting

Beckett never has been much of a hitter, but he tied for the staff lead in sacrifice bunts with five. He is slow to the plate but finds other ways to keep runners guessing. Beckett is a good athlete with good instincts in the field.

2004 Outlook

The cost-conscious Marlins forced Beckett to take the maximum pay cut of 20 percent in 2002, but this time around they gladly will pay him the $2 million or so he is due. He won't qualify for salary arbitration until next winter, but he stands as the unquestioned ace of the staff.

Position: SP
Bats: R **Throws:** R
Ht: 6' 5" **Wt:** 218

Opening Day Age: 23
Born: 5/15/80 in Spring, TX
ML Seasons: 3

Florida

Overall Statistics

	W	L	Pct.	ERA	G	GS	Sv	IP	H	BB	SO	HR	Avg
'03	9	8	.529	3.04	24	23	0	142.0	132	56	152	9	.246
Car.	17	17	.500	3.32	51	48	0	273.2	239	111	289	25	.233

2003 Pitching Profile

	Josh Beckett	NL Average
Overall Strike %	63.5	62.4
1st Pitch Strike %	62.0	58.4
Ratio	1.32	1.38
Strikeouts per 9 IP	9.63	6.65
Walks per 9 IP	3.55	3.42
Home Runs per 9 IP	0.57	1.05
Strikeout/Walk Ratio	2.71	1.94
Groundball/Flyball Ratio	1.33	1.29

2003 Situational Stats

	W	L	ERA	Sv	IP		AB	H	HR	RBI	Avg
Home	7	3	2.67	0	84.1	LHB	241	53	3	15	.220
Road	2	5	3.59	0	57.2	RHB	296	79	6	29	.267
First Half	3	4	3.86	0	53.2	Sc Pos	125	24	2	32	.192
Scnd Half	6	4	2.55	0	88.1	Clutch	30	9	2	4	.300

2003 Rankings (National League)

- 4th in lowest ERA at home
- Led the Marlins in ERA, strikeouts, runners caught stealing (5), highest strikeout-walk ratio (2.7), lowest slugging percentage allowed (.352), highest groundball-flyball ratio allowed (1.3), lowest stolen-base percentage allowed (50.0), lowest ERA at home, lowest ERA on the road, lowest batting average allowed with runners in scoring position, fewest home runs allowed per nine innings (.57) and most strikeouts per nine innings (9.6)

Miguel Cabrera

2003 Season

The Marlins' top prospect, Miguel Cabrera got extra playing time in spring training as incumbent third baseman Mike Lowell battled a lower back problem. That exposure proved invaluable when Cabrera was promoted to the majors on June 20 to replace a struggling Todd Hollandsworth in left field. Despite playing the position in just three games at Double-A Carolina, Cabrera looked surprisingly natural in the outfield over the next two-plus months. When Lowell suffered a broken hand on August 30, Cabrera moved back to third and looked like a perennial All-Star. All of this at age 20.

Hitting

Cabrera absolutely kills lefties. Against quality righthanders he tends to be somewhat mortal, especially when they feed him a steady diet of breaking balls. Fastballs don't bother him, as he showed in the World Series when he took Roger Clemens deep after an early dusting. He has power to all fields but does tend to be streaky. He went into a couple of different funks where he chased breaking balls in the dirt, but worked his way out of them each time.

Baserunning & Defense

Cabrera is an average runner at best and no threat to steal. Defensively, he moved to right field during the playoffs and showed remarkable skill out there. His arm is strong and fairly accurate in the outfield. At third he is agile and capable of making plays to both his right and left. A tremendous natural athlete, Cabrera even played three playoff innings at shortstop, his original position.

2004 Outlook

Cabrera will be in the Marlins' lineup. At the end of the 2003 season, the only question was where he would play. It won't be at third base, where he says he feels most comfortable, because Mike Lowell and the Marlins agreed to a long-term deal in December. So Cabrera will play one of the corner outfield spots in 2004. Long term, he could wind up at first, but that appears years away.

Position: LF/3B
Bats: R **Throws:** R
Ht: 6' 2" **Wt:** 185

Opening Day Age: 20
Born: 4/18/83 in Maracay, VZ
ML Seasons: 1

Overall Statistics

	G	AB	R	H	D	T	HR	RBI	SB	BB	SO	Avg	OBP	Slg
'03	87	314	39	84	21	3	12	62	0	25	84	.268	.325	.468
Car.	87	314	39	84	21	3	12	62	0	25	84	.268	.325	.468

Where He Hits the Ball

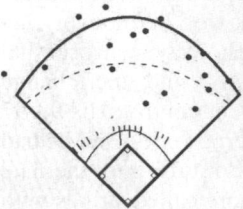 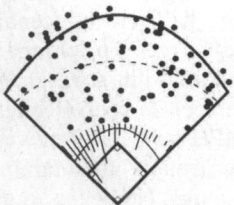

Vs. LHP   **Vs. RHP**

2003 Situational Stats

	AB	H	HR	RBI	Avg		AB	H	HR	RBI	Avg
Home	151	44	7	35	.291	LHP	55	20	3	11	.364
Road	163	40	5	27	.245	RHP	259	64	9	51	.247
First Half	76	17	4	14	.224	Sc Pos	96	36	4	48	.375
Scnd Half	238	67	8	48	.282	Clutch	49	9	2	7	.184

2003 Rankings (National League)

- 2nd in home runs among rookies and RBI among rookies
- 4th in batting average with runners in scoring position and most GDPs per GDP situation (21.4%)
- 5th in batting average among rookies
- 9th in batting average with the bases loaded (.500)
- Led the Marlins in batting average with runners in scoring position and batting average with the bases loaded (.500)

Luis Castillo

Gold Glover

2003 Season

Coming off a 2002 season highlighted by a 35-game hitting streak, Luis Castillo posted his second straight All-Star season. The former leadoff man assumed an unfamiliar role as the No. 2 hitter behind Juan Pierre, but set single-season highs for hits, home runs and slugging percentage.

Hitting

Castillo grasps his limitations and works hard to keep the ball on the ground. He's an excellent bunter and regularly ranks among the leaders in infield hits. A natural righthanded hitter, he's belted all but one of his 14 career homers from that side. From the left side, he slashes and dashes, cutting down on his swing and taking balls the other way. When he gets into occasional funks, he will chase high fastballs. He can be jammed with quality inside fastballs and quality breaking balls on the hands, more so from the left side. He has worked hard to improve his situational hitting and no longer breaks out in a cold sweat with runners in scoring position.

Baserunning & Defense

Following offseason surgery to repair a torn labrum in his left hip, Castillo wasn't quite as dangerous on the bases. The two-time stolen-base champion saw his success rate fall to 53 percent, a huge dropoff from the career mark of 73 percent he carried into the season. Blessed with perhaps the strongest arm of any second baseman, Castillo combined with shortstop Alex Gonzalez for countless flashy double plays. He won his first Gold Glove while playing error-free ball over his final 65 games during the regular season.

2004 Outlook

A free agent for the first time, Castillo enjoyed significant interest in his services around the majors. He wanted to remain in Florida, and he and the Marlins worked out a three-year, $16 million deal to stay with the team. The contract has a club option for 2007, which would push its total value to more than $21 million. Because Castillo never has played under more than a one-year contract, it will be interesting to see how he reacts to his newfound security.

Position: 2B
Bats: B **Throws:** R
Ht: 5'11" **Wt:** 190

Opening Day Age: 28
Born: 9/12/75 in San Pedro de Macoris, DR
ML Seasons: 8
Pronunciation: ca-STEE-yo

Florida

Overall Statistics

	G	AB	R	H	D	T	HR	RBI	SB	BB	SO	Avg	OBP	Slg
'03	152	595	99	187	19	6	6	39	21	63	60	.314	.381	.397
Car.	856	3344	512	977	106	31	14	194	250	393	529	.292	.367	.355

Where He Hits the Ball

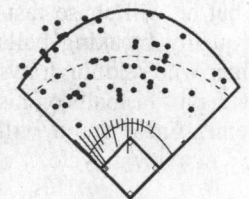 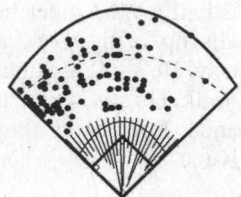

Vs. LHP   **Vs. RHP**

2003 Situational Stats

	AB	H	HR	RBI	Avg		AB	H	HR	RBI	Avg
Home	288	94	2	20	.326	LHP	172	55	6	13	.320
Road	307	93	4	19	.303	RHP	423	132	0	26	.312
First Half	354	110	6	26	.311	Sc Pos	133	38	1	31	.286
Scnd Half	241	77	0	13	.320	Clutch	88	27	1	9	.307

2003 Rankings (National League)

- 1st in sacrifice bunts (15), highest groundball-flyball ratio (2.8) and lowest stolen-base percentage (52.5)
- 2nd in singles, caught stealing (19) and fielding percentage at second base (.986)
- 3rd in lowest percentage of swings that missed (7.5) and batting average with two strikes (.286)
- Led the Marlins in batting average, sacrifice bunts (15), on-base percentage, highest groundball-flyball ratio (2.8), highest percentage of pitches taken (61.0), batting average vs. righthanded pitchers, batting average at home, batting average on the road and batting average with two strikes (.286)

Juan Encarnacion

2003 Season

After coming to Florida in a midseason trade with Cincinnati in 2002, Juan Encarnacion was expected to flourish in his first full season with the Marlins. While Encarnacion set a career high with 94 RBI and 37 doubles, he somehow left onlookers wanting more. His five-tool talent helped the team make the playoffs, but he didn't do much once there, as rookie Miguel Cabrera usually played ahead of him in right field. Encarnacion's .184 postseason average was one of the poorest on the club.

Hitting

A classic mistake hitter, Encarnacion will punish hanging breaking balls. He can handle the average fastball on the inner half, but he will chase fastballs up in the zone and quality breaking balls away. He's an impatient hitter who seldom draws a walk. He can be tied up with plus fastballs on his hands. Streaky as they come, Encarnacion will give at-bats away when he's in a down cycle.

Baserunning & Defense

Encarnacion had his share of misplays in right but managed to make it through the whole year without being charged with an error. Encarnacion has gone 220 games without an outfield error, the third-longest streak in the majors. He has a plus arm and plus range, but his concentration lags at times. His throwing accuracy isn't the best, in part because he throws the ball with just one finger. On the bases, he is an above-average runner who just missed out on his second straight 20/20 season. He had just seven stolen bases in his final 114 games, however.

2004 Outlook

As a fifth-year arbitration candidate, Encarnacion stands to receive a raise into the $5.5 million range. The cost-cutting Marlins are expected to deal or non-tender him, forcing him to start over yet again. He didn't make the front office happy when he complained about playing time during the postseason.

Position: RF
Bats: R **Throws:** R
Ht: 6' 3" **Wt:** 215

Opening Day Age: 28
Born: 3/8/76 in Las Matas de Farfan, DR
ML Seasons: 7
Pronunciation: en-car-NAH-see-own

Overall Statistics

	G	AB	R	H	D	T	HR	RBI	SB	BB	SO	Avg	OBP	Slg
'03	156	601	80	162	37	6	19	94	19	37	82	.270	.313	.446
Car.	752	2855	379	770	143	35	96	403	108	161	534	.270	.313	.445

Where He Hits the Ball

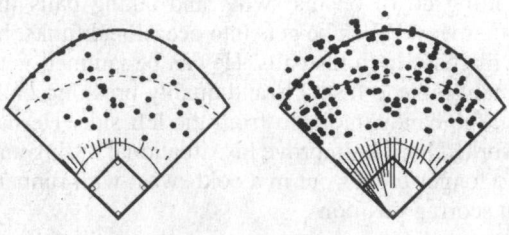

Vs. LHP   **Vs. RHP**

2003 Situational Stats

	AB	H	HR	RBI	Avg		AB	H	HR	RBI	Avg
Home	292	74	9	49	.253	LHP	116	31	2	19	.267
Road	309	88	10	45	.285	RHP	485	131	17	75	.270
First Half	357	101	12	58	.283	Sc Pos	164	43	4	68	.262
Scnd Half	244	61	7	36	.250	Clutch	90	23	2	10	.256

2003 Rankings (National League)

- 1st in fielding percentage in right field (1.000)
- 8th in lowest stolen-base percentage (70.4)
- 9th in triples
- 10th in at-bats
- Led the Marlins in doubles and sacrifice flies (6)

Alex Gonzalez

2003 Season

Coming off a frustrating 2002 season in which he missed the final four-and-a-half months with a shoulder injury that required surgery, Alex Gonzalez began 2003 with a positive attitude. He played with the visible joy demanded of him by fellow Venezuelan and Marlins third-base coach Ozzie Guillen. The result was a big first half. Alas, Gonzalez slumped badly after the break, and his problems carried into the postseason.

Hitting

Notoriously impatient, Gonzalez drew just 20 unintentional walks in 582 plate appearances, while striking out 106 times. When he's in one of his funks he can be easy to pitch to, often carrying the failure of one at-bat over to the next. His most common sin is becoming too pull-conscious, trying to hit home runs when singles will do. He is a zone fastball hitter who can punish mistake pitches over the heart of the plate. Gonzalez knows what to do with a hanger as well, as he reminded the Yankees' Jeff Weaver in the 12th inning of World Series Game 4.

Baserunning & Defense

Along with second baseman Luis Castillo, Gonzalez forms one of the most breathtaking double-play combinations in recent memory. While Gonzalez still boots the odd routine ball or makes a flip throw to first that sails too far wide, he seems to bear down on the tougher chances. His arm is above average. On the bases, he is slower than you would expect and not particularly instinctive. He is no threat to steal bases.

2004 Outlook

His arbitration-fed salary is likely to rise into the $3 million range, and Gonzalez soon could see his price tag outstrip his production. For now, the Marlins are likely to stick with him for lack of a better, cheaper alternative. It will be interesting to see how his attitude evolves now that Guillen has moved on to manage the White Sox.

Position: SS
Bats: R **Throws:** R
Ht: 6' 0" **Wt:** 200

Opening Day Age: 27
Born: 2/15/77 in Cagua, VZ
ML Seasons: 6

Florida

Overall Statistics

	G	AB	R	H	D	T	HR	RBI	SB	BB	SO	Avg	OBP	Slg
'03	150	528	52	135	33	6	18	77	0	33	106	.256	.313	.443
Car.	607	2225	251	543	123	20	53	251	15	112	465	.244	.291	.389

Where He Hits the Ball

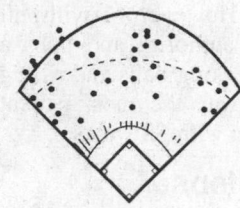

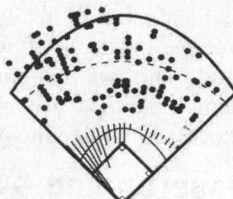

Vs. LHP **Vs. RHP**

2003 Situational Stats

	AB	H	HR	RBI	Avg		AB	H	HR	RBI	Avg
Home	256	61	7	34	.238	LHP	113	31	4	18	.274
Road	272	74	11	43	.272	RHP	415	104	14	59	.251
First Half	316	91	12	53	.288	Sc Pos	138	36	2	54	.261
Scnd Half	212	44	6	24	.208	Clutch	85	16	2	8	.188

2003 Rankings (National League)

- 4th in lowest groundball-flyball ratio (0.7)
- 5th in errors at shortstop (16) and fielding percentage at shortstop (.976)
- 6th in hit by pitch (13), lowest percentage of pitches taken (48.7) and lowest batting average at home
- 7th in intentional walks (13)
- Led the Marlins in intentional walks (13) and hit by pitch (13)

Derrek Lee

2003 Season

Derrek Lee, perhaps the most subtle star in the game, set career marks for home runs, RBI and stolen bases in 2003. He also claimed the Marlins' franchise lead for career homers and extra-base hits. His club-record playing streak of 315 games ended in late July after he fell on his shoulder trying to field a groundball, but Lee fought through the setback and finished strong.

Hitting

Lee has been penalized by his home stadium as much as any player in the majors. Just 41 of his 129 homers with the Marlins came at home. Like most tall hitters, Lee likes to get his long arms extended and can struggle with plus fastballs on his hands and in his eyes. However, he will pull average inside stuff with authority and does a good job of waiting out breaking balls and rifling them the other way. He was the most patient Marlins hitter, leading them with 88 walks.

Baserunning & Defense

After being worthy of the honor for several years, Lee finally won his first Gold Glove last season. With his massive wingspan and soft hands, he saves countless errors for his teammates on throws that are high, wide and low. He has excellent range and is accurate and aggressive with his throws, preferring to nab the lead runner whenever possible. For a big man, he moves well on the bases and set a career high with 21 stolen bases. He is an instinctive and intelligent baserunner.

2004 Outlook

As a fifth-year arbitration-eligible, Lee was slated to move into the $7.5 million range. That made him too expensive for the Marlins, who traded him to the Cubs in late November in a deal that landed them a younger and cheaper first baseman, Hee Seop Choi. Lee should see his home-run totals rise in Wrigley Field, a park better suited for him.

Position: 1B
Bats: R **Throws:** R
Ht: 6' 5" **Wt:** 248

Opening Day Age: 28
Born: 9/6/75 in Sacramento, CA
ML Seasons: 7

Overall Statistics

	G	AB	R	H	D	T	HR	RBI	SB	BB	SO	Avg	OBP	Slg
'03	155	539	91	146	31	2	31	92	21	88	131	.271	.379	.508
Car.	866	2884	431	760	162	18	130	421	51	372	758	.264	.353	.467

Where He Hits the Ball

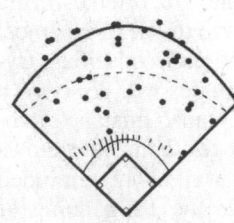 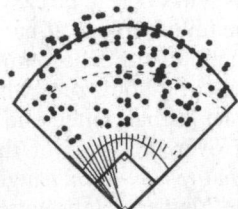

Vs. LHP   **Vs. RHP**

2003 Situational Stats

	AB	H	HR	RBI	Avg		AB	H	HR	RBI	Avg
Home	260	63	11	43	.242	LHP	105	35	6	23	.333
Road	279	83	20	49	.297	RHP	434	111	25	69	.256
First Half	338	89	19	52	.263	Sc Pos	160	43	8	62	.269
Scnd Half	201	57	12	40	.284	Clutch	76	15	0	4	.197

2003 Rankings (National League)

- 3rd in fielding percentage at first base (.996)
- 4th in lowest batting average with the bases loaded (.083)
- 7th in lowest batting average at home
- 8th in strikeouts and most pitches seen per plate appearance (4.05)
- Led the Marlins in total bases (274), sacrifice flies (6), walks, strikeouts, pitches seen (2,604) and most pitches seen per plate appearance (4.05)

Mike Lowell

Position: 3B
Bats: R **Throws:** R
Ht: 6' 3" **Wt:** 215

Opening Day Age: 30
Born: 2/24/74 in San Juan, PR
ML Seasons: 6

2003 Season

When a lower back strain plagued Mike Lowell throughout spring training, it appeared he was in for a long year. Instead, he built on the gains of 2002 and forged his second straight All-Star campaign. What's more, he won the league's Silver Slugger award at third base despite missing the final month of the season with a broken left hand. Lowell showed why he's one of the most respected players in the league when he never made a peep while sitting behind rookie Miguel Cabrera during the Division Series.

Hitting

Lowell was on pace for a monster year with 28 home runs by the All-Star break, but had just four the rest of the way. He played with a nagging groin pull from the middle of June on, but insisted it did not bother his swing. A marked flyball hitter, Lowell has made great strides in terms of pitch selection. He also drove more balls to center and right-center than in the past. He likes the ball middle-in and thigh high. A low-ball hitter, Lowell can have trouble with high fastballs and breaking balls away.

Baserunning & Defense

Lowell is painfully slow but rarely makes mistakes on the basepaths. His defense continues to improve, and he now rates behind only Scott Rolen in Gold Glove consideration. He makes the routine plays, charges in to make barehanded grabs and goes back on balls well. His arm is solid and accurate.

2004 Outlook

The Marlins, eager as they have been to turn third base over to Cabrera, signed Lowell to a four-year, $32 million deal on December 1. With budgetary issues hanging over the Marlins in recent years, Lowell's departure from Florida via a trade had been imminent for months, but now he's not going anywhere. Lowell will be at third base when the Marlins defend their world title in 2004.

Overall Statistics

	G	AB	R	H	D	T	HR	RBI	SB	BB	SO	Avg	OBP	Slg
'03	130	492	76	136	27	1	32	105	3	56	78	.276	.350	.530
Car.	681	2471	335	676	161	1	108	435	12	244	394	.274	.341	.471

Where He Hits the Ball

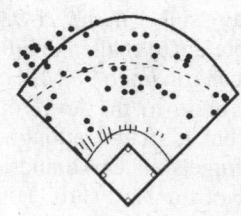
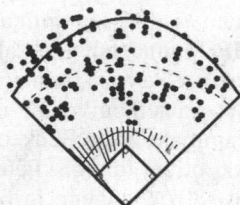

Vs. LHP   **Vs. RHP**

2003 Situational Stats

	AB	H	HR	RBI	Avg		AB	H	HR	RBI	Avg
Home	234	66	14	50	.282	LHP	112	33	12	35	.295
Road	258	70	18	55	.271	RHP	380	103	20	70	.271
First Half	353	97	28	76	.275	Sc Pos	159	48	11	76	.302
Scnd Half	139	39	4	29	.281	Clutch	59	17	7	16	.288

2003 Rankings (National League)

- 1st in fielding percentage at third base (.973) and lowest groundball-flyball ratio (0.6)
- 9th in HR frequency (15.4 ABs per HR)
- 10th in errors at third base (9) and lowest cleanup slugging percentage (.509)
- Led the Marlins in home runs, RBI, sacrifice flies (6), slugging percentage, HR frequency (15.4 ABs per HR) and cleanup slugging percentage (.509)
- Led NL third basemen in home runs

Brad Penny

2003 Season

Nearly traded in a package for Bartolo Colon in January, Brad Penny overcame a slow start to put together the best season of his uneven career. Long accused of "radar love," Penny encountered some not-so-subtle conditioning by the Marlins at midseason when the club turned off the radar gun for a couple of his home starts. He seemed to get the message in the second half, varying his pitches for the most part instead of just humping up and throwing fastballs. Dropped from the rotation at times during the National League playoffs, he wound up starting and winning two games in the World Series.

Pitching

Penny is blessed with a heavy sinker in the 91-93 MPH range, but generally prefers to challenge hitters with a four-seamer he can run up to 98 MPH. His power curveball isn't quite to the level of teammate Josh Beckett's, but it's close enough. Too often, though, Penny forgets his curve and a low-80s changeup in favor of the hard stuff. His weight now on the north side of 250 pounds, Penny tends to run out of gas in the middle innings.

Defense & Hitting

Penny doesn't get cheated at the plate. He hit two of the three home runs by Marlins pitchers and tied for the staff lead with five sacrifice bunts. However, his poor conditioning has made him a poor fielder, and a lack of attention to opposing baserunners has made him one of the easier marks on the staff.

2004 Outlook

Thanks to arbitration, Penny's salary could rise into the $2.8 million range. That could cause the Marlins to dangle him on the trade market as they seek to deal with a roster-wide explosion in payroll cost. Wherever Penny pitches, he should do so with increased maturity and the confidence that he already has succeeded on his sport's grandest stage.

Position: SP
Bats: R **Throws:** R
Ht: 6' 4" **Wt:** 250

Opening Day Age: 25
Born: 5/24/78 in Broken Arrow, OK
ML Seasons: 4

Overall Statistics

	W	L	Pct.	ERA	G	GS	Sv	IP	H	BB	SO	HR	Avg
'03	14	10	.583	4.13	32	32	0	196.1	195	56	138	21	.264
Car.	40	34	.541	4.22	110	109	0	650.1	646	220	465	67	.261

2003 Pitching Profile

	Brad Penny	NL Average
Overall Strike %	65.7	62.4
1st Pitch Strike %	59.7	58.4
Ratio	1.28	1.38
Strikeouts per 9 IP	6.33	6.65
Walks per 9 IP	2.57	3.42
Home Runs per 9 IP	0.96	1.05
Strikeout/Walk Ratio	2.46	1.94
Groundball/Flyball Ratio	1.21	1.29

2003 Situational Stats

	W	L	ERA	Sv	IP		AB	H	HR	RBI	Avg
Home	6	3	3.48	0	85.1	LHB	360	97	8	40	.269
Road	8	7	4.62	0	111.0	RHB	380	98	13	52	.258
First Half	8	6	4.55	0	116.2	Sc Pos	166	47	5	65	.283
Scnd Half	6	4	3.50	0	79.2	Clutch	43	16	1	4	.372

2003 Rankings (National League)

- 1st in balks (4)
- 3rd in GDPs induced (26)
- 7th in most GDPs induced per GDP situation (19.7%) and most run support per nine innings (6.1)
- Led the Marlins in wins, games started, home runs allowed, balks (4), GDPs induced (26) and most run support per nine innings (6.1)

Juan Pierre

2003 Season

Acquired from Colorado in the three-way offseason deal that sent Mike Hampton to Atlanta, Juan Pierre proved he was more than just the hardest-working player in the majors. In squeezing every ounce of ability out of his slight frame, Pierre practically shamed his new teammates into giving their all. Local baseball writers voted him the club's MVP, and he finished 10th in National League MVP balloting.

Hitting

Pierre replaced Luis Castillo in the leadoff role a week into the season and never gave it up. He ranked last among the club's regulars in pitches seen per plate appearance (3.44) and his .361 on-base percentage was 20 points lower than Castillo's, but somehow the dynamic worked. Pierre rarely struck out, littered the infield with bunts and put constant pressure on the defense with his little-ball approach. Pierre actually hit eight points higher against lefties, hanging in against the nastiest of portsiders. Timed as fast as 3.6 seconds to first base, he liked to lean Ichiro-style as he slashed pitches the other way. Plus fastballs on Pierre's hands could tie him up and he sometimes had trouble catching up with hard stuff away.

Baserunning & Defense

With his long strides and awkward gait, Pierre evoked a young Mickey Rivers on the bases. He won his second stolen-base title and combined with Castillo to essentially give the Marlins a two-headed leadoff man. Defensively, Pierre made tremendous strides during the season and did a marvelous job covering Pro Player Stadium's center-field expanse. He made a handful of leaping catches at the wall, took away plenty of hits with all-out dives and compensated for a below-average arm with excellent positioning.

2004 Outlook

Pierre's price tag soon could become an issue. He will make $2.5 million this season and $3.6 million in 2005, but for the now the Marlins remain enamored with his rare brand of ball.

Position: CF
Bats: L **Throws:** L
Ht: 6' 0" **Wt:** 180

Opening Day Age: 26
Born: 8/14/77 in Mobile, AL
ML Seasons: 4
Pronunciation: pee-AIR

Overall Statistics

	G	AB	R	H	D	T	HR	RBI	SB	BB	SO	Avg	OBP	Slg
'03	162	668	100	204	28	7	1	41	65	55	35	.305	.361	.373
Car.	521	2077	324	638	76	23	4	151	165	140	131	.307	.357	.372

Where He Hits the Ball

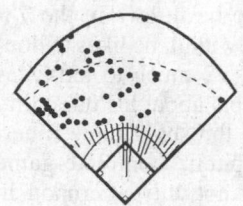
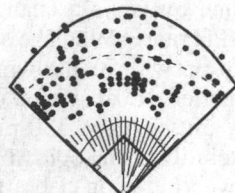

Vs. LHP **Vs. RHP**

2003 Situational Stats

	AB	H	HR	RBI	Avg		AB	H	HR	RBI	Avg
Home	324	103	1	21	.318	LHP	206	64	0	8	.311
Road	344	101	0	20	.294	RHP	462	140	1	33	.303
First Half	393	117	0	25	.298	Sc Pos	115	31	0	40	.270
Scnd Half	275	87	1	16	.316	Clutch	94	33	0	11	.351

2003 Rankings (National League)

- 1st in at-bats, singles, sacrifice bunts (15), stolen bases, caught stealing (20), plate appearances (747), games played, bunts in play (90), lowest percentage of swings that missed (6.0), highest percentage of swings put into play (58.4), steals of third (11) and lowest HR frequency (668.0 ABs per HR)
- 2nd in highest groundball-flyball ratio (2.7) and fielding percentage in center field (.993)
- 3rd in hits
- 4th in batting average with two strikes (.281)
- Led the Marlins in runs scored, hits, singles, triples, stolen bases, caught stealing (20), times on base (264), games played, stolen-base percentage (76.5), steals of third (11), batting average in the clutch

Mark Redman

2003 Season

Written off during previous stops in Minnesota and Detroit as soft and uncompetitive, Mark Redman quieted his doubters with a breakout season in South Florida. Acquired from the Tigers for three pitching prospects in January, Redman was the staff's most consistent starter for long stretches of the first half. The only negative came in the postseason, where his final two starts were clunkers, including a Game 7 shelling in the NLCS.

Pitching

Despite his large stature, Redman is a soft tosser. His fastball sits in the 84-88 MPH range, but he isn't afraid to bust hitters on the hands with it. He features a looping curveball as well, but his best pitch by far is a changeup he throws in the 78-MPH range. When he's on with it, he likes to double up with it, throwing it as much to lefties as righties. He answered doubts about his durability by crossing the 130-pitch threshold three times, including an epic 140-pitch, complete-game seven-hitter on a brutally hot July afternoon in Philadelphia. He allowed just one home run during an 11-start span in the first half but became more susceptible to the longball as the season progressed.

Defense & Hitting

One of the worst hitters (and bunters) in the game, Redman went 1-for-61 (.016) for the year. He broke the thumb on his pitching hand trying to squeeze bunt in Arizona, and the fluke injury cost him nearly a full month. Redman lumbers around the mound and is a poor fielder, but allowed just three successful steals (in four attempts) all year.

2004 Outlook

Because of arbitration, Redman's salary could blow past $3 million. That could make him an expensive luxury for a Marlins club with serious payroll concerns. Whether he returns or not, Redman took a major step forward last season and should carry his newfound confidence forward.

Position: SP
Bats: L **Throws:** L
Ht: 6' 5" **Wt:** 245

Opening Day Age: 30
Born: 1/5/74 in San Diego, CA
ML Seasons: 5

Overall Statistics

	W	L	Pct.	ERA	G	GS	Sv	IP	H	BB	SO	HR	Avg
'03	14	9	.609	3.59	29	29	0	190.2	172	61	151	16	.239
Car.	37	39	.487	4.27	107	95	0	615.2	636	187	421	63	.265

2003 Pitching Profile

	Mark Redman	NL Average
Overall Strike %	62.5	62.4
1st Pitch Strike %	58.5	58.4
Ratio	1.22	1.38
Strikeouts per 9 IP	7.13	6.65
Walks per 9 IP	2.88	3.42
Home Runs per 9 IP	0.76	1.05
Strikeout/Walk Ratio	2.48	1.94
Groundball/Flyball Ratio	0.94	1.29

2003 Situational Stats

	W	L	ERA	Sv	IP		AB	H	HR	RBI	Avg
Home	6	4	2.88	0	93.2	LHB	140	28	4	13	.200
Road	8	5	4.27	0	97.0	RHB	581	144	12	64	.248
First Half	7	4	3.26	0	99.1	Sc Pos	162	43	5	58	.265
Scnd Half	7	5	3.94	0	91.1	Clutch	37	8	1	3	.216

2003 Rankings (National League)

- 4th in most pitches thrown per batter (3.96)
- 5th in balks (2)
- 6th in lowest ERA at home
- 7th in complete games (3)
- 8th in lowest groundball-flyball ratio allowed (0.9)
- 9th in lowest on-base percentage allowed (.301) and lowest batting average allowed vs. lefthanded batters
- 10th in fewest home runs allowed per nine innings (.76)
- Led the Marlins in wins, complete games (3), walks allowed, wild pitches (8), pitches thrown (3,178), lowest batting average allowed (.239) and lowest on-base percentage allowed (.301)

Ivan Rodriguez

2003 Season

After averaging just 103 games per year and landing on the disabled list four times in his final three seasons in Texas, Ivan Rodriguez had much to prove after passing up a three-year offer from Baltimore to sign a one-year, $10 million deal with the Marlins. Rodriguez had a rough May, but caught fire in June and then carried the Marlins all the way to their second World Series title. His leadership as the games grew more important was undeniable.

Hitting

There's a reason Rodriguez has a career .304 batting average. His short, compact swing is a thing of beauty when he's in the groove, as he regularly takes quality outside pitches the other way. When he was struggling early in the year, he was too pull-conscious. Once he resigned himself to the fact Pro Player Stadium isn't nearly the home-run park that the Ballpark at Arlington is, Rodriguez concentrated on making quality contact. Although he set a career high with 92 strikeouts, part of that was attributable to his willingness to run more deep counts.

Baserunning & Defense

Rodriguez won 10 straight Gold Gloves in Texas but has been shut out the past two years. His throwing percentage dipped to 32 percent against opposing basestealers and he had 10 passed balls, his highest total in five years, but he remains a feared gunslinger behind the plate. No one throws behind runners as often. After some early problems, Rodriguez worked well with the Marlins' young pitching staff and put to rest some growing doubts about his interest in game-calling.

2004 Outlook

A free agent for the second time in as many winters, Rodriguez hoped to stay with Florida, but that isn't going to happen after the two sides couldn't come to terms and the Marlins didn't offer salary arbitration. Wherever he winds up, Rodriguez has reestablished his Hall of Fame credentials with one of the all-time great walk-year showings.

Position: C
Bats: R **Throws:** R
Ht: 5' 9" **Wt:** 218

Opening Day Age: 32
Born: 11/30/71 in Vega Baja, PR
ML Seasons: 13
Pronunciation: rod-RI-gez
Nickname: Pudge

Overall Statistics

	G	AB	R	H	D	T	HR	RBI	SB	BB	SO	Avg	OBP	Slg
'03	144	511	90	152	36	3	16	85	10	55	92	.297	.369	.474
Car.	1623	6167	942	1875	380	31	231	914	90	359	855	.304	.344	.488

Where He Hits the Ball

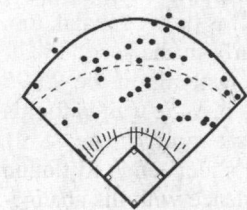
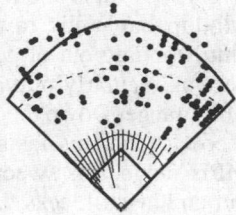

Vs. LHP   **Vs. RHP**

2003 Situational Stats

	AB	H	HR	RBI	Avg		AB	H	HR	RBI	Avg
Home	249	79	8	45	.317	LHP	117	44	3	18	.376
Road	262	73	8	40	.279	RHP	394	108	13	67	.274
First Half	293	88	13	59	.300	Sc Pos	144	54	6	69	.375
Scnd Half	218	64	3	26	.294	Clutch	72	14	2	16	.194

2003 Rankings (National League)

- 4th in batting average with runners in scoring position and batting average vs. lefthanded pitchers
- 5th in errors at catcher (8)
- 6th in lowest batting average with the bases loaded (.100)
- 7th in lowest fielding percentage at catcher (.992)
- Led the Marlins in GDPs (18), batting average with runners in scoring position and batting average vs. lefthanded pitchers

Dontrelle Willis

2003 Season

After opening the year with six starts at Double-A Carolina, Dontrelle Willis rocketed to the majors on May 10 on his way to the National League Rookie of the Year Award. Along the way, he captivated the nation, energized a dormant baseball market, made the All-Star team, picked up a fancy nickname (D-Train) and appeared on countless magazine covers with his distinctive, high-kicking delivery and trademark smile. He pitched out of the bullpen in the World Series but recorded several key outs. As he maintained in thousands of interviews, it was "all a blessing."

Pitching

Everybody talks about the deceptive nature of his windup, but Willis' raw stuff is pretty special, too. Until running out of gas early in the second half, he was regularly pumping fastballs in the 93-96 MPH range. Down the stretch, as he waited for his second wind, his fastball sat more in the 88-91 MPH range. His sweeping slider tends to flatten out and he still lacks confidence with his change-up. Willis dominates lefties, who don't pick up the ball against him until it's almost on top of them.

Defense & Hitting

Willis had one of three home runs by Marlins pitchers in 2003, and his .241 batting average was better than several Florida reserves. Although gangly and somewhat awkward, Willis is a good fielder and a deceptively smooth athlete. He does a good job controlling the running game, sacrificing some of his delivery antics with runners on base. He has a good pickoff move and once nabbed Rickey Henderson after a leadoff walk to start the game.

2004 Outlook

It will be hard to replicate the magic Willis produced as a rookie, but he'll give it a try. He remains a low-cost option in the middle of the Marlins' rotation, though long term some club insiders wonder whether he wouldn't be more valuable in a short-relief role.

Position: SP
Bats: L **Throws:** L
Ht: 6' 4" **Wt:** 195

Opening Day Age: 22
Born: 1/12/82 in Oakland, CA
ML Seasons: 1
Nickname: D-Train

Overall Statistics

	W	L	Pct.	ERA	G	GS	Sv	IP	H	BB	SO	HR	Avg
'03	14	6	.700	3.30	27	27	0	160.2	148	58	142	13	.245
Car.	14	6	.700	3.30	27	27	0	160.2	148	58	142	13	.245

2003 Pitching Profile

	Dontrelle Willis	NL Average
Overall Strike %	62.6	62.4
1st Pitch Strike %	54.3	58.4
Ratio	1.28	1.38
Strikeouts per 9 IP	7.95	6.65
Walks per 9 IP	3.25	3.42
Home Runs per 9 IP	0.73	1.05
Strikeout/Walk Ratio	2.45	1.94
Groundball/Flyball Ratio	1.12	1.29

2003 Situational Stats

	W	L	ERA	Sv	IP		AB	H	HR	RBI	Avg
Home	7	3	3.05	0	88.2	LHB	88	19	1	6	.216
Road	7	3	3.63	0	72.0	RHB	515	129	12	49	.250
First Half	9	1	2.08	0	82.1	Sc Pos	136	34	1	41	.250
Scnd Half	5	5	4.60	0	78.1	Clutch	34	4	1	1	.118

2003 Rankings (National League)

- 2nd in wins among rookies
- 3rd in errors at pitcher (4)
- 4th in shutouts (2)
- 6th in winning percentage
- Led the Marlins in wins, shutouts (2), winning percentage and lowest stolen-base percentage allowed (50.0)

Armando Almanza

Position: RP
Bats: L **Throws:** L
Ht: 6' 3" **Wt:** 240

Opening Day Age: 31
Born: 10/26/72 in El Paso, TX
ML Seasons: 5

Overall Statistics

	W	L	Pct.	ERA	G	GS	Sv	IP	H	BB	SO	HR	Avg
'03	4	5	.444	6.08	51	0	0	50.1	59	25	49	10	.296
Car.	13	12	.520	4.79	235	0	2	199.0	175	126	217	30	.241

2003 Situational Stats

	W	L	ERA	Sv	IP		AB	H	HR	RBI	Avg
Home	3	4	6.15	0	26.1	LHB	65	18	3	12	.277
Road	1	1	6.00	0	24.0	RHB	134	41	7	21	.306
First Half	4	5	4.65	0	40.2	Sc Pos	59	16	3	24	.271
Scnd Half	0	0	12.10	0	9.2	Clutch	74	22	4	12	.297

2003 Season

Confidence and health again were problems for Armando Almanza, whose raw stuff alone would rank him among the game's top lefthanded relievers. Almanza struggled to command his curveball, lost a couple of games on late home runs and had been relegated to mopup duty when elbow pain ended his season in late August. He underwent arthroscopic surgery to remove bone spurs and did not make the playoff roster.

Pitching, Defense & Hitting

When he's on, Almanza can overpower hitters with a live fastball between 92-96 MPH. He always has been a flyball pitcher, and that can get him in trouble when his stuff tails off. His slow curve upsets hitters when he can throw it for strikes. When he can't, they lay off it or pound it for hits. Almanza has a thick frame but is a decent fielder who holds runners well. He rarely bats.

2004 Outlook

Eligible for arbitration, Almanza could become an expensive luxury for a team with severe payroll problems. If he's not non-tendered, he could be moved in a deal for middling prospects. He should be healthy by spring training, when he'll need to reestablish himself as a top situational lefty.

Nate Bump

Position: RP
Bats: R **Throws:** R
Ht: 6' 2" **Wt:** 185

Opening Day Age: 27
Born: 7/24/76 in Towanda, PA
ML Seasons: 1

Overall Statistics

	W	L	Pct.	ERA	G	GS	Sv	IP	H	BB	SO	HR	Avg
'03	4	0	1.000	4.71	32	0	0	36.1	34	20	17	3	.248
Car.	4	0	1.000	4.71	32	0	0	36.1	34	20	17	3	.248

2003 Situational Stats

	W	L	ERA	Sv	IP		AB	H	HR	RBI	Avg
Home	1	0	8.25	0	12.0	LHB	48	11	2	6	.229
Road	3	0	2.96	0	24.1	RHB	89	23	1	18	.258
First Half	2	0	3.86	0	9.1	Sc Pos	29	11	0	19	.379
Scnd Half	2	0	5.00	0	27.0	Clutch	46	10	0	4	.217

2003 Season

After spending parts of four straight seasons at Double-A Portland, Nate Bump was no longer considered much of a prospect. The former Giants first-rounder had a surgically repaired shoulder and middling numbers. However, a strong first half at Triple-A Albuquerque earned him a promotion to the big league bullpen, whereupon he became a valued setup man.

Pitching, Defense & Hitting

Bump doesn't overpower hitters, but he keeps them off balance with a sinker-slider repertoire that produces numerous groundballs. His two-seam fastball sits in the low 90s and has good life. His slider has late break and can pick up strikes for him as well. His solid changeup is effective against lefthanded hitters. A good athlete, Bump fields his position well, holds runners and is quick enough to the plate. He had just one career plate appearance, dropping down a sacrifice bunt.

2004 Outlook

With just three relief outings in 110 minor league appearances, Bump has a starter's training. He could return to the role if the Marlins need to excise a hefty salary from the rotation. More likely, he will return in a middle-relief role. His versatility and low salary are considered big pluses.

A.J. Burnett

Position: SP
Bats: R **Throws:** R
Ht: 6' 4" **Wt:** 232

Opening Day Age: 27
Born: 1/3/77 in North Little Rock, AR
ML Seasons: 5

Overall Statistics

	W	L	Pct.	ERA	G	GS	Sv	IP	H	BB	SO	HR	Avg
'03	0	2	.000	4.70	4	4	0	23.0	18	18	21	2	.217
Car.	30	32	.484	3.86	82	80	0	524.2	433	260	442	45	.227

2003 Situational Stats

	W	L	ERA	Sv	IP		AB	H	HR	RBI	Avg
Home	0	1	4.97	0	12.2	LHB	47	11	1	5	.234
Road	0	1	4.35	0	10.1	RHB	36	7	1	8	.194
First Half	0	2	4.70	0	23.0	Sc Pos	25	8	1	12	.320
Scnd Half	0	0	—	0	0.0	Clutch	4	1	0	1	.250

2003 Season

After walking off a spring-training mound clutching his arm in agony, A.J. Burnett rushed back to start the ninth game of the regular season. While he showed flashes of his old high-90s velocity, he was done for the year after four starts. He underwent Tommy John surgery on April 29 to repair a complete tear of the ulnar collateral ligament.

Pitching, Defense & Hitting

Burnett never reached 101 MPH the way he did several times in 2002, but he still was among the game's hardest-throwing starters. His command suffered as he tried to negotiate bone spurs in his elbow, and his over-the-top knuckle curve wasn't the same weapon as in the past. His changeup continued to develop into a plus pitch. Burnett is an average fielder and handles the bat pretty well. Holding runners remains somewhat of a weak point.

2004 Outlook

Eligible for arbitration and expected to remain in the same $2.5 million range, Burnett was a potential non-tender candidate. That's not likely now that the Marlins have dealt Derrek Lee and his salary. The Marlins anticipate a mid-May return at the latest for Burnett. A cautious return to well-regulated bullpen work may make more sense than an immediate jump back into the rotation.

Jeff Conine

Position: 1B/LF
Bats: R **Throws:** R
Ht: 6' 1" **Wt:** 220

Opening Day Age: 37
Born: 6/27/66 in Tacoma, WA
ML Seasons: 13
Pronunciation: COH-nine

Overall Statistics

	G	AB	R	H	D	T	HR	RBI	SB	BB	SO	Avg	OBP	Slg
'03	149	577	88	163	36	3	20	95	5	50	70	.282	.338	.459
Car.	1510	5356	694	1538	291	28	181	852	40	518	931	.287	.349	.453

2003 Situational Stats

	AB	H	HR	RBI	Avg		AB	H	HR	RBI	Avg
Home	266	76	11	51	.286	LHP	125	36	3	13	.288
Road	311	87	9	44	.280	RHP	452	127	17	82	.281
First Half	354	101	12	63	.285	Sc Pos	175	44	5	71	.251
Scnd Half	223	62	8	32	.278	Clutch	95	21	2	11	.221

2003 Season

An August 31 trade necessitated by Mike Lowell's broken hand put ex-Marlin Jeff Conine back in the middle of a pennant race with his former team. Conine, whose popularity never waned in South Florida, justified the deal by delivering numerous clutch hits down the stretch and in the postseason.

Hitting, Baserunning & Defense

Conine is known for his professional approach and ability to produce with runners in scoring position. His bat has slowed and he can look bad against above-average fastballs, but he prepares well and has gap power. He battles pitchers and will take quality offspeed stuff to the opposite field. Conine doesn't steal much, but he is a smart if limited baserunner. In left, Conine made several acrobatic catches during the championship run and threw out J.T. Snow at home to end the Division Series, against the Giants.

2004 Outlook

Before the Marlins finalized the trade, they insisted that Conine restructure his contract. He is now under contract for the next two seasons at $3 million per year. With Derrek Lee traded to the Cubs for payroll reasons, Conine is expected to return to first base and battle new arrival Hee Seop Choi for playing time.

Rick Helling

Position: SP/RP
Bats: R **Throws:** R
Ht: 6' 3" **Wt:** 241

Opening Day Age: 33
Born: 12/15/70 in Devils Lake, ND
ML Seasons: 10

Overall Statistics

	W	L	Pct.	ERA	G	GS	Sv	IP	H	BB	SO	HR	Avg
'03	8	8	.500	5.17	35	24	0	155.0	167	45	98	31	.277
Car.	90	78	.536	4.77	266	225	0	1442.1	1476	529	984	239	.266

2003 Situational Stats

	W	L	ERA	Sv	IP		AB	H	HR	RBI	Avg
Home	3	5	3.44	0	70.2	LHB	302	85	16	49	.281
Road	5	3	6.62	0	84.1	RHB	300	82	15	32	.273
First Half	6	6	5.65	0	102.0	Sc Pos	138	37	7	52	.268
Scnd Half	2	2	4.25	0	53.0	Clutch	10	2	0	1	.200

2003 Season

Signed to a one-year deal by the Orioles just before the start of spring training, Rick Helling assumed a spot in the Baltimore rotation and did what he's done for most of his career: eat innings. Helling struggled to make those quality innings, however, as the longball remained his nemesis. Waived by the O's, he joined the Marlins on August 22 and became a useful middle reliever, providing a veteran presence for the team's surprising run to the World Series title.

Pitching, Defense & Hitting

Helling throws four pitches for strikes, but none is much above average. His fastball sits in the 89-91 MPH range and doesn't have much natural movement. At times he appears to be putting the ball on a tee for eager hitters. Helling is a good fielder who is quick to the plate and mindful of baserunners. He isn't much of a factor with the bat.

2004 Outlook

Helling was not expected to return to the Marlins, and it's even less likely after the club didn't offer him salary arbitration. A free agent, Helling figures to catch on again as a back-of-the-rotation starter, most likely with a non-contender. He must reestablish himself as something more than a glorified batting practice pitcher.

Todd Hollandsworth

Position: LF
Bats: L **Throws:** L
Ht: 6' 2" **Wt:** 225

Opening Day Age: 30
Born: 4/20/73 in Dayton, OH
ML Seasons: 9
Pronunciation: HAHL-enz-worth

Overall Statistics

	G	AB	R	H	D	T	HR	RBI	SB	BB	SO	Avg	OBP	Slg
'03	93	228	32	58	23	3	3	20	2	22	55	.254	.317	.421
Car.	840	2516	370	695	151	17	77	308	70	212	557	.276	.333	.442

2003 Situational Stats

	AB	H	HR	RBI	Avg		AB	H	HR	RBI	Avg
Home	124	32	1	10	.258	LHP	32	8	0	1	.250
Road	104	26	2	10	.250	RHP	196	50	3	19	.255
First Half	192	50	3	15	.260	Sc Pos	60	14	1	18	.233
Scnd Half	36	8	0	5	.222	Clutch	42	8	1	2	.190

2003 Season

Signed as a free agent for $1.5 million to replace Kevin Millar, Todd Hollandsworth got off to a slow start and never turned things around. He took a permanent seat on the bench after the June 20 promotion of highly touted prospect Miguel Cabrera, but Hollandsworth hit .350 as a pinch-hitter.

Hitting, Baserunning & Defense

Hollandsworth is a professional hitter who studies opposing pitchers, but his bat has slowed. He has trouble catching up to plus fastballs, especially up in the zone and out over the plate, and he struggles with quality breaking stuff as well. His speed, once above average, is barely average in the wake of a 2001 injury that saw him suffer nerve damage and stress fractures in his right shin. A center fielder as recently as 2002 in Texas, he showed above-average range in left. His arm is average, but accurate.

2004 Outlook

To his credit, Hollandsworth never complained after being tossed aside. He stayed ready, supported Cabrera and only increased his reputation as a solid professional. The Marlins were willing to have him back at a lower salary, but that won't happen after the club didn't offer salary arbitration. A bench role elsewhere is in the cards.

Braden Looper ⟨Rubber Arm⟩

Position: RP
Bats: R **Throws:** R
Ht: 6' 3" **Wt:** 220

Opening Day Age: 29
Born: 10/28/74 in
Weatherford, OK
ML Seasons: 6

Overall Statistics

	W	L	Pct.	ERA	G	GS	Sv	IP	H	BB	SO	HR	Avg
'03	6	4	.600	3.68	74	0	28	80.2	82	29	56	4	.264
Car.	19	17	.528	3.70	372	0	46	391.1	390	155	246	31	.261

2003 Situational Stats

	W	L	ERA	Sv	IP		AB	H	HR	RBI	Avg
Home	4	2	2.85	16	47.1	LHB	143	40	3	22	.280
Road	2	2	4.86	12	33.1	RHB	168	42	1	16	.250
First Half	4	2	2.28	17	51.1	Sc Pos	88	23	1	34	.261
Scnd Half	2	2	6.14	11	29.1	Clutch	198	48	3	26	.242

2003 Season

For the first time in his career, Braden Looper opened the year as the Marlins' unquestioned closer. Looper enjoyed a strong first half but faded, and then hit the wall in mid-September. Manager Jack McKeon lost confidence in Looper and made mid-season pickup Ugueth Urbina the closer. Looper saw little meaningful work from then on, but did pick up a key win in Game 4 of the World Series.

Pitching, Defense & Hitting

Before his late-season troubles, Looper pounded the strike zone with 94-97 MPH fastballs and produced nearly two-and-a-half groundballs for every flyball he allowed. He used a cutter and, at times, a split-finger fastball to neutralize lefties, who have always been his nemesis. He controls the running game well with a solid pickoff move, but his defense is just average. He got his first career hit last year.

2004 Outlook

Coming off a three-year contract as a fifth-year arbitration-eligible, Looper could jump into the $3 million territory. His status with the club depends on whether late additions Urbina and Chad Fox are re-signed. Fox was retained, so it remains unclear whether Looper will be traded to cut payroll.

Carl Pavano

Position: SP
Bats: R **Throws:** R
Ht: 6' 5" **Wt:** 235

Opening Day Age: 28
Born: 1/8/76 in New
Britain, CT
ML Seasons: 6
Pronunciation:
pa-VAH-no

Overall Statistics

	W	L	Pct.	ERA	G	GS	Sv	IP	H	BB	SO	HR	Avg
'03	12	13	.480	4.30	33	32	0	201.0	204	49	133	19	.265
Car.	39	50	.438	4.59	136	118	0	715.1	773	222	478	79	.277

2003 Situational Stats

	W	L	ERA	Sv	IP		AB	H	HR	RBI	Avg
Home	9	4	3.44	0	117.2	LHB	341	91	7	31	.267
Road	3	9	5.51	0	83.1	RHB	430	113	12	56	.263
First Half	6	10	4.41	0	118.1	Sc Pos	177	45	3	66	.254
Scnd Half	6	3	4.14	0	82.2	Clutch	65	20	3	6	.308

2003 Season

Carl Pavano fought off challengers and the occasional trade rumor to win the final rotation spot out of spring training. He then put together the best season of his injury-marred career, posting career highs in wins and innings. Dropped from the playoff rotation, he pitched so well out of the bullpen that he earned a key start in Game 6 of the NLCS against the Cubs. He then out-dueled his idol, Roger Clemens, in Game 4 of the World Series.

Pitching, Defense & Hitting

Pavano relies on strong command of a fastball-slider-change repertoire. His 91-93 MPH sinker is heavy, but he threw more four-seamers than in the past. His late-breaking slider was a putaway pitch against righthanders, while his plus changeup enabled him to neutralize lefties. Pavano is a below-average fielder who fared the worst among all Marlins pitchers against basestealers. He had a miserable year with the bat but did help himself with five sacrifice bunts.

2004 Outlook

One of 15 Marlins eligible for arbitration, Pavano figures to receive a substantial raise over his $1.5 million salary. His solid work all year—especially in the postseason—figured to make him a mainstay of the Marlins' rotation.

Michael Tejera

Position: RP
Bats: L **Throws:** L
Ht: 5' 9" **Wt:** 190

Opening Day Age: 27
Born: 10/18/76 in Havana, Cuba
ML Seasons: 3
Pronunciation: te-HAIR-ah

Overall Statistics

	W	L	Pct.	ERA	G	GS	Sv	IP	H	BB	SO	HR	Avg
'03	3	4	.429	4.67	50	6	2	81.0	82	36	58	6	.267
Car.	11	12	.478	4.72	100	25	3	227.0	236	101	160	24	.272

2003 Situational Stats

	W	L	ERA	Sv	IP		AB	H	HR	RBI	Avg
Home	3	2	2.76	1	42.1	LHB	79	31	2	21	.392
Road	0	2	6.75	1	38.2	RHB	228	51	4	24	.224
First Half	1	3	5.46	1	57.2	Sc Pos	88	26	1	35	.295
Scnd Half	2	1	2.70	1	23.1	Clutch	35	13	0	8	.371

2003 Season

All six of Michael Tejera's 2003 starts came in the first two months, with unimpressive results. Thereafter he was a long reliever until elbow surgery robbed the bullpen of lefthander Armando Almanza. Despite a .392 average allowed to left-handed batters, Tejera was the club's only situational lefty through the September wild-card push. He gave up an epic home run to Jim Thome, but that was the only longball he allowed in his final 35 regular-season outings.

Pitching, Defense & Hitting

Having come back from Tommy John surgery while in the minors, Tejera gets by on guts and grit more than pure stuff. His fastball sits at 88-91 MPH and tends to stray from the strike zone. His change-up is his best pitch, enabling him to hold righthanded hitters at bay. He also throws a big-breaking curve and a tight slider. Tejera was a center fielder in Cuba and is an aggressive fielder on the mound. He limits the running game well enough.

2004 Outlook

Tejera was eligible for salary arbitration and could receive a bump into the $400,000 range. Considering his lack of a profile for situational relief, it's possible the Marlins could cut him loose or deal him in a minor trade.

Ugueth Urbina

Position: RP
Bats: R **Throws:** R
Ht: 6' 0" **Wt:** 205

Opening Day Age: 30
Born: 2/15/74 in Caracas, VZ
ML Seasons: 9
Pronunciation: oo-get oor-bee-NAH
Nickname: Oogy

Overall Statistics

	W	L	Pct.	ERA	G	GS	Sv	IP	H	BB	SO	HR	Avg
'03	3	4	.429	2.81	72	0	32	77.0	56	31	78	8	.204
Car.	35	37	.486	3.32	448	21	206	563.2	445	236	661	67	.214

2003 Situational Stats

	W	L	ERA	Sv	IP		AB	H	HR	RBI	Avg
Home	2	3	3.30	21	46.1	LHB	143	26	2	15	.182
Road	1	1	2.05	11	30.2	RHB	131	30	6	21	.229
First Half	0	4	4.08	26	39.2	Sc Pos	87	18	4	30	.207
Scnd Half	3	0	1.45	6	37.1	Clutch	180	37	3	26	.206

2003 Season

Ugueth Urbina spent the first half of 2003 closing for the bottom-feeding Texas Rangers after signing a one-year, $4.5 million deal. When the Marlins surprised the industry by giving up three top prospects for Urbina on July 11, he found himself setting up for Braden Looper for the next two-and-a-half months. When Looper hit a rough patch in late September, Urbina took over the closer's role and held it through the end of the World Series.

Pitching, Defense & Hitting

Spacious Pro Player Stadium was a great fit for Urbina, the most pronounced flyball pitcher on the staff. He pumped four-seam fastballs into the strike zone at 93-96 MPH and held both right- and lefthanded batters to low averages. His sweeping slider was a putaway pitch against righties, and he mixed his changeup and splitter to keep lefties guessing. He pays little attention to baserunners, but is an agile fielder. He can't hit.

2004 Outlook

While the Marlins were hoping to re-sign Urbina, a deal didn't get done and he wasn't offered salary arbitration. He will move on, and with a career save percentage of .848, the fiery Venezuelan has proven that he can handle closer duties.

Other Florida Marlins

Chad Allen (**Pos**: LF, **Age**: 29, **Bats**: R)

	G	AB	R	H	D	T	HR	RBI	SB	BB	SO	Avg	OBP	Slg
'03	12	24	2	5	1	1	0	0	0	0	5	.208	.240	.333
Car.	226	740	93	200	39	6	14	73	15	59	147	.270	.326	.396

Despite carrying a .297 lifetime average in the minors, Allen has just 259 major league at-bats in this millenium. He will try his luck with Texas this season, his fifth organization since the end of 2001. 2004 Outlook: C

Juan Alvarez (**Pos**: LHP, **Age**: 30)

	W	L	Pct.	ERA	G	GS	Sv	IP	H	BB	SO	HR	Avg
'03	0	0	–	3.09	9	0	0	11.2	8	8	6	2	.216
Car.	0	5	.000	5.22	80	0	0	60.1	58	40	42	12	.262

Alvarez has been kicking around the minors since 1995, yet has not pitched as many as 40 innings in a big league season. In 448 professional appearances, the 30-year-old has made just one start. 2004 Outlook: C

Brian Banks (**Pos**: LF/1B, **Age**: 33, **Bats**: B)

	G	AB	R	H	D	T	HR	RBI	SB	BB	SO	Avg	OBP	Slg
'03	92	149	14	35	6	2	4	23	2	25	38	.235	.348	.383
Car.	273	495	65	122	19	3	13	64	8	62	129	.246	.330	.376

Banks has compiled just 495 at-bats in parts of six major league seasons. He has a lifetime average of .287 in the minors and has hit as many as 23 HR in a season. He can catch in an emergency, too. 2004 Outlook: C

Toby Borland (**Pos**: RHP, **Age**: 34)

	W	L	Pct.	ERA	G	GS	Sv	IP	H	BB	SO	HR	Avg
'03	0	0	–	1.86	7	0	0	9.2	3	8	4	0	.097
Car.	10	8	.556	4.08	189	0	8	251.1	245	134	193	20	.254

Borland's season was almost completely wiped out by a mid-May appendectomy. The submariner has a 2.69 ERA over his last three years in Triple-A. 2004 Outlook: C

Ramon Castro (**Pos**: C, **Age**: 28, **Bats**: R)

	G	AB	R	H	D	T	HR	RBI	SB	BB	SO	Avg	OBP	Slg
'03	40	53	6	15	2	0	5	8	0	4	11	.283	.333	.604
Car.	175	370	31	86	14	0	15	45	0	45	86	.232	.313	.392

In his last season in Triple-A in 2001, Castro hit .336 with 27 home runs and 90 RBI in only 390 at-bats, yet has totalled just 370 at-bats in the bigs. If he can get past his legal troubles, Pudge, etc. . . 2004 Outlook: C

Andy Fox (**Pos**: 2B, **Age**: 33, **Bats**: L)

	G	AB	R	H	D	T	HR	RBI	SB	BB	SO	Avg	OBP	Slg
'03	70	108	12	21	5	1	0	8	1	7	29	.194	.269	.259
Car.	730	1870	244	456	65	17	29	167	74	196	388	.244	.330	.343

After playing almost full-time in 2002, Fox got only 31 post-break at-bats from Jack McKeon last year. He has played every position except pitcher and catcher and will be reunited with Buck Showalter in Texas this year. 2004 Outlook: C

Chad Fox (**Pos**: RHP, **Age**: 33)

	W	L	Pct.	ERA	G	GS	Sv	IP	H	BB	SO	HR	Avg
'03	3	3	.500	3.12	38	0	3	43.1	35	31	46	3	.224
Car.	10	10	.500	3.28	191	0	5	205.2	176	112	233	18	.229

Fox missed two months with a strained oblique muscle, then was released as part of Boston's bullpen nip-and-tuck. Opponents hit just .219 against him after the All-Star break, and the Marlins re-signed him in December. 2004 Outlook: B

Lenny Harris (**Pos**: 3B, **Age**: 39, **Bats**: L)

	G	AB	R	H	D	T	HR	RBI	SB	BB	SO	Avg	OBP	Slg
'03	88	145	14	28	3	0	1	8	1	16	21	.193	.272	.234
Car.	1741	3759	448	1013	152	21	35	339	131	269	318	.269	.319	.349

Harris topped off a 16-year career by winning a ring after being released by the Cubs in August. He has collected more than 200 at-bats just once in the last five seasons. 2004 Outlook: C

Allen Levrault (**Pos**: RHP, **Age**: 26)

	W	L	Pct.	ERA	G	GS	Sv	IP	H	BB	SO	HR	Avg
'03	1	0	1.000	3.86	19	0	0	28.0	38	15	21	3	.333
Car.	7	11	.389	5.59	56	21	0	170.2	194	81	110	30	.287

Levrault posted a 1.40 ERA in 21 relief appearances for Triple-A Albuquerque last season. Just 26, the former Brewers prospect will try to make the Cardinals' staff this year. 2004 Outlook: C

Mike Mordecai (**Pos**: SS/2B/3B, **Age**: 36, **Bats**: R)

	G	AB	R	H	D	T	HR	RBI	SB	BB	SO	Avg	OBP	Slg
'03	65	89	11	19	4	0	2	8	3	8	21	.213	.276	.326
Car.	722	1276	150	314	72	7	23	127	13	106	242	.246	.305	.368

Mordecai came through with some big hits for the World Champs down the stretch, but had a total of 89 at-bats all season. He played every position in the infield and will be back with the club. 2004 Outlook: C

Blaine Neal (**Pos**: RHP, **Age**: 25)

	W	L	Pct.	ERA	G	GS	Sv	IP	H	BB	SO	HR	Avg
'03	0	0	–	8.14	18	0	0	21.0	38	9	10	2	.413
Car.	3	0	1.000	5.01	54	0	0	59.1	77	28	46	3	.316

After posting a 2.73 ERA in 2002, Neal got banged around a bit last year. In seven minor league seasons, he has a 2.72 ERA with 72 saves. He will turn 26 in April and might get a shot at the closer spot. 2004 Outlook: B

Vladimir Nunez (**Pos**: RHP, **Age**: 29)

	W	L	Pct.	ERA	G	GS	Sv	IP	H	BB	SO	HR	Avg
'03	0	3	.000	16.03	14	0	0	10.2	21	7	10	7	.396
Car.	17	29	.370	4.68	208	27	21	382.2	370	164	280	47	.257

Nunez had almost twice as many saves (20) in 2002 as he had innings (10.2) last year. He gave up two or more runs in seven of his 14 relief appearances and was sent to the minors three different times as a result. 2004 Outlook: C

Kevin Olsen (Pos: RHP, Age: 27)

	W	L	Pct.	ERA	G	GS	Sv	IP	H	BB	SO	HR	Avg
'03	0	0	—	12.75	7	0	0	12.0	25	4	12	2	.431
Car.	0	5	.000	5.12	28	10	0	82.2	93	37	63	7	.288

Olsen's season was rudely interrupted when he was struck in the head by a line drive in late June. When healthy, he posted a 2.11 ERA with a 4-1 strikeout-walk ratio in seven starts at Triple-A. 2004 Outlook: C

Tommy Phelps (Pos: LHP, Age: 30)

	W	L	Pct.	ERA	G	GS	Sv	IP	H	BB	SO	HR	Avg
'03	0	0	.600	4.00	27	7	0	63.0	70	23	43	3	.282
Car.	3	2	.600	4.00	27	7	0	63.0	70	23	43	0	.000

After toiling in the minors since 1993, Phelps finally got his first taste of the good life last year. He held opposing lefties to a .233 average and posted a 2.12 ERA out of the bullpen. 2004 Outlook: C

Mike Redmond (Pos: C, Age: 32, Bats: R)

	G	AB	R	H	D	T	HR	RBI	SB	BB	SO	Avg	OBP	Slg
'03	59	125	12	30	7	1	0	11	0	7	16	.240	.302	.312
Car.	404	1092	99	317	52	2	9	107	0	85	132	.290	.355	.366

The durability of Pudge Rodriguez gave Redmond his fewest at-bats since 1998. Still, Redmond has hit .300 in four of his six seasons and has a lifetime average of .332 versus lefties. 2004 Outlook: C

Tim Spooneybarger (Pos: RHP, Age: 24)

	W	L	Pct.	ERA	G	GS	Sv	IP	H	BB	SO	HR	Avg
'03	1	2	.333	4.07	33	0	0	42.0	27	11	32	1	.190
Car.	2	3	.400	3.24	88	0	1	97.1	70	39	68	5	.205

Spooneybarger's season ended when he was put on the DL in June, and he eventually had Tommy John surgery. Just 24 years old, he may return to the form of a future closer, but not this year. 2004 Outlook: D

Justin Wayne (Pos: RHP, Age: 24)

	W	L	Pct.	ERA	G	GS	Sv	IP	H	BB	SO	HR	Avg
'03	0	2	.000	11.81	2	2	0	5.1	9	5	1	1	.375
Car.	2	5	.286	6.52	7	7	0	29.0	31	18	17	4	.272

Wayne went 4-12 with a 4.24 ERA in 23 starts at Triple A last season and lasted just 5.1 innings combined in his two starts for the Marlins. He turns 25 in April and needs more time in the minors. 2004 Outlook: C

Gerald Williams (Pos: LF, Age: 37, Bats: R)

	G	AB	R	H	D	T	HR	RBI	SB	BB	SO	Avg	OBP	Slg
'03	27	31	5	4	1	0	0	3	3	2	5	.129	.182	.161
Car.	1072	2900	448	743	173	16	80	351	102	171	497	.256	.302	.410

Since hitting .274 with 21 homers and 89 RBI for Tampa Bay in 2000, Williams has hit .183 over the last three seasons. The end of the road appears to be near for the 37-year-old, but the Marlins inked him to a minor league contract in December. 2004 Outlook: C

Florida Marlins Minor League Prospects

Organization Overview:

En route to the World Series title, the Marlins dipped liberally into their system. They dealt three of their top 11 prospects to Texas (Adrian Gonzalez, Will Smith and Ryan Snare) in the Ugueth Urbina deal, and gave up three young pitchers (Rob Henkel, Gary Knotts and Nate Robertson) to get 14-game winner Mark Redman. When they desperately needed to replace the injured Mike Lowell on August 31, they parted with righthanders Denny Bautista and Don Levinski for Jeff Conine. What's left? Plenty, although not as much as before. Drafting 16th overall, the Marlins got a top-five talent in righthander Jeff Allison. They also saw four members of their 2002 draft class take major steps forward: outfielders Jeremy Hermida and Eric Reed, righthander Trevor Hutchinson and lefty Scott Olsen.

Chris Aguila

Position: OF   **Opening Day Age:** 25
Bats: R **Throws:** R   **Born:** 2/23/79 in
Ht: 5' 11" **Wt:** 180   Redwood City, CA

Recent Statistics

	G	AB	R	H	D	T	HR	RBI	SB	BB	SO	Avg
2002 AA Portland	130	429	62	126	28	4	6	46	14	48	101	.294
2003 R Marlins	1	4	1	3	0	0	1	2	0	0	1	.750
2003 AA Carolina	93	337	58	108	21	3	11	55	6	36	67	.320

Aguila re-established himself in 2003 with a Double-A Southern League batting title. He won the crown despite missing 41 games after an errant pitch left him with a hairline fracture in his right wrist. Even before the injury, Aguila had remade his swing, going from an extreme inside-out stroke to a more power-laden stroke that accented his ability to pull inside mistakes with authority. He pounds fastballs, especially middle-in. Aguila has plus bat speed, a strong situational approach and average power. He is an average runner but an excellent defender who can handle all three outfield spots. He takes good routes and has a plus arm on the corners. Aguila is known for being upbeat, unselfish and a good teammate.

Jeremy Hermida

Position: OF   **Opening Day Age:** 20
Bats: L **Throws:** R   **Born:** 1/30/84 in
Ht: 6' 4" **Wt:** 200   Marietta, GA

Recent Statistics

	G	AB	R	H	D	T	HR	RBI	SB	BB	SO	Avg
2002 R Marlins	38	134	15	30	7	3	0	14	5	15	25	.224
2002 A Jamestown	13	47	8	15	2	1	0	7	1	7	10	.319
2003 A Greensboro	133	468	73	133	23	5	6	49	28	80	100	.284
2003 AAA Albuquerque	1	3	0	0	0	0	0	0	0	0	3	.000

Some scouts called Hermida the best high school hitter since Eric Chavez. Hermida himself identifies more

with Shawn Green. His polished hitting approach and advanced maturity are undeniable. He has a smooth, quick stroke, good plate discipline, a strong work ethic and solid makeup. A natural righthanded hitter, he was converted to the left side at age 4 by his father. Hermida began practicing with a wood bat at 13 and received lessons from former Braves outfielder Terry Harper. Hermida should start out at high Class-A Jupiter, but a promotion to Double-A Carolina isn't hard to envision.

Lincoln Holdzkom

Position: P   **Opening Day Age:** 22
Bats: R **Throws:** R   **Born:** 3/23/82 in Yuma,
Ht: 6' 4" **Wt:** 240   AZ

Recent Statistics

	W	L	ERA	G	GS	Sv	IP	H	R	BB	SO	HR
2002 A Kane County	1	5	2.53	30	0	11	32.0	21	11	29	42	0
2003 A Greensboro	1	4	2.84	43	0	4	57.0	36	24	27	74	0
2003 A Jupiter	0	2	3.07	13	0	2	14.2	9	6	7	20	0

Kicked off his college team for violating team rules, Holdzkom spent his first two-and-a-half professional seasons showing little more than obstinacy. He finally got the message, thanks in part to a midseason shouting match with Class-A Greensboro manager Steve Phillips. Holdzdom pitches in the mid-90s and has touched 97 MPH with his fastball, which he complements with a hard-breaking curve. While he appears to have closer stuff, some in the system wonder whether he has the makeup to go beyond setup status. Holdzkom was added to the 40-man roster for the first time and could begin the year at Double-A Carolina.

Trevor Hutchinson

Position: P   **Opening Day Age:** 24
Bats: R **Throws:** R   **Born:** 10/8/79 in
Ht: 6' 5" **Wt:** 220   Boulder, CO

Recent Statistics

	W	L	ERA	G	GS	Sv	IP	H	R	BB	SO	HR
2003 A Jupiter	9	2	2.88	14	13	0	84.1	77	30	16	58	3
2003 AA Carolina	3	3	3.86	8	6	0	35.0	32	21	13	18	1

Drafted as a college senior from Cal-Berkeley, Hutchinson (the younger brother of Dallas Cowboys quarterback Chad Hutchinson) held out for more than eight months before signing for $375,000 just before the start of spring training. He throws a heavy sinker at 90-92 MPH. He complements that with a slider and changeup, both major league average. He has a good feel for pitching and outthinks young hitters. Hutchinson had a midyear scare after an allergic reaction to a bee sting landed him in the hospital for about a week. He lost 10 pounds and valuable momentum, but came back to earn MVP honors in the Double-A Southern League playoffs.

Eric Reed

Position: OF   **Opening Day Age:** 23
Bats: L **Throws:** L   **Born:** 12/2/80 in Little
Ht: 5' 10" **Wt:** 170   Rock, AR

Recent Statistics

	G	AB	R	H	D	T	HR	RBI	SB	BB	SO	Avg
2002 A Jamestown	60	250	35	77	5	1	0	17	19	17	30	.308
2002 A Kane County	12	50	11	18	1	0	0	2	7	3	11	.360
2003 A Jupiter	134	514	86	154	15	8	0	25	53	52	83	.300

The Marlins' Minor League Player of the Year in 2003, Reed understands his limitations and doesn't even try to lift balls in search of his first professional homer. Widely considered the best defender in the system, he shows great range and jumps and has an average to above-average arm. After mastering the high Class-A Florida State League, Reed figures to move up to Double-A Carolina. Reed is a former high school power-lifting champion who squatted 450 pounds in college. The speedster out of Texas A&M is an excellent bunter, even with two strikes. With Juan Pierre signed for another two seasons, Reed's arrival could dovetail nicely with the end of Pierre's contract.

Jason Stokes

Position: 1B   **Opening Day Age:** 22
Bats: R **Throws:** R   **Born:** 1/23/82 in Irving,
Ht: 6' 4" **Wt:** 225   TX

Recent Statistics

	G	AB	R	H	D	T	HR	RBI	SB	BB	SO	Avg
2002 A Kane County	97	349	73	119	25	0	27	75	1	47	96	.341
2003 A Jupiter	121	462	67	119	31	3	17	89	6	36	135	.258

Now that Adrian Gonzalez is gone, dealt to the Rangers in the Ugueth Urbina package, Stokes is the top first baseman in the system. Stokes, who signed for $2.027 million out of high school, challenged for the Class-A Midwest League Triple Crown in 2002 despite a painful cyst on his left wrist. He underwent wrist surgery in August 2002, but the complicated procedure, which included a bone graft, kept him from letting his swing fly until two months into the 2003 campaign. He should start 2004 at Double-A Carolina, where his natural power should be rewarded more often than it was last year in the high Class-A Florida State League. He could challenge for a big league job sometime in 2005.

Wilson Valdez

Position: SS   **Opening Day Age:** 25
Bats: R **Throws:** R   **Born:** 5/20/78 in Nizao,
Ht: 5' 11" **Wt:** 150   DR

Recent Statistics

	G	AB	R	H	D	T	HR	RBI	SB	BB	SO	Avg
2002 AA Portland	114	375	51	98	19	5	1	30	18	15	47	.261
2003 AA Carolina	37	144	28	45	6	2	0	14	16	15	17	.313
2003 AAA Albuquerque	90	338	45	97	12	4	0	18	33	19	37	.287

Grabbed off waivers from the Expos in the spring of 2002, Valdez has good bat speed with a little gap power and a good understanding of his limitations. Wiry strong, he slaps the ball around, bunts often, moves runners, makes contact and projects as a solid No. 2 or No. 8 hitter. He has shown the ability to convert his above-average speed into a high stolen-base percentage. He is a plus defender at shortstop with a solid-average arm and plus range. Valdez started at Double-A Carolina but earned an early season callup to Triple-A Albuquerque. A late-season thumb injury on his glove hand required surgery, but Valdez should challenge for a big league job in the spring. He could break in as a utilityman.

Josh Willingham

Position: C   **Opening Day Age:** 25
Bats: R **Throws:** R   **Born:** 2/17/79 in
Ht: 6' 1" **Wt:** 200   Florence, AL

Recent Statistics

	G	AB	R	H	D	T	HR	RBI	SB	BB	SO	Avg
2002 A Jupiter	107	376	72	103	21	4	17	69	18	63	88	.274
2003 A Jupiter	59	193	46	51	17	1	12	34	9	46	42	.264
2003 R Marlins	2	7	3	3	1	0	1	3	0	1	2	.429
2003 AA Carolina	22	67	15	20	2	1	5	14	0	13	20	.299

Blocked at both corner infield spots, Willingham agreed to try catching at instructional league after the 2002 season. He showed enough potential behind the plate to rocket up the organizational charts. He ripped up the high Class-A Florida State League to earn a June promotion to Double-A Carolina, but a knee injury interrupted his surge. Arthroscopic surgery caused him to miss a total of seven weeks, slowing his catching conversion for the rest of the season. Having gained valuable experience behind the plate in the Arizona Fall League, Willingham should start 2004 back at Carolina.

Others to Watch

Compared to World Series MVP Josh Beckett for his repertoire, demeanor and confidence, righthander **Jeff Allison** (19) could enjoy a smooth path to the majors as well. Allison's fastball is 93-97 MPH, and he complements it with a big-breaking curve. He also has a tight slider and a changeup that needs work. . . Signed for $85,000 out of Venezuela, righthander **Yorman Bazardo** (19) has an electric arm. Tall and long-limbed, Bazardo pitches at 92-94 MPH and has touched 97. He projects as either a top-of-the-rotation sort or perhaps a closer. He has a plus changeup but his power curve needs work. . . Picked up last winter in the minor league Rule 5 draft, **Frank Gracesqui** (24) is a tall, lefty reliever. He has a plus fastball that gets on hitters late. He pitches at 93-94 MPH and touches 96. Thanks to some deception in his funky three-quarters delivery, he has averaged better than a strikeout per inning in his career. He lacks a second plus pitch and should start the year at Triple-A. . . Virtually unknown in high school, **Scott Olsen** (20) signed for $160,000 as a tall, projectable lefty with a loose arm and an easy delivery. Olsen pitched at 90-92 MPH in his first full season and topped out at 94, showing a plus slider and workable change.

Minute Maid Park

Offense

The Crawford Boxes in left field are among the most inviting in baseball, with their 315-foot dimensions staring at hitters. But the 326 to right field is just as alluring to lefties. However, Minute Maid's home-run reputation is greatly exaggerated. The big expanse in center field and the jutting seats down the left-field line, which caused balls to career wildly back into the playing field, made a bigger impact on triples last season.

Defense

Tal's Hill, a 30-degree incline in the back of center field, has long been feared by center fielders because it takes their legs out from under them. Many have predicted injuries will come from it, but so far no serious ones have occurred. The flagpole also came into play for the first time last season, robbing a visiting player of a home run. But that's the only time in four seasons that has happened.

Who It Helps the Most

Jeff Kent loved the cozy confines of Minute Maid, hitting .317 there—a full 36 points better than on the road. But oddly, he had nine homers at home and 13 on the road. The two Astros' third basemen, Morgan Ensberg and Geoff Blum, also hit much better at home. Tim Redding and Jeriome Robertson profited most at home among the pitchers, both posting much better won-lost records and ERAs there.

Who It Hurts the Most

Octavio Dotel gave up more homers at home, including three in four games in one stretch in July at Minute Maid. Brad Ausmus batted 68 points higher on the road, and Craig Biggio hit 20 points better.

Rookies & Newcomers

Jason Lane is expected to move into Minute Maid on a more permanent basis and should prosper. Colin Porter hit lots of doubles and triples in the minors, and should be able to use his speed to continue that at Minute Maid. Andy Pettitte produced a much better winning percentage and ERA at Yankee Stadium than on the road. Will he be as successful at Minute Maid Park?

Dimensions: LF-315, LCF-362, CF-435, RCF-373, RF-326

Capacity: 40,950

Elevation: 22 feet

Surface: Grass

Foul Territory: Average

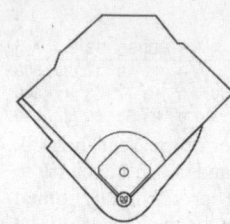

Park Factors

2003 Season

| | Home Games | | | Away Games | | | |
	Astros	Opp	Total	Astros	Opp	Total	Index
G	72	72	144	72	72	144	
Avg	.266	.244	.255	.253	.254	.253	101
AB	2388	2432	4820	2560	2388	4948	97
R	365	301	666	331	299	630	106
H	635	593	1228	647	607	1254	98
2B	131	103	234	137	123	260	92
3B	18	18	36	6	7	13	284
HR	82	79	161	82	66	148	112
BB	251	222	473	250	273	523	93
SO	417	507	924	493	500	993	96
E	40	45	85	39	54	93	91
E-Infield	37	38	75	31	48	79	95
LHB-Avg	.255	.251	.253	.241	.272	.259	98
LHB-HR	16	21	37	16	26	42	89
RHB-Avg	.269	.239	.256	.257	.243	.251	102
RHB-HR	66	58	124	66	40	106	121

2001-2003

| | Home Games | | | Away Games | | | |
	Astros	Opp	Total	Astros	Opp	Total	Index
G	222	222	444	219	219	438	
Avg	.275	.252	.264	.250	.258	.254	104
AB	7427	7652	15079	7612	7270	14882	100
R	1153	979	2132	1000	922	1922	109
H	2046	1932	3978	1906	1875	3781	104
2B	421	365	786	404	386	790	98
3B	55	41	96	29	40	69	137
HR	266	254	520	241	221	462	111
BB	804	659	1463	770	765	1535	94
SO	1414	1702	3116	1548	1550	3098	99
E	128	152	280	129	145	274	101
E-Infield	112	124	236	110	123	233	100
LHB-Avg	.289	.267	.276	.256	.266	.262	105
LHB-HR	78	101	179	64	88	152	118
RHB-Avg	.271	.243	.258	.248	.252	.250	103
RHB-HR	188	153	341	177	133	310	108

2003 Rankings (National League)

- Highest triple factor
- Second-lowest walk factor

Jimy Williams

2003 Season

The Astros started strong and were in first place much of the season. But injuries to ace Roy Oswalt and Jeff Kent hurt them in the middle and late parts of the season, and they ultimately came up short in the Central Division for the second straight year. Houston followers thought if either or both of those mainstays had been healthy all year, it might not have been close at the end.

Offense

The Astros were in the middle of the pack offensively, and their 191 home runs were no better than fifth in the National League. That's not saying much for a team built for power. Some criticized Williams for not pushing some players who were hurt. But he's very protective of injured players and gladly took the heat for not playing Kent in some key spots shortly after the second baseman returned from his injury.

Pitching & Defense

Williams continued his pattern of going to his bullpen early, and the Astros again had the fewest complete games (one) in the majors even though they had the fifth best ERA (3.86) overall in the National League. The bullpen was the most used in the NL as well, which led sometimes to fatigue on some of the relief arms. The defense was fourth in the NL, just 200ths of a point behind the tri-leaders.

2004 Outlook

When he was hired after the Astros had gone to four playoffs in five seasons, the club said Williams was there to "bring us to the next level." That's why some observers were surprised that he was given a contract extension despite the fact that Houston failed to make it to the postseason for the second straight year in 2003. The young players still love Williams, who works with them personally before almost every game. The pitchers, however, are starting to grow weary of his quick yanks and ponderous use of the bullpen. Williams probably needs to have some considerable playoff success this year to stay in good favor with management.

Born: 10/4/43 in Santa Maria, CA

Playing Experience: 1966-1967, StL

Managerial Experience: 11 seasons

Manager Statistics

Year	Team, Lg	W	L	Pct	GB	Finish
2003	Houston, NL	87	75	.537	1.0	2nd Central
11 Seasons		866	746	.537	–	–

2003 Starting Pitchers by Days Rest

	<=3	4	5	6+
Astros Starts	1	83	46	20
Astros ERA	5.06	4.25	4.47	3.43
NL Avg Starts	2	84	43	23
NL ERA	5.00	4.23	4.42	4.68

2003 Situational Stats

	Jimy Williams	NL Average
Hit & Run Success %	23.2	32.7
Stolen Base Success %	68.8	68.9
Platoon Pct.	42.5	52.0
Defensive Subs	8	19
High-Pitch Outings	1	8
Quick/Slow Hooks	40/5	20/12
Sacrifice Attempts	77	93

2003 Rankings (National League)

- 1st in pitchouts with a runner moving (10), quick hooks and relief appearances (502)
- 2nd in 2+ pitching changes in low-scoring games (43)
- 3rd in pinch-hitters used (291)

Houston

Brad Ausmus

2003 Season

Brad Ausmus fell into an early slump at the plate that he never really shook. He recovered slightly in the second half, but his final .229 average was the second-worst of his career, and marked the second time in the last three seasons he has hit south of .240. But his fielding was equal to, and in some ways better than, the previous two years, when he won Gold Gloves.

Hitting

Including a disastrous .138 May, Ausmus hit only .201 before the All-Star break. He tried switching to a heavier bat, as he had done successfully the previous season, but it didn't help. He had a strong .296 August but fell back to .243 in September. Never blessed with a real quick bat, Ausmus appeared to be slowing down even further at the plate. Never a power hitter, he hit with less pop last year than any other of his career, managing only 12 doubles after averaging 21 two-baggers a season the previous six years.

Baserunning & Defense

Ausmus' overall stats were equal to or better then those of his Gold Glove seasons of 2001 and 2002. His 31.3 (31 of 99) caught-stealing percentage was better than the figure he posted in '02. He also had a .997 fielding average, tying his two Gold Glove marks, and he again kept the Astros' young pitching staff on an even keel by calling excellent games, framing pitches well and always thinking behind the plate. Ausmus still has a strong arm and a quick release. As a baserunner, he has above-average speed.

2004 Outlook

For the most part, the young pitchers have grown up, and helping them along had been one of Ausmus' biggest jobs. After Ausmus' difficult season at the plate in 2003, maybe it was time to make a change, especially with a young, offensive-minded catcher like John Buck knocking on the door. But in November, the Astros re-signed Ausmus to a two-year, $4 million contract. He's still one of the top defensive catchers in the game.

Position: C
Bats: R **Throws:** R
Ht: 5'11" **Wt:** 200

Opening Day Age: 34
Born: 4/14/69 in New Haven, CT
ML Seasons: 11
Pronunciation: AHHS-muss

Overall Statistics

	G	AB	R	H	D	T	HR	RBI	SB	BB	SO	Avg	OBP	Slg
'03	143	450	43	103	12	2	4	47	5	46	66	.229	.303	.291
Car.	1314	4327	542	1107	191	29	63	430	85	431	708	.256	.328	.357

Where He Hits the Ball

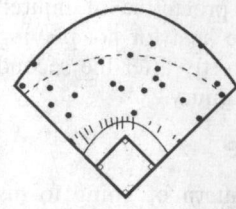
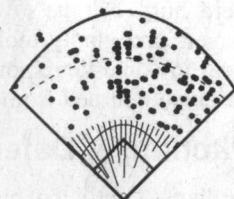

Vs. LHP   **Vs. RHP**

2003 Situational Stats

	AB	H	HR	RBI	Avg		AB	H	HR	RBI	Avg
Home	208	40	1	22	.192	LHP	76	18	1	11	.237
Road	242	63	3	25	.260	RHP	374	85	3	36	.227
First Half	264	53	2	26	.201	Sc Pos	125	31	1	44	.248
Scnd Half	186	50	2	21	.269	Clutch	81	15	1	5	.185

2003 Rankings (National League)

- 1st in lowest slugging percentage
- 2nd in fielding percentage at catcher (.997)
- Led the Astros in sacrifice flies (5), highest groundball-flyball ratio (1.5) and lowest percentage of swings that missed (14.6)

Jeff Bagwell

2003 Season

For the third straight season, Jeff Bagwell failed to hit .300, something that used to be almost automatic. While he still had 100 RBI, scored 109 runs and walked 88 times, it was not the Bagwell of old. His shoulder problems seemed to affect him less this season, though they clearly were still present.

Hitting

Bagwell's annual early-season slump, which he knows to expect because of his complicated stance and swing, didn't take affect until May. But then it took hold and didn't let go for the rest of the season. It included his longest stretch ever without a home run—140 at-bats and more than five weeks. Bagwell still has incredible strength in his forearms, and he came on strong to finish with 39 home runs. Age and wear and tear seem to be getting to the once rock of the franchise, but he's still better than most players in the game.

Baserunning & Defense

Bagwell seemed considerably stronger on defense than he had the previous season. In 2002, he couldn't make the cross-field throws and had trouble just starting the double play to second base while still suffering from the affects of shoulder surgery following the 2001 campaign. This year, however, the shoulder injury didn't seem to affect him as badly or as often. Bagwell's baserunning instincts remain among the best in the game. He knows when to take the extra base and when to hold up, and uses his minimal speed to maximum efficiency.

2004 Outlook

Bagwell, who surpassed the 2,000-hit and 400-homer plateaus last season, isn't the franchise player he once was, but he's still very good. When he works out the kinks of his complicated swing, he is a dangerous power hitter who can help bring a team from behind quickly. He continues to learn how to play with the nagging pain of the shoulder, and he is undaunted by hitting slumps and team slumps. He is also one of the clubhouse's most steadying influences and one of the most respected players in the game.

Position: 1B
Bats: R **Throws:** R
Ht: 6' 0" **Wt:** 215

Opening Day Age: 35
Born: 5/27/68 in Boston, MA
ML Seasons: 13
Pronunciation: BAG-well

Overall Statistics

G	AB	R	H	D	T	HR	RBI	SB	BB	SO	Avg	OBP	Slg
160	605	109	168	28	2	39	100	11	88	119	.278	.373	.524
1955	7125	1402	2137	455	30	419	1421	196	1287	1406	.300	.411	.549

Where He Hits the Ball

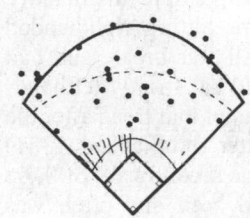 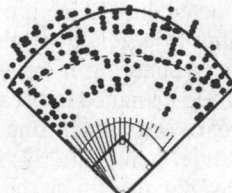

Vs. LHP   **Vs. RHP**

2003 Situational Stats

	AB	H	HR	RBI	Avg		AB	H	HR	RBI	Avg
Home	290	80	22	50	.276	LHP	107	35	7	20	.327
Road	315	88	17	50	.279	RHP	498	133	32	80	.267
First Half	354	96	17	47	.271	Sc Pos	130	43	11	65	.331
Scnd Half	251	72	22	53	.287	Clutch	95	24	1	8	.253

2003 Rankings (National League)

- 2nd in GDPs (25)
- 4th in games played, errors at first base (9) and highest percentage of swings on the first pitch (38.6)
- 6th in plate appearances (702) and fielding percentage at first base (.994)
- Led the Astros in home runs, hits, total bases (317), RBI, stolen bases, strikeouts, GDPs (25), pitches seen (2,675), games played, stolen-base percentage (73.3) and steals of third (3)

Houston

Lance Berkman

2003 Season

It was not a Lance Berkman-like season. He missed winning All-Star honors for the first time in three years and ended up hitting .288, his worst full season in the majors. Berkman's RBI total of 93 was way off his two All-Star campaigns (126 and 128) and his 25 homers fell far below his 42 and 34 of the previous two years, respectively.

Hitting

Berkman got off to a terrible start, going the first 10 games without an RBI or homer. That carried over through much of the season, as he was neither the hitter nor the power hitter he had been in previous years. Club officials felt he was trying to do too much, and that the pressure might have affected him. His problems hitting righthanded came to a zenith by the All-Star break, and had him wondering if he should bat strictly lefthanded. He managed to break out of that trend after the break, actually hitting better righthanded (.351) than lefthanded (.284) in the second half. Still, he was not the threat he had been and often was dropped to the sixth spot in the lineup during his slumps.

Baserunning & Defense

Berkman's defense continued to improve, as it has each year since he switched from first base full-time four years ago. His 10 assists were nearly double his previous best, and toward the end of the season, fewer runners were testing his arm. Berkman also made some spectacular diving catches and proved his athletic ability belies his large, big-boned frame. Though he's not particularly fast, he is a smart baserunner who will take the extra base occasionally.

2004 Outlook

Most in the organization think 2003 was an aberration. They believe Berkman will return to his All-Star form, and will remain at that level for years to come. He has the right balance between intensity and keeping a clear-headed perspective; he never seems to get too down during slumps nor too high during hitting streaks. Look for him to have a big bounce-back in 2004.

Position: LF
Bats: B **Throws:** L
Ht: 6' 1" **Wt:** 220

Opening Day Age: 28
Born: 2/10/76 in Waco, TX
ML Seasons: 5

Overall Statistics

	G	AB	R	H	D	T	HR	RBI	SB	BB	SO	Avg	OBP	Slg
'03	153	538	110	155	35	6	25	93	5	107	108	.288	.412	.515
Car.	615	2139	412	642	155	14	126	429	31	374	441	.300	.407	.562

Where He Hits the Ball

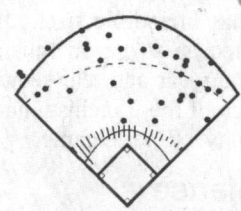
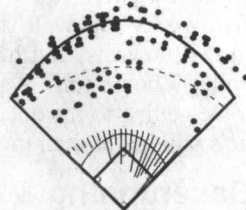

Vs. LHP	Vs. RHP

2003 Situational Stats

	AB	H	HR	RBI	Avg		AB	H	HR	RBI	Avg
Home	278	76	11	45	.273	LHP	117	33	4	26	.282
Road	260	79	14	48	.304	RHP	421	122	21	67	.290
First Half	312	87	17	59	.279	Sc Pos	139	40	6	63	.288
Scnd Half	226	68	8	34	.301	Clutch	84	23	1	7	.274

2003 Rankings (National League)

- 4th in fielding percentage in left field (.989)
- 5th in walks
- 7th in runs scored, intentional walks (13) and on-base percentage
- Led the Astros in runs scored, triples, walks, intentional walks (13), times on base (271), on-base percentage, most pitches seen per plate appearance (3.94), highest percentage of pitches taken (60.8) and cleanup slugging percentage (.564)

Craig Biggio

2003 Season

Switching to center field from second base wasn't all roses for Craig Biggio. The veteran, who was the first player to make the All-Star team at both catcher (1991) and second base (six times), struggled mightily at times playing defense in Minute Maid Park's cavernous center field. He also returned to the leadoff role full-time last season after batting second most of the previous year and had mixed results at the plate.

Hitting

As a leadoff hitter, Biggio now has his limitations. He doesn't have the speed to bunt his way on or steal many bases. He did lead the majors in hit by pitches with 27, but he walked a measly 57 times and registered a career-high 116 strikeouts, further adding to the talk that his bat is slowing down with age. He simply does not get on base as much as he had in the past, with only a .350 on-base percentage to show for his efforts in 2003. Both his batting average and OBP were slightly better than 2002, but still far below Biggio standards.

Baserunning & Defense

Defensively, Biggio was competent athletically, with a .997 fielding average and only one error. But the stats don't tell the whole story. He was a liability trying to play center field, particularly at home, where the large center-field expanse and the silly hill and pole at the back of the field makes it hazardous for anyone. His biggest problem is the lack of a serious throwing arm, and teams routinely advance bases on flies to center. Biggio doesn't have the baserunning speed he once had, and stole only eight bases last year.

2004 Outlook

Early on, some thought Biggio's hitting problems last season were due to his concentration on learning the new position. Now there are serious concerns that after two straight poor seasons at the plate he is fast approaching the end of his career. He's signed through 2004, but unless he takes a turn for the better, it's unlikely the club will exercise its option for 2005.

Position: CF
Bats: R **Throws:** R
Ht: 5'11" **Wt:** 185

Opening Day Age: 38
Born: 12/14/65 in Smithtown, NY
ML Seasons: 16
Pronunciation: BIDG-ee-oh

Overall Statistics

	G	AB	R	H	D	T	HR	RBI	SB	BB	SO	Avg	OBP	Slg
	153	628	102	166	44	2	15	62	8	57	116	.264	.350	.412
	2253	8588	1503	2461	517	51	210	931	389	1020	1373	.287	.375	.432

Where He Hits the Ball

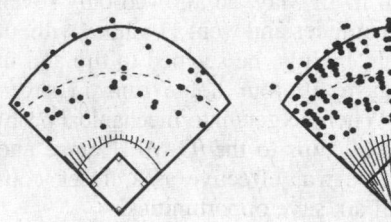

Vs. LHP   **Vs. RHP**

2003 Situational Stats

	AB	H	HR	RBI	Avg		AB	H	HR	RBI	Avg
Home	311	79	6	30	.254	LHP	120	32	2	10	.267
Road	317	87	9	32	.274	RHP	508	134	13	52	.264
First Half	373	102	9	34	.273	Sc Pos	128	35	2	46	.273
Scnd Half	255	64	6	28	.251	Clutch	94	24	2	11	.255

2003 Rankings (National League)

- 1st in hit by pitch (27) and fielding percentage in center field (.997)
- 3rd in at-bats
- 4th in plate appearances (717)
- 9th in doubles and steals of third (3)
- 10th in runs scored and fewest GDPs per GDP situation (5.6%)
- Led the Astros in at-bats, singles, doubles, hit by pitch (27), plate appearances (717), steals of third (3), fewest GDPs per GDP situation (5.6%) and on-base percentage for a leadoff hitter (.350)

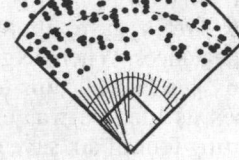

Houston

Octavio Dotel

2003 Season

Octavio Dotel had his second straight superb season in the primary role of eighth-inning setup man in front of closer Billy Wagner. Dotel was the major league leader in holds with 33, and his .172 batting average against was the best among big league setup men and sixth among all relievers. His explosive fastball enabled him to rack up more than a strikeout an inning.

Pitching

Dotel throws a fastball in the 94-97 MPH range and a slider that is in the low 80s. He throws the fastball 80-85 percent of the time, and the pitch normally has so much movement that hitters can't get around on it. In May, he allowed only seven hits in 15 appearances and went 11 games without allowing a run. In July, he seemed to tire and in one stretch gave up four home runs in seven appearances. When he gets into mechanical problems, his fastball dips to the 93-MPH range and loses its life. He was effective as a closer, converting four of six save opportunities.

Defense & Hitting

Dotel completed his second consecutive season without an error, but that stat might be misleading. He strikes out so many batters that he rarely has a chance to show his fielding prowess. Dotel does not pay much attention to opposing baserunners, and that likely won't change as he moves into his new role as stopper. He is capable of coming off the mound well, and his throwing has been consistent. His frequent one-inning stints allowed him only six hitless at-bats in 2003.

2004 Outlook

Club officials have long said that Dotel is their closer of the future, and that future became the present in November when Houston traded Wagner to Philadelphia. Dotel has the stuff to be one of the game's best closers, though he won't have as strong a setup crew to bring him to those opportunities. Team officials still think he can learn some of the finer points of pitching, and become an even better overall pitcher with time.

Position: RP
Bats: R **Throws:** R
Ht: 6' 0" **Wt:** 200

Opening Day Age: 30
Born: 11/25/73 in Santo Domingo, DR
ML Seasons: 5
Pronunciation:
OC-tay-vee-oh dough-TEL

Overall Statistics

	W	L	Pct.	ERA	G	GS	Sv	IP	H	BB	SO	HR	Avg
'03	6	4	.600	2.48	76	0	4	87.0	53	31	97	9	.172
Car.	30	23	.566	3.62	289	34	28	499.2	386	215	587	59	.213

2003 Pitching Profile

	Octavio Dotel	NL Average
Overall Strike %	66.6	62.4
1st Pitch Strike %	58.8	58.4
Ratio	0.97	1.38
Strikeouts per 9 IP	10.03	6.65
Walks per 9 IP	3.21	3.42
Home Runs per 9 IP	0.93	1.05
Strikeout/Walk Ratio	3.13	1.94
Groundball/Flyball Ratio	0.76	1.29

2003 Situational Stats

	W	L	ERA	Sv	IP		AB	H	HR	RBI	Avg
Home	6	3	3.02	2	44.2	LHB	132	20	3	10	.152
Road	0	1	1.91	2	42.1	RHB	177	33	6	20	.186
First Half	6	3	2.52	3	53.2	Sc Pos	66	13	2	22	.197
Scnd Half	0	1	2.43	1	33.1	Clutch	199	33	5	22	.166

2003 Rankings (National League)

- 1st in holds (33)
- 2nd in lowest batting average allowed vs. lefthanded batters
- 4th in relief innings (87.0)
- 5th in fewest baserunners allowed per nine innings in relief (9.0)
- 9th in most strikeouts per nine innings in relief (10.0)
- 10th in relief wins (6)
- Led the Astros in holds (33), lowest batting average allowed vs. lefthanded batters, relief wins (6), relief losses (4) and relief innings (87.0)

Richard Hidalgo

2003 Season

Astros officials said the way Richard Hidalgo played last season was like adding a star free agent. That was because the Hidalgo they signed to the opulent four-year contract after an amazing 2000 season had disappeared for two years. He hit .275 in 2001 and plummeted to .235 in 2002. Last year, he led the team in hitting, and while his home-run and RBI numbers weren't quite to the level of his 2000 stats, he was consistent at the plate and a standout in the field. All this in spite of the fact that Hidalgo had been shot in his left forearm during an apparent carjacking in his native Venezuela in November 2002.

Hitting

After his breakout 2000 season and big contract, Hidalgo wanted to match those stats so badly he went on an ill-advised and intensive weights program. The added bulk slowed him down, and with the added pressure of the contract, he got worse by the month. Last season, he developed better exercise routines to add flexibility. He also quit trying to pull the ball so much, and as soon as the team saw him hitting to right field, they knew he was back. Hidalgo said he was just seeing the ball out of the pitcher's hand better and was more comfortable at the plate.

Baserunning & Defense

Hidalgo's defense also returned last season. He led the majors in outfield assists with 22 and had only four errors. His arm was so dangerous, many teams simply quit testing him late in the season. Hidalgo capably covered ground in right field and occasionally made spectacular catches. He's not as fast as he once was, but he never had blazing speed. He's only an average baserunner.

2004 Outlook

So which Richard Hidalgo will show up in 2004? He's in his contract year with a club option for 2005, so many observers think he will have another good season, as he did when faced with that kind of challenge in 2000. The Astros have no doubt Hidalgo is a quality major league player who will be around for years to come. They just don't know if he will be in Houston that long.

Position: RF
Bats: R **Throws:** R
Ht: 6' 3" **Wt:** 220

Opening Day Age: 28
Born: 7/2/75 in Caracas, VZ
ML Seasons: 7
Pronunciation:
HUH-dahl-go

Overall Statistics

	G	AB	R	H	D	T	HR	RBI	SB	BB	SO	Avg	OBP	Slg
'03	141	514	91	159	43	4	28	88	9	58	104	.309	.385	.572
Car.	755	2628	421	736	176	16	130	435	43	288	534	.280	.359	.508

Where He Hits the Ball

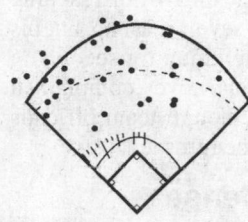
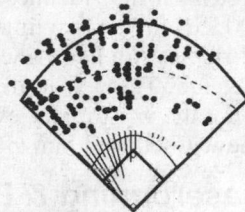

Vs. LHP   **Vs. RHP**

2003 Situational Stats

	AB	H	HR	RBI	Avg		AB	H	HR	RBI	Avg
Home	251	78	11	44	.311	LHP	88	27	7	14	.307
Road	263	81	17	44	.308	RHP	426	132	21	74	.310
First Half	278	88	14	50	.317	Sc Pos	142	32	1	52	.225
Scnd Half	236	71	14	38	.301	Clutch	85	26	2	13	.306

2003 Rankings (National League)

- 3rd in fielding percentage in right field (.987) and lowest groundball-flyball ratio (0.7)
- 6th in errors in right field (4)
- 7th in slugging percentage
- Led the Astros in batting average, sacrifice flies (5), caught stealing (7), slugging percentage, batting average vs. righthanded pitchers, batting average on the road and batting average with two strikes (.233)

Jeff Kent

Position: 2B
Bats: R **Throws:** R
Ht: 6' 1" **Wt:** 215

Opening Day Age: 36
Born: 3/7/68 in
Bellflower, CA
ML Seasons: 12

2003 Season

Injuries and a suspension kept Jeff Kent out of 30 games last season, but he still was close to his old self, and the Astros couldn't have been happier. Kent was leading the team in hitting with a .313 mark in mid-June when wrist tendinitis arose, sidelining him for nearly a month. He came back and continued to produce big hits through the end of the season.

Hitting

Kent is a mature hitter who can handle almost any pitch and hits to all fields. He also became more patient at the plate last season, striking out only 85 times—his lowest figure since 1996. The long stretch on the sidelines kept him from reaching 100 RBI for the first time in seven seasons, but his 93 ribbies still tied Lance Berkman for second on the club. Through it all, Kent never complained about the wrist injury even though team officials knew it bothered him after he returned.

Baserunning & Defense

Kent never will be a dazzling fielder, but he knows his limitations and has adjusted adequately. He goes to his right very well, makes the off-balance throw superbly and has good enough arm strength to be dependable on the double play. But he is stiff on plays right at him and doesn't have very good quickness. He has very average to below-average speed. As a big, lumbering baserunner, he sometimes makes bad decisions but is aggressive and occasionally surprises by taking the extra base.

2004 Outlook

Kent is showing no signs of slowing down, but he also has accomplished nearly everything he could want, with one big exception: a World Series championship. A ring was something he thought this Astros team might be capable of providing when he came over from San Francisco last season. Houston missed the playoffs by a game, but he's undaunted and still has high hopes for 2004. Something probably needs to happen soon in that regard, however, as this is the last year of his current contract. The Astros hold an option for 2005.

Overall Statistics

G	AB	R	H	D	T	HR	RBI	SB	BB	SO	Avg	OBP	Slg
130	505	77	150	39	1	22	93	6	39	85	.297	.351	.509
1632	6064	943	1754	404	34	275	1100	79	543	1159	.289	.352	.503

Where He Hits the Ball

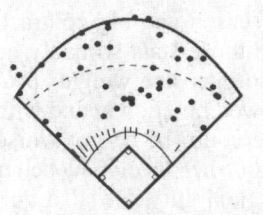
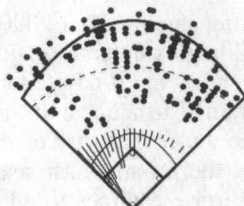

Vs. LHP   **Vs. RHP**

2003 Situational Stats

	AB	H	HR	RBI	Avg		AB	H	HR	RBI	Avg
Home	224	71	9	50	.317	LHP	97	35	2	17	.361
Road	281	79	13	43	.281	RHP	408	115	20	76	.282
First Half	265	83	11	50	.313	Sc Pos	134	48	6	69	.358
Scnd Half	240	67	11	43	.279	Clutch	87	24	4	14	.276

2003 Rankings (National League)

- 3rd in batting average with the bases loaded (.600)
- 5th in errors at second base (11) and fielding percentage at second base (.983)
- Led the Astros in batting average with runners in scoring position, batting average with the bases loaded (.600) and batting average vs. lefthanded pitchers
- Led NL second basemen in home runs and RBI

Wade Miller

2003 Season

Wade Miller again was the workhorse of the Astros' staff, making the most starts (33) and piling up a team-high 187.1 innings. And while he was second on the club in victories, his 14-13 record was nowhere near the consistency and dominance he had shown the previous two years, when he posted 16-8 and 15-4 marks, respectively. He struggled through much of the season to find that edge and seemed to gain it in August, when he went 4-1 with a 1.69 ERA. But in September, he again struggled and had a poor outing in one of the season's biggest games against the Giants.

Pitching

Miller is a hard-nosed, no-excuses battler who fought hard in every game and led the team with 161 strikeouts. He throws a two-seam and a four-seam fastball that run in the 92-94 MPH range. He has a very good curve, slider and changeup when his delivery is smooth. But he also has a complicated delivery that sometimes gets out of whack. His command wasn't always as pinpoint as it had been in the past. Astros officials also believe he was playing hurt with nagging injuries to his shoulder and elbow much of last season, but he never complained about them or missed any extensive time.

Defense & Hitting

Miller is an athletic player who can field reasonably well, but that area still can take some improvement. His pickoff move is nothing special, but he is conscientious about keeping opposing baserunners in check and has benefited from having the strong-armed Brad Ausmus behind the plate. Miller hit .159 in 2003, though his 10 hits last year did tie Tim Redding for most on the pitching staff.

2004 Outlook

The Astros hope that an offseason of rest will help Miller work out the problems he had with his elbow. Doctors don't believe it is serious, and that it only needs rest. Team officials still believe he can be among the top pitchers in the league if he puts together an injury-free season.

Position: SP
Bats: R **Throws:** R
Ht: 6' 2" **Wt:** 210

Opening Day Age: 27
Born: 9/13/76 in Reading, PA
ML Seasons: 5

Overall Statistics

	W	L	Pct.	ERA	G	GS	Sv	IP	H	BB	SO	HR	Avg
'03	14	13	.519	4.13	33	33	0	187.1	168	77	161	17	.242
Car.	51	32	.614	3.93	112	108	0	679.1	623	262	585	80	.246

2003 Pitching Profile

	Wade Miller	NL Average
Overall Strike %	61.8	62.4
1st Pitch Strike %	53.4	58.4
Ratio	1.31	1.38
Strikeouts per 9 IP	7.73	6.65
Walks per 9 IP	3.70	3.42
Home Runs per 9 IP	0.82	1.05
Strikeout/Walk Ratio	2.09	1.94
Groundball/Flyball Ratio	1.27	1.29

2003 Situational Stats

	W	L	ERA	Sv	IP		AB	H	HR	RBI	Avg
Home	7	4	3.94	0	89.0	LHB	329	85	10	39	.258
Road	7	9	4.30	0	98.1	RHB	366	83	7	41	.227
First Half	6	9	4.66	0	116.0	Sc Pos	149	40	4	59	.268
Scnd Half	8	4	3.28	0	71.1	Clutch	27	7	1	4	.259

2003 Rankings (National League)

- 6th in losses and most pitches thrown per batter (3.92)
- 8th in games started
- 9th in hit batsmen (10) and most strikeouts per nine innings (7.7)
- 10th in most run support per nine innings (5.5) and highest walks per nine innings (3.7)
- Led the Astros in games started, innings pitched, batters faced (797), walks allowed, hit batsmen (10), strikeouts, pitches thrown (3,126), fewest home runs allowed per nine innings (.82) and most strikeouts per nine innings (7.7)

Roy Oswalt

2003 Season

Roy Oswalt's season can only be described as utterly frustrating. He was on the disabled list three times with the same injury—a strained groin—and it bothered him to the very end of the season. Just after the season, he finally had surgery to repair it. All things considered, his 10-5 record, 2.97 ERA and 108 strikeouts were remarkable totals for a staff ace who likely ended up missing 13-14 starts.

Pitching

Oswalt could have had the surgery early on, but he gamely kept trying to come back knowing how much the team depended on him physically and emotionally. He finished the year with the help of a halter-like device that limited his movement but allowed him to pitch. When he is on, he has a nasty 94-MPH fastball that is contrasted by a curve and a changeup, both of which are at least 20 MPH slower than the heater. When he occasionally tried to throw harder, especially during the middle of the season when he was hurting, he tended to lose his exceptional control.

Defense & Hitting

As a fielder, Oswalt handled a perfect 23 of 23 chances last year, and he smoothly executes the 3-1 putout. He fields bunts adeptly and takes his defense very seriously. He works fast and has a reasonably good pickoff move, and opposing big league basestealers are just .500 (13-for-13) against him in his career. The Astros don't expect Oswalt to be much of a threat at the plate, but he works hard on his bunting and in 48 plate appearances he had seven sacrifices last year.

2004 Outlook

Oswalt still seems like a Cy Young Award waiting to happen. His repertoire is varied, and he keeps hitters off-balance as well as any pitcher in baseball when he's on. He has great instincts and studies the game well, but he still could improve on his work habits and preparation. The Astros would also like him to work more on his changeup, but overall, it's hard to find fault with him.

Position: SP
Bats: R **Throws:** R
Ht: 6' 0" **Wt:** 175

Opening Day Age: 26
Born: 8/29/77 in Weir, MS
ML Seasons: 3
Pronunciation: OWES-walt

Overall Statistics

	W	L	Pct.	ERA	G	GS	Sv	IP	H	BB	SO	HR	Avg
'03	10	5	.667	2.97	21	21	0	127.1	116	29	108	15	.246
Car.	43	17	.717	2.92	84	75	0	502.0	457	115	460	45	.243

2003 Pitching Profile

	Roy Oswalt	NL Average
Overall Strike %	67.0	62.4
1st Pitch Strike %	64.7	58.4
Ratio	1.14	1.38
Strikeouts per 9 IP	7.63	6.65
Walks per 9 IP	2.05	3.42
Home Runs per 9 IP	1.06	1.05
Strikeout/Walk Ratio	3.72	1.94
Groundball/Flyball Ratio	1.35	1.29

2003 Situational Stats

	W	L	ERA	Sv	IP		AB	H	HR	RBI	Avg
Home	5	3	2.45	0	69.2	LHB	198	52	3	13	.263
Road	5	2	3.59	0	57.2	RHB	274	64	12	33	.234
First Half	5	5	3.15	0	85.2	Sc Pos	87	22	3	31	.253
Scnd Half	5	0	2.59	0	41.2	Clutch	36	10	1	5	.278

2003 Rankings (National League)

- 7th in winning percentage
- Led the Astros in ERA, winning percentage, highest strikeout-walk ratio (3.7), lowest slugging percentage allowed (.375), lowest on-base percentage allowed (.296), highest groundball-flyball ratio allowed (1.3), lowest stolen-base percentage allowed (16.7), lowest ERA at home, lowest ERA on the road and fewest walks per nine innings (2.0)

Tim Redding

2003 Season

Last season, Tim Redding took his biggest strides yet towards being the reliable pitcher the Astros thought he could be. Overall, he was the team's most consistent starter from beginning to end. Club officials were most pleased with his maturity. Once a pitcher who would blow up when things weren't going his way, Redding kept his composure, pitched through tough stretches and ate up the most innings of his career. His won-lost record would have been much better had it not been for poor run support.

Pitching

Redding's stuff is as good as any pitcher in the organization. He throws a four-seam and two-seam fastball, a curve and slider—all effectively. His fastball averages 91-92 MPH and tops out at 94 MPH. He got his hard-breaking curve over for strikes last year, and his still-developing slider was very good at times. He has been working on a changeup, and the Astros are encouraging him to use that pitch more. When he didn't have his best stuff last year, Redding learned to fight through it and stay in the game by changing speeds and moving the ball around the strike zone.

Defense & Hitting

Redding's defensive style is much like the rest of his game, aggressive, and sometimes that gets him into trouble. He comes off the mound well to field bunts, however, and has the dexterity to start double plays. He works slowly and has a below-average move to first—last year, opposing bases-stealers were 17 of 19 on his watch. Redding is a fairly competent hitter who is aggressive at the plate.

2004 Outlook

Astros officials believe Redding can be one of the top pitchers in the league, and if he reaches that potential, they would have one of the best starting trios in baseball. He needs to continue to learn the subtleties of the game, and he still loses focus. But if he makes as big an improvement this season as he did in 2003, he could be a major winner in '04.

Position: SP
Bats: R **Throws:** R
Ht: 6' 0" **Wt:** 195

Opening Day Age: 26
Born: 2/12/78 in Rochester, NY
ML Seasons: 3

Overall Statistics

	W	L	Pct.	ERA	G	GS	Sv	IP	H	BB	SO	HR	Avg
'03	10	14	.417	3.68	33	32	0	176.0	179	65	116	16	.261
Car.	16	21	.432	4.43	64	55	0	305.0	319	124	234	37	.269

2003 Pitching Profile

	Tim Redding	NL Average
Overall Strike %	62.1	62.4
1st Pitch Strike %	53.4	58.4
Ratio	1.39	1.38
Strikeouts per 9 IP	5.93	6.65
Walks per 9 IP	3.32	3.42
Home Runs per 9 IP	0.82	1.05
Strikeout/Walk Ratio	1.78	1.94
Groundball/Flyball Ratio	1.19	1.29

2003 Situational Stats

	W	L	ERA	Sv	IP		AB	H	HR	RBI	Avg
Home	7	7	3.49	0	95.1	LHB	316	94	8	41	.297
Road	3	7	3.90	0	80.2	RHB	371	85	8	34	.229
First Half	6	8	3.80	0	106.2	Sc Pos	175	41	3	56	.234
Scnd Half	4	6	3.50	0	69.1	Clutch	18	5	0	2	.278

2003 Rankings (National League)

- 1st in least run support per nine innings (3.7)
- 3rd in highest stolen-base percentage allowed (89.5)
- 4th in losses
- 6th in lowest winning percentage
- 9th in stolen bases allowed (17)
- Led the Astros in losses, pickoff throws (65), stolen bases allowed (17) and lowest batting average allowed with runners in scoring position

Jeriome Robertson

2003 Season

Jeriome Robertson had a puzzling season, finishing as the Astros' winningest pitcher despite having the highest ERA of anyone on the staff with more than 21 innings pitched. He benefited from good run support, especially early in the season, as he went 8-3 with a 4.87 ERA before the All-Star break. But he also pitched intelligently, going after hitters aggressively and never getting rattled when things weren't going well.

Pitching

Robertson doesn't have great velocity or lots of movement on his pitches, but he does have good control and knows how to move his offerings around the zone. His primary pitch is a sinker that averages 86-88 MPH. When it hits over 90 MPH, it usually doesn't have the same precision or sinking ability. When it doesn't sink sharply, he gets hit hard. Robertson's curve breaks straight down on righthanded hitters. When he gets his slider in on righties, he gets in trouble. He's still learning a changeup, but had good success with it when he threw it correctly.

Defense & Hitting

Robertson is an average fielder. He comes off the mound well, but as a lefty has trouble fielding and throwing balls hit to the third-base side. He has reasonably good reactions to balls hit right at him, but he covers first too slowly. He possesses the best pickoff move on the staff, a very sneaky slide step. He nailed seven runners last year and kept opponents honest at first. Robertson is overmatched against major league pitching. He was fairly adept at getting the bunt down, though he has mediocre speed and doesn't run the bases well.

2004 Outlook

Astros officials want to see Robertson make big improvements in several areas. They realize he can't always count on good run support. He particularly needs work on his changeup and slider, and while his work habits got better last season, he could improve there as well. He'll never be a dominating starter, but if he continues along his present learning curve, he can be a steady, reliable No. 4.

Position: SP
Bats: L **Throws:** L
Ht: 6' 1" **Wt:** 200

Opening Day Age: 27
Born: 3/30/77 in San Jose, CA
ML Seasons: 2
Pronunciation: JER-oh-mee

Overall Statistics

	W	L	Pct.	ERA	G	GS	Sv	IP	H	BB	SO	HR	Avg
'03	15	9	.625	5.10	32	31	0	160.2	180	64	99	23	.287
Car.	15	11	.577	5.18	43	32	0	170.1	193	69	105	27	.292

2003 Pitching Profile

	Jeriome Robertson	NL Average
Overall Strike %	62.0	62.4
1st Pitch Strike %	60.8	58.4
Ratio	1.52	1.38
Strikeouts per 9 IP	5.55	6.65
Walks per 9 IP	3.59	3.42
Home Runs per 9 IP	1.29	1.05
Strikeout/Walk Ratio	1.55	1.94
Groundball/Flyball Ratio	1.16	1.29

2003 Situational Stats

	W	L	ERA	Sv	IP		AB	H	HR	RBI	Avg
Home	7	4	4.93	0	80.1	LHB	152	37	3	19	.243
Road	8	5	5.27	0	80.1	RHB	476	143	20	64	.300
First Half	8	3	4.87	0	94.1	Sc Pos	133	44	6	63	.331
Scnd Half	7	6	5.43	0	66.1	Clutch	7	2	0	0	.286

2003 Rankings (National League)

- 1st in wins among rookies
- 2nd in losses among rookies
- 3rd in errors at pitcher (4) and highest batting average allowed with runners in scoring position
- 5th in balks (2)
- 8th in highest batting average allowed vs. righthanded batters
- 9th in wins
- Led the Astros in wins, hits allowed, home runs allowed, balks (2), runners caught stealing (7), GDPs induced (14), fewest pitches thrown per batter (3.64) and most run support per nine innings (6.8)

Billy Wagner

2003 Season

Billy Wagner had the finest year of his impressive career, breaking his own club record for saves with 44. Wagner also set career highs for games and innings, while striking out 105 opponents. But he lashed out at management on the final day of the season for being too frugal and not making more moves to help Houston reach the playoffs, and six weeks later he was gone to Philadelphia.

Pitching

Wagner improved as a pitcher last season, adding some subtle elements that helped advance his game. Primarily, he pitched better to both sides of the plate, moving the ball in and out on hitters more intelligently and using his slider more. His explosive fastball regularly is clocked at 99-100 MPH, though he varies the speed of that pitch, easing off it occasionally to a mere 96-97 MPH. When his slider is working, it makes his fastball look like a 105-MPH pitch. In spring training, the Astros had wanted Wagner to experiment with a cutter, but he turned it into a slider and used it much more effectively to get hitters off his fastball.

Defense & Hitting

Wagner is adept at coming off the mound and fielding bunts, and also covers first well when balls are hit to the right side. He does a decent job of controlling the running game with a good, quick move to first, though he rarely finds himself in situations where he is tested. Wagner has has only one career hit (1998), and scored his first career run in a June 4 matchup against the Orioles.

2004 Outlook

Wagner will become the closer the Phillies didn't have last year. And they didn't get him for just this season. They've made it clear they expect to pick up his $9 million option after 2004. He dramatically improves the Philadelphia bullpen and will see as many innings this season as he did last, if not more.

Position: RP
Bats: L **Throws:** L
Ht: 5'11" **Wt:** 195

Opening Day Age: 32
Born: 7/25/71 in Tannersville, VA
ML Seasons: 9

Overall Statistics

	W	L	Pct.	ERA	G	GS	Sv	IP	H	BB	SO	HR	Avg
'03	1	4	.200	1.78	78	0	44	86.0	52	23	105	8	.169
Car.	26	29	.473	2.53	464	0	225	504.1	333	191	694	48	.186

2003 Pitching Profile

	Billy Wagner	NL Average
Overall Strike %	66.9	62.4
1st Pitch Strike %	63.2	58.4
Ratio	0.87	1.38
Strikeouts per 9 IP	10.99	6.65
Walks per 9 IP	2.41	3.42
Home Runs per 9 IP	0.84	1.05
Strikeout/Walk Ratio	4.57	1.94
Groundball/Flyball Ratio	1.14	1.29

2003 Situational Stats

	W	L	ERA	Sv	IP		AB	H	HR	RBI	Avg
Home	1	3	3.32	24	40.2	LHB	74	16	1	1	.216
Road	0	1	0.40	20	45.1	RHB	234	36	7	16	.154
First Half	1	3	2.26	25	51.2	Sc Pos	64	6	0	7	.094
Scnd Half	0	1	1.05	19	34.1	Clutch	192	34	6	13	.177

2003 Rankings (National League)

- 1st in games finished (67) and lowest batting average allowed vs. righthanded batters
- 3rd in saves, save percentage (93.6) and fewest baserunners allowed per nine innings in relief (8.2)
- 4th in most strikeouts per nine innings in relief (11.0)
- 5th in games pitched and relief innings (86.0)
- Led the Astros in games pitched, saves, games finished (67), lowest batting average allowed vs. righthanded batters, save percentage (93.6), relief ERA (1.78), relief losses (4), lowest batting average allowed in relief (.169), fewest baserunners allowed per nine innings in relief (8.2) and most strikeouts per nine innings in relief (11.0)

Houston

Geoff Blum

Position: 3B/2B/SS
Bats: B **Throws:** R
Ht: 6' 3" **Wt:** 200

Opening Day Age: 30
Born: 4/26/73 in
Redwood City, CA
ML Seasons: 5
Pronunciation:
bluhm

Overall Statistics

	G	AB	R	H	D	T	HR	RBI	SB	BB	SO	Avg	OBP	Slg
'03	123	420	51	110	19	0	10	52	0	20	50	.262	.295	.379
Car.	570	1717	214	450	91	8	48	217	13	155	299	.262	.326	.408

2003 Situational Stats

	AB	H	HR	RBI	Avg		AB	H	HR	RBI	Avg
Home	203	61	6	34	.300	LHP	37	5	0	6	.135
Road	217	49	4	18	.226	RHP	383	105	10	46	.274
First Half	272	76	9	33	.279	Sc Pos	104	24	2	37	.231
Scnd Half	148	34	1	19	.230	Clutch	68	16	2	6	.235

2003 Season

Geoff Blum was one of baseball's most versatile players last season, spending time at six different positions (every one but pitcher, catcher and center field). He played most of those games (83) at third base, where he largely split time with Morgan Ensberg. Blum is a career .262 hitter who hit exactly that last season.

Hitting, Baserunning & Defense

Blum looked like he might be off to a career year during the first six weeks of 2003. Then he went into a horrendous 3-for-32 slump, as he played in fewer games in the middle of the season. His glove was invaluable to the team, however. A shortstop early in his career, Blum has soft hands and a lightning release on the double play. His .971 fielding average at third was better than Ensberg's.

2004 Outlook

Blum again will be one of the most valuable players on the team, since he can play so many positions. He assumed the role of primary utilityman after Jose Vizcaino went down with a broken wrist and never relinquished the role. Ensberg still appears to be the third baseman of the present and future, so Blum will have to grow accustomed to being in and out of the lineup.

Morgan Ensberg

Position: 3B
Bats: R **Throws:** R
Ht: 6' 2" **Wt:** 220

Opening Day Age: 28
Born: 8/26/75 in
Hermosa Beach, CA
ML Seasons: 3

Overall Statistics

	G	AB	R	H	D	T	HR	RBI	SB	BB	SO	Avg	OBP	Slg
'03	127	385	69	112	15	1	25	60	7	48	60	.291	.377	.530
Car.	180	524	83	146	22	3	28	79	9	66	86	.279	.368	.492

2003 Situational Stats

	AB	H	HR	RBI	Avg		AB	H	HR	RBI	Avg
Home	188	66	16	36	.351	LHP	98	31	7	20	.316
Road	197	46	9	24	.234	RHP	287	81	18	40	.282
First Half	199	62	17	44	.312	Sc Pos	100	28	4	36	.280
Scnd Half	186	50	8	16	.269	Clutch	59	19	2	12	.322

2003 Season

After a slow start, Morgan Ensberg seemed to finally come into his own as the Astros' regular third baseman, a year *after* the job had been handed to him and he had flopped miserably. Ensberg looked strong from spring training in 2003, and finished with a .291 average and 25 home runs—tying the club record for homers by a third baseman.

Hitting, Baserunning & Defense

Ensberg's hitting is his forte, but he's a slow starter. Knowing that, the club platooned him the first month of the season intentionally trying to bring him along slowly. He caught fire in May and June, hitting .321 and .328, respectively, and though he tailed off considerably in July and August, he came back strong in September. He's a power-hitter and a pull-hitter who hits mostly to left field. Enberg's defense is average. He has a strong arm, but his range is limited and his reactions ordinary. He's also an average baserunner.

2004 Outlook

Ensberg is the starter at third until he plays himself out of the role. Astros officials believe he can be one of the best-hitting third basemen in the game once he finds consistency and a little more maturity. They also think his defense will improve as he settles into the majors.

Adam Everett

Position: SS
Bats: R **Throws:** R
Ht: 6' 0" **Wt:** 160

Opening Day Age: 27
Born: 2/2/77 in Austell, GA
ML Seasons: 3

Overall Statistics

	G	AB	R	H	D	T	HR	RBI	SB	BB	SO	Avg	OBP	Slg
'03	128	387	51	99	18	3	8	51	8	28	66	.256	.320	.380
Car.	177	478	63	116	21	3	8	55	12	40	86	.243	.314	.349

2003 Situational Stats

	AB	H	HR	RBI	Avg		AB	H	HR	RBI	Avg
Home	205	54	5	29	.263	LHP	74	24	3	16	.324
Road	182	45	3	22	.247	RHP	313	75	5	35	.240
First Half	189	48	5	25	.254	Sc Pos	111	29	3	43	.261
Scnd Half	198	51	3	26	.258	Clutch	51	8	1	2	.157

2003 Season

Adam Everett took over at shortstop in much the same fashion as Morgan Ensberg took over at third last year. The previous season, both had been handed the jobs out of spring training and both fell flat at the plate and were sent down. This time around, both were up to the task. Everett hit .256 and even flashed a little pop with his bat.

Hitting, Baserunning & Defense

Everett never will be a strong hitter, but the Astros will be happy if he can bat around .260. Sharing the shortstop job in May, Everett hit only .247, but when handed the job full-time, he responded by hitting .273 in June. What was surprising was that the superb glove he reputedly had wasn't nearly as dependable. His 17 errors led the team in 2003. He looked dazzling on the difficult plays, but often booted the simple ones. He is an excellent baserunner with good speed, and was caught stealing only once in nine tries.

2004 Outlook

Everett will be the Astros' shortstop for a while. He has proven he can hit adequately at the major league level, and that was his only question mark. Team officials believe with a full year behind him, Everett will only get better.

Mike Gallo

Position: RP
Bats: L **Throws:** L
Ht: 6' 0" **Wt:** 175

Opening Day Age: 26
Born: 3/18/78 in Long Beach, CA
ML Seasons: 1

Overall Statistics

	W	L	Pct.	ERA	G	GS	Sv	IP	H	BB	SO	HR	Avg
'03	1	0	1.000	3.00	32	0	0	30.0	28	10	16	3	.267
Car.	1	0	1.000	3.00	32	0	0	30.0	28	10	16	3	.267

2003 Situational Stats

	W	L	ERA	Sv	IP		AB	H	HR	RBI	Avg
Home	0	0	4.15	0	13.0	LHB	44	10	1	3	.227
Road	1	0	2.12	0	17.0	RHB	61	18	2	9	.295
First Half	0	0	0.00	0	3.0	Sc Pos	29	6	1	10	.207
Scnd Half	1	0	3.33	0	27.0	Clutch	14	3	0	1	.214

2003 Season

Mike Gallo probably was the biggest pitching surprise in the Astros' organization last season. At the beginning of the year, he wasn't even a blip on the radar, just trying to make it to Double-A. He arrived with the big club in early July and didn't allow a run his first 11 appearances. By the end of the season, he was putting in regular appearances out of the Houston bullpen.

Pitching, Defense & Hitting

The Astros loved Gallo's laid-back, carefree style and his iron-willed composure. He never appeared nervous or intimidated by big league hitters. He has a fastball that runs 89-90 MPH that he uses frequently, with a good curve to complement it. His ability to keep the ball down is excellent, and even when he does get in trouble, he never seemed fazed. He made one error in the field last year, but countered that miscue with a pair of pickoffs.

2004 Outlook

It's hard to tell if Gallo is the real deal, but the Astros think they have a keeper. While club officials want him to work on getting ahead of hitters more and demonstrate better command of both of his primary pitches, they feel with his mental approach to the game, he just might stick.

Carlos Hernandez

Position: SP
Bats: B **Throws:** L
Ht: 5'10" **Wt:** 185

Opening Day Age: 23
Born: 4/22/80 in Guacara, VZ
ML Seasons: 2

Overall Statistics

	W	L	Pct.	ERA	G	GS	Sv	IP	H	BB	SO	HR	Avg
'03				Did Not Play									
Car.	8	5	.615	3.92	26	24	0	128.2	123	68	110	12	.251

2003 Situational Stats

	W	L	ERA	Sv	IP		AB	H	HR	RBI	Avg
Home	–	–	–	–	–	LHB	–	–	–	–	–
Road	–	–	–	–	–	RHB	–	–	–	–	–
First Half	–	–	–	–	–	Sc Pos	–	–	–	–	–
Scnd Half	–	–	–	–	–	Clutch	–	–	–	–	–

2003 Season

After two seasons of promising performances, both marred by injuries to his shoulder, Carlos Hernandez finally gave up on rehab and underwent surgery in February 2003. That knocked him out of the entire 2003 season, but not out of the Astros' thoughts. The player who once was likened to a young Fernando Valenzuela worked very hard on a comeback, and pitched well in the instructional league in October.

Pitching, Defense & Hitting

Officials were impressed with how hard Hernandez rehabbed after the surgery and hope that the feisty lefty will claim one of the five spots in the rotation. He has a sneaky fastball that runs 90-91 MPH. The way he hides it and delivers it, it jumps on hitters as if it were faster. He then comes in with a very good curve and changeup, and he can throw a decent slider as well. Hernandez is a capable fielder who also holds his own at the plate.

2004 Outlook

The Astros want this 23-year-old to continue to learn the game and mature as a professional, and they believe with his intensity and dedication he will move towards those goals. Hernandez could solve a huge problem in the rotation if he returns to his 2001 form.

Brad Lidge

Position: RP
Bats: R **Throws:** R
Ht: 6' 5" **Wt:** 210

Opening Day Age: 27
Born: 12/23/76 in Sacramento, CA
ML Seasons: 2

Overall Statistics

	W	L	Pct.	ERA	G	GS	Sv	IP	H	BB	SO	HR	Avg
'03	6	3	.667	3.60	78	0	1	85.0	60	42	97	6	.202
Car.	7	3	.700	3.84	84	1	1	93.2	72	51	109	6	.216

2003 Situational Stats

	W	L	ERA	Sv	IP		AB	H	HR	RBI	Avg
Home	2	1	3.86	0	39.2	LHB	135	31	3	18	.230
Road	4	2	3.38	1	45.1	RHB	162	29	3	14	.179
First Half	4	1	2.52	1	53.2	Sc Pos	79	19	3	27	.241
Scnd Half	2	2	5.46	0	31.1	Clutch	168	36	2	18	.214

2003 Season

Brad Lidge proved he could go an entire season without a major injury. He settled into a regular pattern of pitching the seventh inning, while Octavio Dotel pitched the eighth and Billy Wagner the ninth. Lidge finished second in the National League in holds with 28, behind only Dotel's 33.

Pitching, Defense & Hitting

Lidge has long been thought of as perhaps the most talented arm in the organization, but injuries held him back his first four seasons in the minors. His fastball hits 97-98 MPH at the top, and regularly goes 95-96 MPH. He also has a good slider. Lidge appeared to tire a little in midseason, but he rallied in September and finished with more than a strikeout per inning. Lidge did a fine job in the field and has a sneaky pickoff move for a righty. He rarely came to the plate last year.

2004 Outlook

The Astros feel Lidge has a tendency to overthrow when he falls behind and think he needs to work on his focus. With Billy Wagner traded to Phiadelphia, he'll be called on for the eighth-inning role that Dotel filled in recent seasons, so Lidge will play under a more intense spotlight. The club now believes he is the closer of the future, when Dotel is done with that job.

Orlando Merced

Position: RF/1B/LF
Bats: L **Throws:** R
Ht: 6' 1" **Wt:** 195

Opening Day Age: 37
Born: 11/2/66 in San Juan, PR
ML Seasons: 13
Pronunciation: mer-SAID

Overall Statistics

	G	AB	R	H	D	T	HR	RBI	SB	BB	SO	Avg	OBP	Slg
'03	123	212	20	49	17	2	3	26	3	15	33	.231	.283	.373
Car.	1391	3998	564	1108	229	28	103	585	57	487	661	.277	.355	.426

2003 Situational Stats

	AB	H	HR	RBI	Avg		AB	H	HR	RBI	Avg
Home	83	19	1	11	.229	LHP	27	8	1	6	.296
Road	129	30	2	15	.233	RHP	185	41	2	20	.222
First Half	155	39	1	21	.252	Sc Pos	61	13	1	22	.213
Scnd Half	57	10	2	5	.175	Clutch	56	13	0	6	.232

2003 Season

Orlando Merced dropped way off the impressive figures of the previous two seasons, but his versatility still proved valuable, as he started at DH, first base and left and right fields. Richard Hidalgo's big season probably affected Merced as much as anything. Merced had earned the assignment of platooning in right field with Hidalgo in 2002, but Hidalgo kept him on the bench much more last year.

Hitting, Baserunning & Defense

Merced is a contact hitter who always has hit to all fields. A lefthanded batter, he plays almost exclusively against righthanders. He exhibited less pop at the plate last year than he had had the previous two seasons, collecting only three homers. He is a capable right fielder with an average arm. He also can play first and third in a pinch. As a baserunner, he has deceptive speed and is smart enough to know when to take extra bases.

2004 Outlook

The Astros like Merced's versatility and probably will need a backup at first and right field, especially if youngster Jason Lane takes over in right. But Merced will need to come around at the plate if he is to stay around very long.

Ricky Stone

Position: RP
Bats: R **Throws:** R
Ht: 6' 1" **Wt:** 170

Opening Day Age: 29
Born: 2/28/75 in Hamilton, OH
ML Seasons: 3

Overall Statistics

	W	L	Pct.	ERA	G	GS	Sv	IP	H	BB	SO	HR	Avg
'03	6	4	.600	3.69	65	0	1	83.0	76	31	47	11	.247
Car.	9	7	.563	3.59	149	0	2	168.0	162	67	114	21	.256

2003 Situational Stats

	W	L	ERA	Sv	IP		AB	H	HR	RBI	Avg
Home	4	1	3.57	1	40.1	LHB	124	36	6	24	.290
Road	2	3	3.80	0	42.2	RHB	184	40	5	26	.217
First Half	5	3	3.52	1	53.2	Sc Pos	99	24	5	41	.242
Scnd Half	1	1	3.99	0	29.1	Clutch	41	11	0	3	.268

2003 Season

Ricky Stone worked just 5.2 innings more in 2003 than he did when he set the club rookie record with 78 appearances in 2002, and he enjoyed just about the same success. He was used a little more often to pitch a full inning or more, though he remained primarily a one- or two-out role player.

Pitching, Defense & Hitting

Stone uses a sinker that tops out at only about 88 MPH, but he has good command of the pitch. He also can throw his breaking ball for strikes consistently. He's a groundball pitcher who has a good changeup and a "slurve" that is effective. Stone is a competent fielder, though he's not very fast off the mound. His short appearances lead to few chances against opposing basestealers and even fewer chances at the plate. He's still looking for his first big league hit.

2004 Outlook

Stone is good when he gets ahead of hitters but suffers whenever he falls behind. The Astros want him to learn to get ahead more often and be able to settle down better when he's behind. A 29-year-old who spent eight seasons in the minors, he likely will get a chance to play the same role for the Astros this season as he did in '03.

Ron Villone

Position: SP
Bats: L **Throws:** L
Ht: 6' 3" **Wt:** 243

Opening Day Age: 34
Born: 1/16/70 in Englewood, NJ
ML Seasons: 9
Pronunciation: vill-OWN

Overall Statistics

	W	L	Pct.	ERA	G	GS	Sv	IP	H	BB	SO	HR	Avg
'03	6	6	.500	4.13	19	19	0	106.2	91	48	91	16	.233
Car.	39	43	.476	4.91	338	83	5	765.2	746	403	589	96	.258

2003 Situational Stats

	W	L	ERA	Sv	IP			AB	H	HR	RBI	Avg
Home	4	3	4.17	0	58.1	LHB		101	27	5	9	.267
Road	2	3	4.10	0	48.1	RHB		289	64	11	30	.221
First Half	1	0	2.70	0	30.0	Sc Pos		67	15	2	21	.224
Scnd Half	5	6	4.70	0	76.2	Clutch		14	6	2	3	.429

2003 Season

Ron Villone signed with the team as a free agent in May and pitched well almost immediately on a staff that was desperate for a starter to eat up innings. He kept the team in almost every game he pitched, posting a 6-3 record with a 3.28 ERA in his first 14 starts, but he tired in September, when he went 0-3 with a 7.03 ERA.

Pitching, Defense & Hitting

Astros officials thought Villone was a much better pitcher last season than he was when he was with them in 2001. He had better command and more confidence. He throws a cut fastball in the high 80s that is his best pitch. He also has a good slider, changeup and slider-curve. Houston also loved his tough approach and willingness to take the ball in any situation. Villone had the first home run of his nine-year career last season, but he's no real threat at the plate. He's an average fielder.

2004 Outlook

A journeyman lefthander who has been with eight teams (including twice with the Astros), Villone will get a chance to win a spot in spring training. He's no lock, but the Astros like his approach to the game and believe he's a strong influence in the clubhouse.

Jose Vizcaino

Position: SS/2B
Bats: B **Throws:** R
Ht: 6' 1" **Wt:** 185

Opening Day Age: 36
Born: 3/26/68 in San Cristobal, DR
ML Seasons: 15
Pronunciation: vis-kie-ee-no

Overall Statistics

	G	AB	R	H	D	T	HR	RBI	SB	BB	SO	Avg	OBP	Slg
'03	91	189	14	47	7	3	3	26	0	8	22	.249	.281	.365
Car.	1504	4692	565	1276	167	42	30	416	71	326	636	.272	.319	.345

2003 Situational Stats

	AB	H	HR	RBI	Avg		AB	H	HR	RBI	Avg
Home	85	20	2	11	.235	LHP	36	8	0	0	.222
Road	104	27	1	15	.260	RHP	153	39	3	26	.255
First Half	143	35	2	19	.245	Sc Pos	54	17	3	25	.315
Scnd Half	46	12	1	7	.261	Clutch	45	12	1	6	.267

2003 Season

It was a miserable season for Jose Vizcaino, who got off to a slow start at the plate and then broke his left wrist. He was out nearly two months and even when he returned, he never achieved the effectiveness he had in 2002, when he had been one of the league's top utilitymen. Last season, after hitting .125 in April and breaking his arm in late June, he struggled to hit .249 overall.

Hitting, Baserunning & Defense

Vizcaino is a contact hitter who sprays the ball to all fields. He's a smart player who hits behind the runner and can go to the opposite field. He hits few homers but can bunt well. Vizcaino has average speed, but he is a solid defensive player who is as comfortable at shortstop as he is at first base. His baserunning is smart, and he'll occasionally surprise with a stolen base.

2004 Outlook

Vizcaino is not getting any younger, and the injury last year stole precious time from his career. The Astros re-signed him for 2004, but with Geoff Blum playing so well as a utility infielder last season, Vizcaino will need to perform well early on to get as much playing time as he has in the past.

Other Houston Astros

Nate Bland (Pos: LHP, Age: 29)

	W	L	Pct.	ERA	G	GS	Sv	IP	H	BB	SO	HR	Avg
'03	1	2	.333	5.75	22	0	0	20.1	22	12	18	3	.286
Car.	1	2	.333	5.75	22	0	0	20.1	22	12	18	3	.286

Bland split the first half of the 2003 campaign between Triple-A New Orleans and Houston, appearing in 39 games. He was sidelined most of the second half of the season with elbow soreness. 2004 Outlook: C

Eric Bruntlett (Pos: SS, Age: 26, Bats: R)

	G	AB	R	H	D	T	HR	RBI	SB	BB	SO	Avg	OBP	Slg
'03	31	54	3	14	3	0	1	4	0	0	10	.259	.255	.370
Car.	31	54	3	14	3	0	1	4	0	0	10	.259	.255	.370

Bruntlett made his major league debut in 2003, filling in for injured regulars in the middle of the Astros' infield. He batted .303 against righthanders, but hit just .190 facing lefthanders. 2004 Outlook: C

Kirk Bullinger (Pos: RHP, Age: 34)

	W	L	Pct.	ERA	G	GS	Sv	IP	H	BB	SO	HR	Avg
'03	0	0	–	6.75	7	0	0	8.0	7	1	5	2	.219
Car.	1	0	1.000	7.08	22	0	0	20.1	27	3	11	3	.310

Bullinger served as the primary closer for Triple-A New Orleans in 2003, posting 20 saves and a 1.94 ERA. With a career 2.12 ERA in 535 minor league games, he should get some looks this offseason. 2004 Outlook: C

Raul Chavez (Pos: C, Age: 31, Bats: R)

	G	AB	R	H	D	T	HR	RBI	SB	BB	SO	Avg	OBP	Slg
'03	19	37	5	10	1	1	1	4	0	1	6	.270	.289	.432
Car.	53	116	10	30	4	1	2	11	2	6	18	.259	.296	.362

Chavez is solid defensively, but his lack of power and consistency with the bat have prevented him from hanging on to a job. He could make the Astros' squad as Brad Ausmus' backup in 2004. 2004 Outlook: C

Tripp Cromer (Pos: 2B, Age: 36, Bats: R)

	G	AB	R	H	D	T	HR	RBI	SB	BB	SO	Avg	OBP	Slg
'03	3	4	0	1	0	1	0	1	0	0	0	.250	.250	.750
Car.	196	524	54	118	22	1	12	48	0	27	101	.225	.266	.340

Cromer made his pro debut in 1989, but has appeared in just 196 major league games in his career. The infielder spent most of 2003 with Triple-A New Orleans, batting .252 with four homers in 84 games. 2004 Outlook: C

Jared Fernandez (Pos: RHP, Age: 32)

	W	L	Pct.	ERA	G	GS	Sv	IP	H	BB	SO	HR	Avg
'03	3	3	.500	3.99	12	6	0	38.1	37	12	19	2	.259
Car.	4	7	.364	4.26	31	16	0	101.1	109	42	60	8	.277

Fernandez was in the hunt for a starting job last spring, but was slowed by a back injury and spent most of 2003 in the minors. He had surgery to repair the problem, but should be ready for 2004. 2004 Outlook: C

Brian L. Hunter (Pos: RF/CF, Age: 33, Bats: R)

	G	AB	R	H	D	T	HR	RBI	SB	BB	SO	Avg	OBP	Slg
'03	56	98	13	23	6	1	0	13	0	6	21	.235	.278	.316
Car.	1000	3347	500	882	146	28	25	241	260	243	581	.264	.313	.346

Hunter, whose best attribute is his speed, did not record a stolen base in 56 games with the Astros last season. The team released the outfielder in July after he batted just .235 in 98 at-bats, and San Diego signed him to a minor league deal in the offseason. 2004 Outlook: C

Jonathan Johnson (Pos: RHP, Age: 29)

	W	L	Pct.	ERA	G	GS	Sv	IP	H	BB	SO	HR	Avg
'03	0	1	.000	5.87	4	3	0	15.1	20	15	7	2	.323
Car.	2	4	.333	6.63	42	4	0	77.1	96	53	68	9	.307

Johnson spent a couple of months with Triple-A New Orleans, going 5-4 with a 3.92 ERA in 13 starts. However, he left a game in July and later told the Astros that he was retiring from baseball. 2004 Outlook: D

Jason Lane (Pos: CF, Age: 27, Bats: R)

	G	AB	R	H	D	T	HR	RBI	SB	BB	SO	Avg	OBP	Slg
'03	18	27	5	8	2	0	4	10	0	0	2	.296	.296	.815
Car.	62	96	17	28	5	1	8	20	1	10	14	.292	.355	.615

Lane struggled with a groin injury most of last season and was unable to break the Astros' lineup. The outfielder, who hit .316 with 38 homers at Double-A in 2001, has a shot at making the team in 2004 despite October surgery to treat a sports hernia. 2004 Outlook: C

Dave Matranga (Pos: 2B, Age: 27, Bats: R)

	G	AB	R	H	D	T	HR	RBI	SB	BB	SO	Avg	OBP	Slg
'03	6	5	1	1	0	0	1	1	0	0	2	.200	.200	.800
Car.	6	5	1	1	0	0	1	1	0	0	2	.200	.200	.800

Matranga spent most of last season with Triple-A New Orleans, batting .241 with three homers and 25 RBI. He was called up for a short stint in June and homered in his first major league at-bat. 2004 Outlook: C

Mitch Meluskey (Pos: C, Age: 30, Bats: B)

	G	AB	R	H	D	T	HR	RBI	SB	BB	SO	Avg	OBP	Slg
'03	12	9	1	1	1	0	0	2	0	2	2	.111	.250	.222
Car.	155	414	56	117	24	0	15	75	2	68	89	.283	.386	.449

Meluskey was released by the A's last April, then sat out nearly four months before signing a minor league deal with the Astros. The catcher likely will spend most, if not all, of 2004 in the minors. 2004 Outlook: C

Dan Miceli (Pos: RHP, Age: 33)

	W	L	Pct.	ERA	G	GS	Sv	IP	H	BB	SO	HR	Avg
'03	2	4	.333	3.20	57	0	1	70.1	59	25	58	13	.223
Car.	35	42	.455	4.59	505	9	33	572.2	566	250	512	78	.258

Miceli bounced around last season, spending time with the Indians, Yankees, Rockies and Astros. Despite the movement, he stayed focused and posted a respectable 3.20 ERA in 57 appearances. He agreed to a one-year, $600,000 deal with Houston in November. 2004 Outlook: B

Houston

Brian Moehler (Pos: RHP, Age: 32)

	W	L	Pct.	ERA	G	GS	Sv	IP	H	BB	SO	HR	Avg
'03	0	0	–	7.90	3	3	0	13.2	22	6	5	4	.379
Car.	50	56	.472	4.57	144	143	0	866.0	986	244	469	110	.287

Moehler, who battled shoulder problems the previous two years, underwent surgery to repair a partially torn ligament in his pitching elbow last May. He likely will be sidelined until at least the middle of 2004. 2004 Outlook: C

Pete Munro (Pos: RHP, Age: 28)

	W	L	Pct.	ERA	G	GS	Sv	IP	H	BB	SO	HR	Avg
'03	3	4	.429	4.67	40	2	0	54.0	63	26	27	7	.294
Car.	9	12	.429	4.76	99	21	0	215.2	260	88	126	19	.304

Munro, who started and pitched in relief, struggled with his control at times in 2003. In 45 appearances with the Astros and Triple-A New Orleans, he allowed 91 hits and 38 walks in 76.1 innings. 2004 Outlook: C

Colin Porter (Pos: CF, Age: 28, Bats: L)

	G	AB	R	H	D	T	HR	RBI	SB	BB	SO	Avg	OBP	Slg
'03	24	32	5	6	0	0	0	0	1	1	17	.188	.212	.188
Car.	24	32	5	6	0	0	0	0	1	1	17	.188	.212	.188

Porter turned in a solid season at Triple-A in 2003, batting .320 with 11 homers, 50 RBI and 22 stolen bases in 102 games. But due to the logjam in the Astros' outfield, he saw just 32 at-bats with Houston. 2004 Outlook: C

Brandon Puffer (Pos: RHP, Age: 28)

	W	L	Pct.	ERA	G	GS	Sv	IP	H	BB	SO	HR	Avg
'03	0	0	–	5.14	13	0	0	21.0	24	16	10	2	.300
Car.	3	3	.500	4.60	68	0	0	90.0	91	54	58	5	.268

After 55 appearances with the Astros in 2002, Puffer pitched in just 13 games with Houston last year. His struggles against lefthanders might be preventing him from earning a full-time shot in the majors. 2004 Outlook: C

Rodrigo Rosario (Pos: RHP, Age: 26)

	W	L	Pct.	ERA	G	GS	Sv	IP	H	BB	SO	HR	Avg
'03	1	0	1.000	1.13	2	2	0	8.0	5	3	6	0	.172
Car.	1	0	1.000	1.13	2	2	0	8.0	5	3	6	0	.172

Rosario debuted in impressive fashion last June, but shoulder surgery soon ended his season and he eventually was released. If healthy, he could return to compete for a spot in somebody's rotation. 2004 Outlook: B

Kirk Saarloos (Pos: RHP, Age: 24)

	W	L	Pct.	ERA	G	GS	Sv	IP	H	BB	SO	HR	Avg
'03	2	1	.667	4.93	36	4	0	49.1	55	17	43	4	.281
Car.	8	8	.500	5.61	53	21	0	134.2	155	44	97	16	.294

Saarloos posted a 2.97 ERA in relief last season, compared to a 10.38 ERA as a starter. The righthander is young, and the Astros still plan on working him into their starting rotation down the line. 2004 Outlook: B

Rick White (Pos: RHP, Age: 35)

	W	L	Pct.	ERA	G	GS	Sv	IP	H	BB	SO	HR	Avg
'03	1	2	.333	5.78	49	0	1	67.0	74	21	54	13	.280
Car.	28	40	.412	4.17	390	18	12	606.0	633	193	400	61	.270

White began last season with the Chicago White Sox, but he was waived after going 1-2 with a 6.61 ERA in 34 games. He was claimed by the Astros and improved his numbers, posting a 3.72 ERA in 15 appearances. 2004 Outlook: C

Houston Astros Minor League Prospects

Organization Overview:

The Jeff Bagwell and Craig Biggio era clearly has been Houston's most successful period in franchise history. However, the Astros never won a playoff series during their glory years, and that era looks like it soon will end. While replacements need to be found, they're unlikely to emerge within the organization, at least in the near future. The system has pushed players to the big leagues in recent years, thinning its ranks at the upper levels. The Astros appear more set at Class-A and below, where, unlike its top two teams, Houston's four lowest affiliates each finished with winning records in 2003. The Astros fielded a team in high Class-A last season, moving one of the two low-A affiliates they had been utilizing. The move figures to pay off in the long run. In the near term, catcher John Buck might have the best chance of contributing in 2004. A pitching prospect or two also may be ready to break through.

Jimmy Barrett

Position: P
Bats: R **Throws:** R
Ht: 6' 2" **Wt:** 190

Opening Day Age: 22
Born: 6/7/81 in Cumberland, MD

Recent Statistics

	W	L	ERA	G	GS	Sv	IP	H	R	BB	SO	HR
2002 A Lexington	9	5	2.81	27	22	1	134.1	112	53	40	131	13
2003 A Salem	7	10	5.33	26	26	0	138.1	160	87	56	75	13

Barrett seemed to turn a corner in 2002, when he fanned nearly a batter per inning while fashioning a sub-3.00 ERA in the Class-A South Atlantic League. But he failed to build on that success last season, at least in its early stages. Nevertheless, he pitched well late in the year at high Class-A. It isn't hard to see what intrigues the Astros. Barrett's fastball will touch 95 MPH, and he blends in good breaking balls and off-speed stuff. All the tools are there, so it appears to be a question of whether he'll harness them. If he can continue improving his consistency and command, as he did late in 2003, he has a chance.

Taylor Buchholz

Position: P
Bats: R **Throws:** R
Ht: 6' 3" **Wt:** 220

Opening Day Age: 22
Born: 10/3/81 in Lower Merion, PA

Recent Statistics

	W	L	ERA	G	GS	Sv	IP	H	R	BB	SO	HR
2002 A Clearwater	10	6	3.29	23	23	0	158.2	140	66	51	129	11
2002 AA Reading	0	2	7.43	4	4	0	23.0	29	19	6	17	5
2003 AA Reading	9	11	3.55	25	24	0	144.2	136	62	33	114	14

The Astros remembered Buchholz from their evaluation of him prior to the 2000 draft. They had been intrigued by his arm, but thought there were signability issues, considering his commitment to North Carolina.

And sure enough, Buchholz slipped to the sixth round that year before his hometown Phillies swooped in and inked him to a big contract. Three years later, the Astros managed to land him as part of the package for Billy Wagner. Buchholz is a big guy who has thrown in the low 90s in the past, complemented by a curveball and changeup. He probably will be the standard by which the Wagner trade will be judged in the future.

John Buck

Position: C
Bats: R **Throws:** R
Ht: 6' 3" **Wt:** 220

Opening Day Age: 23
Born: 7/7/80 in Kemmerer, WY

Recent Statistics

	G	AB	R	H	D	T	HR	RBI	SB	BB	SO	Avg
2002 AA Round Rock	120	448	48	118	29	3	12	89	2	31	93	.263
2003 AAA New Orl'ns	78	274	32	70	18	2	2	39	1	14	53	.255

Buck has been considered one of the top catching prospects in baseball the last few years. But after launching 22 homers in the Class-A South Atlantic League in 2001, he hasn't hit with as much gusto the past couple years. Buck still boasts plus raw power; it just hasn't been demonstrated with great frequency recently. A broken hand derailed his 2003 season, helping explain part of the slide. Still, he remains defensively sound behind the plate. He calls a good game and handles pitchers well. His hands are fine and he has an above-average arm, though he sometimes tends to get a bit long with his throws. While Buck may be back at Triple-A to begin the new season, a spot on Houston's roster later in 2004 isn't out of the question.

Chris Burke

Position: 2B
Bats: R **Throws:** R
Ht: 5' 11" **Wt:** 190

Opening Day Age: 24
Born: 3/11/80 in Louisville, KY

Recent Statistics

	G	AB	R	H	D	T	HR	RBI	SB	BB	SO	Avg
2002 AA Round Rock	136	481	66	127	19	8	3	37	16	39	61	.264
2003 AA Round Rock	137	549	88	165	23	8	3	41	34	57	57	.301

Burke returned to Double-A last year, where he ranked fourth in the Texas League with a .301 average. In addition to his improved average, Burke sharpened his batting eye and doubled his stolen-base total from the previous year. He had led the Southeastern Conference in a number of offensive categories, including home runs, before getting picked with the 10th overall selection in 2001. Nevertheless, he profiles as a top-of-the-order hitter, with nice bat control, a decent on-base percentage, and the ability to steal 30-40 bases. His arm is a bit short for shortstop, but he has the hands and actions afield to handle second base. After two years at Double-A, he should be ready to test Triple-A at age 24.

Hector Gimenez

Position: C   **Opening Day Age:** 21
Bats: B **Throws:** R   **Born:** 9/27/82 in
Ht: 5' 10" **Wt:** 180   Varacuy, VZ

Recent Statistics

	G	AB	R	H	D	T	HR	RBI	SB	BB	SO	Avg
2002 A Lexington	85	297	41	78	16	1	11	42	2	25	78	.263
2003 A Salem	109	381	41	94	17	1	7	54	2	29	75	.247

The Astros signed Gimenez in 1999. After playing the next two seasons in the Venezuelan League, he jumped to the Class-A South Atlantic League in 2002, where he impressed both behind the plate and with the bat. Gimenez' numbers weren't quite as strong at high Class-A Salem last season, though he still has a chance to be an offensive catcher. He's a switch-hitter who's shown extra-base power. His walk rate declined in 2003, though he compensated a bit with fewer strikeouts. His defense also is getting better. He catches well, and his strongest tool is an outstanding throwing arm. If Gimenez continues to progress, the Astros will face a happy dilemma when choosing between him and John Buck as their long-term receiving option.

Fernando Nieve

Position: P   **Opening Day Age:** 21
Bats: R **Throws:** R   **Born:** 7/15/82 in Puerto
Ht: 6' 0" **Wt:** 170   Cabello, Carabobo, VZ

Recent Statistics

	W	L	ERA	G	GS	Sv	IP	H	R	BB	SO	HR
2002 R Martinsville	4	1	2.39	13	13	0	67.2	46	23	27	60	5
2002 A Lexington	0	1	6.00	1	1	0	3.0	6	5	0	2	0
2003 A Lexington	14	9	3.65	28	28	0	150.1	133	69	65	144	10

The Astros have had success developing pitchers like Roy Oswalt and Tim Redding, righthanders who don't exceed six feet in height. Such short stature has tended to stigmatize righthanders in other organizations, but Nieve may be the next Astros six-footer who follows in the Oswalt-Redding mold. Nieve possesses plus stuff, with a mid-90s fastball, hard slider and the makings of a serviceable changeup. His command improved in 2003, and he threw more strikes. He has the potential to be yet another Astros success story who was signed out of Venezuela, a fertile pipeline for the organization. Although Nieve doesn't have much experience above rookie ball, the Astros say he could come on quickly.

Chad Qualls

Position: P   **Opening Day Age:** 25
Bats: R **Throws:** R   **Born:** 8/17/78 in Harbor
Ht: 6' 5" **Wt:** 205   City, CA

Recent Statistics

	W	L	ERA	G	GS	Sv	IP	H	R	BB	SO	HR
2002 AA Round Rock	6	13	4.36	29	29	0	163.0	174	92	67	142	9
2003 AA Round Rock	8	11	3.85	28	28	0	175.1	174	85	61	132	12

Houston's Double-A affiliate at Round Rock really struggled last year, finishing 48 games under .500. So Qualls' 8-11 record is a bit deceiving. In reality, the Astros are pleased with the way he stepped up in the second half. He gained a little bit better command of his low-to-mid 90s fastball, and his slider was thrown with a higher arm angle. The fastball features plus movement, and Qualls has worked on his changeup. He's a big, strong hurler who has pitched at least 162 innings each of the past three seasons. Selected in the second round of the 2000 draft, Qualls almost certainly was the Astros' best pitching prospect at Double-A last year. He would seem to be very much in their future plans.

Tom Whiteman

Position: SS   **Opening Day Age:** 24
Bats: R **Throws:** R   **Born:** 7/14/79 in
Ht: 6' 3" **Wt:** 175   Oklahoma City, OK

Recent Statistics

	G	AB	R	H	D	T	HR	RBI	SB	BB	SO	Avg
2002 AA Round Rock	15	56	3	10	2	1	0	5	1	4	17	.179
2002 A Lexington	90	350	50	106	29	2	10	49	6	36	66	.303
2003 AA Round Rock	133	532	65	139	18	2	13	70	3	35	102	.261

Whiteman has encountered some difficulty making the adjustment to Double-A. He had ranked second in the Class-A South Atlantic League with a .319 average in 2001, but struggled in 15 games at Round Rock in 2002. He tried mastering the Texas League again last year, but endured an up-and-down campaign. Whiteman continues to carry loads of offensive potential. The Astros think he can slug 20 homers and hit in the .280-.290 range. If he manages to pull that off while playing shortstop, he clearly would be a valuable commodity. He has played some third base in the past, but profiles at short, with enough range, arm and actions for the position. He is just an average runner. It'll be interesting to see how he handles the jump to Triple-A.

Others to Watch

Third baseman **Jason Alfaro** (26) might have the best infield arm in the organization and seemingly has played better the higher he's gone. He doesn't run well, but could be a decent offensive option. . . Righthander **Jared Gothreaux'** (24) size and makeup remind some of Jeff Brantley. Gothreaux isn't yet as polished, but he features a low-to-mid 90s fastball and a hard slider with bite. He went 13-4 at high Class-A, mostly as a starter, though a setup role may be in his future. . . Righthander **D.J. Houlton** (24) possesses only average stuff across the board, but succeeds with good intangibles. He's an innings eater who works up and down and throws strikes. His velocity has picked up to the 89-90 MPH range. . . Righthander **Tony Pluta** (21) underwent Tommy John surgery and isn't expected back until the middle of 2004. He has reached the upper 90s in the past and shown an improving breaking ball and good feel for a changeup. . . First baseman **Todd Self** (25) and has hit nothing but .300 the past three years. Even better, he walks a lot, so he's always on base. The problem is that he's a bit overaged for the level he's reached.

Dodger Stadium

Offense

Dodger Stadium continues to be one of the most pitcher-friendly parks in baseball. It is not a huge park, but the outfield walls angle sharply from the foul poles to the gaps, so it takes a good shot to leave the yard. The ball travels much better during the day; the night air tends to be moist and heavy as it rolls in from the Pacific Ocean. There is usually a left-to-right field breeze, giving lefties a slight advantage.

Defense

There are not too many funny bounces off Dodger Stadium's concentric outfield walls. The only tricky spots are down the left and right-field lines; twice last season seemingly routine doubles down the line took crazy hops and ended up becoming inside-the-park homers. As the summer sun grows hotter, the infield surface gets harder and harder, resulting in some bad hops.

Who It Helps the Most

Almost any pitcher becomes better in Dodger Stadium, as balls that might be three-run homers elsewhere end up falling harmlessly into outfielders' mitts. Kaz Ishii and Odalis Perez have been especially effective at Dodger Stadium during their two seasons with the club.

Who It Hurts the Most

As might be expected, flyball hitters are the ones most hurt by the heavy air. Not only do their shots stay in the yard, but their at-bats are often terminated by foul pops that would reach the third row in other cities. Adrian Beltre has hit nearly 50 points higher on the road than at home during his Dodger career.

Rookies & Newcomers

The Dodgers have a lot of fine young pitchers rapidly rising through their minor league system. Whether they be a hard-thrower like Edwin Jackson or more finesse-types like Greg Miller and Joel Hanrahan, they will get every chance to succeed by pitching half their games in Los Angeles.

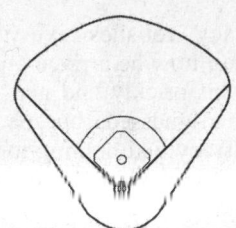

Dimensions: LF-330, LCF-385, CF-395, RCF-385, RF-330

Capacity: 56,000

Elevation: 340 feet

Surface: Grass

Foul Territory: Large

Park Factors

2003 Season

| | Home Games | | | Away Games | | | |
	Dodgers	Opp	Total	Dodgers	Opp	Total	Index
G	72	72	144	72	72	144	
Avg	.241	.222	.231	.252	.247	.250	93
AB	2316	2373	4689	2551	2378	4929	95
R	243	222	465	279	281	560	83
H	557	526	1083	643	587	1230	88
2B	114	74	188	119	111	230	86
3B	8	4	12	14	20	34	37
HR	59	62	121	54	51	105	121
BB	170	230	400	201	246	447	94
SO	425	607	1032	450	534	984	110
E	56	46	102	52	52	104	98
E-Infield	44	43	87	41	41	82	106
LHB-Avg	.249	.215	.235	.245	.238	.242	97
LHB-HR	29	19	48	27	15	42	117
RHB-Avg	.231	.226	.228	.259	.252	.255	89
RHB-HR	30	43	73	27	36	63	124

2001-2003

| | Home Games | | | Away Games | | | |
	Dodgers	Opp	Total	Dodgers	Opp	Total	Index
G	216	216	432	219	219	438	
Avg	.247	.231	.239	.265	.252	.259	92
AB	7034	7313	14347	7774	7212	14986	97
R	812	779	1591	1043	949	1992	81
H	1734	1692	3426	2060	1818	3878	90
2B	329	279	608	403	373	776	82
3B	30	16	46	45	48	93	52
HR	205	212	417	235	206	441	99
BB	613	719	1332	618	737	1355	103
SO	1299	1699	2998	1392	1562	2954	106
E	152	146	298	140	163	303	100
E-Infield	125	126	251	117	128	245	104
LHB-Avg	.242	.228	.235	.257	.247	.253	93
LHB-HR	71	83	154	91	79	170	95
RHB-Avg	.249	.234	.241	.270	.255	.263	92
RHB-HR	134	129	263	144	127	271	101

2003 Rankings (National League)

- Third-highest strikeout factor
- Third-highest LHB home-run factor
- Lowest batting-average factor
- Lowest hit factor
- Lowest RHB batting-average factor
- Second-lowest run factor
- Second-lowest triple factor

Jim Tracy

2003 Season

A true tactician, Jim Tracy relishes every opportunity to explain in detail how he arrived at each decision. He can be a bit prickly and gets defensive when he is second-guessed, but he sticks to his guns. In 2003, Tracy had nothing to work with except pitching and defense, and every decision he made had that in mind. He stuck with slick-fielding Cesar Izturis as his everyday shortstop despite the lack of offensive production.

Offense

Tracy was truly hamstrung on the offensive side last year, especially when injuries slowed down or sidelined several of his key weapons. He knew that any run he could wring out of the lowest-scoring team in baseball was precious, given the strength of his pitching staff. He called for the sacrifice with the bottom of the order, though the Dodgers have become a notoriously poor bunting club. The team attempted 116 stolen bases, but almost half of them (54) were by leadoff man Dave Roberts.

Pitching & Defense

Tracy watches pitch counts like a hawk and would rather pull a guy too soon than too late. Of course, that is an easier decision to make when having a deep and talented bullpen at one's disposal. Once he goes to the 'pen, Tracy plays the percentages fairly religiously. He rode Eric Gagne pretty hard at times, but obviously did not cause any harm. Tracy utilizes pitchouts and intentional walks only when they provide his club with a definite advantage.

2004 Outlook

Fairly or not, Tracy looked to be on the hot seat even before the Dodgers' ownership change. Should Tracy be calling the shots again in 2004, he likely will be bobbing and weaving for any run he can get. And while he definitely would prefer to have more interchangeable parts, deep down, that's probably just the way he likes it.

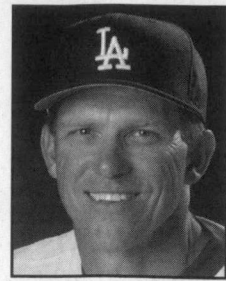

Born: 12/31/55 in Hamilton, OH

Playing Experience: 1980-1981, ChC

Managerial Experience: 3 seasons

Manager Statistics

Year	Team, Lg	W	L	Pct	GB	Finish
2003	Los Angeles, NL	85	77	.525	15.5	2nd West
3 Seasons		263	223	.541	–	–

2003 Starting Pitchers by Days Rest

	<=3	4	5	6+
Dodgers Starts	2	82	44	24
Dodgers ERA	2.77	3.42	3.17	3.80
NL Avg Starts	2	84	43	23
NL ERA	5.00	4.23	4.42	4.68

2003 Situational Stats

	Jim Tracy	NL Average
Hit & Run Success %	33.9	32.7
Stolen Base Success %	69.0	68.9
Platoon Pct.	61.8	52.0
Defensive Subs	51	19
High-Pitch Outings	5	8
Quick/Slow Hooks	20/8	20/12
Sacrifice Attempts	98	93

2003 Rankings (National League)

- 1st in defensive substitutions, saves with over 1 inning pitched (11) and 2+ pitching changes in low-scoring games (49)
- 3rd in one-batter pitcher appearances (49)

Adrian Beltre

Position: 3B
Bats: R **Throws:** R
Ht: 5'11" **Wt:** 170

Opening Day Age: 24
Born: 4/7/79 in Santo Domingo, DR
ML Seasons: 6
Pronunciation:
BELL-tray

2003 Season

Once again in 2003, Adrian Beltre failed to live up to his limitless potential. He only got hot in the last three weeks, averaging .323 from September 5 on after hitting 100 points less up until then. To be fair, he led the punchless Dodgers with 47 RBI after the All Star break.

Hitting

A patient hitter while coming up through the Dodgers minor league system, Beltre has developed a free-swinging approach in the majors. In fact, his on-base percentage has dropped in each successive season this millennium. While he is capable of covering every inch of the strike zone, pitchers now know that they can get him out without throwing many strikes. Beltre can go deep to any part of the park, and when he is in a groove, he drives balls on the outer half into the right-center field gap.

Baserunning & Defense

Beltre bulked up over the last few seasons and is no longer a steal threat. He remains a good baserunner, however, and looks to take the extra base whenever possible. Beltre is an enigma in the field. He has all the tools: soft hands, fine range in every direction and a strong throwing arm. Yet he will make poor decisions at times and has averaged 21-plus errors over the last five campaigns.

2004 Outlook

The Dodgers face a tough decision with Beltre, who is now arbitration-eligible. While many media types blame the third baseman for the team's woes and feel the club should non-tender him, the Dodgers have only Robin Ventura available to take his place, and he is likely to play a reserve role that includes some time at first base. Beltre has lots of room for improvement in all aspects of the game. It's easy to forget how young he is. At an age when many so-called prospects are just getting their feet wet, Beltre already has five full big league seasons under his belt.

Overall Statistics

	G	AB	R	H	D	T	HR	RBI	SB	BB	SO	Avg	OBP	Slg
'03	158	559	50	134	30	2	23	80	2	37	103	.240	.290	.424
Car.	810	2864	352	749	144	18	99	389	55	233	503	.262	.320	.428

Where He Hits the Ball

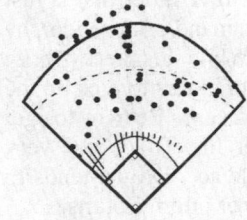
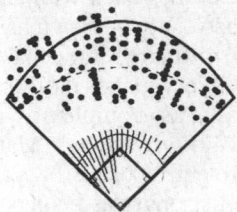

Vs. LHP   **Vs. RHP**

2003 Situational Stats

	AB	H	HR	RBI	Avg		AB	H	HR	RBI	Avg
Home	253	53	13	38	.209	LHP	138	32	7	21	.232
Road	306	81	10	42	.265	RHP	421	102	16	59	.242
First Half	306	69	6	33	.225	Sc Pos	126	35	6	58	.278
Scnd Half	253	65	17	47	.257	Clutch	111	28	5	15	.252

2003 Rankings (National League)

- 2nd in errors at third base (19) and lowest batting average at home
- 4th in lowest on-base percentage and lowest fielding percentage at third base (.957)
- 7th in lowest batting average and lowest batting average vs. lefthanded pitchers
- Led the Dodgers in home runs and sacrifice flies (6)

Kevin Brown

2003 Season

After missing most of the previous two seasons with back and elbow problems, Kevin Brown looked like a man on a mission in 2003. He got roughed up a bit early in the year, then reeled off a string of 11 starts in which he went 9-0 with a 1.38 ERA. Though Brown was sidelined for a couple of weeks in July with an abdominal strain, he ended up posting the third-lowest ERA of his career.

Pitching

Brown probably could get by with just his two-seamer. It bores down and in on righthanded hitters and routinely registers in the low 90s. Then he comes back with an 88-MPH slider that is just nasty. When Brown has command of the slider, he is virtually untouchable. While his herky-jerky delivery makes it difficult for hitters to pick up the ball, its complexity can cause Brown to get off-kilter. Though Manager Jim Tracy was very protective of his 38-year-old ace, Brown tends to get stronger as he gets deeper into his starts.

Defense & Hitting

Brown's follow-through takes him down the first-base slope, so he is vulnerable to balls hit back through the box. What he lacks in agility, he makes up for by chasing after everything he can reach. Brown keeps a close eye on opposing baserunners, but his move is just fair. He takes a big cut at the plate, usually to no avail, and can get the bunt down.

2004 Outlook

The Dodgers have to be encouraged not only by Brown's superb performance, but also by the fact that he tossed more than 200 innings after working less than 200 in the previous two seasons combined. The club is on the hook for a lot of money to Brown over the next couple of seasons, so it needs him to keep pitching the way he did in 2003.

Position: SP
Bats: R **Throws:** R
Ht: 6' 4" **Wt:** 200

Opening Day Age: 39
Born: 3/14/65 in McIntyre, GA
ML Seasons: 17

Overall Statistics

W	L	Pct.	ERA	G	GS	Sv	IP	H	BB	SO	HR	Avg
14	9	.609	2.39	32	32	0	211.0	184	56	185	11	.236
197	131	.601	3.16	451	441	0	3051.0	2840	847	2264	189	.246

2003 Pitching Profile

	Kevin Brown	NL Average
Overall Strike %	65.0	62.4
1st Pitch Strike %	62.9	58.4
Ratio	1.14	1.38
Strikeouts per 9 IP	7.89	6.65
Walks per 9 IP	2.39	3.42
Home Runs per 9 IP	0.47	1.05
Strikeout/Walk Ratio	3.30	1.94
Groundball/Flyball Ratio	3.37	1.29

2003 Situational Stats

	W	L	ERA	Sv	IP		AB	H	HR	RBI	Avg
Home	10	8	2.40	0	139.0	LHB	374	95	0	23	.254
Road	4	1	2.38	0	72.0	RHB	407	89	11	37	.219
First Half	10	4	2.30	0	117.1	Sc Pos	180	32	2	45	.178
Scnd Half	4	5	2.50	0	93.2	Clutch	58	13	1	5	.224

2003 Rankings (National League)

- 2nd in ERA, highest groundball-flyball ratio allowed (3.4) and fewest home runs allowed per nine innings (.47)
- 3rd in lowest slugging percentage allowed (.318) and lowest ERA at home
- 4th in runners caught stealing (9) and lowest batting average allowed with runners in scoring position
- 5th in lowest on-base percentage allowed (.290)
- 6th in strikeouts and GDPs induced (23)
- 7th in highest strikeout-walk ratio (3.3)
- 8th in most strikeouts per nine innings (7.9) and least run support per nine innings (4.1)
- 10th in errors at pitcher (3)
- Led the Dodgers in strikeouts, GDPs induced (23), highest groundball-flyball ratio allowed (3.4), fewest pitches thrown per batter (3.63), lowest ERA at home and fewest home runs allowed per nine innings (.47)

Jeromy Burnitz

2003 Season

The 2003 season was quickly interrupted for Jeromy Burnitz when a Billy Wagner fastball broke his left hand on April 22. After missing exactly a month, Burnitz came back and was putting together a solid season when the Mets traded him to the Dodgers in mid July. He looked to be pressing during his stay in Los Angeles, hitting just .204 after heading West.

Hitting

No one takes a bigger cut than Burnitz. He pays the price for it, striking out more than 100 times in each of the past seven seasons. Then again, he also has homered 30-plus times in five of those campaigns. Burnitz looks to pull the first fastball that he sees, leaving him vulnerable to any offspeed pitch. Back in 1999, he had a .402 on-base percentage, but his walks have decreased each year since 2000.

Baserunning & Defense

Burnitz plays like a bull in a china shop in every phase of the game. He has better-than-average speed, but is not a good basestealer and is as likely to run into an out as take an extra base. He played some center field for both the Mets and Dodgers last season, but he is clearly miscast there. Right field is his best position, as Burnitz has a strong and accurate throwing arm. As with other areas of the game, his misplays in the outfield usually come from over-aggressiveness.

2004 Outlook

Burnitz went into the winter looking for a new deal. He had better temper his expectations, as the market has changed a great deal since his last contract. The Dodgers liked the intensity that he brought to the field and clubhouse. Though Burnitz also brings a lot of pop to a lineup, a low average and frequent lack of contact are part of the package. Let the buyer beware.

Position: LF/RF/CF
Bats: L **Throws:** R
Ht: 6' 0" **Wt:** 213

Opening Day Age: 34
Born: 4/15/69 in Westminster, CA
ML Seasons: 11
Pronunciation: ber-NITS

Overall Statistics

G	AB	R	H	D	T	HR	RBI	SB	BB	SO	Avg	OBP	Slg
126	464	63	111	22	0	31	77	5	35	112	.239	.299	.487
1273	4252	704	1066	225	23	238	735	63	602	1069	.251	.350	.482

Where He Hits the Ball

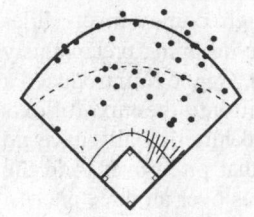

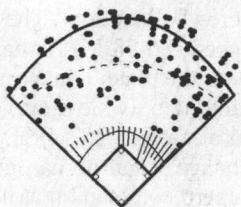

Vs. LHP   **Vs. RHP**

2003 Situational Stats

	AB	H	HR	RBI	Avg		AB	H	HR	RBI	Avg
Home	227	49	10	27	.216	LHP	136	34	8	24	.250
Road	237	62	21	50	.262	RHP	328	77	23	53	.235
First Half	234	64	18	45	.274	Sc Pos	132	32	6	46	.242
Scnd Half	230	47	13	32	.204	Clutch	78	21	6	14	.269

2003 Rankings (National League)

- 5th in fewest GDPs per GDP situation (4.6%)
- 6th in errors in left field (4), lowest batting average (.239) and lowest groundball-flyball ratio (0.7)
- 7th in lowest on-base percentage (.299) and highest percentage of swings on the first pitch (37.9)
- 8th in HR frequency (15.0 ABs per HR)
- 9th in highest percentage of swings that missed (28.3)
- Led the Dodgers in batting average in the clutch (.286)

Eric Gagne

2003 Season

After posting eye-popping numbers in his first season as the Dodgers' closer in 2002, Eric Gagne had a season for the ages last year. Not only did he convert every one of his 55 save opportunities, but he also allowed the lowest batting average (.133) of anyone who has tossed 75 or more innings in a season. He was rewarded after the season with the first Cy Young Award for a reliever since Dennis Eckersley in 1992.

Pitching

Gagne's arsenal begins with a 95-98 MPH fastball. His trademark pitch is a vulcan changeup; he holds it back towards his palm with two fingers on either side of the ball, then gives it a little screwball action. The pitch comes in at slider speed (86-88 MPH) before dropping precipitously near the plate. Last season, Gagne re-introduced a tantalizingly slow curveball into the mix. It floats in at around 70 MPH, and hitters really have no chance when he can get that pitch over. Add the superb command that he has over all three pitches, and there is little wonder as to why Gagne has had so much success.

Defense & Hitting

The former hockey player is a good athlete and has not made an error in the last two seasons. Though his move is just average, Gagne has a compact delivery and the ball gets to the plate in a hurry.

2004 Outlook

If they are not careful, Dodger fans are going to lose their reputation of leaving after the seventh-inning stretch. When the club has a lead heading into the ninth, there is an anticipatory buzz in the stands, which is obliterated by the blaring "Welcome to the Jungle" soundtrack that accompanies Gagne's arrival. Eligible for arbitration for the first time, Gagne will earn big bucks this season, but there is no reason to believe that he will fail to earn them.

Position: RP
Bats: R **Throws:** R
Ht: 6' 2" **Wt:** 195

Opening Day Age: 28
Born: 1/7/76 in Montreal, PQ, Canada
ML Seasons: 5
Pronunciation: gahn-yay

Overall Statistics

	W	L	Pct.	ERA	G	GS	Sv	IP	H	BB	SO	HR	Avg
'03	2	3	.400	1.20	77	0	55	82.1	37	20	137	2	.133
Car.	17	18	.486	3.50	212	48	107	447.2	360	157	490	55	.220

2003 Pitching Profile

	Eric Gagne	NL Average
Overall Strike %	69.5	62.4
1st Pitch Strike %	65.4	58.4
Ratio	0.69	1.38
Strikeouts per 9 IP	14.98	6.65
Walks per 9 IP	2.19	3.42
Home Runs per 9 IP	0.22	1.05
Strikeout/Walk Ratio	6.85	1.94
Groundball/Flyball Ratio	1.75	1.29

2003 Situational Stats

	W	L	ERA	Sv	IP		AB	H	HR	RBI	Avg
Home	2	2	1.54	35	46.2	LHB	138	18	1	2	.130
Road	0	1	0.76	20	35.2	RHB	141	19	1	8	.135
First Half	1	3	1.99	31	45.1	Sc Pos	51	6	1	9	.118
Scnd Half	1	0	0.24	24	37.0	Clutch	210	29	1	8	.138

2003 Rankings (National League)

- 1st in saves, games finished (67), lowest batting average allowed vs. lefthanded batters, save percentage (100.0), most strikeouts per nine innings in relief (15.0), fewest baserunners allowed per nine innings in relief (6.6), and fewest GDPs induced per GDP situation (0.0%)
- 9th in games pitched
- Led the Dodgers in saves, games finished (67), lowest batting average allowed vs. lefthanded batters, lowest batting average allowed vs. righthanded batters, save percentage (100.0), relief ERA (1.20), lowest batting average allowed in relief (.133), fewest baserunners allowed per nine innings in relief (6.6) and most strikeouts per nine innings in relief (15.0)

Shawn Green

2003 Season

Shawn Green had a very disappointing 2003 season, finishing with his lowest home-run and RBI totals since 1997. The explanation for his power outage did not come until August, when it was revealed that Green had been playing almost all season with a damaged right shoulder. Ironically, his performance improved after he no longer carried around the secret of his hidden injury. Only Jim Thome (30) had more ribbies in the final month of the season than Green's 24.

Hitting

Green has a long, complicated swing, which makes him vulnerable to prolonged slumps. When he gets locked in, however, look out. He is much more patient against righthanders than versus lefties; the latter can bust him up-and-in, then fool him with breaking stuff just off the outer edge. He will sometimes give up too soon on tailing fastballs just under his hands. Opponents often employ the shift against him, but Green has enough power to leave any part of the park.

Baserunning & Defense

Though no longer much of a basestealer, Green is an excellent baserunner who looks for the extra base, yet seldom is thrown out trying to take it. Green often gets weak jumps on flyballs and seems to have lost a step or two defensively over the last couple of years. Though a little slow to get rid of the ball, he has a good arm and his throws are almost always on line. Responding to recurring rumors about a change in position, Green has shown a willingness to move to first base. He just wants the change made in the spring so he does not embarass himself out there.

2004 Outlook

Green had his shoulder repaired after the season and should be good to go when spring training rolls around. If the Dodgers' offense is going to improve on its pathetic production of a year ago, the club desperately needs Green to return to his previous norm.

Position: RF
Bats: L **Throws:** L
Ht: 6' 4" **Wt:** 200

Opening Day Age: 31
Born: 11/10/72 in Des Plaines, IL
ML Seasons: 11

Overall Statistics

	G	AB	R	H	D	THR	RBI	SB	BB	SO	Avg	OBP	Slg
'03	160	611	84	171	49	2 19	85	6	68	112	.280	.355	.460
Car.	1357	4935	815	1403	319	26 253	799	134	529	962	.284	.357	.513

Where He Hits the Ball

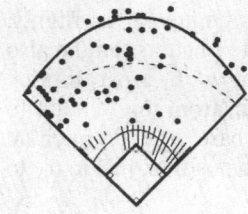
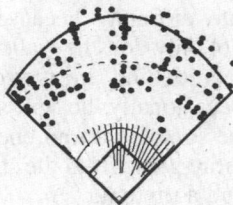

Vs. LHP   **Vs. RHP**

2003 Situational Stats

	AB	H	HR	RBI	Avg		AB	H	HR	RBI	Avg
Home	293	78	10	42	.266	LHP	214	54	8	41	.252
Road	318	93	9	43	.292	RHP	397	117	11	44	.295
First Half	364	93	10	45	.255	Sc Pos	150	44	4	64	.293
Scnd Half	247	78	9	40	.316	Clutch	103	25	4	18	.243

2003 Rankings (National League)

- 2nd in doubles
- 3rd in highest percentage of swings on the first pitch (39.7)
- 4th in games played, errors in right field (5) and lowest fielding percentage in right field (.982)
- 6th in at-bats
- Led the Dodgers in at-bats, runs scored, hits, doubles, total bases (281), RBI, sacrifice flies (6), walks, times on base (245), strikeouts, pitches seen (2,561), plate appearances (691), games played, slugging percentage, on-base percentage, batting average vs. righthanded pitchers and batting average on the road

Kazuhisa Ishii

2003 Season

Perhaps a bit gun-shy after his 2002 season was ended by a line shot that hit him in the face, Kaz Ishii got knocked around in his first start last season. In his next 16 starts, however, he went 7-2 with a 2.37 ERA. Late in July, Ishii sprained his left MCL and spent a month on the disabled list. Perhaps still bothered by the injury, he struggled late in the year.

Pitching

Except perhaps for Randy Johnson, Ishii's stuff is as good as any lefthanded starter in baseball. His fastball registers in the low 90s and has a good deal of movement. His curveball has a lot of break to it, and his changeup is solid as well. Ishii runs into difficulty because his command is flighty. Not only does he walk a lot of batters, but he also gets behind in the count with most hitters. Occasionally, he will switch from the windup to the stretch with no one on base, or even pitch an entire game from the stretch position, just to try to find a rhythm.

Defense & Hitting

Ishii's compact frame serves him well in getting off the mound, as well as making a throw after fielding grounders. He is not afraid to toss over to first and controls the running game adequately. He pretty much flails helplessly at the plate, but somehow got nine bunts down last season despite looking awkward doing so.

2004 Outlook

Assuming that Ishii's knee is sound, there is no reason to believe that he will not be a solid contributor at the back end of the Dodgers' rotation. He is signed to a reasonable contract for the next two seasons, and if he can make 30 starts for the first time, Ishii should post double-digit wins for the club.

Position: SP
Bats: L **Throws:** L
Ht: 6' 0" **Wt:** 200

Opening Day Age: 30
Born: 9/9/73 in Chiba, Japan
ML Seasons: 2
Pronunciation: kaz-u-heesa ee-shee-ee

Overall Statistics

	W	L	Pct.	ERA	G	GS	Sv	IP	H	BB	SO	HR	Avg
'03	9	7	.563	3.86	27	27	0	147.0	129	101	140	16	.238
Car.	23	17	.575	4.07	55	55	0	301.0	266	207	283	36	.239

2003 Pitching Profile

	Kazuhisa Ishii	NL Average
Overall Strike %	57.5	62.4
1st Pitch Strike %	50.1	58.4
Ratio	1.56	1.38
Strikeouts per 9 IP	8.57	6.65
Walks per 9 IP	6.18	3.42
Home Runs per 9 IP	0.98	1.05
Strikeout/Walk Ratio	1.39	1.94
Groundball/Flyball Ratio	0.85	1.29

2003 Situational Stats

	W	L	ERA	Sv	IP		AB	H	HR	RBI	Avg
Home	5	2	3.12	0	78.0	LHB	125	24	4	12	.192
Road	4	5	4.70	0	69.0	RHB	416	105	12	45	.252
First Half	8	3	2.94	0	104.0	Sc Pos	151	25	2	38	.166
Scnd Half	1	4	6.07	0	43.0	Clutch	8	1	0	0	.125

2003 Rankings (National League)

- 2nd in walks allowed, runners caught stealing (13) and lowest batting average allowed with runners in scoring position
- 5th in balks (2) and lowest batting average allowed vs. lefthanded batters
- 8th in stolen bases allowed (18)
- 10th in wild pitches (10)
- Led the Dodgers in walks allowed, hit batsmen (6), balks (2), lowest batting average allowed with runners in scoring position and most strikeouts per nine innings (8.6)

Cesar Izturis

2003 Season

Designated as the everyday starting shortstop from Opening Day last season, Cesar Izturis quickly established himself as the unofficial captain of the Dodgers' infield. While his offense was anemic, it was at least consistent. Izturis never had a monthly batting average below .234 nor one higher than .265 the entire season.

Hitting

After hitting just .195 from the left side in 2002, Izturis had to be persuaded to continue switch-hitting last season. It paid off, as he raised his average versus righthanders by more than 50 points, though his swing from that side still has a loop in it. From his natural right side, Izturis looks much more confident and hits more balls on the line. He does not have a good feel for the strike zone and has three times as many strikeouts as walks over his young career. He needs to hit more balls on the ground to take advantage of his speed.

Baserunning & Defense

Izturis is very quick and has good instincts on the basepaths, though he has not been asked to be much of a basestealer in the bigs. He is an absolute wizard with the glove. Izturis has great range in both directions, turns the double play easily and has plenty of arm for the position. He is the kind of shortstop who makes every other infielder better, and there are a few Gold Gloves in his future if he can hit enough to stay in the lineup.

2004 Outlook

As long as the Dodgers can increase their offensive production at other positions, they can live with Izturis' weak output. He will be just 24 years old when the 2004 season begins, so there is plenty of time for his offense to improve. He was regarded highly enough to be mentioned in trade offers by opposing teams during the offseason.

Position: SS
Bats: B **Throws:** R
Ht: 5' 9" **Wt:** 175

Opening Day Age: 24
Born: 2/10/80 in Barquisimeto, VZ
ML Seasons: 3
Pronunciation:
IS-tur-is

Overall Statistics

	G	AB	R	H	D	T	HR	RBI	SB	BB	SO	Avg	OBP	Slg
'03	158	558	47	140	21	6	1	40	10	25	70	.251	.282	.315
Car.	339	1131	109	278	51	10	4	80	25	41	124	.246	.270	.319

Where He Hits the Ball

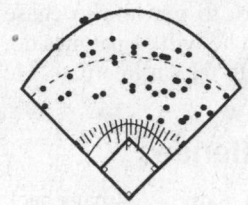 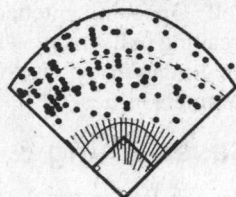

Vs. LHP   **Vs. RHP**

2003 Situational Stats

	AB	H	HR	RBI	Avg		AB	H	HR	RBI	Avg
Home	255	62	0	14	.243	LHP	156	41	0	12	.263
Road	303	78	1	26	.257	RHP	402	99	1	28	.246
First Half	321	82	0	21	.255	Sc Pos	134	28	1	38	.209
Scnd Half	237	58	1	19	.245	Clutch	92	25	0	9	.272

2003 Rankings (National League)

- 1st in lowest on-base percentage and fewest pitches seen per plate appearance (3.21)
- 2nd in lowest slugging percentage and lowest HR frequency (558.0 ABs per HR)
- 3rd in fielding percentage at shortstop (.977)
- 5th in highest groundball-flyball ratio (2.0) and errors at shortstop (16)
- 6th in bunts in play (29)
- 8th in lowest batting average at home
- 9th in triples and games played
- 10th in highest percentage of swings put into play (52.2)
- Led the Dodgers in singles, triples, intentional walks (8) and batting average with the bases loaded (.462)

Brian Jordan

2003 Season

After a busy winter in which he had knee surgery and also demanded a trade in a thinly-disguised attempt to get a contract extension, Brian Jordan put it all aside and started hitting right from the get-go. He stayed in the lineup until the balky left knee got too painful, and was shut down for the season in late June.

Hitting

Jordan is essentially a gap hitter who looks "dead red," and it is tough to sneak a fastball past him. When he gets one on the inner half, no one in the left-field bleachers is safe. He can get too pull-happy, resulting in a lot of grounders to short, but Jordan uses the entire field when things are going well. Opposing pitchers try to get him to chase breaking balls away, which he will sometimes do, but Jordan also is willing to take a free pass. He hammers lefties.

Baserunning & Defense

Though Jordan grabbed as many as 24 bags back in 1995, his legs have gotten old quickly and his stolen base total has decreased in each of the last five seasons. He still plays the game like an ex-defensive back, running aggressively both on the bases and into outfield walls if necessary. Jordan is a good outfielder who can play all three spots, and his arm is above-average.

2004 Outlook

Jordan is a free agent and probably will not be back with the Dodgers. While they appreciated his leadership both on and off the field, he has not been able to stay in the lineup enough to justify the big bucks. If Jordan is willing to accept a reduction in salary, he has enough left to help any club in baseball. However, a platoon situation might be warrented to keep the 37-year-old fresh.

Position: LF/CF
Bats: R **Throws:** R
Ht: 6' 1" **Wt:** 205

Opening Day Age: 37
Born: 3/29/67 in Baltimore, MD
ML Seasons: 12

Overall Statistics

	G	AB	R	H	D	T	HR	RBI	SB	BB	SO	Avg	OBP	Slg
'03	66	224	28	67	9	0	6	28	1	23	30	.299	.372	.420
Car.	1271	4626	692	1329	244	34	173	764	115	316	738	.287	.339	.467

Where He Hits the Ball

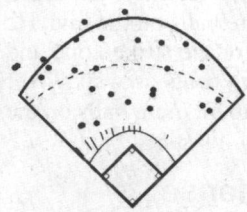 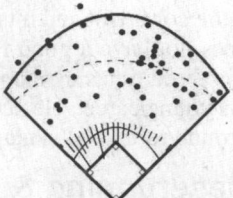

Vs. LHP   **Vs. RHP**

2003 Situational Stats

	AB	H	HR	RBI	Avg		AB	H	HR	RBI	Avg
Home	116	31	3	13	.267	LHP	58	23	4	12	.397
Road	108	36	3	15	.333	RHP	166	44	2	16	.265
First Half	224	67	6	28	.299	Sc Pos	65	19	1	22	.292
Scnd Half	0	0	0	0	–	Clutch	42	7	0	5	.167

2003 Rankings (National League)

- Did not rank near the top or bottom in any category

Paul Lo Duca

Position: C/1B
Bats: R **Throws:** R
Ht: 5'10" **Wt:** 185

Opening Day Age: 31
Born: 4/12/72 in Brooklyn, NY
ML Seasons: 6
Pronunciation:
lah-duke-uh

2003 Season

Paul Lo Duca had a typically hot first half in 2003, and with injuries depleting the already weak Dodger offense, Manager Jim Tracy kept writing Lo Duca's name on the lineup card. As has been his habit, the diminutive catcher eventually wore down, hitting just .226 after the All-Star break.

Hitting

Lo Duca has a compact build and a compact swing. He feasts on high fastballs, even ones up around the shoulders, and may have expanded his strike zone a bit last year, as he had 54 strikeouts after fanning a total of 61 times in the previous two years combined. Lo Duca generally hits the ball where it is pitched and has gap power to all fields. While he may be a bit stronger versus left-handers, his approach is the same regardless of who is on the hill: try to hit the ball hard back through the box.

Baserunning & Defense

While a heady baserunner, Lo Duca is essentially a station-to-station guy at this point in his career. After a rough 2002 season behind the plate, his defense was much improved last season. Opposing basestealers were successful on 66 percent of their attempts, down 10 percent from the year before, and he cut his passed balls in half. In an effort to keep Lo Duca's bat in the lineup, Tracy also used him in left field and at first base, and he was adequate at both positions.

2004 Outlook

A very popular Dodger, Lo Duca is signed through the 2004 season. However, the club must have concerns that his average, home runs and RBI all have dropped each year since he first became a regular in 2001. If nothing else, the Dodgers need to find a platoon mate to allow Lo Duca to take some time off without severely hurting the club's chances for victory.

Overall Statistics

	G	AB	R	H	D	T	HR	RBI	SB	BB	SO	Avg	OBP	Slg
'03	147	568	64	155	34	2	7	52	0	44	54	.273	.335	.377
Car.	497	1782	228	507	104	3	47	226	6	133	133	.285	.341	.425

Where He Hits the Ball

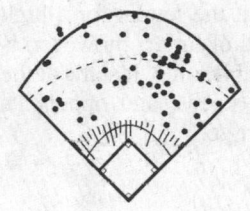 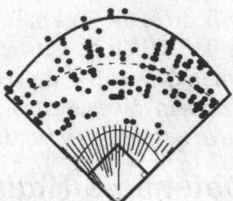

Vs. LHP   **Vs. RHP**

2003 Situational Stats

	AB	H	HR	RBI	Avg		AB	H	HR	RBI	Avg
Home	278	82	4	27	.295	LHP	153	43	3	13	.281
Road	290	73	3	25	.252	RHP	415	112	4	39	.270
First Half	329	101	6	34	.307	Sc Pos	121	37	1	42	.306
Scnd Half	239	54	1	18	.226	Clutch	98	23	0	5	.235

2003 Rankings (National League)

- 1st in errors at catcher (15) and highest percentage of runners caught stealing as a catcher (34.1)
- Led the Dodgers in singles, GDPs (21), batting average with runners in scoring position and batting average at home

Hideo Nomo

2003 Season

Last season saw the continuation of Hideo Nomo's amazing comeback in Los Angeles. After four seasons in which he was a combined 39-42 with a 4.66 ERA, the prodigal son has won 16 games in each of the past two seasons for the Dodgers, while posting a 3.24 ERA. Nomo was solid all year before a damaged shoulder limited him to just four starts in September.

Pitching

Nomo makes the most out of his two pitches. He spots his 88-89 MPH fastball in every quadrant of the strike zone and beyond. What lurks behind every offering is the threat of the devastating splitter. When he is behind in the count, Nomo will drop the forkball in at the letters for a high strike. When he gets ahead of hitters, however, is when the pitch is most troublesome. It starts at the belt and dives below the knees, and opponents have a tough time letting it go.

Defense & Hitting

Nomo's tornado-like windup leaves him vulnerable to comebackers, not to mention opposing basestealers, who have a 75-percent success rate against him over his career. His approach at the plate is to swing as hard as possible, so the ball will go far on the rare occasions that he makes contact. He is not a good bunter.

2004 Outlook

Whether general manager Dan Evans makes it through the ownership change or not, he will be able to look back at the Nomo signing as one of the best moves of his tenure. The 35-year-old has another year on his contract and will occupy one of the top two spots in the Dodgers' rotation this season. He had his labrum and rotator cuff cleaned up right after the season and should be ready to chew up 200 quality innings again in 2004.

Position: SP
Bats: R **Throws:** R
Ht: 6' 2" **Wt:** 210

Opening Day Age: 35
Born: 8/31/68 in Osaka, Japan
ML Seasons: 9
Pronunciation: hih-DAY-oh NO-mo

Overall Statistics

	W	L	Pct.	ERA	G	GS	Sv	IP	H	BB	SO	HR	Avg
'03	16	13	.552	3.09	33	33	0	218.1	175	98	177	24	.223
Car.	114	90	.559	3.85	283	281	0	1787.1	1526	811	1802	213	.231

2003 Pitching Profile

	Hideo Nomo	NL Average
Overall Strike %	63.1	62.4
1st Pitch Strike %	57.2	58.4
Ratio	1.25	1.38
Strikeouts per 9 IP	7.30	6.65
Walks per 9 IP	4.04	3.42
Home Runs per 9 IP	0.99	1.05
Strikeout/Walk Ratio	1.81	1.94
Groundball/Flyball Ratio	1.00	1.29

2003 Situational Stats

	W	L	ERA	Sv	IP		AB	H	HR	RBI	Avg
Home	8	8	3.48	0	111.1	LHB	357	76	10	27	.213
Road	8	5	2.69	0	107.0	RHB	427	99	14	43	.232
First Half	9	8	2.97	0	142.1	Sc Pos	168	34	3	47	.202
Scnd Half	7	5	3.32	0	76.0	Clutch	66	17	3	6	.258

2003 Rankings (National League)

- 1st in runners caught stealing (14)
- 4th in shutouts (2) and walks allowed
- 5th in wins, lowest batting average allowed (.223) and lowest ERA on the road
- 6th in ERA, losses, innings pitched, wild pitches (11), lowest batting average allowed with runners in scoring position and highest walks per nine innings (4.0)
- 7th in stolen bases allowed (19) and least run support per nine innings (4.1)
- 8th in games started, strikeouts and lowest slugging percentage allowed (.357)
- 10th in batters faced (897)
- Led the Dodgers in wins, losses, games started, complete games (2), shutouts (2), innings pitched, batters faced (897), wild pitches (11), pitches thrown (3,272), pickoff throws (117), runners caught stealing (14), and lowest stolen-base percentage allowed (57.6)

Odalis Perez.

2003 Season

After his superb breakout year in 2002, much was expected of Odalis Perez last season. And though he had only three wins to show for it after his first eight starts, his ERA stood at 2.93. From late May through the end of the season, however, Perez was a sub-.500 pitcher (9-10) with a 5.19 ERA. Though they never sent him to the disabled list, the club shut their young lefty down late in the season, due to a cranky shoulder and a blister on the middle finger of his pitching hand.

Pitching

Perez has superb stuff. His fastball routinely reaches the low 90s and tails off as it nears the plate. Righthanded hitters who try to pull this pitch usually end up with a 6-3 on the scorecard. He complements the heater with a fine changeup and curveball that has a nice downward slope. There is concern that Perez sometimes tips his pitches by holding his glove in different spots, but nothing definitive has been discerned and/or disclosed. Of more concern is his lack of focus; no one with his repertoire should give up 28 longballs, as Perez did last season.

Defense & Hitting

Perez has a weak pickoff move and is very slow to deliver to the plate; as a result, no southpaw in baseball allowed more stolen bases. He fields his position well, showing fine reflexes on comebackers and quickness in getting off the hill. At bat, Perez generally makes contact and is a solid bunter.

2004 Outlook

Perez has a loosey-goosey attitude that is infectious when things are going well, but he made some ill-timed comments last year about the club's lack of offense, which were not well-received. It is conceivable that the arbitration-eligible Perez could be dealt over the winter, but the Dodgers will hold out for top value in return for their immensely talented 26-year-old lefty.

Position: SP
Bats: L **Throws:** L
Ht: 6' 0" **Wt:** 150

Opening Day Age: 26
Born: 6/11/77 in Las Matas de Farfan, DR
ML Seasons: 5
Pronunciation: oh-DALL-iss

Overall Statistics

	W	L	Pct.	ERA	G	GS	Sv	IP	H	BB	SO	HR	Avg
'03	12	12	.500	4.52	30	30	0	185.1	191	46	141	28	.267
Car.	38	37	.507	4.24	114	95	0	606.2	591	180	454	69	.257

2003 Pitching Profile

	Odalis Perez	NL Average
Overall Strike %	66.1	62.4
1st Pitch Strike %	60.0	58.4
Ratio	1.28	1.38
Strikeouts per 9 IP	6.85	6.65
Walks per 9 IP	2.23	3.42
Home Runs per 9 IP	1.36	1.05
Strikeout/Walk Ratio	3.07	1.94
Groundball/Flyball Ratio	1.99	1.29

2003 Situational Stats

	W	L	ERA	Sv	IP		AB	H	HR	RBI	Avg
Home	6	3	2.73	0	69.1	LHB	149	30	3	12	.201
Road	6	9	5.59	0	116.0	RHB	566	161	25	81	.284
First Half	6	7	4.25	0	114.1	Sc Pos	148	44	8	65	.297
Scnd Half	6	5	4.94	0	71.0	Clutch	52	15	2	7	.288

2003 Rankings (National League)

- 3rd in stolen bases allowed (25)
- 4th in runners caught stealing (9) and highest ERA on the road
- 6th in highest groundball-flyball ratio allowed (2.0) and most home runs allowed per nine innings (1.36)
- 7th in home runs allowed
- 10th in highest strikeout-walk ratio (3.1) and lowest batting average allowed vs. lefthanded batters
- Led the Dodgers in sacrifice bunts (10), hits allowed, home runs allowed, stolen bases allowed (25) and most run support per nine innings (4.6)

Dave Roberts

2003 Season

Entrenched at the top of the Dodgers' lineup on an everyday basis, Dave Roberts got off to a strong start last season. Through the sixth of May, he was hitting .321 with a .390 on-base percentage. However, he hit just .223 with a .309 OBP the rest of the way, as he struggled with a strained right hamstring that landed him on the disabled list twice.

Hitting

In an attempt to perfect his slap-and-dash style, Roberts has worked extensively with Dodgers legend Maury Wills. The lightning-quick Roberts is always looking to lay one down, and if he can drag one past the pitcher, forget it. Roberts has good bat control and just tries to hit the ball where it is pitched. While he knows that his job is to work the pitcher, Roberts has just a good knowledge of the strike zone. He will chase both inside breaking stuff as well as high fastballs, however, and the harder throwers can overpower him.

Baserunning & Defense

Over the last two seasons, only two players have stolen more bases than Roberts, who studies opposing pitchers constantly. He is fundamentally sound in the outfield, but is only average out there. Fortunately, his speed makes up for the occasional poor break. Roberts has a weak throwing arm and opponents can take the extra base on him.

2004 Outlook

Though some in the local media believe that Roberts is not the answer as the Dodgers' leadoff man, the team's unproductive offense had many bigger problems. The chronic hamstring strain raises red flags for a guy who lives and dies on his legs, but when he is at full speed, Roberts puts a lot of pressure on opposing defenses. He should be back with the club this season and at the top of the lineup card almost every day.

Position: CF
Bats: L **Throws:** L
Ht: 5'10" **Wt:** 180

Opening Day Age: 31
Born: 5/31/72 in Okinawa, Japan
ML Seasons: 5

Overall Statistics

	G	AB	R	H	D	T	HR	RBI	SB	BB	SO	Avg	OBP	Slg
'03	107	388	56	97	6	5	2	16	40	43	39	.250	.331	.307
Car.	309	975	149	254	25	12	7	64	97	103	110	.261	.334	.332

Where He Hits the Ball

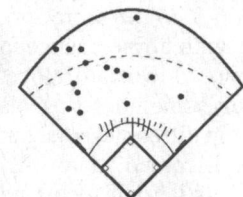 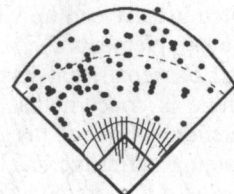

Vs. LHP   **Vs. RHP**

2003 Situational Stats

	AB	H	HR	RBI	Avg		AB	H	HR	RBI	Avg
Home	179	50	1	9	.279	LHP	83	22	0	3	.265
Road	209	47	1	7	.225	RHP	305	75	2	13	.246
First Half	220	55	1	10	.250	Sc Pos	76	16	1	15	.211
Scnd Half	168	42	1	6	.250	Clutch	66	14	1	6	.212

2003 Rankings (National League)

- 2nd in bunts in play (51)
- 3rd in stolen bases, caught stealing (14), highest percentage of swings put into play (56.7) and errors in center field (5)
- 4th in highest percentage of pitches taken (64.1)
- Led the Dodgers in stolen bases, caught stealing (14), highest groundball-flyball ratio (2.1), stolen-base percentage (74.1), most pitches seen per plate appearance (3.94), highest percentage of pitches taken (64.1), lowest percentage of swings that missed (10.1), highest percentage of swings put into play (56.7), steals of third (3), fewest GDPs per GDP situation (0.0%), on-base percentage for a leadoff hitter (.333)

Wilson Alvarez

Position: SP
Bats: L **Throws:** L
Ht: 6' 1" **Wt:** 255

Opening Day Age: 34
Born: 3/24/70 in Maracaibo, VZ
ML Seasons: 12

Overall Statistics

	W	L	Pct.	ERA	G	GS	Sv	IP	H	BB	SO	HR	Avg
'03	6	2	.750	2.37	21	12	1	95.0	80	23	82	5	.231
Car.	94	82	.534	3.93	294	246	3	1603.0	1484	767	1212	171	.247

2003 Situational Stats

	W	L	ERA	Sv	IP		AB	H	HR	RBI	Avg
Home	4	0	0.57	0	47.2	LHB	68	16	1	7	.235
Road	2	2	4.18	1	47.1	RHB	278	64	4	17	.230
First Half	1	1	4.18	1	23.2	Sc Pos	57	11	0	15	.193
Scnd Half	5	1	1.77	0	71.1	Clutch	18	3	0	0	.167

2003 Season

Wilson Alvarez excelled for Triple-A Las Vegas over the first couple months of the season, then filled the long relief role for the big club in June and July. When he finally got a chance to start, Alvarez went 5-0 with a 1.06 ERA over a stretch of nine starts from early August to late September.

Pitching, Defense & Hitting

Though the former fireballer's four-seamed fastball now tops out in the upper 80s, Alvarez is not afraid to come inside with it. The key for Alvarez is to have good command of two other pitches, both of which have good downward movement. He gets righthanders out with a turnover change and hammers lefties with an excellent 12-to-six curveball. Alvarez gets off the mound pretty well for a big guy and takes a decent cut at the plate. He controls the running game very effectively.

2004 Outlook

Alvarez and Dodgers general manager Dan Evans go way back, and the lefty has expressed his desire to repay the club for the comeback opportunity. That may change if Evans loses his job, but the free-agent Alvarez should be a solid fit at the back end of someone's rotation. It still could be with Los Angeles, as the Dodgers offered him salary arbitration.

Andy Ashby

Position: SP
Bats: R **Throws:** R
Ht: 6' 1" **Wt:** 202

Opening Day Age: 36
Born: 7/11/67 in Kansas City, MO
ML Seasons: 13

Overall Statistics

	W	L	Pct.	ERA	G	GS	Sv	IP	H	BB	SO	HR	Avg
'03	3	10	.231	5.18	21	12	0	73.0	90	17	41	8	.311
Car.	98	110	.471	4.13	307	285	1	1808.2	1856	540	1171	205	.268

2003 Situational Stats

	W	L	ERA	Sv	IP		AB	H	HR	RBI	Avg
Home	2	5	5.54	0	39.0	LHB	131	44	6	22	.336
Road	1	5	4.76	0	34.0	RHB	158	46	2	17	.291
First Half	2	6	5.57	0	42.0	Sc Pos	71	21	0	27	.296
Scnd Half	1	4	4.65	0	31.0	Clutch	24	7	1	3	.292

2003 Season

Expecting to be a member of the Dodgers' starting rotation, Andy Ashby was not happy when he opened the year in the bullpen. A spot finally opened up in early June, but Ashby went 3-7 with a 4.95 ERA in 11 starts before a torn elbow ligament ended his season in early September.

Pitching, Defense & Hitting

At this point in his career, Ashby is a shadow of his former self. His sinking fastball now tops out in the upper 80s, and there were games last season when it never got above 85 MPH. He complements that with a slider that also breaks downward, and when Ashby is on his game, the infielders stay busy. He tries to keep runners close by throwing over often, but his move is nothing special. He is a bit gangly both in the field and at the plate, where he went hitless last season.

2004 Outlook

Ashby had Tommy John surgery last September, so he will not pitch in 2004. If Ashby, who will turn 37 in July, is able to make a comeback, it will not be in Los Angeles.

Jolbert Cabrera

Position: 2B/CF/LF
Bats: R **Throws:** R
Ht: 6' 1" **Wt:** 195

Opening Day Age: 31
Born: 12/8/72 in
Cartagena, Colombia
ML Seasons: 6
Pronunciation:
HOLE-bert kah-brair-RAH

Overall Statistics

	G	AB	R	H	D	T	HR	RBI	SB	BB	SO	Avg	OBP	Slg
'03	128	347	43	98	32	2	6	37	6	17	62	.282	.332	.438
Car.	448	932	134	236	54	6	9	98	26	49	142	.253	.303	.353

2003 Situational Stats

	AB	H	HR	RBI	Avg		AB	H	HR	RBI	Avg
Home	151	41	4	17	.272	LHP	137	42	2	12	.307
Road	196	57	2	20	.291	RHP	210	56	4	25	.267
First Half	169	44	6	27	.260	Sc Pos	76	17	0	28	.224
Scnd Half	178	54	0	10	.303	Clutch	67	16	0	6	.239

2003 Season

After totaling just 12 at-bats for the Dodgers in 2002, little was expected of Jolbert Cabrera at the beginning of last season. He started the year as half of a second-base platoon, but he kept hitting and Jim Tracy kept finding a spot for him. In the last two months of the season, Cabrera hit .312.

Hitting, Baserunning & Defense

Cabrera takes a big cut and has enough power to reach either gap or yank a pitch over the left-field wall. Righthanders can beat him with breaking stuff off the plate, but he handles just about everything that lefties have to offer. The 31-year-old has above-average speed and can swipe the occasional bag. Cabrera played every position but pitcher and catcher last year and held his own wherever he went.

2004 Outlook

While many utility players tend to get overexposed with more playing time, Cabrera actually hit better as the season moved along. At times last year, he was the best righthanded hitter on the club, and now looks to have at least a part-time job locked up for this coming campaign.

Alex Cora

Position: 2B/SS
Bats: L **Throws:** R
Ht: 6' 0" **Wt:** 180

Opening Day Age: 28
Born: 10/18/75 in
Caguas, PR
ML Seasons: 6

Overall Statistics

	G	AB	R	H	D	T	HR	RBI	SB	BB	SO	Avg	OBP	Slg
'03	148	477	39	119	24	3	4	34	4	16	59	.249	.287	.338
Car.	546	1556	156	375	75	17	17	126	15	101	220	.241	.301	.344

2003 Situational Stats

	AB	H	HR	RBI	Avg		AB	H	HR	RBI	Avg
Home	227	53	3	13	.233	LHP	65	20	0	5	.308
Road	250	66	1	21	.264	RHP	412	99	4	29	.240
First Half	288	69	1	20	.240	Sc Pos	98	28	0	28	.286
Scnd Half	189	50	3	14	.265	Clutch	91	24	0	7	.264

2003 Season

Alex Cora teamed up with Cesar Izturis as one of baseball's slickest double-play combos last season. Though he hit just .193 from May 22 to August 29, Cora's glove kept him in the lineup enough to receive a career-high 477 at-bats.

Hitting, Baserunning & Defense

Cora is a slap hitter, but he occasionally will hit a low inside fastball like a three-iron into the right-field corner and beyond. He can be overpowered by hard throwers and has a rough time handling breaking pitches. Though he has totaled only 128 at-bats versus lefties over the last three seasons, he has hit .305 against them over that time. Though slow for a middle infielder, Cora is an excellent second baseman. He also can fill in at shortstop, though his arm is not strong enough to play there on an everyday basis.

2004 Outlook

While the Dodgers' middle infielders were fun to watch last year, the club desperately needs to upgrade its offense, and second base would be a likely candidate. Cora is a heady player who gets as much out of his limited ability as anyone on the club, but he is better suited for a part-time role.

Darren Dreifort

Position: SP
Bats: R **Throws:** R
Ht: 6' 2" **Wt:** 211

Opening Day Age: 31
Born: 5/3/72 in Wichita, KS
ML Seasons: 8
Pronunciation: DRY-fort

Overall Statistics

	W	L	Pct.	ERA	G	GS	Sv	IP	H	BB	SO	HR	Avg
'03	4	4	.500	4.03	10	10	0	60.1	58	25	67	6	.250
Car.	47	56	.456	4.36	214	113	10	822.0	783	353	739	85	.252

2003 Situational Stats

	W	L	ERA	Sv	IP		AB	H	HR	RBI	Avg
Home	4	1	2.25	0	40.0	LHB	108	33	3	14	.306
Road	0	3	7.52	0	20.1	RHB	124	25	3	11	.202
First Half	4	4	4.03	0	60.1	Sc Pos	66	13	1	17	.197
Scnd Half	0	0	—	0	0.0	Clutch	11	4	0	1	.364

2003 Season

After sitting out the entire 2002 campaign recovering from his second Tommy John surgery, Darren Dreifort began last season full of promise. He allowed three or fewer earned runs in eight of his 10 starts, but a balky right knee became too painful and Dreifort's season ended in late May. He underwent knee surgery in June, and then had hip surgery in September.

Pitching, Defense & Hitting

Dreifort cannot throw a ball straight, so he just aims for the middle of the plate and ends up on one edge or the other. His low to mid-90s fastball has explosive sinking action, and his 88-MPH slider breaks just as nastily in the other direction. He rattles quite easily, so it is not unusual to see Dreifort cruise along for several innings, then fall apart when a few batters reach base. He is a fine athlete who holds runners, and he can handle both the bat and glove.

2004 Outlook

Dreifort has another two years on his massive contract, so the Dodgers can only hope that he returns to health and gives them a full season. That might be asking for the moon, however, as he has tossed a total of 154.2 innings in the last three seasons combined.

Fred McGriff

Position: 1B
Bats: L **Throws:** L
Ht: 6' 3" **Wt:** 225

Opening Day Age: 40
Born: 10/31/63 in Tampa, FL
ML Seasons: 18
Nickname: Crime Dog

Overall Statistics

	G	AB	R	H	D	T	HR	RBI	SB	BB	SO	Avg	OBP	Slg
'03	86	297	32	74	14	0	13	40	0	31	66	.249	.322	.428
Car.	2433	8685	1342	2477	438	24	491	1543	72	1296	1863	.285	.378	.511

2003 Situational Stats

	AB	H	HR	RBI	Avg		AB	H	HR	RBI	Avg
Home	164	41	7	20	.250	LHP	93	18	5	11	.194
Road	133	33	6	20	.248	RHP	204	56	8	29	.275
First Half	237	59	10	35	.249	Sc Pos	72	22	6	30	.306
Scnd Half	60	15	3	5	.250	Clutch	54	9	3	5	.167

2003 Season

Fred McGriff got off to a slow start in his first month with the Dodgers, but hit solidly in May. He strained his right groin in mid-June and ended up missing almost two months. Though he appeared healthy upon his return, McGriff was not a factor down the stretch.

Hitting, Baserunning & Defense

The Crime Dog still has some pop in his bat, though he has to cheat a bit to catch up to better fastballs. While he generally looks for something on the inner half that he can yank over the fence, McGriff is able to line balls into the left-center field gap if that is what is given to him. After handling lefthanders quite well over most of his career, he now struggles against them. McGriff is one of the slowest runners in baseball, and his reaction time with the glove is alarmingly slow.

2004 Outlook

McGriff badly wants the nine homers he needs to reach 500, but he will not get that opportunity with the Dodgers. Though he turned 40 on Halloween, he appears to have enough left in the tank to help a club—especially an AL team in need of a DH.

Guillermo Mota

Position: RP
Bats: R **Throws:** R
Ht: 6' 4" **Wt:** 205

Opening Day Age: 30
Born: 7/25/73 in San
Pedro de Macoris, DR
ML Seasons: 5
Pronunciation:
mo-TAH

Overall Statistics

	W	L	Pct.	ERA	G	GS	Sv	IP	H	BB	SO	HR	Avg
'03	6	3	.667	1.97	76	0	1	105.0	78	26	99	7	.206
Car.	11	14	.440	3.53	252	0	1	300.2	255	108	230	28	.230

2003 Situational Stats

	W	L	ERA	Sv	IP		AB	H	HR	RBI	Avg
Home	1	1	2.62	0	44.2	LHB	138	25	3	18	.181
Road	5	2	1.49	1	60.1	RHB	241	53	4	17	.220
First Half	2	2	1.57	1	57.1	Sc Pos	76	21	3	29	.276
Scnd Half	4	1	2.45	0	47.2	Clutch	117	24	4	12	.205

2003 Season

Serving in both long and middle relief, Guillermo Mota was the workhorse of the Dodgers' superb 2003 bullpen. Mota wore down a bit down the stretch, posting a 4.00 ERA in September, but still was the first reliever in more than 10 years to pitch 100-plus innings while maintaining a sub-2.00 ERA.

Pitching, Defense & Hitting

Mota is long-limbed and has a real easy delivery, so his 95-98 MPH fastball just explodes upon the hitter. He also throws a nasty slider that registers in the high 80s. Last season, Eric Gagne taught Mota his vulcan change, which almost made things unfair for the hitters. A former shortstop, he is a .278 lifetime hitter and gets off the mound very quickly. He still could use some improvement at holding runners.

2004 Outlook

Short of Gagne, Mota is perhaps the most coveted member of the Dodgers' bullpen. No wonder, as he can work multiple innings several days per week and throws as hard as anyone on the staff. With Paul Quantrill joining the Yankees via free agency, Mota will take on an even more significant role in Los Angeles this season.

Paul Quantrill

Position: RP
Bats: L **Throws:** R
Ht: 6' 1" **Wt:** 195

Opening Day Age: 35
Born: 11/3/68 in
London, ON, Canada
ML Seasons: 12
Pronunciation:
KWAN-trill

Overall Statistics

	W	L	Pct.	ERA	G	GS	Sv	IP	H	BB	SO	HR	Avg
'03	2	5	.286	1.75	89	0	1	77.1	61	15	44	2	.227
Car.	59	73	.447	3.65	705	64	20	1091.1	1225	302	652	99	.287

2003 Situational Stats

	W	L	ERA	Sv	IP		AB	H	HR	RBI	Avg
Home	1	3	1.86	0	38.2	LHB	96	19	1	6	.198
Road	1	2	1.63	1	38.2	RHB	173	42	1	19	.243
First Half	1	2	1.40	1	45.0	Sc Pos	73	14	1	24	.192
Scnd Half	1	3	2.23	0	32.1	Clutch	163	37	2	20	.227

2003 Season

Ace setup man Paul Quantrill led the National League in appearances for the second straight season in 2003. For a guy used as much as he was, Quantrill was amazingly consistent, never posting a monthly ERA higher than 2.00 the entire season.

Pitching, Defense & Hitting

Quantrill lives and dies with his sinker. It tops out in the upper 80s, but moves a good eight inches from side to side and drops as well. He starts every hitter with a sinker that looks to be outside to righthanders and inside to lefties, then drops in and nicks the corner. He occasionally will showcase a little slider and a straight four-seamed fastball, but only to keep hitters honest. Quantrill makes up for a rather slow delivery by tossing over to first base quite often. He fields his position well.

2004 Outlook

Quantrill will take the ball every day. The more he works, the more his trademark pitch moves. Early in the offseason, the 35-year-old declined a $3.1 million option that he controlled. In early December he signed a two-year, $6.8 million deal to join the Yankees. He'll be a critical part of a New York bullpen that was a weakness in 2003.

Paul Shuey

Position: RP
Bats: R **Throws:** R
Ht: 6' 3" **Wt:** 215

Opening Day Age: 33
Born: 9/16/70 in Lima, OH
ML Seasons: 10
Pronunciation: SHOE-ee

Overall Statistics

	W	L	Pct.	ERA	G	GS	Sv	IP	H	BB	SO	HR	Avg
'03	6	4	.600	3.00	62	0	0	69.0	50	33	60	6	.207
Car.	45	27	.625	3.57	451	0	22	504.1	438	256	534	40	.233

2003 Situational Stats

	W	L	ERA	Sv	IP		AB	H	HR	RBI	Avg
Home	2	0	3.19	0	31.0	LHB	107	24	2	9	.224
Road	4	4	2.84	0	38.0	RHB	135	26	4	14	.193
First Half	3	2	1.88	0	38.1	Sc Pos	47	7	0	14	.149
Scnd Half	3	2	4.40	0	30.2	Clutch	108	23	4	9	.213

2003 Season

Paul Shuey began 2003 as one of the Dodgers' principal setup men, but manager Jim Tracy lost confidence in Shuey as the season progressed. He made his annual trip to the DL in late April with a sprained right knee, then had shoulder and hip problems later in the year. Sporadic usage in addition to the physical problems led to a 4.40 ERA after the All-Star break.

Pitching, Defense & Hitting

There is no question that Shuey has great stuff. He regularly registers in the 92-94 range with his fastball and hits the high 80s with his splitter. He will mix in a changeup as well as a curveball, both of which are serviceable. Shuey's delivery is rather complex and can lead to control problems. Opposing basestealers were just 2-for-10 against him in 2003. He is an average fielder.

2004 Outlook

Shuey's name comes up rather often in trade rumors, but his contract is hefty for a setup man ($3.25 million), and there are questions as to whether he has the tenacity to handle a closer's role. For now, Shuey is yet another component in the Dodgers' stable of powerful bullpen arms.

Robin Ventura

Position: 3B/1B
Bats: L **Throws:** R
Ht: 6' 1" **Wt:** 190

Opening Day Age: 36
Born: 7/14/67 in Santa Maria, CA
ML Seasons: 15

Overall Statistics

	G	AB	R	H	D	T	HR	RBI	SB	BB	SO	Avg	OBP	Slg
'03	138	392	42	95	18	1	14	55	0	58	87	.242	.340	.401
Car.	1977	6912	987	1848	335	14	289	1154	24	1053	1148	.267	.363	.445

2003 Situational Stats

	AB	H	HR	RBI	Avg		AB	H	HR	RBI	Avg
Home	179	46	8	27	.257	LHP	51	11	3	5	.216
Road	213	49	6	28	.230	RHP	341	84	11	50	.246
First Half	261	62	9	37	.238	Sc Pos	112	22	0	29	.196
Scnd Half	131	33	5	18	.252	Clutch	54	10	0	2	.185

2003 Season

Robin Ventura hit .292 through the first of June, but a midseason slump reduced his playing time on the deep Yankees' squad. When the Dodgers called in search of offensive help, the veteran third sacker went home to California. Though Ventura provided a little sock down the stretch, it was as a part-timer.

Hitting, Baserunning & Defense

One of the last remaining graduates from the Charlie Lau school of hitting, Ventura's top hand flies off the bat as he finishes his swing. His approach varies with the mound opponent. Against righthanders, Ventura takes whatever is given to him and uses the whole field; he is much more pull-conscious versus southpaws. Ventura is strictly a station-to-station guy on the basepaths, but remains a solid glove man at both third and first.

2004 Outlook

Ventura is unanimously endorsed as a clubhouse guy, so he wasn't going to have a problem finding a job for 2004. As half of a platoon at both corners of the infield, he can help a club both offensively and defensively. He re-signed with Los Angeles in December and will assume a reserve role, playing both first and third base.

Other Los Angeles Dodgers

Victor Alvarez (Pos: LHP, Age: 27)

	W	L	Pct.	ERA	G	GS	Sv	IP	H	BB	SO	HR	Avg
'03	0	1	.000	12.71	5	0	0	5.2	9	6	3	1	.391
Car.	0	2	.000	7.31	9	1	0	16.0	18	8	10	2	.295

Though Alvarez looked overmatched in five appearances for the Dodgers, he has a 2.7 strikeout-walk ratio in six minor league seasons. The little lefty's upside is probably as a situational reliever. 2004 Outlook: C

Larry Barnes (Pos: 1B, Age: 29, Bats: L)

	G	AB	R	H	D	T	HR	RBI	SB	BB	SO	Avg	OBP	Slg
'03	30	38	2	8	2	0	0	2	0	1	9	.211	.231	.263
Car.	46	78	4	12	2	0	1	4	0	2	18	.154	.175	.218

Barnes is a professional hitter, at least at the minor league level. He has spent most of the last four years in Triple-A, with an average season of .286, 15 HR, 70 RBI over that span. 2004 Outlook: C

Troy Brohawn (Pos: LHP, Age: 31)

	W	L	Pct.	ERA	G	GS	Sv	IP	H	BB	SO	HR	Avg
'03	2	0	1.000	3.86	12	0	0	11.2	10	4	13	2	.227
Car.	4	4	.500	4.86	82	0	1	66.2	70	28	46	8	.273

Brohawn has pitched for the D'backs, Giants and Dodgers in the last three seasons as he tours the NL West. Opposing lefthanders have hit .309 against the situational southpaw in his career. 2004 Outlook: C

Steve Colyer (Pos: LHP, Age: 25)

	W	L	Pct.	ERA	G	GS	Sv	IP	H	BB	SO	HR	Avg
'03	0	0	—	2.75	13	0	0	19.2	22	9	16	0	.297
Car.	0	0	—	2.75	13	0	0	19.2	22	9	16	0	.297

Colyer has racked up 44 saves as he has moved through the Dodgers' organization the last two years. The 25-year-old lefthander has good stuff, but he needs to throw more strikes. 2004 Outlook: C

Ron Coomer (Pos: 1B/3B, Age: 37, Bats: R)

	G	AB	R	H	D	T	HR	RBI	SB	BB	SO	Avg	OBP	Slg
'03	69	125	11	30	4	0	4	15	0	10	19	.240	.299	.368
Car.	911	3019	333	827	151	8	92	449	13	177	429	.274	.313	.421

Coomer missed a month last year with a strange bout with dizziness. He hit .355 against lefties and plays good defense at either infield corner, so he still could help some clubs. 2004 Outlook: C

Bubba Crosby (Pos: LF, Age: 27, Bats: L)

	G	AB	R	H	D	T	HR	RBI	SB	BB	SO	Avg	OBP	Slg
'03	9	12	0	1	0	0	0	1	0	0	3	.083	.083	.083
Car.	9	12	0	1	0	0	0	1	0	0	3	.083	.083	.083

The former first-round draft pick had failed to live up to expectations before he hit .350 in Triple-A last year. Crosby was traded to the Yankees in the Robin Ventura deal. 2004 Outlook: C

Rickey Henderson (Pos: LF, Age: 45, Bats: R)

	G	AB	R	H	D	T	HR	RBI	SB	BB	SO	Avg	OBP	Slg
'03	30	72	7	15	1	0	2	5	3	11	16	.208	.321	.306
Car.	3081	10961	2295	3055	510	66	297	1115	1406	2190	1694	.279	.401	.419

The Dodgers signed Henderson at the All-Star break last year in an unsuccessful attempt to energize their moribund offense. The sooner Rickey hangs them up, the sooner he can get to Cooperstown. 2004 Outlook: D

Chad Hermansen (Pos: LF, Age: 26, Bats: R)

	G	AB	R	H	D	T	HR	RBI	SB	BB	SO	Avg	OBP	Slg
'03	11	25	2	4	1	0	0	2	0	2	9	.160	.222	.200
Car.	185	485	49	96	23	2	13	34	9	38	165	.198	.258	.334

The former Pirates wunderkind hit .353 in Triple-A Las Vegas last season, but still has more strikeouts (897) than games (878) in his minor league career. Now 26, he is running out of chances. 2004 Outlook: C

Todd Hundley (Pos: C, Age: 34, Bats: B)

	G	AB	R	H	D	T	HR	RBI	SB	BB	SO	Avg	OBP	Slg
'03	21	33	2	6	1	0	2	11	0	8	13	.182	.341	.394
Car.	1225	3769	495	883	167	7	202	599	14	453	988	.234	.320	.443

Back surgery cost Hundley most of the season, but he posted an .863 OPS versus righthanders in limited at-bats. If he is pain-free, he should relieve Paul LoDuca of some of his heavy load. 2004 Outlook: C

Masao Kida (Pos: RHP, Age: 35)

	W	L	Pct.	ERA	G	GS	Sv	IP	H	BB	SO	HR	Avg
'03	0	1	.000	3.00	3	2	0	12.0	15	3	8	0	.300
Car.	1	1	.500	5.90	54	2	1	79.1	93	33	58	7	.294

Kida filled in quite respectably when injuries created a hole in the Dodgers' rotation, going 0-1 with a 2.70 ERA in his two starts. The 35-year-old journeyman has been bouncing around for years, but LA re-signed him in October. 2004 Outlook: C

Mike Kinkade (Pos: LF/1B, Age: 30, Bats: R)

	G	AB	R	H	D	T	HR	RBI	SB	BB	SO	Avg	OBP	Slg
'03	88	162	25	35	7	0	5	14	1	13	38	.216	.335	.352
Car.	222	429	56	110	20	1	13	48	5	34	89	.256	.350	.399

Kinkade followed up his surprising 2002 campaign in which he hit .380 with a frustrating 2003 season. He is a lifetime .314 hitter versus lefthanders who can play almost anywhere on the field, and he'll take those attributes to Japan in 2004. 2004 Outlook: D

Tom Martin (Pos: LHP, Age: 33)

	W	L	Pct.	ERA	G	GS	Sv	IP	H	BB	SO	HR	Avg
'03	1	2	.333	3.53	80	0	0	51.0	36	24	51	6	.198
Car.	9	7	.563	4.92	202	0	2	183.0	190	88	138	20	.269

After making the Dodger club with an impressive spring, Martin tied for the third most appearances in baseball last season. He signed a two-year, $3.2 million deal with LA over the winter. 2004 Outlook: B

Scott Mullen (Pos: LHP, Age: 29)

	W	L	Pct.	ERA	G	GS	Sv	IP	H	BB	SO	HR	Avg
'03	0	0	–	13.50	3	1	0	7.1	13	10	4	2	.382
Car.	4	5	.444	4.66	75	1	0	67.2	76	35	35	9	.285

Acquired from the Royals in July, Mullen got hammered in his three appearances for the Dodgers. The 29-year-old lefty is 60-42 in eight minor league seasons, mostly working as a starter. 2004 Outlook: C

Rodney Myers (Pos: RHP, Age: 34)

	W	L	Pct.	ERA	G	GS	Sv	IP	H	BB	SO	HR	Avg
'03	0	0	–	6.00	4	0	0	0.0	10	4	5	1	.270
Car.	7	5	.583	5.11	166	1	1	207.2	264	110	100	20	.000

Myers has compiled a respectable 3.45 ERA in 13 minor league seasons, but he never has been able to stick in the bigs. The Dodgers let him go at season's end. 2004 Outlook: C

Jason Romano (Pos: CF, Age: 24, Bats: R)

	G	AB	R	H	D	T	HR	RBI	SB	BB	SO	Avg	OBP	Slg
'03	37	36	3	3	0	0	0	0	2	1	8	.083	.108	.083
Car.	84	127	20	26	4	1	0	8	8	8	32	.205	.250	.252

Romano has a .282 average with 154 stolen bases in his minor league career. Now with his third organization in the last two years, he must get stronger if he hopes to be more than a utilityman. 2004 Outlook: C

Dave Ross (Pos: C, Age: 27, Bats: R)

	G	AB	R	H	D	T	HR	RBI	SB	BB	SO	Avg	OBP	Slg
'03	40	124	19	32	7	0	10	18	0	13	42	.258	.336	.556
Car.	48	134	21	34	8	0	11	20	0	15	46	.254	.340	.560

Ross hit 10 HR in just 124 at-bats for the Dodgers last year, though he also struck out 42 times. With Todd Hundley returning from injury, Ross will have to make contact to get more playing time. 2004 Outlook: C

Wilkin Ruan (Pos: CF, Age: 25, Bats: R)

	G	AB	R	H	D	T	HR	RBI	SB	BB	SO	Avg	OBP	Slg
'03	21	41	2	9	2	1	0	2	1	0	7	.220	.220	.317
Car.	22	52	4	12	3	1	0	5	1	0	9	.231	.231	.327

Ruan hit .308 and stole 41 bases in Triple-A last season, but he walked just 10 times. Though he plays a nice center field, he needs to get on base more often if he hopes to stick in the bigs. 2004 Outlook: C

Daryle Ward (Pos: 1B/LF, Age: 28, Bats: L)

	G	AB	R	H	D	T	HR	RBI	SB	BB	SO	Avg	OBP	Slg
'03	52	109	6	20	1	0	9	9	0	3	19	.183	.211	.193
Car.	470	1192	116	311	63	2	49	197	1	80	243	.261	.306	.440

Picked up to provide some lefthanded pop, Ward was a complete bust with the Dodgers. He knocked in 72 runs for the Astros in 2002 but will have to fight his way back to the majors. He'll get a chance with the Pirates after signing a minor league contract in December. 2004 Outlook: C

Los Angeles Dodgers Minor League Prospects

Organization Overview:

General Manager Dan Evans has the Dodgers' minor league system headed in the right direction. After a decade of failed high-round draft picks, the lower levels are now packed with impact players, especially on the pitching side. So far, Evans has resisted the temptation to exchange any of those riches for a late-season fix. The offensive woes will have to be patched from the outside, however, as there are no impact hitters on the immediate horizon. The loss of Director of Player Development Bill Bavasi to become the Mariners' GM is a big blow, but there is a lot of experience among the braintrust, including former big league managers Terry Collins and John Boles. So they should be able to fill the gaps.

Reggie Abercrombie

Position: OF	Opening Day Age: 22
Bats: R Throws: R	Born: 7/15/81 in
Ht: 6' 3" Wt: 210	Columbus, GA

Recent Statistics

	G	AB	R	H	D	T	HR	RBI	SB	BB	SO	Avg
2002 A Vero Beach	132	526	80	145	23	13	10	56	41	27	158	.276
2002 AA Jacksnville	1	4	1	1	0	0	0	0	1	0	1	.250
2003 AA Jacksnville	116	448	59	117	25	7	15	54	28	16	164	.261

Abercrombie is a five-tool player whose lack of plate discipline has greatly hindered his progress on the diamond. In his first full season in Double-A last year, he struck out (164) ten times more often than he walked (16). He's got a lot of pop in his bat, however, and has averaged 37 stolen bases in his four minor league seasons. Abercrombie can play anywhere in the outfield, but his strong arm tickets him for right field. The Dodgers love his raw ability, but he will have to make more contact if he hopes to keep moving up the organizational ladder.

Franklin Gutierrez

Position: OF	Opening Day Age: 21
Bats: R Throws: R	Born: 2/21/83 in
Ht: 6' 2" Wt: 175	Caricuao, VZ

Recent Statistics

	G	AB	R	H	D	T	HR	RBI	SB	BB	SO	Avg
2002 A S Georgia	92	361	61	102	18	4	12	45	13	31	88	.283
2002 AAA Las Vegas	2	10	2	3	2	0	0	2	0	1	4	.300
2003 A Vero Beach	109	424	65	120	28	5	20	68	17	39	110	.283
2003 AA Jacksnville	18	67	12	21	3	2	4	12	3	7	20	.313

After flying a bit under the radar in his first two professional seasons, Gutierrez had a breakout campaign last year. The Dodgers' Minor League Player of the Year has a lot of pop in his bat; he banged out 62 extra-base hits at two levels in 2003. While his aggressiveness at the plate has served him well, it also led to 130 strike-outs last year, nearly matching the total of his first two seasons. Gutierrez is solid in the outfield, but his arm is just average, and he was 20-for-28 in the stolen-base department. The 21-year-old has improved all his numbers each season so far and will begin 2004 at Double-A Jacksonville.

Joel Hanrahan

Position: P	Opening Day Age: 22
Bats: R Throws: R	Born: 10/6/81 in Des
Ht: 6' 3" Wt: 215	Moines, IA

Recent Statistics

	W	L	ERA	G	GS	Sv	IP	H	R	BB	SO	HR
2002 A Vero Beach	10	6	4.20	25	25	0	143.2	129	74	51	139	11
2002 AA Jacksonville	1	1	10.64	3	3	0	11.0	15	14	7	10	1
2003 AA Jacksonville	10	4	2.43	23	23	0	133.1	117	44	53	130	5
2003 AAA Las Vegas	1	2	10.08	5	5	0	25.0	36	28	20	13	2

In each of the last two seasons, Hanrahan has posted solid numbers at one level only to be sandblasted upon receiving a late-season promotion. Though he does not possess dominating stuff, the big righthander has good command over three pitches. He throws a sinking fastball in the low 90s, as well as a decent slider and solid changeup. Hanrahan needs work on the finer points of the game, but he has the look of a workhorse, as he has made 82 starts over the last three seasons. He will have to prove himself for a full year at Triple-A Las Vegas this season, but it is just a matter of time before he is in the Dodgers' rotation.

Koyie Hill

Position: C	Opening Day Age: 25
Bats: B Throws: R	Born: 3/9/79 in Tulsa,
Ht: 6' 0" Wt: 190	OK

Recent Statistics

	G	AB	R	H	D	T	HR	RBI	SB	BB	SO	Avg
2003 AA Jacksonville	25	101	9	23	7	0	0	7	2	6	19	.228
2003 AAA Las Vegas	85	312	48	98	18	0	3	36	5	15	39	.314
2003 NL Los Angeles	3	3	0	1	1	0	0	0	0	0	2	.333

Hill continued his steady progress through the Dodgers' system last season. In two minor league stops, he hit .293 and totaled 25 doubles. Converted to catcher after playing third base in college at Wichita State, Hill is still learning the nuances of the position. However, he has quick feet and a strong arm, two tools that cannot be taught. The switch-hitter has a decent knowledge of the strike zone and usually makes contact, with gap power from both sides of the slab. While no speed burner, he runs the bases well. Hill is a heady ballplayer who has a keen understanding of all aspects of the game. He will start the year at Triple-A Las Vegas, but it won't be long before he is at least sharing time behind the plate in Los Angeles.

Edwin Jackson

Position: P
Bats: R **Throws:** R
Ht: 6' 1" **Wt:** 190

Opening Day Age: 20
Born: 9/9/83 in Neu-Ulm, West Germany

Recent Statistics

	W	L	ERA	G	GS	Sv	IP	H	R	BB	SO	HR
2003 AA Jacksnville	7	7	3.70	27	27	0	148.1	121	68	53	157	9
2003 NL Los Angeles	2	1	2.45	4	3	0	22.0	17	6	11	19	2

Drafted in the sixth round in 2001, Jackson has exploded to the top of the Dodgers' prospect list. His fastball has gained velocity in his two-plus pro seasons and now reaches the mid-90s with regularity. Neither of his breaking pitches is big league quality at this point, but Jackson made great strides with his changeup last season. The strong second option enabled him to post a 3-1 strikeout-walk ratio. He is a superb athlete who can handle the bat as well as the glove, and has a commanding presence on the mound. Though he has just 297 professional innings under his belt, Jackson will be pitching in the majors at some point this season.

James Loney

Position: 1B
Bats: L **Throws:** L
Ht: 6' 3" **Wt:** 205

Opening Day Age: 19
Born: 5/7/84 in Missouri City, TX

Recent Statistics

	G	AB	R	H	D	T	HR	RBI	SB	BB	SO	Avg
2002 R Great Falls	47	170	33	63	22	3	5	30	5	25	18	.371
2002 A Vero Beach	17	67	6	20	6	0	0	5	0	6	10	.299
2003 A Vero Beach	125	468	64	129	31	3	7	46	9	43	80	.276

Loney did not post the eye-popping numbers of his first pro season, but he quieted concerns that there would be any long-term problems with the broken wrist that ended his 2002 campaign. The lanky first baseman has a picture-perfect swing, but it can get a bit long and the pitchers in high Class-A fanned him 80 times. Loney has not yet fully developed his power stroke, but his 31 doubles should lead to more longballs as he fills out. The former pitcher has the soft hands and solid instincts to be an above-average first sacker, and will only get better as he plays there full-time. He will make the challenging jump to Double-A this season.

Greg Miller

Position: P
Bats: L **Throws:** L
Ht: 6' 5" **Wt:** 195

Opening Day Age: 19
Born: 11/3/84 in Orange, CA

Recent Statistics

	W	L	ERA	G	GS	Sv	IP	H	R	BB	SO	HR
2002 R Great Falls	3	2	2.37	11	7	0	38.0	27	14	13	37	1
2003 A Vero Beach	11	4	2.49	21	21	0	115.2	103	40	41	111	5
2003 AA Jacksnville	1	1	1.01	4	4	0	26.2	15	5	7	40	1

Just two years out of high school, Miller ranks among the best on the Dodgers' prospect list. The lanky left-hander does not have an overpowering heater, as it registers in the 89-92 MPH range. His best pitch is a knuckle-curve that drops off the table, and he also has a serviceable circle change. Everything comes out of a herky-jerky delivery that makes Miller very difficult to decipher. Despite being the youngest player in the Double-A Southern League upon his promotion, he struck out 40 hitters in only 26.2 innings. The team's Minor League Pitcher of the Year did not turn 19 until after the season ended, but Miller could make a cameo appearance in Chavez Ravine as soon as this September.

Joe Thurston

Position: 2B
Bats: L **Throws:** R
Ht: 5' 11" **Wt:** 175

Opening Day Age: 24
Born: 9/29/79 in Fairfield, CA

Recent Statistics

	G	AB	R	H	D	T	HR	RBI	SB	BB	SO	Avg
2003 AAA Las Vegas	132	538	77	156	27	6	7	68	1	31	48	.290
2003 NL Los Angeles	12	10	2	2	0	0	0	0	0	1	1	.200

Expected to be the starting second baseman for the Dodgers in 2003, Thurston did not produce in the spring and spent the entire season in Las Vegas. Though he did not reproduce his sterling 2002 numbers, he had a solid campaign and showed a better sense of the strike zone than he had in the past. He is a line-drive hitter who needs to keep the ball on the ground in order to take advantage of his speed, though his 1-for-13 stolen-base performance does not bode well. The former shortstop is a solid glove man. Thurston appears to be more than ready for the bigs, but he may need a trade to get the opportunity.

Others to Watch

Once a top prospect, outfielder **Chin-Feng Chen** (26) has put up almost identical numbers while playing the last two seasons for Triple-A Las Vegas. If he can continue to cut down on his strikeouts, he could earn a job as a righthanded power bat on the LA bench this season. . . Seemingly on the fast track after posting a 1.42 ERA at two stops in 2002, lefthander **Jonathan Figueroa** (20) ran into arm trouble last season. He went 1-8 and pitched just 78.1 innings in 17 starts for the Class-A South Georgia club. The Dodgers probably will ask him to improve those numbers before they move him up a notch. . . The sky is the limit for **Joel Guzman** (19), a big shortstop with all the tools in the world. He has hit just .242 in his two pro seasons, however, and has not yet learned to hit anything with a wrinkle in it. . . As might be expected from Bert Blyleven's nephew, righty **Brian Pilkington's** (21) best pitch is his curveball. He has walked just 36 batters in 305 professional innings and will make the tough jump to Double-A this season. . . Second baseman **Delwyn Young** (21) is a free-swinging switch-hitter who can put a charge into the ball. He now has hit .300+ in both of his pro seasons and banged out 60 extra-base hits in Class-A ball last year.

Miller Park

Offense

Miller Park seems to have a reputation as a band-box, even though it hasn't come close to earning such a label. While it is one of the better home-run parks in the National League, its overall effect on scoring has been almost negligible. It gives up home runs in the gaps but takes some of them back down the lines. Both the small foul territory and the ability to shut out the April chill help the hitters, but the reflected glare can help the pitchers.

Defense

With minimal foul territory down the lines, the corner infielders don't need to be able to gallop over half the earth to chase down a popup (as they would in, say, Oakland). The relatively deep outfield corners and shallow alleys serve to spread the outfielders. The center fielder has less real estate behind him and can afford to play a little shallower, but must cover more ground laterally. The right fielder needs a good arm in order to make a throw from the right-field corner.

Who It Helps the Most

Flyball hitters whose power is to the alleys. Wes Helms hit 16 of his 23 home runs here and batted more than 100 points higher than he did on the road. Keith Ginter showed better power at Miller Park.

Who It Hurts the Most

A pitcher who likes to pitch up in the zone, but doesn't have the stuff to get away with it, can get hurt here. Wayne Franklin and Ruben Quevedo fit that bill.

Rookies & Newcomers

Junior Spivey hit exceptionally well at Bank One Ballpark and could fall off somewhat. His power is down the line, which is the deepest part of Miller Park. Chad Moeller could lose some points on his average, but Craig Counsell and Lyle Overbay shouldn't be affected much. Lefthander Chris Capuano has kept the ball in the park in the minors—despite pitching in some tough places—and has a fair chance to succeed here. Homegrown southpaw Luis Martinez hasn't been vulnerable to the home run, either.

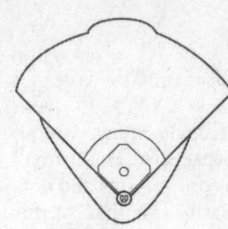

Dimensions: LF-344, LCF-371, CF-400, RCF-374, RF-345

Capacity: 41,900

Elevation: 635 feet

Surface: Grass

Foul Territory: Small

Park Factors

2003 Season

| | Home Games | | | Away Games | | | |
	Brewers	Opp	Total	Brewers	Opp	Total	Index
G	75	75	150	75	75	150	
Avg	.255	.273	.264	.252	.285	.268	98
AB	2531	2741	5272	2585	2546	5131	103
R	318	426	744	329	387	716	104
H	646	747	1393	651	726	1377	101
2B	120	144	264	126	141	267	96
3B	8	20	28	13	20	33	83
HR	100	110	210	82	87	169	121
BB	260	282	542	257	254	511	103
SO	545	497	1042	583	461	1044	97
E	58	38	96	49	60	109	88
E-Infield	51	35	86	40	53	93	92
LHB-Avg	.280	.284	.283	.271	.260	.266	106
LHB-HR	30	41	71	24	24	48	138
RHB-Avg	.244	.266	.255	.242	.298	.270	94
RHB-HR	70	69	139	58	63	121	114

2001-2003

| | Home Games | | | Away Games | | | |
	Brewers	Opp	Total	Brewers	Opp	Total	Index
G	222	222	444	225	225	450	
Avg	.254	.265	.260	.249	.275	.262	99
AB	7339	7815	15154	7749	7492	15241	101
R	936	1137	2073	968	1147	2115	99
H	1864	2071	3935	1928	2062	3990	100
2B	359	417	776	389	406	795	98
3B	33	48	81	43	54	97	84
HR	250	299	549	246	251	497	111
BB	715	873	1588	733	900	1633	98
SO	1644	1481	3125	1791	1380	3171	99
E	145	120	265	150	137	287	94
E-Infield	129	102	231	123	113	236	99
LHB-Avg	.266	.277	.272	.258	.263	.260	104
LHB-HR	91	132	223	85	95	180	124
RHB-Avg	.247	.258	.253	.244	.283	.263	96
RHB-HR	159	167	326	161	156	317	104

2003 Rankings (National League)

- Second-highest LHB home-run factor

Ned Yost

2003 Season

Ned Yost's most significant accomplishment in his first season as manager was to restore a positive attitude to a team that had lost a National League-high 106 games the year before amid a poisonous clubhouse atmosphere. He did just that by holding players accountable for their effort and attitude, such as when he decisively pulled the plug on longtime problem child Alex Sanchez. The won-lost record wasn't pretty, but Yost successfully wove a lot of new faces into the lineup, some of whom may turn out to be keepers.

Offense

Yost's tactics on offensive were dictated mostly by the talent at hand. Within those confines, he generally was conventional, giving the green light to those who could run, pinch-hitting for the weaker hitters and calling for a sacrifice or hit-and-run when appropriate. He used a set line-up, as opposed to riding the hot hand from day-to-day. It never was hard to figure what a given player's role was.

Pitching & Defense

Yost did as well as could have been expected with a staff that was in a constant state of flux. Injuries repeatedly forced him to remake his rotation and redefine his bullpen roles. He moved players in and out; some were better than expected, and some were worse. The one thing that was constant throughout was that he never overreacted—he always gave a struggling player a fair chance to turn things around. If he had any input into the decisions to sign Royce Clayton and Eddie Perez, it shows that he puts great value on defense up the middle.

2004 Outlook

The Brewers' best prospects still are a year or two away from the majors. If Yost can ease them into the lineup as painlessly as he did with last year's newcomers, the results could be impressive. For the shorter term, he will continue to focus on keeping his crew positive yet accountable. Yost can do that in confidence, after the Brewers exercised their 2005 option on Yost. The team also added an option for 2006 to his contract.

Born: 8/19/55 in Eureka, CA

Playing Experience: 1980-1985, Mil, Tex, Mon

Managerial Experience: 1 season

Manager Statistics

Year	Team, Lg	W	L	Pct	GB	Finish
2003	Milwaukee, NL	68	94	.420	20.0	6th Central
1 Season		68	94	.420	–	–

2003 Starting Pitchers by Days Rest

	<=3	4	5	6+
Brewers Starts	2	95	28	26
Brewers ERA	4.66	5.11	5.78	6.39
NL Avg Starts	2	84	43	23
NL ERA	5.00	4.23	4.42	4.68

2003 Situational Stats

	Ned Yost	NL Average
Hit & Run Success %	38.1	32.7
Stolen Base Success %	71.7	68.9
Platoon Pct.	44.2	52.0
Defensive Subs	16	19
High-Pitch Outings	5	8
Quick/Slow Hooks	17/21	20/12
Sacrifice Attempts	86	93

2003 Rankings (National League)

- 1st in steals of second base (89), steals of home plate (1), squeeze plays (9) and slow hooks
- 3rd in stolen base attempts (138)

Royce Clayton

2003 Season

The Brewers signed Royce Clayton to improve their infield defense and buy some time until their prospects developed. The move accomplished both aims, despite the fact that Clayton failed to reach even his own modest norms at the plate. For the first three weeks of the season, he was one of Milwaukee's hottest hitters. Then, he fell into a brutal slump that had him well below .200 by the end of May, and he never really recovered. He was benched in favor of youngster Bill Hall in September. Clayton hadn't really been expected to contribute with the bat, however, and his glove-work did prove to be as good as advertised.

Hitting

Clayton swings big but rarely connects big. Those big cuts, combined with generally poor pitch selection, often puts him at the mercy of the pitcher. When he does make contact, it usually results in a groundball to the right side. This leads to him grounding into more double plays than someone with his speed should. Clayton is capable of hitting well for weeks at a time, but he also is prone to long slumps, as he showed last year. Having spent most of his career near the bottom of the order, he knows how to get a bunt down.

Baserunning & Defense

Despite his offensive limitations, Clayton never has had trouble finding work, thanks to his defensive prowess. A smooth, agile shortstop with cat-like quickness and soft hands, he makes all the plays, and makes them gracefully. His arm is just average, however. He still runs well and is capable of stealing a base, but doesn't always get the best jumps.

2004 Outlook

Clayton became a free agent after the season. He'll hope to find a team that's looking for a good glove and can afford to carry a weak bat. The time soon may be approaching when he won't be able to hold down a regular job, and when that time comes, he also may have trouble holding down a spot as a reserve.

Position: SS
Bats: R **Throws:** R
Ht: 6' 0" **Wt:** 185

Opening Day Age: 34
Born: 1/2/70 in Burbank, CA
ML Seasons: 13

Overall Statistics

G	AB	R	H	D	T	HR	RBI	SB	BB	SO	Avg	OBP	Slg
146	483	49	110	16	1	11	39	5	49	92	.228	.301	.333
1605	5634	708	1438	255	46	97	573	192	435	1047	.255	.310	.368

Where He Hits the Ball

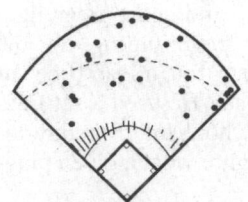

Vs. LHP

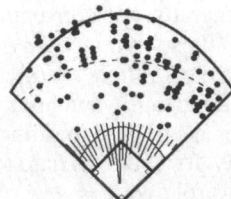

Vs. RHP

2003 Situational Stats

	AB	H	HR	RBI	Avg		AB	H	HR	RBI	Avg
Home	239	52	5	14	.218	LHP	96	23	1	8	.240
Road	244	58	6	25	.238	RHP	387	87	10	31	.225
First Half	305	64	9	26	.210	Sc Pos	116	21	5	33	.181
Scnd Half	178	46	2	13	.258	Clutch	90	18	0	2	.200

2003 Rankings (National League)

- 1st in most GDPs per GDP situation (23.6%)
- 2nd in GDPs (25) and lowest batting average with the bases loaded (.063)
- 3rd in lowest slugging percentage, lowest batting average with runners in scoring position, lowest batting average vs. righthanded pitchers and lowest batting average at home
- 4th in fielding percentage at shortstop (.977) and lowest batting average
- 6th in highest groundball-flyball ratio (1.9)
- 8th in lowest on-base percentage and lowest batting average on the road
- 9th in errors at shortstop (14)
- Led the Brewers in intentional walks (10), GDPs (25) and highest groundball-flyball ratio (1.9)

Wayne Franklin

2003 Season

Lefthander Wayne Franklin had pitched well in four late-season starts in 2002 after coming over in a trade from Houston, and opened 2003 in the Brewers' rotation. He held his starting spot all year and gave Milwaukee innings, but had his share of rough outings, especially toward the end of the season. No pitcher in the majors gave up more home runs, and only five issued more walks. And while Franklin ended up winning 10 games for a last-place team, six of his victories came against Cincinnati and Pittsburgh, the other two sub-.500 clubs in the National League Central Division.

Pitching

Franklin doesn't have exceptional velocity, command or movement, but has just enough of each to get by. His outings always seem to be a high-wire act, however, as his high-80s cutter and short slider are hittable. He tends to leave them up in the zone, inducing a lot of flyballs, many of which can't be tracked down. He throws a changeup, but he simply doesn't fool hitters often enough and they are able to make solid contact against him, even with two strikes—lefthanded and righthanded swingers alike. Franklin converted from relief only two years ago, and he tends lose effectiveness after his first trip through the order.

Defense & Hitting

Franklin's pitching style doesn't produce many comebackers, but he flags down an acceptable number of balls hit back through the box. For a lefthander, his pickoff move is unremarkable, and he isn't especially tough to run on. He's a decent hitter, capable of getting the bat on the ball or bunting a runner over.

2004 Outlook

Franklin is a borderline talent with little upside, and his hold on a rotation spot may never be secure. Last year, he was able to remain in the rotation mostly because several of his worst games came late in the year, rather than early on. If he struggles early this year, he may not be given all that many chances to bring his ERA back into line.

Position: SP
Bats: L **Throws:** L
Ht: 6' 2" **Wt:** 211

Opening Day Age: 30
Born: 3/9/74 in Wilmington, DE
ML Seasons: 4

Overall Statistics

	W	L	Pct.	ERA	G	GS	Sv	IP	H	BB	SO	HR	Avg
'03	10	13	.435	5.50	36	34	0	194.2	201	94	116	36	.268
Car.	12	14	.462	5.29	76	38	0	252.0	258	132	163	43	.265

2003 Pitching Profile

	Wayne Franklin	NL Average
Overall Strike %	60.7	62.4
1st Pitch Strike %	59.9	58.4
Ratio	1.52	1.38
Strikeouts per 9 IP	5.36	6.65
Walks per 9 IP	4.35	3.42
Home Runs per 9 IP	1.66	1.05
Strikeout/Walk Ratio	1.23	1.94
Groundball/Flyball Ratio	0.75	1.29

2003 Situational Stats

	W	L	ERA	Sv	IP		AB	H	HR	RBI	Avg
Home	5	9	5.64	0	91.0	LHB	145	37	8	32	.255
Road	5	4	5.38	0	103.2	RHB	606	164	28	87	.271
First Half	5	6	4.81	0	119.2	Sc Pos	175	48	7	72	.274
Scnd Half	5	7	6.60	0	75.0	Clutch	18	4	0	1	.222

2003 Rankings (National League)

- 1st in home runs allowed, balks (4), fielding percentage at pitcher (1.000), highest ERA, lowest strikeout-walk ratio (1.2), highest ERA at home and most home runs allowed per nine innings (1.66)
- 2nd in lowest groundball-flyball ratio allowed (0.8)
- 3rd in games started, highest slugging percentage allowed (.499), highest on-base percentage allowed (.355) and highest walks per nine innings (4.3)
- 4th in sacrifice bunts (12)
- 5th in walks allowed
- Led the Brewers in sacrifice bunts (12), losses, games started, home runs allowed, walks allowed, hit batsmen (10), balks (4), GDPs induced (18), lowest batting average allowed (.268) and most run support per nine innings (5.4)

Keith Ginter

2003 Season

Keith Ginter failed to win the Brewers' third-base job in spring training, but he did good work as a reserve infielder and eventually wound up as the club's starting second baseman after Eric Young was traded. Ginter was fairly productive at the plate, and more importantly, he showed that he might be able to handle the defensive demands of second base full-time.

Hitting

Ginter has developed a power hitter's approach, taking a full cut and looking for something to pull in the air. He especially likes fastballs on the inner half of the plate. He has decent power, but can be fooled by offspeed pitches and gets in trouble when he gets too pull-conscious. Patience is a virtue of his, although he largely negates it by swinging through so many pitches. Standing on top of the plate does allow him to reach base via the hit-by-pitch, though. He was one of the most productive pinch-hitters in baseball last year, with a .310 average and a pair of home runs in 29 such at-bats.

Baserunning & Defense

Finding a position Ginter could play adequately had impeded his progress. Second base is his least unnatural position, but his range is below-average. He was surehanded there last year and proved capable on the double play, but it remains to be seen if he can make it there. His range, reaction time and arm strength have proven less than ideal for third. He can fill in in left field. His speed is average at best and he isn't much of a factor on the bases.

2004 Outlook

When the season ended, Ginter looked like the Brewers' starting second baseman heading into 2004. That rosy picture changed when the Brewers traded Richie Sexson to Arizona and acquired a pair of infielders, Junior Spivey and Craig Counsell, in the package. Ginter should continue to hit as he did last year, but it appears he'll again be playing a number of positions as a reserve.

Position: 2B/3B
Bats: R **Throws:** R
Ht: 5'10" **Wt:** 195

Opening Day Age: 27
Born: 5/5/76 in Norwalk, CA
ML Seasons: 4
Pronunciation: GHIN-ter

Overall Statistics

	G	AB	R	H	D	T	HR	RBI	SB	BB	SO	Avg	OBP	Slg
'03	127	358	51	92	15	2	14	44	1	37	87	.257	.352	.427
Car.	161	448	61	113	24	2	16	55	1	55	105	.252	.354	.422

Where He Hits the Ball

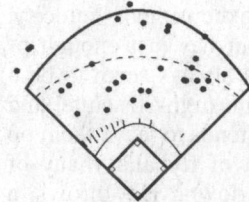
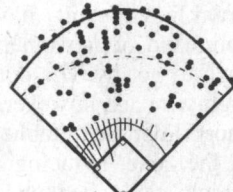

Vs. LHP   **Vs. RHP**

2003 Situational Stats

	AB	H	HR	RBI	Avg		AB	H	HR	RBI	Avg
Home	180	44	9	24	.244	LHP	85	19	4	6	.224
Road	178	48	5	20	.270	RHP	273	73	10	38	.267
First Half	162	43	5	19	.265	Sc Pos	75	19	2	28	.253
Scnd Half	196	49	9	25	.250	Clutch	66	18	1	9	.273

2003 Rankings (National League)

- 1st in home runs among rookies
- 4th in hit by pitch (17)
- 7th in highest percentage of pitches taken (62.2)
- Led the Brewers in hit by pitch (17) and most pitches seen per plate appearance (4.23)

Wes Helms

2003 Season

The Brewers traded for Wes Helms before the 2003 season and gave him their third-base job, making him a major league regular for the first time. Helms hit well enough to keep the post, and showed some improvement over the course of the season. A strained hamstring sidelined him for a couple of weeks in August, but he was a fixture in the lineup the rest of the time.

Hitting

Helms has very good raw power, which he demonstrated with a 465-foot shot onto Bernie Brewer's slide during Milwaukee's last home game of the season. A flyball hitter, he has the juice to reach the fences anywhere from right-center to the left-field line, although he tends to pull the ball. A fairly aggressive batsman who's never afraid to swing and miss, he does his best hitting early in the count and is vulnerable with two strikes. Helms has been streaky, something he may be able to smooth out as he gains experience.

Baserunning & Defense

Helms has below-average range, but makes up for his lack of coverage somewhat with sure hands and a strong, accurate throwing arm. He's decent enough overall to be a regular third baseman but won't ever be a Gold Glover. He's also had some experience at first base and the outfield. He doesn't run well, and the only thing that keeps him from grounding into more double plays is his tendency to hit the ball in the air.

2004 Outlook

If Helms can continue to hit the way he did last year, he could hold Milwaukee's third-base job for a while longer. On the other hand, his past performance suggests that his 2003 season may have been at the top of his range. Plus, he'll turn 28 this May, so it's quite possible that he already is as good as he's going to get. He may top out as the kind of hitter who can hold his own in the lower half of the order.

Position: 3B
Bats: R **Throws:** R
Ht: 6' 4" **Wt:** 230

Opening Day Age: 27
Born: 5/12/76 in Gastonia, NC
ML Seasons: 5

Overall Statistics

	G	AB	R	H	D	T	HR	RBI	SB	BB	SO	Avg	OBP	Slg
'03	134	476	56	124	21	0	23	67	0	43	131	.261	.330	.450
Car.	332	920	106	228	48	3	40	127	2	75	250	.248	.310	.437

Where He Hits the Ball

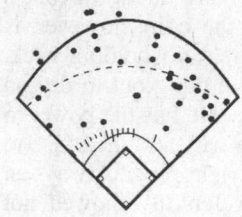 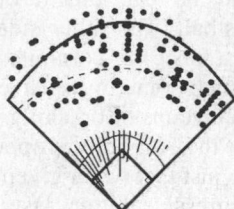

Vs. LHP   **Vs. RHP**

2003 Situational Stats

	AB	H	HR	RBI	Avg		AB	H	HR	RBI	Avg
Home	240	76	16	45	.317	LHP	86	27	6	18	.314
Road	236	48	7	22	.203	RHP	390	97	17	49	.249
First Half	313	80	16	51	.256	Sc Pos	111	24	7	43	.216
Scnd Half	163	44	7	16	.270	Clutch	81	10	2	9	.222

2003 Rankings (National League)

- 1st in lowest batting average on the road
- 2nd in errors at third base (19) and lowest fielding percentage at third base (.945)
- 7th in sacrifice flies (7)
- 8th in strikeouts and lowest batting average with two strikes (.137)
- Led the Brewers in sacrifice flies (7) and batting average at home

Geoff Jenkins

2003 Season

When Geoff Jenkins suffered his devastating, season-ending ankle injury in 2002, one had to wonder if he'd be the same player when he came back. Luckily for the Brewers, he was. He was perhaps a half-step slower and a tad less full-throttle, but he hit like the Jenkins of old before a broken thumb ended his season in late August—just as he was in the midst of a hot streak that had seen him homer in five of his last six games. Still, the best news had to be that the thumb injury was the only serious malady of the season for him.

Hitting

Jenkins' bat speed is among the best in the majors, and he can turn around just about anyone's fastball. The other side of the coin, however, is that once he commits, there's no holding back, which sometimes leaves him hung out to dry on changeups or breaking balls. He has the power to hit the ball out the opposite way and the sense to do just that when given the right pitch. Always an aggressive hitter, last year Jenkins showed not only better plate discipline than he had in the past, but better strike-zone judgment as well, working himself into favorable counts more often. Lefthanders still take a bite out of his power.

Baserunning & Defense

On the bases or in the field, Jenkins is hustling, fearless and maximum-effort. He dialed back his aggression a bit on the bases last year, attempting no steals, even though he still runs fairly well. He continued to play an excellent left field, though, catching everything he could reach, diving for everything close, and throwing as well as anyone at his position. He posted 11 assists as an outfielder last year.

2004 Outlook

The outlook for Jenkins is the same as it's been for years: If he can only stay healthy from start to finish, he could have a very big year. His more mature plate approach last year is a good sign, but he'll need to show even more restraint if teams start pitching around him the way they used to pitch around Richie Sexson.

Position: LF
Bats: L **Throws:** R
Ht: 6' 1" **Wt:** 213

Opening Day Age: 29
Born: 7/21/74 in Olympia, WA
ML Seasons: 6

Overall Statistics

	G	AB	R	H	D	T	HR	RBI	SB	BB	SO	Avg	OBP	Slg
'03	124	487	81	144	30	2	28	95	0	58	120	.296	.375	.538
Car.	650	2348	379	663	159	12	122	391	22	204	583	.282	.349	.516

Where He Hits the Ball

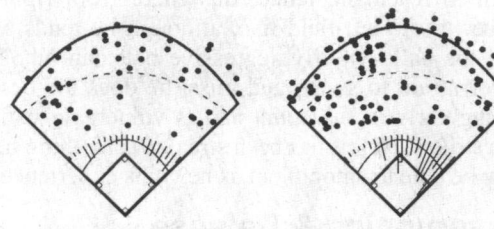

Vs. LHP   **Vs. RHP**

2003 Situational Stats

	AB	H	HR	RBI	Avg		AB	H	HR	RBI	Avg
Home	233	66	16	51	.283	LHP	159	43	4	22	.270
Road	254	78	12	44	.307	RHP	328	101	24	73	.308
First Half	338	93	20	68	.275	Sc Pos	134	41	8	66	.306
Scnd Half	149	51	8	27	.342	Clutch	81	17	3	13	.210

2003 Rankings (National League)

- 1st in fielding percentage in left field (1.000)
- 5th in highest percentage of swings that missed (29.7)
- 8th in highest percentage of swings on the first pitch (37.7)
- 9th in lowest percentage of swings put into play (35.5)
- 10th in slugging percentage
- Led the Brewers in doubles and intentional walks (10)

Matt Kinney

2003 Season

Acquired from the Twins in a minor offseason deal, righthander Matt Kinney was one of Milwaukee's more pleasant surprises in 2003. He won the job as their fifth starter coming out of spring training and solidified his rotation spot with a hot streak in April and May. Though he ran out of gas late in the year, Kinney had more than his share of strong outings and pitched better overall than his ERA would suggest.

Pitching

Kinney has good stuff; when he takes the mound, the only question is whether he'll be able to put the ball where he wants to. When he has command of his good overhand curve, he can be quite effective, mixing it with his low-90s fastball and two-seamer. One would expect a big, strong guy like Kinney to have good stamina, but he doesn't—his effectiveness drops off markedly after the first few innings, a pattern he's shown over the last three years. Still, the Brewers often needed him to stay in and save their bullpen, and it ended up hurting his numbers considerably.

Defense & Hitting

One area where Kinney needs a lot of work is combating the running game. He has a poor pick-off move and is slow to the plate, and he compounds the problem by sometimes failing to pay proper attention to baserunners. He's a capable enough fielder otherwise. Kinney came into the year with almost no experience as a hitter, and it showed. He had only two hits all season and struck out nearly half the time. Even getting a bunt down was a challenge for him.

2004 Outlook

There are a lot of reasons to expect improvement from Kinney in 2004. He has shown that he's capable of being quite effective when he has his command and is at full strength. Now it's just a matter of refining his control and building his stamina. He will go into the season as the Brewers' No. 2 starter.

Position: SP
Bats: R **Throws:** R
Ht: 6' 5" **Wt:** 225

Opening Day Age: 27
Born: 12/16/76 in Bangor, ME
ML Seasons: 0

Overall Statistics

	W	L	Pct.	ERA	G	GS	Sv	IP	H	BB	SO	HR	Avg
'03	10	13	.435	5.19	33	31	0	190.2	201	80	152	27	.272
Car.	14	22	.389	5.06	55	51	0	299.0	320	138	221	47	.276

2003 Pitching Profile

	Matt Kinney	NL Average
Overall Strike %	62.2	62.4
1st Pitch Strike %	58.2	58.4
Ratio	1.47	1.38
Strikeouts per 9 IP	7.17	6.65
Walks per 9 IP	3.78	3.42
Home Runs per 9 IP	1.27	1.05
Strikeout/Walk Ratio	1.90	1.94
Groundball/Flyball Ratio	0.91	1.29

2003 Situational Stats

	W	L	ERA	Sv	IP		AB	H	HR	RBI	Avg
Home	4	7	5.11	0	98.2	LHB	359	102	12	47	.284
Road	6	6	5.28	0	92.0	RHB	381	99	15	63	.260
First Half	6	7	4.72	0	116.1	Sc Pos	196	48	13	89	.245
Scnd Half	4	6	5.93	0	74.1	Clutch	15	3	0	0	.200

2003 Rankings (National League)

- 3rd in highest ERA at home
- 4th in stolen bases allowed (24)
- 5th in balks (2) and highest ERA
- 6th in losses and lowest groundball-flyball ratio allowed (0.9)
- 7th in highest stolen-base percentage allowed (85.7)
- 8th in most home runs allowed per nine innings (1.27)
- 9th in home runs allowed and highest walks per nine innings (3.8)
- 10th in wild pitches (10), lowest winning percentage, highest on-base percentage allowed (.343) and highest ERA on the road
- Led the Brewers in losses, wild pitches (10), pickoff throws (111), stolen bases allowed (24) and most strikeouts per nine innings (7.2)

Danny Kolb

2003 Season

In a season when Scott Podsednik was the Brewers' most pleasant surprise, Danny Kolb ran a very creditable second. Kolb had been signed to a minor league contract after being cut by the Rangers in the final days of spring training. After pitching lights-out for two and a half months as a setup man at Triple-A, he was called up in mid-June and became the closer within weeks. In the second half, he had a 1.27 ERA and converted 21 of 22 save chances.

Pitching

In 2002, Kolb was fairly effective, despite often pitching from behind, thanks to his sinking fastball that reached the mid-90s. Last year, he not only was throwing harder—often getting into the high 90s—but he also was able to throw strikes a little more consistently. The pitch is so nasty that it's hard to drive on any count, and usually produces little more than groundballs. Kolb had missed the first half of 2002 with rotator cuff surgery, which may have had something to do with his increase in velocity in 2003. He also has a slider. Lefthanded hitters had troubled him in the past, but last year he throttled all comers.

Defense & Hitting

Kolb gets the ball to the plate quickly and is tough to get a good jump against. This helps him control the running game well, even though his stuff makes it hard for a catcher to come up firing. He is an average fielder, but is exceptionally surehanded—he hasn't committed an error at any level since 1999. His next plate appearance will be his first as a pro.

2004 Outlook

Kolb goes into 2004 with the closer's job firmly in hand. He's no sure thing, however, despite his success last year. He didn't pitch quite as well as his ERA suggested, and it was the first season in four years that he'd gotten through without a major arm injury. Kolb can be a quality closer if he stays healthy, but he might not ever post a sub-2.00 ERA again.

Position: RP
Bats: R **Throws:** R
Ht: 6' 4" **Wt:** 215

Opening Day Age: 29
Born: 3/29/75 in Sterling, IL
ML Seasons: 5

Overall Statistics

	W	L	Pct.	ERA	G	GS	Sv	IP	H	BB	SO	HR	Avg
'03	1	2	.333	1.96	37	0	21	41.1	34	19	39	2	.221
Car.	6	9	.400	3.96	105	0	22	120.1	114	68	89	7	.248

2003 Pitching Profile

	Danny Kolb	NL Average
Overall Strike %	63.4	62.4
1st Pitch Strike %	59.4	58.4
Ratio	1.28	1.38
Strikeouts per 9 IP	8.49	6.65
Walks per 9 IP	4.14	3.42
Home Runs per 9 IP	0.44	1.05
Strikeout/Walk Ratio	2.05	1.94
Groundball/Flyball Ratio	3.33	1.29

2003 Situational Stats

	W	L	ERA	Sv	IP		AB	H	HR	RBI	Avg
Home	1	2	1.57	9	23.0	LHB	67	14	1	3	.209
Road	0	0	2.45	12	18.1	RHB	87	20	1	7	.230
First Half	0	0	3.46	0	13.0	Sc Pos	40	5	0	7	.125
Scnd Half	1	2	1.27	21	28.1	Clutch	105	23	2	8	.219

2003 Rankings (National League)

- 5th in save percentage (91.3)
- Led the Brewers in saves, lowest batting average allowed vs. lefthanded batters, save percentage (91.3), relief ERA (1.96), lowest batting average allowed in relief (.221) and fewest baserunners allowed per nine innings in relief (11.8)

Eddie Perez

2003 Season

Eddie Perez spent three years in near-oblivion before emerging as the Brewers' first-string catcher last year. He had missed most of 2000 and 2001 recovering from surgeries on his throwing shoulder. Milwaukee signed him in hopes that his experience and defensive skills would help the team's young pitching staff. He was as solid as ever behind the plate and was a pleasant surprise with a bat in his hands, especially in the first half.

Hitting

Perez is an aggressive hitter who hits the ball where it's pitched. Something of a bad-ball hitter, he'll chase pitches off the plate but generally still is able to make decent contact. His occasional extra-base hits come when he happens to hit the ball down either foul line. He hit lefties very well last year but has had very balanced platoon splits for most of his career. Since he hits the ball on ground more than average, and runs poorly, he can be a rally killer in double-play situations.

Baserunning & Defense

Shoulder problems have cost Perez some arm strength—he threw out just 16 of 77 (20.8 percent) of potential basestealers last year—but he still throws accurately. His good defensive reputation rests largely on his ability to block balls in the dirt—which is impressive—and his pitch-calling. Last year, he usually was assigned to catch the youngest and most inexperienced members of the starting rotation, and while he was praised for his work with them, his influence couldn't prevent almost all of them from struggling at one point or another. He is one of the slower runners in the majors, and usually advances only a base at a time.

2004 Outlook

Perez is a free agent, but the Brewers may bring him back if he'll return at the right price. It might be hard for him to find as many at-bats elsewhere. No matter where he ends up, he also might be hard-pressed to match last year's offensive numbers, but his playing time shouldn't be affected much unless he stops hitting altogether.

Position: C
Bats: R **Throws:** R
Ht: 6' 1" **Wt:** 220

Opening Day Age: 35
Born: 5/4/68 in Ciudad Ojeda, VZ
ML Seasons: 9

Overall Statistics

	G	AB	R	H	D	T	HR	RBI	SB	BB	SO	Avg	OBP	Slg
'03	107	350	26	95	17	1	11	45	0	17	47	.271	.304	.420
Car.	474	1317	120	339	71	2	35	153	1	72	200	.257	.300	.394

Where He Hits the Ball

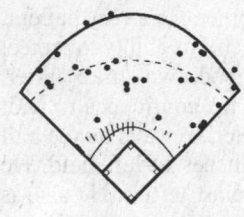 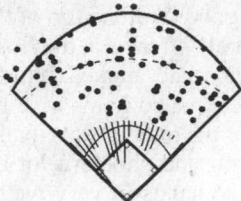

Vs. LHP	**Vs. RHP**

2003 Situational Stats

	AB	H	HR	RBI	Avg		AB	H	HR	RBI	Avg
Home	175	45	5	20	.257	LHP	76	26	2	11	.342
Road	175	50	6	25	.286	RHP	274	69	9	34	.252
First Half	206	64	9	37	.311	Sc Pos	82	24	3	34	.293
Scnd Half	144	31	2	8	.215	Clutch	57	17	3	13	.298

2003 Rankings (National League)

- 3rd in most GDPs per GDP situation (21.6%) and lowest percentage of runners caught stealing as a catcher (20.8)
- Led the Brewers in batting average vs. lefthanded pitchers

Scott Podsednik

2003 Season

When the Brewers finally lost patience with Alex Sanchez in May, they gave his center field job to Scott Podsednik, a veteran minor leaguer with little big league experience who'd made the club as a backup outfielder. Podsednik quickly proved to be everything Sanchez was not: intelligent, hustling, overachieving and well-suited to bat leadoff. In a year with several strong rookie performers, Podsednik was perhaps the most impressive, and he finished second in the National League Rookie of the Year balloting behind Florida's Dontrelle Willis.

Hitting

It's little wonder that Podsednik proved to be such a good fit at the top of the order. He's very patient, rarely offering at the first pitch. His ability to protect the plate makes him a good two-strike hitter, which also helps give him the confidence to wait for his pitch. A low-ball hitter, he waits on the ball well and shoots a lot of pitches to left field. He also hangs in very well against lefties. He also is quite capable of bunting for a hit or a sacrifice.

Baserunning & Defense

Podsednik has good speed, but he seems faster than he is because he uses his legs so well. He's a good basestealer, which results as much from smart jumps and good technique than from pure foot speed. He is less apt to try to steal against a southpaw. In center, Podsednik has good range and gives maximum effort without being reckless. He made a number of circus catches over the course of the season. His throwing arm grades out as average.

2004 Outlook

Though it's true Podsednik never showed this kind of offensive ability in the minors, he had been held back by injuries more than a lack of skill. However, at age 28, he is more of a finished product than a youngster on the way up. The Brewers will be thrilled if he simply continues to play at the same level, which he very well might do. His average may lose a few points, but with his nice collection of other skills, he'll remain a valuable player.

Position: CF/RF
Bats: L **Throws:** L
Ht: 6' 0" **Wt:** 170

Opening Day Age: 28
Born: 3/18/76 in West, TX
ML Seasons: 3
Pronunciation: puh-SED-nik

Overall Statistics

	G	AB	R	H	D	T	HR	RBI	SB	BB	SO	Avg	OBP	Slg
'03	154	558	100	175	29	8	9	58	43	56	91	.314	.379	.443
Car.	173	584	103	180	29	9	10	66	43	60	98	.308	.375	.440

Where He Hits the Ball

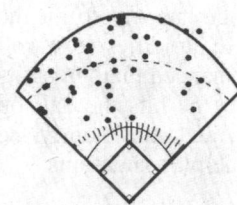
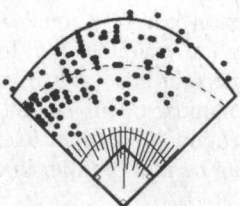

Vs. LHP   **Vs. RHP**

2003 Situational Stats

	AB	H	HR	RBI	Avg		AB	H	HR	RBI	Avg
Home	288	87	7	23	.302	LHP	148	40	4	22	.270
Road	270	88	2	35	.326	RHP	410	135	5	36	.329
First Half	284	91	3	25	.320	Sc Pos	105	40	2	49	.381
Scnd Half	274	84	6	33	.307	Clutch	83	33	2	16	.398

2003 Rankings (National League)

- 1st in batting average among rookies
- 2nd in stolen bases, batting average with runners in scoring position, batting average in the clutch and on-base percentage for a lead off hitter (.399)
- 3rd in triples, bunts in play (35), lowest percentage of swings on the first pitch (15.7) and RBI among rookies
- Led the Brewers in batting average, runs scored, hits, singles, triples, stolen bases, caught stealing (10), on-base percentage, bunts in play (35), highest percentage of pitches taken (62.9), steals of third (4),batting average with runners in scoring position
- Led NL center fielders in batting average

Richie Sexson

Position: 1B
Bats: R **Throws:** R
Ht: 6' 8" **Wt:** 236

Opening Day Age: 29
Born: 12/29/74 in Portland, OR
ML Seasons: 7
Pronunciation: SECKS-un

2003 Season

After seeing his home-run production dip in 2002, Richie Sexson bounced back with his finest season in 2003. He matched his career high with 45 homers, and he just missed tying his career high in RBI as well. He also became the first Brewer to play every inning of every game in a season—despite suffering at times from tendinitis behind his left knee, an ailment that had hobbled him much more severely in the second half of 2002.

Hitting

The lanky, long-armed Sexson has terrific power to all fields. He seemingly can reach anything, so pitchers try to keep him from extending his arms by tying him up inside. Even that approach has its drawbacks; those who miss by even a little might not get a second chance. Though he draws walks, he isn't tremendously patient. He simply swings through a lot of pitches, keeping at-bats going. Plus, he was pitched around more often than ever last year. He remains a power threat even with two strikes.

Baserunning & Defense

Sexson is one of the more underrated defensive first basemen in baseball. With his build, he won't ever impress anyone as graceful, but he makes all the plays. . . and then some. He's one of the best at handling throws in the dirt and corralling pop-ups, and his throwing arm is so good that he serves as a cutoff man on certain plays. His knee problems limited him at times last year, both in the field and on the bases. When healthy, he's an average runner who rarely runs into outs.

2004 Outlook

With the Brewers slashing their payroll significantly and Sexson signed for 2004 only, the team traded its star first baseman to Arizona in a nine-player December deal. Coming to Milwaukee for Sexson and two minor leaguers were infielders Junior Spivey and Craig Counsell, first baseman Lyle Overbay, catcher Chad Moeller and left-handers Chris Capuano and Jorge de la Rosa. Arizona acquired a steady, productive and durable veteran who should hit plenty of longballs from the No. 4 spot at Bank One Ballpark.

Overall Statistics

	G	AB	R	H	D	T	HR	RBI	SB	BB	SO	Avg	OBP	Slg
'03	162	606	97	165	28	2	45	124	2	98	151	.272	.379	.548
Car.	813	2975	467	811	150	16	191	593	10	327	785	.273	.349	.526

Where He Hits the Ball

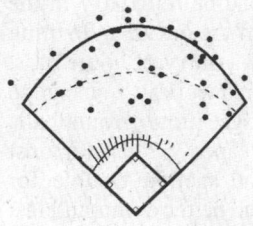 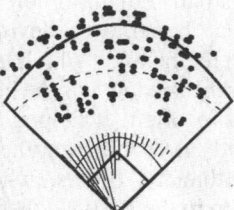

Vs. LHP **Vs. RHP**

2003 Situational Stats

	AB	H	HR	RBI	Avg		AB	H	HR	RBI	Avg
Home	303	78	23	62	.257	LHP	122	34	10	23	.279
Road	303	87	22	62	.287	RHP	484	131	35	101	.271
First Half	353	93	25	70	.263	Sc Pos	175	51	13	83	.291
Scnd Half	253	72	20	54	.285	Clutch	96	21	4	9	.219

2003 Rankings (National League)

- 1st in games played
- 2nd in home runs, errors at first base (11) and lowest fielding percentage at first base (.993)
- 3rd in plate appearances (718)
- 4th in total bases (332), RBI, strikeouts and pitches seen (2,838)
- 5th in HR frequency (13.5 ABs per HR)
- Led the Brewers in home runs, at-bats, total bases (332), RBI, walks, times on base (272), strikeouts, pitches seen (2,838), plate appearances (718), games played, slugging percentage, HR frequency (13.5 ABs per HR), and cleanup slugging percentage (.568)

Milwaukee

Ben Sheets

2003 Season

On the surface, it didn't seem like Ben Sheets made much improvement in 2003. Most of his numbers were no better than the year before, and his ERA rose by three-tenths of a run. He did show some subtle but significant signs of improvement, however. He worked more efficiently, was a bit less hittable and cut his walks by a significant amount. If it hadn't been for a sore back and a mild case of shoulder tendinitis that contributed to a late slump, his season likely would have been his best yet.

Pitching

Sheets' hard overhand curve and low to mid-90s fastball remain his bread and butter. Early in the year, batters were laying off the curve and sitting on the fastball, which led to a flurry of home runs. In the second half, he began to work in a changeup more often. It helped him get more groundballs and gave him another weapon to use against lefthanded hitters, who had spelled trouble for him in the past. He displayed better command last year, and perhaps as a result of being more economical with his pitches, he was able to maintain effectiveness later into games.

Defense & Hitting

Sheets has a better pickoff move than most righthanders, and he does a fairly good job of slowing the running game overall, though he slipped in that department a bit last year. He does a good job in the field overall. The same can't be said of his hitting—he still goes down on strikes more than half the time and is lucky even to get a bunt down.

2004 Outlook

Sheets is a quality pitcher, something that would be a lot more obvious if he had a stronger team behind him. Even so, he hasn't yet reached his full potential, and he's getting to the age when he should start to put it all together. There's every reason to think he could take a significant step forward in 2004.

Position: SP
Bats: R **Throws:** R
Ht: 6' 1" **Wt:** 200

Opening Day Age: 25
Born: 7/18/78 in Baton Rouge, LA
ML Seasons: 3

Overall Statistics

	W	L	Pct.	ERA	G	GS	Sv	IP	H	BB	SO	HR	Avg
'03	11	13	.458	4.45	34	34	0	220.2	232	43	157	29	.268
Car.	33	39	.458	4.42	93	93	0	588.2	635	161	421	73	.277

2003 Pitching Profile

	Ben Sheets	NL Average
Overall Strike %	65.7	62.4
1st Pitch Strike %	64.1	58.4
Ratio	1.25	1.38
Strikeouts per 9 IP	6.40	6.65
Walks per 9 IP	1.75	3.42
Home Runs per 9 IP	1.18	1.05
Strikeout/Walk Ratio	3.65	1.94
Groundball/Flyball Ratio	1.23	1.29

2003 Situational Stats

	W	L	ERA	Sv	IP		AB	H	HR	RBI	Avg
Home	4	8	4.21	0	117.2	LHB	396	98	9	40	.247
Road	7	5	4.72	0	103.0	RHB	469	134	20	76	.286
First Half	7	7	4.19	0	141.2	Sc Pos	197	57	5	76	.289
Scnd Half	4	6	4.90	0	79.0	Clutch	47	10	1	4	.213

2003 Rankings (National League)

- 3rd in games started, hits allowed and fewest walks per nine innings (1.8)
- 4th in innings pitched and batters faced (931)
- 6th in losses, home runs allowed and highest strikeout-walk ratio (3.7)
- 8th in highest ERA at home
- 9th in pitches thrown (3,365)
- 10th in most home runs allowed per nine innings (1.18)
- Led the Brewers in ERA, wins, losses, games started, innings pitched, hits allowed, batters faced (931), strikeouts, pitches thrown (3,365), highest strikeout-walk ratio (3.7), lowest slugging percentage allowed (.430), lowest on-base percentage allowed (.305), highest groundball-flyball ratio allowed (1.2), fewest pitches thrown per batter (3.61), lowest ERA at home, lowest ERA on the road and fewest walks per nine innings (1.8)

John Vander Wal

Position: RF
Bats: L **Throws:** L
Ht: 6' 1" **Wt:** 210

Opening Day Age: 37
Born: 4/29/66 in Grand Rapids, MI
ML Seasons: 13

2003 Season

John Vander Wal was expected to serve as a fourth outfielder and pinch-hitter for the Brewers, but he got more at-bats than planned. After projected right fielder Jeffrey Hammonds got hurt and was released, Vander Wal wound up forming a loose platoon with Brady Clark in right field. Vander Wal got semi-regular playing time in that capacity until September, when he strained a groin muscle. He was fairly productive, especially in the first half.

Hitting

A low-ball hitter, Vander Wal has respectable straightaway power. He never has faced lefties extensively in the majors, and he's done little to change that in the limited trials he's had against them. He'll take a walk, but he'll also swing through a lot of pitches and strikes out frequently. He's especially vulnerable with two strikes. What he does best is pinch-hit—there are few players in the majors with better credentials coming off the bench, although he didn't fare as well in that regard last year as he had in the past.

Baserunning & Defense

Vander Wal can get by in left field, right field and first base, but defense never has been a strength of his, and he is getting up in years. Knee problems have further eroded his below-average range in the outfield, where he plays it safe and limits his mistakes. His arm is a little short for right field but isn't a major liability. His speed is below-average at this point, and he's mostly a station-to-station baserunner. He's stolen just one base in each of the past two seasons.

2004 Outlook

Vander Wal once again is looking to catch on with a team in need of a pinch-hitter and fourth outfielder. Despite his age, he remains a useful pinch-hitter, so he probably will land a spot somewhere. It would be a surprise, though, if he were to wind up in a situation that allowed him to get nearly as many at-bats as he did last year.

Overall Statistics

	G	AB	R	H	D	T	HR	RBI	SB	BB	SO	Avg	OBP	Slg
'03	117	327	50	84	25	1	14	45	1	46	104	.257	.350	.468
Car.	1330	2700	372	711	168	18	95	426	38	381	678	.263	.354	.444

Where He Hits the Ball

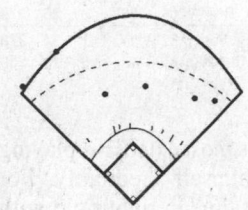
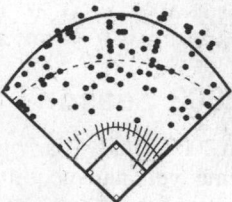

Vs. LHP   **Vs. RHP**

2003 Situational Stats

	AB	H	HR	RBI	Avg		AB	H	HR	RBI	Avg
Home	158	44	7	22	.278	LHP	38	6	0	2	.158
Road	169	40	7	23	.237	RHP	289	78	14	43	.270
First Half	219	62	9	31	.283	Sc Pos	80	16	4	29	.200
Scnd Half	108	22	5	14	.204	Clutch	55	16	2	6	.291

2003 Rankings (National League)

- 5th in lowest percentage of swings put into play (34.0)
- 6th in highest percentage of swings that missed (28.9) and lowest batting average with runners in scoring position
- Led the Brewers in fewest GDPs per GDP situation (7.2%)

Brady Clark

Position: RF/LF
Bats: R **Throws:** R
Ht: 6' 2" **Wt:** 195

Opening Day Age: 30
Born: 4/18/73 in
Portland, OR
ML Seasons: 4

Overall Statistics

	G	AB	R	H	D	T	HR	RBI	SB	BB	SO	Avg	OBP	Slg
'03	128	315	33	86	21	1	6	40	13	21	40	.273	.330	.403
Car.	289	533	65	138	29	1	12	70	18	50	69	.259	.331	.385

2003 Situational Stats

	AB	H	HR	RBI	Avg		AB	H	HR	RBI	Avg
Home	171	46	5	26	.269	LHP	114	30	3	14	.263
Road	144	40	1	14	.278	RHP	201	56	3	26	.279
First Half	144	39	2	23	.271	Sc Pos	87	24	1	34	.276
Scnd Half	171	47	4	17	.275	Clutch	66	17	0	13	.258

2003 Season

In 2003, Brady Clark got his most extensive playing time yet, and acquitted himself creditably. For most of the season, he split time in right field with John Vander Wal, and he later took over in left after Geoff Jenkins broke his thumb. Clark also served as a useful righthanded bat off the bench, batting .286 in 35 at-bats as a pinch-hitter.

Hitting, Baserunning & Defense

Clark is a patient hitter who usually takes the first pitch. Still, he rarely walks, since he makes such good contact that he consistently puts the ball in play. He's good at protecting the plate with two strikes, has moderate power to left field and has shown good pinch-hitting ability. He runs well enough to steal a few bases and play all three outfield positions competently, although his arm is a little short for right field.

2004 Outlook

Being a righthanded hitter, it always will be an uphill battle for Clark to maintain a roster spot as a reserve. He may never see as many at-bats again, although he may continue to contribute at the big league level.

Mike Crudale

Position: RP
Bats: R **Throws:** R
Ht: 6' 0" **Wt:** 220

Opening Day Age: 27
Born: 1/3/77 in San
Diego, CA
ML Seasons: 2
Pronunciation:
CREW-dale

Overall Statistics

	W	L	Pct.	ERA	G	GS	Sv	IP	H	BB	SO	HR	Avg
'03	0	1	.000	2.61	22	0	0	20.2	12	18	13	1	.167
Car.	3	1	.750	2.09	71	1	0	73.1	55	32	60	4	.211

2003 Situational Stats

	W	L	ERA	Sv	IP		AB	H	HR	RBI	Avg
Home	0	0	3.29	0	13.2	LHB	19	2	0	3	.105
Road	0	1	1.29	0	7.0	RHB	53	10	1	6	.189
First Half	0	1	1.00	0	9.0	Sc Pos	17	3	1	8	.176
Scnd Half	0	0	3.86	0	11.2	Clutch	17	3	0	4	.176

2003 Season

Mike Crudale had a fine rookie season in 2002 and was expected to play a key role in St. Louis' bullpen in 2003, but then everything seemed to go wrong. He was hit hard in spring training and began the season in the minors, missed most of April with a broken toe and was recalled in May. Given inconsistent work, he bounced up and down between the majors and Triple-A, and just never got into a groove. After being traded to the Brewers in late August, he came around somewhat.

Pitching, Defense & Hitting

A big-breaking slider is Crudale's bread and butter. In 2002, he had been able to coax hitters into chasing the offering, but last year his command wavered and hitters were better able to lay off it. His low-90s fastball is decent but not enough on its own. Crudale is an adequate fielder but is fairly easy to run on—only one of seven major league basestealers have been caught on his watch during his career. He's hitless in two pro at-bats.

2004 Outlook

Crudale could establish himself as a capable setup man for the Brewers, but to do so he'll need to regain the command of his out pitch.

Doug Davis

Position: SP
Bats: R **Throws:** L
Ht: 6' 4" **Wt:** 190

Opening Day Age: 28
Born: 9/21/75 in
Sacramento, CA
ML Seasons: 5

Overall Statistics

	W	L	Pct.	ERA	G	GS	Sv	IP	H	BB	SO	HR	Avg
'03	7	8	.467	4.03	21	20	0	109.1	123	51	62	16	.285
Car.	28	29	.491	4.79	93	73	0	456.1	531	200	274	54	.294

2003 Situational Stats

	W	L	ERA	Sv	IP		AB	H	HR	RBI	Avg
Home	3	4	5.47	0	49.1	LHB	92	27	5	11	.293
Road	4	4	2.85	0	60.0	RHB	339	96	11	34	.283
First Half	4	6	5.37	0	57.0	Sc Pos	89	19	2	25	.213
Scnd Half	3	2	2.58	0	52.1	Clutch	15	5	2	3	.333

2003 Season

The Brewers got some fine work out of Doug Davis late last year, especially considering that he already had been released by two clubs since the start of the season. He was signed to a minor league deal in July, called up and inserted into the Milwaukee rotation in mid-August, and was effective nearly every time he took the hill the rest of the way.

Pitching, Defense & Hitting

Davis' stuff isn't much to look at, but he hides the ball well. He relies heavily on a cutter with average velocity while mixing in a slow curve. He's hittable, even for lefthanded batters, and he has trouble finishing hitters off with two strikes. Davis cuts off the running game with a slide step that he varies, but he otherwise does little to help himself in the field. His inexperience at the plate is obvious.

2004 Outlook

Davis didn't pitch nearly as well for Milwaukee as his ERA suggested—it would have been a lot worse if he hadn't been able to wriggle out of quite so many jams. He'll head into camp with the inside track on a rotation spot, but he's just as likely to pitch his way off the club as he is to help.

Jayson Durocher

Position: RP
Bats: R **Throws:** R
Ht: 6' 3" **Wt:** 229

Opening Day Age: 29
Born: 8/18/74 in
Hartford, CT
ML Seasons: 2
Pronunciation:
der-o-sher

Overall Statistics

	W	L	Pct.	ERA	G	GS	Sv	IP	H	BB	SO	HR	Avg
'03	2	0	1.000	11.05	6	0	0	7.1	9	2	7	4	.300
Car.	3	1	.750	3.09	45	0	0	55.1	36	23	51	7	.185

2003 Situational Stats

	W	L	ERA	Sv	IP		AB	H	HR	RBI	Avg
Home	1	0	21.00	0	3.0	LHB	9	3	2	5	.333
Road	1	0	4.15	0	4.1	RHB	21	6	2	6	.286
First Half	2	0	11.05	0	7.1	Sc Pos	12	3	2	9	.250
Scnd Half	0	0	—	0	0.0	Clutch	8	3	1	5	.375

2003 Season

Jayson Durocher, who had pitched so brilliantly out of the bullpen in the second half of 2002, never got out of the blocks in 2003. He'd had elbow surgery in early March and began the year on rehab, but he hurt his shoulder in his final rehab outing. The Brewers activated him anyway, but his velocity was off and there was no fooling the hitters. He was shut down in mid-June, made no progress, and didn't throw another major league pitch all year.

Pitching, Defense & Hitting

The only thing that's special about Durocher is his mid-90s fastball, so he has to be healthy to be effective. When he's feeling good, he can come in and blow high heat past hitters for an inning at a time. Without the velocity, he's left with an ordinary splitter and slider, and iffy command. He fields his position capably, and makes good use of a slide step. Hitting is not part of his job, and it shows.

2004 Outlook

Health issues have dotted Durocher's career, so it hardly was surprising when his arm came up lame. He easily could rebound, but he never will be a good bet to stay effective for more than a few months at a time.

Bill Hall

Position: 2B/SS
Bats: R **Throws:** R
Ht: 6' 0" **Wt:** 198

Opening Day Age: 24
Born: 12/28/79 in Nettleton, MS
ML Seasons: 2

Overall Statistics

	G	AB	R	H	D	T	HR	RBI	SB	BB	SO	Avg	OBP	Slg
'03	52	142	23	37	9	2	5	20	1	7	28	.261	.298	.458
Car.	71	178	26	44	10	3	6	25	1	10	41	.247	.289	.438

2003 Situational Stats

	AB	H	HR	RBI	Avg		AB	H	HR	RBI	Avg
Home	65	13	2	9	.200	LHP	27	5	0	1	.185
Road	77	24	3	11	.312	RHP	115	32	5	19	.278
First Half	0	0	0	0	–	Sc Pos	36	11	2	15	.306
Scnd Half	142	37	5	20	.261	Clutch	23	3	1	3	.130

2003 Season

Middle-infield prospect Bill Hall was rushed up to Triple-A and suffered through a dismal season in 2002, and his struggles continued early in 2003. He suddenly turned it around, though, and was called up after the All-Star Break. He garnered semi-regular playing time at second base and shortstop from August through the end of the season, and showed enough skills to revive his prospect status.

Hitting, Baserunning & Defense

Hall is gifted but raw in almost every phase of the game. At the plate, he has decent power potential, but needs to work on his discipline and pitch recognition. He has good speed but has to learn how to translate it into basestealing success. In the field, he can range afar and make a difficult throw on one play, only to boot an easy chance the next. It's an open question whether his glovework has become consistent enough at second or short for him to hold a major league job.

2004 Outlook

The Brewers cut loose shortstop Royce Clayton, so Hall had a chance to open 2004 as the starting shortstop. Now newly acquired infielders Craig Counsell and Junior Spivey may push Hall back to the minors, as Counsell may take over at short. Hall needs a good season to not get lost in the shuffle.

Brooks Kieschnick

Position: RP/OF
Bats: L **Throws:** R
Ht: 6' 4" **Wt:** 230

Opening Day Age: 31
Born: 6/6/72 in Robstown, TX
ML Seasons: 5
Pronunciation: KEESH-nick

Overall Statistics

	W	L	Pct.	ERA	G	GS	Sv	IP	H	BB	SO	HR	Avg
'03	1	1	.500	5.26	42	0	0	53.0	66	13	39	5	.299
Car.	1	1	.500	5.26	42	0	0	53.0	66	13	39	5	.299

2003 Situational Stats

	W	L	ERA	Sv	IP		AB	H	HR	RBI	Avg
Home	1	1	4.33	0	27.0	LHB	88	21	3	12	.239
Road	0	0	6.23	0	26.0	RHB	133	45	2	21	.338
First Half	1	1	4.35	0	31.0	Sc Pos	81	20	2	27	.247
Scnd Half	0	0	6.55	0	22.0	Clutch	15	3	1	2	.200

2003 Season

It was one of the great stories of the 2003 season. Brooks Kieschnick, who had starred as a two-way player in college but had dead-ended in Triple-A as a position player, returned to the mound and made the Brewers as a two-way player. He was more than a mere novelty, becoming one of the best pinch-hitters in the league. As a pitcher, he was little more than a mopup man, but he managed to post a higher batting average (.300) than the opponents he faced on the mound (.299).

Pitching, Defense & Hitting

Kieschnick is a sinker-slider pitcher with average velocity. He throws strikes and gets groundballs. His best asset is his lefthanded batting stroke; he has legitimate 20-homer power. Last year, he showed the ability to come off the bench and hit (and then go in to pitch). He also can play left field, right field and first base. He is not a fast runner.

2004 Outlook

While Kieschnick may have earned himself a longer look as a hitter, it remains to be seen whether he's anything more than a novelty on the mound. Even if he proves unable to make a real contribution as a pitcher, he still may make it solely on his offensive talents.

Nick Neugebauer

Position: SP
Bats: R **Throws:** R
Ht: 6' 3" **Wt:** 221

Opening Day Age: 23
Born: 7/15/80 in
Riverside, CA
ML Seasons: 2
Pronunciation:
NEW-ga-bower

Overall Statistics

	W	L	Pct.	ERA	G	GS	Sv	IP	H	BB	SO	HR	Avg
'03						Did Not Play							
Car.	2	8	.200	4.99	14	14	0	61.1	62	50	58	11	.263

2003 Situational Stats

	W	L	ERA	Sv	IP		AB	H	HR	RBI	Avg
Home	–	–	–	–	–	LHB	–	–	–	–	–
Road	–	–	–	–	–	RHB	–	–	–	–	–
First Half	–	–	–	–	–	Sc Pos	–	–	–	–	–
Scnd Half	–	–	–	–	–	Clutch	–	–	–	–	–

2003 Season

Hard-throwing Nick Neugebauer suddenly found his control in 2001 and progressed steadily up to the majors by the end of the year, only to hurt his shoulder in his second major league start. He then had surgery to repair a torn labrum and partially torn rotator cuff. He pitched inconsistently in 2002 and missed half the year with continuing shoulder problems, which eventually required a second surgery that idled him for all of 2003.

Pitching, Defense & Hitting

Before his shoulder problems surfaced, Neugebauer had an upper-90s fastball and a slurvy slider, a combination that made him incredibly tough to hit. He was starting to find the strike zone enough that his walks had become an obstacle rather than a fatal flaw. He'd proven to be an adequate fielder but not much of a hitter.

2004 Outlook

For obvious reasons, it's impossible to know what to expect from Neugebauer in 2004. Even if he comes back at 100 percent, he'll still need time in the minors to rebuild his arm strength and work on the control issues that he never really conquered. But if he still can throw above 96 MPH, that's a great place to be starting over from, especially at age 23.

Keith Osik

Position: C
Bats: R **Throws:** R
Ht: 6' 0" **Wt:** 200

Opening Day Age: 35
Born: 10/22/68 in Port Jefferson, NY
ML Seasons: 8
Pronunciation:
OH-sick

Overall Statistics

	G	AB	R	H	D	T	HR	RBI	SB	BB	SO	Avg	OBP	Slg
'03	80	241	22	60	12	0	2	21	0	31	44	.249	.342	.324
Car.	439	1094	96	257	55	4	13	108	6	111	193	.235	.314	.328

2003 Situational Stats

	AB	H	HR	RBI	Avg		AB	H	HR	RBI	Avg
Home	115	29	1	10	.252	LHP	37	14	0	7	.378
Road	126	31	1	11	.246	RHP	204	46	2	14	.225
First Half	146	33	1	10	.226	Sc Pos	64	10	0	19	.156
Scnd Half	95	27	1	11	.284	Clutch	34	9	1	2	.265

2003 Season

The Brewers brought in Keith Osik last year, expecting him to be a capable backup, and he was. He logged a career-high 80 games and handled a larger share of the catching than he had in the past. Simply put, he made a solid all-around contribution in a low-profile role.

Hitting, Baserunning & Defense

Osik takes a line-drive approach, hitting the ball to all fields. He has little power beyond an occasional double. Never notably patient, he did a much better job of waiting out walks. His success against lefthanders likely was a fluke, however. He's is a competent defensive catcher, throwing fairly accurately. He nabbed a higher percentage of basestealers (26.4 Percent) than teammate Eddie Perez (20.8) did last year. Osik is a good athlete and has played some third base in the past, although he doesn't run nearly well enough to be any sort of factor on the bases.

2004 Outlook

A free agent, Osik will look to hook on somewhere as a backup. He's a known quantity who can help plug a hole, but he is not cut out for a larger role. There are many players with comparable skills, so it may be hard for him to distinguish himself from cheaper alternatives.

Milwaukee

Glendon Rusch

Position: SP/RP
Bats: L **Throws:** L
Ht: 6' 1" **Wt:** 223

Opening Day Age: 29
Born: 11/7/74 in Seattle, WA
ML Seasons: 7
Pronunciation: RUSH

Overall Statistics

	W	L	Pct.	ERA	G	GS	Sv	IP	H	BB	SO	HR	Avg
'03	1	12	.077	6.42	32	19	1	123.1	171	45	93	11	.331
Car.	42	76	.356	5.11	193	167	2	1033.2	1215	313	760	133	.295

2003 Situational Stats

	W	L	ERA	Sv	IP		AB	H	HR	RBI	Avg
Home	0	6	7.44	0	55.2	LHB	127	39	2	21	.307
Road	1	6	5.59	1	67.2	RHB	390	132	9	57	.338
First Half	1	11	7.90	0	84.1	Sc Pos	138	49	4	63	.355
Scnd Half	0	1	3.23	1	39.0	Clutch	32	14	1	7	.438

2003 Season

Few pitchers ever go through as hellish a stretch as Glendon Rusch did in the first half of 2003. He was given an embarrassing demotion to the minors in June, to which he humbly assented. Recalled in July, he seemed to be on the road to reestablishing himself when he pulled a groin muscle. He returned in late August but never got his rotation spot back. His 6.42 ERA would have been the highest figure in all of baseball had he pitched enough innings to qualify.

Pitching, Defense & Hitting

Rusch, who never has been overpowering, suddenly became alarmingly hittable last year. Part of the problem might have been that he couldn't seem to get his curve over the plate, although he always had relied mostly on his cutter and changeup. With a slide step that he varies and a good pickoff move, he's one of the toughest pitchers to run against. He's become a pretty good hitter in the past two years.

2004 Outlook

The Brewers, as expected, declined their option on Rusch, making him a free agent. Because he's a lefty, he probably will catch on somewhere, though he may have to go back to the minors to re-establish himself.

Luis Vizcaino

Position: RP
Bats: R **Throws:** R
Ht: 5'11" **Wt:** 180

Opening Day Age: 29
Born: 8/6/74 in Bani, DR
ML Seasons: 5
Pronunciation: vis-ki-ee-no

Overall Statistics

	W	L	Pct.	ERA	G	GS	Sv	IP	H	BB	SO	HR	Avg
'03	4	3	.571	6.39	75	0	0	62.0	64	25	61	16	.263
Car.	11	8	.579	4.80	200	0	6	202.2	185	81	191	33	.241

2003 Situational Stats

	W	L	ERA	Sv	IP		AB	H	HR	RBI	Avg
Home	1	1	6.52	0	29.0	LHB	83	21	5	16	.253
Road	3	2	6.27	0	33.0	RHB	160	43	11	30	.269
First Half	2	3	8.05	0	34.2	Sc Pos	75	17	4	30	.227
Scnd Half	2	0	4.28	0	27.1	Clutch	69	19	5	16	.275

2003 Season

Luis Vizcaino had been the Brewers' most effective reliever, and one of the best setup men in baseball, in 2002, but 2003 couldn't have been more different. He blew an eighth-inning lead on Opening Day and continued to get hammered for the rest of the first half. A drop in velocity led to rumors of arm problems, but nothing ever was confirmed. He rebounded somewhat in the second half after being reduced to being essentially a mopup man.

Pitching, Defense & Hitting

Vizcaino works up in the zone. He could get away with that in 2002, when he was throwing in the mid- to high 90s, but last year, his dropoff in velocity led to an explosion of longballs. The slider he developed in 2002 wasn't as consistent last year, either. Throwing so many high fastballs helps him keep the running game in check. He's an adequate fielder who hasn't yet erred in the majors, but he's no hitter.

2004 Outlook

Vizcaino still is a major question mark, and it remains to be seen whether his second-half performance was enough to convince the Brewers to stick with him. If their options are limited enough, they just might choose to cross their fingers and do so.

Other Milwaukee Brewers

Dave Burba (Pos: RHP, Age: 37)

	W	L	Pct.	ERA	G	GS	Sv	IP	H	BB	SO	HR	Avg
'03	1	1	.500	3.53	17	2	0	43.1	42	19	35	5	.250
Car.	111	86	.563	4.50	460	234	1	1700.2	1707	736	1348	194	.261

In Burba's 14-year career, he has become best known for his versatility and durability. The righthander has a 4.61 ERA in 234 starts, while posting a 4.06 ERA in 226 appearances out of the bullpen. 2004 Outlook: C

Jason Conti (Pos: RF, Age: 29, Bats: L)

	G	AB	R	H	D	T	HR	RBI	SB	BB	SO	Avg	OBP	Slg
'03	30	48	3	11	2	0	2	7	0	2	18	.229	.255	.396
Car.	160	365	41	90	21	5	6	43	7	28	105	.247	.303	.381

The Brewers acquired Conti from the Devil Rays during spring training in exchange for catcher Javier Valentin. The outfielder spent most of the year in Triple-A, batting .248 in 121 games. He heads to Texas this spring. 2004 Outlook: C

Enrique Cruz (Pos: SS, Age: 22, Bats: R)

	G	AB	R	H	D	T	HR	RBI	SB	BB	SO	Avg	OBP	Slg
'03	60	71	6	6	1	0	0	2	0	4	30	.085	.145	.099
Car.	60	71	6	6	1	0	0	2	0	4	30	.085	.145	.099

Despite not playing above Class-A previously, Cruz spent the entire season with the Brewers, but batted just .085 in 60 games. The team was impressed enough to re-sign the infielder through 2005, but they outrighted him to Triple-A in December. 2004 Outlook: C

Leo Estrella (Pos: RHP, Age: 29)

	W	L	Pct.	ERA	G	GS	Sv	IP	H	BB	SO	HR	Avg
'03	7	3	.700	4.36	58	0	3	66.0	75	21	25	10	.290
Car.	7	3	.700	4.46	60	0	3	70.2	84	21	28	11	.301

Estrella served as a setup man for the Brewers this past season, and was even called upon in a few save situations. However, he struggled with elbow problems after the break, posting a 6.59 ERA. 2004 Outlook: B

Matt Ford (Pos: LHP, Age: 22)

	W	L	Pct.	ERA	G	GS	Sv	IP	H	BB	SO	HR	Avg
'03	0	3	.000	4.33	25	4	0	43.2	46	21	26	5	.264
Car.	0	3	.000	4.33	25	4	0	43.2	46	21	26	5	.264

After posting a 10.32 ERA in three July starts, Ford was placed on the disabled list with bone fragments in his elbow. Surgery was required, but the young lefthander should be ready for spring training. 2004 Outlook: C

John Foster (Pos: LHP, Age: 25)

	W	L	Pct.	ERA	G	GS	Sv	IP	H	BB	SO	HR	Avg
'03	2	0	1.000	4.71	23	0	0	21.0	00	8	16	5	.341
Car.	3	0	1.000	5.88	28	0	0	26.0	36	14	22	8	.330

Acquired from Atlanta in an offseason trade, Foster was expected to supply the Brewers with a dependable left-hander out of the bullpen. Inconsistency limited him to just 23 appearances with Milwaukee. 2004 Outlook: C

David Manning (Pos: RHP, Age: 31)

	W	L	Pct.	ERA	G	GS	Sv	IP	H	BB	SO	HR	Avg
'03	0	2	.000	16.20	2	2	0	6.2	11	8	2	1	.393
Car.	0	2	.000	16.20	2	2	0	6.2	11	8	2	1	.393

After 11 seasons in the minors, Manning made his big league debut late in the 2003 season. He was signed by Florida in November. 2004 Outlook: C

Shane Nance (Pos: LHP, Age: 26)

	W	L	Pct.	ERA	G	GS	Sv	IP	H	BB	SO	HR	Avg
'03	0	2	.000	4.81	26	0	0	24.1	34	10	25	5	.327
Car.	0	2	.000	4.70	30	0	0	30.2	38	14	30	6	.299

Nance has posted a 5-4 record and 1.04 ERA in 44 appearances at Triple-A since coming over from the Dodgers in 2002. The D'backs, who acquired Nance in the Richie Sexson trade, hope he can mirror those numbers in the majors next season. 2004 Outlook: C

Wes Obermueller (Pos: RHP, Age: 27)

	W	L	Pct.	ERA	G	GS	Sv	IP	H	BB	SO	HR	Avg
'03	2	5	.286	5.07	12	11	0	65.2	81	25	34	10	.301
Car.	2	7	.222	5.77	14	13	0	73.1	95	27	39	13	.310

The Royals traded Obermueller to Milwaukee in July. In a dozen appearances with the Brewers, he showed he might need another year in Triple-A. 2004 Outlook: C

Ruben Quevedo (Pos: RHP, Age: 25)

	W	L	Pct.	ERA	G	GS	Sv	IP	H	BB	SO	HR	Avg
'03	1	4	.200	6.75	9	8	0	42.2	53	23	19	12	.314
Car.	14	30	.318	6.15	66	58	0	326.1	364	175	237	70	.282

Quevedo spent much of the 2003 season on the disabled list, battling tendinitis in his pitching shoulder. The righthander never lived up to his potential with Milwaukee and was released in October. 2004 Outlook: C

Todd Ritchie (Pos: RHP, Age: 32)

	W	L	Pct.	ERA	G	GS	Sv	IP	H	BB	SO	HR	Avg
'03	1	2	.333	5.08	5	5	0	28.1	36	10	15	4	.319
Car.	43	52	.453	4.67	180	118	0	827.1	917	256	512	100	.280

Ritchie struggled in five starts with the Brewers before undergoing surgery on his rotator cuff in June. He plans to be ready for spring training. 2004 Outlook: C

Mark Smith (Pos: LF, Age: 33, Bats: R)

	G	AB	R	H	D	T	HR	RBI	SB	BB	SO	Avg	OBP	Slg
'03	33	63	8	15	4	0	3	10	0	4	13	.238	.275	.444
Car.	414	959	125	233	51	3	32	130	15	97	211	.243	.316	.403

Smith, who will turn 34 in May, has spent the bulk of his pro career at the Triple-A level. He signed with the Phils in November. 2004 Outlook: C

Pete Zoccolillo (Pos: RF, Age: 27, Bats: L)

	G	AB	R	H	D	T	HR	RBI	SB	BB	SO	Avg	OBP	Slg
'03	20	37	0	4	1	0	0	3	0	2	13	.108	.154	.135
Car.	20	37	0	4	1	0	0	3	0	2	13	.108	.154	.135

Zoccolillo's skill as a contact hitter quickly moved him up through the Brewers' farm system. He needs work, but a good spring could land him a bench job. 2004 Outlook: C

Milwaukee

Milwaukee Brewers Minor League Prospects

Organization Overview:

Coming off a nightmarish 56-106 season, the Brewers showed signs of recovery in 2003. The team is ready to go as far as its pitching will take it, but that's a problem for an organization with little recent success in developing pitchers. Even if Ben Sheets and Nick Neugebauer can pitch at the top of the rotation, the No. 3-5 slots are a crapshoot, and no team can win 75 games that way, even in the always-humorous National League Central. When they have a third and fourth starter, they may be in position to contend. It seems unlikely that any 2004 rookie position player will play a major role with the Brewers, but any pitcher having success in Double-A or Triple-A will likely get a look at Miller Park.

Prince Fielder

Position: 1B   **Opening Day Age:** 19
Bats: L **Throws:** R   **Born:** 5/9/84 in Ontario,
Ht: 5' 11" **Wt:** 286   CA

Recent Statistics

	G	AB	R	H	D	T	HR	RBI	SB	BB	SO	Avg
2002 R Ogden	41	146	35	57	12	0	10	40	3	37	27	.390
2002 A Beloit	32	112	15	27	7	0	3	11	0	10	27	.241
2003 A Beloit	137	502	81	157	22	2	27	112	2	71	80	.313

At age 19, Fielder tore up the Class-A Midwest League in his first full pro season. The son of Cecil Fielder, Prince may again be consorting with major leaguers by the end of 2005. The Brewers selected him with the seventh overall pick in 2002, and he's been hitting for power ever since, with 40 homers in 760 professional at-bats. Fielder may skip high Class-A ball and move directly to Double-A Huntsville to start 2004. A good 2004 season would mark him as the heir apparent at first base now that Richie Sexson has moved on to Arizona, and perhaps Fielder will be a source of new power generation in Milwaukee before he turns 21. Defense will not be a plus—he's a big man with limited range who committed 18 errors at Beloit—but his hitting should compensate for that.

J.J. Hardy

Position: SS   **Opening Day Age:** 21
Bats: R **Throws:** R   **Born:** 8/19/82 in Tucson,
Ht: 6' 1" **Wt:** 170   AZ

Recent Statistics

	G	AB	R	H	D	T	HR	RBI	SB	BB	SO	Avg
2002 A High Desert	84	335	53	98	19	1	6	48	9	19	38	.293
2002 AA Huntsville	38	145	14	33	7	0	1	13	1	9	19	.228
2003 AA Huntsville	114	416	67	116	26	0	12	62	6	58	54	.279

Hardy's stock continued to rise in 2003. A second-round choice in the 2001 draft, Hardy returned to Huntsville at age 20, adding some pop and a big improvement in plate discipline to his solid defensive skills. Last season Hardy more than matched his previous career total of nine home runs over 625 at-bats, and by walking more than he struck out in 2003 he countered the 71-44 strikeout-walk ratio of his first two professional seasons. He does not run much, with six stolen bases in 10 attempts. Hardy is seen as the Brewers' shortstop of the future, and may get a look in the second half of the 2004 season.

Corey Hart

Position: 3B   **Opening Day Age:** 22
Bats: R **Throws:** R   **Born:** 3/24/82 in
Ht: 6' 6" **Wt:** 190   Lawrenceburg, TN

Recent Statistics

	G	AB	R	H	D	T	HR	RBI	SB	BB	SO	Avg
2002 A High Desert	100	393	76	113	26	10	22	84	24	37	101	.288
2002 AA Huntsville	28	94	16	25	3	0	2	15	3	7	16	.266
2003 AA Huntsville	130	493	70	149	40	1	13	94	25	28	101	.302

At age 21, Hart led the Double-A Southern League in hits, doubles and RBI, and was named the league MVP. He earned that distinction while the Stars were at bat. When the Stars took the field, however, Hart struggled, with 32 errors, worse even than his 2002 campaign for high Class-A High Desert, in which he recorded a fielding average of .866 as a third baseman. To win at Miller Park, a pitcher needs groundball outs, so a move to the outfield may be necessary. Hart is a good young player with obvious strengths and equally obvious weaknesses. Players of that description have not tended to do well for Milwaukee in the past 10 years.

Mike Jones

Position: P   **Opening Day Age:** 20
Bats: R **Throws:** R   **Born:** 4/23/83 in
Ht: 6' 5" **Wt:** 210   Phoenix, AZ

Recent Statistics

	W	L	ERA	G	GS	Sv	IP	H	R	BB	SO	HR
2002 A Beloit	7	7	3.12	27	27	0	138.2	135	63	62	132	3
2003 AA Huntsville	7	2	2.40	17	17	0	97.2	87	35	47	63	4

Jones has battled injury throughout his pro career. Selected out of high school with the 12th overall pick in 2001, he experienced shoulder problems that year, and in 2003 developed elbow problems that kept him out of the Arizona Fall League and may yet require Tommy John surgery. An impressive 2002 season in the Class-A Midwest League led to a promotion to Double-A Huntsville in 2003 at age 20. At Huntsville, he pitched well until the elbow problem virtually ended his season at the end of June. Jones averaged nearly a strikeout per inning in his first two professional seasons, but in 2003 that average dipped to .65 K-IP. Until the status of his elbow is resolved, it's impossible to tell what contribution Jones may be able to make for the Brewers this year and next.

Dave Krynzel

Position: OF   **Opening Day Age:** 22
Bats: L **Throws:** L   **Born:** 11/7/81 in Dayton,
Ht: 6' 1" **Wt:** 180   OH

Recent Statistics

	G	AB	R	H	D	T	HR	RBI	SB	BB	SO	Avg
2002 A High Desert	97	365	76	98	13	12	11	45	29	64	100	.268
2002 AA Huntsville	31	129	13	31	2	3	2	13	13	4	30	.240
2003 AA Huntsville	124	457	72	122	13	11	2	34	43	60	119	.267

Krynzel got off to a good start in his first full season at Double-A Huntsville, but slumped badly in the final six weeks. Selected 11th overall in the 2000 draft, Krynzel is an excellent defensive center fielder who is unlikely to hit many home runs. His problems in 2003 can be summarized by three figures: 119, 21, and 2, respectively his strikeouts, caught stealing, and home runs. Also, his slugging average was off nearly 75 points from his 2002 level. Scott Podsednik's development may afford the Brewers the luxury of giving Krynzel more time in the high minors to cut down on his strikeouts and improve his stolen-base percentage.

Luis Martinez

Position: P   **Opening Day Age:** 24
Bats: L **Throws:** L   **Born:** 1/20/80 in Santo
Ht: 6' 7" **Wt:** 200   Domingo, DR

Recent Statistics

	W	L	ERA	G	GS	Sv	IP	H	R	BB	SO	HR
2003 AA Huntsville	8	5	2.58	20	20	0	115.0	93	46	54	116	4
2003 AAA Indianapolis	4	0	0.99	7	7	0	45.2	37	5	19	46	0
2003 NL Milwaukee	0	3	9.92	4	4	0	16.1	25	18	15	10	3

The 2003 campaign was the best of Martinez' seven seasons in the Brewers' system. Martinez has always impressed scouts with his fluid motion, 92-93 MPH fastball and good changeup, but he struggled in 2001 and 2002 after an encouraging 2000 season at Class-A Beloit. Last year, the lefthander cut his BB-IP ratio considerably from his 2001-2002 level, and bettered his previous best single-season strikeout total by 28. Martinez struggled in a September look with the big club, but given the lack of depth at the major league level, a good spring training in 2004 likely would land him in the Brewers' rotation.

Brad Nelson

Position: OF-1B   **Opening Day Age:** 21
Bats: L **Throws:** R   **Born:** 12/23/82 in
Ht: 6' 2" **Wt:** 220   Algona, IA

Recent Statistics

	G	AB	R	H	D	T	HR	RBI	SB	BB	SO	Avg
2002 A Beloit	106	417	70	124	38	2	17	99	4	34	86	.297
2002 A High Desert	26	102	24	26	11	0	3	17	0	12	28	.255
2003 A High Desert	41	167	23	52	9	1	1	18	2	12	22	.311
2003 AA Huntsville	39	143	15	30	12	0	1	14	2	11	34	.210

Nelson's 2003 season appears to be another instance of the Brewers' determination to get their prospects to Double-A before they turn 21. In 2002, Nelson led all minor leaguers with 116 RBI while swatting 20 homers. Highly regarded for his potential as a power hitter, the Algona, Iowa native returned to high Class-A High Desert after a late-2002 promotion. But he suffered a broken hamate bone, which cost him two months on the DL, and hit only one homer in 167 at-bats. Then he was promoted to Huntsville, where he swatted one in 143 at-bats. If Prince Fielder develops as hoped, Nelson may have to play the outfield in order to secure a long-running role with the Brewers.

Rickie Weeks

Position: 2B   **Opening Day Age:** 21
Bats: R **Throws:** R   **Born:** 9/13/82 in
Ht: 6' 0" **Wt:** 195   Daytona Beach, FL

Recent Statistics

	G	AB	R	H	D	T	HR	RBI	SB	BB	SO	Avg
2003 R Brewers	1	4	0	2	0	0	0	4	1	0	2	.500
2003 A Beloit	20	63	13	22	8	1	1	16	2	15	9	.349
2003 NL Milwaukee	7	12	1	2	1	0	0	0	0	1	6	.167

With the second choice in last June's draft, the Brewers selected Weeks, a hitting star for Southern University. He was signed to a major league contract in time to get 63 at-bats at Class-A Beloit before a September callup. At Beloit he showed good plate discipline and good gap power. Weeks is relatively new to the second-base position, having played center field and shortstop for much of his college career; his seven errors at Beloit probably reflect inexperience rather than his true level of athletic ability. Weeks figures to start 2004 at Double-A Huntsville, and will be on the fast track to Milwaukee if he hits well there.

Others to Watch

Acquired in December's Richie Sexson trade, southpaw **Chris Capuano** (25) recovered rapidly from Tommy John surgery in May 2002, going 9-5 (3.34) with Triple-A Tucson and 2-4 (4.64) with Arizona. He throws a low-90s fastball and a reliable slider. If he can't cut it as a starter, he could join the Brewers' pen. . . Lefty **Jorge de la Rosa** (22) arguably was Boston's best pitching prospect before moving to Arizona and Milwaukee in the Curt Schilling and Richie Sexson trades. He was 9-5 with a 2.98 ERA at Double-A and Triple-A stops last year, calling on a low-90s fastball, hard curve and changeup. . . Righthander **Ben Hendrickson** (23) posted ERAs under 3.00 at three levels in 2001 and 2002, but an inflamed elbow limited him to 13 IP for Huntsville before a late-June return. For the season, he went 7-6 with a 3.45 ERA and 56 strikeouts. . . Despite a broken ankle suffered in mid-August, catcher **Lou Palmisano** (21) was the MVP in the Rookie-level Pioneer League, where he hit six homers and drove in 43 runs in 174 at-bats, and stole 13 bases. His defensive skills are excellent. . . Lefty **Manny Parra** (21), signed as a draft-and-follow for $1.55 million, went 11-2 for Class-A Beloit, striking out 117 while walking only 24, and posting a 2.73 ERA.

Olympic Stadium

Offense

Although its dimensions are larger than many ballparks, Stade Olympique is a decent hitters' park. The spacious alleys and fast turf turn singles into extra bases. Hiram Bithorn Stadium is by any professional standard, a bandbox. It is 315 feet down the foul lines, and the power-alley walls are a mere 340-350 feet away from the plate.

Defense

Even though the field at Olympic is artificial turf, there are so many dead spots and seams that it plays as unpredictably as grass. The stadium's speaker system also is in play, so balls headed foul can ricochet back into fair territory. Bithorn's outfield dimensions are only slightly larger than a regulation softball field, but the park has more foul territory than the Hanford Nuclear Reservation, allowing defenders an almost end-less stretch of turf to pursue foul popups.

Who It Helps the Most

Orlando Cabrera hit 67 points higher in home games than he did away, and his slugging per-centage went up more than 100 points. Brad Wilkerson also hit significantly higher. Bithorn Stadium is good for all hitters, but Anaheim Angel outfielder Jeff DaVanon particularly enjoyed it, hitting four of his 12 home runs in back-to-back games.

Who It Hurts the Most

Zach Day's ERA was nearly a run higher at home. Relievers T.J. Tucker and Joe Eischen also weren't fond of home-cooking. Javier Vazquez gave up more than two-thirds of his home runs at home and Tomo Ohka gave up 17 of his 24 long-balls at his home parks.

Rookies & Newcomers

Two good young outfielders, Terrmel Sledge and Val Pascucci, will move up from Triple-A. Sledge will take over left field and is one of the early leading candidates for the 2004 Rookie of the Year Award. Both Nick Johnson and Juan Rivera, acquired from the Yankees, should enjoy hitting at Olympic Stadium, as well as getting 22 games at Bithorn.

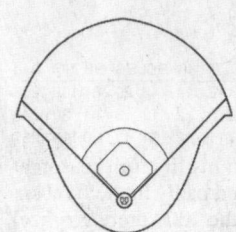

Dimensions: LF-325, LCF-375, CF-404, RCF-375, RF-325

Capacity: 46,338

Elevation: 90 feet

Surface: Turf

Foul Territory: Large

Park Factors

2003 Season

	Home Games			Away Games			
	Expos	Opp	Total	Expos	Opp	Total	Index
G	56	56	112	72	72	144	
Avg	.280	.260	.270	.239	.265	.252	107
AB	1856	1963	3819	2441	2373	4814	102
R	307	251	558	237	287	524	137
H	520	511	1031	583	630	1213	109
2B	135	121	256	99	127	226	143
3B	14	6	20	8	12	20	126
HR	50	62	112	57	54	111	127
BB	179	149	328	223	214	437	95
SO	306	366	672	477	439	916	92
E	31	33	64	42	46	88	94
E-Infield	24	29	53	36	33	69	99
LHB-Avg	.267	.254	.261	.231	.289	.258	101
LHB-HR	17	20	37	21	21	42	117
RHB-Avg	.291	.264	.277	.246	.248	.247	112
RHB-HR	33	42	75	36	33	69	131

2001-2003

	Home Games			Away Games			
	Expos	Opp	Total	Expos	Opp	Total	Index
G	200	200	400	216	216	432	
Avg	.269	.263	.266	.244	.270	.257	103
AB	6607	7026	13633	7350	7160	14510	101
R	956	944	1900	825	955	1780	115
H	1776	1846	3622	1796	1931	3727	105
2B	445	423	868	349	371	720	128
3B	37	28	65	41	44	85	81
HR	180	225	405	181	207	388	111
BB	660	575	1235	679	702	1381	95
SO	1236	1369	2605	1506	1392	2898	96
E	148	140	288	149	150	299	104
E-Infield	116	118	234	127	121	248	102
LHB-Avg	.263	.272	.268	.238	.281	.258	104
LHB-HR	69	83	152	73	90	163	102
RHB-Avg	.273	.256	.264	.250	.262	.256	103
RHB-HR	111	142	253	108	117	225	117

2003 Rankings (National League)

- Highest run factor
- Highest double factor
- Second-highest batting-average factor
- Second-highest hit factor
- Second-highest home-run factor
- Second-highest RHB batting-average factor
- Second-highest RHB home-run factor
- Third-lowest strikeout factor

Frank Robinson

2003 Season

As has been the case with any recent Expos season, Frank Robinson faced adversity that no other manager would ever have to deal with. The major problem was salary, although this year it was because the 29 competing owners of the Expos did not want to pay the $50,000 for any minor league callups. He also had to split his "home games" between Montreal and San Juan, Puerto Rico, an inconvenience that stuck the Expos with essentially a midseason 22-game road trip that covered more than 10,000 miles.

Offense

Robinson's success as a manager is due in part to his ability to sell his hitting philosophy to his players. He asks his players to be selective, but be aggressive. He recognized that his team couldn't match the home-run power of his opponents, but he knew he possessed plenty of good fastball hitters who could make contact and run well. So once his hitters were on base, Robinson liked movement—the Expos were one of the most prolific NL clubs in stealing bases (both by volume and success percentage) and hit-and-run plays.

Pitching & Defense

Robinson is old school when it comes to handling his starting pitchers, so as long as they throw strikes, they stay in the game. As a result, only Dusty Baker's Cubs racked up more 120 plus pitch outings than Montreal in all of baseball. Robinson also has no patience for relievers who nibble. In large part because of Brian Schneider's arm, Robinson felt little need to pitch out, but he did put in the extreme infield shift for dangerous lefthanded hitters like Jim Thome and Barry Bonds.

2004 Outlook

That Montreal was in contention for the wild-card as late as the middle of September—despite the unprecedented adversity the club faced—is a testament to Robinson's own strength of character, as well as his ability to uncover that strength in his players. The Expos' situation makes it difficult for them to contend, but with Robinson, they are a strong candidate to again surprise.

Born: 8/31/35 in Beaumont, TX

Playing Experience: 1956-1976, Cin, Bal, LA, Cal, Cle

Managerial Experience: 13 seasons

Manager Statistics

Year	Team, Lg	W	L	Pct	GB	Finish
2003	Montreal, NL	83	79	.512	18.0	4th East
13 Seasons		846	909	.482	–	–

2003 Starting Pitchers by Days Rest

	<=3	4	5	6+
Expos Starts	2	101	31	17
Expos ERA	3.86	3.84	3.35	4.32
NL Avg Starts	2	84	43	23
NL ERA	5.00	4.23	4.42	4.68

2003 Situational Stats

	Frank Robinson	NL Average
Hit & Run Success %	30.5	32.7
Stolen Base Success %	71.9	68.9
Platoon Pct.	58.8	52.0
Defensive Subs	20	19
High-Pitch Outings	25	8
Quick/Slow Hooks	16/10	20/12
Sacrifice Attempts	90	93

2003 Rankings (National League)

- 1st in steals of third base (19)
- 2nd in stolen base attempts (139), fewest caught stealings of third base (1), hit-and-run attempts (95) and starts with over 120 pitches (25)
- 3rd in stolen-base percentage, steals of second base (81) and starting lineups used (133)

Tony Armas Jr.

2003 Season

It looked like 2003 was going to be a break-through season for Tony Armas Jr. He began last year as the team's Opening Day starter, shutting down the Braves in Atlanta, 10-2. But the break-through turned into a breakdown after he was diagnosed with tears in his right labrum and rotator cuff in mid-May that required season-ending surgery. Before the injury, Armas was an early leading contender for the National League Cy Young Award, with a 2.61 ERA while allowing barely more than a baserunner per inning (1.065).

Pitching

Armas uses two pitches—a low-90s moving fast-ball and a sharp-breaking curve—to establish what he wants to do with each hitter. He'll mix in a decent slider, splitter and change to keep opponents guessing. In his brief showing this season, Armas demonstrated significant improvement against lefties, holding them to a lower OPS than he did righthanders. The improvement was due to pitching more aggressively inside and reducing the number of walks he surrendered to them. He also successfully addressed his other major weakness: the longball. He did not allow a home run until he gave up for longballs in what ended up being his final start.

Defense & Hitting

Armas Jr. is naturally athletic and quick as a fielder, and he has a great arm. But unlike his All-Star father, he's not a good hitter at all. He has drawn just two walks in 157 career plate appearances. Armas' slide step has improved to the point where opposing baserunners no longer take him for granted.

2004 Outlook

Armas' rehab is going very well and all signs point to him being completely healthy for spring training. Assuming all goes according to plan and he resumes where he left off in 2003, Armas will be a significant player in the Expos' effort to contend for a playoff spot in 2004. If he does return to his 2003 form, he also might be a significant player in the NL Cy Young race.

Position: SP
Bats: R **Throws:** R
Ht: 6' 3" **Wt:** 225

Opening Day Age: 25
Born: 4/29/78 in Puerto Piritu, VZ
ML Seasons: 5
Pronunciation: ar-MUS

Overall Statistics

	W	L	Pct.	ERA	G	GS	Sv	IP	H	BB	SO	HR	Avg
'03	2	1	.667	2.61	5	5	0	31.0	25	8	23	4	.225
Car.	30	37	.448	4.11	86	86	0	493.0	436	229	391	54	.240

2003 Pitching Profile

	Tony Armas	NL Average
Overall Strike %	62.2	62.4
1st Pitch Strike %	60.5	58.4
Ratio	1.06	1.38
Strikeouts per 9 IP	6.68	6.65
Walks per 9 IP	2.32	3.42
Home Runs per 9 IP	1.16	1.05
Strikeout/Walk Ratio	2.88	1.94
Groundball/Flyball Ratio	0.67	1.29

2003 Situational Stats

	W	L	ERA	Sv	IP		AB	H	HR	RBI	Avg
Home	0	0	3.46	0	13.0	LHB	44	11	0	4	.250
Road	2	1	2.00	0	18.0	RHB	67	14	4	5	.209
First Half	2	1	2.61	0	31.0	Sc Pos	20	2	0	4	.100
Scnd Half	0	0	—	0	0.0	Clutch	3	0	0	0	.000

2003 Rankings (National League)

- Did not rank near the top or bottom in any category

Orlando Cabrera

2003 Season

Back troubles slowed Orlando Cabrera in 2002, but the injury did not affect his performance in 2003. He finished second among National League shortstops in batting average, slugging and RBI. He also finished second in stolen-base percentage among all players who snagged at least 20 bags. Only four Montreal players have ever played all 162 games in a season, and last year Cabrera became the first to do it twice. To top it all off, his 17 homers were the most ever by an Expos shortstop.

Hitting

Cabrera is a very good fastball hitter who doesn't get cheated when he swings. He especially likes pitches that are up in the zone, which is both a strength and a weakness. He crushes most anything belt high but can't seem to handle or lay off anything at the letters. Cabrera is not particularly patient, but he has surprisingly good bat control for a guy who swings the way he does. He makes contact and uses all fields, although his home runs come from pulling the ball.

Baserunning & Defense

Even though he plays in Montreal, Cabrera gets league-wide recognition for his superb defense. He has excellent range, good hands and a strong arm, though he is capable of both the truly spectacular play and the two-base throwing error. His instincts as to when to go for the great play and when to pocket the ball are improving. Cabrera is a significant basestealing threat, having swiped at least 19 in each of the last three seasons, with a high degree of success. Twice in the minors he stole at least 30 bases, including one season in which he stole 51, so he could become even more dangerous.

2004 Outlook

The Expos are set at shortstop for the near future. Cabrera is durable and excels in all aspects of the game. The concerns that dimmed his 2002 performance were not apparent in 2003, leaving his near-term salary increases as the only subject of long-term intrigue for the Expos.

Position: SS
Bats: R **Throws:** R
Ht: 5' 9" **Wt:** 180

Opening Day Age: 29
Born: 11/2/74 in Cartagena, Colombia
ML Seasons: 7
Pronunciation: kah-BRAY-rah

Overall Statistics

	G	AB	R	H	D	T	HR	RBI	SB	BB	SO	Avg	OBP	Slg
'03	162	626	95	186	47	2	17	80	24	52	64	.297	.347	.460
Car.	801	2898	366	781	195	20	62	350	81	205	267	.269	.318	.415

Where He Hits the Ball

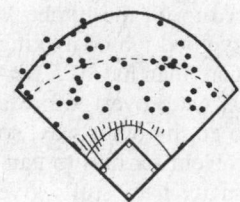 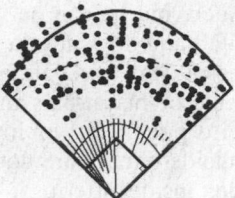

Vs. LHP   **Vs. RHP**

2003 Situational Stats

	AB	H	HR	RBI	Avg		AB	H	HR	RBI	Avg
Home	301	100	8	48	.332	LHP	148	46	2	20	.311
Road	325	86	9	32	.265	RHP	478	140	15	60	.293
First Half	360	108	13	51	.300	Sc Pos	149	43	1	57	.289
Scnd Half	266	78	4	29	.293	Clutch	100	30	4	21	.300

2003 Rankings (National League)

- 1st in games played
- 2nd in sacrifice flies (9), stolen-base percentage (92.3) and errors at shortstop (18)
- 4th in steals of third (6)
- 5th in at-bats
- 6th in doubles and fielding percentage at shortstop (.975)
- Led the Expos in at-bats, runs scored, hits, singles, doubles, total bases (288), RBI, sacrifice flies (9), stolen bases, times on base (239), GDPs (18), plate appearances (691), games played, stolen-base percentage (92.3), steals of third (6) and batting average with two strikes (.270)

Endy Chavez

2003 Season

Endy Chavez cemented the Opening Day center-field and leadoff spots with a solid September in 2002. For the first month of the 2003 season, he looked like a long-term solution at both outposts. But beginning in May, pitchers took advantage of his free-swinging ways and by the end of the campaign, Chavez had lost both jobs to Brad Wilkerson, and he finished with an on-base percentage that was south of .300.

Hitting

Chavez does not possess home-run power. He's strictly a slap-hitter who puts the ball on the ground and uses his speed to leg out extra-base hits. He makes contact and doesn't strike out much, but he can be induced to hit the pitcher's pitch and does not do a very good job of making the pitcher work. In fact, more than half (55 percent) of his at-bats in 2003 were over before a third pitch. Chavez likes to go the other way, so outside pitches are not a problem for him to handle. Inside offerings, especially hard stuff, give him fits.

Baserunning & Defense

Blessed with excellent foot speed, Chavez simply does not get on base enough to be a legitimate basestealer. If he drew a few more walks, he could steal 30-40 bases annually just on pure speed alone. The steals he does register largely are due to his talent, but his ability to read pitchers is improving. In the outfield, he can cover a lot of ground and his arm, though average, is accurate.

2004 Outlook

With his weaknesses as a hitter exposed, Chavez was moved down on the depth chart and may have a tough time finding playing time in Montreal this year. He has value as a pinch-runner and defensive replacement, but unless Terrmel Sledge and Val Pascucci fail, he might only make the team as a fifth outfielder. If Chavez can become more disciplined at the plate, however, his value could soar.

Position: CF
Bats: L **Throws:** L
Ht: 5' 9" **Wt:** 170

Opening Day Age: 26
Born: 2/7/78 in Valencia, VZ
ML Seasons: 3
Pronunciation: shah-VEZ

Overall Statistics

	G	AB	R	H	D	T	HR	RBI	SB	BB	SO	Avg	OBP	Slg
'03	141	483	66	121	25	5	5	47	18	31	59	.251	.294	.354
Car.	206	685	90	174	35	10	6	61	21	39	83	.254	.293	.361

Where He Hits the Ball

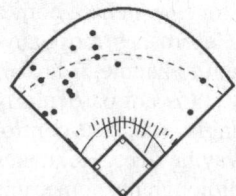 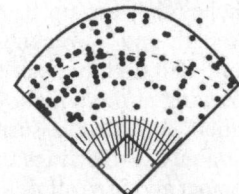

Vs. LHP   **Vs. RHP**

2003 Situational Stats

	AB	H	HR	RBI	Avg		AB	H	HR	RBI	Avg
Home	243	63	4	27	.259	LHP	92	28	0	13	.304
Road	240	58	1	20	.242	RHP	391	93	5	34	.238
First Half	327	85	4	29	.260	Sc Pos	100	32	1	40	.320
Scnd Half	156	36	1	18	.231	Clutch	86	23	2	15	.267

2003 Rankings (National League)

- 2nd in lowest on-base percentage for a leadoff hitter (.292)
- 3rd in highest groundball-flyball ratio (2.2)
- 4th in bunts in play (32)
- 5th in lowest on-base percentage
- 6th in lowest fielding percentage in center field (.990)
- Led the Expos in triples, bunts in play (32), highest percentage of swings put into play (50.7) and batting average with runners in scoring position

Wil Cordero

Position: 1B
Bats: R **Throws:** R
Ht: 6' 2" **Wt:** 215

Opening Day Age: 32
Born: 10/3/71 in Mayaguez, PR
ML Seasons: 12
Pronunciation: cor-DARE-oh

2003 Season

After a slow start, Wil Cordero managed to have one of his most productive seasons in 2003. His output took off when it became clear that the Jeff Leifer platoon idea wasn't going to work, and Cordero assumed full-time duty at first base in May. From that point on, he hit .290 with an on base mark above .360. An injury to his left wrist from an errant pitch slowed his summer, but did not deter him from a strong finish: he batted .311 with a .982 OPS in September.

Hitting

As he's matured, Cordero has developed more patience. But he's still a free-swinger, sometimes chasing pitches a foot outside the strike zone. Like most free-swingers, the count doesn't seem to affect him; if he sees a pitch he likes, he swings regardless. Whether it's due to coaching or familiarity with the pitchers, he did show a hefty improvement in his walk rate last season. Cordero has average power for a corner fielder, but he is a good contact hitter, able to put the ball in play and move runners along.

Baserunning & Defense

Cordero has decent speed, but he isn't a bases-stealing threat. He advances around the diamond as the situation dictates, rarely trying to stretch out an extra base. The former Expos shortstop is versatile in the field, able to play outfield or either corner-infield position, but first base easily is his best position. He has soft hands and digs balls out of the dirt very well, saving his infielders numerous errors.

2004 Outlook

Cordero seemed to find his way into Frank Robinson's doghouse a number of times for perceived lackadaisical play, and he won't be back after the Expos didn't offer him salary arbitration. Cordero will be replaced by first baseman Nick Johnson, who was acquired from the Yankees in the Javier Vazquez trade. As for Cordero, his Kevin Millar-like production and defense will attract some attention. If he's given regular playing time, his signing could pay off with a nice season in 2004.

Overall Statistics

	G	AB	R	H	D	T	HR	RBI	SB	BB	SO	Avg	OBP	Slg
'03	130	436	57	121	27	0	16	71	1	49	90	.278	.354	.450
Car.	1191	4194	579	1159	256	19	121	558	48	319	742	.276	.333	.433

Where He Hits the Ball

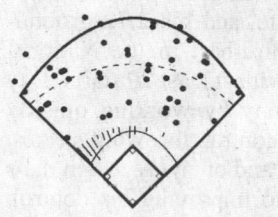
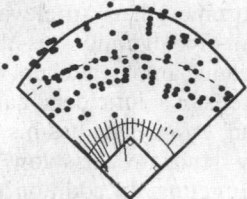

Vs. LHP **Vs. RHP**

2003 Situational Stats

	AB	H	HR	RBI	Avg		AB	H	HR	RBI	Avg
Home	205	59	8	40	.288	LHP	108	35	4	19	.324
Road	231	62	8	31	.268	RHP	328	86	12	52	.262
First Half	251	70	9	39	.279	Sc Pos	134	39	6	57	.291
Scnd Half	185	51	7	32	.276	Clutch	80	22	3	10	.275

2003 Rankings (National League)

- 4th in fielding percentage at first base (.996)

Zach Day

2003 Season

When Orlando Hernandez came up lame in spring training with shoulder trouble, Zach Day found himself in the rotation. Day pitched brilliantly in April, but a cyst above his right kneecap, followed by a slight tear of his rotator cuff that sent him to the disabled list, derailed what might have been a breakout season. After his return, he struggled with his control and never quite got back on track. His season peaked on May 1, when he threw a three-hit shutout in Milwaukee.

Pitching

Day relies on a hard sinker that ranges from 88-92 MPH. He'll mix in a slow curve that has a medium break, a slider and changeup. His sinker is extremely hard to elevate, and his 2.72 groundball-flyball ratio was third-best in the National League among pitchers with at least 20 starts. Day keeps his infielders happy by working quickly and, on days he has his control, throwing strikes. He tends to miss low and/or away when he's struggling. In addition to improving his control, he will need to refine one of his other pitches to keep hitters off-balance on days his sinker isn't there.

Defense & Hitting

As would be expected of a sinkerballer, Day is an agile fielder off the mound, but he lets his infielders do most of the work. Baserunners have a hard time getting a good jump off him because he's relatively quick to the plate and doesn't have much leg kick in his delivery. Even for a pitcher, Day is not a good hitter and could use plenty of extra work on his bunting skills if he's to help himself at the plate.

2004 Outlook

There could be plenty of movement this winter in Montreal, making Day a good bet to begin the 2004 season in the rotation. However, he will need to improve his control significantly to remain there. While he won't ever be more than a No. 3 starter, his repertoire offers an excellent contrast to the rest of the Expos' power/flyball staff.

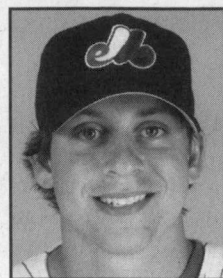

Position: SP
Bats: R **Throws:** R
Ht: 6' 4" **Wt:** 210

Opening Day Age: 25
Born: 6/15/78 in Cincinnati, OH
ML Seasons: 2

Overall Statistics

	W	L	Pct.	ERA	G	GS	Sv	IP	H	BB	SO	HR	Avg
'03	9	8	.529	4.18	23	23	0	131.1	132	59	61	8	.262
Car.	13	9	.591	4.06	42	25	1	168.2	160	74	86	11	.250

2003 Pitching Profile

	Zach Day	NL Average
Overall Strike %	59.4	62.4
1st Pitch Strike %	54.4	58.4
Ratio	1.45	1.38
Strikeouts per 9 IP	4.18	6.65
Walks per 9 IP	4.04	3.42
Home Runs per 9 IP	0.55	1.05
Strikeout/Walk Ratio	1.03	1.94
Groundball/Flyball Ratio	2.72	1.29

2003 Situational Stats

	W	L	ERA	Sv	IP		AB	H	HR	RBI	Avg
Home	5	3	4.54	0	69.1	LHB	234	66	4	24	.282
Road	4	5	3.77	0	62.0	RHB	270	66	4	32	.244
First Half	4	3	3.44	0	65.1	Sc Pos	136	35	2	45	.257
Scnd Half	5	5	4.91	0	66.0	Clutch	20	5	0	1	.250

2003 Rankings (National League)

- 1st in wild pitches (13)
- 9th in hit batsmen (10)
- Led the Expos in walks allowed, hit batsmen (10), wild pitches (13), highest groundball-flyball ratio allowed (2.7) and fewest home runs allowed per nine innings (.55)

Vladimir Guerrero

2003 Season

The 2003 campaign was a landmark season for Vladimir Guerrero. Despite the fact that he missed 39 games due to a herniated disc, he became the Expos' all-time leader in home runs on August 21, passing Andre Dawson, and on September 14, he became the sixth Montreal player to hit for the cycle. Guerrero also established his status as the premier free agent heading into 2004 by hitting .353 and smacking 17 homers upon his return after the All-Star break.

Hitting

Guerrero has legendary power, and not just because of the 500-foot bombs he hits. With his long arms and powerful wrists, anything he can reach is a potential home run. His discipline continues to improve, but he gets overeager on breaking pitches outside and fastballs on his hands. He has a long swing, but his bat speed and bat control are such that he still makes contact with almost everything he swings at. Most pitchers try to get ahead of Guerrero and then throw him junk in the hope that he'll get himself out.

Baserunning & Defense

Guerrero gobbles up basepaths with his huge strides, but he can be reckless trying to take extra bases, though his excellent speed affords him some leeway. Many observers have gone on record as saying that Guerrero has the best outfield arm since Roberto Clemente, and he loves to show it off, sometimes to the cutoff man's dismay. His errors have dropped in each of the last two years, however, and his 51 assists from right since 2000 is the best figure in baseball.

2004 Outlook

With the current financial climate in baseball, it's unlikely that Guerrero will be offered a $20 million-per-year contract, and he wasn't finding many suitors when the free-agent season began. There was an outside chance that Guerrero would stay in Montreal, as his mother wields significant influence over his life and she likes living in Montreal, but that hope died when the Expos didn't offer him salary arbitration. Whichever team ends up with him significantly improves its postseason chances.

Position: RF
Bats: R **Throws:** R
Ht: 6' 3" **Wt:** 220

Opening Day Age: 28
Born: 2/9/76 in Nizao Bani, DR
ML Seasons: 8
Pronunciation: guh-RAR-oh
Nickname: Miqueas

Overall Statistics

	G	AB	R	H	D	T	HR	RBI	SB	BB	SO	Avg	OBP	Slg
'03	112	394	71	130	20	3	25	79	9	63	53	.330	.426	.586
Car.	1004	3763	641	1215	226	34	234	702	123	381	484	.323	.390	.588

Where He Hits the Ball

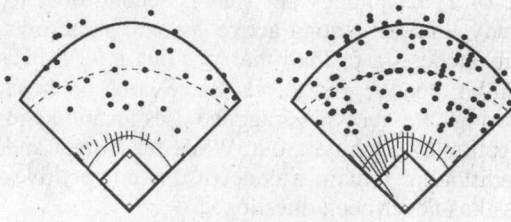

Vs. LHP   **Vs. RHP**

2003 Situational Stats

	AB	H	HR	RBI	Avg		AB	H	HR	RBI	Avg
Home	208	68	15	56	.327	LHP	84	33	9	22	.393
Road	186	62	10	23	.333	RHP	310	97	16	57	.313
First Half	176	53	8	33	.301	Sc Pos	105	33	5	48	.314
Scnd Half	218	77	17	46	.353	Clutch	58	17	4	14	.290

2003 Rankings (National League)

- 1st in errors in right field (7) and lowest fielding percentage in right field (.970)
- 2nd in intentional walks (22)
- 5th in cleanup slugging percentage (.607)
- 6th in most GDPs per GDP situation (19.1%)
- 8th in lowest percentage of pitches taken (48.9)
- Led the Expos in batting average, home runs, intentional walks (22), GDPs (18), slugging percentage, on-base percentage, HR frequency (15.8 ABs per HR), batting average vs. lefthanded pitchers, batting average vs. righthanded pitchers, cleanup slugging percentage (.607) and batting average on the road

Montreal

Livan Hernandez

2003 Season

Livan Hernandez came to the Expos via a spring trade that was ostensibly a salary dump by the Giants, but he turned the tables on the deal with perhaps his best year in the majors. He posted the second-best ERA of his career, and in 17 of his 33 starts allowed two or fewer earned runs. Had Hernandez not tired in September, he also might have topped his career best in wins and winning percentage.

Pitching

The resilience of Hernandez' arm continues to amaze observers. He racked up 13 outings of at least 120 pitches this season, and his career average of 110.3 pitches per start is second only to Randy Johnson among active starters. He throws four pitches—a fastball that tops out at 92 MPH, a slider, change and curve. Since none of those offerings are above average, he uses location and selection to get hitters out. While his weight and conditioning remain a concern, his competitiveness has never been questioned.

Defense & Hitting

While he doesn't possess great range, Hernandez is a surehanded fielder and was tops in the majors among pitchers in turning double plays. His ability to control the running game seems to be largely dependent upon who's catching him. In three of the last four years, he's had an excellent rate of stifling the running game. However, in 2002, basestealers ran wild on him, suggesting that his own skills are nothing spectacular. Hernandez is one of the best hitting pitchers in the game. This year marked the first full season in his career in which he did not record at least three extra-base hits, however, and he had his worst batting average (.189) since 1997.

2004 Outlook

In September, Hernandez surpassed the 217-inning requirement for his option to kick in, so he will start for Montreal next year while earning $6 million. Because Hernandez was so effective in 2003, the Expos might be able to move his contract and turn their efforts to keeping their premier offensive players.

Position: SP
Bats: R **Throws:** R
Ht: 6' 2" **Wt:** 240

Opening Day Age: 29
Born: 2/20/75 in Villa Clara, Cuba
ML Seasons: 8
Pronunciation: lee-VAHN her-NAN-dezz

Overall Statistics

	W	L	Pct.	ERA	G	GS	Sv	IP	H	BB	SO	HR	Avg
'03	15	10	.600	3.20	33	33	0	233.1	225	57	178	27	.253
Car.	84	79	.515	4.22	214	213	0	1449.1	1554	506	995	157	.277

2003 Pitching Profile

	Livan Hernandez	NL Average
Overall Strike %	63.2	62.4
1st Pitch Strike %	61.0	58.4
Ratio	1.21	1.38
Strikeouts per 9 IP	6.87	6.65
Walks per 9 IP	2.20	3.42
Home Runs per 9 IP	1.04	1.05
Strikeout/Walk Ratio	3.12	1.94
Groundball/Flyball Ratio	1.48	1.29

2003 Situational Stats

	W	L	ERA	Sv	IP		AB	H	HR	RBI	Avg
Home	11	5	3.04	0	130.1	LHB	388	108	11	37	.278
Road	4	5	3.41	0	103.0	RHB	502	117	16	49	.233
First Half	9	6	3.63	0	129.0	Sc Pos	191	39	3	53	.204
Scnd Half	6	4	2.67	0	104.1	Clutch	63	14	1	2	.222

2003 Rankings (National League)

- 1st in complete games (8), innings pitched and batters faced (967)
- 3rd in pitches thrown (3,582)
- 4th in hits allowed
- 7th in strikeouts and lowest batting average allowed with runners in scoring position
- 8th in games started and highest strikeout-walk ratio (3.1)
- 9th in ERA, wins, home runs allowed and hit batsmen (10)
- 10th in lowest on-base percentage allowed (.304) and lowest ERA at home
- Led the Expos in ERA, wins, complete games (8), innings pitched, batters faced (967), hit batsmen (10), GDPs induced (21), lowest ERA at home, most run support per nine innings (5.4) and lowest batting average allowed with runners in scoring position

Tomo Ohka

2003 Season

Tomo Ohka was not able to improve on his 2002 season, when he finished with the seventh-best ERA in the National League, but he did manage to hold his ground. He tied for the team lead in starts in 2003, and the highlight of his season was a two-hit shutout against the Blue Jays on June 29. He struggled mightily with his consistency. In his 10 wins, Ohka's ERA was 1.22, in his 12 losses, it was 8.54.

Pitching

Ohka throws five different pitches, but only his curve is above average. His fastball is straight and averages in the high 80s, but he can tune it up to 91 MPH. He spots it on both sides of the plate and complements it with his curve, a change, splitter and slider. Most of his struggles came in the first inning of games, when batters hit .326 against him and eight of the 24 home runs were surrendered. Ohka is prepared and has a game plan for each hitter, pitching specifically to his opponents' weaknesses. He works quickly and throws strikes, perhaps *too many* strikes at times, resulting in a substantial increase in the number of hits he gave up over last year.

Defense & Hitting

Ohka's defense is solid if unspectacular. He varies his timing to the plate, making it very difficult for would-be base stealers to get a good jump. He also has a good pickoff move to keep them from getting comfortable. At the plate, he moves his feet around the box quite a bit and tends to lunge with his swing, yet still manages to be a proficient bunter.

2004 Outlook

Ohka will be in the Montreal rotation next year, probably penciled into the fourth spot, depending on whether the Expos move one of their top starters. He could jockey with Orlando Hernandez for the third spot if El Duque returns. Ohka's strong showing after the All-Star break boosted optimism that he will continue to improve in 2004.

Position: SP
Bats: R **Throws:** R
Ht: 6' 1" **Wt:** 180

Opening Day Age: 28
Born: 3/18/76 in Kyoto, Japan
ML Seasons: 5
Pronunciation: TOE-mo-KAH-zoo OH-kah

Overall Statistics

	W	L	Pct.	ERA	G	GS	Sv	IP	H	BB	SO	HR	Avg
'03	10	12	.455	4.16	34	34	0	199.0	233	45	118	24	.292
Car.	30	37	.448	4.00	109	100	0	581.0	652	151	352	67	.285

2003 Pitching Profile

	Tomo Ohka	NL Average
Overall Strike %	66.0	62.4
1st Pitch Strike %	64.5	58.4
Ratio	1.40	1.38
Strikeouts per 9 IP	5.34	6.65
Walks per 9 IP	2.04	3.42
Home Runs per 9 IP	1.09	1.05
Strikeout/Walk Ratio	2.62	1.94
Groundball/Flyball Ratio	1.36	1.29

2003 Situational Stats

	W	L	ERA	Sv	IP		AB	H	HR	RBI	Avg
Home	6	5	3.93	0	110.0	LHB	318	99	6	26	.311
Road	4	7	4.45	0	89.0	RHB	481	134	18	57	.279
First Half	7	9	4.51	0	105.2	Sc Pos	186	51	5	55	.274
2nd Half	0	0	0.70	0	00.1	Clutch	33	17	2	6	.515

2003 Rankings (National League)

- 1st in lowest stolen-base percentage allowed (20.0)
- 2nd in hits allowed
- 3rd in games started, fewest pitches thrown per batter (3.44) and errors at pitcher (4)
- 5th in fewest walks per nine innings (2.0) and lowest fielding percentage at pitcher (.918)
- 6th in highest batting average allowed (.292)
- 7th in pickoff throws (123) and runners caught stealing (8)
- Led the Expos in losses, games started, hits allowed, pickoff throws (123), runners caught stealing (8), lowest stolen-base percentage allowed (20.0), fewest pitches thrown per batter (3.44) and fewest walks per nine innings (2.0)

Brian Schneider

2003 Season

Brian Schneider opened the season as Michael Barrett's backup at catcher, but Barrett's struggles at the plate provided Schneider an opportunity to start. After a solid first half, Schneider struggled after being hit in the head with an Aramis Ramirez back-swing on June 25. Fatigue also played a role in his second-half slump, as he surpassed his previous career high in plate appearances by more than 50 percent. Although his defense remained steady, his batting average, power and strikeout-walk ratio all suffered as a result of the extra workload.

Hitting

Schneider is a good contact hitter who will turn on inside fastballs. He has a very good eye for pitches on the outer half of the plate and lays off anything that is tailing out of his reach. Breaking pitches down and in are about the only things that consistently give him trouble. He doesn't have great patience, but he can wear out a pitcher by fouling off borderline offerings.

Baserunning & Defense

The game behind the plate is Schneider's greatest strength. His Catcher's ERA (3.75) was fourth-best among National League regulars despite the fact that he was calling pitches for one of the league's youngest staffs. He has quick feet and blocks pitches in the dirt extremely well, yielding the lowest number of passed balls in the league among regulars. Schneider absolutely shuts down the running game with a plus arm, throwing out a league-best 46.7 percent of opposing basestealers. Like most catchers, he is a station-to-station runner and no threat to steal.

2004 Outlook

Barrett showed some signs of life in the second half of '03, but Schneider virtually is assured of getting the starting nod to open 2004. Manager Frank Robinson likes the way Schneider handles the staff and his offensive upside is similar to that of Barrett's, although his ceiling probably is lower. However, Schneider's defensive contributions are unmatched, so unless he struggles like he did last September (.185), his position in the line-up should be secure.

Position: C
Bats: L **Throws:** R
Ht: 6' 1" **Wt:** 200

Opening Day Age: 27
Born: 11/26/76 in Jacksonville, FL
ML Seasons: 4

Overall Statistics

	G	AB	R	H	D	T	HR	RBI	SB	BB	SO	Avg	OBP	Slg
'03	108	335	34	77	26	1	9	46	0	37	75	.230	.309	.394
Car.	253	698	65	174	54	3	15	92	1	71	143	.249	.318	.400

Where He Hits the Ball

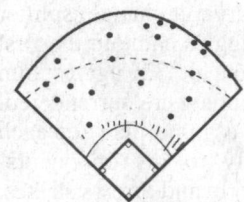

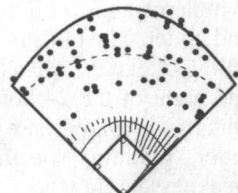

Vs. LHP   **Vs. RHP**

2003 Situational Stats

	AB	H	HR	RBI	Avg		AB	H	HR	RBI	Avg
Home	183	48	9	37	.262	LHP	67	12	3	9	.179
Road	152	29	0	9	.191	RHP	268	65	6	37	.243
First Half	161	40	6	25	.248	Sc Pos	85	19	3	35	.224
Scnd Half	174	37	3	21	.213	Clutch	70	16	3	13	.229

2003 Rankings (National League)

• 5th in fielding percentage at catcher (.996)

Javier Vazquez

Position: SP
Bats: R **Throws:** R
Ht: 6' 2" **Wt:** 205

Opening Day Age: 27
Born: 7/25/76 in Ponce, PR
ML Seasons: 6
Pronunciation: VAS-kez

2003 Season

In 2003, Javier Vazquez continued his improvement, posting a career low in ERA (3.20) and a career-high 241 strikeouts. He almost certainly would have finished with more than his 13 wins had he received better run support. He struggled some in May and June, though how much of that was due to his increased workload—he averaged 110 pitches per start, four more than his previous season high—or to the complications his wife was experiencing during their first pregnancy is unknown. Whatever it was, it did not affect him in the second half of the season, as his 2.39 ERA after the break was among the league's best.

Pitching

Vazquez works hitters in and out with four pitches he throws for strikes. He can cut or sink his 93-MPH fastball, and he gives batters plenty to think about with a good slider, curve and above-average changeup. He continued last year's trend of getting batters to hit the ball in the air—his 0.83 groundball-flyball ratio was third lowest in the NL.

Defense & Hitting

Were he in a different league than Greg Maddux, Vazquez might have won a couple of Gold Gloves by now. He used to be among the pitching leaders in turning double plays, but his development as a flyball pitcher has taken that skill out of play. Vazquez is quick to the plate and has an effective slide step to stymie basestealers. His hitting was a mixed bag in 2003; he registered his lowest batting average, but most RBI, of his career. He is an excellent bunter.

2004 Outlook

With Vazquez due for a substantial raise in arbitration, the ace righthander was dealt to the Yankees in December for first baseman Nick Johnson, outfielder Juan Rivera and lefthander Randy Choate. It's with New York that Vazquez will strive to break the up-year/down-year cycle that he's been on the last four seasons, while continuing to establish himself as one of the game's premier starters with a contending Yankees squad.

Overall Statistics

	W	L	Pct.	ERA	G	GS	Sv	IP	H	BB	SO	HR	Avg
'03	13	12	.520	3.24	34	34	0	230.2	198	57	241	28	.229
Car.	64	68	.485	4.16	192	191	0	1229.1	1235	331	1076	155	.260

2003 Pitching Profile

	Javier Vazquez	NL Average
Overall Strike %	65.8	62.4
1st Pitch Strike %	65.4	58.4
Ratio	1.11	1.38
Strikeouts per 9 IP	9.40	6.65
Walks per 9 IP	2.22	3.42
Home Runs per 9 IP	1.09	1.05
Strikeout/Walk Ratio	4.23	1.94
Groundball/Flyball Ratio	0.83	1.29

2003 Situational Stats

	W	L	ERA	Sv	IP		AB	H	HR	RBI	Avg
Home	9	4	3.29	0	126.0	LHB	377	88	10	35	.233
Road	4	8	3.18	0	104.2	RHB	488	110	18	53	.225
First Half	6	6	3.95	0	125.1	So Pos	162	36	7	57	.222
Scnd Half	7	6	2.39	0	105.1	Clutch	69	15	1	9	.217

2003 Rankings (National League)

- 1st in pitches thrown (3,741)
- 2nd in innings pitched
- 3rd in games started, batters faced (938), strikeouts, lowest on-base percentage allowed (.278), lowest groundball-flyball ratio allowed (0.8) and most pitches thrown per batter (3.99)
- 4th in sacrifice bunts (12), highest strikeout-walk ratio (4.2) and most strikeouts per nine innings (9.4)
- Led the Expos in sacrifice bunts (12), losses, games started, home runs allowed, strikeouts, pitches thrown (3,741), highest strikeout-walk ratio (4.2), lowest batting average allowed (.229), lowest slugging percentage allowed (.380), lowest on-base percentage allowed (.278), lowest ERA on the road, lowest batting average allowed vs. lefthanded batters and most strikeouts per nine innings (9.4)

Montreal

Jose Vidro

2003 Season

It's hard to say that a middle infielder had a down year when he hit as well as Jose Vidro did in 2003, but that is the standard he set for himself. One of just eight active batters who has hit .300 or better in each of the last five seasons, Vidro's overall power numbers tailed off from 2002 due to nagging knee and shoulder injuries. One positive development was the significant improvement in his walk rate, as 2003 marked the first time in his career that Vidro walked more than he struck out.

Hitting

Vidro is a very good contact hitter with a level, easy swing from both sides of the plate. He has home-run power to all fields, but most of his extra base hits are line-drive doubles off the wall. He has excellent plate coverage and is very good at fouling off borderline pitches outside. Pitches on his hands tend to tie him up, but anything that tails back over the plate usually finds the fat part of the bat. Vidro remains one of the more dangerous two-strike hitters in the game, and he was particularly tough with the count full, hitting .348 with an OPS of 1.153 in such situations in 2003.

Baserunning & Defense

Vidro is smart on the bases, but his below-average foot speed prevents him from being much more than a station-to-station runner. His strong arm allows him to play deeper than most second basemen, making his range better than average. His strained knee limited his effectiveness, however, and prompted Frank Robinson to remove him late in games for a defensive replacement more often as the season progressed.

2004 Outlook

As with every Expos offseason, rumors of players being dealt for salary reasons are flying, and Vidro is one of the targets this year. Despite what appears to be a down year, the improved patience at the plate was a significant development. If the switch-hitting Vidro can stay healthy in 2004, a big power year is imminent, wherever he ends up.

Position: 2B
Bats: B **Throws:** R
Ht: 5'11" **Wt:** 195

Opening Day Age: 29
Born: 8/27/74 in Mayaguez, PR
ML Seasons: 7
Pronunciation: VEE-droe

Overall Statistics

	G	AB	R	H	D	T	HR	RBI	SB	BB	SO	Avg	OBP	Slg
'03	144	509	77	158	36	0	15	65	3	69	50	.310	.397	.470
Car.	863	3073	473	940	233	9	87	411	17	276	342	.306	.367	.473

Where He Hits the Ball

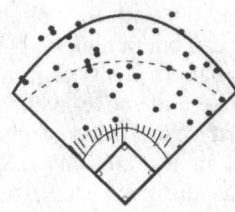 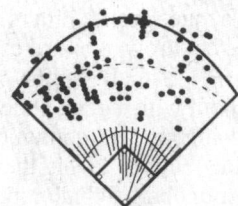

Vs. LHP   **Vs. RHP**

2003 Situational Stats

	AB	H	HR	RBI	Avg		AB	H	HR	RBI	Avg
Home	249	83	7	38	.333	LHP	127	40	7	22	.315
Road	260	75	8	27	.288	RHP	382	118	8	43	.309
First Half	316	105	11	47	.332	Sc Pos	118	36	3	47	.305
Scnd Half	193	53	4	18	.275	Clutch	84	28	4	14	.333

2003 Rankings (National League)

- 4th in fielding percentage at second base (.983)
- 6th in errors at second base (10)
- Led the Expos in hit by pitch (7), lowest percentage of swings that missed (11.5), batting average in the clutch, batting average with the bases loaded (.667) and batting average at home

Brad Wilkerson

2003 Season

The 2003 season was somewhat of a breakthrough for Brad Wilkerson. Although his overall numbers were similar to 2002, there were several developments that bode well for his continued growth into an All-Star, including career highs in doubles, walks and steals. On June 24, he became the fifth Expo to hit for the cycle. Manager Frank Robinson moved him up and down the lineup throughout the year, but finally found him a home in the leadoff spot. On August 17, he put an exclamation point on a season sweep of the Giants and provided a spark for Montreal's wild-card push with a game-ending grand slam.

Hitting

Wilkerson has a good eye for balls and strikes and is comfortable going deep in the count. He rarely swings at the first offering, but when he does, it usually means the pitcher made a mistake. He prefers pitches on the inner half so he can pull the ball, but he has good plate coverage and will go the other way. He's a student of hitting and always is looking to improve.

Baserunning & Defense

Although not blessed with great speed, Wilkerson is a good baserunner, aggressively taking extra bases when available and breaking up double plays with textbook efficiency. In the field, Wilkerson's versatility is a huge asset, as he is an above-average defender at any of the outfield positions as well as at first base. He has a strong, accurate arm, which he used to great effect at the University of Florida as one of the best two-way players in NCAA history.

2004 Outlook

With Vladimir Guerrero's departure virtually assured, Wilkerson may find himself starting in center field. It won't be between Guerrero and outstanding prospect Terrmel Sledge, but more likely between Sledge and another inexperienced player, Juan Rivera, who arrived in the Javier Vazquez trade. Wilkerson's success in the leadoff spot likely will keep him at the top of the lineup, though his power and selectivity probably are better suited for an RBI spot.

Position: LF/CF/1B/RF
Bats: L **Throws:** L
Ht: 6' 0" **Wt:** 205

Opening Day Age: 26
Born: 6/1/77 in Daviess, KY
ML Seasons: 0

Overall Statistics

	G	AB	R	H	D	T	HR	RBI	SB	BB	SO	Avg	OBP	Slg
'03	146	504	78	135	34	4	19	77	13	89	155	.268	.380	.464
Car.	346	1128	181	294	68	14	40	141	22	187	357	.261	.368	.452

Where He Hits the Ball

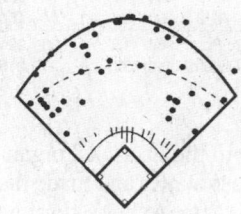 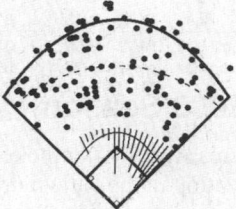

Vs. LHP   **Vs. RHP**

2003 Situational Stats

	AB	H	HR	RBI	Avg		AB	H	HR	RBI	Avg
Home	249	72	9	51	.289	LHP	128	36	3	19	.281
Road	255	63	10	26	.247	RHP	376	99	16	58	.263
First Half	277	76	10	47	.274	Sc Pos	130	36	7	59	.277
Scnd Half	227	59	9	30	.260	Clutch	78	13	3	12	.167

2003 Rankings (National League)

- 1st in most pitches seen per plate appearance (4.37)
- 2nd in lowest stolen-base percentage (56.5)
- 3rd in strikeouts
- 6th in caught stealing (10), errors in left field (4) and lowest percentage of swings put into play (34.3)
- 8th in fewest GDPs per GDP situation (4.8%)
- Led the Expos in caught stealing (10), walks, strikeouts, pitches seen (2,628), most pitches seen per plate appearance (4.37), highest percentage of pitches taken (60.7), fewest GDPs per GDP situation (4.8%), on-base percentage for a leadoff hitter (.424) and lowest percentage of swings on the first pitch (17.4)

Montreal

Luis Ayala

Position: RP
Bats: R **Throws:** R
Ht: 6' 2" **Wt:** 170

Opening Day Age: 26
Born: 1/12/78 in Los Mochis, Mexico
ML Seasons: 1
Pronunciation: eye-YA-lah

Overall Statistics

	W	L	Pct.	ERA	G	GS	Sv	IP	H	BB	SO	HR	Avg
'03	10	3	.769	2.92	65	0	5	71.0	65	13	46	8	.244
Car.	10	3	.769	2.92	65	0	5	71.0	65	13	46	8	.244

2003 Situational Stats

	W	L	ERA	Sv	IP		AB	H	HR	RBI	Avg
Home	6	1	2.75	4	39.1	LHB	101	34	5	14	.337
Road	4	2	3.13	1	31.2	RHB	165	31	3	14	.188
First Half	6	2	3.09	2	35.0	Sc Pos	68	15	4	23	.221
Scnd Half	4	1	2.75	3	36.0	Clutch	149	32	6	20	.215

2003 Season

Luis Ayala was plucked from the D'backs' organization in the Rule 5 draft last winter and made the team out of spring training. After a shaky start, he posted a streak of retiring 28 straight batters that spanned eight games from early to late May. In late June, he struggled through some inflammation in his right shoulder, but he was back to form in August. His 10 victories fell just one shy of the Expos' rookie record for a reliever.

Pitching, Defense & Hitting

Combined with a low-90s fastball, Ayala's short-armed delivery makes him very tough for righthanders to pick up. Lefthanders, however, had no trouble seeing his pitches and hit him very hard this year. He can cut or sink his fastball and his slider has a late, sharp break. He's an average fielder who almost never steps up to the plate.

2004 Outlook

The Expos' closing situation is a little cloudy, but Ayala, along with Rocky Biddle and Chad Cordero, will be the primary contenders. Ayala was comfortable in any role, so he probably will end up as the righthanded setup man. But if Biddle falters or Cordero proves he's not ready, Ayala shouldn't have much trouble in the stopper role.

Michael Barrett

Position: C
Bats: R **Throws:** R
Ht: 6' 2" **Wt:** 200

Opening Day Age: 27
Born: 10/22/76 in Atlanta, GA
ML Seasons: 6

Overall Statistics

	G	AB	R	H	D	T	HR	RBI	SB	BB	SO	Avg	OBP	Slg
'03	70	226	33	47	9	2	10	30	0	21	37	.208	.280	.398
Car.	542	1801	200	456	111	9	38	193	8	144	236	.253	.310	.388

2003 Situational Stats

	AB	H	HR	RBI	Avg		AB	H	HR	RBI	Avg
Home	102	19	5	15	.186	LHP	78	16	3	11	.205
Road	124	28	5	15	.226	RHP	148	31	7	19	.209
First Half	169	32	8	17	.189	Sc Pos	57	14	3	21	.246
Scnd Half	57	15	2	13	.263	Clutch	42	10	2	9	.238

2003 Season

Michael Barrett opened as the Expos' starting catcher, but self-imposed expectations of living up to a big salary increase appeared to cause him to press at the plate when he got off to a slow start. A bruised right index finger only made things worse. He straightened himself out in July, only to be sidelined by a strained hip flexor. Brian Schneider's solid play pushed Barrett to a backup role when he returned.

Hitting, Baserunning & Defense

Barrett's natural swing produces line drives to all fields, but his desire to hit more home runs fouled his swing and it wasn't until halfway through the season that he got it straightened out. He never lost his discipline at the plate, however. He has good speed for a catcher, but primarily runs station-to-station. He doesn't have a very strong arm and is nothing special when it comes to handling pitchers.

2004 Outlook

Despite hitting very well in July, Barrett and his offensive potential lost the starting job to Schneider's superior defensive skills in manager Frank Robinson's mind. Barrett may get the job back with a strong spring, but his best bet to get regular playing time in 2004 might be to return to third base.

Rocky Biddle

Position: RP
Bats: R **Throws:** R
Ht: 6' 3" **Wt:** 230

Opening Day Age: 27
Born: 5/21/76 in Las Vegas, NV
ML Seasons: 4

Overall Statistics

	W	L	Pct.	ERA	G	GS	Sv	IP	H	BB	SO	HR	Avg
'03	5	8	.385	4.65	73	0	34	71.2	71	40	54	10	.254
Car.	16	22	.421	5.09	151	32	35	300.2	311	139	210	44	.265

2003 Situational Stats

	W	L	ERA	Sv	IP		AB	H	HR	RBI	Avg
Home	5	3	4.07	19	42.0	LHB	120	29	3	15	.242
Road	0	5	5.46	15	29.2	RHB	159	42	7	29	.264
First Half	3	4	3.97	22	45.1	Sc Pos	93	22	3	37	.237
Scnd Half	2	4	5.81	12	26.1	Clutch	194	48	3	31	.247

2003 Season

When the Expos traded Bartolo Colon in order to pare salary in January 2003, Rocky Biddle was regarded as an afterthought in the deal. However, with a strong spring and no one else establishing themselves in the pen, Biddle found himself as the unlikely closer soon after the season began. He quickly became a fan favorite, and the team went so far as to arrange a hard-rock fanfare typical for elite closers like Trevor Hoffman or Mariano Rivera whenever he entered the game. Biddle pitched reasonably well until August, when he struggled and lost some closing opportunities.

Pitching, Defense & Hitting

Biddle throws a straight fastball that runs in the low 90s. He complements it with an 80-82 MPH big-breaking curve. He works quickly and relies on his infield to get most of his outs. His experience as a starter helped him become a decent defender off the mound, but his experience pitching in the American League did nothing to help him hit.

2004 Outlook

After Biddle's dreadful August, Robinson looked elsewhere for his closer and found two candidates in Luis Ayala and 2003 draftee Chad Cordero. Biddle likely will open 2004 as the closer, but he will face serious competition.

Ron Calloway

Position: LF/RF
Bats: L **Throws:** L
Ht: 6' 1" **Wt:** 210

Opening Day Age: 27
Born: 9/4/76 in San Jose, CA
ML Seasons: 1

Overall Statistics

	G	AB	R	H	D	T	HR	RBI	SB	BB	SO	Avg	OBP	Slg
'03	126	340	36	81	17	1	9	52	9	20	80	.238	.282	.374
Car.	126	340	36	81	17	1	9	52	9	20	80	.238	.282	.374

2003 Situational Stats

	AB	H	HR	RBI	Avg		AB	H	HR	RBI	Avg
Home	161	37	5	29	.230	LHP	59	10	1	7	.169
Road	179	44	4	23	.246	RHP	281	71	8	45	.253
First Half	197	47	8	36	.239	Sc Pos	101	30	3	38	.297
Scnd Half	143	34	1	16	.238	Clutch	72	14	4	13	.194

2003 Season

Ron Calloway got his big league chance when Vladimir Guerrero went down with back troubles. Calloway played pretty well initially, especially in Puerto Rico, where he had his best game on June 5, a 3-for-7 performance with a homer and five RBI. Unfortunately, he wasn't able to sustain that pace and was moved to the bench as a fourth outfielder once Guerrero returned.

Hitting, Baserunning & Defense

Calloway is not an overly toolsy player, but he has enough speed and power to be an effective fourth outfielder. He's capable of double-digit totals in homers and steals, but doesn't yet have the skills to translate that ability into regular playing time. He's not patient or overly selective and will chase pitches well out of the zone. Calloway does have very good instincts on the basepaths and is a low risk to make an out if given the green light. His defense in the outfield is solid but unremarkable.

2004 Outlook

With Terrmel Sledge and Val Pascucci slated to join the team next year, Calloway may find a tough time getting at-bats. The pressure will lighten some because Guerrero is gone, but only in the short term. Calloway will have to hone his skills to stay in the big leagues.

Montreal

Joey Eischen

Position: RP
Bats: L **Throws:** L
Ht: 6' 0" **Wt:** 215

Opening Day Age: 33
Born: 5/25/70 in West Covina, CA
ML Seasons: 7
Pronunciation: EYE-shen

Overall Statistics

	W	L	Pct.	ERA	G	GS	Sv	IP	H	BB	SO	HR	Avg
'03	2	2	.500	3.06	70	0	1	53.0	57	13	40	7	.282
Car.	9	6	.600	3.41	224	0	3	227.0	229	93	179	20	.264

2003 Situational Stats

	W	L	ERA	Sv	IP		AB	H	HR	RBI	Avg
Home	2	1	4.21	1	25.2	LHB	98	25	3	12	.255
Road	0	1	1.98	0	27.1	RHB	104	32	4	24	.308
First Half	1	1	2.34	0	34.2	Sc Pos	58	21	0	27	.362
Scnd Half	1	1	4.42	1	18.1	Clutch	68	12	2	9	.176

2003 Season

Joey Eischen followed up an excellent 2002 season with another strong performance in 2003. He battled through a deltoid strain in June and July, but was outstanding when healthy. He was second on the team in appearances despite the injury, and his ERA in the other four months was 2.12.

Pitching, Defense & Hitting

Groomed as a starter when he was an Expos prospect, Eischen uses his full repertoire as a reliever. He throws a fastball around 90 MPH, a two-plane slider, a curve and change, although he rarely uses the latter. He aggressively goes after hitters, pitching to all quadrants of the strike zone, but gets most of his outs on the ground. There doesn't appear to be any situation that intimidates him. However, becoming the regular closer or moving into the rotation don't appear to be options because righthanders simply hit him too well. He doesn't have much range off the mound, but is surehanded and has improved against the running game. He rarely finds a bat in his hands.

2004 Outlook

Eischen supplanted Scott Stewart as Montreal's primary late-inning lefty. Based on Eischen's numbers from the last two seasons, he has become one of the most effective lefthanded relievers.

Orlando Hernandez

Position: SP
Bats: R **Throws:** R
Ht: 6' 2" **Wt:** 220

Opening Day Age: 34
Born: 10/11/69 in Havana, Cuba
ML Seasons: 5
Pronunciation: her-NAN-dezz
Nickname: El Duque

Overall Statistics

	W	L	Pct.	ERA	G	GS	Sv	IP	H	BB	SO	HR	Avg
'03					Did Not Play								
Car.	53	38	.582	4.04	124	121	1	791.2	707	268	619	105	.237

2003 Situational Stats

	W	L	ERA	Sv	IP		AB	H	HR	RBI	Avg
Home	–	–	–	–	–	LHB	–	–	–	–	–
Road	–	–	–	–	–	RHB	–	–	–	–	–
First Half	–	–	–	–	–	Sc Pos	–	–	–	–	–
Scnd Half	–	–	–	–	–	Clutch	–	–	–	–	–

2003 Season

The Expos acquired Orlando Hernandez from the Yankees as part of the Bartolo Colon deal last winter. However, a tear in both the muscle and the rotator cuff in Hernandez' pitching shoulder sidelined him early in the spring. He spent the first month and a half of 2003 trying to rehab back into playing shape, but he finally decided in May that surgery was the only option. He felt he could return in September, but doctors thought otherwise.

Pitching, Defense & Hitting

Hernandez' repertoire—fastball, curve, slider and change—doesn't feature any outstanding pitches, but he is able to throw them all for strikes with so many different arm angles that it looks like he has about 20 pitches from which to choose. He's an agile fielder, but because of his high leg kick, he struggles to slow the running game. He has just one career hit.

2004 Outlook

As expected, Hernandez' rehab is progressing slowly, but he should be ready to pitch by spring. His salary should keep him in Montreal, and depending upon who remains after the impending salary purge, he could be anything from the Expos' No. 3 guy to their Opening Day starter.

Jose Macias

Position: LF/3B/CF
Bats: B **Throws:** R
Ht: 5' 8" **Wt:** 190

Opening Day Age: 32
Born: 1/25/72 in
Panama City, Panama
ML Seasons: 5
Pronunciation:
muh-SEE-us

Overall Statistics

	G	AB	R	H	D	T	HR	RBI	SB	BB	SO	Avg	OBP	Slg
'03	111	272	31	65	15	2	4	22	4	11	45	.239	.273	.353
Car.	449	1275	163	325	63	14	22	138	35	82	181	.255	.302	.378

2003 Situational Stats

	AB	H	HR	RBI	Avg			AB	H	HR	RBI	Avg
Home	149	43	3	15	.289	LHP		112	28	2	11	.250
Road	123	22	1	7	.179	RHP		160	37	2	11	.231
First Half	160	42	3	12	.263	Sc Pos		76	19	0	18	.250
Scnd Half	112	23	1	10	.205	Clutch		60	15	3	9	.250

2003 Season

Jose Macias was the Expos' top utilityman, playing second base, third base and all three outfield positions. He had a strong April in limited playing time, but that was offset by a dreadful August and September where he posted an on-base percentage under .200.

Hitting, Baserunning & Defense

Macias is a slap-hitter who starts swinging once he steps out of the dugout. He does make contact and is an excellent bunter, so his bat does have value in certain situations. And unlike many slap-hitters, he's not completely devoid of power; if given regular playing time he could reach double digits in homers and hit 25-30 doubles. He has decent speed, but his inability to read pitchers prevents him from getting the green light. His defense at five positions ranges from average to very good, with second base and center field being his best. He has a strong arm and good instincts for the ball.

2004 Outlook

While Macias isn't overly productive at the plate, his defensive versatility will keep him in the majors. He needs to develop more patience if he's to take advantage of his physical tools, which could make him one of the better utility players in the league.

Scott Stewart

Position: RP
Bats: R **Throws:** L
Ht: 6' 2" **Wt:** 225

Opening Day Age: 28
Born: 8/14/75 in
Stoughton, MA
ML Seasons: 3

Overall Statistics

	W	L	Pct.	ERA	G	GS	Sv	IP	H	BB	SO	HR	Avg
'03	3	1	.750	3.98	51	0	0	43.0	52	13	29	5	.306
Car.	10	4	.714	3.55	180	0	20	154.2	144	48	135	14	.247

2003 Situational Stats

	W	L	ERA	Sv	IP			AB	H	HR	RBI	Avg
Home	1	1	4.07	0	24.1	LHB		60	17	2	7	.283
Road	2	0	3.86	0	18.2	RHB		110	35	3	16	.318
First Half	3	1	3.35	0	37.2	Sc Pos		53	14	1	18	.264
Scnd Half	0	0	8.44	0	5.1	Clutch		68	21	2	9	.309

2003 Season

Scott Stewart's recovery from offseason elbow surgery went unexpectedly slow, and he wasn't able to pitch at all during spring training. His season was a roller-coaster ride that crashed at the end. He pitched very well in April, only to sour in May. He returned to form in June, only to undergo an appendectomy in July that sidelined him until September. Once back, he struggled terribly.

Pitching, Defense & Hitting

Whether it was due to the elbow surgery or Stewart's reluctance to let himself go when he threw, his sinking fastball simply didn't have the same life or velocity it once showed. He thus was forced to use his cutter and slider more. He also lacked the aggressiveness to put hitters away when he was ahead in the count, often nibbling at the corners in search of the perfect pitch. He does a very good job at holding runners, but his glovework is just average. He almost never comes to the plate, with no hits in four career at-bats.

2004 Outlook

Stewart slipped behind Joey Eischen as the primary lefty out of the pen. The Expos are hoping that Stewart's struggles were only the temporary results of his injuries, and not a cause for long-term concern.

Montreal

Claudio Vargas

Position: SP
Bats: R **Throws:** R
Ht: 6' 3" **Wt:** 225

Opening Day Age: 25
Born: 6/19/78 in
Valverde Mao, DR
ML Seasons: 1

Overall Statistics

	W	L	Pct.	ERA	G	GS	Sv	IP	H	BB	SO	HR	Avg
'03	6	8	.429	4.34	23	20	0	114.0	111	41	62	16	.255
Car.	6	8	.429	4.34	23	20	0	114.0	111	41	62	16	.255

2003 Situational Stats

	W	L	ERA	Sv	IP		AB	H	HR	RBI	Avg
Home	3	3	5.01	0	50.1	LHB	196	53	4	16	.270
Road	3	5	3.82	0	63.2	RHB	240	58	12	37	.242
First Half	6	5	3.59	0	92.2	Sc Pos	99	25	3	35	.253
Scnd Half	0	3	7.59	0	21.1	Clutch	15	7	3	7	.467

2003 Season

Claudio Vargas was called up from Triple-A after Tony Armas Jr. went down for the season. Vargas was brilliant for his first three months, winning five games and posting an ERA of 2.74. However, the good times came to a crashing end in July and August, and a sore shoulder landed him on the disabled list. He rediscovered his early form in September and finished the season with six score-less innings.

Pitching, Defense & Hitting

Vargas showed surprising maturity for a young pitcher. He is poised, varies the speed on his pitch-es and works all quadrants of the strike zone. His fastball is straight, but he keeps hitters off-stride by running it anywhere between 90-94 MPH. He also throws a tight curve and a decent change. His glovework is mechanical, but because most of his outs come on flyballs, that usually doesn't come into play. A bat has little value in Vargas' hands.

2004 Outlook

Montreal was very high on Vargas, and he did nothing in 2003 to disappoint. His performance in September went a long way towards assuring that he will get a shot at the rotation in 2004, and that the Expos' staff won't be crippled when manage-ment traded Javier Vazquez.

Todd Zeile

Position: 3B/1B
Bats: R **Throws:** R
Ht: 6' 1" **Wt:** 200

Opening Day Age: 38
Born: 9/9/65 in Van Nuys, CA
ML Seasons: 15
Pronunciation: ZEAL

Overall Statistics

G	AB	R	H	D	T	HR	RBI	SB	BB	SO	Avg	OBP	Slg
100	299	40	68	10	2	11	42	1	34	54	.227	.308	.385
2021	7225	956	1923	381	23	244	1075	53	901	1196	.266	.347	.427

2003 Situational Stats

	AB	H	HR	RBI	Avg		AB	H	HR	RBI	Avg
Home	150	36	7	29	.240	LHP	98	23	7	21	.235
Road	149	32	4	13	.215	RHP	201	45	4	21	.224
First Half	169	33	6	22	.195	Sc Pos	82	17	3	30	.207
Scnd Half	130	35	5	20	.269	Clutch	49	6	1	5	.122

2003 Season

Released on August 18 by the Yankees due to over-crowding at the corners, Todd Zeile found quick employment when the Expos called two days later. He got off to a very hot start in Montreal and played a significant role in the team's wild-card push. This season will be memorable for Zeile because he broke two long-standing major league records: most teams for whom he hit a home run (11) and most home runs for a player with a last name begin-ning with the letter Z (244), formerly held by Gus Zernial.

Hitting, Baserunning & Defense

Zeile's guess-hitting is sometimes mistaken for dis-cipline at the plate. His primary instinct is to pull everything, but he will wait back and go the other way when the count goes deep. The one-time catch-er has below-average speed and runs station to sta-tion. His third-base defense on the turf was better than expected, but his best position still is first, where his below-average arm is not regularly tested.

2004 Outlook

Zeile showed that he still could be a valuable play-er, although he seemed to wear down a bit after only a month of playing every day. The Expos may try to bring him back, but his value is strictly as a bench player.

Other Montreal Expos

Hector Almonte (Pos: RHP, Age: 28)

	W	L	Pct.	ERA	G	GS	Sv	IP	H	BB	SO	HR	Avg
'03	1	2	.333	7.12	35	0	0	36.2	43	24	32	5	.295
Car.	1	4	.200	6.27	50	0	0	51.2	63	30	40	6	.307

Almonte had an 8.22 ERA in seven relief appearances for Boston when he cleared waivers and opted for free agency in July. The Expos signed him shortly thereafter. He was only slightly better in Montreal. 2004 Outlook: C

Jamey Carroll (Pos: 3B/2B/SS, Age: 30, Bats: R)

	G	AB	R	H	D	T	HR	RBI	SB	BB	SO	Avg	OBP	Slg
'03	105	227	31	59	10	1	1	10	5	19	39	.260	.323	.326
Car.	121	298	47	81	15	4	2	16	6	23	51	.272	.328	.369

Carroll took over as Montreal's starting third baseman in July and early August, but hit .258 with only one homer and three RBI in the two months. He hit .353 as a pinch-hitter in 17 at-bats. 2004 Outlook: C

Matt Cepicky (Pos: LF, Age: 26, Bats: L)

	G	AB	R	H	D	T	HR	RBI	SB	BB	SO	Avg	OBP	Slg
'03	5	8	0	2	1	0	0	0	0	0	2	.250	.250	.375
Car.	37	82	7	18	4	0	3	15	0	4	23	.220	.256	.378

The Expos were looking for Cepicky to win a job as a reserve, but he hit just .220 in the spring. He went on to hit .301 at Triple-A Edmonton, but had just seven homers and 31 walks in 442 at-bats. 2004 Outlook: C

Vic Darensbourg (Pos: LHP, Age: 33)

	W	L	Pct.	ERA	G	GS	Sv	IP	H	BB	SO	HR	Avg
'03	0	0	—	8.00	9	0	0	9.0	17	1	4	2	.386
Car.	7	15	.318	5.10	280	0	2	273.2	293	116	219	31	.275

Injury prevented Darensbourg from competing for a job out of spring training. He appeared in three games for the Rockies before he was released in July. The Expos signed him a couple of weeks later. 2004 Outlook: C

Scott Downs (Pos: LHP, Age: 28)

	W	L	Pct.	ERA	G	GS	Sv	IP	H	BB	SO	HR	Avg
'03	0	1	.000	15.00	1	1	0	3.0	5	3	4	2	.357
Car.	4	4	.500	5.58	20	20	0	100.0	127	44	67	15	.314

Downs allowed just one run in 6.2 innings in the spring but failed to make the club in his second year back from Tommy John surgery. He made it back to the majors for the first time since 2000 in August. 2004 Outlook: C

Tim Drew (Pos: RHP, Age: 25)

	W	L	Pct.	ERA	G	GS	Sv	IP	H	BB	SO	HR	Avg
'03	0	2	.000	12.46	6	1	0	8.2	12	8	3	3	.343
Car.	2	4	.333	7.60	24	11	2	68.2	92	34	33	14	.323

Drew looked like one of the better bets for saves on the Expos after recording two saves with a 2.81 ERA in 2002, but he did not make the team out of the spring. He did not fare well in his callup. 2004 Outlook: B

Anthony Ferrari (Pos: LHP, Age: 25)

	W	L	Pct.	ERA	G	GS	Sv	IP	H	BB	SO	HR	Avg
'03	0	0	—	6.75	4	0	0	4.0	4	5	1	1	.267
Car.	0	0	—	6.75	4	0	0	4.0	4	5	1	1	.267

Ferrari made four appearances with the Expos after being called up in June to help fill a need for their tired bullpen. He was 7-2 with five saves in relief for Double-A Harrisburg and Triple-A Edmonton. 2004 Outlook: C

Edwards Guzman (Pos: 3B/1B, Age: 27, Bats: L)

	G	AB	R	H	D	T	HR	RBI	SB	BB	SO	Avg	OBP	Slg
'03	52	146	15	35	5	0	1	14	0	5	17	.240	.263	.295
Car.	127	276	23	63	11	0	4	21	0	10	37	.228	.253	.312

Guzman was traded from San Francisco to Montreal before the season. He was the starting third baseman in the middle of the season and hit .240 with a .558 OPS in 146 at-bats. Tampa Bay signed him in November. 2004 Outlook: C

Bryan Hebson (Pos: RHP, Age: 28)

	W	L	Pct.	ERA	G	GS	Sv	IP	H	BB	SO	HR	Avg
'03	0	0	—	13.50	2	0	0	2.0	4	1	1	1	.444
Car.	0	0	—	13.50	2	0	0	2.0	4	1	1	1	.444

The Red Sox and Expos basically traded righthanded relievers in July when Hector Almonte signed with Montreal after being let go by Boston, and the Red Sox used the open 40-man roster spot to snare Hebson. 2004 Outlook: C

Sun-Woo Kim (Pos: RHP, Age: 26)

	W	L	Pct.	ERA	G	GS	Sv	IP	H	BB	SO	HR	Avg
'03	0	1	.000	8.36	4	3	0	14.0	24	8	5	6	.407
Car.	3	3	.500	5.66	43	10	0	105.0	130	43	61	12	.308

Kim gave up 12 earned runs and walked seven in three starts with the Expos. He was blasted by manager Frank Robinson after one of those games in July and was sent down for good. 2004 Outlook: C

Eric Knott (Pos: LHP, Age: 29)

	W	L	Pct.	ERA	G	GS	Sv	IP	H	BB	SO	HR	Avg
'03	1	2	.333	5.12	13	1	0	19.1	23	6	17	2	.295
Car.	1	3	.250	4.50	16	2	0	24.0	31	6	21	2	.307

Knott spent his career in the Diamondbacks' organization before signing with Montreal prior to last year. He had a 5.12 ERA in 13 appearances for the Expos. The Dodgers signed him in November. 2004 Outlook: C

Henry Mateo (Pos: 2B, Age: 27, Bats: B)

	G	AB	R	H	D	T	HR	RBI	SB	BB	SO	Avg	OBP	Slg
'03	100	154	29	37	3	1	0	7	11	11	38	.240	.304	.273
Car.	127	186	31	44	4	2	0	7	13	13	45	.237	.297	.280

Mateo hit .451 in spring training and reached career-highs in virtually every category with the Expos. He went 3-for-5 on May 1 to raise his average to .474, but hit just .207 the rest of the way. 2004 Outlook: C

Jose Mercedes (Pos: RHP, Age: 33)

	W	L	Pct.	ERA	G	GS	Sv	IP	H	BB	SO	HR	Avg
'03	0	0	–	0.00	5	0	0	7.1	6	5	3	0	.231
Car.	33	39	.458	4.75	145	79	0	583.0	617	223	310	75	.274

The Expos signed Mercedes, an eight-year veteran journeyman, in September. The 33-year-old went 14-6 with an ERA of 3.71 in 22 starts with Saltillo of the Mexican League before he was picked up by Montreal. 2004 Outlook: C

Britt Reames (Pos: RHP, Age: 30)

	W	L	Pct.	ERA	G	GS	Sv	IP	H	BB	SO	HR	Avg
'03	0	0	–	27.00	2	0	0	1.1	4	2	1	0	.500
Car.	7	13	.350	5.00	93	26	0	205.0	205	111	194	28	.261

Reames hasn't pitched well since the Expos acquired him from the Cardinals prior to 2001. After spending most of the previous three seasons in the majors, he was only up for a week and a half in 2003. 2004 Outlook: C

Dan Smith (Pos: RHP, Age: 28)

	W	L	Pct.	ERA	G	GS	Sv	IP	H	BB	SO	HR	Avg
'03	2	2	.500	5.26	32	0	0	37.2	42	18	35	11	.280
Car.	7	12	.368	5.23	87	17	2	177.1	182	81	142	29	.270

Smith had rough stretches starting in late April and again in early June, when he gave up a total of 14 runs in 7.2 innings. Otherwise, he had a 2.40 ERA before undergoing season-ending shoulder surgery. 2004 Outlook: C

Fernando Tatis (Pos: 3B, Age: 29, Bats: R)

	G	AB	R	H	D	T	HR	RBI	SB	BB	SO	Avg	OBP	Slg
'03	53	175	15	34	6	0	2	15	2	18	40	.194	.281	.263
Car.	663	2317	339	604	127	8	90	339	43	258	560	.261	.344	.439

It was another injured-riddled campaign for Tatis, who missed three and a half months with a strained groin and then later with chest inflammation. He became a free agent after the season. 2004 Outlook: C

T.J. Tucker (Pos: RHP, Age: 25)

	W	L	Pct.	ERA	G	GS	Sv	IP	H	BB	SO	HR	Avg
'03	2	3	.400	4.73	45	7	0	80.0	90	20	47	8	.278
Car.	8	7	.533	4.79	104	9	4	148.1	170	54	91	18	.286

Tucker enjoyed a promising rookie season in 2002, and despite decent enough stuff, the righthander hasn't been able to establish himself in a role. A little more tenacity and fire might help. 2004 Outlook: C

Joe Vitiello (Pos: LF/1B, Age: 33, Bats: R)

	G	AB	R	H	D	T	HR	RBI	SB	BB	SO	Avg	OBP	Slg
'03	38	76	12	26	6	0	3	13	0	7	14	.342	.407	.539
Car.	282	693	76	172	35	1	26	104	2	80	165	.248	.335	.414

Vitiello made the most of his first major league action since 2000 by batting .342 with a .946 OPS in 38 games. Montreal acquired Vitiello from the Giants for Ben Washburn in May. 2004 Outlook: C

Montreal Expos Minor League Prospects

Organization Overview:

When it came time to call up the organization's top prospects for the September playoff run, the Expos' 29 competing owners cried poverty and denied the team reinforcements. Angered by the lack of support, the major league players leveraged their split schedule next season for an agreement with the owners that will assure both callups and enough salary cap to keep most of the team. Despite unprecedented salary restraints, the Expos still manage to keep their farm system fairly healthy. Last year's top pick, Clint Everts, had a strong season, further refining his fastball and changeup to accompany one of the best curveballs in the minors. The organization also added 19-year-old Caribbean phenom Francisco Guzman, who some compare to a young Bernie Williams.

Chad Cordero

Position: P **Opening Day Age:** 22
Bats: R **Throws:** R **Born:** 3/18/82 in Upland,
Ht: 6' 0" **Wt:** 195 CA

Recent Statistics

	W	L	ERA	G	GS	Sv	IP	H	R	BB	SO	HR
2003 A Brevard Cty	1	1	2.05	19	0	6	26.1	17	8	10	17	1
2003 NL Montreal	1	0	1.64	12	0	1	11.0	4	2	3	12	1

The organization felt it needed a quick return on its 2003 draft. By taking Cordero with the 20th overall pick, the Expos felt they could get a major league-ready reliever with their first choice. Cordero proved their assessment correct by spending fewer than two months in the high Class-A Florida State League before a promotion to the majors. He showed no rookie jitters in his debut, posting scoreless outings in all but one of his 12 appearances. Cordero has a low-90s fastball and a terrific slider that's been compared to that of Anaheim's Francisco Rodriguez. He was a closer throughout his college career and his opportunity to close in the majors should come soon.

Shawn Hill

Position: P **Opening Day Age:** 22
Bats: R **Throws:** R **Born:** 4/28/81 in
Ht: 6' 2" **Wt:** 185 Mississauga, ON,
Canada

Recent Statistics

	W	L	ERA	G	GS	Sv	IP	H	R	BB	SO	HR
2002 A Clinton	12	7	3.44	25	25	0	146.2	149	75	35	99	7
2003 A Brevard Cty	9	4	2.62	21	20	0	123.2	118	47	26	63	3
2003 AA Harrisburg	3	1	3.54	4	4	0	20.1	23	12	11	12	0

Hill struggled with mechanics his first few starts in 2003 at high Class-A Brevard County, but once he stopped rushing forward on his delivery, he ran off a

solid 7-3 record and a 2.25 ERA. The former high school shortstop is a very good athlete and should be able to help himself as he advances up the minor league ladder. He throws a 90-91 MPH sinking fastball, complemented by a good curve and change. Like fellow extreme groundballer Zach Day, Hill is very hard to elevate and should benefit from Montreal's excellent infield defense once he makes the team, probably no later than spring 2005.

Josh McKinley

Position: 2B **Opening Day Age:** 24
Bats: B **Throws:** R **Born:** 9/14/79 in York, PA
Ht: 6' 2" **Wt:** 190

Recent Statistics

	G	AB	R	H	D	T	HR	RBI	SB	BB	SO	Avg
2002 AA Harrisburg	103	325	40	76	17	0	7	33	2	42	81	.234
2003 AA Harrisburg	126	458	82	132	33	2	15	75	17	60	86	.288

The Expos' first-round pick in 1998 was drafted as a shortstop, but McKinley has been moved to third, then to second base in 2002, and finally to catcher in the Arizona Fall League. Despite having no previous experience behind the plate, he impressed the front office with his fall performance. He has quick feet, an accurate arm—although it's probably below average strength-wise—and a good feel for calling a game. After working extensively with Expos hitting instructors this spring, his second season at Double-A showed considerable improvement, largely due to taking a more aggressive approach at the plate. He could get his big league chance as soon as mid- to late 2004.

Val Pascucci

Position: OF **Opening Day Age:** 25
Bats: R **Throws:** R **Born:** 11/17/78 in
Ht: 6' 6" **Wt:** 235 Bellflower, CA

Recent Statistics

	G	AB	R	H	D	T	HR	RBI	SB	BB	SO	Avg
2002 AA Harrisburg	137	459	73	108	14	1	27	82	2	93	115	.235
2003 AAA Edmonton	138	459	80	129	29	1	15	85	3	101	132	.281

After struggling to hit Double-A pitching for two seasons, Pascucci showed he was ready to pit his skills against major league hurlers with an excellent 2003 campaign in Triple-A. His strike-zone judgment improved to the point of being voted the best in the Pacific Coast League by opposing managers. While his home-run totals dropped this season, he was able to maintain his slugging percentage by increasing his doubles output. Pascucci covers the plate well and generates line-drive power to all fields. He has a very good arm and enough speed for either outfield corner. Pascucci should battle newly acquired Juan Rivera in spring for the starting right-field spot in 2004.

Juan Rivera

Position: OF   **Opening Day Age:** 25
Bats: R **Throws:** R   **Born:** 7/3/78 in Caracas,
Ht: 6' 2" **Wt:** 170   VZ

Recent Statistics

	G	AB	R	H	D	T	HR	RBI	SB	BB	SO	Avg
2003 AAA Columbus	79	308	47	100	21	0	7	37	1	26	37	.325
2003 AL New York	57	173	22	46	14	0	7	26	0	10	27	.266

Signed in 1996 by the Yankees, Rivera led the Rookie-level Gulf Coast League in homers and RBI in 1998. Then he didn't make much noise until a .322-28-98 season between Double-A Norwich and Triple-A Columbus in 2001. After a fast start at Columbus in 2002, Rivera took over right field in New York, but fractured a kneecap three days later and Raul Mondesi was acquired. A starting job in the majors has been elusive ever since—until Rivera was dealt to Montreal in December's Javier Vazquez trade. An excellent fielder with a strong arm, Rivera will compete for the Expos' right-field job this spring. While he hasn't had much success as a big league hitter, he may thrive playing regularly without the pressures of New York.

Terrmel Sledge

Position: OF   **Opening Day Age:** 27
Bats: L **Throws:** L   **Born:** 3/18/77 in
Ht: 6' 0" **Wt:** 180   Fayetteville, NC

Recent Statistics

	G	AB	R	H	D	T	HR	RBI	SB	BB	SO	Avg
2002 AA Harrisburg	102	396	74	119	18	6	8	43	11	55	70	.301
2002 AAA Ottawa	24	80	12	21	5	2	1	11	1	11	15	.263
2003 AAA Edmonton	131	497	95	161	26	9	22	92	13	61	93	.324

Sledge certainly would have been a big boost to the Expos in September. After a strong 2002 and AFL season, he followed up by leading the Triple-A Pacific Coast League in runs scored. The Expos asked him to stay back from the plate a little more this year and concentrate on driving the ball. The result was that he doubled his home runs and showed much better plate coverage. The one-time player to be named in the Chris Widger trade has above-average tools across the board and projects to be a solid regular outfielder. Barring a disastrous spring, he will open in left field in Montreal.

Seung Song

Position: P   **Opening Day Age:** 23
Bats: R **Throws:** R   **Born:** 6/29/80 in Pusan,
Ht: 6' 1" **Wt:** 192   South Korea

Recent Statistics

	W	L	ERA	G	GS	Sv	IP	H	R	BB	SO	HR
2002 AA Trenton	7	7	4.39	21	21	0	108.2	106	61	37	116	11
2002 AA Harrisburg	0	0	0.00	1	1	0	5.0	5	2	0	5	0
2003 AA Harrisburg	5	2	2.35	13	13	0	72.2	55	26	24	44	5
2003 AAA Edmonton	7	2	3.79	13	13	0	73.2	69	34	33	40	6

Before the 2002 season, Song was viewed as Boston's best pitching prospect, but a deadline deal for Cliff Floyd brought him to Montreal. This year was a landmark year for Song, as he not only participated in the Futures Game, but threw a no-hitter versus Double-A Erie on 119 pitches. Brent Strom, the Expos' minor league pitching instructor, revamped his delivery to put less stress on his shoulder, and the results were positive. Song posted career highs in innings pitched and wins. His fastball is in the low 90s, and he complements it with a high-70s curve and an average change. He has good pitching instincts, a consistent release point and excellent command of his fastball and curve.

Chris Young

Position: P   **Opening Day Age:** 24
Bats: R **Throws:** R   **Born:** 5/25/79 in Dallas,
Ht: 6' 11" **Wt:** 255   TX

Recent Statistics

	W	L	ERA	G	GS	Sv	IP	H	R	BB	SO	HR
2002 A Hickory	11	9	3.11	26	26	0	144.2	127	57	34	136	11
2003 A Brevard Cty	5	2	1.62	8	8	0	50.0	26	9	5	39	3
2003 AA Harrisburg	4	4	4.01	15	15	0	83.0	83	39	22	64	9

Young began the season on the disabled list with shoulder tendinitis, but he was dominant when he returned, capping off his high Class-A Florida State League season with seven innings of one-hit ball versus Palm Beach. He continued to pitch well upon his promotion to Double-A, but his home-run rate was somewhat troubling. Young has excellent command of a low-90s heater and an above-average curve. Acquired from the Pirates in December 2002 in exchange for Matt Herges, he returned to his natural delivery and made a case for a 2004 major league debut.

Others to Watch

First baseman **Larry Broadway** (23) won the home-run derby at the Class-A South Atlantic League All-Star game before finishing at Double-A Harrisburg. He makes good contact and drives the ball a long way with an easy swing that has natural loft. . . Righty **Roy Corcoran** (23) has very quick arm action similar to that of Chad Cordero's. Corcoran also possesses good command down in the zone of a 91-92 MPH fastball that both runs and sinks. . . Lefthanded starter **Mike Hinckley** (21) ranked No. 2 in the Expos' farm system coming into the season. After a sluggish start, he finished the year on a 4-0, 0.72 ERA tear. He rates above average in maturity, work ethic and three pitches (fastball, change, curve). . . Righthanded starter **Josh Karp** (24) battled strep throat and didn't make his first start until mid-April. He struggled in his second season in Double-A, but his combination of a 94-MPH fastball, tight 12-to-6 curve and circle change still intrigues the Expos. . . Righthander **Chris Schroder** (25) has become a prospect as a reliever. The former academic All-American at Oklahoma City University gets hitters out with good deception, a moving low-90s fastball, a slider and an excellent changeup.

Shea Stadium

Offense

Only one National League ballpark surrendered fewer home runs per game than Shea Stadium's paltry 1.7 dingers per contest. The ballpark, which seats 57,393 and was designed to expand to 90,000, remains unenclosed beyond the outfield walls, thereby allowing games early and late in the season to be affected by the frequent strong winds from Flushing Bay. Lefthanded hitters fare better than righthanded hitters at Shea, particularly in the power department, since the scoreboard, nestled in right-center, blocks some of the wind and allows lefties to pull pitches for home runs.

Defense

Shea offers symmetrical fences on natural grass that produces one of the slowest surfaces in the major leagues. The foul lines are relatively deep at 338 feet, which leads to bloop doubles and a better-than-average chance for triples on balls hit down the right-field line.

Who It Helps the Most

Shea has been one of the top four pitchers' parks for the past four years. The facility features above-average strikeout rates and below-average walk rates, which tends to shave a couple of points off batting averages over the course of the campaign. Cliff Floyd, a lefthanded hitter, thrived in his new home park.

Who It Hurts the Most

Righthanded power hitters continue to curse Shea. Mike Piazza likely would have 30 or more additional career home runs if not for playing half his games here for almost six full seasons. Piazza ranks third all-time for homers by a Met at Shea with just 76 (compared to 105 longballs during that time on the road).

Rookies & Newcomers

Tom Glavine admitted last year that Shea's generous dimensions played a role in his decision to sign with the Mets. While the Mets are suddenly crowded at first base, lefthanded hitter Craig Brazell will add some punch to the lineup when given the opportunity.

Dimensions: LF-338, LCF-378, CF-410, RCF-378, RF-338

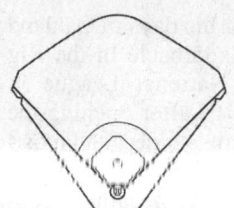

Capacity: 57,393

Elevation: 20 feet

Surface: Grass

Foul Territory: Average

Park Factors

2003 Season

	Home Games			Away Games			
	Mets	Opp	Total	Mets	Opp	Total	Index
G	74	74	148	68	68	136	
Avg	.256	.266	.261	.239	.275	.257	102
AB	2415	2564	4979	2279	2244	4523	101
R	291	336	627	276	308	584	99
H	618	683	1301	544	617	1161	103
2B	128	155	283	107	120	227	113
3B	9	14	23	14	25	39	54
HR	48	71	119	56	70	126	86
BB	229	266	495	219	231	450	100
SO	447	458	905	463	353	816	101
E	59	50	109	40	52	92	109
E-Infield	49	45	94	35	42	77	112
LHB-Avg	.270	.255	.263	.257	.250	.254	103
LHB-HR	24	23	47	27	15	42	96
RHB-Avg	.246	.273	.260	.226	.287	.258	101
RHB-HR	24	48	72	29	55	84	81

2001-2003

	Home Games			Away Games			
	Mets	Opp	Total	Mets	Opp	Total	Index
G	218	218	436	211	211	422	
Avg	.248	.258	.253	.253	.269	.261	97
AB	7177	7649	14826	7255	7000	14255	101
R	848	961	1809	904	961	1865	94
H	1770	1972	3751	1839	1881	3720	98
2B	340	378	718	356	373	729	95
3B	29	44	73	30	54	84	84
HR	177	230	407	194	225	419	93
BB	689	693	1382	685	666	1351	98
SO	1365	1548	2913	1430	1292	2722	103
E	175	156	331	144	153	297	108
E-Infield	146	133	279	122	125	247	109
LHB-Avg	.256	.255	.256	.250	.255	.253	101
LHB-HR	79	81	160	70	67	137	112
RHB-Avg	.242	.259	.252	.256	.276	.266	95
RHB-HR	98	149	247	124	158	282	84

2003 Rankings (National League)
- Second-highest infield-error factor
- Third-highest double factor
- Third-lowest triple factor
- Third-lowest RHB home-run factor

Art Howe

2003 Season

Art Howe may be longing for his days in Oakland after experiencing last year's debacle in the Big Apple. The Mets led the National League in games started by rookies (510) after opening the campaign with one of the game's oldest and most-expensive rosters. The team alleviated the problem at midseason when turnover became a constant, with New York discarding Roberto Alomar, Armando Benitez, Rey Sanchez and Jeromy Burnitz. The Mets ended the season with 19 losses in their final 23 games and finished in last place in the NL East with 95 defeats, their most setbacks since 1993.

Offense

With Mike Piazza sidelined for most of last year and numerous veterans failing to earn their keep, Howe had little to work with. The Mets scored only 642 runs, the second fewest in the NL, good for an average of 4.0 runs per game. Known for his willingness to wait for three-run homers instead of taking chances, Howe felt helpless guiding a team that tied the Dodgers for last in the majors in home runs.

Pitching & Defense

Although Howe said he thought the starting pitching was one of the lone positives of the 2003 season, the Mets reassigned pitching coach Vern Ruhle at the end of the campaign. Still, there were many times last year in which the Mets' starters tried to be too perfect with their pitches. Only four NL teams made more errors than the Mets' 118 miscues, most of which can be attributed to poor fundamentals.

2004 Outlook

Howe never had security with Oakland and should feel the same way in New York, even though he has three years remaining on his $9.4 million contract. The departure of some high-priced underachievers should give him some time and more freedom to work with a younger group of players trying to prove themselves. While the pressure is always on to win in New York, the Mets will have difficulty reaching the break-even mark in 2004.

Born: 12/15/46 in Pittsburgh, PA

Playing Experience: 1974-1985, Pit, Hou, StL

Managerial Experience: 13 seasons

Manager Statistics

Year	Team, Lg	W	L	Pct	GB	Finish
2003	New York, NL	66	95	.410	34.5	5th East
13 Seasons		1058	1046	.503	–	–

2003 Starting Pitchers by Days Rest

	<=3	4	5	6+
Mets Starts	3	76	49	23
Mets ERA	1.45	4.17	4.94	5.25
NL Avg Starts	2	84	43	23
NL ERA	5.00	4.23	4.42	4.68

2003 Situational Stats

	Art Howe	NL Average
Hit & Run Success %	26.2	32.7
Stolen Base Success %	69.3	68.9
Platoon Pct.	58.9	52.0
Defensive Subs	39	19
High-Pitch Outings	6	8
Quick/Slow Hooks	16/16	20/12
Sacrifice Attempts	108	93

2003 Rankings (National League)

- 1st in intentional walks (56) and saves with over 1 inning pitched (11)
- 2nd in sacrifice bunt attempts and defensive substitutions
- 3rd in sacrifice-bunt percentage (83.3%), starting lineups used (133), slow hooks and starts on three days rest

Pedro Astacio

2003 Season

Throughout the 2002 campaign, the Mets held their breath regarding Pedro Astacio's lingering shoulder troubles that included a frayed labrum. Despite the ailment, he threw more than 190 innings to guarantee a $6 million contract for 2003. Everything unraveled, however, early last year when the righthander missed most of April with biceps tendinitis and sat out the final four months of the season after undergoing surgery to repair torn cartilage in his right shoulder.

Pitching

Astacio is at his best when he trusts his stuff, which leads to plus command of his 90-MPH sinking fastball and a big-breaking curveball. He also throws a good changeup with solid depth and fade and mixes his three offerings well to keep hitters off-balance. The righthander is capable of being an innings-eater when he keeps his pitches down in the strike zone, resulting in numerous groundball outs. As effective as Astacio can be, he also can falter by trying to be too fine with his pitches, especially when his command is inconsistent. He is prone to surrendering a plethora of longballs when he leaves his heater up and his breaking ball falls flat.

Defense & Hitting

Despite his injuries, Astacio remains an above-average athlete. He covers his position well with good range from the mound. Astacio has soft hands, fast reflexes and good overall quickness. He holds runners well with his quick delivery and a solid pickoff move that will be called a balk a couple times per season. Astacio was one of the best bunters among the Mets' pitchers, and registered 10 hits during the 2002 season.

2004 Outlook

Astacio is a free agent and is not expected to re-sign with the Mets. For the second time in three years, he must prove his shoulder is healthy in order to receive an extended look in spring training. With the dearth of pitching in the major leagues, he will find a taker, although a long-term deal will not be forthcoming.

Position: SP
Bats: R **Throws:** R
Ht: 6' 2" **Wt:** 210

Opening Day Age: 34
Born: 11/28/69 in Hato Mayor, DR
ML Seasons: 12
Pronunciation: ah-STAH-see-oh

Overall Statistics

	W	L	Pct.	ERA	G	GS	Sv	IP	H	BB	SO	HR	Avg
'03	3	2	.600	7.36	7	7	0	36.2	47	18	20	8	.311
Car.	118	109	.520	4.58	346	303	0	1971.0	2037	653	1538	258	.269

2003 Pitching Profile

	Pedro Astacio	NL Average
Overall Strike %	60.0	62.4
1st Pitch Strike %	62.3	58.4
Ratio	1.77	1.38
Strikeouts per 9 IP	4.91	6.65
Walks per 9 IP	4.42	3.42
Home Runs per 9 IP	1.96	1.05
Strikeout/Walk Ratio	1.11	1.94
Groundball/Flyball Ratio	0.85	1.29

2003 Situational Stats

	W	L	ERA	Sv	IP			AB	H	HR	RBI	Avg
Home	3	0	3.38	0	24.0	LHB		71	23	4	10	.324
Road	0	2	14.92	0	12.2	RHB		80	24	4	18	.300
First Half	3	2	7.36	0	36.2	Sc Pos		44	15	4	21	.341
Scnd Half	0	0	—	0	0.0	Clutch		0	0	0	0	—

2003 Rankings (National League)

- Did not rank near the top or bottom in any category

Roger Cedeno  Overrated

2003 Season

Roger Cedeno did little last season to erase the memories of a miserable 2002 campaign with the Mets. His effort was questioned on numerous occasions, and his mental approach was nothing short of disappointing. The outfielder's lone contributions came during his final 58 appearances, when he batted at a .295 clip and put together a pair of 10-game hitting streaks.

Hitting

The switch-hitting Cedeno has decent power for a leadoff hitter but does not possess the patience nor the discipline necessary to register a respectable on-base percentage from the top spot. His strikeout-walk ratio last season was a poor 2.3-1. The free swinger is prone to chasing high pitches, and he often is caught looking on pitches in the lower reaches of the strike zone. Cedeno is a much better hitter from the left side, although he drives the ball better as a righthanded swinger.

Baserunning & Defense

Cedeno continues to have good speed even though he appears to have lost a step in the past two years. His baserunning instincts, meanwhile, continue to be suspect. He was successful on just 14 of 23 stolen-base attempts last season, although his 105 swipes as a Met rank eighth on the franchise's career list. Defensively, Cedeno saw the vast majority of activity in right field last year. Regardless of where he is stationed, he misplays balls by frequently overrunning them and continues to take the wrong path on flyballs. While his arm strength is considered slightly above-average, the accuracy of his throws remains suspect.

2004 Outlook

Cedeno's unruly contract does not expire until after the 2005 campaign, which is the only reason the Mets have not parted company with the declining outfielder. The organization has considered eating the remainder of the deal, but that scenario is not likely until next year. While New York would prefer to find enough parts to make Cedeno a reserve, he likely will find his name in the lineup more often than not this season.

Position: RF/CF
Bats: B **Throws:** R
Ht: 6' 1" **Wt:** 205

Opening Day Age: 29
Born: 8/16/74 in Valencia, VZ
ML Seasons: 9
Pronunciation: sid-AIN-yo

Overall Statistics

	G	AB	R	H	D	T	HR	RBI	SB	BB	SO	Avg	OBP	Slg
'03	148	484	70	129	25	4	7	37	14	38	86	.267	.320	.378
Car.	968	2917	452	803	117	30	37	243	208	298	566	.275	.343	.374

Where He Hits the Ball

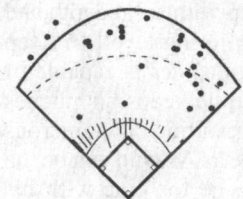 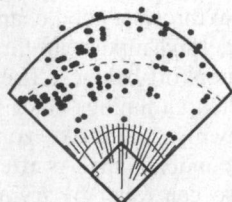

Vs. LHP   **Vs. RHP**

2003 Situational Stats

	AB	H	HR	RBI	Avg		AB	H	HR	RBI	Avg
Home	242	61	5	16	.252	LHP	108	26	3	12	.241
Road	242	68	2	21	.281	RHP	376	103	4	25	.274
First Half	246	62	4	19	.252	Sc Pos	111	23	1	29	.207
Scnd Half	238	67	3	18	.282	Clutch	63	13	0	6	.206

2003 Rankings (National League)

- 3rd in lowest stolen-base percentage (60.9)
- 4th in highest groundball-flyball ratio (2.1)
- 5th in fielding percentage in right field (.985)
- Led the Mets in singles, stolen bases, caught stealing (9) and highest groundball-flyball ratio (2.1)

Cliff Floyd

2003 Season

Ailments have been synonymous with Cliff Floyd for the past several seasons. That proved to be the case again in 2003, his first season as a Met. Floyd missed time with a sore right wrist before opting to get a head start on the four-month recovery from surgery on his right Achilles' tendon on August 19, but not before going 11-for-15 with six RBI in his final four games.

Hitting

With Mike Piazza and Mo Vaughn out of the lineup for most of the season's first half, Floyd was one of the lone offensive forces for the Mets. A solid No. 3 hitter and cleanup man, Floyd was pitched around most of last year. The aggressive lefthanded hitter has become more patient at the plate in recent seasons, and he continues to drive the ball to all fields against both righthanders and lefties. He thrived at Shea Stadium, batting .330 in a ballpark where hitters rarely excel.

Baserunning & Defense

Floyd's ailing Achilles' heel not only sidelined him for many day games after night contests, but prevented the normally fleet-footed standout from stealing bases and limited his ability to track down balls in the outfield. Floyd is a smart baserunner who has learned to read pitchers and pick the opportune time to steal a base. When healthy, he is an above-average left fielder with good arm strength, as evidenced by his leading the Mets with eight outfield assists. With knee and ankle problems limiting him in recent seasons, Floyd could benefit by moving to first base, but the position is becoming crowded in New York.

2004 Outlook

Floyd sacrificed the latter part of last season in order to obtain an extra six weeks to recover from surgery. He and the Mets are hopeful that the procedure and a full winter of rest will enable him to repeat his 2001 season at Florida, where he hit .317 with 31 homers and 103 RBI.

Position: LF
Bats: L **Throws:** R
Ht: 6' 4" **Wt:** 230

Opening Day Age: 31
Born: 12/5/72 in Chicago, IL
MI Seasons: 11

Overall Statistics

	G	AB	R	H	D	T	HR	RBI	SB	BB	SO	Avg	OBP	Slg
'03	108	365	57	106	25	2	18	68	3	51	66	.290	.376	.518
Car.	1063	3497	567	997	250	19	150	576	118	398	693	.285	.363	.496

Where He Hits the Ball

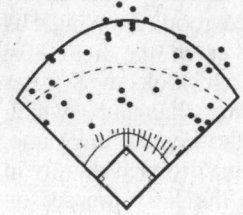 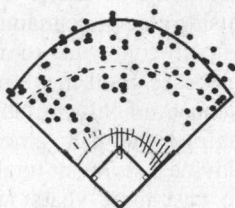

Vs. LHP   **Vs. RHP**

2003 Situational Stats

	AB	H	HR	RBI	Avg		AB	H	HR	RBI	Avg
Home	179	59	10	30	.330	LHP	122	32	7	19	.262
Road	186	47	8	38	.253	RHP	243	74	11	49	.305
First Half	276	75	15	47	.272	Sc Pos	106	29	8	55	.274
Scnd Half	89	31	3	21	.348	Clutch	42	10	2	4	.238

2003 Rankings (National League)

- 5th in errors in left field (5)
- 8th in cleanup slugging percentage (.574)
- Led the Mets in home runs, walks, slugging percentage, on-base percentage, HR frequency (20.3 ABs per HR), batting average with the bases loaded (.600), batting average vs. righthanded pitchers and cleanup slugging percentage (.574)

Tom Glavine

2003 Season

Tom Glavine did not appear to be himself for much of the 2003 season. Not only did he fail to receive as much support as he had with Atlanta, but he also appeared to be unnerved in four starts versus his old team, going 0-4 with a 10.35 ERA. Against everyone else, his ERA was 3.80. His 14 losses represent his most in a season since 1988, his first full year in the major leagues.

Pitching

Despite his difficulties last year, including a bone spur in his left elbow, blister problems on his fingers and the controversial QuesTec system, Glavine threw the ball nearly as well as he ever has. While he failed to get as many calls on the outside corner, he maintained good command. His fastball continues to register in the high 80s, possesses good movement and looks even faster because of his outstanding changeup, which continues to rank among the best in the game. Glavine's strikeout totals have dropped sharply in the past three years while the lefty focuses on moving his pitches around in the strike zone with the hope of inducing groundballs.

Defense & Hitting

Glavine helps himself with his glove and bat. His days as a hockey goalie are obvious with his quick reflexes and soft hands. His pickoff move is average for a lefty, but he does a good job of holding baserunners with his short, quick delivery to home. Offensively, the four-time Silver Slugger recipient leads all active players in career sacrifices with 178. He came through with eight hits to finish the season one shy of 200 career safeties.

2004 Outlook

A former draft pick of the Los Angeles Kings, Glavine was invited to a 10-day tryout with the New York Rangers after the 2003 baseball season. His future remains on the mound, where he must make the necessary adjustments to the redefined strike zone. At 38, he is one of the more competitive pitchers in the game, and is determined to post 49 more triumphs to reach 300 wins.

Position: SP
Bats: L **Throws:** L
Ht: 6' 0" **Wt:** 185

Opening Day Age: 38
Born: 3/25/66 in Concord, MA
ML Seasons: 17
Pronunciation: GLA-vin

Overall Statistics

W	L	Pct.	ERA	G	GS	Sv	IP	H	BB	SO	HR	Avg
9	14	.391	4.52	32	32	0	183.1	205	66	82	21	.288
251	157	.615	3.43	537	537	0	3528.0	3379	1206	2136	268	.254

2003 Pitching Profile

	Tom Glavine	NL Average
Overall Strike %	59.6	62.4
1st Pitch Strike %	54.1	58.4
Ratio	1.48	1.38
Strikeouts per 9 IP	4.03	6.65
Walks per 9 IP	3.24	3.42
Home Runs per 9 IP	1.03	1.05
Strikeout/Walk Ratio	1.24	1.94
Groundball/Flyball Ratio	1.40	1.29

2003 Situational Stats

	W	L	ERA	Sv	IP		AB	H	HR	RBI	Avg
Home	3	9	5.22	0	91.1	LHB	144	41	0	16	.285
Road	6	5	3.82	0	92.0	RHB	567	164	21	71	.289
First Half	6	9	4.73	0	110.1	Sc Pos	166	50	4	66	.301
Scnd Half	3	5	4.19	0	73.0	Clutch	35	15	0	5	.429

2003 Rankings (National League)

- 2nd in lowest strikeout-walk ratio (1.2), highest ERA at home and fewest strikeouts per nine innings (4.0)
- 3rd in least run support per nine innings (3.8)
- 4th in losses and lowest winning percentage
- 6th in GDPs induced (23)
- 7th in runners caught stealing (8) and highest on-base percentage allowed (.349)
- 8th in highest batting average allowed (.288) and highest batting average allowed with runners in scoring position
- 9th in pickoff throws (120) and highest slugging percentage allowed (.457)
- Led the Mets in losses, hits allowed, GDPs induced (23) and highest groundball-flyball ratio allowed (1.4)

Al Leiter

2003 Season

An inflamed right knee that caused him to miss three starts at midseason proved to be the dividing point between good and bad for Al Leiter in 2003. After posting an 8.51 ERA in his six starts prior to going on the disabled list in early July, the lefty surrendered only 11 earned runs in his first 10 starts after the All-Star break and gave up more than two earned runs in only two of his final 13 outings.

Pitching

Leiter is an intelligent pitcher who is a capable of dominating hitters even though his stuff is not overpowering. His hard, cut fastball sits in the 90-92 MPH range and possesses incredible sinking action just prior to reaching the plate, making it most difficult for righthanded hitters to hit. He uses his slider and regular fastball mostly against lefthanded hitters, always working the outside half of the dish. His changeup also is an effective offering, provided it stays low in the strike zone. Leiter gets in trouble when he fails to complete the follow-through in his delivery, which causes his pitches to rise.

Defense & Hitting

No pitcher throws more often to first base than Leiter. Despite that tendency, he surrenders as many stolen bases as any lefthander in recent memory besides Randy Johnson, due in part to his slow delivery to the plate. Defensively, he fields his position adequately and has soft hands on balls hit back through the box. Leiter is one of the worst hitters in baseball. Though capable of dropping down a bunt when necessary, he recorded just one hit last year in 53 at-bats to lower his career batting average nine points, to .087.

2004 Outlook

Leiter remains the ace of the Mets' pitching staff. Entering the final season of his contract, he has admitted in years past that his career could be coming to a close, yet he remains one of the most consistent lefthanders in the game. He has shown nothing to suggest there aren't at least another couple seasons left in the tank.

Position: SP
Bats: L **Throws:** L
Ht: 6' 3" **Wt:** 220

Opening Day Age: 38
Born: 10/23/65 in Toms River, NJ
ML Seasons: 17
Pronunciation: LIGH-ter

Overall Statistics

W	L	Pct.	ERA	G	GS	Sv	IP	H	BB	SO	HR	Avg
15	9	.625	3.99	30	30	0	180.2	176	94	139	15	.260
145	112	.564	3.69	356	326	2	2075.0	1860	968	1760	169	.241

2003 Pitching Profile

	Al Leiter	NL Average
Overall Strike %	58.8	62.4
1st Pitch Strike %	52.7	58.4
Ratio	1.49	1.38
Strikeouts per 9 IP	6.92	6.65
Walks per 9 IP	4.68	3.42
Home Runs per 9 IP	0.75	1.05
Strikeout/Walk Ratio	1.48	1.94
Groundball/Flyball Ratio	0.99	1.29

2003 Situational Stats

	W	L	ERA	Sv	IP		AB	H	HR	RBI	Avg
Home	8	2	3.46	0	80.2	LHB	117	35	3	11	.299
Road	7	7	4.41	0	100.0	RHB	560	141	12	61	.252
First Half	8	5	5.57	0	97.0	Sc Pos	181	46	4	60	.254
Scnd Half	7	4	2.15	0	83.2	Clutch	32	8	0	0	.250

2003 Rankings (National League)

- 1st in fielding percentage at pitcher (1.000), most pitches thrown per batter (4.07) and highest walks per nine innings (4.7)
- 2nd in pickoff throws (175)
- 3rd in runners caught stealing (11)
- 4th in highest on-base percentage allowed (.355)
- 5th in walks allowed
- 6th in stolen bases allowed (21)
- Led the Mets in walks allowed, hit batsmen (9), strikeouts, wild pitches (5), stolen bases allowed (21), runners caught stealing (11), winning percentage, lowest batting average allowed (.260), lowest slugging percentage allowed (.396), lowest ERA at home, lowest batting average allowed vs. righthanded batters, fewest home runs allowed per nine innings (.75) and most strikeouts per nine innings (6.9)

Timo Perez

2003 Season

Timo Perez was manager Art Howe's most versatile outfielder, starting 41 times in center field, 36 in left and eight in right. He hit at a .278 clip and produced 16 of his 21 doubles and 28 of his 42 RBI in his last 63 games with an at-bat. Perez' inability to hit lefthanders continued to cost him a full-time starting job, with the outfielder batting just .172 against southpaws last year.

Hitting

Perez is a solid contact hitter with little patience. He walked only 18 times last year and had only seven at-bats in which he put a 2-0 pitch into play. Nevertheless, Perez rarely strikes out. He owns a smooth line-drive stroke with good pop and has learned how to drive pitches against righthanders over the past two seasons after slapping at most offerings early on in his career. Perez also does a good job with runners in scoring position by shortening his swing to keep a rally intact.

Baserunning & Defense

Perez is the Mets' best all-around defensive outfielder. He owns above-average arm strength and good accuracy, enabling him to accumulate six outfield assists last year—second-best on the team. He plays one of the more shallow center fields in the game because of his speed and ability to read balls off the bat. Despite his above-average wheels, which helped him hit 64 points higher last year on turf compared to grass, Perez is only an average baserunner and is not a serious basestealing threat. He swiped only five bags in 11 attempts last year.

2004 Outlook

The Mets are not sold on Perez' ability to handle the center-field duties on a full-time basis. The team looks for the position to also serve as the leadoff hitter, but Perez is not ideal in that role, either. New York is expected to hold auditions for the starting job in the middle garden in spring training, and Perez will be a leading candidate to either earn the nod or serve as the club's fourth outfielder.

Position: LF/CF/RF
Bats: L **Throws:** L
Ht: 5' 9" **Wt:** 167

Opening Day Age: 28
Born: 4/8/75 in Bani, DR
ML Seasons: 4

Overall Statistics

	G	AB	R	H	D	T	HR	RBI	SB	BB	SO	Avg	OBP	Slg
'03	127	346	32	93	21	0	4	42	5	18	29	.269	.301	.364
Car.	372	1078	121	297	61	8	18	114	17	56	95	.276	.312	.397

Where He Hits the Ball

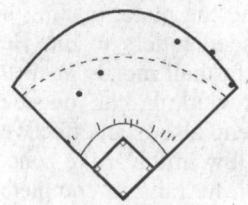

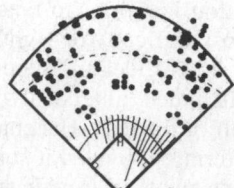

Vs. LHP   **Vs. RHP**

2003 Situational Stats

	AB	H	HR	RBI	Avg		AB	H	HR	RBI	Avg
Home	163	42	1	24	.258	LHP	29	5	0	3	.172
Road	183	51	3	18	.279	RHP	317	88	4	39	.278
First Half	157	42	2	18	.268	Sc Pos	77	21	0	35	.273
Scnd Half	189	51	2	24	.270	Clutch	54	13	0	6	.241

2003 Rankings (National League)

- 2nd in sacrifice flies (9)
- Led the Mets in sacrifice flies (9), lowest percentage of swings that missed (8.8) and highest percentage of swings put into play (52.4)

Jason Phillips

2003 Season

After spending three short stints with the Mets during the season's first six weeks, Jason Phillips stuck in New York after being recalled May 17. Splitting his time between first base and catcher, Phillips ranked among the top five National League rookies in several offensive categories. He put together hitting streaks of 14 and 10 games during the season, and hit the 5,000th home run in Mets history on August 30.

Hitting

Over the past three years, Phillips has developed into a good hitter with decent power. While the majority of his power numbers came against righthanders last season, he handles pitchers from both sides of the plate equally well. Phillips is an aggressive hitter who batted .369 when putting the first pitch of an at-bat in play last year. He also showed the ability to rise to the occasion in 2003, including a .348 clip with runners in scoring position and two outs. Phillips admits he sees the ball well at Shea Stadium, where he batted .354, 110 points higher than on the road.

Baserunning & Defense

Phillips filled a major void in the absence of Mo Vaughn and Mike Piazza last year. He is a steady all-around receiver whose strengths are his catch-and-throw skills and his game-calling ability. He moves well behind the plate and has a take-charge attitude that can be infectious for the pitching staff. His arm strength is also good, enabling him to retire one-third of would-be basestealers last season. Phillips' defense at first base is steady as well, despite his limited experience at the position. Though not a blazer, he does not clog the basepaths.

2004 Outlook

With his performance last season, Phillips has forced himself into the Mets' plans. Provided Vaughn does not return, Phillips should open the slate as the starting first baseman, and he could share that position and catcher with Piazza and Vance Wilson. His presence is one of the brighter spots for the team's future.

Position: 1B/C
Bats: R **Throws:** R
Ht: 6' 1" **Wt:** 177

Opening Day Age: 27
Born: 9/27/76 in La Mesa, CA
ML Seasons: 3

Overall Statistics

	G	AB	R	H	D	T	HR	RBI	SB	BB	SO	Avg	OBP	Slg
'03	119	403	45	120	25	0	11	58	0	39	50	.298	.373	.442
Car.	136	429	51	128	26	0	12	61	0	40	52	.298	.371	.443

Where He Hits the Ball

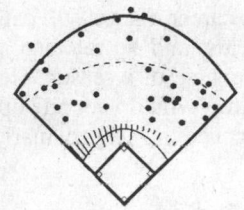
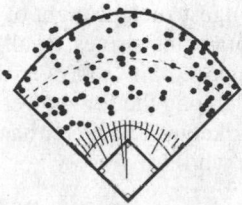

Vs. LHP   **Vs. RHP**

2003 Situational Stats

	AB	H	HR	RBI	Avg		AB	H	HR	RBI	Avg
Home	198	70	7	36	.354	LHP	117	36	2	18	.308
Road	205	50	4	22	.244	RHP	286	84	9	40	.294
First Half	186	58	5	22	.312	Sc Pos	116	37	2	44	.319
Scnd Half	217	62	6	36	.286	Clutch	53	12	0	7	.226

2003 Rankings (National League)

- 2nd in most GDPs per GDP situation (22.8%)
- 3rd in batting average among rookies, home runs among rookies and RBI among rookies
- 6th in GDPs (21), errors at first base (7) and batting average with two strikes (.279)
- Led the Mets in hit by pitch (10), GDPs (21), batting average vs. lefthanded pitchers, batting average at home and batting average with two strikes (.279)

Mike Piazza

2003 Season

Any hope the Mets had of recording a winning season disappeared when Mike Piazza succumbed to a strained right groin on May 16 and missed the next three months. Prior to the injury, he batted .333 with seven home runs during the season's first six weeks. He struggled after a quick start following his comeback, yet still become only the ninth catcher in history to reach 1,100 career RBI.

Hitting

Piazza remains determined to break Carlton Fisk's record of 351 home runs by a catcher, and is within four of achieving the feat. There is no question that Piazza's bat has declined of late. He did not homer in his final 88 at-bats last year, the longest such drought of his career. Piazza still can spray line drives to all fields, and he remains a threat to hit .300 over the course of a season. He is among the few power hitters who do not pile up strikeouts and never has reached the century mark in whiffs.

Baserunning & Defense

It's no secret that Piazza has been one of weakest defensive catchers in the game for most of the past decade. He is a poor thrower with minimal arm strength, and his defense is borderline clumsy. Still, his determination to remain behind the plate has been the sole reason he has stayed there, although changes appear to be in store. He made his Mets debut at first base on September 25, marking only the second time in 1,380 contests he had manned the position. Once the possessor of average speed, Piazza's ability to round the bases has slowed due to his years of crouching behind the plate.

2004 Outlook

The Mets are expected to encourage Piazza to split his time between first base and catcher in an effort to maintain his power production. The rebuilding club would love to unload the catcher, but the $30 million he is owed for the next two seasons is prohibitive, particularly for a player whose production is declining.

Position: C
Bats: R **Throws:** R
Ht: 6' 3" **Wt:** 215

Opening Day Age: 35
Born: 9/4/68 in Norristown, PA
ML Seasons: 12
Pronunciation: pee-AH-zuh

Overall Statistics

G	AB	R	H	D	T	HR	RBI	SB	BB	SO	Avg	OBP	Slg
68	234	37	67	13	0	11	34	0	35	40	.286	.377	.483
1461	5350	888	1708	264	6	358	1107	17	598	841	.319	.388	.572

Where He Hits the Ball

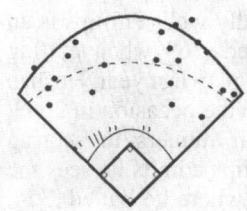 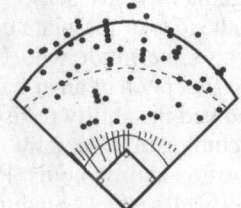

Vs. LHP   **Vs. RHP**

2003 Situational Stats

	AB	H	HR	RBI	Avg		AB	H	HR	RBI	Avg
Home	109	32	4	16	.294	LHP	49	13	1	7	.265
Road	125	35	7	18	.280	RHP	185	54	10	27	.292
First Half	111	37	7	15	.333	Sc Pos	59	17	4	24	.288
Scnd Half	123	30	4	19	.244	Clutch	44	14	1	4	.318

2003 Rankings (National League)

- 1st in lowest cleanup slugging percentage (.403)
- 4th in highest percentage of runners caught stealing as a catcher (22.4)

Jose Reyes

2003 Season

When the Mets promoted Jose Reyes to New York on June 10, they hoped the shortstop would hit at least .200 while providing an instant upgrade to the team's defense. He batted .207 during his first four weeks then exceeded expectations in every phase of the game, including batting .339 following the All-Star break before missing September due to a sprained left ankle. His 17-game hitting streak was the longest for a Mets' rookie since Mike Vail hit in 23 straight contests in 1975.

Hitting

Reyes is one of the exciting young stars in the game. He showed no difficulty in making the adjustments to the speed of the game at the major league level. He can bunt for base hits and has the ability to hit for power. The switch-hitter is more effective from the right side of the plate than the left side. While opponents try to retire the aggressive Reyes by working him outside, he has discovered the discipline to lay off those offerings and wait for his pitch.

Baserunning & Defense

Reyes is not only fast, but a plus-plus baserunner who was leading the Triple-A International League in steals last year at the time of his promotion to New York. He routinely turns singles into doubles with his speed and instincts on the basepaths. Defensively, he has steady hands and his arm is one of the strongest in the league with excellent accuracy, allowing him to throw out batters at first from deep in the hole. He maintains full control of his fluid actions and makes plays that leave mouths agape, thanks to his incredible baseball instincts.

2004 Outlook

Reyes needs to become more disciplined at the plate, as evidenced by his two walks in his first 100 at-bats in the big leagues last year. Nevertheless, the natural ability is obvious, and the confident Reyes is a star in the making. He will move to second base in 2004, in order to accommodate the offseason signing of star Japanese shortstop Kazuo Matsui. Look for Reyes to become a mainstay near the top of the Mets' batting order.

Position: SS
Bats: B **Throws:** R
Ht: 6' 0" **Wt:** 160

Opening Day Age: 20
Born: 6/11/83 in Villa Gonzalez, DR
ML Seasons: 1
Pronunciation: RAY-ess

Overall Statistics

	G	AB	R	H	D	T	HR	RBI	SB	BB	SO	Avg	OBP	Slg
'03	69	274	47	84	12	4	5	32	13	13	36	.307	.334	.434
Car.	69	274	47	84	12	4	5	32	13	13	36	.307	.334	.434

Where He Hits the Ball

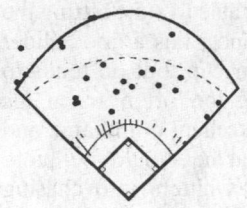
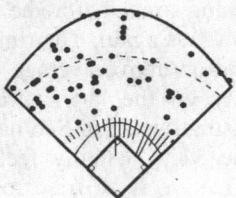

Vs. LHP   **Vs. RHP**

2003 Situational Stats

	AB	H	HR	RBI	Avg		AB	H	HR	RBI	Avg
Home	131	44	1	12	.336	LHP	80	18	3	17	.225
Road	143	40	4	20	.280	RHP	194	66	2	15	.340
First Half	100	25	1	20	.250	Sc Pos	54	19	1	27	.352
Scnd Half	174	59	4	12	.339	Clutch	32	10	1	6	.313

2003 Rankings (National League)

- 3rd in fewest GDPs per GDP situation (1.8%)
- 5th in batting average with the bases loaded (.556)
- 9th in steals of third (3)
- Led the Mets in batting average, steals of third (3), fewest GDPs per GDP situation (1.8%) and batting average with runners in scoring position

Jae Weong Seo

2003 Season

Jae Weong Seo stepped into the Mets' rotation last April and produced a streaky season that created higher expectations for the future. Seo won four straight games from May 31 through June 17 before dropping six straight decisions over a five-week period. He then won three consecutive starts before suffering four straight setbacks. He concluded the season by registering a 1.71 ERA in September.

Pitching

Seo is at his best when he moves his pitches around in the strike zone. He went through a minor dead-arm period at midseason, causing his fastball to lose some juice during his six-game losing streak before he was able to start hitting the low 90s again. The righthander has a good slider and an above-average changeup, but he tends to rely on the latter offering too often when his fastball gets hit. Seo has excellent command, and the Mets actually feel that he would be more effective if he tried to coax hitters into chasing some pitches instead of being so fine around the plate. He was reluctant to take manager Art Howe's advice to add a two-seam fastball to run inside on righthanded hitters, but Seo realized as the season progressed that he needed more bullets in his holster.

Defense & Hitting

Seo is not a superior athlete. His conditioning has been questioned in the past due to improper eating habits. He is an average fielder, but he does an excellent job of holding runners. Seo is capable of swinging the bat, as evidenced by his five hits, although his ability to drop down a bunt needs work.

2004 Outlook

After watching his stock fall following Tommy John surgery in 1999, Seo has rebounded and could become a solid middle-of-the-rotation pitcher for the Mets. His strong finish should give him an advantage over fellow challengers, such as Aaron Heilman and Jeremy Griffiths, for the fifth spot in the rotation. That scenario should land Seo with at least as many starts as he received in 2003.

Position: SP
Bats: R **Throws:** R
Ht: 6' 1" **Wt:** 210

Opening Day Age: 26
Born: 5/24/77 in Kwanju, South Korea
ML Seasons: 2
Pronunciation: jay wong sew

Overall Statistics

	W	L	Pct.	ERA	G	GS	Sv	IP	H	BB	SO	HR	Avg
'03	9	12	.429	3.82	32	31	0	188.1	193	46	110	18	.260
Car.	9	12	.429	3.80	33	31	0	189.1	193	46	111	18	.259

2003 Pitching Profile

	Jae Weong Seo	NL Average
Overall Strike %	65.0	62.4
1st Pitch Strike %	63.8	58.4
Ratio	1.27	1.38
Strikeouts per 9 IP	5.26	6.65
Walks per 9 IP	2.20	3.42
Home Runs per 9 IP	0.86	1.05
Strikeout/Walk Ratio	2.39	1.94
Groundball/Flyball Ratio	0.94	1.29

2003 Situational Stats

	W	L	ERA	Sv	IP		AB	H	HR	RBI	Avg
Home	3	6	4.43	0	91.1	LHB	336	75	6	37	.223
Road	6	6	3.25	0	97.0	RHB	406	118	12	51	.291
First Half	5	5	3.64	0	108.2	Sc Pos	178	44	4	66	.247
Scnd Half	4	7	4.07	0	79.2	Clutch	23	8	1	2	.348

2003 Rankings (National League)

- 1st in losses among rookies
- 2nd in ERA among rookies
- 3rd in lowest stolen-base percentage allowed (36.4)
- 4th in pickoff throws (132)
- 6th in highest ERA at home
- Led the Mets in highest strikeout-walk ratio (2.4), lowest on-base percentage allowed (.307), lowest stolen-base percentage allowed (36.4), fewest pitches thrown per batter (3.65), lowest ERA on the road, and fewest walks per nine innings (2.2)

Steve Trachsel

2003 Season

For the second straight season, Steve Trachsel was the Mets' best starting pitcher from start to finish. He battled inconsistency during the first half before finding his rhythm down the stretch. The righthander won seven of his last 10 decisions and had a 2.20 ERA during August and September. He established a new career high in wins, and became the first Mets pitcher to throw two one-hitters in the same season.

Pitching

Trachsel is an unheralded hurler who keeps his team in games every time he pitches. He does an excellent job of mixing his two-seam fastball, curveball and changeup, and has plus command of all three offerings while keeping them down in the strike zone. He wastes few pitches, which allows him to go deep into games and eat innings. The righthander is determined to get ahead in the count with first-pitch strikes and is not afraid of hitters making contact and putting his fielders to work. His stuff is far from outstanding, with his heater rarely breaking 90 MPH, but his methodical pace can be irritating to opposing hitters.

Defense & Hitting

Trachsel helps himself in a variety of ways. A good all-around athlete with quick feet, he mans his position with sure hands and covers first base well. Although he allowed 17 stolen bases in 2003, he also does a good job of holding runners for a righthander. He was one of the best-hitting pitchers in the National League last year, posting 11 hits, 11 sac bunts and a sac fly in 58 at-bats.

2004 Outlook

Not surprisingly, Trachsel emerged as one of manager Art Howe's favorites down the stretch. He has reached double figures in wins for three straight seasons for the first time in his career, and has been one of the few bright spots for the Mets since joining the team in 2001. Combined with Al Leiter and Tom Glavine, Trachsel gives New York a formidable top three in the rotation.

Position: SP
Bats: R **Throws:** R
Ht: 6' 4" **Wt:** 205

Opening Day Age: 33
Born: 10/31/70 in Oxnard, CA
ML Seasons: 11
Pronunciation: track-s'l

Overall Statistics

	W	L	Pct.	ERA	G	GS	Sv	IP	H	BB	SO	HR	Avg
'03	16	10	.615	3.78	33	33	0	204.2	204	65	111	26	.264
Car.	106	118	.473	4.26	312	311	0	1899.0	1933	667	1299	265	.265

2003 Pitching Profile

	Steve Trachsel	NL Average
Overall Strike %	61.4	62.4
1st Pitch Strike %	59.1	58.4
Ratio	1.31	1.38
Strikeouts per 9 IP	4.88	6.65
Walks per 9 IP	2.86	3.42
Home Runs per 9 IP	1.14	1.05
Strikeout/Walk Ratio	1.71	1.94
Groundball/Flyball Ratio	0.85	1.29

2003 Situational Stats

	W	L	ERA	Sv	IP		AB	H	HR	RBI	Avg
Home	6	9	3.97	0	113.1	LHB	327	65	6	18	.199
Road	10	1	3.55	0	91.1	RHB	446	139	20	65	.312
First Half	8	6	4.61	0	111.1	Sc Pos	159	36	4	52	.226
Scnd Half	8	4	2.80	0	93.1	Clutch	31	5	0	0	.161

2003 Rankings (National League)

- 1st in pickoff throws (189)
- 4th in shutouts (2)
- 5th in wins, balks (2), lowest groundball-flyball ratio allowed (0.9) and fewest strikeouts per nine innings (4.9)
- 7th in sacrifice bunts (11), runners caught stealing (8) and highest batting average allowed vs. righthanded batters
- 8th in games started and lowest batting average allowed vs. lefthanded batters
- Led the Mets in ERA, sacrifice bunts (11), wins, games started, complete games (2), shutouts (2), innings pitched, batters faced (857), home runs allowed, wild pitches (5), balks (2), pitches thrown (3,324), pickoff throws (189), lowest batting average allowed vs. lefthanded batters and most run support per nine innings (5.4)

Ty Wigginton

2003 Season

After losing Edgardo Alfonzo to free agency, the Mets searched for a replacement at third base before Ty Wigginton earned the job with a blistering performance in spring training. Wigginton, who was productive enough to find his name in the lineup nearly every game, led New York in RBI and set the franchise rookie record for doubles, hits and extra-base hits. His RBI, doubles and extra-base hits paced all National League rookies.

Hitting

Wigginton wrestled with his confidence while trying to prove himself for much of last year. When he finally determined he was going to stick, the third baseman became more comfortable and patient at the plate. He has good power that should enable him to hit at least 20 homers a year, a level he reached on two occasions during his five seasons in the minor leagues. While Wigginton hits lefties well, he batted nearly 60 points lower versus righthanded pitchers. Strikeouts continue to be his downfall, resulting in an average of one whiff per 4.62 at-bats last season.

Baserunning & Defense

Wigginton not only hit for power, but also displayed above-average speed. He is aggressive on the basepaths and does an excellent job of taking the extra base when available. Milwaukee's Scott Podsednik was the only NL rookie to hit more triples than Wigginton's six three-baggers. With 12 swipes, Wigginton joined Jose Reyes as the first pair of Mets rookies to reach double digits in swipes in the same season in franchise history. Wigginton exceeded expectations with his defense. Though only an average fielder, he showed decent range, consistent hands and an accurate arm with good zip at the hot corner.

2004 Outlook

The Mets opened last season having used 31 third basemen since Opening Day 1995. The position has been a virtual revolving door through the franchise's 42 years. Wigginton must continue to prove himself as a potential long-term answer, and he will have plenty of opportunity to do that once again this season as the Mets' starter.

Position: 3B
Bats: R **Throws:** R
Ht: 6' 0" **Wt:** 200

Opening Day Age: 26
Born: 10/11/77 in San Diego, CA
ML Seasons: 2

Overall Statistics

	G	AB	R	H	D	T	HR	RBI	SB	BB	SO	Avg	OBP	Slg
'03	156	573	73	146	36	6	11	71	12	46	124	.255	.318	.396
Car.	202	689	91	181	44	6	17	89	14	54	143	.263	.324	.418

Where He Hits the Ball

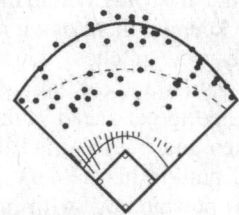
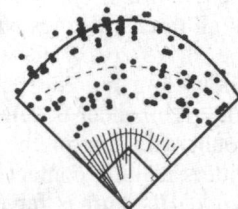

Vs. LHP   **Vs. RHP**

2003 Situational Stats

	AB	H	HR	RBI	Avg		AB	H	HR	RBI	Avg
Home	276	69	4	30	.250	LHP	155	46	4	17	.297
Road	297	77	7	41	.259	RHP	418	100	7	54	.239
First Half	348	93	6	41	.267	Sc Pos	153	44	2	60	.288
Scnd Half	225	53	5	30	.236	Clutch	86	20	4	14	.233

2003 Rankings (National League)

- 1st in RBI among rookies
- 3rd in home runs among rookies
- 5th in errors at third base (16), highest percentage of swings on the first pitch (38.6) and lowest fielding percentage at third base (.962)
- Led the Mets in at-bats, runs scored, hits, singles, doubles, triples, total bases (227), RBI, times on base (201), strikeouts, pitches seen (2,355), plate appearances (633), games played and stolen-base percentage (85.7)

Tony Clark

Position: 1B
Bats: B **Throws:** R
Ht: 6' 7" **Wt:** 245

Opening Day Age: 31
Born: 6/15/72 in
Newton, KS
ML Seasons: 9

Overall Statistics

	G	AB	R	H	D	T	HR	RBI	SB	BB	SO	Avg	OBP	Slg
'03	125	254	29	59	13	0	16	43	0	24	73	.232	.300	.472
Car.	987	3360	482	899	181	8	175	586	6	388	851	.268	.344	.482

2003 Situational Stats

	AB	H	HR	RBI	Avg		AB	H	HR	RBI	Avg
Home	130	34	9	27	.262	LHP	68	19	4	10	.279
Road	124	25	7	16	.202	RHP	186	40	12	33	.215
First Half	148	32	10	27	.216	Sc Pos	68	13	1	19	.191
Scnd Half	106	27	6	16	.255	Clutch	60	12	3	10	.200

2003 Season

Signed by the Mets early in spring training after a dismal showing with the Red Sox in 2002, Tony Clark proved to be a valuable reserve and a consistent replacement at first base for the injured Mo Vaughn. In 50 starts, Clark produced 11 doubles, 12 homers and 30 RBI.

Hitting, Baserunning & Defense

Clark continues to offer power from both sides of the plate. The majority of his pop comes from the left side, while he relies on line drives as a righthanded hitter. He is one of the streakier hitters in the game, as evidenced by his five home runs in as many games to open August. Last season he went deep twice in a game for the 13th time as a major leaguer. A good baserunner for his size, Clark is steady defensively with his solid range and soft hands.

2004 Outlook

Clark entered the offseason as a free agent and was not expected to return to the Mets, due to the emergence of Jason Phillips and some possible activity at first base by Mike Piazza. Clark remains a decent power producer from both sides of the plate, a trait that could attract a suitor from the American League.

John Franco

Position: RP
Bats: L **Throws:** L
Ht: 5'10" **Wt:** 185

Opening Day Age: 43
Born: 9/17/60 in
Brooklyn, NY
ML Seasons: 19

Overall Statistics

W	L	Pct.	ERA	G	GS	Sv	IP	H	BB	SO	HR	Avg
0	3	.000	2.62	38	0	2	34.1	35	13	16	5	.265
88	79	.527	2.74	1036	0	424	1184.2	1097	462	923	75	.247

2003 Situational Stats

	W	L	ERA	Sv	IP		AB	H	HR	RBI	Avg
Home	0	1	2.55	0	17.2	LHB	45	12	2	7	.267
Road	0	2	2.70	2	16.2	RHB	87	23	3	6	.264
First Half	0	1	3.14	0	14.1	Sc Pos	36	8	0	8	.222
Scnd Half	0	2	2.25	2	20.0	Clutch	45	15	3	10	.333

2003 Season

Most pitchers would have retired to the links or the lakes after blowing out their arm on the wrong side of 40. Not John Franco. He rehabbed his way back from the Tommy John surgery that cost him all of the 2002 season to appear in 38 contests, beginning in late May. The lefthander did not allow a run in 18 of his last 21 outings.

Pitching, Defense & Hitting

Franco's overall stuff improved as the season progressed last year. That situation was most notable with his 88-90 MPH fastball, which displayed more command and better life as his arm gained strength. A nasty slider that acts like a cutter remains a decent offering, while his best pitch is a darting changeup that produces groundball outs and the majority of his whiffs. A good fielder, Franco's job responsibilities rarely include hitting.

2004 Outlook

Franco, who ranks second on the all-time saves list with 424 and sixth in pitching appearances with 1,036, made known his desire to continue pitching. Considering the fact that Franco still is productive out of the pen, the Mets would be remiss if they fail to give the lefty a shot to make the roster in spring training.

Jeremy Griffiths

Position: SP
Bats: R **Throws:** R
Ht: 6' 6" **Wt:** 240

Opening Day Age: 26
Born: 3/22/78 in
Fairview, OH
ML Seasons: 1

Overall Statistics

	W	L	Pct.	ERA	G	GS	Sv	IP	H	BB	SO	HR	Avg
'03	1	4	.200	7.02	9	6	0	41.0	57	19	25	5	.328
Car.	1	4	.200	7.02	9	6	0	41.0	57	19	25	5	.328

2003 Situational Stats

	W	L	ERA	Sv	IP		AB	H	HR	RBI	Avg
Home	1	0	3.10	0	20.1	LHB	81	28	3	21	.346
Road	0	4	10.89	0	20.2	RHB	93	29	2	11	.312
First Half	0	1	9.00	0	15.0	Sc Pos	61	18	1	26	.295
Scnd Half	1	3	5.88	0	26.0	Clutch	6	2	0	0	.333

2003 Season

Jeremy Griffiths made three trips to New York last season in between spending most of the campaign at Triple-A Norfolk, where he was named the Tides' MVP. In addition to pacing International League starters with a 2.76 ERA, the righthander put together solid showings in a pair of big league starts on August 3 and September 6.

Pitching, Defense & Hitting

A third-round draft pick in 1999, Griffiths has made steady progress in his development over the past three years. The righthander has ironed out his delivery and become more consistent with his command. His fastball is in the low 90s with an excellent downward plane from his 6-foot-6 frame. His slider and changeup have developed into solid-average pitches. The Mets want Griffiths to improve his mound presence and become more aggressive. Griffiths went hitless with one sacrifice in nine at-bats.

2004 Outlook

Griffiths will be in the running for a starting job at the end of the Mets' rotation this year. The team believes Griffiths will continue to get better with experience and some adjustments, and he should emerge as a steady middle-of-the-rotation hurler in 2005.

Aaron Heilman

Position: SP
Bats: R **Throws:** R
Ht: 6' 5" **Wt:** 220

Opening Day Age: 25
Born: 11/12/78 in
Logansport, IN
ML Seasons: 1

Overall Statistics

	W	L	Pct.	ERA	G	GS	Sv	IP	H	BB	SO	HR	Avg
'03	2	7	.222	6.75	14	13	0	65.1	79	41	51	13	.300
Car.	2	7	.222	6.75	14	13	0	65.1	79	41	51	13	.300

2003 Situational Stats

	W	L	ERA	Sv	IP		AB	H	HR	RBI	Avg
Home	1	4	5.95	0	39.1	LHB	117	35	8	23	.299
Road	1	3	7.96	0	26.0	RHB	146	44	5	27	.301
First Half	0	2	7.17	0	21.1	Sc Pos	82	22	3	38	.268
Scnd Half	2	5	6.55	0	44.0	Clutch	4	1	1	1	.250

2003 Season

Aaron Heilman debuted with the Mets last year and joined his teammates by struggling through most of the campaign. Averaging just under five innings per start, he received limited run support while surrendering four earned runs or more in six of his 14 appearances.

Pitching, Defense & Hitting

Heilman depends heavily upon the location of his pitches. He had difficulty in that area last year and got hurt by being too fine while trying to get ahead in the count. The result was five home runs and a .594 batting average for opponents on Heilman's first pitch in the count. He is not a hard thrower, possessing a fastball in the low 90s that must stay down in the strike zone to be effective. His slider and changeup can be good pitches but lack consistency. An average fielder at best, he struggled at the plate with one hit in 22 at-bats.

2004 Outlook

After a less than overwhelming debut, Heilman will get another shot this spring. He will compete with at least two other young pitchers for the No. 5 spot. If he finds more consistency with his pitches, he could develop into a decent No. 3 starter.

Kazuo Matsui

Position: SS
Bats: B **Throws:** R
Ht: 5' 9" **Wt:** 183

Opening Day Age: 28
Born: 10/23/75 in Osaka, Japan
ML Seasons: 0
Pronunciation: mat-soo-ee

Career Statistics (Seibu, Japan Pacific League)

	G	AB	R	H	D	T	HR	RBI	SB	BB	SO	Avg	OBP	Slg
'95	69	204	25	45	9	1	2	15	21	7	26	.221	.245	.304
'96	130	473	51	134	22	5	1	29	50	14	93	.283	.307	.357
'97	135	576	91	178	23	13	7	63	62	44	89	.309	.362	.431
'98	135	575	92	179	38	5	9	58	43	55	89	.311	.370	.442
'99	135	539	87	178	29	4	15	67	32	56	75	.330	.389	.482
'00	135	550	99	177	40	11	23	90	26	46	60	.322	.372	.560
'01	140	552	94	170	28	2	24	76	26	46	83	.308	.365	.496
'02	140	582	119	193	46	6	36	87	33	53	112	.332	.389	.617
'03	140	587	104	179	36	4	33	84	13	55	124	.305	.365	.549
Car.	1159	4638	762	1433	271	51	150	569	306	376	751	.309	.361	.486

2003 Season

The Mets surprised many observers by outlasting several clubs in the wooing of Kazuo Matsui. Signed in December to a three-year deal worth $20.1 million, he hit .305 with 33 home runs last year with Seibu. He earned four Gold Gloves and two stolen-base crowns in Japan's Pacific League, and was tabbed MVP in 1998.

Hitting, Baserunning & Defense

The 28-year-old Matsui supplants shortstop Jose Reyes, who moves to second base to give the Mets a spectacular double-play combination. Matsui is a smooth fielder with plus range, a strong arm and great quickness. Offensively, he is a top-of-the-lineup contributor who is capable of driving pitches from gap to gap. While the Mets do not expect him to hit 30-plus homers in the major leagues, Matsui reminds some of Rickey Henderson with his speed/power combination.

2004 Outlook

When the Mets added veteran scout and player development guru Al Goldis to the front office this past fall, he said the team needed to get plus-plus defenders up the middle. New York now has that with Matsui and Reyes. Based on his tools and overall confidence, "Little Matsui" could be everything to New York that Ichiro is to Seattle.

Grant Roberts

Position: RP
Bats: R **Throws:** R
Ht: 6' 3" **Wt:** 205

Opening Day Age: 26
Born: 9/13/77 in El Cajon, CA
ML Seasons: 4

Overall Statistics

	W	L	Pct.	ERA	G	GS	Sv	IP	H	BB	SO	HR	Avg
'03	0	3	.000	3.79	18	0	1	19.0	19	3	10	0	.257
Car.	4	4	.500	3.62	72	1	1	97.0	97	31	76	5	.258

2003 Situational Stats

	W	L	ERA	Sv	IP			AB	H	HR	RBI	Avg
Home	0	2	5.40	0	10.0		LHB	26	6	0	1	.231
Road	0	1	2.00	1	9.0		RHB	48	13	0	4	.271
First Half	0	0	—	0	0.0		Sc Pos	14	6	0	5	.429
Scnd Half	0	3	3.79	1	19.0		Clutch	41	11	0	3	.268

2003 Season

Grant Roberts spent the last two months of the season in the major leagues after missing all of the campaign's first four months while battling tendinitis in his right shoulder. He pitched well out of the Mets' bullpen, allowing no runs in 13 of his 18 appearances. The righthander also picked up his first major league save.

Pitching, Defense & Hitting

Injuries have halted Roberts' progress over the past two seasons. He was a starter in the minors, but the Mets are hoping the righthander can avoid his constant battles with tendinitis as a reliever. Roberts' repertoire—a low-90s fastball with plus movement and a hard slider—is also more conducive to relief, especially since he has had difficulty finding a consistent release point with his curveball. He is not afraid to challenge hitters and will pitch up in the strike zone. He is a good fielder and has shown that he is capable of swinging the bat in his limited opportunities.

2004 Outlook

The Mets would like to see Roberts remain healthy for an entire season. If he can do that, his stuff is good enough for him to become a mainstay in the New York bullpen and develop into the team's righthanded setup man.

Mike Stanton

Position: RP
Bats: L **Throws:** L
Ht: 6' 1" **Wt:** 215

Opening Day Age: 36
Born: 6/2/67 in
Houston, TX
ML Seasons: 15

Overall Statistics

	W	L	Pct.	ERA	G	GS	Sv	IP	H	BB	SO	HR	Avg
'03	2	7	.222	4.57	50	0	5	45.1	37	19	34	6	.219
Car.	55	44	.556	3.81	885	1	76	869.0	822	327	722	76	.252

2003 Situational Stats

	W	L	ERA	Sv	IP		AB	H	HR	RBI	Avg
Home	2	1	3.38	2	24.0	LHB	63	13	0	4	.206
Road	0	6	5.91	3	21.1	RHB	106	24	6	19	.226
First Half	2	3	4.57	0	21.2	Sc Pos	38	11	1	17	.289
Scnd Half	0	4	4.56	5	23.2	Clutch	112	25	5	20	.223

2003 Season

Mike Stanton put together a strong second half last season after battling knee problems that cost him nearly seven weeks during the first half. He underwent surgery to repair a torn meniscus in his left knee in early June before returning to action on July 12. He shared the closer's job with David Weathers after Armando Benitez was traded and saved five games.

Pitching, Defense & Hitting

Stanton appeared to have lost a foot on his fastball early in the season before regaining most of his low-90s velocity. With his drop-and-drive delivery, he was unable to generate as much power when his knee was hurting. Batters posted only a .219 batting average against Stanton, who mixes his hard splitter and slider extremely well. Walks were his primary downfall last year. Stanton fields his position well and is difficult to run on due to his quick move to first.

2004 Outlook

The Mets believe Stanton can resume his role as one of the game's better setup men. He benefits a team with his ability to pitch frequently and shut down opposing clubs in the late innings. Provided he remains healthy, he gives New York one more solid, consistent performer.

Mo Vaughn

Position: 1B
Bats: L **Throws:** R
Ht: 6' 1" **Wt:** 275

Opening Day Age: 36
Born: 12/15/67 in
Norwalk, CT
ML Seasons: 12
Nickname: The Hit Dog

Overall Statistics

	G	AB	R	H	D	T	HR	RBI	SB	BB	SO	Avg	OBP	Slg
	27	79	10	15	2	0	3	15	0	14	22	.190	.323	.329
	1512	5532	861	1620	270	10	328	1064	30	725	1429	.293	.383	.523

2003 Situational Stats

	AB	H	HR	RBI	Avg		AB	H	HR	RBI	Avg
Home	39	8	1	9	.205	LHP	15	2	0	4	.133
Road	40	7	2	6	.175	RHP	64	13	3	11	.203
First Half	79	15	3	15	.190	Sc Pos	28	6	0	12	.214
Scnd Half	0	0	0	0	–	Clutch	7	1	0	2	.143

2003 Season

The Mets hoped that a rededicated Mo Vaughn would discover lightning in a bottle and return to his hard-hitting ways of yore. It didn't happen. After driving in 15 runs in April, Vaughn was shelved with inflammation of the left knee on May 3, underwent surgery and did not return.

Hitting, Baserunning & Defense

Vaughn is nothing more than a shadow of his former All-Star self. He entered last season slightly slimmer, yet he remained too massive to be productive. Offensively, Vaughn is capable of making hard contact, but his bat speed has slowed considerably. His power also is not what it used to be, although that can be difficult to judge because of his inability to hit the ball consistently. His defense has become a liability due to his lack of range and flexibility, and his baserunning clogs the bases.

2004 Outlook

The Mets hope to move forward by having Vaughn opt for retirement. Vaughn, however, is attempting a comeback, even though the arthritis in the left knee can make it difficult for the first baseman to walk, not to mention play pro ball. The chances of Vaughn contributing to the Mets in a positive way this year are not promising.

Dave Weathers (Rubber Arm)

Position: RP
Bats: R **Throws:** R
Ht: 6' 3" **Wt:** 230

Opening Day Age: 34
Born: 9/25/69 in Lawrenceburg, TN
ML Seasons: 13

Overall Statistics

	W	L	Pct.	ERA	G	GS	Sv	IP	H	BB	SO	HR	Avg
'03	1	6	.143	3.08	77	0	7	87.2	87	40	75	6	.264
Car.	45	55	.450	4.49	548	67	14	933.2	1019	421	673	82	.282

2003 Situational Stats

	W	L	ERA	Sv	IP		AB	H	HR	RBI	Avg
Home	1	3	3.00	5	45.0	LHB	109	26	2	10	.239
Road	0	3	3.16	2	42.2	RHB	221	61	4	23	.276
First Half	1	4	3.00	1	51.0	Sc Pos	99	21	2	27	.212
Scnd Half	0	2	3.19	6	36.2	Clutch	196	50	5	22	.255

2003 Season

David Weathers was one of the few hurlers manager Art Howe maintained confidence in throughout 2003. He was among the league leaders in holds and innings pitched out of the bullpen. While he lost his last six decisions, Weathers set a career high for saves, and allowed only four runs in his last 18 outings.

Pitching, Defense & Hitting

Weathers is a rubber-armed reliever with good sinking action on his low-90s fastball. While he is particularly effective against righthanded hitters, he throws his sharp slider that sits at 82-84 MPH to batters from both sides of the plate and is superb at inducing groundballs in double-play situations. He has emerged as the Mets' primary setup man due to his ability to strand inherited runners. Weathers' slide-step delivery is effective at holding runners close. He is an average fielder with decent quickness for a big man, and rarely is called upon to hit.

2004 Outlook

Weathers is more effective the more often he pitches. After playing for seven different teams in his first 11 years in the big leagues, Weathers has found stability in the New York bullpen.

Vance Wilson

Position: C
Bats: R **Throws:** R
Ht: 5'11" **Wt:** 190

Opening Day Age: 31
Born: 3/17/73 in Mesa, AZ
ML Seasons: 5

Overall Statistics

	G	AB	R	H	D	T	HR	RBI	SB	BB	SO	Avg	OBP	Slg
'03	96	268	28	65	9	1	8	39	1	15	56	.243	.293	.373
Car.	207	492	50	122	19	1	13	71	1	22	106	.248	.299	.370

2003 Situational Stats

	AB	H	HR	RBI	Avg		AB	H	HR	RBI	Avg
Home	139	31	3	16	.223	LHP	74	18	2	8	.243
Road	129	34	5	23	.264	RHP	194	47	6	31	.242
First Half	187	53	7	31	.283	Sc Pos	61	17	3	33	.279
Scnd Half	81	12	1	8	.148	Clutch	32	9	1	4	.281

2003 Season

With Mike Piazza missing nearly half the season due to a groin injury, Vance Wilson led the Mets by starting 71 games at catcher in 2003. The situation proved to be a blessing, with Wilson guiding a staff filled with young pitchers. He also established his single-game bests by registering five RBI on June 12 and four hits on September 27.

Hitting, Baserunning & Defense

Wilson is an intelligent, defensive-minded catcher who gives the Mets a steady presence behind the plate. He calls an excellent game, moves well defensively and quiets the running game by throwing out 32.6 percent of would-be basestealers last year. Wilson provides decent power near the bottom of the batting order. Although his batting average is nothing spectacular, he tends to come through in the clutch, batting .279 with teammates in scoring position in 2003. His speed is not unlike that of most catchers, with Wilson swiping the first base of his career last season.

2004 Outlook

Wilson's opportunity for playing time figures to increase substantially if Piazza winds up playing more often at first base. While Jason Phillips is in the picture as well, Wilson again should catch the majority of Mets games this season.

Other New York Mets

Edwin Almonte (Pos: RHP, Age: 27)

	W	L	Pct.	ERA	G	GS	Sv	IP	H	BB	SO	HR	Avg
'03	0	0	–	11.12	12	0	0	11.1	21	5	7	3	.412
Car.	0	0	–	11.12	12	0	0	11.1	21	5	7	3	.412

Almonte was traded from the White Sox to the Mets in July. He had outstanding minor league numbers as a closer in 2001 and 2002, but posted some disappointing stats in 2003. The Red Sox claimed Almonte off waivers in November. 2004 Outlook: C

Jason Anderson (Pos: RHP, Age: 24)

	W	L	Pct.	ERA	G	GS	Sv	IP	H	BB	SO	HR	Avg
'03	1	0	1.000	4.88	28	0	0	31.1	33	19	16	5	.273
Car.	1	0	1.000	4.88	28	0	0	31.1	33	19	16	5	.273

Anderson was traded by the Yankees to the Mets in July. For the season, lefties hit .354 off Anderson, while righties hit .219. He had a 2.19 ERA during the day, but a 6.63 ERA at night. 2004 Outlook: C

Mike Bacsik (Pos: LHP, Age: 26)

	W	L	Pct.	ERA	G	GS	Sv	IP	H	BB	SO	HR	Avg
'03	1	2	.333	10.19	5	3	0	17.2	28	8	12	5	.368
Car.	4	4	.500	6.12	19	12	0	82.1	104	30	46	13	.311

Bacsik gave up nine earned runs in three innings as a reliever in March and April and 11 earned runs in 14.2 innings in three starts in June. The Mets optioned him in late June and he did not return. 2004 Outlook: C

Jay Bell (Pos: 1B/2B/3B/SS, Age: 38, Bats: R)

	G	AB	R	H	D	T	HR	RBI	SB	BB	SO	Avg	OBP	Slg
	72	116	11	21	1	0	0	3	0	22	38	.181	.319	.190
	2063	7398	1123	1963	394	67	195	860	91	853	1443	.265	.343	.416

Bell hit just .181 with three RBI in 116 at-bats in his final year. He may retire with a career .265 batting average to go with 195 homers and 860 RBI in 18 seasons. 2004 Outlook: D

Jaime Cerda (Pos: LHP, Age: 25)

	W	L	Pct.	ERA	G	GS	Sv	IP	H	BB	SO	HR	Avg
'03	1	1	.500	5.85	27	0	0	32.1	32	20	19	4	.267
Car.	1	1	.500	4.34	59	0	0	58.0	54	34	40	4	.251

Cerda wore a trail from New York to Triple-A Norfolk last season as the Mets recalled and demoted him on four different occasions. He struggled in the majors, but had a 1.67 ERA at Norfolk. 2004 Outlook: C

David Cone (Pos: RHP, Age: 41)

	W	L	Pct.	ERA	G	GS	Sv	IP	H	BB	SO	HR	Avg
	1	3	.250	6.50	5	4	0	18.0	20	13	13	4	.282
	194	126	.606	3.46	450	419	1	2898.2	2504	1137	2668	258	.232

After posting a 1-3 record and 6.50 ERA during an injury-plagued start to the season, Cone announced his retirement in May. He finishes his career at 194-126 with a 3.46 ERA. 2004 Outlook: D

Joe DePastino (Pos: C, Age: 30, Bats: R)

	G	AB	R	H	D	T	HR	RBI	SB	BB	SO	Avg	OBP	Slg
'03	2	2	0	0	0	0	0	0	0	0	1	.000	.000	.000
Car.	2	2	0	0	0	0	0	0	0	0	1	.000	.000	.000

The 30-year-old DePastino worked as Vance Wilson's backup for two days in August while Jason Phillips left to attend the birth of his child. The 6-foot-2 catcher was hitless in two at-bats with the Mets. 2004 Outlook: C

Pedro Feliciano (Pos: LHP, Age: 27)

	W	L	Pct.	ERA	G	GS	Sv	IP	H	BB	SO	HR	Avg
'03	0	0	–	3.35	23	0	0	48.1	52	21	43	5	.269
Car.	0	0	–	3.81	29	0	0	54.1	61	22	47	5	.280

Feliciano, who pitched in six September games for the Mets in 2002, gave the Mets four lefties in the pen when he was called up in May. He had a 1.93 ERA in day games, but a 4.25 ERA at night. 2004 Outlook: C

Mike Glavine (Pos: 1B, Age: 31, Bats: L)

	G	AB	R	H	D	T	HR	RBI	SB	BB	SO	Avg	OBP	Slg
'03	6	7	0	1	0	0	0	0	0	0	2	.143	.143	.143
Car.	6	7	0	1	0	0	0	0	0	0	2	.143	.143	.143

Tom's brother hit .266 with five homers and 17 RBI in 169 at-bats for Triple-A Norfolk in 2003. The Mets purchased his contract in early September in what was widely viewed as a publicity ploy. 2004 Outlook: C

Raul Gonzalez (Pos: LF/CF/RF, Age: 30, Bats: R)

	G	AB	R	H	D	T	HR	RBI	SB	BB	SO	Avg	OBP	Slg
'03	107	217	28	50	12	2	2	21	3	27	34	.230	.317	.332
Car.	161	337	41	80	15	2	5	33	7	34	61	.237	.307	.338

Gonzalez was 4-for-6 with a home run in his first two games after a callup from Triple-A in April, but was hitting .235 when the Mets sent him down in June. He later hit .205 in August and September. 2004 Outlook: C

Joe McEwing (Pos: 2B/SS/LF, Age: 31, Bats: R)

	G	AB	R	H	D	T	HR	RBI	SB	BB	SO	Avg	OBP	Slg
'03	119	278	31	67	11	0	1	16	3	25	57	.241	.309	.291
Car.	589	1443	184	365	79	9	23	136	25	98	283	.253	.308	.368

McEwing has been a Mets staple as a utilityman, and he secured a fair share of the playing time at second after Robbie Alomar was traded. While McEwing hasn't been as productive offensively of late, he'll still probably find a 2004 spot with the Mets. 2004 Outlook: C

Jason Middlebrook (Pos: RHP, Age: 28)

	W	L	Pct.	ERA	G	GS	Sv	IP	H	BB	SO	HR	Avg
'03	0	0	–	10.29	5	0	0	7.0	13	4	3	0	.433
Car.	4	4	.500	5.33	24	8	0	77.2	75	36	55	8	.260

Middlebrook had a chance to claim a rotation spot in spring training, but pitched poorly. He was used in relief by the Mets in April and May, when righties hit 10-for-22 against him. 2004 Outlook: C

Orber Moreno (Pos: RHP, Age: 26)

	W	L	Pct.	ERA	G	GS	Sv	IP	H	BB	SO	HR	Avg
'03	0	0	–	7.88	7	0	0	8.0	10	3	5	1	.313
Car.	0	0	–	6.75	14	0	0	16.0	14	9	12	2	.233

The Mets signed Moreno in March and a September callup marked his first return to the majors since he was Kansas City's closer of the future in 1999. Tommy John surgery sidetracked his career in 2000. 2004 Outlook: C

Jason Roach (Pos: RHP, Age: 27)

	W	L	Pct.	ERA	G	GS	Sv	IP	H	BB	SO	HR	Avg
'03	0	2	.000	12.00	2	2	0	0.0	14	4	2	3	.350
Car.	0	2	.000	12.00	2	2	0	9.0	14	4	2	3	.350

Roach, a former third baseman, had two spot starts for the Mets and took the loss in both. He had a 5.07 ERA in 20 starts and 11 relief appearances for Triple-A Norfolk. 2004 Outlook: C

Marco Scutaro (Pos: 2B, Age: 28, Bats: R)

	G	AB	R	H	D	T	HR	RBI	SB	BB	SO	Avg	OBP	Slg
'03	48	75	10	16	4	0	2	6	2	13	14	.213	.333	.347
Car.	75	111	12	24	4	1	3	12	2	13	25	.216	.299	.351

The Mets signed the 28-year-old Scutaro in February. The infielder was recalled in May and hit .213 in 48 games for New York, before Oakland claimed him off waivers in October. 2004 Outlook: B

Tsuyoshi Shinjo (Pos: CF, Age: 32, Bats: R)

	G	AB	R	H	D	T	HR	RBI	SB	BB	SO	Avg	OBP	Slg
'03	62	114	10	22	3	0	1	7	0	6	12	.193	.238	.246
Car.	303	876	98	215	41	4	20	100	9	55	128	.245	.299	.370

Shinjo hit .167 in April and .114 in June and was optioned to Triple-A. He hit 2-for-33 against right-handers. He spent the second half in the minors and is headed back to Japan for 2004. 2004 Outlook: D

Pat Strange (Pos: RHP, Age: 23)

	W	L	Pct.	ERA	G	GS	Sv	IP	H	BB	SO	HR	Avg
'03	0	0	–	11.00	6	0	0	9.0	13	11	5	4	.351
Car.	0	0	–	6.35	11	0	0	17.0	19	12	9	4	.288

Strange was 3-1 with a 3.34 ERA at Triple-A Norfolk when the Mets promoted him in May. Big league hitters hit .351 off him. In his third appearance, he yielded six runs while recording only one out. 2004 Outlook: C

Scott Strickland (Pos: RHP, Age: 27)

	W	L	Pct.	ERA	G	GS	Sv	IP	H	BB	SO	HR	Avg
'03	0	2	.000	2.25	19	0	0	20.0	16	10	16	1	.219
Car.	12	21	.364	3.28	231	0	20	236.0	197	111	241	23	.224

Strickland gave up just three earned runs in his final 17 appearances before leaving a game in May with a strained groin. He later had Tommy John surgery in June and will miss much of next season. 2004 Outlook: C

Jorge Velandia (Pos: SS, Age: 29, Bats: R)

	G	AB	R	H	D	T	HR	RBI	SB	BB	SO	Avg	OBP	Slg
'03	23	58	6	11	3	1	0	8	0	10	15	.190	.304	.276
Car.	100	178	18	37	7	1	0	12	2	17	45	.151	.231	.200

Velandia, a six-year veteran, was signed by the Mets in July. He had a cup of coffee with the team that month and spent most of September as the starting shortstop, when he hit just .190 in 23 games. 2004 Outlook: C

Matt Watson (Pos: LF, Age: 25, Bats: L)

	G	AB	R	H	D	T	HR	RBI	SB	BB	SO	Avg	OBP	Slg
'03	15	23	0	4	2	0	0	2	0	1	5	.174	.208	.261
Car.	15	23	0	4	2	0	0	2	0	1	5	.174	.208	.261

Watson hit .295 with 11 HR and 55 RBI in 74 games for Triple-A Norfolk, before he was claimed off waivers by Oakland. The 25-year-old outfielder should compete for a reserve spot in spring training with the A's, who claimed Watson off waivers in October. 2004 Outlook: C

Dan Wheeler (Pos: RHP, Age: 26)

	W	L	Pct.	ERA	G	GS	Sv	IP	H	BB	SO	HR	Avg
'03	1	3	.250	3.71	35	0	2	51.0	49	17	35	6	.253
Car.	3	8	.273	5.30	65	8	2	122.1	143	46	96	18	.291

Wheeler made his first appearance in the majors since pitching for Tampa Bay in 2001. He was 4-2 with four saves and a 3.94 ERA at Norfolk when he was called up to the Mets in June. 2004 Outlook: C

New York Mets Minor League Prospects

Organization Overview:

The overhaul experienced at the major league level midway through last year, including the ouster of GM Steve Phillips, should bode well for the long-term future of the Mets. After Phillips depleted the farm system by trading minor leaguers for overrated major league help, the Mets added considerable mid-level depth in deals that shipped such veterans as Roberto Alomar and Jeromy Burnitz out of town. The strength of the New York farm system is its pitching and athletic outfielders. Scouting director Gary LaRocque nabbed four high-ceiling hurlers in as many drafts from 1999-2002 before selecting outfielder Lastings Milledge, possibly the best all-around athlete in the 2003 process, with the 12th overall pick last year.

Craig Brazell

Position: 1B   **Opening Day Age:** 23
Bats: L **Throws:** R   **Born:** 5/10/80 in
Ht: 6' 3" **Wt:** 185   Montgomery, AL

Recent Statistics

	G	AB	R	H	D	T	HR	RBI	SB	BB	SO	Avg
2002 A St. Lucie	100	402	38	107	25	3	16	82	2	13	78	.266
2002 AA Binghamton	35	130	14	40	8	0	6	19	0	1	28	.308
2003 AA Binghamton	111	432	58	126	23	2	17	76	2	23	97	.292
2003 AAA Norfolk	12	46	4	12	3	0	0	1	1	1	8	.261

Brazell made the full-season jump to the Double-A Eastern League last year and continued to prove he is the best lefthanded power hitter the Mets have developed in many years. He has a smooth and easy swing that enables him to hit for average, and New York officials believe he will produce 30 home runs annually in the major leagues. Brazell eventually should be a productive middle-of-the-lineup run producer, but his offensive approach needs some refinements—he tends to try to pull too many pitches and his strike-zone judgment is lacking. A former catcher, Brazell is an above-average first baseman with soft hands and good range.

Jeff Duncan

Position: OF   **Opening Day Age:** 25
Bats: L **Throws:** L   **Born:** 12/9/78 in Harvey,
Ht: 6' 2" **Wt:** 188   IL

Recent Statistics

	G	AB	R	H	D	T	HR	RBI	SB	BB	SO	Avg
2003 AA Binghamton	76	278	49	80	11	5	4	23	24	36	59	.288
2003 AAA Norfolk	4	15	2	4	1	0	2	4	1	1	7	.267
2003 NL New York	56	139	13	27	0	2	1	10	4	17	41	.194

Duncan was toiling at the Class-A level in early 2002, yet reached the big leagues a little more than a year later. A plus runner with good baseball instincts, he impressed the Mets with his outstanding defense and baserunning skills. He is a potential leadoff hitter due to his excellent plate discipline and his ability to hit pitches the other way. The lefthanded hitter also has some pop in his bat. Duncan struggled with injuries during his first two professional seasons before blossoming the past two years. If he can avoid the prolonged slumps that affected him in 2003, he could emerge as the Mets' starting center fielder.

Danny Garcia

Position: 2B   **Opening Day Age:** 23
Bats: R **Throws:** R   **Born:** 4/12/80 in
Ht: 6' 0" **Wt:** 174   Riverside, CA

Recent Statistics

	G	AB	R	H	D	T	HR	RBI	SB	BB	SO	Avg
2003 AA Binghamton	31	116	21	38	12	1	3	21	2	10	20	.328
2003 AAA Norfolk	101	388	45	102	23	3	4	54	11	22	60	.263
2003 NL New York	19	56	5	12	2	0	2	6	0	2	11	.214

Garcia has the grittiness and desire that will allow him to compete for a job on the 25-man roster, possibly as the starting second baseman. He stands his ground and makes the pivot on double plays very well and gives every ounce of energy he has on every play. The first graduate of the Class-A Brooklyn Cyclones to play for the Mets, Garcia is not loaded with tools, yet the total package is greater than the sum of the individual parts. He is a surehanded defender and a good baserunner who drives the ball into the gaps. He singled twice in his major league debut, including a line drive up the middle in his first at-bat.

Justin Huber

Position: C   **Opening Day Age:** 21
Bats: R **Throws:** R   **Born:** 7/1/82 in
Ht: 6' 2" **Wt:** 190   Melbourne, Australia

Recent Statistics

	G	AB	R	H	D	T	HR	RBI	SB	BB	SO	Avg
2002 A St. Lucie	28	100	15	27	2	1	3	15	0	11	18	.270
2002 A Capital City	95	330	49	96	22	2	11	78	1	45	81	.291
2003 A St. Lucie	50	183	26	52	15	0	9	36	1	17	30	.284
2003 AA Binghamton	55	193	16	51	13	0	6	36	0	19	54	.264

More than a few scouts believe Huber is on track toward becoming the next Mike Piazza. The Australia native continues to develop into a productive hitter with above-average power and run-producing abilities, but his progress behind the plate has lagged over the past year. Huber can drive the ball to all fields with his strong and quick wrists, and he should become a consistent home-run producer at higher levels. Defensively, however, Huber has below-average arm strength and is only an average catch-and-throw receiver. The Mets still believe that with some seasoning, he has the tools to be an average catcher with above-average offensive production.

Scott Kazmir

Position: P
Opening Day Age: 20
Bats: L **Throws:** L
Born: 1/24/84 in
Ht: 6' 0" **Wt:** 175
Houston, TX

Recent Statistics

	W	L	ERA	G	GS	Sv	IP	H	R	BB	SO	HR
2002 A Brooklyn	0	1	0.50	5	5	0	18.0	5	2	7	34	0
2003 A Capital City	4	4	2.36	18	18	0	76.1	50	26	28	105	6
2003 A St. Lucie	1	2	3.27	7	7	0	33.0	29	15	16	40	0

Kazmir may be the top lefthanded pitching prospect in the minor leagues. Tabbed the High School Player of the Year in 2002 by *Baseball America*, he dominated the Class-A South Atlantic League during the first half of 2003 by averaging 12.4 strikeouts per nine innings while limiting opposing hitters to a .185 clip. Kazmir's fastball has incredible movement while sitting at 94 MPH and climbing as high as 97 MPH. He also throws a hard slider in the upper 80s that overwhelms left-handed hitters. He made significant strides with his changeup over the course of last season and is on the verge of becoming a solid three-pitch hurler.

Matt Peterson

Position: P
Opening Day Age: 22
Bats: R **Throws:** R
Born: 2/11/82 in
Ht: 6' 5" **Wt:** 185
Alexandria, LA

Recent Statistics

	W	L	ERA	G	GS	Sv	IP	H	R	BB	SO	HR
2002 A St. Lucie	1	0	1.50	1	1	0	6.0	5	2	2	5	0
2002 A Capital City	8	10	3.86	26	26	0	137.2	109	67	61	153	13
2003 AA Binghamton	1	2	3.45	6	6	0	31.1	29	18	20	23	2
2003 A St. Lucie	0	2	1.71	15	15	0	84.0	65	24	24	73	2

The Mets' second-round pick in 2000, Peterson was tabbed the organization's Pitcher of the Year in 2003. Among other accomplishments, the righthander helped lead high Class-A St. Lucie to the Florida State League championship. Peterson succeeds with a 92-93 MPH fastball that he throws on an excellent downhill plane. He also has a plus overhand curveball with an 11-to-5 break, and his changeup showed significant improvement with its depth and fade over the course of last season. Peterson's mind used to drift at times, but he now wants the ball in big-game situations, which has him on the verge of knocking on the door to the major leagues.

Royce Ring

Position: P
Opening Day Age: 23
Bats: L **Throws:** L
Born: 12/21/80 in La
Ht: 6' 0" **Wt:** 220
Mesa, CA

Recent Statistics

	W	L	ERA	G	GS	Sv	IP	H	R	BB	SO	HR
2002 R White Sox	0	0	0.00	3	0	0	5.0	2	0	0	9	0
2002 A Winston-Sal	2	0	3.91	21	0	5	23.0	20	11	11	22	2
2003 AA Birmingham	1	4	2.52	36	0	19	35.2	31	14	14	44	1
2003 AA Binghamton	3	0	1.66	18	0	7	21.2	13	4	11	18	2

The Mets acquired Ring from the White Sox last summer in exchange for Roberto Alomar. The strong-armed lefthander has the power and makeup to be a premier setup man or possibly a closer at the game's top level. An aggressive pitcher who is not afraid to challenge hitters, he throws a good fastball in the 89-92 MPH range with above-average movement, along with a sharp slider and a decent changeup. He also possesses a rubber arm and performs better the more often he pitches. Chicago's first-round draft pick in 2002 out of San Diego State, Ring has struggled with walks on occasion, yet he still managed to go 4-4 with a 2.20 ERA and 26 saves between two Double-A teams in 2003.

David Wright

Position: 3B
Opening Day Age: 21
Bats: R **Throws:** R
Born: 12/20/82 in
Ht: 6' 0" **Wt:** 195
Chesapeake, VA

Recent Statistics

	G	AB	R	H	D	T	HR	RBI	SB	BB	SO	Avg
2002 A Capital City	135	496	85	132	30	2	11	93	21	76	114	.266
2003 A St. Lucie	133	466	69	126	39	2	15	75	19	72	98	.270

The 38th overall pick in the 2001 draft, Wright has made a methodical climb through the Mets' organization. A superior defensive third baseman who charges balls extremely well, he is a pure hitter who makes solid contact. He possesses a smooth and easy swing from his compact stride, and should develop into a high-average batter due to his solid plate discipline. Wright also drives the ball well into the gaps and is expected to produce more than 20 home runs annually in the majors. He overcame an early '03 slump that was caused in part by his tremendous work ethic to hit at a .323 clip in the final six weeks.

Others to Watch

Victor Diaz (22) will get a long look at second base after arriving from the Dodgers last summer in exchange for Jeromy Burnitz. Diaz hits for both power and average but raises concerns about his glove. Some scouts question his desire due to his excess weight and suggest that he would be better served at third base. . . Catcher **Mike Jacobs** (23) was named the Mets' Organizational Player of the Year in 2003 after leading the Double-A Eastern League with a .548 slugging percentage. He is intriguing because of the power potential in his lefthanded bat, and has made impressive defensive strides behind the plate last year. . . **Bob Keppel** (21) threw the first regular-season no-hitter for the Double-A Binghamton franchise last year and continues to make steady progress along the organizational ladder. Keppel has good sinking action on his low 90s fastball along with a good curveball and changeup. He simply needs to refine all of his pitches while locating them better in the strike zone. . . Outfielder **Prentice Redman** (24) is one of the best baserunners in the organization with superb range and a good arm in the field. His bat has improved due to his willingness to hit to all fields, yet his batting average is not exceptional due to his difficulties against lefthanders.

Citizens Bank Park

Offense

The dimensions of new Citzens Bank Park are similar to Veterans Stadium, which was generally a pitchers' park early in the season and then became more hitter-friendly when the weather warmed. Still, the changes should favor the offense—instead of being a uniform 12 feet, the fence will be as low as six feet in some places, just over 13 feet above the out-of-town scoreboard in right and as high as 19 feet just left of center field. There will also be less foul territory. The wind patterns should be altered, as the new park is much more open, so the wind direction should affect batted balls directly.

Defense

The biggest difference will be the move from artificial turf to natural grass. With a solid infield and a staff full of pitchers who can get groundballs, that should work in the Phillies' favor. It remains to be seen how the grass will be manicured. Will it be kept short, making it a fast field similar to the old NexTurf? Or will it be allowed to grow, slowing down groundballs and giving infielders a better chance to make plays?

Who It Helps the Most

The softer playing surface will be a boon for all the Phillies, especially Jim Thome and David Bell, who have had lower back problems. It should also be good for groundball pitchers like Vicente Padilla and Brett Myers, if they become more consistent keeping their pitches down in the strike zone.

Who It Hurts the Most

Jimmy Rollins has been a prototypical turf shortstop, so he'll have an adjustment to make. It also doesn't help that his mission this season is to hit the ball on the ground more. The addition of a cut-out in left-center will be a challenge for Pat Burrell.

Rookies & Newcomers

Lefthander Eric Milton, an extreme flyball pitcher who gave up plenty of home runs with Minnesota, should enjoy pitching at home more than he did in the cozy Hubert H. Humphrey Metrodome. New relievers Billy Wagner and Tim Worrell will prefer the new park's grass over the Vet's artificial turf.

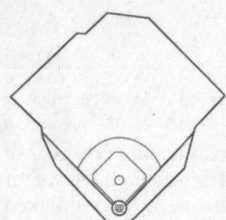

Dimensions: LF-329, LCF-369, CF-401, RCF-369, RF-330

Capacity: 43,000

Elevation: 20 feet

Surface: Grass

Foul Territory: Average

Park Factors

2003 Season (Veterans Stadium)

	Home Games			Away Games			
	Phillies	Opp	Total	Phillies	Opp	Total	Index
G	72	72	144	75	75	150	
Avg	.264	.235	.250	.259	.273	.266	94
AB	2379	2446	4825	2625	2482	5107	98
R	349	266	615	373	369	742	86
H	628	576	1204	681	678	1359	92
2B	148	135	283	145	157	302	99
3B	15	11	26	12	15	27	102
HR	68	54	122	76	76	152	85
BB	302	233	535	282	247	529	107
SO	496	555	1051	539	403	942	118
E	38	34	72	54	42	96	78
E-Infield	33	32	65	42	32	74	91
LHB-Avg	.270	.231	.252	.262	.282	.271	93
LHB-HR	40	13	53	38	27	65	83
RHB-Avg	.259	.238	.248	.257	.268	.263	94
RHB-HR	28	41	69	38	49	87	86

2001-2003 (Veterans Stadium)

	Home Games			Away Games			
	Phillies	Opp	Total	Phillies	Opp	Total	Index
G	215	215	430	219	219	438	
Avg	.256	.239	.248	.266	.273	.269	92
AB	7059	7321	14380	7709	7316	15025	97
R	963	848	1811	1057	1074	2131	87
H	1809	1752	3561	2049	1995	4044	90
2B	409	394	803	435	448	883	95
3B	50	38	88	40	51	91	101
HR	212	190	402	225	224	449	94
BB	822	708	1530	816	742	1558	103
SO	1470	1598	3068	1538	1282	2820	114
E	101	117	218	151	152	303	73
E-Infield	88	99	187	117	120	237	80
LHB-Avg	.251	.242	.247	.274	.281	.277	89
LHB-HR	107	63	170	102	76	178	97
RHB-Avg	.261	.238	.248	.259	.268	.264	94
RHB-HR	105	127	232	123	148	271	92

2003 Rankings (National League)

- Highest strikeout factor
- Lowest error factor
- Second-lowest batting-average factor
- Second-lowest hit factor
- Third-lowest run factor
- Third-lowest LHB batting-average factor
- Third-lowest RHB batting-average factor

Larry Bowa

2003 Season

In Larry Bowa's third season, the Phillies failed to make the playoffs for the ninth straight year despite raising expectations by signing free agents Jim Thome and David Bell, and trading for Kevin Millwood. Even the second winning season in three years—the first time since the mid 1980s that's happened—didn't make up for the disappointment. For the third straight year, coaching-staff changes were made at the end of the season.

Offense

Bowa used 119 different lineups last season. That was partly because he was searching for a leadoff hitter until settling on rookie Marlon Byrd, and partly because Pat Burrell's season-long slump caused him to move up and down the order all year. Bowa has fundamentally changed his approach from trying to manufacture runs to waiting for home runs. Last season, the Phillies attempted just 101 stolen bases and had only 71 sacrifice bunt attempts. He lacks patience with hitters in slumps and generally tries to play the hot hand.

Pitching & Defense

Bowa earned a reputation for having a quick hook, but situations most often dictated his moves last season. With the offense struggling, he was forced to pinch-hit for his starter when trailing in the middle innings in an attempt to get back into the game. At the same time, he became enamored of his bullpen after a strong first half, and the relievers' relative lack of effectiveness in the second half could have been a result of heavy workloads after the break. He prefers set roles for his relievers, but Jose Mesa's struggles forced him to use a committee approach for most of the last month.

2004 Outlook

Bowa has unqualified public support from the front office, although problems within the clubhouse have been well documented. That didn't stop management from picking up his 2005 option and added two more option years to his contract. With the Phillies moving into a new stadium, making the 2004 playoffs is almost imperative, especially with the higher payroll. Bowa remains popular with the fans, but that could change with a poor start.

Born: 12/6/45 in Sacramento, CA

Playing Experience: 1970-1985, Phi, ChC, NYM

Managerial Experience: 5 seasons

Manager Statistics

Year	Team, Lg	W	L	Pct	GB	Finish
2003	Philadelphia, NL	86	76	.531	15.0	3rd East
5 Seasons		333	360	.481	–	–

2003 Starting Pitchers by Days Rest

	<=3	4	5	6+
Phillies Starts	0	95	41	18
Phillies ERA	–	4.05	4.52	3.83
NL Avg Starts	2	84	43	23
NL ERA	5.00	4.23	4.42	4.68

2003 Situational Stats

	Larry Bowa	NL Average
Hit & Run Success %	45.7	32.7
Stolen Base Success %	71.3	68.9
Platoon Pct.	54.0	52.0
Defensive Subs	14	19
High-Pitch Outings	5	8
Quick/Slow Hooks	17/6	20/12
Sacrifice Attempts	71	93

2003 Rankings (National League)

- 1st in hit-and-run success percentage
- 2nd in pitchouts with a runner moving (9)
- 3rd in fewest caught stealings of second base (24)

Bobby Abreu

2003 Season

Bobby Abreu continues to be an enigma. After becoming the first 30-30 player in franchise history in 2001, he was signed to a five-year, $64 million contract extension that included escalator clauses for winning the Most Valuable Player Award. Club officials said they believed he had only begun to tap his potential. Yet Abreu, who will play at 30 this season, hasn't come close to even making an All-Star team yet.

Hitting

Is Abreu a power hitter? Or is he a line drive hitter who is a threat to steal bases? It sometimes seems neither he nor the Phillies can decide. He walked 109 times and scored 99 runs. . . but also struck out 126 times. He has a career .409 on-base percentage. . . but was unhappy when asked to lead off for five games last season. He is on record as saying his goal is to win a batting title. . . but batted just .274 before the All-Star break.

Baserunning & Defense

Abreu is a fast baserunner, but not necessarily a good one. He has a green light most of the time but doesn't take advantage of that as often as he probably should. He is considered an average outfielder, despite a strong arm and the speed to cover a lot of ground. He has problems going back on the ball, and last season often appeared tentative coming in on shallows flyballs just over the infield. His biggest strength is that baserunners rarely try to take an extra base on him.

2004 Outlook

Abreu will remain a fixture as the Phillies move into their new ballpark, at least in part because of his contract. General manager Ed Wade "discovered" him while scouting the Astros and helped convince then-GM Lee Thomas to trade for him at the expansion draft in 1997. Abreu gives the team a potent lefthanded bat to go along with Jim Thome in the middle of the lineup. If he ever has the breakthrough season that has been envisioned for years, that will be a plus.

Position: RF
Bats: L **Throws:** R
Ht: 6' 0" **Wt:** 200

Opening Day Age: 30
Born: 3/11/74 in Aragua, VZ
ML Seasons: 8
Pronunciation: ah-BRAY-you

Overall Statistics

	G	AB	R	H	D	T	HR	RBI	SB	BB	SO	Avg	OBP	Slg
'03	158	577	99	173	35	1	20	101	22	109	126	.300	.409	.468
Car.	1008	3566	631	1091	250	40	136	569	170	635	793	.306	.409	.513

Where He Hits the Ball

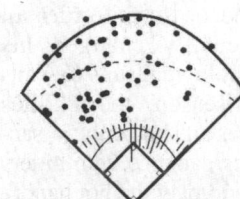
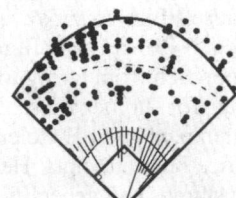

Vs. LHP   **Vs. RHP**

2003 Situational Stats

	AB	H	HR	RBI	Avg		AB	H	HR	RBI	Avg
Home	281	98	11	56	.349	LHP	180	49	3	31	.272
Road	296	75	9	45	.253	RHP	397	124	17	70	.312
First Half	332	91	14	56	.274	Sc Pos	155	56	7	83	.361
Scnd Half	245	82	6	45	.335	Clutch	88	28	2	14	.318

2003 Rankings (National League)

- 1st in pitches seen (2,994)
- 2nd in most pitches seen per plate appearance (4.31), highest percentage of pitches taken (65.6), lowest percentage of swings on the first pitch (9.7) and errors in right field (6)
- 3rd in lowest fielding percentage in right field (.981)
- 4th in walks and times on base (284)
- Led the Phillies in hits, singles, sacrifice flies (7), stolen bases, intentional walks (13), times on base (284), on-base percentage, most pitches seen per plate appearance (4.31), batting average with runners in scoring position, batting average vs. righthanded pitchers, batting average at home

David Bell

Position: 3B
Bats: R **Throws:** R
Ht: 5'10" **Wt:** 195

Opening Day Age: 31
Born: 9/14/72 in Cincinnati, OH
ML Seasons: 0

2003 Season

David Bell was the first free agent the Phillies signed before last season. He was given a four-year, $17 million contract in part to replace Scott Rolen at third and in part to bring some veteran leadership to the clubhouse. Unfortunately, he was bothered by a herniated disc in his back during much of the first half of the season and played only two games after July 10. Manager Larry Bowa said repeatedly that Phillies fans didn't get a chance to see the real Bell.

Hitting

With the benefit of hindsight, the Phillies say they should have known something was wrong with Bell. After a strong spring training his numbers went straight downhill. He batted .138 in July before he finally admitted that his back was bothering him. The original diagnosis was that he would return after two weeks, but complications kept setting in and the pain eventually extended to his hip. He could begin his swing without a problem but would feel pain as he tried to follow through. When healthy, he can usually be counted on to bat around .260 with about 15 homers.

Baserunning & Defense

Bell is the son of former big leaguer Buddy Bell, also a third baseman, and inherited his father's defensive skills. He may not have the strongest arm but he can fire the ball when he has to. Normally, however, he relies on a quick release and accuracy. He is fundamentally sound receiving the ball, with good footwork around the base. He is a smart, heady runner who uses good instincts to make up for a lack of speed.

2004 Outlook

Since Bell's back injury lingered so much longer than originally expected, and because he still wasn't fully recovered at the end of the season, there will be a natural concern about his health until he proves he's 100 percent. The Phillies expect Bell to be at full strength this season, which would allow Placido Polanco to remain at second base, his more natural position.

Overall Statistics

	G	AB	R	H	D	T	HR	RBI	SB	BB	SO	Avg	OBP	Slg
'03	85	297	32	58	14	0	4	37	0	41	40	.195	.296	.283
Car.	965	3232	407	810	176	12	85	388	15	274	475	.251	.312	.391

Where He Hits the Ball

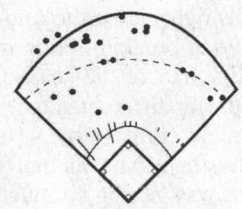
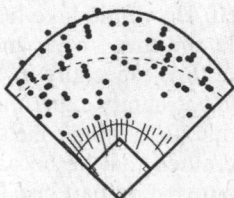

Vs. LHP　　　　**Vs. RHP**

2003 Situational Stats

	AB	H	HR	RBI	Avg		AB	H	HR	RBI	Avg
Home	144	23	1	16	.160	LHP	71	12	3	10	.169
Road	153	35	3	21	.229	RHP	226	46	1	27	.204
First Half	293	58	4	37	.198	Sc Pos	90	20	1	31	.222
Scnd Half	4	0	0	0	.000	Clutch	38	9	0	6	.237

2003 Rankings (National League)

- 10th in lowest batting average with the bases loaded (.111)

Pat Burrell

2003 Season

Pat Burrell was the Phillies' biggest disappointment last season. After he batted .282 with 37 homers and 116 RBI in 2002, he was rewarded with a six-year, $50 million contract extension even though he wasn't even eligible for salary arbitration. That looked pretty smart until Burrell suffered through a season-long slump that led to his being booed at home. He periodically was benched, and clashed at times with manager Larry Bowa.

Hitting

Burrell was the first player drafted in 1998 and had never experienced failure until last season. He started off slowly and couldn't seem to find himself. He would take fastballs right down the middle and then swing and miss at breaking balls in the dirt, especially in the first half of the season. He constantly experimented with different stances without finding one that felt comfortable. He admitted that he became frustrated and mentally confused, in part because he was getting so much advice from so many different people.

Baserunning & Defense

Burrell has worked hard to make himself a more-than-adequate left fielder. Last season, however, he seemed to take his hitting problems into the field. He has an extremely strong arm, and opposing teams have learned not to try to run on him. That accounts for the fact that he doesn't get as many assists as he has in previous years. He has turned himself into a good baserunner despite limited speed, though definitely not a basestealing threat.

2004 Outlook

Philadelphia needs Burrell to find himself again. To that end, he agreed to an intensive hitting tutorial in the offseason, with the goal of rebuilding his swing from the ground up. Since there is no apparent physical reason for Burrell's problems last season, the Phillies are taking the stance that they see no reason why he shouldn't bounce back. If he does, it will allow Bowa to use him between the two lefthanded bats—Bobby Abreu and Jim Thome—in the middle of the order.

Position: LF
Bats: R **Throws:** R
Ht: 6' 4" **Wt:** 222

Opening Day Age: 27
Born: 10/10/76 in Eureka Springs, AR
ML Seasons: 4
Pronunciation: BURL

Overall Statistics

	G	AB	R	H	D	T	HR	RBI	SB	BB	SO	Avg	OBP	Slg
'03	146	522	57	109	31	4	21	64	0	72	142	.209	.309	.404
Car.	569	2055	280	519	126	9	103	348	3	294	596	.253	.348	.473

Where He Hits the Ball

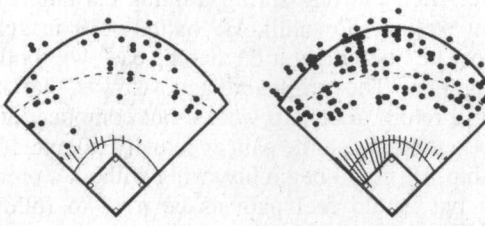

Vs. LHP   **Vs. RHP**

2003 Situational Stats

	AB	H	HR	RBI	Avg		AB	H	HR	RBI	Avg
Home	253	52	9	33	.206	LHP	111	22	4	6	.198
Road	269	57	12	31	.212	RHP	411	87	17	58	.212
First Half	317	61	12	34	.192	Sc Pos	145	29	6	44	.200
Scnd Half	205	48	9	30	.234	Clutch	72	16	5	10	.222

2003 Rankings (National League)

- 1st in lowest batting average, lowest batting average vs. lefthanded pitchers, lowest batting average vs. righthanded pitchers and lowest batting average at home
- 3rd in errors in left field (6), lowest batting average on the road and lowest fielding percentage in left field (.976)
- 4th in most pitches seen per plate appearance (4.14)
- 6th in strikeouts and lowest batting average with runners in scoring position
- Led the Phillies in GDPs (18)

Marlon Byrd

2003 Season

Marlon Byrd overcame early skepticism to have one of the best seasons of any National League rookie. He struggled through the first two months, batting .193 while spending two weeks on the disabled list with a knee laceration suffered when sliding into home plate. There were rumors he would be sent back to Triple-A Scranton/Wilkes-Barre. But he responded by batting .364 in June on his way to finishing with a .303 average.

Hitting

Byrd is a free swinger who wouldn't seem ideally suited to the leadoff spot, but he blossomed after being moved to the top of the order in July. He has the ability to chop a ball over the infield or beat out a grounder with his speed. He also showed some gap power, though he wasn't the home-run threat that might have been suggested by his 28 longballs at Double-A Reading in 2001. Strong and solidly-built, with a body reminiscent of Kirby Puckett, Byrd should be more of a power threat as he gains experience.

Baserunning & Defense

Byrd uses his great speed to cover up a lack of fundamentals both in the field and on the bases. He sometimes doesn't get a good jump on flyballs but still is able to make most plays. His arm is average at best. He stole 11 bases and was caught only once, but did it all on raw talent. Manager Larry Bowa made teaching him better techniques for getting a lead and reading pitchers a top priority for spring training this year, hoping he can become the type of legitimate threat who will become a distraction to opposing teams.

2004 Outlook

The Phillies haven't had a prototype leadoff hitter since Lenny Dykstra. In Byrd, they may have found another. He's two years away from being eligible for arbitration, which helps the front office balance some of the big, long-term contracts given to other players. He also has the sort of inner drive that allows him to rise to a challenge; the more others doubt him, the more determined he becomes.

Position: CF
Bats: R **Throws:** R
Ht: 6' 0" **Wt:** 230

Opening Day Age: 26
Born: 8/30/77 in Boynton Beach, FL
ML Seasons: 2

Philadelphia

Overall Statistics

	G	AB	R	H	D	T	HR	RBI	SB	BB	SO	Avg	OBP	Slg
'03	135	495	86	150	28	4	7	45	11	44	94	.303	.366	.418
Car.	145	530	88	158	30	4	8	46	11	45	102	.298	.359	.415

Where He Hits the Ball

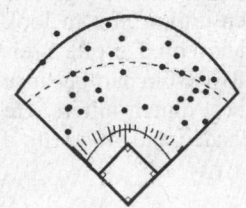

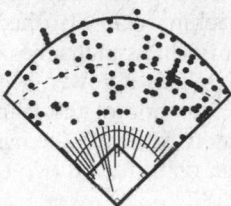

Vs. LHP   **Vs. RHP**

2003 Situational Stats

	AB	H	HR	RBI	Avg		AB	H	HR	RBI	Avg
Home	219	73	3	22	.333	LHP	111	35	1	10	.315
Road	276	77	4	23	.279	RHP	384	115	6	35	.299
First Half	198	57	2	18	.288	Sc Pos	116	30	3	39	.259
Scnd Half	297	93	5	27	.313	Clutch	72	19	2	11	.264

2003 Rankings (National League)

- 2nd in batting average among rookies
- 3rd in on-base percentage for a leadoff hitter (.374) and errors in center field (5)
- 4th in lowest fielding percentage in center field (.984)
- 7th in highest groundball-flyball ratio (1.9)
- 8th in batting average at home
- Led the Phillies in highest groundball-flyball ratio (1.9), stolen-base percentage (91.7) and on-base percentage for a leadoff hitter (.374)

Mike Lieberthal

2003 Season

Mike Lieberthal batted a career-high .313 and, just as significantly, played in at least 130 games for the second straight year. That was particularly important last season after Johnny Estrada, the catcher at Triple-A Scranton/Wilkes-Barre in 2002, was traded to the Braves to acquire righthander Kevin Millwood. That left the organization with nobody they thought was capable of playing regularly if Lieberthal was injured.

Hitting

Lieberthal hit 31 homers in 1999 but hasn't come close to matching that since. One explanation was that he made a slight adjustment in his swing, extending his arms more when he swung. The coaching staff also had been urging him to look for fastballs in that he could turn on. Despite a relative lack of power, he had 81 RBI in part because he was one of the team's best clutch hitters. He batted .563 with the bases loaded and .406 with a man on third and two outs.

Baserunning & Defense

Lieberthal takes pride in his defensive arsenal, which includes a strong, accurate arm. So it bothered him that he threw out only 18 of 102 baserunners, even though that was more a reflection of pitching coach Joe Kerrigan's emphasis on focusing on the hitters and not worrying about the runners. That led to some tension during the season. But an understanding appeared to have been reached by the end of the year, as Kerrigan relented somewhat and agreed to allow pitchers to occasionally use a slide step to keep runners honest. Possibly the slowest runner on the team, he's no threat to steal.

2004 Outlook

Lieberthal is the senior Phillies player, with continuous service since late 1995. While his game-calling has been questioned, he has a good rapport with most of the starters. The question remains how long he can remain healthy and productive at age 32, a point in the career of many catchers where the demands of the position start to catch up with them. With no heir apparent, the Phillies are counting on a couple more years left in his tank.

Position: C
Bats: R **Throws:** R
Ht: 6' 0" **Wt:** 195

Opening Day Age: 32
Born: 1/18/72 in Glendale, CA
ML Seasons: 10
Pronunciation: LEE-ber-thal

Overall Statistics

	G	AB	R	H	D	T	HR	RBI	SB	BB	SO	Avg	OBP	Slg
'03	131	508	68	159	30	1	13	81	0	38	59	.313	.373	.453
Car.	858	3064	400	848	185	9	112	465	7	251	437	.277	.340	.453

Where He Hits the Ball

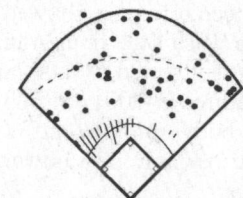
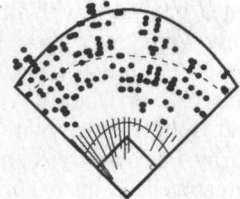

Vs. LHP   **Vs. RHP**

2003 Situational Stats

	AB	H	HR	RBI	Avg		AB	H	HR	RBI	Avg
Home	251	80	6	38	.319	LHP	116	37	1	12	.319
Road	257	79	7	43	.307	RHP	392	122	12	69	.311
First Half	286	95	6	44	.332	Sc Pos	144	46	4	67	.319
Scnd Half	222	64	7	37	.288	Clutch	81	22	0	8	.272

2003 Rankings (National League)

- 1st in lowest percentage of runners caught stealing as a catcher (17.6)
- 4th in batting average with the bases loaded (.563) and errors at catcher (9)
- Led the Phillies in batting average, hit by pitch (12), batting average with the bases loaded (.563), batting average vs. lefthanded pitchers and batting average on the road

Kevin Millwood

2003 Season

Kevin Millwood had a Jekyll-and-Hyde season after being acquired in a trade from the Braves for minor league catcher Johnny Estrada. Millwood was counted on to become the ace of the Phillies' staff and, in the beginning, performed that way. Through May 29 he was 7-1, including a no-hitter against the Giants, with a 2.84 ERA. After that, he was 7-11, including a 5.94 ERA in September.

Pitching

Millwood has a running fastball in the 92-94 MPH range, and also throws a two-seamer with a heavy, sinking action. He has an above-average changeup and a backdoor slider that he uses to freeze hitters. While he's a borderline power pitcher, he needs to command his pitches, and that command was lacking for much of the final four months of the season. Since he was coming off a successful season with the Braves, he also was allowed to prepare himself as he saw fit, and that became an issue late in the season when he seemed to lack endurance. Still, he ended up leading the staff with 222 innings pitched.

Defense & Hitting

Millwood is average defensively. He has a big, deliberate windup that allows runners to get a good jump. He must compensate by keeping runners close, but has an adequate pickoff move at best. Hitting may well have been the most disappointing aspect of his game in 2003. In his last year with the Braves, he batted .200 with five doubles, a home run, 11 RBI and 11 sacrifice bunts. Last season he was feeble, batting .059 with one ribbie and six sacrifices.

2004 Outlook

Millwood insisted all last season that he hadn't made up his mind about his future. But by the end of the year, it was apparent that he didn't have much interest in returning to Philadelphia. The Phillies, for their part, didn't seem upset after he filed for free agency. Still, given Millwood's workload and reputation for mentoring younger pitchers, few doubt that he will end up with a lucrative contract somewhere.

Position: SP
Bats: R **Throws:** R
Ht: 6' 4" **Wt:** 220

Opening Day Age: 29
Born: 12/24/74 in Gastonia, NC
ML Seasons: 7

Philadelphia

Overall Statistics

	W	L	Pct.	ERA	G	GS	Sv	IP	H	BB	SO	HR	Avg
'03	14	12	.538	4.01	35	35	0	222.0	210	68	169	19	.250
Car.	89	58	.605	3.78	203	195	0	1226.1	1128	371	1009	124	.243

2003 Pitching Profile

	Kevin Millwood	NL Average
Overall Strike %	62.7	62.4
1st Pitch Strike %	60.1	58.4
Ratio	1.25	1.38
Strikeouts per 9 IP	6.85	6.65
Walks per 9 IP	2.76	3.42
Home Runs per 9 IP	0.77	1.05
Strikeout/Walk Ratio	2.49	1.94
Groundball/Flyball Ratio	1.04	1.29

2003 Situational Stats

	W	L	ERA	Sv	IP		AB	H	HR	RBI	Avg
Home	6	6	3.76	0	105.1	LHB	362	89	6	40	.246
Road	8	6	4.24	0	116.2	RHB	479	121	13	55	.253
First Half	10	6	3.60	0	127.2	Sc Pos	197	54	3	66	.274
Scnd Half	4	6	4.58	0	94.1	Clutch	67	10	3	5	.149

2003 Rankings (National League)

- 1st in shutouts (3) and stolen bases allowed (41)
- 2nd in games started, complete games (5) and highest stolen-base percentage allowed (91.1)
- 3rd in innings pitched
- 5th in batters faced (930)
- 6th in pitches thrown (3,490)
- 9th in hits allowed
- Led the Phillies in losses, games started, complete games (5), shutouts (3), innings pitched, hits allowed, batters faced (930), pitches thrown (3,490), stolen bases allowed (41), highest strikeout-walk ratio (2.5), lowest slugging percentage allowed (.388), lowest on-base percentage allowed (.307) and fewest home runs allowed per nine innings (.77)

Brett Myers

2003 Season

As far as the Phillies were concerned, everything Brett Myers did last season should have been marked with an asterisk indicating that he was in his first full big league season and didn't turn 23 until August. By that yardstick, 14 wins was an extremely successful campaign, even though he had a 3.65 ERA in the first half and a 5.72 mark after the All-Star break.

Pitching

Myers has an electric arm. His fastball routinely hits 94 MPH, his curve buckles the knees of even the best hitters and his changeup improved as the year went on. He's a pure power pitcher out of the Curt Schilling mold who should improve as he gets older, but Myers also owns a splitter and a slider. At this point of his career, he has a tendency to overthrow—he allowed a .256 average with the bases empty versus a .296 mark with runners on. He occasionally has lapses of concentration and needs to be reminded to pay attention to his mechanics. Yet he's also a dogged competitor and one of the hardest-working pitchers on the team.

Defense & Hitting

Myers is very athletic and fundamentally sound. He is quick to get off the mound to make a fielding play or to cover first. He also is aware of the importance of holding runners and has an above-average move to first. A decent bunter, Myers doesn't hit for a high average. But he can be dangerous because he isn't afraid to take a big swing at the plate.

2004 Outlook

The only things holding Myers back are experience and maturity. At times last season, he butted heads with pitching coach Joe Kerrigan, and like many young pitchers, when he got into jams his first inclination was to try to throw even harder. When he does that, his pitches straighten out and stay up in the strike zone. Once he learns to harness his emotions, Myers should be one of the best pitchers in baseball.

Position: SP
Bats: R **Throws:** R
Ht: 6' 4" **Wt:** 215

Opening Day Age: 23
Born: 8/17/80 in Jacksonville, FL
ML Seasons: 2

Overall Statistics

	W	L	Pct.	ERA	G	GS	Sv	IP	H	BB	SO	HR	Avg
'03	14	9	.609	4.43	32	32	0	193.0	205	76	143	20	.272
Car.	18	14	.563	4.38	44	44	0	265.0	278	105	177	31	.273

2003 Pitching Profile

	Brett Myers	NL Average
Overall Strike %	63.9	62.4
1st Pitch Strike %	61.2	58.4
Ratio	1.46	1.38
Strikeouts per 9 IP	6.67	6.65
Walks per 9 IP	3.54	3.42
Home Runs per 9 IP	0.93	1.05
Strikeout/Walk Ratio	1.88	1.94
Groundball/Flyball Ratio	1.85	1.29

2003 Situational Stats

	W	L	ERA	Sv	IP		AB	H	HR	RBI	Avg
Home	8	5	3.71	0	99.1	LHB	333	90	10	40	.270
Road	6	4	5.19	0	93.2	RHB	421	115	10	48	.273
First Half	9	6	3.65	0	120.2	Sc Pos	176	47	2	59	.267
Scnd Half	5	3	5.72	0	72.1	Clutch	28	11	1	3	.393

2003 Rankings (National League)

- 8th in highest groundball-flyball ratio allowed (1.9)
- 9th in fewest pitches thrown per batter (3.56) and highest on-base percentage allowed (.344)
- Led the Phillies in pickoff throws (117), runners caught stealing (5), highest ground ball-flyball ratio allowed (1.9) and fewest pitches thrown per batter (3.56)

Vicente Padilla

2003 Season

Vicente Padilla remains an enigma. He made the All-Star team in 2002, but faltered in the second half with stiffness in his shoulder and elbow. He skipped winter ball and came back strong, but was inconsistent enough to finish with a so-so 14-12 record despite a 3.62 ERA —lowest among Phillies starters. He had a good year, yet there was a sense that he should have been better.

Pitching

Padilla's arm never has been questioned. He has a fastball that lights up radar guns at 96 MPH, though he sometimes seems to fall in love with the heater. He clashed with manager Larry Bowa and pitching coach Joe Kerrigan at times last season when he refused to throw his slider, curve or changeup. Padilla also frustrated the staff by occasionally dropping down and throwing sidearm for no apparent reason, and there were two occasions when team officials were convinced he was tipping his pitches. His preparation also was called into question because of the startling difference in his ERA between day starts (4.85) and night games (3.13). Despite all that, he was the only full-time starter whose second half ERA was lower than in the first half.

Defense & Hitting

The first time Padilla stood in lefthanded at the plate against a righthanded pitcher, it surprised everybody because he had never switch-hit before. He is not a hitting threat, batting just .060 last season, but he almost always takes a healthy swing at the plate. He is only a fair bunter and is also average at holding runners—he has yet to register a big league pickoff—and fielding his position.

2004 Outlook

Padilla was eligible for salary arbitration for the first time this season, which means that his compensation will begin to rise. . . as will his expectations. He clearly has the physical ability to be a dominant starter, but he's reached the point where he's going to have to put things together to justify the financial commitment the team is making.

Position: SP
Bats: R **Throws:** R
Ht: 6' 2" **Wt:** 215

Opening Day Age: 26
Born: 9/27/77 in Chinandega, Nicaragua
ML Seasons: 5
Pronunciation: pa-DEE-ya

Overall Statistics

	W	L	Pct.	ERA	G	GS	Sv	IP	H	BB	SO	HR	Avg
'03	14	12	.538	3.62	32	32	0	208.2	196	62	133	22	.251
Car.	35	32	.522	3.61	147	64	2	516.2	509	158	341	43	.259

2003 Pitching Profile

	Vicente Padilla	NL Average
Overall Strike %	64.8	62.4
1st Pitch Strike %	59.8	58.4
Ratio	1.24	1.38
Strikeouts per 9 IP	5.74	6.65
Walks per 9 IP	2.67	3.42
Home Runs per 9 IP	0.95	1.05
Strikeout/Walk Ratio	2.15	1.94
Groundball/Flyball Ratio	1.32	1.29

2003 Situational Stats

	W	L	ERA	Sv	IP		AB	H	HR	RBI	Avg
Home	8	6	3.14	0	111.2	LHB	344	92	7	40	.267
Road	6	6	4.18	0	97.0	RHB	436	104	15	45	.239
First Half	8	8	3.81	0	115.2	Sc Pos	168	40	4	57	.238
Scnd Half	6	4	3.39	0	93.0	Clutch	49	14	0	4	.286

2003 Rankings (National League)

- 2nd in hit batsmen (16)
- 3rd in errors at pitcher (4)
- 5th in balks (2)
- 6th in GDPs induced (23) and lowest fielding percentage at pitcher (.922)
- Led the Phillies in ERA, losses, hit batsmen (16), balks (2), GDPs induced (23), lowest stolen-base percentage allowed (55.6), lowest ERA at home, lowest ERA on the road and fewest walks per nine innings (2.7)

Placido Polanco

2003 Season

Placido Polanco might be the Phillies' most underrated regular. He is the best situational hitter in the lineup and one of the most complete players in the league. Despite being limited to 122 games last season, much of that due to a deep thigh bruise suffered late in the year, he reached career highs in home runs and RBI.

Hitting

Polanco is a classic No. 2 hitter, but he was willing to lead off or bat further down in the order when asked. He not only has the ability to bunt or advance a runner by hitting to the right side, but he also can turn on a pitch. Best of all, he is intelligent enough to know which approach best suits the circumstances. He has become a more patient hitter, walking 42 times—also a career best. There simply aren't many holes in his swing, as evidenced by the fact that he struck out just once every 13 at-bats.

Baserunning & Defense

Polanco's unselfish style is demonstrated in the field as well as at the plate. When first acquired from the Cardinals in July 2002, he played third base. He started last season at second, his more natural position, but moved back to third without complaint after David Bell went on the DL in July. Polanco has an adequate arm and decent range, but compensates by rarely making a mistake at either position. While not the fastest runner, he can take the extra base and stole 14 bases while being thrown out only twice.

2004 Outlook

The Phillies have second baseman Chase Utley, their No. 1 draft pick in 2000, ready to step into the lineup. Not so fast. Polanco will be back with the club this year even though, as an arbitration-eligible player who's a year away from free agency, he'll be in line for a healthy raise. Utley will have to wait his turn—or could even be traded—because Polanco is so valuable to the team.

Position: 2B/3B
Bats: R **Throws:** R
Ht: 5'10" **Wt:** 185

Opening Day Age: 28
Born: 10/10/75 in Santo Domingo, DR
ML Seasons: 6
Pronunciation: PLAH-si-doh poh-LAHN-co

Overall Statistics

	G	AB	R	H	D	T	HR	RBI	SB	BB	SO	Avg	OBP	Slg
'03	122	492	87	142	30	3	14	63	14	42	38	.289	.352	.447
Car.	664	2261	333	665	112	17	33	219	38	129	181	.294	.337	.402

Where He Hits the Ball

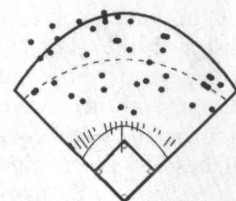 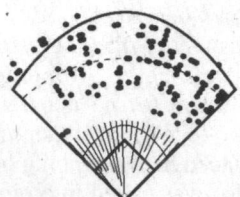

Vs. LHP   **Vs. RHP**

2003 Situational Stats

	AB	H	HR	RBI	Avg		AB	H	HR	RBI	Avg
Home	228	64	7	24	.281	LHP	96	28	5	14	.292
Road	264	78	7	39	.295	RHP	396	114	9	49	.288
First Half	294	84	7	33	.286	Sc Pos	107	34	2	50	.318
Scnd Half	198	58	7	30	.293	Clutch	74	20	3	11	.270

2003 Rankings (National League)

- 2nd in lowest percentage of swings that missed (7.4) and highest percentage of swings put into play (57.6)
- 6th in fewest pitches seen per plate appearance (3.43)
- 9th in steals of third (3)
- Led the Phillies in sacrifice bunts (8), lowest percentage of swings that missed (7.4), highest percentage of swings put into play (57.6), steals of third (3) and batting average with two strikes (.268)

Jimmy Rollins

2003 Season

Jimmy Rollins was a National League All-Star in each of his first two full seasons in the big leagues. But he barely received any such consideration last season, leaving the impression that his career has hit a roadblock. He remained a durable player, appearing in 156 games, but Rollins still has an undisciplined approach at the plate. A speedy switch-hitter who should ignite the offense, he's not yet been able to consistently handle that role.

Hitting

Rollins goes into spring training penciled in as the No. 6 hitter. He has an uppercut swing that too often leads to popups instead of keeping the ball on the ground and using his speed. He is susceptible to pitchers who go up the ladder with fastballs. He batted everywhere in the order but third and fourth last year and, interestingly, his best average (.360) was from the sixth spot. It's actually considered a good sign that his homers have decreased in each of his three full seasons while his doubles have increased.

Baserunning & Defense

Rollins' defense is the strongest part of his game. He has excellent range, especially to his right, and possesses the kind of arm that allows him to throw out a runner even after making a play deep in the hole. He also is steady on the routine plays. Rollins has not become the basestealer that many expected him to be after he tied for the league lead with 46 thefts as a rookie in 2001. He swiped just 20 last season, partly as a result of nagging leg problems and partly because of a team approach that de-emphasized the running game.

2004 Outlook

Rollins rejected an offer for a multiyear contract before last season and now is eligible for salary arbitration. He must continue to improve or the Phillies will have to start considering their options. To his credit, the fact that he agreed to work on his game with future Hall of Famer Tony Gwynn during the offseason demonstrates that he understands the immediacy of his situation.

Position: SS
Bats: B **Throws:** R
Ht: 5' 8" **Wt:** 165

Opening Day Age: 25
Born: 11/27/78 in Oakland, CA
ML Seasons: 4

Overall Statistics

	G	AB	R	H	D	T	HR	RBI	SB	BB	SO	Avg	OBP	Slg
'03	156	628	85	165	42	6	8	62	20	54	113	.263	.320	.387
Car.	482	1974	269	518	105	29	33	181	100	158	331	.262	.317	.395

Where He Hits the Ball

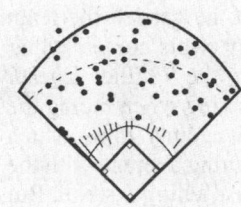   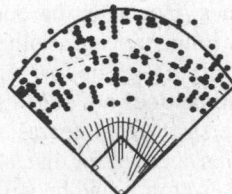

Vs. LHP   **Vs. RHP**

2003 Situational Stats

	AB	H	HR	RBI	Avg		AB	H	HR	RBI	Avg
Home	306	85	5	34	.278	LHP	145	38	2	11	.262
Road	322	80	3	28	.248	RHP	483	127	6	51	.263
First Half	390	101	5	38	.259	Sc Pos	152	41	4	53	.270
Secnd Half	238	64	3	24	.269	Clutch	85	22	2	8	.259

2003 Rankings (National League)

- 2nd in fielding percentage at shortstop (.979)
- 3rd in at-bats
- 4th in caught stealing (12) and lowest stolen-base percentage (62.5)
- 5th in lowest on-base percentage for a leadoff hitter (.314)
- 9th in triples, steals of third (3) and errors at shortstop (14)
- 10th in lowest HR frequency (78.5 ABs per HR)
- Led the Phillies in at-bats, doubles, triples, caught stealing (12), bunts in play (14) and steals of third (3)

Jim Thome

2003 Season

Manager Larry Bowa frequently offered the opinion that Jim Thome was the best free agent the Phillies ever signed. That's saying a lot considering that Bowa was a teammate of Pete Rose, who generally is considered the key acquisition to the Phillies only World Championship club in 1980. All Thome did was lead the National League with 47 homers, drive in 131 runs and become the middle-of-the-lineup threat that Philadelphia had needed for years.

Hitting

Thome is a home-run hitter who displays the classic strengths and weaknesses of a modern slugger. He is prone to lengthy slumps and struck out 182 times. But when he got hot, he carried the team for long stretches, with many of his homers either tying the game or putting the Phillies ahead. Thome does not adjust his swing when facing the overshift most teams used against him, which helps account for his .247 batting average with the bases empty, and he will chase a high fastball. But when a pitcher makes a mistake, he doesn't often miss it.

Baserunning & Defense

Thome came to the National League with a reputation for being a barely adequate defensive first baseman, but he exceeded those expectations. He doesn't have much range around the base, but he is surehanded with what he gets to and is proficient at digging low throws out of the dirt. And he did that playing a majority of his games on artificial turf; moving to natural grass at the new Citizens Bank Park should only help. His arm is accurate. On the bases he runs hard, but has below-average speed.

2004 Outlook

Thome became a fan favorite in Philadelphia almost instantly. He also led by example, always taking the same approach no matter what he had done the game before. While it remains possible that Thome could improve statistically in some categories now that he has a year in the National League behind him, the Phillies gladly would settle for a carbon copy of last year's production.

Position: 1B
Bats: L **Throws:** R
Ht: 6' 4" **Wt:** 240

Opening Day Age: 33
Born: 8/27/70 in Peoria, IL
ML Seasons: 13
Pronunciation: TOE-mee

Overall Statistics

G	AB	R	H	D	T	HR	RBI	SB	BB	SO	Avg	OBP	Slg
159	578	111	154	30	3	47	131	0	111	182	.266	.385	.573
1536	5218	1028	1486	289	23	381	1058	18	1108	1559	.285	.411	.568

Where He Hits the Ball

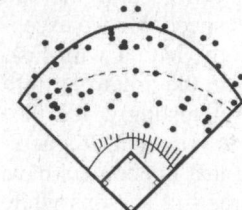 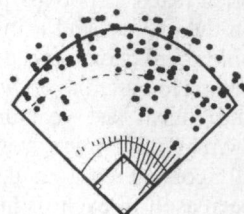

Vs. LHP **Vs. RHP**

2003 Situational Stats

	AB	H	HR	RBI	Avg		AB	H	HR	RBI	Avg
Home	291	73	28	73	.251	LHP	177	45	10	34	.254
Road	287	81	19	58	.282	RHP	401	109	37	97	.272
First Half	331	88	23	67	.266	Sc Pos	159	44	13	81	.277
Scnd Half	247	66	24	64	.267	Clutch	76	19	6	16	.250

2003 Rankings (National League)

- 1st in home runs, strikeouts and highest percentage of swings that missed (32.9)
- 2nd in walks, pitches seen (2,870) and fielding percentage at first base (.997)
- 3rd in RBI, HR frequency (12.3 ABs per HR) and cleanup slugging percentage (.655)
- 4th in fewest GDPs per GDP situation (3.0%) and lowest percentage of swings put into play (32.4)
- Led the Phillies in home runs, runs scored, total bases (331), RBI, walks, strikeouts, plate appearances (698), games played, slugging percentage, HR frequency (12.3 ABs per HR), fewest GDPs per GDP situation (3.0%), and cleanup slugging percentage (.655)
- Led NL first basemen in home runs and RBI

Randy Wolf

2003 Season

Randy Wolf made his first All-Star team last year. The problem was that, unlike previous seasons, he faded down the stretch. Wolf threw 136 pitches while working a four-hit shutout against the Cubs on July 23, improving his record to 11-5 with a 3.07 ERA. He was never the same after that, going 5-5 with a 6.61 the rest of the way, though he still finished with a career-high 16 wins.

Pitching

Wolf's fastball rarely tops 90 MPH, but he sets it up nicely with an excellent changeup and a slow curve that can be clocked as low as 76 MPH. Those offspeed pitches make his fastball appear to get on hitters more quickly than it actually does. He also has a sharp-breaking curve. Wolf changes speeds well, uses both sides of the plate and is equally successful against righthanded hitters as lefties. His walks were up somewhat from his career norms, and that's a problem for a finesse pitcher. Still, for a pitcher who is relatively inexperienced, he has tremendous poise on the mound and isn't afraid to throw any of his pitches in any situation.

Defense & Hitting

Wolf is an excellent athlete who helps himself at the plate and in the field. He is far from an automatic out, batting .200 with six doubles and 11 RBI. He is conscious of holding runners on base with an above-average pickoff move. He has a decent slide step, although pitching coach Joe Kerrigan prefers that his pitchers focus on the hitter. He fields his position well, but did make three errors last year.

2004 Outlook

Wolf is counted on to be the Phillies' No. 1 starter going into this season. He is durable, having pitched at least 200 innings in three of the last four years. The organization has been reluctant to make long-term commitments to pitchers, but made an exception when it gave Wolf a four-year, $23 million deal going into last season. At 27, he should be reaching his peak years.

Position: SP
Bats: L **Throws:** L
Ht: 6' 0" **Wt:** 194

Opening Day Age: 27
Born: 8/22/76 in Canoga Park, CA
ML Seasons: 5

Overall Statistics

	W	L	Pct.	ERA	G	GS	Sv	IP	H	BB	SO	HR	Avg
'03	16	10	.615	4.23	33	33	0	200.0	176	78	177	27	.233
Car.	54	48	.529	4.10	146	142	0	901.2	834	342	777	110	.246

2003 Pitching Profile

	Randy Wolf	NL Average
Overall Strike %	64.2	62.4
1st Pitch Strike %	58.7	58.4
Ratio	1.27	1.38
Strikeouts per 9 IP	7.97	6.65
Walks per 9 IP	3.51	3.42
Home Runs per 9 IP	1.22	1.05
Strikeout/Walk Ratio	2.27	1.94
Groundball/Flyball Ratio	1.06	1.29

2003 Situational Stats

	W	L	ERA	Sv	IP		AB	H	HR	RBI	Avg
Home	6	4	3.63	0	96.2	LHB	125	29	7	13	.232
Road	10	6	4.79	0	103.1	RHB	629	147	20	74	.234
First Half	10	4	3.31	0	119.2	Sc Pos	153	37	4	52	.242
Scnd Half	6	6	5.60	0	80.1	Clutch	35	8	1	2	.229

2003 Rankings (National League)

- 3rd in most run support per nine innings (6.7)
- 4th in shutouts (2)
- 5th in wins
- 7th in most strikeouts per nine innings (8.0)
- 8th in games started, strikeouts and lowest fielding percentage at pitcher (.927)
- 9th in home runs allowed and most home runs allowed per nine innings (1.22)
- 10th in errors at pitcher (3)
- Led the Phillies in wins, home runs allowed, walks allowed, strikeouts, winning percentage, lowest batting average allowed (.233), most run support per nine innings (6.7) and most strikeouts per nine innings (8.0)

Terry Adams

Position: RP
Bats: R **Throws:** R
Ht: 6' 3" **Wt:** 220

Opening Day Age: 31
Born: 3/6/73 in Mobile, AL
ML Seasons: 9

Overall Statistics

	W	L	Pct.	ERA	G	GS	Sv	IP	H	BB	SO	HR	Avg
'03	1	4	.200	2.65	66	0	0	68.0	68	23	51	1	.268
Car.	45	56	.446	3.97	497	41	39	786.0	781	342	631	50	.260

2003 Situational Stats

	W	L	ERA	Sv	IP			AB	H	HR	RBI	Avg
Home	1	0	2.31	0	35.0	LHB		110	29	0	9	.264
Road	0	4	3.00	0	33.0	RHB		144	39	1	15	.271
First Half	1	3	2.72	0	46.1	Sc Pos		85	22	1	24	.259
Scnd Half	0	1	2.49	0	21.2	Clutch		100	29	0	10	.290

2003 Season

Terry Adams was on his way to a career high in appearances when his elbow locked up on August 26. He pitched only once after that and eventually underwent arthroscopic elbow surgery to remove five bone chips and a spur. Despite that, he still led the bullpen with 66 games and was the Phillies' most consistent righthanded reliever.

Pitching, Defense & Hitting

Adams throws a 92-MPH fastball and a sharp-breaking slider. When he's hitting his spots and keeping his pitches down, he can be extremely effective. He's also been a durable pitcher, although manager Larry Bowa may have over-done it by pitching him nine times in 12 days from August 12-23. In his subsequent appearance, he began experiencing elbow problems that ended his season. Adams is a below-average hitter and fielder, factors that are less significant now that he's no longer being used as a starter.

2004 Outlook

The Phillies were very interested in re-signing Adams the free agent, expecting him to be completely recovered by the start of spring training. But he wasn't offered salary arbitration and will move on. At age 31 come Opening Day, Adams should have many productive seasons left.

Rheal Cormier

Position: RP
Bats: L **Throws:** L
Ht: 5'10" **Wt:** 195

Opening Day Age: 36
Born: 4/23/67 in Moncton, NB, Canada
ML Seasons: 12
Pronunciation: ree-AL cor-mee-AY
Nickname: Frenchy

Overall Statistics

	W	L	Pct.	ERA	G	GS	Sv	IP	H	BB	SO	HR	Avg
'03	8	0	1.000	1.70	65	0	1	84.2	54	25	67	4	.182
Car.	61	54	.530	4.04	472	108	2	1042.1	1070	257	660	99	.266

2003 Situational Stats

	W	L	ERA	Sv	IP			AB	H	HR	RBI	Avg
Home	7	0	0.86	1	42.0	LHB		84	10	0	5	.119
Road	1	0	2.53	0	42.2	RHB		213	44	4	15	.207
First Half	2	0	1.52	0	47.1	Sc Pos		70	13	1	16	.186
Scnd Half	6	0	1.93	1	37.1	Clutch		155	27	0	8	.174

2003 Season

After surviving rumors in spring training that he might be released with a year to go on his contract, Rheal Cormier responded with a career season. He was one of the most effective setup relievers in baseball. Pitching coach Joe Kerrigan, who was with him in Montreal and Boston, helped by rebuilding his mechanics from scratch.

Pitching, Defense & Hitting

Cormier is a finesse pitcher who relies on hitting his spots with his splitter, slider and changeup. His fastball tops out in the high 80s. Unlike previous seasons, when he struggled to retire lefthanded hitters, he was devastating against lefties last year, holding them to a .119 batting average. He also had the ability to turn the ball over to get inning-ending double plays. He is best used in short stints. Cormier is fundamentally sound at holding runners and covering first, and he fields his position well. He does not hurt himself at the plate.

2004 Outlook

The Phillies were quick to exercise their $3 million option on Cormier's contract for this season, and he comes to camp counted on as an integral part of the bullpen. The question, of course, is whether he can duplicate his success, as he turns 37 in April.

Brandon Duckworth

Traded To ASTROS

Position: SP
Bats: R **Throws:** R
Ht: 6' 2" **Wt:** 195

Opening Day Age: 28
Born: 1/23/76 in Salt Lake City, UT
ML Seasons: 3

Overall Statistics

	W	L	Pct.	ERA	G	GS	Sv	IP	H	BB	SO	HR	Avg
'03	4	7	.364	4.94	24	18	0	93.0	98	44	68	12	.272
Car.	15	18	.455	4.87	65	58	0	325.0	322	142	275	40	.259

2003 Situational Stats

	W	L	ERA	Sv	IP		AB	H	HR	RBI	Avg
Home	2	2	4.61	0	41.0	LHB	175	43	4	20	.246
Road	2	5	5.19	0	52.0	RHB	185	55	8	30	.297
First Half	3	3	4.76	0	58.2	Sc Pos	100	27	2	38	.270
Scnd Half	1	4	5.24	0	34.1	Clutch	4	1	0	0	.250

2003 Season

For the second straight season, Brandon Duckworth pitched his way out of the rotation and into the bullpen. That's particularly puzzling since he was considered a top prospect in 2001, when he was recalled from Triple-A Scranton/Wilkes-Barre and went 3-2, 3.52 in 11 starts down the stretch.

Pitching, Defense & Hitting

Duckworth has big league stuff—a moving fastball in the low 90s, a sharp curve and a nice changeup—but he has been unable to put the package together with any consistency. He too often gets ahead of hitters, then is unable to put them away. As a result, he had such high pitch counts that he often didn't last past the fifth inning. Lack of confidence is frequently mentioned as another problem. He is a decent hitter who fields his position well. He pays very little attention to opposing baserunners, and it shows.

2004 Outlook

Coming off two poor seasons, Duckworth has reached the point of his career where he needs to start showing results quickly. There was a growing perception that he wouldn't reach his potential in Philadelphia, so being traded to the Astros in the Billy Wagner deal is a much-needed opportunity for a fresh start.

Ricky Ledee

Position: CF/LF
Bats: L **Throws:** L
Ht: 6' 1" **Wt:** 200

Opening Day Age: 30
Born: 11/22/73 in Ponce, PR
ML Seasons: 6
Pronunciation: la-DAY

Overall Statistics

	G	AB	R	H	D	T	HR	RBI	SB	BB	SO	Avg	OBP	Slg
'03	121	255	37	63	15	2	13	46	0	34	59	.247	.334	.475
Car.	562	1496	220	363	86	16	46	234	24	186	367	.243	.327	.414

2003 Situational Stats

	AB	H	HR	RBI	Avg		AB	H	HR	RBI	Avg
Home	138	37	6	23	.268	LHP	20	5	0	4	.250
Road	117	26	7	23	.222	RHP	235	58	13	42	.247
First Half	164	38	7	26	.232	Sc Pos	73	17	3	32	.233
Scnd Half	91	25	6	20	.275	Clutch	47	10	1	5	.213

2003 Season

Ricky Ledee has developed into a valued reserve who ended up making 54 starts, largely because rookie center fielder Marlon Byrd got off to a slow start and left fielder Pat Burrell endured a season-long slump. Ledee's 13 home runs matched a career high, and his 46 RBI led all Phillies' role players.

Hitting, Baserunning & Defense

Ledee was considered an up-and-coming star in the Yankees' system, but has settled into a niche as a fourth outfielder. He went out of his way to help Byrd early in the season, even though they were competing for playing time. Ledee can hit a fastball but struggles as a pinch-hitter, batting just .224 in those situations last season. He's an above-average outfielder with a good arm who can play left or center. He has good speed, although it doesn't translate into stolen bases; amazingly, he didn't even attempt a single steal last season.

2004 Outlook

Manager Larry Bowa made it clear he wanted Ledee back for this season. Ledee has proven he can be productive in two to three starts a week and also is a competent defensive replacement. He's also not the kind of player who will create a problem because he's not playing regularly.

Philadelphia

Jose Mesa

Position: RP
Bats: R **Throws:** R
Ht: 6' 3" **Wt:** 230

Opening Day Age: 37
Born: 5/22/66 in Azua, DR
ML Seasons: 15
Pronunciation: MAY-sa
Nickname: Joe Table

Overall Statistics

	W	L	Pct.	ERA	G	GS	Sv	IP	H	BB	SO	HR	Avg
'03	5	7	.417	6.52	61	0	24	58.0	71	31	45	7	.296
Car.	70	91	.435	4.32	762	95	249	1299.2	1364	544	896	120	.271

2003 Situational Stats

	W	L	ERA	Sv	IP		AB	H	HR	RBI	Avg
Home	4	5	7.76	13	26.2	LHB	94	20	1	9	.213
Road	1	2	5.46	11	31.1	RHB	146	51	6	29	.349
First Half	4	5	4.73	18	40.0	Sc Pos	74	24	4	33	.324
Scnd Half	1	2	10.50	6	18.0	Clutch	141	39	4	20	.277

2003 Season

Jose Mesa became the Phillies' all-time career saves leader last season, but he also pitched himself out of the closer's role—twice—and ultimately out of the organization. After he posted a 6.52 ERA and worked just twice after September 12, his $5.95 million option was not exercised.

Pitching, Defense & Hitting

Pitching coach Joe Kerrigan said after Mesa was removed from the closer's role the first time that his arm was "too good not to save." Despite completely overhauled mechanics, which were supposed to help him hide the ball better during his delivery, he was never able to attain any consistency. Location with both his fastball and slider was a problem. He often appeared to lose his composure when something went wrong, hardly ideal for a veteran pitching with the game on the line. Mesa doesn't always get a good break to first on a grounder hit to the right side. Because of his slow delivery, he doesn't hold runners well.

2004 Outlook

Mesa still throws hard, but a team would have to make a leap of faith to consider him as a closer in 2004. He's 37 years old and, while he has no apparent physical problems, would have to be viewed as a major reclamation project.

Todd Pratt

Position: C
Bats: R **Throws:** R
Ht: 6' 3" **Wt:** 235

Opening Day Age: 37
Born: 2/9/67 in Bellevue, NE
ML Seasons: 11

Overall Statistics

	G	AB	R	H	D	T	HR	RBI	SB	BB	SO	Avg	OBP	Slg
'03	43	125	16	34	10	1	4	20	0	22	38	.272	.400	.464
Car.	495	1174	147	299	69	3	35	166	5	159	323	.255	.353	.408

2003 Situational Stats

	AB	H	HR	RBI	Avg		AB	H	HR	RBI	Avg
Home	52	16	3	12	.308	LHP	30	8	1	4	.267
Road	73	18	1	8	.247	RHP	95	26	3	16	.274
First Half	66	17	1	13	.258	Sc Pos	22	8	1	16	.364
Scnd Half	59	17	3	7	.288	Clutch	13	3	1	3	.231

2003 Season

Todd Pratt is one of the better backup catchers in baseball. Despite getting only 125 at-bats, he was productive at the plate with power: 15 of his 34 hits went for extra bases. He also came through in the clutch, batting .364 with runners in scoring position.

Hitting, Baserunning & Defense

Pratt swings for the fences, but he also is a pretty good situational hitter. He looks for a fastball he can hit and, until he gets two strikes, takes a healthy rip. His greatest strength, however, is as a receiver. Manager Larry Bowa has used him to help break in his young pitchers. Pratt has a good arm and can throw out a runner if the pitchers give him a chance. He is a below-average runner who is astute enough to take an extra base and tough enough to break up a double play.

2004 Outlook

Pratt is a veteran of winning teams who helps keep the clubhouse loose with a loud, outgoing personality. As long as the Phillies carry two catchers, his role will be limited to making occasional starts when Mike Lieberthal gets a rest. And that's not often, since Lieberthal was behind the plate for the third-most innings of any catcher in the league last year.

Carlos Silva

Traded To TWINS

Position: RP
Bats: R **Throws:** R
Ht: 6' 4" **Wt:** 240

Opening Day Age: 24
Born: 4/23/79 in Bolivar, VZ
ML Seasons: 2

Overall Statistics

	W	L	Pct.	ERA	G	GS	Sv	IP	H	BB	SO	HR	Avg
'03	3	1	.750	4.43	62	1	1	87.1	92	37	48	7	.280
Car.	8	1	.889	3.83	130	1	2	171.1	180	59	89	11	.281

2003 Situational Stats

	W	L	ERA	Sv	IP		AB	H	HR	RBI	Avg
Home	2	0	3.27	1	44.0	LHB	130	39	2	22	.300
Road	1	1	5.61	0	43.1	RHB	199	53	5	32	.266
First Half	3	1	3.62	1	54.2	Sc Pos	97	29	1	44	.299
Scnd Half	0	0	5.79	0	32.2	Clutch	44	12	1	6	.273

2003 Season

Carlos Silva's season can be described in one word: inconsistent. He had ERAs of 1.86 in April, 3.31 in June and 1.69 in September. He also had ERAs of 9.31 in May, 6.17 in July and 5.50 in August. He was a workhorse, however. Sixteen of his 35 relief appearances after the break were for more than one inning.

Pitching, Defense & Hitting

Silva's 90-MPH fastball has a heavy, sinking action, and he needs to keep it down in the strike zone, or even slightly under it, to be effective. Silva also throws a changeup and a curve, but he relies on his fielders; he had just 48 strikeouts in 87.1 innings. It's worth remembering that he'll be just 24 on Opening Day and made the jump from being a Double-A starter in 2001 to major league middle relief in 2002. He's an average fielder who rarely comes to the plate.

2004 Outlook

Silva took a step backward last season, but the Twins believe he has the talent to get his career back on track. Silva, infielder Nick Punto and a player to be named were shipped to Minnesota for lefthanded starter Eric Milton in December. Silva could end up starting for the Twins.

Amaury Telemaco

Position: SP
Bats: R **Throws:** R
Ht: 6' 3" **Wt:** 222

Opening Day Age: 30
Born: 1/19/74 in Higuey, DR
ML Seasons: 7
Pronunciation: ah-MARR-ee tel-ah-MAH-ko

Overall Statistics

	W	L	Pct.	ERA	G	GS	Sv	IP	H	BB	SO	HR	Avg
'03	1	4	.200	3.97	8	8	0	45.1	41	11	29	5	.238
Car.	23	32	.418	5.03	170	64	0	496.0	516	171	324	78	.269

2003 Situational Stats

	W	L	ERA	Sv	IP		AB	H	HR	RBI	Avg
Home	1	1	2.79	0	29.0	LHB	73	21	2	5	.288
Road	0	3	6.06	0	16.1	RHB	99	20	3	12	.202
First Half	0	0	–	0	0.0	Sc Pos	51	8	1	13	.157
Scnd Half	1	4	3.97	0	45.1	Clutch	6	2	0	1	.333

2003 Season

Amaury Telemaco was the best starter available at Triple-A Scranton/Wilkes-Barre by the time Brandon Duckworth had pitched his way out of the rotation in mid-August. Telemaco stuck the rest of the year with the parent club and pitched better than his record would indicate. The Phillies were shut out twice in his eight starts, but he allowed fewer hits than innings pitched.

Pitching, Defense & Hitting

Telemaco has made a complete recovery from reconstructive shoulder surgery in 2002. While his fastball tops out around 90 MPH, he has become a savvy pitcher instead of simply trying to throw fastballs past hitters as he did earlier in his career. He throws a slider and a changeup, and has a good grasp of changing speeds and using both sides of the plate. At the plate he can put his bat on the ball. He is an average fielder who is conscious of holding runners.

2004 Outlook

Telemaco will be given a chance to defend his spot in the rotation, but he figures to have competition from the likes of Ryan Madson, Josh Hancock and Bud Smith. If nothing else, Telemaco remains a valuable insurance policy at Triple-A and has a future as an instructor in the organization.

Philadelphia

Turk Wendell

Position: RP
Bats: L **Throws:** R
Ht: 6' 2" **Wt:** 205

Opening Day Age: 36
Born: 5/19/67 in Pittsfield, MA
ML Seasons: 10
Pronunciation: WEN-del

Overall Statistics

	W	L	Pct.	ERA	G	GS	Sv	IP	H	BB	SO	HR	Avg
'03	3	3	.500	3.38	56	0	1	64.0	54	28	27	6	.235
Car.	36	33	.522	3.85	540	6	33	629.0	562	312	504	69	.240

2003 Situational Stats

	W	L	ERA	Sv	IP		AB	H	HR	RBI	Avg
Home	2	1	2.57	1	35.0	LHB	86	26	3	11	.302
Road	1	2	4.34	0	29.0	RHB	144	28	3	19	.194
First Half	1	2	1.59	0	34.0	Sc Pos	77	15	2	24	.195
Scnd Half	2	1	5.40	1	30.0	Clutch	89	22	4	21	.247

2003 Season

Turk Wendell was a strong candidate for Comeback Player of the Year early in the season. After missing all of 2002 following reconstructive elbow surgery, he had an 0.67 ERA going into July. He couldn't sustain that level, however, as his ERA jumped to 4.70 in July and 5.82 in August and September.

Pitching, Defense & Hitting

Wendell's best pitch is a slider, and he needs it to be working in order to be successful. His fastball occasionally will hit 90 MPH. What has become clear is that he wasn't ready to carry the heavy workload that characterized the early years of his career. In the first half, he was used on back-to-back days three times and had a 1.59 ERA. After the break, he also was used consecutively four times but had a 5.40 ERA. Wendell knows how to field his position and is aware of the running game. He gives his catcher a chance by holding runners close, usually by stepping off.

2004 Outlook

A free agent, Wendell is unlikely to be back with the Phillies. He was unhappy after being traded from the Mets in 2001 and clashed with the fans before being sidelined by elbow problems. His early success shows that he still has something left.

Mike Williams

Position: RP
Bats: R **Throws:** R
Ht: 6' 2" **Wt:** 200

Opening Day Age: 35
Born: 7/29/68 in Radford, VA
ML Seasons: 12

Overall Statistics

	W	L	Pct.	ERA	G	GS	Sv	IP	H	BB	SO	HR	Avg
'03	1	7	.125	6.14	68	0	28	63.0	66	41	39	5	.268
Car.	32	54	.372	4.45	468	55	144	768.1	764	343	584	89	.260

2003 Situational Stats

	W	L	ERA	Sv	IP		AB	H	HR	RBI	Avg
Home	0	3	6.87	13	36.2	LHB	112	31	3	19	.277
Road	1	4	5.13	15	26.1	RHB	134	35	2	26	.261
First Half	1	3	6.44	25	36.1	Sc Pos	92	25	1	37	.272
Scnd Half	0	4	5.74	3	26.2	Clutch	138	39	4	35	.283

2003 Season

It all fell apart for Mike Williams last season. A year after setting a Pirates record for saves, he was traded to the Phillies on July 20 with a 6.27 earned run average in tow. A change of scenery and moving to a setup role didn't help, and his ERA was 5.96 in 28 games after the trade.

Pitching, Defense & Hitting

Williams still throws the sharp-breaking slider that made him a successful closer for most of five seasons in Pittsburgh. He just didn't locate it as well as he needs to. While 66 hits in 63 innings might not be a problem, it becomes one when you factor in 41 walks. His fastball rarely reaches 90 MPH, which means he needs to locate all his pitches with surgical precision. His greatest strength is his composure, but that didn't help much last season. Williams is adept at fielding his position. He also keeps runners honest with frequent throws to first. He's a below-average hitter.

2004 Outlook

The Phillies didn't pick up Williams' $4 million option for this season. Since he's a 35-year-old finesse pitcher coming off a terrible season, it's likely he'll have to accept a contract with a low base plus incentives—or even a minor league contract—if he wants to extend his career.

Other Philadelphia Phillies

Valerio de los Santos (**Pos**: LHP, **Age**: 31)

	W	L	Pct.	ERA	G	GS	Sv	IP	H	BB	SO	HR	Avg
'03	4	3	.571	4.50	51	0	1	52.0	45	25	39	8	.241
Car.	8	10	.444	4.28	189	2	1	214.1	183	94	171	32	.234

The Phillies took advantage of some Milwaukee salary-dumping and got de los Santos from the Brewers in September. Lefties have hit 25 points higher than righties against him over his career. 2004 Outlook: B

Geoff Geary (**Pos**: RHP, **Age**: 27)

	W	L	Pct.	ERA	G	GS	Sv	IP	H	BB	SO	HR	Avg
'03	0	0	–	4.50	5	0	0	6.0	8	3	3	0	.333
Car.	0	0	–	4.50	5	0	0	6.0	8	3	3	0	.333

The acquisition of Mike Williams delayed his debut in Philadelphia, but Geary finally was recalled in August. He was 9-4 with a 2.16 ERA and 80 strikeouts in 87.2 innings at Scranton/Wilkes-Barre. 2004 Outlook: C

Tyler Houston (**Pos**: 3B, **Age**: 33, **Bats**: L)

	G	AB	R	H	D	T	HR	RBI	SB	BB	SO	Avg	OBP	Slg
'03	54	97	7	27	6	0	3	14	0	6	19	.278	.320	.402
Car.	700	1805	197	479	84	6	63	253	10	119	408	.265	.312	.423

Houston led the NL with a .448 average in 29 pinch-at-bats when he was released in September. He hit only .226 in August, but his public spat with manager Larry Bowa likely led to his release. 2004 Outlook: B

Andy Machado (**Pos**: 3B, **Age**: 23, **Bats**: B)

	G	AB	R	H	D	T	HR	RBI	SB	BB	SO	Avg	OBP	Slg
'03	1	0	0	0	0	0	0	0	1	0	0	–	–	–
Car.	1	0	0	0	0	0	0	0	1	0	0	–	–	–

Machado batted just .196 in 423 at-bats at Double-A Reading. However, the switch-hitting prospect walked 108 times for an OBP of .360. He's a solid batting average away from becoming a regular in the majors. 2004 Outlook: C

Hector Mercado (**Pos**: LHP, **Age**: 29)

	W	L	Pct.	ERA	G	GS	Sv	IP	H	BB	SO	HR	Avg
'03	0	0	–	5.79	13	0	1	18.2	18	12	15	5	.254
Car.	5	4	.556	4.55	112	3	1	124.2	117	75	127	15	.249

Mercado gave up six earned runs in his first nine innings of work. He made the fewest appearances since his rookie year and his 5.79 ERA was a career-high. The Phillies sent him down in July. 2004 Outlook: C

Jason Michaels (**Pos**: LF/RF, **Age**: 27, **Bats**: R)

	G	AB	R	H	D	T	HR	RBI	SB	BB	SO	Avg	OBP	Slg
'03	76	109	20	36	11	0	5	17	0	15	22	.330	.416	.569
Car.	163	220	36	65	21	3	7	29	1	28	57	.295	.377	.514

Michaels reached career marks in virtually every category. He batted 63 points higher than he did in 2002 with 11 fewer strikeouts in four more at-bats. Michaels hit .400 in August and September. 2004 Outlook: B

Tomas Perez (**Pos**: 3B/2B, **Age**: 30, **Bats**: B)

	G	AB	R	H	D	T	HR	RBI	SB	BB	SO	Avg	OBP	Slg
'03	125	298	39	79	18	1	5	33	0	23	54	.265	.316	.383
Car.	502	1310	135	327	64	11	16	121	4	106	224	.250	.307	.352

Perez and Jason Michaels became the third set of teammates in Phillies history to hit two grand slams in a game on September 9. Perez reached a career-high in at-bats and was hitting .344 in July until fading late. 2004 Outlook: B

Dan Plesac (**Pos**: LHP, **Age**: 42)

	W	L	Pct.	ERA	G	GS	Sv	IP	H	BB	SO	HR	Avg
'03	2	1	.667	2.70	58	0	2	33.1	29	11	37	3	.228
Car.	65	71	.478	3.64	1064	14	158	1072.0	977	402	1041	105	.242

Plesac, a 41-year-old free agent, decided to put off retirement for another year. He had a 2.70 ERA last season, his best since 1989. The southpaw held lefties to a .224 batting average and hung up his cleats in December. 2004 Outlook: D

Nick Punto (**Pos**: 2B, **Age**: 26, **Bats**: B)

	G	AB	R	H	D	T	HR	RBI	SB	BB	SO	Avg	OBP	Slg
'03	64	92	14	20	2	0	1	4	2	7	22	.217	.273	.272
Car.	77	103	14	23	2	0	1	4	2	7	25	.223	.273	.272

When various injuries hit the Phillies, Punto often was the first player called up to fill in as a utility infielder and pinch-hitter. He racked up career-highs in most statistical categories in 2003 and was sent to the Twins in the Eric Milton deal. 2004 Outlook C

Kelly Stinnett (**Pos**: C, **Age**: 34, **Bats**: R)

	G	AB	R	H	D	T	HR	RBI	SB	BB	SO	Avg	OBP	Slg
'03	67	186	14	44	13	0	3	19	0	14	52	.237	.302	.355
Car.	588	1672	190	394	81	4	54	197	10	169	464	.236	.319	.386

The Phillies got Stinnett from the Reds at the end of August. The catcher went 3-for-7 with Philadelphia after enduring a 3-for-33 August. He became a free agent after the season. 2004 Outlook: C

Chase Utley (**Pos**: 2B, **Age**: 25, **Bats**: L)

	G	AB	R	H	D	T	HR	RBI	SB	BB	SO	Avg	OBP	Slg
'03	43	134	13	32	10	1	2	21	2	11	22	.239	.322	.373
Car.	43	134	13	32	10	1	2	21	2	11	22	.239	.322	.373

Utley had 18 home runs, 77 RBI and a .323 average in 431 at-bats at Triple-A. He wasn't very productive with the Phillies, but Placido Polanco is arbitration-eligible this offseason. 2004 Outlook: C

Philadelphia Phillies Minor League Prospects

Organization Overview:

Several years ago, the Phillies made a decision to emphasize pitching in the draft, and the results are now apparent. It's not far-fetched to imagine that the team could have a rotation comprised entirely of homegrown talent in the not-too-distant future. Lefthander Randy Wolf and righthander Brett Myers are already in place, and the majority of the top prospects coming through the pipeline are pitchers. The flip side of that, though, is that the system is painfully thin on position players. There is no heir apparent to catcher Mike Lieberthal, for example, and few prospects with plus speed or power. It didn't help that the 2003 draft is widely considered to be weak, in part because the organization forfeited its No. 1 and 2 draft choices as compensation for signing Jim Thome and David Bell.

Keith Bucktrot

Position: P **Opening Day Age:** 23
Bats: L **Throws:** R **Born:** 11/27/80 in
Ht: 6' 3" **Wt:** 195 Claremore, OK

Recent Statistics

		W	L	ERA	G	GS	Sv	IP	H	R	BB	SO	HR
2002 A Clearwater		8	9	4.88	27	24	0	160.1	167	101	78	84	10
2003 A Clearwater		7	7	3.33	19	17	0	110.2	104	50	29	68	8
2003 AA Reading		3	1	2.56	7	7	0	45.2	34	17	15	30	3

Bucktrot, a third-round pick in the 2000 draft, was in danger of having his career stall at Class-A before showing signs of putting it all together last season. He returned to high Class-A Clearwater for a second straight year but finished with a flourish at Double-A Reading. He always has had good stuff—a sinking fastball that he throws consistently at 92 MPH, an above-average changeup and a developing slider—but in his fourth professional season began to demonstrate the necessary command and consistency. That made him one of the most improved players in the system. He was selected for the Arizona Fall League and could be at Triple-A Scranton/Wilkes-Barre by the end of this season.

Gavin Floyd

Position: P **Opening Day Age:** 21
Bats: R **Throws:** R **Born:** 1/27/83 in
Ht: 6' 6" **Wt:** 210 Annapolis, MD

Recent Statistics

		W	L	ERA	G	GS	Sv	IP	H	R	BB	SO	HR
2002 A Lakewood		11	10	2.77	27	27	0	166.0	119	59	64	140	13
2003 A Clearwater		7	8	3.00	24	20	0	138.0	128	61	45	115	9

Despite some whispers that his stock had slipped last season, Floyd remains one of the Phillies' untouchable prospects, although it's true that he's fallen behind left-hander Cole Hamels on the organizational depth chart.

The 2001 first-rounder, fourth overall, has a fastball that hits 95 MPH and a 12-to-6 curve, and his change-up projects as a solid major league average. He has good mound presence and composure. The Phillies are particularly impressed with his strong work ethic. Now he just needs to refine his tools, develop his change and becoming more consistent with all his pitches. He's expected to join the rotation no later than Opening Day 2006, but he won't be rushed.

Cole Hamels

Position: P **Opening Day Age:** 20
Bats: L **Throws:** L **Born:** 12/27/83 in San
Ht: 6' 3" **Wt:** 175 Diego, CA

Recent Statistics

		W	L	ERA	G	GS	Sv	IP	H	R	BB	SO	HR
2003 A Lakewood		6	1	0.84	13	13	0	74.2	32	8	25	115	0
2003 A Clearwater		0	2	2.73	5	5	0	26.1	29	9	14	32	0

Hamels, the Phillies' No. 1 draft choice in 2002 out of Rancho Bernardo High School in San Diego, is on the fast track to the majors after only one year of pro experience. He won the Paul Owens Award as the top pitcher in the organization, and while he'll start this year at high Class-A Clearwater, it wouldn't be a surprise to see him at Double-A Reading by midseason. His 92-MPH fastball and changeup already are considered plus pitches. His curve is improving and could be another plus pitch by the time he arrives in Philadelphia. He has excellent control for a young pitcher and a feel for pitching that could get him to the big leagues by the middle of 2005.

Josh Hancock

Position: P **Opening Day Age:** 25
Bats: R **Throws:** R **Born:** 4/11/78 in
Ht: 6' 3" **Wt:** 217 Cleveland, MS

Recent Statistics

		W	L	ERA	G	GS	Sv	IP	H	R	BB	SO	HR
2003 AAA Scran-WB		10	9	3.86	28	27	0	165.2	147	78	46	122	14
2003 NL Philadelphia		0	0	3.00	2	0	0	3.0	2	1	0	4	0

The Phillies believe Hancock will be a serviceable member of a big league pitching staff some day, either as a bottom-of-the-rotation starter or pitching out of the bullpen in middle relief. He has an average fastball with good movement and an average changeup. The organization worked with him last season on tightening up his breaking ball to the point where it now has action that more resembles a slider. Acquired from the Red Sox' organization for Jeremy Giambi before last season, he'll compete with righthanders Ryan Madson and Amaury Telemaco for the fifth spot in the rotation this spring, and could earn consideration as a long reliever if he doesn't start.

Ryan Howard

Position: 1B   **Opening Day Age:** 24
Bats: L **Throws:** L   **Born:** 11/19/79 in
Ht: 6' 4" **Wt:** 220   Wildwood, MO

Recent Statistics

	G	AB	R	H	D	T	HR	RBI	SB	BB	SO	Avg
2002 A Lakewood	135	493	56	138	20	6	19	87	5	66	145	.280
2003 A Clearwater	130	490	67	149	32	1	23	82	0	50	151	.304

Howard was the 2003 Paul Owens Award winner as the top position player in the system. He is projected to be a legitimate power hitter while hitting for a solid average. Like most power hitters, he strikes out a lot, but he should cut down on his whiffs as he improves his approach. He has been adept in the field, but the problem is that he plays first base and his path to the big leagues is blocked by Jim Thome. Since he doesn't run well enough to make the transition to another position, his long-term future could be with another organization, although the Phillies still list him as one of their untouchable prospects.

Eric Junge

Position: P   **Opening Day Age:** 27
Bats: R **Throws:** R   **Born:** 1/5/77 in
Ht: 6' 5" **Wt:** 215   Manhasset, NY

Recent Statistics

	W	L	ERA	G	GS	Sv	IP	H	R	BB	SO	HR
2003 AAA Scran-WB	1	0	3.06	10	8	0	47.0	38	20	16	42	2
2003 NL Philadelphia	0	0	3.52	6	0	0	7.2	5	3	1	5	1

Acquired from the Dodgers before the 2002 season, the biggest thing holding Junge's career back to this point has been injuries. Last season, he had a torn tendon in his thumb and later underwent arthroscopic shoulder surgery. He's expected to be fully recovered by the start of spring training and has a chance to make the team out of the bullpen. He has a plus fastball with movement and a decent breaking ball. He's shown signs of maturing into a pitcher instead of simply trying to throw the ball harder when he gets in trouble. It still hasn't been determined whether his future is as a reliever or as a bottom-of-the-rotation starter.

Ryan Madson

Position: P   **Opening Day Age:** 23
Bats: L **Throws:** R   **Born:** 8/28/80 in Long
Ht: 6' 6" **Wt:** 180   Beach, CA

Recent Statistics

	W	L	ERA	G	GS	Sv	IP	H	R	BB	SO	HR
2003 A Clearwater	0	0	5.63	2	2	0	8.0	11	5	2	9	0
2003 AAA Scran-WB	12	8	3.50	26	26	0	157.0	157	70	42	138	9
2003 NL Philadelphia	0	0	0.00	1	0	0	2.0	0	0	0	0	0

The improvement he showed last season, plus his impressive outings for the United States Olympic qualifying team, make Madson a legitimate candidate to win the fifth starting spot out of spring training. He'll face challenges from righthanders Josh Hancock and Amaury Telemaco, however. Madson's progress is attributed to an improved breaking ball. His fastball rarely tops 90 MPH, but he throws a two-seamer with good life. His best pitch is a changeup that's rated double-plus by the organization. He appeared to tire somewhat late in the season at Triple-A Scranton/Wilkes-Barre, so he may need to work on his durability. Eventually he projects as a solid middle-of-the-rotation starter.

Jorge Padilla

Position: OF   **Opening Day Age:** 24
Bats: R **Throws:** R   **Born:** 8/11/79 in Rio
Ht: 6' 2" **Wt:** 200   Piedras, PR

Recent Statistics

	G	AB	R	H	D	T	HR	RBI	SB	BB	SO	Avg
2002 AA Reading	127	484	71	124	30	2	7	65	32	40	77	.256
2003 AA Reading	46	173	21	51	13	1	2	23	11	18	29	.295

Padilla's career, which appeared so promising when he was drafted in the third round in 1998, has been slowed by injuries. Last year it was a stress fracture of the foot which caused him to miss half the season. He showed what he could do in 2002 when he became the first 30-doubles/30-steals player in history at Double-A Reading. While he hasn't shown the kind of home-run stroke that's normally associated with corner outfielders, he's a good contact hitter who runs well and has gap power. Defensively, he has legitimate right-field tools. While the organization still lists him among its top prospects, Padilla needs to have a healthy and productive year at Triple-A Scranton/Wilkes-Barre in 2004 to maintain that status.

Others to Watch

Outfielder **Michael Bourn** (21), the fourth-round pick last year, is projected as a Kenny Lofton-type outfielder. He utilizes his great speed both in the outfield and on the bases. It's hoped that he can develop into a prototype leadoff hitter. . . Third baseman **Terry Jones** (21) could be in a position to compete for a spot in the big leagues after David Bell's contract expires following the 2006 season. Jones still relies on his athleticism, but began to show signs of developing his baseball skills in the second half of last season at Class-A Lakewood. . . Righthander **Elizardo Ramirez** (21) posted sensational numbers as he jumped from the Rookie-level Gulf Coast League to high Class-A Clearwater, and his 101-33 strikeout-walk ratio was impressive. He has excellent mound presence. . . Righthander **Alfredo Simon** (22) played as Carlos Cabrera for his first three years in the organization. When Simon had visa problems, the Phillies found out his real name and also that he was 20 months older than they had thought. While inconsistent with his breaking ball, his fastball hits 96-97 MPH. He's developing a Roberto Hernandez-type body, filling out to 215 pounds on a 6-foot-4 frame.

PNC Park

Offense

Lefthanded pull-hitters thrive at PNC Park, as the distance down the right-field line is just 320 feet. The seats in right-center also are reachable. However, it is a different story for righthanded batters. While it is only 325 down the left-field line, the fence quickly juts out all the way until it reaches 410 feet in the notch in left-center. The prevailing winds also can knock down balls hit to left and left-center, while aiding those hit to right and right-center.

Defense

Going against the grain, the Pirates play their better corner outfielder in left field instead of right because of the big gap in left-center at PNC Park. Right is easier to play because there is much less ground to cover. The infield now plays much truer than during PNC Park's inaugural season in 2001, when opposing infielders routinely complained about wicked hops created by the hard dirt surface.

Who It Helps the Most

Craig Wilson slugged .581 at PNC Park as a part-time player. Tike Redman enjoyed hitting there after he was recalled on August 1, batting .361 with 10 doubles in just 27 games. Kip Wells has learned how to pitch to the park, as his 2.12 home ERA was tops in the league. Joe Beimel took advantage of the natural advantage lefthanded pitchers have at PNC, posting a 2.57 home ERA compared to 8.23 on the road.

Who It Hurts the Most

Jason Kendall hasn't enjoyed the move from Three Rivers Stadium. The grass slows down many of his line drives that used to shoot through the gaps on artificial turf and the deep left field has cut down on his home-run totals.

Rookies & Newcomers

The Pirates are hoping that young first baseman Carlos Rivera can take advantage of the short porch in right. Rookie outfielder J.J. Davis is hurt by the fact he is a righthanded hitter, but he is strong enough to hit the ball out to any part of the park.

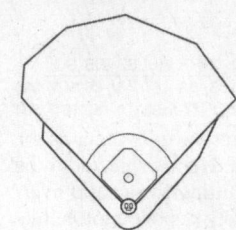

Dimensions: LF-325, LCF-389, CF-399, RCF-375, RF-320

Capacity: 37,898

Elevation: 730 feet

Surface: Grass

Foul Territory: Small

Park Factors

2003 Season

| | Home Games | | | Away Games | | | |
	Pirates	Opp	Total	Pirates	Opp	Total	Index
G	75	75	150	75	75	150	
Avg	.278	.269	.274	.257	.267	.262	105
AB	2510	2655	5165	2615	2482	5097	101
R	342	357	699	343	356	699	100
H	699	714	1413	671	663	1334	106
2B	135	139	274	111	138	249	109
3B	17	10	27	23	12	35	76
HR	74	73	147	76	86	162	90
BB	231	224	455	248	234	482	93
SO	442	436	878	534	426	960	90
E	66	43	109	47	52	99	110
E-Infield	60	37	97	40	47	87	111
LHB-Avg	.298	.294	.296	.273	.276	.274	108
LHB-HR	34	26	60	29	32	61	98
RHB-Avg	.267	.251	.259	.246	.261	.253	102
RHB-HR	40	47	87	47	54	101	84

2001-2003

| | Home Games | | | Away Games | | | |
	Pirates	Opp	Total	Pirates	Opp	Total	Index
G	224	224	448	222	222	444	
Avg	.262	.269	.266	.242	.270	.256	104
AB	7388	7857	15245	7546	7275	14821	102
R	981	1119	2100	892	1068	1960	106
H	1936	2112	4048	1828	1965	3793	106
2B	390	433	823	335	403	738	108
3B	33	38	71	49	43	92	75
HR	201	227	428	230	236	466	89
BB	715	743	1458	699	756	1455	97
SO	1360	1313	2673	1677	1248	2925	89
E	194	160	354	152	147	299	117
E-Infield	163	140	303	129	129	258	116
LHB-Avg	.275	.284	.280	.255	.283	.270	104
LHB-HR	88	88	176	85	96	181	93
RHB-Avg	.255	.259	.257	.236	.262	.248	104
RHB-HR	113	139	252	145	140	285	87

2003 Rankings (National League)

- Third-highest LHB batting-average factor
- Second-lowest strikeout factor
- Third-lowest walk factor

Lloyd McClendon

2003 Season

In the final year of his contract, Lloyd McClendon entered the season under a cloud of uncertainty. Though the Pirates underachieved in the first half, McClendon received a one-year extension for 2004 just before the All-Star break, with a club option for 2005. He then held the Pirates together as they produced a respectable 33-35 mark from July 20 on despite the trades of Brian Giles, Mike Williams, Aramis Ramirez, Kenny Lofton, Scott Sauerbeck, Jeff Suppan and Randall Simon in budget-slashing moves.

Offense

Given a more powerful lineup last season, McClendon shifted his offensive philosophy slightly. He still forced the issue and called for plenty of steal attempts and hit-and-runs, but he also waited more often for the big inning. The Pirates were third in the National League in hitting after finishing last in McClendon's first two seasons. He loves double switches, going to the move so often that he will at times hurt his lineup by taking out some of his top hitters.

Pitching & Defense

McClendon is extremely protective of his young pitchers, watching their pitch counts closely and yanking them at the first sign of fatigue. He will give his veteran pitchers more leeway, however, and stick with them longer if they are effective. McClendon took heat for the way he handled the bullpen last season, as the Pirates lost 24 games in which they led or were tied after six innings. However, much of the heat was unjust, as Williams, Sauerbeck and Brian Boehringer all failed to repeat their fine performances of 2002.

2004 Outlook

McClendon is growing into the job after three seasons. While he still tends to overdo it at times with double switches and late-inning bullpen matchups, and also tends to be wound a bit too tight, he has gotten away from his tendency to overmanage. McClendon's teams always play hard, and he did a great job of holding things together last season after his roster was gutted by the trades.

Born: 1/11/59 in Gary, IN

Playing Experience: 1987-1994, Cin, ChC, Pit

Managerial Experience: 3 seasons

Manager Statistics

Year	Team, Lg	W	L	Pct	GB	Finish
2003	Pittsburgh, NL	75	87	.463	13.0	4th Central
3 Seasons		209	276	.431	–	–

2003 Starting Pitchers by Days Rest

	<=3	4	5	6+
Pirates Starts	0	60	58	34
Pirates ERA	–	4.64	3.87	5.45
NL Avg Starts	2	84	43	23
NL ERA	5.00	4.23	4.42	4.68

2003 Situational Stats

	Lloyd McClendon	NL Average
Hit & Run Success %	39.2	32.7
Stolen Base Success %	69.9	68.9
Platoon Pct.	54.2	52.0
Defensive Subs	26	19
High-Pitch Outings	4	8
Quick/Slow Hooks	26/14	20/12
Sacrifice Attempts	104	93

2003 Rankings (National League)

- 1st in hit-and-run attempts (102) and pitchouts (79)
- 2nd in double steals (5) and quick hooks
- 3rd in steals of third base (16), sacrifice bunt attempts, hit-and-run success percentage, defensive substitutions and saves with over 1 inning pitched (10)

Jason Bay

2003 Season

Jason Bay made his major league debut with San Diego on May 23 but suffered a broken right wrist when hit by a pitch two days later and wound up back at Triple-A Portland once healthy. He got the opportunity he needed August 26 as he was one of three players traded to Pittsburgh for star outfielder Brian Giles. Bay saw regular duty, primarily in left field, for the remainder of the season and reached base safely in his last 14 games.

Hitting

Bay has an advanced approach to hitting despite his lack of big league experience. He is willing to take pitches and work the count. Though he was more prone to strikeouts against advanced pitching, he also drew his share of walks. Bay has the ability to hit for average and power, though he tended to try to pull too many pitches in his first taste of the majors. He looks to be a solid clutch hitter, and his eight-RBI game against the Chicago Cubs on September 19 was one short of the Pirates' record.

Baserunning & Defense

Bay has good speed and baserunning instincts. He picks his spots well to steal and was rarely thrown out in the minor leagues. He has enough range to play center field and his arm is good enough for right, but he figures to settle in as a left fielder with the Pirates. Left field is more difficult to play than right at PNC Park, with the spacious gap in left-center.

2004 Outlook

The Pirates aren't ready to completely commit to the rookie, but it seems certain Bay will be the everyday left fielder this year while batting sixth or seventh in the lineup. He is with his fourth organization but is a late-bloomer. He doesn't figure to be a superstar, but he looks like the type of player who can have a long and solid career. His 2004 may get off to a slow start after labrum surgery on his shoulder in November. Bay will begin throwing in mid-February and should be ready close to Opening Day.

Position: LF
Bats: R **Throws:** R
Ht: 6' 2" **Wt:** 200

Opening Day Age: 25
Born: 9/20/78 in Trail, BC, Canada
ML Seasons: 1

Overall Statistics

	G	AB	R	H	D	T	HR	RBI	SB	BB	SO	Avg	OBP	Slg
'03	30	87	15	25	7	1	4	14	3	19	29	.287	.421	.529
Car.	30	87	15	25	7	1	4	14	3	19	29	.287	.421	.529

Where He Hits the Ball

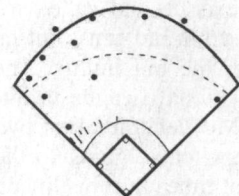 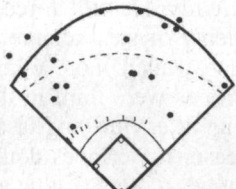

Vs. LHP   **Vs. RHP**

2003 Situational Stats

	AB	H	HR	RBI	Avg		AB	H	HR	RBI	Avg
Home	36	12	2	11	.333	LHP	32	9	1	1	.281
Road	51	13	2	3	.255	RHP	55	16	3	13	.291
First Half	8	2	1	2	.250	Sc Pos	33	9	2	12	.273
Scnd Half	79	23	3	12	.291	Clutch	10	2	0	0	.200

2003 Rankings (National League)

- Did not rank near the top or bottom in any category

Kris Benson

2003 Season

Early on in the year, Kris Benson appeared on his way to finally fulfilling his vast potential. After missing 2001 because of reconstructive elbow surgery, he followed up a 9-2 finish to the 2002 campaign by going 3-3 with a 2.90 ERA in his first six starts of '03. However, his season began to unravel after that. He felt pain in his shoulder and missed a start in June before being shut down for good one game after the All-Star break.

Pitching

Benson seemingly has everything it takes to be a premier starting pitcher. His arsenal includes a fastball that reaches 95 MPH along with a curveball, slider and changeup. All four pitches are above-average when Benson is right. However, he has yet to show consistency, and injuries have played a major part in that. He left too many fastballs over the heart of the plate last season, particularly to lefthanders, and he continually had problems keeping his curveball down in the strike zone.

Defense & Hitting

Benson understands the importance of helping himself with the glove, and is surehanded and attentive in the field. He slows the running game as well, with the help of a quick delivery to the plate and a decent pickoff move. His hitting skills have deteriorated in recent years, and he went 0-for-30 last season. He is a decent bunter, however.

2004 Outlook

Benson has something to prove after a promising 2003 turned into disaster and some teammates privately, and probably unfairly, questioned his heart. Despite all the hype surrounding him ever since he was selected first overall in the 1996 draft, Benson's career record is just 35-41, and he isn't getting any younger. His window of opportunity to develop into a staff ace is closing, and he needs to re-establish himself with a healthy showing in 2004. Benson should be 100-percent ready when he begins throwing in preparation for spring training in mid-December. He is eligible for free agency at the end of this season.

Position: SP
Bats: R **Throws:** R
Ht: 6' 4" **Wt:** 195

Opening Day Age: 29
Born: 11/7/74 in Superior, WI
ML Seasons: 4

Overall Statistics

	W	L	Pct.	ERA	G	GS	Sv	IP	H	BB	SO	HR	Avg
'03	5	9	.357	4.97	18	18	0	105.0	127	36	68	14	.295
Car.	35	41	.461	4.27	106	106	0	649.2	669	255	470	72	.266

2003 Pitching Profile

	Kris Benson	NL Average
Overall Strike %	62.0	62.4
1st Pitch Strike %	55.0	58.4
Ratio	1.55	1.38
Strikeouts per 9 IP	5.83	6.65
Walks per 9 IP	3.09	3.42
Home Runs per 9 IP	1.20	1.05
Strikeout/Walk Ratio	1.89	1.94
Groundball/Flyball Ratio	0.79	1.29

2003 Situational Stats

	W	L	ERA	Sv	IP		AB	H	HR	RBI	Avg
Home	1	6	4.92	0	60.1	LHB	189	64	9	37	.339
Road	4	3	5.04	0	44.2	RHB	242	63	5	26	.260
First Half	5	8	4.63	0	103.0	Sc Pos	115	31	5	50	.270
Scnd Half	0	1	22.50	0	2.0	Clutch	14	4	0	0	.286

2003 Rankings (National League)

- 6th in highest batting average allowed vs. lefthanded batters
- Led the Pirates in wild pitches (7)

Jeff D'Amico

2003 Season

The Pirates signed Jeff D'Amico to a minor league contract less than a month before the start of spring training, and he wound up spending the season as the team's No. 5 starter. He struggled late in the year and was 3-6 with a 7.10 ERA in nine starts over the final two months as he led the National League with 16 losses. However, after a career marred by shoulder and elbow injuries, D'Amico did establish personal bests with 29 starts and 175.1 innings, thanks in part to careful handling by manager Lloyd McClendon and pitching coach Spin Williams.

Pitching

The 6-foot-7 D'Amico has the look of a power pitcher. In reality, he is a finesse pitcher, especially following all his injuries. His best pitch is a big-breaking slow curveball that he will throw for strikes at any point in the count to either left- or righthanded hitters. D'Amico's fastball tops out at 88 MPH and doesn't have enough movement to consistently get batters out. He also throws a changeup. He has excellent control and walked only 2.2 hitters per nine innings last season.

Defense & Hitting

D'Amico fields his position well for a big man. He gets off the mound quickly to field bunts and cover first base. He has trouble with the running game, however, since he relies on his curveball and also has a slow delivery. D'Amico is awkward at the plate and doesn't make consistent contact, though he did hit his second career home run last season and usually is reliable in sacrifice situations. He is a patient hitter who drew six walks last year.

2004 Outlook

D'Amico's poor finish doomed his chances of coming back to the Pirates, and they released him four days after last season ended. Once a first-round draft pick by Milwaukee, he no longer has star potential. That said, he is young enough to be a serviceable starter at the back end of a rotation.

Position: SP
Bats: R **Throws:** R
Ht: 6' 7" **Wt:** 255

Opening Day Age: 28
Born: 12/27/75 in St. Petersburg, FL
ML Seasons: 7
Pronunciation: duh-MEEK-oh

Overall Statistics

	W	L	Pct.	ERA	G	GS	Sv	IP	H	BB	SO	HR	Avg
'03	9	16	.360	4.77	29	29	0	175.1	204	42	100	23	.291
Car.	44	50	.468	4.49	132	124	0	753.1	787	215	482	114	.269

2003 Pitching Profile

	Jeff D'Amico	NL Average
Overall Strike %	65.4	62.4
1st Pitch Strike %	61.6	58.4
Ratio	1.40	1.38
Strikeouts per 9 IP	5.13	6.65
Walks per 9 IP	2.16	3.42
Home Runs per 9 IP	1.18	1.05
Strikeout/Walk Ratio	2.38	1.94
Groundball/Flyball Ratio	0.95	1.29

2003 Situational Stats

	W	L	ERA	Sv	IP		AB	H	HR	RBI	Avg
Home	5	7	4.79	0	92.0	LHB	311	91	7	33	.293
Road	4	9	4.75	0	83.1	RHB	389	113	16	56	.290
First Half	6	9	3.97	0	104.1	Sc Pos	165	48	7	70	.291
Scnd Half	3	7	5.96	0	71.0	Clutch	11	7	0	2	.636

2003 Rankings (National League)

- 1st in losses
- 3rd in lowest winning percentage
- 4th in fewest pitches thrown per batter (3.47), highest slugging percentage allowed (.469), highest stolen-base percentage allowed (88.9) and highest ERA at home
- 7th in highest batting average allowed (.291)
- 8th in fewest walks per nine innings (2.2)
- 9th in highest ERA and lowest groundball-flyball ratio allowed (1.0)
- Led the Pirates in losses, hits allowed and GDPs induced (18)

Josh Fogg

2003 Season

Josh Fogg struggled in his second full major league season, spending a little more than a month on the disabled list from April 21 through May 26 with a strained muscle in his left ribcage and showing little consistency until late in the season. After failing to record an out in an August 12 outing against St. Louis, Fogg went 4-2 in his last eight games. Fogg finished one game above .500 after a 12-12 rookie showing, but he was the beneficiary of the Pirates scoring 6.2 runs per game in his 2003 starts.

Pitching

Fogg doesn't have a dominant offering and tries to fool hitters with an assortment of pitches, location and control. He rarely touches 90 MPH with his fastball, instead usually hovering in the 87-MPH range. He also has a curveball, slider and a changeup that can be his best pitch when he consistently throws strikes with it. While Fogg rarely hurts himself with walks, he also rarely helps himself with a strikeout because of his lack of stuff. He tends to struggle after one turn through the batting order.

Defense & Hitting

Fogg is conscientious in the field and rarely hurts himself with misplays as he has sure hands and makes accurate throws. His pickoff move is nothing spectacular, but he usually pays attention to runners and opponents don't run wild on him. He improved his hitting in his second season but remains below average in that area, struggling just to make consistent contact. He is an adequate bunter.

2004 Outlook

Since going 9-6 with a 3.56 ERA in 17 starts in the first half of his 2002 rookie season, Fogg is 13-15 with a 5.26 ERA in 42 starts. He is a bright guy who tries to compensate for his lack of overwhelming stuff with guile. However, he really has not produced significant numbers in more than a year, and his struggles in the middle and late innings suggest his long-term future may be in middle relief.

Position: SP
Bats: R **Throws:** R
Ht: 6' 0" **Wt:** 202

Opening Day Age: 27
Born: 12/13/76 in Lynn, MA
ML Seasons: 3

Overall Statistics

	W	L	Pct.	ERA	G	GS	Sv	IP	H	BB	SO	HR	Avg
'03	10	9	.526	5.26	26	26	0	142.0	166	40	71	22	.293
Car.	22	21	.512	4.63	70	59	0	349.2	375	112	201	50	.276

2003 Pitching Profile

	Josh Fogg	NL Average
Overall Strike %	62.8	62.4
1st Pitch Strike %	57.3	58.4
Ratio	1.45	1.38
Strikeouts per 9 IP	4.50	6.65
Walks per 9 IP	2.54	3.42
Home Runs per 9 IP	1.39	1.05
Strikeout/Walk Ratio	1.78	1.94
Groundball/Flyball Ratio	1.19	1.29

2003 Situational Stats

	W	L	ERA	Sv	IP		AB	H	HR	RBI	Avg
Home	6	4	5.71	0	64.2	LHB	247	79	8	38	.320
Road	4	5	4.89	0	77.1	RHB	319	87	14	44	.273
First Half	5	4	4.68	0	73.0	Sc Pos	136	34	6	56	.250
Scnd Half	5	5	5.87	0	69.0	Clutch	15	2	0	1	.133

2003 Rankings (National League)

- Led the Pirates in wins, hit batsmen (9), fewest pitches thrown per batter (3.40) and most run support per nine innings (6.2)

Jose Hernandez

2003 Season

Jose Hernandez toured the National League in 2003. He began the season as Colorado's starting shortstop after signing as a free agent in January. He then was traded to the Cubs on June 19. On July 22, Chicago sent him to the Pirates in a deal that netted the Cubs both Aramis Ramirez and Kenny Lofton. Hernandez was the Pirates' primary starter at third base after the swap, but his playing time was limited in September when he hit .148. He did not have an extra-base hit in his last 23 games and was released three days after the season ended.

Hitting

Hernandez' propensity to strike out has become almost legendary in recent years. Playing for Milwaukee in 2002, he came within one whiff of tying the major league single-season strikeout record of 189 set by Bobby Bonds in 1970. Hernandez again challenged that mark last season until his playing time was curtailed in the final month. He simply seems unable to lay off high fastballs, breaking balls and offspeed pitches in the dirt. Hernandez isn't a total zero offensively, however. He has very good pop as his strong hands and wrists allow him to drive balls to the opposite field. Still, Hernandez was horrible with teammates on base last season, batting a paltry .190 with runners in scoring position, including .157 with two outs.

Baserunning & Defense

Hernandez is an average runner who rarely takes chances on the basepaths. He can play all four infield spots as well as center field. While he prefers playing shortstop, his range is limited at that position. However, his strong arm and good first-step quickness, particularly to his backhand side, make him a good third baseman.

2004 Outlook

Hernandez struggled last season, and the time may be coming when he settles into more of a utility role. His ability to play five positions while also hitting with power make him an attractive bench player, though he will look for a starting job as a free agent.

Position: 3B/SS
Bats: R **Throws:** R
Ht: 6' 1" **Wt:** 188

Opening Day Age: 34
Born: 7/14/69 in Vega Alta, PR
ML Seasons: 12
Pronunciation: her-NAN-dezz

Overall Statistics

G	AB	R	H	D	T	HR	RBI	SB	BB	SO	Avg	OBP	Slg
150	519	58	117	18	3	13	57	2	46	177	.225	.287	.347
1323	4021	551	1011	170	31	146	524	37	332	1230	.251	.310	.418

Where He Hits the Ball

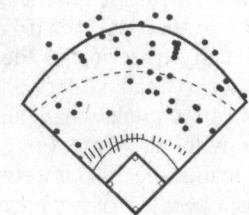 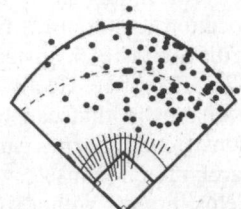

Vs. LHP　　　**Vs. RHP**

2003 Situational Stats

	AB	H	HR	RBI	Avg		AB	H	HR	RBI	Avg
Home	269	62	7	36	.230	LHP	153	36	9	29	.235
Road	250	55	6	21	.220	RHP	366	81	4	28	.221
First Half	315	72	10	33	.229	Sc Pos	158	30	1	42	.190
Scnd Half	204	45	3	24	.221	Clutch	79	23	3	11	.291

2003 Rankings (National League)

- 2nd in strikeouts (177), lowest batting average (.225), highest percentage of swings that missed (32.8), lowest batting average vs. righthanded pitchers (.221) and lowest batting average with two strikes (.122)
- 3rd in lowest on-base percentage (.287) and lowest percentage of swings put into play (32.2)
- 4th in lowest batting average on the road (.220)
- 5th in lowest slugging percentage (.347), lowest batting average with runners in scoring position (.190) and lowest batting average at home (.230)
- 8th in lowest batting average vs. lefthanded pitchers (.235)

Jason Kendall

2003 Season

Jason Kendall had a fine comeback season, notching a career high with 191 hits after batting just .266 and .283 the previous two years while being hampered by a torn ligament in his left thumb. He finished strong in 2003, hitting .388 in his last 45 games. He also hit .449 from May 28 until the end of the season, raising his overall batting average from .270 to .325.

Hitting

When healthy, Kendall sprays line drives to all fields, and that is just what he did last season. He makes consistent contact, as evidenced by the fact that he did not strike out twice in a game last season after July 20. He also exhibits outstanding patience. Never a big home-run hitter, Kendall has been robbed of some of his gap power by the hand injury. He thrived in the No. 3 spot of the batting order last season after Brian Giles was traded, but his bat-handling ability and lack of power make him better suited to batting second.

Baserunning & Defense

Kendall was once one of the top basestealing catchers in history, but he has slowed considerably since dislocating his ankle in 1999. He will take the occasional extra base but rarely tries to steal and was successful on barely 50 percent of his tries last season. Kendall's defense is average at best. He went through a stretch last season in which he struggled to block pitches in the dirt. He doesn't have a strong arm and teams will run on him.

2004 Outlook

Kendall was nearly traded to San Diego along with Giles. However, the two sides couldn't agree on how much the Pirates would assume of the $42 million left on the final four years on Kendall's six-year, $60 million contract. The cost-cutting Pirates would love to unload Kendall and he, too, would prefer to move on after seeing the team gutted by trades last season. Regardless of where he is playing, he remains a formidable hitter in terms of average, and someone who can get on base.

Position: C
Bats: R **Throws:** R
Ht: 6' 0" **Wt:** 197

Opening Day Age: 29
Born: 6/26/74 in San Diego, CA
ML Seasons: 0

Overall Statistics

	G	AB	R	H	D	T	HR	RBI	SB	BB	SO	Avg	OBP	Slg
'03	150	587	84	191	29	3	6	58	8	49	40	.325	.399	.416
Car.	1105	4032	620	1226	224	29	64	420	129	394	362	.304	.385	.422

Where He Hits the Ball

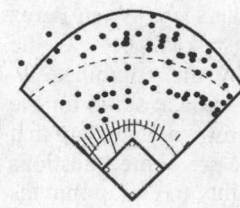
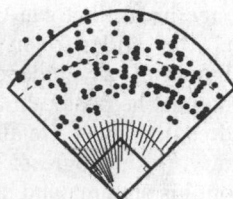

Vs. LHP   **Vs. RHP**

2003 Situational Stats

	AB	H	HR	RBI	Avg		AB	H	HR	RBI	Avg
Home	292	92	3	24	.315	LHP	158	49	1	14	.310
Road	295	99	3	34	.336	RHP	429	142	5	44	.331
First Half	334	103	4	34	.308	Sc Pos	140	44	1	47	.314
Scnd Half	253	88	2	24	.348	Clutch	99	37	2	15	.374

2003 Rankings (National League)

- 1st in lowest percentage of swings on the first pitch (7.8)
- 2nd in hit by pitch (25), batting average with two strikes (.292) and lowest percentage of runners caught stealing as a catcher (20.3)
- 3rd in singles and errors at catcher (10)
- Led the Pirates in batting average, at-bats, runs scored, hits, singles, caught stealing (7), hit by pitch (25), times on base (265), pitches seen (2,622), plate appearances (666), games played, highest percentage of pitches taken (63.0), highest percentage of swings put into play (56.7), batting average with runners in scoring position, batting average with the bases loaded (.556)
- Led NL catchers in batting average

Oliver Perez

2003 Season

Oliver Perez was the key to a three-player package the Pirates received from San Diego in the August 26 trade that shipped star outfielder Brian Giles to the Padres. Perez struggled after the trade, going 0-3 with a 5.87 ERA in five starts before being forced to miss his last turn in the rotation because of a blister on the thumb of his pitching hand. In all, he finished the season on a big league career-worst six-game losing streak and did not win after July 22.

Pitching

Perez has an excellent arm with a fastball that reaches 96 MPH and regularly sits in the 92-94 MPH range. His best pitch is a wicked slider with a huge break that can tie hitters up. When Perez gets the slider over for strikes, he can be dominating, as evidenced by the combined 24 strikeouts he posted in back-to-back starts for the Padres in August. He also throws a changeup that is a work in progress. There are some questions about his stamina and his ability to eat up innings over the grind of a 162-game season, and some scouts fear his violent delivery will lead to arm problems.

Defense & Hitting

Perez is athletic and he pounces off the mound to field bunts and slow rollers. As a lefthander, he has the natural advantage of holding baserunners on. Like many young pitchers, he needs to refine that skill and pay closer attention to runners. Perez makes decent contact at the plate, though he has no power and needs work on his bunting.

2004 Outlook

PNC Park is made for lefthanded pitchers, but the Pirates haven't had a quality southpaw starter since moving into their new digs in 2001. Perez will begin the season in the starting rotation, and the Pirates believe he will blossom in his new home. He is a competitor who has the chance to be a consistent 15-game winner with his stuff, but he first must learn to throw strikes.

Position: SP
Bats: L **Throws:** L
Ht: 6' 3" **Wt:** 160

Opening Day Age: 22
Born: 8/15/81 in Culiacan, Mexico
ML Seasons: 2

Overall Statistics

	W	L	Pct.	ERA	G	GS	Sv	IP	H	BB	SO	HR	Avg
'03	4	10	.286	5.47	24	24	0	126.2	129	77	141	22	.263
Car.	8	15	.348	4.65	40	39	0	216.2	200	125	235	35	.245

2003 Pitching Profile

	Oliver Perez	NL Average
Overall Strike %	61.4	62.4
1st Pitch Strike %	54.2	58.4
Ratio	1.63	1.38
Strikeouts per 9 IP	10.02	6.65
Walks per 9 IP	5.47	3.42
Home Runs per 9 IP	1.56	1.05
Strikeout/Walk Ratio	1.83	1.94
Groundball/Flyball Ratio	0.93	1.29

2003 Situational Stats

	W	L	ERA	Sv	IP		AB	H	HR	RBI	Avg
Home	2	8	6.68	0	63.1	LHB	72	21	3	8	.292
Road	2	2	4.26	0	63.1	RHB	419	108	19	65	.258
First Half	3	3	5.40	0	63.1	Sc Pos	117	33	4	49	.282
Scnd Half	1	7	5.54	0	63.1	Clutch	23	6	0	2	.261

2003 Rankings (National League)

- Did not rank near the top or bottom in any category

Pokey Reese

Position: 2B
Bats: R **Throws:** R
Ht: 5'11" **Wt:** 180

Opening Day Age: 30
Born: 6/10/73 in Columbia, SC
MI Seasons: 7

2003 Season

Pokey Reese got off to an awful start, hitting .215 and making an uncharacteristic six errors in his first 19 games. Then, things got worse. Reese tore a ligament in his left thumb while stealing second base in a May 13 game against Houston and wound up missing the rest of the season. He went 4-for-29 (.138) in his last 13 games.

Hitting

Hitting never has been Reese's strong point, and he was on his way to another poor year with the bat in 2003 before the thumb injury. He lacks power but fails to compensate, as he refuses to play the little man's game. He is an impatient hitter who swings at too many offerings out of the strike zone. Reese also hits too many balls in the air rather than utilizing his speed by hitting more grounders and bunting more frequently.

Baserunning & Defense

Reese has above-average speed, and he uses it well once he's on base. He's a high-percentage basestealer who always looks to take the extra base, but he is not able to take full advantage of that skill because of his inability to get on base consistently. Reese is a top-notch defensive second baseman with outstanding range and a strong arm. He seemingly sucks up every ball hit between first and second base. His slow start in the field last season appears to be an aberration, as he did not commit an error in his last 18 games.

2004 Outlook

The Pirates decided not to exercise a $5 million club option in Reese's contract for this season and paid him a $1.5 million buyout. Reese might scramble to find a starting job as a free agent after his injury-marred season. His best bet would be to catch on with a good-hitting team that can afford to carry a glove man. The time may be nearing when Reese, who came up through Cincinnati's farm system as a shortstop, moves into a utility infielder's role.

Overall Statistics

	G	AB	R	H	D	T	HR	RBI	SB	BB	SO	Avg	OBP	Slg
'03	37	107	9	23	2	0	1	12	6	9	31	.215	.271	.262
Car.	760	2589	334	650	121	15	41	242	138	209	471	.251	.310	.357

Where He Hits the Ball

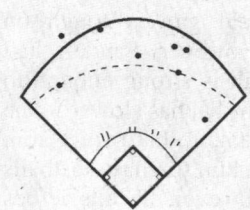
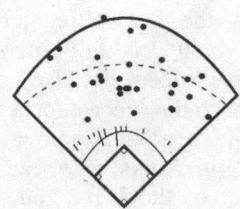

Vs. LHP   **Vs. RHP**

2003 Situational Stats

	AB	H	HR	RBI	Avg		AB	H	HR	RBI	Avg
Home	55	13	0	5	.236	LHP	31	5	1	4	.161
Road	52	10	1	7	.192	RHP	76	18	0	8	.237
First Half	107	23	1	12	.215	Sc Pos	27	7	0	11	.259
Scnd Half	0	0	0	0	—	Clutch	18	6	0	1	.333

2003 Rankings (National League)

- Did not rank near the top or bottom in any category

Reggie Sanders

2003 Season

Despite being the starting right fielder for the previous two National League pennant winners— Arizona in 2001 and San Francisco in 2002— Reggie Sanders had to wait until spring training began before signing a one-year, $1 million contract with the Pirates as a free agent. He proved to be quite a bargain as he led the club in home runs with 31, just two short of his career best, and RBI despite missing the final 11 games with a strained muscle in his left ribcage. He finished strong, hitting .337 in his last 50 games with 15 doubles, 15 homers and 47 RBI.

Hitting

PNC Park seemed like a bad match for Sanders, as the big left-center field gap is tough on righthanded pull-hitters. However, Sanders had no problem because he still is strong enough to reach the deepest fences. His bat has slowed some with age, and he is vulnerable to hard stuff from righthanders, who can get him to chase fastballs out of the strike zone. However, he hits lefties extremely well and still crushes mistakes from righties. Sanders strikes out too much and doesn't walk enough, but he makes up for those deficiencies with his power and knack for delivering clutch hits.

Baserunning & Defense

Sanders has lost a step over the years but still is in excellent physical shape and has above-average speed. He also is an extremely smart baserunner who knows how to take the extra base and when to pick his spots to steal. He has good range and a decent arm in the outfield, though he doesn't get to as many balls in the gap as he used to.

2004 Outlook

Sanders has been a nomad, playing for six teams in the past six seasons, but he still is a good player. He became a free agent at the end of last season, and wherever he lands, he will be a positive addition as a productive player on the field and a steadying veteran presence off it.

Position: RF/LF
Bats: R **Throws:** R
Ht: 6' 1" **Wt:** 205

Opening Day Age: 36
Born: 12/1/67 in Florence, SC
ML Seasons: 13

Overall Statistics

G	AB	R	H	D	T	HR	RBI	SB	BB	SO	Avg	OBP	Slg
130	453	74	129	27	4	31	87	15	38	110	.285	.345	.567
1437	5102	867	1367	270	54	249	802	262	574	1320	.268	.347	.488

Where He Hits the Ball

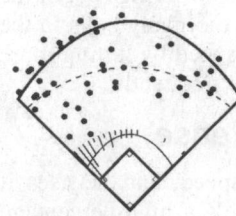 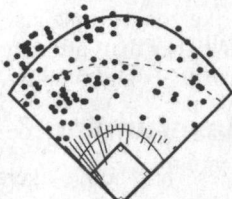

Vs. LHP   **Vs. RHP**

2003 Situational Stats

	AB	H	HR	RBI	Avg		AB	H	HR	RBI	Avg
Home	233	61	17	37	.262	LHP	136	41	12	33	.301
Road	220	68	14	50	.309	RHP	317	88	19	54	.278
First Half	250	65	15	37	.260	Sc Pos	133	41	12	66	.308
Scnd Half	203	64	16	50	.315	Clutch	74	21	6	10	.284

2003 Rankings (National League)

- 2nd in cleanup slugging percentage (.679)
- 3rd in steals of third (7)
- 4th in lowest percentage of pitches taken (48.2)
- 10th in stolen-base percentage (75.0)
- Led the Pirates in home runs, total bases (257), RBI, strikeouts, slugging percentage, HR frequency (14.6 ABs per HR), steals of third (7) and cleanup slugging percentage (.679)

Kip Wells

Position: SP
Bats: R **Throws:** R
Ht: 6' 3" **Wt:** 205

Opening Day Age: 26
Born: 4/21/77 in Houston, TX
ML Seasons: 6

2003 Season

Following a public tongue-lashing from Pirates manager Lloyd McClendon on the mound during an August 22 start at Milwaukee, Kip Wells went on to an excellent finish by going 5-2 with a 1.50 ERA in his last seven starts. During that stretch, he pitched six shutout innings against World Series champion Florida, tossed an eight-inning complete game against the NL East champion Braves and retired the first 17 batters in a start against Cincinnati. Wells was outstanding at PNC Park, and his 2.12 home ERA was tops in the National League. He should have had more than 10 wins, but the Pirates' bullpen blew seven leads for him.

Pitching

Wells always has had a great arm, but he now is figuring out the nuances of pitching. His fastball tops out at 96 MPH and sits comfortably in the 91-93 range with outstanding movement. He is gaining confidence in throwing his other pitches for strikes, including a curveball, slider and changeup. Wells has a tendency to run up high pitch counts in the early innings, but he improved his efficiency during the latter stages of last season. He also is developing a reputation of being tough with the game on the line, as opponents hit just .169 with runners in scoring position last season.

Defense & Hitting

Wells is a good athlete who has been used as both a pinch-hitter and pinch-runner, but he needs work on both his defense and hitting. He made five errors last season and tends to get flustered on bunt plays. He goes up to the plate swinging hard and drilled a 457-foot home run in 2003, but he is a terrible bunter and hurts himself in sacrifice situations.

2004 Outlook

Wells has improved markedly during his two seasons with the Pirates and seems poised for a breakthrough season. He hasn't been helped much by his defense or bullpen during his time in Pittsburgh, but he has the stuff to develop into a No. 1 or 2 starter and should be on the mound for the first pitch of the opener for the Pirates this year.

Overall Statistics

	W	L	Pct.	ERA	G	GS	Sv	IP	H	BB	SO	HR	Avg
'03	10	9	.526	3.28	31	31	0	197.1	171	76	147	24	.233
Car.	42	44	.488	4.12	131	111	0	663.1	672	281	480	76	.264

2003 Pitching Profile

	Kip Wells	NL Average
Overall Strike %	61.9	62.4
1st Pitch Strike %	58.1	58.4
Ratio	1.25	1.38
Strikeouts per 9 IP	6.70	6.65
Walks per 9 IP	3.47	3.42
Home Runs per 9 IP	1.09	1.05
Strikeout/Walk Ratio	1.93	1.94
Groundball/Flyball Ratio	1.55	1.29

2003 Situational Stats

	W	L	ERA	Sv	IP		AB	H	HR	RBI	Avg
Home	5	3	2.12	0	85.0	LHB	314	79	10	34	.252
Road	5	6	4.17	0	112.1	RHB	421	92	14	36	.219
First Half	3	4	3.76	0	105.1	Sc Pos	172	29	3	43	.169
Scnd Half	7	5	2.74	0	92.0	Clutch	53	17	2	5	.321

2003 Rankings (National League)

- 1st in lowest ERA at home and errors at pitcher (5)
- 3rd in lowest batting average allowed with runners in scoring position and lowest fielding percentage at pitcher (.886)
- 5th in highest stolen-base percentage allowed (87.5)
- Led the Pirates in ERA, wins, games started, innings pitched, batters faced (835), home runs allowed, walks allowed, strikeouts, wild pitches (7), pitches thrown (3,201), pickoff throws (92), stolen bases allowed (14), lowest batting average allowed (.233), lowest slugging percentage allowed (.376), lowest on-base percentage allowed (.310), lowest ERA at home, lowest ERA on the road, lowest batting average allowed with runners in scoring position, and most strikeouts per nine innings (6.7)

Craig Wilson

2003 Season

Craig Wilson started at four different positions for the Pirates. He made 29 starts at first base, 28 in right field, 15 at catcher and four in left field. In a bit of a surprise, the Pirates decided to make him their No. 2 catcher in spring training. While he was primarily a catcher in the minor leagues, he played sparingly at the position in his first two big league seasons.

Hitting

While Wilson racks up his share of strikeouts, he has made progress as a hitter since breaking into the major leagues in 2001. He has learned to use the whole field, and now realizes he is strong enough to go the other way and still hit the ball out of the park. He can be pitched to, however, and opponents often put him away with two strikes by throwing offspeed stuff and fastballs out of the strike zone. Wilson shows patience early in the count but tends to get too aggressive with two strikes.

Baserunning & Defense

Wilson does not run well but understands his limitations. He rarely takes chances, preferring to go station-to-station on the basepaths. He is shedding the reputation of having an iron glove. He has made himself into a decent right fielder with improving range and an accurate, though ordinary, arm. He is decent behind the plate and has the aptitude to improve, but at first base, his footwork and range are lacking.

2004 Outlook

Wilson has been a productive power hitter in part-time duty for three major league seasons, hitting 47 home runs. The Pirates have fretted about his strikeouts and defense, but he showed improvement in those areas last season and finally could see more regular duty this year. The Pirates may have vacancies at catcher, first base and right field, giving Wilson plenty of opportunities to show what he can do with 500 at-bats in a season.

Position: RF/1B/C
Bats: R **Throws:** R
Ht: 6' 2"   **Wt:** 218

Opening Day Age: 27
Born: 11/30/76 in Fountain Valley, CA
ML Seasons: 3

Overall Statistics

	G	AB	R	H	D	T	HR	RBI	SB	BB	SO	Avg	OBP	Slg
'03	116	309	49	81	15	4	18	48	3	35	89	.262	.360	.511
Car.	335	835	124	227	34	6	47	137	8	82	258	.272	.363	.496

Where He Hits the Ball

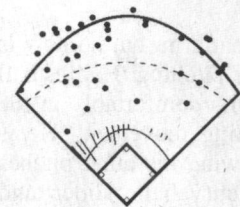
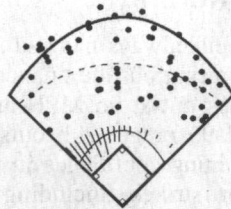

Vs. LHP   **Vs. RHP**

2003 Situational Stats

	AB	H	HR	RBI	Avg		AB	H	HR	RBI	Avg
Home	148	43	9	23	.291	LHP	107	33	11	26	.308
Road	161	38	9	25	.236	RHP	202	48	7	22	.238
First Half	140	34	4	16	.243	Sc Pos	83	19	5	32	.229
Scnd Half	169	47	14	32	.278	Clutch	55	6	2	2	.109

2003 Rankings (National League)

- 3rd in lowest batting average in the clutch
- 6th in hit by pitch (13)

Jack Wilson

2003 Season

Jack Wilson had the best of his three major league seasons in 2003, as he established career highs with 143 hits, nine homers and 62 RBI. He went on his best stretch of the year, putting together a career-best 17-game hitting streak from August 10-30, not long after the Pirates acquired young middle infielders Bobby Hill and Freddy Sanchez in trades. Wilson also finished the season by hitting .333 over his final 48 at-bats.

Hitting

Wilson doesn't get on base enough or hit with very much power, which is a bad combination. However, he did show signs of improvement last season as he increased his power output and learned to turn on certain inside pitches. While he handles the bat well in hit-and-run situations and is very a decent-to-outstanding bunter, he doesn't put those skills to use enough. He chases too many bad pitches and too often gets pull-happy. Wilson is very good with runners in scoring position and admits his concentration is much higher in meaningful plate appearances.

Baserunning & Defense

Wilson is an average runner who rarely steals bases and too often gets reckless on the basepaths while trying to make things happen. He stole five bases last year, but also was thrown out five times. He is developing into a top-notch defensive shortstop. He has very good range and is particularly adept at going into the hole. Wilson's arm is fine, though he still has a tendency to force throws even when he has no chance of making the play.

2004 Outlook

Wilson has performed marginally better in each of his three major league seasons, but he is far from being an upper-echelon shortstop. He will need to put up better offensive numbers to keep his starting job for very much longer, unless he can land with a team that has enough hitting depth to carry a glove man.

Position: SS
Bats: R **Throws:** R
Ht: 6' 0"   **Wt:** 193

Opening Day Age: 26
Born: 12/29/77 in Westlake Village, CA
ML Seasons: 3

Overall Statistics

	G	AB	R	H	D	T	HR	RBI	SB	BB	SO	Avg	OBP	Slg
'03	150	558	58	143	21	3	9	62	5	36	74	.256	.303	.353
Car.	405	1475	179	363	60	8	16	134	11	89	218	.246	.292	.330

Where He Hits the Ball

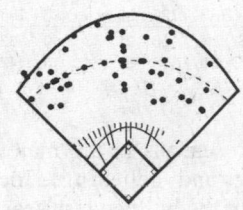   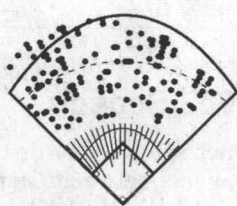

Vs. LHP   **Vs. RHP**

2003 Situational Stats

	AB	H	HR	RBI	Avg		AB	H	HR	RBI	Avg
Home	286	78	2	36	.273	LHP	134	35	2	11	.261
Road	272	65	7	26	.239	RHP	424	108	7	51	.255
First Half	324	77	5	33	.238	Sc Pos	120	37	2	52	.308
Scnd Half	234	66	4	29	.282	Clutch	88	20	2	8	.227

2003 Rankings (National League)

- 3rd in errors at shortstop (17)
- 6th in lowest slugging percentage and lowest fielding percentage at shortstop (.975)
- 7th in sacrifice bunts (11) and bunts in play (27)
- Led the Pirates in sacrifice bunts (11), games played and bunts in play (27)

Joe Beimel

Position: RP
Bats: L **Throws:** L
Ht: 6' 3" **Wt:** 220

Opening Day Age: 26
Born: 4/19/77 in St. Marys, PA
ML Seasons: 3
Pronunciation: BYE-muhl

Overall Statistics

	W	L	Pct.	ERA	G	GS	Sv	IP	H	BB	SO	HR	Avg
'03	1	3	.250	5.05	69	0	0	62.1	69	33	42	7	.299
Car.	10	19	.345	5.00	164	23	0	263.0	288	127	153	28	.284

2003 Situational Stats

	W	L	ERA	Sv	IP		AB	H	HR	RBI	Avg
Home	0	0	2.57	0	35.0	LHB	106	33	3	22	.311
Road	1	3	8.23	0	27.1	RHB	125	36	4	23	.288
First Half	1	2	3.57	0	40.1	Sc Pos	58	21	3	40	.362
Scnd Half	0	1	7.77	0	22.0	Clutch	73	25	4	15	.342

2003 Season

After splitting his first two seasons in the major leagues between starting and relieving, Joe Beimel worked solely out of the bullpen last year. Despite the reduced workload in terms of innings, he seemed to feel the strain of pitching in a career-high 69 games. He posted a 7.77 ERA after the All-Star break and gave up runs in nine of his final 15 appearances.

Pitching, Defense & Hitting

Beimel's fastball tops out at 92 MPH and he has a solid slider. However, he has trouble with command and leaves too many pitches over the heart of the plate. He has made five errors in 52 major league chances but has one of the best pick-off moves in the bigs, making him extremely difficult to run on—only one of six would-be thieves were successful on his watch last year. Beimel is a good athlete who can handle the bat, though he gets few chances in relief.

2004 Outlook

The Pirates asked Beimel to become their top lefthanded reliever after trading Scott Sauerbeck to Boston in July. Beimel wasn't up to the task. While he is young enough to turn things around, he has shown little improvement in three major league seasons and seems unprepared for a major role.

Brian Boehringer

Position: RP
Bats: B **Throws:** R
Ht: 6' 2" **Wt:** 192

Opening Day Age: 34
Born: 1/8/70 in St. Louis, MO
ML Seasons: 9
Pronunciation: BOH-ring-uhr

Overall Statistics

	W	L	Pct.	ERA	G	GS	Sv	IP	H	BB	SO	HR	Avg
'03	5	4	.556	5.49	62	0	0	62.1	64	30	47	11	.267
Car.	25	31	.446	4.35	335	21	3	509.1	495	257	412	62	.255

2003 Situational Stats

	W	L	ERA	Sv	IP		AB	H	HR	RBI	Avg
Home	3	0	3.48	0	33.2	LHB	88	17	3	11	.193
Road	2	4	7.85	0	28.2	RHB	152	47	8	29	.309
First Half	4	2	6.44	0	36.1	Sc Pos	71	15	4	28	.211
Scnd Half	1	2	4.15	0	26.0	Clutch	82	19	4	15	.232

2003 Season

Brian Boehringer came into the season as the Pirates' primary setup reliever from the right side, but his role gradually was reduced due to ineffectiveness. He had an 8.44 ERA in April and 9.64 in May. Though he improved on those numbers, he never pitched well enough to fully regain the Pirates' trust.

Pitching, Defense & Hitting

Boehringer is a hard thrower whose fastball can reach 95-96 MPH and routinely sits in the 92-93 zone. However, he needs very good location because the heater lacks much movement and his command of a hard slider is erratic. Boehringer is quick off the mound and surehanded in fielding bunts—he has committed just one error in his career. He rarely bats, and that's just as well. Over the past three seasons, opposing basestealers are 15 of 19 (78.9 percent) when he is on the mound.

2004 Outlook

Boehringer was a major disappointment last season, but he will be back again as he has one year and $2 million left on his two-year, $3.8 million contract. The Pirates need him to bounce back this season, but that might be wishful thinking, as he really hasn't been effective since the first half of the 2002 campaign.

J.J. Davis

Position: RF
Bats: R **Throws:** R
Ht: 6' 5" **Wt:** 240

Opening Day Age: 25
Born: 10/25/78 in Glendora, CA
ML Seasons: 2

Overall Statistics

	G	AB	R	H	D	T	HR	RBI	SB	BB	SO	Avg	OBP	Slg
'03	19	35	1	7	0	0	1	4	0	3	13	.200	.263	.286
Car.	28	45	2	8	0	0	1	4	0	3	17	.178	.245	.244

2003 Situational Stats

	AB	H	HR	RBI	Avg		AB	H	HR	RBI	Avg
Home	18	5	1	3	.278	LHP	19	4	1	2	.211
Road	17	2	0	1	.118	RHP	16	3	0	2	.188
First Half	0	0	0	0	–	Sc Pos	8	2	0	3	.250
Scnd Half	35	7	1	4	.200	Clutch	8	1	0	0	.125

2003 Season

J.J. Davis continued his career turnaround after looking like a first-round bust early in his pro career. He enjoyed a breakout season with Double-A Altoona in 2002, and then hit .284 with 26 home runs and 67 RBI in 122 games for Triple-A Nashville in 2003 while leading the Pacific Coast League with a .554 slugging percentage. He was third in the PCL in homers and fourth with 59 extra-base hits.

Hitting, Baserunning & Defense

Davis tries to pull too many pitches and can be prone to strikeouts. However, he is getting better at using the opposite field and showing more patience. He produces his fair share of doubles. Davis is an above-average runner for a big man and has the ability to steal some bases. He has a strong-average arm in right field but needs some work on tracking flyballs.

2004 Outlook

Davis is out of minor league options, meaning he will be kept in the major leagues this season. The Pirates are likely to ease him into the lineup by platooning him in right field and playing him mainly against lefthanded pitchers. He has a chance to eventually turn into an impact player.

Bobby Hill

Position: 2B
Bats: B **Throws:** R
Ht: 5'10" **Wt:** 190

Opening Day Age: 25
Born: 4/3/78 in San Jose, CA
ML Seasons: 2

Overall Statistics

	G	AB	R	H	D	T	HR	RBI	SB	BB	SO	Avg	OBP	Slg
'03	6	7	1	2	0	0	0	0	0	2	2	.286	.444	.286
Car.	65	197	27	50	7	2	4	20	6	19	44	.254	.332	.371

2003 Situational Stats

	AB	H	HR	RBI	Avg		AB	H	HR	RBI	Avg
Home	6	2	0	0	.333	LHP	4	1	0	0	.250
Road	1	0	0	0	.000	RHP	3	1	0	0	.333
First Half	4	1	0	0	.250	Sc Pos	2	1	0	0	.500
Scnd Half	3	1	0	0	.333	Clutch	1	0	0	0	.000

2003 Season

Bobby Hill went to spring training as the favorite to win the Chicago Cubs' starting second-base job, but he was beaten out by Mark Grudzielanek and sent to Triple-A Iowa. Hill was traded to the Pirates on August 15 and assigned to Triple-A Nashville. The Pirates recalled him September 13, but he played in just one game because of lower back soreness.

Hitting, Baserunning & Defense

Hill is a top-of-the-order type hitter who plays the little man's game by working the count and looking to make contact. The switch-hitter has been much more productive from the right side in his limited major league at-bats, but he has the reputation of also swinging well from the left. Hill has outstanding speed, good instincts on the bases and always is a threat to steal. He is a solid second baseman with good range and hands who hangs tough on the double play.

2004 Outlook

Hill will battle Freddy Sanchez in spring training for the starting job at the keystone for Pittsburgh. Hill needed a change of scenery after things went sour in Chicago, but the question of whether he will be able to fully develop into the star the Cubs once projected remains unanswered.

Mike Lincoln

Position: RP
Bats: R **Throws:** R
Ht: 6' 2" **Wt:** 213

Opening Day Age: 28
Born: 4/10/75 in
Carmichael, CA
ML Seasons: 5

Overall Statistics

	W	L	Pct.	ERA	G	GS	Sv	IP	H	BB	SO	HR	Avg
'03	3	4	.429	5.20	36	0	5	36.1	38	13	28	5	.277
Car.	10	22	.313	5.16	148	19	5	246.0	290	90	144	36	.297

2003 Situational Stats

	W	L	ERA	Sv	IP		AB	H	HR	RBI	Avg
Home	1	2	5.82	3	17.0	LHB	45	15	0	2	.333
Road	2	2	4.66	2	19.1	RHB	92	23	5	15	.250
First Half	0	0	2.57	0	7.0	Sc Pos	38	8	0	9	.211
Scnd Half	3	4	5.83	5	29.1	Clutch	78	23	2	11	.295

2003 Season

Mike Lincoln missed the first three months with a bruised pitching shoulder after a freak spring training accident in which he tripped over a golf ball while jogging. He wound up being the Pirates' closer for a three-week stretch after Mike Williams was traded to Philadelphia on July 20. Lincoln converted his first three save opportunities, but then was taken out of the role after blowing three of his next five chances.

Pitching, Defense & Hitting

Lincoln relies heavily on an outstanding curveball that drops off the table. His fastball hits 92 MPH but is more of a secondary pitch. Lincoln, despite his jogging mishap, is a good athlete who fields his position well and does a good job of holding runners. In fact, seven of the 12 big league basestealers who have tried to run on him during his career have been caught. Lincoln doesn't bat often and struggles to make contact when he does.

2004 Outlook

Lincoln found himself in over his head as a closer last season and had his confidence shaken. However, he will move back into a middle-relief role this year, and he has enjoyed some success in that spot in the past.

Abraham O. Nunez

Position: 2B/SS
Bats: B **Throws:** R
Ht: 5'11" **Wt:** 186

Opening Day Age: 28
Born: 3/16/76 in Santo
Domingo, DR
ML Seasons: 7
Pronunciation:
NOON-yez

Overall Statistics

	G	AB	R	H	D	T	HR	RBI	SB	BB	SO	Avg	OBP	Slg
'03	118	311	37	77	8	7	4	35	9	26	53	.248	.310	.357
Car.	518	1307	139	311	46	14	9	104	34	132	242	.238	.311	.315

2003 Situational Stats

	AB	H	HR	RBI	Avg		AB	H	HR	RBI	Avg
Home	151	41	2	16	.272	LHP	43	7	0	3	.163
Road	160	36	2	19	.225	RHP	268	70	4	32	.261
First Half	145	32	1	14	.221	Sc Pos	75	15	0	28	.200
Scnd Half	166	45	3	21	.271	Clutch	60	9	0	7	.150

2003 Season

Abraham Nunez wound up getting the most playing time of his career as he shared the second-base job with Jeff Reboulet after Pokey Reese went down May 13 with a season-ending thumb injury. Nunez' playing time grew as the season wore on, and the increased at-bats agreed with him as he hit .271 after the All-Star break.

Hitting, Baserunning & Defense

Nunez is a switch-hitter in name only. He struggled from the right side and rarely is asked to face a lefthanded pitcher. He has gotten consistently stronger in recent years and now is able to drive some balls into the gap after being almost solely a singles hitter earlier in his career. Nunez has good speed, runs the bases well and is a threat to steal. He is a solid glove man at both middle-infield spots, though his range and arm play better at the keystone.

2004 Outlook

Nunez likely had his best year in 2003, but he has yet to live up to the great expectations that were placed on him when he came to the major leagues. Once heralded as a potential top-notch shortstop, it has taken Nunez a long time to finally develop into simply a solid utility infielder.

Tike Redman

Position: CF
Bats: L **Throws:** L
Ht: 5'11" **Wt:** 166

Opening Day Age: 27
Born: 3/10/77 in Tuscaloosa, Al
ML Seasons: 3

Overall Statistics

	G	AB	R	H	D	T	HR	RBI	SB	BB	SO	Avg	OBP	Slg
'03	56	230	36	76	16	5	3	19	7	14	18	.330	.374	.483
Car.	102	373	46	110	21	6	5	24	11	19	50	.295	.332	.424

2003 Situational Stats

	AB	H	HR	RBI	Avg		AB	H	HR	RBI	Avg
Home	108	39	2	12	.361	LHP	73	24	0	6	.329
Road	122	37	1	7	.303	RHP	157	52	3	13	.331
First Half	0	0	0	0	—	Sc Pos	41	14	2	18	.341
Scnd Half	230	76	3	19	.330	Clutch	37	14	2	8	.378

2003 Season

Tike Redman was dropped off the Pirates' 40-man roster in December 2002. However, he hit .294 with four homers, 29 RBI and 42 steals in 100 games at Triple-A Nashville, prompting Pittsburgh to call him up August 1 after the club traded Kenny Lofton to the Cubs. Redman had 76 hits—tied for the most in the major leagues—over the final two months of the season.

Hitting, Baserunning & Defense

Redman has learned to utilize his speed and looked like a legitimate major league leadoff man by the end of last season. He is increasingly patient, works the count and is willing to hit the ball on the ground, though he does have enough pop to reach the gaps. Redman has outstanding speed and his instincts on the bases have improved, making him a legitimate stolen-base threat. His range is outstanding in center field, which offsetts his habit of sometimes taking the wrong first step on flyballs and his below-average arm.

2004 Outlook

Redman will go into spring training as the Pirates' center fielder and leadoff man. He looked lost during major league trials in 2000 and 2001 but has improved, though nothing in his past suggests he can duplicate the final two months of last season.

Matt Stairs

Position: RF/1B
Bats: L **Throws:** R
Ht: 5' 9" **Wt:** 210

Opening Day Age: 36
Born: 2/27/68 in Saint John, NB, Canada
ML Seasons: 11

Overall Statistics

	G	AB	R	H	D	T	HR	RBI	SB	BB	SO	Avg	OBP	Slg
'03	121	305	49	89	20	1	20	57	0	45	64	.292	.389	.561
Car.	1046	3060	488	813	175	7	176	568	23	439	634	.266	.362	.500

2003 Situational Stats

	AB	H	HR	RBI	Avg		AB	H	HR	RBI	Avg
Home	157	55	13	40	.350	LHP	32	6	2	4	.188
Road	148	34	7	17	.230	RHP	273	83	18	53	.304
First Half	158	43	10	23	.272	Sc Pos	91	26	7	41	.286
Scnd Half	147	46	10	34	.313	Clutch	53	15	5	11	.283

2003 Season

Signed as a free agent at the 2002 winter meetings, Matt Stairs looked like a bust when he went on the disabled list May 23 with a finger injury, as he was hitting .185 with one homer and five RBI in 37 games. However, Stairs came back to hit .330 with 18 doubles, one triple, 19 homers and 52 ribbies over his last 84 games, while manning both right field and first base against righthanded pitchers.

Hitting, Baserunning & Defense

The stocky Stairs has a compact stroke that enables him to turn on inside pitches for power, sometimes connecting on tape-measure shots, while also handling stuff on the outer half of the plate. He has a good eye at the plate and rarely gets fooled. Stairs lost 25 pounds prior to last season but still is strictly a station-to-station runner. He is a below-average defender at both first base and right field, though his arm is adequate in right. While he catches what he gets to, his range is extremely limited.

2004 Outlook

Stairs showed in the second half of 2003 that he has something left in the tank. He hammers righthanded pitching, making him a valuable platoon option and pinch-hitter. The Royals signed him to a one-year contract in December.

Pittsburgh

Julian Tavarez

Position: RP
Bats: L **Throws:** R
Ht: 6' 2" **Wt:** 195

Opening Day Age: 30
Born: 5/22/73 in Santiago, DR
ML Seasons: 11
Pronunciation: JOOL-ee-en tah-VAR-rez

Overall Statistics

	W	L	Pct.	ERA	G	GS	Sv	IP	H	BB	SO	HR	Avg
'03	3	3	.500	3.66	64	0	11	83.2	75	27	39	1	.244
Car.	63	48	.568	4.52	491	79	13	951.1	1047	375	531	76	.284

2003 Situational Stats

	W	L	ERA	Sv	IP		AB	H	HR	RBI	Avg
Home	2	2	2.37	6	49.1	LHB	113	33	0	12	.292
Road	1	1	5.50	5	34.1	RHB	195	42	1	26	.215
First Half	0	3	4.38	0	39.0	Sc Pos	99	27	0	35	.273
Scnd Half	3	0	3.02	11	44.2	Clutch	157	31	1	16	.197

2003 Season

After failing to make the starting rotation in spring training, Julian Tavarez began the season as a middle reliever for the Pirates. He got off to a poor start and had a 4.38 ERA at the All-Star break. However, he was thrown into the closer's role when the Pirates could not find anyone else to succeed the traded Mike Williams, and Tavarez wound up converting 11 of 14 save opportunities, including his last seven in a row.

Pitching, Defense & Hitting

Tavarez is a sinker-slider pitcher, whose fastball can reach 95 MPH but usually sits around 90. The sinking action results in plenty of groundballs and few home runs. He is effective in relief, where he thrives in pressure situations and doesn't need to throw his below-average changeup much. Tavarez is quick off the mound but has a tendency to rush his throws to bases on occasion. He holds runners well, but his hitting isn't much to get excited about.

2004 Outlook

Tavarez did an admirable job as a closer late last season, but he lacks a dominant pitch and is better suited as a setup man. He is fearless, a good attribute in a reliever, and he could get a lot of holds while working the eighth inning. Tavarez will change teams after the Pirates didn't offer salary arbitration.

Salomon Torres

Position: RP/SP
Bats: R **Throws:** R
Ht: 5'11" **Wt:** 210

Opening Day Age: 32
Born: 3/11/72 in San Pedro de Macoris, DR
ML Seasons: 7

Overall Statistics

	W	L	Pct.	ERA	G	GS	Sv	IP	H	BB	SO	HR	Avg
'03	7	5	.583	4.76	41	16	2	121.0	128	42	84	19	.276
Car.	20	31	.392	5.24	114	64	2	434.2	464	203	255	59	.277

2003 Situational Stats

	W	L	ERA	Sv	IP		AB	H	HR	RBI	Avg
Home	4	4	5.25	0	58.1	LHB	202	62	10	36	.307
Road	3	1	4.31	2	62.2	RHB	262	66	9	25	.252
First Half	5	2	4.48	2	70.1	Sc Pos	105	26	2	37	.248
Scnd Half	2	3	5.15	0	50.2	Clutch	48	18	1	6	.375

2003 Season

Salomon Torres continued his amazing comeback, spending his first full season in the major leagues six years after he retired from Montreal and became a pitching coach in the Expos' farm system. Torres was forced to split time between the rotation and bullpen because of injuries to the Pirates' pitching staff, and he finished the season by winning his last two starts after going nine in a row without a victory.

Pitching, Defense & Hitting

Torres relies on power. His fastball reaches 95-96 MPH and sits comfortably at 91-92 MPH. He also works with a good slider and throws a curveball and changeup that are average at best. Torres is very athletic and an excellent fielder, but he doesn't do much with the bat. He does not have much in the way of a pickoff move, but he did a decent job of controlling the running game last year.

2004 Outlook

Torres will have a chance to compete for a spot at the back end of the Pirates' rotation, but he seems better suited for relief work with two reliable pitches. Some scouts believe his power arm may be geared towards closing, though the Pirates aren't ready to commit to him in that role.

Other Pittsburgh Pirates

Mark Corey (**Pos**: RHP, **Age**: 29)

	W	L	Pct.	ERA	G	GS	Sv	IP	H	BB	SO	HR	Avg
'03	1	2	.333	5.34	22	0	0	30.1	29	11	27	2	.252
Car.	1	5	.167	7.00	50	0	0	54.0	66	30	51	11	.300

Corey pitched better at Triple-A in 2003 than his 4.34 ERA would indicate. He struck out 63 and walked just 18 in 45.2 innings and ended the season tied for the Pacific Coast League lead with 29 saves. 2004 Outlook: C

Humberto Cota (**Pos**: C, **Age**: 25, **Bats**: R)

	G	AB	R	H	D	T	HR	RBI	SB	BB	SO	Avg	OBP	Slg
'03	10	16	1	4	1	0	0	1	0	1	5	.250	.294	.313
Car.	24	42	3	11	2	0	0	2	0	2	14	.262	.295	.310

Cota battled pain in his surgically-repaired left hand most of the 2003 campaign and batted just .205 in 62 games at Triple-A. Unless he has a great spring, another year in the minors is likely. 2004 Outlook: C

Nelson Figueroa (**Pos**: RHP, **Age**: 29)

	W	L	Pct.	ERA	G	GS	Sv	IP	H	BB	SO	HR	Avg
'03	2	1	.667	3.31	12	3	0	35.1	28	13	23	8	.220
Car.	7	14	.333	4.52	64	30	0	233.0	236	92	142	38	.266

Figueroa posted impressive numbers in 12 appearances with the Pirates last season, despite dealing with control problems at times. He was called up after going 12-5 with a 2.97 ERA at Triple-A and re-signed with Pittsburgh in November. 2004 Outlook: C

John Grabow (**Pos**: LHP, **Age**: 25)

	W	L	Pct.	ERA	G	GS	Sv	IP	H	BB	SO	HR	Avg
'03	0	0	—	3.60	5	0	0	5.0	6	0	9	0	.273
Car.	0	0	—	3.60	5	0	0	5.0	6	0	9	0	.273

Not known as an overpowering pitcher, Grabow fanned nine batters in just five innings in his first taste of the major leagues. The lefthander probably could use another season at Triple-A. 2004 Outlook: C

Adam Hyzdu (**Pos**: CF/RF, **Age**: 32, **Bats**: R)

	G	AB	R	H	D	T	HR	RBI	SB	BB	SO	Avg	OBP	Slg
'03	51	63	16	13	5	0	1	8	0	10	21	.206	.320	.333
Car.	173	308	49	71	14	0	18	55	0	35	87	.231	.312	.451

Although he has had flashes of power, Hyzdu never has displayed enough consistency at the plate to make it as an everyday player in the majors. He will try to change that with the Red Sox next season. 2004 Outlook: C

Rob Mackowiak (**Pos**: 3B/2B/RF, **Age**: 27, **Bats**: L)

	G	AB	R	H	D	T	HR	RBI	SB	BB	SO	Avg	OBP	Slg
'03	77	174	20	47	4	4	6	19	6	15	53	.270	.342	.443
Car.	296	773	107	198	41	6	26	88	19	72	229	.256	.329	.420

Primarily a third baseman, Mackowiak saw time at second base and all three outfield positions with Pittsburgh in 2003. His versatility alone could land him a spot on the Pirates' roster next season. 2004 Outlook: B

Pat Mahomes (**Pos**: RHP, **Age**: 33)

	W	L	Pct.	ERA	G	GS	Sv	IP	H	BB	SO	HR	Avg
'03	0	1	.000	4.84	9	1	0	22.1	19	12	13	2	.241
Car.	42	39	.519	5.47	308	63	5	709.0	738	392	452	116	.272

Mahomes has posted a career 3.13 ERA in 255 minor league games, but he has been unable to produce similar numbers in the majors. 2004 Outlook: C

Jim Mann (**Pos**: RHP, **Age**: 29)

	W	L	Pct.	ERA	G	GS	Sv	IP	H	BB	SO	HR	Avg
'03	0	0	—	10.80	2	0	0	1.2	5	1	1	1	.455
Car.	0	1	.000	4.83	25	0	0	31.2	33	13	25	5	.268

Mann spent most of 2003 in Triple-A. In 51 relief appearances with Nashville, he was 3-2 with a 3.06 ERA and five saves. 2004 Outlook: C

Brian Meadows (**Pos**: RHP, **Age**: 28)

	W	L	Pct.	ERA	G	GS	Sv	IP	H	BB	SO	HR	Avg
'03	2	1	.667	4.72	34	7	1	76.1	91	11	38	8	.290
Car.	39	51	.433	5.24	150	122	1	738.1	896	204	329	110	.302

Meadows went 7-0 with a 1.41 ERA at Triple-A last season. Pirates manager Lloyd McClendon preferred Meadows in a relief role, but the righthander could challenge for a rotation spot in 2004. 2004 Outlook: B

Jeff Reboulet (**Pos**: 2B, **Age**: 39, **Bats**: R)

	G	AB	R	H	D	T	HR	RBI	SB	BB	SO	Avg	OBP	Slg
'03	93	261	37	63	10	2	3	25	2	27	47	.241	.321	.330
Car.	1018	2229	310	536	100	6	20	202	22	292	401	.240	.332	.318

Reboulet spent spring training with the Orioles, was released, and then signed with Pittsburgh. He is going on 40, but could get a couple of looks because of his experience. 2004 Outlook: C

Carlos Rivera (**Pos**: 1B, **Age**: 25, **Bats**: L)

	G	AB	R	H	D	T	HR	RBI	SB	BB	SO	Avg	OBP	Slg
'03	78	95	12	21	5	0	3	10	0	8	28	.221	.283	.368
Car.	78	95	12	21	5	0	3	10	0	8	28	.221	.283	.368

Although Rivera still is a bit green, the first baseman has some power and could challenge for a starting job next year. 2004 Outlook: B

Duaner Sanchez (**Pos**: RHP, **Age**: 24)

	W	L	Pct.	ERA	G	GS	Sv	IP	H	BB	SO	HR	Avg
'03	1	0	1.000	16.50	6	0	0	6.0	15	1	3	2	.500
Car.	1	0	1.000	12.75	15	0	0	12.0	21	8	9	4	.389

Sanchez has a fastball that was clocked as high as 102 MPH in the minor leagues. With some work, Sanchez could become a solid closer, and the Dodgers made him a waiver claim. 2004 Outlook: C

Kevin Young (**Pos**: 1B, **Age**: 34, **Bats**: R)

	G	AB	R	H	D	T	HR	RBI	SB	BB	SO	Avg	OBP	Slg
'03	52	84	8	17	4	0	2	7	1	12	25	.202	.302	.321
Car.	1205	3897	536	1007	235	17	144	606	83	336	882	.258	.324	.438

The Pirates released Young midway through last season. He inked a minor league deal with the Twins, but later was released to be with his ill wife. 2004 Outlook: C

Pittsburgh

617

Pittsburgh Pirates Minor League Prospects

Organization Overview:

The Pirates' farm system has undergone a dramatic turnaround during Brian Graham's two seasons as the player development director. Before Graham, a former major league coach with Cleveland and Baltimore, took over in 2002, the Pirates' minor league affiliates had combined to have just a single plus-.500 year in the previous 33 seasons. In 2002, Pittsburgh farm clubs had the second-best winning percentage in the minors. Last year, the Pirates ranked first with a .581 (399-288) winning percentage. Pittsburgh has emphasized pitching at the minor league level, and the organization led the minor leagues with the lowest batting average allowed (.248) and fewest walks (1,943) in 2003.

Bryan Bullington

Position: P
Bats: R **Throws:** R
Ht: 6' 5" **Wt:** 220

Opening Day Age: 23
Born: 9/30/80 in Madison, IN

Recent Statistics

	W	L	ERA	G	GS	Sv	IP	H	R	BB	SO	HR
2003 A Hickory	5	1	1.39	8	7	0	45.1	25	10	11	46	3
2003 A Lynchburg	8	4	3.05	17	17	0	97.1	101	39	27	67	5

The Pirates used the first overall pick in the 2002 first-year player draft to select Bullington from Ball State. He did not sign until October 30, however, and he was not able to begin his professional career until last season. After dominating at times in the Class-A South Atlantic League last year, he had a tougher time in the high Class-A Carolina League. Bullington is a power pitcher with a fastball that reaches 95 MPH. He also can throw a curveball and slider for strikes, though the Pirates will ask him to settle on one or the other. His changeup is a work in progress, but once he begins mastering that pitch, he should make a quick rise through the farm system.

Sean Burnett

Position: P
Bats: L **Throws:** L
Ht: 6' 1" **Wt:** 179

Opening Day Age: 21
Born: 9/17/82 in Dunedin, FL

Recent Statistics

	W	L	ERA	G	GS	Sv	IP	H	R	BB	SO	HR
2002 A Lynchburg	13	4	1.80	26	26	0	155.1	118	46	33	96	4
2003 AA Altoona	14	6	3.21	27	27	0	159.2	158	60	29	86	2

Many thought pitching at Double-A Altoona would be a litmus test for Burnett last season, but he had another fine year and was named both the Eastern League Pitcher of the Year and the Pirates' Minor League Pitcher of the Year. Burnett's fastball can reach 93 MPH but usually sits in the 88-89 MPH range, and he gets by more on location and changing speeds than overpowering

hitters. His best pitch is a changeup that drops off the table. He also has a good curveball and added a slider to his arsenal last season to give him a harder breaking pitch. Burnett will compete for the fifth slot in the Pittsburgh rotation in spring training, but he likely will get some seasoning at Triple-A before coming to the majors.

Jose Castillo

Position: 2B-SS
Bats: R **Throws:** R
Ht: 6' 0" **Wt:** 180

Opening Day Age: 23
Born: 3/19/81 in Las Mercedes, VZ

Recent Statistics

	G	AB	R	H	D	T	HR	RBI	SB	BB	SO	Avg
2002 A Lynchburg	134	503	82	151	25	2	16	81	27	49	95	.300
2003 AA Altoona	126	498	68	143	24	6	5	66	19	40	81	.287

Castillo struggled initially in his first taste of Double-A last year before hitting .300 from May 1 on. He did not display the same power he showed at high Class-A Lynchburg the previous season, however, and also did not improve his weak plate discipline. The Pirates began playing Castillo at second base in mid-May after Pokey Reese went down with season-ending thumb surgery. Castillo wound up splitting time between second base and shortstop, his natural position, the rest of the season. He will play shortstop at Triple-A in 2004, and likely be ready to challenge Jack Wilson for the starting job at the big league level in 2005.

Mike Gonzalez

Position: P
Bats: R **Throws:** L
Ht: 6' 2" **Wt:** 213

Opening Day Age: 25
Born: 5/23/78 in Corpus Christi, TX

Recent Statistics

	W	L	ERA	G	GS	Sv	IP	H	R	BB	SO	HR
2003 A Lynchburg	0	1	5.14	5	0	0	7.0	7	9	5	9	0
2003 AA Altoona	0	0	1.23	5	0	1	7.1	4	1	2	10	1
2003 AAA Pawtucket	0	0	0.00	2	0	1	1.2	2	0	1	2	0
2003 AAA Nashville	0	0	4.50	7	0	2	10.0	9	5	4	10	0
2003 NL Pittsburgh	0	1	7.56	16	0	0	8.1	7	7	6	6	4

Gonzalez had a wild season in 2003 that saw him get traded to Boston on July 22, only to be returned to the Pittsburgh organization nine days later as part of a reworked deal in which the Pirates sent reliever Brandon Lyon back to Boston because they believed he had a bad elbow. Gonzalez spent the final seven weeks of the campaign with the parent club and struggled with his control. When he is throwing strikes, he is tough to hit with a 95-MPH fastball and sharp slider. He needs a little more time at Triple-A to sharpen his control. The other factor that could hold him back is health—he has had back, shoulder and knee problems in his career.

J.R. House

Position: C **Opening Day Age:** 24
Bats: R **Throws:** R **Born:** 11/11/79 in
Ht: 6' 1" **Wt:** 202 Charleston, WV

Recent Statistics

	G	AB	R	H	D	T	HR	RBI	SB	BB	SO	Avg
2003 R Pirates	19	65	16	26	9	0	4	23	0	12	5	.400
2003 AA Altoona	20	63	12	21	6	0	2	11	0	5	11	.333
2003 NL Pittsburgh	1	1	0	1	0	0	0	0	0	0	0	1.000

House unexpectedly ended last season in the major leagues, spending the final week with the Pirates when they needed an extra bat because of a spate of injuries. He had a hit in his only big league at-bat. After sitting out the first half of 2003 while recovering from reconstructive elbow surgery, House played well at Double-A Altoona and in the playoffs for Triple-A Nashville before being moved up to the majors. The Pirates continue to be more intrigued by House's bat than his glovework behind the plate. He finally is healthy after also undergoing two abdominal surgeries to repair a sports hernia in 2002, but he needs to log more at-bats at Triple-A.

Freddy Sanchez

Position: SS-2B **Opening Day Age:** 26
Bats: R **Throws:** R **Born:** 12/21/77 in
Ht: 5' 11" **Wt:** 185 Hollywood, CA

Recent Statistics

	G	AB	R	H	D	T	HR	RBI	SB	BB	SO	Avg
2003 AAA Pawtucket	58	211	46	72	17	0	5	25	8	31	36	.341
2003 AAA Nashville	1	5	1	2	1	0	0	0	0	0	1	.400
2003 AL Boston	20	34	6	8	2	0	0	2	0	0	8	.235

The Pirates acquired Sanchez from Boston in a deadline deal for Jeff Suppan. Sanchez was sent to Triple-A Nashville with the idea he would join the major league club in a couple of weeks after the deal, but he was shut down for the year after only one game because of a stress fracture in his right ankle. He hit for a high average in the Red Sox' farm system and projects as a potential .300 hitter in the majors with good speed, but marginal power. Sanchez will compete with another young infielder acquired in a trade last season, Bobby Hill, for the starting second-base job in spring training.

John VanBenschoten

Position: P **Opening Day Age:** 23
Bats: R **Throws:** R **Born:** 4/14/80 in Milford,
Ht: 6' 4" **Wt:** 215 OH

Recent Statistics

	W	L	ERA	G	GS	Sv	IP	H	R	BB	SO	HR
2002 A Hickory	11	4	2.80	27	27	0	148.0	119	57	62	145	6
2003 A Lynchburg	6	0	2.22	9	9	0	48.2	33	14	18	49	1
2003 AA Altoona	7	6	3.69	17	17	0	90.1	95	46	34	78	5

Despite a five-game losing streak at Double-A Altoona late last season, VanBenschoten again showed that former Pittsburgh scouting director Mickey White made a prudent move in 2001 with the Pirates' first-round pick. White projected VanBenschoten as a pitcher when nearly every other club thought his future was either at first base or right field. VanBenschoten has yet to develop one dominant pitch, but he has an array of offerings he can throw for strikes, including a fastball that tops out at 95 MPH. He also has a curveball, slider and changeup. He needs one more full season at Triple-A before reaching the majors.

Ryan Vogelsong

Position: P **Opening Day Age:** 26
Bats: R **Throws:** R **Born:** 7/22/77 in
Ht: 6' 3" **Wt:** 205 Charlotte, NC

Recent Statistics

	W	L	ERA	G	GS	Sv	IP	H	R	BB	SO	HR
2003 AAA Nashville	12	8	4.29	26	26	0	149.0	142	75	54	146	12
2003 NL Pittsburgh	2	2	6.55	6	5	0	22.0	30	19	9	15	1

Vogelsong has had more than his share of frustration since the Pirates acquired him in a four-player trade from San Francisco during the 2001 season. He tore an elbow ligament in his second start with Pittsburgh that year and underwent reconstructive surgery. He spent 2002 rehabbing the elbow in the minor leagues and was dispatched to Triple-A Nashville last season to continue building arm strength. His fastball now reaches 94 MPH, and he also has two breaking pitches: a sharp slider and an erratic curveball. Vogelsong won two of three starts with the parent club in September to put himself in position to compete for the No. 5 rotation spot this spring.

Others to Watch

Outfielder **Tony Alvarez** (24) did not get a September callup last year after spending the final month with the Pirates in 2002. Alvarez has some speed and power and hits for a decent average, making him a candidate to win a bench job this season. . . Catcher **Ryan Doumit** (22) finally stayed healthy for a full season and was productive at high Class-A Lynchburg. He missed the second half of the 2002 season with a broken index finger and also has had back spasms at various points in his career. If he can improve his durability, he has the look of a No. 1 catcher in the major leagues. . . Righthander **Ian Oquendo** (22) is on the small side, but he pitches like a big man with a fastball that sits comfortably at 92-93 MPH and a sharp-breaking curveball. Oquendo is one of the best-conditioned athletes in the Pirates' system and seems to be overcoming some maturity issues now that he is married with a child. . . **Chris Shelton** (23) has done nothing but hit for average and power since Pittsburgh found him in the 33rd round in 2001 from the University of Utah. Shelton is below average defensively at both catcher and first base, and the Pirates had him play third base and left field in instructional league last fall to improve his versatility.

Busch Stadium

Offense

Busch Stadium is rather vanilla in terms of its dimensions and field aspects. Fences are reachable, but the ballpark is hardly a bandbox. The infield, baked hard by the hot Midwest summer sun, is fast. There rarely are any unusual wind patterns for players to worry about and no unusual angles in the outfield gaps or down the lines. It is, in other words, as fair a park as there is the majors.

Defense

The St. Louis infield always is well-maintained. So while the ball can shoot through quickly, the hops usually are true and infielders with good range are rewarded. It's no coincidence that the Cardinals had two Gold Glove infielders in Scott Rolen and Edgar Renteria. The outfield requires good speed to cover the gaps and the walls allow players to make leaping attempts, aspects that are well-exploited by Gold Glove outfielder Jim Edmonds.

Who It Helps the Most

Both Rolen and Renteria are suited to the dimensions of Busch Stadium. Albert Pujols also is extremely comfortable at home, especially with his ability to hit to all fields. Cardinals pitchers almost to a man pitch better at home.

Who It Hurts the Most

Jim Edmonds struggled at home last year, one reason perhaps being his difficulties in hitting the ball to the opposite field, an important part of Edmonds' game. The great St. Louis fans can be tough on players who struggle, and slumping pitchers especially can hear it from the Cardinals Nation. There is a segment of Cardinals fans who will never forgive La Russa for not being Whitey Herzog.

Rookies & Newcomers

Hustling players like last year's rookie second baseman, Bo Hart, tend to thrive in St. Louis. It's a place that appreciates effort and good fundamental play. Overall, St. Louis remains one of the best places in the majors to play.

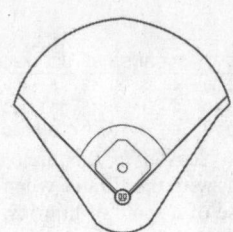

Dimensions: LF-330, LCF-372, CF-402, RCF-372, RF-330

Capacity: 50,354

Elevation: 535 feet

Surface: Grass

Foul Territory: Large

Park Factors

2003 Season

	Home Games Cardinals	Opp	Total	Away Games Cardinals	Opp	Total	Index
G	72	72	144	72	72	144	
Avg	.283	.251	.267	.267	.284	.276	97
AB	2433	2525	4958	2572	2497	5069	98
R	368	314	682	387	356	743	92
H	688	634	1322	688	709	1397	95
2B	161	133	294	138	148	286	105
3B	5	13	18	21	12	33	56
HR	77	79	156	94	102	196	81
BB	253	219	472	270	229	499	97
SO	373	449	822	462	429	891	94
E	33	49	82	34	49	83	99
E-Infield	28	38	66	27	38	65	102
LHB-Avg	.256	.257	.256	.264	.296	.280	92
LHB-HR	30	30	60	33	30	63	100
RHB-Avg	.297	.247	.273	.270	.277	.273	100
RHB-HR	47	49	96	61	72	133	73

2001-2003

	Home Games Cardinals	Opp	Total	Away Games Cardinals	Opp	Total	Index
G	220	220	440	221	221	442	
Avg	.276	.246	.261	.264	.272	.268	97
AB	7317	7552	14869	7748	7382	15130	99
R	1125	867	1992	1104	1027	2131	94
H	2022	1856	3878	2049	2009	4058	96
2B	415	379	794	401	415	816	99
3B	31	23	54	50	33	83	66
HR	245	228	473	269	263	532	90
BB	768	723	1491	748	720	1468	103
SO	1269	1480	2749	1444	1327	2771	101
E	123	162	285	135	149	284	101
E-Infield	99	128	227	105	124	229	100
LHB-Avg	.272	.249	.260	.271	.272	.271	96
LHB-HR	110	90	200	103	99	202	104
RHB-Avg	.279	.244	.261	.260	.272	.266	98
RHB-HR	135	138	273	166	164	330	82

2003 Rankings (National League)

- Lowest RHB home-run factor
- Second-lowest home-run factor
- Second-lowest LHB batting-average factor

Tony La Russa

2003 Season

With his pitching staff reeling from injuries all season, Tony La Russa never had the luxury of a stable rotation or bullpen in 2003. Compounding the pitching problems was the steady erosion due to injuries of what was projected to be the deepest roster in the National League. Despite that, St. Louis remained in contention until the final week. However, for La Russa, the biggest disappointment was watching how short his club came up in several key September series. By then, there were indications that a group of Cardinals veterans was taking private potshots at their manager.

Offense

With more of a power club in recent years, La Russa has played more often for big innings rather than trying to manufacture runs. However, he remains aggressive in picking his spots for hit and runs or steal attempts. La Russa never lets his bench players get stale and is remarkably adept at finding the right spots for his reserves to have the optimum chance at success.

Pitching & Defense

Even with a completely healthy staff, La Russa wheels pitchers in and out according to matchups as actively as any manager in the game. However, last season he let his top starters go deeper into games in order to better cover up his bullpen woes. Defensively, La Russa's teams always are fundamentally sound, and no coaching staff better prepares its fielders in terms of positioning and the opposition's trends.

2004 Outlook

After another stressful season which included confrontations with some of his players, it would not have been a surprise if a worn-down La Russa announced he wouldn't be back. However, he was buoyed by the respect of GM Walt Jocketty and the Cardinals' ownership, which is likely to try and weed out some of the unhappy Cardinals and also try to stabilize their pitching. La Russa demands much from his players, but he pays the price with his own intensity.

Born: 10/4/44 in Tampa, FL

Playing Experience: 1963-1973, Oak, Atl, ChC

Managerial Experience: 25 seasons

Manager Statistics

Year	Team, Lg	W	L	Pct	GB	Finish
2003	St. Louis, NL	85	77	.525	3.0	3rd Central
25 Seasons		2009	1789	.529	–	–

2003 Starting Pitchers by Days Rest

	<=3	4	5	6+
Cardinals Starts	0	93	35	26
Cardinals ERA	–	4.53	4.59	4.92
NL Avg Starts	2	84	43	23
NL ERA	5.00	4.23	4.42	4.68

2003 Situational Stats

	Tony La Russa	NL Average
Hit & Run Success %	37.4	32.7
Stolen Base Success %	71.9	68.9
Platoon Pct.	46.8	52.0
Defensive Subs	17	19
High-Pitch Outings	12	8
Quick/Slow Hooks	14/9	20/12
Sacrifice Attempts	116	93

2003 Rankings (National League)

- 1st in double steals (10), sacrifice bunt attempts and squeeze plays (9)
- 2nd in steals of third base (17), pinch-hitters used (296) and mid-inning pitching changes (185)
- 3rd in fewest caught stealings of second base (24), hit-and-run attempts (91) and starts with over 120 pitches (12)

St. Louis

J.D. Drew

2003 Season

It was the same old story for J.D. Drew, who spent much of yet another season on the sidelines. Drew missed the first five weeks due to the aftereffects of offseason knee surgery and was still less than 100 percent after his return. He later landed on the disabled list for the sixth time in his brief career with a ribcage pull that cost him most of August and early September. Drew ended up making only 70 starts all season, though he produced decent numbers in his limited action.

Hitting

When he was able to play, Drew demonstrated excellent progress toward finally becoming a complete hitter. He did struggle against left-handers, posting a career-low .218 average in limited action against southpaws. But Drew has matured physically, and he has begun showing more consistent power to all fields. He has exceptional power to right and the bat speed to handle inside hard stuff. Where he has improved most is in his ability to take fastballs away and drive them to left-center. He has become a much better hitter against breaking stuff, though he still will chase breaking balls out of the strike zone. He also is becoming a more patient hitter.

Baserunning & Defense

At one point in his checkered career, Drew was viewed as a potential 30-30 player. But his physical troubles have made him only an occasional basestealer, and he also is less aggressive on the bases. He stole just two bases in four tries last year. When healthy, Drew has a center fielder's range and a right fielder's arm.

2004 Outlook

Few players generate more debate than Drew. No one questions his physical tools, and certain baseball people still believe he eventually will realize the stardom long predicted for him. However, many in the Cardinals' organization remain unconvinced that Drew will ever fully blossom, pointing to his china-doll history. He was the subject of numerous offseason trade rumors.

Position: RF/CF
Bats: L **Throws:** R
Ht: 6' 1" **Wt:** 200

Opening Day Age: 28
Born: 11/20/75 in Valdosta, GA
ML Seasons: 6

Overall Statistics

	G	AB	R	H	D	T	HR	RBI	SB	BB	SO	Avg	OBP	Slg
'03	100	287	60	83	13	3	15	42	2	36	48	.289	.374	.512
Car.	597	1897	355	535	86	18	96	280	59	271	413	.282	.377	.498

Where He Hits the Ball

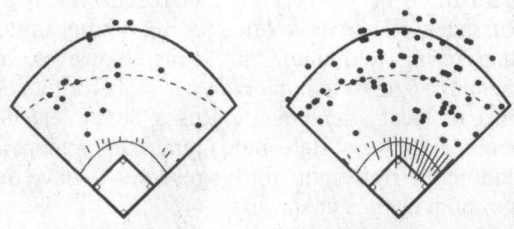

Vs. LHP   **Vs. RHP**

2003 Situational Stats

	AB	H	HR	RBI	Avg		AB	H	HR	RBI	Avg
Home	132	38	7	18	.288	LHP	55	12	3	7	.218
Road	155	45	8	24	.290	RHP	232	71	12	35	.306
First Half	164	50	10	27	.305	Sc Pos	74	25	4	27	.338
Scnd Half	123	33	5	15	.268	Clutch	51	15	3	7	.294

2003 Rankings (National League)

- Did not rank near the top or bottom in any category

Jim Edmonds

2003 Season

What at one point seemed like a career year fell apart in more ways than one for Jim Edmonds. Edmonds had launched 28 home runs by the All-Star break. However, a shoulder injury which he apparently suffered in the All-Star Game Home Run Derby contributed to a sharp drop-off in his production in the second half, when he often was unavailable to play.

Hitting

Edmonds has the blue-chip combination of high on-base percentage and slugging percentage attained by only an elite few hitters. And few left-handed batters have better opposite-field power than Edmonds. However, there always is the sense that he could be even better. He gives away far too many at-bats for a player of his caliber, and he also is as streaky as any top echelon player in the game. Edmonds annually is among league leaders in strikeouts, many of them coming in bunches when he starts chasing high pitches.

Baserunning & Defense

Edmonds is no steal threat, and you can count on him for at least one baserunning gaffe every couple of weeks. However, he remains one of the game's premier outfielders and won his sixth Gold Glove last year. Edmonds has outstanding range and a strong, accurate throwing arm that annually produces double-figure totals in outfield assists. At the same time, he will have lapses in concentration and occasionally seems to time his leaps and dives for dramatic effect.

2004 Outlook

There were whispers last September that Edmonds was among a group of Cardinals veterans who quit on Tony La Russa down the stretch. True or not, tension has become obvious between the hard-driving manager and the laid-back center fielder. Whether that translates into a change of scenery could depend on whether St. Louis can find a market for Edmonds' hefty contract. However, he remains one of the game's premier talents—with several prime seasons still ahead.

Position: CF
Bats: L **Throws:** L
Ht: 6' 1" **Wt:** 212

Opening Day Age: 33
Born: 6/27/70 in Fullerton, CA
ML Seasons: 11
Pronunciation: ED-muns

Overall Statistics

G	AB	R	H	D	T	HR	RBI	SB	BB	SO	Avg	OBP	Slg
137	447	89	123	32	2	39	89	1	77	127	.275	.385	.617
1292	4592	873	1346	287	17	260	798	46	633	1122	.293	.380	.533

Where He Hits the Ball

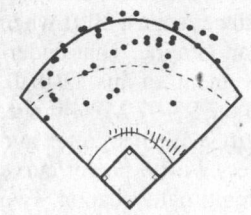
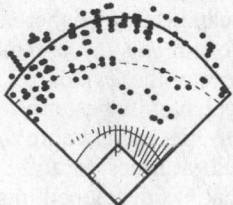

Vs. LHP   **Vs. RHP**

2003 Situational Stats

	AB	H	HR	RBI	Avg		AB	H	HR	RBI	Avg
Home	224	57	17	34	.254	LHP	111	25	11	22	.225
Road	223	66	22	55	.296	RHP	336	98	28	67	.292
First Half	307	93	28	67	.303	Sc Pos	121	26	10	47	.215
Scnd Half	140	30	11	22	.214	Clutch	63	15	6	12	.238

2003 Rankings (National League)

- 2nd in HR frequency (11.5 ABs per HR)
- 3rd in errors in center field (5)
- 4th in slugging percentage and cleanup slugging percentage (.624)
- 5th in most pitches seen per plate appearance (4.13), lowest batting average vs. lefthanded pitchers and lowest fielding percentage in center field (.986)
- 7th in home runs and lowest groundball-fly ball ratio (0.7)
- Led the Cardinals in strikeouts, HR frequency (11.5 ABs per HR), highest percentage of pitches taken (58.0) and cleanup slugging percentage (.624)
- Led NL center fielders in home runs

St. Louis

Jason Isringhausen

2003 Season

One of the major reasons the Cardinals came up short in the National League Central race was the absence of closer Jason Isringhausen for the first 63 games due to an unexpectedly lengthy recovery from shoulder surgery. The Cardinals' bullpen suffered a meltdown while he was out, and with Isringhausen's workload often limited for cautionary reasons related to his shoulder, the bullpen never really stabilized even after he returned. He wound up with only 25 save opportunities after averaging 40 save opportunities per year from 2000-03.

Pitching

Isringhausen was nicked for two home runs last year, his first gopherballs since August 2001 when he still was in the American League. That underscores the explosive movement of his fastball, which at its best arrives in the 95-97 MPH range. He hits comparable velocity with his cutter and will at times paralyze hitters with a power curve that has developed into a legitimate weapon. Two things continue to prevent Isringhausen from joining the game's elite group of closers. One is inconsistent command, which causes him to fall behind in too many counts. The other is conditioning. Isringhausen has had a career full of physical troubles, some real, some imagined and some kept secret from his manager.

Defense & Hitting

Isringhausen is vulnerable to stolen bases. In fact, over the last five years, only three basestealers in 43 attempts have been caught stealing against him. He also is slow coming off the mound to cover first and has a career fielding percentage of just .897. He rarely gets to bat.

2004 Outlook

St. Louis is waiting for a completely healthy season from Isringhausen. The Cardinals have two more contract years invested in him, and they need him to become more of a constant in what has become a revolving-door bullpen. If Isringhausen is available for the entire year, he's capable of a 40-save season.

Position: RP
Bats: R **Throws:** R
Ht: 6' 3" **Wt:** 230

Opening Day Age: 31
Born: 9/7/72 in Brighton, IL
ML Seasons: 8
Pronunciation: IS-ring-how-zin
Nickname: Izzy

Overall Statistics

	W	L	Pct.	ERA	G	GS	Sv	IP	H	BB	SO	HR	Avg
'03	0	1	.000	2.36	40	0	22	42.0	31	18	41	2	.200
Car.	31	32	.492	3.83	311	52	130	606.2	580	251	485	44	.252

2003 Pitching Profile

	Jason Isringhausen	NL Average
Overall Strike %	64.5	62.4
1st Pitch Strike %	64.4	58.4
Ratio	1.17	1.38
Strikeouts per 9 IP	8.79	6.65
Walks per 9 IP	3.86	3.42
Home Runs per 9 IP	0.43	1.05
Strikeout/Walk Ratio	2.28	1.94
Groundball/Flyball Ratio	1.57	1.29

2003 Situational Stats

	W	L	ERA	Sv	IP		AB	H	HR	RBI	Avg
Home	0	1	3.04	11	23.2	LHB	67	17	2	6	.254
Road	0	0	1.47	11	18.1	RHB	88	14	0	5	.159
First Half	0	0	1.32	5	13.2	Sc Pos	50	9	0	8	.180
Scnd Half	0	1	2.86	17	28.1	Clutch	94	18	1	8	.191

2003 Rankings (National League)

- 8th in save percentage (88.0)
- Led the Cardinals in saves, games finished (31), wild pitches (6), save percentage (88.0), relief ERA (2.36), lowest batting average allowed in relief (.200) and fewest baserunners allowed per nine innings in relief (10.5)

Eli Marrero

2003 Season

Eli Marrero is not a marquee name, but the Cardinals were not the same after he slipped on the wet Wrigley Field outfield in early May and suffered a serious ankle injury. For all intents and purposes, the injury ended his season, though Marrero did return in September for limited action. He had become a valuable part of the Cardinals' lineup, playing roughly 60 percent of the time in right field and providing a good RBI bat in his limited action.

Hitting

Marrero was just emerging from a slow start last year when he was injured. Over the last two years, he has learned to make adjustments as a hitter. Marrero is at his best when uses a short stroke and thinks about taking the ball up the middle. At times, he can have fragile confidence as a hitter, and he is prone to strikeouts and long slumps when he starts trying to pull the ball too much. Marrero has matured physically and his added strength makes him a home-run threat.

Baserunning & Defense

Though he went without a steal last year, Marrero is an above-average baserunner and a high-percentage basestealer. He has reached double-digit stolen-base totals in a season twice during his big league career. Few players have his versatility. Though working mostly in the outfield the past couple of years, Marrero still has the skills to be a very good catcher with a good arm. His outfield range is solid in both right and left, and he also has played center competently. Marrero can fill in at first without hurting his team's defense.

2004 Outlook

When Marrero went down last year, manager Tony La Russa was robbed of much of the flexibility he loves in fielding his lineups day to day. The Cardinals are counting on Marrero to be a valuable part of their mix this year, especially with some of the other St. Louis veterans unlikely to return.

Position: RF/LF
Bats: R **Throws:** R
Ht: 6' 1" **Wt:** 180

Opening Day Age: 30
Born: 11/17/73 in Havana, Cuba
ML Seasons: 7
Pronunciation: muh-RARE-ro

Overall Statistics

	G	AB	R	H	D	T	HR	RBI	SB	BB	SO	Avg	OBP	Slg
'03	41	107	10	24	4	2	2	20	0	7	18	.224	.267	.355
Car.	525	1425	195	339	70	9	43	187	46	119	253	.238	.295	.390

Where He Hits the Ball

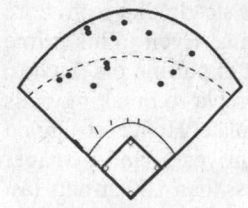 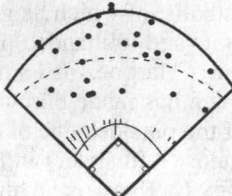

Vs. LHP   **Vs. RHP**

2003 Situational Stats

	AB	H	HR	RBI	Avg		AB	H	HR	RBI	Avg
Home	56	11	1	10	.196	LHP	26	6	0	4	.231
Road	51	13	1	10	.255	RHP	81	18	2	16	.222
First Half	75	17	2	15	.227	Sc Pos	29	11	1	18	.379
Scnd Half	32	7	0	5	.219	Clutch	20	0	0	3	.261

2003 Rankings (National League)

- Did not rank near the top or bottom in any category

Tino Martinez

Traded To DEVIL RAYS

2003 Season

The large majority of moves made by St. Louis GM Walt Jocketty have been successful. However, one glaring disappointment was the expensive free-agent signing of Tino Martinez. He had a second straight mediocre season for the Cardinals, his production dropping in most major categories from what was a lackluster 2002. That was enough for the Cardinals, who dealt Martinez to Tampa Bay after the season while agreeing to pick up a good chunk of his salary.

Hitting

With his bat speed deteriorating, Martinez' power has dissipated over the last three years. He consistently has been unable to catch up with high fastballs, of which he gets a steady diet from both right- and lefthanded pitching. Even in his prime years, Martinez had a habit of pulling off pitches, which has made him vulnerable to breaking balls off the outside edge of the plate. He has struggled against lefthanders in recent years, and manager Tony La Russa gave him less than 100 at-bats last year against southpaws.

Baserunning & Defense

There are few slower runners than Martinez, but he almost always makes the right decisions on the bases. His range at first base is subpar, but he is otherwise a very good defensive player with excellent hands and outstanding ability to pick up low throws. Martinez has an accurate throwing arm and a quick release.

2004 Outlook

Martinez' poor production alone would have been enough to sour the Cardinals. However, the club's management also felt he had become something of a clubhouse whisperer whose target was La Russa. Martinez widely was perceived as being at the center of a group of veterans who seemed to lay down for the Cards down the stretch. Nonetheless, the Devil Rays felt that Martinez had something left and swung a deal for the Tampa native in November. He'll be reunited with his former Seattle manager, Lou Piniella.

Position: 1B
Bats: L **Throws:** R
Ht: 6' 2" **Wt:** 230

Opening Day Age: 36
Born: 12/7/67 in Tampa, FL
ML Seasons: 14

Overall Statistics

G	AB	R	H	D	T	HR	RBI	SB	BB	SO	Avg	OBP	Slg
138	476	66	130	25	2	15	69	1	53	71	.273	.352	.429
1754	6350	902	1732	336	20	299	1146	22	676	943	.273	.344	.473

Where He Hits the Ball

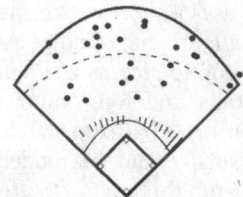 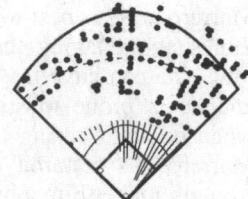

Vs. LHP	Vs. RHP

2003 Situational Stats

	AB	H	HR	RBI	Avg		AB	H	HR	RBI	Avg
Home	234	67	6	32	.286	LHP	81	19	2	12	.235
Road	242	63	9	37	.260	RHP	395	111	13	57	.281
First Half	292	82	10	43	.281	Sc Pos	138	29	5	53	.210
Scnd Half	184	48	5	26	.261	Clutch	72	13	2	9	.181

2003 Rankings (National League)

- 1st in fielding percentage at first base (.997)
- 7th in sacrifice flies (7)
- 10th in fewest pitches seen per plate appearance (3.50)
- Led the Cardinals in sacrifice flies (7)

Mike Matheny

2003 Season

Mike Matheny firmly established his role as the Cardinals' No. 1 catcher with the best season of his career. He set personal highs in nearly all major categories, including games, home runs, runs batted in and runs scored. He also led all National League catchers with a perfect 1.000 fielding percentage.

Hitting

Matheny is no threat to duplicate Mike Piazza's offensive numbers. Matheny is a very streaky hitter, as witnessed by his August (.109) and September (.328) batting averages. However, he has quickened his bat with a shorter stroke and a slightly open stance that has helped him become less vulnerable against inside fastballs. He also has developed some gap power to the opposite field. Matheny can be overpowered with hard stuff and he will chase high pitches, contributing to his increased strikeout total. He has become a good offspeed hitter and has become especially dangerous versus lefthanded pitchers, against whom he hit 114 points higher than versus righthanders.

Baserunning & Defense

There are few catchers in the game more solid defensively than Matheny, who was awarded the second Gold Glove of his career following the 2003 campaign. He frames pitches very well and blocks balls in the dirt as well as anyone. He has textbook mechanics, with his quick throwing release that makes opponents reluctant to attempt a steal against him, even though his caught-stealing perecentage last year was subpar at 23 percent. Matheny also has grown as a handler of pitchers under Cardinals pitching coach Dave Duncan.

2004 Outlook

Matheny is a solid pro who is an asset to the Cardinals in a number of ways. On a club that has had constant turnover in its pitching staff, he has been a rock of stability behind the plate. And he has made himself into a competitive enough hitter to earn everyday status for the next few years.

Position: C
Bats: R **Throws:** R
Ht: 6' 3" **Wt:** 220

Opening Day Age: 33
Born: 9/22/70 in Reynoldsburg, OH
ML Seasons: 10
Pronunciation: ma-THEE-nee

Overall Statistics

	G	AB	R	H	D	T	HR	RBI	SB	BB	SO	Avg	OBP	Slg
'03	141	441	43	111	18	2	8	47	1	44	81	.252	.320	.356
Car.	1002	2889	273	686	126	8	46	316	8	205	591	.237	.293	.334

Where He Hits the Ball

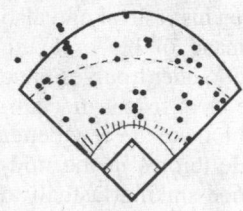 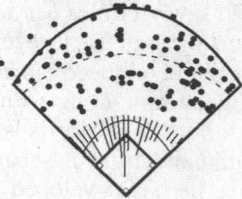

Vs. LHP   **Vs. RHP**

2003 Situational Stats

	AB	H	HR	RBI	Avg		AB	H	HR	RBI	Avg
Home	214	63	4	22	.294	LHP	100	34	3	15	.340
Road	227	48	4	25	.211	RHP	341	77	5	32	.226
First Half	283	78	4	28	.276	Sc Pos	126	35	1	39	.278
Scnd Half	158	33	4	19	.209	Clutch	65	12	1	8	.185

2003 Rankings (National League)

- 1st in fielding percentage at catcher (1.000)
- 2nd in lowest batting average on the road
- 4th in lowest batting average vs. righthanded pitchers
- 5th in intentional walks (16)
- Led the Cardinals in intentional walks (16)

St. Louis

Matt Morris

2003 Season

After establishing himself as an elite starting pitcher with 39 wins in 2001-02, Matt Morris suffered through a disappointing 2003 season. Shoulder problems and faulty mechanics set him back throughout much of June and July. After returning to the regular rotation, he had a bone in his right hand broken by a line drive on July 21. He didn't pitch again until August 23, his return delayed an extra week by an ankle injury foolishly suffered during hotel horseplay with teammates. Morris finished with four strong starts in five September outings.

Pitching

Morris was out of sync much of last year, costing him several miles per hour on his fastball and also causing him to lose command of his breaking stuff and offspeed pitches. Shoulder troubles have dogged him along with the inconsistent mechanics, but when Morris is right, there are few better righthanders in baseball. He throws in the mid-90s, he has developed a good sinking fastball to go with his four-seamer, his changeup is as good as anybody's and he at times will show an effective power curve. Morris is an excellent competitor, but will sometimes be his own toughest critic and start to lose aggressiveness on the mound.

Defense & Hitting

Morris has learned to hold runners much better, and only six stolen bases were attempted against him in 2003. He is a good athlete who handles most defensive plays well, and he occasionally can do some damage swinging the bat.

2004 Outlook

For the Cardinals to return to the playoffs, they need Morris to be the ace he was in 2001-02. He was over his shoulder troubles by last September, and he now should be just entering his prime. Morris can be a free agent after this season, and the timing couldn't be better for him to re-establish himself as one of baseball's best starting pitchers.

Position: SP
Bats: R **Throws:** R
Ht: 6' 5" **Wt:** 220

Opening Day Age: 29
Born: 8/9/74 in Middletown, NY
ML Seasons: 6

Overall Statistics

	W	L	Pct.	ERA	G	GS	Sv	IP	H	BB	SO	HR	Avg
'03	11	8	.579	3.76	27	27	0	172.1	164	39	120	20	.252
Car.	72	42	.632	3.28	174	143	4	982.2	954	285	738	72	.257

2003 Pitching Profile

	Matt Morris	NL Average
Overall Strike %	66.0	62.4
1st Pitch Strike %	64.1	58.4
Ratio	1.18	1.38
Strikeouts per 9 IP	6.27	6.65
Walks per 9 IP	2.04	3.42
Home Runs per 9 IP	1.04	1.05
Strikeout/Walk Ratio	3.08	1.94
Groundball/Flyball Ratio	1.44	1.29

2003 Situational Stats

	W	L	ERA	Sv	IP		AB	H	HR	RBI	Avg
Home	6	4	4.32	0	106.1	LHB	271	69	4	22	.255
Road	5	4	2.86	0	66.0	RHB	381	95	16	48	.249
First Half	8	6	4.19	0	124.2	Sc Pos	134	32	4	46	.239
Scnd Half	3	2	2.64	0	47.2	Clutch	54	12	1	3	.222

2003 Rankings (National League)

- 1st in shutouts (3) and fielding percentage at pitcher (1.000)
- 2nd in complete games (5)
- 4th in sacrifice bunts (12)
- 6th in lowest on-base percentage allowed (.297) and fewest walks per nine innings (2.0)
- 7th in highest ERA at home
- 8th in lowest stolen-base percentage allowed (50.0)
- Led the Cardinals in ERA, sacrifice bunts (12), complete games (5), shutouts (3), GDPs induced (17), highest strikeout-walk ratio (3.1), lowest batting average allowed (.252), lowest on-base percentage allowed (.297), highest groundball-flyball ratio allowed (1.4), fewest pitches thrown per batter (3.57), lowest ERA on the road, most strikeouts per nine innings (6.3) and fewest walks per nine innings (2.0)

Albert Pujols

2003 Season

After his enormous third major league season, Albert Pujols has set a clear course for Cooperstown. Pujols dwarfed even the lofty standards he set for himself in his two years by winning a National League batting title, flirting with a Triple Crown and becoming the only player ever to hit 30 homers, drive in 100 and score 100 in each of his first three seasons. He also tied the all-time record for home runs in a player's first three seasons. As remarkable as his numbers were, equally eye-popping was Pujols' consistency. He batted over .310 and had at least five homers in every month of the season en route to a runner-up showing in the final NL MVP vote.

Hitting

Said Cardinals manager Tony La Russa last summer, "The amazing thing about Albert is that he has no holes. There is no one way you can get him out." Indeed, Pujols can turn around any fastball and waits on pitches so well that he is not often fooled by offspeed or breaking balls. Pujols has power to all fields and has improved every year in cutting down on his strikeouts. He is very aggressive early in counts, but still has continued to add to his walk totals.

Baserunning & Defense

Pujols has below-average speed, but he displays good judgment on the bases and will steal a base if ignored. He played the majority of time last year in left, where he is competent, if unspectacular, with a decent arm. Pujols also played a lot of first base—where he has good instincts—and that could end up being his regular position.

2004 Outlook

Pujols' work ethic seems unaffected by his remarkable success, and if he does no more than simply maintain the level he's already established, he is headed for immortality. In the shorter term, he likely is headed for a big pay raise as the Cardinals contemplate signing him to a long-term contract that will keep him in St. Louis as the club's irreplaceable star.

Position: LF/1B
Bats: R **Throws:** R
Ht: 6' 3" **Wt:** 225

Opening Day Age: 24
Born: 1/16/80 in Santo Domingo, DR
ML Seasons: 3
Pronunciation: POO-holes

Overall Statistics

	G	AB	R	H	D	T	HR	RBI	SB	BB	SO	Avg	OBP	Slg
'03	157	591	137	212	51	1	43	124	5	79	65	.359	.439	.667
Car.	475	1771	367	591	138	7	114	381	8	220	227	.334	.412	.613

Where He Hits the Ball

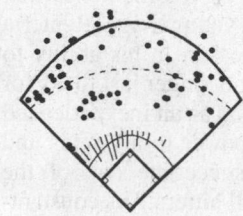
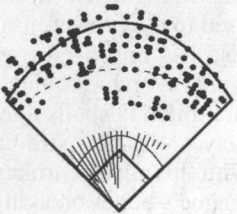

Vs. LHP   **Vs. RHP**

2003 Situational Stats

	AB	H	HR	RBI	Avg		AB	H	HR	RBI	Avg
Home	286	111	21	66	.388	LHP	142	55	11	32	.387
Road	305	101	22	58	.331	RHP	449	157	32	92	.350
First Half	348	128	27	86	.368	Sc Pos	131	49	12	76	.374
Scnd Half	243	84	16	38	.346	Clutch	82	32	6	19	.390

2003 Rankings (National League)

- 1st in batting average, runs scored, hits, doubles and total bases (394)
- 2nd in times on base (301), slugging percentage, batting average vs. lefthanded pitchers, batting average vs. righthanded pitchers and batting average at home
- 3rd in on-base percentage and batting average in the clutch
- 4th in home runs and RBI
- Led the Cardinals in home runs, at-bats, total bases (394), RBI, plate appearances (685), games played, on-base percentage, batting average with runners in scoring position, batting average in the clutch, batting average vs. righthanded pitchers, batting average at home and batting average on the road

St. Louis

Edgar Renteria

2003 Season

The rise of Edgar Renteria into the upper echelon of shortstops continued with a career year. Renteria became the first National League shortstop to drive in 100 runs in 18 years and fell just six hits short of being the first NL shortstop in more than 90 years to have 200 hits and 100 RBI in the same season. He helped carry the Cardinals through their rocky start, driving in 24 runs in March/April. He also continued to sparkle in the field, earning his second straight Gold Glove.

Hitting

Renteria's evolution into one of the league's best hitters coincides with his improved conditioning and strength. He now can fight off pitches that used to overpower him at a younger age. Renteria also has improved every season in his ability to work favorable counts. He no longer just looks for first-pitch fastballs like he did as an inexperienced player. He has extra-base power to all fields and with his short stroke, has become one of the league's better breaking-ball hitters. His constantly improving bat speed has made him a legitimate home-run threat.

Baserunning & Defense

Usually hitting from the sixth or seventh spot in the order, Renteria had free rein to steal bases. He used his good speed and instincts for one of his best stolen-base seasons in 2003. He is one of the best defensive shortstops in the game, possessing fluid range and excellent hands. He will occasionally air-mail throws and try to do too much with difficult plays.

2004 Outlook

Entering what should be his prime years, Renteria clearly has matured into one of the game's best shortstops. He is eligible for free agency after this season, and it seems certain that St. Louis will try to sign him to a multiyear deal, not only for his playing ability but for his solid presence in the clubhouse.

Position: SS
Bats: R **Throws:** R
Ht: 6' 1" **Wt:** 200

Opening Day Age: 28
Born: 8/7/75 in Barranquilla, Colombia
ML Seasons: 8
Pronunciation: ren-ter-ee-AH

Overall Statistics

	G	AB	R	H	D	T	HR	RBI	SB	BB	SO	Avg	OBP	Slg
'03	157	587	96	194	47	1	13	100	34	65	54	.330	.394	.480
Car.	1147	4336	650	1255	227	17	73	493	220	395	597	.289	.348	.400

Where He Hits the Ball

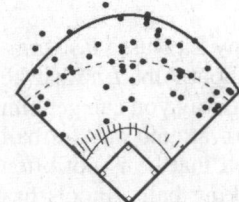 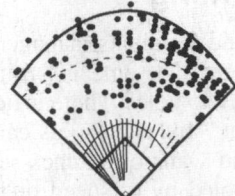

Vs. LHP   **Vs. RHP**

2003 Situational Stats

	AB	H	HR	RBI	Avg		AB	H	HR	RBI	Avg
Home	289	103	4	54	.356	LHP	115	45	5	34	.391
Road	298	91	9	46	.305	RHP	472	149	8	66	.316
First Half	357	118	9	60	.331	Sc Pos	180	57	2	84	.317
Scnd Half	230	76	4	40	.330	Clutch	77	22	1	10	.286

2003 Rankings (National League)

- 1st in batting average vs. lefthanded pitchers
- 2nd in steals of third (8)
- 3rd in stolen-base percentage (82.9)
- 4th in batting average, hits, stolen bases and batting average at home
- 5th in errors at shortstop (16) and lowest fielding percentage at shortstop (.975)
- 6th in singles, doubles and GDPs (21)
- Led the Cardinals in singles, sacrifice flies (7), stolen bases, caught stealing (7), GDPs (21), games played, stolen-base percentage (82.9), steals of third (8), batting average with the bases loaded (.500), batting average vs. lefthanded pitchers, and batting average with two strikes (.251)
- Led NL shortstops in batting average and RBI

Scott Rolen

2003 Season

A sluggish September marred an otherwise solid season for Scott Rolen, who nonetheless drove in 100 runs for the third consecutive season. Rolen was streaky all year, possibly because he was hampered at times by neck and back troubles. He had several lengthy RBI droughts, and drove in many of his runs in bunches—he had 13 games in which he had three or more RBI. On defense, Rolen won his fifth Gold Glove at third base.

Hitting

Rolen is vulnerable to hard stuff that crowds him, and that remains the best strategy to get him out. He often will get himself out by chasing eye-high fastballs, pitches that he has difficulty laying off. He gets many of his home runs on fastballs down in the strike zone, and National League pitchers also try to avoid throwing changeups over the plate to Rolen. He has good plate coverage and displays consistent extra-base power to the opposite field. He also has shown more consistent patience at the plate, last year earning the second-highest walk total of his career.

Baserunning & Defense

Many opponents around the NL consider Rolen the best all-around baserunner in the league. No one is more aggressive going from first to third, and he always has been a high-percentage bases-stealer, last year returning to double figures in thefts. No third baseman is Rolen's equal in the field. He makes the spectacular play look routine and makes the routine plays consistently, last year committing only five errors after the All-Star break.

2004 Outlook

Along with Albert Pujols, Rolen is part of the St. Louis foundation for the coming decade. He is a solid citizen, someone who plays hard every night, and the best all-around player at his position in the game. Rolen will turn 29 this April, and his best years could be ahead of him.

Position: 3B
Bats: R **Throws:** R
Ht: 6' 4" **Wt:** 240

Opening Day Age: 28
Born: 4/4/75 in Jasper, IN
ML Seasons: 8
Pronunciation: ROH-len

Overall Statistics

	G	AB	R	H	D	T	HR	RBI	SB	BB	SO	Avg	OBP	Slg
'03	154	559	98	160	49	1	28	104	13	82	104	.286	.382	.528
Car.	1053	3889	668	1097	264	24	192	707	87	528	852	.282	.374	.510

Where He Hits the Ball

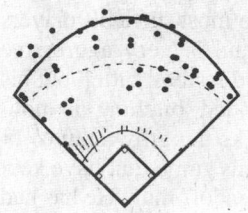 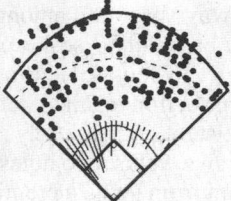

Vs. LHP   **Vs. RHP**

2003 Situational Stats

	AB	H	HR	RBI	Avg		AB	H	HR	RBI	Avg
Home	281	85	12	61	.302	LHP	113	32	7	27	.283
Road	278	75	16	43	.270	RHP	446	128	21	77	.287
First Half	320	89	18	62	.278	Sc Pos	155	41	9	76	.265
Scnd Half	239	71	10	42	.297	Clutch	82	24	7	22	.293

2003 Rankings (National League)

- 2nd in doubles
- 3rd in most pitches seen per plate appearance (4.15) and fielding percentage at third base (.969)
- 6th in pitches seen (2,728)
- 7th in sacrifice flies (7), steals of third (4), cleanup slugging percentage (.579) and errors at third base (13)
- Led the Cardinals in sacrifice flies (7), walks and pitches seen (2,728)

St. Louis

Fernando Vina

2003 Season

It was a disastrous season for Fernando Vina, whose year basically was wiped out by a hamstring injury suffered in late May. He did not return until late August. By then, the Cardinals had become enamored of rookie Bo Hart, and Vina spent the last month platooning with Hart. Losing his full-time job did not set well with Vina, who had a fiery confrontation with manager Tony La Russa in the season's final week, which sealed Vina's certain departure from St. Louis.

Hitting

Vina hit four home runs in his abbreviated 2003 campaign, but he is at his best when sending line drives up the middle and on the ground. He always has been among the most difficult players in baseball to strike out and is very aggressive early in counts. He is a good fastball hitter, but his production against lefthanded pitching is non-existent. Vina rarely works lengthy counts or draws walks, two holes in his game that have kept him from being a premier leadoff man. He has had a knack for getting hit by pitches to help his on-base percentage.

Baserunning & Defense

Vina has above-average speed but does not always show the best judgment on the bases. He is a very mediocre basestealer who had his green light taken away by La Russa. When healthy, Vina is an outstanding second baseman with good range, a quick and accurate arm and a fearlessness when turning double plays.

2004 Outlook

It was a foregone conclusion that the Cardinals would not pick up their 2004 option on Vina, making him a free agent. His struggles against lefties and frequent hamstring troubles likely will make him a liability in many teams' eyes, especially at his age. However, Vina's solid defense play and pesky offensive talent convinced the Tigers he was worth a two-year, $6 million contract. While Vina's on-base numbers are down the last couple of seasons, he is almost certain to take over as Detroit's leadoff man.

Position: 2B
Bats: L **Throws:** R
Ht: 5' 9" **Wt:** 180

Opening Day Age: 34
Born: 4/16/69 in Sacramento, CA
ML Seasons: 11
Pronunciation: VEEN-yah

Overall Statistics

	G	AB	R	H	D	T	HR	RBI	SB	BB	SO	Avg	OBP	Slg
'03	61	259	35	65	14	4	4	23	4	11	24	.251	.309	.382
Car.	1119	4125	606	1170	189	49	40	336	114	279	283	.284	.350	.382

Where He Hits the Ball

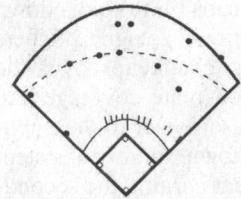
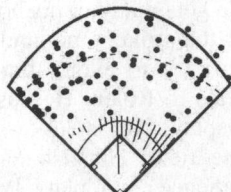

Vs. LHP   **Vs. RHP**

2003 Situational Stats

	AB	H	HR	RBI	Avg		AB	H	HR	RBI	Avg
Home	119	33	2	12	.277	LHP	49	8	0	5	.163
Road	140	32	2	11	.229	RHP	210	57	4	18	.271
First Half	172	45	4	19	.262	Sc Pos	63	13	2	21	.206
Scnd Half	87	20	0	4	.230	Clutch	44	10	0	5	.227

2003 Rankings (National League)

- 3rd in lowest on-base percentage for a leadoff hitter (.302)
- 8th in errors at second base (8)
- 9th in hit by pitch (11)
- Led the Cardinals in hit by pitch (11), lowest percentage of swings that missed (8.9), highest percentage of swings put into play (55.7) and batting average with the bases loaded (.500)

Woody Williams

2003 Season

In a season in which St. Louis' pitching staff was beset with any number of problems, the rock of stability was Woody Williams. Re-signed as a free agent the previous winter, Williams set career highs in wins and innings pitched. He had one dead-arm stretch around the All-Star break but otherwise kept the Cardinals in most of his starts. He finished the year by winning four of his last five starts as the Cards struggled to stay in the race.

Pitching

Williams has developed into a winner in his mid-30s, largely thanks to a cut fastball that when at its best stays in the low 90s with heavy movement. Under Cardinals pitching coach Dave Duncan, Williams also has developed consistent command of a good changeup that he will confidently throw at any point in the count. Williams shows an occasional curveball, but when he's right, he wins with the cutter and the change. His strength needs to be monitored, because when his arm is fatigued, the cutter loses velocity and often sits over the middle of the plate instead of diving to the corners. However, Williams is one of those gamers who will try and make the best out of days in which he doesn't have his best stuff.

Defense & Hitting

Williams has developed a decent slide step to help hold runners, and he permitted only eight stolen bases last season. He's a fine fielder and a solid hitting pitcher who frequently helps himself with the bat.

2004 Outlook

Without Williams last year, the Cardinals never would have stayed in contention until the final week. He is one of those rare starting pitchers who not only is a staff leader but also is a leader for all his teammates. With the great St. Louis defense behind him, Williams should run off some more big seasons in his late-developing career as an ace.

Position: SP
Bats: R **Throws:** R
Ht: 6' 0" **Wt:** 200

Opening Day Age: 37
Born: 8/19/66 in Houston, TX
ML Seasons: 11

Overall Statistics

	W	L	Pct.	ERA	G	GS	Sv	IP	H	BB	SO	HR	Avg
'03	18	9	.667	3.87	34	33	0	220.2	220	55	153	20	.256
Car.	92	76	.548	4.04	307	216	0	1533.2	1482	514	1070	209	.254

2003 Pitching Profile

	Woody Williams	NL Average
Overall Strike %	64.3	62.4
1st Pitch Strike %	61.4	58.4
Ratio	1.25	1.38
Strikeouts per 9 IP	6.24	6.65
Walks per 9 IP	2.24	3.42
Home Runs per 9 IP	0.82	1.05
Strikeout/Walk Ratio	2.78	1.94
Groundball/Flyball Ratio	0.97	1.29

2003 Situational Stats

	W	L	ERA	Sv	IP		AB	H	HR	RBI	Avg
Home	12	3	3.00	0	126.0	LHB	385	103	8	36	.268
Road	6	6	5.04	0	94.2	RHB	476	117	12	55	.246
First Half	12	3	3.01	0	134.2	Sc Pos	197	51	6	68	.259
Scnd Half	6	6	5.23	0	86.0	Clutch	45	13	0	5	.289

2003 Rankings (National League)

- 1st in most run support per nine innings (7.0)
- 2nd in wins, batters faced (944) and pitches thrown (3,647)
- 4th in innings pitched
- 6th in hits allowed
- 7th in hit batsmen (11) and winning percentage
- 8th in games started, lowest ERA at home and fewest GDPs induced per GDP situation (4.3%)
- Led the Cardinals in wins, games started, innings pitched, batters faced (944), strikeouts, pitches thrown (3,647), winning percentage, lowest slugging percentage allowed (.394) and fewest home runs allowed per nine innings (.82)

Miguel Cairo

Position: 2B/LF/3B
Bats: R **Throws:** R
Ht: 6' 1" **Wt:** 208

Opening Day Age: 29
Born: 5/4/74 in Anaco, VZ
ML Seasons: 8
Pronunciation: KI-row

Overall Statistics

	G	AB	R	H	D	T	HR	RBI	SB	BB	SO	Avg	OBP	Slg
'03	92	261	41	64	15	2	5	32	4	13	30	.245	.289	.375
Car.	707	2012	265	542	94	17	19	189	76	125	225	.269	.317	.361

2003 Situational Stats

	AB	H	HR	RBI	Avg		AB	H	HR	RBI	Avg
Home	121	28	2	12	.231	LHP	78	19	2	11	.244
Road	140	36	3	20	.257	RHP	183	45	3	21	.246
First Half	161	41	2	15	.255	Sc Pos	67	13	1	25	.194
Scnd Half	100	23	3	17	.230	Clutch	53	11	1	6	.208

2003 Season

When Fernando Vina went down last May, Miguel Cairo got the chance to play every day for the Cardinals. However, Cairo's timing proved unlucky days later. After driving in seven runs over two successive games June 17-18, he suffered a broken finger that sidelined him for nearly six weeks. In the interim, rookie Bo Hart wowed St. Louis, and Cairo returned to his reserve role when reactivated.

Hitting, Baserunning & Defense

Cairo is a good fastball hitter who usually is aggressive early in counts, especially when serving as a pinch-hitter. Cairo's power is negligible. He has decent speed and good instincts on the bases. His best position is second, where he has good range and turns the double play well. However, Cairo can adequately play both short and third, and also has the ability to play left field without hurting his club.

2004 Outlook

The Cardinals' entire bench, including Cairo, became free agents after the season, with St. Louis uncertain as to whom would fit its budget. While manager Tony La Russa appreciates Cairo's professionalism and versatility, it was the Yankees who secured his services with a one-year contract in '04.

Mike DeJean

Position: RP
Bats: R **Throws:** R
Ht: 6' 4" **Wt:** 217

Opening Day Age: 33
Born: 9/28/70 in Baton Rouge, LA
ML Seasons: 7
Pronunciation: DAY-zhan

Overall Statistics

	W	L	Pct.	ERA	G	GS	Sv	IP	H	BB	SO	HR	Avg
'03	5	8	.385	4.68	76	0	19	82.2	86	39	71	13	.269
Car.	24	24	.500	4.26	443	1	52	498.1	516	227	334	54	.271

2003 Situational Stats

	W	L	ERA	Sv	IP		AB	H	HR	RBI	Avg
Home	5	4	4.33	6	43.2	LHB	149	49	9	28	.329
Road	0	4	5.08	13	39.0	RHB	171	37	4	20	.216
First Half	2	7	5.44	17	46.1	Sc Pos	93	21	3	33	.226
Scnd Half	3	1	3.72	2	36.1	Clutch	215	63	6	37	.293

2003 Season

Acquired from Milwaukee in late August to bolster the reeling Cardinals bullpen, Mike DeJean did not have a major impact on St. Louis' unsuccessful playoff drive during his five weeks with the club. DeJean had begun the year as the Brewers' closer, but he lost his job after blowing eight of his 26 save opportunities and posting an ERA close to 5.00. His work for the Cardinals was only slightly better.

Pitching, Defense & Hitting

A good competitor, DeJean is at his best when he's getting groundballs with his 90-92 MPH sinker and strikeouts with his splitter. However, he too often is a fine-line pitcher who gets behind in the count and robs himself of using all his weapons. DeJean does not do a good job of holding runners and is easy pickings for basestealers. He is steady with the glove, and he has not committed an error since his 1997 rookie campaign. He rarely hits.

2004 Outlook

DeJean's durability and ability to pitch in pressure situations should make him attractive to many clubs, though he clearly is not among the elite closers. St. Louis elected not to pick up the 2004 option in his contract and did not offer him salary arbitration in December.

Cal Eldred

Position: RP
Bats: R **Throws:** R
Ht: 6' 4" **Wt:** 235

Opening Day Age: 36
Born: 11/24/67 in
Cedar Rapids, IA
ML Seasons: 12
Pronunciation:
EL-dred

Overall Statistics

	W	L	Pct.	ERA	G	GS	Sv	IP	H	BB	SO	HR	Avg
'03	7	4	.636	3.74	62	0	8	67.1	62	31	67	9	.248
Car.	81	72	.529	4.52	258	191	8	1264.0	1234	541	856	159	.256

2003 Situational Stats

	W	L	ERA	Sv	IP		AB	H	HR	RBI	Avg
Home	5	1	3.41	6	31.2	LHB	78	23	2	11	.295
Road	2	3	4.04	2	35.2	RHB	172	39	7	21	.227
First Half	3	2	3.96	8	38.2	Sc Pos	72	17	2	22	.236
Scnd Half	4	2	3.45	0	28.2	Clutch	148	38	6	17	.257

2003 Season

Though he worked largely under the radar, Cal Eldred engineered one of the best comeback stories of the year. Sidelined for two years with arm trouble, he earned a job in spring training as a non-roster player and then became one of the Cardinals' most consistent relievers. He led the St. Louis bullpen in relief wins, had eight saves as fill-in closer and finished strong by allowing only two runs in his final 11 appearances.

Pitching, Defense & Hitting

Eldred's dogged effort to put his arm troubles behind him finally paid dividends. In a less taxing bullpen role after starting for most of his career, his velocity was back in the low 90s and he developed good cutting movement on his hard stuff. He also mixed in a decent change. Eldred rarely hits and his delivery is slow, making him vulnerable to steals.

2004 Outlook

Eldred clearly exceeded all of St. Louis' expectations, and the Cards re-signed him to a one-year, $900,000 contract in December. There is every reason to believe he can be even better this year, with an offseason to condition and the rust of his inaction long gone.

Danny Haren

Position: SP
Bats: R **Throws:** R
Ht: 6' 5" **Wt:** 220

Opening Day Age: 23
Born: 9/17/80 in
Monterey Park, CA
ML Seasons: 1

Overall Statistics

	W	L	Pct.	ERA	G	GS	Sv	IP	H	BB	SO	HR	Avg
'03	3	7	.300	5.08	14	14	0	72.2	84	22	43	9	.293
Car.	3	7	.300	5.08	14	14	0	72.2	84	22	43	9	.293

2003 Situational Stats

	W	L	ERA	Sv	IP		AB	H	HR	RBI	Avg
Home	0	3	4.73	0	32.1	LHB	126	35	7	16	.278
Road	3	4	5.36	0	40.1	RHB	161	49	2	18	.304
First Half	0	2	5.27	0	13.2	Sc Pos	60	19	3	28	.317
Scnd Half	3	5	5.03	0	59.0	Clutch	1	1	0	0	1.000

2003 Season

Desperate for starting pitching, the Cards rushed Danny Haren to the majors in late June after only eight starts at the Triple-A level. After picking up his first major league victory with a strong six-inning performance against Kevin Brown and the Dodgers on July 19, the former second-round draft pick had mixed results the rest of the way. St. Louis won only four of his 14 starts.

Pitching, Defense & Hitting

Haren's herky-jerky delivery and deceiving arm angle makes his stuff difficult to pick up. However, hitters can adjust to his release point, and he needs to enhance his repertoire. His fastball tops out in the low 90s, but he showed a promising change and splitter, plus a cutter. Haren's command is uneven, and he needs to improve at holding runners. He handled all eight of his chances in the field without incident last year, and he also showed he can handle the bat fairly well.

2004 Outlook

Haren, who wasn't even in spring training with the Cardinals, had his share of problems last year, but also showed competitiveness and the potential to be a useful starting pitcher. He'll likely have a spot to lose in the rotation this spring. The Cardinals think he could become a 12-15 game winner.

Bo Hart

Position: 2B
Bats: R **Throws:** R
Ht: 5'11" **Wt:** 170

Opening Day Age: 27
Born: 9/27/76 in Creswell, OR
ML Seasons: 1

Overall Statistics

	G	AB	R	H	D	T	HR	RBI	SB	BB	SO	Avg	OBP	Slg
'03	77	296	46	82	13	5	4	28	3	12	64	.277	.317	.395
Car.	77	296	46	82	13	5	4	28	3	12	64	.277	.317	.395

2003 Situational Stats

	AB	H	HR	RBI	Avg		AB	H	HR	RBI	Avg
Home	160	46	1	12	.288	LHP	90	27	0	8	.300
Road	136	36	3	16	.265	RHP	206	55	4	20	.267
First Half	106	39	1	11	.368	Sc Pos	73	20	1	23	.274
Scnd Half	190	43	3	17	.226	Clutch	37	10	0	1	.270

2003 Season

Virtual unknown Bo Hart burst onto the St. Louis stage with a bang last June, hitting .391 in his first two weeks as the Cardinals' second baseman. The rookie predictably fell back to earth, but he held his own overall, batting .285 in his 62 games as a leadoff hitter.

Hitting, Baserunning & Defense

Hart has a big swing for a small player, and while it did produce three leadoff home runs in 2003, he also struck out far too often for someone projected to lead off. He doesn't walk much, either. He can hit a fastball but needs to learn better pitch recognition. Hart plays a solid second base, showing good range and hanging in well on the double play, and he also can fill in at short or third. Hart has above-average speed, though he probably won't steal more 15-20 bases in a full season.

2004 Outlook

With Fernando Vina gone, Hart will have a chance to win the St. Louis second-base job. The jury still is out on whether he is a long-term answer at the position. If not, his hustle and versatility at least should make him a solid utility player.

Sterling Hitchcock

Position: RP
Bats: L **Throws:** L
Ht: 6' 0" **Wt:** 200

Opening Day Age: 32
Born: 4/29/71 in Fayetteville, NC
ML Seasons: 12

Overall Statistics

	W	L	Pct.	ERA	G	GS	Sv	IP	H	BB	SO	HR	Avg
'03	6	4	.600	4.72	35	7	0	87.2	91	32	68	14	.265
Car.	74	73	.503	4.77	277	196	3	1264.1	1352	463	983	176	.273

2003 Situational Stats

	W	L	ERA	Sv	IP		AB	H	HR	RBI	Avg
Home	4	2	5.16	0	52.1	LHB	99	20	1	13	.202
Road	2	2	4.08	0	35.1	RHB	244	71	13	29	.291
First Half	0	2	4.78	0	32.0	Sc Pos	64	19	1	25	.297
Scnd Half	6	2	4.69	0	55.2	Clutch	18	6	0	1	.333

2003 Season

Sterling Hitchcock was a virtual non-entity for most of the season in the Yankees' bullpen. But after being acquired late in the season to bolster the Cards' depleted rotation, Hitchcock breathed some life into his career by winning five games in his brief stint with St. Louis, including his last three starts in succession.

Pitching, Defense & Hitting

Hitchcock finally seems to be over the arm and back problems that had derailed him since the 2000 season, when he was San Diego's Opening Day starter. His velocity is back into the high 80s, and he is throwing some effective splitters and changeups with more aggressiveness than he'd shown in recent years. He was particularly effective against left-handed hitters last year, allowing only four hits in 34 at-bats to lefties after joining the Cardinals. Hitchcock always has been a lefty who is easy to run on and is no factor as a hitter.

2004 Outlook

A free agent, Hitchcock no longer is untouchable due to the excessive contract given him by New York. St. Louis declined to offer him salary arbitration, but he could end up being a serviceable pitcher for a team needing depth in its rotation.

Steve Kline

Position: RP
Bats: B **Throws:** L
Ht: 6' 1" **Wt:** 215

Opening Day Age: 31
Born: 8/22/72 in
Sunbury, PA
ML Seasons: 7

Overall Statistics

	W	L	Pct.	ERA	G	GS	Sv	IP	H	BB	SO	HR	Avg
'03	5	5	.500	3.82	78	0	3	63.2	56	30	31	5	.237
Car.	25	28	.472	3.46	522	1	33	473.1	442	204	372	41	.249

2003 Situational Stats

	W	L	ERA	Sv	IP		AB	H	HR	RBI	Avg
Home	2	2	2.64	2	30.2	LHB	107	26	1	12	.243
Road	3	3	4.91	1	33.0	RHB	129	30	4	15	.233
First Half	3	4	3.93	3	36.2	Sc Pos	62	13	1	19	.210
Scnd Half	2	1	3.67	0	27.0	Clutch	126	33	4	16	.262

2003 Season

As usual, the durable Steve Kline was among the National League leaders in appearances last year. He had another solid season as a lefty setup man, earning 18 holds. The highlight of his year may have been working three perfect innings to earn the win in a 20-inning, 7-6 victory against Florida on April 27.

Pitching, Defense & Hitting

Kline makes his living with two pitches, a good sinker and hard slider. He will not give into hitters and is willing to walk someone rather than leave a hittable pitch over the plate. He is a tireless competitor who has appeared in at least 70 games in five of the last six years, and he is solid against both left- and righthanded pitching. Kline holds runners fairly well for a reliever and is steady afield. Last year, he actually did some rare damage with the bat, hitting a two-run double.

2004 Outlook

Kline was another of the Cardinals' many free agents, but tireless lefties like him are valuable to a contending club. St. Louis re-signed him to a one year, $1.7 million contract in December, and he should be good for another 70-plus games this season.

Orlando Palmeiro

Position: RF/LF/CF
Bats: L **Throws:** L
Ht: 5'11" **Wt:** 180

Opening Day Age: 35
Born: 1/19/69 in
Hoboken, NJ
ML Seasons: 9
Pronunciation:
pal-MAIR-oh

Overall Statistics

	G	AB	R	H	D	T	HR	RBI	SB	BB	SO	Avg	OBP	Slg
'03	141	317	37	86	13	1	3	33	3	32	31	.271	.336	.347
Car.	786	1776	241	496	82	11	6	171	32	210	163	.279	.357	.348

2003 Situational Stats

	AB	H	HR	RBI	Avg		AB	H	HR	RBI	Avg
Home	132	34	1	13	.258	LHP	55	10	0	3	.182
Road	185	52	2	20	.281	RHP	262	76	3	30	.290
First Half	198	54	1	19	.273	Sc Pos	72	16	0	27	.222
Scnd Half	119	32	2	14	.269	Clutch	50	16	0	8	.320

2003 Season

Signed to a one-year, $700,000 free-agent contract after spending eight seasons with the Angels, Orlando Palmeiro was the sort of versatile spare part manager Tony La Russa loves having on his teams. Appearing in a career-high 141 games, Palmeiro also reached career marks in home runs and RBI while playing all three outfield positions. He was the Cardinals' most reliable pinch-hitter with 13 hits off the bench.

Hitting, Baserunning & Defense

Palmeiro can be overpowered by hard stuff, but he is a good contact hitter who can line the ball to all fields. He usually works decent counts but is more aggressive as a pinch-hitter, a role in which he has a lot of experience. He can play any of the three outfield positions with decent range, but his arm is better suited to left or center. Palmeiro is just an average baserunner and not much of a threat to steal.

2004 Outlook

Palmeiro is one of those bench pieces that can help a winning club, and the Cardinals offered him salary arbitration in December. If St.Louis doesn't re-sign him, he certainly will show up on someone's roster this year.

Garrett Stephenson

Position: SP
Bats: R **Throws:** R
Ht: 6' 5" **Wt:** 215

Opening Day Age: 32
Born: 1/2/72 in Takoma Park, MD
ML Seasons: 7

Overall Statistics

	W	L	Pct.	ERA	G	GS	Sv	IP	H	BB	SO	HR	Avg
'03	7	13	.350	4.59	32	27	0	174.1	167	60	91	30	.255
Car.	39	39	.500	4.55	123	104	0	651.1	662	237	408	91	.267

2003 Situational Stats

	W	L	ERA	Sv	IP		AB	H	HR	RBI	Avg
Home	4	6	5.19	0	76.1	LHB	268	75	12	38	.280
Road	3	7	4.13	0	98.0	RHB	386	92	18	49	.238
First Half	4	9	4.58	0	118.0	Sc Pos	136	29	5	57	.213
Scnd Half	3	4	4.63	0	56.1	Clutch	42	5	0	1	.119

2003 Season

Each time Garrett Stephenson seemed on his way out of the Cardinals' rotation last season, someone else would get hurt to save his spot. At times, Stephenson pitched better than his record, and he received the worst run support of any of the St. Louis starters. That said, the Cards were just 10-17 in his 27 starts.

Pitching, Defense & Hitting

There is little margin for error with Stephenson, who lacks an out pitch that he can rely on from start to start. He needs to hit spots with his average fastball and stay ahead in counts in order to make his good changeup effective. Stephenson is a very steady fielder, with just one career error on his big league resumé. He holds runners fairly well but is slow to the plate. He's useless as a hitter.

2004 Outlook

Stephenson has been on thin ice with St. Louis for a few years, and he didn't help matters by often complaining about his lack of run support and then whining when he was dropped from the rotation. With a 16-win season on his resumé and a return to health, he likely will get a shot to fill a spot in someone's rotation, but it won't be in St. Louis.

Brett Tomko

Position: SP
Bats: R **Throws:** R
Ht: 6' 4" **Wt:** 215

Opening Day Age: 30
Born: 4/7/73 in Euclid, OH
ML Seasons: 7
Pronunciation: TOM-koh

Overall Statistics

	W	L	Pct.	ERA	G	GS	Sv	IP	H	BB	SO	HR	Avg
'03	13	9	.591	5.28	33	32	0	202.2	252	57	114	35	.305
Car.	62	51	.549	4.62	197	155	1	1042.2	1077	343	710	154	.267

2003 Situational Stats

	W	L	ERA	Sv	IP		AB	H	HR	RBI	Avg
Home	4	4	2.88	0	103.0	LHB	329	107	14	47	.325
Road	9	5	7.77	0	99.2	RHB	496	145	21	72	.292
First Half	5	6	5.80	0	118.0	Sc Pos	194	58	8	80	.299
Scnd Half	8	3	4.57	0	84.2	Clutch	29	10	0	2	.345

2003 Season

After joining the Cardinals in an offseason trade with San Diego, Brett Tomko's first 14 appearances of 2003 included three separate outings in which he allowed *nine* earned runs. Despite his early struggles, Tomko was a much-improved pitcher from midseason on, winning eight of his last 11 decisions.

Pitching, Defense & Hitting

Tomko has an array of good stuff, including a moving fastball that hits 95 MPH, a hard slider, serviceable curve and sinking change. He lacks command and the ability to pitch to the inner half of the plate, but those were two areas in which he showed some improvement as last season wore on. Tomko induces more groundballs these days, so he gets more chances in the field and holds his own in that regard. He is easy to run on, though he continues to work on a slide step. He is a good-hitting pitcher who last year had three two-hit games.

2004 Outlook

Tomko was yet another St. Louis free agent after the Cardinals failed to offer him salary arbitration in December. There is the belief that he could be on the verge of realizing his long-delayed potential and become a solid 15-game winner, but it probably won't happen in St. Louis.

Other St. Louis Cardinals

Pedro Borbon (**Pos**: LHP, **Age**: 36)

	W	L	Pct.	ERA	G	GS	Sv	IP	H	BB	SO	HR	Avg
'03	0	1	.000	20.25	7	0	0	4.0	14	2	0	2	.560
Car.	16	16	.500	4.68	368	0	6	271.0	259	134	224	33	.252

Borbon signed a minor league deal with the Dodgers last January, but was released. He then played in the Independent League until signing with St. Louis in late July and appeared in just seven games. 2004 Outlook: C

Kiko Calero (**Pos**: RHP, **Age**: 29)

	W	L	Pct.	ERA	G	GS	Sv	IP	H	BB	SO	HR	Avg
'03	1	1	.500	2.82	26	1	1	38.1	29	20	51	5	.212
Car.	1	1	.500	2.82	26	1	1	38.1	29	20	51	5	.212

Seeing his first major league action, Calero posted a respectable 2.82 ERA in 26 appearances with the Cardinals in 2003. However, his season was cut short after tearing a tendon in his right knee in June. 2004 Outlook: C

Jeff Fassero (**Pos**: LHP, **Age**: 41)

	W	L	Pct.	ERA	G	GS	Sv	IP	H	BB	SO	HR	Avg
'03	1	7	.125	5.68	62	6	3	77.2	93	34	55	17	.296
Car.	113	108	.511	4.00	621	223	25	1815.2	1832	641	1516	194	.261

At 40 years of age, Fassero appeared in 62 games with the Cardinals last season, including six starts. The left-hander's versatility and willingness to pitch in any role could land him a job in 2004. 2004 Outlook: C

Joe Girardi (**Pos**: C, **Age**: 39, **Bats**: R)

	G	AB	R	H	D	T	HR	RBI	SB	BB	SO	Avg	OBP	Slg
'03	16	23	1	3	0	0	0	1	0	3	4	.130	.231	.130
Car.	1277	4127	454	1100	186	26	36	422	44	279	607	.267	.315	.350

A herniated disc in Girardi's neck limited him to just 16 games in 2003. If the veteran catcher is unable to find a job as a player this offseason, several teams could consider him for a coaching position. 2004 Outlook: C

Gabe Molina (**Pos**: RHP, **Age**: 28)

	W	L	Pct.	ERA	G	GS	Sv	IP	H	BB	SO	HR	Avg
'03	0	0	—	13.50	3	0	0	2.2	5	1	1	1	.385
Car.	2	2	.500	6.58	46	0	0	52.0	61	33	28	9	.295

Molina struggled in three appearances with the Cardinals last season and spent most of the year in Triple-A. At one time considered to be a future closer, Molina likely is stuck in middle relief. 2004 Outlook: C

Kevin Ohme (**Pos**: LHP, **Age**: 32)

	W	L	Pct.	ERA	G	GS	Sv	IP	H	BB	SO	HR	Avg
'03	0	0	—	0.00	2	0	0	4.1	3	1	2	0	.200
Car.	0	0	—	0.00	2	0	0	4.1	3	1	2	0	.200

Ohme was the Triple-A Memphis co-leader (with Gabe Molina) with 56 appearances in 2002 and was second on the team last season, pitching in 49 games. The left-hander spent 2000 and 2001 playing in the Japanese League. 2004 Outlook: C

Lance Painter (**Pos**: LHP, **Age**: 36)

	W	L	Pct.	ERA	G	GS	Sv	IP	H	BB	SO	HR	Avg
'03	0	1	.000	5.50	22	0	0	18.0	17	7	11	3	.246
Car.	25	18	.581	5.24	314	28	3	450.0	496	178	331	66	.283

Painter missed the entire 2002 campaign after undergoing Tommy John surgery, but returned to action last spring. A fractured pelvis and strained left calf limited him to just 22 games in 2003. 2004 Outlook: C

Jason Pearson (**Pos**: LHP, **Age**: 28)

	W	L	Pct.	ERA	G	GS	Sv	IP	H	BB	SO	HR	Avg
'03	0	0	—	63.00	2	0	0	1.0	4	3	1	1	.571
Car.	0	0	—	23.63	4	0	0	2.2	5	3	4	1	.385

Besides two outings with St. Louis, Pearson split 2003 between Double-A and Triple-A. He posted respectable numbers, going 4-4 with a 2.56 ERA in 53 games with the two minor league clubs. 2004 Outlook: C

Eduardo Perez (**Pos**: RF/3B, **Age**: 34, **Bats**: R)

	G	AB	R	H	D	T	HR	RBI	SB	BB	SO	Avg	OBP	Slg
'03	105	253	47	72	16	0	11	41	5	29	53	.285	.365	.478
Car.	584	1415	191	349	70	3	58	226	19	146	321	.247	.322	.423

Perez spent the 2001 season in Japan, but returned to the majors in 2002. He has been solid as a reserve for St. Louis the past two seasons, batting .253 with 21 homers and 67 RBI in 407 at-bats. He signed a two-year, $1.7 million deal with Tampa in December. 2004 Outlook: B

Kerry Robinson (**Pos**: RF/LF/CF, **Age**: 30, **Bats**: L)

	G	AB	R	H	D	T	HR	RBI	SB	BB	SO	Avg	OBP	Slg
'03	116	208	19	52	6	3	1	16	6	8	27	.250	.281	.322
Car.	365	579	84	152	19	8	3	46	24	31	78	.263	.301	.339

Robinson has served as the Cardinals' fourth outfielder most of the last three seasons. He is solid defensively and has good speed, but he lacks power, hitting just three homers in 579 career at-bats. 2004 Outlook: C

Jason Simontacchi (**Pos**: RHP, **Age**: 30)

	W	L	Pct.	ERA	G	GS	Sv	IP	H	BB	SO	HR	Avg
'03	9	5	.643	5.56	46	16	1	126.1	153	41	74	21	.299
Car.	20	10	.667	4.74	70	40	1	269.2	287	95	146	39	.276

Simontacchi struggled in 16 starts last season, posting a 6.33 ERA. Comparably, the righthander had a 3.95 ERA in 30 relief appearances. He could compete for a spot in the rotation in 2004. 2004 Outlook: B

Russ Springer (**Pos**: RHP, **Age**: 35)

	W	L	Pct.	ERA	G	GS	Sv	IP	H	BB	SO	HR	Avg
'03	1	1	.500	8.31	17	0	0	17.1	19	6	11	8	.271
Car.	20	33	.377	5.18	368	27	8	549.0	564	252	496	85	.264

After missing all of 2002 recovering from shoulder surgery, Springer was limited to just 17 games in 2003 due to elbow problems. He has played with seven different major league teams in 11 years. 2004 Outlook: C

So Taguchi (Pos: CF/LF/RF, **Age**: 34, **Bats**: R)

	G	AB	R	H	D	T	HR	RBI	SB	BB	SO	Avg	OBP	Slg
'03	43	54	9	14	3	1	3	13	0	4	11	.259	.310	.519
Car.	62	69	13	20	3	1	3	15	1	6	12	.290	.347	.493

Taguchi, a former Japanese League All-Star, has yet to make a significant impact in the major leagues. With a saturated outfield, Taguchi will have a hard time breaking the Cardinals' everyday lineup. 2004 Outlook: C

Chris Widger (Pos: C, **Age**: 32, **Bats**: R)

	G	AB	R	H	D	T	HR	RBI	SB	BB	SO	Avg	OBP	Slg
'03	44	102	9	24	9	0	0	14	0	6	20	.235	.279	.324
Car.	532	1592	156	385	93	7	50	202	10	120	338	.242	.299	.403

Widger participated in spring training with the Yankees, but was released a week into the season. The catcher got 102 at-bats with St. Louis, even though he missed nearly a month with a bruised thumb. 2004 Outlook: C

Esteban Yan (Pos: RHP, **Age**: 28)

	W	L	Pct.	ERA	G	GS	Sv	IP	H	BB	SO	HR	Avg
'03	2	1	.667	6.35	54	0	1	66.2	84	23	53	13	.308
Car.	28	32	.467	5.41	327	23	43	504.1	564	188	415	81	.283

Yan, who was Tampa Bay's closer in 2001 and 2002, began the 2003 season with the Rangers, but was traded to St. Louis in May. He served as a setup man for both teams, posting a gaudy 6.35 ERA. 2004 Outlook: B

St. Louis Cardinals Minor League Prospects

Organization Overview:

The 2003 season may have been the year when a questionable farm system finally bit the Cardinals. The National League Central was there for the taking, were it not for injury problems to key players and a bullpen that often poured gasoline on the fire. Unfortunately, the best the Cardinals' system could offer was second baseman Bo Hart, a classic overachiever, and righthanded starter Dan Haren, who was shut down after mid-September. In years past, the Cardinals swapped minor league talent for help down the stretch. That didn't occur last season, but whether that was due to organizational restraint or dubious talent is open to debate. The Cardinals have taken steps to address their organizational needs. John Mozeliak has added scouting director duties to his job description, and it looks like the team might use more of a performance-based approach to evaluating players. For now, impact players are scarce.

John Gall

Position: 1B   **Opening Day Age:** 25
Bats: R **Throws:** R   **Born:** 4/2/78 in Stanford,
Ht: 6' 0" **Wt:** 195   CA

Recent Statistics

	G	AB	R	H	D	T	HR	RBI	SB	BB	SO	Avg
2002 AA New Haven	135	526	82	166	45	3	20	81	4	38	75	.316
2003 AA Tennessee	12	52	6	17	1	0	3	12	0	3	4	.327
2003 AAA Memphis	123	461	62	144	24	1	16	73	5	39	56	.312

Gall has been a consistent .300 hitter at every level he's played the past three years. An 11th-round pick out of Stanford in 2000, Gall swings the kind of bat you'd like to write into your lineup, as he's shown the ability to hit for average and drive in runs. But while he's also displayed decent extra-base totals at the upper levels, he doesn't possess the home-run power you hope to get from a first baseman. He's tried third base in the past, but that didn't work out. He also can play the outfield, and his best chance to stick in the big leagues may come as a utilityman or stick off the bench. In the best of all worlds, he gets a crack to be the next Mark Grace.

Reid Gorecki

Position: OF   **Opening Day Age:** 23
Bats: R **Throws:** R   **Born:** 12/22/80 in East
Ht: 6' 1" **Wt:** 180   Rockaway, NY

Recent Statistics

	G	AB	R	H	D	T	HR	RBI	SB	BB	SO	Avg
2002 A New Jersey	73	274	55	77	8	13	8	52	22	20	57	.281
2003 A Peoria	128	480	77	128	19	8	15	61	23	51	90	.267

Gorecki played his college ball at Delaware, where he led the Colonial Athletic Association in runs scored and triples his final season there. As you might suspect, he runs well and has stolen over 20 bases in each of his first two professional seasons. He's also a pretty good defensive center fielder with a decent arm. Although Gorecki drew his share of walks last year, the Cardinals would like to see a few more free passes, which would make him even more valuable at the top of a lineup. He might develop more power as he matures. The Cardinals don't appear to be loaded with legitimate outfield prospects, so an opportunity awaits Gorecki.

Blake Hawksworth

Position: P   **Opening Day Age:** 21
Bats: R **Throws:** R   **Born:** 3/1/83 in North
Ht: 6' 3" **Wt:** 195   Vancouver, BC

Recent Statistics

	W	L	ERA	G	GS	Sv	IP	H	R	BB	SO	HR
2002 R Johnson City	2	4	3.14	13	12	0	66.0	58	31	18	61	8
2002 A New Jersey	1	0	0.00	2	2	0	9.2	6	0	2	8	0
2003 A Peoria	5	1	2.30	10	10	0	54.2	37	16	12	57	0
2003 A Palm Beach	1	3	3.94	6	6	0	32.0	28	14	11	32	2

Hawksworth has outstanding stuff, the best in the organization. Selected in the 28th round of the 2001 draft out of a high school in Washington state, Hawksworth signed late and didn't debut professionally until 2002. His fastball can hit 95 MPH and complements a good changeup. He can get by with just those two pitches in the low minors, but he'll need to improve his breaking ball as he moves up the chain. He'll also need to show that he can remain durable. An ankle injury shut him down towards the end of last season, and he has yet to throw 100 innings in a minor league campaign. But he probably has the highest ceiling of any Cardinals pitching prospect.

Tyler Johnson

Position: P   **Opening Day Age:** 22
Bats: L **Throws:** L   **Born:** 6/7/81 in Newbury
Ht: 6' 3" **Wt:** 190   Park, CA

Recent Statistics

	W	L	ERA	G	GS	Sv	IP	H	R	BB	SO	HR
2002 A Peoria	15	3	2.00	22	18	0	121.1	96	35	42	132	7
2003 A Palm Beach	5	5	3.08	22	10	0	79.0	79	29	38	81	2
2003 AA Tennessee	1	0	1.65	20	0	0	27.1	16	7	15	39	1

Johnson had a breakout season in 2002, when he finished second to Dontrelle Willis in the Class-A Midwest League with a 2.00 ERA. While Johnson's followup last season wasn't quite as impressive as Willis', Johnson continued to strike out over a batter an inning as he rose to Double-A. Johnson moved from a starting to a relief role in 2003. While his 87-89 MPH fastball might be a tick below what you'd like, his curveball is way above average. His changeup also can be useful. The Cardinals envision him as a lefty specialist out of the bullpen, though it may be too early to typecast him at age 22. A big league job this season is possible.

Jimmy Journell

Position: P

Bats: R **Throws:** R

Ht: 6' 4" **Wt:** 205

Opening Day Age: 26

Born: 12/29/77 in Springfield, OH

Recent Statistics

	W	L	ERA	G	GS	Sv	IP	H	R	BB	SO	HR
2003 AAA Memphis	6	6	3.92	40	7	5	78.0	80	38	32	70	3
2003 NL St. Louis	0	0	6.00	7	0	0	9.0	10	7	11	8	0

Journell made the switch to relief at Triple-A last season, which is where he had excelled as a college pitcher at Illinois. The Cardinals think it's a role where he'll be more comfortable and enjoy success with his power arm. Featuring a fastball that hits 95 MPH at times, Journell appears dominant when he's on. He comes at hitters with a lower arm angle, and can be downright nasty on righthanded batters. Considering all the problems the Cardinals endured with their imploding bullpen in 2003, it might be surprising that Journell did not get more of a look. But his command wasn't as good in the majors as it had been at Memphis. He should get another chance to prove himself at some point this season.

Yadier Molina

Position: C

Bats: R **Throws:** R

Ht: 5' 11" **Wt:** 187

Opening Day Age: 21

Born: 7/13/82 in Bayamon, PR

Recent Statistics

	G	AB	R	H	D	T	HR	RBI	SB	BB	SO	Avg
2002 A Peoria	112	393	39	110	20	0	7	50	2	21	36	.280
2003 AA Tennessee	104	364	32	100	13	1	2	51	0	25	45	.275

Early last year, when the Cardinals experienced a rash of injuries among their big league receivers, there was some speculation about Molina's preparedness. Even though he was only 20 and hadn't played above Class-A entering the season, Molina's defense may have been worthy of a promotion. His brothers Bengie and Jose are catchers for the Angels, so the defensive skills may be second nature. And even though he was four or five years younger than some of the pitchers he worked with at Double-A, Molina showed the ability to take charge. He didn't tear up the Southern League with the bat, but he was quite young for the level. Molina projects to be at least an average offensive catcher in the majors.

Chris Narveson

Position: P

Bats: L **Throws:** L

Ht: 6' 3" **Wt:** 180

Opening Day Age: 22

Born: 12/20/81 in Englewood, CO

Recent Statistics

	W	L	ERA	G	GS	Sv	IP	H	R	BB	SO	HR
2002 R Johnson City	0	2	4.91	6	6	0	18.1	23	12	6	16	2
2002 A Peoria	2	1	4.46	9	9	0	42.1	49	24	8	36	5
2003 A Palm Beach	7	7	2.86	15	14	0	91.1	83	34	19	65	4
2003 AA Tennessee	4	3	3.00	10	10	0	57.0	56	21	26	34	6

Narveson was selected in the second round of the 2000 draft out of a North Carolina high school. At the time, the Cardinals had a couple other highly touted young lefthanders in their system. While Narveson didn't possess the velocity of Rick Ankiel or the control of Bud Smith, he did exhibit perhaps the best combination of the two talents. Another year removed from the Tommy John surgery he underwent in 2001, Narveson increased his workload last season as he reached Double-A at age 21. His fastball will touch the low 90s, which isn't bad for a southpaw. He also throws a good breaking pitch and a decent changeup. He and Rhett Parrott rank as the Cardinals' top two prospects among those starting pitchers closest to the big leagues.

Rhett Parrott

Position: P

Bats: R **Throws:** R

Ht: 6' 2" **Wt:** 185

Opening Day Age: 24

Born: 11/12/79 in Dalton, GA

Recent Statistics

	W	L	ERA	G	GS	Sv	IP	H	R	BB	SO	HR
2002 A Potomac	8	5	2.71	19	19	0	113.0	91	42	41	82	6
2002 AA New Haven	4	1	2.86	9	9	0	66.0	53	24	13	38	3
2003 AA Tennessee	8	9	3.27	21	21	0	124.0	122	52	40	112	11
2003 AAA Memphis	2	3	3.54	7	7	0	40.2	39	16	19	25	2

The Cardinals selected Parrott in the ninth round of the 2001 draft, seven rounds after grabbing Dan Haren in the second. While Parrott appeared to be ahead of Haren in 2002, it was Haren who reached the majors last year. Parrott may not be far behind, however, as he's been added to the Cardinals' 40-man roster. He throws a 90-92 MPH fastball and a changeup that's major league average, though his breaking ball needs work. Like Haren, Parrott is a workhorse who projects as a No. 3 type of pitcher in the big leagues. He's started 28 games each of the past two years while logging over 340 innings. He could be battling Haren and others for a spot in the Cards' rotation at some point in '04.

Others to Watch

Shaun Boyd (22) moved to the outfield last season, in part to relieve the recurring throwing problems he had experienced at second base. He shows a quick bat and nice discipline, as well as good speed. . . Third baseman **Travis Hanson** (23) was on fire with the bat early last season, but eventually leveled off, when fatigue might have been an issue. He's a line-drive hitter who needs to learn to lay off chase pitches. . . Righthander **Josh Pearce** (26) produced an outstanding strikeout-walk ratio in three minor league stops last season, and got into seven games in relief with the Cardinals. He may be no better than a "4-A" type of pitcher, however. . . An undrafted college pitcher signed by Tampa Bay, **Evan Rust** (25) has progressed steadily with a low-90s fastball he keeps low in the zone. In 2003, he posted 12 saves and a 2.96 ERA in the high minors before he was acquired for Tino Martinez in November. . . A supplemental No. 1 choice in 1999, righty **Nick Stocks** (25) re-opened some eyes last year. He has good stuff and was more consistent in '03, but needs to improve his command.

Petco Park

Offense

The Padres are hoping Petco Park's deep power alleys will play like a pitchers' park. With a location near the water, the heavy sea air at night also should help keep balls inside the fences. During the day, the air won't prevent hitters from taking advantage of the short foul lines and a center-field wall less than 400 feet away.

Defense

The light standards are significantly taller at Petco than at Qualcomm, which will help outfielders who couldn't see the low line drives hit right at them due to the glare. The infield should be a significant improvement with state of the art drainage and landscaping. There doesn't appear to be as much foul ground as at the Q, so range at the corners should be less of a factor.

Who It Helps the Most

Pull hitters should be able to take advantage of the short porches down the line: 322 feet in right, 334 feet and only a four-foot outfield wall to clear in left. Pitchers who can keep the ball in the middle of the field should fare well, especially in night games. Similarly, the improved playing surface in the infield should help groundball pitchers like Brian Lawrence.

Who It Hurts the Most

If the ball carries during the day, flyball pitchers like Jake Peavy, Scott Linebrink and Ben Howard will probably miss Qualcomm's spacious outfield. Line-drive hitters like Mark Kotsay and Mark Loretta might lose out in the home-run department due to the deep power alleys, but that should be offset somewhat by an increase in doubles to the gaps.

Rookies & Newcomers

Khalil Greene will open 2004 as the everyday shortstop in his first full big league season. The Padres are optimistic that his combination of solid defense and extra-base power will be a good fit in the new park. New catcher Ramon Hernandez may have trouble building on his career-high 21 homers in 2003.

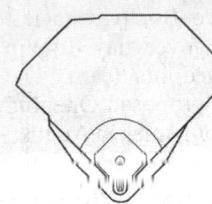

Dimensions: LF-334, LCF-367, CF-396, RCF-387, RF-322

Capacity: 42,000

Elevation: 0 feet

Surface: Grass

Foul Territory: Small

Park Factors

2003 Season (Qualcomm Stadium)

	Home Games			Away Games			
	Padres	Opp	Total	Padres	Opp	Total	Index
G	72	72	144	72	72	144	
Avg	.256	.256	.256	.264	.277	.270	95
AB	2404	2527	4931	2508	2394	4902	101
R	270	342	612	331	415	746	82
H	615	647	1262	661	664	1325	95
2B	96	115	211	126	125	251	84
3B	18	17	35	12	20	32	109
HR	48	87	135	63	101	164	82
BB	265	272	537	238	281	519	103
SO	484	513	997	482	473	955	104
E	46	47	93	41	39	80	116
E-Infield	37	37	74	38	28	66	112
LHB-Avg	.243	.264	.253	.277	.293	.284	89
LHB-HR	17	33	50	28	38	66	74
RHB-Avg	.267	.251	.258	.252	.267	.260	99
RHB-HR	31	54	85	35	63	98	87

2001-2003 (Qualcomm Stadium)

	Home Games			Away Games			
	Padres	Opp	Total	Padres	Opp	Total	Index
G	216	216	432	219	219	438	
Avg	.251	.257	.254	.258	.283	.270	94
AB	7178	7593	14771	7632	7382	15014	100
R	855	998	1853	1045	1218	2263	83
H	1803	1949	3752	1969	2091	4060	94
2B	300	345	645	391	438	829	79
3B	48	48	96	33	56	89	110
HR	161	258	419	216	294	510	84
BB	806	716	1522	790	786	1576	98
SO	1492	1551	3043	1597	1408	3005	103
E	176	137	313	154	149	303	105
E-Infield	156	108	264	128	118	246	109
LHB-Avg	.263	.267	.265	.267	.293	.278	95
LHB-HR	74	111	185	97	129	226	82
RHB-Avg	.240	.249	.245	.250	.277	.264	93
RHB-HR	87	147	234	119	165	284	85

2003 Rankings (National League)

- Second-highest error factor
- Third-highest infield-error factor
- Lowest run factor
- Lowest LHB batting-average factor
- Second-lowest LHB home-run factor
- Third-lowest batting-average factor
- Third-lowest double factor

Bruce Bochy

2003 Season

Just as he did in 2002, Bruce Bochy was left trying to patch together an everyday lineup because injuries had decimated his team. The Padres were able to field their proposed Opening Day lineup for only a handful of games in August. Worse still, injuries to Trevor Hoffman and Jay Witasick left his bullpen short on quality, forcing him to play Russian roulette nightly before the Rod Beck signing stabilized the situation.

Offense

Bochy makes most of his moves before the game, adjusting the lineup to suit the individual matchups. For the most part, he will let his players play. Bochy's biggest strength is his openness and candor with his players. He earns their trust, and in return, they very rarely fail to give him 100 percent of their effort.

Pitching & Defense

When it comes to the bullpen, Bochy is a creature of habit. He likes to have a specific role for each reliever so that each move he makes in the end-game is relatively automatic. He has become much more circumspect regarding pitch counts, especially with his young starters. After finishing near the bottom defensively in each of the previous three years, Bochy focused on fundamentals last spring and the team responded.

2004 Outlook

When Bochy admitted in a midseason interview that he might look elsewhere after his contract ran out after the season, it was clear that five consecutive losing seasons had worn thin on him. But the Padres' trade for Brian Giles and their promise to bring in some quality free agents this offseason appear to have changed his tune. He has never had a great deal of success with young teams, so an infusion of veterans who can shoulder the mentoring load might be just the remedy the Padres need to fully take advantage of his strengths.

Born: 4/16/55 in Landes de Boussac, France

Playing Experience: 1978-1987, Hou, NYM, SD

Managerial Experience: 9 seasons

Manager Statistics

Year	Team, Lg	W	L	Pct	GB	Finish
2003	San Diego, NL	64	98	.395	36.5	5th West
9 Seasons		694	746	.482	–	–

2003 Starting Pitchers by Days Rest

	<=3	4	5	6+
Padres Starts	0	74	54	21
Padres ERA	–	5.23	4.41	4.96
NL Avg Starts	2	84	43	23
NL ERA	5.00	4.23	4.42	4.68

2003 Situational Stats

	Bruce Bochy	NL Average
Hit & Run Success %	27.3	32.7
Stolen Base Success %	66.1	68.9
Platoon Pct.	56.1	52.0
Defensive Subs	11	19
High-Pitch Outings	2	8
Quick/Slow Hooks	17/16	20/12
Sacrifice Attempts	67	93

2003 Rankings (National League)

- 1st in pinch-hitters used (307) and mid-inning pitching changes (199)
- 2nd in starting lineups used (135) and one-batter pitcher appearances (51)
- 3rd in slow hooks and first-batter platoon percentage

Rod Beck

2003 Season

Rod Beck began the season pitching for the Triple-A Iowa Cubs, living in his trailer in the ballpark parking lot and sharing postgame brews and stories with the local fans. He finished the season as one of the most effective closers in the league, saving all 20 of his opportunities and posting the second-best ERA of his career. After the Cubs released him from his Triple-A contract at the end of May, he joined the Padres in June and immediately brought order to a bullpen that was in complete disarray. He was named closer just two weeks later and pitched brilliantly down the stretch, posting a scoreless August and a 1.31 ERA after the break.

Pitching

Beck throws a fastball that rarely tops 86 MPH, but he spots it well and pitches fearlessly in all quadrants of the strike zone. He also has a very good forkball that he locates just as well, and when ahead in the count will get hitters to chase it. His changeup and slider are average and are more for show, but that doesn't stop him from throwing them in any situation.

Defense & Hitting

Beck moves off the mound surprisingly well for a pitcher with a regular-guy body and has not made an error since 1997. He does not hold runners very well, but in his role few players try to steal.

2004 Outlook

Beck was grateful to the Padres for the opportunity to resurrect his major league career. So the veteran righthander was open to returning as a setup man for Trevor Hoffman in 2004. Undoubtedly he would get plenty of offers, but Beck signed a one-year contract with the Padres early in the offseason. He stays in San Diego, which will delay his pursuit of 300 career saves.

Position: RP
Bats: R **Throws:** R
Ht: 6' 1" **Wt:** 235

Opening Day Age: 35
Born: 8/3/68 in Burbank, CA
ML Seasons: 12
Nickname: Shooter

Overall Statistics

	W	L	Pct.	ERA	G	GS	Sv	IP	H	BB	SO	HR	Avg
'03	3	2	.600	1.78	36	0	20	35.1	25	11	32	4	.197
Car.	38	43	.469	3.21	678	0	286	744.0	676	182	629	89	.241

2003 Pitching Profile

	Rod Beck	NL Average
Overall Strike %	64.6	62.4
1st Pitch Strike %	69.3	58.4
Ratio	1.02	1.38
Strikeouts per 9 IP	8.15	6.65
Walks per 9 IP	2.80	3.42
Home Runs per 9 IP	1.02	1.05
Strikeout/Walk Ratio	2.91	1.94
Groundball/Flyball Ratio	1.50	1.29

2003 Situational Stats

	W	L	ERA	Sv	IP		AB	H	HR	RBI	Avg
Home	2	2	1.71	10	21.0	LHB	69	11	2	4	.159
Road	1	0	1.88	10	14.1	RHB	58	14	2	6	.241
First Half	1	1	2.45	8	14.2	Sc Pos	27	2	0	5	.074
Scnd Half	2	1	1.31	12	20.2	Clutch	94	18	3	9	.191

2003 Rankings (National League)

- 1st in save percentage (100.0)
- Led the Padres in saves, games finished (30), lowest batting average allowed vs. lefthanded batters, save percentage (100.0), relief ERA (1.78), lowest batting average allowed in relief (.197) and fewest baserunners allowed per nine innings in relief (9.4)

Sean Burroughs

2003 Season

Sean Burroughs' sophomore season was a considerable improvement over his initial exposure, but it suffered some of the same concerns: namely, nagging injuries. He battled through strains to his hamstrings, elbows, groin, hip flexors and two fastball-caused bruises to his right ankle. When healthy, Burroughs displayed the hitting prowess that made him a top hitting prospect, topping .320 in May, June and August. He was also second on the team with 42 multi-hit games, including his first four-hit effort. All but one of his multi-hit games came after April, when he was still recovering from offseason shoulder surgery.

Hitting

Burroughs is a prototypical line-drive hitter, going with the pitch to all fields. His swing still doesn't generate a lot of drive through his hips and lower body, but he could easily develop home-run power with some minor adjustments. There really isn't any pitch that he struggles with, but he can be induced into swinging at the pitcher's pitch deep in the count. That should be cured with more experience.

Baserunning & Defense

Although he didn't have many steals, Burroughs is surprisingly fast and, with a little more knowledge of the league, might develop into a legitimate basestealing threat. He's made significant strides on the defensive side: he's less tentative on balls hit in front of him and is unafraid to try for the great play, of which he made several last season. This marked improvement is a good omen for those who predicted multiple Gold Gloves in his future.

2004 Outlook

Burroughs will be the Padres' third baseman and their leadoff hitter against righthanders. Staying healthy has been the biggest obstacle in his young career—one that has been a major problem for the Padres in general the last several seasons. If Burroughs can stay relatively free from injury, he will battle for a batting title.

Position: 3B
Bats: L **Throws:** R
Ht: 6' 2" **Wt:** 200

Opening Day Age: 23
Born: 9/12/80 in Atlanta, GA
ML Seasons: 2

Overall Statistics

	G	AB	R	H	D	T	HR	RBI	SB	BB	SO	Avg	OBP	Slg
'03	146	517	62	148	27	6	7	58	7	44	75	.286	.352	.402
Car.	209	709	80	200	32	7	8	69	9	56	105	.282	.343	.381

Where He Hits the Ball

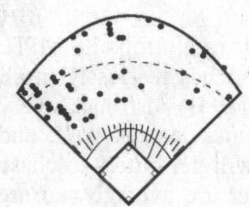
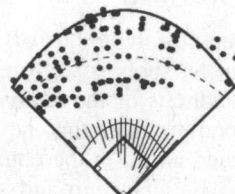

Vs. LHP   **Vs. RHP**

2003 Situational Stats

	AB	H	HR	RBI	Avg		AB	H	HR	RBI	Avg
Home	261	71	2	32	.272	LHP	146	38	3	23	.260
Road	256	77	5	26	.301	RHP	371	110	4	35	.296
First Half	298	91	5	39	.305	Sc Pos	117	28	1	44	.239
Scnd Half	219	57	2	19	.260	Clutch	84	28	1	13	.333

2003 Rankings (National League)

- 5th in fielding percentage at third base (.966)
- Led the Padres in triples, hit by pitch (11) and on-base percentage for a leadoff hitter (.362)
- Led NL third basemen in batting average

Adam Eaton

2003 Season

Adam Eaton returned last season after missing most of 2002 while recovering from reconstructive surgery on his pitching elbow. With the exception of May, when he was battling through a groin strain, Eaton pitched very well. He got his first win of the season on April 23 when he shut out the Cubs for seven innings while striking out 12. He was 2-7 when June ended, but went 7-5 with a 3.56 ERA the rest of the way. His overall record would have been much better if not for poor run support—the Padres scored two or fewer runs for Eaton in 16 of his 31 starts.

Pitching

Eaton seems to start slowly and gain strength as the game progresses, holding back a little extra for tough situations. His fastball ranges from 90-95 MPH, and he can vary the speed of his big-breaking curve from 68-78 MPH. He also features a solid changeup and a serviceable slider. He gets into trouble when he tries to be too fine with his location. He has good poise and control and has no fear of pitching inside.

Defense & Hitting

Eaton is a good hitter for a pitcher and an excellent bunter, giving his manager a number of options at the plate. This year, he hit his first two career home runs, although oddly enough neither one came in games the Padres won. He fields his position well and allowed only 10 steals in 183 innings last year.

2004 Outlook

Although the final results appear mediocre, the Padres were very encouraged by Eaton's season. Despite injuries and poor run support, he managed to throw quality starts in more than half of his outings. With the promise of better run support, he should have a strong 2004 season.

Position: SP
Bats: R **Throws:** R
Ht: 6' 2" **Wt:** 190

Opening Day Age: 26
Born: 11/23/77 in Seattle, WA
ML Seasons: 4

Overall Statistics

	W	L	Pct.	ERA	G	GS	Sv	IP	H	BB	SO	HR	Avg
'03	9	12	.429	4.08	31	31	0	183.0	173	68	146	20	.246
Car.	25	22	.532	4.25	76	76	0	468.0	443	186	370	59	.248

2003 Pitching Profile

	Adam Eaton	NL Average
Overall Strike %	63.0	62.4
1st Pitch Strike %	57.7	58.4
Ratio	1.32	1.38
Strikeouts per 9 IP	7.18	6.65
Walks per 9 IP	3.34	3.42
Home Runs per 9 IP	0.98	1.05
Strikeout/Walk Ratio	2.15	1.94
Groundball/Flyball Ratio	1.26	1.29

2003 Situational Stats

	W	L	ERA	Sv	IP		AB	H	HR	RBI	Avg
Home	4	6	3.58	0	93.0	LHB	315	87	10	40	.276
Road	5	6	4.60	0	90.0	RHB	388	86	10	41	.222
First Half	4	7	4.21	0	102.2	Sc Pos	171	42	5	61	.246
Scnd Half	5	5	3.92	0	80.1	Clutch	39	9	0	2	.231

2003 Rankings (National League)

- 8th in lowest winning percentage
- 9th in highest stolen-base percentage allowed (83.3)
- 10th in errors at pitcher (3) and most pitches thrown per batter (3.88)
- Led the Padres in ERA, pickoff throws (75), highest strikeout-walk ratio (2.1), lowest slugging percentage allowed (.405) and fewest home runs allowed per nine innings (.98)

San Diego

Brian Giles

2003 Season

It wasn't clear whether it was a strain or a slight tear to his medial collateral ligament, but the April injury to Brian Giles' right knee appeared to affect his play in 2003. His home runs were down by almost half from his 2002 total, and his speed all but disappeared. Still, the Padres liked him enough to trade three very good young players to bring Giles back to his hometown of San Diego.

Hitting

Over the last five years, Giles has arguably been the National League's second best hitter, behind only Barry Bonds. His patience and discerning eye forces pitchers to throw him pitches he can handle; he'll accept a free pass if they don't. He hits the ball to all fields, but really drives pitches when he gets his arms extended. Pitching him to extremes—in on his hands, low and away—is how most opponents go after him, but their mistakes often end up as souvenirs.

Baserunning & Defense

Although his speed is only average, Giles will steal on any pitcher who forgets about him, and is always looking to take an extra base if the opposition is careless. Giles is not blessed with great defensive tools, but he hustles on everything and has a flair for the spectacular, as evidenced by his over-the-wall catch against the Indians on June 21 which was voted by ESPN viewers as the best defensive play of the year. He's also versatile, playing all three outfield positions ably, and rarely makes a bad throw.

2004 Outlook

How much the Padres miss Oliver Perez, Jason Bay and Cory Stewart won't be known for several years. What they do know is that for the next two years they will have an excellent hitter and gutsy veteran on a team that was in desperate need of both in 2003. With the trade that moves Mark Kotsay to Oakland, Giles will be the center fielder unless the Padres sign a free agent during the offseason.

Position: LF/CF
Bats: L **Throws:** L
Ht: 5'10" **Wt:** 205

Opening Day Age: 33
Born: 1/20/71 in El Cajon, CA
ML Seasons: 9
Pronunciation: JYLES

Overall Statistics

	G	AB	R	H	D	T	HR	RBI	SB	BB	SO	Avg	OBP	Slg
'03	134	492	93	147	34	6	20	88	4	105	58	.299	.427	.514
Car.	1043	3502	674	1056	226	32	208	681	70	694	487	.302	.417	.563

Where He Hits the Ball

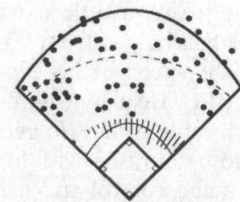
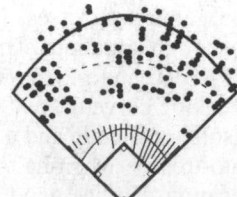

Vs. LHP **Vs. RHP**

2003 Situational Stats

	AB	H	HR	RBI	Avg		AB	H	HR	RBI	Avg
Home	241	76	12	42	.315	LHP	161	46	3	31	.286
Road	251	71	8	46	.283	RHP	331	101	17	57	.305
First Half	248	76	10	45	.306	Sc Pos	121	36	4	59	.298
Scnd Half	244	71	10	43	.291	Clutch	64	13	1	5	.203

2003 Rankings (National League)

- 4th in on-base percentage (.427) and lowest fielding percentage in left field (.984)
- 5th in lowest groundball-flyball ratio (0.7)
- 6th in walks (105) and errors in left field (4)
- 7th in lowest percentage of swings that missed (9.3)

Ryan Klesko

2003 Season

Ryan Klesko's season began promisingly enough, with seven home runs in the first month. But a beanball in May and shoulder pains in August put a damper on what might have been a big year. Klesko's season ended in September when he underwent surgery on his shoulder to shave away a bone impingement that was affecting his rotator cuff and bicipital tendon.

Hitting

After making significant progress hitting lefties the previous two years, Klesko struggled terribly against them in 2003. Part of the problem had to do with his ailing shoulder; being hit in the head by a LHP Horacio Ramirez fastball in May probably didn't help. Klesko is a disciplined hitter who crushes fastballs on the inner half. Almost all of his home runs are pulled to right field. He has good plate coverage and will take the ball on the outer half the other way, although he occasionally will flail at outside sliders.

Baserunning & Defense

Klesko is a good baserunner with above-average speed who took advantage of pitchers ignoring him to rack up some nice steal totals in 2000 and 2001. The last two years, pitchers were more mindful of him, effectively reigning in his freewheeling ways. His glovework at first is not especially notable other than his ability to consistently make perfect throws to the pitcher on infield grounders. In the outfield, he sometimes takes awkward routes, but the former high school pitcher has a strong and accurate arm.

2004 Outlook

The tentative plan is for Klesko to move to left field in order to open up first base for Phil Nevin. Although Klesko is more comfortable at first, it is in left that he has the most major league experience. With the Padres showing an inclination to be active during the offseason, a trade involving Klesko is not completely out of the question.

Position: 1B
Bats: L **Throws:** L
Ht: 6' 3" **Wt:** 220

Opening Day Age: 32
Born: 6/12/71 in Westminster, CA
ML Seasons: 12

Overall Statistics

	G	AB	R	H	D	T	HR	RBI	SB	BB	SO	Avg	OBP	Slg
'03	121	397	47	100	18	0	21	67	2	65	83	.252	.354	.456
Car.	1350	4400	704	1240	264	27	245	817	80	621	862	.282	.370	.521

Where He Hits the Ball

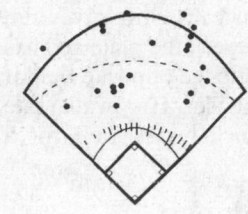 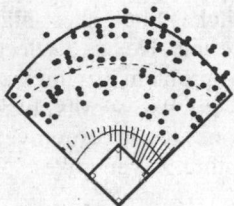

Vs. LHP   **Vs. RHP**

2003 Situational Stats

	AB	H	HR	RBI	Avg		AB	H	HR	RBI	Avg
Home	186	42	8	26	.226	LHP	103	20	4	11	.194
Road	211	58	13	41	.275	RHP	294	80	17	56	.272
First Half	271	71	19	52	.262	Sc Pos	93	22	6	48	.237
Scnd Half	126	29	2	15	.230	Clutch	72	17	5	15	.236

2003 Rankings (National League)

- 2nd in sacrifice flies (9)
- 5th in lowest fielding percentage at first base (.994)
- 7th in errors at first base (6)
- Led the Padres in home runs, sacrifice flies (9), caught stealing (5), walks, intentional walks (5) and HR frequency (18.9 ABs per HR)

Mark Kotsay

2003 Season

Hobbled by nagging injuries, Mark Kotsay had his worst season since breaking into the majors in 1997. Beginning in April with a strained lower back and a protruding disk which required a cortisone injection, followed by a strained elbow in July, the former Golden Spikes award winner's season was one long trip to the trainer's table. His bat did show some signs of life after the break, but even that was tempered by continuing flare-ups with his back.

Hitting

Kotsay is a line-drive hitter who makes contact with a very high percentage of his swings. He's shown continued improvement turning on inside pitches, but chest-high fastballs still give him trouble. He has a selective eye at the plate and has no problem driving the ball to the opposite field if a pitcher works him outside. His walk rate continues to improve, which bodes well for a future power spike.

Baserunning & Defense

Normally a brilliant baserunner, Kotasy was overly aggressive at times last year, resulting in some needless outs. Perhaps it was an effort to compensate for his injury-induced struggles at the plate. He has above-average footspeed and will steal an occasional base. In the field, he is textbook-perfect, taking efficient routes and rarely getting fooled by any batted ball. He has a strong, accurate arm and has averaged nearly 14 assists a season for the last six years.

2004 Outlook

Last year's struggles along probably motivate Kotsay to be ready for 2004. On top of that, he'll go to camp with a new team. He'll start in center for Oakland, after the Padres dealt him in November for catcher Ramon Hernandez and outfielder Terrence Long. Kotsay joins a rebuilt Oakland outfield that wasn't productive offensively. He is a good bet to bat at the top of the lineup.

Position: CF
Bats: L **Throws:** L
Ht: 6' 0" **Wt:** 201

Opening Day Age: 28
Born: 12/2/75 in Whittier, CA
ML Seasons: 7
Pronunciation: KAH-tsay

Overall Statistics

	G	AB	R	H	D	T	HR	RBI	SB	BB	SO	Avg	OBP	Slg
'03	128	482	64	128	28	4	7	38	6	56	82	.266	.343	.384
Car.	868	3121	434	878	164	34	65	336	69	272	393	.281	.338	.418

Where He Hits the Ball

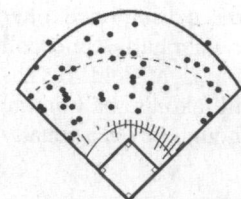
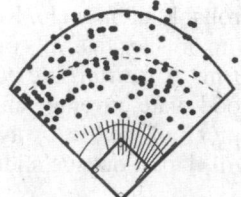

Vs. LHP   **Vs. RHP**

2003 Situational Stats

	AB	H	HR	RBI	Avg		AB	H	HR	RBI	Avg
Home	241	64	1	14	.266	LHP	140	33	1	9	.236
Road	241	64	6	24	.266	RHP	342	95	6	29	.278
First Half	265	65	4	22	.245	Sc Pos	105	23	1	27	.219
Scnd Half	217	63	3	16	.290	Clutch	74	13	1	5	.176

2003 Rankings (National League)

- 4th in fielding percentage in center field (.991) and lowest batting average with two strikes (.127)
- 8th in errors in center field (3)
- 9th in lowest batting average vs. lefthanded pitchers
- Led the Padres in doubles

Brian Lawrence

2003 Season

The 2003 season will not be among Brian Lawrence's favorites when his career is done. It marked only the second time in his professional career that he lost more games than he won, he posted his highest major league ERA by half a run, and his home run rate nearly doubled. However, the year was not a total loss. Lawrence won five of his final seven decisions while posting an ERA of 2.66 over the final two months of the season.

Pitching

Lefties had become increasingly comfortable against Lawrence in 2001-02 (.821 OPS allowed), so he added a sidearm fastball that tails away to complement the cutter he throws in on their hands. Although he has not completely neutralized the lefty advantage, he enjoyed a noticeable improvement in 2003. He uses a sinking fastball down in the zone to get most of his grounders, and he features a solid changeup and a hard-breaking slider as strikeout pitches. Both manager Bruce Bochy and GM Kevin Towers attributed his strong performance over the final two months to Lawrence going back to pitching off his sinker rather than his slider.

Defense & Hitting

Lawrence is a good-fielding pitcher with above-average range off the mound. He does a solid job holding runners, with a quick delivery home. Lawrence has improved as a hitter and can help himself bunting and swinging away.

2004 Outlook

Lawrence's improvement against lefties is encouraging, but there are still some signs that the Padres' 17th-round draft pick in 1998 might continue to struggle: his walk rate was up slightly while his strikeout rate and groundball-flyball ratio were down significantly. Still, his strong finish gave the Padres reason for optimism that Lawrence will pitch capably out of one of the middle spots in the rotation in 2004.

Position: SP
Bats: R **Throws:** R
Ht: 6' 0" **Wt:** 195

Opening Day Age: 27
Born: 5/14/76 in Fort Collins, CO
ML Seasons: 3

Overall Statistics

	W	L	Pct.	ERA	G	GS	Sv	IP	H	BB	SO	HR	Avg
'03	10	15	.400	4.19	33	33	0	210.2	206	57	116	27	.258
Car.	27	32	.458	3.83	95	79	0	535.1	543	143	349	53	.264

2003 Pitching Profile

	Brian Lawrence	NL Average
Overall Strike %	64.4	62.4
1st Pitch Strike %	62.7	58.4
Ratio	1.25	1.38
Strikeouts per 9 IP	4.96	6.65
Walks per 9 IP	2.44	3.42
Home Runs per 9 IP	1.15	1.05
Strikeout/Walk Ratio	2.04	1.94
Groundball/Flyball Ratio	1.61	1.29

2003 Situational Stats

	W	L	ERA	Sv	IP		AB	H	HR	RBI	Avg
Home	6	8	3.18	0	127.1	LHB	360	99	12	35	.275
Road	4	7	5.72	0	83.1	RHB	439	107	15	60	.244
First Half	5	10	4.45	0	129.1	Sc Pos	177	46	7	69	.260
Scnd Half	5	5	3.76	0	81.1	Clutch	50	16	2	10	.320

2003 Rankings (National League)

- 2nd in losses
- 3rd in highest ERA on the road
- 5th in lowest winning percentage
- 6th in GDPs induced (23)
- 7th in hit batsmen (11), fewest pitches thrown per batter (3.52) and fewest strikeouts per nine innings (5.0)
- Led the Padres in losses, games started, innings pitched, hits allowed, batters faced (884), hit batsmen (11), stolen bases allowed (11), runners caught stealing (6), GDPs induced (23), lowest on-base percentage allowed (.314), highest groundball flyball ratio allowed (1.6), fewest pitches thrown per batter (3.52), lowest ERA at home, most run support per nine innings (4.6) and fewest walks per nine innings (2.4)

San Diego

Mark Loretta

2003 Season

Mark Loretta entered the 2003 season with a mission to disprove two notions: that his range had declined to the point where he could only be a utility player, and that he didn't have the bat to play every day. He succeeded on both counts, posting career highs in home runs, RBI and OPS, while steadying the infield with one of his best defensive seasons. He boosted his profile and trade value substantially in June and July, hitting .364 and slugging almost .500. The Padres weren't persuaded by the trade offers, so in August, they signed him to a two-year extension.

Hitting

Loretta is a patient contact hitter who sprays the ball to all fields. Any strike that's down in the zone, particularly on the inner half, is likely to be hit hard. The only part of the hitting zone that he appears to struggle with is above the belt inside. He's an excellent bunter, hits behind the runners well and is comfortable going deep in the count, making him an ideal No. 2 hitter.

Baserunning & Defense

The surehanded Loretta has average range and a decent arm, but turns the double play surprisingly well. He's versatile, able to play short, second or third with above-average competence. Loretta is not an especially fast baserunner, but he is smart and efficient in taking extra bases when opposing outfielders misjudge his speed.

2004 Outlook

Although there was much speculation that Loretta would be traded to a contender at the deadline, the Padres decided to hold on to their batting leader. Not only will Loretta provide a veteran solution to two concerns for next year—second base and the No. 2 hitter—but the signing also allows San Diego to take its time bringing along quality second-base prospects Jake Gautreau, Bernie Castro and California League MVP Josh Barfield.

Position: 2B
Bats: R **Throws:** R
Ht: 6' 0" **Wt:** 186

Opening Day Age: 32
Born: 8/14/71 in Santa Monica, CA
ML Seasons: 9

Overall Statistics

	G	AB	R	H	D	T	HR	RBI	SB	BB	SO	Avg	OBP	Slg
'03	154	589	74	185	28	4	13	72	5	54	62	.314	.372	.441
Car.	971	3251	433	964	167	17	44	352	28	310	371	.297	.361	.399

Where He Hits the Ball

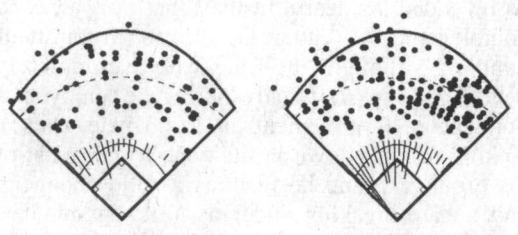

Vs. LHP   **Vs. RHP**

2003 Situational Stats

	AB	H	HR	RBI	Avg		AB	H	HR	RBI	Avg
Home	278	87	10	31	.313	LHP	189	58	4	20	.307
Road	311	98	3	41	.315	RHP	400	127	9	52	.318
First Half	335	104	6	37	.310	Sc Pos	136	47	1	57	.346
Scnd Half	254	81	7	35	.319	Clutch	84	30	2	17	.357

2003 Rankings (National League)

- 1st in fielding percentage at second base (.990)
- 4th in singles
- Led the Padres in batting average, at-bats, runs scored, hits, singles, doubles, total bases (260), RBI, times on base (242), GDPs (17), pitches seen (2,601), plate appearances (653), games played, on-base percentage, most pitches seen per plate appearance (3.98), lowest percentage of swings that missed (10.5), highest percentage of swings put into play (48.3), batting average with runners in scoring position

Xavier Nady

2003 Season

When Phil Nevin went down in spring training, Xavier Nady became the obvious choice as his replacement in the outfield. Nady made the choice rather easy for the Padres, hitting .333 in the spring and carrying the hot bat over through the first two months of the regular season. But a slump which started in mid-June sent him to the bench, and ultimately to the minors upon Nevin's return. Season ending surgery for Ryan Klesko in September afforded Nady another chance. He didn't disappoint, hitting .385 and slugging .564 in the final month.

Hitting

Nady is an aggressive hitter and likes to swing at the first pitch he can handle. He has enough power to hit 25-30 home runs given regular duty and makes enough contact to hit .275-.280. He's not a wild swinger, but his eagerness to swing can be used against him, inducing him to offer at marginal pitches rather than good ones to hit. He could benefit tremendously by learning more selectivity from hitting coach Dave Magadan.

Baserunning & Defense

Nady has average speed, but he runs hard and is fundamentally sound on the bases. In the field, his range and arm are average and his routes are occasionally geometric. The outfield is still fairly new to him—he was a corner infielder in college and the minors—but he learns quickly and could mature into a slightly above-average outfielder.

2004 Outlook

Nady was one of the players rumored to be going to Pittsburgh in exchange for Brian Giles, but after his strong September, the Padres are glad they didn't move him. Nady will vie for a starting outfield spot in 2004, competing with newly acquired Terrence Long and Gene Kingsale. Nady has the most potent bat of the three, so if he shows improvement on defense in spring training, he should secure the right-field spot. At worst, he will be a fourth outfielder and a backup at first base.

Position: RF
Bats: R **Throws:** R
Ht: 6' 0" **Wt:** 180

Opening Day Age: 25
Born: 11/14/78 in Salinas, CA
ML Seasons: 2
Pronunciation: ZAV-yer NAY-dee

Overall Statistics

	G	AB	R	H	D	T	HR	RBI	SB	BB	SO	Avg	OBP	Slg
'03	110	371	50	99	17	1	9	39	6	24	74	.267	.321	.391
Car.	111	372	51	100	17	1	9	39	6	24	74	.269	.323	.392

Where He Hits the Ball

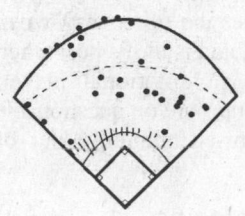 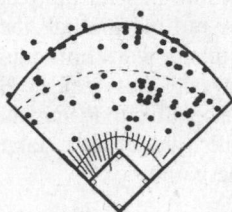

Vs. LHP   **Vs. RHP**

2003 Situational Stats

	AB	H	HR	RBI	Avg		AB	H	HR	RBI	Avg
Home	191	54	5	20	.283	LHP	106	33	1	8	.311
Road	180	45	4	19	.250	RHP	265	66	8	31	.249
First Half	319	83	7	31	.260	Sc Pos	101	22	2	27	.218
Scnd Half	52	16	2	8	.308	Clutch	59	13	2	6	.220

2003 Rankings (National League)

- 2nd in errors in right field (6)
- 10th in lowest batting average with the bases loaded (.111)
- Led the Padres in highest groundball-flyball ratio (1.7) and batting average vs. lefthanded pitchers

Phil Nevin

2003 Season

Phil Nevin's season nearly ended before it began when he separated his shoulder diving for a catch in a spring training game against the White Sox. The separation was severe enough to require surgery, and the general consensus was that he would be out for the season. Nevin used those doubts to accelerate his rehab and returned to the field on July 23. He proved he was all the way back from the injury by hitting .298 and slugging .585 in September.

Hitting

Nevin is very aggressive on inside pitches, taking savage cuts on just about anything that's middle-in over the plate. Despite his predilection for pulling the ball, he goes the other way when pitchers work him outside, and is at his best when he uses all fields. He's an emotional player, susceptible to losing his composure on questionable calls, which can take himself mentally out of the game.

Baserunning & Defense

Although he played the outfield for Detroit in 1997, Nevin does not look comfortable there, even on routine plays. He's tentative breaking on the ball and doesn't have the foot speed to cover much ground. He does have a strong and accurate arm. He's more comfortable in the infield, either at third or first, where he can simply react to the play. Nevin's lack of speed relegates him to station-to-station baserunning, but no one in the majors breaks up a double play with more enthusiasm.

2004 Outlook

General manager Kevin Towers has suggested that the Padres will undergo a number of changes this offseason. Reportedly, one of them involves moving Nevin to first base and returning Ryan Klesko to the outfield. Nevin should thrive in the No. 4 spot between lefties Brian Giles and Klesko. With an improved top of the lineup, he might be among the league leaders in RBI in 2004.

Position: 1B/RF
Bats: R **Throws:** R
Ht: 6' 2" **Wt:** 231

Opening Day Age: 33
Born: 1/19/71 in Fullerton, CA
ML Seasons: 9

Overall Statistics

	G	AB	R	H	D	T	HR	RBI	SB	BB	SO	Avg	OBP	Slg
'03	59	226	30	63	8	0	13	46	2	21	44	.279	.339	.487
Car.	839	2864	406	788	149	4	148	515	15	308	695	.275	.348	.485

Where He Hits the Ball

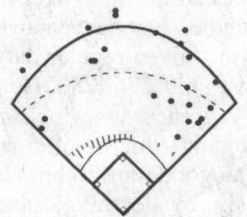 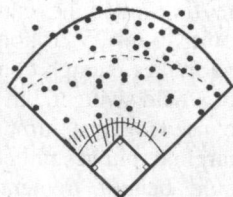

Vs. LHP   **Vs. RHP**

2003 Situational Stats

	AB	H	HR	RBI	Avg		AB	H	HR	RBI	Avg
Home	107	27	6	18	.252	LHP	63	22	9	27	.349
Road	119	36	7	28	.303	RHP	163	41	4	19	.252
First Half	0	0	0	0	–	Sc Pos	73	22	6	35	.301
Scnd Half	226	63	13	46	.279	Clutch	27	9	1	5	.333

2003 Rankings (National League)

- 6th in lowest cleanup slugging percentage (.487)

Jake Peavy

2003 Season

Jake Peavy was having an excellent sophomore season until July, when trade rumors putting him in a proposed deal to Pittsburgh began to surface. Once the deadline passed and he was assured by the Padres both publicly and privately that he wouldn't be going anywhere, Peavy resumed his strong season. Without his July struggles, Peavy's season ERA drops to 3.53. Peavy held opposing hitters to three hits or less in six of his 32 starts.

Pitching

Peavy can throw four pitches for strikes, the best of which is probably his changeup—a pitch GM Kevin Towers has gone on record as saying he'd like to see Peavy throw more. He also features a moving fastball that ranges from 91-95 MPH, as well as a slider and curve. He throws slightly across his body, but has good leg drive and generally solid pitching mechanics. Peavy is an intense competitor and possesses tremendous poise on the mound. If he has one flaw, it is that he can be too aggressive in the strike zone: two-thirds of the 33 home runs he surrendered were solo shots.

Defense & Hitting

Peavy looks like a major league hitter when he swings the bat, but he doesn't make much contact because it's always on the same plane. Ironically, he's a solid bunter, almost always putting the ball on the ground. He's an agile defender, but occasionally takes chances on balls that he'd be better off just pocketing. He controls the running game, allowing only seven steals in nearly 200 innings last year.

2004 Outlook

Because he is a few years younger, Peavy has a slight edge on Adam Eaton as the Padres' ace of the future. Like Kerry Wood and Mark Prior in Chicago, and Josh Beckett and Brad Penny in Florida, these two will anchor an excellent young staff for years to come.

Position: SP
Bats: R **Throws:** R
Ht: 6' 1" **Wt:** 180

Opening Day Age: 22
Born: 5/31/81 in Mobile, AL
ML Seasons: 2
Pronunciation: PEE-vee

Overall Statistics

	W	L	Pct.	ERA	G	GS	Sv	IP	H	BB	SO	HR	Avg
'03	12	11	.522	4.11	32	32	0	194.2	173	82	156	33	.238
Car.	18	18	.500	4.25	49	49	0	292.1	279	115	246	44	.250

2003 Pitching Profile

	Jake Peavy	NL Average
Overall Strike %	63.2	62.4
1st Pitch Strike %	58.8	58.4
Ratio	1.31	1.38
Strikeouts per 9 IP	7.21	6.65
Walks per 9 IP	3.79	3.42
Home Runs per 9 IP	1.53	1.05
Strikeout/Walk Ratio	1.90	1.94
Groundball/Flyball Ratio	0.97	1.29

2003 Situational Stats

	W	L	ERA	Sv	IP		AB	H	HR	RBI	Avg
Home	3	3	3.57	0	90.2	LHB	362	89	16	40	.246
Road	9	8	4.59	0	104.0	RHB	365	84	17	46	.230
First Half	8	7	4.55	0	116.2	Sc Pos	147	36	5	51	.245
Scnd Half	4	4	3.46	0	78.0	Clutch	40	13	1	3	.325

2003 Rankings (National League)

- 3rd in home runs allowed
- 5th in highest stolen-base percentage allowed (87.5) and most home runs allowed per nine innings (1.53)
- 7th in lowest fielding percentage at pitcher (.925)
- 8th in most pitches thrown per batter (3.90) and highest walks per nine innings (3.8)
- 10th in walks allowed, errors at pitcher (3) and lowest groundball-flyball ratio allowed (1.0)
- Led the Padres in sacrifice bunts (8), wins, home runs allowed, walks allowed, strikeouts, pitches thrown (3,226), lowest batting average allowed (.238), lowest ERA on the road and lowest batting average allowed with runners in scoring position

Ramon Vazquez

2003 Season

Ramon Vazquez was supposed to be the Padres' starting shortstop in 2003, but an abdominal strain limited him to just 116 games. Overall, his season was somewhat of a disappointment, in large part because of his continuing struggles to hit lefthanded pitching. The Padres were hoping that, like Ryan Klesko, he would be able to make the necessary adjustments to stay in the lineup everyday, but that just hasn't happened yet.

Hitting

With his inside-out swing, Vazquez prefers to guide the ball to the opposite field and use his speed to get extra bases on balls that find the seams of the outfield defense. He's a fairly disciplined hitter, rarely offering at balls out of the zone, and he rarely swings and misses. More than a third of his strikeouts come on called strikes, well above the MLB average. He looks outside and makes solid contact on just about anything on the outer half. Not surprisingly, fastballs inside give him the most trouble. He is fairly helpless against lefthanded pitching, making him more of a platoon player than a regular. He'll draw some walks and is a viable option as a leadoff hitter.

Baserunning & Defense

Vazquez has slightly above-average speed, but is an excellent baserunner and very efficient at going first to third on singles. His high success rate at stealing bases is more attributable to his ability to read pitchers than his footspeed. Vazquez' defense is about average. He doesn't have much range and doesn't charge balls in front of him particularly well, but he's surehanded and comfortable playing either short or second.

2004 Outlook

Vazquez will begin the 2004 season as the Padres' primary utility infielder and backup plan should Khalil Greene struggle at shortstop. They might also test Vazquez' versatility and let him play some center field.

Position: SS
Bats: L **Throws:** R
Ht: 5'11" **Wt:** 170

Opening Day Age: 27
Born: 8/21/76 in Aibonito, PR
ML Seasons: 3

Overall Statistics

	G	AB	R	H	D	T	HR	RBI	SB	BB	SO	Avg	OBP	Slg
'03	116	422	56	110	17	4	3	30	10	52	88	.261	.342	.341
Car.	261	880	111	234	38	9	5	66	17	97	170	.266	.339	.347

Where He Hits the Ball

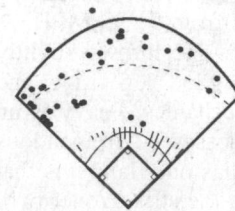 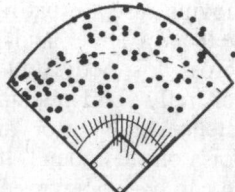

Vs. LHP   **Vs. RHP**

2003 Situational Stats

	AB	H	HR	RBI	Avg		AB	H	HR	RBI	Avg
Home	196	47	1	11	.240	LHP	116	26	0	7	.224
Road	226	63	2	19	.279	RHP	306	84	3	23	.275
First Half	232	64	3	22	.276	Sc Pos	90	19	0	24	.211
Scnd Half	190	46	0	8	.242	Clutch	64	17	0	9	.266

2003 Rankings (National League)

- 2nd in lowest fielding percentage at shortstop (.969)
- 4th in lowest batting average vs. lefthanded pitchers
- 9th in steals of third (3) and lowest on-base percentage for a leadoff hitter (.330)
- Led the Padres in strikeouts, stolen-base percentage (76.9), bunts in play (19) and steals of third (3)

Gary Bennett

Position: C
Bats: R **Throws:** R
Ht: 6' 0" **Wt:** 208

Opening Day Age: 31
Born: 4/17/72 in Waukegan, IL
ML Seasons: 8

Overall Statistics

	G	AB	R	H	D	T	HR	RBI	SB	BB	SO	Avg	OBP	Slg
'03	96	307	26	73	15	0	2	42	3	24	48	.238	.296	.306
Car.	315	939	86	237	40	3	11	108	4	75	155	.252	.313	.337

2003 Situational Stats

	AB	H	HR	RBI	Avg		AB	H	HR	RBI	Avg
Home	161	38	1	21	.236	LHP	101	22	1	15	.218
Road	146	35	1	21	.240	RHP	206	51	1	27	.248
First Half	163	31	1	16	.190	Sc Pos	92	27	1	40	.293
Scnd Half	144	42	1	26	.292	Clutch	52	11	1	6	.212

2003 Season

In 2003, Gary Bennett established himself as one of the best signal callers in the game. The Padres' top starters—Brian Lawrence, Jake Peavy and Adam Eaton—were a combined 29-22 with Bennett calling the pitches.

Hitting, Baserunning & Defense

Weak hitting probably will relegate Bennett to backup status for the majority of his career, but his game-calling skills should keep him on a big league roster. He's excellent at framing strikes and blocking pitches in the dirt, and he always seems to be in sync with what the pitcher wants to do. Basestealers have had success running on his arm. He's not a particularly dangerous hitter, as he has very little power and will chase pitches out of the zone. However, he generally makes contact with anything over the plate, so he's not a bad option on hit and run plays.

2004 Outlook

If Bennett re-ups with the Padres, it most likely will be as a backup. More likely, he will find work as a regular on a team that doesn't require his offensive contributions, much the way Joe Girardi did with the Yankees in the late 1990s.

Brian Buchanan

Position: RF/1B/LF
Bats: R **Throws:** R
Ht: 6' 4" **Wt:** 230

Opening Day Age: 30
Born: 7/21/73 in Miami, FL
ML Seasons: 4

Overall Statistics

	G	AB	R	H	D	T	HR	RBI	SB	BB	SO	Avg	OBP	Slg
'03	115	198	29	52	10	2	8	29	6	24	51	.263	.346	.455
Car.	306	704	98	186	35	3	30	97	9	66	190	.264	.332	.450

2003 Situational Stats

	AB	H	HR	RBI	Avg		AB	H	HR	RBI	Avg
Home	103	31	3	16	.301	LHP	106	32	6	18	.302
Road	95	21	5	13	.221	RHP	92	20	2	11	.217
First Half	136	41	7	25	.301	Sc Pos	68	16	3	22	.235
Scnd Half	62	11	1	4	.177	Clutch	43	10	3	7	.233

2003 Season

Perhaps best-known as NBA Hall of Famer John Havlicek's son-in-law, Brian Buchanan was a quality bench player in his first full season with the Padres. When a rash of injuries forced the club into a rebuilding mode early, Buchanan got an opportunity to work on his hitting fundamentals and demonstrate his versatility. He was tremendous in June, hitting five home runs and batting .289 with a 1.021 OPS.

Hitting, Baserunning & Defense

Buchanan's impressive power is generated almost solely from his arms and shoulders. Though pitchers still can climb the ladder against him, his strike-zone judgment improved dramatically under the tutelage of hitting coach Dave Magadan. He still has holes in his swing, but those holes no longer extend outside the strike zone. Buchanan is a slow runner, which makes him a liability on the basepaths and in the outfield. He did manage to swipe six bases in eight tries last year, however. His defense at first is adequate.

2004 Outlook

Although Buchanan's 2003 season looks statistically very similar to his previous campaigns, the improvements to his strike-zone judgment should make him a more valuable bench player in 2004.

Luther Hackman

Position: RP
Bats: R **Throws:** R
Ht: 6' 4" **Wt:** 195

Opening Day Age: 29
Born: 10/10/74 in
Columbus, MS
ML Seasons: 5

Overall Statistics

	W	L	Pct.	ERA	G	GS	Sv	IP	H	BB	SO	HR	Avg
'03	2	2	.500	5.17	65	0	0	76.2	78	36	48	7	.261
Car.	9	10	.474	5.09	149	9	1	212.0	226	105	128	26	.274

2003 Situational Stats

	W	L	ERA	Sv	IP		AB	H	HR	RBI	Avg
Home	1	2	6.25	0	40.1	LHB	122	29	4	12	.238
Road	1	0	3.96	0	36.1	RHB	177	49	3	34	.277
First Half	2	2	3.73	0	50.2	Sc Pos	87	28	2	39	.322
Scnd Half	0	0	7.96	0	26.0	Clutch	91	26	1	15	.286

2003 Season

Luther Hackman came to the Padres in a cost-cutting trade with the Cardinals last winter in exchange for Brett Tomko. Hackman was supposed to fill a long-relief role, but injuries in the bullpen never allowed him to settle in. He did post sub-3.00 ERAs in April, June and August, but his good work was offset by a woeful May (8.03) and a horrific September (18.90).

Pitching, Defense & Hitting

Hackman has a tendency to nibble on the edges of the plate, despite having a fastball that ranges from 92-95 MPH that he can cut or sink. He'll also show a breaking pitch, but it doesn't break very sharply, and batters will hit it hard when it's in the strike zone. He has a slow delivery and a tendency to ignore baserunners, resulting in a 100 percent stolen-base rate against him. He's a weak hitter but adequate defensively.

2004 Outlook

It is unlikely that Hackman will return to the Padres, but he throws hard enough and has been effective enough at times over the last three years to warrant someone offering him a major league roster spot.

Trevor Hoffman

Position: RP
Bats: R **Throws:** R
Ht: 6' 0" **Wt:** 205

Opening Day Age: 36
Born: 10/13/67 in
Bellflower, CA
ML Seasons: 11

Overall Statistics

	W	L	Pct.	ERA	G	GS	Sv	IP	H	BB	SO	HR	Avg
'03	0	0	–	2.00	9	0	0	9.0	7	3	11	1	.212
Car.	45	44	.506	2.78	641	0	352	710.0	533	217	808	66	.205

2003 Situational Stats

	W	L	ERA	Sv	IP		AB	H	HR	RBI	Avg
Home	0	0	3.00	0	6.0	LHB	22	4	1	1	.182
Road	0	0	0.00	0	3.0	RHB	11	3	0	1	.273
First Half	0	0	–	0	0.0	Sc Pos	12	1	0	1	.083
Scnd Half	0	0	2.00	0	9.0	Clutch	4	1	0	0	.250

2003 Season

A season without AC/DC's "Hells Bells" blaring through the speakers in the ninth inning? It was a reality that both the Padres and their fans nearly had to deal with when Trevor Hoffman went down in spring training with more problems with his surgically repaired shoulder. After a second surgery, he returned in September and his performance was classic Hoffman.

Pitching, Defense & Hitting

Despite a fastball that rarely reaches 90 MPH, Hoffman is still one of the best closers in history. His changeup is widely considered the best in the game. Hoffman will throw it in any count and will double or triple up on it to the same hitter. He also throws a slider and curve to give batters something else to think about. Hoffman began his professional career as a shortstop, so he can handle the bat. His high leg kick hinders his ability to field, and he does not hold runners particularly well.

2004 Outlook

Hoffman's option was bought out in early November, and the Padres signed him to a one-year, $2.5 million incentive-laden contract with a 2005 option. He will open the new Petco Park as the team's closer. . . Get ready to fire up the AC/DC.

Kevin Jarvis

Position: SP
Bats: L **Throws:** R
Ht: 6' 2" **Wt:** 200

Opening Day Age: 34
Born: 8/1/69 in Lexington, KY
ML Seasons: 9

Overall Statistics

	W	L	Pct.	ERA	G	GS	Sv	IP	H	BB	SO	HR	Avg
'03	4	8	.333	5.87	16	16	0	92.0	113	32	49	15	.304
Car.	33	46	.418	5.83	164	114	1	734.1	868	239	431	140	.294

2003 Situational Stats

	W	L	ERA	Sv	IP		AB	H	HR	RBI	Avg
Home	2	3	5.27	0	41.0	LHB	163	47	5	18	.288
Road	2	5	6.35	0	51.0	RHB	209	66	10	40	.316
First Half	2	2	4.84	0	35.1	Sc Pos	96	33	2	42	.344
Scnd Half	2	6	6.51	0	56.2	Clutch	20	3	0	1	.150

2003 Season

Kevin Jarvis missed the first two months of the season recovering from offseason surgery on his pitching elbow. His first four starts were shaky, but when rumors started floating around in July that he was on the trading block, Jarvis suddenly became one of the best pitchers in baseball, posting a 2.20 ERA for the month. However, his elbow started hurting again in August, and Jarvis lost his last six decisions.

Pitching, Defense & Hitting

Jarvis pitches aggressively, spotting his mid- to high-80s fastball in all quadrants of the strike zone. He'll pitch to both edges of the plate with his assortment of average breaking pitches, daring hitters to expand their zone. He's a solid fielder off the mound and a good hitter for a pitcher, but easy to run on.

2004 Outlook

Not blessed with great talent, Jarvis maximizes his ability with headiness and guile. He's due another year on his contract, but the Padres have an increasingly crowded starting rotation picture. Ideally, they would like to move him, giving Jarvis a chance to start elsewhere and making room for younger pitchers.

Scott Linebrink

Position: RP
Bats: R **Throws:** R
Ht: 6' 2" **Wt:** 200

Opening Day Age: 27
Born: 8/4/76 in Austin, TX
ML Seasons: 4

Overall Statistics

	W	L	Pct.	ERA	G	GS	Sv	IP	H	BB	SO	HR	Avg
'03	3	2	.600	3.31	52	6	0	92.1	93	36	68	9	.270
Car.	3	2	.600	4.14	94	6	0	139.0	148	63	107	15	.277

2003 Situational Stats

	W	L	ERA	Sv	IP		AB	H	HR	RBI	Avg
Home	3	0	3.99	0	47.1	LHB	149	41	3	13	.275
Road	0	2	2.60	0	45.0	RHB	196	52	6	28	.265
First Half	1	2	2.94	0	64.1	Sc Pos	93	19	1	30	.204
Scnd Half	2	0	4.18	0	28.0	Clutch	52	15	2	7	.288

2003 Season

Scott Linebrink opened the season as Houston's sixth option for their rotation. He got his opportunity when Brian Moehler was injured in late April. While moderately effective in the role, he made it to the sixth inning just once. The Astros tried to send him to the minors for refinement, but the Padres claimed him off waivers on May 29. San Diego put Linebrink back in the pen, where he re-asserted himself as a solid major league pitcher.

Pitching, Defense & Hitting

Linebrink throws a straight fastball in the low 90s, but can tune it up to 94-95 MPH. He complements it with a cut fastball that tails away from lefties, and a slider that is effective down and away to righties. He has better velocity up in the zone. At the plate, he takes professional-looking swings and will hit a fastball hard. He is an average fielder who doesn't log many chances and is so-so at holding runners.

2004 Outlook

Linebrink had some trouble with his knee in September, but it doesn't figure to affect his performance in 2004. He pitched well enough to return as one of the Padres' long relievers, but his flyball tendencies might not play well at Petco.

Gary Matthews Jr.

Position: CF/RF/LF
Bats: B **Throws:** R
Ht: 6' 3" **Wt:** 225

Opening Day Age: 29
Born: 8/25/74 in San Francisco, CA
ML Seasons: 5

Overall Statistics

	G	AB	R	H	D	T	HR	RBI	SB	BB	SO	Avg	OBP	Slg
'03	144	468	71	116	31	2	6	42	12	43	95	.248	.314	.361
Car.	510	1412	216	341	72	9	31	145	40	170	301	.242	.324	.371

2003 Situational Stats

	AB	H	HR	RBI	Avg		AB	H	HR	RBI	Avg
Home	236	54	3	20	.229	LHP	129	37	1	9	.287
Road	232	62	3	22	.267	RHP	339	79	5	33	.233
First Half	306	74	3	30	.242	Sc Pos	112	26	3	36	.232
Scnd Half	162	42	3	12	.259	Clutch	83	20	1	7	.241

2003 Season

The Padres plucked Gary Matthews Jr. from the waiver wire in May after the Orioles tried to send him down to work on his swing. Once one of the Padres' top prospects, he posted one of the team's better on-base percentages and led the club in steals.

Hitting, Baserunning & Defense

The switch-hitting Matthews uses the same approach from both sides of the plate: look for something down in the zone that he can lift and drive. He especially likes fastballs on the inner half. He's an excellent hitter when ahead early in the count, but gets panicky if he falls behind. He will get himself out on sliders away. In the outfield, Matthews takes good routes, covers a lot of ground and has a strong, accurate arm. His above-average speed is an asset on the basepaths, but he needs to improve his reads as a basestealer.

2004 Outlook

Matthews is due a raise through arbitration, and keeping him as a fourth outfielder with a multi-million-dollar salary wasn't in the Padres' plans. In November, Matthews was claimed off waivers by Atlanta. He would be a part-time player there.

Miguel Ojeda

Position: C
Bats: R **Throws:** R
Ht: 6' 2" **Wt:** 190

Opening Day Age: 29
Born: 1/29/75 in Sonora, Mexico
ML Seasons: 1

Overall Statistics

	G	AB	R	H	D	T	HR	RBI	SB	BB	SO	Avg	OBP	Slg
'03	61	141	13	33	6	0	4	22	1	18	26	.234	.331	.362
Car.	61	141	13	33	6	0	4	22	1	18	26	.234	.331	.362

2003 Situational Stats

	AB	H	HR	RBI	Avg		AB	H	HR	RBI	Avg
Home	70	16	3	12	.229	LHP	43	10	2	6	.233
Road	71	17	1	10	.239	RHP	98	23	2	16	.235
First Half	67	16	2	17	.239	Sc Pos	39	13	1	19	.333
Scnd Half	74	17	2	5	.230	Clutch	25	7	1	6	.280

2003 Season

Miguel Ojeda tormented Mexican League pitchers for the first couple of months of the season, hitting .327 with power, before the Padres signed him and put him on the major league roster. The transition wasn't easy, but Ojeda showed some promise when given an opportunity to play regularly in July and August. However, he was relegated to a backup role in September because of Gary Bennett's superior game-calling skills.

Hitting, Baserunning & Defense

Ojeda does an adequate job behind the plate, framing pitches and keeping the ball in front of him. He has an average arm and needs help from his pitchers to control the running game. His calling card is his bat. He has a good knowledge of the strike zone, doesn't often chase pitches and is a surprisingly good contact hitter. He's a good mistake hitter as well, but his slider speed bat leaves him vulnerable to being overpowered by the better fastballs in the league.

2004 Outlook

Ojeda will open the 2004 season as Ramon Hernandez' backup. Ojeda's defense can continue to develop under a talented mentor, and the Mexican League veteran should provide some offensive punch off the bench.

Brandon Villafuerte

Position: RP
Bats: R **Throws:** R
Ht: 5'11" **Wt:** 165

Opening Day Age: 28
Born: 12/17/75 in Hilo, HI
ML Seasons: 4
Pronunciation: vila-FERT-tee

Overall Statistics

	W	L	Pct.	ERA	G	GS	Sv	IP	H	BB	SO	HR	Avg
'03	0	2	.000	4.20	31	0	2	40.2	39	26	34	7	.252
Car.	1	4	.200	4.14	71	0	3	82.2	84	46	64	12	.265

2003 Situational Stats

	W	L	ERA	Sv	IP		AB	H	HR	RBI	Avg
Home	0	1	2.42	2	22.1	LHB	60	12	3	9	.200
Road	0	1	6.38	0	18.1	RHB	95	27	4	15	.284
First Half	0	2	4.60	2	29.1	Sc Pos	41	11	0	13	.268
Scnd Half	0	0	3.18	0	11.1	Clutch	46	13	2	6	.283

2003 Season

After a sensational 2002 season, much was expected of Brandon Villafuerte in 2003. When Trevor Hoffman and Jay Witasick both went down with injuries in spring training, it was expected that Villafuerte would assume the closer's role. Unfortunately, he struggled with both his control and the longball, so much so that the Padres optioned him to Triple-A Portland before the end of May. A proposed trade to Montreal never materialized, and Villafuerte was recalled to finish September in San Diego.

Pitching, Defense & Hitting

Villafuerte is not overpowering. His fastball sits around 92 MPH and tails into righthanders. He also throws a sharp-breaking slider that breaks away from them. His delivery commits him to the first base side of the mound, but he's quick on his feet and does a decent job fielding his position.

2004 Outlook

The Hawaii native struggled with a shoulder strain for part of the season, but did not pitch particularly well even when healthy. One of the Padres' publicly stated priorities this winter will be to upgrade their bullpen, virtually assuring that Villafuerte will be pitching in a new city in 2004.

Jay Witasick

Position: RP
Bats: R **Throws:** R
Ht: 6' 4" **Wt:** 235

Opening Day Age: 31
Born: 8/28/72 in Baltimore, MD
ML Seasons: 8
Pronunciation: wi-TASS-ik

Overall Statistics

	W	L	Pct.	ERA	G	GS	Sv	IP	H	BB	SO	HR	Avg
'03	3	7	.300	4.53	46	0	2	45.2	42	25	42	6	.244
Car.	29	35	.453	4.89	245	56	3	552.1	609	261	474	80	.280

2003 Situational Stats

	W	L	ERA	Sv	IP		AB	H	HR	RBI	Avg
Home	1	3	4.44	0	24.1	LHB	65	19	1	11	.292
Road	2	4	4.64	2	21.1	RHB	107	23	5	20	.215
First Half	1	1	3.21	2	14.0	Sc Pos	68	18	1	25	.265
Scnd Half	2	6	5.12	0	31.2	Clutch	133	29	5	24	.218

2003 Season

When Trevor Hoffman went down in spring training, Jay Witasick was the frontrunner for the Padres' closer role. But in late March, an elbow strain caused by an inflamed ligament ended that opportunity, and Witasick didn't return to regular duty until mid-June. By then, Rod Beck was establishing himself as the closer, and Witasick was left to less glamorous duty.

Pitching, Defense & Hitting

All of Witasick's pitches have above-average movement, making it hard for him not only to throw strikes, but to get calls on pitches that somehow break back into the zone. His fastball runs consistently around 94 MPH and he can sink or tail it into righthanders. His curve has a late tail into lefties. He is a suspect fielder who will rush his throws, and he does not hold runners very well. At the plate, he has little value.

2004 Outlook

General manager Kevin Towers has made building a strong bullpen a priority this winter and a healthy Witasick is a solid piece to that puzzle. If he returns to his 2001-2002 form, he could vie for the primary setup role.

San Diego

Other San Diego Padres

Mike Bynum (Pos: LHP, Age: 26)

	W	L	Pct.	ERA	G	GS	Sv	IP	H	BB	SO	HR	Avg
'03	1	4	.200	8.75	13	5	0	36.0	44	15	35	14	.297
Car.	2	4	.333	7.25	27	8	0	63.1	77	30	52	17	.302

Bynum has had some success as a starter in the minors, but he has been used mostly out of the bullpen in the bigs. He has an electric slider, but little else, and may be destined for situational usage. 2004 Outlook: C

Jermaine Clark (Pos: LF, Age: 27, Bats: L)

	G	AB	R	H	D	T	HR	RBI	SB	BB	SO	Avg	OBP	Slg
'03	25	48	2	8	2	0	0	7	2	6	5	.167	.250	.208
Car.	28	48	3	8	2	0	0	7	2	6	5	.167	.250	.208

After hitting better than .300 in his first three minor league seasons, Clark has not reached that mark in this millennium. He could help a club with his speed, but full-time play looks to be a reach. 2004 Outlook: C

Clay Condrey (Pos: RHP, Age: 28)

	W	L	Pct.	ERA	G	GS	Sv	IP	H	BB	SO	HR	Avg
'03	1	2	.333	8.47	9	6	0	34.0	43	21	25	7	.305
Car.	2	4	.333	5.49	18	9	0	60.2	63	29	41	8	.270

After four years working out of the bullpen, Condrey went 10-4 as a starter in Triple-A in 2002. He battled a left oblique strain last year, but should contend for a spot on the Padres' staff in 2004. 2004 Outlook: C

Roger Deago (Pos: LHP, Age: 26)

	W	L	Pct.	ERA	G	GS	Sv	IP	H	BB	SO	HR	Avg
'03	0	1	.000	7.84	2	2	0	10.1	11	8	10	0	.282
Car.	0	1	.000	7.84	2	2	0	10.1	11	8	10	0	.282

The Padres signed Deago out of the Mexican League, and he got knocked around in two starts for the big club. The 26-year-old knows how to pitch and could find himself in the rotation mix this year. 2004 Outlook: C

Wiki Gonzalez (Pos: C, Age: 29, Bats: R)

	G	AB	R	H	D	T	HR	RBI	SB	BB	SO	Avg	OBP	Slg
'03	24	65	1	13	5	0	0	10	0	5	13	.200	.264	.277
Car.	269	756	65	180	36	3	17	99	3	74	104	.238	.312	.361

Apparently expecting to be handed the full-time catching job, Gonzalez came to spring training out of shape. He was shipped out in May and never came back. His days as a Padre probably are over. 2004 Outlook: C

Dave Hansen (Pos: 1B/3B, Age: 35, Bats: L)

	G	AB	R	H	D	T	HR	RBI	SB	BB	SO	Avg	OBP	Slg
'03	110	135	13	33	4	1	2	15	1	23	25	.244	.358	.333
Car.	1084	1612	167	427	74	6	31	199	4	253	292	.265	.365	.376

In his debut season with the Padres, Hansen batted just .164 as a pinch-hitter. He will continue to serve as one of their first choices off the bench and play a bit at both infield corners. 2004 Outlook: C

Randy Keisler (Pos: LHP, Age: 28)

	W	L	Pct.	ERA	G	GS	Sv	IP	H	BB	SO	HR	Avg
'03	0	1	.000	12.00	2	2	0	6.0	7	7	5	3	.292
Car.	2	3	.400	7.62	16	13	0	67.1	75	49	47	16	.279

The one-time hotshot Yankees prospect never has achieved any major league success. Recovering from 2002 shoulder surgery, Keisler bounced through four organizations last year. 2004 Outlook: C

Keith Lockhart (Pos: 2B, Age: 39, Bats: L)

	G	AB	R	H	D	T	HR	RBI	SB	BB	SO	Avg	OBP	Slg
'03	62	95	18	23	5	1	3	8	0	13	19	.242	.339	.411
Car.	979	2268	290	591	117	17	44	268	30	195	268	.261	.319	.385

After six seasons with Atlanta, Lockhart returned to his original club only to total his fewest at-bats since his debut year. Released by the Padres, the end is near for the 39-year-old. 2004 Outlook: D

Carlton Loewer (Pos: RHP, Age: 30)

	W	L	Pct.	ERA	G	GS	Sv	IP	H	BB	SO	HR	Avg
'03	1	2	.333	6.65	5	5	0	21.2	35	8	11	3	.368
Car.	10	18	.357	6.12	48	41	0	238.1	302	76	118	32	.314

Shoulder woes have allowed Loewer to pitch just 26 innings over the last four major league seasons. No longer a prospect at age 30, he will have a rough time making a big league roster this season. 2004 Outlook: C

Mike Matthews (Pos: LHP, Age: 30)

	W	L	Pct.	ERA	G	GS	Sv	IP	H	BB	SO	HR	Avg
'03	6	4	.600	4.45	77	0	0	64.2	65	29	44	4	.271
Car.	11	9	.550	4.14	189	10	1	208.2	197	101	158	22	.254

Snagged off the waiver wire right before Opening Day, Matthews played a significant role in the Padres' bullpen. After holding lefties to a .172 average coming in, they hit .294 off him last year. 2004 Outlook: C

Donaldo Mendez (Pos: SS, Age: 25, Bats: R)

	G	AB	R	H	D	T	HR	RBI	SB	BB	SO	Avg	OBP	Slg
'03	26	84	10	19	6	0	2	9	1	7	32	.226	.298	.369
Car.	72	202	21	37	8	1	3	14	2	12	69	.183	.245	.277

A lifetime .230 hitter in the minors, Mendez will have to field his position brilliantly to stay in the show. He would appear to have a future as a utility infielder, but not with the Padres, who released him in December. 2004 Outlook: C

Charles Nagy (Pos: RHP, Age: 36)

	W	L	Pct.	ERA	G	GS	Sv	IP	H	BB	SO	HR	Avg
'03	0	2	.000	4.38	5	0	0	12.1	15	3	7	0	.313
Car.	129	105	.551	4.51	318	297	0	1954.2	2188	586	1242	217	.284

Since winning 17 games for the Indians in 1999, Nagy has tossed a total of 188.1 innings with a record of 8-19 and a 7.46 ERA. Recurring elbow problems probably have finished his career. 2004 Outlook: D

Michael Rivera (Pos: C, Age: 27, Bats: R)

	G	AB	R	H	D	T	HR	RBI	SB	BB	SO	Avg	OBP	Slg
'03	19	53	2	9	1	0	1	2	0	5	11	.170	.241	.245
Car.	62	197	15	43	11	1	2	14	0	9	48	.218	.255	.315

Rivera moved from the Tigers to the Padres in November 2002 and then to the White Sox last year. He has hit 65 homers in the minors over the last three seasons, but has had trouble making contact in the bigs. 2004 Outlook: C

Joe Roa (Pos: RHP, Age: 32)

	W	L	Pct.	ERA	G	GS	Sv	IP	H	BB	SO	HR	Avg
'00	1	3	.250	6.14	28	4	0	51.1	60	10	29	11	.610
Car.	7	13	.350	5.10	72	19	0	196.0	246	48	107	30	.313

Roa pitched for four clubs in 2003, three in the majors and one in Triple-A. Despite posting a 121-66 lifetime record in 14 seasons in the minors, he has not had much major league success. The Twins signed him to a minor league deal in December. 2004 Outlook: C

Todd Sears (Pos: 1B, Age: 28, Bats: L)

	G	AB	R	H	D	T	HR	RBI	SB	BB	SO	Avg	OBP	Slg
'03	33	73	9	18	3	0	2	11	0	7	18	.247	.317	.370
Car.	40	85	11	22	5	0	2	11	0	7	19	.259	.319	.388

Acquired from the Twins in a September trade, Sears will fight for playing time with the Padres. He not only is a lifetime .293 hitter in the minors, but also is slick around the first-base bag as well. 2004 Outlook: C

Brian Tollberg (Pos: RHP, Age: 31)

	W	L	Pct.	ERA	G	GS	Sv	IP	H	BB	SO	HR	Avg
'03	0	2	.000	6.97	3	3	0	10.1	9	4	2	1	.231
Car.	15	16	.484	4.48	53	52	0	307.1	356	83	182	40	.292

Tollberg went 10-4 for the Padres in 2001 but has suffered with a fractured finger and a bum elbow in the two years since then. While his stuff is average at best, he has the savvy to succeed in the majors. 2004 Outlook: C

Shane Victorino (Pos: CF/LF, Age: 23, Bats: B)

	G	AB	R	H	D	T	HR	RBI	SB	BB	SO	Avg	OBP	Slg
'03	36	73	8	11	2	0	0	4	7	7	17	.151	.232	.178
Car.	36	73	8	11	2	0	0	4	7	7	17	.151	.232	.178

Victorino rode the Rule 5 highway from the Dodgers to the Padres and back again last year. The fleet-footed center fielder is a righthanded version of Dave Roberts and could contend for playing time in 2004. 2004 Outlook: C

Kevin Walker (Pos: LHP, Age: 27)

	W	L	Pct.	ERA	G	GS	Sv	IP	H	BB	SO	HR	Avg
'03	0	0	–	5.40	11	0	0	6.2	5	5	5	1	.200
Car.	7	2	.778	4.24	108	0	0	93.1	71	56	89	8	.209

Elbow troubles have allowed Walker to pitch just 26.2 innings over the last three seasons. He has talent when healthy; opponents have hit just .209 against him in his 108 big league games. The Pads re-signed him in December. 2004 Outlook: C

San Diego

663

San Diego Padres Minor League Prospects

Organization Overview:

Like the major league team, the Padres' minor league clubs did not fare well in the face of adversity. None of the upper level teams finished with a winning record in 2003, and several top prospects suffered down seasons and/or serious injuries. The Triple-A Portland Beavers' season was marred when an unruly Las Vegas fan hit Tagg Bozied in the head with a promotional stress-relief ball, inciting a brawl in which 19 Beaver players were later suspended. The year wasn't a complete disaster, however, as two of San Diego's top 10 draft picks in 2003—catcher Colt Morton and third baseman Billy Hogan—showed considerable promise in their professional debuts.

Josh Barfield

Position: 2B   **Opening Day Age:** 21
Bats: R **Throws:** R   **Born:** 12/17/82 in
Ht: 6' 0" **Wt:** 185   Spring, TX

Recent Statistics

	G	AB	R	H	D	T	HR	RBI	SB	BB	SO	Avg
2002 A Ft. Wayne	129	536	73	164	22	3	8	57	26	26	105	.306
2002 A Lk Elsinore	6	23	2	2	0	0	0	4	0	1	4	.087
2003 A Lk Elsinore	135	549	99	185	46	6	16	128	16	50	122	.337

Barfield was viewed as a slap-hitting infielder with strike-zone deficiencies. That was before the son of former big league slugger Jesse Barfield led the minor leagues in hits, doubles, total bases and RBI, on his way to the 2003 California League MVP *despite* playing the season with ligament damage in his right wrist that required season-ending surgery in August. The prognosis is good for a full recovery by spring training. Although Barfield is a very good athlete with good instincts and soft hands, unless he continues to improve his play around second, a move to left field might be in his future. He'll open 2004 in Double-A and challenge for a regular major league job no later than 2005.

Bernie Castro

Position: 2B   **Opening Day Age:** 24
Bats: B **Throws:** R   **Born:** 7/14/79 in Santo
Ht: 5' 10" **Wt:** 165   Domingo, DR

Recent Statistics

	G	AB	R	H	D	T	HR	RBI	SB	BB	SO	Avg
2002 AA Mobile	109	419	61	109	13	3	0	32	53	52	67	.260
2003 AAA Portland	105	424	57	131	17	5	2	24	49	25	43	.309

Castro was acquired in 2002 from the Yankees in exchange for outfielder Kevin Reese, and he has been among the league leaders in stolen bases each year since. This year, Castro lifted 49 bags before a knee injury ended his season in August. He won consecutive batting titles in the Dominican League in each of the last two winters and has posted on-base figures of at least .345 in each of the last four minor league campaigns. He's a very disruptive force from the left side of the plate, and may need to abandon switch-hitting as he moves up. Although only an average fielder, Castro looks like another steal in GM Kevin Towers' trading record.

Justin Germano

Position: P   **Opening Day Age:** 21
Bats: R **Throws:** R   **Born:** 8/6/82 in
Ht: 6' 2" **Wt:** 197   Pasadena, CA

Recent Statistics

	W	L	ERA	G	GS	Sv	IP	H	R	BB	SO	HR
2002 A Ft. Wayne	12	5	3.18	24	24	0	155.2	166	63	19	119	14
2002 A Lk Elsinore	2	0	0.95	3	3	0	19.0	12	3	5	18	1
2003 A Lk Elsinore	9	5	4.23	19	19	0	110.2	127	61	25	78	4
2003 AA Mobile	2	5	4.34	9	9	0	58.0	60	34	13	44	6

Like Brian Lawrence, Germano does not have overpowering stuff. But he does have excellent command of an 88-MPH fastball with movement, a changeup and a big, sharp-breaking curve. Germano gets into trouble when he throws too many strikes, but he has good poise and is effective at keeping the ball in the park. Once he learns how to set up hitters to chase his breaking pitches, he'll become a solid No. 3-type starter. A 13th-round pick out of high school in 2000, Germano is on target for a permanent spot in the 2005 Padres' rotation, although he probably will make an appearance this year.

Khalil Greene

Position: SS   **Opening Day Age:** 24
Bats: R **Throws:** R   **Born:** 10/21/79 in Butler,
Ht: 5' 10" **Wt:** 210   PA

Recent Statistics

	G	AB	R	H	D	T	HR	RBI	SB	BB	SO	Avg
2003 AA Mobile	59	229	20	63	17	2	3	20	2	16	55	.275
2003 AAA Portland	76	319	42	92	19	0	10	47	5	20	52	.288
2003 NL San Diego	20	65	8	14	4	1	2	6	0	4	19	.215

Greene has rocketed through the system and is penciled in as the Padres' Opening Day shortstop in 2004. The 13th overall pick of the 2002 draft is blessed with above-average ability in all facets of the game, yet his off-the-charts makeup and poise allow him to play above his tools. Greene is a line-drive hitter with 20-homer potential, though he gets himself into trouble when he becomes too pull-conscious. In the field, he has good range to his left, and what he may lack going to his right he makes up for with a strong, accurate arm. Although his discipline at the plate needs work, Greene is coachable—Padres hitting coach Dave Magadan has worked wonders with lesser talents.

Ben Howard

Position: P **Opening Day Age:** 25
Bats: R **Throws:** R **Born:** 1/15/79 in
Ht: 6' 2" **Wt:** 190 Danville, IL

Recent Statistics

	W	L	ERA	G	GS	Sv	IP	H	R	BB	SO	HR
2003 AAA Portland	7	9	4.55	22	22	0	130.2	118	69	49	68	17
2003 NL San Diego	1	3	3.63	6	6	0	34.2	31	17	15	24	10

Howard is a fireballing righthander capable of generating mid-90s heat. He also works with a hard-breaking slider and improving changeup to keep hitters from hitting dead red. In 2002, he tried to pitch through elbow troubles and suffered from poor control and a significant reduction in velocity. This year, he struggled with control before tearing a cartilage in his right knee, causing him to miss more than a month of the season. The Padres gave him a look in September, and he gave them something to consider for next season with two excellent starts against division rivals and playoff contenders Arizona and Los Angeles.

Jon Knott

Position: OF-1B **Opening Day Age:** 25
Bats: R **Throws:** R **Born:** 8/4/78 in
Ht: 6' 3" **Wt:** 230 Manassas, VA

Recent Statistics

	G	AB	R	H	D	T	HR	RBI	SB	BB	SO	Avg
2002 A Ft. Wayne	37	126	19	42	12	3	3	18	2	17	33	.333
2002 A Lk Elsinore	93	367	55	125	33	8	8	73	5	46	68	.341
2003 AA Mobile	127	432	83	109	32	0	27	82	5	82	117	.252
2003 AAA Portland	7	26	5	9	1	0	1	5	0	4	3	.346

Knott pushed himself into the Padres' long-term outfield picture with another solid season in 2003. After winning the high Class-A California League batting title and being named the Padres' co-Minor League Player of the Year in 2002, the non-drafted signee from Mississippi State was a Double-A Southern League All-Star this year. The line-drive hitter with excellent plate discipline and improving power has only average range in the outfield, but he possesses a strong enough arm to play anywhere. Wherever he ends up in the field, he won't be a liability because his work ethic is second to none.

Tim Stauffer

Position: P **Opening Day Age:** 21
Bats: R **Throws:** R **Born:** 6/2/82 in Saratoga
Ht: 6' 2" **Wt:** 205 Springs, NY

Recent Statistics: No major or minor league playing experience.

A 2002 All-American from the University of Richmond, Stauffer was the fourth overall pick in the 2003 draft. He reported a weakness in his shoulder before signing with the Padres, which probably cost him a couple million dollars in signing bonus, but his honesty earned him far more in moral capital within the organization. Stauffer has excellent control of a moving

four-seam fastball that runs 89-94 MPH, a lively two-seamer he can cut around 92 MPH, a change and a knuckle curve. With excellent poise and pitching instincts, and a mechanically sound delivery, he should push for a spot in the rotation no later than 2005.

Dennis Tankersley

Position: P **Opening Day Age:** 25
Bats: R **Throws:** R **Born:** 2/24/79 in Troy,
Ht: 6' 2" **Wt:** 185 MO

Recent Statistics

	W	L	ERA	G	GS	Sv	IP	H	R	BB	SO	HR
2003 AAA Portland	8	11	4.65	27	27	0	151.0	149	82	67	148	15
2003 NL San Diego	0	1	—	1	1	0	0.0	3	7	4	0	0

In 2002, Tankersley was neck-and-neck with Jake Peavy for the honor of most promising Padres pitching prospect. But struggles with mechanics and some off-the-field issues left Tankersley thinking about too many things, and he was demoted back to the minors. Overthinking continued to plague him in his disastrous start against the Giants this year, as he tried to throw too many sinking two-seamers down in the zone to get groundballs, instead of challenging the hitters with his mid-90s four-seamer up. Still, the Padres hope his solid performance at Triple-A this year gives reason for optimism. In addition to two plus fastballs, Tankersley features an excellent slider that he'll overuse sometimes, as well as an improving changeup.

Others to Watch

Righty **Brad Baker** (23) had struggled with control since coming from the Red Sox in 2002, but he may have found his niche with an early season switch to relief work. He put himself back on the prospect map with a dominating season at high Class-A Lake Elsinore. . . After setting an Arizona Fall League record for most home runs in 2002, first baseman **Tagg Bozied** (24) opened the 2003 season battling a sprained ankle. Once healthy, he rebounded with 15 multihit games in June. He still has stretches where he looks lost in the field and at the plate, so he may have a hard time breaking into the major league lineup, but his power bat is still intriguing. . . GM Kevin Towers found **Chris Oxspring** (26) in the independent Frontier League. The Aussie works in the low 90s with his fastball and features a plus curve. After initially resisting the idea of starting, he has taken to the role after adding a slider and a change. . . **Humberto Quintero** (24) was voted the best defensive catcher in the Double-A Southern League and improved his offense dramatically this season. His September callup may be a prelude to a back-up role next season. . . Lefthander **Rusty Tucker** (23) required Tommy John surgery in late August when he tore the ulnar collateral ligament in his pitching elbow. He won't pitch again until August 2004, but with a fastball that touches 97 MPH to go along with a plus slider, he'll be in the mix for a spot in the Padres' bullpen in 2005.

Pacific Bell Park

Offense

Pacific Bell Park has been in existence only four years, but it's earned a well-deserved reputation for being a hitters' nightmare. Most of the complaints come from lefthanded batters. While the park has an inviting 309-foot fence down the right-field line, it's extremely difficult to get the ball over the high wall because of a wind that usually blows from left to right. Rather than try to pull the ball, it's advantageous for hitters to try to aim for the sizable alleys.

Defense

Hardly anyone complains about the condition of the Pac Bell infield, just the opposite of the team's former home, Candlestick Park. During day games, left field is one of the most difficult positions to play because of the sun. Because of the many quirks of the right-field area, the Giants have employed solid defensive players such as Ellis Burks, Reggie Sanders and Jose Cruz Jr. to play the position.

Who It Helps the Most

Just about any pitcher improves when pitching at Pac Bell. Jason Schmidt, while an ace anywhere, has had a 2.31 ERA at the park over the last two seasons, more than a run better than his road mark. Shortstop Rich Aurilia has been one of the few Giants—aside from Barry Bonds—who hits better at home than on the road.

Who It Hurts the Most

Lefthanded pull hitters such as J.T. Snow struggle at Pac Bell. Infielder Neifi Perez wasn't successful hitting at home, with a .221 batting average, compared with a .285 mark on the road.

Rookies & Newcomers

Rookie Jerome Williams had an easy transition to pitching at Pac Bell, compiling a 2.91 ERA there, almost a run less than his road ERA. A.J. Pierzynski isn't a home-run hitter, so he shouldn't be frustrated by the difficulty of homering at Pac Bell. He could benefit by driving the ball into those expansive gaps. He tripled off the right-field wall there last June.

Dimensions: LF-339, LCF-364, CF-399, RCF-421, RF-309

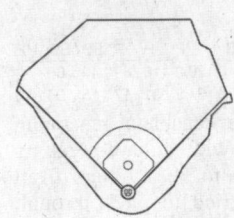

Capacity: 41,503

Elevation: 0 feet

Surface: Grass

Foul Territory: Average

Park Factors

2003 Season

| | Home Games | | | Away Games | | | |
	Giants	Opp	Total	Giants	Opp	Total	Index
G	72	72	144	71	71	142	
Avg	.275	.243	.259	.249	.252	.250	103
AB	2391	2487	4878	2434	2304	4738	102
R	353	259	612	309	296	605	100
H	658	605	1263	605	581	1186	105
2B	120	116	236	128	111	239	96
3B	17	13	30	9	11	20	146
HR	70	55	125	86	63	149	81
BB	278	233	511	259	244	503	99
SO	412	481	893	474	416	890	97
E	42	53	95	29	37	66	142
E-Infield	33	44	77	25	31	56	136
LHB-Avg	.264	.230	.246	.255	.263	.260	95
LHB-HR	27	15	42	35	20	55	75
RHB-Avg	.281	.252	.267	.245	.244	.245	109
RHB-HR	43	40	83	51	43	94	85

2001-2003

| | Home Games | | | Away Games | | | |
	Giants	Opp	Total	Giants	Opp	Total	Index
G	219	219	438	215	215	430	
Avg	.263	.247	.255	.269	.259	.264	97
AB	7243	7572	14815	7579	7075	14654	99
R	1003	844	1847	1109	967	2076	87
H	1906	1873	3779	2037	1833	3870	96
2B	381	361	742	418	343	761	96
3B	62	54	116	35	39	74	155
HR	222	137	359	331	216	547	65
BB	856	709	1565	822	773	1595	97
SO	1283	1445	2728	1461	1295	2756	98
E	138	147	285	124	129	253	111
E-Infield	109	120	229	94	110	204	110
LHB-Avg	.254	.246	.250	.284	.274	.279	90
LHB-HR	98	39	137	139	81	220	61
RHB-Avg	.267	.248	.258	.262	.248	.256	101
RHB-HR	124	98	222	192	135	327	68

2003 Rankings (National League)

- Highest error factor
- Highest infield-error factor
- Third-highest RHB batting-average factor
- Third-lowest home-run factor
- Third-lowest LHB home-run factor

Felipe Alou

Born: 5/12/35 in Haina, Dominican Republic

Playing Experience: 1958-1974, SF, Atl, Oak, NYY, Mon, Mil

Managerial Experience: 11 seasons

2003 Season

In his first season with the Giants after replacing popular manager Dusty Baker, Felipe Alou guided the team to a 100-win season and a postseason berth. But all the goodwill he achieved during the regular season seemed to go up in smoke during a first-round loss to eventual World Series champion Florida. Alou intimated that Jason Schmidt didn't want to pitch on three day's rest for Game 4, when Schmidt had been pitching with a tendon tear in his elbow for most of the season. Schmidt and a handful of others questioned Alou's communication skills after the playoff loss.

Offense

Alou squeezed the most out of a lineup built solely around Barry Bonds. There was only one constant through most of the season: When Bonds played, he hit cleanup. The rest was strictly mix and match. While the club continued to win, some players privately complained that it would have been nice to have more of a set lineup during the season.

Pitching & Defense

Alou is a stickler for defense, and his players did not disappoint. Jose Cruz Jr. won his first Gold Glove, first baseman J.T. Snow played his usual high level of defense, and so did third baseman Edgardo Alfonzo and center fielder Marquis Grissom. With a relatively young rotation and a deep, veteran bullpen, Alou showed a penchant for pulling starters at the first sign of trouble. Only Jason Schmidt was allowed to pitch deep into games.

2004 Outlook

The happy marriage between Alou and the Giants became rocky in the postseason, and it will be interesting to see if there is any carryover from last season. Many of the players who complained about Alou's failure to speak to them directly on issues may not be back next season, so the point could be moot. But if the Giants are slow out of the gate this year, Alou could start feeling some heat.

Manager Statistics

Year	Team, Lg	W	L	Pct	GB	Finish
2003	San Fran, NL	100	61	.621	–	1st West
11 Seasons		791	778	.504	–	–

2003 Starting Pitchers by Days Rest

	<=3	4	5	6+
Giants Starts	0	65	54	30
Giants ERA	–	3.79	3.66	4.02
NL Avg Starts	2	84	43	23
NL ERA	5.00	4.23	4.42	4.68

2003 Situational Stats

	Felipe Alou	NL Average
Hit & Run Success %	36.4	32.7
Stolen Base Success %	58.9	68.9
Platoon Pct.	52.9	52.0
Defensive Subs	19	19
High-Pitch Outings	8	8
Quick/Slow Hooks	26/7	20/12
Sacrifice Attempts	96	93

2003 Rankings (National League)

- 1st in squeeze plays (9) and one-batter pitcher appearances (57)
- 2nd in quick hooks
- 3rd in sacrifice-bunt percentage (83.3%), mid-inning pitching changes (181) and 2+ pitching changes in low-scoring games (42)

San Francisco

667

Edgardo Alfonzo

2003 Season

When Edgardo Alfonzo was hitting .216 on June 28, it appeared the Giants had made a terrible mistake by signing him to a four-year, $26 million contract. His bat looked slow, and he appeared to be lost hitting at Pacific Bell Park. However, Alfonzo got in gear and batted .306 with 54 RBI the rest of the way. He also was the only Giant who hit consistently in the Division Series.

Hitting

Although he struggled for most of the first half, Alfonzo showed he's a patient, selective hitter. He struck out just 41 times, his lowest total since his rookie year (1995). Alfonzo's power numbers have declined every year since 1999, and he hit just 13 homers last season; part of that decline can be attributed to a back injury that has bothered him for years. However, Alfonzo still can drive the ball into the gaps.

Baserunning & Defense

Although Alfonzo's offensive problems were well chronicled, his defense at third was a constant positive. He committed only 11 errors and was steady, if not spectacular, all year. Showing his selfless personality, Alfonzo agreed to move to second base, a position he hadn't played since 2001, for a six-game stretch in August to replace the injured Ray Durham. Alfonzo lacks speed but is an intelligent baserunner who is 16-for-18 stealing the last three years.

2004 Outlook

Considering that he barely was over the Mendoza Line in late June, Alfonzo's .259 average last season was quite an accomplishment. His days of reaching the mid-20 range in homers likely are over, but Alfonzo proved he can be an accomplished run producer and a clutch player, as evidenced by his showing in the playoffs. While Alfonzo admitted he missed playing and living in New York, he's more comfortable with his new surroundings and won't have to endure an adjustment period this season.

Position: 3B
Bats: R **Throws:** R
Ht: 5'11" **Wt:** 187

Opening Day Age: 30
Born: 11/8/73 in St. Teresa, VZ
ML Seasons: 9

Overall Statistics

	G	AB	R	H	D	T	HR	RBI	SB	BB	SO	Avg	OBP	Slg
'03	142	514	56	133	25	2	13	81	5	58	41	.259	.334	.391
Car.	1228	4411	670	1269	237	16	133	619	50	516	539	.288	.363	.439

Where He Hits the Ball

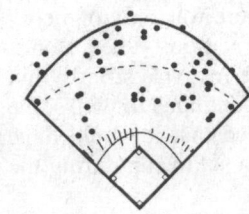
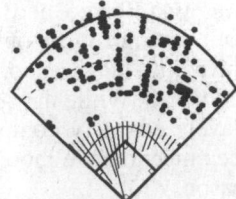

Vs. LHP   **Vs. RHP**

2003 Situational Stats

	AB	H	HR	RBI	Avg		AB	H	HR	RBI	Avg
Home	234	62	6	42	.265	LHP	106	25	4	13	.236
Road	280	71	7	39	.254	RHP	408	108	9	68	.265
First Half	318	75	5	33	.236	Sc Pos	146	43	5	67	.295
Scnd Half	196	58	8	48	.296	Clutch	62	10	1	7	.161

2003 Rankings (National League)

- 6th in fielding percentage at third base (.966)
- Led the Giants in sacrifice flies (7) and highest percentage of swings put into play (54.4)

Rich Aurilia

2003 Season

Rich Aurilia showed once again that he is far removed from his 2001 All-Star season in which he hit .324 with 37 homers and 97 RBI. Unlike the 2002 season, however, he could not use his injured right elbow as an alibi. Aurilia did have a stint on the disabled list after undergoing an emer gency appendectomy August 4. The Giants were encouraged that he hit .312 after the All-Star break after struggling in the first half. Still, he hit only four homers after the break.

Hitting

Aurilia hasn't been a bona fide threat since he was moved out of the No. 2 spot after the 2002 season. He flourished hitting ahead of Barry Bonds and feasting on a steady diet of fastballs. Aurilia can be a free swinger who chases high pitches, and he can lose his patience at times. He is a better hitter when he hits balls in the gap rather trying to yank them over the left-field fence.

Baserunning & Defense

Aurilia has become a dependable fielder over the years after struggling earlier in his career. However, his range has decreased and he's unable to get to balls that quicker shortstops can reach. He compensates for that deficiency with a quick release and accurate throws across the diamond. Aurilia is one of the slowest runners on the team and never has been a threat on the bases. He does not make bonehead moves on the bases.

2004 Outlook

Although Aurilia was drafted by the Texas Rangers, he was bred in the Giants' farm system and has been employed by the Giants longer than anyone except Barry Bonds and Marvin Benard. However, Aurilia's contract ended last season and he became a free agent. The Giants didn't offer him salary arbitration, and with Neifi Perez around, Aurilia won't be returning to San Francisco in 2004.

Position: SS
Bats: R **Throws:** R
Ht: 6' 1" **Wt:** 185

Opening Day Age: 32
Born: 9/2/71 in Brooklyn, NY
ML Seasons: 9
Pronunciation: uh-REEL-yuh
Nickname: Dickie

Overall Statistics

	G	AB	R	H	D	T	HR	RBI	SB	BB	SO	Avg	OBP	Slg
'03	129	505	65	140	26	1	13	58	2	36	82	.277	.325	.410
Car.	993	3598	491	1002	190	14	126	473	16	282	547	.278	.331	.444

Where He Hits the Ball

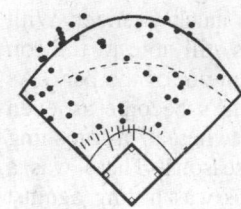 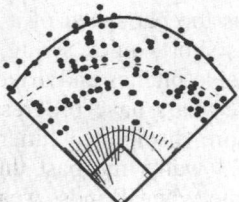

Vs. LHP   **Vs. RHP**

2003 Situational Stats

	AB	H	HR	RBI	Avg		AB	H	HR	RBI	Avg
Home	251	79	6	33	.315	LHP	112	31	8	21	.277
Road	254	61	7	25	.240	RHP	393	109	5	37	.277
First Half	316	81	9	31	.256	Sc Pos	122	31	3	46	.254
Scnd Half	189	59	4	27	.312	Clutch	59	16	2	10	.271

2003 Rankings (National League)

- 4th in lowest fielding percentage at shortstop (.974)
- 8th in batting average with the bases loaded (.545)
- Led the Giants in GDPs (18) and batting average with the bases loaded (.545)

Barry Bonds

2003 Season

Though he again posted amazing numbers while winning his sixth National League MVP Award, it was a difficult season for Barry Bonds, who played most of the season knowing his father, Bobby, was dying of cancer. Bonds was on the bereavement list twice, including a second time when his father passed away on August 23. When he returned, Bonds openly talked about the tough times he was experiencing, saying he was having trouble sleeping. Bonds stayed overnight in a Phoenix hospital with a rapid heartbeat in early September.

Hitting

Although Bonds is approaching 40 years old, he has the bat speed of a man much younger. With his short, quick swing, he's still able to turn on inside pitches and drive them out of the park. As the years have progressed he's become an even more disciplined hitter, drawing an astonishing 523 walks the past three seasons. There was a time when Bonds' weakness was hitting against lefthanders, but that's no longer the case.

Baserunning & Defense

Bonds' days as a Gold Glove left fielder are over. He's bulked up over the years and has lost his agility and foot speed. However, he still can keep runners from taking the extra base with a quick release and intelligent positioning. He also cut his errors from the previous season from eight to two. Bonds no longer is an elite basestealer, but he was 7-for-7 last season, including the 500th of his career.

2004 Outlook

There seems no reason to believe Bonds can't continue his astounding pace, even though he'll turn 40 on July 24. He needs two homers to tie his godfather, Willie Mays, for third place on the all-time list. Bonds has to continue to remain patient at the plate; at times, it appeared he grew frustrated with the walks he constantly received, going into mini-slumps when teams *did* pitch to him.

Position: LF
Bats: L **Throws:** L
Ht: 6' 2" **Wt:** 228

Opening Day Age: 39
Born: 7/24/64 in Riverside, CA
ML Seasons: 18
Nickname: BB

Overall Statistics

G	AB	R	H	D	T	HR	RBI	SB	BB	SO	Avg	OBP	Slg
130	390	111	133	22	1	45	90	7	148	58	.341	.529	.749
2569	8725	1941	2595	536	74	658	1742	500	2070	1387	.297	.433	.602

Where He Hits the Ball

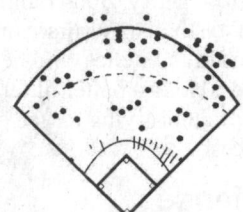 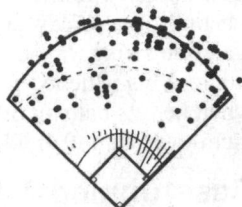

Vs. LHP   **Vs. RHP**

2003 Situational Stats

	AB	H	HR	RBI	Avg		AB	H	HR	RBI	Avg
Home	195	72	23	41	.369	LHP	124	45	16	30	.363
Road	195	61	22	49	.313	RHP	266	88	29	60	.331
First Half	256	81	30	63	.316	Sc Pos	77	26	4	40	.338
Scnd Half	134	52	15	27	.388	Clutch	44	14	5	10	.318

2003 Rankings (National League)

- 1st in walks, intentional walks (61), slugging percentage, on-base percentage, HR frequency (8.7 ABs per HR), highest percentage of pitches taken (65.9) and cleanup slugging percentage (.769)
- 2nd in home runs, fielding percentage in left field (.992) and lowest groundball-flyball ratio (0.7)
- 3rd in batting average, times on base (291) and batting average at home
- Led the Giants in runs scored, total bases (292), RBI, hit by pitch (10), times on base (291), on-base percentage, HR frequency (8.7 ABs per HR)
- Led NL left fielders in batting average and home runs

Jose Cruz Jr.

Position: RF
Bats: B **Throws:** R
Ht: 6' 0" **Wt:** 210

Opening Day Age: 29
Born: 4/19/74 in Arroyo, PR
ML Seasons: 7

2003 Season

Not even a Gold Glove Award in November could erase the stigma of Jose Cruz Jr. dropping a routine flyball off the bat of Jeff Conine in the 11th inning, leading to a crucial Game 3 Division Series loss to Florida. Cruz made just two errors during the regular season, but had a horrible playoff which included an 0-for-11 stint at the plate, a slip while trying to catch a ball in Game 2 and the aforementioned drop.

Hitting

The Giants envisioned Cruz as a 30-homer player who would drive in plenty of runs, especially after he got off to a hot start with seven homers in April. National League pitchers soon figured out that he is an outstanding fastball hitter but much less potent against breaking and offspeed pitches. Cruz had only four home runs and 14 extra-base hits after the break, and while he drew a career-high 102 walks, he also struck out 121 times. He also struggled in pressure situations, turning in one of the poorest averages in the league with runners in scoring position before going hitless in the playoffs.

Baserunning & Defense

Cruz played sensational defense during the regular season, with 18 outfield assists, setting a San Francisco record. He also made diving and running catches time after time. However, he simply wasn't the same player in the postseason. Cruz stole 32 bases with Toronto in 2001, but he regressed in that department last year, stealing just five times in 13 attempts.

2004 Outlook

The Giants declined to exercise Cruz' option after the season and will go in a different direction in right field this season. Although the team was more than happy with his defense, it needs more consistent offensive production than he was able to provide. The Giants also need a player who can come up bigger in clutch situations.

Overall Statistics

	G	AB	R	H	D	T	HR	RBI	SB	BB	SO	Avg	OBP	Slg
'03	158	539	90	135	26	1	20	68	5	102	121	.250	.366	.414
Car.	905	3281	514	824	174	22	154	457	91	431	801	.251	.336	.458

Where He Hits the Ball

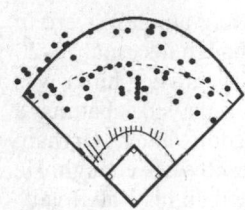
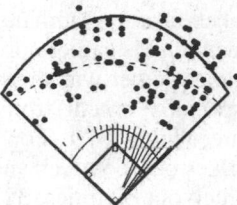

Vs. LHP   **Vs. RHP**

2003 Situational Stats

	AB	H	HR	RBI	Avg		AB	H	HR	RBI	Avg
Home	266	71	9	37	.267	LHP	135	41	7	17	.304
Road	273	64	11	31	.234	RHP	404	94	13	51	.233
First Half	324	85	16	47	.262	Sc Pos	143	27	6	52	.189
Scnd Half	215	50	4	21	.233	Clutch	75	16	4	9	.213

2003 Rankings (National League)

- 1st in lowest batting average with the bases loaded (.000)
- 2nd in fielding percentage in right field (.994)
- 4th in lowest batting average with runners in scoring position
- 6th in lowest batting average on the road
- 7th in sacrifice flies (7), walks and lowest batting average vs. righthanded pitchers
- 9th in games played and lowest batting average
- Led the Giants in sacrifice flies (7), caught stealing (8), strikeouts, pitches seen (2,578), plate appearances (650) and games played

Ray Durham

2003 Season

Signed to a three-year, $20.1 million contract prior to the season, Ray Durham appeared in only 110 games because of ankle, hamstring and hip problems. To his credit, Durham returned from what appeared to be a horrific right ankle sprain suffered May 10 when he slid awkwardly into third base in Atlanta. He was back on the field about two weeks later, but returned to the DL in August when he strained his right hamstring. Durham never seemed to settle into a nice grove, and rather alarmingly, he hit only .256 with 14 RBI in the second half. His 33 RBI were easily his lowest total in his nine-year career.

Hitting

When healthy, Durham's hitting numbers were in line with his career norms, though his usual 15-20 homer power was missing. The switch-hitter was especially potent from the right side, batting a career-high .370. For a leadoff hitter, Durham strikes out too much and doesn't walk enough. He struck out 82 times, 32 more than his walk total.

Baserunning & Defense

The Giants signed Durham to be a disruptive force at the top of the lineup and on the bases, but his injuries destroyed his usefulness as a bases-stealer. His seven steals were a career low by a big margin. Durham is a gifted athlete whom the Giants considered moving to the outfield before they signed Jose Cruz Jr. He has plenty of range at second base, and made only five errors.

2004 Outlook

So far, the Giants' sizable investment in Durham has been a bust, but he could change that this season. He needs to remain healthy and become the leadoff man San Francisco expected him to be. The Giants hope his poor second half was a result of his injuries. If not, they may have to move him out of the leadoff spot.

Position: 2B
Bats: B **Throws:** R
Ht: 5' 8" **Wt:** 180

Opening Day Age: 32
Born: 11/30/71 in Charlotte, NC
ML Seasons: 9

Overall Statistics

	G	AB	R	H	D	T	HR	RBI	SB	BB	SO	Avg	OBP	Slg
'03	110	410	61	117	30	5	8	33	7	50	82	.285	.366	.441
Car.	1310	5108	888	1423	293	62	120	539	232	558	874	.279	.353	.431

Where He Hits the Ball

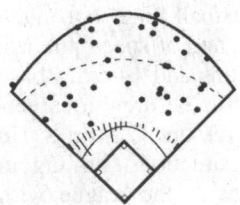
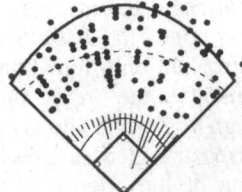

Vs. LHP   **Vs. RHP**

2003 Situational Stats

	AB	H	HR	RBI	Avg		AB	H	HR	RBI	Avg
Home	209	66	3	19	.316	LHP	100	37	1	10	.370
Road	201	51	5	14	.254	RHP	310	80	7	23	.258
First Half	277	83	4	19	.300	Sc Pos	78	16	0	23	.205
Scnd Half	133	34	4	14	.256	Clutch	46	13	1	2	.283

2003 Rankings (National League)

- 6th in on-base percentage for a leadoff hitter (.359)
- Led the Giants in triples, batting average vs. lefthanded pitchers and lowest percentage of swings on the first pitch (17.0)

Marquis Grissom

2003 Season

The Los Angeles Dodgers felt confident that Marquis Grissom was merely a part-time player and allowed him to become a free agent after the 2002 season. Signed by the Giants, Grissom showed he still could be a productive everyday player, though he seemed to tire at times as the season progressed and struggled at the plate in the postseason.

Hitting

Grissom makes no secret of the fact that he's a free swinger, proving that again by striking out 82 times while walking just 20. He will chase fastballs out of the strike zone and swing at breaking pitches off the plate. He always has been a pull hitter and once again feasted on lefthanders. He wasn't nearly as productive against righties, displaying far less power and posting an on-base percentage below .300.

Baserunning & Defense

Grissom may have lost a step in the outfield, but he's still among the most skilled center fielders in the NL. He doesn't have the raw speed he had in his earlier years with Montreal, but he makes up for that deficiency with experience and positioning. He gets good jumps on balls and his arm is adequate, though he occasionally is prone to overthrows. He also dropped a couple of routine balls last year. Grissom once stole more than 70 bases in back-to-back seasons, but he attempts a steal only occasionally these days. He ran a bit more often under Felipe Alou, his old Montreal manager, reaching double figures in steals for the first time in three years.

2004 Outlook

The Giants signed Grissom to a two-year, $4.25 million contract, one of their most cost prudent and important offseason moves. Although he'll turn 37 this season, Grissom appears to have plenty in his tank to produce a season similar to 2003. He's a good clubhouse presence and became friends with Barry Bonds, something players rarely experience.

Position: CF
Bats: R **Throws:** R
Ht: 5'11" **Wt:** 180

Opening Day Age: 36
Born: 4/17/67 in Atlanta, GA
ML Seasons: 13
Pronunciation: mar-KEESE
Nickname: Grip

Overall Statistics

G	AB	R	H	D	T	HR	RBI	SB	BB	SO	Avg	OBP	Slg
149	587	82	176	33	3	20	79	11	20	82	.300	.322	.468
1976	7576	1101	2065	356	54	203	862	425	509	1139	.273	.319	.414

Where He Hits the Ball

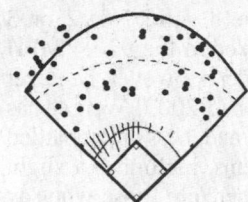
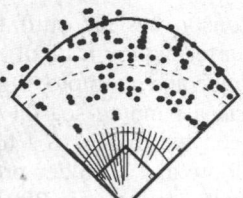

Vs. LHP   **Vs. RHP**

2003 Situational Stats

	AB	H	HR	RBI	Avg		AB	H	HR	RBI	Avg
Home	299	93	10	46	.311	LHP	140	51	9	25	.364
Road	288	83	10	33	.288	RHP	447	125	11	54	.280
First Half	357	111	14	47	.311	Sc Pos	127	42	3	54	.331
Scnd Half	230	65	6	32	.283	Clutch	83	20	1	8	.241

2003 Rankings (National League)

- 1st in on-base percentage for a leadoff hitter (.412), errors in center field (8) and lowest fielding percentage in center field (.977)
- 4th in fewest pitches seen per plate appearance (3.36)
- 7th in batting average vs. lefthanded pitchers and lowest percentage of pitches taken (48.9)
- 10th in singles
- Led the Giants in at bats, hits, singles, doubles, stolen bases, stolen-base percentage (78.6), steals of third (2), on-base percentage for a leadoff hitter (.412) and batting average with two strikes (.257)

San Francisco

673

Sidney Ponson

Position: SP
Bats: R **Throws:** R
Ht: 6' 1" **Wt:** 249

Opening Day Age: 27
Born: 11/2/76 in Noord, Aruba
ML Seasons: 6
Pronunciation: pon-SONE

2003 Season

With a 14-6 record for the lowly Orioles, Sidney Ponson was one of the most attractive pitchers being shopped as the trading deadline approached last July. But after being acquired acquired by the Giants on July 31, he won only three more games. Ponson didn't pitch all that badly for San Francisco, but the club ruined some of his best efforts by blowing late-inning leads. He also lacked consistency. After a good stretch in August and early September, he went 0-3 with a 5.90 ERA in his last five starts, including a Game 2 Division Series no-decision against the Marlins in which he blew a 4-1 lead.

Pitching

Ponson has the stuff to be a solid No. 2 or 3 starter, with a fastball clocked in the 92-94 MPH range and an improving slider. However, he never had a winning season prior to 2003. Weight has been a problem for him, and he's also battled elbow and shoulder problems, including a slight rotator cuff tear in 2002. There are those who say he doesn't have the mental toughness late in games and has too much of a laid-back attitude to become a dominant pitcher.

Defense & Hitting

A big man, Ponson appears slow while coming off the mound, but he is flawless on bunts and slow rollers, and he covers first base adequately. His move to first is so-so, but he compensates by being quick to the plate. Since he has played mostly in the American League, Ponson hasn't hit much, and was just 2-for-27 last season.

2004 Outlook

Because of Ponson's poor finish, the Giants have soured on him. He's a free agent who won't be back after the club chose not to offer him salary arbitration. Ponson likely will receive a lucrative offer from a big-market team. He probably won't come cheap. Ponson turned down a three-year, $21 million contract offer from the Orioles before he was traded to the Giants.

Overall Statistics

	W	L	Pct.	ERA	G	GS	Sv	IP	H	BB	SO	HR	Avg
'03	17	12	.586	3.75	31	31	0	216.0	211	61	134	16	.257
Car.	58	65	.472	4.54	177	166	1	1097.1	1151	366	687	147	.271

2003 Pitching Profile

	Sidney Ponson (NL)	NL Average
Overall Strike %	64.7	62.4
1st Pitch Strike %	59.7	58.4
Ratio	1.21	1.38
Strikeouts per 9 IP	4.50	6.65
Walks per 9 IP	2.38	3.42
Home Runs per 9 IP	0.79	1.05
Strikeout/Walk Ratio	1.89	1.94
Groundball/Flyball Ratio	1.85	1.29

2003 Situational Stats

	W	L	ERA	Sv	IP		AB	H	HR	RBI	Avg
Home	7	6	4.35	0	91.0	LHB	410	111	5	40	.271
Road	10	6	3.31	0	125.0	RHB	411	100	11	42	.243
First Half	12	5	3.64	0	126.0	Sc Pos	187	50	5	65	.267
Scnd Half	5	7	3.90	0	90.0	Clutch	55	20	1	9	.364

2003 Rankings (National League)

- 2nd in most GDPs induced per GDP situation (31.3%)
- Led the Giants in most GDPs induced per GDP situation (31.3%)

Kirk Rueter

2003 Season

Entering the 2003 season, Kirk Rueter had never had a serious arm injury during his 10-year major league career. But then came 2003, when Rueter had two stays on the DL with left shoulder injuries. He finished with only 27 starts and 10 wins, his lowest season totals since his first full season with the Giants in 1997. Despite his injuries, Rueter was able to reach double figures in victories for a seventh consecutive season, the longest streak for a Giants' lefthander since Hall of Famer Carl Hubbell had at least 10 victories for 15 straight seasons (1928-42). Rueter looked to be completely recovered from his injuries in September, when he was 3-0 in five starts.

Pitching

Rueter has been compared to Tom Glavine—pitchers who don't throw hard but make their living hitting the corners. Rueter won't impress anyone with his velocity, but he'll challenge hitters with an occasional inside fastball. He generally lives on the outside corner, and hitters usually are powerless to do anything about it. Most of his problems last season came against righthanded hitters, who batted .326 against him—the worst performance of his career vs. righties.

Defense & Hitting

Rueter is a fierce competitor and among the team's best fielders. With his quick move to first base, he's difficult to run on. He also can hit a little, slapping balls the other way and helping himself with a bunt. Last season, Rueter had six sacrifices and struck out just eight times in 53 at-bats.

2004 Outlook

The front office loves Rueter, signing him to a two-year extension in February 2003, meaning he'll be a Giant through the 2005 season. The team knows that if he remains healthy, Rueter can be counted on to win 14-16 games and stop a losing streak or two. The team hopes that his injuries were just an aberration and not a trend.

Position: SP
Bats: L **Throws:** L
Ht: 6' 3" **Wt:** 212

Opening Day Age: 33
Born: 12/1/70 in Centralia, IL
ML Seasons: 11
Pronunciation: REE-ter
Nickname: Woody

Overall Statistics

	W	L	Pct.	ERA	G	GS	Sv	IP	H	BB	SO	HR	Avg
'03	10	5	.667	4.53	27	27	0	147.0	170	47	41	14	.297
Car.	119	73	.620	4.11	287	285	0	1620.1	1736	469	737	187	.277

2003 Pitching Profile

	Kirk Rueter	NL Average
Overall Strike %	58.6	62.4
1st Pitch Strike %	51.7	58.4
Ratio	1.48	1.38
Strikeouts per 9 IP	2.51	6.65
Walks per 9 IP	2.88	3.42
Home Runs per 9 IP	0.86	1.05
Strikeout/Walk Ratio	0.87	1.94
Groundball/Flyball Ratio	1.49	1.29

2003 Situational Stats

	W	L	ERA	Sv	IP		AB	H	HR	RBI	Avg
Home	6	2	4.08	0	81.2	LHB	146	31	1	13	.212
Road	4	3	5.10	0	65.1	RHB	427	139	13	51	.326
First Half	7	3	4.46	0	105.0	Sc Pos	130	41	4	50	.315
Scnd Half	3	2	4.71	0	42.0	Clutch	8	1	0	0	.125

2003 Rankings (National League)

- 2nd in highest batting average allowed vs. righthanded batters
- 4th in GDPs induced (24)
- 6th in highest batting average allowed with runners in scoring position
- 7th in winning percentage
- 9th in most GDPs induced per GDP situation (19.4%) and highest ERA at home
- Led the Giants in hits allowed, GDPs induced (24) and most run support per nine innings (6.3)

Benito Santiago

Signed By
ROYALS

2003 Season

Benito Santiago was as big a disappointment last season as he was a surprise in 2002. Santiago came to camp complaining that he was under-paid—he made $1.775 million in 2003—and wanted the team to sign him to a contract extension. No deal was reached, and the matter became a distraction. For the year, Santiago actually had a higher batting average than he did in 2002, but he hit only one homer after the All-Star break and could barely field his position. When Santiago was benched in favor of Yorvit Torrealba for the final game of the NLDS, the baton essentially had been passed.

Hitting

Santiago could turn on fastballs in 2002, when he hit 16 homers and was the MVP of the NLCS. But his bat speed slowed noticeably last season, and he was a nonentity at the plate in the second half. Santiago always loved the high pitch, but he couldn't catch up to high offerings most of last season. With his long, looping swing, he became an easy out at times.

Baserunning & Defense

Santiago played a lot the previous two seasons after getting his career back on track following a horrific automobile accident in 1998. The cumulative effect of catching so many games for a man his age appeared to have caught up to him. Santiago used to throw out baserunners from his knees, but he could hardly throw out anybody from any position last season. He also had eight passed balls. On the bases, Santiago continued to use poor judgment.

2004 Outlook

The front office privately was not happy with Santiago's early-season attitude and his defense, and he'll be playing elsewhere in 2004 after the Giants acquired catcher A.J. Pierzynski from Minnesota. Santiago will remain a starter as a 39-year-old, however, after signing a two-year, $4.3 million deal with the Royals.

Position: C
Bats: R **Throws:** R
Ht: 6' 1" **Wt:** 200

Opening Day Age: 39
Born: 3/9/65 in Ponce, PR
ML Seasons: 18
Pronunciation: sahn-tee-AH-go

Overall Statistics

G	AB	R	H	D	T	HR	RBI	SB	BB	SO	Avg	OBP	Slg
108	401	53	112	21	2	11	56	0	29	69	.279	.329	.424
1923	6753	739	1776	312	40	211	897	90	422	1235	.263	.307	.415

Where He Hits the Ball

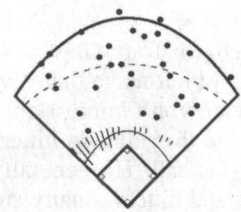 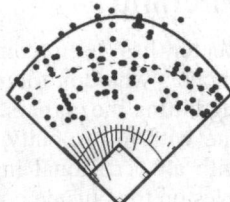

Vs. LHP **Vs. RHP**

2003 Situational Stats

	AB	H	HR	RBI	Avg		AB	H	HR	RBI	Avg
Home	188	53	2	20	.282	LHP	100	29	4	12	.290
Road	213	59	9	36	.277	RHP	301	83	7	44	.276
First Half	256	74	10	41	.289	Sc Pos	116	31	1	38	.267
Scnd Half	145	38	1	15	.262	Clutch	59	18	3	11	.305

2003 Rankings (National League)

• 8th in fielding percentage at catcher (.993)

Jason Schmidt

2003 Season

The breakout season that had long been expected of Jason Schmidt finally materialized in 2003. Despite season-long elbow problems and the death of his mother, Vicki, in April, Schmidt led the league in ERA and finished second in the National League CY Young Award voting. He was 8-1 with a 2.29 ERA in the second half, a remarkable achievement considering he was pitching with a tear in his elbow tendon that required surgery after the season.

Pitching

Schmidt has become one of the dominant pitchers in the NL. Although he was hurt most of the season, he struck out more than a batter an inning and issued only 46 walks in 207.2 innings. He continued to throw his fastball in the upper-90 MPH range and used a hard slider as a strikeout pitch. A man who once had a reputation for wilting in tough situations, Schmidt returned after the death of his mother by throwing a three-hit shutout with 12 strikeouts against the Cubs. He also hurled a three-hit shutout in Game 1 of the Division Series.

Defense & Hitting

Schmidt has a reputation as a poor fielder, but he has committed just two errors the past two seasons. Perhaps because of his gangly 6-foot-5 frame, he has problems controlling the running game. After improving his hitting in 2001 and 2002, Schmidt regressed last season as he tried to protect his torn tendon. He did help himself by tying for the league lead with 15 sacrifice bunts.

2004 Outlook

Schmidt seems ready to move into the 20-win class, but elbow surgery performed in October puts his availability for Opening Day in question. Schmidt believes he'll be ready for the start of the season, but the Giants as a rule don't like to rush their pitchers back. If all goes well, they can look forward to another dominating season from their ace starter.

Position: SP
Bats: R **Throws:** R
Ht: 6' 5" **Wt:** 205

Opening Day Age: 31
Born: 1/29/73 in Lewiston, ID
ML Seasons: 9

Overall Statistics

	W	L	Pct.	ERA	G	GS	Sv	IP	H	BB	SO	HR	Avg
'03	17	5	.773	2.34	29	29	0	207.2	152	46	208	14	.200
Car.	86	67	.562	4.02	220	211	0	1342.2	1284	524	1132	124	.251

2003 Pitching Profile

	Jason Schmidt	NL Average
Overall Strike %	68.2	62.4
1st Pitch Strike %	64.7	58.4
Ratio	0.95	1.38
Strikeouts per 9 IP	9.01	6.65
Walks per 9 IP	1.99	3.42
Home Runs per 9 IP	0.61	1.05
Strikeout/Walk Ratio	4.52	1.94
Groundball/Flyball Ratio	0.84	1.29

2003 Situational Stats

	W	L	ERA	Sv	IP		AB	H	HR	RBI	Avg
Home	7	1	2.24	0	100.2	LHB	401	79	7	27	.197
Road	10	4	2.44	0	107.0	RHB	358	73	7	23	.204
First Half	9	4	2.37	0	133.0	Sc Pos	146	32	1	33	.010
Scnd Half	8	1	2.29	0	74.2	Clutch	64	13	0	4	.203

2003 Rankings (National League)

- 1st in ERA, sacrifice bunts (15), shutouts (3), winning percentage, lowest batting average allowed (.200) and lowest on-base percentage allowed (.250)
- 2nd in complete games (5), lowest slugging percentage allowed (.316) and lowest ERA at home
- 3rd in highest strikeout-walk ratio (4.5)
- 4th in wins, strikeouts, lowest ERA on the road, fewest walks per nine innings (2.0) and lowest groundball-flyball ratio allowed (0.8)
- Led the Giants in wins, games started, innings pitched, batters faced (819), strikeouts, pitches thrown (3,097), stolen bases allowed (17), lowest batting average allowed (.200), lowest on-base percentage allowed (.250), lowest ERA on the road, lowest batting average allowed vs. lefthanded batters, fewest home runs allowed per nine innings (.61), most strikeouts per nine innings (9.0)

J.T. Snow

2003 Season

J.T. Snow improved his 2002 batting average by 27 points to .273 in 2003, but his homers and RBI continued to be on the low side for a first baseman. It was the third straight season in which Snow failed to reach double figures in home runs or collect at least 54 RBI. A left groin strain put him on the disabled list twice, contributing to his 12-RBI total in the second half.

Hitting

While Pacific Bell Park has been a godsend for the Giants, it's been a nightmare for Snow. He's hit just 16 homers there in the park's first four seasons. Snow's bat speed has slowed noticeably in recent years, though he always seems to come up big during the postseason. He draws a fair number of walks, but he sometimes can be a little too selective at the plate. Snow was once a full-time player, but weakness against lefties has made him a platoon player.

Baserunning & Defense

Snow was thrown out at the plate to end Game 4 of the Division Series against Florida, though it wasn't because of bad baserunning. He might be the slowest runner on the Giants, which is why he was thrown out so easily by left fielder Jeff Conine to end the team's season. Snow isn't winning Gold Gloves these days, but that's not to say he's undeserving. A six-time Gold Glove winner, Snow probably has won more games for the Giants in recent years with his glove than his bat.

2004 Outlook

The Giants declined to exercise the $6.5 million option for 2004 on Snow's contract, but they turned around and re-signed him to a one-year deal for $1.5 million. The contract also includes a club option for 2005, and the Giants, without a bona fide replacement in the farm system, could have him around for two years.

Position: 1B
Bats: L **Throws:** L
Ht: 6' 2" **Wt:** 209

Opening Day Age: 36
Born: 2/26/68 in Long Beach, CA
ML Seasons: 12
Nickname: Snowball

Overall Statistics

G	AB	R	H	D	T	HR	RBI	SB	BB	SO	Avg	OBP	Slg
103	330	48	90	18	3	8	51	1	55	55	.273	.387	.418
1453	4884	691	1286	244	16	173	773	15	662	1012	.263	.353	.426

Where He Hits the Ball

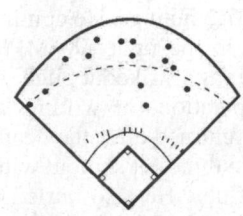 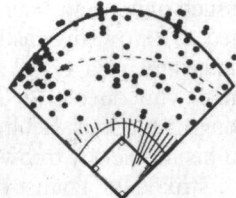

Vs. LHP   **Vs. RHP**

2003 Situational Stats

	AB	H	HR	RBI	Avg		AB	H	HR	RBI	Avg
Home	180	48	2	25	.267	LHP	48	10	0	6	.208
Road	150	42	6	26	.280	RHP	282	80	8	45	.284
First Half	224	62	5	39	.277	Sc Pos	81	27	1	39	.333
Scnd Half	106	28	3	12	.264	Clutch	47	16	3	9	.340

2003 Rankings (National League)

- 10th in batting average in the clutch
- Led the Giants in most pitches seen per plate appearance (4.10)

Tim Worrell

Signed By
PHILLIES

2003 Season

Tim Worrell was ready to begin another season as the Giants' setup man when things changed dramatically last spring. Closer Robb Nen was placed on the disabled list with a right shoulder injury, then underwent two surgeries and didn't pitch at all during the season. Worrell, who'd had just seven career saves prior to 2003 and none the previous two years, was given first crack at the closer's job. He quickly established himself as Nen's replacement, recording 38 of the team's 43 saves. Though he had a fine year overall, Worrell faded a bit as the season wore on; his ERA was 1.57 through July 6, but 4.73 from then on.

Pitching

Worrell had a lively fastball in the first half, but lost velocity and movement in the latter stretches of the season. In truth, velocity hasn't been the key to Worrell's success the last few years. With his fastball and more-than-adequate slider, Worrell relies primarily on location to succeed. When his location is off, he's in trouble. At his best last year he was keeping the ball down in the zone, getting a fair number of groundball outs and double plays.

Defense & Hitting

Worrell can be run on, but that wasn't much of a problem in his closer's role last season. He's solid defensively and competent coming off the mound to field bunts. Worrell doesn't get paid to hit, and it shows.

2004 Outlook

The Giants received three commendable seasons from Worrell after he was acquired from the Chicago Cubs for popular third baseman Bill Mueller. However, Worrell's days with San Francisco are over. The righthander signed a two-year, $5.5 million contract to join fellow newcomer Billy Wagner in the Philadelphia bullpen. He'll return to recording just the occasional save with the Phillies.

Position: RP
Bats: R **Throws:** R
Ht: 6' 4" **Wt:** 230

Opening Day Age: 36
Born: 7/5/67 in Pasadena, CA
ML Seasons: 11
Pronunciation: wor-RELL

Overall Statistics

	W	L	Pct.	ERA	G	GS	Sv	IP	H	BB	SO	HR	Avg
'03	4	4	.500	2.87	76	0	38	78.1	74	28	65	5	.246
Car.	39	49	.443	3.90	527	49	45	826.1	801	326	643	80	.252

2003 Pitching Profile

	Tim Worrell	NL Average
Overall Strike %	64.5	62.4
1st Pitch Strike %	58.3	58.4
Ratio	1.30	1.38
Strikeouts per 9 IP	7.47	6.65
Walks per 9 IP	3.22	3.42
Home Runs per 9 IP	0.57	1.05
Strikeout/Walk Ratio	2.32	1.94
Groundball/Flyball Ratio	1.41	1.29

2003 Situational Stats

	W	L	ERA	Sv	IP		AB	H	HR	RBI	Avg
Home	4	1	2.64	19	44.1	LHB	145	35	2	22	.241
Road	0	3	3.18	19	34.0	RHB	156	39	3	23	.250
First Half	2	3	2.12	20	46.2	Oc Pos	88	28	2	41	.302
Scnd Half	2	1	3.98	18	31.2	Clutch	226	47	3	34	.208

2003 Rankings (National League)

- 2nd in blown saves (7)
- 3rd in games finished (64)
- 4th in saves
- 7th in lowest save percentage (84.4)
- Led the Giants in saves, games finished (64), save percentage (84.4), blown saves (7) and relief losses (4)

San Francisco

Pedro Feliz

Position: 3B/LF/1B
Bats: R **Throws:** R
Ht: 6' 1" **Wt:** 205

Opening Day Age: 28
Born: 4/27/75 in Azua, DR
ML Seasons: 4

Overall Statistics

	G	AB	R	H	D	T	HR	RBI	SB	BB	SO	Avg	OBP	Slg
'03	95	235	31	58	9	3	16	48	2	10	53	.247	.278	.515
Car.	264	608	69	147	22	5	25	83	4	26	131	.242	.274	.418

2003 Situational Stats

	AB	H	HR	RBI	Avg		AB	H	HR	RBI	Avg
Home	120	29	6	21	.242	LHP	52	12	4	14	.231
Road	115	29	10	27	.252	RHP	183	46	12	34	.251
First Half	124	28	8	27	.226	Sc Pos	70	19	7	34	.271
Scnd Half	111	30	8	21	.270	Clutch	42	13	4	11	.310

2003 Season

Filling his usual part-time role, Pedro Feliz had his best season with the Giants, compiling a career-high 16 home runs and 48 RBI in just 235 at-bats. For the first time, he began to show glimpses of the player who hit 33 homers and drove in 105 runs at Triple-A Fresno in 2000.

Hitting, Baserunning & Defense

Once considered a player who struck out too much and wasn't selective at the plate, Feliz stopped trying to pull every pitch and began using right field more. Patience is a problem for him, as he walked only 10 times in nearly 250 plate appearances. Feliz is competent at his natural position, third base, and he played a handful of games in left field without making an error or embarrassing himself. He also was fine at first base. Feliz is not blessed with great speed, and his baserunning is unexceptional.

2004 Outlook

Just when it appeared Feliz might be nothing more than a role player in the major leagues, he proved last season that he could be a starter. The chance to be a full-time first baseman was there until the Giants re-signed first baseman J.T. Snow in December. So Felix will continue as a part-timer at first base.

Andres Galarraga

Position: 1B
Bats: R **Throws:** R
Ht: 6' 3" **Wt:** 265

Opening Day Age: 42
Born: 6/18/61 in Caracas, VZ
ML Seasons: 18
Pronunciation:
ON-dress Gahl-la-RAH-ga
Nickname: Big Cat

Overall Statistics

G	AB	R	H	D	T	HR	RBI	SB	BB	SO	Avg	OBP	Slg
110	272	36	82	15	0	12	42	1	19	61	.301	.352	.489
2250	8086	1194	2330	444	32	398	1423	128	583	2000	.288	.347	.499

2003 Situational Stats

	AB	H	HR	RBI	Avg		AB	H	HR	RBI	Avg
Home	133	41	6	23	.308	LHP	94	29	7	17	.309
Road	139	41	6	19	.295	RHP	178	53	5	25	.298
First Half	132	39	7	21	.295	Sc Pos	77	27	2	30	.351
Scnd Half	140	43	5	21	.307	Clutch	41	14	3	7	.341

2003 Season

When the Giants signed Andres Galarraga to a minor league deal before the season, there were questions about whether he could even make the team. Those concerns were quickly erased. Although Galarraga turned 42 last June, he added 41 points to his batting average from the previous season and hit three more home runs.

Hitting, Baserunning & Defense

At this point, Galarraga is best suited as a pinch-hitter and occasional starter. When he had to fill in for injured J.T. Snow for long stretches, his offense suffered. Overall, he was productive against both right- and lefthanders, though he showed more power vs. southpaws. Galarraga's added weight in his advancing years has made him much less nimble at first base, and he's become a below-average fielder. He also can clog the bases.

2004 Outlook

Galarraga returned last season to try to reach the 400-homer level. He's two short of that goal, but he hinted last season about the desire to retire and grew frustrated when manager Felipe Alou pinch-hit for him late in the season. However, it appears Galarraga could be back for his 19th season, though probably not with the Giants.

Jeffrey Hammonds

Position: LF/CF/RF
Bats: R **Throws:** R
Ht: 6' 0" **Wt:** 207

Opening Day Age: 33
Born: 3/5/71 in Scotch Plains, NJ
ML Seasons: 11

Overall Statistics

	G	AB	R	H	D	T	HR	RBI	SB	BB	SO	Avg	OBP	Slg
'03	46	132	22	32	12	0	4	13	1	16	28	.242	.329	.424
Car.	904	2905	458	797	166	17	107	416	66	275	570	.274	.339	.454

2003 Situational Stats

	AB	H	HR	RBI	Avg		AB	H	HR	RBI	Avg
Home	50	14	3	8	.280	LHP	25	9	0	0	.360
Road	82	18	1	5	.220	RHP	107	23	4	13	.215
First Half	38	6	1	3	.158	Sc Pos	30	3	0	5	.100
Scnd Half	94	26	3	10	.277	Clutch	20	2	1	2	.100

2003 Season

Released by the Brewers on June 4, Jeffrey Hammonds signed a minor league contract with the Giants and was promoted to the big club on July 30. Hammonds had played in just 10 games for Milwaukee, hitting .158, before spraining his right ankle April 14. Healthy again, he was a productive bench player in his 36 games with the Giants.

Hitting, Baserunning & Defense

A major disappointment in his two-plus seasons with Milwaukee, Hammonds showed glimpses of the gifted player he's supposed to be during his stint with the Giants. He hit the ball with authority and even showed some selectivity at the plate—a problem for him during much of his career. Hammonds also played well in the outfield. He doesn't have a great arm, and no longer is a stolen-base threat.

2004 Outlook

Hammonds showed enough with the Giants that the club re-signed the free agent for 2004. He could get a lot more at-bats than he did last year, especially if the Giants don't sign a replacement for Jose Cruz Jr. in right field. Getting more at-bats also means the injury-prone Hammonds has to stay healthy.

Matt Herges

Position: RP
Bats: L **Throws:** R
Ht: 6' 0" **Wt:** 205

Opening Day Age: 34
Born: 4/1/70 in Champaign, IL
ML Seasons: 5
Pronunciation: hur-JISS

Overall Statistics

	W	L	Pct.	ERA	G	GS	Sv	IP	H	BB	SO	HR	Avg
'03	3	2	.600	2.62	67	0	3	79.0	68	29	68	3	.233
Car.	25	20	.556	3.33	280	4	11	378.0	369	149	287	33	.259

2003 Situational Stats

	W	L	ERA	Sv	IP		AB	H	HR	RBI	Avg
Home	2	0	1.40	2	45.0	LHB	115	24	1	9	.209
Road	1	2	4.24	1	34.0	RHB	177	44	2	23	.249
First Half	2	2	2.86	3	44.0	Sc Pos	91	15	1	28	.165
Scnd Half	1	0	2.31	0	35.0	Clutch	110	27	2	20	.245

2003 Season

Matt Herges was one of several in-season acquisitions who helped the Giants win the National League West. Acquired from the Padres on July 13, Herges had a 0.71 ERA in his last 11 games and didn't allow a run in three games in the Division Series.

Pitching, Defense & Hitting

After struggling with his control in Montreal the season before, especially with his hard curveball, Herges walked only nine in 35 innings with the Giants. He displayed excellent velocity on his fastball, throwing in the mid-90s at times. A ground-ball pitcher, he permitted only three home runs after allowing 10 in 2002. Herges does not stand out as a fielder, but he is hard to run on because of his quick move to first base. He is a .222 lifetime hitter in the major leagues.

2004 Outlook

For a pitcher with his talent, Herges has bounced around the league the last few years, playing with four teams in three seasons. Although he was arbitration-eligible, his next relocation was delayed when the Giants signed him to a one-year deal in December. Herges has nine saves the past two seasons, and he seems more than adequate in late-game setup situations.

Joe Nathan

Traded To TWINS

Position: RP
Bats: R **Throws:** R
Ht: 6' 4" **Wt:** 207

Opening Day Age: 29
Born: 11/22/74 in Houston, TX
ML Seasons: 4

Overall Statistics

	W	L	Pct.	ERA	G	GS	Sv	IP	H	BB	SO	HR	Avg
'03	12	4	.750	2.96	78	0	0	79.0	51	33	83	7	.186
Car.	24	10	.706	4.12	121	29	1	266.1	225	142	200	36	.229

2003 Situational Stats

	W	L	ERA	Sv	IP		AB	H	HR	RBI	Avg
Home	7	1	1.99	0	40.2	LHB	98	27	2	14	.276
Road	5	3	3.99	0	38.1	RHB	176	24	5	22	.136
First Half	7	3	3.73	0	50.2	Sc Pos	67	14	4	31	.209
Scnd Half	5	1	1.59	0	28.1	Clutch	113	22	3	14	.195

2003 Season

Joe Nathan was one of San Francisco's biggest surprises while getting significant major league work for the first time since the 2000 season. Nathan had been a promising young starter before a right shoulder injury nearly ended his career. After spending two seasons in the minors, he was converted to relief and excelled in his role.

Pitching, Defense & Hitting

Nathan won a spot in spring training and began the season with a 22.1-inning scoreless streak that wasn't snapped until May 8. He went into a funk before regaining his confidence and control in July. Nathan throws a hard fastball with little movement, and when he doesn't spot it well, allows home runs. He gave up seven last season. A converted shortstop, he fields his position well. He had only one at-bat last season, but has hit two homers in the majors.

2004 Outlook

Though Nathan was a key member of the bullpen, the Giants shipped him to the Twins in a December deal for catcher A.J. Pierzynski. Nathan had ascended to the setup role, but there are those who believe he has the stuff to become a closer. He may get his first chance in 2004, as the Twins lost Eddie Guardado and LaTroy Hawkins to free agency.

Robb Nen

Position: RP
Bats: R **Throws:** R
Ht: 6' 5" **Wt:** 222

Opening Day Age: 34
Born: 11/28/69 in San Pedro, CA
ML Seasons: 10

Overall Statistics

	W	L	Pct.	ERA	G	GS	Sv	IP	H	BB	SO	HR	Avg
'03					Did Not Play								
Car.	45	42	.517	2.98	643	4	314	715.0	607	260	793	51	.227

2003 Situational Stats

	W	L	ERA	Sv	IP		AB	H	HR	RBI	Avg
Home	–	–	–	–	–	LHB	–	–	–	–	–
Road	–	–	–	–	–	RHB	–	–	–	–	–
First Half	–	–	–	–	–	Sc Pos	–	–	–	–	–
Scnd Half	–	–	–	–	–	Clutch	–	–	–	–	–

2003 Season

After undergoing arthroscopic surgery to repair a frayed labrum to his right shoulder following the 2002 season, Robb Nen appeared to be on schedule to pitch on Opening Day. However, a setback late in spring training resulted in a trip to the disabled list, followed by additional arthroscopic surgery April 18. When there was little improvement, Nen opted for a more comprehensive procedure to repair a rotator cuff tear in early May, ending his season.

Pitching, Defense & Hitting

The Giants won 100 games and made the playoffs without Nen throwing a pitch, but they need their closer to return to his old form. When healthy, he's one of the best in the game, featuring a high-90s fastball and a 90-92 MPH slider. With an awkward toe-tap in his delivery, Nen isn't always in position to handle comebackers or line drives. He's easy to run on.

2004 Outlook

The Giants expect Nen to be at full health before the regular season, but that's what they thought last year. This is his second major operation in four years, and there are no guarantees that Nen will have his full velocity by Opening Day, if at all this year.

Neifi Perez

Position: 2B/SS
Bats: B **Throws:** R
Ht: 6' 0" **Wt:** 175

Opening Day Age: 30
Born: 6/2/73 in Villa Mella, DR
ML Seasons: 8
Pronunciation: NAY-fee

Overall Statistics

	G	AB	R	H	D	T	HR	RBI	SB	BB	SO	Avg	OBP	Slg
'03	120	328	27	84	19	4	1	31	3	14	23	.256	.285	.348
Car.	982	3809	505	1032	171	58	48	361	47	177	382	.271	.301	.384

2003 Situational Stats

	AB	H	HR	RBI	Avg		AB	H	HR	RBI	Avg
Home	149	33	1	18	.221	LHP	75	19	1	14	.253
Road	179	51	0	13	.285	RHP	253	65	0	17	.257
First Half	208	59	0	21	.284	Sc Pos	84	20	0	28	.238
Scnd Half	120	25	1	10	.208	Clutch	51	6	1	5	.118

2003 Season

The Giants signed Neifi Perez to be a backup middle infielder, but because of injuries to second baseman Ray Durham and shortstop Rich Aurilia, he wound up appearing in 120 games. Perez came to the Giants with a reputation as a guy who could create clubhouse problems, but if that side of Perez ever existed, it did not surface last season. He was a contributor on the field and a cheery presence in the clubhouse.

Hitting, Baserunning & Defense

Perez is an aggressive line-drive hitter who makes contact but doesn't walk or hit with power. The switch-hitter has a little bit more extra-base pop from the right side. Perez plays Gold Glove-caliber defense at shortstop, displaying tremendous range and one of the most powerful arms of any infielder in the National League. He also is very adept at second base. He has decent speed but is not a good baserunner.

2004 Outlook

The Giants signed Perez to a two-year contract prior to 2003, and he could replace the departing Rich Aurilia as the regular shortstop this year. Perez would be an upgrade defensively over Aurilia, but the team would have to make up for Aurilia's offense elsewhere.

Felix Rodriguez

Position: RP
Bats: R **Throws:** R
Ht: 6' 1" **Wt:** 198

Opening Day Age: 31
Born: 9/9/72 in Montecristi, DR
ML Seasons: 8

Overall Statistics

	W	L	Pct.	ERA	G	GS	Sv	IP	H	BB	SO	HR	Avg
'03	8	2	.800	3.10	68	0	2	61.0	59	29	46	5	.259
Car.	32	17	.653	3.43	422	1	10	459.0	400	218	420	35	.235

2003 Situational Stats

	W	L	ERA	Sv	IP		AB	H	HR	RBI	Avg
Home	6	0	2.55	1	35.1	LHB	91	24	1	4	.264
Road	2	2	3.86	1	25.2	RHB	137	35	4	21	.255
First Half	5	0	3.48	2	41.1	Sc Pos	66	14	3	22	.212
Scnd Half	3	2	2.29	0	19.2	Clutch	138	36	4	18	.261

2003 Season

Although Felix Rodriguez improved on his 2002 numbers, his critics continued to grow last season. Giants fans will never forgive Rodriguez for allowing a three-run homer to Anaheim's Scott Spiezio late in Game 6 of the 2002 World Series, and he gave up a two-run single to Florida's Miguel Cabrera that proved to be the game-winner in Game 4 of last season's Division Series.

Pitching, Defense & Hitting

Rodriguez has tried to integrate an offspeed pitch into his repertoire, but he remains strictly a fastball pitcher. His velocity was down early in the season and he struggled, losing his setup job to Joe Nathan. With a less-pressured role, his work improved. A former minor league catcher, Rodriguez is an accomplished hitter. He rarely has to field his position because of his high strikeout and flyball totals, but he's effective at controlling the running game.

2004 Outlook

Despite his ups and downs, the Giants picked up the $3.05 million option on Rodriguez' contract. There was once a time when he was considered possible closer material, but he'll probably have to settle for his current role as seventh-inning specialist for the time being.

Jerome Williams

Top Prospect

Position: SP
Bats: R **Throws:** R
Ht: 6' 3" **Wt:** 180

Opening Day Age: 22
Born: 12/4/81 in Honolulu, HI
ML Seasons: 1

Overall Statistics

	W	L	Pct.	ERA	G	GS	Sv	IP	H	BB	SO	HR	Avg
'03	7	5	.583	3.30	21	21	0	131.0	116	49	88	10	.242
Car.	7	5	.583	3.30	21	21	0	131.0	116	49	88	10	.242

2003 Situational Stats

	W	L	ERA	Sv	IP		AB	H	HR	RBI	Avg
Home	3	3	2.91	0	68.0	LHB	228	49	1	13	.215
Road	4	2	3.71	0	63.0	RHB	252	67	9	28	.266
First Half	5	1	2.64	0	58.0	Sc Pos	87	24	1	26	.276
Scnd Half	2	4	3.82	0	73.0	Clutch	17	7	1	3	.412

2003 Season

After beginning the season at Triple-A Fresno, Jerome Williams made his debut in Philadelphia on April 26 when Jason Schmidt went on the bereavement list. Sent back to Fresno after a so-so outing, Williams was promoted again on June 3. He pitched much better in this go-round and remained with the Giants the rest of the season.

Pitching

Williams was advertised as having a fastball that reached 95 MPH, but that rarely materialized. More often, he threw in the low 90s, though with precise control. He complemented his fastball with an effective slider. Williams is a natural athlete who is agile and quick off the mound. He also displayed a fine pickoff move, but his slow delivery to the plate helped runners. His hitting is subpar, but he showed he could lay down a bunt.

2004 Outlook

Williams wasn't expected to reach the majors, much less have a prominent role in the rotation last season, but injuries forced the Giants to alter their plans. Now that he's had almost a full year under his belt, he should only improve. Manager Felipe Alou marveled at the maturity and intelligence Williams exhibited. The Giants will have to be wary of overuse at this point in his career.

Eric Young

Position: 2B
Bats: R **Throws:** R
Ht: 5' 8" **Wt:** 186

Opening Day Age: 36
Born: 5/18/67 in New Brunswick, NJ
ML Seasons: 12
Nickname: E.Y.

Overall Statistics

	G	AB	R	H	D	T	HR	RBI	SB	BB	SO	Avg	OBP	Slg
'03	135	475	80	119	20	1	15	34	28	57	44	.251	.336	.392
Car.	1510	5495	899	1565	287	43	73	489	436	585	405	.285	.360	.393

2003 Situational Stats

	AB	H	HR	RBI	Avg		AB	H	HR	RBI	Avg
Home	225	56	7	18	.249	LHP	114	28	6	8	.246
Road	250	63	8	16	.252	RHP	361	91	9	26	.252
First Half	307	77	12	27	.251	Sc Pos	80	16	1	19	.200
Scnd Half	168	42	3	7	.250	Clutch	76	18	2	5	.237

2003 Season

With second baseman Ray Durham bothered by injuries, the Giants acquired Eric Young from Milwaukee on August 19 for minor league pitcher Greg Bruso. They didn't receive much from Young, who hit .197 with no homers and three RBI in 26 games. Young also was left off the roster for the Division Series.

Hitting, Baserunning & Defense

Young is considered a contact hitter, but he had hit a career high 15 homers with the Brewers prior to the trade. The power—and pretty much everything else—was totally lacking in his short stint with the Giants. At second base, Young has good range, but he bobbles too many balls and is average at best on the double play. Despite a strained quad muscle, Young continued to run, stealing a combined 28 bases with the Brewers and Giants.

2004 Outlook

The Giants declined to exercise the option on Young's contract, making him a free agent. He appears to be on the downward side of his career, and at age 36, his days as an everyday player may be over. He'll probably have to settle for signing a minor league contract before spring training begins.

Other San Francisco Giants

Manny Aybar (Pos: RHP, Age: 31)

	W	L	Pct.	ERA	G	GS	Sv	IP	H	BB	SO	HR	Avg
'03	0	0	–	6.00	3	0	0	3.0	4	3	2	1	.333
Car.	17	18	.486	5.05	186	28	3	365.2	382	165	246	45	.269

Though Aybar has a 3.41 lifetime ERA in the minors, he has pitched a total of 40 big league innings over the last three seasons. The Giants are his sixth organization in parts of seven seasons. 2004 Outlook: C

Marvin Benard (Pos: LF, Age: 34, Bats: L)

	G	AB	R	H	D	T	HR	RBI	SB	BB	SO	Avg	OBP	Slg
'03	46	71	5	14	3	1	0	4	1	4	9	.197	.237	.268
Car.	891	2630	441	714	138	21	54	260	105	265	454	.271	.343	.402

Since hitting .290 with 16 HR in 1999, Benard has had fewer at-bats in each season. Both of the 34-year-old's knees have given him trouble, and his days as a Giant probably are over. 2004 Outlook: C

Jim Brower (Pos: RHP, Age: 31)

	W	L	Pct.	ERA	G	GS	Sv	IP	H	BB	SO	HR	Avg
'03	8	5	.615	3.96	51	5	2	100.0	90	39	65	8	.249
Car.	23	21	.523	4.44	175	28	3	397.1	393	172	266	51	.261

Acquired just before Opening Day, Brower was a staff-saver for the Giants, pitching 100 innings in both starting and relief roles. He loved his new home park, posting a 2.06 ERA in Pac Bell. 2004 Outlook: C

Alberto Castillo (Pos: C, Age: 34, Bats: R)

	G	AB	R	H	D	T	HR	RBI	SB	BB	SO	Avg	OBP	Slg
'03	11	15	2	3	1	0	1	4	0	0	5	.200	.200	.467
Car.	343	805	68	176	26	1	9	73	2	74	177	.219	.287	.287

Castillo has a .219 lifetime average and never has gotten more than 255 at-bats in a season. He was re-signed by the Giants to hold down the third catcher spot. 2004 Outlook: C

Jason Christiansen (Pos: LHP, Age: 34)

	W	L	Pct.	ERA	G	GS	Sv	IP	H	BB	SO	HR	Avg
'03	0	0	–	5.19	40	0	0	26.0	25	11	22	3	.243
Car.	17	22	.436	4.17	400	0	13	352.0	320	174	341	30	.243

The classic situational southpaw, Christiansen has no starts among his 400 appearances. Despite shoulder and elbow surgeries in recent years, he held opposing lefties to a .208 average in 2003. 2004 Outlook: C

Kevin Correia (Pos: RHP, Age: 23)

	W	L	Pct.	ERA	G	GS	Sv	IP	H	BB	SO	HR	Avg
'03	3	1	.750	3.66	10	7	0	39.1	41	18	28	6	.275
Car.	3	1	.750	3.66	10	7	0	39.1	41	18	28	6	.275

Correia was called up from the minors five different times last year and held his own in seven starts for the Giants. The big righthander has not yet reached 200 innings in his pro career. 2004 Outlook: C

Scott Eyre (Pos: LHP, Age: 31)

	W	L	Pct.	ERA	G	GS	Sv	IP	H	BB	SO	HR	Avg
'03	2	1	.667	3.32	74	0	1	57.0	60	26	35	4	.268
Car.	14	21	.400	4.94	239	32	3	359.0	398	191	251	53	.281

Since he was acquired on waivers from Toronto in August of 2002, Eyre has played an important role in the Giants' pen. Last year, he held opposing lefties to a .219 average. 2004 Outlook: C

Jesse Foppert (Pos: RHP, Age: 23)

	W	L	Pct.	ERA	G	GS	Sv	IP	H	BB	SO	HR	Avg
'03	8	9	.471	5.03	23	21	0	111.0	103	69	101	16	.249
Car.	8	9	.471	5.03	23	21	0	111.0	103	69	101	16	.249

With barely 200 professional innings under his belt, Foppert suffered the usual growing pains in his rookie season. His elbow pains were more serious, and he had Tommy John surgery late in the year. 2004 Outlook: D

Dustin Hermanson (Pos: RHP, Age: 31)

	W	L	Pct.	ERA	G	GS	Sv	IP	H	BB	SO	HR	Avg
'03	3	3	.500	4.06	32	6	1	68.2	70	24	39	9	.271
Car.	65	65	.500	4.28	247	162	5	1088.0	1101	396	734	139	.265

After pitching for four teams in the last four years, Hermanson was re-signed by the Giants in December. He might be considered for a rotation spot, as he had a 2.97 ERA in six starts last season. 2004 Outlook: C

Ryan Jensen (Pos: RHP, Age: 28)

	W	L	Pct.	ERA	G	GS	Sv	IP	H	BB	SO	HR	Avg
'03	0	0	–	10.80	6	2	0	13.1	21	5	3	6	.404
Car.	14	10	.583	4.83	48	39	0	227.1	248	96	134	32	.284

Jensen started the year in the Giants' rotation, but a lower back strain sent him to the DL after two poor starts. It all went downhill from there, and he went 1-10 with a 5.30 ERA for Triple-A Fresno. 2004 Outlook: C

Trey Lunsford (Pos: C, Age: 24, Bats: R)

	G	AB	R	H	D	T	HR	RBI	SB	BB	SO	Avg	OBP	Slg
'03	1	1	0	0	0	0	0	0	0	0	0	.000	.000	.000
Car.	4	4	0	2	1	0	0	1	0	0	1	.500	.500	.750

Lunsford has hit .271 in just 473 at-bats above Class-A ball. At 24, he simply needs experience, but there are several catchers in front of him who will make progress difficult. 2004 Outlook: C

Brian Powell (Pos: RHP, Age: 30)

	W	L	Pct.	ERA	G	GS	Sv	IP	H	BB	SO	HR	Avg
'03	0	1	.000	13.50	1	1	0	4.2	8	1	3	3	.381
Car.	6	16	.273	6.14	42	32	0	180.1	212	74	96	40	.290

Powell is 78-56 with a 3.82 ERA in his nine minor league seasons, but he has not been able to succeed in the majors. He ended last season in the Phillies' organization. 2004 Outlook: C

Cody Ransom (Pos: SS, Age: 28, Bats: R)

	G	AB	R	H	D	T	HR	RBI	SB	BB	SO	Avg	OBP	Slg
'03	20	27	7	6	1	0	1	1	0	1	11	.222	.250	.370
Car.	36	37	10	8	1	0	1	2	0	2	17	.216	.256	.324

The Giants' perennial shortstop of the future is now 28 years old. In the last three years at Triple-A Fresno, Ransom has hit .233 with an average season of 16 home runs and 58 RBI. 2004 Outlook: C

Ruben Rivera (Pos: CF, Age: 30, Bats: R)

	G	AB	R	H	D	T	HR	RBI	SB	BB	SO	Avg	OBP	Slg
'03	31	50	6	9	2	0	2	4	1	5	14	.180	.255	.340
Car.	662	1586	237	343	67	11	64	203	50	185	510	.216	.307	.393

Once a hot Yankees prospect, Rivera has been with six teams in the last four seasons. While he has all the tools, he has a lifetime average of .216 in 1,586 at-bats. 2004 Outlook: C

Francisco Santos (Pos: RF, Age: 30, Bats: L)

	G	AB	R	H	D	T	HR	RBI	SB	BB	SO	Avg	OBP	Slg
'03	8	15	2	3	2	0	1	1	0	0	3	.200	.200	.533
Car.	8	15	2	3	2	0	1	1	0	0	3	.200	.200	.533

Santos has compiled a .286 average in the minors and has stolen as many as 16 bases in a season. He has enough tools to compete for a spot on the big league bench this year. 2004 Outlook: C

Tony Torcato (Pos: LF, Age: 24, Bats: L)

	G	AB	R	H	D	T	HR	RBI	SB	BB	SO	Avg	OBP	Slg
'03	14	16	0	3	1	0	0	1	0	0	4	.188	.235	.250
Car.	19	27	0	6	2	0	0	1	0	0	6	.222	.250	.296

Torcato has hit .305 in his six seasons in the Giants' minor league system. Now 24 years old, he should get a shot at winning at least a bench job in the majors this year. 2004 Outlook: C

Yorvit Torrealba (Pos: C, Age: 25, Bats: R)

	G	AB	R	H	D	T	HR	RBI	SB	BB	SO	Avg	OBP	Slg
'03	66	200	22	52	10	2	4	29	1	14	39	.260	.312	.390
Car.	122	340	39	92	20	3	6	45	1	28	59	.271	.332	.400

Torrealba had two stints on the bereavement list last year. He will continue to serve as the Giants' back-up catcher, this year to newcomer A. J. Pierzynski. 2004 Outlook: C

Carlos Valderrama (Pos: LF, Age: 26, Bats: R)

	G	AB	R	H	D	T	HR	RBI	SB	BB	SO	Avg	OBP	Slg
'03	7	7	0	1	0	0	0	0	1	0	3	.143	.143	.143
Car.	7	7	0	1	0	0	0	0	1	0	3	.143	.143	.143

With only 202 Triple-A at-bats under his belt, Valderrama needs more seasoning, but he has hit exactly .300 in seven minor league seasons. The speedy center fielder stole 54 bases back in 2000. 2004 Outlook: C

Chad Zerbe (Pos: LHP, Age: 31)

	W	L	Pct.	ERA	G	GS	Sv	IP	H	BB	SO	HR	Avg
'03	1	1	.500	4.71	33	1	0	49.2	60	14	17	3	.311
Car.	6	1	.857	3.87	114	2	0	151.0	159	46	70	10	.278

Though most of his minor league experience has been as a starter, Zerbe has worked almost exclusively out of the pen in the bigs. Opposing lefthanders batted .365 against him last year, so his future is cloudy. 2004 Outlook: C

San Francisco Giants Minor League Prospects

Organization Overview:

In recent years the Giants have made a habit of trading young pitching talent in order to acquire major leaguers. Last season was no exception, when they included Kurt Ainsworth and Ryan Hannaman in the deal that netted Sidney Ponson for the stretch drive. This offseason, Boof Bonser and Francisco Liriano were sacrificed as part of the trade that landed A.J. Pierzynski. Such a purge of pitching talent would be alarming were it not for the fact that the system also spat out Jerome Williams and Jesse Foppert in 2003, and they may not be going anywhere. Even more high-caliber performers could be surfacing in the near future. Still, ownership doesn't mind seeing youngsters earning a minimal salary make the roster. Don't be surprised if the Giants start retaining more of their homegrown products.

David Aardsma

Position: P
Opening Day Age: 22
Bats: R **Throws:** R
Born: 12/27/81
Ht: 6' 5" **Wt:** 200

Recent Statistics

	W	L	ERA	G	GS	Sv	IP	H	R	BB	SO	HR
2003 A San Jose	1	1	1.96	18	0	8	18.1	14	4	7	28	2

The Giants used one of the picks obtained as compensation for the loss of free agent Jeff Kent to choose Aardsma with the 22nd overall selection last June. Aardsma had been the closer at Rice, and he moved seamlessly into a similar role at high Class-A San Jose. As you'd expect with a first-round pick, Aardsma has good stuff, with a 96-97 MPH fastball and a hard breaking ball. But perhaps his best trait is his ability to throw strikes. He's also a workaholic who loves the game and is very hungry to succeed. He's actually older than a couple of the Giants' other top pitching prospects. Despite his professional inexperience, Aardsma may move quickly.

Matthew Cain

Position: P
Opening Day Age: 19
Bats: R **Throws:** R
Born: 10/1/84 in Dothan,
Ht: 6' 3" **Wt:** 185
AL

Recent Statistics

	W	L	ERA	G	GS	Sv	IP	H	R	BB	SO	HR
2002 R Giants	0	1	3.72	8	7	0	19.1	19	10	11	20	1
2003 A Hagerstown	4	4	2.55	14	14	0	74.0	57	24	24	90	5

Cain lost a good part of 2003 due to a stress fracture in his elbow, but showed considerable promise at Class-A Hagerstown. A first-round selection in 2002 out of a Tennessee high school, Cain worked last season at age 18. But he still struck out nearly 11 batters per nine innings in the South Atlantic League. Any lingering concerns about his arm injury were allayed when he was throwing 96-97 MPH in the instructional league. Cain complements his fastball with a hard breaking ball and an excellent changeup. He's a smart, competitive hurler who asks the right questions, so he would seem to have the aptitude for making adjustments. He'll likely pitch at Double-A this season while still just a teenager.

Fred Lewis

Position: OF
Opening Day Age: 23
Bats: L **Throws:** R
Born: 12/9/80 in
Ht: 6' 2" **Wt:** 190
Wiggins, MS

Recent Statistics

	G	AB	R	H	D	T	HR	RBI	SB	BB	SO	Avg
2002 A Salem-Keiz	58	239	43	77	9	3	1	23	9	26	58	.322
2003 A Hagerstown	114	420	61	105	17	8	1	27	30	68	112	.250

Lewis played collegiately at Southern University before getting taken in the second round of the 2002 draft. While he debuted in impressive fashion that summer, batting .322 at short-season Salem-Keizer, he found the going a bit tougher in his first crack at a full-season league. Nevertheless, the Giants say Lewis has made tremendous strides in his overall game. With over 170 professional games under his belt, he's learned how to make better use of his speed when stealing bases, taking the extra base, and when taking routes to balls in the outfield. If he can improve last year's batting average while maintaining his walk rate, Lewis would present an exciting package at the top of a lineup.

Todd Linden

Position: OF
Opening Day Age: 23
Bats: B **Throws:** R
Born: 6/30/80 in
Ht: 6' 2" **Wt:** 210
Edmonds, WA

Recent Statistics

	G	AB	R	H	D	T	HR	RBI	SB	BB	SO	Avg
2003 AAA Fresno	125	471	75	131	24	3	11	56	14	40	105	.278
2003 NL San Fran	18	38	2	8	1	0	1	6	0	1	8	.211

Linden has been on the fast track since signing as a supplemental first-round pick in 2001. He made his professional debut at Double-A in 2002, reached Triple-A that season, and was promoted to the majors in the midst of the Giants' pennant race last year. Linden possesses many of the physical tools you look for. He's a switch-hitter with power potential from both sides of the plate. While his walk rate declined last season, he has shown a willingness to take a free pass in the past. He also boasts surprising speed for his size. Depending on the roster moves the Giants make this winter, it isn't out of the question that Linden could open in their outfield in 2004.

Noah Lowry

Position: P **Opening Day Age:** 23
Bats: L **Throws:** L **Born:** 10/10/80 in
Ht: 6' 2" **Wt:** 190 Ventura, CA

Recent Statistics

	W	L	ERA	G	GS	Sv	IP	H	R	BB	SO	HR
2003 AA Norwich	9	6	4.72	23	23	0	118.1	127	66	47	97	7
2003 AAA Fresno	1	0	2.37	4	4	0	19.0	15	5	6	13	0
2003 NL San Fran	0	0	0.00	4	0	0	6.1	1	0	2	5	0

Lowry and Dan Haren formed quite a duo for Pepperdine in 2001. Lowry led the West Coast Conference in wins, ERA and strikeouts that spring, before being chosen by the Giants in the first round of the June draft. Haren was selected a round later by the Cardinals, and both made their big league debuts last season. Lowry's pitching arm may have been abused a bit in college, but he features an excellent changeup that can make his fastball look even more sneaky quick. While he didn't exactly dominate at Double-A last year, he did nothing wrong in limited exposure at Triple-A and in four September appearances with San Francisco. He has a chance of securing a big league job in '04.

Lance Niekro

Position: 3B **Opening Day Age:** 25
Bats: R **Throws:** R **Born:** 1/29/79 in Winter
Ht: 6' 3" **Wt:** 210 Haven, FL

Recent Statistics

	G	AB	R	H	D	T	HR	RBI	SB	BB	SO	Avg
2003 AAA Fresno	98	381	43	115	15	2	4	41	3	19	39	.302
2003 NL San Fran	5	5	2	1	1	0	0	2	0	0	1	.200

Niekro is the son and nephew of former big leaguers Joe and Phil, respectively. Lance has demonstrated an interesting blend of strengths and weaknesses since being chosen in the second round of the 2000 draft. He's hit .300 at nearly every level and doesn't strike out a lot for someone who plays a corner position. But those talents have been balanced by disappointing home-run power and a seeming unwillingness to take any walks. He's also had problems staying healthy, as 2003 marked the first time he played 80 games. Hoping to fortify his power, Niekro has been working on getting stronger this winter. Since almost all of his offensive value has been tied to his batting average, improved slugging could be critical.

Daniel Ortmeier

Position: OF **Opening Day Age:** 22
Bats: B **Throws:** L **Born:** 5/11/81 in
Ht: 6' 4" **Wt:** 220 Highland Village, TX

Recent Statistics

	G	AB	R	H	D	T	HR	RBI	SB	BB	SO	Avg
2002 A Salem-Keiz	49	195	32	57	9	1	5	31	3	18	37	.292
2003 A San Jose	115	408	62	124	32	6	8	56	13	39	89	.304

From a physical standpoint, Ortmeier is almost identical to Linden. Like Linden, Ortmeier is a switch-hitting outfielder with good size and power potential. He was the Giants' third-round selection in 2002, one round after Lewis. But Ortmeier injured his throwing shoulder diving for a ball that summer, and hasn't yet converted his power into home runs. Still, he has looked like a .300 hitter, posting an average that ranked in the top 10 of the high Class-A California League last season. He also delivered lots of extra-base hits. In time, the doubles may start clearing the fences. He arguably had a better 2003 than Lewis, at a higher level, and Ortmeier's next logical step would be Double-A.

Merkin Valdez

Position: P **Opening Day Age:** 21
Bats: R **Throws:** R **Born:** 8/26/82 in San
Ht: 6' 3" **Wt:** 171 Cristobal, DR

Recent Statistics

	W	L	ERA	G	GS	Sv	IP	H	R	BB	SO	HR
2002 R Braves	7	3	1.98	12	8	0	68.1	47	18	12	76	0
2003 A Hagerstown	9	5	2.25	26	26	0	156.0	119	42	49	166	11

The Giants acquired Valdez, along with Damian Moss, when they dealt Russ Ortiz to the Braves after the 2002 season. Valdez looks like a keeper. He was named Pitcher of the Year in the Giants' system last season, ranking second in the Class-A South Atlantic League in ERA. Tall, with arms like a spider, Valdez has great stuff, including a good slider and a fastball that can reach 97 MPH. Even though he has yet to work at the upper levels of the system, the Giants aren't ruling out a leap to the big leagues in 2004. They've learned that pitchers with Valdez' delivery, arm strength and ability to handle pressure have a way of forcing their way into a team's plans.

Others to Watch

Shortstop **Jamie Athas** (24) won't knock your socks off, but he's a solid player who can run and play either middle-infield position. He bats lefthanded, which may add to his value. . . Likewise, outfielder **Jason Ellison** (25) isn't an upper-echelon prospect, but since 2002 he has hit .300 in over 600 Triple-A at-bats. He might be a useful bat off the bench. . . Lefthander **Josh Habel** (23), a 14th-round pick out of Northern Iowa in 2002, has drawn comparisons to Jamie Moyer. Habel's best offering is a plus-plus changeup, and he thrived at Class-A last year. Still, he may be tested when he works at higher levels. . . First baseman **Travis Ishikawa** (20) was a highly touted football prospect in high school. The Giants had to pay a lot to sign him, but feel he was worth it. He's struck out quite a bit in the minors, but began to flash his power potential in the instructional league. . . While catcher **Justin Knoedler** (23) has pitched in the past, his future is behind the plate. As you might guess, his arm might be his best defensive tool, and he can hit the longball. . . Lefthander **Erick Threets** (22) continues to tease with his power arm. For Threets, 98 MPH is only an average fastball. Unfortunately, control and consistency are problems.

2003 American League Leaders

Batters

Batting Average
minimum 502 PA

Bill Mueller	**.326**
Manny Ramirez	.325
Derek Jeter	.324

Home Runs

Alex Rodriguez	**47**
Carlos Delgado	42
Frank Thomas	42

Runs Batted In

Carlos Delgado	**145**
Alex Rodriguez	118
2 players tied with	117

Games Played

Hideki Matsui	**163**
Aubrey Huff	162
Miguel Tejada	162

At-Bats

Alfonso Soriano	**682**
Ichiro Suzuki	679
Vernon Wells	678

Runs Scored

Alex Rodriguez	**124**
Nomar Garciaparra	120
Vernon Wells	118

Hits

Vernon Wells	**215**
Ichiro Suzuki	212
Michael Young	204

Singles

Ichiro Suzuki	**162**
Michael Young	148
Carl Crawford	145

Doubles

Garret Anderson	**49**
Vernon Wells	**49**
Aubrey Huff	47

Triples

Cristian Guzman	**14**
Nomar Garciaparra	13
Carlos Beltran	10

Stolen Bases

Carl Crawford	**55**
Alex Sanchez	44
Carlos Beltran	41

Caught Stealing

Alex Sanchez	**18**
3 players tied with	10

Walks

Jason Giambi	**129**
Carlos Delgado	109
2 players tied with	100

Intentional Walks

Manny Ramirez	**28**
Carlos Delgado	23
Aubrey Huff	17

Hit by Pitch

Jason Giambi	**21**
Reed Johnson	20
Carlos Delgado	19

Strikeouts

Jason Giambi	**140**
Mike Cameron	137
Carlos Delgado	137

GDP

Paul Konerko	**28**
Hideki Matsui	25
Manny Ramirez	22

Sacrifice Hits

Ramon Santiago	**18**
Angel Berroa	13
Cristian Guzman	12

Sacrifice Flies

Jeff Conine	**12**
Shannon Stewart	11
3 players tied with	10

Plate Appearances

Vernon Wells	**735**
Alfonso Soriano	734
Ichiro Suzuki	725

Times on Base

Carlos Delgado	**300**
Manny Ramirez	290
Jason Giambi	284

Total Bases

Vernon Wells	**373**
Alex Rodriguez	364
Alfonso Soriano	358

Slugging Percentage
minimum 502 PA

Alex Rodriguez	**.600**
Carlos Delgado	.593
David Ortiz	.592

Slugging vs. LHP
minimum 125 PA

Frank Thomas	**.732**
Alex Rodriguez	.652
Milton Bradley	.634

Slugging vs. RHP
minimum 377 PA

David Ortiz	**.654**
Carlos Delgado	.649
Trot Nixon	.635

Cleanup Slugging
minimum 150 PA

Carlos Delgado	**.593**
Manny Ramirez	.587
Garret Anderson	.583

On-Base Percentage
minimum 502 PA

Manny Ramirez	**.427**
Carlos Delgado	.426
Jason Giambi	.412

OBP vs. LHP
minimum 125 PA

Milton Bradley	**.500**
Manny Ramirez	.476
Edgar Martinez	.457

OBP vs. RHP
minimum 377 PA

Carlos Delgado	**.439**
Jason Giambi	.430
Trot Nixon	.423

Leadoff Hitters OBP
minimum 150 PA

Jerry Hairston Jr.	**.389**
Aaron Guiel	.387
Shannon Stewart	.363

AB per HR
minimum 502 PA

Alex Rodriguez	**12.9**
Frank Thomas	13.0
Jason Giambi	13.0

Ground/Fly Ratio
minimum 502 PA

Jacque Jones	**2.58**
Ken Harvey	2.49
Derek Jeter	2.41

% Extra Bases Taken
minimum 40 Opp to Advance

Carlos Beltran	**66.0**
Raul Ibanez	64.5
Randy Winn	63.0

% Runs/Time on Base
minimum 502 PA

Nomar Garciaparra	**48.4**
Alfonso Soriano	46.0
Randy Winn	45.6

SB Success %
minimum 20 SB Attempts

Carlos Beltran	**91.1**
Marlon Anderson	86.4
Alex Rodriguez	85.0

Steals of Third

Ichiro Suzuki	**12**
Carl Crawford	9
Alex Sanchez	7

AVG Scoring Position
minimum 100 PA

Mike Sweeney	**.398**
Carlos Delgado	.357
Edgar Martinez	.352

AVG Late & Close
minimum 50 PA

Larry Bigbie	**.426**
Magglio Ordonez	.425
Doug Mientkiewicz	.397

AVG Bases Loaded
minimum 10 PA

Mike Sweeney	**.667**
Rocco Baldelli	.600
Mike Bordick	.600

GDP/GDP Opp
minimum 50 PA

Chris Singleton	**0.03**
Ichiro Suzuki	0.03
Trot Nixon	0.03

AVG vs. LHP
minimum 125 PA

Milton Bradley	.402
Manny Ramirez	.385
Ichiro Suzuki	.359

AVG vs. RHP
minimum 377 PA

Bill Mueller	.342
Trot Nixon	.330
Hank Blalock	.329

AVG at Home
minimum 251 PA

N. Garciaparra	.359
Michael Young	.353
Luis Matos	.350

AVG on the Road
minimum 251 PA

Edgar Martinez	.339
Garret Anderson	.339
Derek Jeter	.330

AVG on 3-1 Count
minimum 10 PA

Troy Glaus	.857
Darin Erstad	.750
Carlos Pena	.727

AVG with Two Strikes
minimum 150 PA

B.J. Surhoff	.270
Tony Graffanino	.268
Derek Jeter	.264

AVG on 0-2 Count
minimum 20 PA

David Ortiz	.364
Aubrey Huff	.322
Carlos Lee	.304

AVG on Full Count
minimum 40 PA

N. Garciaparra	.467
Reed Johnson	.429
Josh Bard	.429

Pitches Seen

Jason Giambi	2916
Johnny Damon	2850
Frank Thomas	2824

Pitches per PA
minimum 502 PA

Edgar Martinez	4.02
Frank Thomas	4.27
Jason Giambi	4.23

% Pitches Taken
minimum 1500 Pitches Seen

Scott Hatteberg	67.1
Edgar Martinez	65.0
Nick Johnson	64.3

% Swings that Missed
minimum 1500 Pitches Seen

Brian Roberts	6.8
David Eckstein	7.7
Scott Hatteberg	8.8

% Swings Put in Play
minimum 1500 Pitches Seen

Scott Hatteberg	60.5
Hideki Matsui	55.5
John Olerud	53.6

Bunts in Play

Alex Sanchez	71
Ramon Santiago	49
Coco Crisp	37

Pitchers

Earned Run Average
minimum 162 IP

Pedro Martinez	2.22
Tim Hudson	2.70
Esteban Loaiza	2.90

Wins

Roy Halladay	22
3 players tied with	21

Losses

Mike Maroth	21
Jeremy Bonderman	19
Nate Cornejo	17

Won-Lost Percentage
minimum 15 decisions

Johan Santana	.800
Pedro Martinez	.778
Roy Halladay	.759

Games

Trever Miller	79
Jamie Walker	78
2 players tied with	76

Games Started

Roy Halladay	36
3 players tied with	35

Complete Games

Bartolo Colon	9
Roy Halladay	9
Mark Mulder	9

Shutouts

5 players tied with	2

Games Finished

Keith Foulke	67
Mike MacDougal	61
Eddie Guardado	60

Innings Pitched

Roy Halladay	266.0
Bartolo Colon	242.0
Tim Hudson	240.0

Hits Allowed

Roy Halladay	253
Mark Buehrle	250
2 players tied with	242

Batters Faced

Roy Halladay	1071
Bartolo Colon	984
Mark Buehrle	978

Runs Allowed

Cory Lidle	133
Mike Maroth	131
John Thomson	125

Earned Runs Allowed

Cory Lidle	123
Mike Maroth	123
John Thomson	117

Home Runs Allowed

Ryan Franklin	34
Mike Maroth	34
Jarrod Washburn	34

Walks Allowed

Victor Zambrano	106
Barry Zito	88
Jason Johnson	80

Hit Batsmen

Victor Zambrano	20
6 players tied with	12

Strikeouts

Esteban Loaiza	207
Pedro Martinez	206
Roy Halladay	204

Wild Pitches

Victor Zambrano	15
Jeremy Bonderman	12
2 players tied with	11

Balks

Ted Lilly	4
Kenny Rogers	4
4 players tied with	3

Run Support per 9 IP
minimum 162 IP

Derek Lowe	7.26
Andy Pettitte	7.04
Brian Anderson	6.42

Baserunners per 9 IP
minimum 162 IP

Pedro Martinez	9.8
Mike Mussina	9.9
Roy Halladay	9.9

Opposition AVG
minimum 162 IP

Pedro Martinez	.215
Barry Zito	.219
Tim Hudson	.223

Opposition SLG
minimum 162 IP

Tim Hudson	.308
Pedro Martinez	.314
Barry Zito	.324

Opposition OBP
minimum 162 IP

Pedro Martinez	.272
Mike Mussina	.275
Roy Halladay	.275

Home Runs per 9 IP
minimum 162 IP

Pedro Martinez	0.34
Tim Hudson	0.56
Esteban Loaiza	0.68

Strikeouts per 9 IP
minimum 162 IP

Pedro Martinez	9.93
Esteban Loaiza	8.23
Mike Mussina	8.18

Walks per 9 IP
minimum 162 IP

David Wells	0.8
Roy Halladay	1.1
Brad Radke	1.2

K/BB Ratio
minimum 162 IP

Roy Halladay	6.38
David Wells	5.05
Mike Mussina	4.88

Fielding

Steals Allowed

Jason Johnson	32
Jeremy Bonderman	25
2 players tied with	24

Caught Stealing Off

Mike Maroth	11
Mark Mulder	10
Mike Mussina	10

SB % Allowed
minimum 162 IP

Brian Anderson	11.1
Bartolo Colon	14.3
Mark Buehrle	20.0

GDPs Induced

Bartolo Colon	31
Nate Cornejo	30
Jake Westbrook	26

GDPs per 9 IP
minimum 162 IP

Nate Cornejo	1.4
Bartolo Colon	1.2
Brian Anderson	1.1

GDP/GDP Opp
minimum 30 BFP

S. Hasegawa	0.25
Jose Santiago	0.23
2 players tied with	0.21

Ground/Fly Ratio Off
minimum 162 IP

Derek Lowe	3.9
Roy Halladay	2.7
Tim Hudson	2.3

AVG Allowed Sc Pos
minimum 125 BFP

Johan Santana	.165
Roger Clemens	.186
Esteban Loaiza	.192

Pitches Thrown

Barry Zito	3747
Roy Halladay	3630
Bartolo Colon	3529

Pitches per Batter
minimum 162 IP

David Wells	3.39
Roy Halladay	3.39
Mark Mulder	3.51

Pickoff Throws

Bartolo Colon	184
Mike Maroth	182
Andy Pettitte	165

ERA at Home
minimum 81 IP

Scot Shields	1.83
Mark Mulder	2.18
Tim Hudson	2.32

ERA on the Road
minimum 81 IP

Pedro Martinez	1.57
Esteban Loaiza	2.46
Roger Clemens	2.53

AVG vs. LHB
minimum 125 BFP

David Riske	.145
Keith Foulke	.158
Damaso Marte	.168

AVG vs. RHB
minimum 225 BFP

Pedro Martinez	.179
Esteban Loaiza	.191
Victor Zambrano	.206

Relief ERA
minimum 50 relief IP

S. Hasegawa	1.48
Rafael Soriano	1.53
Brendan Donnelly	1.58

Relief Wins

Keith Foulke	9
LaTroy Hawkins	9
2 players tied with	8

Relief Losses

Danys Baez	9
Francisco Cordero	8
Travis Harper	8

Saves

Keith Foulke	43
Eddie Guardado	41
Mariano Rivera	40

Blown Saves

Danys Baez	10
Francisco Cordero	10
2 players tied with	8

Save Opportunities

Keith Foulke	48
Mariano Rivera	46
Eddie Guardado	45

Save Percentage
minimum 20 SvOp

Eddie Guardado	91.1
Keith Foulke	89.6
Troy Percival	89.2

Holds

Brendan Donnelly	29
Jason Grimsley	28
LaTroy Hawkins	28

Relief Innings

Steve Sparks	107.0
Travis Harper	93.0
Keith Foulke	86.2

Relief AVG Allowed
minimum 50 relief IP

Rafael Soriano	.162
Fr. Rodriguez	.172
Keith Foulke	.184

Relief Runners/9 IP
minimum 50 relief IP

Rafael Soriano	7.6
Keith Foulke	8.7
Eddie Guardado	8.8

Relief Strikeouts/9 IP
minimum 50 relief IP

Rafael Soriano	11.5
B.J. Ryan	11.3
Tom Gordon	11.1

% Inh Runners Scored
minimum 30 inh runners

Buddy Groom	14.6
Chad Bradford	16.4
S. Hasegawa	16.7

1st Batter AVG
minimum 40 relief first BFP

Jason Kershner	.114
Tom Gordon	.133
Eddie Guardado	.136

Errors by Pitcher

Jason Davis	6
Andy Pettitte	6
3 players tied with	4

Errors by Catcher

Toby Hall	9
Miguel Olivo	9
Jason Varitek	9

Errors by First Base

Carlos Pena	13
Ken Harvey	11
2 players tied with	10

Errors by Second Base

Alfonso Soriano	19
Todd Walker	16
Marlon Anderson	15

Errors by Third Base

Eric Hinske	22
Tony Batista	20
2 players tied with	19

Errors by Shortstop

Angel Berroa	24
Miguel Tejada	21
2 players tied with	20

Errors by Left Field

Carlos Lee	7
Hideki Matsui	7
Jacque Jones	5

Errors by Center Field

Alex Sanchez	6
3 players tied with	5

Errors by Right Field

Aubrey Huff	6
Tim Salmon	6
2 players tied with	5

% CS by Catchers
minimum 70 SB Attempts

Toby Hall	41.3
Bengie Molina	40.8
Einar Diaz	31.0

Enclosed is an appointment reminder for your **Dental Service** visit at the Syracuse VA Medical Center. If you cannot keep this appointment, please contact the **Dental Service** secretary as soon as possible at 800-792-4334, extension 52090 (FROM INSIDE THE 315 AREA CODE). Call 800-221-2883, extension 52090, from outside the 315 area code. We will contact another veteran from our waiting list and offer them the visit. Thank you.

...Bases

...e	65
...dnik	43
...ts	40

...Stealing

...e	20
...	19
...ts	14

...alks

...ds	148
...	111
	111

...al Walks

...ds	61
...errero	22
...	21

...y Pitch

...io	27
...dall	25
...ue	20

...keouts

...e	182
...andez	177
...rson	155

...GDP

...n	27
...ll	25
...yton	25

...ifice Hits

...tillo	15
...rre	15
...chmidt	15

...rifice Flies

...Ramirez	11
...s tied with	9

Triples

Steve Finley	10
Rafael Furcal	10
2 players tied with	8

Plate Appearances

Juan Pierre	747
Rafael Furcal	734
Richie Sexson	718

Times on Base

Todd Helton	322
Albert Pujols	301
Barry Bonds	291

Total Bases

Albert Pujols	394
Todd Helton	367
Gary Sheffield	348

Slugging Percentage
minimum 502 PA

Barry Bonds	.749
Albert Pujols	.667
Todd Helton	.630

Slugging vs. LHP
minimum 125 PA

Barry Bonds	.790
Albert Pujols	.732
Craig Wilson	.692

Slugging vs. RHP
minimum 377 PA

Barry Bonds	.729
Javy Lopez	.677
Albert Pujols	.646

Cleanup Slugging
minimum 150 PA

Barry Bonds	.769
Reggie Sanders	.679
Jim Thome	.655

On-Base Percentage
minimum 502 PA

Barry Bonds	.529
Todd Helton	.458
Albert Pujols	.439

OBP vs. LHP
minimum 125 PA

Barry Bonds	.509
Edgar Renteria	.503
Todd Helton	.470

OBP vs. RHP
minimum 377 PA

Barry Bonds	.537
Luis Gonzalez	.459
Todd Helton	.452

Leadoff Hitters OBP
minimum 150 PA

Marquis Grissom	.412
Scott Podsednik	.399
Marlon Byrd	.374

AB per HR
minimum 502 PA

Barry Bonds	8.7
Jim Edmonds	11.5
Jim Thome	12.3

Ground/Fly Ratio
minimum 502 PA

Luis Castillo	2.81
Juan Pierre	2.67
Endy Chavez	2.17

% Extra Bases Taken
minimum 40 Opp to Advance

Orlando Cabrera	68.5
Preston Wilson	65.1
Kenny Lofton	62.0

% Runs/Time on Base
minimum 502 PA

Rafael Furcal	50.6
Sammy Sosa	46.9
Kenny Lofton	45.8

SB Success %
minimum 20 SB Attempts

Rafael Furcal	92.6
Orlando Cabrera	92.3
Edgar Renteria	82.9

Steals of Third

Juan Pierre	11
Edgar Renteria	8
Reggie Sanders	7

AVG Scoring Position
minimum 100 PA

Todd Helton	.414
Scott Podsednik	.381
Gary Sheffield	.379

AVG Late & Close
minimum 50 PA

Carlos Baerga	.407
Scott Podsednik	.398
Albert Pujols	.390

AVG Bases Loaded
minimum 10 PA

Ronnie Belliard	.625
Chris Stynes	.615
Jeff Kent	.600

GDP/GDP Opp
minimum 50 PA

Rafael Furcal	0.01
Orlando Palmeiro	0.02
Jose Reyes	0.02

AVG vs. LHP
minimum 125 PA

Edgar Renteria	**.391**
Albert Pujols	.387
Todd Helton	.387

AVG vs. RHP
minimum 377 PA

Luis Gonzalez	**.354**
Albert Pujols	.350
Todd Helton	.344

AVG at Home
minimum 251 PA

Todd Helton	**.391**
Albert Pujols	.388
Barry Bonds	.369

AVG on the Road
minimum 251 PA

Gary Sheffield	**.343**
Luis Gonzalez	.342
Marcus Giles	.342

AVG on 3-1 Count
minimum 10 PA

Ricky Ledee	**.857**
Fernando Tatis	.750
2 players tied with	.700

AVG with Two Strikes
minimum 150 PA

Todd Helton	**.324**
Jason Kendall	.292
Luis Castillo	.286

AVG on 0-2 Count
minimum 20 PA

Rondell White	**.333**
Phil Nevin	**.333**
Orlando Palmeiro	**.333**

AVG on Full Count
minimum 40 PA

Jason Michaels	**.583**
Eddie Perez	.450
Juan Pierre	.404

Pitches Seen

Bobby Abreu	**2994**
Jim Thome	2870
Rafael Furcal	2845

Pitches per PA
minimum 502 PA

Brad Wilkerson	**4.37**
Bobby Abreu	4.31
Scott Rolen	4.15

% Pitches Taken
minimum 1500 Pitches Seen

Barry Bonds	**65.9**
Bobby Abreu	65.6
Craig Counsell	64.3

% Swings that Missed
minimum 1500 Pitches Seen

Juan Pierre	**6.0**
Placido Polanco	7.4
Luis Castillo	7.5

% Swings Put in Play
minimum 1500 Pitches Seen

Juan Pierre	**58.4**
Placido Polanco	57.6
Dave Roberts	56.7

Bunts in Play

Juan Pierre	**90**
Dave Roberts	51
Scott Podsednik	35

Pitchers

Earned Run Average
minimum 162 IP

Jason Schmidt	**2.34**
Kevin Brown	2.39
Mark Prior	2.43

Wins

Russ Ortiz	**21**
Mark Prior	18
Woody Williams	18

Losses

Jeff D'Amico	**16**
Danny Graves	15
Brian Lawrence	15

Won-Lost Percentage
minimum 15 decisions

Jason Schmidt	**.773**
4 players tied with	.750

Games

Paul Quantrill	**89**
Oscar Villarreal	86
2 players tied with	80

Games Started

Greg Maddux	**36**
Kevin Millwood	35
5 players tied with	34

Complete Games

Livan Hernandez	**8**
3 players tied with	5

Shutouts

Kevin Millwood	**3**
Matt Morris	**3**
Jason Schmidt	**3**

Games Finished

Eric Gagne	**67**
Billy Wagner	**67**
2 players tied with	64

Innings Pitched

Livan Hernandez	**233.1**
Javier Vazquez	230.2
Kevin Millwood	222.0

Hits Allowed

Brett Tomko	**252**
Tomo Ohka	233
Ben Sheets	232

Batters Faced

Livan Hernandez	**967**
Woody Williams	944
Javier Vazquez	938

Runs Allowed

Wayne Franklin	**129**
Brett Tomko	126
Ben Sheets	122

Earned Runs Allowed

Wayne Franklin	**119**
Brett Tomko	**119**
Matt Kinney	110

Home Runs Allowed

Wayne Franklin	**36**
Brett Tomko	35
Jake Peavy	33

Walks Allowed

Russ Ortiz	**102**
Kazuhisa Ishii	101
Kerry Wood	100

Hit Batsmen

Kerry Wood	**21**
Vicente Padilla	16
Matt Clement	14

Strikeouts

Kerry Wood	**266**
Mark Prior	245
Javier Vazquez	241

Wild Pitches

Matt Clement	**13**
Zach Day	**13**
3 players tied with	12

Balks

Wayne Franklin	**4**
Brad Penny	**4**
2 players tied with	3

Run Support per 9 IP
minimum 162 IP

Woody Williams	**6.97**
Brett Tomko	6.75
Randy Wolf	6.71

Baserunners per 9 IP
minimum 162 IP

Jason Schmidt	**8.8**
Curt Schilling	9.6
Javier Vazquez	10.1

Opposition AVG
minimum 162 IP

Jason Schmidt	**.200**
Kerry Wood	.203
Brandon Webb	.212

Opposition SLG
minimum 162 IP

Brandon Webb	**.307**
Jason Schmidt	.316
Kevin Brown	.318

Opposition OBP
minimum 162 IP

Jason Schmidt	**.250**
Curt Schilling	.270
Javier Vazquez	.278

Home Runs per 9 IP
minimum 162 IP

Carlos Zambrano	**0.38**
Kevin Brown	0.47
Brandon Webb	0.60

Strikeouts per 9 IP
minimum 162 IP

Kerry Wood	**11.35**
Mark Prior	10.43
Curt Schilling	10.39

Walks per 9 IP
minimum 162 IP

Greg Maddux	**1.4**
Curt Schilling	1.7
Ben Sheets	1.8

K/BB Ratio
minimum 162 IP

Curt Schilling	**6.06**
Mark Prior	4.90
Jason Schmidt	4.52

Steals Allowed

Kevin Millwood	41
Greg Maddux	26
Odalis Perez	25

Caught Stealing Off

Hideo Nomo	14
Kazuhisa Ishii	13
Al Leiter	11

SB % Allowed
minimum 162 IP

Tomo Ohka	20.0
Mike Hampton	33.3
Jae Weong Seo	36.4

GDPs Induced

Horacio Ramirez	29
Shawn Estes	27
Brad Penny	26

GDPs per 9 IP
minimum 162 IP

Horacio Ramirez	1.4
Brad Penny	1.2
Tom Glavine	1.1

GDP/GDP Opp
minimum 30 BFP

Paul Quantrill	0.33
Sidney Ponson	0.31
Kevin Gryboski	0.28

Ground/Fly Ratio Off
minimum 162 IP

Brandon Webb	3.4
Kevin Brown	3.4
Carlos Zambrano	2.3

AVG Allowed Sc Pos
minimum 125 BFP

Kerry Wood	.157
Kazuhisa Ishii	.166
Kip Wells	.169

Pitches Thrown

Javier Vazquez	3741
Woody Williams	3647
Livan Hernandez	3582

Pitches per Batter
minimum 162 IP

Greg Maddux	3.26
Danny Graves	3.35
Tomo Ohka	3.44

Pickoff Throws

Steve Trachsel	189
Al Leiter	175
Greg Maddux	163

ERA at Home
minimum 81 IP

Kip Wells	2.12
Jason Schmidt	2.24
Kevin Brown	2.40

ERA on the Road
minimum 81 IP

Mark Prior	2.08
Curt Schilling	2.18
Brandon Webb	2.27

AVG vs. LHB
minimum 125 BFP

Eric Gagne	.130
Octavio Dotel	.152
Mike Hampton	.164

AVG vs. RHB
minimum 225 BFP

Billy Wagner	.154
Brandon Webb	.167
Russ Ortiz	.187

Relief ERA
minimum 50 relief IP

John Smoltz	1.12
Eric Gagne	1.20
Rheal Cormier	1.70

Relief Wins

Joe Nathan	12
Luis Ayala	10
Oscar Villarreal	10

Relief Losses

Rocky Biddle	8
Mike DeJean	8
5 players tied with	7

Saves

Eric Gagne	55
John Smoltz	45
Billy Wagner	44

Blown Saves

Mike DeJean	8
4 players tied with	7

Save Opportunities

Eric Gagne	55
John Smoltz	49
Billy Wagner	47

Save Percentage
minimum 20 SvOp

Eric Gagne	100.0
Rod Beck	100.0
Billy Wagner	93.6

Holds

Octavio Dotel	33
3 players tied with	28

Relief Innings

Guillermo Mota	105.0
Oscar Villarreal	96.0
Dave Weathers	87.2

Relief AVG Allowed
minimum 50 relief IP

Eric Gagne	.133
Jose Valverde	.137
Billy Wagner	.169

Relief Runners/9 IP
minimum 50 relief IP

Eric Gagne	6.6
John Smoltz	7.8
Billy Wagner	8.2

Relief Strikeouts/9 IP
minimum 50 relief IP

Eric Gagne	15.0
Jose Valverde	12.7
Matt Mantei	11.1

% Inh Runners Scored
minimum 30 inh runners

Tom Martin	11.9
Rheal Cormier	13.9
Luis Ayala	16.7

1st Batter AVG
minimum 40 relief first BFP

Tom Martin	.100
Jose Valverde	.114
Luther Hackman	.143

Errors by Pitcher

Curt Schilling	5
Kip Wells	5
7 players tied with	4

Errors by Catcher

Paul Lo Duca	15
Jason LaRue	11
Jason Kendall	10

Errors by First Base

Robert Fick	14
Todd Helton	11
Richie Sexson	11

Errors by Second Base

Eric Young	16
Ronnie Belliard	15
Alex Cora	15

Errors by Third Base

Aramis Ramirez	33
3 players tied with	19

Errors by Shortstop

Rafael Furcal	31
Orlando Cabrera	18
2 players tied with	17

Errors by Left Field

Adam Dunn	9
Chipper Jones	7
2 players tied with	6

Errors by Center Field

Marquis Grissom	8
Preston Wilson	7
4 players tied with	5

Errors by Right Field

Vladimir Guerrero	7
Bobby Abreu	6
Xavier Nady	6

% CS by Catchers
minimum 70 SB Attempts

Paul Lo Duca	34.1
Brad Ausmus	31.3
Javy Lopez	27.8

Projections for 2004 Batters

Batter projections based on transactions through December 15, 2003. Age as of June 30, 2004.

Batter	Age	Avg	G	AB	R	H	2B	3B	HR	RBI	BB	SO	SB	CS	OBP	SLG
Abreu, Bobby, Phi	30	.303	159	578	104	175	41	5	23	93	108	128	26	11	.413	.510
Alfonzo, Edgardo, SF	30	.284	145	528	76	150	29	2	17	73	62	57	4	2	.359	.443
Almonte, Erick, NYY	26	.240	38	104	13	25	4	0	3	15	10	30	2	1	.307	.365
Alomar, Roberto, CWS	36	.288	137	504	77	145	27	3	10	59	58	72	17	4	.361	.413
Alomar Jr., Sandy, CWS	38	.267	88	243	25	65	15	0	5	29	8	24	1	1	.291	.391
Alou, Moises, ChC	37	.294	134	494	66	145	28	2	20	86	52	61	3	2	.361	.480
Amezaga, Alfredo, Ana	26	.256	62	211	27	54	9	2	2	16	11	41	8	5	.293	.346
Anderson, Garret, Ana	32	.296	155	632	82	187	40	2	28	113	29	87	7	5	.327	.498
Anderson, Marlon, TB	30	.271	122	376	44	102	21	3	6	43	29	50	9	4	.323	.391
Aurilia, Rich, SF	32	.278	141	562	77	156	27	2	20	72	41	87	2	2	.327	.440
Ausmus, Brad, Hou	35	.247	119	384	43	95	17	2	4	38	33	61	4	2	.307	.333
Baerga, Carlos, Ari	35	.287	105	216	24	62	19	1	3	32	14	23	2	1	.330	.426
Bagwell, Jeff, Hou	36	.282	157	577	109	163	35	2	35	107	95	130	7	4	.384	.532
Bako, Paul, ChC	32	.236	77	178	18	42	11	1	2	17	20	41	0	0	.313	.343
Baldelli, Rocco, TB	22	.301	148	601	84	181	31	5	12	75	24	121	21	13	.328	.429
Barajas, Rod, Ari	28	.247	95	251	23	62	20	0	6	38	13	43	1	1	.284	.398
Bard, Josh, Cle	26	.273	74	198	21	54	13	0	4	28	14	29	0	0	.321	.399
Barrett, Michael, Oak	27	.258	105	345	43	89	23	1	10	43	29	50	2	1	.316	.417
Batista, Tony, Bal	30	.248	148	564	76	140	27	2	27	89	35	100	4	3	.292	.447
Bautista, Danny, Ari	32	.273	85	227	27	62	10	1	5	29	16	36	3	2	.321	.392
Bell, David, Phi	31	.252	125	429	57	108	24	1	12	55	41	59	1	1	.317	.396
Bellhorn, Mark, Col	29	.226	114	319	53	72	13	3	12	39	51	111	6	3	.332	.398
Belliard, Ronnie, Col	29	.260	87	269	40	70	16	2	5	27	26	44	3	2	.325	.390
Beltran, Carlos, KC	27	.292	152	585	109	171	30	8	27	101	67	109	29	4	.365	.509
Beltre, Adrian, LA	25	.266	159	580	71	154	31	3	24	87	39	96	8	4	.312	.453
Bennett, Gary, SD	32	.254	89	264	24	67	15	0	4	30	18	44	1	0	.301	.356
Berg, Dave, Tor	33	.267	76	206	25	55	12	1	3	20	14	36	1	1	.314	.379
Berkman, Lance, Hou	28	.303	157	567	109	172	42	3	34	116	108	115	8	6	.415	.568
Berroa, Angel, KC	26	.259	150	553	87	143	28	6	15	67	27	115	16	7	.293	.412
Bigbie, Larry, Bal	26	.275	108	353	45	97	20	1	5	35	36	84	7	4	.342	.380
Biggio, Craig, Hou	38	.268	146	571	94	153	33	2	14	57	54	107	8	3	.331	.406
Blake, Casey, Cle	30	.265	146	536	71	142	31	2	14	57	41	105	10	6	.317	.409
Blalock, Hank, Tex	23	.302	147	582	96	176	41	3	22	102	58	95	3	3	.366	.497
Blanco, Henry, Atl	32	.218	45	101	9	22	7	0	2	10	10	22	0	0	.288	.347
Bloomquist, Willie, Sea	26	.242	79	165	20	40	10	1	1	16	11	22	6	2	.290	.333
Blum, Geoff, TB	31	.258	132	403	48	104	23	1	10	50	37	70	3	2	.320	.395
Bonds, Barry, SF	39	.293	136	403	102	118	23	2	41	87	164	65	7	2	.497	.665
Boone, Aaron, NYY	31	.263	144	532	77	140	31	2	22	82	45	97	16	5	.321	.453
Boone, Bret, Sea	35	.271	149	583	87	158	30	2	26	103	50	111	8	4	.329	.463
Bradley, Milton, Cle	26	.270	132	489	74	132	31	3	10	53	67	106	18	11	.358	.407
Branyan, Russell, Cin	28	.239	111	297	46	71	14	1	19	53	42	118	1	1	.333	.485
Broussard, Ben, Cle	27	.260	96	319	54	83	16	1	15	48	39	70	5	2	.341	.458
Brown, Dee, KC	26	.265	35	102	13	27	5	1	3	14	8	24	2	1	.318	.422
Buchanan, Brian, SD	30	.250	121	268	40	67	20	1	12	47	25	73	2	2	.314	.466
Burks, Ellis, Cle	39	.274	99	347	54	95	18	2	17	58	40	75	2	1	.349	.484
Burnitz, Jeromy, LA	35	.234	148	517	75	121	27	2	28	83	58	143	4	4	.311	.456
Burrell, Pat, Phi	27	.263	142	509	77	134	34	3	28	93	75	138	1	0	.358	.507
Burroughs, Sean, SD	23	.288	149	546	70	157	34	3	7	63	49	73	7	5	.346	.399
Byrd, Marlon, Phi	26	.294	134	489	85	144	29	5	15	64	40	95	17	6	.348	.466
Byrnes, Eric, Oak	28	.248	124	403	60	100	26	2	11	46	28	67	13	5	.297	.404
Cabrera, Jolbert, LA	31	.269	117	331	51	89	18	1	3	33	23	54	7	6	.316	.356
Cabrera, Orlando, Mon	29	.270	160	608	73	164	39	3	13	77	50	57	18	6	.325	.408
Cairo, Miguel, NYY	30	.260	109	246	36	64	15	2	4	28	16	34	6	3	.305	.386
Calloway, Ron, Mon	27	.255	83	263	33	67	14	1	8	36	18	58	9	4	.302	.407
Cameron, Mike, NYM	31	.246	151	537	84	132	27	4	21	83	74	157	22	7	.337	.428
Carroll, Jamey, Mon	30	.253	86	229	26	58	13	1	2	20	17	30	2	3	.305	.345
Casey, Sean, Cin	29	.302	147	562	73	170	34	1	14	84	52	61	2	1	.362	.441
Cash, Kevin, Tor	26	.234	116	355	43	83	26	0	10	45	30	92	2	1	.303	.392
Castilla, Vinny, Col	36	.266	139	515	57	137	24	1	18	75	26	87	2	2	.301	.421
Castillo, Luis, Fla	28	.300	153	614	96	184	19	4	4	41	69	79	40	18	.370	.363
Castro, Juan, Cin	32	.221	96	226	19	50	11	1	4	22	13	44	1	1	.264	.332
Catalanotto, Frank, Tor	30	.301	124	429	73	129	25	3	10	52	36	53	8	4	.355	.443
Cedeno, Roger, NYM	29	.280	145	511	75	143	18	4	8	46	41	88	30	11	.333	.378
Chavez, Endy, Mon	26	.298	115	410	60	122	24	3	3	36	26	42	15	8	.339	.393
Chavez, Eric, Oak	26	.284	157	587	99	167	38	3	34	113	60	101	6	3	.351	.533

Batter	Age	Avg	G	AB	R	H	2B	3B	HR	RBI	BB	SO	SB	CS	OBP	SLG
Choi, Hee Seop, Fla	25	.238	82	244	37	58	13	0	11	39	36	67	2	1	.336	.426
Christenson, Ryan, Fla	30	.238	73	231	30	55	12	0	4	22	18	44	5	3	.293	.342
Cintron, Alex, Ari	25	.289	132	501	63	145	29	4	7	42	20	47	6	6	.317	.405
Cirillo, Jeff, Sea	34	.265	130	491	65	130	31	1	9	74	39	65	5	3	.319	.387
Clark, Brady, Mil	31	.274	104	248	32	68	21	1	4	33	20	29	4	3	.328	.415
Clark, Tony, NYM	32	.257	112	230	30	59	12	0	10	37	26	58	0	0	.332	.439
Clayton, Royce, Mil	34	.245	127	400	51	98	20	2	9	44	33	76	6	3	.303	.373
Conine, Jeff, Fla	38	.288	129	489	63	141	23	1	15	73	43	69	5	3	.346	.431
Cora, Alex, LA	28	.249	136	386	40	96	20	4	4	36	26	52	4	3	.296	.352
Cordero, Wil, Mon	32	.266	110	316	41	84	24	1	10	46	33	63	1	1	.335	.443
Counsell, Craig, Mil	33	.269	122	409	61	110	20	2	3	36	50	56	6	4	.349	.350
Crawford, Carl, TB	22	.279	126	523	70	146	22	8	6	60	24	92	33	10	.311	.379
Crede, Joe, CWS	26	.282	150	550	79	155	34	0	27	87	40	91	1	1	.333	.491
Crisp, Coco, Cle	24	.288	98	393	59	113	18	3	5	39	30	55	20	8	.338	.387
Cruz, Deivi, Bal	31	.265	141	499	52	132	30	1	10	60	18	51	2	2	.290	.389
Cruz, Jose, TB	30	.251	141	505	76	127	28	2	22	68	64	118	12	5	.336	.446
Cuddyer, Michael, Min	25	.264	91	288	44	76	18	3	9	36	27	73	4	4	.327	.441
Damon, Johnny, Bos	30	.280	152	624	113	175	32	7	12	66	66	72	30	9	.349	.412
Daubach, Brian, CWS	32	.254	91	201	26	51	14	1	9	33	27	58	1	0	.342	.468
DaVanon, Jeff, Ana	30	.270	106	318	45	86	21	3	11	45	35	73	9	6	.343	.459
Davis, Ben, Sea	27	.240	101	304	37	73	19	0	8	47	35	75	2	2	.319	.382
Delgado, Carlos, Tor	32	.281	152	538	100	151	37	1	36	114	107	133	1	0	.400	.554
Dellucci, David, NYY	30	.245	96	204	25	50	12	3	5	27	23	52	3	2	.322	.407
DeRosa, Mark, Atl	29	.266	110	323	48	86	19	1	4	30	23	41	5	3	.315	.368
Diaz, Einar, Tex	31	.261	120	380	42	99	23	1	4	38	15	36	2	2	.289	.358
DiFelice, Mike, KC	35	.233	80	206	23	48	12	1	3	19	13	46	0	0	.279	.345
Drew, J.D., Atl	28	.286	124	388	71	111	19	3	21	61	56	80	9	4	.376	.513
Dunn, Adam, Cin	24	.273	154	513	99	140	29	1	39	93	100	145	13	6	.392	.561
Durazo, Erubiel, Oak	29	.290	152	555	107	161	29	1	29	99	103	123	1	1	.401	.503
Durham, Ray, SF	32	.272	139	533	93	145	31	5	13	56	64	98	17	9	.350	.422
Dye, Jermaine, Oak	30	.262	111	370	55	97	21	1	15	61	39	75	2	1	.333	.446
Eckstein, David, Ana	29	.276	139	532	83	147	24	2	5	45	42	48	16	8	.329	.357
Edmonds, Jim, StL	34	.273	141	462	89	126	30	1	31	87	85	134	4	3	.386	.543
Ellis, Mark, Oak	27	.247	152	555	74	137	35	2	8	51	52	94	10	4	.311	.360
Encarnacion, Juan, LA	28	.270	144	555	76	150	29	5	19	81	39	99	15	7	.318	.443
Ensberg, Morgan, Hou	28	.288	133	437	74	126	25	1	22	68	63	83	7	7	.378	.501
Erstad, Darin, Ana	30	.284	139	538	78	153	28	3	10	60	39	78	16	6	.333	.403
Estalella, Bobby, Col	29	.224	54	156	21	35	9	0	8	26	18	48	1	0	.305	.436
Everett, Adam, Hou	27	.251	134	430	62	108	20	3	4	37	34	76	11	4	.306	.310
Everett, Carl, Mon	33	.275	124	451	67	124	24	2	22	78	40	94	6	3	.334	.483
Febles, Carlos, KC	28	.259	83	220	35	57	10	2	2	20	19	36	8	3	.318	.350
Feliz, Pedro, SF	29	.238	105	239	30	57	17	2	11	39	11	52	1	0	.272	.464
Fick, Robert, Atl	30	.269	112	360	46	97	22	1	11	54	34	53	1	1	.332	.428
Figgins, Chone, Ana	26	.258	101	356	50	92	17	6	3	31	30	62	18	8	.316	.365
Finley, Steve, Ari	39	.263	135	463	67	122	22	4	18	67	51	74	9	5	.337	.445
Flaherty, John, NYY	36	.242	46	124	11	30	7	0	2	13	6	21	0	0	.277	.347
Floyd, Cliff, NYM	31	.291	138	492	88	143	33	2	25	87	65	94	13	4	.373	.518
Fordyce, Brook, Bal	34	.250	100	284	26	71	17	0	5	29	18	46	1	1	.295	.363
Franco, Julio, Atl	45	.258	87	198	24	51	12	1	3	21	23	46	1	1	.335	.374
Freel, Ryan, Cin	28	.252	62	210	32	53	12	1	4	20	19	27	13	6	.314	.376
Fullmer, Brad, Tex	29	.284	127	426	65	121	31	2	19	72	37	60	5	3	.341	.500
Furcal, Rafael, Atl	26	.287	157	655	112	188	33	6	12	62	54	96	33	12	.341	.411
Galarraga, Andres, SF	43	.256	92	238	25	61	11	0	8	36	20	67	1	1	.314	.403
Garcia, Karim, NYY	28	.263	68	198	27	52	8	1	10	34	14	42	1	2	.311	.465
Garciaparra, Nomar, Bos	30	.320	158	649	111	208	48	6	27	112	41	64	8	4	.361	.538
Gerut, Jody, Cle	26	.289	141	530	79	153	37	3	17	83	55	68	14	12	.356	.466
Giambi, Jason, NYY	33	.292	150	521	100	152	34	1	39	116	121	111	1	1	.425	.585
Giambi, Jeremy, Bos	29	.265	65	166	29	44	9	0	8	26	34	46	0	0	.390	.464
Gibbons, Jay, Bal	27	.271	155	560	82	152	39	1	27	86	49	79	1	1	.330	.489
Gil, Geronimo, Bal	28	.248	99	323	29	80	17	0	6	40	15	71	1	1	.281	.356
Giles, Brian, SD	33	.300	146	510	96	153	31	3	29	93	110	67	7	4	.424	.543
Giles, Marcus, Atl	26	.293	149	546	91	160	35	1	18	74	57	88	15	7	.360	.460
Ginter, Keith, Mil	28	.267	111	307	49	82	24	1	11	43	39	85	4	3	.350	.459
Glanville, Doug, ChC	33	.265	100	340	41	90	16	2	6	28	14	48	11	3	.294	.376
Glaus, Troy, Ana	27	.258	147	523	95	135	31	1	34	96	90	130	9	5	.367	.516
Gomez, Chris, Min	33	.270	84	178	20	48	9	1	3	20	10	19	1	1	.309	.382
Gonzalez, Alex, Fla	27	.249	150	550	62	137	31	6	15	71	36	111	4	3	.295	.409
Gonzalez, Alex S., ChC	31	.241	149	561	70	135	31	3	19	68	46	137	6	5	.298	.408
Gonzalez, Juan, Tex	34	.287	108	408	62	117	24	1	23	78	26	83	1	1	.329	.520
Gonzalez, Luis, Ari	36	.285	146	534	87	152	32	3	28	97	90	73	3	2	.388	.513

Batter	Age	Avg	G	AB	R	H	2B	3B	HR	RBI	BB	SO	SB	CS	OBP	SLG
Gonzalez, Raul, NYM	30	.284	96	222	34	63	20	1	5	31	26	36	3	3	.359	.450
Goodwin, Tom, ChC	35	.252	99	226	34	57	9	2	2	21	18	43	15	5	.307	.336
Graffanino, Tony, KC	32	.269	96	242	44	65	16	2	6	28	24	41	5	2	.335	.426
Green, Shawn, LA	31	.288	157	593	100	171	38	2	32	105	78	109	12	5	.371	.521
Greene, Todd, Col	33	.249	68	209	24	52	11	0	10	31	6	41	1	0	.270	.445
Grieve, Ben, TB	28	.259	82	274	39	71	18	0	9	39	46	73	2	1	.366	.423
Griffey Jr., Ken, Cin	34	.271	138	501	79	136	27	2	33	94	70	111	3	2	.361	.531
Grissom, Marquis, SF	37	.252	128	441	54	111	22	2	15	56	18	86	7	4	.281	.413
Grudzielanek, Mark, ChC	34	.274	134	514	68	141	28	2	7	44	27	81	5	2	.311	.377
Guerrero, Vladimir, Mon	28	.323	152	564	99	182	36	4	36	108	76	73	23	13	.403	.592
Guiel, Aaron, KC	31	.271	116	399	62	108	24	1	14	61	40	82	4	2	.337	.441
Guillen, Carlos, Sea	28	.267	136	468	76	125	22	3	9	59	56	85	5	3	.345	.385
Guillen, Jose, Oak	28	.280	130	429	58	120	26	2	21	75	18	84	3	3	.309	.497
Guzman, Cristian, Min	26	.278	149	600	87	167	26	10	8	59	26	83	22	11	.308	.395
Guzman, Edwards, TB	27	.268	60	164	17	44	9	0	1	18	6	13	1	1	.294	.341
Hafner, Travis, Cle	27	.293	110	358	60	105	23	1	19	65	58	84	2	1	.392	.522
Hairston Jr., Jerry, Bal	28	.260	100	339	46	88	19	2	5	31	30	44	14	6	.320	.372
Hall, Bill, Mil	24	.230	71	243	22	56	11	1	3	19	12	59	6	5	.267	.321
Hall, Toby, TB	28	.291	127	471	57	137	30	0	14	72	26	37	1	1	.328	.444
Halter, Shane, Det	34	.239	98	306	33	73	13	1	8	32	26	70	2	2	.298	.366
Hammock, Robby, Ari	27	.251	73	227	28	57	12	1	5	28	16	43	2	2	.300	.379
Hammonds, Jeffrey, SF	33	.262	56	164	23	43	10	1	5	22	18	34	3	2	.335	.427
Harris, Willie, CWS	26	.264	92	193	27	51	13	2	3	19	17	34	11	4	.324	.399
Hart, Bo, StL	27	.261	117	437	58	114	20	4	7	44	27	93	6	4	.304	.373
Harvey, Ken, KC	26	.283	112	403	56	114	24	1	14	62	25	75	3	2	.325	.452
Hatteberg, Scott, Oak	34	.263	106	357	40	94	20	1	9	42	46	38	0	0	.347	.401
Helms, Wes, Mil	28	.248	129	359	41	89	22	2	16	52	31	96	1	1	.308	.454
Helton, Todd, Col	30	.332	160	578	121	192	47	3	35	122	105	91	4	3	.435	.606
Hernandez, Jose, Pit	34	.232	124	427	48	99	15	2	14	51	38	154	2	3	.295	.375
Hernandez, Ramon, SD	28	.252	145	468	61	118	23	1	16	65	41	73	0	0	.312	.408
Hidalgo, Richard, Hou	28	.278	140	489	79	136	34	2	24	81	56	101	7	5	.352	.503
Higginson, Bobby, Det	33	.276	113	406	57	112	22	2	13	56	51	53	9	5	.357	.436
Hillenbrand, Shea, Ari	28	.275	147	550	69	151	36	2	18	78	22	76	2	2	.302	.445
Hinske, Eric, Tor	26	.258	140	515	81	133	31	3	20	77	61	129	13	5	.337	.447
Hocking, Denny, Min	34	.241	90	220	23	53	11	1	2	21	20	44	2	1	.304	.327
Hollandsworth, Todd, Fla	31	.278	87	234	35	65	14	1	7	28	22	53	6	4	.340	.436
Hudson, Orlando, Tor	26	.278	137	475	66	132	30	6	8	64	45	78	10	6	.340	.417
Huff, Aubrey, TB	27	.300	149	576	85	173	43	2	26	91	45	74	2	2	.351	.517
Hunter, Torii, Min	28	.270	155	585	93	158	34	4	28	100	41	118	13	7	.318	.485
Ibanez, Raul, Sea	32	.271	147	538	76	146	28	3	19	88	46	87	4	3	.329	.441
Infante, Omar, Det	22	.259	64	201	21	52	8	2	1	19	14	25	8	6	.307	.333
Inge, Brandon, Det	27	.220	113	345	37	76	22	2	8	41	27	85	4	4	.277	.365
Izturis, Cesar, LA	24	.250	150	509	52	127	23	4	1	40	17	46	19	8	.274	.316
Jackson, Damian, Bos	30	.249	103	273	39	68	20	2	2	25	25	62	12	5	.312	.359
Jenkins, Geoff, Mil	29	.273	126	479	81	131	32	2	26	81	51	128	4	2	.343	.511
Jeter, Derek, NYY	30	.316	159	594	109	188	30	4	16	73	60	103	19	5	.379	.461
Jimenez, D'Angelo, Cin	26	.269	153	568	84	153	30	3	13	60	70	88	9	7	.350	.401
Johnson, Charles, Col	32	.237	117	375	45	89	20	0	17	62	43	101	1	1	.316	.427
Johnson, Nick, Mon	25	.265	134	441	75	117	26	1	20	66	81	112	5	2	.379	.465
Johnson, Reed, Tor	27	.290	136	500	89	145	26	3	10	61	29	75	15	8	.329	.414
Jones, Andruw, Atl	27	.265	157	593	105	157	32	3	37	105	67	131	9	4	.339	.516
Jones, Chipper, Atl	32	.306	153	545	98	167	33	2	28	98	99	84	7	5	.413	.528
Jones, Jacque, Min	29	.291	146	525	75	153	34	2	19	72	34	109	8	5	.335	.472
Jones, Jason, Tex	27	.272	61	195	27	53	14	0	5	27	25	40	2	2	.355	.421
Jordan, Brian, LA	37	.276	116	416	55	115	21	2	14	64	29	70	3	2	.324	.438
Kapler, Gabe, Bos	28	.275	121	346	48	95	26	2	7	46	38	55	9	4	.346	.422
Karros, Eric, ChC	36	.265	102	310	33	82	15	0	10	45	25	55	2	1	.319	.410
Kata, Matt, Ari	26	.266	80	304	41	81	17	5	5	30	16	46	4	3	.303	.405
Kearns, Austin, Cin	24	.278	140	496	81	138	27	2	23	88	66	109	9	6	.363	.480
Kendall, Jason, Pit	30	.306	152	582	82	178	32	3	7	57	49	40	12	9	.360	.407
Kennedy, Adam, Ana	28	.277	148	487	67	135	31	4	10	55	33	77	16	7	.323	.419
Kent, Jeff, Hou	36	.292	140	548	79	160	33	2	24	94	49	92	5	4	.350	.491
Kielty, Bobby, Oak	27	.258	137	391	60	101	30	2	12	53	57	90	4	2	.353	.437
Kingsale, Gene, SD	27	.232	54	155	19	36	7	1	1	15	11	26	6	2	.283	.310
Klesko, Ryan, SD	33	.282	145	514	84	145	31	2	28	96	81	93	11	5	.380	.514
Konerko, Paul, CWS	28	.282	130	464	68	131	26	1	22	81	43	61	0	0	.343	.485
Koskie, Corey, Min	31	.279	144	513	82	143	33	2	17	77	75	122	12	7	.371	.450
Kotsay, Mark, Oak	28	.276	143	521	77	144	28	5	12	56	61	81	12	7	.352	.418
Laker, Tim, Cle	34	.225	56	178	21	40	9	0	6	25	15	39	1	0	.285	.376
Larkin, Barry, Cin	40	.273	94	311	47	85	18	2	4	28	32	41	6	3	.341	.383

Batter	Age	Avg	G	AB	R	H	2B	3B	HR	RBI	BB	SO	SB	CS	OBP	SLG
LaRue, Jason, Cin	30	.228	128	394	50	90	27	1	14	52	32	121	2	2	.286	.409
Lawton, Matt, Cle	32	.257	102	370	58	95	21	1	12	50	53	46	11	5	.350	.416
LeCroy, Matthew, Min	28	.279	120	405	50	113	20	0	18	69	29	98	1	1	.327	.462
Ledee, Ricky, Phi	30	.253	125	297	44	75	20	2	11	50	38	69	4	3	.337	.444
Lee, Carlos, CWS	28	.283	155	576	97	163	34	2	29	98	54	85	12	5	.344	.500
Lee, Derrek, ChC	28	.269	159	561	88	151	31	2	36	103	83	139	11	6	.363	.524
Lee, Travis, TB	29	.261	140	491	62	128	27	2	15	67	60	93	4	2	.341	.415
Lieberthal, Mike, Phi	32	.280	122	447	53	125	27	1	12	62	36	57	0	0	.333	.425
Liefer, Jeff, TB	29	.250	46	128	17	32	9	0	7	21	12	41	0	0	.314	.484
Lo Duca, Paul, LA	32	.284	141	535	66	152	31	1	11	69	39	39	3	4	.333	.407
Lofton, Kenny, ChC	37	.286	132	507	90	145	24	4	12	56	52	64	21	8	.352	.420
Long, Terrence, SD	28	.268	130	496	72	133	28	3	14	66	40	77	4	3	.323	.421
Lopez, Felipe, Cin	24	.255	88	306	43	78	15	0	5	00	07	111	10	7	.333	.373
Lopez, Javy, Atl	33	.276	127	424	56	117	21	1	25	80	30	83	0	0	.324	.507
Loretta, Mark, SD	32	.288	139	476	58	137	24	2	8	50	43	56	2	2	.347	.397
Lowell, Mike, Fla	30	.279	146	545	78	152	34	0	26	99	56	84	3	2	.346	.484
Ludwick, Ryan, Cle	25	.259	70	251	40	65	16	1	11	42	23	65	2	3	.321	.462
Lugo, Julio, TB	28	.271	132	476	79	129	22	3	13	49	44	102	16	9	.333	.412
Macias, Jose, Mon	32	.243	90	251	30	61	13	3	4	25	15	36	5	3	.286	.367
Mackowiak, Rob, Pit	28	.242	104	293	35	71	20	2	8	33	25	85	5	3	.302	.406
Marrero, Eli, Atl	30	.240	111	350	53	84	17	2	12	49	31	62	8	3	.302	.403
Martin, Al, TB	36	.263	70	160	22	42	11	2	3	17	16	35	3	2	.330	.413
Martinez, Edgar, Sea	41	.280	118	400	54	112	28	0	17	82	77	82	1	1	.396	.478
Martinez, Ramon, ChC	31	.271	115	314	39	85	18	1	5	35	28	47	2	1	.330	.382
Martinez, Tino, TB	36	.266	135	478	62	127	25	1	18	76	46	73	2	1	.330	.435
Martinez, Victor, Cle	25	.321	110	377	60	121	30	0	14	63	38	52	3	3	.383	.512
Mateo, Henry, Mon	27	.251	85	223	29	56	11	4	2	19	13	43	12	5	.292	.363
Mateo, Ruben, Cin	26	.266	89	293	39	78	19	1	7	34	17	57	3	1	.306	.410
Matheny, Mike, StL	33	.238	128	386	38	92	16	1	6	42	36	72	1	1	.303	.332
Matos, Luis, Bal	25	.250	122	428	60	107	20	3	9	54	36	90	18	9	.308	.374
Matsui, Hideki, NYY	30	.289	162	620	81	179	43	1	16	101	64	83	2	2	.355	.439
Matthews Jr., Gary, Atl	29	.240	103	262	39	63	12	1	5	26	33	57	7	3	.325	.351
Mayne, Brent, Ari	36	.259	106	332	31	86	14	0	4	40	29	52	1	2	.319	.337
McCracken, Quinton, Sea	33	.276	58	152	19	42	9	1	1	14	10	28	2	2	.321	.368
McDonald, John, Cle	29	.239	79	205	24	49	12	0	1	18	13	37	4	3	.284	.312
McEwing, Joe, NYM	31	.250	111	240	31	60	19	2	3	26	16	52	5	3	.297	.383
McGriff, Fred, LA	40	.276	103	352	43	97	17	1	18	64	42	74	1	1	.353	.483
McLemore, Mark, Sea	39	.238	86	239	34	57	9	1	3	25	38	51	11	5	.343	.322
McMillon, Billy, Oak	32	.274	53	117	14	32	11	0	3	14	13	23	0	0	.346	.444
Mench, Kevin, Tex	26	.259	87	290	45	75	23	1	14	48	25	55	2	2	.317	.490
Merced, Orlando, Hou	37	.256	78	117	14	30	12	1	2	19	11	23	1	1	.320	.427
Merloni, Lou, Bos	33	.253	83	217	26	55	14	1	3	20	18	45	1	1	.311	.369
Michaels, Jason, Phi	28	.250	99	148	20	37	18	2	4	24	14	45	1	1	.315	.480
Mientkiewicz, Doug, Min	30	.290	147	504	72	146	36	1	12	71	74	73	4	4	.381	.437
Millar, Kevin, Bos	32	.282	141	479	64	135	31	2	20	77	47	88	1	1	.346	.480
Miller, Damian, ChC	34	.250	119	352	40	88	23	0	11	43	39	92	1	1	.325	.409
Mirabelli, Doug, Bos	33	.236	72	165	18	39	12	0	7	24	18	42	0	0	.311	.436
Moeller, Chad, Mil	29	.258	89	275	35	71	15	1	7	33	27	61	1	1	.325	.396
Mohr, Dustan, SF	28	.272	113	320	48	87	23	1	10	40	29	83	4	2	.332	.444
Molina, Bengie, Ana	29	.260	131	446	43	116	22	0	11	61	18	45	1	0	.289	.383
Molina, Jose, Ana	29	.243	40	111	9	27	4	0	1	10	4	26	0	1	.270	.306
Mondesi, Raul, Ari	33	.264	144	545	91	144	30	4	27	85	63	111	20	9	.340	.483
Monroe, Craig, Det	27	.274	108	351	55	96	25	3	15	58	32	69	5	5	.334	.490
Mora, Melvin, Bal	32	.257	130	459	71	118	22	2	14	55	56	95	10	7	.338	.405
Morneau, Justin, Min	23	.263	85	278	37	73	13	1	12	40	21	59	1	1	.314	.446
Morris, Warren, Det	30	.273	70	242	27	66	12	1	3	27	13	31	2	3	.310	.368
Mueller, Bill, Bos	33	.295	137	478	79	141	29	2	13	59	63	60	2	2	.377	.446
Munson, Eric, Det	26	.245	133	441	62	108	24	2	22	74	61	101	2	2	.337	.458
Myers, Greg, Tor	38	.237	92	224	27	53	12	0	9	32	30	49	0	0	.327	411
Nady, Xavier, SD	25	.265	120	422	58	112	17	0	12	53	26	85	2	2	.308	.391
Nevin, Phil, SD	33	.274	131	478	67	131	24	0	24	87	53	115	2	1	.347	.475
Nixon, Trot, Bos	30	.276	146	504	86	139	30	4	25	86	71	107	5	3	.365	.500
Norton, Greg, Col	31	.238	117	189	22	45	15	1	7	33	20	55	1	1	.311	.439
Nunez, Abraham O., Pit	28	.241	128	381	43	92	12	2	3	30	37	68	11	5	.309	.307
O'Leary, Troy, ChC	34	.256	54	125	15	32	9	1	3	19	11	25	0	0	.316	.416
Olerud, John, Sea	35	.291	138	491	69	143	31	1	14	84	81	63	1	1	.392	.444
Olivo, Miguel, CWS	25	.267	113	352	46	94	22	3	9	48	31	73	11	6	.326	.423
Olmedo, Ray, Cin	23	.240	74	229	26	55	10	0	1	17	17	45	4	5	.293	.297
Ordonez, Magglio, CWS	30	.307	159	600	100	184	40	2	32	116	62	75	13	6	.372	.540
Ordonez, Rey, TB	33	.247	87	259	23	64	11	1	2	25	15	26	1	1	.288	.320

Batter	Age	Avg	G	AB	R	H	2B	3B	HR	RBI	BB	SO	SB	CS	OBP	SLG
Ortiz, David, Bos	28	.276	136	463	72	128	36	1	26	85	57	95	1	1	.356	.527
Osik, Keith, Mil	35	.217	82	180	13	39	9	0	2	20	19	35	1	0	.291	.300
Overbay, Lyle, Mil	27	.291	134	429	58	125	33	1	9	59	67	98	3	2	.387	.436
Owens, Eric, Ana	33	.263	102	281	34	74	11	2	2	23	19	33	10	6	.310	.338
Palmeiro, Orlando, StL	35	.271	102	221	27	60	11	1	1	23	24	22	3	2	.343	.344
Palmeiro, Rafael, Tex	39	.270	142	514	85	139	28	1	37	103	86	82	1	1	.375	.545
Patterson, Corey, ChC	24	.254	153	591	85	150	31	5	18	74	30	126	23	9	.290	.415
Payton, Jay, Col	31	.290	149	538	77	156	28	3	21	71	35	71	6	5	.333	.470
Pena, Carlos, Det	26	.261	135	463	63	121	33	2	22	70	65	131	5	3	.352	.484
Pena, Wily Mo, Cin	22	.243	84	181	22	44	14	0	6	22	13	62	2	1	.294	.420
Peralta, Jhonny, Cle	22	.255	72	239	26	61	13	1	4	25	18	54	2	2	.307	.368
Perez, Antonio, TB	24	.250	65	196	30	49	10	1	4	21	17	55	6	3	.310	.372
Perez, Eddie, Mil	36	.256	73	211	15	54	10	0	6	21	8	35	0	0	.283	.389
Perez, Eduardo, TB	34	.256	111	215	34	55	16	0	11	40	25	49	3	2	.333	.484
Perez, Neifi, SF	31	.266	131	473	58	126	24	6	4	44	20	47	5	5	.296	.368
Perez, Timo, NYM	29	.299	115	358	47	107	21	2	6	39	20	33	9	6	.336	.419
Perez, Tomas, Phi	30	.248	77	202	23	50	9	1	4	24	16	36	1	1	.303	.361
Petrick, Ben, Det	27	.278	73	212	32	59	15	2	11	33	25	57	3	2	.354	.524
Phelps, Josh, Tor	26	.278	130	439	75	122	30	0	28	86	50	129	1	1	.352	.538
Phillips, Brandon, Cle	23	.252	71	242	27	61	15	0	5	27	10	42	7	4	.282	.376
Phillips, Jason, NYM	27	.269	128	439	48	118	24	0	13	67	34	44	0	0	.321	.412
Piatt, Adam, TB	28	.259	74	205	26	53	16	1	5	29	20	45	2	1	.324	.420
Piazza, Mike, NYM	35	.300	134	466	73	140	23	0	30	91	60	84	1	1	.380	.543
Pierre, Juan, Fla	26	.316	160	637	106	201	25	6	1	50	45	38	54	18	.361	.378
Pierzynski, A.J., SF	27	.288	142	483	62	139	33	2	9	63	21	63	2	2	.317	.420
Podsednik, Scott, Mil	28	.261	148	547	75	143	25	4	8	57	46	95	31	11	.319	.366
Polanco, Placido, Phi	28	.290	138	534	84	155	25	3	10	54	33	40	9	4	.332	.404
Posada, Jorge, NYY	32	.266	142	493	74	131	30	1	24	92	80	131	2	2	.368	.477
Pratt, Todd, Phi	37	.230	51	100	13	23	6	0	3	11	20	33	0	0	.358	.380
Pujols, Albert, StL	24	.337	158	590	129	199	48	2	41	133	78	74	3	2	.415	.634
Ramirez, Aramis, ChC	26	.278	156	586	75	163	35	1	27	99	39	96	3	2	.323	.480
Ramirez, Manny, Bos	32	.312	140	507	91	158	33	1	34	112	86	112	1	1	.411	.582
Randa, Joe, KC	34	.275	141	530	67	146	29	3	13	79	43	71	2	1	.330	.415
Reboulet, Jeff, Pit	40	.222	61	126	16	28	5	0	1	9	15	26	1	1	.305	.286
Redman, Tike, Pit	27	.267	69	251	29	67	10	3	2	20	15	23	10	5	.308	.355
Redmond, Mike, Fla	33	.286	97	301	28	86	14	0	2	28	24	35	0	0	.338	.352
Reese, Pokey, Pit	31	.244	71	209	25	51	10	1	3	20	19	43	8	2	.307	.344
Relaford, Desi, KC	30	.258	139	418	57	108	23	3	7	51	38	70	11	4	.320	.378
Renteria, Edgar, StL	28	.304	157	566	82	172	33	2	12	82	56	63	23	8	.367	.433
Reyes, Jose, NYM	21	.277	147	542	85	150	25	9	5	55	29	82	39	15	.313	.384
Reyes, Rene, Col	26	.317	67	221	29	70	17	2	6	25	11	31	4	4	.349	.493
Rivas, Luis, Min	24	.259	131	463	69	120	29	6	7	49	32	71	16	7	.307	.393
Rivera, Juan, Mon	25	.297	116	401	57	119	25	1	14	63	21	61	4	4	.332	.469
Roberts, Brian, Bal	26	.261	129	499	70	130	19	3	3	42	55	68	31	10	.334	.329
Roberts, Dave, LA	32	.272	122	423	63	115	16	4	4	34	42	60	27	11	.338	.357
Robinson, Kerry, StL	30	.271	107	188	24	51	10	3	1	15	10	28	7	3	.308	.372
Rodriguez, Alex, Tex	28	.306	162	620	132	190	37	2	49	139	87	125	13	4	.392	.610
Rodriguez, Ivan, Fla	32	.289	127	471	72	136	30	2	19	71	36	83	7	5	.339	.482
Rolen, Scott, StL	29	.287	156	574	101	165	41	3	30	110	81	113	11	4	.376	.526
Rollins, Jimmy, Phi	25	.256	157	644	84	165	32	9	11	65	55	104	30	11	.315	.385
Rolls, Damian, TB	26	.257	73	226	31	58	9	1	4	24	13	44	8	3	.297	.358
Ross, Dave, LA	27	.236	63	178	23	42	8	0	8	28	17	58	0	0	.303	.416
Rowand, Aaron, CWS	26	.277	119	267	40	74	22	1	10	37	17	41	3	1	.320	.479
Sadler, Donnie, Ari	29	.216	78	148	22	32	7	2	1	11	15	29	4	2	.288	.311
Salmon, Tim, Ana	35	.277	137	480	74	133	28	1	20	70	78	107	3	2	.378	.465
Sanchez, Alex, Det	27	.278	141	514	63	143	18	5	1	37	32	72	38	16	.321	.339
Sanchez, Rey, TB	36	.268	102	343	37	92	13	1	0	26	13	34	3	1	.295	.312
Sandberg, Jared, TB	26	.234	68	205	27	48	12	0	8	30	23	68	1	1	.311	.410
Sanders, Reggie, Pit	36	.259	130	452	70	117	23	3	25	77	42	119	14	6	.322	.489
Santiago, Benito, KC	39	.260	119	431	43	112	18	1	10	54	25	73	2	2	.300	.376
Santiago, Ramon, Det	24	.248	117	371	45	92	11	3	3	33	25	61	11	6	.295	.318
Schneider, Brian, Mon	27	.249	122	369	35	92	27	1	8	45	34	68	1	1	.313	.393
Segui, David, Bal	37	.254	57	173	23	44	10	0	4	23	24	38	0	0	.345	.382
Sexson, Richie, Ari	29	.273	161	598	97	163	31	2	40	117	81	157	2	1	.359	.532
Sheffield, Gary, Atl	35	.295	140	508	89	150	26	1	30	94	80	59	8	4	.391	.528
Sierra, Ruben, NYY	38	.260	96	311	36	81	18	1	10	45	23	50	1	1	.311	.421
Simon, Randall, ChC	29	.287	104	352	39	101	16	1	13	57	18	30	1	2	.322	.449
Singleton, Chris, Oak	31	.264	127	368	52	97	23	4	5	43	22	63	11	5	.305	.389
Snow, J.T., SF	36	.246	118	345	45	85	19	1	7	47	55	81	1	1	.350	.368
Soriano, Alfonso, NYY	26	.283	158	654	119	185	40	3	33	94	32	134	31	11	.316	.505

Batter	Age	Avg	G	AB	R	H	2B	3B	HR	RBI	BB	SO	SB	CS	OBP	SLG
Sosa, Sammy, ChC	35	.270	143	526	98	142	22	2	41	105	89	147	2	1	.376	.553
Spencer, Shane, Tex	32	.247	82	259	29	64	13	1	7	32	27	52	2	1	.318	.386
Spiezio, Scott, Sea	31	.270	105	348	48	94	22	2	10	52	36	44	3	3	.339	.431
Spivey, Junior, Mil	29	.260	140	507	80	132	29	4	15	65	59	107	9	6	.337	.422
Stairs, Matt, KC	36	.256	120	301	46	77	19	1	17	55	44	65	2	1	.351	.495
Stewart, Shannon, Min	30	.309	144	593	99	183	39	4	13	62	51	66	14	6	.363	.454
Stinnett, Kelly, Phi	34	.220	66	164	14	36	8	0	3	18	13	50	1	0	.277	.323
Stynes, Chris, Col	31	.268	97	291	43	78	15	1	7	33	26	47	2	2	.328	.399
Surhoff, B.J., Bal	39	.272	87	279	32	76	16	1	5	32	24	27	3	2	.330	.391
Suzuki, Ichiro, Sea	30	.328	159	679	118	223	31	7	10	65	46	60	35	13	.371	.439
Sweeney, Mike, KC	30	.305	126	466	76	142	29	0	21	90	62	55	6	3	.386	.502
Tatis, Fernando, Mon	29	.251	59	187	24	47	11	1	6	27	10	40	1	1	.320	.417
Taylor, Reggie, Cin	27	.235	112	217	24	51	11	0	8	21	11	54	7	3	.272	.418
Teixeira, Mark, Tex	24	.284	151	552	84	157	32	7	32	93	57	120	4	3	.351	.542
Tejada, Miguel, Bal	28	.281	162	640	103	180	35	2	31	118	47	79	7	2	.330	.488
Thomas, Frank, CWS	36	.278	142	503	81	140	31	1	34	102	87	111	1	1	.385	.547
Thome, Jim, Phi	33	.271	150	512	97	139	28	2	44	114	113	168	1	1	.403	.592
Torrealba, Yorvit, SF	25	.250	71	188	22	47	9	0	3	16	10	32	1	1	.288	.346
Torres, Andres, Det	26	.246	51	167	25	41	7	2	1	13	16	39	10	5	.311	.329
Tucker, Michael, SF	33	.255	132	427	63	109	20	4	13	54	47	100	14	8	.329	.412
Uribe, Juan, CWS	24	.277	123	444	56	123	32	9	11	59	21	79	9	5	.310	.464
Utley, Chase, Phi	25	.268	62	209	30	56	16	0	7	31	18	40	3	1	.326	.445
Valentin, Javier, TB	28	.248	61	157	16	39	13	0	5	21	12	40	0	0	.302	.427
Valentin, Jose, CWS	34	.240	134	467	74	112	25	2	25	70	49	112	7	3	.312	.463
Vander Wal, John, Mil	38	.244	116	324	42	79	14	1	11	44	44	96	4	2	.334	.395
Varitek, Jason, Bos	32	.261	130	433	54	113	29	1	16	68	46	95	2	1	.332	.443
Vazquez, Ramon, SD	27	.261	131	448	62	117	24	2	5	52	60	86	5	5	.348	.357
Ventura, Robin, LA	36	.241	109	332	43	80	15	0	15	54	59	76	1	2	.355	.422
Vidro, Jose, Mon	29	.308	151	572	92	176	42	1	18	81	60	60	3	2	.373	.479
Vina, Fernando, Det	35	.277	110	441	59	122	18	3	4	34	25	29	9	6	.315	.358
Vizcaino, Jose, Hou	36	.274	100	252	30	69	11	2	3	21	14	29	2	3	.312	.369
Vizquel, Omar, Cle	37	.260	119	458	65	119	18	2	6	43	46	51	11	6	.327	.347
Walker, Larry, Col	37	.302	134	451	84	136	31	2	21	84	77	86	7	4	.403	.519
Walker, Todd, Bos	31	.292	150	582	89	170	37	2	13	77	51	73	6	4	.349	.430
Ward, Daryle, Pit	29	.277	98	285	28	79	16	0	9	44	20	55	1	0	.325	.428
Wells, Vernon, Tor	25	.283	161	646	100	183	41	4	25	95	38	91	15	8	.323	.475
White, Rondell, Det	32	.278	126	436	58	121	25	2	18	72	28	79	2	2	.321	.468
Wigginton, Ty, NYM	26	.263	154	562	69	148	31	2	12	67	52	109	7	5	.326	.390
Wilkerson, Brad, Mon	27	.247	152	558	95	138	33	3	21	78	107	172	13	9	.368	.430
Williams, Bernie, NYY	35	.299	137	515	88	154	30	3	19	88	74	76	7	3	.387	.480
Wilson, Craig, Pit	27	.265	131	396	63	105	21	2	23	68	38	121	2	2	.329	.503
Wilson, Dan, Sea	35	.250	105	320	31	80	17	1	5	37	16	65	1	1	.286	.356
Wilson, Enrique, NYY	30	.236	66	140	15	33	7	0	3	15	7	22	1	1	.272	.350
Wilson, Jack, Pit	26	.262	152	553	76	145	27	4	6	52	36	78	4	5	.307	.358
Wilson, Preston, Col	29	.276	153	572	93	158	33	2	32	107	58	139	22	10	.343	.509
Wilson, Tom, Tor	33	.250	61	156	20	39	8	0	5	24	19	46	0	0	.331	.397
Wilson, Vance, NYM	31	.236	89	233	22	55	13	0	6	32	11	45	2	2	.270	.369
Winn, Randy, Sea	30	.293	157	587	91	172	37	6	11	71	49	108	19	9	.347	.433
Witt, Kevin, StL	28	.251	87	255	30	64	16	1	11	41	14	74	0	0	.290	.451
Womack, Tony, ChC	34	.262	89	260	36	68	10	2	2	21	14	34	12	5	.299	.338
Woodward, Chris, Tor	28	.263	125	411	57	108	27	3	13	55	32	89	2	1	.316	.438
Wooten, Shawn, Ana	31	.271	55	129	14	35	9	0	3	17	7	25	1	0	.309	.411
Young, Dmitri, Det	30	.293	148	532	69	156	36	3	23	79	45	101	3	2	.348	.502
Young, Eric, SF	37	.271	112	377	56	102	19	2	6	25	33	32	20	7	.329	.379
Young, Michael, Tex	27	.280	160	617	91	173	35	7	15	77	45	113	7	5	.329	.433
Zaun, Gregg, Col	33	.240	64	146	16	35	8	0	3	19	13	21	1	1	.302	.356
Zeile, Todd, Mon	38	.250	109	356	41	89	19	1	11	49	46	69	1	1	.336	.402

Projections for 2004 Pitchers

Pitcher projections based on transactions through December 15, 2003; pitchers with 150 games or 500 innings in the major leagues. Age as of June 30, 2004.

Pitcher	Age	ERA	W	L	Sv	G	GS	IP	H	HR	BB	SO	BR/9
Abbott, Paul, TB	36	4.68	4	5	0	30	12	75	70	9	41	60	13.3
Acevedo, Juan, Pit	34	4.32	2	4	0	48	0	50	51	5	24	33	13.5
Adams, Terry, Phi	31	3.56	5	4	0	59	6	91	90	5	33	71	12.2
Alfonseca, Antonio, ChC	32	4.43	4	4	0	62	0	69	76	6	27	52	13.4
Almanza, Armando, Fla	31	4.59	3	3	0	51	0	49	44	8	26	54	12.9
Alvarez, Wilson, LA	34	3.48	8	6	0	22	20	119	112	13	29	97	10.7
Anderson, Brian, KC	32	4.60	10	11	0	33	29	184	202	30	40	87	11.8
Anderson, Jimmy, SF	28	5.05	4	5	0	15	13	73	86	8	26	24	13.8
Anderson, Matt, Det	27	3.76	4	3	14	58	0	55	53	5	21	44	12.1
Appier, Kevin, KC	36	4.34	9	9	0	26	26	137	133	18	53	86	12.2
Astacio, Pedro, NYM	34	5.44	5	8	0	18	18	101	108	16	50	76	14.1
Baez, Danys, Cle	26	3.63	5	3	16	62	0	72	64	7	31	61	11.9
Baldwin, James, Min	32	4.95	2	2	0	17	8	60	67	11	20	34	13.1
Batista, Miguel, Tor	33	3.75	14	9	0	35	32	199	194	20	57	137	11.4
Beck, Rod, SD	35	3.80	5	4	2	64	0	71	62	12	24	58	10.9
Beimel, Joe, Pit	27	4.76	3	5	0	64	3	70	77	7	34	41	14.3
Benitez, Armando, Sea	31	3.04	6	3	24	67	0	71	49	9	35	81	10.6
Benson, Kris, Pit	29	4.62	7	12	0	28	28	156	167	19	53	97	12.7
Bere, Jason, Cle	33	4.31	8	7	0	22	22	119	120	16	36	85	11.8
Biddle, Rocky, Mon	28	4.62	2	4	21	63	2	74	73	11	35	54	13.1
Boehringer, Brian, Pit	34	4.10	4	5	0	65	0	68	64	8	30	56	12.4
Borowski, Joe, ChC	33	3.16	3	4	29	70	0	77	66	7	24	76	10.5
Bradford, Chad, Oak	29	3.08	6	3	5	73	0	76	69	6	22	61	10.8
Brower, Jim, SF	31	4.16	4	4	0	51	3	93	92	11	40	65	12.8
Brown, Kevin, NYY	39	3.43	14	7	0	27	27	173	168	14	43	149	11.0
Buehrle, Mark, CWS	25	3.75	17	10	0	35	35	233	229	24	62	126	11.2
Burba, Dave, Mil	37	4.32	3	3	0	23	8	77	81	9	31	53	13.1
Burkett, John, Bos	39	4.63	12	10	0	31	30	179	202	23	46	116	12.5
Burnett, A.J., Fla	27	4.66	4	6	0	13	12	83	68	7	65	82	14.4
Carrara, Giovanni, Sea	36	4.14	3	3	0	36	0	50	47	8	17	34	11.5
Carrasco, Hector, Bal	34	4.74	2	3	0	40	0	38	42	4	17	33	14.0
Chen, Bruce, Tor	27	4.93	2	2	0	29	3	42	41	8	19	39	12.9
Clement, Matt, ChC	29	3.72	13	11	0	32	32	203	181	20	79	192	11.5
Colon, Bartolo, Ana	31	3.46	16	11	0	34	34	239	223	22	66	160	10.9
Cordero, Francisco, Tex	29	3.60	3	3	29	62	0	70	65	6	28	71	12.0
Cormier, Rheal, Phi	37	2.84	6	3	0	61	0	76	60	5	30	61	10.7
Cruz, Nelson, Col	31	4.50	3	3	0	28	6	62	64	10	18	50	11.9
Daal, Omar, Bal	32	4.89	6	8	0	26	19	116	131	16	37	72	13.0
D'Amico, Jeff, Pit	28	4.20	8	12	0	29	27	165	174	21	40	104	11.7
DeJean, Mike, StL	33	4.16	5	4	0	73	0	80	76	9	39	68	12.9
de los Santos, Valerio, Phi	31	4.00	4	3	0	51	0	54	47	8	25	38	12.0
Dempster, Ryan, Cin	27	5.45	1	2	0	9	4	33	34	4	20	24	14.7
Dessens, Elmer, Ari	33	4.70	10	12	0	33	30	176	194	22	57	103	12.8
Dotel, Octavio, Hou	30	3.00	3	3	44	73	0	78	60	9	28	97	10.2
Dreifort, Darren, LA	32	4.33	5	5	0	14	14	81	75	11	34	90	12.1
Eischen, Joey, Mon	34	3.57	4	3	7	66	0	53	50	5	18	43	11.5
Elarton, Scott, Col	28	5.51	4	6	0	16	16	80	88	16	31	31	13.4
Eldred, Cal, StL	36	4.57	4	4	0	62	0	67	68	9	31	67	13.3
Embree, Alan, Bos	34	3.79	5	3	0	66	0	57	55	7	18	62	11.5
Escobar, Kelvim, Ana	28	4.17	12	11	0	32	30	190	181	19	82	178	12.5
Estes, Shawn, ChC	31	4.94	8	11	0	29	28	155	163	13	85	105	14.4
Eyre, Scott, SF	32	4.43	4	4	0	73	1	63	70	5	29	47	14.1
Farnsworth, Kyle, ChC	28	3.95	4	4	0	66	0	66	59	9	29	79	12.0
Fassero, Jeff, StL	41	5.52	4	5	0	66	4	75	89	13	31	57	14.4
Foulke, Keith, Bos	31	2.36	4	2	35	70	0	84	64	7	19	73	8.9
Fox, Chad, Fla	33	3.35	4	3	2	48	0	51	38	4	32	57	12.4
Franco, John, NYM	43	4.50	2	2	0	38	0	34	35	5	13	16	12.7
Fultz, Aaron, Tex	30	4.27	4	3	0	57	0	59	61	7	22	49	12.7
Gagne, Eric, LA	28	2.52	3	3	58	77	0	82	57	10	21	109	8.6
Garcia, Freddy, Sea	28	4.00	13	11	0	33	33	209	198	25	74	160	11.7
Garland, Jon, CWS	24	4.59	13	11	0	32	32	192	195	26	74	110	12.6
Glavine, Tom, NYM	38	4.25	11	12	0	33	33	197	200	20	71	101	12.4
Gordon, Tom, NYY	36	2.81	6	2	3	55	0	64	51	4	25	81	10.7
Graves, Danny, Cin	30	3.89	2	3	35	65	0	81	81	10	20	45	11.2

Pitcher	Age	ERA	W	L	Sv	G	GS	IP	H	HR	BB	SO	BR/9
Grimsley, Jason, KC	36	3.89	5	4	0	74	0	74	73	6	33	58	12.9
Groom, Buddy, Bal	38	3.35	4	3	0	63	0	51	48	5	12	39	10.6
Guardado, Eddie, Sea	33	2.91	5	3	6	64	0	65	50	9	18	63	9.4
Guthrie, Mark, ChC	38	3.48	4	3	0	66	0	44	37	4	20	33	11.7
Halama, John, TB	32	4.75	4	5	0	34	12	106	126	13	32	56	13.4
Halladay, Roy, Tor	27	3.12	20	9	0	35	35	257	258	20	31	189	10.1
Hamilton, Joey, SD	33	4.78	2	2	0	15	6	49	59	5	18	33	14.1
Hammond, Chris, NYY	38	2.69	6	2	0	62	0	67	57	3	20	52	10.3
Hampton, Mike, Atl	31	4.65	11	12	0	31	31	186	199	19	76	93	13.3
Hasegawa, Shigetoshi, Sea	35	3.09	5	3	4	61	0	70	61	5	24	39	10.9
Hawkins, LaTroy, ChC	31	3.12	6	4	7	71	0	78	69	5	28	66	11.2
Haynes, Jimmy, Cin	31	5.70	6	10	0	23	23	128	140	15	78	77	15.5
Helling, Rick, Fla	33	4.78	8	11	0	33	26	162	173	27	47	107	12.2
Hentgen, Pat, Tor	35	4.42	7	6	0	20	16	114	111	17	41	70	12.0
Heredia, Felix, NYY	29	3.96	5	3	0	64	0	75	70	9	32	45	12.2
Herges, Matt, SF	34	3.65	5	4	2	65	0	74	70	6	31	59	12.3
Hermanson, Dustin, SF	31	4.75	2	3	0	25	4	53	58	8	20	33	13.2
Hernandez, Livan, Mon	29	4.07	14	12	0	33	33	228	243	23	56	158	11.8
Hernandez, Roberto, Phi	39	4.89	3	4	0	62	0	57	61	8	28	47	14.1
Hitchcock, Sterling, StL	33	5.00	3	3	0	30	5	72	83	10	25	51	13.5
Hoffman, Trevor, SD	36	3.05	2	3	34	59	0	56	47	6	18	62	10.4
Holmes, Darren, Atl	38	3.13	4	2	0	50	0	46	42	4	11	44	10.4
Hudson, Tim, Oak	28	3.13	18	9	0	34	34	239	214	20	61	157	10.4
Isringhausen, Jason, StL	31	2.52	2	2	38	47	0	50	40	3	17	51	10.3
Jarvis, Kevin, SD	34	5.30	4	5	0	13	13	73	80	14	25	42	12.9
Jimenez, Jose, Col	30	4.01	5	4	0	67	5	92	102	7	26	52	12.5
Johnson, Jason, Bal	30	5.08	8	13	0	29	29	170	183	25	72	114	13.5
Johnson, Randy, Ari	40	3.15	16	10	0	33	33	223	192	25	53	274	9.9
Jones, Todd, Bos	36	5.30	4	4	0	66	1	73	88	10	29	62	14.4
Kim, Byung-Hyun, Bos	25	3.13	13	5	0	29	26	144	123	14	45	125	10.5
King, Ray, StL	30	3.10	6	3	0	79	0	61	50	4	26	50	11.2
Kline, Steve, StL	31	3.34	5	3	2	74	0	62	56	4	25	40	11.8
Koch, Billy, CWS	29	4.10	2	3	23	65	0	68	64	7	34	60	13.0
Lawrence, Brian, SD	28	3.90	13	11	0	34	32	210	213	21	57	132	11.6
Leiter, Al, NYM	38	4.52	10	12	0	31	31	189	181	19	98	152	13.3
Leskanic, Curtis, KC	36	3.40	4	3	14	53	0	53	42	6	26	50	11.5
Levine, Al, Det	36	3.65	4	3	0	53	0	69	61	7	30	38	11.9
Lidle, Cory, Tor	32	4.22	13	10	0	31	31	192	199	22	60	112	12.1
Ligtenberg, Kerry, Tor	33	3.66	5	3	2	62	0	64	56	7	27	54	11.7
Lima, Jose, KC	31	6.00	3	6	0	16	13	72	87	15	25	33	14.0
Lloyd, Graeme, KC	37	4.94	3	4	0	57	0	51	65	4	16	30	14.3
Loaiza, Esteban, CWS	32	4.30	13	10	0	31	31	201	219	24	50	157	12.0
Looper, Braden, Fla	29	3.51	5	4	3	75	0	82	78	6	30	56	11.9
Lopez, Albie, KC	32	4.76	2	2	0	20	1	34	38	4	13	23	13.5
Lowe, Derek, Bos	31	3.62	16	9	0	33	33	209	198	14	74	117	11.7
Lowe, Sean, KC	33	4.66	3	3	0	36	0	56	62	7	21	37	13.3
Maddux, Greg, Atl	38	3.35	16	10	0	35	35	212	213	19	32	123	10.4
Mantei, Matt, Ari	30	2.93	2	2	34	44	0	46	35	5	17	54	10.2
Marte, Damaso, CWS	29	2.47	7	2	15	70	0	73	53	5	26	82	9.7
Martin, Tom, LA	34	4.37	3	3	0	54	0	35	32	4	17	32	12.6
Martinez, Pedro, Bos	32	1.98	19	3	0	29	29	191	133	11	48	220	8.5
Matthews, Mike, SD	30	4.03	4	4	0	67	0	58	55	6	26	44	12.6
Meadows, Brian, Pit	28	4.75	2	4	0	26	8	72	86	11	14	34	12.5
Mecir, Jim, Oak	34	3.45	4	2	0	48	0	47	43	3	20	39	12.1
Mendoza, Ramiro, Bos	32	4.08	4	3	0	45	3	75	82	8	17	48	11.9
Mercker, Kent, Atl	36	5.19	3	4	0	64	0	52	52	9	28	44	13.8
Mesa, Jose, Phi	38	4.36	4	4	0	62	0	64	65	6	34	52	13.9
Miceli, Dan, Hou	33	4.14	3	3	0	41	0	50	47	7	18	45	11.7
Miller, Trever, Tor	31	4.91	4	4	0	72	0	55	56	8	29	46	13.9
Miller, Wade, Hou	27	4.00	12	9	0	31	31	180	163	20	74	156	11.9
Millwood, Kevin, Phi	29	3.72	15	11	0	35	35	220	208	23	67	174	11.3
Milton, Eric, Phi	28	3.26	12	7	0	28	28	160	151	25	10	112	9.1
Moehler, Brian, Hou	32	6.00	2	2	0	6	6	30	38	4	13	14	15.3
Morris, Matt, StL	29	3.45	15	9	0	32	32	206	204	16	47	157	11.0
Mota, Guillermo, LA	30	3.00	6	4	0	65	0	90	74	8	30	75	10.4
Moyer, Jamie, Sea	41	3.48	15	10	0	33	33	220	196	23	68	136	10.8
Mulder, Mark, Oak	26	3.50	15	9	0	30	30	211	208	20	45	154	10.8
Mulholland, Terry, Cle	41	5.48	3	5	0	42	3	92	113	17	30	41	14.0
Mussina, Mike, NYY	35	3.14	17	7	0	32	32	215	196	22	40	188	9.9
Myers, Mike, Ari	35	4.14	3	3	0	66	0	37	35	3	20	28	13.4

Pitcher	Age	ERA	W	L	Sv	G	GS	IP	H	HR	BB	SO	BR/9
Nelson, Jeff, NYY	37	3.63	5	2	0	60	0	52	45	4	26	63	12.3
Nen, Robb, SF	34	3.14	4	3	30	62	0	63	57	4	20	66	11.0
Nomo, Hideo, LA	35	3.86	13	13	0	33	33	219	184	26	98	185	11.6
Nunez, Vladimir, Fla	29	4.28	2	2	0	35	0	40	40	5	15	29	12.4
Ohka, Tomo, Mon	28	4.29	12	12	0	33	33	197	219	23	45	119	12.1
Oliver, Darren, Col	33	5.40	8	11	0	28	28	155	189	21	52	78	14.0
Orosco, Jesse, Ari	47	5.34	2	3	0	62	0	32	34	5	19	25	14.9
Ortiz, Ramon, Ana	31	4.55	11	12	0	32	32	192	192	30	67	124	12.1
Ortiz, Russ, Atl	30	3.93	14	11	0	34	34	213	189	18	102	143	12.3
Osuna, Antonio, NYY	31	3.86	4	2	0	52	0	56	55	4	23	55	12.5
Oswalt, Roy, Hou	26	3.14	15	7	0	30	30	189	172	17	43	166	10.2
Padilla, Vicente, Phi	26	3.63	14	10	0	32	32	208	203	17	62	131	11.5
Park, Chan Ho, Tex	31	5.01	9	9	0	26	26	149	128	16	86	116	12.9
Parris, Steve, TB	36	5.83	2	4	0	11	9	54	68	10	16	28	14.0
Pavano, Carl, Fla	28	4.32	10	11	0	34	29	179	198	20	44	120	12.2
Penny, Brad, Fla	26	3.88	11	10	0	29	29	174	173	18	50	123	11.5
Percival, Troy, Ana	34	2.77	2	2	35	54	0	52	37	5	21	60	10.0
Perez, Odalis, LA	27	3.64	12	11	0	31	31	198	189	22	49	144	10.8
Person, Robert, Bos	34	3.65	3	2	0	10	5	37	32	5	17	31	11.9
Pettitte, Andy, Hou	32	3.97	13	10	0	31	31	197	214	15	51	158	12.1
Pineiro, Joel, Sea	25	3.67	14	10	0	34	31	206	188	20	74	146	11.4
Politte, Cliff, Tor	30	3.63	4	3	2	59	0	57	52	7	20	52	11.4
Ponson, Sidney, SF	27	4.17	12	12	0	30	30	203	207	25	57	131	11.7
Powell, Jay, Tex	32	4.66	4	3	0	51	0	56	61	6	27	39	14.1
Quantrill, Paul, NYY	35	3.16	7	3	0	88	0	77	78	3	16	49	11.0
Radke, Brad, Min	31	3.96	13	11	0	32	32	200	220	24	26	110	11.1
Redman, Mark, Oak	30	4.29	12	11	0	29	29	195	205	22	58	125	12.1
Reed, Rick, Min	38	4.47	9	9	0	29	25	153	164	25	33	91	11.6
Reed, Steve, Col	38	3.18	5	3	0	66	0	65	57	5	20	44	10.7
Remlinger, Mike, ChC	38	3.13	5	3	0	73	0	69	51	7	34	76	11.1
Reyes, Carlos, TB	35	4.50	1	2	0	10	3	40	40	10	5	13	10.1
Reyes, Dennys, KC	27	5.25	2	2	0	29	2	36	40	4	20	29	15.0
Reynolds, Shane, Atl	36	4.98	9	11	0	28	28	159	180	21	56	93	13.4
Rhodes, Arthur, Sea	34	2.14	6	2	0	67	0	59	44	4	13	66	8.7
Rincon, Ricardo, Oak	34	2.89	5	2	2	66	0	56	46	4	22	47	10.9
Riske, David, Cle	27	3.49	2	3	23	62	0	67	53	9	32	77	11.4
Ritchie, Todd, Mil	32	5.00	5	8	0	18	17	99	112	13	35	56	13.4
Rivera, Mariano, NYY	34	2.03	3	1	49	58	0	62	49	3	10	59	8.6
Rodriguez, Felix, SF	31	2.91	6	3	2	69	0	65	51	4	26	60	10.7
Rogers, Kenny, Min	39	4.23	13	11	0	33	32	200	217	21	51	110	12.1
Romero, J.C., Min	28	4.43	5	4	0	76	0	69	70	7	34	54	13.6
Rueter, Kirk, SF	33	4.50	9	11	0	29	29	166	180	19	53	55	12.6
Rusch, Glendon, Mil	29	5.03	7	11	0	33	24	152	175	18	55	106	13.6
Ryan, B.J., Bal	28	3.91	4	4	0	73	0	53	46	5	30	57	12.9
Sabathia, C.C., Cle	23	3.56	14	10	0	31	31	202	184	19	67	144	11.2
Santiago, Jose, Cle	29	4.14	2	2	0	31	0	37	41	3	11	19	12.6
Sasaki, Kazuhiro, Sea	36	2.62	3	2	29	57	0	55	42	5	16	56	9.5
Sauerbeck, Scott, Bos	32	3.97	5	3	0	79	0	59	53	4	35	64	13.4
Schilling, Curt, Bos	37	2.81	19	6	0	31	31	221	189	22	39	267	9.3
Schmidt, Jason, SF	31	2.70	16	7	0	29	29	200	168	16	44	206	9.5
Schoeneweis, Scott, CWS	30	4.39	5	4	0	57	5	82	87	9	31	48	13.0
Sele, Aaron, Ana	34	5.04	7	10	0	25	25	134	145	15	64	64	14.0
Service, Scott, Cin	37	4.24	2	2	0	33	0	34	38	4	8	35	12.2
Sheets, Ben, Mil	25	4.11	12	14	0	34	34	219	237	27	43	164	11.5
Shuey, Paul, LA	33	3.13	5	3	0	64	0	69	57	4	32	69	11.6
Smoltz, John, Atl	37	1.93	3	1	45	66	0	70	52	3	15	76	8.6
Sparks, Steve, Oak	38	4.97	5	6	0	45	10	134	160	16	47	69	13.9
Speier, Justin, Tor	30	3.34	6	3	13	69	0	70	61	10	19	61	10.3
Stanton, Mike, NYM	37	3.38	4	3	2	60	0	56	50	5	21	35	11.4
Stephenson, Garrett, StL	32	4.60	8	8	0	25	21	131	133	20	45	75	12.2
Stewart, Scott, Mon	28	3.42	4	3	0	56	0	50	47	5	16	44	11.3
Strickland, Scott, NYM	28	3.50	3	2	0	36	0	36	30	3	18	36	12.0
Sturtze, Tanyon, Tor	33	4.97	5	5	0	38	16	134	151	18	56	79	13.9
Sullivan, Scott, KC	33	4.04	5	4	0	67	0	69	66	8	28	56	12.3
Suppan, Jeff, StL	29	4.13	13	11	0	32	32	205	208	27	55	111	11.5
Tam, Jeff, Tor	33	4.19	3	2	0	43	0	43	47	2	18	23	13.6
Tavarez, Julian, Pit	31	4.21	3	5	0	52	2	77	83	5	33	41	13.6
Telemaco, Amaury, Phi	30	4.26	8	8	0	23	23	129	129	21	31	83	11.2
Thomson, John, Atl	30	3.91	14	11	0	33	33	205	204	25	50	122	11.2
Timlin, Mike, Bos	38	2.97	7	3	0	72	0	88	74	13	11	56	8.7

Pitcher	Age	ERA	W	L	Sv	G	GS	IP	H	HR	BB	SO	BR/9
Tomko, Brett, StL	31	4.92	11	13	0	33	32	203	228	33	57	120	12.6
Trachsel, Steve, NYM	33	4.36	11	12	0	32	32	194	200	25	62	111	12.2
Urbina, Ugueth, Fla	30	3.17	3	3	29	68	0	71	55	9	26	83	10.3
Valdes, Ismael, Tex	30	4.69	10	8	0	25	25	142	157	22	36	68	12.2
Van Poppel, Todd, Cin	32	4.34	2	3	0	27	3	56	55	8	24	60	12.7
Vazquez, Javier, NYY	27	3.74	17	10	0	34	34	231	227	28	53	215	10.9
Veres, Dave, ChC	37	3.86	3	3	0	44	0	49	44	7	19	40	11.6
Villone, Ron, Hou	34	4.94	5	6	0	28	15	102	106	14	46	75	13.4
Vizcaino, Luis, Mil	29	4.10	4	5	2	75	0	68	62	11	25	65	11.5
Wagner, Billy, Phi	32	2.20	4	2	33	75	0	82	54	8	24	106	8.6
Wakefield, Tim, Bos	37	3.48	14	7	0	38	27	189	163	20	66	157	10.9
Walker, Jamie, Det	32	3.41	5	0	0	71	0	58	50	10	14	45	9.9
Washburn, Jarrod, Ana	30	3.70	11	11	0	32	32	207	194	28	54	129	10.8
Weathers, Dave, NYM	34	3.54	6	4	8	75	0	84	75	6	37	68	12.0
Weaver, Jeff, LA	27	3.95	10	10	0	32	24	173	175	15	55	111	12.0
Weber, Ben, Ana	34	3.49	5	4	0	62	0	80	79	5	26	45	11.8
Wells, David, NYY	41	3.63	16	8	0	31	30	211	227	23	20	120	10.5
Wells, Kip, Pit	27	4.45	9	14	0	32	32	198	201	23	76	140	12.6
Wendell, Turk, Phi	37	3.43	5	3	0	56	0	63	53	6	28	27	11.6
White, Gabe, NYY	32	3.49	4	2	0	51	0	49	44	7	13	34	10.5
White, Rick, Hou	35	4.09	4	3	0	53	0	66	68	8	19	48	11.9
Williams, Mike, Phi	35	4.29	4	4	0	63	0	63	60	7	32	47	13.1
Williams, Woody, StL	37	3.40	15	8	0	31	31	201	189	19	50	142	10.7
Williamson, Scott, Bos	28	3.14	6	2	4	65	0	66	51	5	35	76	11.7
Wilson, Paul, Cin	31	4.60	10	11	0	29	29	176	191	23	53	99	12.5
Witasick, Jay, SD	31	4.42	3	3	0	45	0	53	55	6	22	55	13.1
Wolf, Randy, Phi	27	3.93	13	11	0	32	32	204	185	23	79	173	11.6
Wood, Kerry, ChC	27	3.48	14	11	0	32	32	212	161	23	100	241	11.1
Worrell, Tim, Phi	36	3.08	6	3	2	77	0	79	68	5	31	68	11.3
Wright, Jamey, KC	29	4.50	4	4	0	10	10	60	60	7	26	37	12.9
Wright, Jaret, Atl	28	6.34	2	3	0	36	2	44	55	6	30	34	17.4
Wunsch, Kelly, CWS	31	3.34	3	2	0	45	0	35	26	3	20	27	11.8
Yan, Esteban, StL	29	4.97	4	4	0	54	0	67	76	11	21	58	13.0
Zito, Barry, Oak	26	3.16	18	9	0	35	35	231	185	20	88	164	10.6

Index